INDEX to RECORD AND TAPE REVIEWS

A Classical Music Buying Guide

1981

ANTOINETTE O. MALEADY

CHULAINN PRESS

San Anselmo, California 1982

ISBN 0-917600-07-X
Library of Congress Catalog Card No. 72-3355
Manufactured in the United States of America

CHULAINN PRESS
Post Office Box 770
San Anselmo, California 94960

To Donna

CONTENTS

Introduction		vii
Abbreviations		ix
I.	Composers	1
II.	Music in Collections	585
III.	Anonymous Works	697

INTRODUCTION

This Index brings together in one volume a listing of all classical music recordings reviewed in 1981 in the major reviewing media of the United States, England and Canada.

The Index has three sections. Section I is a straight listing by composer. Section II, "Music in Collections", lists records or tapes with several composers on one disc or tape. Section II main entries are arranged alphabeticcally by name of the manufacturer, and then serially by the manufacturer's number within each entry. The work of any composer in each of these collections appears in Section I under the name of that composer, with a reference to the Section II entry. Section III lists, alphabetically by title, anonymous works with a reference to their location in Section I or Section II. Each citation gives, if available, complete entries for each composition; performers; the disc label and number; variant labels and numbers; tape cassette, cartridge or reel numbers; quadraphonic disc or tape numbers; reissues; location of the reviews and the reviewers evaluation of the recording. The main entry for each recording is in upper case letters. Tapes or discs reviewed in 1981 that were also reviewed in 1980, 1979, 1978, 1977, 1976, 1975, 1974, 1973, 1972 and/or 1971 have all the reviews brought together in the 1981 Index.

A key is provided for understanding the entries of the three sections. The entries are fictitious entries to show the various possibilities of form.

Section I

MACONCHY, Elizabeth
1219 Ariadne, soprano and orchestra. WALTON: Songs: Daphne, Old Sir
[entry no.] Faulk; Through gilded trellises. Heather Harper, s [Heather Harper, soprano]; Paul Hamburger, pno [Paul Hamburger, piano]; ECO [English Chamber Orchestra]; Raymond Leppard [conductor]. Columbia M 30443 [disc number] (2) [number of discs in set] Tape (c) MT 30443 [cassette number] (ct) MA 30443 [cartridge number] (r) L 30443 [reel number] (Q) MQ 30443 [quadraphonic disc number] Tape (c) MAQ 30443 [quadraphonic tape cartridge number]. (also CBS 72941) [recording also available on CBS label].

++Gr 9-81 p1025 [evaluation excellent; review in Gramophone, September 1981, page 1025]
+-OV 3-80 p40 [evaluation mixed, review in Ovation, March 1980, page 40]
-MUM 12-79 p50 [evaluation poor, review in Music Magazine, December 1979, page 50]

+NYT 7-23-80 pD38 [evaluation good, review in New York Times, July 23, 1980, page D38]

Section II

LONDON

OS 36577 (also Decca SXL 3315) [label number. Also available on Decca label] (Reissue from OS 3716) [Reissue from London OS 3716]

2395 Baroque flute sonatas. BLAVET: Sonata, flute no. 3, F major. GAULTIER: Suite, G minor. HANDEL: Sonata, flute, op. 1 no. 5, G major. LOEILLET: Sonata, flute, F major. VINCI: Sonata, flute, D major. Jean-Pierre Rampal, flt [Jean-Pierre Rampal, flute]; Raymond Leppard, hpd [Raymond Leppard, harpsichord]; Claude Viala, vlc [Claude Viala, violoncello]; AMF [Academy of St. Martin-in-the-Fields]; Raymond Leppard [conductor]

[entry no.]

+-MQ 4-79 p53 [evaluation mixed, review in Musical Quarterly, April 1979, page 53]

+STL 1-15-81 p30 [evaluation good, review in Sunday Times, London, January 15, 1981, page 30]

Section III

Kyrie trope: Orbis factor. See no. 1315. [Anonymous works, appears in Section I, citation number 1315]

ABBREVIATIONS

Periodicals Indexed

AR	American Recorder
ARG	American Record Guide
ARSC	Association for Recorded Sound Collections Journal
Audio	Audio
CJ	Choral Journal
CL	Clavier
CMJ	Computer Music Journal
FF	Fanfare
FU	Fugue
Gr	Gramophone
GRT	Guitar Review
Ha	Harpers
HF	High Fidelity
HFN	Hi-Fi News & Record Review
HPD	Harpsichord
IN	The Instrumentalist
LAMR	Latin American Music Review
LJ	Library Journal/School Library Journal Previews
MJ	Music Journal
MM	Music & Musicians
MQ	Musical Quarterly
MR	Music Review
MT	Musical Times
MU	Music/American Guild of Organists/American Organist
MUM	Music Magazine
NCM	Nineteenth Century Music
NR	New Record
NYT	New York Times
OC	Opera Canada
ON	Opera News
Op	Opera, London
OR	Opera Review
OV	Ovation
PNM	Perspectives of New Music
PRO	Pro Musica
RR	Records and Recording
SFC	San Francisco Examiner and Chronicle
SR	Saturday Review/World
St	Stereo Review
ST	Strad

STL Sunday Times, London
Te Tempo

Performers

Orchestral

AMF Academy of St. Martin-in-the-Fields
BBO Berlin Bach Orchestra
BeSO Berlin Symphony Orchestra
BPhO Berlin Philharmonic Orchestra
BPO Boston "Pops" Orchestra
Brno PO Brno State Philharmonic Orchestra
BRSO Berlin Radio Symphony Orchestra
BSO Boston Symphony Orchestra
CnSO Cincinnati Symphony Orchestra
CO Cleveland Orchestra
COA Concertgebouw Orchestra, Amsterdam
CPhO Czech Philharmonic Orchestra
CSO Chicago Shymphony Orchestra
DBS Deutsche Bach Solisten
ECO English Chamber Orchestra
FK Frankfurt Kantorei
HCO Hungarian Chamber Orchestra
HRT Hungarian Radio and Television
HSO Hungarian State Symphony Orchestra
LAPO Los Angeles Philharmonic Orchestra
LOL Little Orchestra, London
LPO London Philharmonic Orchestra
LSO London Symphony Orchestra
MB Munich Bach Orchestra
MPAC Munich Pro Arte Chamber Orchestra
MPO Moscow Philharmonic Orchestra
MRSO Moscow Radio Symphony Orchestra
NPhO New Philharmonia Orchestra
NSL New Symphony, London
NWE Netherlands Wind Ensemble
NYP New York Philharmonic Orchestra
ORTF O.R.T.F. Philharmonic Orchestra
OSCCP Orchestre de la Societe des Concerts du Conservatoire du Paris
OSR L'Orchestre de la Suisse Romande
PCO Prague Chamber Orchestra
PH Philharmonia Hungarica
PhO Philharmonia Orchestra, London
PO Philadelphia Orchestra
PSO Prague Symphony Orchestra
ROHO Royal Opera House Orchestra, Covent Garden
RPO Royal Philharmonic Orchestra
SBC Stuttgart Bach Collegium

SCO	Stuttgart Chamber Orchestra
SDR	Stuttgart S.D.R. Symphony Orchestra
SSO	Sydney Symphony Orchestra
VCM	Vienna Concentus Musicus
VPM	Vienna Pro Musica
VPO	Vienna Philharmonic Orchestra
VSO	Vienna Symphony Orchestra
VSOO	Vienna State Opera Orchestra

Instrumental

acc	accordion	mand	mandolin
bal	balalaika	mar	marimba
bs	bass	ob	oboe
bsn	bassoon	ond	ondes martenot
c	celesta	org	organ
cimb	cimbalon	perc	percussion
cld	clavichord	pic	piccolo
clt	clarinet	pno	piano
cor	cornet	rec	recorder
dr	drums	sax	saxophone
Eh	English horn	sit	sitar
flt	flute	tpt	trumpet
Fr hn	French horn	trom	trombone
gtr	guitar	vib	vibraphone
harm	harmonica	v	viol
hn	horn	vla	viola
hp	harp	vlc	violoncello
hpd	harpsichord	vln	violin
lt	lute	z	zither

Vocal

bar	baritone	ms	mezzo-soprano
bs	bass	s	soprano
con	contralto	t	tenor
c-t	countertenor		

Qualitative Evaluation of Recordings

++	excellent or very good	/	fair
+	good	-	poor
+-	mixed	*	no evaluation

Section I

COMPOSERS

ABBIATE, Louis

1 Concerto italien, op. 96. Monaecencis, op. 110. Marcelle Bousquet, pno; Monte Carlo Opera Orchestra; Richard Blareau, Louis Fremaux. Ecce Musica CM 306
-Gr 11-81 p678

Monaecencis, op. 110. See no. 1

2 Sonata, piano, no. 3, op. 34, E flat major. Bernard Ringeissen, pno. Calliope CAL 1872
+Gr 1-81 p966 +HFN 12-80 p131

ABAELARD, Peter

O quanta qualia. See no. 4009

ABEL, Karl

Sonata, G major. See no. 3867

Symphony concertante, B flat major. See no. 3794

ABT

Serenade. See no. 4030

ACHRON, Joseph

3 Hebrew melody, opp. 32 and 35 (orch. Gerhardt). BLOCH (orch. Gerhardt): Baal Shem. Abodah. BRUCH: Kol Nidrei, op. 47. RAVEL (orch. Gerhardt): Melodies hebraiques: Kaddisch. Lydia Mordkovitch, vln; National Philharmonic Orchestra; Charles Gerhardt. RCA RL 2-5370 Tape (c) RK 2-5370
+Gr 12-81 p892 +HFN 12-81 p112 tape
+HFN 11-81 p101

ADAM, Adolphe Charles

Le chalet: Vallons de l'Helvetie. See no. 4025

Giselle: Myrtha's appearance; Giselle's appearance; Giselle's dance; Scene; Albrecht's appearance and scene with Giselle; Willis scene. See no. 3840

Minuits, Chretiens. See no. 3688

4 Le postillon de Longjumeau (sung in German). Stina-Britte Melander, s; John van Kesteren, t; Ernst Krukowski, bar; Ivan Sardi, Fritz Hoppe, bs; Berlin RIAS Choir; Berlin Radio Orchestra; Reinhard Peters. Eurodisc 300073 (2)
+Gr 12-81 p929

Le postillon de Longjumeau: Mes amis ecoutez l'histoire. See no. 3648

Songs: Mariquita. See no. 3758

Le toreador: Ah vous dirai-je Maman. See no. 3649

ADAM DE LA HALLE
Fines amouretes ai. See no. 2096
Play of Robin and Marion, excerpts. See no. 3670
ADAMS
Songs: Thora. See no. 3967
ADAMS, Byron
Nightingales. See no. 3954
ADAMS, John
Apple blossom round. See no. 6
August voices. See no. 6
Evensong. See no. 6
Joyful noise. See no. 6
Meadowdance. See no. 6
Morningfieldsong. See no. 6
Mourning dove. See no. 6
Notquitespringdawn. See no. 6
5 Phrygian gates. Shaker loops. Ridge Quartet. 1750 Arch S 1784
+ARG 12-81 p8 +NR 8-81 p7
++FF 9/10-81 p56 +NYT 6-7-81 pD23
+HF 10-81 p76
Shaker loops. See no. 5
Wood thrush. See no. 6
6 Works, selections: Apple blossom round. August voices. Evensong. Joyful noise. Morningfieldsong. Mourning dove. Meadowdance. Notquitespringdawn. Wood thrush. Anne McFarland, Michael Cook, Kevin Culver, pic and ocarina; Tim Embry, Scott Douglas, John Adams, perc. Opus One 66
+ARG 10-81 p13
ADAMS, Stephen
The holy city. See no. 4100
ADASKIN, Murray
7 Divertimento, no. 3, DANZI: Trio, op. 23, F major. Taras Gabora, vln; Barry Tuckwell, hn; George Zukerman, bsn. Radio Canada RCI 405
*FF 7/8-81 p48
ADLER, Samuel
8 Quartet, strings, no. 6. HODKINSON: Dance variations on a Chopin fragment. Eastman Trio; Jan De Gaetani, ms; Fine Arts Quartet. CRI SD 432
+-ARG 7/8-81 p19 ++NR 1-81 p6
+FF 7/8-81 p113
Songs: A kiss; Strings in the earth. See no. 3951
ADSON, John
Ayres (12). See no. 4002
AGRELL, Johan
9 Sinfonia, op. 1, no. 6, F major. ATTERBERG: Symphony, no. 4. LARSSON: A winter's tale. Norrkoping Symphony Orchestra; Sten Frykberg. Sterling Conifer S 1003
+Gr 8-81 p317
AGUADO, Dionisio
10 Adagio, op. 2, no. 1. Introduction and rondo, op. 2, no. 3. Polonaise, op. 2, no. 2. SOR: Fantaisies, op. 7; op. 30. Variations on a theme by Mozart, op. 9. Julian Bream, gtr. RCA ATC 1-4033 Tape (c) RK 1-4033
+Gr 10-81 p584 ++NR 8-81 p14
++FF 11/12-81 p248 ++SFC 9-27-81 p18

Introduction and rondo, op. 2, no. 3. See no. 10
Polonaise, op. 2, no. 2. See no. 10

AGUILERA DE HEREDIA, Sebastian
Ensalada del 8th tono alto. See no. 3958
Tiento de falsas 4th tono. See no. 3958
Tiento lleno por Gsolreut. See no. 3958

AHO, Kalevi
11 Quintet, oboe and strings. CRUSELL: Divertimento, op. 9. MOZART: Quartet, oboe, K 370, F major. Jauko Teikari, ob; Hannale Segerstam, Olavi Palli, vln; Pentii Mikkonen, vla; Veli-Pekka Bister, Risto Poutanen, vlc. Finlandia FA 320
+FF 3/4-81 p52 +HFN 10-80 p111
+Gr 1-81 p998 +NR 4-81 p8

AITKEN
Maire my girl. See no. 3967

ALABIEFF (Alabiev), Alexander
Die Nachtigall. See no. 3649

ALADOR, Zoltan
12 Symphony, no. 2. BOLDIZSAR: Prelude, chorale-fugue and postlude. CSABA: Variations, orchestra. Tirgu-Mures Philharmonic Orchestra; Szalman Lorant. Electrecord ST ECE 01504
+/FF 5/6-81 p219

ALAIN, Albert
Toccata on "Cantemus domino". See no. 3799

ALAIN, Jehan
Andante. See no. 13. See no. 14
Aria. See no. 13. See no. 14
Ballade en mode Phrygien. See no. 13. See no. 14
Berceuse sur 2 notes qui cornent. See no. 13. See no. 14
Choral Cistercien. See no. 13. See no. 14
Choral Dorien, op. 47. See no. 13. See no. 14
Choral Phrygien. See no. 13. See no. 14
Climat, op. 53. See no. 13. See no. 14
Danses (3). See no. 13. See no. 14
Danses a Agni Yavishta, op. 52. See no. 13. See no. 14
Fantasies, nos. 1 and 2. See no. 13. See no. 14
Grave, op. 32. See no. 13. See no. 14
Intermezzo. See no. 13. See no. 14
Le jardin suspendu, op. 50. See no. 13. See no. 14
Lamento, op. 12. See no. 13. See no. 14
Litanies. See no. 13. See no. 14
Litanies, op. 79. See no. 3744
Litanies, op. 79: Trois mouvement. See no. 4113
Monodie. See no. 13. See no. 14

13 Organ works: Andante. Aria. Berceuse sur 2 notes qui cornent. Ballade en mode Phrygien. Choral Cistercien. Choral Dorien, op. 47. Choral Phrygien. Climat, op. 53. Danses (3). Danses a Agni Yavishta, op. 52. Fantasies, nos. 1 and 2. Grave, op. 32. Intermezzo. Le jardin suspendu, op. 50. Lamento, op. 12. Litanies. Monodie. Petite piece. Preludes profanes, nos. 1 and 2. Prelude and fugue. Postlude pour l'Office de Complies. Suite, organ. Variations sur Lucis Creator, op. 28. Variations sur un theme de Clement Janequin, op. 78. Wolfgang Rubsam, org. Da Camera SM 93264/6 (3)
+HF 10-81 p76

14 Organ works: Andante. Aria. Berceuse sur 2 notes qui cornent. Ballade en mode Phrygien. Choral Cistercien. Choral Dorien. Choral Phrygien. Climat, op. 53. Danses (3). Danses a Agni Yavishta, op. 52 (2). Fantasies, nos. 1 and 2. Grave, op. 32. Intermezzo. Le jardin suspendu, op. 50. Lamento, op. 120. Litanies. Monodie. Petite piece. Preludes profanes, nos. 1 and 2. Prelude and fugue. Postlude pour l'Office de Complies. Suite, organ. Variations sur Lucis Creator, op. 28. Variations sur un theme de Clement Janequin, op. 78. Marie-Claire Alain, org. Musical Heritage Society MHS 804254 (3)
++Gr 4-81 p1343 +HF 10-81 p76
++FF 3/4-81 p52

Petite piece. See no. 13. See no. 14
Postlude pour l'Office de Complies. See no. 13. See no. 14
Prelude and fugue. See no. 13. See no. 14
Preludes profanes, nos. 1 and 2. See no. 13. See no. 14
Suite, organ. See no. 13. See no. 14
Variations sur Lucis Creator, op. 28. See no. 13. See no. 14
Variations sur un theme de Janequin, op. 78. See no. 13. See no. 14

ALBAN, Jean-Baptiste
Variations on a German theme. See no. 3986

ALBENIZ, Isaac
Cantos de Espana, op. 232: Baja la palmera; Cordoba. See no. 3879
Cantos de Espana, op. 232: Cordoba. See no. 22
Cantos de Espana, op. 232: Prelude; Orientale; Sous le Palmier; Cordoba; Seguidillas. See no. 16
Espana, op. 165: Tango. See no. 3993

15 Iberia. Alicia de Larrocha, pno. Turnabout 34750/1 Tape (c) 4750/1
++CL 12-79 p11 ++HF 12-81 p93

Iberia: Carnival in Seville. See no. 3717

16 Iberia: Evocacion; El puerto; Fete-Dieu a Seville; Rondena; Almeria; Triana; El Albaicin; El polo; Lavapies; Malaga; Jerez; Eritana. Navarra. Cantos de Espana, op. 232: Prelude; Orientale; Sous le Palmier; Cordoba; Seguidillas. Alicia de Larrocha, pno. London CSA 2235 (2) Tape (c) OSA 5-2235 (also Decca SXL 6586/7)
++Gr 10-73 p695 +NYT 7-12-81 pD21
+HF 6-74 p79 ++RR 10-73 p32
++HF 7-78 p70 tape ++SFC 2-17-74 p28
++MJ 11-74 p51 +SR 10-5-74 p11
+-NR 6-74 p11 ++St 3-74 p110

Iberia: Fete Dieu a Seville. See no. 3817
Mallorca, op. 202. See no. 22. See no. 3765

17 Navarra. DEBUSSY: La plus que lente. RAVEL: Forlane. SCHUMANN: Arabesque, op. 18, C major. Symphonic etudes, op. 13. Artur Rubinstein, pno. RCA ARL 1-3850 Tape (c) ARK 1-3850
+CL 4-81 p12 +-HFN 6-81 p82
+-FF 5/6-81 p144 +-HFN 9-81 p93 tape
+-Gr 7-81 p178 +NR 4-81 p11
*Gr 10-81 p614 tape +NYT 3-22-81 pD 23
+-HF 11-81 p100 +SFC 3-1-81 p19

Navarra. See no. 16

18 Piezas caracteristicas, op. 92: Torre bermeja. Recuerdos de

viaje, op. 71: Rumores de la caleta. Suite espanola, op. 47: Asturias. FALLA: El amor brujo: El circulo magico; Cancion del fuego fatuo. El sombrero de tres picos: Danza del molinero. GRANADOS: Danzas espanolas, op. 37: Villanesca. TURINA: Fandanguillo, op. 36. Sonata, guitar, op. 61, D major. Narciso Yepes, gtr. DG 2542 157 Tape (c) 3342 157 (From DG 2530 159)
+Gr 9-81 p418

19 Piezas caracteristicas, op. 92: Torre bermeja. BACH: Partita, violin, no. 2, S 1004, D minor: Chaconne (trans. Newman). SAINZ DE LA MAZA: Campanas del alba. TURINA: Fandanguillo, op. 36. Michael Newman, gtr. Sheffield LAB 10
++ARG 11-79 p31 ++HFN 1-81 p104
+FF 11/12-79 p15 +SFC 12-23-79 p40
+FF 7/8-80 p174 ++St 11-79 p104
+-HF 11-79 p116

Piezas caracteristicas: Torre bermeja. See no. 3727
Piezas caracteristicas: Zambra; Torre bermeja. See no. 22
Recuerdos de viaje, op. 71: Rumores de la caleta. See no. 18. See no. 3727

20 Seguidillas, no. 5. CHOPIN: Valse brillante, E flat major. Sonata, piano, no. 2, op. 35, B flat major. GRIEG: Lyric pieces, op. 12: Ariette; Feuille d'album. Lyric pieces, op. 43: To the spring. Papillon. Norwegian bridal procession. MOSZKOWSKI: Waltz, E flat major. Arthur de Greef, pno. Bruno Walter Society RH 2
+/FF 9/10-81 p233

Songs: Besa el aura; Del salon. See no. 3889
Suite espanola, op. 47: Asturias. See no. 18. See no. 3727. See no. 3886
Suite espanola, op. 47: Cadiz. See no. 3694

21 Suite espanola, op. 47: Cataluna. CHABRIER: Espana.* FALLA: El amor brujo.* GRANADOS: Danzas espanolas, op. 37: Villanesca; Asturiana; Mazurca. Ines Rivadeneyra, ms; Spanish Radio and TV Orchestra; Igor Markevitch. Philips 6527 068 Tape (c) 7311 068 (*From SAL 3659)
+-Gr 8-81 p282 +HFN 9-81 p89
+-Gr 8-81 p282 +HFN 9-81 p89

Suite espanola, op. 47: Granada; Sevillanas; Cadiz; Asturias. See no. 22
Tango, op. 163, no. 2. See no. 22

22 Works, selections: Cantos de Espana, op. 232: Cordoba. Mallorca, op. 202. Piezas caracteristicas, op. 92: Zambra; Torre bermeja. Suite espanola, op. 47: Granada; Sevillanas; Cadiz; Asturias. Tango, op. 163, no. 2. John Williams, gtr. CBS 36679 Tape (c) 41-36679
++Gr 11-81 p720

ALBENIZ, Melchior
Sonata, D major. See no. 3701
Sonata, guitar, D major. See no. 4001

d'ALBERT, Eugen
23 Die Abreise. Edda Moser, t; Peter Schreier, t; Hermann Prey, bar; PH; James Kulka. EMI 1C 065 30800
++FF 9/10-81 p56

Tiefland, excerpts. See no. 4122
Tiefland: Schau her das ist ein Taler. See no. 3747. See no. 3966

Tiefland: Wolfserzahlung. See no. 3800

ALBERT, Heinrich

Herbstlied. See no. 3985

24 Songs: Letzte Rede einer vormals stolzen; Quid not praestat amor. KITTEL: Coridon der gieng betrubet; Jetz und kompt die Nacht herbey. NAUWACH: Ach Liebste lass uns eilen. SCHEIN: Amor das blinde Gottelein; Der edle Schafer Coridon; Einsmals wett Coridon; O Scheiden o bitter Scheiden; O Sternenaugelein in grosser Traurigkeit. Rene Jacobs, alto; Konrad Junghanel, lt and theorbo. Accent ACC 8015
+Gr 1-81 p985 +HFN 1-81 p103

ALBERT, Stephen

25 To wake the dead. PERERA: Poems of Gunter Grass (3). Elsa Charlston, s; Sheila Marie Allen, s; Boston Musica Viva, Pro Musica Moderna; Electronic tape; Richard Pittman, Charles Fussell. CRI SD 420
+-ARG 4-81 p31 ++NR 2-81 p12
++FF 1/2-81 p163

ALBERTO, Luys

Piece, 3 parts. See no. 3778

ALBINONI, Tomaso

Adagio, G minor. See no. 3924. See no. 3980. See no. 4115

26 Concerti, op. 2 (12). I Solisti Veneti; Claudio Scimone. Erato STU 71234 (2) (also Musical Heritage Society MHS 4242/3)
+-FF 3/4-81 p54 -MT 12-80 p783
+-Gr 4-80 p1549 +RR 4-80 p52
+-HFN 4-80 p100

Concerto, op. 5, no. 5, A major. See no. 3767

27 Concerti, op. 9, nos. 2, 5, 8, 11. Heinz Holliger, ob; I Musici. Philips 9502 012 Tape (c) 7313 012
+FF 3/4-80 p34 +NR 8-80 p7
++HF 4-80 p104 tape +NYT 12-2-79 pD22
+HFN 7-81 p81

28 Concerto, op. 9, no. 2, D minor (orch. Thilde). Concerto "St Mark" (recon. Thilde). TELEMANN: Concerto, trumpet, D major (ed. Grebe). TORELLI: Sonata, trumpet, D major (arr. Tarr). VIVALDI: Concerto, trumpet, A flat major (trans. and arr. Thilde). Stacy Blair, tpt; Jean-Francois Paillard Chamber Orchestra; Jean-Francois Paillard. Erato STU 71379
+Gr 10-81 p567

29 Concerto, op. 9, no. 2, D minor (trans.). BARSANTI: Concerto grosso, op. 3, no. 10, D major. HANDEL: Sonata, violin, op. 1 no. 12, F major (trans.). OTTO: Concerto, trumpet, E flat major. Maurice Andre, tpt; Wurttemberg Chamber Orchestra; Jorg Faerber. HMV ASD 4030
+Gr 8-81 p282 +-HFN 7-81 p78

30 Concerti, op. 9, nos. 3, 6, 9, 12. Heinz Holliger, Maurice Bourgue, ob; Maria Teresa Garatti, hpd; I Musici. Philips 9502 012 Tape (c) 7313 012 (From AXS 3005)
+Gr 7-81 p151 ++NR 5-81 p8
++HFN 11-81 p105 tape

31 Concerti, op. 10. Piero Toso, Giuliano Carmignola, vln; I Solisti Veneti; Claudio Scimone. Erato STU 71311 (2) (also Musical Heritage Society MHS 824361)
++FF 11/12-91 p80 ++HFN 12-80 p131
+Gr 11-80 p660

Concerto, oboe, D major. See no. 3633
32 Concerto, trumpet, B flat major. HUMMEL: Concerto, trumpet, E major. TELEMANN: Sonata, trumpet, D major. Guy Touvron, tpt; ECO; Jean-Claude Casadesus. Accord ACC 140 001
+-HFN 11-81 p103
33 Concerto, trumpet, B flat major. TARTINI: Concerto, trumpet, D major. TORELLI: Concerti, trumpet, D major (2). Sonata, trumpet, D major. Jean-Luc Dasse, tpt; Bologna Filharmonic; Angelo Ephrikian. Harmonia Mundi HM 1049
+HFN 7-81 p78
Concerto, trumpet, B flat major. See no. 4117
Concerto, "St. Mark". See no. 28
34 Pimpinone. Elena Zilio, ms; Domenico Trimarchi, bar; I Solisti Veneti; Claudio Scimone. Fonit-Cetra Italia ITL 70080
+Gr 9-81 p421 +STL 9-13-81 p41
35 Sonatas, op. 6 (12). Piero Toso, vln; Edoardo Farina, hpd, org; Susan Moses, vlc. Erato STU 71300 (2)
-Gr 10-81 p568 +HFN 11-81 p89
36 Trattenimenti armonici per camera, op. 6, no. 4, D minor (trans. Thilde). MOZART, L.: Concerto, trumpet, D major. TELEMANN: Concerto, oboe, F minor (trans.). VIVALDI: Concerto, oboe and violin, RV 548, B flat major (trans.). Maurice Andre, tpt; Daniele Artur, vln; Rouen Chamber Orchestra; Albert Beaucamp. Philips 6527 082 Tape (c) 7311 082 (From SAL 3662)
+Gr 8-81 p282
ALBRECHTSBERGER, Johann Georg
37 Concerto, organ, B flat major. BACH, C.P.E.: Concerto, organ, E flat major. HAYDN: Concerto, organ, F major. Jane Parker-Smith, org; PCO; Steuart Bedford. Supraphon 110 2624
+FF 9/10-81 p251 ++NR 6-81 p6
38 Partita, harp, F major. HOFFMEISTER: Concerto, flute, D major. Janos Szebenyi, flt; Anna Lelkes, hp; Gyor Philharmonic Orchestra; Janos Sandor. Hungaroton FX 12299
+HFN 5-81 p75
Partita, harp, F major. See no. 1853
ALBRIGHT, William
Chichester mass: Sanctus, Benedictus and Agnus Dei. See no. 3637
39 Dream rags. Grand sonata in rag. Rags (5). William Albright, pno. Musical Heritage Society MHS 4253
++FF 3/4-81 p54 +HF 8-81 p65
Grand sonata in rag. See no. 39
40 The king of instruments. PERSICHETTI: Chorale prelude. Sonata, organ, op. 86. David Craighead, org. Crystal S 181
+NR 9-81 p15
41 Pianagogog. PHILLIPS: Sonatas, piano, nos. 1 and 2. WATTS: Sonata, piano. Dean Sanders, pno. Trilogy Records/ Composers Theatre Series CTS 1003
+FF 5/6-81 p206
Rags (5). See no. 39
ALCOCK, John
Voluntary, D major. See no. 3905
ALCOCK, Walter
42 Out of the deep. BYRD: Exalt thyself O God, anthem. EAST: O Lord of whom I do depend; When Israel came out of Egypt; When David heard that Absalom was slain. Magnificat: Nunc Dimittis.

HARRIS, W.: Almighty and most merciful father; I was glad when they said unto me; Come down O lord divine; King of glory king of peace. Lichfield Cathedral Choir; Peter King, org; Jonathan Rees-Williams. Abbey Alpha APS 311
+-Gr 11-80 p728 +-NR 3-81 p10

ALEXANDER, R.
The southerner march. See no. 3817

ALEXIUS, Carl
43 Sonatina. GERSHWIN: Rhapsody in blue (arr. Dokschitzer). HINDEMITH: Sonata, trumpet and piano. MARTINU: Sonatina. Edward Tarr, tpt; Elisabeth Westenholz, pno. BIS LP 152
+FF 1/2-81 p225 +HF 3-81 p77
+Gr 1-81 p966

ALFONSO X, King
44 Las cantigas de Santa Maria: Des quando Deus; Des oge mais; A virgen mui gloriosa; Tod aqueste mund'a loar; Tan beeyta foi; Pois que dos reys. MARTIN CODAX: Cantigas de amigo: Ondas do mar de Vigo; Mandad'ey comigo; Mia irmana fremosa; Ay Deus se sab' ora meu amigo; Quantas sabedes amar amigo; Eno sagrado en Vigo; Ay ondasque eu vin veer. Euterpe Ensemble for Old Music Paris. Harmonia Mundi HM 1060
+FF 11/12-81 p80 ++Gr 10-81 p586

45 Las cantigas de Santa Maria: Santa Maria strela do dia; A que pera parayso; Dized ai trobadores; Pero que seja a gente; Quena festa e o dia. Schola Cantorum Basiliensis; Thomas Binkley. Harmonia Mundi 1C 065 99898
++FF 7/8-81 p48 +-HFN 4-81 p77
+Gr 3-81 p1224

46 Las cantigas de Santa Maria, nos. 20, 27, 60, 150, 159, 322, 340, 384, 391. Ester Lamandier, singer, harp, portatif, viele. Astree AS 59
++FF 11/12-81 p80 +HFN 11-81 p89
++Gr 11-81 p728

ALFORD, Harry
Colonel Bogey march. See no. 3699

ALFORD, Kenneth
A step ahead. See no. 3817

ALFVEN, Hugo
Notturno elegiaco, op. 5. See no. 3683

47 Symphony, no. 4, op. 39, C minor. Elizabeth Soderstrom, s; Gosta Winbergh, t; Stockholm Philharmonic Orchestra; Stig Westerberg. Bluebell Bell 107
+FF 3/4-80 p35 +Gr 8-81 p256

48 Synnove solbakken, op. 50. LINDE: Prelude and finale, op. 16. OLANDER: Symphony, E major. SKOLD: Sommar. Vasteras Orchestra; Harry Damgaard. Connoisseur S 1005
/Gr 8-81 p317

ALISON, Richard
Dolorosa pavan. See no. 3945
Go from my windoe. See no. 4059
Lady Francis Sidney's goodmorowe. See no. 4059
Mr. Allisons knell. See no. 4059
Sharp pavin. See no. 3937

ALKAN, Charles
Barcarolle. See no. 51

Barcarollette. See no. 50
Les diablotins. See no. 50
Etudes, A flat major. See no. 50
Etudes dans les tons mineurs, op. 39: Scherzo diabolico. See no. 51
49 Fantasy, G major. Minuet, op. 51, no. 3, G major. Grande sonate, op. 33. Suite, no. 3, op. 65: Barcarolle, G minor. Pierre Reach, pno. RCA RL 3-7243
+-CL 5/6-81 p9
Le frisson. See no. 50
Gigue, op. 24. See no. 51
Grande sonate, op. 33. See no. 49
Gros temps. See no. 50
Heraclite et Democrite. See no. 50
Marche, op. 37, no. 1. See no. 51
Marcia funebre sulla morte d'un pappagallo. See no. 50
Minuet, op. 51, no. 3, G major. See no. 49
Nocturne, no. 2. See no. 51
Petite conte. See no. 50
50 Piano works: Barcarollette. Les diablotins. Etude, A flat major. Le frisson. Gros temps. Heraclite et Democrite. Marcia funebre sulla morte d'un pappagallo. Petite conte. Scherzetto. Les soupirs. Sonatine. Le tambour bat aux champs. Raymond Lewenthal, pno. CBS 61117
+Gr 8-81 p288 +-HFN 9-81 p77
51 Piano works: Barcarolle. Gigue, op. 24. Marche, op. 37, no. 1. Nocturne, no. 2. Saltarelle, op. 23. Etudes dans les tons mineurs, op. 39: Scherzo diabolico. Soantine, op. 61. Zorcico. Bernard Ringeissen, pno. Harmonia Mundi HM 927
+-FF 11/12-81 p81 +Gr 9-78 p500
Saltarelle, op. 23. See no. 51
Scherzetto. See no. 50
52 Sonata, violoncello and piano, op. 47. Yehuda Hanani, vlc; Edward Auer, pno. Finnadar SR 9030
+FF 9/10-81 p57 ++St 9-81 p85
++NR 8-81 p8
Sonatine. See no. 50
Sonatine, op. 61. See no. 51
Les soupirs. See no. 50
Suite, no. 3, op. 65: Barcarolle, G minor. See no. 49
Le tambour bat aux champs. See no. 50
Zorcico. See no. 51

ALLANBROOK, Douglas
53 Naples music. Venice music. BACH: Prelude and fugue, F sharp minor. HAYDN: Sonata, piano, no. 42, D major. Douglas Allanbrook, pno. Richardson RRS 70010
/NR 12-81 p15
Venice music. See no. 53

ALLDAHL, Per-Gunnar
Biceps. See no. 4072

ALLEGRI, Gregorio
54 Miserere. MUNDY: Vox patris caelestis. PALESTRINA: Missa Papae Marcelli. Alison Stamp, treble; Tallis Scholars; Peter Philips. Classics for Pleasure CFP 40339 Tape (c) T C CFP 40339
+Gr 10-80 p523 +HFN 10-80 p110

+Gr 12-80 p889 tape +HFN 12-80 p159 tape
+Gr 12-81 p944 tape

ALLITSEN, Mary Frances
The Lord is my light. See no. 4046
Psalm, no. 27. See no. 3967

ALMEIDA, Laurindo
55 Concerto, guitar, no. 1. Lobiana. GNATTALI: Concerto, guitar, no. 4. Laurindo Almeida, gtr; Los Angeles Orchestra de Camera; Elmer Ramsey. GS 2026 (From Concord CC 2001)
-FF 5/6-81 p38 +-NR 6-81 p7
Lobiana. See no. 55

ALONSO, Lopez Francisco
Maitechu mia. See no. 3983

ALTENBERG, Johann
Concerto a 7. See no. 3979
Concerto, trumpet, D major. See no. 3761

ALVARADO, Diego de
Tiento por Delasolrre. See no. 4098

ALVAREZ
La mantilla. See no. 4031
Suspiros de Espana. See no. 3981

ALVAREZ, Fermin
La partida. See no. 3983

AMALIA, Princess of Prussia
Regimental marches (3). See no. 3814

AMMERBACH, Elias
Ich sag ade. See no. 3676
Wer das Tochterlein haben will. See no. 3622. See no. 4012

AMON, Johann Andreas
56 Sonata, flute, E flat major. SPOHR: Sonata, violoncello and harp, op. 115, G major. Martin Ulrich Senn, flt; Chantal Matheiu, hp. Jecklin 548
+-FF 1/2-81 p162

ANDERSON
Blue tango. See no. 3816
Forgotten dreams. See no. 3816
How firm a foundation. See no. 3809
Syncopated clock. See no. 3816

ANDREE, Elfride
Quintet, E major: Allegro molto vivace. See no. 3814

ANDRIESSEN, Jurriaan
57 Concertino, bassoon and wind ensemble. DOWNEY: The edge of space. JACOB: Concerto, bassoon. Robert Thompson, bsn; LSO, ECO; Geoffrey Simon. Chandos ABRD 1033 Tape (c) ABTD 1033
/Gr 12-81 p883 +HFN 11-81 p101

ANDRIESSEN, Louis
In memoriam. See no. 3728

d'ANGLEBERT, Jean-Henri
Chaconne, D major. See no. 3916
58 Pieces de clavecin. CHAMBONNIERES: Pieces de clavecin. Edward Smith, hpd. Titanic TI 8
+AR 11-81 p133
59 Suites, D minor, G major, G minor. Kenneth Gilbert, hpd. Harmonia Mundi HMU 941
+FF 9/10-81 p57 +MT 11-79 p920

+Gr 1-76 p1221 +RR 3-78 p57
+Gr 9-79 p487 +RR 8-79 p100
++HFN 1-76 p105 +St 6-76 p100
++HFN 9-79 p100

60 Suite, no. 1, G major. Transcriptions of works by Jean-Baptiste Lully: Air d'Apollon du triomphe de l'amour; Chaconne de Phaeton; Courante and double de la courante; Dans nos bois; Gigue; Menuet; Ouverture de Cadmus; Sarabande: Dieu des enfers; Les songes agreable d'Atys. William Neil Roberts, hpd.
+ARG 11-81 p20 +FF 9/10-81 p57

Le tombeau de M. de Chambonnieres. See no. 3916

Transcriptions of works by Jean-Baptiste Lully. See no. 60

ANGUS

Our father which in heaven art. See no. 4101

ANNA AMALIA, Duchess of Saxe Weimar

61 Concerto, 12 instruments and cembalo. Divertimento. CHAMINADE: Concertstuck, piano, op. 40. TAILLEFERRE: Ballade. Rosario Marciano, pno; Vienna Chamber Orchestra; Kurt Rapf. Turnabout TV 34754 Tape (c) CT 2276
+FF 9/10-81 p242 +HFN 11-81 p103

Divertimento. See no. 61

Erwin and Elmore, excerpts. See no. 3814

d'ANNIBALE

Paese d' 'o sole. See no. 3641. See no. 3843

ANSELMI, Giuseppe

Songs: Su l'ocean, fragment; La villanella; La serenata; Pater noster. See no. 4027

ANTHEIL, George

62 Symphony, no. 5. MAXWELL DAVIES: St. Thomas wake. Louisville Orchestra; Richard Duffallo. Louisville LS 770
++ARG 2-81 p12 +NR 11-80 p3
+-FF 11/12-80 p134 +St 3-81 p90

ANTONI, Giovanni Degli

63 Ricercata, no. 8. BOCCHERINI: Concerto, violoncello, no. 5, G major.* Sonata, violoncello, no. 7, B major. GABRIELLI, D.: Canon.* SAMMARTINI: Sonata, 2 violoncelli, no. 3, A minor. Anner Bylsma, vlc; Anthony Woodrow, violone; Gustav Leonhardt, hpd; Jaap Schroder, vln; Dijck Koster, vlc; Concerto Amsterdam, Telefunken AP 6-42653 Tape (c) CR 4-42653 (From SAWT 9473, 9548)
+Gr 10-81 p567

ANTONIOTTI, Giorgio

Sonata, no. 9, C minor. See no. 4096

APPLETON, Jon

In deserto. See no. 64

Mussems sang. See no. 64

The Sydsing camklang. See no. 64

Syntrophia. See no. 64

64 Works, selections: In deserto. Mussems sang. The Sydsing camklang. Syntrophia. Zoetrope. Jon Appleton, synclavier and other digital systems. Folkways 33445
+-ARG 2-79 p10 /NR 2-81 p15
+NR 1-80 p15

Zoetrope. See no. 64

AQUILON, Enar

65 Pieces, piano: Den forverkligande; Jag-initial; Lakande vagspel; Ur hjarte-krafter. Pieces, violin: Sommarsondagssang; Vordnad

verkar vaxande. Songs: Folkvisa; Hostens var. Nicolai Gedda, t; Ulf Ingwall, vln; Barbro Aquilon, pno. Artemis ART 50-103
++FF 3/4-81 p55
Pieces, violin: Sommarsondagssang; Vordnad verkar vaxande. See no. 65
Songs: Folkvisa; Hostens var. See no. 65
ARAUJO, Juan
Los cofla desde la estleya. See no. 3911
ARAUJO, Pedro de
Batalha de 6th tono. See no. 3958
ARCADELT, Jacques
Ancidetimi pur. See no. 3766
Da si felice sorte. See no. 3766
Defecerunt. See no. 3909
Donna quando pietosa. See no. 3766
Madrigals: Ahime ahime dov' e'l bel viso; Il bianco e dolce cigno; Il ciel rado virtu tanta mostra; O felici occhi miei; Ver' infern' el'el mio petto; Voi mi ponest in foco; Voi ve n'andat al cielo. See no. 4010
ARDITI, Luigi
Il bacio. See no. 3721
Parla. See no. 4083
ARFIB, Daniel
66 Musique numerique. Laboratoire de Mecanique et d'Acoustique, Marseille, France.
+CMJ Fall 1981 p84
ARGENTO, Dominick
Trio carmina paschalia. See no. 3925
ARIOSTI, Attilio
La profezio d'Eliseo nel'assedio di Amaria: Ma per destin peggiore...Prole tenera. See no. 3813
67 Sonatas, viola d'amore and harpsichord, E flat major, A major, E minor (2), F major, D major. Nane Calabrese, vla d'amore; Claudio Scimone, hpd. Musical Heritage Society MHS 4337
+FF 9/10-81 p58
ARMA, Paul
Comme une improvisation. See no. 68
Deux structures mouvantes. See no. 68
Lumieres et ombres. See no. 68
Sept transparences. See no. 68
Sonatine. See no. 68
68 Works, selections: Comme un improvisation. Lumieres et ombres. Sonatine. Deux structures mouvantes. Sept transparences. Jean-Pierre Rampal, flt; Roy Christensen, vlc; Jacques Desloges, sax; Marie-Christine and Francois Doublier, pno; Philarte Quartet. Gasparo GS 214
+NR 11-81 p6
ARMENIAN SACRED SONGS. See no. 3974
ARNAUD, Leo
69 Fanfares: Olympic theme; La chasse; Olympiad. GRAINGER: Lincolnshire posy. Shepherd's hey. VAUGHAN WILLIAMS: English folk song suite. Toccata marziale. Cleveland Symphony Winds; Frederick Fennell. Telarc DG 10050
+FF 1/2-81 p228 ++MUM 2-81 p30
+Gr 8-80 p326 +NR 1-81 p15
+HFN 9-80 p114 ++St 1-81 p89

ARNDT, Felix
Marionette. See no. 4104
ARNE, Thomas
70 Artaxerxes. Elizabeth Vaughan, Sandra Browne, Margaret Cable, Sandra Dugdale, John Brecknock, soloists; New Chamber Soloists Orchestra and Chorus; Maurits Sillem. MRF Records MRF 162 (2)
++FF 1/2-81 p56
British Grenadiers. See no. 3699
Concerto, harpsichord, no. 1, F major. See no. 3877
Rule Brittania. See no. 3699
Sonata, harpsichord, no. 3, G major. See no. 3732
Sonata, harpsichord, no. 6, G major. See no. 3733. See no. 4103
Songs: The lass with a delicate air. See no. 3657
Songs: The street intrigue; Whch is the properest day to drink. See no. 4058
Songs: When daisies pied; Where the bee sucks. See no. 3844
Under the greenwood tree. See no. 3853
ARNESTAD, Finn
71 Concerto, violin. Iesus Nazaremus Rex Iudaeorum. Oslo Philharmonic Orchestra; LPO; Okko Kamu, Kjell Ingrebretsen; Ole Bohn, vln. Philips 6578 107
+FF 9/10-81 p58
Iesus Nazeremus Rex Iudaeorum. See no. 71
ARNOLD, Malcolm
Concerto, flute, op. 45. See no. 72
72 Concerto, flute, no. 2, op. 111. Concerto, flute, op. 45. Serenade, small orchestra. Sinfonietta, no. 3, op. 81. Richard Adeney, flt; Bournemouth Sinfonietta; Ronald Thomas. HMV ASD 3868 Tape (c) TC ASD 3868
+FF 1/2-81 p56 +HFN 9-80 p115 tape
++Gr 7-80 p135 +RR 8-80 p36
+Gr 8-80 p548 tape
73 Concerto, guitar, op. 67. BROUWER: Concerto, guitar. John Williams, gtr; London Sinfonietta; Elgar Howarth. CBS 76715 Tape (c) 40-76715 (also CBS M 36680 Tape (c) MT 36680)
*FF 7/8-81 p50 +HFN 10-78 p121
++Gr 9-78 p461 +HFN 1-79 p127 tape
+RR 9-78 p40 ++St 9-81 p85
74 Concerto, guitar, op. 67. GIULIANI: Concerto, guitar, op. 30, A major. Julian Bream, gtr; Melos Ensemble; Malcolm Arnold. RCA AGL 1-3883 Tape (c) GK 1-3883 (From LSC 2847)
+FF 9/10-81 p59 +Gr 11-81 p678
75 English dances (Johnstone). GRAINGER: Over the hills and far away (Erickson). ISRAEL: concerto, piano and wind ensemble. VIVALDI: Concerto, trumpet, G minor (Stith). Brian Israel, pno; Marice Stith, tpt; Cornell University Wind Ensemble; Marice Stith, Mark Taggart. Cornell CUWE 27
/FF 1/2-81 p233
Little suite, brass. See no. 3721
Quintet, brass. See no. 3898
Quintet, brass, op. 73. See no. 3798
Serenade, small orchestra. See no. 72
Sinfonietta, no. 3, op. 81. See no. 72
Sonatina, op. 29. See no. 3714
76 Symphony, brass instruments, op. 123. PREMRU: Music for Harter

Fell. SALZEDO: Capriccio, op. 90. Philip Jones Brass Ensemble; Howard Snell. Argo ZRG 906 Tape (c) KZRC 906
+-FF 1/2-81 p227 +HFN 12-79 p177
++Gr 11-79 p801 ++RR 11-79 p67
+Gr 2-80 p1302
Tam O'Shanter, op. 51. See no. 3722
ARRAS, Thomas
A.B.C. See no. 3728
ARRIAGA Y BALZOLA, Juan de
77 Quartets, strings, nos. 1-3. Chilingirian Quartet. CRD CRD 1012/3 (2) Tape (c) CRDC 4012/3
+Gr 6-75 p56 +RR 6-75 p57
+Gr 11-81 p783 tape +-St 3-76 p108
+HFN 9-75 p91E ++STL 1-4-76 p36
+-HFN 10-81 p95 tape
ARRIEU, Claude
78 Trio, oboe, clarinet and bassoon. FRANCAIX: Impromptus, flute and bassoon (7). GERSTER: Cantata, flute, oboe, clarinet and bassoon. KETTING: Trio, flute, clarinet and bassoon. Soni Ventorum. Crystal S 254
+-FF 9/10-81 p276 +NR 7-81 p6
ARZRUNI, Sahan
Heterophonic suite, excerpts. See no. 3913
Invocation. See no. 3913
Mentations, no. 1. See no. 3913
ASHFIELD, Robert
The fair chivalry. See no. 3615
ASHFORTH, Alden
Sentimental waltz. See no. 3942
ASTVATSATRIAN
Prologue and motet. See no. 3917
ATTAIGNANT, Pierre
Branles (5). See no. 3766
Galliard. See no. 3676
ATTERBERG, Kurt
79 Suite, violin and viola, no. 3. LARSSON: Pastorale suite, op. 19. A winter's tale, op. 18: Vignettes (4). ROMAN: Concerto, oboe d'amore, D major. ROSENBERG: Small piece, violoncello. Alf Nilsson, ob d'amore; Nils Erik Sparf, vln; Juoko Mansnerus, vla; Elemer Lavotha, vlc; Stockholm Sinfonietta; J-O. Wedin. BIS LP 165
++FF 1/2-81 p230 +HFN 1-81 p107
+Gr 3-81 p1237
Symphony, no. 4, op. 14, G minor. See no. 9
Symphony, no. 6, op. 31, C major. See no. 4122
80 Symphony, no. 8, E minor. BUSONI: Overture to a comedy. Helsingborg Symphony Orchestra; Lennart Hedwall. Aries LP 1630
+-FF 1/2-81 p57
ATTWOOD, Thomas
Songs: Come holy ghost. See no. 3873
Songs: Turn thee again, O Lord, at the last. See no. 3824
AUBER, Daniel
81 Le cheval de bronze. OFFENBACH: La chanson de Fortunio. Sonia Nigoghossian, Armand Arapian, Leonard Pezzino, Isabel Garcisanz, Ulrik Cold, Anne-Marie Rodde, Brigitte Bellami, soloists; ORTF, NPhO Orchestra and Chorus, Orchestra; Jean-Pierre Marty,

A. Paris. MRF Records MRF 164 (3)
+FF 1/2-81 p58
Les diamants de la Couronne: Overture. See no. 84
Domino noir: Overture. See no. 84
82 Fra Diavolo. Bernadette Antoine, Remy Corazza, Gerard Friedmann, Tibere Raffalli, Jean Brun, soloists; Strasbourg Opera du Rhin Orchestra and Chorus; Jean-Marc Cochereau. VOCE 26 (2)
+FF 11/12-81 p82
Fra Diavolo: Overture. See no. 84
Fra Diavolo: Pour toujours disait-elle. See no. 3648
83 Manon Lescaut. Mady Mesple, s; Emmy Greger, ms; Jean-Claude Orliac, Gerard Friedmann, t; Peter-Christoph Runge, Yves Bisson, Alain Duverry, bar; Radio France Lyric Orchestra and Chorus; Jean-Pierre Marty. Arabesque 8059-3 (3) Tape (c) 9059-3
+FF 3/4-81 p55 +NR 1-81 p10
+HF 7-81 p71 +St 6-81 p110
Marco Spada: Overture. See no. 84
La muette de Portici: Overture. See no. 84
La part du diable: Overture. See no. 84
Les rendezvous: Allegro non troppo; Allegro. See no. 3840
84 Works, selections (overtures): Diamants de la Couronne. Domino noir. Fra diavolo. Marco Spada. La muette de Portici. La part du diable. Monte Carlo Opera Orchestra; Sylvain Cambreling. HMV ESD 7096 Tape (c) TC ESD 7096
-Gr 4-81 p1310 +HFN 2-81 p85
AUDRAN, Edmond
La mascotte: Couplets de Fritellini; Couplets du tambour. See no. 4051
AUFDERHEIDE, May
Pelham waltzes. See no. 4104
AULIN, Tor
85 Aquarelles (4). BRAHMS: Sonata movement (Scherzo), violin and piano. SUK: Pieces, violin and piano, op. 17 (4). Nilla Pierrou, vln; Eugene de Cank, pno. Opus 3 7912
+FF 9/10-81 p257
AURIC, Georges
86 Imaginees, nos. 1-6. Michele Debost, flt; Frederic Lodeon, vlc; Claude Desurmont, clt; Michele Command, s; Jean-Philippe Collard, pno; Parrenin Quartet. EMI 2C 069 16287
+Gr 7-81 p164
Songs: Chansons de Lise Hirtz; Printemps. See no. 3687
Trio, oboe, clarinet and bassoon. See no. 3934
AUSTIN, Larry
87 Hybrid musics. Irida 0022
+CMJ Fall 1981 p84
AYLEWARD, Richard
Preces and responses. See no. 3895
AZARASHVILI, Vazha
88 Concerto, viola. GABUNIYA: Elegy. TSINTSADZE: Fantasy, quartet. Yuriy Yurov, vla; Georgia State String Quartet, Georgia State Chamber Orchestra; Eduard Sanadze. Melodiya S10 12791/2
+FF 9/10-81 p284
AZZAIOLO, Filippo
Sentemi la formicula. See no. 3945

BABADJANIAN, Arno

89 Andante. Suite, piano. BEETHOVEN: Sonata, piano, no. 23, op. 57, F minor. LISZT: Mephisto waltz. Seta Tanyel, pno. Golden Age 1010

-FF 9/10-81 p237

Dance of Vagharshapat. See no. 3917

Images: Chorale; Dance of the people of Sassoun. See no. 3917

Prelude. See no. 3917

Suite, piano. See no. 89

BABBITT, Milton

90 Composition, viola and piano. GHENT: Entelechy. PERSICHETTI: Parable, no. 16, op. 130. POLLOCK: Violament. John Graham, vla; Robert Black, pno. CRI SD 446

+-NR 9-81 p7

Minute waltz (or 3/4 ± 1/8). See no. 3942

91 Philomel. SESSIONS: Sonata, piano, no. 3. Bethany Beardslee, s; Robert Helps, pno. New World Records NW 307

+FF 1/2-81 p59 +NYT 4-12-81 pD29

BABELL, William

Concerto a 7, D major. See no. 4095

BABOU, Rene

92 Fantaisie des trompettes basses et hautes. CHAUMONT: Suite sur le 2nd ton. SCRONX: Echo, F major, C major. Jozef Sluys, org. Zephyr ZO 6

+-Gr 7-80 p153 +MT 3-81 p197

+HFN 9-80 p114

BACEWICZ, Grazyna

Ten studies, nos. 2 and 8. See no. 3918

Triptych. See no. 3918

BACH

The sea named solaris. See no. 4003

BACH, Carl Philipp Emanuel

Adagio, D minor. See no. 105

93 Concerti, flute, A minor, B flat major. Stephen Preston, flt; English Concert; Trevor Pinnock, hpd. DG 2533 455

++Gr 7-81 p151 +HFN 8-81 p77

94 Concerto, flute, D minor. STAMITZ: Concerto, flute, op. 29, G minor. VIVALDI: Concerto, flute, op. 10, no. 3, D major. Eugenia Zukerman, flt; ECO; Pinchas Zukerman. Columbia M 35879

+FF 1/2-81 p60 +NR 12-80 p5

95 Concerto, flute, D minor. HOFFMEISTER: Concerto, flute, no. 6, D major. Ingrid Dingfelder, flt; ECO; Charles Mackerras. Nonesuch H 71388

/ARG 6-81 p13 +FF 1/2-81 p61

96 Concerti, harpsichord, A major, D major. Malcolm Hamilton, hpd; Los Angeles Chamber Orchestra; Gerard Schwarz. Nonesuch D 79015 Tape (c) DI 79015

+FF 9/10-81 p60 ++SFC 6-21-81 p18

+HF 10-81 p91 tape +St 10-81 p115

97 Concerto, harpsichord, D minor. Concerto, oboe, E flat major. Gustav Leonhardt, hpd; Helmut Hucke, ob; Collegium Aureum; Franzjosef Maier. Harmonia Mundi 065 99828

+FF 11/12-81 p83 +MT 12-80 p783

+Gr 9-80 p326 +RR 7-80 p48

+-HFN 7-80 p117

98 Concerti, harpsichord, Wq 14, E major; Wq 43, no. 5, G major. MOZART: Concerto, piano, K 107, D major. English Concert; Trevor Pinnock, hpd and cond. Vanguard VSD 71265 (From CRD)
+ARG 5-81 p10 ++NR 1-81 p4
+FF 3/4-81 p57
99 Concerto, harpsichord, Wq 112, no. 1, C major. Sonatas, harpsichord, nos. 1-6, Wq 48. Bob van Asperen, hpd. Telefunken 6-35460 (2)
+FF 3/4-81 p55
100 Concerto, 2 harpsichords. BACH. J. S.: Concerto, harpsichord, S 1052, D minor. Gustav Leonhardt, Alan Curtis, hpd; Collegium Aureum. Harmonia Mundi 065 99785
+HFN 11-80 p131 +MT 6-81 p388
101 Concerti, oboe, B flat major, E flat major. Peter Pongracz, ob; Ferenc Liszt Chamber Orchestra; Janos Sandor. Hungaroton SLPX 12120
+ARG 4-81 p31 +NR 1-81 p4
+FF 5/6-81 p39 +SFC 7-19-81 p19
+HFN 12-80 p131
Concerto, oboe, E flat major. See no. 97
Concerto, organ, E flat major. See no. 37
102 Concerto, violoncello, A major. COUPERIN: Pieces en concert (arr. Bazelaire). VIVALDI: Concerti, violoncello, G minor, G major (arr. Malipiero). Lynn Harrell, vlc; ECO; Pinchas Zukerman. HMV ASD 3899 Tape (c) TC ASD 3899 (also Angel SZ 37738)
+-ARG 7-81 p47 +HFN 12-80 p159 tape
++FF 1/2-81 p59 +-NR 2-81 p6
+-Gr 11-80 p684 +ST 5-81 p46
+HFN 10-80 p111
Fantasias, nos. 1-2. See no. 106
103 Fantasia and fugue, C minor. Prelude, D major. BACH, J. S.: Chorale prelude, S 770, Ach was soll ich Sunder machen. Prelude and fugue, S 545, C major. BACH, W. F.: Fugues, F major, G minor. Rudolf Zartner, org. Pape 10
++NR 4-81 p13
104 Fantasia and fugue, C minor. Sonata, organ, no. 2, B flat major. BACH, J. M.: Wenn wir in hochsten Noten sein. BACH, J. S.: Chorale preludes, S 659, Nun komm der Heiden Heiland; S 671, Kyrie Gott heiliger Geist. Prelude and fugue, S 552, E flat major. Gerald Gifford, org. Vista VPS 1088
+Gr 6-81 p56 ++NR 12-80 p10
Fantasia and fugue, C minor. See no. 105
Fugues, D minor, E flat major. See no. 105
105 Organ works: Adagio, D minor. Fantasia and fugue, C minor. Fugues, D minor, E flat major. Sonatas, organ, nos. 1-6. Prelude, D major. Herbert Tachezi, org. Telefunken EX 6-35453 (2)
+FF 3/4-81 p57 +HFN 8-79 p99
+-Gr 10-79 p672 +RR 7-79 p82
Prelude, D major. See no. 103
Prelude, D minor. See no. 105
106 Rondos, 1-3. Fantasias, nos. 1-2. Sonatas, haprisichord, nos. 1, 3. Inger Grudin-Brandt, cld and fortepiano. BIS LP 142
+ARG 7-81 p10 +HFN 10-80 p102
-FF 1/2-81 p62
107 Sinfonias, nos. 1-4. ECO; Raymond Leppard. Philips 9502 013 (From SAL 3701)

++FF 7/8-80 p42 ++NR 7-80 p3
++Gr 8-81 p261 ++St 6-80 p83
+HFN 9-81 p89 +STL 9-13-81 p41

108 Sinfonias, nos. 1-6; C major, D major. Academy of Ancient Music; Christopher Hogwood. L'Oiseau-Lyre DSLO 557/8 (2) Tape (c) KDSL 2-7064
++ARG 6-81 p14 ++NR 2-81 p2
++FF 5/6-81 p38 ++RR 11-79 p68
+Gr 11-79 p802 +RR 4-80 p128 tape
+HFN 11-79 p133 +STL 12-2-79 p37
+MUM 11/12-81 p32

109 Sinfonias, nos. 1-6. English Concert; Trevor Pinnock. DG 2533 449 Tape (c) 3310 449
++FF 5/6-81 p38 +HFN 10-80 p101
+Gr 10-80 p487 +MT 3-81 p180
++Gr 3-81 p1171 +NR 2-81 p5
+HF 6-81 p69 tape

110 Sinfonias, nos. 2-5. Collegium Aureum. Harmonia Mundi 1C 065 99691
+FF 11/12-81 p83

111 Sonata, G minor. FREDERICK II, King: Sonata, flute, no. 17, A major. GRAUN: Sonata, F major. QUANTZ: Sonata, flute, F major. Nuremberg Chamber Soloists. Intercord INT 120 938
+-HFN 11-81 p101

112 Sonata, flute, A minor. BENDA: Sonata, flute and harpsichord, op. 3, no. 1, G major. KLEINKNECHT: Sonata, flute and oboe, C minor. MUTHEL: Sonata, flute, D major. Manfred Zimmermann, flt; Renate Hildebrand, ob; Christophe Coin, vlc; Philip Swanton, Alina Parker, hpd. Orpheus ORP 0702
+-Gr 5-81 p1493 +-HFN 8-81 p90

113 Sonata, flute, A minor. STAMITZ: Concerti, flute, D major, G major. James Galway, flt; New Irish Chamber Orchestra; Andre Preiur. RCA RL 2-5315 Tape (c) RK 2-5315 (also ARL 1-3858)
+-FF 3/4-81 p155 ++NR 3-81 p6
+Gr 11-80 p660 +SFC 7-19-81 p19
+HFN 1-81 p101

114 Sonatas, flute and harpsichord, D major, E major, G major (2). Andras Adorjan, flt; Huguette Dreyfus, hpd. Denon OX 7082
++HFN 5-81 p75

115 Sonatas, harpsichord, F major, B minor. BACH, J.C.F.: Sonatina, A minor. BACH, W.F.: Sonata, harpsichord, B flat mainor. Rolf Junghanns, cld. Telefunken 6-42073 Tape (c) 4-42073
+FF 5/6-80 p192 +Gr 9-81 p406

116 Sonatas, harpsichord (6). Sonatine nuove (6). Christopher Hogwood, cld. L'Oiseau-Lyre DSLO 589
+Gr 8-81 p290 +HFN 7-81 p70

Sonatas, harpsichord, nos. 1, 3. See no. 106
Sonatas, harpsichord, nos. 1-6. See no. 99
Sonata, harpsichord, no. 1, op. 2, A minor. See no. 3698. See no. 3832
Sonata, harpsichord, no. 5, C major. See no. 3807
Sonatas, organ, nos. 1-6. See no. 105
Sonata, organ, no. 2, B flat major. See no. 104
Sonata, organ, no. 5, D major. See no. 3735

117 Sonata, organ, no. 6, G minor. BALBASTRE: Il est un petit ange.

Noel "Votre bonte grand Dieu". MOZART: Adagio and rondo, K 617, C major. Fugue, K 401, G minor. STANLEY: Voluntary, no. 7. Gunther Kaunzinger, org. Solist 1183
+-FF 9/10-81 p247

118 Sonata, viola, G minor. BACH, W.F.: Sonata, viola, C minor. Karel Spelina, vla; Josef Hala, hpd; Frantisek Slama, vlc. Supraphon 111 2615
+FF 9/10-81 p60 +NR 7-81 p7

119 Sonata, violin and harpsichord, B minor. BACH, J.C.: Sonatas, violin and harpsichord, op. 10 (3). Carol Lieberman, vln; Mark Kroll, hpd. Titanic TI 90
++FF 7/8-81 p51 +St 5-81 p64

120 Sonata, violin and harpsichord, W 73, C major. LEDUC: Sonatas, violin and harpsichord, op. 1, no. 1, D major; op. 4, nos. 1, 4. Carol Lieberman, Baroque vln; Mark Kroll, hpd. AFKA SK 299
+-FF 3/4-81 p34

Sonatine nuove. See no. 116

Songs: Der Fruhling; Passionalied. See no. 3985

121 Trio sonata, A major. BACH, J.S.: Trio sonata, S 525, G major. TELEMANN: Sonata, flute, G major. Suite, flute, D minor. Kuijken Quartet. Accent ACC 8019
+FF 7/8-81 p220 +HFN 6-81 p81
++Gr 8-81 p288 +MUM 7/8-81 p31

122 Trio sonatas, C minor, B flat major, E major. Ars Rediviva. Supraphon 111 1675
++FF 11/12-80 p55 +NR 10-80 p8
+Gr 10-80 p511 *SFC 7-19-81 p19
+HFN 10-80 p102

123 Trio sonata, D minor. FREDERICK II, King: Symphony, D major. GRAUN: Trio sonata, F major. QUANTZ: Concerto, flute, G major. Hans-Ulrich, flt; Kammerorchester Emil Seiler; Stuttgart Kammermusikkreis. DG 2547 014 Tape (c) 3347 014
+HFN 1-81 p190 tape

BACH, Johann Christian

124 Arias: Ach dass ich Wassers g'nug hatte. BUXTEHUDE: Muss der Tod denn nun doch trennen. Jubilate Domino, cantata. TELEMANN: Ach Herr strafe mich nicht. Rene Jacobs, c-t; Kuijken Consort. Accent ACC 7912
+FF 1/2-81 p221 +RR 6-80 p13
++HFN 6-80 p101

125 Quartet, oboe, violin, viola and violoncello, B flat major. HAYDN, M.: Divertimento, P 99. Quartet, P 115, C major. MOZART: Adagio, K 580a, C major. Heinz Holliger, ob, Eng hn; Antonio Salvatore, vln; Massimo Paris, vla; Vito Paternoster, vlc; Lucio Buccarella, bs. Denon OX 7185
++FF 1/2-81 p210 ++St 4-81 p74
+HFN 5-81 p87

126 Sinfonias, op. 3, nos. 1-6. Simon Preston, hpd; AMF; Neville Marriner. Philips 9502 001 Tape (c) 7313 001 (From 6707 013)
++FF 11/12-79 p21 +HFN 1-81 p109 tape
+Gr 11-80 p660 ++SFC 6-10-79 p45
++HF 9-79 p109 ++St 10-79 p146
+HFN 11-80 p129

127 Sinfonias, op. 3, nos. 4, 6; op. 6, no. 3; op. 9, no. 2. Deutsche Bachsolisten; Helmut Winschermann. Arabesque 8078 Tape (c) 9078

+FF 3/4-81 p58 +NR 2-81 p5

Sinfonia, op. 6, no. 3. See no. 127

128 Sinfonias, op. 6, no. 6; op. 18, nos. 4, 6. Collegium Aureum. Harmonia Mundi 065 99759

+FF 9/10-81 p62 +RR 10-79 p75
+HFN 10-79 p167

Sinfonias, op. 9, no. 2. See no. 127

Sinfonias, op. 18, no. 1, E flat major. See no. 129

129 Sinfonia concertante, A major. Sinfonia, op. 18, no. 1, E flat major. Franzjosef Maier, vln; Angelica May, vlc; Collegium Aureum; Reinhard Peters. Harmonia Mundi 1C 065 99827

+FF 3/4-80 p40 +HFN 4-80 p117
+FF 11/12-81 p83 +RR 4-80 p55

130 Sinfonia concertanti, C major, F major, E flat major. Collegium Aureum; Franzjosef Maier. Harmonia Munid 065 99790

+FF 11/12-81 p83 ++RR 2-80 p45
+HFN 2-80 p85

Sonata, harpsichord, op. 5, no. 6, Cminor. See no. 3732

Sonatas, violin and harpsichord, op. 10 (3). See no. 119

BACH, Johann Christoff Friedrich

131 Die Kindheit Jesu. Esther Himmler, s; Ingeborg Russ, alto; Urs Dettwyler, t; Bruce Abel, bs; Trossingen Martin Luther Church Choir; Gerd Witte. Musical Heritage Society MHS 4086 (also FSM 53034)

-FF 7/8-80 p42 +MU 10-81 p8

Sonatina, A minor. See no. 115

BACH, Johann Michael

Wenn wir in hochsten Noten sein. See no. 104

BACH, Johann Sebastian

Adagio, S 968, C major. See no. 3832

Air. See no. 4100

Air with 15 variations, A minor. See no. 4087

132 Anna Magdalena notebook, S 508, excerpts. Judith Blegen, s; Benjamin Luxon, bar; Igor Kipnis, hpd, cld; Catharina Neints, vla da gamba. Nonesuch DB 79020

+NYT 12-6-81 pD27

Anna Magdalena notebook, S 508: Bist du bei mir. See no. 3626. See no. 3844

Anna Magdalena notebook, S 508: Bist du bei mir; Erbauliche Gedanken eines Tabakrauchers. See no. 3985

Allabreve, S 589, D major. See no. 275. See no. 284. See no. 292

Aria, S 587, F major. See no. 276. See no. 284. See no. 291

Ave Maria. See no. 3725. See no. 3753. See no. 3852. See no. 3924. See no. 3967. See no. 3999

133 Brandenburg concerti, nos. 1-6, S 1046-1051. Los Angeles Chamber Orchestra; Gerard Schwarz. Angel DBS 3901 DSSC 4504 (2) Tape (c) 4Z2S 3901 (45 rpm) DSSC 4504

+ARG 12-80 p14 +NR 5-81 p3
+-FF 9/10-80 p52 ++NYT 6-8-80 pD20
+-FF 7/8-81 p52 ++SFC 6-22-80 p36
+-HF 10-80 p71 +-SFC 4-5-81 p18
+-NR 8-80 p6 +St 9-80 p78

134 Brandenburg concerti, nos. 1-6, S 1046-1051. DBS; Helmut Winschermann. Arabesque 8088 (2) Tape (c) 9088

+NR 12-81 p3

135 Brandenburg concerti, nos. 1-6, S 1046-1051. Wendy Carlos, synthesizer. Columbia M2X 35895 (2) Tape (c) M2T 35895 (also CBS 79227 Tape (c) 40-79227. From 73163, 73395 (nos. 2-5)
+FF 9/10-80 p52 +MUM 1/2-81 p30
+Gr 7-80 p167 +NYT 5-25-80 pD21
+-HF 6-80 p67 +-RR 7-80 p49
++HFN 7-80 p105 +SR 8-80 p83
++HFN 9-80 p115 tape +-St 10-80 p108

136 Brandenburg concerti, nos. 1-6, S 1046-1051. BPhO; Herbert von Karajan. DG 2531 332/3 Tape (c) 3301 332/3 (From 2707 112)
+-Gr 8-81 p256 +-HFN 8-81 p92 tape
+Gr 10-81 p614 tape

137 Brandenburg concerti, nos. 1-6, S 1046-1051. BPhO; Herbert von Karajan. DG 2707 112 (2) Tape (c) 3370 030
+ARG 6-81 p12 +HFN 9-81 p89
-FF 11/12-80 p56 +-MUM 2-81 p30
+-Gr 6-80 p31 ++NR 9-80 p2
+Gr 8-80 p275 tape +-RR 6-80 p39
+-HF 10-80 p71 +SFC 7-13-80 p33
+-HF 3-81 p80 tape +SR 8-80 p83
+-HFN 6-80 p102 +-St 9-80 p78
+-HFN 8-80 p109 tape

138 Brandenburg concerti, nos. 1-6, S 1046-1051. Lucerne Festival Strings; Rudolf Baumgartner. Eurodisc 300 086 (2) Tape (c) 500 086
+-FF 11/12-81 p84 +-HF 11-81 p103 tape
+HF 10-81 p78 +-NYT 7-26-81 pD23

139 Brandenburg concerti, nos. 1-6, S 1046-1051. Suites, orchestra, S 1066-1069. Collegium Aureum. Harmonia Mundi 197 53000/3 (4)
+-HFN 12-80 p153 ++ST 2-81 p733

140 Brandenburg concerti, nos. 1-6, S 1046-1051. Bath Festival Orchestra; Yehudi Menuhin, vln and vla. HMV SXDW 3054 (2) Tape (c) TC ASDW 3054 (From ASD 327/8)
+Gr 9-81 p372 +HFN 9-81 p89

141 Brandenburg concerti, nos. 1-6, S 1046-1051. Die Kunst der Fuge, S 1080. Ein musicalische Opfer, S 1079. Suites, orchestra, S 1066-1069. AMF; Neville Marriner. Philips 6786 232 (7)
+FF 9/10-81 p61 +-Gr 11-81 p678

142 Brandenburg concerti, nos. 1-6, S 1046-1051. AMF; Neville Marriner. Philips 9502 014/5 Tape (c) 7313 014/5 (From 6700 045)
+Gr 3-81 p1180 +HFN 7-81 p81 tape
+HFN 4-81 p80

143 Brandenburg concerti, nos. 1-6, S 1046-1051. Leonhardt Consort; Gustav Leonhardt. Pro Arte 2 PAX 2001 (2)
+FF 11/12-81 p96

144 Brandenburg concerti, nos. 1-6, S 1046-1051. Leonhardt Consort; Gustav Leonhardt. RCA RL 3-0400 (2)
+-FF 9/10-80 p51 ++HFN 8-81 p81
-Gr 8-81 p256

145 Brandenburg concerti, nos. 1-6, S 1046-1051. VCM; Nikolaus Harnoncourt. Telefunken 6-35043 Tape (r) N 6-35043
++Audio 11-79 p127 +HF 6-79 p96 tape
+FF 9/10-81 p62

146 Brandenburg concerti, nos. 1-6, S 1046-1051. ECO; Johannes Somary. Vanguard VSD 71208/9 (2) (Q) VSQ 30049/50 Tape (c) 471208/9

++HF 3-76 p79 ++SFC 11-30-75 p34
++HF 6-81 p69 tape ++St 4-76 p110
+NR 2-76 p3

147 Brandenburg concerti, nos. 1-6, S 1046-1051. VSOO Members; Hermann Scherchen. Westminster MCA 2-9500 (2) (From WST 307)
-FF 11/12-80 p57 /-MUM 1/2-81 p30

Brandenburg concerti, nos. 1-6, S 1046-1051. See no. 362

148 Brandenburg concerti, nos. 1, 3-4, S 1046, 1048-1049. VCM; Nikolaus Harnoncourt. Telefunken 6-41191 Tape (c) 4-41191 (From SAWT 9549/60)
+Gr 4-81 p1310 +-HFN 3-81 p95

149 Brandenburg concerti, nos. 2-3, 5, S 1047-1048, 1050. Thomas Stevens, tpt; Anne Diener Giles, flt; David Weiss, ob; Pinchas Zukerman, vln; Zita Carno, hpd; LAPO Members; Pinchas Zukerman. DG 2531 292 Tape (c) 3301 292 (From 2707 098)
+-ARG 12-81 p9 +-NR 5-81 p3
-FF 5/6-81 p40

150 Brandenburg concerto, no. 3, S 1048, G major. Die Kunst der Fuge, S 1080: Contrapuncti (3). Ein musicalische Opfer, S 1079, C major: Ricercar a 6. Prelude and fugue, S 541, G major (arr.). Sofia Chamber Orchestra; Vassil Kasandjiev. Denon OX 7028
+HFN 5-81 p76

Brandenburg concerto, no. 3, S 1048, G major. See no. 360. See no. 3767. See no. 3980

Brandenburg concerto, no. 3, S 1048, G major: 1st movement. See no. 3617

151 Brandenburg concerto, no. 5, S 1050, D major. HANDEL: Sonatas, recorder, op. 1, no. 4, A minor; D minor. HOTTETERRE: Bourree d'Achille. Suite, op. 2: Ecos pour la flute traversiere, B major. Trio sonata, op. 3, C major. MOZART: Concerto, violin, no. 1, K 207, B flat major. Frans Bruggen, rec; Leonhardt Consort; Gustav Leonhardt. RCA RL 3-0333 (2)
+FF 9/10-81 p261 +HFN 9-81 p89

152 Brandenburg concerto, no. 5, S 1050, D major. Suite, orchestra, S 1067, B minor. Marcel Moyse, flt; Adolf Busch, vln; Rudolf Serkin, pno; Busch Chamber Orchestra; Adolf Busch. Seraphim 60357 (From various EMI 78s)
+FF 5/6-81 p42 +MUM 11/12-81 p30
+HF 9-81 p68

Brandenburg concerto, no. 5, S 1050, D major. See no. 261

Canone perpetuo. See no. 3807

153 Cantatas. nos. 5, 26, 38, 70, 80, 96, 115, 116, 130, 139, 140, 180. Edith Mathis, s; Trudeliese Schmidt, ms; Peter Schreier, t; Dietrich Fischer-Dieskau, bar; Munich Bach Orchestra and Choir; Karl Richter. DG 2722 030 (6)
+FF 11/12-81 p88 +-HFN 3-79 p119
+-Gr 4-79 p1750 +-RR 4-79 p107

154 Cantata, no. 11, Lobet Gott in seinen Reichen. Cantata, no. 34, O ewiger Jeuer. Margaret Marshall, s; Alfreda Hodgson, con; Martyn Hill, t; Stephen Roberts, bar; King's College Choir; ECO; Adrian Partington, org; Philip Ledger. HMV ASD 4055 Tape (c) TC ASD 4055
+-Gr 11-81 p728 +-HFN 10-81 p85

155 Cantatas (Advent and Christmas), nos. 13, 28, 58, 61, 63-65, 81-82, 111, 121, 124, 132, 171. Lotte Schadle, Edith Mathis, Sheila

Armstrong, s; Hertha Topper, Anna Reynolds, alto; Peter Schreier, Ernst Hafliger, t; Dietrich Fischer-Dieskau, Theo Adam, bs; MB and Choir; Karl Richter. DG 2722 005 (6). (Reissues)

+Gr 11-72 p935 +RR 10-76 p92
+-HF 2-73 p74 +SFC 12-13-81 p18
+HFN 12-72 p2436 +SR 12-81 p64
++NR 2-73 p8 +St 2-73 p111
+RR 11-72 p93

156 Cantata, no. 21, Ich hatte viel Bekummernis. Indiana University Chamber Singers; Bach Collegium Stuttgart; Helmuth Rilling. Musical Heritage Society MHS 3641 (From Claudius Verlag)

/-MU 4-81 p20

Cantata, no. 29: Sinfonia. See no. 360

Cantata, no. 29: Wir danken dir Gott wir danken dir: Sinfonia. See no. 361

157 Cantatas, nos. 32, 51, 57, 74, 128, 134, 147, 151, 173, 191. Ileana Cotrubas, Elly Ameling, Agnes Giebel, s; Birgit Finnila, Julia Hamari, con; Kurt Equiluz, Dieter Ellenbeck, t; Hermann Prey, William Reimer, bar; Barmen-Gemarke Singers; German Bach Soloists Chorus, Westphalian Singers, Netherlands Vocal Ensemble; Helmut Winschermann. Philips 6770 049 (5) (From From 6500 080, 6500 014, 6500 386)

+Gr 12-81 p912

Cantata, no. 34, O ewiger Feuer. See no. 154

158 Cantata, no 36, Schwingt freudig euch empor. Cantata, no. 209, Non sa che sia dolore. Edith Mathis, s; Peter Schreier, t; Siegfried Lorenz, bs; Berlin Solisten; Berlin Chamber Orchestra; Peter Shcreier. DG 2533 453

++ARG 11-81 p16 +Gr 8-81 p302
++FF 11/12-81 p85 +HFN 9-81 p77

Cantata, no. 50, Nun ist das Heil. See no. 267

159 Cantata, no. 51, Jauchzet Gott in allen Landen. Christmas oratorio, S 248: Grosser Herr und starker Konig. HANDEL: Messiah: The trumpet shall sound. Samson: Let all bright seraphim. TELEMANN: Psalm, no. 111: Ich danke dem Herrn, Er sendent eine Erlosung seinem Volk. Lucia Popp, s; Jorma Hynninen, bs; Carol Dawn Reinhart, tpt; Amsterdam Kammerorchestra; Marinus Voorberg. Acanta EA 23147

+-FF 9/10-81 p273

160 Cantata, no. 51, Jauchzet Gott. Cantata, no. 199, Mein Herze schwimmt. Edita Gruberova, s; Deutsche Bachsolisten; Helmut Winschermann. RCA ARL 1-3715

+-ARG 6-81 p13 +NR 2-81 p8
+-FF 3/4-81 p59

161 Cantata, no. 56, Ich will den Kreuzstab gerne tragen. Cantata, no. 82, Ich habe genug. Michael Schopper, bs; Philippe Huttenlocher, bs; Hanover Boys Choir; Leonhardt Consort, VCM; Gustav Leonhardt, Nikolaus Harnoncourt. Telefunken AQ 6-42579 Tape (c) 4-42579 (From EX 6-35304, EX 6-35363)

+Gr 11-81 p728

162 Cantata, no. 73, Herr wie du willt. Cantata, no. 94, Was frag ich nach der Welt. Jorg Erler, Wilhelm Wiedle, boy sopranos; Paul Esswood, alto; Kurt Equiluz, t; Max van Egmond, Philippe Huttenlocher, bs; Leonhardt Consort, VCM; Hanover Children's Chorus, Collegium Vocale Ghent, Tolzer Boys Choir; Gustav Leon-

hardt, Nikolaus Harnoncourt. Telefunken 6-42664 Tape (c) 6-42664
+Gr 9-81 p460 tape ++HFN 3-81 p97

163 Cantata, no. 78, Wir eilen mit schwachen. Cantata, no. 140, Wachet auf. Concerto, 2 harpsichords, S 1060, C minor. Suite, orchestra, S 1067, B minor. Maurice Andre, Lionel Andre, Janos Rolla, tpt; Franz Liszt Chamber Orchestra; Zsuzsa Pertis, continuo. Angel SZ 37728
*FF 3/4-81 p65 +-NR 2-81 p6

164 Cantata, no. 78, Wir eilen mit schwachen doch emsigen Schritten. Chorale preludes, S 645, Wachet auf ruft uns die Stimme. Prelude and fugue, S 542, G minor. DITTERSDORF: Concerto, harp, A major: Rondeau and allegretto. HANDEL: Concerto, harp, op. 4, no. 6, B flat major: Andante allegro. Walter music: Suite; Allegro; Andante espressiveo; Allegro deciso. MOZART: Serenade, no. 13, K 525, G major. Martin Geliot, hp; Suttgart Chamber Orchestra; Karl Munchinger. Intercord INT 160 824
+-FF 5/6-81 p216 +-HFN 11-81 p100

165 Cantata, no. 82, Ich habe genug. Cantata, no. 169, Gott soll allein mein Herze haben. Janet Baker, ms; Simon Preston, org; Derek Simpson, vlc; John Gray, double bs; Colin Tilney, org, hpd; Ambrosian Singers; Bath Festival Orchestra; Yehudi Menuhin. HMV SXLP 30289 Tape (c) TC SXLP 30289 (From ASD 2302)
++Gr 5-79 p1918 +-HFN 6-79 p117
++Gr 7-79 p259 tape +HFN 7-79 p119 tape
+Gr 12-81 p945 tape +RR 6-79 p110

Cantata, no. 82, Ich habe genug. See no. 161
Cantata, no. 94, Was frag ich nach der Welt. See no. 162
Cantata, no. 98, Wass Gott tut das ist wohlgetan. See no. 3881

166 Cantatas, nos. 99-102. Wilhelm Wiedl, Detlef Bratschke, treble; Paul Esswood, alto; Kurt Equiluz, t; Philippe Huttenlocher, bar; Max van Egmond, bs; Tolzer Boys Choir, Hanover Boys Choir, Ghent Collegium Vocale; VCM, Leonhardt Consort; Nikolaus Harnoncourt, vlc and cond; Gustav Leonhardt. Telefunken EX 6-35443 (2)
+FF 1/2-81 p62 +-HFN 11-80 p115
+Gr 12-80 p859 ++NR 2-81 p8
+HF 11-81 p73

167 Cantatas, nos. 103-106. Wilhelm Wiedle, Marcus Klien, treble; Raphael Harten, alto; Paul Esswood, c-t; Kurt Equiluz, Marius van Altena, t; Max van Egmond, Philippe Huttenlocher, Ruud van der Meer, bs; Knabenchor Hannover, Collegium Vocale, Ghent, Tolzer Knabenchor, VCM; Gustav Leonhardt, Nikolaus Harnoncourt. Telefunken 6-35558 (2)
+-FF 3/4-81 p59 +-HF 11-81 p73
+-Gr 8-81 p299

Cantata, no. 106: Sonatina. See no. 3853

168 Cantatas, nos. 107-110. Kurt Equiluz, t; Max van Egmond, bs; Hanover Boys Choir, Ghent Collegium Vocale; Leonhardt Consort; Gustav Leonhardt. Telefunken 6-35559
+FF 7/8-81 p52 +-HF 11-81 p73
++Gr 5-81 p1501

169 Cantatas, nos. 111-114. Gustav Leonhardt, hpd; Hanover Boys Choir, Collegium Vocale; Sebastian Hennig, s; Rene Jacobs, Detlef Bratschke, alto; Kurt Equiluz, t; Max van Egmond, bs; Leonhardt Consort; Gustav Leonhardt. Telefunken 6-35573 (2)

+FF 11/12-81 p96 +STL 7-12-81 p40
+Gr 7-81 p178

Cantata, no. 112, Der Herr ist mein getreuer Hirt. See no. 3671

Cantata, no. 118, O Jesu Christ mein Lebens Lichts. See no. 267

170 Cantata, no. 140, Wachet auf. Passacaglia and fugue, C minor. Toccata and fugue, S 565, D minor. FRESCOBALDI: Toccata. HANDEL: Water music: Suite. PACHELBEL: Canon. Canadian Brass. RCA RL 1-3654

+Gr 7-81 p195

Cantata, no. 140, Wachet auf. See no. 163. See no. 359

171 Cantata, no. 147, Jesu joy of man's desiring. Cantata, no. 161, Komm Susser Tod. Chorale preludes, S 599, Nun Komm der Heiden Heiland; S 645, Wachet auf ruft uns die Stimme. MOZART: Fantasia, K 396, C minor. Rondo, piano, K 511, A minor. Sonata, piano, no. 15, K 545, C major. Thomas Richner, pno. Towerhill T 1011

-FF 7/8-81 p136 +St 8-81 p96

Cantata, no. 147, Jesu joy of man's desiring. See no. 360. See no. 3700. See no. 3725. See no. 3749. See no. 3796. See no. 3898. See no. 3924. See no. 3992

Cantata, no. 156: Arioso. See no. 363

Cantata, no. 161, Komm du susse Todesstunde. See no. 171

Cantata, no. 169, Gott soll allein mein Herze haben. See no. 165

Cantata, no. 199, Mein Herze schwimmt im Blut. See no. 160

172 Cantata, no. 202, Weichet nur. Cantata, no. 204, Ich bin in mir vergnugt. Edith Mathis, s; Peter Schreier, t; Berlin Solisten and Kammerorchester; Peter Schreier. DG 2533 363

+SFC 12-20-81 p18

173 Cantata, no. 204, Ich bin in mir vergnugt. Cantata, no. 209, Non sa che si dolore. Jana Jonasova, s; Ars Rediviva; Milan Munclinger. Supraphon 112 2453

-FF 3/4-81 p60 +NR 2-81 p8

Cantata, no. 204, Ich bin in mir vergnugt. See no. 172

174 Cantata, no. 207, Vereinigte Zwietracht der wechseinden Saiten. Cantata, no. 214, Tonet ihr Pauken. Edith Mathis, Julia Hamari, s; Peter Schreier, t; Siegfried Lorenz, bar; Theo Adam, bs; Berlin Chamber Orchestra; Berlin Soloists. DG 2533 401

+SFC 12-20-81 p18

Cantata, no. 208, Schafe konnen sicher weiden. See no. 3853

Cantata, no. 209, Non sa che sia dolore. See no. 158. See no. 173

175 Cantata, no. 210, O holder Tag erwunschte Zeit. Judith Nelson, s; Bach Ensemble; Joshua Rifkin. Nonesuch D 79013 Tape (c) DI 79013

+FF 11/12-81 p84 ++St 12-81 p75
++HF 12-81 p93 tape

176 Cantata, no. 211, Schweiget stille plandet nicht. Cantata, no. 212, Mer hahn en neue Oberkeet. Lisa Otto, s; Josef Traxel, t; Dietrich Fischer-Dieskau, bar; St. Hedwig's Cathedral Choir Members; BPhO; Karl Foster. EMI 1C 037 29014

+FF 11/12-81 p85

Cantata, no. 212, Mer hahn en neue Oberkeet. See no. 176

Cantata, no. 214, Tonet ihr Pauken. See no. 174

177 Cantata, S 249a, Entflieht verschwindet entwiechet ihr Sorgen. Edith Mathis, s; Hetty Plumacher, alto; Theo Altmeyer, t;

Jakob Stampfli, bs; Gachinger Kantorei; Figuralchor der Gedachtniskirche; Bach Collegium; Helmuth Rilling. SDG 610204
+Gr 2-81 p972 +HFN 12-80 p132

Canzona, S 588, D minor. See no. 276. See no. 284. See no. 292

Capriccio, S 992, B flat major. See no. 255. See no. 4087

Capriccio, S 993, E major. See no. 285

178 Chorales, 4-part. Regensburg Domspatzen; Collegium St. Emmeram; Hanns-Martin Schneidt. DG 2533 436
+FF 3/4-81 p60

Chorale preludes, Drauf schliess ich mich; Lobet den Herrn. See no. 4060

Chorale preludes, In dulci jubilo; Meine Seele erhebet den Herrn. See no. 3921

179 Chorale prelude, Vater unser im Himmelreich. DAVID: Chaconne, A minor. MENDELSSOHN: Sonata, organ, op. 65, no. 6, D minor. Arno Schonstedt, org. Pape 11
++NR 4-81 p13

Chorale prelude, S 63, Liebster, Jesu, wir sind hier. See no. 3811

Chorale preludes, S 140, Zion hort die Wachter singen; S 147, Wohl mir dass ich Jesum habe, Jesus bleibet meine Freude; S 307, Es ist gewisslich an der Zeit; S 727, Herzlich tut mich verlangen; S 639, Ich ruf zu dir Herr Jesu Christ; S 645, Wachet auf ruft uns die Stimme; S 659, Nun komm der Heiden Heiland; S 727, Herzlich tut mich verlangen; S 734, Nun freut euch lieben Christen g'mein; S 751, In dulci jubilo. See no. 361

Chorale preludes, S 572, 690-713, 736. See no. 273

180 Chorale preludes, S 599-644. Peter Hurford, org; Alban Singers. Argo ZRG 766/8 (3)
+Gr 10-74 p723 +RR 10-74 p83
-HF 5-75 p69 +-SR 6-81 p68
++MT 7-75 p628 ++STL 2-9-75 p37

181 Chorale preludes, S 599-644. Michel Chapuis, org. Telefunken EK 6-35085 (2)
+-Gr 11-76 p837 ++SFC 10-10-76 p32
+-HFN 10-76 p163 +SR 6-81 p68
-RR 10-76 p82

Chorale preludes, S 599, 600, 603, 607, 618-619. See no. 4117

Chorale preludes, S 599, Nun komm der Heiden Heiland; S 645, Wachet auf ruft uns die Stimme. See no. 171

Chorale preludes, S 599, Nun kom der Heiden Heiland; S 639, Ich ruf zu dir Herr Jesu Christ. See no. 3749

Chorale preludes, S 603-615. See no. 289

182 Chorale preludes, S 605, Der Tag der ist so freudenreich; S 615, In dir ist Freude; S 641, Wenn wir in hochsten Noten sein. DISTLER: Nun komm der Heiden Heiland, partita. MENDELSSOHN: Prelude and fugue D minor. Arno Schonstedt, org. Pape 202
+-FF 7/8-80 p169 +NR 2-81 p13

183 Chorale preludes, S 614, Das alte Jahr vergangen ist; S 683, Vater unser im Himmelreich; S 618, O Lamm Gottes unschuldig. Toccata and fugue, S 538, D minor. KREBS: Ach Gott erhor mein Seufzen. Von Gott will ich nicht lassen. Trio, C minor. GHEYN: Prelude and fugue, G minor. VOGLER: Preludes, B minor, E flat major. Rune Engso, org. BIS LP 124
+FF 7/8-81 p214 ++NR 2-81 p13

Chorale prelude, S 615, In dir ist Freude. See no. 288

Chorale preludes, S 618, O Lamm Gottes Unschuldig; S 663, Allein Gott in der Hoh sei Ehr; S 665/666, Jesus Christus unser Heiland; S 710, Wir Christenleut hab'n Jetzund Freud; S 736, Valet will ich dir geben; S 766, Christ der du bist der Helle Tag; S 767, O Gott du frommer Gott. See no. 286

184 Chorale prelude, S 641, Wenn wir in hochsten Noten sein; S 645, Wachet auf ruft uns die Stimme. Passacaglia and fugue, S 582, C minor. KEE: Gedenck-Clanck '76. SWEELINCK: Pavana lachrimae. Variations on "Allein Gott in der Hoh sei Ehr". Piet Kee, org. Guild GRSP 7017

+Gr 11-81 p720

185 Chorale prelude, S 641, Wenn wir in hochsten Noten sein; S 767, O Gott du frommer Gott: Partita. Toccata and fugue, S 565, D minor. DUPRE: Versets pour les Vepres du commun des fetes de la Sainte Vierge, op. 18: Antiphon; Magnificat, nos. 1 and 6. FRANCK: Fantaisia, A major. KARG ELERT: Pastels from the Lake Constance, op. 96: Pastel. Rondo alla campanella, op. 156. Ralph Downes, org. Vista VPS 1089

+Gr 5-80 p1694 -NR 1-81 p12
+MT 11-80 p712 +RR 4-80 p94
++MUM 11-81 p12

Chorale prelude, S 642, Wer nur den lieben Gott lasst walten. See no. 3961

186 Chorale preludes, S 643, Alle Menschen mussen sterben; S 737, Vater unser im Himmelreich. Fantasia and fugue, S 542, G minor. Passacaglia and fugue, S 582, C minor. Toccata, S 540, F major. Michael Murray, org. Telarc DG 10049

-FF 1/2-81 p64 +-HF 2-81 p63
+-Audio 3-81 p66 ++NR 10-80 p12
++Gr 10-80 p517

Chorale preludes, S 643, Alle Menschen mussen sterben. See no. 3673

Chorale preludes, S 645-650. See no. 281. See no. 284

Chorale preludes, S 645-650; S 659-661. See no. 286

Chorale preludes, S 645-650; S 726, Herr Jesu Christ dich zu uns wend; S 729, In dulci jubilo; S 728, Jesus meine Zuversicht; S 730/731, Liebster Jesu wir sind hier; S 732, Lobt Gott ihr Christen allzugleich; S 735, Valet will ich dir geben; S 737, Vater unser im Himmelreich; S 763, Sei gegrusset Jesu gutig: Partita; S 769, Vom Himmel hoch: Variations. See no. 275

187 Chorale preludes, S 645, Wachet auf ruft uns die Stimme; S 650, Kommst du nun Jesu. Fantasia and fugue, S 542, G minor. Prelude and fugue, S 552, E flat major. Toccata and fugue, S 565, D minor. Karl Richter, org. DG 2535 611

+-FF 11/12-81 p88

Chorale prelude, S 645, Wachet auf ruft uns die Stimme. See no. 164. See no. 360. See no. 363

Chorale prelude, S 648, Meine Seele erhebt den Herren. See no 3901

188 Chorale preludes, S 649-650, 645-648, 694-701, 703-704, 710-713, 715, 717-718, 722, 724, 729, 732, 738, 769. Fuga sopra il Magnificat, S 733. Michael Chapuis, org. Telefunken BC 25099-1/1-2 (2)

+AR 5-75 p51 +-NR 9-74 p11
+Gr 6-74 p71 +RR 4-74 p59
+HF 9-74 p85 +SR 6-81 p68

189 Chorale preludes, S 651-668. Peter Hurford, org; Alban Singers. Argo ZRG 843/4 (2)
+ARG 12-76 p10 +-SR 6-81 p68
+MT 6-77 p485 ++St 2-77 p112
+MU 9-77 p14

190 Chorale preludes, S 651-688. Michael Chapuis, org. Telefunken EK 6-35083 (2)
++Gr 10-75 p652 +RR 10-75 p69
+-HFN 10-75 p136 +SR 6-81 p68
-MU 10-76 p18

191 Chorale preludes, S 651-668, 653b. Clavierubung, S 552, 669-689, 683a, 802-5. Marie Claire Alain, org. Erato STU 71356 (4)
+Gr 7-81 p172

Chorale preludes, S 653, An Wasserflussen Babylon; S 656, O Lamm Gottes unschuldig; S 741, Ach Gott vom Himmel sich darein. See no. 291

192 Chorale preludes, S 654, Schmucke dich; S 658, Von Gott will ich nicht lassen; S 659, Nun komm der Heiden Heiland; S 662, Allein Gott in der Hoh (2); S 665, Jesus Christus unser Heiland; S 667, Komm Gott Schopfer. Hermann Harassowitz, org. Motette M 1011
+-FF 1/2-81 p79 /MU 11-80 p18

193 Chorale preludes, S 656, O Lamm Gottes unschuldig; S 658, Von Gott will ich nicht lassen; S 659, Nun komm der Heiden Heiland; S 668, Vor deinen Thron tret' ich hiermit; S 769, Vom Himmel hoch: Canonic variations. Fugue sopra il Magnificat, S 733. Preludes and fugues, S 533, E minor; S 544, B minor; S 547, C major; S 548, E minor. Gustav Leonhardt, org. RCA RL 3-0382 (2)
-Gr 10-81 p580

194 Chorale prelude, S 659, Nun komm der Heiden Heiland. Pastorale, S 590, F major. Toccata, S 540, F major. Toccata and fugue, S 565, D minor. Gabor Lehotka, org. Hungaroton SLPX 12198
+FF 5/6-81 p46 -NR 4-81 p12

Chorale preludes, S 659, Nun komm der Heiden Heiland. See no. 104

195 Chorale preludes, S 662-664, 651-666, 667-668. Alban Singers; Peter Hurford, org. Argo ZRG 843/4 (2)
++Gr 6-76 p71 +RR 9-76 p78
+HFN 8-76 p76 +-SR 6-81 p68

Chorale preludes, S 669/672, 670/673, 671/674, 675/676/677/716, 678/679, 680/681, 682/683, 684/685, 686/687, 688/689, 714, 719, 721, 723, 724, 733. See no. 274

Chorale preludes, S 671, Kyrie Gott heiliger Geist. See no. 104

Chorale preludes, S 690-1, 694-741, 743-745, 747, 751, 754, 762, 765, 891a, Anh 55. See no. 285

196 Chorale preludes, S 700/701, Vom Himmel hoch: Fugue. Chorale prelude, S 769, Vom himmel hoch: Variations. SCHOLZ: In paradisum. THIEME: Invocation. Viktor Scholz, org. Pape 6
+NR 4-81 p12

197 Chorale preludes, 714, 690-1, 706, 709, 720-721, 725-728, 730-1, 734, 736-737, 766-768. Michael Chapuis org. Telefunken BC 25103/1-2
+-NR 4-75 p10 +SR 6-81 p68

Chorale preludes, S 715, Allein Gott in der Hoh sei Ehr; S 720, Ein feste Burg ist unser Gott; S 722, Gelobet seist du Jesu Christ; S 738, Von Himmel hoch; S 766, Christ der du bist: Partita. See no. 277

Chorale preludes, S 717, 725, 740, 741, 747, 755, 758, 739, 765, Anh 55. See no. 278

Chorale prelude, S 720, Ein feste Burg ist unser Gott. See no. 363

Chorale preludes, S 727, Herzlich tut mich verlangen; S 734, Nun freut euch; S 736, Valet will ich dir geben. See no. 293

Chorale prelude, S 729, In dulci jubilo: Fantasia. See no. 289

198 Chorale prelude, S 767, O Gott du frommer Gott. MENDELSSOHN: Prelude and fugue, op. 37, no. 3, D minor. Sonata, organ, op. 65, no. 3, A major. REGER: Choral fantasies, op. 67: Meinen Jesum lass ich nicht; Wachet aur ruft uns die Stimme. Matthias Janz, org. Pape 16

+NR 4-81 p13

199 Chorale prelude, S 768, Sei gegrusset Jesu gutig: Partita. Passacaglia and fugue, S 582, C minor. Toccata and fugue, S 538, D minor. Karl Richter, org. DG 2533 441

+-FF 3/4-81 p64 +-NR 3-81 p14
+-Gr 8-80 p240 +-RR 8-80 p67
+-HFN 9-80 p99

Chorale prelude, S 769, Vom himmel hoch: Variations. See no. 196. See no. 289

200 Chorale prelude, S 770, Ach was soll ich Sunder machen: Partita. Prelude and fugue, S 532, D major. GARDONYI: Hommage a Marcel Dupre. KLUGE: Vater unser. Klaus Uwe Ludwig, org. Motette M 1024

+-FF 1/2-81 p222

Chorale prelude, S 770, Ach was soll ich Sunder machen. See no. 103

Chorale preludes, S 770, Ach was soll ich Sunder machen; S 771, Allein Gott in der Hoh sei Ehr. See no. 276

Christmas oratorio, S 248: Grosser Herr und Starker Konig. See 159

201 Christmas oratorio, S 248: Jauchzet frohlocket; Bereite dich Zion; Er ist auf Erden kommen arm...Wer will die Liebe recht erhohen; Symphony; Brich an o schones Morgenlicht; Frohe Hirten eilt ach eilet; Schaut hin dort liegt im finstern Stall; Schlafe mein Liebster geniesse der Ruh; Wir singen dir in deinem Herr; Flosst mein Heiland flosst dein Namen; Erleucht auch meine finstern Sinnen; Ach wenn wird die Zeit erscheinen; Ich steh an deiner Krippe hier. Elly Ameling, s; Brigitte Fassbaender, con; Horst Laubenthal, t; Hermann Prey, bs; Tolzer Boys Choir, Bavarian Radio Chorus; Bavarian Symphony Orchestra; Eugen Jochum. Philips 6527 070 Tape (c) 7311 070 (From 7603 037)

+Gr 11-81 p728 +-HFN 12-81 p109

202 Charomatic fantasia and fugue, S 903, D minor. Concerto, harpsichord, S 971, F major. Fantasia, S 906, C minor. Prelude and fugue, S 894, A minor. Huguette Dreyfus, hpd. Denon OX 7083

+HFN 5-81 p76

203 Chromatic fantasia and fugue, S 903, D minor. Concerto, harpsichord, S 971, F major. Partita, harpsichord, no. 1, S 825, B flat major. Ralph Kirkpatrick, hpd. DG 2535 213 (From 198003, 198 032, 198185)

+ARG 11-81 p14 +FF 9/10-81 p66

204 Chromatic fantasia and fugue, S 903, D minor. Suites, lute, S 995, G minor. Suite solo violoncello, S 1010, E flat major. Gustav Leonhardt, hpd. Pro Arte 1010 (also RCA RL 3-0391)

+FF 11/12-81 p97 ++Gr 11-81 p720

205 Chromatic fantasia and fugue, S 903, D minor. HAYDN: Fantasia, C

major. MOZART: Fantasia, K 397, D minor. SCHUBERT: Fantasia, op. 15, D 760, C major. Lili Kraus, pno. Vanguard VA 25003
+NR 12-81 p15

Chromatic fantasia and fugue, S 903, D minor. See no. 255

206 Clavierubung, Pt 3. Michel Chapuis, org. Telefunken 6-35084 (2)
+Gr 4-76 p1628 +SR 6-81 p68
+HFN 2-76 p91 +-St 12-76 p72
+RR 5-76 p63

Clavierubung, S 552, 669-689, 683a, 802-5. See no. 191

Concert movement, S 1045, D major. See no. 240

Concerto, flute and harpsichord, D minor (fragment of Sonata, S 1030, B minor: Andante). See no. 363

207 Concerto, flute, violin and harpsichord, S 1044, A minor. Suites, orchestra, S 1066-1068. Stephen Preston, flt; Simon Standage, vln; English Concert; Trevor Pinnock, hpd and cond. DG 2533 410/11 (2) Tape (c) 3310 410/11
++ARG 1-80 p16 +HF 3-81 p80 tape
++ARG 3-81 p8 +-HFN 5-79 p118
+-FF 1/2-80 p40 +NYT 6-8-80 pD20
+Gr 5-79 p1880 +-RR 5-79 p48
++HF 11-79 p88 +St 10-79 p131

208 Concerto, flute, violin and harpsichord, S 1044, A minor. Concerto, oboe, S 1055, A major (trans.). Concerto, 3 harpsichords, S 1064, C major (trans.). Gerhard Hetzel, Walter Forchert, Ruben Gonzales, vln; Aurele Nicolet, flt; Manfred Clement, ob d'amore; Munich Bach Orchestra; Karl Richter, hpd. DG 2533 452 Tape (c) 3310 452
+ARG 11-81 p16 +-HFN 5-81 p75
+-FF 9/10-81 p63 +HFN 6-81 p87 tape
+-Gr 3-81 p1180

209 Concerto, harpsichord, S 971, F major. Duets, harpsichord, S 802-805. Partita, harpsichord, S 831, B minor. Mireille Lagace, hpd. Calliope CAL 1657
+FF 11/12-80 p62 +-HFN 12-81 p91
+HF 4-81 p72

210 Concerto, harpsichord, S 971, F major. Concerto, harpsichord, S 972, D major. Partita, harpsichord, S 831, B minor. Trevor Pinnock, hpd. DG 2533 424 Tape (c) 3310 424
+FF 7/8-80 p44 +NYT 6-8-80 pD20
+Gr 12-79 p1002 +-St 7-80 p78
-HF 4-81 p73 +STL 2-10-80 p40
++NR 5-80 p13

211 Concerto, harpsichord, S 971, F major. Partita, harpsichord, S 831, B minor. Prelude, fugue and allegro, S 998, E major. Gustav Leonhardt, hpd. Harmonia Mundi 065 99867
+FF 11/12-81 p97 +-HFN 10-80 p113

212 Concerto, harpsichord, S 971, F major. Fantasia, S 906, C minor. Fugue, S 944, A minor. Toccata, S 912, D major. Toccata, S 913, D minor. Gustav Leonhardt, hpd. Pro Arte 1025
+FF 11/12-81 p97

213 Concerto, harpsichord, S 971, F major. GRIEG: Concerto, piano, op. 16, A minor. Lyric pieces, op. 43: Erotik. SCARLATTI, D.: Sonatas, harpsichord, B minor, C minor, D minor, D major. Arturo Benedetti Michelangeli, pno; La Scala Orchestra; Alceo Galliera. Rococo RR 2125
+-FF 9/10-81 p230 +-NR 7-81 p4

Concerto, harpsichord, S 971, F major. See no. 202. See no. 203. See no. 255
Concerto, harpsichord, S 971, F major: 1st movement. See no. 359
214 Concerti, harpsichord, S 972, 974-976. Hans Ludwig Hirsch, hpd. Jecklin 5005
+FF 3/4-81 p61
215 Concerto, harpsichord, S 972, D major (after Vivaldi, op. 3, no. 7). PURCELL: The Gordian knot untied: Rondeau minuet. VIVALDI: Concerto, mandolin, RV 425, G major. Concerto, 2 violins, RV 93, D major. Sonata, RV 57, G major. Trios, violin and lute, RV 82, C major, RV 85, G minor. Frederic Hand, gtr; Eric Weissberg, banjo; Andy Statman, mand; Jane Bloom, sax; Robert Bonfiglio, harm; Kermit Moore, Richard Bock, vlc; Paul Dunkel, flt; Keith Underwood, rec; Joe Passaro, temple blocks and cymbal. CBS FM 36687
/FF 9/10-81 p281 +St 10-81 p136
Concerto, harpsichord, S 972, D major. See no. 210
216 Concerti, harpsichord, S 973, G major; S 976, C major; S 978, F major (trans. Zabaleta). HANDEL: Concerti, organ, op. 4, no. 5, F major; op. 7, no. 4, D minor (trans. Zabaleta). Nicanor Zabaleta, hp; ECO; Garcia Navarro. DG 2531 114 Tape (c) 3301 114
+FF 5/6-81 p42 +HFN 3-80 p89
+Gr 3-80 p1379 +RR 3-80 p67
+HF 3-81 p80 tape +NR 11-80 p4
217 Concerto, harpsichord, S 973, G major. Concerto, harpsichord, S 978, F major. Concerto, harpsichord, S 980, G major. Concerto, S 981, C minor. Hans Ludwig Hirsch, hpd. Jecklin 5006
+Gr 4-81 p1310
Concerto, harpsichord, S 976, C major. See no. 216
Concerto, harpsichord, S 978, F major. See no. 216. See no. 217
Concerto, harpsichord, S 980, G major. See no. 217
Concerto, harpsichord, S 981, C minor. See no. 217
218 Concerto, harpsichord, S 986, G major. Fantasia, S 906, C minor. Partita, harpsichord, S 831, B minor. Toccata, S 910, F sharp minor. Rafael Puyana, hpd. Philips 6538 008 (From Mercury)
+-MUM 3/4-81 p31
219 Concerti, harpsichord, S 1052-1058. Concerti, 2 harpsichords, S 1060-1061. Concerti, 3 harpsichords, S 1063-1064*. Concerto, 4 harpsichords, S 1065, A minor. Kenneth Gilbert, Lars Ulrik Mortensen, Nicholas Kraemer, hpd; English Concert, Trevor Pinnock. DG 2723 077 (4) (*also available on 2534 001)
++Gr 10-81 p538 ++HFN 10-81 p84
220 Concerti, harpsichord, S 1052-1058. Concerti, 2 harpsichords, S 1060-1062. Concerti, 3 harpsichords, S 1063-1064. Concerto, 4 harpsichords, S 1065, A minor. Igor Kipnis, Linda Schnell-Pluth, David Schrader, David Hertzberg, hpd; Stuttgart Chamber Orchestra; Karl Munchinger. Intercord INT 185925 (5) Tape (c) INT 485 925
+-FF 3/4-81 p62 +NYT 3-29-81 pD31
+-HF 7-81 p55
Concerti, harpsichord, S 1052-1058. See no. 362
221 Concerti, harpsichord, S 1052, 1053, 1055. ECO; Raymond Leppard. Philips 9502 002 Tape (c) 7313 002
+-Gr 1-81 p948 +HFN 8-80 p109 tape
+HFN 4-80 p119 +RR 4-80 p53

222 Concerti, harpsichord, S 1052, 1055-1056. Andras Schiff, pno; ECO; George Malcolm. Denon OX 7182
+FF 11/12-80 p59 +Gr 4-81 p1310
223 Concerto, harpsichord, S 1052, D minor. MOZART: Concerto, piano, no. 21, K 467, C major. Carl Post, pno; Grand Prix Festival Orchestra; Carl Post, Hans Peeters. Grand Prix GP 9001
-FF 5/6-80 p35 -NR 5-81 p7
224 Concerto, harpsichord, S 1052, D minor. Concerto, 3 harpsichords, S 1064, C major. Concerto, 4 harpsichords, S 1065, A minor. Karl Richter, Eduard Muller, Gerhard Aeschbacher, Heinrich Gurtner, hpd; Ansbach Bach Festival Soloists; Karl Richter. Telefunken 6-41914 Tape (c) 4-41914 (From Decca LXT 5203, LX 3152)
+-Gr 4-81 p1310 +-HFN 5-81 p76
Concerto, harpsichord, S 1052, D minor. See no. 100. See no. 3857
225 Concerto, harpsichord, S 1053, F major. Concerto, oboe, S 1055, A major. Concerto, harpsichord, S 1056, F major (all. trans.). Helmut Winschermann, ob; Saschko Gawriloff, vln; DBS, Frankfurter Bachorchester; Helmut Winschermann. Musicaphom BM 30 4202
+-HFN 5-81 p76
226 Concerto, harpsichord, S 1054, D major. Concerto, harpsichord, S 1058, G minor. Edith Picht-Axenfeld, George Malcolm, hpd; DBS; Helmut Winschermann. Musicaphon BM 30 SL 4203
+-HFN 5-81 p76
227 Concerto, harpsichord, S 1055, A major (trans.). HANDEL: Concerto, oboe, no. 3, G minor. MOZART: Adagio, K 580a, C major. VIVALDI: concerto, oboe, A minor. Jurg Schaeftlein, ob d'amore, cor anglais; VCM; Nikolaus Harnoncourt. Telefunken AP 6-42110 (From 6-41270, 6-41961)
+-Gr 10-78 p678 +MT 3-79 p227
+Gr 9-81 p372 +RR 9-78 p83
+HFN 11-78 p181
228 Concerto, harpsichord, S 1056, A major. HAYDN: Concerto, piano, D major. MOZART: Concerto, piano, no. 12, K 414, A major. Alicia de Larrocha, pno; London Sinfonietta; David Zinman. London OS 7180 (also Decca SXL 6952 Tape (c) KSXC 6952)
+FF 9/10-81 +-NR 8-81 p5
+Gr 5-81 p33 +NYT 7-12-81 pD21
+Gr 11-81 p783 tape ++SFC 6-14-81 p18
+-HFN 5-81 p85
229 Concerto, harpsichord, S 1056, A major. Concerto, 2 harpsichords, S 1060, C minor. Concerto, 2 harpsichords, S 1061, C major. Raymond Leppard, Andrew Davis, hpd; ECO; Raymond Leppard. Philips 9502 017 Tape (c) 7313 017 (From 6747 098)
+-Gr 8-81 p261 +HFN 9-81 p89
Concerto, harpsichord, S 1056, F major. See no. 225
Concerto, harpsichord, S 1056, F major: Largo. See no. 361
Concerto, harpsichord, S 1058, G minor. See no. 226
Concerti, 2 harpsichords, S 1060-1061. See no. 219
Concerti, 2 harpsichords, S 1060-1062. See no. 220. See no. 362
230 Concerto, 2 harpsichords, S 1060, C major; S 1062, C minor. Concerto, 4 harpsichords, S 1065, A minor. Gustav Leonhardt, Eduard Muller. Janny van Wering, Anneke Uittenbosch, hpd;

Leonhardt Consort; Gustav Leonhardt. Telefunken SAWT 9424
+FF 9/10-81 p336

Concerto, 2 harpsichords, S 1060, C minor. See no. 163. See no. 229. See no. 232

Concerto, 2 harpsichords, S 1061, C major. See no. 229. See no. 230

Concerti, 3 harpsichords, S 1063-1064. See no. 219. See no. 220

Concerti, 3 harpsichords, S 1063-1065. See no. 362

Concerto, 3 harpsichords, S 1063, D minor. See no. 236

231 Concerto, 3 harpsichords, S 1064, C major. Concero, 4 harpsichords, S 1065, A minor. Trevor Pinnock, Kenneth Gilbert, Ulrik Mortensen, Nicholas Kramer, hpd; English Consort; Trevor Pinnock. DG 2534 001
+HFN 11-81 p89

232 Concerto, 3 harpsichords, S 1064, C major (trans.). Concerto, 2 harpsichords, S 1060, D minor (trans.). Helmut Winschermann, ob; Georg Friedrich Hendel, vln; Hans Mohring, flt; DBS. Musicaphon BM 30 SL 4201
+-HFN 5-81 p75

Concerto, 3 harpsichords, S 1064, C major. See no. 208. See no. 224

Concerto, 4 harpsichords, S 1065, A minor. See no. 219. See no. 220. See no. 224. See no. 230. See no. 231

Concerto, oboe, S 1055, A major. See no. 208. See no. 225

233 Concerto, organ, S 592, G major. Concerto, organ, S 595, C major. Trio, organ, S 586, G major. Trio, organ, S 1027a, G major. MOZART: Allegro, K 312, G minor. Fantasia, K 397, D minor. Fugue, K 401, G minor. Church sonata, no. 17, K 336, C major. Hanns-Christoph Schuster, org. Pape 3
++NR 4-81 p12

Concerti, organ, S 592-593. See no. 273

Concerti, organ, S 592-597. See no. 284. See no. 291

Concerto, organ, S 594, C major. See no. 277

Concerto, organ, S 595, C major. See no. 233

234 Concerto, organ, S 596, D minor. Prelude and fugue, S 532, D major. Prelude and fugue, S 544, B minor. Trio sonata, S 525, E flat major. James Johnson, org. Ashmont A-1
+FF 11/12-81 p87 +MU 10-81 p12

235 Concerto, organ, S 596, D minor. HANDEL: Sonata, fute, op. 1, no. 11, F major. HINDEMITH: Sonata, organ, no. 3. GEISER: Sonatina, flute, op. 33b. Frank Nagel, flt; Hanspeter Aeschlimann, org. Orpheus ORPO 901
+Gr 12-81 p897

Concerto, organ, S 596, D minor. See no. 277

Concerto, organ, S 597, E flat major. See no. 275

236 Concerti, violin, S 1041-1042. Concerto, 2 violins, S 1043, D minor. Concerto, 3 harpsichords, S 1063, D minor. Concerto, violin and oboe, S 1060, D minor. Christian Altenberger, Ernst Mayer-Schierning, Jurgen Kussmaul, Wolfgang Kussmaul, vln; Ingo Goritzki, ob; German Bach Soloists; Helmut Winschermann. Arabesque 8075-2 Tape (c) 9075-2
-FF 1/2-81 p64 ++NR 11-80 p4
+-HF 12-80 p66

237 Concerto, violin, S 1041, A minor. Concerto, violin, S 1042, E major. Concerto, 2 violins, S 1043, D minor. Jean-Jacques

Kantorow, Sigrid Cenariu, vln; Munich Chamber Orchestra; Hans Stadlmair. Denon OX 7196
+FF 5/6-81 p43

238 Concerto, violin, S 1041, A minor. Concerto, violin, S 1042, E major. Concerto, 2 violins, S 1043, D minor. Peter Rybar, Henryk Szeryng, vln; Winterthur Collegium Musicum; Henryk Szeryng. Philips 9502 016 Tape (c) 7313 016 (From SAL 3540)
+Gr 4-81 p1310

239 Concerto, violin, S 1042, E major. Sonata, violin and harpsichord, S 1025, A mjor. Sonata, violin and harpsichord, S 1023, E minor (arr. Respighi). Gidon Kremer, vln; Leningrad Philharmonic Orchestra Ensembles; Arvid Jansons. Chant du Monde LDX 78674
+-HFN 9-81 p77

240 Concerto, violin, S 1042, E major (orch. Respighi). Partita, violin, S 1002, B minor. Partita, violin, S 1006, E major. Concerto movement, S 1045, D major. Sonata, 2 violins, S 1023, E minor. Gidon Kremer, vln; Leningrad Philharmonia Academic Symphony Orchestra; Maris Yansons. Musical Heritage Society MHS 824324 (2)
+-ARG 10-81 p14 +FF 7/8-81 p54

Concerto, violin, S 1042, E major. See no. 237. See no. 238. See no. 4091

241 Concerto, 2 violins, S 1043, D minor. MOZART: Sinfonia concertante, K 364, E flat major. VIVALDI: Concerto, 3 violins, F major. Isaac Stern, Itzhak Perlman, Pinchas Zukerman, vln; Pinchas Zukerman, vla; NYP; Zubin Mehta. CBS IM 36692 Tape (c) 36692
+-FF 7/8-81 p219 ++NR 4-81 p6
+HF 11-81 p74 +SFC 4-26-81 p18
+MUM 7/8-81 p35 +-St 6-81 p132

242 Concerto, 2 violins, S 1043, D minor. BRUCH: Concerto, violin, no. 1, op. 26, G minor. Igor Oistrakh, David Oistrakh, vln; RPO; Eugene Goossens. DG 2535 176 Tape (c) 3335 176 (From 138714, 135039)
+-Gr 8-81 p256 +HFN 9-81 p93 tape
+HFN 8-81 p91

Concerto, 2 violins, S 1043, D minor. See no. 236. See no. 237. See no. 238

Concerto, violin, oboe and strings, S 1060, D minor. See no. 236

Duets, S 802-805. See no. 209

243 English suites, S 806-811. Kenneth Gilbert, hpd. Harmonia Mundi HM 1074/5 (2) Tape (c) HM 40-1074
++Gr 11-81 p720 +HFN 12-81 p91

244 English suites, S 806-811. French suites, S 812-817. Alan Curtis, hpd. Telefunken 6-35452 (4)
+-FF 11/12-80 p60 ++HF 1-81 p65

English suite, S 807, A minor: Bourree. See no. 359

English suite, S 807, A minor: Bourrees, nos. 1 and 2, Gigue. See no. 358

English suite, S 808, G minor: Gavottes, nos 1 and 2. See no. 358

English suite, S 808, G minor: Gavotte and musette. See no. 359

245 English suite, S 811, D minor. BEETHOVEN: Sonata, piano, no. 15, op. 28, D major. SCHUBERT: Sonata, piano, no. 18, D 894, G major. Walter Gieseking, pno. Bruno Walter Society IGI 380
+*NR 6-81 p14

Fantasia, C minor. See no. 285

Fantasias, S 562-563, 570-572. See no. 283
Fantasia, S 562, C minor. See no. 276. See no. 287. See no. 4110
Fantasia, S 563, B minor. See no. 274. See no. 279. See no. 290
Fantasia, S 570, C major. See no. 277. See no. 279. See no. 281. See no. 290
Fantasia, S 571, G major. See no. 276. See no. 293
246 Fantasia, S 572, G major. Prelude and fugue, S 544, B minor. FRANCK: Prelude, fugue and variation, op. 18, B minor. LISZT: Prelude and fugue, on the name B-A-C-H, S 260. Richard Seal, org. Meridian E 77045
+-Gr 8-81 p288
247 Fantasia, S 572, G major: Gravement (arr. Goldman and Leist). HANDEL: Royal fireworks music (ed. Baines and Mackerras). HOLST: Suite, no. 1, op. 28. Suite no. 2, op. 28, F major. Cleveland Symphonic Winds; Frederick Fennell. Telarc 5038
++ARG 12-78 p6 ++HFN 12-79 p60
+Audio 1-79 p125 +IN 1-79 p98
+Audio 3-79 p97 +NR 1-81 p15
++FF 11/12-78 p75 +RR 12-79 p60
+HF 12-78 p134 +SFC 12-3-78 p55
Fantasia, S 572, G major. See no. 273. See no. 286. See no. 287. See no. 288. See no. 292
Fantasia, S 573, C major. See no. 291. See no. 3735
Fantasia, S 906, C minor. See no. 202. See no. 212. See no. 218. See no. 255
Fantasia, S 917. See no. 285
248 Fantasias and fugues, S 537, C minor; S 542, G minor. Preludes and fugues, S 534, F minor; S 536, A major; S 539, D minor, S 541, G major; S 543, A minor; S 545, C major; S 546, C minor. Toccata and fugue, S 538, D minor. Michael Chapuis, org. Telefunken BC 25100 (2)
+-Gr 7-74 p229 +RR 6-74 p63
+HF 9-74 p83 +SR 6-81 p68
+-NR 9-74 p11
Fantasia and fugue, S 537, C minor. See no. 277. See no. 282. See no. 291
Fantasia and fugue, S 542, G minor. See no. 186. See no. 187. See no. 248. See no. 273. See no. 282. See no. 3811
Fantasia and fugue, S 561, A minor. See no. 283
249 Fantasia and fugue, S 562, C minor. BOHM: Ach wie fluchtig ach wie nichtig. BUXTEHUDE: Prelude and fugue, no. 21, D minor. PACHELBEL: Chaconne, F minor. Hans Helmut Tillmanns, org. Pape 14
+NR 3-81 p14
250 Fantasia and fugue, S 562, C minor, excerpt. Preludes and fugues, S 531-533, 535, 547-550. Toccata and fugue, S 540, F major. Michael Chapuis, org. Telefunken BC 25101/1-2
+AR 5-75 p51 +RR 9-74 p70
++Gr 9-74 p543 +SR 6-81 p68
+NR 11-74 p9 +St 1-75 p106
French suites, S 812-817. See no. 244
French suites, S 814, B minor: Minuet; Trio. See no. 358
French suites, S 816, G major. See no. 4087

French suites, S 816, G major: Gavottes; Bouree; Gigue. See no. 358
French suites, S 816, G major: Gigue. See no. 359
French suites, S 817, E major: Allemande. See no. 359
French suites, S 817, E major: Allemande and courrante. See no. 3643
French suites, S 817, E major: Minuet; Bouree; Gigue. See no. 358
Fugue, G minor. See no. 3627. See no. 3737
Fugues, S 574-579, 581. See no. 283
Fugues, S 574, C minor. See no. 276. See no. 280. See no. 292
Fugues, S 575, C minor. See no. 278. See no. 279. See no. 290
Fugues, S 576, G major. See no. 276

251 Fugues, S 577, G major. Toccata and fugue, S 565, D minor. MOZART: Fantasia, K 608, F minor. PIERNE: Scherzando. WIDOR: Symphony, organ, no. 5, op. 42, no. 1, F major: Toccata. Symphony, no. 6, op. 42, no. 2, G major: Finale. Carlo Curley, org. Chalfont SDG 77021
-FF 5/6-81 p207

Fugues, S 577, G major. See no. 277. See no. 291. See no. 359
Fugues, S 578, G minor. See no. 276. See no. 279. See no. 281. See no. 288. See no. 290. See no. 293. See no. 363
Fugues, S 579, B minor. See no. 275. See no. 292
Fugues, S 944, A minor. See no. 212
Fugues, S 946, C major. See no. 285
Fugues, S 949, A major. See no. 285

252 Fugues, S 952, 953, 961. Preludes, S 924-928, 930, 933-938. Preludes and fugues, S 899, 902, 895, 900. Glenn Gould, pno. CBS M 35891 Tape (c) MT 35891 (also 76985 tape (c) 41-76985)
+ARG 4-81 p10 +HFN 8-81 p92 tape
+FF 1/2-81 p69 ++MUM 3/4-81 p31
+-Gr 6-81 p56 +St 3-81 p83
+Gr 8-81 p324 ++STL 5-10-81 p41
+HFN 7-81 p70

Fugues, S 961, C minor. See no. 358

253 Fugues, S 1026, G minor. Sonata, 2 violins, S 1021, G major. Sonata, violin, S 1024, C major. Sonata, 2 violins, S 1023, E minor. Daniel Stepner, vln; John Gibbons, hpd; Laura Jeppesen, vla da gamba. Titanic TI 80
+ARG 5-81 p9 /FF 1/2-81 p63

254 Fugue, lute, S 1000, G minor. Prelude, S 999, C minor. Prelude, fugue and allegro, S 998, E flat major. Suite, lute, S 995, G minor. Gergeley Sarkozy, lt. Hungaroton SLPX 12157
+-NR 11-81 p15

Fugue, lute, S 1000, G minor. See no. 4015
Fugue sopra il Magnificat, S 733. See no. 188. See no. 193

255 Harpsichord works: Capriccio, S 992, B flat major. Chromatic fantasia and fugue, S 903, D minor. Concerto, harpsichord, S 971, F major. Fantasia, S 906, C minor. Toccata and fugue, S 916, G major. Ralph Kirkpatrick, hpd. DG 2547 031 Tape (c) 3347 031 (From SAPM 198565, 198183, 198185)
+-Gr 12-80 p847 +-HFN 12-80 p153
+Gr 2-81 p1122 tape

256 Hercules auf dem Scheidewege, S 213. Carolyn Watkinson, alto; Edith Mathis, s; Peter Schreier, t; Siegfried Lorenz, bs; Berlin Chamber Orchestra and Soloists; Peter Schreier. DG 2533 447

++Gr 6-81 p66 +NR 6-81 p8
++HFN 8-81 p81 +St 6-81 p110

Inventions, 2 part, F major, B flat major, D minor. See no. 360

Inventions, 2 part, S 772, 774-775, 777, 779, 781, 784, 786. See no. 358

257 Inventions and sinfonias, S 772-801. Huguette Dreyfus, hpd. Denon OX 7150
++HFN 5-81 p76

Joy. See no. 3816

Kleines harmonisches Labyrinth, S 591, C major. See no. 277. See no. 284. See no. 291

258 Die Kunst der Fuge, S 1080. Gustav Leonhardt, hpd. Pro Arte 2PAL 2000 (2)
+FF 11/12-81 p97

Die Kunst der Fuge, S 1080. See no. 141

Die Kunst der Fuge, S 1080: Contrapuncti (3). See no. 150

Die Kunst der Fuge, S 1080: Contrapuncti, 1 and 9. See no. 4002

Die Kunst der Fuge, S 1080: Contrapuncti, nos. 3 and 9. See no. 3762

Die Kunst der Fuge, S 1080: Contrapunctus, no. 9. See no. 3898

Lobet den Herrn. See no. 3925

259 Magnificat, S 243, D major (with additional Christmas music). Arleen Auger, s; Ann Murray, ms; Helen Watts, con; Adalbert Kraus, t; Philippe Huttenlocher, bar; Wolfgang Schone, bs; Gachinger Singers; Bach Collegium; Helmuth Rilling. CBS 76884
+Gr 3-81 p1217 +HFN 3-81 p85

260 Magnificat, S 243, D major. STRAVINSKY: Symphony of psalms (rev. version). Anna Tomova-Sintow, s; Agnes Baltsa, ms; Peter Schreier, t; Benjamin Luxon, bs; German Opera Chorus; BPhO; Herbert von Karajan. DG 2531 048 Tape (c) 3301 048
-ARG 5-80 p15 +NR 3-80 p10
+-FF 3/4-80 p44 +-NYT 1-20-80 pD22
-Gr 11-79 p886 +-RR 12-79 p105
-HF 3-80 p86 -SFC 3-9-80 p39
+-HF 3-81 p80 tape +-St 4-80 p123
+-HFN 12-79 p157

261 Magnificat, S 243, D major. Brandenburg concerto, no. 5, S 1050, D major. Anna Bathy, Judit Sandor, s; Magda Tiszay, con; Lajos Somogyvari, t; Gyorgy Littasy, bs; Budapest Chorus; Tibor Ney, vln; Janos Szebenyi, flt; Annie Fischer, pno; Budapest Symphony Orchestra and Chorus; Otto Klemperer. Hungaroton LPX 12160
+-FF 5/6-81 p44 +HFN 12-80 p149
+Gr 12-80 p881 +NR 3-81 p4
-HF 4-81 p73

262 Magnificat, S 243, D major. KUHNAU (Bach): Der Gerechte kommt um. Judith Nelson, Emma Kirkby, s; Carolyn Watkinson, con; Paul Elliott, t; David Thomas, bs; Christ Church Cathedral Choir; Academy of Ancient Music; Simon Preston. L'Oiseau-Lyre DSLO 572 Tape (c) KDSLC 572
+Gr 1-80 p1182 ++HFN 1-80 p101
+Gr 12-81 p945 tape +RR 1-80 p106

Magnificat, S 243, D major: Arioso, fanfare and fugue. See no. 3796

Magnificat, S 243, D major: Esurientes. See no. 3853

Magnificat, S 243, D major: Sicut locatus est. See no. 3671

263 Mass, S 232, B minor: Gloria in excelsis Deo; Et in terra pax; Domine Deus; Qui tollis peccata mundi; Quoniam tu solus sanctus; Cum Sancto Spiritu; Credo in unam Deum; Et incarnatus est; Et resurrexit; Pleni sunt coeli; Dona nobis pacem. Margaret Marshall, s; Janet Baker, ms; Robert Tear, t; Samuel Ramey, bs; AMF and Chorus; Neville Marriner. Philips 6527 099 Tape (c) 7311 099 (From 6769 002)
+Gr 11-81 p728

A mighty fortress is our God. See no. 3700

264 Motets, S 225-226,228-229. Hungarian Radio and Television Chorus; Gabor Lehotka, org; Ferenc Sapszon. Hungaroton SLPX 12104
-ARG 6-81 p10 -HF 1-81 p66
-FF 1/2-81 p66 +NR 1-81 p7

265 Motets, S 225-230. Hannover Knabenchor; Collegium Aureum. Harmonia Mundi 157 99901/2 (2)
+HFN 4-81 p67

266 Motets, S 225-230. Stockholm Bach Choir; VCM; Nikolaus Harnoncourt. Telefunken 6-35470 Tape (c) 4-42663
+FF 1/2-81 p66 ++St 3-81 p83
++Gr 5-81 p1502 +STL 3-8-81 p38
+HF 1-81 p66

267 Motets, S 225-231. Cantata, no. 50, Nun ist das Heil. Cantata, no. 118, O Jesu Christ mein Lebens Lichts. Monteverdi Choir; English Baroque Soloists; Eliot Gardiner. Erato STU 71337 (2)
+-Gr 10-81 p586 +HFN 12-81 p91

268 Motets, S 227, Jesu priceless treasure. Songs (partsongs): God liveth still, S 461; Breadth of God life giving, S 445; It is finished, S 458; Jesus is this dark world's light, S 474; Lord pour not thy vengeance on me, S 463; Now is the mournful time, S 450; O Jesu so meek O Jesu so kind, S 49. King's College Chapel Choir; Bernard Richards, vlc; Francis Baines, bs; Simon Preston, org; David Willcocks. Argo ZK 67 Tape (r) KZKC 67
+Gr 10-80 p523 +-HFN 10-80 p115
+Gr 2-81 p1122 tape

269 Ein musicalischesOpfer, S 1079. Musica Antiqua Cologne; Reinhard Goebel. DG 2533 422 Tape (c) 3310 422
+FF 3/4-80 p46 +-MT 4-80 p248
+-Gr 11-79 p854 +-NR 2-80 p7
+HF 6-80 p71 +-NYT 6-8-80 pD20
+-HF 3-81 p80 tape +RR 11-79 p110
++HFN 11-79 p133

270 Ein musicalisches Opfer, S 1079. Tilford Ensemble. Everest SP 3478
-ARG 5-81 p8 -NR 2-81 p5
+-FF 3/4-81 p62

271 Ein musicalisches Opfer, S 1079. Yorkshire Sinfonia Members; Manoug Parikian. Nonesuch H 71384
+-FF 1/2-81 p67 +SFC 7-19-81 p19

272 Ein musicalisches Opfer, S 1079. Leonhardt Consort. Pro Arte 1000
+FF 11/12-82 p97

Ein musicalisches Opfer, S 1079. See no. 141

Ein musikalisches Opfer, S 1079, C minor: Fugue (orch. Webern). See no. 3580

Ein musikalisches Opfer, S 1079: Ricercar a 3 voce. See no. 3807
Ein musicalisches Opfer, S 1079, C minor: Ricercare a 6. See no. 150
Ein musicalisches Opfer, S 1079: Trio sonata, C minor. See no. 324

273 Organ works: Chorale preludes S 572, 690-713, 727, 736. Concerti, organ, S 592-593. Fantasia, S 572, G major. Fantasia and fugue, S 542, G minor. Preludes and fugues, S 533, 536, 541, Sonata, organ, S 528, E minor. Sonata, organ, S 529, C major. Peter Hurford, org. Argo D120D3 (3) Tape (c) K120K32
+Audio 4-79 p81 ++HFN 4-79 p133 tape
+FF 3/4-80 p47 +MT 3-79 p224
++Gr 11-78 p921 +RR 12-78 p87
+Gr 5-79 p1940 tape +SFC 7-13-80 p33
+HFN 11-78 p163 +-SR 6-81 p68

274 Organ works: Chorale preludes, S 669/672, Kyrie Gott Vater in Ewigkeit; S 670/673, Christe aller Welt trost; S 671/674, Kyrie Gott heiliger Geist; S 675/676/677/716, Allein Gott in der Hoh sei Ehr; S 678/679, Diess sind die heil'gen zehn Gebot; S 680/681, Wir glauben all an einen Gott; S 682/683, Vater unser in Himmelreich; S 684/685, Christ unser Herr zum Jordam kam; S 686/687, Aus tiefer Not schrei ich zu dir; S 688/689, Jesus Christus unser Heiland; S 714, Ach Gott und Herr; S 719, Der Tag der ist so freudenreich; S 721, Erbarm dich mein, O Herre Gott; S 723, Gelobet seist du Jesu Christ; S 724, Gottes Sohn ist kommen; S 733, Meine Seele erhebt den Herren. Fantasia, S 563, B minor. Prelude and fugue, S 552, E flat major. Prelude and fugue, S 543, A minor. Toccata and fugue, S 566, E major. Peter Hurford, org. Argo D138D3 (3) Tape (c) K138K32
++Gr 5-79 p1913 +HFN 7-79 p119 tape
++Gr 9-79 p534 tape ++SFC 7-13-80 p33
++HFN 5-79 p118 +SR 6-81 p68

275 Organ works: Allabreve, S 589, D major. Chorale preludes, S 645-650; S 726, Herr Jesu Christ dich zu uns wend; S 729, In dulci jubilo; S 728, Jesus meine Zuversicht; S 730/731, Liebster Jesu wir sind hier; S 732, Lobt Gott ihr Christen allzugleich; S 735, Valet will ich dir geben; S 737, Vater unser im Himmelreich; S 763, Sei gegrusset Jesu gutig: Partita; S 769, Vom Himmel hoch: Variations. Concerto, organ, S 597, E flat major. Fugue, S 579, B minor. Preludes and fugues, S 544, B minor; S 545, C major. Sonatas, organ, S 525, 527. Trio, S 583, D minor. Peter Hurford, org. Argo D150D3 (3) Tape (c) K150K32
+FF 1/2-81 p67 +MT 2-80 p105
+Gr 7-79 p224 ++RR 5-79 p79
++Gr 12-79 p1065 tape +-SR 6-81 p68
++HFN 9-79 p100 ++RR 8-79 p100

276 Organ works: Aria, S 587. Canzona, S 588, D minor. Chorale preludes, S 770, Ach was soll ich Sunder machen; S 771, Allein Gott in der Hoh sei Ehr. Fantasias, S 562, C minor; S 571, G major. Fugues, S 574, C minor; S 578, G minor; S 576, G major. Passacaglia and fugue, S 582, C minor. Pastorale, S 590, F major. Pedal-Exercitium, S 598. Preludes, S 567, C major; S 569, A minor. Preludes and fugues, S 546, C minor; S 547, C major. Sonata, viola da gamba and harpsichord, S 1027, G major. Peter Hurford, org. Argo D177D3 (3) Tape (c) K177K32

+FF 5/6-81 p45 +MT 9-80 p565
+Gr 12-79 p1027 +-RR 12-79 p91
++HFN 12-79 p157 +-SR 6-81 p68

277 Organ works: Chorale preludes, S 715, Allein Gott in der Hoh sei Ehr; S 720, Ein feste Burg ist unser Gott; S 722, Gelobet seist du Jesu Christ; S 738, Von Himmel; S 766, Christ der du bist: Partita. Concerti, organ, S 594, C major; S 596, D minor. Fantasia and fugue, S 537, C minor. Fantasia, S 570, C major. Fugue, S 577, G major. Kleines harmonisches Labyrinth, S 591, C major. Preludes and fugues, S 532, D major; S 534, F minor; S 553-560. Sonata, organ, S 530, G major. Toccatas and fugues, S 538, D minor; S 565, D mionr. Trio, S 584, G minor. Peter Hurford, org. Argo D207D3 (3) Tape (c) K207K33
+-FF 7/8-81 p55 +HFN 11-80 p115
++Gr 11-80 p698 +MT 3-81 p195
+Gr 2-81 p1122 tape +NR 7-81 p14

278 Organ works: Chorale preludes, S 717, Allein Gott in der Hoh sei Ehr; S 725, Herr Gott dich loben wir; S 740, Wir glauben all an einen Gott; S 741, Acht Gott vom Himmel sieh darein; S 747, Christus der uns selig macht; S 755, Nun freut euch; S 758, O Vater allmachtiger Gott; S 739, Wie schon leuchtet der Morgenstern; S 765, Wir glauben all an einen Gott; Anh 55, Herr Christ der einig Gottes Sohn. Fugue, S 575, C minor. Preludes and fugues, S 531, 535, 548, 550-551. Toccata, adagio and fugue, S 564, C major. Toccata and fugue, S 540, F major. Sonata, organ, S 526, C minor. Trio, S 585, C minor. Peter Hurford, org. Argo D226D3 (3) Tape (c) K226K33
+Gr 5-81 p1493 +Gr 6-81 p94 tape

279 Organ works: Fantasia, S 563, B minor. Fantasia, S 570, C major. Fugue, S 575, C minor. Fugue, S 578, G minor. Prelude, S 568, G major. Prelude, S 569, A minor. Trio, S 584, G minor. Trio sonata, S 528, E minor. Trio Sonata, S 530, G major. Michael Chapuis, org. Astree MB 342
+FF 11/12-81 p85

280 Organ works: Fugue, S 574, C minor. Prelude and fugue, S 551, A minor. Toccata, adagio and fugue, S 564, C major. Toccata, S 566, E major. Toccata and fugue, S 565, D minor. Trio, S 583, D minor. Michel Chapuis, org. Astree MB 343
+FF 11/12-81 p86

281 Organ works: Chorale preludes, S 645-650. Fantasia, S 570, C major. Fugue, S 578, G minor. Prelude and fugue, S 535, G minor. Prelude and fugue, S 545, C major. Toccata and fugue, S 565, D minor. Trios, S 583, D minor; S 585, C minor. Hans Otto, org. Denon OX 7184
+FF 1/2-81 p65 ++HFN 6-81 p82
+HF 2-81 p63

282 Organ works: Fantasias and fugues, S 537, C minor; S 542, G minor. Trio sonatas, S 525-530. Preludes and fugues, S 531-536, 539, 541, 543-545. Toccatas and fugues, S 538, D minor; S 540, F major. Marie Claire Alain, org. Erato STU 71341 (4)
+Gr 7-81 p172

283 Organ works: Fantasias, S 562-563, 570-572. Fantasia and fugue, S 561, A minor. Fugues, S 574-579, 581. Passacaglia and fugue, S 582, C minor. Preludes, S 568-569. Preludes and fugues, 546-551, 553-560. Toccata, adagio and fugue, S 564, C major.

Toccatas and fugues, S 565-566. Marie-Claire Alain, org. Erato STU 71346 (4)
+Gr 7-81 p172

284 Organ works: Allabreve, S 589, D major. Aria, S 587, F major. Canzona, S 588, D minor. Chorale preludes, S 645-650. Concerti, organ, S 592-597. Kleines harmonisches Labyrinth, S 591, C major. Orgelbuchlein, S 599-644. Pastorale, S 590, F major. Pedal-Exercitium, S 598. Trios, S 583-584, 586. Marie-Claire Alain, org. Erato STU 71351 (4)
+Gr 7-81 p172

285 Organ works: Capriccio, S 993, E major. Chorale preludes, S 690-1, 694-741, 743-745, 747, 751, 754, 762, 765, 891a, Anh. 55. Fantasia, C minor. Fantasia, S 917. Fugues, S 946, C major; S 949, A major. Partitas, S 766-770. Prelude, S 943, C major. Sonata, viola da gamba and harpsichord, S 1027-1028. Marie-Claire Alain, org. Erato STU 71361 (5)
+Gr 7-81 p172

286 Organ works: Chorale preludes, S 645-650; S 659-661. Fantasia, S 572, G major. Passacaglia and fugue, S 582, C minor. Preludes and fugues, S 536, A major; S 541, G major; S 548, E minor. Almut Rossler, org. Motette M 1019 (2)
+ARG 6-81 p8 +-FF 1/2-81 p71

287 Organ works: Chorale preludes, S 618, O Lamm Gottes unschuldig; S 663, Allein Gott in der Hoh sei Ehr; S 665/666, Jesus Christus unser Heiland; S 710, Wir Christenleut hab'n Jetzund Freud; S 736, Valet will ich dir geben; S 766, Christ der du bist der Helle Tag; S 767, O Gott do frommer Gott. Fantasia, S 562, C minor. Fantasia, S 572, G minor. Prelude and fugue, S 546, C minor. Toccata and fugue, S 565, D minor. Gustav Leonhardt, org. Musical Heritage Society MHS 824335 (2)
+-FF 11/12-81 p92 +St 11-81 p77

288 Organ works: Chorale prelude, S 615, In dir ist Freude. Fantasia, S 572, G major. Fugue, S 578, G minor. Pedal-Exercitium, S 598, G minor. Prelude and fugue, S 544, B minor. Toccata, adagio and fugue, S 564, C major. Carlo Curley, org. RCA RL 2-5369 Tape (c) RK 2-5369
+Gr 10-81 p580 +-HFN 11-81 p89

289 Organ works: Chorale preludes, S 603-615. Choral prelude, S 729, In dulci jubilo: Fantasia. Chorale prelude, S 769, Vom Himmel hoch: Variations. Pastorale, S 590, F major. Nicholas Jackson, org. Spectrum SR 117 Tape (c) SC 117
+FF 11/12-80 p59 +-HF 3-81 p80 tape

290 Organ works: Fantasias, S 563, B minor; S 570, C major. Fugues, S 578, G minor; S 575, C minor. Preludes, S 569, A minor; S 568, G major. Trio, S 584, G minor. Trio sonatas, S 525-530. Michael Chapuis, org. Telefunken BC 25098/1-2 (2)
+AR 5-75 p51 +-NR 3-74 p14
+Gr 4-74 p1876 ++PRO 1/2-76 p20
+HF 9-74 p83 +RR 3-74 p51
++HFN 3-74 p22 ++SFC 1-6-74 p32
++MJ 5-74 p52 +SR 6-81 p68
+MQ 10-74 p685 +-St 6-74 p115

291 Organ works: Aria, S 587, F major. Concerti, organ, S 592-597. Chorale preludes, S 741, Ach Gott vom Himmel sich darein; S 653, An Wasserflussen Babylon; S 656, O Lamm Gottes unschuldig. Fantasia, S 573, C major. Fantasia and fugue, S 537, C minor.

Fugue, S 577, G major. Kleines harmonisches Labyrinth, S 591, C major. Prelude, trio and fugue, S 545, B major. Trio, S 586, G major. Trio, S 1027, G major. Michael Chapuis, org. Telefunken BC 25102/1-2
+AR 5-75 p51 +RR 2-75 p47
+Gr 2-75 p1515 +SR 6-81 p68
+-NR 2-75 p13

292 Organ works: Allabreve, S 589, D major. Canzona, S 588, D minor. Fantasia, S 572, C major. Fugues, S 574, C minor; S 579, B minor. Passacaglia and fugue, S 582, C minor. Pastorale, S 590, F major. Prelude and fugue, S 551, A minor. Toccatas (3). Michael Chapuis, org. Telefunken BC 25104 (2)
+NR 7-75 p15 ++SFC 10-26-74 p24
+SR 6-81 p68

293 Organ works: Chorale preludes, S 727, Herzlich tut mich verlangen; S 734, Nun freut euch; S 736, Valet will ich dir geben. Fugue, S 578, G minor. Fantasia, S 571, C major. Pastoral, S 590, F major. Toccata and fugue, S 565, D minor. Bernard Lagace, org. Titanic TI 14
++FF 9/10-81 p67 +St 11-81 p77

294 Orgelbuchlein, S 599-644. Andre Isoir, org. Calliope CAL 1710/11 (2) Tape (c) CAL 4710/11
++Gr 5-80 p1690 +MT 3-81 p195
+HFN 5-80 p117 +RR 6-80 p71

295 Orgelbuchlein, S 599-644. Paul Jordan, org. Pape 1001 (2)
+-FF 11/12-81 p86 +NR 3-81 p14

Orgelbuchlein, S 599-644. See no. 284

Partita, flute, S 1013, A minor: Bourree anglaise, Corrente, Sarabande. See no. 363

296 Partitas, harpsichord, S 825-830. Joao Carlos Martins, pno. Arabesque 6501-3 (3) Tape (c) 7501-3
+-ARG 9-81 p9 +NR 5-81 p14
+FF 9/10-81 p64 +-SFC 12-27-81 p18
-HF 10-81 p79 ++St 6-81 p76
+HF 11-81 p103 tape

297 Partitas, harpsichord, S 825-830. Mireille Lagace, hpd. Calliope CAL 1654/6 (3)
+-HFN 12-81 p91

298 Partita, harpsichord, S 825, B flat major. CHOPIN: Waltzes (13). MOZART: Sonata, piano, no. 8, K 310, A minor. SCHUBERT: Impromptus, op. 90, no. 2, D 899, E flat major; no. 3, G flat major. Dinu Lipatti, pno. HMV RLS 761 Tape (c) TC RLS 761 (From 33CX 1499, 33CX 1500)
+Gr 6-81 p65 +MT 12-81 p826
+Gr 9-81 p460 tape

Partita, harpsichord, S 825, B flat major. See no. 203. See no. 3749

Partita, harpsichord, S 825, B flat major: Minuets, nos. 1 and 2, Gigue. See no. 358

Partita, harpsichord, S 831, B minor. See no. 209. See no. 210. See no. 211. See no. 218

Partitas, organ, S 766-770. See no. 285

299 Partitas, violin, S 1002, 1004, 1006. Gidon Kremer, vln. Chant du Monde LDX 78688
+-HFN 4-81 p67

Partita, violin, S 1002, B minor. See no. 240

300 Partita, violin, S 1004, D minor: Chaconne (arr. Busoni). FRANCK: Prelude, chorale and fugue. MOZART: Rondo, piano, K 511, A minor. Artur Rubinstein, pno. RCA RL 1-3342 Tape (c) RK 1-3342

+Gr 6-80 p53 +-HFN 2-81 p97
+Gr 10-80 p548 tape +RR 6-80 p78
+HFN 6-80 p115

Partita, violin, S 1004, D minor: Chaconne. See no. 19. See no. 363. See no. 365. See no. 1460

301 Partita, violin, S 1006, E major. SCARLATTI, D.: Sonatas, guitar (5). Eliot Fisk, gtr. Levinson MAL 6

+FF 5/6-79 p10 +NYT 6-1-80 pD19
-FF 1/2-81 p68

Partita, violin, S 1006, E major. See no. 240

Partita, violin, S 1006, E major: Gavotte. See no. 365

Partita, violin, S 1006, E major: Preludio. See no. 363

Passacaglia and fugue, C minor. See no. 170

302 Passacaglia and fugue, S 582, C minor. Prelude and fugue, S 547, C major. Toccata and fugue, S 565, D minor. Trio sonata, S 525, E flat major. Kjell Johnsen, org. Polyhymnia 7801

+-FF 9/10-81 p62

Passacaglia and fugue, S 852, C minor. See no. 184. See no. 186. See no. 199. See no. 276. See no. 283. See no. 286. See no. 292. See no. 3812

Pastorale S 590, F major. See no. 194. See no. 276. See no. 284. See no. 289. See no. 292. See no. 293

Pastorale, S 590, F major: Adagio. See no. 359

Pedal-Exercitium, S 598, G minor. See no. 276. See no. 284. See no. 288

Praise the Lord all ye heathen. See no. 3614

Prelude, S 567, C major. See no. 276

Preludes, S 568-569. See no. 283

Prelude, S 568, G major. See no. 279. See no. 290

Prelude, S 569, A minor. See no. 276. See no. 279. See no. 290

Preludes, S 924-928, 930, 933-938. See no. 252

Preludes, S 924, C major. See no. 358

Preludes, S 926, D minor. See no. 365

Preludes, S 929, G minor. See no. 365

Preludes, S 933-934. See no. 358

Preludes, S 934, E minor. See no. 365

Preludes, S 940, D minor. See no. 365

Preludes, S 943, C major. See no. 285

Preludes, S 999, C minor. See no. 254. See no. 365. See no. 4015

Prelude and fugue, F sharp minor. See no. 53

Preludes and fugues, S 531-533, 535, 547-550. See no. 250

Preludes and fugues, S 531-536, 539, 541, 543-545. See no. 282

Preludes and fugues, S 531, 535, 548, 550, 551. See no. 278

303 Preludes and fugues, S 531, C major; S 536, A major. Toccata and fugue, S 540, F major. Trio sonata, S 529, C major. Kjell Johnsen, org. Polyhymnia 7805

+-FF 9/10-81 p64

304 Preludes and fugues, S 532, D major; 544, B minor. Toccata, adagio and fugue, S 564, C major. Trio sonata, S 529, C major.

Hans Heintze, org. Nonesuch H 71321 (also SDB 610705)
+-HFN 6-81 p69 +-St 12-76 p72
+-NR 7-76 p10

Preludes and fugues, S 532, D major. See no. 200. See no. 234. See no. 277. See no. 3674. See no. 3806

Preludes and fugues, S 533, E minor. See no. 193. See no. 273

305 Preludes and fugues, S 534, F minor; S 535, G minor; S 548, E minor. Trio sonata, S 527, D minor. Kjell Johnsen, org. Polyhymnia 7803
+-FF 9/10-81 p64

Preludes and fugues, S 534, F minor. See no. 248. See no. 277

Preludes and fugues, S 535, G minor. See no. 281

Preludes and fugues, S 536, A major. See no. 248. See no. 273. See no. 286. See no. 303

306 Preludes and fugues, S 539, D minor; S 541, G major; S 543, A minor; S 546, C minor. Toccata and fugue, S 538, D minor. Michael Chapuis, org. Astree AB 345
-FF 11/12-81 p86

Preludes and fugues, S 539, D minor. See no. 248

Preludes and fugues, S 541, G major. See no. 150. See no. 248. See no. 273. See no. 286. See no. 306. See no. 4116

Preludes and fugues, S 542, G minor. See no. 164. See no. 4113

307 Preludes and fugues, S 543, A minor; S 549, C minor; S 552, E flat major. Trio sonata, S 526, C minor. Kjell Johnsen, org. Polyhymnia 7802
+-FF 9/10-81 p64

Preludes and fugues, S 543, A minor. See no. 248. See no. 274. See no. 306

Preludes and fugues, S 544, B minor. See no. 193. See no. 234. See no. 246. See no. 275. See no. 288. See no. 304

Preludes and fugues, S 545, C major. See no. 103. See no. 248. See no. 275. See no. 281

308 Preludes and fugues, S 546, C minor; S 551, A minor. Toccata and fugue, S 538, D minor. Trio sonata, S 528, E minor. Kjell Johnsen, org. Polyhymnia 7804
+-FF 9/10-81 p64

Preludes and fugues, S 546-551, 553-560. See no. 283

Preludes and fugues, S 546, C minor. See no. 248. See no. 276. See no. 287. See no. 306

Preludes and fugues, S 547, C major. See no. 193. See no. 276. See no. 302. See no. 4117

309 Preludes and fugues, S 548, E minor. Trio sonata, S 528, E minor. COUPERIN, F.: Messe pour les paroisses, excerpts. SWEELINCK: Fantasia, D minor. Rudolf Heinemann, org. Motette M 1004
+FF 1/2-81 p222

Preludes and fugues, S 548, E minor. See no. 193. See no. 286. See no. 305

Preludes and fugues, S 549, C minor. See no. 307

Preludes and fugues, S 551, A minor. See no. 280. See no. 292. See no. 308

310 Preludes and fugues, S 552, E flat major. CLERAMBAULT: Suite du 2nd ton. FLEURY: Variations sur un noel bourguignon (7). MESSIAEN: La nativite du Seigneur: Dieu parmi nous. Hanns Brendel, Johannes Ricken, Herbert Heine, Dick Klomp, org. Motette M 1014
/-FF 1/2-81 p202

Preludes and fugues, S 552, E flat major. See no. 104. See no. 187. See no. 274. See no. 307
Preludes and fugues, S 553-560. See no. 277
Preludes and fugues, S 553, C major. See no. 3961
Preludes and fugues, S 555, E minor. See no. 3671
Preludes and fugues, S 848, C sharp major. See no. 4101
Preludes and fugues, S 849, C sharp minor. See no. 4101
Preludes and fugues, S 894, A minor. See no. 202
Preludes and fugues, S 895, 899, 900, 902. See no. 252
Preludes and fugues, S 895, A minor. See no. 365

311 Prelude, fugue and allegro, S 998, E flat major. Suites, lute, S 995, G minor; S 996, E minor. Hopkinson Smith, lt. Astree AS 61
++Gr 10-81 p580

312 Prelude, fugue and allegro, S 998, E flat major. BUXTEHUDE: Suite, E minor. CORBETTA: La guitarre royalle: Suite, A minor. WEISS: Suite, D major. Jukka Savijoki, gtr. BIS LP 176
+FF 9/10-81 p253 ++HFN 4-81 p79

Prelude, fugue and allegro, S 998, E flat major. See no. 211. See no. 254. See no. 3832
Prelude, fugue and variation, op. 18, B minor. See no. 246
Prelude, trio and fugue, S 545, B major. See no. 291

313 St. John Passion, S 245 (with choruses and arias of the 1725 version). Arleen Auger, s; Doris Soffel, alto; Adalbert Kraus, t; Lutz-Michael Harder, t; Arthur Loosli, bs; Kurt Widmer, bs; Bern Bach Chamber Orchestra and Choir; Theo Loosli. EMI 1C 157 99860/2 (3)
+-FF 11/12-81 p88

314 St. Matthew Passion, S 244 (sung in English). Felicity Lott, s; Alfreda Hodgson, ms; Robert Tear, Neil Jenkins, t; John Shirley-Quirk, Stephen Roberts, bar; Bach Choir; St. Paul's Cathedral Boys Choir; Thames Chamber Orchestra; David Willcocks. Decca D139D4 (4) Tape (c) K139K44
+Audio 12-79 p100 +-RR 5-79 p93
+Gr 3-79 p1594 +-MT 10-80 p633
+Gr 12-81 p945 tape +-RR 5-79 p93

315 St. Matthew Passion, S 244. Edith Mathis, s; Janet Baker, ms; Peter Schreier, t; Dietrich Fischer-Dieskau, bar; Matti Salminen, bs; Munich Bach Choir, Regensburg Cathedral Choir; Munich Bach Orchestra; Karl Richter. DG 2723 067 (4) Tape (c) 3376 016 (also DG 2712 005 Tape (c) 3376 016)
+ARG 1-81 p15 +-HFN 7-80 p105
+FF 9/10-80 p56 +-HFN 8-80 p109 tape
+Gr 5-80 p1699 ++NR 7-80 p8
++Gr 7-80 p166 tape +-NYT 6-8-80 pD20
+Gr 12-81 p945 tape +-RR 4-80 p106
+-HF 9-80 p82 +St 10-80 p108
+-HF 3-81 p80 tape ++STL 6-8-80 p38

316 St. Matthew Passion, S 244: Kommt ihr Tochter helft mir klagen; Blute nur du liebes Herz; Ich will bei meinem Jesu wachen; O Mensch bewein dein Sunde gross; Erbarme dich mein Gott; Und von der sechsten Stunde; Wenn ich einmal soll scheiden; Und siehe da der Vorhang im Tempel zerriss; Mache dich mein Herze rein; Wir setzen uns mit Tranen nieder. Edith Mathis, s; Janet Baker, ms; Peter Schreier, t; Dietrich Fischer-Dieskau, bar;

Matti Salminen, bs; Munich Bach Orchestra and Chorus; Karl Richter. DG 2531 317 Tape (c) 3301 317 (From 2723 067)
+-FF 9/10-81 p66 +-HFN 4-81 p81 tape
+-Gr 3-81 p1218 -HFN 6-81 p87

St. Matthew Passion, S 244: Wenn ich einmal soll scheiden. See no. 3881

Sonata, flute and harpsichord, A minor. See no. 3730

317 Sonata, flute and harpsichord, S 1020, G minor. HANDEL: Sonata, oboe, op. 1, no. 6, G minor. VIVALDI: Sonata, oboe, RV 53, C minor. Heinz Holliger, ob; Edith Picht-Axenfeld, hpd; Marcal Cervera, vlc. Philips 9502 019 (From SAL 3772)
++FF 5/6-80 p88 +NR 5-80 p7
+Gr 4-81 p1343

318 Sonatas, flute and harpsichord, S 1030, 1032, 1034-1035. Marc Beaucoudray, flt; William Christie, hpd. Harmonia Mundi HM 10065
+SFC 4-5-81 p18

Sonatas, flute and harpsichord, S 1032, 1034-1035. See no. 363

Sonatas, flute and harpsichord, S 1031, E flat major: Siciliano. See no. 361. See no. 3749. See no. 4113

Sonatas, harpsichord, S 965, A minor. See no. 3783

Sonatas, organ, S 525, S 527. See no. 275

Sonatas, organ, S 526, C minor. See no. 278

Sonatas, organ, S 528, E minor. See no. 273

Sonatas, organ, S 529, C major. See no. 273

Sonatas, organ, S 530, G major. See no. 277

319 Sonatas, viola and harpsichord, S 1027-1029. Catharina Meints, vla da gamba; Doris Ornstein, hpd. Gasparo GS 212
+ARG 3-81 p9 +NR 10-80 p7
/FF 1/2-81 p72 +St 2-81 p103
+HF 3-81 p63

320 Sonatas, viola and harpsichord, S 1027-1029. Marcal Cervera, vla da gamba; Rafael Puyana, hpd. Philips 9502 003 (From 6500 005)
++FF 11/12-79 p27 ++SFC 6-10-79 p45
-Gr 11-80 p684 +-ST 6-81 p124
+HFN 11-80 p129

321 Sonatas, viola and harpsichord, S 1027-1029. Janos Starker, vlc; Zuzana Ruzickova, hpd. Surpaphon 111 2485
+-ARG 3-81 p9 +-HFN 10-80 p101
+FF 11/12-80 p64 ++NR 10-80 p8
-HF 3-81 p63 ++St 2-81 p103

Sonatas, viola and harpsichord, S 1027-1028. See no. 285

Sonatas, viola and harpsichord, S 1027, G major. See no. 276

Sonatas, violin, S 1003, A minor: Andante. See no. 3643

Sonatas, violin and harpsichord, S 1017, C minor: Adagio. See no. 359

322 Sonatas, violin and harpsichord, S 1019-1023. Arthur Grumiaux, vln; Christiane Jaccottet, hpd; Philippe Mermoud, vlc. Philips 9500 905 Tape (c) 7300 905
+FF 9/10-81 p66 +NR 7-81 p7

Sonatas, violin and harpsichord, S 1023, E minor. See no. 239

Sonatas, violin and harpsichord, S 1025, A major. See no. 239

Sonatas, 2 violins, S 1021, 1023. See no. 253

Sonatas, 2 violins, S 1023, E minor. See no. 240

323 Sonatas, 2 violins and harpsichord, S 1036-1039. Musica Antiqua Koln. DG 2533 448
++HFN 6-81 p82
Sonatas, 2 violins and harpsichord, S 1037, C major. See no. 3763
324 Sonatas, 2 violins and harpsichord, S 1038, G major; S 1039, G major. Ein Musicalische Opfer, S 1079: Trio sonata, C minor. James Galway, flt; Kyung-Wha Chung, vln; Phillip Moll, hpd; Morey Welsh, vlc. RCA RL 2-5280 Tape (c) RK 2-5280
+Gr 9-81 p396 +-HFN 8-81 p81
325 Sonatas and partitas, solo violin, S 1001-1006. Sergiu Luca, vln. Nonesuch 73030 (3)
++AR 2-81 p187 +MJ 1-79 p46
+ARG 9-78 p19 ++NR 2-78 p13
+-Gr 4-78 p1744 ++RR 4-78 p76
+HF 3-78 p92 ++St 4-78 p86
+-HFN 4-78 p109
326 Sonatas and partitas, solo violin, S 1001-1006. Gidon Kremer, vln. Philips 6769 053 (3) Tape (c) 7654 053
+-Gr 10-81 p580 ++SFC 12-27-81 p18
+-HFN 11-81 p89
327 Songs (from the Schemelli songbook): Die goldne Sonne, S 451; O Jesulein suss, S 493; Ich steh an deiner Krippen hier, S 469; Die bittre Leidenszeit, S 450; Mein Jesu was fur Seelenweh, S 487; Jesus unser Trost und Leben, S 475; Gott lebet noch, S 461; Kommt wieder aus der finstern Gruft, S 480; Der Tag ist hin die Sonne gehet nieder, S 447; Der lieben Sonnen, S 446; Beschrankt ihr Weisen, S 443; Was bist du doch o Seele, so betrubet, S 506; Eins ist not, S 453; Brunnquell aller Guter, S 445; Ich halte treulich still und liebe, S 466; Dich bet ich an mein hochster Gott, S 449; Gieb dich zufrieden und sei stille, S 460; Liebster Herr Jesu wo bleibest du, S 484; O wie selig seid ihr doch, S 495; Komm susser Tod kom, S 478. Peter Schreier, t; Karl Richter, org. DG 2533 458
-Gr 12-81 p912 +-STL 12-13-81 p39
+HFN 11-81 p90
Songs: All glory, laud and honour. See no. 4107
Songs (partsongs): God liveth still, S 461; Breath of God life giving, S 445; It is finished, S 458; Jesus is this dark world's light, S 474; Lord pour not thy vengeance on me, S 463; Now is the mournful time, S 450; O Jesu so meek O Jesu so kind, S 49. See no. 268
Songs: Lasset uns mit Jesu ziehan, S 481. See no. 3985
Suite, harp, S 814, B minor. See no. 3877
Suite, lute, S 995, G minor. See no. 204. See no. 254. See no. 311
328 Suite, lute, S 996, E minor. BRITTEN: Nocturnal, op. 70. BROUWER: La espiral eterna. Sharon Isbin, gtr. Sound Environment TR 1013
+St 8-81 p102
Suite, lute, S 996, E minor. See no. 311
Suites, orchestra, S 1066-1068. See no. 207
329 Suites, orchestra, S 1066-1069. English Concert; Trevor Pinnock. DG 2723 072 (2) Tape (c) 3310 175 (From 2533 410/11, 2533 440)
+-ARG 9-81 p8 +HFN 4-81 p81 tape
+-FF 7/8-81 p56 +-MT 5-81 p317

+-Gr 12-80 p824 +-NR 5-81 p4
+-HFN 12-80 p132

330 Suites, orchestra, S 1066-1069. German Bach Soloists; Helmut Winschermann. Musical Heritage Society MHS 4203/4 Tape (c) MHC 6203/4
+-FF 1/2-81 p72 +HF 12-80 p66

331 Suites, orchestra, S 1066-1069. Busch Chamber Players; Marcel Moyse, flt; Fritz Busch. WRC SHB 68 (2)
+Gr 1-81 p998 +HFN 12-80 p132

Suites, orchestra, S 1066-1069. See no. 139. See no. 141. See no. 362

332 Suites, orchestra, S 1066, C major. Suites, orchestra, S 1067, B minor. Leopold Stastny, flt; VCM; Nikolaus Harnoncourt. Telefunken AQ 6-41228 Tape (c) CQ 4-41228 (From SAWT 9509)
+Gr 3-81 p1180 +HFN 3-81 p94

333 Suites, orchestra, S 1067, B minor. TELEMANN: Suite, flute, A minor. Ransom Wilson, flt; Los Angeles Chamber Orchestra; Gerard Schwarz. Angel DS 37330 Tape (c) 42S 37330 (also HMV ASD 3948)
+ARG 12-80 p16 +NR 9-80 p12
+FF 9/10-80 p61 +RR 9-80 p100
+-Gr 9-80 p326 +SFC 7-6-80 p27
+-HF 1-81 p78 ++St 12-80 p116

334 Suites, orchestra, S 1067, B minor. Suites, orchestra, S 1068, D major. BPhO; Herbert von Karajan. DG 2535 138 (From SLPM 138 978)
+-ARG 11-81 p14 +-Gr 4-76 p1588
+-FF 9/10-81 p66 +HFN 3-76 p109
+-FU 9-79 p46 +-RR 3-76 p33

335 Suites, orchestra, S 1067, B minor. GLUCK: Orfeo ed Euridice: Dance of the blessed spirits. MOZART: Concerto, flute, no. 2, K 314, D major. Claude Monteux, flt; LSO; Pierre Monteux. London STS 15493 (Also Contour CC 7504 Tape (c) CCT 7504)
+-FF 3/4-80 p120 +-HFN 8-81 p91
+Gr 8-81 p316

Suites, orchestra, S 1067, B minor. See no. 152. See no. 163. See no. 332

Suites, orchestra, S 1068, D major. See no. 334

336 Suites, orchestra, S 1068, D major: Air on the G string. HANDEL: Berenice: Minuet. Solomon: Arrival of the Queen of Sheba. Water Music: Air and hornpipe. HAYDN: Concerto, trumpet, E flat major. MOZART: Divertimento, no. 17, D 334, D major: Minuet. Serenade, no. 13, K 525, G major. AMF; Neville Marriner. Argo ZRG 902 Tape (c) KZRC 902 (From ZRG 442, 697, 543, 679)
*-FF 5/6-81 p216 +NR 2-81 p2
+-Gr 8-80 p233 +RR 8-80 p49
+HFN 8-80 p103

Suites, orchestra, S 1068, D major: Air on the G string. See no. 360. See no. 363. See no. 3736

337 Suites, solo violoncello, S 1007-1012. Enrico Mainardi, vlc. Eurodisc 25403 (3)
-HFN 12-81 p91

338 Suites, solo violoncello, S 1007-1012. Anner Bylsma, vlc. Pro Arte PAL 3001 Tape (c) 3 PAC 3001

+FF 11/12-81 p88 +HF 9-81 p46 tape

339 Suites, solo violoncello, S 1007-1012. Anner Bylsma, vlc. RCA RL 3-0369 (3)
+FF 9/10-81 p67 +HFN 8-81 p81
++Gr 7-81 p170

Suites, solo violoncello, S 1007, G minor: Prelude. See no. 365
Suites, solo violoncello, S 1010, E flat major. See no. 204
Toccatas (3). See no. 292
Toccatas, S 540, F major. See no. 186
Toccatas, S 566, E major. See no. 280
Toccatas, S 910, F sharp minor. See no. 218

340 Toccatas, S 911, C minor; S 914, E minor; S 915, G minor; S 916, G major. Glenn Gould, pno. Columbia M 35831 Tape (c) MT 35831 (also CBS 76984 Tape (c) 41-76984)
+ARG 11-80 p15 +-NR 5-80 p11
+FF 7/8-80 p49 +NYT 6-8-80 pD20
+Gr 6-81 p56 +St 8-80 p92
+-HF 11-80 p61 ++STL 5-10-81 p41
+-HFN 6-81 p69

Toccatas, S 912, D major. See no. 212
Toccatas, S 913, D minor. See no. 212. See no. 4087
Toccatas, S 914, E minor. See no. 4020
Toccatas, S 916, C major. See no. 3949. See no. 4087
Toccata, adagio and fugue, S 564, C major. See no. 278. See no. 280. See no. 283. See no. 288. See no. 304. See no. 341. See no. 3744. See no. 3902
Toccata and fugue, D minor. See no. 3817

341 Toccatas and fugues, S 538, D minor; S 540, F major; S 565, D minor. Toccata, adagio and fugue, S 564, C major. Joan Lippincott, org. Gothic 68005
+-ARG 6-81 p10 +MU 4-81 p20
+CL 2-81 p13 -NR 12-80 p10
+-FF 1/2-81 p72

Toccatas and fugues, S 538, D minor. See no. 183. See no. 199. See no. 248. See no. 277. See no. 282. See no. 306. See no. 308
Toccatas and fugue, S 540, F major. See no. 186. See no. 194. See no. 250. See no. 278. See no. 282. See no. 303. See no. 341. See no. 3615
Toccatas and fugue, S 565, D minor. See no. 170. See no. 185. See no. 187. See no. 194. See no. 251. See no. 277. See no. 280. See no. 281. See no. 283. See no. 287. See no. 293. See no. 302. See no. 341. See no. 3725. See no. 3744. See no. 3745. See no. 3799. See no. 4111
Toccatas and fugue, S 566, E major. See no. 274. See no. 283
Toccatas and fugue, S 916, G minor. See no. 255
Trios, S 583-584, 586. See no. 284
Trios, S 583, D minor. See no. 275. See no. 280. See no. 281
Trios, S 584, G minor. See no. 277. See no. 279. See no. 290
Trios, S 585, C minor. See no. 278. See no. 281
Trios, S 586, G major. See no. 291. See no. 233
Trios, S 1027, G major. See no. 233. See no. 291. See no. 359
Trio sonata. See no. 3807

342 Trio sonatas, S 525-530. Jean-Pierre Rampal, flt; Robert Veyron-Lacroix, hpd. RCA ARL 1-3580 Tape (c) ARK 1-3580

+ARG 1-81 p16 +NR 7-80 p7
+FF 9/10-80 p64 +SFC 6-15-80 p36
+HF 3-81 p80 tape

Trio sonatas, S 525-530. See no. 282. See no. 290

343 Trio sonatas, S 525-527, 529. Michel Chapuis, org. Valois Astree MB 341
++FF 3/6-81 p46

Trio sonatas, S 525, E flat major. See no. 121. See no. 234. See no. 302. See no. 4087

Trio sonatas, S 526, C minor. See no. 307. See no. 4087

Trio sonatas, S 527, D minor. See no. 305

Trio sonatas, S 528, E minor. See no. 279. See no. 308. See no. 309. See no. 4110

Trio sonatas, S 529, C major. See no. 303. See no. 304

Trio sonatas, S 530, G major. See no. 279. See no. 359

344 Trio sonatas, S 1036-1039. Cologne Musica Antiqua. DG 2533 448
+Gr 6-81 p46 +ST 9-81 p351
++FF 11/12-81 p91

345 Variations, harpsichord, S 988. BEETHOVEN: Variations on a theme by Diabelli, op. 120. Daniel Varsano, pno. CBS M2X 36925 (2)
+-FF 3/4-81 p81 -NR 5-81 p15
-HF 8-81 p56 -NYT 3-8-81 pD34
+-MUM 9/10-81 p30

346 Variations, harpsichord, S 988. Trevor Pinnock, hpd. DG 2533 425 Tape (c) 3310 425
+ARG 10-81 p16 +-HFN 12-80 p132
+-FF 7/8-81 p54 +NR 5-81 p15
+Gr 12-80 p847 +St 7-81 p73
+HF 8-81 p56

347 Variations, harpsichord, S 988. Ralph Kirkpatrick, hpd. DG 2547 050 Tape (c) 3347 050 (From SAPM 198020)
+Gr 4-81 p1343 +HFN 7-81 p81 tape
+Gr 9-81 p460 tape +-HFN 9-81 p89

348 Variations, harpsichord, S 988. Liisa Soinne, pno. Finlandia FA 315
-FF 5/6-81 p44 +NR 3-81 p13

349 Variations, harpsichord, S 988. John Gibbons, hpd. Titanic TI 30/1 (2) Tape (c) AAGAX 01
+-FF 5/6-80 p36 ++NYT 1-27-80 pD20
++HF 8-81 p56

350 Variations, harpsichord, S 988. Pamela Resch, pno. WRS 580
+CL 5/6-81 p8

Variations, harpsichord, S 988. See no. 358

351 Das wohltemperierte Clavier, S 846-869. Mieczyslaw Horszowski, pno. Vanguard VCS 10138/40 (3)
++NR 8-81 p13 +SFC 12-27-81 p18

352 Das wohltemperierte Clavier, S 846-869: Preludes and fugues, nos. 1-3, 5-8, 15-17, 21-22. Wilhelm Kempff, pno. DG 2530 807 Tape (c) 3300 807
+CL 3-81 p12 +NR 3-81 p13
+-FF 3/4-81 p65 *SFC 9-6-81 p18
+-HF 10-81 p79

353 Das wohltemperierte Clavier, S 846-893. Glenn Gould, hpd. CBS 77427 (From 77225, 78277)
+-Gr 6-81 p56 +-MT 11-81 p753
+-HFN 7-81 p70

354 Das wohltemperierte Clavier, S 846-893. Gustav Leonhardt, hpd. Harmonia Mundi 1C 153 99752/6 (5)
+FF 11/12-81 p97

Das wohltemperierte Clavier, S 846-869: Preludes and fugues, C major, B flat major. See no. 4087

Das wohltemperierte Clavier, S 846-869: Preludes and fugues, nos. 1, 5, 21. See no. 358

355 Das wohltemperierte Clavier, S 870-893. Betty Oberacker, pno. Klavier KS 567 (2)
+ARG 1-81 p14 +HF 10-81 p79
+ARG 7/8-81 p8

356 Das wohltemperierte Clavier, S 870-893. Sviatoslav Richter, pno. Musical Heritage Society MHS 834314 (3)
+-ARG 10-81 p14 +-FF 7/8-81 p56

357 Das wohltemperierte Clavier, Bk I: Preludes and fugues, nos. 4, 9-13; Bk II, nos. 3, 6-7, 15, 24. Wilhelm Kempff, pno. DG 2531 299 Tape (c) 3301 299
+CL 12-81 p11 +-HF 10-81 p79
+-FF 5/6-81 p46 +-HFN 1-81 p91
+-Gr 1-81 p966 +HFN 1-81 p109 tape
+Gr 1-81 p1001 tape +NR 5-81 p14

Das wohltemperierte Clavier, Bk I: Prelude. See no. 365. See no. 3290

Das wohltemperierte Clavier, Bk I: Prelude and fugue, no. 7, E flat major. See no. 360

358 Works, selections: English suite, S 807, A minor: Bourees, nos. 1 and 2; Gigue. English suite, S 808, G minor: Gavottes, nos. 1 and 2. French suite, S 841, B minor: Minuet; Trio. French suite, S 816, G major: Gavottes, Bouree, Gigue. French suite, S 817, E major: Minuet; Bouree; Gigue. Fugue, S 961, C minor. Inventions, 2-part, S 772, 774-775, 777, 779, 781, 784-786. Partita, harpsichord, S 825, B flat major: Minuets, nos. 1 and 2; Gigue. Preludes, S 924, C major; S 933-934. Variations, harpsichord, S 988. Das wohltemperierte Clavier, Bk I, S 846-869: Preludes and fugues, nos. 1, 5, 21. Glenn Gould, pno. CBS 36672 Tape (c) MT 36672 (also CBS 67986)
+-ARG 6-81 p9 +-HFN 7-81 p70
+FF 3/4-81 p66 +St 6-81 p126
+-Gr 6-81 p56 +-STL 5-10-81 p41

359 Works selections (trans. for guitar and organ): Cantata, no. 140, Wachet auf ruft uns die Stimme. Concerto, harpsichord, S 971, F major: 1st movement. English suite, S 807, A minor: Bourree. English suite, S 808, G minor: Gavotte and musette. French suite, S 816, G major: Gigue. French suite, S 817, E major: Allemande. Fugue, S 577, G major. Pastorale, S 590, F major: Adagio. Sonata, violin and harpsichord, S 1017, C minor: Adagio. Trio, S 1027, G major. Trio sonata, S 530, G major. John Williams, gtr; Peter Hurford, org. CBS 37250 Tape (c) 40-37250
+Gr 12-81 p895

360 Works, selections: Brandenburg concerto, S 1048, G major. Cantata, no. 29: Sinfonia. Cantata, no. 147, Jesu joy of man's desiring. Chorale prelude, S 645, Wachet auf. Inventions, 2 part, F major, B flat major, D minor. Suite, orchestra, S 1068, D major: Air on the G string. Das wohltemperierte Clavier, Bk

I: Prelude and fugue, no. 7, E flat major. Electronic realizations and performances by Walter Carlos. CBS 47194
+-FF 5/6-81 p47

361 Works, selections: Cantata, no. 29, Wir danken dir Gott wir danken dir: Sinfonia. Chorale preludes, S 140, Zion hort die Wachter singen; S 147, Wohl mir dass ich Jesum habe, Jesus bleibet meine Freude; S 307, Es ist gewisslich an der Zeit; S 727, Herzlich tut mich verlangen; S 639, Ich ruf zu dir Herr Jesu Christ; S 645, Wachet auf ruft uns die Stimme; S 659, Nun komm der Heiden Heiland; S 727, Herzlich tut mich verlangen; S 734, Nun freut euch lieben Christen g'mein; S 751, In dulci jubilo. Concerto, harpsichord, S 1056, F major: Largo. Sonata, flute and harpsichord, S 1031, E flat major: Siciliano (attrib.). GLUCK: Orfeo ed Euridice: Ballet music. HANDEL: Aylesford pieces: Minuet, G minor. (trans. Kempff). Wilhelm Kempff, pno. DG 2542 158 Tape (c) 3342 158 (From 2530 647)
+Gr 9-81 p418

362 Works, selections: Brandenburg concerti, S 1046-1051. Concerti, harpsichord, S 1052-1058. Concerti, 2 harpsichords, S 1060-1062. Concerti, 3 harpsichords, S 1063-1065. Suites, orchestra, S 1066-1069. Aurele Nicolet, flt; Manfred Clement, ob; Hermann Baumann, Werner Meyendorf, hn; Karl Kolbinger, bsn; Hansheinz Schneeberger, vln; Hedwig Bilgram, Karl Richter, Iwona Futterer, Ulrike Schott, hpd; Pierre Thibaud, tpt; Hans-Martin Linde, Gunther Holler, Peter Jenne, rec; Kurt-Christian Stier, Ingo Sinnhoffer, vla; Oswald Uhl, Johannes Fink, vla da gamba; Fritz Kishalt, vlc; Herbert Duft, bs; Munich Bach Orchestra; Karl Richter. DG 2722 033 (9)
+FF 3/4-81 p63

363 Works, selections: Cantata, no. 156: Arioso. Chorale preludes, S 645, Wachet auf ruft uns die Stimme; S 720; Ein feste Burg. Fugue, S 578, G minor. Partita, violin, S 1004, D minor: Chaconne. Partita, violin, S 1006, E major: Preludio. Suite, orchestra, S 1068, D major: Air on the G string. LSO; Leopold Stokowski. RCA GL 4-2921 (also AGL 1-3656) (From ARL 1-0880)
+-FF 9/10-81 p67 +-RR 4-80 p55
+HFN 4-80 p117

364 Works, selections: Concerto, flute and harpsichord, D minor (fragment of Sonata, S 1030, B minor: Andante). Partita, flute, S 1013, A minor: Bourree anglaise, Corrente; Sarabande. Partita, flute, S 1013, A minor (alternative instrumentation). Sonatas, flute and harpsichord, S 1030, 1032, 1034-1035. Frans Bruggen, rec, flt; Gustav Leonhardt, hpd; Anner Bylsma, vlc; Lucy van Dael, vla, vln; Sigiswalk Kuijken, vln; Adelheid Glatt, Wieland Kuijken, vla; Anthony Woodrow, violone. RCA RL 3-0426 (2)
+-Gr 12-81 p895

365 Works, selections: Partita, violin, S 1004, D minor: Chaconne. Partita, violin, S 1006, E major: Gavotte. Preludes, S 926, D minor; S 929, C minor; S 934, E minor; S 940, D minor; S 999, C minor. Prelude and fugue, S 895, A minor. Suite, solo violoncello, S 1007, G minor: Prelude. Das wohltemperierte Clavier, Bk I: Prelude. (all arr. Zelenka, Segovia). Milan Zelanka, gtr. Supraphon 111 2263
+FF 11/12-80 p62 +St 11-80 p78
+NR 7-81 p15

BACH, P.D.Q.
366 Liebeslieder polkas. Quite heavenly songs (12). Anne Epperstein, Peter Schickele, pno; John Ferrante, c-t; David Oei, chord organ, calliope, hpd, pno; Swarthmore College Chorus; Peter Gram Swing. Vanguard VSD 79438
+FF 5/6-81 p47 +NR 4-81 p16
Quite heavenly songs. See no. 366
BACH, Wilhelm Friedemann
Air. See no. 3841
367 Concerto, harpsichord, no. 4, F major. Concerto, harpsichord, no. 5, A minor. Brigitte Haudebourg, hpd; Pro Arte Orchestra; Kurt Redel. Arion ARN 38349 (also Musical Heritage Society MHS 4305)
+FF 5/6-81 p48 +RR 6-79 p67
+Gr 7-79 p191
Concerto, harpsichord, no. 5, A minor. See no. 367
Fugues, F major, G minor. See no. 103
Sonata, harpsichord, B flat minor. See no. 115
Sonata, viola, C minor. See no. 118
BACHARACH, Bert
Wives and lovers. See no. 4114
BACHELET, Alfred
Chere nuit. See no. 4038
BACHILER, Daniell
The Lady Walsinghams conceites. See no. 5049
BACK, Sven-Erik
368 Motets. Swedish Radio Choir, Swedith Chamber Choir; Eric Ericson, Sven-Erik Back. Phono Suecia PS 10
++FF 7/8-81 p57
Som hjorten torstar. See no. 3991
Time present. See no. 4072
Tollo. See no. 4072
BACON, Ernst
Billy in the Darbies. See no. 3932
BADINGS, Henk
Dialogues. See no. 3681
BAERMANN, Heinrich
Quintet, clarinet, op. 23: Adagio. See no. 3793
BAGLEY, E.
National emblem. See no. 3699
BAINTON, Edgar
And I saw a new heaven. See no. 3636
BAIRD, Tadeusz
369 Elegeia. LUTOSLAWSKI: Mi-Parti. PENDERECKI: Anaklasis. Awakening of Jacob. Prague Radio Orchestra; Jacek Kasprzyk. Supraphon 410 2734
+-Gr 11-81 p678 ++SFC 10-18-81 p18
+HFN 11-81 p100
BAIRSTOW, Edward
Allegro giocoso. See no. 3806
Scherzo. See no. 4116
Songs: Let all mortal flesh keep silence. See no. 3618
Songs: Lord I call upon thee. See no. 3875
Songs: Though I speak with the tongues of men and of angels. See no. 3619
Toccata prelude on "Pange lingua". See no. 3625

BAKER, Ernest
Cantilena. See no. 3731
BAKFARK, Balint
Fantasia. See no. 4016
BALAKIREV, Mily
Islamey. See no. 3723
Romance. See no. 3789
BALANCHIVADZE, Andrej
Fugue. See no. 3910
BALASSA, Sandor
370 The man outside. Hungarian Radio Chorus; Budapest Symphony Orchestra; Gyorgy Lehel. Hungaroton SLPX 12052/3 (2)
+FF 1/2-81 p73 +NR 8-80 p10
+-HF 4-81 p74 ++SFC 11-23-80 p21
+HFN 2-81 p85 +St 1-81 p18
BALBASTRE, Claude
Au jo deu de pubelle. See no. 3812
371 La courteille. La d'hericourt. La lugeac. La malesherbe. La Suzanne. COUPERIN, F.: Livres de clavecin, Bk IV, Ordre, no. 23. DUPHLY, J.: La de belombre. La felix. La vanlo. Mark Kroll, hpd. AFKA SK 298
+-FF 3/4-81 p34
La d'hericourt. See no. 371. See no. 3763
Grand dei ribon ribeine. See no. 3812
Il est un petit ange. See no. 117
La lugeac. See no. 371
La malesherbe. See no. 371
Noel "Votre bonte grand Dieu". See no. 117
Suzanne. See no. 371
BALDELLI
A suon di baci. See no. 4032
BALFE, Michael
The Bohemian girl: When other lips. See no. 3967. See no. 3972
Killarney. See no. 4046
BANCHIERI, Adirano
Fantasia. See no. 3921
Sonata sopra l'aria musicale del Gran Duca. See no. 3938
Udite ecco le trombe fantasia. See no. 3663
BANTOK, Granville
372 Fifine at the fair. DELIUS: Songs of sunset. Maureen Forrester, con; John Cameron, bar; Beecham Choral Society; RPO; Thomas Beecham. HMV SXLP 30440 Tape (c) TC SXLP 30440 (From HMV DB 21145/8, ALP 1983)
+Gr 10-80 p523 +MT 4-81 p246
+-HFN 10-80 p115
Songs: Desolation; A dream of spring. See no. 4043
Songs: Love's secret; Songs from the Chinese poets, op. 2; A dream of spring; Desolation. See no. 3967
BARAB, Seymour
Bits and pieces. See no. 3957
BARBER, Samuel
Adagio. See no. 4082
373 Adagio, strings, op. 11. BARTOK: Rumanian folk dances, op. 8a. BRITTEN: Simple symphony, op. 4. RESPIGHI: Antiche danze ed arie per liuto: Suite, no. 3. I Musici. Philips 6570 181

Tape (c) 7310181 (From SABL 216)
+-Gr 1-81 p1002 +-HFN 4-81 p83 tape
+-HFN 1-81 p107

374 Adagio, strings, op. 11. ELGAR: Introduction and allegro, op. 47. TCHAIKOVSKY: Serenade, op. 48, C major. BSO; Charles Munch. RCA AGL 1-3790 Tape (c) AGK 1-3790
-FF 7/8-81 p227

375 Ballade, op. 46. Excursions, op. 20. Nocturne, op. 33. Sonata, piano, op. 26. Angela Brownridge, pno. Hyperion A66016
/-FF 9/10-81 p68 ++HFN 3-81 p85
+Gr 3-81 p1212 +St 8-81 p91

376 Essay, no. 3, op. 47. CORIGLIANO: Concerto, clarinet. Stanley Drucker, clt; NYP; Zubin Mehta. New World Records NW 309
++ARG 10-81 p21 ++NYT 4-12-81 pD29
++Audio 10-81 p28 +OV 12-81 p38
+FF 5/6-81 p49 ++St 5-81 p57
+-HF 4-81 p77

Excursions, op. 20. See no. 375
Nocturne, op. 33. See no. 375
Reincarnation, op. 16. See no. 3931

377 Serenade, op. 1. CARTER: Elegy. DIAMOND: Rounds. FINE: Serious song: A lament for string orchestra. Los Angeles Chamber Orchestra; Gerard Schwarz. Nonesuch D 79002
+-FF 3/4-81 p232 ++St 2-81 p111
+NYT 3-29-81 pD31

378 Sonata, piano, op. 26, E minor. RILEY: A rainbow in curved air. SHAW (Krimsky): Epilogue. Specs. SHAW: Katrina ballerina. Katrina Krimsky, pno. Transonic Records 3008
+FF 9/10-81 p238

Sonata, piano, op. 26, E minor. See no. 375. See no. 3723

BARBINGANT (c 1470)
L'Omme bany de sa plaisance. See no. 3948

BARBIREAU, Jacques
Songs: En frolyk weson. See no. 3853

BARBLAN, Otto

379 Chaconne sur BACH, op. 10, G minor. Fantasie, op. 16. Toccata, op. 23. GAGNEBIN: Dialogue et passacaille. Toccata, no. 3. Pierre Cochereau, org. Motette M 1035
+-FF 9/10-81 p69

Fantasie, op. 16. See no. 379
Toccata, op. 23. See no. 379

BARDOS, Lajos

380 Sounds of Bakony, Folk songs for mixed chorus: The big bell of Mikohaza. KODALY: Evening song; Evening; Norwegian girls; Szekeley lament; Te deum of Sandor Sik; Those who are always late. NAGY: The orphan bird. SZERVANSZKY: The river has overflown. Veszprem Liszt Ferenc Chorus; Kalman Kollar. Hungaroton SLPX 12202
+ARG 2-81 p43 +-FF 9/10-81 p221

BARKHUDARIAN
Maz-Par. See no. 3917

BARNARD, Charlotte
Come back to Erin. See no. 4046

BARON, Ernst

381 Concerto, guitar, no. 1, C major. GALILEI: Studies, guitar (6).

GIULIANI: Sonata, violin and guitar, op. 25, E minor. SCHEIDLER: Sonata, flute and guitar, D major. Diego Blanco, gtr; Gunilla von Bahr, flt. BIS LP 90
+FF 7/8-80 p78 ++NR 5-80 p7
+-HFN 4-80 p115 ++RR 3-80 p80
+MUM 9/10-81 p30

BARRAQUE, Jean
382 ...au dela du hasard. Ensemble 2E 2M; Paul Mefano. Astree AS 50
*+FF 3/4-81 p66

BARRE, Michel de la
Meslanges de musique: Tendres plaisirs. See no. 4067
Suite, no. 3, E minor: Sarabande. See no. 4067
Suite, no. 7, E minor. See no. 4067

BARRERA SAAVEDRA, Tomas
Granadinas. See no. 4054

BARRERA Y CALLEJA
Adios Granada. See no. 3642

BARRIOS MANGORE, Agustin
Aire de zambal. See no. 3929
Choro do Saudade. See no. 3765
383 Danza paraguaya. Sarita mazurka. BROUWER: Elogio de la danza. GIULIANI: Grand overture, op. 61. Alan Rinehart, gtr, lt. Dulcian 1001
-MUM 9/10-81 p36
Danza paraguaya. See no. 3929
Maxixa. See no. 3929
Sarita mazurka. See no. 383

BARROCLOUGH
Simoraine. See no. 3955

BARSANTI, Francesco
384 Concerto, 2 horns, op. 3, no. 4, D major. HANDEL: Concerto, 2 horns, F major. TELEMANN: Concerto, horn, D major. Concerto, 3 horns, D major. Suite, 2 horns, F major. James Stagliano, Arthur Berv, hn; Kapp Sinfonietta; Richard Dunn. Westminster MCA 1422 Tape (c) 1422
+FF 5/6-81 p170 +NR 12-80 p6
Concerto grosso, op. 3, no. 10, D major. See no. 29. See no. 3978
Sonata, recorder, G minor. See no. 4056

BARTEVIAN, Ara
For children. See no. 3913

BARTHE
Passacaille. See no. 4019

BARTHELEMY
Songs: Adorables tourments; Triste ritorno. See no. 3995
Songs: Sulla bocca amorosa; Triste ritorno; Serenamente. See no. 4032

BARTOK, Bela
Allegro barbaro. See no. 430. See no. 431
385 Andante. Hungarian folk songs. Rhapsodies, violin, nos. 1, 2. Sonatas, violin and piano, nos. 1, 2. Gyorgy Pauk, vln; Peter Frankl, pno. Hungaroton SLPX 12318/9 (2)
++FF 9/10-81 p72 +NR 9-81 p7
++Gr 6-81 p48 +NYT 8-2-81 pD19
++HFN 5-81 p69 ++St 12-81 p113
Bagatelle, op. 6, no. 2. See no. 432

386 Blubeard's castle, op. 11. Tatiana Troyanos, ms; Siegmund Nimsgern, bs; BBC Symphony Orchestra; Pierre Boulez. CBS 76518 Tape (c) 40-76518 (also Columbia M 34217)
++Gr 9-76 p466 ++NR 2-77 p11
+HF 2-77 p96 +-ON 2-12-77 p41
++HFN 9-76 p114 ++RR 9-76 p26
++HFN 11-76 p175 tape ++RR 1-77 p87 tape
+MJ 4-77 p50 ++St 2-77 p81
++MT 3-77 p214 +ST 1-77 p775
+MUM 5/6-81 p34
387 Bluebeard's castle, op. 11. Dance suite. The miraculous Mandarin, op. 17. The wooden prince, op. 13. Tatiana Troyanos, con; Siegmund Nimsgern, bs; BBC Symphony Orchestra, NYP; Pierre Boulez. CBS 79338 (3) Tape (c) 41-79338 (From 76518, 76625, 73031)
+Gr 6-81 p33 +-HFN 7-81 p81
388 Bluebeard's castle, op. 11. Sylvia Sass, s; Kolos Kovats, bs-bar; LPO; Georg Solti. London OSA 1174
+-FF 3/4-81 p67 +ON 4-4-81 p28
+HF 1-81 p66 +SR 3-81 p91
Burlesques, op. 8c. See no. 430
389 Cantata profana. Hungarian folksongs (5). Village scenes. Choruses (7). Laura Farago, Anna Adam, s; Julia Hamari, alto; Jozsef Reti, t; Andras Farago, bar; Budapest Chorus; Gyor Girls Chorus; Ferenc Liszt Academy Chamber Chorus; Budapest Symphony Orchestra, Hungarian State Symphony Orchestra, Budapest Chamber Ensemble; Janos Ferencsik, Andras Korody, Antal Dorati. Hungaroton SLPX 11510
+CJ 9-75 p30 +-MUM 5/6-81 p35
++Gr 7-74 p244 +RR 4-74 p73
Choruses (7). See no. 389
390 Concerto, orchestra. BPhO; Herbert von Karajan. Angel S 37059 (also HMV ASD 3046)
+Gr 1-75 p1335 +NYT 11-10-74 pD1
-HF 2-75 p87 +-RR 1-75 p25
+MUM 5/6-81 p36 ++St 3-75 p96
+NR 12-74 p4
391 Concerto, orchestra. NYP; Pierre Boulez. CBS HM 42132
+-FF 11/12-81 p97
392 Concerto, orchestra. Dance suite. LSO; Georg Solti. Decca SXDL 7536 Tape (c) KSXDC 7536 (also London LDR 71036)
+Gr 9-81 p372 ++HFN 9-81 p78
+Gr 11-81 p783 tape ++SFC 10-11-81 p19
393 Concerto, orchestra. Images, op. 10. BPhO; Lorin Maazel. DG 2531 269 Tape (c) 3301 269
+ARG 9-81 p13 ++NR 6-81 p2
+-FF 7/8-81 p58 +NYT 8-2-81 pD19
+Gr 2-81 p1079 ++SFC 6-14-81 p18
+Gr 4-81 p1376 tape ++St 7-81 p78
+HFN 3-81 p85 +STL 2-8-81 p40
+HFN 3-81 p97 tape
394 Concerto, orchestra. BPhO; Herbert von Karajan. DG 2535 202 (From SLPM 139003)
+-FF 9/10-81 p70 ++MUM 5/6-81 p36
+-Gr 12-76 p989 +RR 12-76 p51
++HFN 12-76 p151

395 Concerto, orchestra. CPhO; Karel Ancerl. Quintessence PMC 7152 Tape (c) 7152
+ARG 1-81 p20 +FF 11/12-80 p67

396 Concerto, orchestra. CSO; Fritz Reiner. RCA AGL 1-2909
++FF 3/4-79 p25 +SR 3-81 p91

397 Concerto, orchestra. PO; Eugene Ormandy. RCA ARC 1-3421 Tape (c) ARK 1-3421
++Gr 7-80 p135 +NYT 3-30-80 pD23
-HF 12-79 p79 ++RR 7-80 p50
+-HF 3-81 p80 tape ++SFC 9-16-79 p61
+-HFN 7-80 p105 +-St 11-79 p86

398 Concerto, orchestra. Budapest Symphony Orchestra; Arpad Joo. Sefel SEFD 5009
+MUM 11/12-81 p36

Concerto, orchestra. See no. 460

399 Concerti, piano, nos. 1 and 2. Maurizio Pollini, pno; CSO; Claudio Abbado. DG 2530 901 Tape (c) 3301 901
+-ARG 1-80 p18 ++HFN 8-79 p99
+FF 3/4-80 p50 ++MUM 5/6-81 p35
++FU 4-80 p44 ++NYT 3-30-80 pD24
+Gr 7-79 p191 ++RR 9-79 p68
+Gr 9-79 p533 tape ++SFC 9-16-79 p61
+HF 2-80 p83 ++St 1-80 p95

Concerti, piano, nos. 1 and 2. See no. 460. See no. 3785

400 Concerti, piano, nos. 2 and 3. Vladimir Ashkenazy, pno; LPO; Georg Solti. Decca SXL 6937 Tape (c) KSXC 6937 (also London 7167 Tape (c) 5-7167)
+-ARG 9-81 p14 +MT 8-81 p539
+CL 10-81 p8 +SFC 2-22-81 p18
+-FF 7/8-81 p59 ++St 7-81 p75
+Gr 3-81 p1180 ++STL 4-12-81 p40
++HFN 3-81 p85

401 Concerto, piano, no. 3, E major. SHOSTAKOVICH: Concerto, piano, no. 2, op. 101, F major. John Ogdon, pno; NPhO; Malcolm Sargent, Lawrence Foster. HMV SXLP 30514 Tape (c) TC SXLP 30514 (From ASD 2347, 2709)
+Gr 6-81 p34 +HFN 7-81 p79
+Gr 11-81 p783 tape

402 Concerto, viola (completed Serly). HINDEMITH: Der Schwanendreher. Daniel Benyamini, vla; Orchestre de Paris; Daniel Barenboim. DG 2531 249
+-ARG 12-80 p18 +MT 12-80 p783
+-FF 9/10-80 p69 -NR 7-80 p2
+Gr 4-80 p1549 +MUM 5/6-81 p35
+HFN 5-80 p117 +RR 5-80 p52
+/HFN 10-80 p109

403 Concerti, violin, nos. 1 and 2. Yehudi Menuhin, vln; NPhO; Antal Dorati. HMV SXLP 30533 Tape (c) TC SXLP 30533 (From ASD 2323, 2281)
+Gr 8-81 p261 +HFN 8-81 p91
+Gr 11-81 p783 tape

404 Concerto, violin, no. 1. Concerto, violin, no. 2, B minor. Nell Gotkovsky, vln; National Philharmonic Orchestra; Charles Gerhardt. RCA RL 3-7444
+Gr 10-81 p538

405 Concerto, violin, no. 2, B minor. Peter Zazofsky, vln; Orchestre National de Belgique; Georges Octors. DG 2535 012
++ARG 12-81 p9
+NR 7-81 p2
+-NYT 8-2-81 pD19
+SFC 6-7-81 p19
++St 9-81 p86

406 Concerto, violin, no. 2, B minor. Pinchas Zukerman, vln; LAPO; Zubin Mehta. Columbia M 35156 Tape (c) MT 35156 (also CBS 76831 Tape (c) 40-76831)
+-FF 7/8-80 p52
/Gr 3-80 p1379
+Gr 5-80 p1717 tape
++HF 7-80 p60
+HFN 3-80 p86
+HFN 6-80 p119 tape
+MUM 5/6-81 p35
+NR 5-80 p4
+NYT 3-30-80 pD24
++RR 4-80 p56
++St 7-80 p76
+-ST 9-80 p339

407 Concerto, violin, no. 2, B minor. Kyung Wha Chung; LPO; Georg Solti. Decca SXL 6802 Tape (c) KSXC 6802 (also London 7023 Tape (c) 5-7023)
+-FF 7/8-78 p14
+Gr 4-78 p1707
+Gr 9-78 p558 tape
++HF 4-78 p85
+HFN 4-78 p110
+HFN 7-78 p109 tape
+MUM 5/6-81 p35
++NR 6-78 p5
++RR 5-78 p27
+RR 7-78 p95 tape
+-St 6-78 p138

408 Concerto, violin, no. 2, B minor. Itzhak Perlman, vln; LSO; Andre Previn. HMV ASD 3014 (also Angel S 37014)
++Gr 10-74 p676
+HF 1-75 p75
*MUM 5/6-81 p35
+NR 12-74 p6
+-RR 11-74 p34
++St 3-75 p97

409 Concerto, violin, no. 2, B minor. Andre Gertler, vln; CPhO; Karel Ancerl. Quintessence PMC 7181 (From Supraphon)
-FF 7/8-81 p60

Concerto, violin, no. 2, B minor. See no. 404. See no. 460

410 Contrasts. Bela Bartok, pno; Joseph Szigeti, vln; Benny Goodman, clt. Odyssey 32160220E
+-MUM 5/6-81 p34
+St 5-77 p72

Contrasts. See no. 423

411 Dance suite. Hungarian peasant songs (15). Rondos on folk tunes (3). Rumanian folk dances. Andras Schiff, pno. Denon OX 7215
+-FF 11/12-81 p99
+St 11-81 p78

412 Dance suite. The miraculous Mandarin, op. 19. Budapest Philharmonic Orchestra; Arpad Joo. Sefel SEFD 5008
++MUM 11/12-81 p36

Dance suite. See no. 387. See no. 392. See no. 424. See no. 460

413 Dances in Bulgarian rhythm (6). Pieces, 2 pianos (7). Mikrokosmos, excerpts. Ditta Pasztory-Bartok, Maria Comensoli, pno. Hungaroton SLPX 12283
+-FF 9/10-81 p70
+St 11-81 p78

Divertimento, strings. See no. 460

414 Duos, 2 violins, nos. 1-44. Itzhak Perlman, Pinchas Zukerman, vln. Angel SZ 37540 (also HMV ASD 4011)
++FF 7/8-81 p60
+Gr 5-81 p1485
+HF 10-81 p80
+HFN 7-81 p71
+NYT 8-2-81 pD19
++SFC 5-10-81 p18
+St 7-81 p78
++ST 10-81 p431

++MUM 7/8-81 p31 +STL 6-12-81 p40
++NR 7-81 p6

Elegies, op. 8b. See no. 430
Esquisses, op. 9b. See no. 431
Etudes, op. 18. See no. 3869

415 For children, Bks I and II. Ten easy pieces. Sonatina. Michel Beroff, pno. EMI 2C 167 16246/7 (2)
+Gr 5-81 p1494

416 For children, Bks I and II. Zoltan Kocsis, pno. Hungaroton SLPX 12304/5 (2)
+FF 11/12-81 p97 +NR 12-81 p16
+Gr 8-81 p290 +NYT 8-2-81 pD19
+HFN 8-81 p82 ++St 11-81 p78

For children, Bk I, nos. 1-4, 13-15, 18, 21-22, 25-26, 28, 30-32, 40; Bk II, nos. 1-3, 8, 13, 18, 26, 28, 34, 36-37. See no. 430
For children: Children at play; Play; Old Hungarian tune; Andante con moto; Teasing song; Farewell. See no. 3680
Hungarian folksongs. See no. 389. See no. 432. See no. 4119
Hungarian folksongs from the Csik district. See no. 431
Hungarian peasant songs. See no. 411. See no. 430. See no. 431
Images, op. 10. See no. 393

417 Improvisations on Hungarian peasant songs, op. 20. Out of doors. Sonata, piano. Suite, op. 14. Murray Perahia, pno. CBS M 36704 Tape (c) MT 36704 (also CBS 76650)
+FF 9/10-81 p71 +NR 8-81 p12
++Gr 9-81 p406 +NYT 8-2-81 pD19
+HFN 12-81 p92 +SFC 6-7-81 p19
+MUM 9/10-81 p33 +St 10-81 p116

Improvisations on Hungarian peasant songs, op. 20. See no. 430. See no. 431
Improvisations on Hugarian peasant songs, op. 20, nos. 1-2, 6-8. See no. 432

418 Kossuth. Pieces, orchestra, op. 12. Budapest Philharmonic Orchestra; Arpad Joo. Sefel SEFD 5005
+MUM 11/12-81 p36

Kossuth, op. 2. See no. 458
Little piano pieces. See no. 430

419 Mikrokosmos. Homero Francesch, pno. DG 2740 239 (3)
+-FF 11/12-81 p98 +NYT 8-2-81 pD19
+Gr 5-81 p1494 -St 11-81 p78
+HFN 5-81 p77

420 Mikrokosmos. Dezso Ranki, pno. Telefunken 6-35369 (3)
+FF 9/10-78 p15 +MUM 5/6-81 p34
+Gr 1-79 p1305 +RR 11-78 p85
++HF 10-78 p102 ++SFC 9-16-79 p61
+HFN 11-78 p165

421 Mikrokosmos, excerpts. Ditta Bartok Pasztory, Maria Comensoli, pno. Hungaroton LSPX 12283
+NR 12-81 p16 +NYT 8-2-81 pD19

Mikrokosmos, excerpts. See no. 413. See no. 432
Mikrokosmos, nos. 97, 100, 102, 108, 113, 115, 122, 125-128, 130, 137, 139-143, 146, 148-153. See no. 430

422 Mikrokosmos: 5 pieces (arr.). JANACEK: Quartet, strings, no. 2. STRAVINSKY: Pieces, string quartet (3). WEBERN: Bagatelles, op. 9 (6). Dornbusch Quartet. Musical Heritage Society MHS

3883 (also Da Camera SM 92414)
+-FF 5/6-79 p128 +HFN 11-81 p100

423 Mikrokosmos: Tale; In the style of a folk song; Wrestling; From the island of Bali; Bulgarian rhythm; Fifth chords; Peasant dance; Alternating thirds; Fourths; Syncopation; Bagpipe; Free variations; From the diary of a fly; Dances, nos. 1-6 in Bulgarian rhythm. Contrasts. Bela Bartok, pno; Joseph Szigeti, vln; Benny Goodman, clt. CBS 61882 (also CBS 235484)
+Gr 2-80 p1276 +HFN 2-80 p86
++Gr 3-81 p1170 ++RR 2-80 p70

424 The miraculous Mandarin, op. 19. Dance suite. NYP; Pierre Boulez. Columbia M 31368 Tape (c) MT 31368 (Q) MQ 31368 (also CBS 73031)
+-Gr 1-73 p1319 +-NR 11-72 p3
+-HF 12-72 p74 +-RR 1-73 p37
+HFN 2-73 p333 -SFC 4-29-73 p31
++MUM 5/6-81 p34 ++St 1-73 p104

425 The miraculous Mandarin, op. 19. Music, strings, percussion and celesta. PO; Eugene Ormandy. HMV ASD 3655 Tape (c) TC ASD 3655 (also Angel SZ 37608)
-FF 1/2-80 p43 +HFN 9-79 p123 tape
+FU 5-80 p46 +MUM 5/6-81 p35
+Gr 7-79 p191 +NYT 3-30-80 pD23
+Gr 9-79 p533 tape ++RR 7-79 p46
+HF 12-79 p79 ++SFC 9-16-79 p61
+HFN 9-79 p101

The miraculous Mandarin, op. 19. See no. 387. See no. 412

426 The miraculous Mandarin, op. 19: Suite. The wooden prince, op. 13: Suite. Minnesota Orchestea; Stanislaw Skrowaczewski. Candide QCE 31097
+ARG 12-77 p20 +MUM 5/6-81 p34
+-FF 1-78 p8 ++NR 10-77 p4
+HF 11-77 p104 ++SFC 8-14-77 p50

427 The miraculous Mandarin, op. 19: Suite. Portraits, op. 5 (2). VPO; Christoph von Dohnanyi. Decca SXL 6882
+-Gr 6-81 p33 +-MT 11-81 p753
+HFN 6-81 p69

428 The miraculous Mandarin, op. 19: Suite. Music, strings, percussion and celesta. BSO; Seiji Ozawa. DG 2535 454 Tape (c) 3335 454 (From 2530 887)
+-Gr 8-81 p261 +HFN 8-81 p91

429 Music, strings, percussion and celesta. STRAVINSKY: Apollon musagete. BPhO; Herbert von Karajan. DG 2530 065
+-Gr 5-73 p2042 +-RR 5-73 p45
+HFN 5-73 p979 +-SFC 11-18-73 p33
+-HF 6-73 p100 +SR 3-81 p91
/NR 6-73 p2 -St 4-73 p107
+-NYT 2-1-73 pD42

Music, strings, percussion and celesta. See no. 425. See no. 428. See no. 460

Nenies, op. 9a. See no. 431

Nine little pieces, no. 9: All Ungherese, Preludio. See no. 432

Out of doors. See no. 417. See no. 430

Petite suite. See no. 432

430 Piano works: Allegro barbaro. Burlesques, op. 8c (3). Elegies, op. 8b (2). For children, Bk I, nos. 1-4, 13-15, 18, 21-22,

25-26, 28, 30-32, 40; Bk II, nos. 1-3, 8, 13, 18, 26, 28, 34, 36-37. Hungarian peasant songs (15). Improvisations on Hungarian peasant songs, op. 20. Mikrokosmos, nos. 97, 100, 102, 108, 113, 115, 122, 125-128, 130, 137, 139-143, 146, 148-153. Little piano pieces. Out of doors. Pieces, piano: Fantasy, no. 2. Rondos on folk tunes (3). Rumanian Christmas carols. Rumanian folk dances (6). Sketches (7). Sonatina. Sonata. Suite. Ten easy piano pieces. Andor Foldes, pno. DG 2740 232 (4) (From DGM 18270, 18271, 18272, 17283)
+Gr 8-81 p290 +HFN 5-81 p91

431 Piano works: Allegro barbaro. Esquisses, op. 9b. Hungarian folksongs from the Csik district. Hungarian peasant songs (15). Improvisations on Hungarian peasant songs, op. 20. Nenies, op. 9a (4). Zoltan Kocsis, pno. Philips 9500 876 Tape (c) 7300 876
+ARG 10-81 p17 +NR 7-81 p13
++FF 9/10-81 p69 ++NYT 8-2-81 pD19
+Gr 8-81 p290 +St 9-81 p86
+HFN 8-81 p82

432 Piano works: Nine little pieces, no. 9: All Ungherese, Preludio. Bagatelle, op. 6, no. 2. Hungarian folksongs. Improvisations on Hungarian peasant songs, op. 20, nos. 1-2, 6-8. Mikrokosmos, excerpts. Petite suite. Rondo on folk tunes, no. 1. Bela Bartok, Ditta Pasztory Bartok, pno. Turnabout THS 65010
+HF 10-74 p88 +NR 9-74 p9
*MUM 5/6-81 p34 +St 3-75 p96

Pictures, op. 10 (2). See no. 457
Pieces, orchestra, op. 12. See no. 418
Pieces, piano: Fantasy, no. 2. See no. 430
Pieces, 2 pianos (7). See no. 413
Portraits, op. 5 (2). See no. 427. See no. 456. See no. 460

433 Quartets, strings, nos. 1-6. Juilliard Quartet. Columbia D3S 717
++HF 4-71 p62 +SR 3-81 p91
+MUM 5/6-81 p35

434 Quartets, strings, nos. 1-6. Tokyo Quartet. DG 2740 235 (3) (also 2562 237/9) (nos. 2, 6 from DG 2530 658)
++ARG 9-81 p12 ++NR 5-81 p10
++Gr 4-81 p1330 ++NYT 8-2-81 pD19
++HF 11-81 p74 ++SFC 5-10-81 p18
+HFN 5-81 p76 ++St 7-81 p77
+MT 12-81 p826 ++ST 9-81 p349

435 Quartets, strings, nos. 1-6. Guarnieri Quartet. RCA RL 2412 (3) (also RCA RL 3-2412)
+-ARG 5-78 p12 +-MJ 2-78 p28
++FF 1-78 p9 +-MUM 5/6-81 p35
+Gr 9-78 p491 +NR 1-78 p8
+-HF 3-78 p93 +RR 11-78 p79
+-HFN 9-78 p139 -St 2-78 p148

436 Quartet, strings, nos. 1-6. Vegh Quartet. Telefunken 6-35023
+MUM 5/6-81 p35 ++St 2-78 p148
+-NYT 10-23-77 pD15

437 Quartet, strings, no. 1, op. 7, A minor. Quartet, strings, no. 2, op. 17, A minor. Lindsay Quartet. ASV DCA 510 Tape (c) ZCDCA 510
+Gr 10-81 p568 +HFN 10-81 p85

438 Quartet, strings, no. 1, op. 7, A minor. Quartet, strings, no. 2, op. 17, A minor. Fine Arts Quartet. Saga 5203 (From STXID 5203)
+-Gr 6-81 p46

Quartet, strings, no. 2, op. 17, A minor. See no. 437. See no. 438

439 Quartet, strings, no. 3, C sharp major. Quartet, strings, no. 4, C major. Lindsay Quartet. ASV DCA 509 Tape (c) ZCDCA 509
+Gr 9-81 p396 +HFN 8-81 p81
+Gr 9-81 p460 tape

440 Quartet, strings, no. 3, C sharp major. RAVEL: Quartet, strings, F major. Sequoia String Quartet. Delos DMS 3004
+Audio 9-81 p84 ++NYT 3-30-80 pD24
+HF 8-80 p80 +RR 4-80 p88
+HFN 4-80 p101 ++St 6-80 p120
+NR 2-80 p6

441 Quartet, strings, no. 3, C major. Quartet, strings, no. 4, C major. Fine Arts Quartet. Saga 5402 (From STXID 5204)
+Gr 6-81 p46 +HFN 5-81 p9

442 Quartet, strings, no. 4, C major. CRAWFORD: Quartet, strings. Vaghy Quartet. Canadian Braodcasting Corp. SM 325
+FF 7/8-81 p92

Quartet, strings, no. 4, C major. See no. 439. See no. 441

443 Quartet, strings, no. 5, B flat major. Quartet, strings, no. 6, D major. Lindsay Quartet. ASV DCA 504 Tape (c) ZCDCA 504
+Gr 7-81 p196 tape ++HFN 7-81 p71
+Gr 6-81 p48

444 Quartet, strings, no. 5, B flat major. Quartet, strings, no. 6, D major. Fine Arts Quartet. Saga 5205 (From STXID 5205)
+Gr 6-81 p46 +HFN 5-81 p91

Quartet, strings, no. 6, D major. See no. 443. See no. 444

445 Quintet, piano. Sylvia Glickman, pno; Alard Quartet. Leonarda LPL 108
+-FF 9/10-81 p70 +/St 10-81 p115
++NYT 8-2-81 pD19

446 Quintet, piano. Quintetto Italiano. Ricordi RCL 27021
+FF 11/12-81 p98

Rhapsody, piano. See no. 460

447 Rhapsodies, violin (2). BERG: Concerto, violin. Yehudi Menuhin, vln; BBC Symphony Orchestra; Pierre Boulez. Arabesque 8009 Tape (c) 9009
+FF 1/2-81 p83 ++MUM 7/8-81 p35
++HF 1-81 p69 +NR 3-81 p6

Rhapsodies, violin, nos. 1, 2. See no. 385

Rondos on folk tunes (3). See no. 411. See no. 430

Rondos on folk tunes, no. 1. See no. 432

Rumanian Christmas carols. See no. 430

Rumanian folk dances. See no. 411. See no. 430. See no. 3704. See no. 3847

Rumanian folk dances, op. 8a. See no. 373

Scherzo. See no. 458

Sketches (7). See no. 430

Sonata, piano. See no. 417. See no. 430

448 Sonata, 2 pianos and percussion. STRAVINSKY: Concerto, 2 solo pianos. Sonata, 2 pianos. Alfons and Aloys Kontarsky, pno;

Christoph Caskel, Heinz Konig, perc. DG 2530 964
+-ARG 10-78 p49 ++MJ 3/4-79 p46
+-FF 9/10-78 p113 +MUM 5/6-81 p35
+Gr 6-78 p76 ++NR 8-78 p10
+HF 11-78 p105 +RR 6-78 p75
+HFN 6-78 p117 +St 8-78 p126

449 Sonata, 2 pianos and percussion. DEBUSSY: En blanc et noir. MOZART: Andante with variations, K 501, G major. Martha Argerich, Stephen Bishop-Kovacevich, pno; Willy Goudswaard, Michael de Roo, perc. Philips 9500 434 Tape (c) 7300 664
++CL 1-79 p10 +MM 3-79 p36
++FF 3/4-79 p25 +MUM 5/6-81 p35
++Gr 8-78 p347 ++NR 2-79 p13
+-Gr 12-78 p1178 tape -RR 8-78 p84
+HFN 8-78 p101 ++RR 1-79 p90 tape
+HFN 10-78 p139 tape ++St 12-78 p144
++MJ 3/4-79 p45

450 Sonata, solo violin. HONEGGER: Sonata, solo violin. PROKOFIEV: Sonata, solo violin, op. 115, D major. Lydia Mordkovich, vln. RCA RL 2-5311
+Gr 4-81 p1343 +ST 7-81 p204
+HFN 3-81 p94

Sonata, solo violin. See no. 4072
Sonata, violin and piano. See no. 453
Sonatas, violin and piano, nos. 1, 2. See no. 385

451 Sonata, violin and piano, no. 1. Sonata, violin and piano, no. 2. Yehudi Menuhin, vln; Jeremy Menuhin, pno. Ades 14021
+Gr 9-81 p396 +HFN 8-81 p81

Sonata, violin and piano, no. 1. See no. 452
Sonata, violin and piano, no. 2. See no. 451
Sonatina. See no. 415
Sonatina, piano. See no. 430
Songs, op. 16 (5). See no. 455

452 Songs: Hungarian peasant songs (15). Sonata, violin and piano, no. 1. David Oistrakh, vln; Sviatoslav Richter, pno. CBS M 36712 Tape (c) MT 36712
+-FF 9/10-81 p73 ++SFC 7-5-81 p19
+-NR 9-81 p7 ++St 12-81 p113

453 Songs: Hungarian peasant songs (15). Sonata, violin and piano. David Oistrakh, vln; Sviatoslav Richter, pno. Chant du Monde LDX 78673
+HFN 5-81 p76

454 Songs: Hungarian folksongs, op. 16 (5). LISZT: Songs: Die drei Zigeuner, S 320; Es muss ein Wunderbares sein, S 314; Es war ein Konig in Thule, S 278; Kling leise mein Lied, S 301; Die Loreley, S 273; Ne brany menya moy drug; Enfant si j'etais roi, S 283; Vergiftet sind meine Lieder, G 289. Sylvia Sass, s; Andras Schiff, pno. Decca SXL 6984
+Gr 5-81 p1502 /STL 6-14-81 p40
+HFN 4-81 p67

455 Songs, op. 15 (5). Songs, op. 16 (5). Eszter Kovacs, s; Adam Fellegi, pno. Hungaroton LSPX 11603
+-Gr 8-76 p324 +NR 6-76 p14
+-HF 8-76 p79 +-RR 6-76 p77
+MUM 5/6-81 p35 ++SFC 8-14-77 p50

Suite. See no. 430
456 Suite, no. 1, op. 3. Portraits, op. 5 (2). Budapest Symphony Orchestra; Arpad Joo. Sefel SEFD 5006
+MUM 11/12-81 p36
457 Suite, no. 2, op. 4. Pictures, op. 10 (2). Budapest Symphony Orchestra; Arpad Joo. Sefel SEFD 5007
++MUM 11/12-81 p36
Suite, op. 14. See no. 417
458 Symphony, E flat major: Scherzo. Kossuth, op. 2. Scherzo. Erzsebet Tusa, pno; Budapest Symphony Orchestra; Gyorgy Lehel. Hungaroton SLPX 11517 (also Qualiton LPX 11517)
+-Gr 6-72 p39
+-HF 5-72 p84
+-HFN 8-72 p1453
+MUM 5/6-81 p34
+-SFC 10-21-73 p28
Ten easy pieces. See no. 415. See no. 430
Village scenes. See no. 389
459 The wooden prince, op. 13. NYP; Pierre Boulez. Columbia M 34514 Tape (c) MT 34514 (also CBS SQ 76625)
++ARG 7-77 p16
++Gr 10-77 p618
+HF 11-77 p104
+HFN 10-77 p147
+-MJ 2-78 p28
+MT 8-78 p686
++MUM 5/6-81 p34
+NR 6-77 p3
++RR 10-77 p37
+SFC 8-14-77 p50
++St 10-77 p86
The wooden prince, op. 13. See no. 387
The wooden prince, op. 13: Suite. See no. 426
460 Works, selections: Concerto, orchestra. Concerti, piano, nos. 1 and 2. Concerto, violin, no. 2, B minor. Dance suite. Divertimento, strings. Music, strings, percussion and celesta. Portraits, op. 5 (2). Rhapsody, piano. Geza Anda, pno; Tibor Varga, vln; RIAS Symphony Orchestra Berlin, BRSO, BPhO; Ferenc Fricsay. DG 2740 233 (5) (From 18377, 18493, 18153, 138708, 138111, 18006)
+-Gr 8-81 p261
+HFN 6-81 p83

BARTOLINO DA PADOVA
Per un verde boschetto. See no. 4102

BASSANO, Giovanni
Songs: Anchor che co'l partire; La bella netta ignuda e bianca mano; Frais et gaillard; Io canterei d'amor; Ricercata prima; Susanne un jour; Tirsi morir volea; Un gay bergier. See no. 3835

BASSETT, Leslie
461 Concerto, 2 pianos. HODKINSON: November voices. MOSS: Omaggio II. Fernando Laires, Nelita True, Sheryl Seltzer, Joel Sachs, pno; Midland Symphony Orchestra, Eastman Musica Nova Ensemble; Don Jaeger, Sidney Hodkinson. Advance FGR 26
+NR 7-81 p3
462 Echoes from an invisible world. LAZAROF: Concerto, orchestra. Baltimore Symphony Orchestra; Sergiu Comissiona. CRI SD 429
-FF 3/4-81 p68
+-NR 5-81 p2
++SFC 2-1-81 p18

BASSI, Luigi
Fantasia di concerto on Verdi's "Rigoletto". See no. 3715

BATCHELOR, Daniel
Songs: To plead with my faith. See no. 3946

BATTEN, Adrian
O sing joyfully. See no. 3824
Out of the deep. See no. 3637
BATTISHILL, Jonathan
O Lord look down from heaven. See no. 3824
BAUDAC
South Rampart Street parade (Haggart). See no. 3976
BAUER, Marion
Pieces, piano (4). See no. 3918
BAUR, Jean-Pierre
463 Sonatas, harp and harpsichord, op. 6, nos. 3-4, op. 7, nos. 1-2; op. 8, nos. 3-4. Marielle Nordmann, hp; Brigitte Haudebourg, hpd. Arion ARN 38533 (also Musical Heritage Society MHS 4317)
+FF 7/8-81 p60 +RR 7-80 p75
++HFN 8-80 p94
BAUR, John
464 The moon and the yew tree. CHATMAN: Whisper baby. RHODES: Visions of remembrance. Carol Wilson, Christine Anderson, s; Lorraine Manz, ms; Elizabeth Baur, flt; Robert Weirich, pno; John Burton, vlc; Maura Chatman, pno; Carleton Contemporary Ensemble; Univ. of British Columbia Chamber Singers; William Wells, Cortland Hultberg. CRI SD 426
+ARG 2-81 p46 +NR 10-80 p11
+FF 5/6-81 p222
BAUSZNERN, Dietrich von
Veni creator spiritus. See no. 1082
BAX, Arnold
Burlesque. See no. 4055
465 Irish songs (3). LISZT: Es war ein Konig in Thule, S 278; Mignon's Lied. SCHUBERT: Mignons Gesang, op. 19, no. 2; Der Konig in Thule, D 367. SCHUMANN: Frauenliebe und Leben, op. 42. Mary O'Brien, s; Lincoln Mayorga, pno. Townhall S22
-FF 9/10-81 p208
466 Sonata, viola and piano. Lionel Tertis, vla; Arnold Bax, pno. Pearl GEMM 201
+HFN 9-81 p78
Sonata, viola and piano. See no. 3971
Songs: Far in a western brookland. See no. 3893
Songs: Morning song. See no. 3857
467 Three small pieces, orchestra: Dance in the sunlight. BUTTERWORTH: A Shropshire lad. The banks of green willow: Idyll. BRIDGE: There is a willow grows aslant a brook. HARTY: John Field suite. English Sinfonia; Neville Dilkes. HMV ESD 7100 Tape (c) TC ESD 7100 (From CSD 3696)
+-Gr 11-81 p713 +-HFN 11-81 p103
468 Tintagel. DELIUS: Irmelin. A song of summer. A village Romeo and Juliet: The walk to the paradise garden (arr. Beecham). IRELAND: A London overture. LSO; John Barbirolli. HMV ESD 7092 Tape (c) TC ESD 7092 (From ASD 2305)
++FF 1/2-81 p131 +Gr 12-80 p899 tape
+Gr 11-80 p234 +HFN 9-80 p115
BAZIN, Francois
Maitre pathelin: Je pense a vous quand je m'eveille. See no. 4049
BEACH, Amy
469 Theme and variations, op. 80. FOOTE: A night piece. HOOVER:

Divertimento. Diane Gold, flt; Alard Quartet. Leonarda LPI 105
+ARG 2-81 p42 ++NR 9-80 p4
+FF 11/12-80 p68 ++St 1-81 p78

Variations on Balkan themes, op. 60. See no. 3918

BEACH, Bennie

Music, brass quintet. See no. 3671

BEAT, Jane

Dancing on moonbeams. See no. 4062

BEDYNGHAM, John

Songs: Mon seul plaisir ma doulce joye; Zentil madona. See no. 3948

BEESON, Jack

470 Dr. Heidegger's fountain of youth. Carol Wilcox s; Judith Christin, ms; Grayson Hirst, t; Robert Shiesley, bar; Alfred Anderson, bs-bar; Chamber Orchestra; Thomas Martin. CRI SD 406
+ARG 9-80 p18 +ON 4-11-81 p52
+FF 3/4-80 p51 ++St 5-80 p82
+NR 2-80 p11

BEETHOVEN, Ludwig van

471 Adagio and allegretto, WoO 33. HAYDN: Divertimento, B flat major. Pieces, mechanical clock: Minuet, C major; Andante, C major; Allegretto, G major; Marcia, D major; Andante and allegro, E major; Fugue, C major; Allegro, C major. MOZART: Adagio and allegro, K 594, F major. Andante, K 616, F major. Fantasia, K 608, F minor. Vienna Wind Soloists. Decca SDD 576
+HFN 10-81 p93

472 Ah perfido, op. 65. Fidelio, op. 72: Abscheulicher wo eilst du bin...Komm Hoffung. MOZART: Don Giovanni, K 527: Or sai chi l'onore. WEBER: Oberon: Ozean du Ungeheuer. Birgit Nilsson, s; PhO; Heinz Wallberg. Seraphim S 60353
+MUM 11/12-81 p30 +-NYT 5-31-81 pD23

Andante favori, F major. See no. 477

473 Bagatelle, no. 25, A minor. Sonata, piano, no. 17, op. 31, no. 2, D minor. Sonata, piano, no. 28, op. 101, A major. Oxana Yablonskaya, pno. Orion Tape (c) In Sync C 4037
+ARG 9-81 p17 +NR 9-80 p10 tape

474 Bagatelle, no. 25, A minor. Sonata, piano, no. 14, op. 27, no. 2, C sharp minor. Sonata, piano, no. 18, op. 31, no. 3, E flat major. Bella Davidovich, pno. Philips 9500 665 Tape (c) 7300 763
+ARG 2-80 p18 +-HF 1-80 p73
+-FF 7/8-80 p56 +HFN 3-81 p86
+-FU 5-80 p47 +NR 1-80 p14
+-Gr 2-81 p1101

Bagatelle, no. 25, A minor. See no. 3680. See no. 3695. See no. 3764

475 Bagatelles, op. 33, nos. 1-7. MOZART: Sonata, piano, no. 4, K 282, E flat major. Sonata, piano, no. 8, K 310, A minor. Alicia de Larrocha, pno. London CS 7179 (also Decca SXL 6951 Tape (c) KSXC 6951)
+Audio 10-81 p30 ++NR 1-81 p14
+FF 11/12-80 p141 +-NYT 7-12-81 pD21
+Gr 1-81 p976 +SFC 10-19-80 p20
+HFN 1-81 p99 +St 10-80 p114

476 Bagatelles, op. 126. Polonaise, op. 89, C major. Sonata, piano, no. 32, op. 111, C minor. Julius Katchen, pno. London STS 15508 (From CS 6599)
+FF 3/4-81 p73

477 Concerti, piano, nos. 1-5. Andante favori, F major. Polonaise, op. 89, C major. Artur Schnabel, pno; LSO, LPO; Malcolm Sargent. Arabesque 8103/4 (4) Tape (c) 9103/4 (From RCA LCT 6700)
+-ARG 12-81 p50 +HF 11-81 p103 tape
+HF 10-81 p68 -NR 7-81 p4

478 Concerti, piano, nos. 1-5. Claudio Arrau, pno; PhO; Alceo Galliera. Quintessence 4PMC 4701 (4) (From various Angel originals)
+FF 5/6-81 p51

Concerto, piano, nos. 1-5. See no. 721

479 Concerto, piano, no. 1, op. 15, C major. Fantasia, op. 80, C minor. John Lill, pno; Scottish National Orchestra and Chorus; Alexander Gibson. Classics for Pleasure CFP 40232 Tape (c) CT 40232
+-Gr 11-75 p802 +-HFN 5-81 p93 tape
+HFN 10-75 p136 +RR 11-75 p41

480 Concerto, piano, no. 1, op. 15, C major. Concerto, piano, no. 2, op. 19, B flat major. Radu Lupu, pno; Israel Philharmonic Orchestra; Zubin Mehta. Decca SXDL 7502 Tape (c) KSXCD 7502 (also London LDR 10006 Tape (c) LDRS 10006)
+ARG 5-81 p11 +HF 10-80 p98 tape
+-FF 11/12-80 p69 +HFN 4-80 p101
+Gr 4-80 p1550 ++RR 4-80 p59
+-HF 12-80 p68

481 Concerto, piano, no. 1, op. 15, C major. Arturo Benedetti Michelangeli, pno; VSO; Carlo Maria Giulini. DG 2531 302 Tape (c) 3301 302
++ARG 6-81 p16 +HFN 10-80 p102
+-Audio 3-81 p60 +HFN 11-80 p131 tape
+CL 2-81 p12 +SFC 10-19-80 p20
++FF 1/2-81 p74 ++St 1-81 p68
+Gr 10-80 p487 +STL 9-14-80 p40
+HF 1-81 p68

482 Concerto, piano, no. 2, op. 19, B flat major. Concerto, piano, no. 4, op. 58, G major. John Lill, pno; Scottish National Orchestra; Alexander Gibson. Classics for Pleasure CFP 40271 Tape (c) CT 40271
+Gr 1-78 p1248 +-HFN 5-81 p93 tape
+HFN 12-77 p165 +-RR 1-78 p40

483 Concerto, piano, no. 2, op. 19, B flat major. Concerto, piano, no. 4, op. 58, G major. Wilhelm Kempff, pno; BPhO; Ferdinand Leitner. DG 2542 136 Tape (c) 3342 136
+-HFN 12-80 p153 +-HFN 3-81 p97 tape

484 Concerto, piano, no. 2, op. 19, B flat major. Concerto, piano, no. 4, op. 58, G major. Emil Gilels, pno; CO; Georg Szell. HMV SXLP 30515 Tape (c) TC SXLP 30515 (From World SM 156/160)
++Gr 7-81 p151 +HFN 7-81 p79

485 Concerto, piano, no. 2, op. 19, B flat major. Concerto, piano, no. 4, op. 58, G major. Stephen Bishop-Kovacevich, pno; BBC Symphony Orchestra; Colin Davis. Philips 6570 059 Tape (c) 7310 059
+Gr 3-81 p1184 ++HFN 5-81 p93 tape
++HFN 2-81 p97

486 Concerto, piano, no. 2, op. 19, B flat major. Fantasia, op. 80, C minor. LPO and Chorus; Alfred Brendel, pno; Bernard Haitink. Philips 9500 471 Tape (c) 7300 628 (r) G 9500 471 (From 6767 002)
+-FF 3/4-79 p28
++Gr 3-79 p1561
+Gr 8-79 p382 tape
+HF 8-81 p69 tape
++HFN 7-79 p119 tape
++HFN 3-79 p139
+NR 9-78 p7
+RR 3-79 p61
+-RR 9-79 p134 tape

Concerto, piano, no. 2, op. 19, B flat major. See no. 480

487 Concerto, piano, no. 3, op. 37, C minor. Malcolm Frager, pno; Hamburg State Philharmonic Orchestra; Gary Bertini. Acanta DG 22460
+-HFN 9-81 p78

488 Concerto, piano, no. 3, op. 37, C minor. Sonata, piano, no. 13, op. 27, no. 1, E flat major. Jeremy Menuhin, pno; RPO; Yehudi Menuhin. Ades 14 016
+-HFN 6-81 p69

489 Concerto, piano, no. 3, op. 37, C minor. Christoph Eschenbach, pno; LSO; Hans Werner Henze. Contour CC 7509 Tape (c) CCT 7509
+-Gr 8-81 p316

490 Concerto, piano, no. 3, op. 37, C minor. Rondos, op. 51, nos. 1, 2. Radu Lupu, pno; Israel Philharmonic Orchestra; Zubin Mehta. Decca SXDL 7507 Tape (c) KSXDC 7507
+-FF 7/8-81 p60
+-Gr 2-81 p1079
+HFN 2-81 p85
+NR 7-81 p3
++SFC 6-21-81 p18

491 Concerto, piano, no. 3, op. 37, C minor. Concerto, piano, no. 4, op. 58, G major. Ernst Groschel, pno; Bamberg Philharmonic Orchestra; Hans Zanotelli. Intercord INT 120932/3 (2)
/-HFN 12-81 p92

492 Concerto, piano, no. 3, op. 37, C minor. Clara Haskil, pno; Lamoureux Concerts Orchestra; Igor Markevitch. Philips 6527 090 Tape (c) 7311 090 (From SABL 172)
+Gr 8-81 p264
+-HFN 7-81 p81 tape
+STL 5-10-81 p41

493 Concerto, piano, no. 3, op. 37, C minor. Artur Rubinstein, pno; LPO; Daniel Barenboim. RCA ARL 1-1418 Tape (c) ARK 1-1418 (ct) ARS 1-1418 (From CRL 5-1415)
+ARG 7-79 p22
+-Gr 2-81 p1122 tape
+-HFN 9-80 p115
+-HFN 11-80 p131 tape
+-NR 6-79 p7
++RR 8-80 p37

494 Concerto, piano, no. 4, op. 58, G major. Leonore overture, no. 2, op. 72. Conrad Hansen, pno; BPhO; Wilhelm Furtwangler. DG 2535 807 Tape (c) 3335 807 (From LPM 18742, Unicorn UN 1106)
+-FF 9/10-79 p43
+Gr 7-78 p187
+-HF 2-81 p81 tape
+HFN 6-78 p121
+NR 6-79 p7
+-RR 6-78 p48

495 Concerto, piano, no. 4, op. 58, G major. MOZART: Concerto, piano, no. 23, K 488, A major. Wilhelm Kempff, pno. DG Tape (c) 3583 016
+Gr 8-81 p324 tape

Concerto, piano, no. 4, op. 58, G major. See no. 482. See no. 483. See no. 484. See no. 485. See no. 491. See no. 4122

Concerto, piano, no. 4, op. 58, G major: 1st movement. See no. 3684

496 Concerto, piano, no. 5, op. 73, E flat major. Paul Badura-Skoda, pno; North German Radio Orchestra; Hans Knappertsbusch. Bruno Walter Society RR 483
+FF 11/12-81 p100 +NR 11-81 p5
497 Concerto, piano, no. 5, op. 73, E flat major. Rudolf Serkin, pno; NYP; Leonard Bernstein. CBS MY 37223
+FF 11/12-81 p106 -NYT 9-27-81 pD22
498 Concerto, piano, no. 5, op. 73, E flat major. Walter Gieseking, pno. NYP; Guido Cantelli. Cetra LO 521
++CL 5/6-81 p8
499 Concerto, piano, no. 5, op. 73, E flat major. Claudio Arrau, pno; COA; Bernard Haitink. Philips 6527 055 Tape (c) 7311 055 (From SAL 3567)
+Gr 4-81 p1312 +-HFN 5-81 p89
+Gr 7-81 p196 tape +-HFN 7-81 p81
500 Concerto, piano, no. 5, op. 73, E flat major. Vladimir Horowitz, pno; RCA Symphony Orchestra; Fritz Reiner. RCA 1-3690 Tape (c) ARK 1-3690 (From LM 1718)
+HF 5-81 p57 +HF 2-81 p81 tape
501 Concerto, piano, no. 5, op. 73, E flat major. Hanae Nakajima, pno; Nurnberg Symphony Orchestra; Rato Tschupp. Saphir INT 120830
-FF 7/8-81 p61
502 Concerto, piano, no. 5, op. 73, E flat major. Rudolf Serkin, pno; BSO; Seiji Ozawa. Telarc DG 10065
+-FF 9/10-81 073 ++MUM 11/12-81 p30
++Gr 10-81 p538 +NR 7-81 p3
+HF 10-81 p80 ++NYT 9-27-81 pD22
+-HFN 10-81 p86 +St 9-81 p88
Concerto, piano, no. 5, op. 73, E flat major. See no. 4017
503 Concerto, violin, op. 61, D major. Itzhak Perlman, vln; PhO; Carlo Maria Giulini. Angel DS 37471 (also HMV ASD 4059 Tape (c) TCC ASD 4059)
++Gr 9-81 p372 +-NR 12-81 p6
+-HFN 10-81 p85 +SFC 11-22-81 p18
504 Concerto, violin, op. 61, D major. Iona Brown, vln; AMF; Neville Marriner. Argo ZRG 929 Tape (c) KZRC 929
+Gr 11-81 p682 +HFN 11-81 p90
505 Concerto, violin, op. 61, D major. Isaac Stern, vln; NYP; Leonard Bernstein. CBS MY 37224
++FF 11/12-81 p106
506 Concerto, violin, op. 61, D major. Kyung-Wha Chung, vln; VPO; Kiril Kondrashin. Decca SXDL 7508 Tape (c) KSXDC 7508 (also London LDR 10010 Tape (c) 5-10010)
+-ARG 3-81 p10 +HF 12-80 p68
++FF 11/12-80 p70 +-HFN 7-80 p105
+-Gr 8-80 p214 ++NR 10-80 p6
*Gr 10-80 p548 tape ++RR 7-80 p50
+Gr 9-80 p413 tape +St 11-80 p78
507 Concerto, violin, op. 61, D major. Anne-Sophie Mutter, vln; BPhO; Herbert von Karajan. DG 2531 250 Tape (c) 3301 250
+-ARG 7/8-81 p10 +-HFN 9-80 p100
+-FF 1/2-81 p75 +HFN 10-80 p117 tape
+Gr 9-80 p331 +-MT 3-81 p181
++Gr 10-80 p548 tape +-NR 12-80 p6
+HF 2-81 p63 +-SR 11-81 p62

508 Concerto, violin, op. 61, D major. Erich Gruenberg, vln; NPhO; Jascha Horenstein. Nonesuch H 71381
+ARG 3-81 p12
+FF 11/12-80 p70
++St 11-80 p78

509 Concerto, violin, op. 61, D major. Hermann Krebbers, vln; COA; Bernard Haitink. Philips Import 6580 115 (From 6580 115)
++Gr 6-81 p34

Concerto, violin, op. 61, D major. See no. 721

510 Concerto, violin, violoncello and piano, op. 56, C major. Anne-Sophie Mutter, vln; Yo Yo Ma, vlc; Mark Zeltser, pno; BPhO; Herbert von Karajan. DG 2531 262 Tape (c) 3301 262
+-ARG 12-80 p20
++FF 9/10-80 p70
+Gr 5-80 p1632
++HF 9-80 p84
+HFN 5-80 p118
+MT 3-81 p181
+-NR 7-80 p5
+NYT 9-21-80 pD22
++RR 5-80 p53
++RR 8-80 p93 tape
++SFC 4-27-80 p35
+SR 11-81 p62
++STL 5-11-80 p38

Consecration of the house, op. 124: Overture. See no. 528. See no. 653. See no. 665. See no. 666. See no. 721

Consecration of the house, op. 124: Overture; Wo sich die Pulse. See no. 722

Coriolan overture, op. 62. See no. 526. See no. 527. See no. 528. See no. 644. See no. 645. See no. 646. See no. 688. See no. 690. See no. 721. See no. 722

511 Deutsche Tanze (12). Minuets (12). Vienna Bella Musica Ensemble. Harmonia Mundi HM 1017
+-FF 9/10-80 p73
+Gr 4-80 p1567
+HFN 3-80 p86
+NR 6-80 p8
+RR 3-80 p46
+SFC 4-26-81 p18
+St 8-80 p92

Deutsche Tanze (6). See no. 3693

Deutsche Tanze, no. 12. See no. 3964

Duo, viola and violoncello, E flat major. See no. 3971

Egmont, op. 84, excerpts. See no. 721

Egmont, op. 84: Overture. See no. 526. See no. 527. See no. 528. See no. 645. See no. 646. See no. 667. See no. 675. See no. 722. See no. 3781

Fantasia, op. 80, C minor. See no. 479. See no. 486. See no. 721

512 Fidelio, op. 72. Gundula Janowitz, Lucia Popp, s; Rene Kollo, Adolf Dallapozza, t; Dietrich Fischer-Dieskau, bar; Hans Sotin, Manfred Jungwirth, bs; Vienna State Opera Chorus; VPO; Leonard Bernstein. DG 2709 082 Tape (c) 3371 039 (also 2740 191)
+-ARG 2-79 p13
+-FF 7/8-79 p22
+-Gr 10-78 p727
+Gr 2-79 p1473 tape
+-HF 2-79 p68
+HFN 11-78 p165
++MJ 1-79 p50
+-NR 2-79 p10
+-NYT 11-19-78 pD21
+OC Winter 1981 p55
+-ON 12-23-78 p40
+-Op 3-79 p251
+RR 11-78 p40
++St 2-79 p99

513 Fidelio, op. 72. Leonie Rysanek, Irmgard Seefried, s; Ernst Hafliger, Friedrich Lenz, t; Dietrich Fischer-Dieskau, bar; Keith Engen, Gottlob Frick, bs; Bavarian State Opera Orchestra and Chorus; Ferenc Fricsay. DG 2726 088 Tape (c) 3372 088

+-ARG 4-81 p47 +NYT 6-29-80 pD18
+FF 5/6-80 p44

514 Fidelio, op. 72. Ingeborg Hallstein, s; Christa Ludwig, ms; Gerhard Unger, Jon Vickers, Kurt Wehofschitz, t; Raymond Wolansky, bar; Gottlob Frick, Walter Berry, Franz Crass, bs; PhO and Chorus; Otto Klemperer. HMV SLS 5006 Tape (c) TC SLS 5006 (also Angel S 3625) (From Columbia SAX 2451/3)
+ARG 4-81 p47 ++HFN 12-75 p173 tape
++Gr 5-75 p2010 ++RR 5-75 p18
+Gr 11-81 p783 tape ++RR 12-75 p99 tape
++HFN 7-75 p76 +SFC 8-6-78 p45

515 Fidelio, op. 72. Helga Dernesch, Helen Donath, s; Jon Vickers, Horst Laubenthal, Werner Hollweg, t; Jose van Dam, Zoltan Keleman, bar; Karl Ridderbusch, bs; German Opera Chorus; BPhO; Herbert von Karajan. HMV SLS 5231 (2) Tape (c) TC SLS 5231 (From SAN 280/2).
+-Gr 8-81 p309 +HFN 8-81 p92
+Gr 11-81 p783 tape

516 Fidelio, op. 72. Hildegard Behrens, Sona Ghazarian, s; Peter Hofmann, David Kubler, Robert Johnson, t; Theo Adam, Gwynne Howell, Philip Kraus, bar; Hans Sotin, bs; CSO and Chorus; Georg Solti. London 3LDR 10017 (3) (also Decca D178D3 Tape (c) K178K32)
+-ARG 4-81 p47 +OC Summer 1981 p50
+-FF 9/10-80 p71 +-ON 3-7-81 p28
+-Gr 4-80 p1584 ++Op 6-80 p575
+Gr 9-80 p413 tape +RR 4-80 p38
+-HF 8-80 p61 +SFC 4-27-80 p35
+-HFN 5-80 p117 ++St 8-80 p98
+-NYT 6-29-80 pD18 +STL 4-13-80 p39

517 Fidelio, op. 72. Martha Modl, Sena Jurinac, s; Wolfgang Windgassen, t; Otto Edelmann, Gottlob Frick, bs; Vienna State Opera Chorus; VPO; Wilhelm Furtwangler. Replica RPL 2439/41 (3)
-FF 11/12-81 p101

518 Fidelio, op. 72. Sena Jurinac, Maria Stader, s; Jan Peerce, t; Gustav Neidlinger, bs; Bavarian State Opera Orchestra and Chorus; Hans Knappertsbusch. Westminster MCA 3-14300
+-ARG 4-81 p47 ++SFC 6-15-80 p36
+FF 11/12-80 p70

Fidelio, op. 72. See no. 721

519 Fidelio, op. 72, excerpts. HAYDN: Pieces, musical clock: Auswahl. HUMMEL: Partita, E flat major. KROL: Linzer Harmoniemusik, op. 67. Linzer Holzblaser. Intercord INT 120 931
+-HFN 11-81 p101

Fidelio, op. 72: Abscheulicher. See no. 3989

Fidelio, op. 72: Abscheulicher wo eilst du hin...Komm Hoffung. See no. 472

Fidelio, op. 72: Gott welch Dunkel hier...In des Lebens Fruhlingstagen. See no. 3648

520 Fidelio, op. 72: Mir ist so wunderbar; Hat man nich auch Gold beineben; Ha welch ein Augenblick; Abscheulicher; O welche Lust; Euch werde Lohn; Er sterbe; O namenlose Freude; Heil sei dem Tag. Hildegard Behrens, Sona Ghazarian, s; Peter Hofmann, David Kubler, Robert Johnson, t; Philip Kraus, bar; Hans Sotin, Gwynne Howell, bs; Theo Adam, bs-bar; CSO and Chorus; Georg Solti. Decca SXDL 7529 Tape (c) DSXDC 7529 (From D 178D3)
+-Gr 4-81 p1361 +-HFN 4-81 p81

Fidelio, op. 72: Overture. See no. 526. See no. 527. See no. 528. See no. 644. See no. 645. See no. 670. See no. 721. See no. 722. See no. 3792. See no. 3858
Die Geschopfe des Prometheus, op. 43, excerpts. See no. 721
Die Geschopfe des Prometheus, op. 43: Overture. See no. 526. See no. 642. See no. 645. See no. 722
Grosse Fuge, op. 133, B flat major. See no. 555. See no. 556. See no. 721
Heiligenstadt testament. See no. 602
Konig Stefan, op. 117: Overture. See no. 526. See no. 528. See no. 721. See no. 722
Leonore overtures, nos. 1-3, opp. 72, 138. See no. 528. See no. 721. See no. 722
Leonore overture, no. 1, op. 72. See no. 653
Leonore overtures, nos. 2 and 3, op. 72. See no. 644
Leonore overture, no. 2, op. 72. See no. 494. See no. 668
521 Leonore overture, no. 3, op. 72. BERLIOZ: Le carnaval romain, op. 9. BRAHMS: Academic festival overture, op. 80. WAGNER: Rienzi: Overture. Netherlands Radio Philharmonic Orchestra; Carlos Paita. Lodia LOD 771 Tape (c) LOC 771
+-Gr 7-81 p195 +HFN 8-81 p92 tape
+HFN 7-81 p79
Leonore overture, no. 3, op. 72. See no. 526. See no. 527. See no. 691. See no. 3760
Leonore Prohaska funeral march. See no. 722
522 Mass, op. 123, D major. Symphony, no. 4, op. 60, B flat major. Birgit Nilsson, s; Lisa Tunnel, alto; Gosta Bockelin, t; Sigurd Bjorling, bs; Stockholm Philharmonic Orchestra and Chorus, COA; Erich Kleiber. Bruno Walter Society IGI 366 (2)
+-FF 11/12-81 p102 -NR 4-81 p9
523 Mass, op. 123, D major. Anna Tomova, s; Annelies Burmeister, ms; Peter Schreier, t; Hermann Polster, bs; Hannes Kastner, org; Leipzig Radio Chorus; Leipzig Gewandhaus Orchestra; Kurt Masur. Eurodisc 85760
+-HF 12-81 p68 +NYT 7-26-81 pD23
524 Mass, op. 123, D major. Sylvia Geszty, s; Doris Soffel, con; David Randall, t; Kurt Widmer, bs; South German Madrigal Choir, Collegium Aureum; Wolfgang Gonnenwein. Harmonia Mundi 157 99668/9 (2) (also Pro Arte 2PAL 2005 (2) Tape (c) 2 PAC 2005)
-Gr 3-79 p1594 +HFN 3-79 p119
+HF 9-81 p46 tape +-MM 6-79 p32
+HF 12-81 p68 +-RR 4-79 p109
525 Mass, op. 123, D major. Elisabeth Schwarzkopf, s; Christa Ludwig, ms; Nicolai Gedda, t; Nicolas Zaccaria, bs; Vienna Singverein, PhO; Herbert von Karajan. HMV SLS 5198 (2) Tape (c) TC SLS 5198 (From 33CS 1634/5, World Records ST 914/5)
+Gr 7-80 p157 +-HFN 1-81 p109 tape
+-HFN 7-80 p117
Mass, op. 123, D major. See no. 721
Meerestille und Gluckliche Fahrt, op. 112. See no. 722
Minuet, G major. See no. 3695
Minuets (12). See no. 511
Minuet of congratulations. See no. 722
Namensfeier, op. 115: Overture. See no. 722
526 Overtures: Coriolan overture, op. 62. Egmont, op. 84: Overture.

Fidelio, op. 72: Overture. Die Geschopfe des Prometheus, op. 43: Overture. Konig Stefan, op. 117: Overture. Leonore overture, no. 3, op. 72. VPO; Leonard Bernstein. DG 2531 347 Tape (c) 3301 347 (From 2709 082, 2531 309)
+Gr 12-81 p883 ++HFN 12-81 p92

527 Overtures: Egmont, op. 84. Coriolan, op. 62. Fidelio, op. 72b. Leonore, no. 3, op. 72a. Ruinen von Athens, op. 113. BPhO; Herbert von Karajan. DG 2542 141 Tape (c) 3342 141 (From SLPM 13900, 64362B/30)
+Gr 10-80 p487 +-ST 6-81 p123
+HFN 11-80 p129

528 Overtures: Consecration of the house, op. 124. Coriolan, op. 62. Egmont, op. 84. Fidelio, op. 72. Leonore overtures, nos. 1-3, opp. 72, 138. Konig Stefan, op. 117. PhO; NPhO; Otto Klemperer. EMI Electrola 1C 197 03103/4 (2)
+-FF 11/12-81 p111

Polonaise, op. 89, C major. See no. 476. See no. 477. See no. 619

529 Quartets, strings, nos. 1-6, op. 18. Alban Berg Quartet. HMV SLS 5217 Tape (c) TC SLS 5217
+-HFN 12-81 p92
+-RR 10-81 p80

530 Quartets, strings, nos. 1-6, op. 18, Cleveland Quartet. RCA ARL 3-3486 (3) Tape (c) ARK 3-3486
+-ARG 9-80 p18 +-HFN 12-81 p92
+-FF 9/10-80 p74 ++NR 3-80 p9
+-Gr 9-80 p354 +NYT 2-10-80 pD24
+-HF 8-80 p65 +-SFC 2-17-80 p44
+-HFN 10-80 p102 ++St 6-80 p111
+ST 1-81 p647

531 Quartets, strings, nos. 1-6, op. 18. Smetana Quartet. Supraphon 111 2731/3 (3)
+FF 9/10-81 p74 ++NR 6-81 p5
+-Gr 9-81 p401 ++St 8-81 p91
+-HFN 8-81 p82

532 Quartet, strings, no. 1, op. 18, F major. Quartet, strings, no. 3, op. 18, D major. Vegh Quartet. Astree MB 301
+FF 11/12-81 p104

533 Quartet, strings, no. 1, op. 18, F major. Quartet, strings, no. 3, op. 18, D major. Orford Quartet. CBC SM 357
+MUM 9/10-81 p30

534 Quartet, strings, no. 1, op. 18, F major. Quartet, strings, no. 9, op. 59, C major. Quartet, strings, no. 11, op. 95, F minor. Sonata, violin and piano, no. 5, op. 24, F major. Busch Quartet; Adolph Busch, vln; Rudolf Serkin, pno. DaCapo 1C 181 01822/3 (2)
+ARG 12-81 p50 ++FF 3/4-81 p69

535 Quartet, strings, no. 1, op. 18, F major. Quartet, strings, no. 5, op. 18, A major. Smetana Quartet. Denon OX 7150
+FF 1/2-81 p75

536 Quartet, strings, no. 1, op. 18, F major. Pro Arte Quartet. Laurel LR 116
+FF 11/12-81 p102 ++NR 8-81 p7

537 Quartet, strings, no. 2, op. 18, G major. Quartet, strings, no. 5, op. 18, A major. Vegh Quartet. Astree MB 302
+FF 11/12-81 p104

538 Quartet, strings, no. 2, op. 18, G major. Quartet, strings, no. 6, op. 18, B flat major. Orford Quartet. CBC SM 358
++MUM 9/10-81 p30

539 Quartet, strings, no. 2, op. 18, G major. Quartet, strings, no. 4, op. 18, C minor. Smetana Quartet. Denon 7077
+FF 1/2-81 p75

540 Quartets, strings, no. 3, op. 18, D major. Quartet, strings, no. 6, op. 18, B flat major. Smetana Quartet. Denon OX 7138
+FF 1/2-81 p75

Quartet, strings, no. 3, op. 18, D major. See no. 532. See no. 533

541 Quartets, strings, nos. 4, 6, 7. Vegh Quartet. Astree Valois MB 303/4
+FF 5/6-81 p51

542 Quartet, strings, no. 4, op. 18, C minor. Quartet, strings, no. 6, op. 18, B flat major. Vegh Quartet. Astree Valois MB 303
+FF 5/6-81 p51

Quartet, strings, no. 4, op. 18, Cminor. See no. 539

543 Quartet, strings, no. 4, op. 18, C minor: Allegro. HAYDN: Quartet, strings, op. 3, no. 5, F major: Presto and andante cantabile. Quartet, strings, op. 20, no. 4, D major: Un poco adagio. MOZART: Quartet, strings, no. 6, K 159, B major: Andante. Quintet, clarinet, K 581, A major: Allegretto con variazioni. Trio, piano, no. 5, K 564, G major: Allegretto. SCHUBERT: Quartet, strings, no. 13, D 804, A minor: Andante. Quartet, strings, no. 8, D 112, B major: Menuetto. Dimitre Kozev, vlc. Harmonia Mundi HM 1038
-FF 7/8-81 p219

Quartet, strings, no. 5, op. 18, A major. See no. 535. See no. 537

Quartet, strings, no. 6, op. 18, B flat major. See no. 538. See no. 540. See no. 542

544 Quartets, strings, nos. 7-9, op. 59. Gabrieli Quartet. Decca D214D2 (2)
++Gr 2-81 p1095 +HFN 2-81 p85

545 Quartets, strings, nos. 7-9, op. 59. Quartet, strings, no. 10, op. 74, E flat major. Quartet, strings, no. 11, op. 95, F minor. Vegh Quartet. Astree Valois CMB 32 (3)
+HFN 12-81 p92

546 Quartets, strings, nos. 7-1, opp. 59, 74, 95. Talich Quartet. Calliope CAL 1634/6 (3)
++Gr 9-81 p401

547 Quartets, strings, nos. 7-11, opp. 59, 74, 95. Vegh Quartet. Telefunken EX 6-35041 (3)
++Gr 9-81 p401 +Gr 8-76 p311

548 Quartet, strings, no. 7, op. 59, F major. Vegh Quartet. Astree Valois MB 304
+FF 5/6-81 p51

549 Quartet, strings, no. 7, op. 59, F major. HAYDN: Quartet, strings, op. 103, D major: Minuet. Busch Quartet. CBS 61888
+Gr 4-80 p1567 +RR 5-80 p75
+HFN 4-80 p101 +STL 4-13-80 p39
+-MT 1-81 p33

550 Quartet, strings, no. 7, op. 59, F major. Quartet, strings, no. 10, op. 74, E flat major. Quartet, strings, no. 11, op. 95, F minor. Melos Quartet. Intercord 25759/2 (2)

+-HFN 12-81 p92

551 Quartet, strings, no. 8, op. 59, E minor. Quartet, strings, no. 1, op. 95, F minor. Talich Quartet. Calliope CAL 1634
+-HFN 8-81 p82

552 Quartet, strings, no. 9, op. 59, C major. Quartet, strings, no. 10, op. 74, E flat major. Talich Quartet. Calliope CAL 1636 Tape (c) CAL 4636
+-FF 1/2-81 p77
+Gr 1-81 p959
-HFN 12-80 p132

553 Quartet, strings, no. 9, op. 59, C major. Quartet, strings, no. 10, op. 74, E flat major. Smetana Quartet. Denon OX 7188
+FF 3/4-81 p70
+HFN 5-81 p77

Quartet, strings, no. 9, op. 59, C major. See no. 534

Quartet, strings, no. 10, op. 74, E flat major. See no. 545. See no. 550. See no. 552. See no. 553

Quartet, strings, no. 11, op. 95, F minor. See no. 534. See no. 545. See no. 550. See no. 551

554 Quartet, strings, no. 12, op. 127, E flat major. Quartet, strings, no. 16, op. 135, F major. Talich Quartet. Calliope CAL 1640 Tape (c) CAL 4640
+Gr 6-80 p44
+Gr 12-80 p842
+-HFN 6-80 p102
+-HFN 11-80 p115
+RR 6-80 p65
+ST 9-80 p342
+ST 1-81 p647

555 Quartet, strings, no. 13, op. 130, B flat major. Grosse Fuge, op. 133, B flat major. Vegh Quartet. Astree MB 308
+FF 11/12-81 p104

556 Quartet, strings, no. 13, op. 130, B flat major. Grosse Fuge, op. 133, B flat major. Talich Quartet. Calliope CAL 1637 Tape (c) 4637
+-HFN 11-80 p115
+ST 1-81 p647

557 Quartet, strings, no. 13, op. 130, B flat major. Busch Quartet. CBS 61664
+ARG 12-81 p50
++FF 1/2-81 p77
++Gr 11-75 p846
++HFN 11-75 p155
+-RR 11-75 p59

558 Quartet, strings, no. 13, op. 130, B flat major (original version). Smetana Quartet. Quintessence PMC 7176 (From Crossroads 2216 0056)
+FF 3/4-81 p71

559 Quartet, strings, no. 14, op. 131, C sharp minor. Talich Quartet. Calliope CAL 1638
+Gr 12-80 p842
+HFN 8-80 p94
+-HFN 11-80 p115
+RR 7-80 p69
+ST 1-81 p647

560 Quartet, strings, no. 15, op. 132, A minor. Talich Quartet. Calliope CAL 1639 Tape (c) CAL 4639
+Gr 6-80 p44
+Gr 12-80 p842
+-HFN 6-80 p102
+-HFN 11-80 p115
+RR 6-80 p65
+ST 9-80 p342
+ST 1-81 p647

Quartet, strings, no. 16, op. 135, F major. See no. 554

561 Quintet, piano, op. 16, E flat major. DUKAS: Villanelle. MALIPIERO: Dialogue, no. 4. MARAIS: Le Basque. Dennis Brain, hn; Wilfrid Parry, pno; Dennis Brain Wind Ensemble. Arabesque 8071

Tape (c) 9071
+HF 5-81 p64 +NR 11-80 p8
+MUM 3/4-81 p31

562 Quintet, piano, op. 16, E flat major. Sonata, horn and piano, op. 17, F major. MOZART: Divertimento, no. 14, K 270, B flat major (arr. Baines). MILHAUD: La cheminee du Roi Rene, op. 205. Benjamin Britten, Conrad Hansen, pno; Dennis Brain, hn; Dennis Brain Wind Quintet. Bruno Walter Society IGI 370
+-NR 4-81 p7

Quintet, piano, op. 16, E flat major. See no. 574

563 Romance, no. 1, op. 40, G major. Romance, no. 2, op. 50, F major. MENDELSSOHN: Concerto, violin, op. 64, E minor. Isaac Stern, vln; BSO; Seiji Ozawa. CBS IM 37204
+SFC 11-29-81 p18

564 Romance, no. 1, op. 40, G major. Romance, no. 2, op. 50, F major. BERLIOZ: Romance, reverie et caprice, op. 8. CHAUSSON: Poeme, op. 25. WIENIAWSKI: Legende, op. 17. Yehudi Menuhin, vln; PhO; John Pritchard. Classics for Pleasure CFP 40365 Tape (c) TC CFP 40365 (From ASD 618)
++Gr 9-81 p386 +HFN 12-81 p112 tape
+-HFN 9-81 p89

565 Romance, no. 1, op. 40, G major. Romance, no. 2, op. 50, F major. MOZART: Concerto, violin, no. 5, K 219, A major. Shmuel Ashkenazi, vln; Zurich Chamber Orchestra; Edmond de Stoutz. Tudor 73026
+HFN 8-81 p82

Romance, no. 2, op. 50, F major. See no. 563. See no. 564. See no. 565. See no. 1040

Rondos, op. 51, nos. 1 and 2. See no. 490

Die Ruinen von Athens, op. 113: Overture. See no. 527. See no. 3726

Die Ruinen von Athens, op. 113: Overture; Turkish march. See no. 722

Die Ruinen von Athens, op. 113: Turkish march. See no. 3695

566 Septet, op. 20, E flat major. Trio, clarinet, op. 11, B flat major. New Vienna Octet Members. Decca SDD 528 Tape (c) KSDC 528
+Gr 5-81 p1485 +-HFN 5-81 p77

567 Septet, op. 20, E flat major. Berlin Philharmonic Octet. Philips 6527 066 Tape (c) 7311 066 (From 6500 543)
+-Gr 8-81 p282 +HFN 11-81 p105 tape
+-HFN 6-81 p85

568 Septet, op. 20, E flat major. AMF Chamber Ensemble. Philips 9500 873 Tape (c) 7300 873
+FF 7/8-81 p62 ++MUM 7/8-81 p35
+Gr 3-81 p1208 +NR 7-81 p8
+Gr 6-81 p94 ++SFC 6-21-81 p18
++HFN 3-81 p86 ++St 7-81 p78
+HFN 4-81 p81 tape

569 Serenade, op. 8, D major. KODALY: Duo, violin and violoncello, op. 7. Jascha Heifetz, vln; William Primrose, vla; Gregor Piatigorsky, vlc. RCA LSC 2550
+-FF 3/4-81 p256

570 Serenade, op. 25, D major. Trio, strings, op. 3, E flat major. Trio, op. 8, D major. Trios, strings, op. 9, nos. 1-3. Arthur

Grumiaux, vln; Georges Janzer, vla; Eva Czako, vlc; Maxence Larrieu, flt. Philips 6770 159 (3) Tape (c) 7699 159
+FF 5/6-81 p56 +St 8-81 p92
+SFC 5-10-81 p18

571 Sonata, flute and paino, B flat major. Variations on "Air russe", op. 107, no. 7. Variations on "Air de la petite Russie", op. 107, no. 3. MOZART: Sonata, flute and harpsichord, no. 4, K 13, F major. SCHUBERT: Introduction and variations, op. 160, D 802, E minor. Richard Adeney, flt; Ian Brown, pno and hpd. ASV ACM 2024 Tape (c) ZCACM 2024 (From Enigma VAR 1029)
+Gr 8-81 p284 /HFN 6-81 p81

572 Sonata, horn and piano, op. 17, F major. Trio, clarinet, op. 11, B flat major. Variations on Mozart's "Bei Mannern welche Liebe fuhlen" (7). Music Group of London. ASV ACA 1005 (From Enigma 53579)
+Gr 9-81 p396 +-HFN 9-81 p90

573 Sonata, horn and piano, op. 17, F major. Trio, piano, flute and bassoon, G major. Daniel Barenboim, pno; Michel Debost, flt; Andre Sennedat, bsn; Myron Bloom, hn. DG 2531 293
+-FF 7/8-81 p63 +NR 7-81 p8
+-Gr 3-81 p1208 +St 10-81 p118
+HFN 4-81 p68

574 Sonata, horn and piano, op. 17, F major. Quintet, piano, op. 16, E flat major. MILHAUD: Le cheminee du Roi Rene, op. 205. MOZART: Divertimento, no. 14, K 270, B flat major (arr. Baines). Dennis Brain, hn; Conrad Hansen, Benjamin Britten, pno; Dennis Brain Wind Quintet. Bruno Walter Society IGI 370
+HF 5-81 p64 +-NR 4-81 p7

575 Sonata, horn and piano, op. 17, F major. CHERUBINI: Sonata, horn and piano, no. 1, E flat major. Sonata, horn, no. 2, F major. DANZI: Sonata, horn and piano, op. 28, E flat major. Ifor James, hn; Jennifer Partridge, pno. Phoenix DGS 1002
+Gr 7-81 p164

Sonata, horn and piano, op. 17, F major. See no. 562

576 Sonatas, piano, nos. 1-3, 15. Glenn Gould, pno. CBS M2 35911 (2)
+-FF 5/6-81 p53 +St 5-81 p64

577 Sonatas, piano, nos. 1-7. Artur Schnabel, pno. HMV RLS 753 (3) Tape (c) TC RLS 753
+FF 7/8-81 p63 +HFN 12-80 p153
+Gr 10-80 p542 +-MT 4-81 p245

578 Sonatas, piano, nos. 1-7. Malcolm Binns, fortepiano. L'Oiseau-Lyre D182D3 (3)
+Gr 10-80 p517 -MT 6-81 p388
+HFN 9-80 p100

579 Sonatas, piano, nos. 1-32. Wilehlm Kempff, pno. DG 2740 228 (10)
+HFN 1-81 p107

580 Sonatas, piano, nos. 1, 13, 17, 19, 24, 28. John Lill, pno. ASV ACM 2028/9 Tape (c) ZCACM 2028/9 (From Enigma K 53521, 53525)
+-Gr 10-81 p580 +-HFN 9-81 p90
+Gr 10-81 p614 +HFN 9-81 p93 tape

581 Sonatas, piano, nos. 1, 17, 20. Daniel Barenboim, pno. Angel RL 32005
+NYT 9-27-81 pD22

582 Sonata, piano, no. 1, op. 2, no. 1, F minor. Sonata, piano, no. 7, op. 10, no. 3, D major. Vladimir Ashkenazy, pno. London CS

7190 (also Decca SXL 6960 Tape (c) KSXC 6960)
+FF 11/12-81 p105 +-HFN 6-81 p70
+Gr 6-81 p58 +NYT 9-27-81 pD22

583 Sonata, piano, no, 2, op. 2, no. 2, A major. Sonata, piano, no. 3, op. 2, no. 3, C major. John Lill, pno. ASV ACM 2023 Tape (c) ZCACM 2023 (From Enigma VAR 1005)
+Gr 4-81 p1343 +-HFN 4-81 p80
+Gr 7-81 p196 tape +-HFN 6-81 p87 tape

584 Sonata, piano, no. 2, op. 2, no. 2, A major. Sonata, piano, no. 21, op. 53, C major. Steven De Groote, pno. Finlandia FA 319
+-FF 9/10-81 p75 +-NR 7-81 p13

585 Sonatas, piano, nos. 3, 7, 14, 17-18, 23, 25. Rudolf Buchbinder, pno. Telefunken 6-35472 (3)
+FF 3/4-81 p71 ++SFC 3-8-81 p19

Sonata, piano, no, 3, op. 2, no. 3, C major. See no. 583

586 Sonata, piano, no. 4, op. 7, E flat major. Sonata, piano, no. 21, op. 53, C major. John Lill, pno. ASV ACM 2018 Tape (c) ZCACM 2018
+Gr 7-81 p196 tape +HFN 5-81 p79

587 Sonata, piano, no. 4, op. 7, E flat major. Sonata, piano, no. 9, op. 14, no. 1, E major. Sonata, piano, no. 10, op. 14, no. 2, G major. Vladimir Ashkenazy, pno. Decca SXL 6961 Tape (c) KSXC 6961 (also London 7191)
+Gr 12-80 p847 +-FF 1/2-81 p78
+-Gr 4-81 p1376 tape +-HFN 12-80 p133

588 Sonata, piano, no. 5, op. 10, no. 1, C minor. Sonata, piano, no. 6, op. 10, no. 2, F major. Sonata, piano, no. 7, op. 10, no. 3, D major. John Lill, pno. ASV ACM 2031 Tape (c) ZCACM 2031 (From Enigma K 53561)
+-Gr 12-81 p898 +-HFN 10-81 p95

589 Sonata, piano, no. 6, op. 10, no. 2, F major. BUSONI: Elegien: Turantos Frauengemach. LISZT (Busoni): Paraphrase on themes from "Le nozze di Figaro". RACHMANINOFF: Etudes tableaux, op. 33, nos. 1 and 2. Etudes tableaux, op. 39, no. 5. Lilacs, op. 21, no. 5 (arr. Rachmaninoff). Vocalise, op. 34, no. 14. Boris Bloch, pno. DG 2535 006
+CL 2-81 p12 ++NR 1-81 p15
+FF 5/6-81 p203 +NYT 3-8-81 pD34
+HF 1-81 p59 +-St 2-81 p54

590 Sonata, piano, no. 6, op. 10, no. 2, F major. Sonata, piano, no. 17, op. 31, no. 2, D minor. Malcolm Bilson, fortepiano. Nonesuch N 78008
+FF 7/8-81 p64 ++NYT 9-27-81 pD22
++NR 7-81 p13

Sonata, piano, no. 6, op. 10, no. 2, F major. See no. 588

591 Sonatas, piano, nos. 7-8, 23, 31-32. Edwin Fischer, pno. DaCapo 1C 147 01674/5 (2)
+FF 9/10-81 p75

Sonata, piano, no. 7, op. 10, no. 3, D major. See no. 582. See no. 588

592 Sonatas, piano, nos. 8, 13, 14. Emil Gilels, pno. DG 2532 008 Tape (c) 3302 008
+FF 11/12-81 p106 +-HFN 8-81 p82
+-Gr 8-81 p292 -NYT 9-27-81 pD22
++Gr 9-81 p460 tape +-SFC 10-25-81 p21

593 Sonatas, piano, nos. 8, 14, 19, 20. John O'Conor, pno. Denon OX 7075
+HFN 5-81 p79
594 Sonatas, piano, nos. 8, 14, 21. Rudolf Firkusny, pno. Contour CC 7529 Tape (c) CCT 7529
+Gr 8-81 p316
595 Sonatas, piano, nos. 8, 14, 21. Radu Lupu, pno. Decca JB 105 Tape (c) KJBC 105 (From SXL 6576)
+Gr 11-81 p720
596 Sonatas, piano, nos. 8, 14, 23. Inger Sodergren, pno. Calliope CAL 1683
-FF 7/8-81 p65 -HFN 4-81 p68
-Gr 4-81 p1345
597 Sonatas, piano, nos. 8, 14, 23. Rudolf Serkin, pno. CBS 61937 Tape (c) 40-61937 (From SBRG 72148) (also CBS MY 37219)
-FF 11/12-81 p105 +-HFN 2-80 p107 tape
++Gr 12-79 p1028 +NYT 9-27-81 pD22
+-HFN 12-79 p179 ++RR 12-79 p93
598 Sonatas, piano, nos. 8, 14, 23. Daniel Chorzempa, pno. Classics for Pleasure CFP 40352 Tape (c) TC CFP 40352 (From CFP 192)
+Gr 4-81 p1345 +HFN 5-81 p93 tape
+HFN 4-81 p80
599 Sonatas, piano, nos. 8, 14, 23. Ivan Moravec, pno. Connoisseur Tape (c) In Sync C 4047
+Gr 8-81 p324 tape ++St 1-81 p90 tape
+HFN 8-81 p92 tape
600 Sonatas, piano, nos, 8, 14, 23. Alfred Brendel, pno. Philips 9500 899 Tape (c) 7300 899 (From 9500 077, 6500 417, 6500 138)
+-CL 10-81 p10 ++Gr 9-81 p460 tape
+-FF 5/6-81 p55 +HFN 6-81 p85
+Gr 5-81 p1494 +HFN 9-81 p93 tape
601 Sonata, piano, no. 8, op. 13, C minor. Sonata, piano, no. 14, op. 27, no. 2, C sharp minor. Sonata, piano, no. 23, op. 57, F minor. John Lill, pno. ASV ACM 2015 Tape (c) ZCACM 2015 (From Enigma VAR 1001)
+Gr 5-81 p1498 +HFN 5-81 p91
+Gr 7-81 p196 tape +HFN 6-81 p87 tape

Sonata, piano, no. 8, op. 13, C minor. See no. 3697. See no. 3866

602 Sonata, piano, no. 8, op. 13, C minor: 2nd movement. Sonata, piano, no. 32, op. 111, C minor. Variations on "Nel cor piu non mi sento". Heiligenstadt testament. Elly Ney, pno and reader. DaCapo 1C 047 29148 (From EMI originals)
+FF 5/6-81 p55
603 Sonatas, piano, nos. 8-15. Artur Schnabel, pno. HMV RLS 754 (3) Tape (c) TC RLS 754
++Gr 1-81 p998 +HFN 1-81 p107
+FF 7/8-81 p63 +HFN 4-81 p81 tape
604 Sonatas, piano, nos. 8-15. Bernard Roberts, pno. Nimbus D/C 902 (4)
+Gr 1-81 p966 +-RR 2-80 p71
605 Sonatas, piano, nos. 8-15. Malcolm Binns, pno; L'Oiseau-Lyre D183D3 (3)
++Gr 9-81 p406
606 Sonatas, piano, nos. 9-10, 12, 22, 25, 30-31. John Lill, pno. ASV ACM 2026/7 (2) Tape (c) ZCACM 2026/7

+Gr 6-81 p58 +HFN 7-81 p71
+Gr 7-81 p196 tape

Sonata, piano, no. 9, op. 14, no. 1, E major. See no. 587

Sonata, piano, no. 10, op. 14, no. 2, G major. See no. 587

607 Sonata, piano, no. 11, op. 22, B flat major. Sonata, piano, no. 32, op. 111, C minor. John Lill, pno. ASV ACM 2013
+HFN 12-81 p92

608 Sonata, piano, no. 11, op. 22, B flat major. Sonata, piano, no. 12, op. 26, A flat major. Vladimir Ashkenazy, pno. London CS 7162 (also Decca SXL 6929 Tape (c) KSXC 6929)
++FF 3/4-81 p73 +Gr 9-81 p460 tape
+-Gr 5-81 p1494 +HFN 5-81 p79

Sonata, piano, no. 12, op. 26, A flat major. See no. 608

609 Sonata, piano, no. 13, op. 27, no. 1, E flat major. Sonata, piano, no. 14, op. 27, no. 2, C sharp minor. MOZART: Rondo, piano, K 485, D major. Rondo, piano, K 511, A minor. Malcolm Bilson, fortepiano. Nonesuch H 71377 Tape (c) Advent E 1056
+FF 9/10-80 p167 +NYT 7-27-80 pD20
+HF 2-81 p61 ++St 11-80 p79

Sonata, piano, no. 13, op. 27, no. 1, E flat major. See no. 488

610 Sonata, piano, no. 14, op. 27, no. 2, C sharp minor. Sonata, piano, no. 15, op. 28, D major: Andante. Sonata, piano, no. 23, op. 57, F minor. Paul Badura-Skoda, pno. Harmonia Mundi 1C 065 99769 (also Pro Arte PAL 1017)
+FF 1/2-80 p51 +NYT 7-27-80 pD20
+-FF 11/12-81 p105 +RR 5-80 p82
+HFN 6-80 p117

Sonata, piano, no. 14, op. 27, no. 2, C sharp minor. See no. 474. See no. 601. See no. 609. See no. 3816. See no. 3866

611 Sonata, piano, no. 15, op. 28, D major. Sonata, piano, no. 26, op. 81a, E flat major. Sonata, piano, no. 27, op. 90, E minor. John Lill, pno. ASV ACM 2014 Tape (c) ZCACM 2014 (From Enigma VAR 1004)
+Gr 11-81 p720 +HFN 9-81 p90

Sonata, piano, no. 15, op. 28, D major. See no. 245

Sonata, piano, no. 15, op. 28, D major: Andante. See no. 610

612 Sonatas, piano, nos. 16-18, 21, 23, 24, 26. Charles Rosen, pno. Nonesuch 78010 (3)
+NYT 9-27-81 pD22

613 Sonatas, piano, nos. 16-22, 24. Artur Schnabel, pno. HMV RLS 755 (3) Tape (c) TC RLS 755
++Gr 4-81 p1374 +HFN 4-81 p68
+Gr 7-81 p196 tape

614 Sonatas, piano, nos. 16-23. Malcolm Binns, fortepiano. L'Oiseau-Lyre D184D3 (3)
+Gr 12-81 p897

615 Sonata, piano, no. 16, op. 31, no. 1, G major. Sonata, piano, no. 18, op. 31, no. 3, E flat major. Sonata, piano, no. 20, op. 49, no. 2, G major. John Lill, pno. ASV ACM 2022 Tape (c) ZCAC 2022 (From Enigma VAR 1003)
+Gr 5-81 p1498 +HFN 5-81 p91
+Gr 7-81 p196 tape +HFN 6-81 p87 tape

616 Sonata, piano, no. 17, op. 31, no. 2, D minor. Sonata, piano, no. 21, op. 53, C major. Claudio Arrau, pno. Philips 6570 190 Tape (c) 7310 190 (From SAL 3603, 3517)

+FF 1/2-81 p78 +HFN 9-81 p90
++Gr 9-81 p411

Sonata, piano, no. 17, op. 31, no. 2, D minor. See no. 473. See no. 590

Sonata, piano, no. 18, op. 31, no. 3, E flat major. See no. 474. See no. 615

Sonata, piano, no. 20, op. 49, no. 2, G major. See no. 615

Sonata, piano, no. 21, op. 53, C major. See no. 584. See no. 586. See no. 616

617 Sonatas, piano, nos. 22, 24-25, 27. Vladimir Ashkenazy, pno. Decca SXL 6962 Tape (c) KSXC 6962 (also London 7192)
+CL 10-81 p8 +HF 9-81 p14
+FF 7/8-81 p66 +HFN 3-81 p86
++Gr 3-81 p1212 +STL 4-12-81 p40

618 Sonatas, piano, nos. 23, 29-32. Artur Schnabel, pno. HMV RLS 758 Tape (c) TC RLS 758
+Gr 9-81 p446 +HFN 9-81 p78

619 Sonata, piano, no. 23, op. 57, F minor. Sonata, piano, no. 26, op. 81, E flat major. Polonaise, op. 89, C major. Emanuel Ax, pno. RCA ARL 1-2752 Tape (c) ARK 1-2752
+-FF 7/8-81 p67 ++SFC 5-31-81 p22
+-NR 6-81 p13 ++SFC 5-10-81 p18
+NYT 9-27-81 pD22 +-St 9-81 p88

Sonata, piano, no. 23, op. 57, F minor. See no. 89. See no. 601. See no. 610

620 Sonatas, piano, nos. 24-32. Malcolm Binns, fortepiano. L'Oiseau-Lyre D185D3 (3)
+Gr 8-81 p292 +HFN 8-81 p82

621 Sonata, piano, no. 24, op. 78, F sharp major. Sonata, piano, no. 29, op. 106, B flat major. Claudio Arrau, pno. Philips 6570 055 Tape (c) 7310 055 (From SAL 3600, 3484)
+Gr 1-81 p966 +-HFN 5-81 p93 tape
+HFN 2-81 p97

622 Sonatas, piano, nos. 26-32. Bernard Roberts, pno. Nimbus DC 904
+HFN 6-81 p70

Sonata, piano, no. 26, op. 81, E flat major. See no. 611. See no. 619

623 Sonata, piano, no. 27, op. 90, E minor. Sonata, piano, no. 29, op. 106, B flat major. Alfred Brendel, pno. Vox Tape (c) CT 23009
+HF 9-81 p46 tape

Sonata, piano, no. 27, op. 90, E minor. See no. 611

624 Sonatas, piano, nos. 28-30. Paul Badura-Skoda, pno. Astree AS 47/8 (2)
++FF 1/2-81 p78 +RR 5-80 p82
+Gr 5-80 p1690 +St 5-81 p64

625 Sonatas, piano, nos. 28-32. Paul Badura-Skoda, pno. Astree AS 909 (3)
++HFN 12-81 p92

626 Sonata, piano, no. 28, op. 101, A major. Sonata, piano, no. 30, op. 109, E major. Paul Badura-Skoda, pno. Astree AS 48
+HFN 9-81 p78 ++FF 1/2-81 p78

627 Sonata, piano, no. 28, op. 101, A major. RAVEL: Gaspard de la nuit. SCHUMANN: Toccata, op. 7, C major. Jorge Luis Prats, pno. DG 2535 010
+HF 6-81 p52 ++NR 8-81 p12

Sonata, piano, no. 28, op. 101, A major. See no. 473
Sonata, piano, no. 28, op. 101, A major: Allegretto ma non troppo. See no. 3866
628 Sonata, piano, no. 29, op. 106, B flat major. John Lill, pno. ASV ACM 2032
+-Gr 10-81 p580 -HFN 9-81 p78
629 Sonata, piano, no. 29, op. 106, B flat major. Zdenek Hnat, pno. Supraphon 111 2618
-FF 7/8-81 p67 -NR 4-81 p12
Sonata, piano, no. 29, op. 106, B flat major. See no. 621. See no. 623
Sonata, piano, no. 30, op. 109, E major. See no. 626
630 Sonata, piano, no. 31, op. 110, A flat major. Sonata, piano, no. 32, op. 111, C minor. Paul Badura-Skoda, fortepiano. Astree AS 49
++FF 3/4-81 072 +SFC 7-19-81 p19
+Gr 10-81 p582 +-St 5-81 p64
+HFN 5-81 p79
Sonata, piano, no. 32, op. 111, C minor. See no. 476. See no. 602. See no. 607. See no. 630
631 Sonatas, violin and piano, nos. 1-10. Henryk Szeryng, vln; Ingrid Haebler, pno. Philips 6769 011 (5)
+-ARG 5-81 p12 +-HF 3-81 p63
+-Audio 3-81 p60 ++HFN 10-80 p102
+-FF 3/4-81 p74 ++NR 11-80 p6
+Gr 10-80 p511 +SFC 2-15-81 p19
632 Sonatas, violin and piano, no. 2, op. 12, A major. Sonata, violin and piano, no. 4, op. 23, A minor. Arthur Grumiaux, vln; Claudio Arrau, pno. Philips 9500 263 Tape (c) 7300 785
+FF 9/10-80 p77 ++NR 6-80 p8
+Gr 8-77 p313 +-NYT 7-6-80 pD15
+HF 3-81 p63 ++RR 9-77 p81
++HFN 7-77 p107
Sonata, violin and piano, no. 4, op. 23, A minor. See no. 632
633 Sonata, violin and piano, no. 5, op. 24, F major. Sonata, violin and piano, no. 9, op. 47, A major. Itzhak Perlman, vln; Vladimir Ashkenazy, pno. Decca SXL 6990
+STL 12-13-81 p39
634 Sonata, violin and piano, no. 5, op. 24, F major. Sonata, violin and piano, no. 9, op. 47, A major. Yehudi Menuhin, vln; Wilhelm Kempff, pno. DG 2531 300 Tape (c) 3301 300
+FF 5/6-81 p56 ++St 9-81 p89
+-NR 5-81 p9
635 Sonata, violin and piano, no. 5, op. 24, F major. Sonata, violin and piano, no. 9, op. 47, A major. Denes Kovacs, vln; Mihaly Bacher, pno. Hungaroton SLPX 12279
-FF 5/6-81 p57 +-St 9-81 p89
++NR 5-81 p9
Sonata, violin and piano, no. 5, op. 24, F major. See no. 534
636 Sonata, violin and piano, no. 8, op. 30, no. 3, G major. MOZART: Sonatas, violin and piano, K 304, 376-377, 526. SCHUBERT: Sonatina, violin and piano, no. 3, op. 137, D 408, G minor. Norbert Brainin, vln; Lamar Crowson, Lili Kraus, pno. BBC 22313 (2)
+-FF 3/4-81 p165

Sonata, violin and piano, no. 9, op. 47, A major. See no. 633. See no. 634. See no. 635

637 Songs: Ich liebe dich; Kennst du das Land, op. 75, no. 1; Lieder von Gellert, op. 48, no. 1, Bitten; no. 2, Die Liebe des Nachsten; no. 3, Vom Tode; no. 4, Die Ehre Gottes aus der Natur; no. 5, Gottes Macht und Versehung; no. 6, Busslied; Wonne der Wehmut, op. 83, no. 1. SCHUBERT: Songs: An die Musik, D 547; Die Allmacht, D 852; Du bist die Ruh, D 776; Der Jungling an der Quelle, D 300; Lachen und Weinen, D 777; Nacht und Traume, D 827; Nachtviolen, D 752; Rastlose Liebe, D 138. Heather Harper, s; Paul Hamburger, pno. BBC REB 170 (also BBC 22170)
+-FF 3/4-81 p166 +-RR 2-75 p58
+Gr 2-75 p1541

638 Songs: Abendlied unterm gesternten Himmel; Adelaide, op. 46; An die ferne Geliebte, op. 98; An die Hoffnung, op. 94; Andenken; Bitten, op. 48, no. 1; Die Ehre Gottes aus der Natur, op. 48, no. 4; Flohlied, op. 75, no. 3; Der Kuss, op. 128; Lied aus der Ferne; Der Liebende; Maigesang, op. 52, no. 4; Neue Liebe neues Leben, op. 75, no. 2; Resignation; Songs, op. 83; Songs, WoO 118; Der Wachtelschlag; Zartlich Liebe; Der Zufriedene, op. 75, no. 6. Peter Schreier, t; Jorg Demus, pno. Eurodisc 300 760 (2)
+Gr 12-81 p917

639 Songs: Scotch (5) and Irish airs (4). Jean-Pierre Rampal, flt; Robert Veyron-Lacroix, pno. Everest 3473
-ARG 4-81 p13 -NR 5-81 p9
-FF 3/4-81 p71

640 Songs: An die ferne Geliebte, op. 98. HAYDN: Schottische und Walisische Lieder. STRAUSS: Orchesterlieder (5). Fritz Wunderlich, t; Walter Weller, vln; Ludwig Beinl, vlc; Heinrich Schmidt, pno; Bavarian Radio Orchestra; Jan Koetsier. Philips 6520 022
+-ON 3-81 p28 +RR 8-80 p14

641 Songs: Irish songs: The British Light Dragoons; Come draw we round the cheerful ring; The kiss dear maid thy lip has left; O harp of Erin; On the massacre of Glencoe; The pulse of an Irishman; The return to Ulster; Tis sunshine at last. Scottish songs: Cease your funning; O Mary at thy window be; Sally in our alley. Welsh songs: Cupid's kindness; Good night; The vale of the Clwyd; When mortals all to rest retire. Songs of various nationality: The soldier. Robert White, t; Samuel Sanders, pno; Ani Kavafian, vln; Yo Yo Ma, vlc. RCA ARL 1-3417
+ARG 1-80 p20 +NR 12-79 p11
++FF 3/4-80 p52 +NYT 10-14-79 pD24
+Gr 2-80 p1282 +ON 2-2-80 p28
+HF 12-79 p88 +RR 2-80 p49
+-HFN 2-81 p95 +SFC 9-9-79 p45
+-MT 3-81 p181 +St 5-80 p86

Songs: Ich liebe dich. See no. 3639
Songs: In questa tomba oscura. See no. 4026
Songs: Nei campi e nelle selve. See no. 3845
Songs: There once was a king, op. 75, no. 3. See no. 3801

642 Symphonies, nos. 1-9.* Die Geschopfe des Prometheus, op. 43: Overture. Gwyneth Jones, s; Hanna Schwarz, con; Rene Kollo, t; Kurt Moll, bs; Vienna State Opera Chorus; VPO; Leonard Bern-

stein. DG 2531 308/313, 2707 124 Tape (c) 3301 308/313, 3370 037. (*From 2740 216)
+Gr 2-81 p1079 ++HFN 4-81 p81 tape
+HFN 3-81 p94 +-MUM 11/12-81 p32

643 Symphonies, nos. 1-9. Gundula Janowitz, s; Hilde Rossel-Madjan, alto; Waldemar Kmentt, t; Walter Berry, bar; Wiener Singverein; BPhO; Herbert von Karajan. DG 2740 242 (8)
+-FF 9/10-81 p76

644 Symphonies, nos. 1-9. Fidelio, op. 72: Overture. Coriolan overture, op. 62. Leonore overtures, nos. 2 and 3, op. 72. Elisabeth Schwarzkopf, Elisabeth Hongen, s; Hans Hopf, Otto Edelmann, bar; Bayreuth Festival Orchestra and Chorus, VPO, BPhO, Stockholm Philharmonic orchestra; Wilhelm Furtwangler. Electrola 149 53432/9 (8)
+FF 3/4-81 p76 ++NYT 4-27-80 pD25
+-Gr 12-80 p881

645 Symphonies, nos. 1-9. Fidelio, op. 72: Overture. Coriolan overture, op. 62. Die Geschopfe des Prometheus, op. 43. Egmont, op. 84: Overture. Sheila Armstrong, s; Linda Finney, ms; Robert Tear, t; John Tomlinson, bs; PhO and Chorus; Kurt Sanderling. HMV SLS 5239 Tape (c) TCC SLS 5239
++Gr 11-81 p680

646 Symphonies, nos. 1-9. Coriolan overture, op. 62. Egmont, op. 84: Overture. Ingeborg Wenglor, s; Annelies Burmeister, alto; Martin Ritzmann, t; Rolf Kuhne, bs; CPhO and Chorus; Paul Kletzki. Supraphon 110 2461/8 (8)
+-ARG 3-81 p11 +SFC 8-31-80 p31
+NR 8-80 p2

Symphonies, nos. 1-9. See no. 721

647 Symphony, no. 1, op. 21, C major. Symphony, no. 2, op. 36, D major. CO; Lorin Maazel. CBS 76854 Tape (c) 40-76854 (From 79800)
+Gr 8-80 p214 +Gr 2-81 p1122 tape

648 Symphony, no. 1, op. 21, C major. Symphony, no. 4, op. 60, B flat major. VPO; Leonard Bernstein. DG 2531 308
+ST 6-81 p124

649 Symphony, no. 1, op. 21, C major. Symphony, no. 9, op. 125, D minor. Helen Donath, s; Teresa Berganza, con; Wieslaw Ochman, t; Thomas Stewart, bar; LSO, Bavarian Radio Orchestra and Chorus; Rafael Kubelik. DG 2726 112 (2) Tape (c) 3372 112 (From 2740 155)
+-Gr 4-81 p1312 +HFN 8-81 p92 tape
+-HFN 5-81 p89

650 Symphony, no. 1, op. 21, C major. Symphony, no. 2, op. 36, D major. AMF; Neville Marriner. Philips 6527 074 Tape (c) 7311 074 (From 6707 013)
++Gr 4-81 p1312 +-HFN 5-81 p89
+Gr 7-81 p196 tape +-HFN 7-81 p81 tape

651 Symphony, no. 2, op. 36, D major. Symphony, no. 4, op. 60, B flat major. COA, Israel Philharmonic Orchestra; Rafael Kubelik. DG 2535 441 Tape (c) 3335 441 (From 2740 155)
+Gr 3-81 p1184 +HFN 8-81 p92 tape

652 Symphony, no. 2, op. 36, D major. HAYDN: Symphony, no. 93, D major. Symphony, no. 99, E flat major. Symphony, no. 104, D major. LPO; Thomas Beecham. HMV RLS 734 (2) (From Columbia LX 586/9, 721/3, 505/7, 856/8)

+ARSC Vol 12, no. 3 1980 p247
+-FF 3/4-81 p140
+-Gr 6-79 p41
+HFN 6-79 p115
+RR 6-79 p80

653 Symphony, no. 2, op. 36, D major. Consecration of the house, op. 124: Overture. Leonore overture, no. 1, op. 72. Leipzig Gewandhaus Orchestra; Kurt Masur. Philips 6570 130 Tape (c) 7310 130 (From 6747 135)
+Gr 5-81 p1472
+-HFN 6-81 p83

654 Symphony, no. 2, op. 36, D major. VPO; Wilhelm Furtwangler. La Voix de Son Maitre C 051 03649
+FF 11/12-81 p107

Symphony, no. 2, op. 36, D major. See no. 647. See no. 650

655 Symphony, no. 3, op. 55, E flat major. Halle Orchestra; James Loughran. ASV Tape (c) ZCALH 901
+-HFN 11-81 p105 tape

656 Symphony, no. 3, op. 55, E flat major. Stuttgart Radio Orchestra; Erich Kleiber. Bruno Walter Society RR 392
-FF 7/8-81 p68
+-NR 4-81 p2

657 Symphony, no. 3, op. 55, E flat major. NYP; Zubin Mehta. CBS 35883 Tape (c) HMT 35883
+ARG 4-81 p14
+Audio 4-81 p59
+-FF 1/2-81 p80
+-Gr 9-80 p326
-HF 1-81 p69
-HF 4-81 p93 tape
+-HFN 10-80 p103
+-HFN 12-80 p159 tape
+SFC 2-22-81 p19
+St 5-81 p66
+STL 9-14-80 p40

658 Symphony, no. 3, op. 55, E flat major. CO; Georg Szell. CBS MY 37222 (From Odyssey 34622)
+FF 11/12-81 p109

659 Symphony, no. 3, op. 55, E flat major. Berlin State Orchestra; Otmar Suitner. Denon OX 7202
+-HF 6-81 p52
+St 5-81 p66

660 Symphony, no. 3, op. 55, E flat major. Scottish National Symphony Orchestra; Carlos Paita. Lodia Tape (c) LOC 774 (From Decca SXL 4367)
+-HFN 6-81 p87 tape

661 Symphony, no. 3, op. 55, E flat major. COA; Pierre Monteux. Philips 6570 204 Tape (c) 7310 204 (From World WS 9137)
+ARG 10-81 p18
+FF 7/8-81 p68
+Gr 10-81 p540
+-HFN 10-81 p95

662 Symphony, no. 3, op. 55, E flat major. Collegium Aureum; Franz-josef Maier. Pro Arte PAL 1029 Tape (c) PAC 1029
+FF 11/12-81 p107
+HF 11-81 p76
+NYT 10-11-81 pD31

663 Symphony, no. 3, op. 55, E flat major. PO; Eugene Ormandy. RCA ATC 1-4032 Tape (c) ATK 1-4032
+-FF 11/12-82 p108
+-HF 11-81 p76

664 Symphony, no. 3, op. 55, E flat major. Warsaw National Philharmonic Orchestra; Witold Rowicki. Stolat SZM 0101
-FF 11/12-81 p108
+-NYT 7-26-81 pD23

665 Symphony, no. 3, op. 55, E flat major. Consecration of the house, op. 124: Overture. Southwest German Radio Orchestra, VSO; Jascha Horenstein. Turnabout TV 34758
-ARG 1-81 p20

666 Symphony, no. 4, op. 60, B flat major. Consecration of the house,

op. 124: Overture. VPO; Hans Schmidt-Isserstedt. Decca JB 7 Tape (c) KJBC 7 (From SXL 6274) (also London STS 15528. From 6512)
+FF 3/4-81 p79
+Gr 1-78 p1248
+Gr 4-78 p1771 tape
+HFN 12-77 p185
+HFN 3-78 p155 tape
+-RR 12-77 p44
+RR 4-78 p103 tape

667 Symphony, no. 4, op. 60, B major. Egmont, op. 84: Overture. Leipzig Gewandhaus Orchestra; Kurt Masur. Philips 6570 132 Tape (c) 7310 132 (From 6747 135)
++Gr 1-81 p948
+HFN 2-81 p97
+HFN 3-81 p97tape

668 Symphony, no. 4, op. 60, B flat major. Leonore overture, no. 2, op. 72. BPhO; Eugen Jochum. Quintessence PMC 7139 (From DG 138694)
++Audio 1-81 p82
++FF 5/6-80 p48

Symphony, no. 4, op. 60, B flat major. See no. 522. See no. 648. See no. 651

669 Symphony, no. 5, op. 67, C minor. Symphony, no. 8, op. 93, F major. BPhO, VPO; Wilhelm Furtwangler. Bruno Walter Society RR 522
-FF 7/8-81 p69
+NR 4-81 p2

670 Symphony, no. 5, op. 67, C minor. SCHUBERT: Symphony, no. 8, D 759, B minor. NYP; Leonard Bernstein. CBS MY 36719
+-FF 11/12-81 p110
-NR 11-81 p2

671 Symphony, no. 5, op. 67, C minor. LSO; Loris Tjeknavorian. Chalfont SDG 314
-FF 11/12-81 p110
-HF 11-81 p76

672 Symphony, no. 5, op. 67, C minor. Fidelio, op. 72: Overture. Bavarian Radio Symphony Orchestra; Eugen Jochum. Contour CC 7526 Tape (c) CCT 7526
+Gr 8-81 p316

673 Symphony, no. 5, op. 67, C minor. Symphony, no. 8, op. 93, F major. BSO, CO Members; Rafael Kubelik. DG 2535 407 Tape (c) 3335 407
++FF 11/12-80 p77
+-Gr 8-81 p264
+/HFN 12-80 p159 tape
+-HFN 6-81 p83

674 Symphony, no. 5, op. 67, C minor. BPhO; Wilhelm Furtwangler. Pathe 2C 051 03587
+FF 11/12-81 p110

675 Symphony, no. 5, op. 67, C minor. Egmont, op. 84: Overture. BSO; Seiji Ozawa. Telarc DG 10060
+-FF 9/10-81 p77
+HF 11-81 p76
++HFN 11-81 p90
+-MUM 11/12-81 p30
++NR 8-81 p2
++SFC 6-21-81 p18
+-St 11-81 p80

Symphony, no. 5, op. 67, C minor. See no. 3781

676 Symphony, no. 6, op. 68, F major. Halle Orchestra; James Loughran. ASV ALH 902 Tape (c) ZCALH 902 (From Enigma VAR 1036)
+Gr 12-81 p883
+HFN 11-81 p105 tape

677 Symphony, no. 6, op. 68, F major. PFITZNER: Palestrina: Preludes (3). BPhO; Wilhelm Furtwangler. Bruno Walter Society RR 477
+-FF 7/8-81 p69
+NR 4-81 p2

678 Symphony, no. 6, op. 68, F major. National Arts Centre Orchestra; Mario Bernardi. CBS SM 5008
++MUM 11/12-81 p36

679 Symphony, no. 6, op. 68, F major. Columbia Symphony Orchestra; Bruno Walter. CBS MY 36720 (From CBS MS 6012, Odyssey Y 33924)
-FF 9/10-81 p77
+SFC 8-30-81 p18

680 Symphony, no. 6, op. 68, F major. Berlin State Orchestra; Otmar Suitner. Denon OX 7222
+-FF 11/12-81 p111
+-HF 11-81 p76

681 Symphony, no. 6, op. 68, F major. LAPO; Carlo Maria Giulini. DG 2531 266 Tape (c) 3301 266
+-FF 3/4-81 p80
+-Gr 6-80 p32
+-HF 3-81 p64
+HFN 6-80 p102
+HFN 8-80 p109 tape
++NR 3-81 p4
-RR 6-80 p40

682 Symphony, no. 6, op. 68, F major. PO; Riccardo Muti. HMV ASD 3854 Tape (c) TC ASD 3854 (also Angel S 36739 Tape (c) 4ZS 37639)
+-FF 9/10-80 p77
+-Gr 5-80 p1652
+-HF 3-81 p64
+-HFN 5-80 p118
+HFN 8-80 p109 tape
++NR 7-80 p3
+-NYT 5-11-80 pD24
+-RR 5-80 p53
+St 11-80 p79

683 Symphony, no. 6, op. 68, F major. Stuttgart Classical Philharmonic; Karl Munchinger. Intercord INT 160 828
+FF 3/4-81 p80
+HF 3-81 p64
+HFN 9-81 p78
+NYT 3-29-81 pD31

684 Symphony, no. 6, op. 68, F major. COA; Eugen Jochum. Philips 6570 159 (also 6527 045 Tape (c) 7311 045. From ASX 9000/1-9)
+-FF 1/2-80 p55
+Gr 6-81 p34
+-HFN 6-81 p83
+-HFN 10-81 p95 tape

Symphony, no. 6, op. 68, F major: 1st movement. See no. 3698

685 Symphony, no. 7, op. 92, A major. STRAUSS, R.: Don Juan, op. 20. BPhO; Wilhelm Furtwangler. Bruno Walter Society RR 476
-FF 7/8-81 p69
+NR 4-81 p2

686 Symphony, no. 7, op. 92, A major. BPhO; Herbert von Karajan. Contour CC 7502 Tape (c) CCT 7502
+-Gr 8-81 p316

687 Symphony, no. 7, op. 92, A major. VPO; Leonard Bernstein. DG 2531 313
+ST 6-81 p124

688 Symphony, no. 7, op. 92, A major. Coriolan overture, op. 62. BPhO; Karl Bohm. DG 2535 147 (From SLPM 138018)
-Gr 2-76 p1331
+HFN 5-76 p115
+-RR 3-76 p36
+SFC 2-15-81 p19

689 Symphony, no. 7, op. 92, A major. VPO; Rafael Kubelik. DG 2535 472 Tape (c) 3335 472 (From 2740 155)
+Gr 10-81 p540

690 Symphony, no. 7, op. 92, A major. Coriolan overture, op. 62. BSO; Erich Leinsdorf. RCA AGL 1-3966 (From LSC 2969)
-FF 9/10-81 p78

691 Symphony, no. 7, op. 92, A major. Leonore overture, no. 3, op. 72a. Orchestra; Sergiu Celibidache. Rococo 2148
+-NR 3-81 p1

Symphony, no. 7, op. 92, A major. See no. 963. See no. 3943

692 Symphony, no. 8, op. 93, F major. Symphony, no. 9, op. 125, D minor. Kiri Te Kanawa, s; Julia Hamari, con; Stuart Burrows, t; Robert Holl, bs; LSO and Chorus; Eugen Jochum. Angel SZB 3880 (2)
+-FF 3/4-81 p80

693 Symphony, no. 8, op. 93, F major. BRUCKNER: Symphony, no. 8, C minor. VPO, NDR Symphony Orchestra; Hans Knappertsbusch. Bruno Walter Society IGI 375 (2)
+-FF 7/8-81 p84 -NR 5-81 p4

694 Symphony, no. 8, op. 93, F major. SCHUBERT: Symphony, no. 8, D 759, B minor. VPO; Claudio Abbado, Josef Krips. Contour CC 7503 Tape (c) CCT 7503
++Gr 8-81 p316

695 Symphony, no. 8, op. 93, F major. STRAUSS, R.: Don Juan, op. 20. WEILL: Die Dreigroschenoper: Suite. BPhO, Berlin State Opera Orchestra; Hans Pfitzner, Otto Klemperer. Past Master PM 31 (From Parlophone and Polydor 78s)
+FF 5/6-81 p221

Symphony, no. 8, op. 93, F major. See no. 669. See no. 673
Symphony, no. 8, op. 93, F major: Allegretto. See no. 3964

696 Symphony, no. 9, op. 125, D minor. Isobel Buchanan, s; Alfreda Hodgson, ms; John Mitchinson, t; Gwynne Howell, bs; Halle Orchestra and Chorus; James Loughran. ASV ALH 903 Tape (c) ZCALH 903
+-Gr 12-81 p884 +STL 10-11-81 p41
+-HFN 11-81 p105 tape

697 Symphony, no. 9, op. 125, D minor. Elisabeth Schwarzkopf, s; Elsa Cavelti, ms; Ernst Hafliger, t; Otto Edelmann, bs; Lucerne Festival Choir; PhO; Wilhelm Furtwangler. Bruno Walter Society RR 390
-FF 7/8-81 p69 +NR 4-81 p2

698 Symphony, no. 9, op. 125, D minor. Gre Brouwenstijn, s; Kerstin Meyer, con; Nicolai Gedda, t; Frederick Guthrie, bs; St. Hedwig's Cathedral Choir; BPhO; Andre Cluytens. Classics for Pleasure CFP 40019 Tape (c) TC 40019 (From HMV SXLP 30085)
+Gr 8-73 p375 /RR 8-73 p35
+-HFN 5-81 p93 tape

699 Symphony, no. 9, op. 125, D minor. Elisabeth Schwarzkopf, s; Marga Hoffgen, alto; Ernst Hafliger, t; Otto Edelmann, bs; Musikfreunde Gesellschaft Chorus; VPO; Herbert von Karajan. DaCapo 1C 063 01200 (From Angel 3544)
+-FF 3/4-81 p81

700 Symphony, no. 9, op. 125, D minor. Soloists; Prague Philharmonic Choir; CPhO; Vaclav Neumann. Denon PCM OB 7333/4 (2)
+HF 10-77 p112 +HFN 5-81 p77

701 Symphony, no. 9, op. 125, D minor. Jessye Norman, s; Brigitte Fassbaender, ms; Placido Domingo, t; Walter Berry, bs; Vienna State Opera Concert Choir; VPO; Karl Bohm. DG 2741 009 (2) Tape (c) 3382 009
+Gr 11-81 p680 +SFC 12-20-81 p18

702 Symphony, no. 9, op. 125, D minor. Pilar Lorengar, s; Yvonne Minton, ms; Stuart Burrows, t; Martti Talvela, bs; CSO and Chorus; Georg Solti. Mobile Fidelity MFSL 2-516
+NR 12-81 p3

703 Symphony, no. 9, op. 125, D minor. Janet Price, s; Birgit Finnila, alto; Horst Laubenthal, t; Marius Rintzler, bs; COA and Chorus; Bernard Haitink. Philips 6769 067 (2) Tape (c) 7654 067
+-Gr 11-81 p680 +-MUM 9/10-81 p33
+HF 11-81 p76 ++SFC 5-31-81 p22
+HFN 10-81 p85 +STL 10-11-81 p41

704 Symphony, no. 9, op. 125, D minor. Leontyne Price, s; Maureen Forrester, con; David Poleri, t; Giorgio Tozzi, bs; New England Conservatory Chorus; BSO; Charles Munch. RCA AGL 1-3007 (From LSC 6066, VICS 1660)
-FF 9/10-81 p78

705 Symphony, no. 9, op. 125, D minor. Elisabeth Soderstrom, s; Regina Resnik, con; Jon Vickers, t; David Ward, bs; LSO; London Bach Choir; Pierre Monteux. Westminster WG 8364/2 (2)
-ARG 3-80 p18 +MUM 1/2-81 p31
+FF 1/2-80 p54

Symphony, no. 9, op. 125, D minor. See no. 649. See no. 692. See no. 3791

Tarpeja, trumphal march. See no. 722

706 Trio, clarinet, op. 11, B flat major. Trio, piano, no. 4, op. 70, no. 1, D major. Franzjosef Maier, vln; Hans Deinzer, clt; Rudolf Mandalka, vlc; Jorg Demus, pno. Harmonia Mundi 1C 065 99839
+FF 5/6-80 p52 +-RR 4-80 p84
+-HFN 5-80 p118 +-ST 9-80 p342
+MT 3-81 p181

707 Trio, clarinet, op. 11, B flat major. BRAHMS: Trio, clarinet, violoncello and piano, op. 114, A minor.* George Pieterson, clt; Bernard Greenhouse, vlc; Menahem Pressler, pno. Philips 9500 670 Tape (c) 7300 826 (*From 6768 146)
++ARG 4-81 p18 ++HF 2-81 p59
+Audio 3-81 p60 ++HFN 3-81 p86
++FF 3/4-81 p92 ++NR 2-81 p7
+Gr 4-81 p1332 ++St 3-81 p92
+Gr 7-81 p196 tape

708 Trio, clarinet, op. 11, B flat major. BRAHMS: Trio, clarinet, op. 114, A minor. Bob Wilber, clt; Leo Winland, vlc; Janos Solyom, pno. Phontastic Artemis ARTE 7107
+FF 5/6-80 p52 +Gr 11-80 p691
+FF 1/2-81 p81

Trio, clarinet, op. 11, B flat major. See no. 566. See no. 572. See no. 711

709 Trio, piano, no. 1, op. 1, no. 1, E flat major. Trio, piano, no. 3, op. 1, no. 3, C minor. George Malcolm Piano Trio. Crescent ARS 108 Tape (c) Libra Realsound LRS 108
+-Gr 5-77 p1704 +-HFN 5-77 p119
+Gr 6-81 p94 tape +RR 5-77 p62
+Gr 7-81 p196 tape

Trio, piano, no. 3, op. 1, no. 3, C minor. See no. 709

710 Trio, piano, no. 4, op. 70, no. 1, D major. SCHUBERT: Quintet, piano, op. 114, D 667, A major. Hephzibah Menuhin, pno; Yehudi Menuhin, vln; Maurice Gendron, vlc; Amadeus Quartet; James Edward Merrett, double bass. HMV SXLP 30523 Tape (c) TC SXLP 30523 (From ASD 2258, 322)
+Gr 7-81 p164

711 Trio, piano, no. 4, op. 70, no. 1, D major. Trio, piano, op. 11, B flat major. Variations on "Ich bin der Schneider Kakadu", op. 121a, G major. Beaux Arts Trio. Philips 6527 077 Tape (c) 7311 077 (From SAL 3527/30)
+Gr 8-81 p282

Trio, piano, no. 4, op. 70, no. 1, D major. See no. 706

712 Trio, piano, no. 6, op. 97, B flat major. Kantorow Trio. Accord ACC 140 002
+HFN 9-81 p78

713 Trio, piano, no. 6, op. 97, B flat major. William Murdoch, pno; Albert Sammons, vln; W. H. Squire, vlc. Bruno Walter Society RH 1
+ARG 12-81 p50 +-NR 5-81 p9
+FF 9/10-81 p78

714 Trio, piano, no. 6, op. 97, B flat major. Beaux Arts Trio. Philips 9500 895 Tape (c) 7300 895)
+-FF 7/8-81 p71 ++MUM 7/8-81 p32
+-Gr 6-81 p48 +-NR 4-81 p7
+-Gr 9-81 p460 tape ++NYT 6-21-81 pD23
+HFN 5-81 p79 ++SFC 2-15-81 p19
+HFN 9-81 p93 tape +-ST 10-81 p429

715 Trio, piano, no. 10, op. posth., B flat major. GOLDMARK: Trio, piano, op. 1, D minor. HAYDN: Trio, piano, no. 27, C major. Western Arts Trio. Laurel LR 112
+/FF 11/12-81 p294 ++NR 9-81 p6

Trio, piano, flute and bassoon, G major. See no. 573
Trio, strings, no. 3, E flat major. See no. 570
Trio, strings, op. 8, D major. See no. 570
Trio, string, op. 9, nos. 1-3. See no. 570

716 Trio, strings, op. 9, no. 1, G major. MOZART: Quartet, piano, K 493, E flat major. Richard Goode, pno; Charles Treger, vln; Walter Trampler, vla; Leslie Parnas, vlc. Musical Heritage Society MHS 4291 Tape (c) MHC 6291
+-FF 5/6-81 p114 +-HF 11-81 p94

717 Variations and fugue, op. 34, F major (6). MENDELSSOHN: Variations serieuses, op. 54, D minor. MOZART: Variations on "Unser Dummer Pobel", K 455 (10). HAYDN: Variations, F minor. Lydia Artymiw, pno. Chandos ABR 1013 Tape (c) ABT 1013
+-FF 1/2-81 p221 +HFN 10-80 p117 tape
+-Gr 10-80 p548 tape +MT 4-81 p246
+Gr 9-80 p380 +-STL 9-14-80 p40
+HFN 9-80 p113

718 Variations and fugue, op. 35, E flat major. SCHUMANN: Symphonic etudes, op. 13. Steven de Groote, pno. DG 2535 007
+-CL 2-81 p12 +NR 1-81 p14
+FF 1/2-81 p81 -NYT 3-8-81 pD34
+-HF 1-81 p58 +-St 2-81 p54

719 Variations on a theme by Diabelli, op. 120. Bernard Roberts, pno. Nimbus DC 906
+HFN 6-81 p70

Variations on a theme by Diabelli, op. 120. See no. 345
Variations on "Air de la petite Russie", op. 107, no. 3. See no. 571
Variations on "Air Russe", op. 107, no. 7. See no. 571
Variations on "Ich bin der Schneider Kakadu", op. 121a, G major. See no. 711
Variations on Mozart's "Be Mannern welche Liebe fuhlen" (7). See no. 572

720 Variations on Mozart's "Se vuol ballare". MOZART, F.X.: Sonata, op. 19, E major. SCHUBERT: Fantasia, op. 159, D 934, C major. Gidon Kremer, vln; Elena Kremer, pno. Philips 9500 904 Tape

(c) 7300 904
+FF 11/12-81 p292 ++NR 7-81 p7
+Gr 8-81 p284 +SFC 7-12-81 p18
+HFN 8-81 p90 ++St 9-81 p78

Variations on "Nel cor piu non mi sento". See no. 602

721 Works, selections: Concerti piano, nos. 1-5. Concerto, violin, op. 61, D major. Consecration of the house, op. 124: Overture. Coriolan overture, op. 62. Egmont, op. 84, excerpts. Fantasia, op. 80, C minor. Fidelio, op. 72. Fidelio, op. 72: Overture. Dei Geschopfe des Prometheus, op. 43, excerpts. Grosse Fuge, op. 133, B flat major. Konig Stefan, op. 117: Overture. Leonore overtures, nos. 1-3, opp. 72, 138. Mass, op. 123, D major. Symphonies, nos. 1-9. Various vocalists; Daniel Barenboim, pno; Yehudi Menuhin, vln; PhO and Chorus, NPhO; Otto Klemperer. EMI Electrola 1C 197 53400/19 (20)
+-FF 11/12-81 p111

722 Works, selections: Consecration of the house, op. 124: Overture; Wo sich die Pulse. Coriolan overture, op. 62. Egmont, op. 84: Overture. Fidelio, op. 72: Overture. Die Geschopfe des Prometheus, op. 43: Overture. Konig Stefan, op. 117: Overture. Leonore overtures, nos. 1-3. Leonore Prohaska funeral march. Meerestille und Gluckliche Fahrt, op. 112. Minuet of congratulations. Namensfeier, op. 115: Overture. Die Ruinen von Athens, op. 113: Overture; Turkish march. Tarpeja, triumphal march. Phyllis Bryn-Julson, s; Minnesota Bach Society Chorus; Minnesota Orchestra; Stanislaw Skrowaczewski. Vox SVBX 5156 (3)
+-FF 7/8-81 p61 ++SFC 3-29-81 p18
*NYT 5-31-81 pD23 +St 11-81 p80

BELARSKY-KACERGINSKY

Zol Shoin Kumin di Geula. See no. 3897

BELCHER, Supply

Carol. See no. 3911

BELLINI, Vincenzo

Beatrice di Tenda: Angiol de pace. See no. 3890

723 Bianca e Fernando: Ove son; Che m'avvenne...Sorgi o padre. Norma: Dormono entrambi...Mira o Norma...Si find all'ore. MERCADANTE: Le due illustri rivali: Leggio gia nel vostro cor. MOZART: Le nozze di Figaro, K 492: Cosa mi narri...Sull' arial. Renata Scotto, Mirella Freni, s; NPhO; Leone Magiera, Lorenzo Anselmi. Decca SXL 6970 Tape (c) KSXC 6970 (also London OS 26652 Tape (c) OS5 26652)
+FF 7/8-81 p206 +-ON 5-81 p44
+-Gr 1-81 p993 +Op 6-81 p649
+HFN 1-81 p104 +SFC 5-24-81 p19
+NR 6-81 p9 +St 8-81 p101
+-NYT 4-5-81 pD33

I Capuleti ed i Montecchi: Deh tu bell'anima. See no. 3838

I Capuleti ed i Montecchi: Oh quante volte; Ah crudel d'onor ragioni. See no. 3640

724 Norma. Renata Scotto, s; Tatiana Troyanos, Ann Murray, ms; Giuseppe Giacomini, Paul Crook, t; Paul Plishka, bs; Ambrosian Opera Chorus; National Philharmonic Orchestra; James Levine. Columbia M 3 35902 (3) (also CBS 79327 Tape (c) 40-79327)
+-ARG 10-80 p10 +NYT 3-23-80 pD25

+-FF 7/8-80 p61
+-Gr 7-80 p161
+-HF 7-80 p64
+-HFN 7-80 p106
+MT 6-81 p388
+OC Summer 1980 p47
+ON 5-80 p44
+-Op 9-80 p910
+RR 7-80 p42
+St 7-80 p76

725 Norma. Maria Callas, s; Ebe Stignani, ms; Mario Del Monaco, t; Orchestra; Tullio Serafin. Replica 6 RPL 24 16/8 (3)
+FF 9/10-81 p79

Norma: Al del tebro. See no. 3968
Norma: Casta diva. See no. 3713. See no. 4026
Norma: Dormono entrambi...Mira o Norma...Si find all'ore. See no. 723
Norma: Duet. See no. 4021
Norma: Meco al altar. See no. 3839
Norma: Meco al altar di venere...Me protegge me difende. See no. 3646
Norma: Mira Norma. See no. 3849
Norma: Scena and duet, Act 1; Finale, Act 1. See no. 3890
"Norma" variations (Alban). See no. 3986
Il pirata: Cor sorriso d'innocenza. See no. 3647

726 I puritani. Montserrat Caballe, s; Julia Hamari, ms; Alfredo Kraus, t; Matteo Manuguerra, bar; Ambrosian Opera Chorus; PhO; Riccardo Muti. Angel SZCX 3881 (3) (also HMV SLS 5201 Tape (c) TC SLS 5021)
++ARG 5-81 p42
+-FF 3/4-81 p83
+Gr 1-81 p986
+-HF 5-81 p54
+-HFN 1-81 p91
+-HFN 4-81 p81 tape
+-MT 5-81 p317
+-NR 2-81 p9
++OC Summer 1981 p51
+-ON 2-14-81 p44
++Op 2-81 p159
+SFC 12-7-80 p33
+STL 1-11-81 p38

727 I puritani, abridged. Joan Sutherland, s; Alfredo Kraus, t; Rolando Panerai, bar; Nicolai Ghiuselev, bs; Orchestra and Chorus; Richard Bonynge. Historical Recording HRE 335 (2)
+FF 11/12-81 p113

I puritani: A te o cara. See no. 3759. See no. 3885
I puritani: Cinta di fiori. See no. 3968
I puritani: Vien diletto. See no. 3647

728 La sonnambula. Renata Scotto, Marisa Zotti, s; Rosa Laghezza, ms; Alfredo Kraus, t; Ivo Vinco, bs; La Fenice Teatro Orchestra and Chorus; Nello Santi. Historical Recordings HRE 337 (2)
+-FF 5/6-81 p57

La sonnambula: Ah perche non posso odiarti; Prendi l'anel ti dono; Son geloso. See no. 4032
La sonnambula: Prendi l'anel; Son geloso; D'un pensiero. See no. 4047
La sonnambula: Va ravviso. See no. 4029
Songs: Dolente immagine di fille mia; Malinconia ninfa gentile; Vaga luna che inargenti. See no. 3758
Songs: Dolente immagine di felle mia; Vaga luna che inargenti. See no. 3838
Songs: Fenesta che lucive. See no. 3641. See no. 3843
Songs: Vanne o rosa fortunata. See no. 3759
La straniera: Sono all'ara...Ciel pietoso...Or sei pago. See no. 4014

729 Zaira. Renata Scotto, s; Maria Luisa Nave, Giovanna Collica, Carmelo Mollica; Luigi Roni, bs; Giorgio Casellato Lamberti, Nino Valori; Teatro Massimo Bellini; Danilo Balardinelli. BJR Records 146-3 (3)
+-FF 7/8-81 p73

BEMBERG, Herman
Le soupir. See no. 4029

BENATZKY, Ralph
Ich muss wieder einmal. See no. 3823

BENDA, Franz (Frantisek)
Sonata, flute and harpsichord, op. 3, no. 1, G major. See no. 112
Sonata, violoncello and bass, F major. See no. 4096

BENDA, Jiri (Georg)

730 Concerti, harpsichord, G major, D major, C major, G minor, F major. Divertimento, G major. Josef Hala, hpd; Antonin Nôvak, Vojtech Jouza, vln; Karel Spelina, vla; Frantisek Slama, vlc; Frantisek Posta, violone. Supraphon 111 2671/2 (2)
+-Gr 7-81 p164 +NR 9-81 p4
+HFN 8-81 p82

Divertimento, G major. See no. 730

BENEDICT, Julius
Il carnevale di Venezi. See no. 3649
The lily of Killarney: The moon has raised her lamp above. See no. 3967

BENET, John
Songs: All creatures. See no. 3876

BENJAMIN, Arthur
Fanfare for a festive occasion. See no. 4006
Fanfares: For a state occasion; For a brilliant occasion; For a gala occasion. See no. 4006

BENNET, John
Weep o mine eyes. See no. 3677

BENNETT
Symphonic songs. See no. 3817

BENNETT, John
Songs: Luer falconer; Round about a fair ring. See no. 4093

BENNETT, Richard Rodney

731 Aubade. Spells. Jane Manning, s; Bach Choir; PhO; David Willcocks, David Atherton. ARgo ZRG 907
+FF 1/2-81 p82 ++HFN 1-80 p102
+Gr 1-80 p1181 +MT 4-80 p248

Out of your sleep. See no. 3685
Spells. See no. 731

BENNETT, William Sterndale
Take oh take those lips away. See no. 3967

BENSON, Warren

732 Capriccio. Dream net. Quartet, strings, no. 1. Frederick Hemke, sax; Kronos Quartet, Chester Quartet, Eastman Quartet. CRI SD 433
+ARG 12-81 p12 -NR 8-81 p7
+FF 9/10-81 p79

Dream net. See no. 732
Quartet strings. no. 1. See no. 732

BENTZON, Niels
Variations on "Volga boatmen's song". See no. 4072

BERBERIAN
Prelude. See no. 3912
BERCHAM, Jacquet de
O Jesu Christe. See no. 3634
BERG, Alban
Arias: Der Wein. See no. 738
733 Chamber concerto. STRAVINSKY: Agon. London Sinfonietta; David Atherton. Argo ZRG 937
++Gr 7-81 p151 +-HFN 7-81 p71
734 Chamber concerto. Sviatoslav Richter, pno; Oleg Kagan, vln; Moscow Conservatory Ensemble; Yuri Nikolaiewski. EMI 1C 065 03672
++FF 1/2-81 p83
735 Chamber concerto. Concerto, violin. Josef Suk, Ivan Strauss, vln; Zdenek Kozina, pno; CPhO; Prague Chamber Harmony; Karel Ancerl, Libor Pesek. Quintessence PMC 7179
+MUM 5/6-81 p30
736 Concerto, violin. STRAVINSKY: Concerto, violin, D major. Itzhak Perlman, vln; BSO; Seiji Ozawa. DG 2531 110 Tape (c) 3301 110
++FF 9/10-80 p78 +MUM 10-80 p32
++Gr 3-80 p1385 ++NR 5-80 p4
++Gr 5-80 p1717 tape ++NYT 7-6-80 pD15
++HF 7-80 p60 ++RR 3-80 p47
++HF 6-81 p69 tape ++SFC 4-6-80 p31
+HFN 3-80 p87 ++St 7-80 p82
+HFN 8-80 p109 tape ++ST 9-80 p340
+MT 10-80 p633 ++STL 3-9-80 p41
737 Concerto, violin, Pieces, orchestra, op. 6. Ulf Hoelscher, vln; Cologne Radio Orchestra; Hiroshi Wakasugi. Harmonia Mundi 1C 065 99848
+-FF 9/10-80 p79 +-HFN 1-81 p91
+-Gr 10-80 p494 +-ST 5-81 p44
Concerto, violin. See no. 447. See no. 735
738 Lulu: Suite. Arias: Der Wein. Judith Blegen, Jessye Norman, s; NYP; Pierre Boulez. CBS 76575 (also CBS M 35849 Tape (c) MT 35849)
+-ARG 4-81 p15 +-MUM 7/8-81 p32
+FF 11/12-80 p78 +NR 1-81 p8
+Gr 8-79 p327 +RR 9-79 p69
+HF 1-81 p69 ++SFC 8-10-80 p29
+HFN 8-79 p101 +St 2-81 p104
Pieces, orchestra, op. 6. See no. 737
Seven early songs: Die Nachtigall. See no. 3709
739 Wozzeck. Anja Silja, s; Gertrude Jahn, ms; Heinz Zednik, Horst Laubenthal, t; Eberhard Waechter, bar; Alexander Malta, bs; VPO; Christoph von Dohnanyi. Decca D231D2 Tape (c) K231K22 (also London LDR 72007)
+FF 11/12-81 p114 +NR 12-81 p6
+Gr 6-81 p81 +Op 11-81 p1150
+Gr 10-81 p614 tape +STL 7-12-81 p40
+HFN 6-81 p70 ++SFC 9-20-81 p18
+-MT 12-81 p826
BERG, Gunnar
Songs: Ave Maria; Miserere; Sig frojde nu var kristen man; Veni creator spiritus. See no. 3991

BERGER, Arthur

740 Pieces, piano (5). Septet. WOLPE: Form for piano. Piece in two parts, solo violin. Russell Sherman, Robert Miller, pno; Rose Mary Harbison, vln; Contemporary Chamber Players; Arthur Weisberg. New World Records NW 308 (From Acoustic Research)
+FF 1/2-81 p84 ++St 5-81 p80
+NYT 4-12-81 pD29

Septet. See no. 740

BERGER, Jean

Songs: Snake baked a hoe-cake; The Frisco whale. See no. 3951

BERGER, Theodor

Rondino giocoso, op. 4. See no. 3791

BERGH, Sverre

Pan. See no. 3683

BERGMAN, Erik

741 Aubade, op. 48. SIBELIUS: Finlandia, op. 26. Legends, op. 22: Lemminkainen and the maidens of Saari. Helsinki Philharmonic Orchestra; Jorma Panula. Finlandia FA 314 (also Decca (Swedish) SXL 6434)
-FF 11/12-80 p175 +-HFN 1-81 p101
+-FF 3/4-81 p196 ++NR 3-81 p2
+-Gr 4-81 p1312

Junibastu. See no. 3805

BERIO, Luciano

742 Children's play, op. no. Zoo. KLUGHARDT: Quintet, winds, op. 79. MATHIAS: Quintet, winds, op. 22. Westwood Wind Quintet. Crystal S 250
+NR 12-81 p11

743 Coro. Cologne Radio Orchestra and Choir; Luciano Berio. DG 2531 270
+-FF 3/4-81 p84 ++HFN 11-80 p116
+Gr 9-80 p380 ++NR 1-81 p8
+HF 3-81 p56 +STL 8-10-80 p30

BERKELEY, Lennox

744 Mass, op. 64. Pieces, organ, op. 72, no. 1. BRITTEN: Festival te deum, op. 32; Hymn to St. Peter, op. 56a; Hymn of St. Colomba; Antiphon, op. 56b. Prelude and fugue on a theme by Vittoria. WALTON: Chichester service: Magnificat; Nunc dimittis. Norwich Cathedral Choir; Malcolm Archer, org; Michael Nicholas, org and dir. Vista VPS 1096
+Gr 12-81 p924

Pieces, organ, op. 72, no. 1. See no. 744

Sonatina. See no. 4001

Songs: I sing of a maiden. See no. 3685

Songs: Poems of St. Teresa of Avila. See no. 3654

BERLIN, Johan Daniel

745 Concerto, violin, A major. Minuets, F major, G major, C major (4). Sinfonia, 2 clarinets and 2 flutes. Sinfonia, cornetto, D major. Arve Tellefsen, vln; Kejll Jonnun, tpt; Gayle Mosand, hpd, cld; Trondheim Chamber Orchestra Members; Arve Tellefsen. Norsk Kulturrads NKF 30027
/FF 7/8-81 p74 -HFN 6-81 p70
+Gr 8-81 p317

Minuets, F major, G major, C major. See no. 745

Sinfonia, 2 clarinets and 2 flutes. See no. 745

Sinfonia, cornetto, D major. See no. 745
BERLINSKY, Herman
Psalm, no. 23. See no. 3953
BERLIOZ, Hector
Beatrice et Benedict: Dieu, Que viens-je d'entendre...Il m'en souvient. See no. 3710
746 Beatrice et Benedict: Overture. Le carnaval romain, op. 9. La damnation de Faust, op. 24: Hungarian march. DUKAS: L'apprenti sorcier. SAINT-SAENS: Le deluge, op. 45: Prelude. Samson et Dalila: Bacchanale. Danse macabre, op. 40. Orchestre de Paris; Daniel Barenboim. DG 2531 331 Tape (c) 3301 331
+-Gr 7-81 p195 +-HFN 8-81 p92 tape
+-HFN 8-81 p90
747 Benvenuto Cellini, op. 23: Overture. Le Corsaire, op. 21. LISZT: Tasso lamento e trionfo, S 96. WEBER: Turandot: Overture. MRSO; Gennady Rozhdestvensky. Quintessence PMC 7190 (also HMV ASD 3714)
+FF 7/8-81 p228 +-MT 2-80 p106
+Gr 8-79 p327 ++RR 8-79 p83
+HFN 8-79 p119
Benvenuto Cellini, op. 23: Overture. See no. 3684
748 Le carnaval romain, op. 9. TCHAIKOVSKY: Romeo and Juliet: Fantasy overture. VERDI: La forza del destino: Overture. Halle Orchestra; NPhO; John Barbirolli. Barbirolli Society SJB 103
+ARG 6-81 p55 +RR 2-80 p62
+HFN 1-80 p115
749 Le carnaval romain, op. 9. LISZT Les preludes, S 97. RESPIGHI: Pines of Rome. PhO; Herbert von Karajan. HMV SXLP 30450 Tape (c) TC SXLP 30450 (From Columbia 33CX 1548, SLS 5019)
++Gr 2-81 p1080 +HFN 4-81 p81 tape
+HFN 3-81 p95
Le carnaval romain, op. 9. See no. 521. See no. 746. See no. 3656. See no. 3709. See no. 3717. See no. 3760. See no. 4122
750 Le Corsaire, op. 21. ENESCO: Rumanian rhapsody, no. 1, op. 11. RAVEL: Bolero. RIMSKY-KORSAKOV: Capriccio espagnol, op. 34. Baltimore Symphony Orchestra; Sergiu Comissiona. Vanguard VS 25005 Tape (c) CVS 25005
+-FF 9/10-81 p287 ++NR 5-81 p5
+-HF 12-81 p93 tape
Le Corsaire, op. 21. See no. 747. See no. 3726
La damnation de Faust, op. 24: D'amour l'ardente flamme. See no. 3710
751 La damnation de Faust, op. 24: Hungarian march; Dance of the sylphys; Minuet of the will-o-the-wisps. Les Troyens: Royal hunt and storm; Trojan march. IBERT: Divertissement. Bacchanale. SATIE (Debussy): Gymnopedies, nos. 1, 3. Birmingham Symphony Orchestra and Chorus; Louis Fremaux. HMV ESD 7097 Tape (c) TC ESD 7097 (From ASD 2989, 3176, 3080)
+FF 9/10-81 p288 +-HFN 4-81 p80
+Gr 4-81 p1328
La damnation de Faust, op. 24: Hungarian march. See no. 746
La damnation de Faust, op. 24: Hungarian march; Dance of the sylphs; Minuet of the will-o-the-wisps. See no. 4121
La damnation de Faust, op. 24: Marche hongroise. See no. 3817
La damnation de Faust, op. 24: Nature immense. See no. 3688

752 La damnation de Faust, op. 24: Rakoczy march. BIZET: L'Arlesienne: Suite, no. 2. CHABRIER: Espana. GOUNOD: Faust: Ballet music. BPhO; Herbert von Karajan. HMV ASD 3761 Tape (c) TC ASD 3761 (also Angel SZ 37687)
++FF 1/2-81 p85 ++HFN 11-80 p127
++Gr 9-80 p352 +NR 1-81 p2

La damnation de Faust, op. 24: Rakoczy march. See no. 3699. See no. 3792. See no. 3863. See no. 3964

La damnation de Faust, op. 24: Serenade. See no. 4025. See no. 4034

La damnation de Faust, op. 24: Une puce gentille; Serenade; Voici des roses. See no. 4029

753 L'Enfance du Christ, op. 25. Janet Baker, ms; Eric Tappy, Philip Langridge, t; Thomas Allen, Raimund Herincx, bar; Joseph Rouleau, Jules Bastin, bs; John Alldis Choir; LSO; Colin Davis. Philips 6700 106 (2) Tape (c) 7699 058
+ARG 1-78 p12 +NR 12-77 p8
+Gr 10-77 p677 +-NYT 10-2-77 pD19
+Gr 3-78 p1622 tape ++RR 10-77 p81
+HF 1-78 p92 +-RR 4-78 p104 tape
+HF 3-78 p111 tape ++SFC 10-9-77 p40
+HFN 10-77 p152 +SR 12-81 p64
++HFN 2-78 p119 tape ++St 12-77 p133
+-MT 8-78 p687

L'Enfance du Christ, op. 25: Dance of the Ishmaelites. See no. 3921

754 Harold in Italy, op. 16 (trans. Liszt). Aldo Bennici, vla; Daniel Rivera, pno. Dischi Ricordi RCL 27054
+-FF 11/12-81 p225 +HFN 12-80 p133
+-Gr 11-80 p691

755 Harold in Italy, op. 16. Nobuko Imai, vla; LSO; Colin Davis. Philips 9500 026 Tape (c) 7300 441 (r) B-C G 9500 026
+Gr 3-76 p1463 +MT 6-77 p485
+-HF 10-76 p103 ++NR 6-76 p4
+-HF 2-77 p118 tape +RR 2-76 p26
+HF 6-81 p70 tape ++SFC 5-23-76 p36
+HFN 2-76 p92 ++St 9-76 p118

Herminie. See no. 757

756 La mort de Cleopatre. ELGAR: Sea pictures, op. 37. Yvonne Minton, s; BBC Symphony Orchestra, LPO; Pierre Boulez, Daniel Barenboim. CBS 71891 Tape (c) 40-61891 (From 76576, 76579)
++Gr 8-80 p247 +-HFN 10-80 p117 tape
+Gr 2-81 p1122 tape +RR 8-80 p78
+-HFN 8-80 p107

757 La mort de Cleopatre. Herminie. Janet Baker, ms; LSO; Colin Davis. Philips 9500 683 Tape (c) 7300 778
+ARG 1-81 p21 +MUM 11/12-80 p32
+FF 11/12-80 p78 ++NR 7-80 p11
++Gr 8-80 p247 +NYT 6-15-80 pD29
+-HF 9-80 p86 +RR 8-80 p77
+HFN 7-80 p106 ++SFC 6-8-80 p36
+HFN 9-80 p115 tape +-St 11-80 p80
+MT 1-81 p33 +STL 6-8-80 p38

758 Les nuits d'ete, op. 7. RAVEL: Sheherazade. Jessye Norman, s; LSO; Colin Davis. Philips 9500 783 Tape (c) 7300 857

++FF 9/10-81 p80 +-NR 7-81 p12
+-Gr 6-81 p66 +-SFC 9-19-81 p18
+-Gr 10-81 p614 tape ++St 8-81 p96
+HFN 6-81 p70 +-STL 7-12-81 p40

759 Nuits d'ete, op. 7. FALLA: El amor brujo. Leontyne Price, s; CSO; Fritz Reiner. RCA AGL 1-3792 Tape (c) AGK 1-3792 (From SB 6566)
-FF 7/8-81 p98 +-HFN 11-81 p90
+-Gr 11-81 p682

760 Requiem, op. 5. Robert Tear, t; LPO and Chorus; Andre Previn. Angel DSB 3907 (2) (also HMV SLS 5209 Tape (c) TCC SLS 5209)
-FF 9/10-81 p81 +HFN 9-81 p93 tape
+-Gr 7-81 p180 -MUM 9/10-81 p30
+Gr 8-81 p324 tape ++STL 7-12-81 p40

761 Requiem, op. 5. Placido Domingo, t; Paris Orchestra and Chorus; Daniel Barenboim. DG 2531 240 (2) (also DG 2707 119)
+-FF 11/12-81 p115 +-HFN 8-81 p82
+-Gr 7-81 p180

762 Requiem, op. 5. Peter Schreier, t; Bavarian Radio Orchestra and Chorus; Charles Munch. DG 2726 050 (2) Tape (c) 3372 050 (From SLPM 139264/5)
+Gr 3-77 p1437 +-HFN 1-81 p109 tape
+HFN 8-77 p95 +RR 3-77 p86

Romance, reverie et caprice, op. 8. See no. 564

763 Romeo et Juliette, op. 17. Yvonne Minton, ms; Francisco Araiza, t; Jules Bastin, bs; Orchestre de Paris and Chorus; Daniel Barenboim. DG 2707 115 (2) Tape (c) 3370 036
+-FF 3/4-81 p85 +NR 2-81 p2
+-Gr 11-80 p717 +NYT 12-14-80 pD38
+HFN 11-80 p117 +-ON 2-28-81 p36
+HFN 1-81 p109 tape

764 Romeo and Juliet, op. 17: Love scene. PROKOFIEV: Romeo and Juliet, op. 64: Montagues and Capulets; Dance; Romeo at Juliet's grave; Dance of the girls from Antilles; Tybalt's death. TCHAIKOVSKY: Romeo and Juliet: Fantasy overture. San Francisco Symphony Orchestra; Seiji Ozawa. DG 2535 422 Tape (c) 3335 422 (From 2530 308)
+Gr 4-81 p1377 +-HFN 12-80 p153

765 Romeo and Juliet, op. 17: 3rd scene (trans.). GEOGHEGHAN, T.: Duos, guitar, nos. 1 and 2. Spanish folk songs (4) (arr.). GRANADOS: Danza lenta. SCARLATTI, D.: Sonatas, guitar (2). Hugh and Thomas Geoghegan, gtr. Sail Records 1700
+GTR Fall 1981 p27 +NR 11-81 p14

766 Symphonie fantastique, op. 14. CO; Lorin Maazel. CBS M 35867 Tape (c) MT 35867
+-ARG 7-81 p12 +-HF 3-81 p64
-FF 3/4-81 p181 ++St 6-81 p110

767 Symphonie fantastique, op. 14 (trans. Liszt). Bruno Mezzena, pno. CBS 76861 (also Ricordi RCL 2-7006)
-FF 11/12-81 p225 /-HFN 10-80 p102
+Gr 10-80 p517 /-MT 4-81 p245

768 Symphonie fantastique, op. 14. VPO; Bernard Haitink. Decca SXL 6938 Tape (c) KSXC 6938 (also Decca DKL 14; London CS 7168)
+Gr 12-79 p1007 +RR 12-79 p49
+HF 4-81 p93 tape ++SFC 7-5-81 p19
+HFN 12-79 p158 ++SFC 8-9-81 p18

769 Symphonie fantastique, op. 14. NYP; Zubin Mehta. Decca SXDL 7512 Tape (c) KSXDC 7512 (also London LDR 10013)
+ARG 3-81 p12
+-FF 9/10-80 p31
+Gr 6-80 p32
+-Gr 12-80 p889 tape
++HF 8-80 p66
++HFN 6-80 p103
+RR 6-80 p42
+SFC 6-22-80 p36
+-St 11-80 p80

770 Symphonie fantastique, op. 14 (trans. Liszt). Francois Duchable, pno. EMI 2C 069 73004
+Gr 1-81 p967
+HFN 12-80 p133

771 Symphonie fantastique, op. 14. Lille Philharmonic Orchestra; Jean-Claude Casadesus. Harmonia Mundi HM 10072
+-FF 7/8-81 p75
++HFN 5-81 p79

772 Symphonie fantastique, op. 14. LSO; Carlos Paita. Lodia LOD 777 Tape (c) LOC 777 (From Decca 7659)
+HFN 6-81 p87 tape
-HFN 7-81 p79

773 Symphonie fantastique, op. 14. BSO; Charles Munch. RCA AGL 1-2706
+FF 7/8-81 p74

Les Troyens: Royal hunt and storm. See no. 3787
Les Troyens: Royal hunt and storm; Trojan march. See no. 751
Waverly overture, op. 2. See no. 3722

BERNARD DE VENTADORN
Can vei la lauzeta mover. See no. 4086

BERNARDI, Steffano
Il bianco e dolce cigno. See no. 4010

BERNERS (Gerald Hugh Tyrwhitt-Wilson)
Wedding bouquet: Tango and waltz. See no. 3840

BERNIA, Vincenzo
Toccata chromatica. See no. 3937

BERNSTEIN, Charles Harold

774 Apologyana. Glory of Samothrace. In appreciation. Poem tones, violoncello and bassoon. Trilogy, flute. The woman speaks. Toby Saks, vlc; Arthur Grossman, bsn; Felix Skowronek, flt; Gary Gray, clt; Milton Thomas, vla; Soni Ventorum. Laurel LR 113
/FF 5/6-81 p57
+NR 11-80 p6

Glory of Samothrace. See no. 774
In appreciation. See no. 774
Poem tones, violoncello and bassoon. See no. 774
Trilogy, flute. See no. 774
The woman speaks. See no. 774

BERNSTEIN, Leonard

775 Dybbuk: Suites, nos. 1 and 2. Paul Sperry, t; Bruce Fifer, bs-bar; NYP; Leonard Bernstein. DG 2531 348
+Gr 12-81 p884
+HFN 12-81 p92

776 Fancy free. CHAVEZ Y RAMIREZ: Daughter of Colchis. Ballet Theatre Orchestra, National Symphony Orchestra of Mexico; Leonard Bernstein, Carlos Chavez. Varese VC 81055 (From Decca DL 6023, 7512)
-FF 7/8-81 p75
+HF 6-80 p73
++NR 4-79 p4

777 West side story: Ballet music. TCHAIKOVSKY: Romeo and Juliet: Overture. Atlanta Symphony Orchestra; Robert Shaw. Vox VCL 9002 Tape (c) VCS 9002

+-FF 9/10-81 p82 +SFC 7-5-81 p19
+HF 11-81 p103 tape +St 10-81 p135
++NR 8-81 p3

778 West side story: Suite (arr. Gale). GERSHWIN: Porgy and Bess: Suite (arr. Gale). JOPLIN: Paragon rag (arr. Pilafian). SOUSA: Washington Post. Empire Brass Quintet. Digitech DIGI 104
+ARG 11-81 p51 +-FF 9/10-81 p282

BERTALOT, John
Lord of the dance. See no. 4061

BERWALD, Franz
779 Quartet, strings, G minor. WIKMANSON: Quartet, strings, op. 1, no. 2, E minor. Chilingirian Quartet. CRD CRD 1061 Tape (c) CRDC 4061
+Gr 5-80 p1678 +MT 5-80 p321
+HFN 3-80 p87 +RR 3-80 p71
+HFN 11-81 p105 tape

BESARD, Jean
Air de cour. See no. 4016
Branle. See no. 4016
Branles de village (4). See no. 4097
Guillemette. See no. 4016
Volte. See no. 4016

BEST
Make we joy now in this fest. See no. 3685

BIALAS, Gunther
Haiku, Bk 2. See no. 4119
Puss in boots. See no. 3789

BIBALO, Antonio
780 Miss Julie. Gertrud Spliid, s; Edith Guillaume, ms; Ingolf Olsen, t; Aarhus City Orchestra; Francesco Cristofoli. Nordisc NORLP 501/2 (2)
+-FF 11/12-81 p116

781 Sonatina, no. 1a. FERNSTROM: Quintet, winds, op. 59. NIELSEN: Quintet, winds, op. 43. Norwegian Wind Quintet. Simax PS 1003
+-Gr 3-81 p1237 ++HFN 2-81 p95

BIBER, Carl Heinrich
Sonatas, trumpet (2). See no. 3979
Sonata, trumpet, C major. See no. 3761
Sonata sancti polycarpi. See no. 3936. See no. 3979

BIBER, Heinrich
Battalia, D major. See no. 4091
Harmonia artificosa ariosa, no. 1, D minor. See no. 3833

782 Serenade, C major. BOCCHERINI: Quintet, strings, op. 30, no. 6, C major. MOZART: Serenade, no. 13, K 525, G major. VIVALDI: Concerto, op. 10, no. 2, G minor. James Galway, flt; Karl Ridderbusch, bs; Lucerne Festival Strings; Rudolf Baumgartner. Vanguard VSD 71266 (also RCA GL 2-5309 Tape (c) GK 2-5309. From LRL 1-5085)
+-Audio 11-80 p86 +NR 9-80 p6
++FF 3/4-81 p235 +SFC 8-31-80 p31
+Gr 11-80 p139 +St 12-80 p137
+HFN 1-81 p109 tape

Sonata, solo violin, no. 6. See no. 3813
Sonata a 4, A 5. See no. 3979

783 Sonata a 6. NERUDA: Concerto, trumpet, E flat major. ROSETTI: Concerto, horn, no. 1, E flat major. RYBA: Concerto, horn, D sharp major. Josef Svejkovsky, tpt; Stanislav Suchanek, French hn; Plzen Radio Orchestra; Stanislav Macura. Supraphon 110 2434
/FF 9/10-81 p271 +NR 6-81 p7
+Gr 4-81 p1328 +HFN 4-81 p79
784 Sonata a 6, B flat major. HAYDN: Concerto, trumpet, E flat major. HUMMEL: Concerto, trumpet, E flat major. Timofei Dokshitser, tpt; Moscow Chamber Orchestra. Quintessence PMC 7135 (From Angel SR 40123)
++ARG 6-80 p52 ++FF 5/6-80 p88
+Audio 8-81 p66 +HF 1-80 p100
Sonata a 7. See no. 3979
BIBERIAN, Gilbert
785 Monogram. COUPERIN, L.: Tombeau de M. Blancrochet. McGUIRE: Suite, no. 2, in popular style. PONCE: Variations and fugue on "Las folias de Espana". John Holmquist, gtr. Cavata CV 5001
++St 12-81 p129
BILLINGS, William
Songs: Bethlehem; Boston; Judea. See no. 3911
When Jesus wept. See no. 3817
BINCHOIS, Gilles de
786 Songs (vocal works) Adieu adieu; Amoureux suy; C'est assez; De plus en plus; Dueil angoisseus; Filles a marier; Jeloymors; Joyeux penser; Magnificat; Missa; Mon cuer; Triste plaisir. Clemencic Consort; Rene Clemencic. Harmonia Mundi HM 10069
+-FF 11/12-81 p117 +-Gr 10-81 p586
Songs: Dueil angoisseus. See no. 3896
Songs: Je ne veis onques la pareille. See no. 3948
BINGHAM
Passacaglia, op. 40. See no. 3674
BINGHAM, Seth
Roulade. See no. 3806
BIRTWISTLE, Harrison
787 Punch and Judy. Jan DeGaetani, ms; Phyllis Bryn-Julson, s; Stephen Roberts, bs-bar; Philip Langridge, t; London Sinfonietta; David Atherton. Decca HEAD 24/5 (2)
+FF 3/4-81 p86 +Op 2-81 p202
+Gr 9-80 p391 +-St 3-81 p96
++Gr 3-81 p1171 +STL 9-18-80 p40
+HF 12-81 p68 +STL 12-14-80 p38
++HFN 8-80 p94 +Te 3-81 p27
+MT 3-81 p182
BIXIO
Songs: Vola vola; Canto ma sotto voce. See no. 3843
BIZET, Georges
Agnus Dei. See no. 3999
L'Arlesienne: Intermezzo. See no. 3969
788 L'Arlesienne: Suites, nos. 1 and 2. Jeux d'enfants, op. 22. Toronto Symphony Orchestra; Andrew Davis. CBS IM 36713
+MUM 11/12-81 p30 +SFC 11-1-81 p18
789 L'Arlesienne: Suites, nos. 1 and 2. Jeux d'enfants, op. 22. CO; Lorin Maazel. Decca SXL 6903 Tape (c) KSXC 6903 (also London CS 7127)

+FF 5/6-81 p58 +-HFN 12-80 p133
+Gr 12-80 p824 +NR 5-81 p6

790 L'Arlesienne: Suites, nos. 1 and 2. Carmen: Suite, no. 1. LSO; Claudio Abbado. DG 2531 329 Tape (c) 3301 329
++Gr 9-81 p378 +HFN 11-81 p105 tape
+HFN 10-81 p86

791 L'Arlesienne: Suites, nos. 1 and 2. Silesian Philharmonic Orchestra; Karol Stryja. Stolat SZM 0102
/FF 11/12-81 p122

L'Arlesienne: Suites, nos. 1 and 2. See no. 4121
L'Arlesienne: Suite, no. 1. See no. 800
L'Arlesienne: Suite, no. 2. See no. 752

792 Carmen. Grace Bumbry, ms; Mirella Freni, Eliane Lublin, s; Grace Bumbry, Viorica Cortez, ms; Jon Vickers, t; Kostas Paskalis, Michel Trempont, bar; Albert Voli, t; Claude Meloni, bar; Bernard Gontcharenki, bs; Les Petits Chanteurs a la Croix de Bois, Paris National Opera Theatre Orchestra and Chorus; Rafael Fruhbeck de Burgos. EMI 1C 197 02072/4 (3) (From SLS 952/3)
+-Gr 4-81 p1361

793 Carmen. Anna Moffo, Helen Donath, Arleen Auger, s; Jane Berbie, ms; Franco Corelli, Karl-Ernst Mercker, t; Piero Cappuccilli, Barry McDaniel, Jean-Christopher Benoit, bar; Jose van Dam, bs; German Opera Orchestra; Lorin Maazel. Eurodisc 300 197 440 (3)
-FF 11/12-81 p122

794 Carmen. Irina Arkhopova, ms; Mario Del Monaco, t; Ernest Blanc, bar; San Carlo Theatre Orchestra and Chorus; Peter Maag. Movimento Musica 03 002 (3)
-HFN 12-81 p93

Carmen: Air du toreador. See no. 4029
Carmen: Flower song. See no. 3885. See no. 3944
Carmen: Flower song; Finale, Act 3. See no. 3839
Carmen: Habanera; Seguidilla. See no. 3642
Carmen: Il fior che avevi a me; Flower song. See no. 3657
Carmen: Il fior che avevi a me; La tua madre...Mia madre vedo ancor. See no. 4032
Carmen: Je dis que rien ne m'epouvante. See no. 3837
Carmen: La fleur que tu m'avais jetee. See no. 3747. See no. 3759. See no. 3769. See no. 4050. See no. 4053
Carmen: La fleur que tu m'avais jetee; Il fior che avevi a me dato. See no. 3996

795 Carmen: L'amour est un oiseau rebelle; Pres des remparts de Seville; En vain pour evitar. VERDI: Don Carlo: O don fatale. Macbeth: La luce langue; Una macchia e qui tutt' ora. WAGNER: Gotterdammerung: Starke Scheite schichet mir. Tristan und Isolde: Mild und leise. Martha Modl, s. Preiser PR 135012
+Gr 1-81 p998

Carmen: L'amour est un oiseau rebelle. See no. 3752
Carmen: March of the toreadors. See no. 3699
Carmen: Micaela's aria. See no. 4042
Carmen: Parle-moi di ma mere; Flower song. See no. 3966
Carmen: Parle-moi de ma mere; Il fior che avevi. See no. 3967

796 Carmen: Suite, no. 1. MASSENET: Suites, orchestra: Scenes pittoresques. STRAUSS, R.: Der Rosenkavalier, op. 59: Suite. Toronto Symphony Orchestra; Andrew Davis. CBC SM 5003
+-MUM 7/8-81 p32

Carmen: Suite, no. 1. See no. 790. See no. 4121

Carmen: Toreador song. See no. 3968
797 Ivan IV. Jeanette Scovotti, Patricia Kern, Barbara Rebotham, John Noble, John Brecknock, Nielsen Taylor, Richard Angas, David Lennox, Dennis Nelson, soloists; BBC Northern Orchestra and Chorus; Bryden Thomson. VOCE 22 (3) (also MRF Records MRF 166)
-ARG 3-81 p13 ++FF 3/4-81 p87
Jeux d'enfants, op. 22. See no. 788. See no. 789. See no. 3665
La jolie fille de Perth: Suite. See no. 4121
798 Les pecheurs de perles. Pierrette Alarie, s; Leopold Simoneau, t; Rene Bianco, bar; Xavier Depraz, bs; Elisabeth Brasseur Chorus; Lamoureux Concerts Orchestra; Jean Fournet. Philips 6747 404 (2) (From Epic)
+FF 9/10-80 p81 +-HFN 11-81 p105
+Gr 10-81 p598
Les pecheurs de perles: C'etait le soir...Au fond du temple saint. See no. 3849
Les pecheurs de perles: Del tempio al limitar. See no. 3995. See no. 4048
Les pecheurs de perles: Del tempio al limitar; Mi par d'udir ancora. See no. 3967
Les pecheurs de perles: Del tempio al limitar; Mi par d'udir ancora; Della mia vita. See no. 4047
Les pecheurs de perles: Della mia vita; Mi par d'udir ancora; Non hai compreso. See no. 4032
Les pecheurs de perles: Je crois entendre. See no. 3769
Les pecheurs de perles: Me voila seule dans la nuit...Come autrefois. See no. 3850
Les pecheurs de perles: Mi par d'udir ancora. See no. 4022. See no. 4027. See no. 4045
Songs: Pastorale. See no. 3758
799 Symphony, C major. PROKOFIEV: Symphony, no. 1, op. 25, D major. NYP; Leonard Bernstein. CBS MY 36725
+FF 11/12-81 p222
800 Symphony, C major. L'Arlesienne: Suite, no. 1. PO; Eugene Ormandy. RCA ARL 1-3640 Tape (c) ARK 1-3640
+ARG 4-81 p16 ++NR 11-80 p2
-FF 1/2-81 p85 ++SFC 11-23-80 p21

BLACKWOOD, Easley
801 Twelve microtonal etudes for electronic music media. Easley Blackwood, heyboard. Department of Music, University of Chicago, no. E 639
+CMJ Fall 1981 p81 +FF 5/6-81 p59

BLAKE, David
802 Concerto, violin, In praise of Krishna. Teresa Cahill, s; Iona Brown, vln; PhO, Northern Sinfonia; Norman Del Mar, David Blake. Argo ZRG 922
+Gr 3-81 p1218 +MT 12-81 p826
+HFN 3-81 p86 +ST 7-81 p205
In praise of Krishna. See no. 802

BLATNY
803 Movements (3). DVORACEK: Music. REINER: Drawings. TAUSINGER: Au dernier amour. Sasa Vectomov, vlc; Jiri Stengl, clt; Milos Petr, French hn; Josef Kodousek, vla; Jarmila Kozderkova, Josef Hala, Kveta Novotna, pno; Prague Wind Quintet. Supraphon

1112658
+NR 8-81 p9

BLECH, Leo
Telefonische Bestellung. See no. 3823

BLISS, Arthur
Adam Zero: Dance of summer. See no. 3840
Checkmate: Dances (5). See no. 2848

804 Concerto, piano, March, homage to a great man, op. 99. Welcome to the queen march. Philip Fowke, pno; Royal Liverpool Philharmonic Orchestra; David Atherton. Unicorn DKP 9006
+Gr 9-81 p378 +MT 12-81 p827
+HFN 8-81 p83

Fanfare for a coming of age. See no. 4006
Fanfare for a dignified occasion. See no. 4006
Fanfare for heroes. See no. 4006
Fanfare for the bride. See no. 4006
Fanfare for the Lord Mayor of London. See no. 3660. See no. 4006
Fanfare, homage to Shakespeare. See no. 4006
Interlude. See no. 4006
March, homage to a great man, op. 99. See no. 804

805 Morning heroes. John Westbrook orator; Liverpool Philharmonic Choir; Royal Liverpool Philharmonic Orchestra; Charles Groves. HMV SAN 365
+ARG 1-81 p38 ++HFN 7-75 p77
+Gr 3-75 p1687 +RR 6-75 p77

806 Morning heroes. John Westbrook, narrator; Liverpool Philharmonic Choir; Royal Liverpool Philharmonic Orchestra; Charles Groves. HMV ESD 7133 Tape (c) TC ESD 7133 (From SAN 365)
+Gr 12-81 p917 +HFN 12-81 p109

Prelude. See no. 4118

807 Quintet, clarinet. COLERIDGE-TAYLOR: Quintet, clarinet, op. 15, F sharp minor. Ramon Kireilis, clt; Lamont String Quartet. Spectrum SR 127
+FF 9/10-81 p83

Royal fanfare. See no. 4006
Royal fanfare, no. 1: Sovereign's fanfare. See no. 4006
Royal fanfares, nos. 5, 6. See no. 4006
Salute. See no. 3745
Things to come: Epilogue. See no. 4105
Welcome the queen march. See no. 804

BLITHEMAN, John
In pace. See no. 3636. See no. 3637

BLITHEMAN, William
Etere rerum. See no. 3622. See no. 4012

BLOCH, Ernest
A bodah. See no. 3
Baal Shem. See no. 3

808 Five sketches in sepia. Poems of the sea. MACDOWELL: Sonata, piano, no. 1, op. 45, G minor. Emily Corbato, pno. Orion ORS 80383
+-FF 5/6-81 p60 +-NR 1-81 p14

809 Four episodes. CRESTON: Choric dances, op. 17a. MUCZYNSKI: Dance movements, op. 17. Serenade for summer, op. 38. Arizona Chamber Orchestra; Robert Hull. Laurel LR 110
+-ARG 2-81 p45 +-NR 7-79 p5
+FF 9/10-79 p72 +SFC 10-12-80 p21

810 Nocturnes (3). JUON: Litaniae, op. 70. MALIPIERO: Sonata, piano trio. SCHOENBERG (Greissle): Serenade, no. 24: 4th movement. Gobel Trio. Thorofon MTH 203
+FF 9/10-81 p275
Poems of the sea. See no. 808
811 Quintet, piano, no. 1, Grant Johannesen, pno; New World Quartet. Golden Crest CRDG 4193
+ARG 6-81 p18 +FF 5/6-81 p60
+CL 9-81 p18 +NR 7-81 p6
812 Sacred service. Louis Berkman, bar; Zemel Choir, London Chorale, London Concord Singers; LSO; Geoffrey Simon. Chandos ABR 1001 Tape (c) ABT 1001
++FF 1/2-81 p86 +HFN 2-80 p87
+-Gr 1-80 p1182 +MT 9-80 p565
+-Gr 7-80 p166 tape +RR 3-80 p91
813 Sonata, violin and piano, no. 1. ENESCO: Sonata, violin and piano, no. 3, op. 25, A minor. Kees Kooper, vln; Mary Louise Boehm, pno. Golden Crest CRDG 4199
+NR 11-81 p7
BLONDEL DE NESLE
Quant je plus. See no. 3670
BLOW, John
Chloe found Amyntas. See no. 4058
Mortlack's ground. See no. 3733. See no. 4103
814 No Lesbia no. PURCELL: Songs: Come ye sons of art; High on a throne glitt'ring ore; O dive custos Auricae Domus; Incassum Lesbia incassum rogas. New York Ensemble for Early Music's Grande Bande; Frederick Lenz. Musicmasters MM 20005 Tape (c) MMC 40005 (also Musical Heritage Society MHS 4234)
+-FF 7/8-81 +NYT 4-12-81 pD28
*HF 12-81 p93 tape
No Lesbia no. See no. 2673
815 Salvator mundi. HUMFREY: O Lord my god. LOCKE: How doth the city sit solitary. PURCELL: Motet: Jehova quam multi sunt. Anthems: Hear my prayer; My beloved spake; O God thou hast cast us out. Monteverdi Choir; English Baroque Soloists; John Eliot Gardiner. Erato STU 71276
++FF 7/8-81 p145 +MUM 12-80 p35
Salvator mundi. See no. 3620
BLUME
Grun ist die Heide. See no. 4083
BOCCHERINI, Luigi
816 Concerto, violoncello, B flat major (ed. Grutzmacher). TARTINI: Concerto, violoncello, A major. VIVALDI: Concerto, violoncello, RV 401, C minor. Pierre Fournier, Enrico Mainardi, Klaus Storck, vlc; Lucerne Festival Strings, Emil Seiler Chamber Orchestra; Rudolf Baumgartner, Wolfgang Hofmann. DG 2547 046 Tape (c) 3347 046 (From SLPM 138816, SAP 195001, SAPM 198318)
+Gr 4-81 p1312 +-HFN 9-81 p89
+/HFN 7-81 p83 tape
817 Concerto, violoncello, B flat major. Concerto, violoncello, op. 34, D major. Frederic Lodeon, vlc; Bournemouth Sinfonietta; Theodor Guschlbauer. Musical Heritage Society MHS 3879 (also Erato STU 70997)
+FF 3/4-79 p41 +-HFN 9-79 p104
+Gr 10-81 p540 +RR 11-79 p82

818 Concerti, violoncello, nos. 2 and 3. Frederic Lodeon, vlc; Lausanne Chamber Orchestra; Armin Jordan. Erato STU 71369
+Gr 3-81 p1184

Concerto, violoncello, no. 4, op. 34, D major. See no. 817

Concerto, violoncello, no. 5, G major. See no. 63

819 Concerto, violoncello, no. 7, B flat major. HAYDN: Concerto, violoncello, op. 101, D major. Pierre Fournier, vlc; Lucerne Festival Strings; Rudolf Baumgartner. DG 2535 179 Tape (c) 3335 179
+-FF 1/2-81 p121

Fugues, C major, E major, E flat major. See no. 4096

820 Quartet, strings, op. 33, no. 6, A major. Quintets, oboe, op. 45, nos. 3, 5-6. Allan Vogel, ob; Sequoia String Quartet. Nonesuch D 79004
+-FF 3/4-81 p88

821 Quartet, strings, op. 58, no. 2, E flat major. VERDI: Quartet, strings, E minor. Moravian Quartet. Supraphon 111 0573
+Gr 1-71 p1172 -HFN 3-81 p95
/-Gr 4-81 p1332

822 Quintets, flute, op. 17 (6). Christian Larde, flt; Via Nova Quartet. Musical Heritage Society MHS 4290
++FF 5/6-81 p61

823 Quintet, guitar, D major. DVORAK: Trio, piano, no. 4, op. 90, E minor. David Starobin, gtr; Bruno Canino, pno; Daniel Phillips, Pina Carmirelli, Joseph Genualdi, vln; Jerry Grossman, Marcy Rosen, vlc; Philipp Naegele, vla. Marlboro Recording MRS 13
+ARG 5-80 p9 +NYT 6-21-81 pD23
+FF 1/2-81 p109

824 Quintets, guitar, nos. 1-2, 7. Pepe Romero, gtr; AMF Chamber Ensemble. Philips 9500 985 Tape (c) 7300 985
+Gr 11-81 p714 +HFN 11-81 p90

825 Quintets, guitar, nos. 1-7, 9. Pepe Romero; AMF Chamber Ensemble. Philips 6768 268 (3) (From 9500 789, 9500 621, 9500 985)
+Gr 12-81 p895

826 Quintet, guitar, no. 3, B flat major. Quintet, guitar, no. 9, C major. Pepe Romero, gtr; AMF Chamber Ensemble. Philips 9500 789 Tape (c) 7300 861
++Gr 10-81 p568 +HFN 9-81 p78

827 Quintets, guitar, nos. 4-6. Pepe Romero, gtr; AMF Chamber Ensemble. Philips 9500 621 Tape (c) 7300 737
++ARG 5-81 p16 +Gr 4-81 p1376 tape
++FF 1/2-81 p87 +HFN 11-80 p116
+Gr 11-80 p691 +NR 12-80 p7

828 Quintet, guitar, no. 5, D major. Quintet, guitar, no. 6, C major. GUASTAVINO: La presencias, no. 6. John Williams, gtr; London String Quartet. CBS 36671 Tape (c) 40-36671
+FF 11/12-81 p123 +HFN 4-81 p68
+Gr 4-81 p1332 +HFN 9-81 p93 tape

Quintet, guitar no. 6, C major. See no. 828

Quintet, guitar, no. 9, C major. See no. 826

829 Quintets, oboe, nos. 1-6. Sarah Francis, ob; Allegri Quartet. Argo ZK 93
+Gr 7-81 p167 +HFN 7-81 p71

Quintets, oboe, op. 45, nos. 3, 5-6, See no. 820

Quintet, strings, A major: Minuet. See no. 3695
Quintet, strings, op. 13, no. 5, E major: Minuet. See no. 3851
Quintet, strings, op. 30, no. 6, C major. See no. 782
Sonata, violoncello, no. 7, B major. See no. 63

BOCHSA, Charles
Sonata, clarinet and piano. See no. 3793

BODENSCHATZ, Erhard
Songs: Joseph lieber Joseph mein. See no. 3963

BODINUS, Sebastian
830 Sonata, flute, horn and violin, D major. Suite, flute, A major. Symphony, 2 horns, F major. Heidelberg Chamber Orchestra. Da Camera SM 91049
/FF 9/10-81 p83
Suite, flute, A major. See no. 830
Symphony, 2 horns, F major. See no. 830

BOEHM, Yohanan
831 Symphony, no. 1, op. 8. Symphony, no. 2, op. 14. Jerusalem Symphony Orchestra; Mendi Rodan, Hans Freudenthal. Aries LP 1627
+-FF 1/2-81 p87
Symphony, no. 2, op. 14. See no. 831

BOELLMANN, Leon
832 Fantasy. Pieces, organ, op. 16, nos. 1-2, 4-5, 11. Suite, no. 2, op. 27. Piet van der Steen, org. Cantilena AG 2461
-Gr 7-81 p172
Pieces, organ, op. 16, nos. 1-2, 4-5, 11. See no. 832
Suite, no. 2, op. 27. See no. 832
Suite, no. 2, op. 27: Toccata, C minor. See no. 3799
833 Suite gothique, op. 25. FRANCK: Cantabile. Piece heroique. SAINT-SAENS: Prelude and fugue, B major. VIERNE: Fantasiestucke, op. 53: Claire de lune; Toccata. John Rose, org. Towerhill T 1010
+FF 9/10-81 p251
Suite gothique, op. 25: Priere a Notre Dame. See no. 3725

BOELY, Alexandre
Fantasy, B flat major. See no. 3799

BOERMAN, Jan
834 Alchemie 1961. Composition 1972. De Zee. Composers Voice CV 7701
++FF 1-78 p14 *Te 6-78 p39
*FF 3/4-81 p30
Composition 1972. See no. 834

BOHM
Grand polonaise, op. 16. See no. 3682

BOHM, Goerg
Choral partitas: Ach wie nichtig ach wie fluchtig. See no. 249. See no. 3903
Prelude and fugue, C major. See no. 3903
Vater unser im Himmelreich. See no. 3720

BOHM, Karl
Still as the night. See no. 3967

BOHME
835 Sextet, op. 30, E flat minor. DVORAK: Waltzes, op. 54 (2). HINDEMITH: Morgenmusik: Acht Stucke (trans.). HOVHANESS: Sharagan and fugue, op. 58. Rolf Smedvig, Charles Lewis,

Timothy Morrison, tpt; David Ohanian, French hn; Donald Sanders, trom; Samuel Pilafian, tuba. Digitech 105
+FF 11/12-81 p295

BOIELDIEU, Francois

836 Concerto, harp, C major. DITTERSDORF: Concerto, harp, op. 4, no. 6 B flat major. Marisa Robles, hp; AMF; Iona Brown. Argo ZRG 930
++FF 3/4-81 p89 +RR 8-80 p45
++Gr 9-80 p331 ++St 4-81 p101
+HFN 8-80 p105 ++STL 7-13-80 p38

La dame blanche: Ah quel plaisir d'etre soldat; Viens gentille dame. See no. 4049

BOISMORTIER, Joseph Bodin de

837 Concerto, op. 15, no. 3, D major. Concerto, op. 28, no. 3, A minor. Sonata, op. 13, no. 1, G minor. Sonata, op. 34, no. 6, A minor. Sonata, op. 7, no. 4, D minor. Trio sonata, op. 50, no. 6, D major. Peter Pongracz, Peter Jagasich, ob; Peter Komlos, Jozsef Sepsey, Sandor Devich, vln; Geza Nemeth, vla; Karoly Botvay, vlc; Zoltan Jeney, Attila Lajos, Gabor Vida, Zoltan Fasang, Jozsef Szarka, flt; Janos Sebestyen, hpd; Budapest Chamber Orchestra; Miklos Erdelyi. Budapest FX 12295
+FF 9/10-81 p83 +NR 9-81 p6
+-HFN 7-81 p79

838 Concerto, op. 26, D major. GUBAIDULINA: Concerto, bassoon and low strings. MALIPIERO: Serenade, bassoon. Valerii Popov, bsn; USSR State Academic Symphony Orchestra Solo Ensemble; Petr Meschaninov, Gennady Rozhdestvensky. Melodiya C10 12749/50
+FF 9/10-81 p266

Concerto, op. 28, no. 3, A minor. See no. 837

839 Concerto, op. 37, no. 6, E minor. Trio sonata, op. 50, no. 6, D major. COUPERIN, F.: Concert royaux, no. 3, A major. LECLAIR: Sonata, flute, op. 2, no. 8, D major. Hamburg Telemann Society Instrumental Camerata. DG 2547 048 Tape (c) 3347 048 (From SAPM 198031)
+Gr 4-81 p1332 +HFN 7-81 p83 tape
+Gr 9-81 p460 tape

Concerto, op. 37, no. 6, E minor. See no. 3631

Sonata, op. 7, no. 4, D minor. See no. 837

Sonata, op. 13, no. 1, G minor. See no. 837

840 Sonata, op. 23, no. 2. HANDEL: Sonata, oboe, op. 1, no. 6, G minor. MOZART: Divertimenti, no. 12, K 252, E flat major; no. 9, K 240, B flat major. TELEMANN: Sonata, bassoon, A flat major. Ensemble Baroque de Paris. Denon OX 7030
+-HFN 5-81 p85

Sonata, op. 34, no. 6, A minor. See no. 837

Trio sonata, E minor. See no. 3867

Trio sonata, op. 50, no. 6, D major. See no. 837. See no. 839

BOITO, Arrigo

841 Mefistofele. Renata Tebaldi, Elena Suliotis, s; Mary MacKenzie, Margaret Roggero, alto; Alfredo Kraus, Herbert Kraus, t; Nicolai Ghiaurov, bs; Orchestra and Chorus; Nino Sanzogno. Historical Recording Enterprises HRE 333 (3)
+-FF 5/6-81 p62

Mefistofele: Ave signor; Son io spirito che nega. See no. 3968. See no. 4064

842 Mefistofele: Dai campi dai prati. GOUNOD: Faust: Quel trouble inconnu...Salut demeure. PUCCINI: Manon Lescaut: Tra voi belle brune e bionde; Donna non vidi mai; Ah Manon mi tradisce. Tosca: Dammi i colori...Recondita armonia; E lucevan le stelle. VERDI: Aida: Se quel guerrier io fossi...Celeste Aida. Un ballo in maschera: La rivedra nell'estasi; Di tu se fedele; Forse la soglia attinse...Ma se m'e forza perdierti. Don Carlo: Fontainebleau; Foresta immense...Io la vidi al suo sorriso. Giovanni d'Arco: Sotto una quercia parvemi...Pondo e letal martiro. Placido Domingo, t; LSO,NPhO, ROHO, Paris Opera Orchestra; PhO; James Levine, Riccardo Muti, Carlo Maria Giulini, Georges Pretre, Julius Redel, Bruno Bartoletto. Angel S 37835 (also HMV 4031 Tape (c) TCA SD 4031)
+Gr 5-81 p1515 +SFC 9-20-81 p18
+NR 9-81 p12

Mefistofele: Dai camp dai prati; Giunto sul passo estremo. See no. 3965. See no. 3967. See no. 4022. See no. 4023. See no. 4045

Mefistofele: Dai campi dai prati; Ogni mortal mister gustai... Giunto sul passo estremo. See no. 3757

Mefistofele: L'altra notte. See no. 3647. See no. 3754. See no. 4041

843 Nerone. Bruno Prevedi, Agostino Ferrin, Alessandro Cassis, Ilva Ligabue, Ruza Baldani, Antonio Zerbini, Gianpaolo Corradi, Anna di Stasio, Corinna Vozza; RAI, Turin, Orchestra and Chorus; Gianandrea Gavazzeni. MRF Records MRF 616 (3)
++FF 5/6-81 p63

Nerone: Queste ad un lido; Ecco la Dea. See no. 4037

BOLCOM, William

844 Ghost rags (3). COPLAND: Piano blues (4). RZEWSKI: North American ballads (4). Paul Jacobs, pno. Nonesuch D 79006
+FF 7/8-81 p213 +St 5-81 p68
+HF 8-81 p65

845 Quartet, piano. FINNEY: Trio, piano, no. 2. American Trio; David Ireland, vla. CRI SD 447
+FF 11/12-81 p123 +NR 9-81 p7

BOLDIZSAR

Prelude, chorale-fugue and postlude. See no. 12

BOLLING, Claude

846 California suite. Suite, flute and jazz piano. Elena Duran, Colin Fleming, flt; Laurie Holloway, pno. Allen Walley, double bass; Allan Ganley, drums; Timothy Kain, gtr. RCA RL 2-5348 Tape (c) RK 2-5348
+-Gr 7-81 p195 +HFN 8-81 p92 tape
+Gr 8-81 p324 tape

847 Concerto, guitar and piano. Angel Romero, gtr; George Shearing, pno; Shelly Manne, drum; Ray Brown, bs. HMV EMD 5535 Tape (c) TC EMD 5535 (also Angel DS 37327 Tape (c) 4ZS 37327)
+ARG 1-81 p23 +Gr 10-80 p548 tape
++FF 9/10-80 p85 +HFN 6-80 p103
++Gr 6-80 p69 ++NR 10-80 p5

848 Suite, flute and jazz piano. Jean-Pierre Rampal, flt; Claude Bolling, pno; Max Hediguer, double bs; Marcel Sabiani, drums. Columbia M 33233 Tape (c) MT 33233 (also CBS 73900 Tape (c) 40-73900 (ct) M 33233)

+Gr 3-81 p1238 +NR 10-75 p4
+HF 7-77 p125 tape ++St 2-76 p99
++HFN 3-81 p97 tape

Suite, flute and jazz piano. See no. 846

849 Toot suite. Maurice Andre, tpt; Claude Bolling, pno; Guy Pedersen, bs; Daniel Humair, drums. CBS FM 36731
+FF 11/12-81 p124

BOND, Victoria

850 Monologue. Peter Quince at the clavier. GILBERT: Interrupted suite. Transmutations. Penny Orloff, s; Zita Carno, Delores Stevens, Richard Grayson, Susan Savage, pno; Ronald Leonard, vlc; Thomas Harmon, org; Scott Shepherd, Penny Orloff, perc; Gary Gray, clt. Protone PR 150
+ARG 11-81 p19 +HF 6-81 p55
+-FF 11/12-80 p84 -NR 7-81 p5

Peter Quince at the clavier. See no. 850

BONDON, Jacques

851 Le soleil multicolore. DEBUSSY: Sonata, flute, harp and viola, no. 2. Carter Chamber Ensemble. Sound Storage SSR 2020
+ARG 6-81 p20 ++SFC 7-12-81 p18
+FF 3/4-81 p89

BONONCINI, Giovanni

852 Care luci del mio ben. Ecco Dorinda il giorno. Misero pastorello. Siedi amarilli. Rene Jacobs, alto; Sigiswald Kuijken, Lucy van Dael, vln; Wieland Kuijken, vlc; Robert Kohnen, hpd. DG 2533 450
++FF 3/4-81 p90 +-NR 3-81 p12
+Gr 10-80 p524 +STL 11-9-80 p40
+HFN 11-80 p116

Divertimento, F major. See no. 4056

Ecco Dorinda il giorno. See no. 852

Misero pastorello. See no. 852

Siedi amarilli. See no. 852

Songs: Vado ben spesso. See no. 3838

BONPORTI, Francesco Antonio

853 Concerti, op. 11, nos. 4, 6, 8-9. I Musici. Philips 9502 004 (From 6500 182)
+ARG 6-80 p18 +NR 8-80 p7
++FF 5/6-80 p58 +NYT 5-25-80 pD21
+Gr 3-81 p1184 +ST 8-81 p276
+-HFN 4-81 p80

BORDESE

David chantant devant Saul. See no. 4051

BORG, Kim

854 Songs: East Karelian songs, op. 2; Songs from Saimaa, op. 13; Songs on texts of Aleksis Kivi, op. 27. Kim Borg, bs; Pentti Koskimies, pno. Finlandia FA 901
+-FF 3/4-81 p90 +-NR 2-81 p12
+-Gr 2-81 p1108

BORGES

Vals venezolano. See no. 3727

BORODIN, Alexander

855 In the Steppes of Central Asia. Prince Igor: Polovtsian march. Symphony, no. 2, B minor. USSR Symphony Orchestra; Yevgeny Svetlanov. Quintessence PCM 7165 Tape (c) 7165

++ARG 1-81 p23 +-FF 11/12-80 p85

856 In the Steppes of Central Asia. MUSSORGSKY: A night on the bare mountain. RIMSKY-KORSAKOV: Antar, op. 9. Brno Philharmonic Orchestra; Jiri Belohlavek. Supraphon 110 2279
-FF 5/6-81 p218 +-NR 10-80 p3

Prince Igor: Galitzky's aria; Kontchak's aria. See no. 4064

857 Prince Igor: Overture (arr. Glazunov); Polovtsian dances (orch. Rimsky-Korsakov). STRAVINSKY: The firebird (1919 version). Atlanta Symphony Orchestra and Chorus; Robert Shaw. Telarc DG 10039
++ARG 4-79 p50 +-NR 1-81 p3
++FF 1/2-79 p22 +RR 1-80 p87
+-HF 3-79 p110 ++St 2-79 p136
+-HFN 12-79 p158

Prince Igor: Overture. See no. 1594

858 Prince Igor: Polovtsian dances. RIMSKY-KORSAKOV: Russian Easter overture, op. 36. TCHAIKOVSKY: Overture, the year 1812, op. 49. COA; Igor Marketvitch. Philips 6570 191 Tape (c) 7310 191 (From 6530 022, 6530 009)
+FF 5/6-81 p218 +HFN 4-81 p83 tape
+Gr 1-81 p1002 +NYT 9-7-80 pD29
+HFN 3-81 p95

Prince Igor: Polovtsian dances. See no. 4122

Prince Igor: Polovtsian march. See no. 855

Prince Igor: Vladimir's cavatina. See no. 4030

859 Quartet, strings, no. 2, D major. DVORAK: Quartet, strings, no. 12, op. 96, F major. Concord Quartet. Turnabout TVC 37009 Tape (c) CT 7009
+FF 3/4-81 p111 +St 4-81 p101

860 Symphony, no. 1, E flat major. Symphony, no. 3, A minor. National Philharmonic Orchestra; Loris Tjeknavorian. RCA RL 2-5322 Tape (c) RK 2-5322 (From RL 2-5098)
+Gr 2-81 p1080 +HFN 3-81 p94

861 Symphony, no. 2, B minor. TCHAIKOVSKY: Francesca da Rimini, op. 32. OSR; Silvio Varviso. Contour CC 7533 Tape (c) CCT 7533
+Gr 8-81 p316

Symphony, no. 2, B minor. See no. 855

Symphony, no. 3, A minor. See no. 860

BORRONO DA MILANO, Pietro

Casteliono book: Pieces (3). See no. 3937

BORTZ, Daniel

862 In memoria Di. FRUMERIE: Symphonic variations. LARSSON: Divertimento. Louisville Orchestra; Varujan Kojian. Louisville LS 773
+FF 9/10-81 p286 +-NR 8-81 p4

BOSSI, Marco Enrico

Entree pontificale. See no. 3895

BOTTESINI, Giovanni

863 Elegie, double bass and piano. GLIERE: Prelude and scherzo, op. 32, nos. 1 and 2. Intermezzo and tarantella, op. 9, nos. 1 and 2. MISEK: Sonata, double bass and piano, no. 2, op. 6, E minor. James VanDemark, double bs; Robert Spillman, pno. Musical Heritage Society MHS 4265
+FF 9/10-81 p261

BOULANGER

A spring morning. See no. 3923

BOULANGER, Lili
864 Clairieres dans le ciel. Paulina Stark, s; David Garvey, pno. Spectrum SR 126
+-FF 9/10-81 p84
Clairieres dans le ciel, excerpts. See no. 3814
D'un matin de printemps. See no. 3884
Nocturne. See no. 3814. See no. 3884
BOULEZ, Pierre
865 Le marteau sans maitre. Jean Deroubaix, ms; Severino Gazzelloni, flt; Georges van Gucht, xylorimba; Claude Ricou, vibraphone; Jean Batigne, perc; Anton Stingl, gtr; Serge Collot, vla; Pierre Boulez. Harmonia Mundi 1C 065 99831 (also Ades 14.008. Also Turnabout TV 34081)
+-FF 11/12-80 p86
+FF 9/10-81 p84
+-Gr 5-80 p1700
++HFN 5-80 p135
+RR 5-80 p56
866 Messagesquisse. LEFEBVRE: D'un abre de nuit. Etwas Weiter. MEFANO: Melodies. Dorothy Dorow, s; Paul Mefano, Pierre-Yves Artaud, flt; Lluis Claret, Pierre Pensassou, vlc; Jacqueline Mefano, pno; 2E 2M Ensemble; Paul Mefano. Le Chant du Monde LDX 78686
+-Gr 4-81 p1032
+HFN 1-81 p105
Sonata, piano, no. 2. See no. 3785
BOURGEOIS, Derek
Wine symphony: Hock theme. See no. 3660
BOUTRY, Roger
Pieces a quatre (5). See no. 3742
BOVICELLI, Giovanni
Songs: Anchor che co'l partire; Angelus ad pastores ait; Io son ferito. See no. 3835
BOWEN, Edwin York
867 Sonata, viola and piano, C minor. WALKER: Sonata, viola and piano, C major. Georgiy Bezrukov, vla; Mikhail Muntyan, pno. Melodiya S 10 11563/4
/FF 11/12-81 p124
Sonata, op. 35. See no. 4055
BOWERS, Stacey
868 Pattern study, no. 2. deMARS: Premonitions of Christopher Columbus. STOCKHAUSEN: Set sail for the sun. Zeitgeist. Sound Environment Recordings TR 1015
+FF 9/10-81 p277
BOYCE, William
869 Concerti grossi, B flat major, B minor, E minor. Overture, F major. Cantilena; Adrian Shepherd. Chandos ABR 1005 Tape (c) ABT 1005
+-ARG 7-81 p54
+-Gr 12-79 p1007
+Gr 8-80 p275 tape
-HF 12-80 p70
+HFN 2-80 p91
/RR 1-80 p69
870 Overtures, nos. 1-12. Cantilena; Adrian Shepherd. Chandos DBR 2002 (2) Tape (c) DBT 2002
++FF 9/10-81 p85
+-Gr 6-81 p34
++HFN 6-81 p70
++HFN 7-81 p81 tape
Overture, F major. See no. 869
The prospect before us: Fugue, D major. See no. 3840
871 Songs (choral): I have surely built thee an house; O be joyful; O give thanks; Save me O God; Turn thee unto me. Worcester

Cathedral Academy and Choir; Donald Hunt. Abbey ABY 811
+Gr 3-80 p1424 +MT 3-81 p195
+-HFN 2-80 p87 +RR 3-80 p92
+HFN 12-80 p133

872 Songs (choral): By the waters of Babylon; I have surely built thee an house; O where shall wisdom be found; Turn thee unto me O Lord. Voluntaries, organ, nos. 1-2, 4, 10. Arthur Wills, org; Ely Cathedral Choir; Arthur Wills. Saga 5440 Tape (c) CA 5440
+-ARG 3-81 p15 +-HFN 4-79 p131
+-FF 1/2-81 p87 +HFN 11-77 p187 tape
+Gr 3-77 p1437 +RR 3-77 p88
+-HF 12-80 p70 ++RR 11-77 p119 tape
+-HFN 3-77 p99 +RR 4-79 p109

Songs; I have surely built thee an house. See no. 3824
Songs: On the banks gentle Stour; Orpheus and Euridice. See no. 4058
Voluntary, A minor. See no. 3627
Voluntaries, organ, nos. 1-4, 4, 10. See no. 872

BOYER, Robert

873 Illusions I. MORRILL: Six dark questions. PENNYCOOK: If carillons grew wings. SULLIVAN: Numbers, names. Neva Pilgrim, s; Frank Bennett, perc; Stephen Stalker, vlc; Colgate Computer Music Studio. Redwood Records ES 10
+-FF 5/6-81 p222 +NR 2-81 p15

BOZZA, Eugene

Agrestide. See no. 3668
Aria. See no. 3738
Badinage. See no. 3741
Caprice. See no. 3741
Lied. See no. 3741
Nuages. See no. 3737
Pulcinella, op. 53, no. 1. See no. 3819

BRADE, William

Pavan and galliard a 6. See no. 4092

BRAEIN, Edvard

874 Anne Pedersdotter, excerpts. Capriccio. The merry musicians. Overture. Richard Kjelstrup, clt; Eva Knardahl, pno; Anne Nyborg, s; Jonny Blanc, t; Almar Heggen, bs; Hindar Quartet Members, Norwegian Opera Orchestra and Chorus, Bergan Symphony Orchestra; Arvid Fladmoe, Sverre Bruland. Philips 6507 041
+FF 7/8-81 p159

Capriccio. See no. 874
The merry musicians. See no. 874
Overture. See no. 874

BRAGA, Gaetano

Angel's serenade. See no. 3967

BRAHE, May

Songs: Bless this house. See no. 3852

BRAHMS, Johannes

Academic festival overture, op. 80. See no. 521. See no. 904. See no. 975. See no. 977. See no. 981. See no. 3726
Alto rhapsody, op. 53. See no. 974

875 Ballades, op. 10. SCHUBERT: Sonata, piano, no. 4, D 537, A minor. Arturo Benedetti Michelangeli, pno. DG 2532 017 Tape (c) 3302 017

+-ARG 10-81 p14 ++HFN 11-81 p105 tape
+FF 11/12-81 p233 +HFN 9-81 p79
+Gr 9-81 p411 ++St 11-81 p98
+Gr 11-81 p783 tape ++STL 9-13-81 p41

876 Ballaeds, op. 10. Rhapsodies, op. 79, nos. 1-2. Waltzes, op. 39. Julius Katchen, pno. London STS 15527
+-FF 3/4-81 093

Chorale preludes, op. 122, no. 2. See no. 3901

Chorale preludes, op. 122, no. 6. See no. 3962

877 Chorale preludes, op. 122, nos. 9 and 10. FUCHS: Fantasia, op. 91, E minor. SCHUMANN, C.: Sonata, organ, no. 5, op. 40, G minor. Viktor Scholz, org. Pape 15
+NR 3-81 p15

878 Concerto, piano, no. 1, op. 15, D minor. Lazar Berman, pno; CSO; Erich Leinsdorf. CBS IM 35850 Tape (c) HMT 35850
+-FF 9/10-81 p85 -HFN 9-81 p79
+-Gr 9-81 p378 -SFC 9-19-81 p18
+HF 11-81 p103 tape +St 10-81 p119
-HF 9-81 p69

879 Concerto, piano, no. 1, op. 15, D minor. Daniel Barenboim, pno; NYP; Zubin Mehta. CBS M 35884
+-FF 11/12-81 p125 +-NR 11-81 p5

880 Concerto, piano, no. 1, op. 15, D minor. Concerto, piano, no. 2, op. 83, B flat major. Martino Tirimo, pno; LPO; Kurt Sanderling, Yoel Levi. Classics for Pleasure CFP 40343/4 (2)
+Gr 2-81 p1080 +-HFN 2-81 p86

881 Concerto, piano, no. 1, op. 15, D minor. Clifford Curzon, pno; LSO; Georg Szell. Decca JB 102 Tape (c) KJBC 102 (From SXL 6023)
+Gr 11-81 p682

882 Concerto, piano, no. 1, op. 15, D minor. Maurizio Pollini, pno; VPO; Karl Bohm. DG 2531 294 Tape (c) 3301 294
+CL 3-81 p10 +HFN 11-80 p116
++FF 5/6-81 p64 +HFN 12-80 p159 tape
+-Gr 12-80 p824 +-NR 3-81 p6
+HF 9-81 p69 -SFC 5-31-81 p22

883 Concerto, piano, no. 1, op. 15, D minor. Concerto, piano, no. 2, op. 83, B flat major. Maurizio Pollini, pno; VPO; Karl Bohm, Claudio Abbado. DG 2707 127 (From 2531 294, 2530 790)
+-Gr 8-81 p264 +-MT 11-81 p753
+HFN 8-81 p91

884 Concerto, piano, no. 1, op. 15, D minor. Jakob Gimpel, pno; BPhO; Rudolf Kempe. Pelican LP 2021
+-HF 9-81 p70 +St 10-81 p119

885 Concerto, piano, no. 1, op. 15, D minor. Concerto, piano, no. 2, op, 83, B flat major. Alfred Brendel, pno; COA; Hans Schmidt-Isserstedt, Bernard Haitink. Philips 6770 006 (2) Tape (c) 7650 006 (From 6500 623, 6500 767)
++Gr 9-81 p378 ++HFN 10-81 p95

886 Concerto, piano, no. 1, op. 15, D minor. Stephen Bishop-Kovacevich, pno; LSO; Colin Davis. Philips 9500 871 Tape (c) 7300 871
+ARG 11-81 p20 +HF 9-81 p69
+FF 9/10-81 p85 +-HFN 6-81 p70
+-Gr 6-81 p34 +-HFN 9-81 p93 tape

887 Concerto, piano, no. 1, op. 15, D minor. Artur Rubinstein, pno; CSO; Fritz Reiner. RCA ARL 1-2044 Tape (c) ARK 1-2044 (ct)

ARS 1-2044 (From LM 1831)
++ARG 9-77 p23 +MJ 5-77 p32
+FF 7/8-78 p25 ++NR 6-77 p5
+-Gr 4-81 p1314 ++SFC 3-27-77 p41
+HF 6-77 p84 ++St 6-77 p127
+-HFN 4-81 p81 tape

888 Concerto, piano, no. 2, op. 83, B flat major. Variations on an original theme, op. 21, no. 1, D major. Edwin Fischer, pno; Basel Orchestra; Hans Munch. Bruno Walter Society RR 503
+NR 11-81 p5

889 Concerto, piano, no. 2, op. 83, B flat major. Daniel Barenboim, pno; NYP; Zubin Mehta. CBS M 35885 Tape (c) MT 35885
-FF 9/10-81 p86 -NR 7-81 p4
-HF 9-81 p70 ++St 9-81 p89

890 Concerto, piano, no. 2, op. 83, B flat major. Wilhelm Backhaus, pno; VPO; Karl Bohm. Decca JB 94 Tape (c) KJBC 94 (From SXL 6322)
+Gr 2-81 p1082

891 Concerto, piano, no. 2, op. 83, B flat major. Geza Anda, pno; BPhO; Herbert von Karajan. DG 2535 263 Tape (c) 3335 263 (From 139034)
+-ARG 4-81 p19 +-Gr 12-78 p1094
+FF 11/12-80 p81

892 Concerto, piano, no. 2, op. 83, B flat major. Emil Gilels, pno; BPhO; Eugen Jochum. DG 2542 151 Tape (c) 3342 151 (From 2707 064)
++Gr 4-81 p1314 +HFN 6-81 p87 tape
+HFN 6-81 p85

893 Concerto, piano, no. 2, op. 83, B flat major. Martino Tirimo, pno; LPO; Yoel Levi. Musical Heritage Society MHS 4001 (also Classics for Pleasure CFP 40344)
+-FF 9/10-79 p54 +HFN 2-81 p86
++HF 12-79 p90

894 Concerto, piano, no. 2, op. 83, B flat major. Stephen Bishop-Kovacevich, pno; LSO; Colin Davis. Philips 9500 682 Tape (c) 7300 777
+CL 4-81 p14 +HF 9-81 p70
+-FF 1/2-81 p88 +HFN 12-81 p93
+Gr 12-81 p884 ++NR 12-80 p6

895 Concerto, piano, no. 2, op. 83, B flat major. Gina Bachauer, pno; LSO; Antal Dorati. Quintessence PMC 7178
+FF 5/6-81 p65 -HF 9-81 p70

Concerto, piano, no. 2, op. 83, B flat major. See no. 880. See no. 883. See no. 885. See no. 1006. See no. 4017

896 Concerto, violin, op. 77, D major. BRUCH: Concerto, violin, no. 1, op. 26, G minor. MENDELSSOHN: Concerto, violin, op. 64, E minor. TCHAIKOVSKY: Concerto, violin, op. 35, D major. Itzhak Perlman, vln; PO, CSO, LSO; Eugene Ormandy, Carlo Maria Giulini, Andre Previn. Angel SZC 3912 (3)
++FF 9/10-81 p260 +SFC 7-28-81 p18

897 Concerto, violin, op. 77, D major. Ulf Hoelscher, vln; North German Radio Orchestra; Klaus Tennstedt. Angel DS 37798 (also HMV ASD 3973)
+-FF 7/8-81 p78 +HFN 2-81 p86
+-Gr 2-81 p1080 -NR 5-81 p3
+-HF 9-81 p70 ++St 6-81 p112

898 Concerto, violin, op. 77, D major. Henryk Szeryng, vln; LSO; Antal Dorati. Contour CC 7523 Tape (c) CCT 7523
-Gr 8-81 p316

899 Concerto, violin, op. 77, D major. Pinchas Zukerman, vln; Orchestre de Paris; Daniel Barenboim. DG 2531 251 Tape (c) 3301 251
++ARG 3-81 p16
+-FF 1/2-81 p89
+Gr 4-80 p1553
+Gr 7-80 p166 tape
-HF 12-80 p72
/HFN 6-80 p103
+NR 12-80 p5
++RR 5-80 p56

900 Concerto, violin, op. 77, D major. MOZART: Concerto, violin, no. 5, K 219, A major. TCHAIKOVSKY: Concerto, violin, op. 35, D major. David Oistrakh, vln; Dresden Staatskapelle; Franz Konwitschny. DG 2726 087 (2) Tape (c) 3372 087
+FF 7/8-80 p172
+-Gr 10-81 p567
+-HFN 9-81 p93 tape
+NR 4-80 p5

901 Concerto, violin, op. 77, D major. Salvatore Accardo, vln; Leipzig Gewandhaus Orchestra; Kurt Masur. Philips 9500 624 Tape (c) 7300 729
+-FF 5/6-80 p59
+-Gr 3-81 p1186
+Gr 6-81 p94 tape
++HF 6-80 p73
-HFN 4-81 p68
-NR 5-80 p5
+NYT 7-6-80 pD15
+SFC 2-3-80 p45
+-ST 9-81 p351

902 Concerto, violin, op. 77, D major. Albert Spalding, vln; Vienna Tonkunstler Orchestra; Wilhelm Loibner. Varese VC 81059 (From Remington R 145)
+-ARG 3-81 p16
+-FF 1/2-81 p89
+-HF 12-80 p72
+St 3-81 p98

Concerto, violin, op. 77, D major. See no. 1006. See no. 3841

903 Concerto, violin and violoncello, op. 102, A minor. Itzhak Perlman, vln; Mstislav Rostropovich, vlc; COA; Bernard Haitink. Angel SZ 37680 Tape (c) 4ZS 37680 (also HMV ASD 3905 Tape (c) TC ASD 3905)
++ARG 3-81 p17
++FF 11/12-80 p87
++Gr 4-81 p3176 tape
+Gr 10-80 p494
++HF 12-80 p72
+HFN 12-80 p133
+HFN 12-80 p157 tape
++NR 10-80 p6
++NYT 9-21-80 pD22
++St 1-81 p78
+-ST 5-81 p46

904 Concerto, violin and violoncello, op. 102, A minor. Academic festival overture, op. 80. Pinchas Zukerman, vln; Lynn Harrell, vlc; NYP; Zubin Mehta. CBS M 35894 Tape (c) MT 35894 (also CBS 74003)
+-Gr 9-81 p378
+HF 9-81 p69
+HFN 9-81 p78
+SFC 3-29-81 p18

905 Concerto, violin and violoncello, op. 102, A minor. Primoz Novsak, vln; Susanne Basler, vlc; Bamberg Symphony Orchestra Members; Heinz Wallberg. Musical Heritage Society MHS 3788 (also Claves D 8014)
+FF 11/12-78 p34
-FF 9/10-81 p87

906 Concerto, violin and violoncello, op. 102, A minor. Variations on a theme by Haydn, op. 56a.* Salvatore Accardo, vln; Heinrich Schiff, vlc; Leipzig Gewandhaus Orchestra; Kurt Masur. Philips 9500 623 Tape (c) 7300 728 (*From 6769 009)
+-FF 9/10-80 p87
+Gr 12-80 p824
+-NR 8-80 p7
+NYT 7-6-80 pD15

+HF 6-80 p73 +SFC 7-6-80 p27
+-HFN 12-80 p133 +St 8-80 p83
+-HFN 3-81 p97

Concerto, violin and violoncello, op. 102, A minor. See no. 1006

907 Ein deutsches Requiem, op. 45. Schicksalslied, op. 54. Gundula Janowitz, s; Tom Krause, bar; Vienna State Opera Concert Choir; VPO; Bernard Haitink. Philips 6769 055 (2) Tape (c) 7654 055
-Gr 10-81 p586 +HFN 10-81 p86

Fugue, A flat minor. See no. 3930

Hungarian dances. See no. 1006

908 Hungarian dances (21) (trans. Hidas). Franz Liszt Chamber Orchestra; Janos Rolla. Erato STU 71411
+-Gr 10-81 p540

Hungarian dances, nos. 1, 3, 10. See no. 3792

Hungarian dance, no. 5, G minor. See no. 3693

Hungarian dances, nos. 11-16. See no. 3998

909 Hungarian dances, nos. 17-20. LISZT: Hungarian fantasia, S 123. Hungarian rhapsody, no. 4, S 244, E flat major. Hungarian rhapsody, no. 5, S 244, E minor. Shura Cherkassky, pno; BPhO; Herbert von Karajan. DG 2535 175 Tape (c) 3335 175
+ARG 2-81 p20 +Gr 11-81 p783 tape
+FF 11/12-80 p81

Intermezzo. See no. 3816

Let nothing ever grieve thee, op. 30. See no. 3745

910 Liebeslieder, op. 52. Neue Liebeslieder, op. 65. Los Angeles Vocal Arts Ensemble; Armen Guzelimian, Raul Herrera, pno. Nonesuch DL 79008
+-FF 7/8-81 p78 +SFC 5-10-81 p18
+NR 7-81 p12

911 Liebeslieder, op. 52. Variations on a theme by Schumann, op. 23. Waltzes, op. 39. Michel Beroff, Jean-Philippe Collard, pno. Pathe Marconi C 069 73044 (also HMV ASD 4079)
-FF 9/10-81 p91 +-HFN 9-81 p79
+Gr 9-81 p411

Liebeslieder, op. 52. See no. 958

Motets: Warum ist das Licht gegeben, op. 74, no. 1. See no. 3925

Neue Liebeslieder, op. 65. See no. 910

912 Pieces, piano, op. 116. Variations and fugue on a theme by Handel, op. 24, B flat major. Daniel Graham, pno. Vivace VCR 1101
+-Audio 11-80 p86 -NR 8-80 p12
+CL 9-80 p16 +-St 12-80 p119
+-FF 3/4-81 p93

913 Pieces, piano, op. 116, nos. 5 and 6. DEBUSSY: Images: Reflets dans l'eau; Hommage a Rameau; Mouvement. MOZART: Allegro and andante, K 533, F major. Rondo, K 494, F major. Emil Gilels, pno. Supraphon 111 2550
+Gr 3-81 p1212 -NR 4-81 p12
+-FF 9/10-81 p232 ++SFC 1-4-81 p18
+-HFN 5-81 p87

Pieces, piano, op. 117: Intermezzo. See no. 3866

914 Pieces, piano, op. 118 (6). FRANCK: Prelude, chorale and fugue. Stephanie Brown, pno. Musical Heritage Society MHS 4200
+FF 1/2-81 p90 +-HF 1-81 p58

915 Pieces, piano, op. 119. Variations and fugue on a theme by Handel, op. 24, B flat major. Rudolf Serkin, pno. CBS M 35177 Tape

(c) MT 35177 (also CBS 76913 Tape (c) 40-76913)
+ARG 1-81 p24
+FF 9/10-80 p91
+Gr 2-81 p1101
+Gr 6-81 p94 tape
++HF 8-80 p67
+HFN 2-81 p86
+HFN 4-81 p81 tape
+NYT 6-22-80 pD20
++St 9-80 p77
+-STL 3-8-81 p38

916 Pieces, piano, op. 119. Rhapsodies, op. 79 (2). Variations on a theme by Paganini, op. 35, A minor. Francois-Rene Duchable, pno. Erato STU 71401
+HFN 9-81 p79

Prelude and fugue, E major. See no. 3992

Quartets, piano, nos. 1-3. See no. 1007

917 Quartet, piano, no. 1, op. 25, G minor (orch. Schoenberg). German Philharmonic Youth Orchestra; Hans Zender. DG 2531 198
++FF 3/4-81 p189
+-Gr 5-80 p1659
+HFN 6-80 p103
+-MT 11-81 p753
+NR 3-81 p6
++RR 6-80 p42

918 Quartet, piano, no. 1, op. 25, G minor. Emil Gilels, pno; Amadeus Quartet. DG 2542 140 Tape (c) 3342 140 (From 2530 133)
++Gr 12-80 p842
+HFN 12-80 p153
+HFN 1-81 p109 tape

919 Quartet, piano, no. 1, op. 25, G minor. Les Musiciens. Harmonia Mundi HM 1062 Tape (c) HM 40 1062
+Gr 9-81 p401
+FF 9/10-81 p87
+HFN 9-81 p79

Quartet, piano, no. 1, op. 25, G minor. See no. 1008

Quartet, piano, no. 2, op. 26, A major. See no. 1008

920 Quartets, strings, nos. 1-3. SCHUMANN: Quartets, strings, nos. 1-3. Guarneri Quartet. RCA ARL 3-3834 (3) Tape (c) ARK 3-3834
+-FF 5/6-81 p66
+HF 4-81 p76
++NR 3-81 p8
++SFC 1-11-81 p17
+-St 6-81 p112

Quartets, strings, nos. 1-3. See no. 1007

921 Quartet, strings, no. 1, op. 51, C minor. Quartet, strings, no. 2, op. 51, A minor. Allegri Quartet. Argo ZK 89
+Gr 5-81 p1486
+ST 8-81 p276

922 Quartet, strings, no. 1, op. 51, C minor. Quartet, strings, no. 2, op. 51, A minor. LaSalle Quartet. DG 2531 255 Tape (c) 3301 255
+-FF 5/6-81 p66
+-Gr 12-80 p846
+Gr 2-81 p1122 tape
+HF 4-81 p76
+HFN 12-80 p135
+HFN 1-81 p109 tape
+NR 3-81 p7
+St 6-81 p112
++STL 11-9-80 p40

Quartet, strings, no. 1, op. 51, C minor. See no. 1008

Quartet, strings, no. 2, op. 51, A minor. See no. 921. See no. 922

923 Quartet, strings, no. 3, op. 67, B flat major. LARSSON: Quartet, strings, no. 3, op. 65. Stockholm Quartet. Caprice CAP 1186
+-FF 7/8-81 p79
+-NR 7-81 p8

Quartet, strings, no. 3, op. 67, B flat major. See no. 1008

924 Quintet, clarinet, op. 115, B minor. Sonata, violin and piano, no. 3, op. 108, D minor. Adolf Busch, vln; Rudolf Serkin, pno; Reginald Kell, clt; Busch Quartet. Bruno Walter Society RR 485
+FF 11/12-81 p126
+NR 11-81 p7

925 Quintet, clarinet, op. 115, B minor. Janet Hilton, clt; Lindsay

Quartet. Chandos ABR 1035 Tape (c) ABT 1035
+Gr 11-81 p714 +HFN 11-81 p90

926 Quintet, clarinet, op. 115, B minor. WEBER (attrib.): Variations on a theme from Silvana. Peter Schmidl, clt; New Vienna Octet Members. Decca SDD 575
+Gr 10-81 p568 +-HFN 10-81 p86

927 Quintet, clarinet, op. 115, B minor. Paul Drushler, clt; Tremont String Quartet. Mark Records MES 57579
+*FF 3/4-81 p91

928 Quintet, clarinet, op. 115, B minor. Richard Stoltzman, clt; Cleveland Quartet. RCA ARL 1-1993 Tape (c) ARK 1-1993 (ct) 1-1993
++ARG 4-77 p19 +MJ 4-77 p50
+Gr 8-77 p313 +NR 4-77 p6
+Gr 4-81 p1334 +RR 8-77 p66
+-HF 4-77 p94 ++St 5-77 p104
+HF 5-77 p101 tape +ST 1-78 p843
+-HFN 10-77 p152

Quintet, clarinet, op. 115, B minor. See no. 1007. See no. 1008

929 Quintet, piano, op. 34, F minor. Amadeus Quartet; Christoph Eschenbach, pno. DG 2525 418 Tape (c) 3335 418 (From SLPM 139397)
+Gr 2-81 p1095 +HFN 8-81 p92 tape

930 Quintet, piano, op. 34, F minor. Maurizio Pollini, pno. Quartetto Italiano. DG 2531 197 Tape (c) 3301 197
++Audio 3-81 p60 +HF 4-81 p76
++CL 4-81 p12 +HFN 8-80 p95
++FF 1/2-81 p90 +-HFN 10-80 p117 tape
+Gr 10-80 p548 tape +MUM 2-81 p31
+-Gr 9-80 p359 +RR 8-80 p59
++Gr 3-81 p1170 ++ST 1-81 p647

931 Quintet, piano, op. 34, F minor. Dezso Ranki, pno; Bartok Quartet. Hungaroton SLPX 12280
+-HFN 6-81 p71 ++SFC 12-20-81 p18
++NR 9-81 p6 ++St 12-81 p75

Quintet, piano, op. 34, F minor. See no. 1007. See no. 1008

Quintets, strings, nos. 1-2. See no. 1007

Rhapsodies, op. 79. See no. 876. See no. 916

Schicksalslied, op. 54. See no. 907

932 Serenade, no. 1, op. 11, D major. LSO; Istvan Kertesz. Decca JB 86 Tape (c) KJBC 86 (From SXL 6340)
+Gr 9-81 p382

933 Serenade, no. 1, op. 11, D major. Gewandhaus Orchestra; Kurt Masur. Philips 6514 081 Tape (c) 7337 081
++SFC 12-20-81 p18

934 Serenade, no. 1, op. 11, D major. COA; Bernard Haitink. Philips 9500 322 Tape (c) 7300 584 (r) G 9500 322
+-ARG 5-78 p21 +MJ 9/10-79 p51
+Gr 2-78 p1399 ++NR 3-78 p3
++Gr 1-79 p1339 tape +RR 3-78 p34
++HF 7-78 p70 tape +RR 6-78 p93
+HF 8-81 p69 tape ++RR 9-78 p101 tape
+HFN 2-78 p105 ++SFC 11-20-77 p54
+HFN 5-78 p146 tape ++St 2-78 p145

935 Serenade, no. 2, op. 16, A major. DVORAK: Serenade, op. 44, D minor. LSO; Istvan Kertesz. Decca JB 87 Tape (c) KJBC 87

(From SXL 6368)
+Gr 9-81 p382

Sextets, strings, nos. 1-2. See no. 1007

936 Sextet, strings, no. 1, op. 18, B flat major. Sextet, strings, no. 2, op. 36, G major. Stuttgart Solisten. Intercord INT 180 834
+HFN 12-81 p93

Sextet strings, no. 2, op. 36, G major. See no. 936

Sonatas, clarinet and piano, nos. 1-2. See no. 1007

937 Sonata, clarinet and piano, no. 1, op. 120, F minor. Sonata, clarinet and piano, no. 2, op. 120, E flat major. Mark Walton, clt; Simon Ballard, pno. Chalumeau EBY 002
+-MT 10-81 p677

938 Sonata, clarinet and piano, no. 1, op. 120, F minor. Sonata, clarinet and piano, no. 2, op. 120, E flat major. Janet Hilton, clt; Peter Frankl, pno. Chandos ABR 1020 Tape (c) ABT 1020
+Gr 5-81 p1486 +HFN 6-81 p71

939 Sonata, clarinet and piano, no. 1, op. 120, F minor. Sonata, clarinet and piano, no. 2, op. 120, E flat major. Michel Portal, clt; Georges Pludermacher, pno. Harmonia Mundi HM 904
+FF 11/12-81 p125 +HFN 10-78 p119

940 Sonata, clarinet and piano, no. 1, op. 120, F minor. Sonata, clarinet and piano, no. 2, op. 120, E flat major. Jenny Abel, vln; Roberto Szidon, pno. Harmonia Mundi 1C 065 99787
+Gr 8-81 p292

941 Sonata, clarinet and piano, no. 1, op. 120, F minor. Sonata, clarinet and piano, no. 2, op. 120, E flat major. George Pieterson, clt; Hephzibah Menuhin, pno. Philips 9500 784 Tape (c) 7300 858
++ARG 12-81 p12 +St 10-81 p119
++FF 9/10-81 p87

Sonata, clarinet and piano, no. 2, op. 120, E flat major. See no. 937. See no. 938. See no. 939. See no. 940. See no. 941

942 Sonata, piano, no. 1, op. 1, C major. Sonata, piano, no. 2, op. 2, F sharp minor. Krystian Zimerman, pno. DG 2531 252
++CL 1-81 p12 ++NR 11-80 p9
++FF 1/2-81 p91 ++RR 6-80 p73
+Gr 6-80 p53 ++SR 11-81 p62
++Gr 3-81 p1172 ++St 12-80 p82
+HFN 6-80 p103 ++STL 5-11-80 p38
+MT 1-81 p33

Sonata, piano, no. 2, op. 2, F sharp minor. See no. 942

943 Sonata, 2 pianos, op. 34b, F minor. Maria Tipo, Alessandro Specchi, pno. Dischi Ricordi 27058
+Gr 10-81 p568

944 Sonata, viola and piano, no. 1, op. 120, F minor. Sonata, viola and piano, no. 2, op. 120, E flat major. Bernard Zaslav, vla; Naomi Zaslav, pno. Gasparo GS 215
+FF 7/8-81 p79 ++St 6-81 p112
+IN 11-81 p94 ++ST 7-81 p205
+NR 3-81 p7

Sonata, viola and piano, no. 2, op. 120, E flat major. See no. 944

945 Sonata, violin and piano, nos. 1-3. Trio, horn, op. 40, E flat major. Yehudi Menuhin, vln; Alan Civil, hn; Louis Kentner,

Hephzibah Menuhin, pno. La Voix de Son Maitre 2C 181 03710/1 (2)
+-FF 11/12-81 p125

Sonatas, violin and piano, nos. 1-3. See no. 1007

Sonata, violin and piano, no. 1, op. 78, G major. See no. 1008

946 Sonata, violin and piano, no. 2, op. 100, A major. SCHUBERT: Trio, piano, no. 1, op. 99, D 898, B flat major. Joseph Szigeti, vln; Artur Schnabel, pno; Pierre Fournier, vlc. Bruno Walter Society RR 488
+-NR 11-81 p7

947 Sonata, violin and piano, no. 2, op. 100, A major. SCHUBERT: Sonatina, no. 1, D 384, D major. Sonata, piano, no. 21, D 960, B flat major. Isaac Stern, vln; Myra Hess, pno. Bruno Walter Society RR 524
/-NR 6-81 p14

Sonata, violin and piano, no. 2, op. 100, A major. See no. 1008

948 Sonata, violin and piano, no. 3, op. 108, D minor. TCHEREPNIN: Sonata, violin and piano, F major. Yehudi Menuhin, vln; Hephzibah Menuhin, Alexander Tcherepnin, pno. A portrait in sound narrated by Edward Greenfield. BBC REGL 409 Tape (c) ZCF 409
+Gr 6-81 p55

Sonata, violin and piano, no. 3, op. 108, D minor. See no. 924

949 Sonata, violoncello and piano, D major (trans. from Sonata, violin and piano, no. 1, op. 78, G major). GINASTERA: Pampeana, no. 2. MENDELSSOHN: Variations concertantes, op. 17. Bert Phillips, vlc; Toby Blumenthal, pno. Gasparo GS 208
+-FF 7/8-81 p79 +NR 3-81 p7

Sonatas, violincello and piano, nos. 1 and 2. See no. 1007

950 Sonata, violoncello, no. 1, op. 38, E minor. Sonata, violoncello, no. 2, op. 99, F major. Lynn Harrell, vlc; Vladimir Ashkenazy, pno. Decca SXL 6979 Tape (c) KSXC 6979 (also London 7208)
+Gr 12-81 p896

Sonata, violoncello and piano, no. 2, op. 99, F major. See no. 950

Sonata movement (Scherzo), violin and piano. See no. 85

951 Songs: Fest und Gedenkspruche, op. 109. DEBUSSY: Chansons de Charles d'Orleans (3). TIPPETT: Negro spirituals (5). WOLF: Geistliche Lieder (6). Cambridge University Chamber Choir; Richard Marlow. Cambridge Records CCRS 1002
+-Gr 4-81 p1356

952 Songs: Blinde Kuh, op. 58, no. 1; Madchenlied, op. 95, no. 6; Therese, op. 86, no. 1. GRIEG: Ein Schwan, op. 25, no. 2. LOEWE: Die wandelnde Glocke. WOLF: Auf ein altes Bild; Bei einer Trauung; Elfenlied; Fussreise; Heimweh; Jagerlied; Selbstgestandnis; Mausfallenspruchlein; Nixe Binsefuss; Nimmersatte Liebe; Storchenbotschaft; Das verlassene Magdlein. Elisabeth Schwarzkopf, s; Geoffrey Parsons, pno. Decca SXL 6943 Tape (c) KSXC 6943 (also London OS 26592)
+Gr 1-81 p982 ++SFC 11-29-81 p18
+HFN 1-81 p104 +STL 2-8-81 p40

953 Songs: Lieder und Romanzen, op. 14. Folksongs: Beim Ritt auf dem Knie; Der Mann; Dem Schutzengel; Dornroschen; Heidenroslein; Die Henne; Der Jager in dem Walde; Das Madchen und die Hasel; Marienwurmchen; Die Nachtigall; Sandmannchen; Das Schlaraffenland; Weihnachten; Wiegenlied. Julia Paszthy, s; Laszlo Baranyay, pno. Hungaroton SLPX 12136
+NR 12-81 p14

954 Songs: Madchenlieder, op. 85, no. 3; op. 95, no. 6; op. 107, no. 5; Das Madchen, op. 95, no. 1; Das Madchen spricht, op. 107, no. 3; Madchenfluch, op. 69, no. 9. Zigeunerlieder, op. 103. DVORAK: Folk songs, op. 73 (4). Gypsy songs, op. 55. Sarah Walker, ms; Roger Vignoles, pno. Meridian E 77042
+Gr 11-81 p733 +STL 9-13-81 p41

955 Songs: Der bucklichte Fiedler, op. 93, no. 1; O susser Mai, op. 93, no. 3; Waldesnacht, op. 62, no. 3. MENDELSSOHN: Songs, op. 48 (6). SCHUMANN: Der Konig von Thule, op. 67, no. 1; Im Walde, op. 75, no. 2. REGER: Es waren zwei Konigskinder; Ich hab heut Nacht getraumet. Marburg Vocal Ensemble. Musicaphon BM 30 SL 1337
+-Gr 6-81 p76 +-HFN 10-80 p111

956 Songs: Das Madchen, op. 95, no. 1; Das Madchen spricht, op. 107, no. 3; Madchenlied, op. 85, no. 3; Madchenlied, op. 95, no. 6; Madchenlied, op. 107, no. 5; Madchenfluch, op. 69, no. 9; Gestille Sehnsucht, op. 91, no. 1; Geistliches Wiegenlied. BRITTEN: A charm of lullabies, op. 41. MOERAN: Shakespeare songs: The lover and his lass; Where the bee sucks; When daisies pied; When icicles hang by the wall. RUBBRA: Sonnets, op. 87 (2). Alfreda Hodgson, ms; Keith Swallow, pno; Ludmila Navratil, vla. Pearl SHE 559
+Gr 6-81 p76 ++HFN 8-81 p89

957 Songs: Botschaft, op. 47, no. 1; Geistliches Wiegenlied, op. 91, no. 2; Gestille Sehnsucht, op. 91, no. 1; Immer leise wird mein Schlummer, op. 105, no. 2; Die Mainacht, op. 43, no. 2; Meine Liebe ist grun, op. 63, no. 5; O komme holde Sommernacht, op. 58, no. 2; Standchen, op. 106, no. 1; Therese, op. 86, no. 1; Der Tod das ist die kuhle Nacht, op. 96, no. 1; Von ewiger Liebe, op. 43, no. 1; Wie Melodien zieht es mir, op. 105, no. 1. Jessye Norman, s; Geoffrey Parsons, pno; Ulrich von Wrochem, vla. Philips 9500 785 Tape (c) 7300 859
+-ARG 4-81 p20 ++HFN 10-80 p117 tape
++FF 1/2-81 p92 +-MT 3-81 p183
+Gr 7-80 p158 ++NR 11-80 p8
+Gr 1-81 p1001 tape +-RR 7-80 p87
++HFN 8-80 p95 +-St 2-81 p104

958 Songs: Liebeslieder, op. 42. Zigeunerlieder, op. 104. MARX: Der bescheidene Schafer; Hat dich die Liebe beruhrt; Und gestern hat er mir Rosen gebracht; Valse de Chopin; Wandrader. SCHUBERT: Im Walde, D 834. Ljuba Welitsch, s; Ernest Lush, Frederick Stone, Joseph Marx, pno; Irmgard Seefried, s; Elisabeth Hongen, con; Hugo Meyer-Welfing, t; Hans Hotter, bar; Friedrich Wuhrer, Hermann von Nordberg, pno. World Records SH 373
+Gr 9-80 p408 +-ON 12-20-80 p52
+-MT 6-81 p394 +-RR 8-80 p78

Songs: Auf dem See, op. 59, no. 2; Es Schauen die Blumen, op. 96, no. 3; Der Jager, op. 95, no. 4; Ruhe Sussliebchen im Schatten. See no. 3654

Songs: Dein blaues Auge, op. 59, no. 8. See no. 3653

Songs: Dein blaues Auge, op. 59, no. 8; Vergebliches Standchen, op. 84 no. 4. See no. 3642

Songs: Die Mainacht, op. 43, no. 2; In Waldeinsamkeit. See no. 3657

Songs: Feldeinsamkeit, op. 86, no. 2; Standchen. See no. 3988

Songs: Feldeinsamkeit, op. 86, no. 2; Im Waldeseinsamkeit, op. 85, no. 6, Komm bald; Die Mainacht, op. 43, no. 2. See no. 3967
Songs: Mein Madel hat einen Rosenmund. See no. 3703
Songs: Ninna Nanna. See no. 3753
Songs: Vergebliches Standchen, op. 84, no. 4. See no. 3844
959 Souvenir de la Russie, op. 151. Variations on a theme by Schumann, op. 23. Waltzes, op. 39. Victoria Postnikova, Gennady Rozhdestvensky, pno. Eurodisc 89152
+SFC 11-29-81 p18
960 Symphonies, nos. 1-4. Variations on a theme by Haydn, op. 56a. Tragic overture, op. 81. PhO, NPhO; Carlo Maria Giulini. HMV SLS 5241 (4)
+-HFN 8-81 p83
961 Symphonies, nos. 1-4. Tragic overture, op. 81. SCHUMANN: Manfred overture, op. 115. LSO, BPhO, CPhO; Jascha Horenstein, Rudolf Kempe, Dietrich Fischer-Dieskau. Quintessence 4PMC 4702 (4)
+FF 5/6-81 p67
Symphonies, no. 1-4. See no. 1006
962 Symphony, no. 1, op. 68, C minor. Orchestre de Paris; Charles Munch. Arabesque 8056 Tape (c) 9056
+FF 1/2-81 p92 +-SFC 3-23-80 p35
++NR 5-80 p5
963 Symphony, no. 1, op. 68, C minor. BEETHOVEN: Symphony, no. 7, op. 92, A major: 2nd movement rehearsal fragment. Lucerne Festival Orchestra; Wilhelm Furtwangler. Bruno Walter Society RR 393
-FF 7/8-81 p80
964 Symphony, no. 1, op. 68, C minor. WAGNER: Rienzi: Overture. PO; Leopold Stokowski. Cameo GOCLP 9009 (From Matrix A37483/92, D1499-1503, A37004, A37700/1, DB 1226-7)
++FF 3/4-81 p91 +Gr 8-80 p215
965 Symphony, no. 1, op. 68, C minor. BPhO; Karl Bohm. Contour CC 7514 Tape (c) CCT 7514
+Gr 8-81 p316
966 Symphony, no. 1, op. 68, C minor. CSO; Georg Solti. Decca SXL 6924 Tape (c) KSXC 6924 (From D151D4)
+Gr 8-81 p264
967 Symphony, no. 1, op. 68, C mnor. VPO; Claudio Abbado. DG 2542 138 Tape (c) 3342 138
+Gr 12-80 p831 +-HFN 1-81 p109 tape
+-HFN 12-80 p153
968 Symphony, no. 1, op. 68, C minor. National Philharmonic Orchestra; Carlos Paita. Lodia LOD 779
+HFN 9-81 p78
969 Symphony, no. 1, op. 68, C minor. Berlin State Opera Orchestra; Oskar Fried. Past Masters PM 32
+FF 1/2-81 p93
Symphony, no. 1, op. 68, C minor. See no. 3781
970 Symphony, no. 2, op. 73, D major. WAGNER: Die Meistersinger von Nurnberg: Prelude, Act 1. Berlin Opera Orchestra; Hans Knappertsbusch. Bruno Walter Society RR 388
+-NR 9-81 p2
971 Symphony, no. 2, op. 73, D major. Tragic overture, op. 81. CSO; Georg Solti. Decca SXL 6925 Tape (c) KSXC 6925 (From D151D4)
+Gr 10-81 p540
972 Symphony, no. 2, op. 73, D major. LAPO; Carlo Maria Giulini. DG

2532 014 Tape (c) 3302 014
+Gr 11-81 p686 ++HFN 11-81 p90

973 Symphony, no. 2, op. 73, D major. SCHUBERT: Symphony, no. 8, D 759, B minor. PhO; Herbert von Karajan. HMV SXLP 30513 Tape (c) TC SCLP 30513 (From 33CX1355, 33CX 1349)
+Gr 5-81 p1472 +-HFN 6-81 p85

974 Symphony, no. 2, op. 73, D major. Alto rhapsody, op. 53. Janet Baker, s; LPO; Adrian Boult. HMV SXLP 30529 Tape (c) TC SXLP 30529 (From ASD 2746)
++Gr 12-81 p884

975 Symphony, no. 2, op. 73, D major. Academic festival overture, op. 80. LSO; Pierre Monteux. Philips 6570 108 Tape (c) 7310 108 (From SAL 3435, 9500 035, World 9123)
+Audio 2-80 p42 +HFN 9-79 p121
++FF 7/8-81 p81 ++HFN 11-79 p157 tape
+Gr 11-79 p810 +MUM 7/8-79 p37
+HFN 10-79 p171 tape +-RR 9-79 p80

Symphony, no, 2, op. 73, D major. See no. 3855

976 Symphony, no. 3, op. 90, F major. Houston Symphony Orchestra; Leopold Stokowski. Everest Tape (c) 3030
+HF 10-81 p91 tape

977 Symphony, no. 3, op. 90, F major. Academic festival overture, op. 80. CSO; Georg Solti. London CS 7200 (also Decca SXL 6902 Tape (c) KSXC 6902)
+-FF 9/10-81 p88 +-NR 5-81 p3
+-Gr 8-81 p382

978 Symphony, no. 4, op. 98, E minor. SCHUBERT: Symphony, no. 8, D 759, B minor. BPhO; Wilhelm Furtwanger. Bruno Walter Society RR 394
+-FF 7/8-81 p80 +NR 4-81 p3

979 Symphony, no. 4, op. 98, E minor. CSO; Georg Solti. Decca SXL 6890 Tape (c) KSXC 6890 (also London CS 7201)
+Gr 8-78 p329 +NR 2-81 p4
++Gr 1-79 p1331 tape +-RR 9-78 p49
+-HFN 9-78 p139 +-RR 1-79 p90 tape
+-HFN 11-78 p187 tape +St 11-81 p82

980 Symphony, no. 4, op. 98, E minor. VPO; Carlos Kleiber. DG 2532 003 Tape (c) 3302 003
+-FF 9/10-81 p88 +HFN 6-81 p87 tape
+Gr 4-81 p1312 +-MUM 9/10-81 p33
++Gr 6-81 p93 tape -SFC 8-2-81 p17
+HF 10-81 p82 +-St 11-81 p82
+-HFN 5-81 p79 ++STL 4-12-81 p40

981 Symphony, no. 4, op. 98, E minor. Academic festival overture, op. 80. LSO, BPhO; Claudio Abbado. DG 2542 120 Tape (c) 3342 120 (From 2720 061, 135112) (also DG 2535 360)
-FF 1/2-81 p93 +HFN 8-80 p109 tape
+Gr 7-80 p136 +-RR 5-80 p106 tape
+HFN 5-80 p135 +-RR 6-80 p42

982 Symphony, no. 4, op. 98, E minor. PhO; Herbert von Karajan. HMV SXLP 30505 Tape (c) TC SXLP 30505 (From Columbia 33CS 1361)
+Gr 5-81 p1472 +-HFN 6-81 p85

983 Symphony, no. 4, op. 98, E minor. RPO; Fritz Reiner. Quintessence PMC 7182
+FF 7/8-81 p81

984 Symphony, no. 4, op. 98, E minor. Dresden Staatskapelle Orchestra; Kurt Sanderling. RCA GL 2-5279 Tape (c) GK 2-5279 (From SB 6879)
+-Gr 8-81 p264 +-HFN 8-81 p92 tape
985 Symphony, no. 4, op. 98, E minor. CHERUBINI: Anacreon: Overture. Orchestra; Sergiu Celibidache. Rococo 2150
+NR 3-81 p1
Symphony, no. 4, op. 98, E minor. See no. 3791
986 Theme and variations, D minor. SCHUBERT: Sonata, piano, no. 4, D 537, A minor. Sonata, piano, no. 13, D 664, A major. Sonata, piano, no. 8, D 571, F sharp minor. Luc Devos, pno. Nimbus 2129
+-Gr 8-81 p296 +-HFN 8-81 p83
Tragic overture, op. 81. See no. 960. See no. 961. See no. 971. See no. 3858
987 Trio, clarinet, op. 114, A minor. Trio, horn, op. 40, E flat major. Malcolm Frager, pno; Stoika Milanova, vln; Hermann Baumann, waldhorn, vlc; Piet Honingh, clt. Musical Heritage Society MHS 4347
+FF 11/12-81 p127
988 Trio, clarinet, op. 114, A minor. Trio, piano, no. 2, op. 87, C major. Odeon Trio. Quintessence 7191 Tape (c) P4C 7191
+HF 10-81 p91 tape
Trio, clarinet, op. 114, A minor. See no. 707. See no. 708. See no. 1007. See no. 993
989 Trio, horn, op. 40, E flat major. MARAIS: Le basque. MOZART: Quintet, horn, K 407, E flat major. Dennis Brain, hn; Max Salpeter, vln; Cyril Preedy, pno; Eileen Granger, vla; Wilfrid Parry, pno; Carter String Trio. Everest SDBR 3432 (also BBC 22175)
-FF 3/4-81 p93 ++NR 3-79 p10
990 Trio, horn, op. 40, E flat major. Trios, piano, nos. 1-3. Suk Trio; Zdenek Tylsar, hn. Supraphon 111 2251/1
+-FF 1/2-80 p70 -+HFN 8-79 p101
+-Gr 10-79 p667 ++NR 12-79 p7
-HF 2-81 p61 +-RR 7-79 p73
Trio, horn, op. 40, E flat major. See no. 945. See no. 987. See no. 993. See no. 1007. See no. 1008
991 Trios, piano, nos. 1-3. Pro Arte Trio. BIS LP 98/9 (2)
+-Gr 9-80 p359 ++NR 5-80 p7
+HF 2-81 p60 +RR 3-80 p72
+-HFN 3-80 p87
992 Trios, piano, nos. 1-3. Gyorgy Pauk, vln; Ralph Kirshbaum, vlc; Peter Frankl, pno. HMV SLS 5114 (2)
+FF 7/8-81 p82 ++MT 4-80 p248
+Gr 12-79 p1027 +RR 1-80 p94
+HFN 1-80 p103 ++STL 2-10-80 p40
993 Trios, piano, nos. 1-3. Trio, horn, op. 40, E flat major. Trio, clarinet, op. 114, A minor. Odeon Trio; Rainer Moog, vla. Musical Heritage Society MHS 4215/7 Tape (c) MHC 6215/7
-ARG 3-81 p18 +HF 2-81 p59
+FF 1/2-81 p95
994 Trios, piano, nos. 1-3. Beaux Arts Trio. Philips 6770 007 (2) Tape (c) 7650 007 (From World PHC 2-013)
+Gr 5-81 p1486 +HFN 5-81 p91

+Gr 9-81 p460 tape +HFN 9-81 p93 tape
+HF 2-81 p59

995 Trios, piano, nos. 1-3. Vienna Haydn Trio. Telefunken 6-35471 (2)
+FF 1/2-81 p94 +-HF 2-81 p59

Trios, piano, nos. 1-3. See no. 990. See no. 1007

996 Trio, piano, no. 1, op. 8, B major. Trio, piano, no. 2, op. 87, C major. Wolfgang Schneiderhan, vln; Enrico Mainardi, vlc; Edwin Fischer, pno. Bruno Walter Society BWS 739
++HF 2-81 p59

997 Trio, piano, no. 1, op. 8, B major. Trio, piano, no. 2, op. 87, C major. Trio, piano, no. 3, op. 101, C minor. Les Musiciens. Harmonia Mundi HM 1063/4
/HFN 12-81 p93 ++ST 12-81 p589

998 Trio, piano, no. 2, op. 87, C major. Trio, piano, no. 3, op. 101, C minor. Trio Rouvier. Accord 140 004
+HFN 12-81 p93

999 Trio, piano, no. 2, op. 87, C major. San Francisco Trio. Sound Storage SSR 2010
++ARG 4-81 p17 +SFC 12-9-80 p33
-FF 11/12-80 p89 ++St 5-81 p68
+-HF 2-81 p60

Trio, piano, no. 2, op. 87, C major. See no. 988. See no. 996. See no. 997

1000 Trio, piano, no. 3, op. 101, C minor. MENDELSSOHN: Trio, piano, no. 1, op. 49, D minor. Suk Trio. Quintessence PMC 7148
+FF 3/4-81 p154

Trio, piano, no. 3, op. 101, C minor. See no. 997. See no. 998

1001 Trio, piano, op. posth., A major. Odeon Trio. Quintssence PMC 7186 Tape (c) P4C 7186
+-FF 9/10-81 p90 +HF 10-81 p91 tape

1002 Variations and fugue on a theme by Handel, op. 24. REGER: Variations and fugue on a theme by Telemann, op. 134. Jorge Bolet, pno. Decca SXL 6969
++Gr 11-81 p722 +STL 10-11-81 p41
+HFN 11-81 p90

1003 Variations and fugue on a theme by Handel, op. 24. CHOPIN: Etude, op. 10, no. 12, C minor. Etude, op. 25, no. 1, A flat major. Nocturne, op. 27, no. 2, D flat major. Polonaise, op. 40, no. 1, A major. Prelude, op. 28, no. 17, A flat major. GRANADOS: Goyescas: The maiden and the nightingale. NIEMANN: Evening in Seville, op. 55, no. 2. Jean Carrington Cook, pno. Golden Age 1018
-NR 6-81 p13

1004 Variations and fugue on a theme by Handel, op. 24, B flat major. CHOPIN: Mazurka, op. 17, no. 4, A minor. HANDEL: Air with variations, B flat major. Lincoln Mayorga, pno. Sheffield LAB 4
+-HFN 1-81 p104 +MJ 7-77 p70

Variations and fugue on a theme by Handel, op. 24, B flat major. See no. 912. See no. 915

1005 Variations on a theme by Haydn, op. 56b. Variations on a theme by Schumann, op. 23. Waltzes, op. 39. Alfons and Aloys Kontarsky, pno. Musicaphon BM 30 SL 3004
+Gr 12-81 p896

Variations on a theme by Haydn, op. 56a. See no. 906. See no. 960. See no. 1006

Variations on a theme by Paganini, op. 35, A minor. See no. 916
Variations on a theme by Schumann, op. 23. See no. 911. See no. 959. See no. 1005
Variations on an original theme, op. 21, no. 1, D major. See no. 888
Waltzes, op. 39. See no. 876. See no. 911. See no. 959. See no. 1005. See no. 3749
Waltz, op. 39, no. 15, A flat major. See no. 3645

1006 Works, selections: Concerto, piano, no. 2, op. 83, B flat major.* Concerto, violin, op. 77, D major.* Concerto, violin and violoncello, op. 102, A minor. Hungarian dances. Symphonies, nos. 1-4.* Variations on a theme by Haydn, op. 56a. Yehudi Menuhin, vln; Willi Boskovsky, vln; Emanuel Brabec, vlc; Edwin Fischer, pno; BPhO, VPO; Wilhelm Furtwangler. EMI Electrola 159 53240/6 (7) (*From Turnabout TV 4342, TV 4476, Seraphim 60232)
+-Gr 12-81 p880 +NYT 6-22-80 pD20
+HF 4-80 p69

1007 Works, selections: Quartets, piano, nos. 1-3. Quartet, strings, nos. 1-3. Quintet, clarinet, op. 115, B minor. Quintet, piano, op. 34, F minor. Quintets, strings, nos. 1-2. Sextets, nos. 1-2. Sonatas, clarinet and piano, nos. 1-2. Sonatas, violin and piano, nos. 1-3. Sonatas, violoncello and piano, nos. 1, 2. Trio, clarinet, op. 114, A minor. Trio, horn, op. 40, E flat major. Trios, piano, nos. 1-3. Arthur Grumiaux, Daniel Gullet, Alfred Malacek, Rudolf Hartmann, vln; Gyorgy Sebok, Hephzibah Menuhin, Menahem Pressler, pno; Janos Starker, Bernard Greenhouse, Peter Steiner, vlc; Kunio Tsuchiya, vla; Beaux Arts Trio, BPhO Octet, Quartetto Italiano. Philips 6768 146 (15)
+-Gr 9-80 p356 +-ST 6-81 p119
+HFN 11-80 p116

1008 Works, selections: Quartet, piano, no. 1, op. 25, G minor. Quartet, piano, no. 2, op. 26, A major. Quintet, clarinet, op. 115, B minor. Quintet, piano, op. 34, F minor. Quartet, strings, no. 1, op. 51, C minor. Quartet, strings, no. 3, op. 67, B flat major.* Sonata, violin and piano, no. 1, op. 78, G major. Sonata, violin and piano, no. 2, op. 100, A major. Trio, horn, op. 40, E flat major. Adolf Busch, vln; Rudolf Serkin, pno; Reginald Kell, clt; Aubrey Brain, hn; Busch Quartet. World Records SHB 61 (7) (From EMI originals, *Columbia ML 4330)
+FF 7/8-81 p76 +Gr 4-81 p1372

Zigeunerlieder, op. 103. See no. 958

BREHM, Alvin

1009 Cycle of six songs on poems of Garcia Lorca. CLARK: Concerto, clarinet and chamber orchestra. FOLEY: Four pieces for Saturday afternoon. WATTS: Signals, soprano and chamber orchestra. Catherine Rowe, Jan DeGaetani, s; Jerome Bunke, clt; Composers Festival Orchestra; Alvin Brehm. Trilogy Records CTS 1002
/FF 9/10-81 p278 +MJ 3-74 p10

1010 Theme, syllogism and epilogue. KRAFT, L.: Sestina. KUPFERMAN: Second thought. Short suite. WALLOWITCH: Snappy pieces (4). John Wallowitch, Dwight Peltzer, Kazuko Hayami, pno. Serenus SRS 12085
+-FF 9/10-81 p238

BREMNER, Robert

Miscellany: Tunes from Colonial Williamsburg. See no. 4111

BRETAN, Nicolae
1011 Hungarian songs (9). Romanian songs (9). Ludovic Konya, bar; Martin Berkofsky, Ferdinand Weiss, pno. Musical Heritage Society MHS 3572
+ON 12-5-81 p60 ++St 5-78 p92
Romanian songs (9). See no. 1011
BREVELLE-SMITH
The witch of Bowden. See no. 4074
BREWER, Alfred Herbert
Magnificat and nunc dimittis, D major. See no. 3895
Marche heroique. See no. 4112
BRIAN, Havergal
1012 Festal dance. For valour. In memoriam. Hull Youth Symphony Orchestra; Geoffrey Heald-Smith. Cameo GOCLP 9012
+Gr 4-81 p1314
Festival fanfare. See no. 4006
For valour. See no. 1012
In memoriam. See no. 1012
1013 Symphony, no. 2, E minor. Dresden Symphony Orchestra; Ernest Weir. Aries LP 1631
+-FF 1/2-81 p96
1014 Symphony, no. 10, C minor. Symphony, no. 21, E flat major. Leicestershire School Symphony Orchestra; James Loughran, Eric Pinkett. Unicorn RHS 265 (From RHS 313)
+-FF 3/4-81 p93 +HFN 12-80 p153
+Gr 12-80 p831 +-St 5-81 p72
+HF 8-81 p85
Symphony, no. 21, E flat major. See no. 1014
BRIDGE, Frank
Adagio, E major. See no. 3875
Cherry ripe. See no. 1020
1015 Divertimenti, wind quartet. Lament, 2 violas. Songs: Love went a'riding; So perverse; Strew no more red roses; Where she lies asleep. Part-songs (ed. Hindmarsh): Autumn; The bee; Hilly-ho Hilly-ho; Music when soft voices die; O weary hearts. David Johnston, t; Michael Ponder, Thomas Tichauer, vla; Jonathan Hinden, pno; Louis Halsey Singers; Phoenix Wind Ensemble; Louis Halsey. Pearl SHE 551
+Gr 6-81 p69 +-HFN 9-81 p79
1016 Elegy. BRITTEN: Suite, violoncello, no, 3, op. 87, IRELAND: Sonata, violoncello and piano, G minor. Julian Lloyd Webber, vlc; John McCabe, pno. ASV ACA 1001 Tape (c) ZCACZ 1001
+Gr 5-81 p1486 +MT 6-81 p388
+Gr 7-81 p196 tape +ST 7-81 p206
+-HFN 5-81 p85 ++STL 3-8-81 p38
+-HFN 6-81 p87 tape
Enter spring. See no. 1020
First book of organ pieces. See no. 1017
Lament. See no. 1015. See no. 1020
1017 Lento, "In memoriam CHHP". First book of organ pieces. Second book of organ pieces. Pieces, 1905 (3). Pieces, 1939 (3). Stuart Campbell, org. Pearl SHE 545
++FF 9/10-81 p91 -HFN 1-81 p91
Pieces, organ, 1905 and 1939. See no. 1017
1018 Quartet, strings, no. 1, E minor. MOERAN: Trio, strings, G major.

Hanson Quartet. Pearl SHE 563
+Gr 4-81 p1332 /HFN 6-81 p71
The sea. See no. 1020
Second book of organ pieces. See no. 1017
Sketches (3). See no. 4055
1019 Sonata, piano. DECAUX: Clairs de lune. WEBERN: Piece, piano. Sonata movement. Kinderstuck. Meral Guneyman, pno. Finnadar SR 9031
+FF 11/12-81 p99 +SFC 11-15-81 p18
+NR 9-81 p14
Songs: Love went a'riding; So perverse; Strew no more red roses; Where she lies asleep. Part-songs: Autumn; The bee; Hilly-ho Hilly-ho; Music when soft voices die; O weary hearts. See no. 1015
Summer. See no. 1020
There is a willow grows aslant a brook. See no. 467
1020 Works, selections: Cherry ripe. Enter spring. Lament. The sea. Summer. Royal Liverpool Philharmonic Orchestra; Charles Groves. HMV SQ ASD 3190
+ARG 2-78 p42 +HFN 5-76 p97
++FF 1/2-79 p159 ++MT 9-76 p744
++FF 7/8-81 p83 ++RR 5-76 p39
+Gr 5-76 p1749 ++Te 9-76 p31
BRIDGE, Frederick
God's goodness. See no. 3615
BRISTOL, Lee Jr.
Let your bearing in life. See no. 3810
BRITTEN, Benjamin
Antiphon. See no. 3616
The eagle has two heads. See no. 3660
Festival De Deum, op. 32. See no. 3620
1021 Gloriana: Morris dance (arr. Bream). GRAINGER: Molly on the shore. Shepherd's hey (arr. Wilson). VAUGHAN WILLIAMS: Prelude on Welsh hymn tunes: Rhosymedre. Suite de ballet: Passepied. TRAD. (arr./orch. Wilson): Chanter's song. The cuckoo. Greensleeves. The plough boy. Scottish dance tunes. Sweet Jane. Scarborough fair. Tomorrow shall be my dancing day. Ransom Wilson, flt; Nancy Allen, hp; Chamber Orchestra; Ransom Wilson. Angel DS 37333
+NR 6-81 p15
1022 Les illuminations, op. 18. SUDERBURG: Concerto (Voyage de nuit d'apres Baudelaire). Elizabeth Suderburg, s; Piedmont Chamber Orchestra; Nicholas Harsanyi. Turnabout TV 34776
+-FF 9/10-81 p92 +SFC 10-4-81 p17
+NR 7-81 p12 +-St 10-81 p122
Jubilate Deo, C major. See no. 3618. See no. 4061
1023 Lacrymae, op. 48. CLARKE: Sonata, viola. ECCLES: Sonata, viola, C minor. Josef Kodousek, vla; Kveta Novotna, pno. Supraphon 111 2694
++Gr 7-81 p167 ++St 11-81 p84
+HFN 8-81 p89 +STL 6-14-81 p40
++NR 8-81 p8
Nocturnal, op. 70. See no. 328
1024 Peter Grimes, op. 33: Four sea interludes. TIPPETT: The midsummer marriage: Ritual dances.* Joan Carlyle, s; Elizabeth Bainbridge, ms; Alberto Remedios, t; Stafford Dean, bs; ROHO and

Chorus; Colin Davis. Philips 6527 112 Tape (c) 7311 112 (*From 6703 027)
+Gr 11-81 p753 +HFN 10-81 p86
Prelude and fugue on a theme by Vittoria. See no. 744
1025 Quartet, strings, no. 1, op. 25, D major. SHOSTAKOVICH: Quintet, piano, op. 57, G minor. Clifford Benson, pno; Alberni Quartet. CRD CRD 1051 Tape (c) CRDC 4051
+Gr 11-78 p915 +HFN 10-81 p95 tape
+Gr 11-81 p783 tape +MT 2-79 p135
+HFN 11-78 p168 +RR 10-78 p89
1026 The rape of Lucretia, op. 37, excerpts. Joan Cross, Kathleen Ferrier, Peter Pears, Otakar Kraus, Owen Brannigan, soloists; English Opera Group; Benjamin Britten. I Grandi Interpreti IGI 369
+FF 11/12-81 p128
The rape of Lucretia, op. 37: Duet. See no. 3654
Russian funeral. See no. 3660
Simple symphony, op. 4. See no. 373
1027 Sinfonia da requiem, op. 20.* COPLAND: The red pony. St. Louis Symphony Orchestra; Andre Previn. CBS 61167 Tape (c) 40-61167 (*From 61427) (also Odyssey Y 31016)
/Gr 9-81 p382 +-HFN 9-81 p89
+-HFN 10-81 p86
1028 Songs: A charm of lullabies, op. 41; On this island, op. 11; Our hunting fathers, op. 8. Helen Watts, con; Peter Pears, t; LSO; Benjamin Britten, pno and cond. BBC REGL 417
+STL 12-13-81 p39
Songs: A charm of lullabies, op. 41. See no. 956
Songs: Come you not from Newcastle; The foggy foggy dew; The holy sonnets of John Donne, op. 35; The king is gone a-hunting; O waly waly; The plougboy; Sonnets of Michelangelo, op. 22. See no. 3842
Songs: Festival Te deum, op. 32; Hymn to St. Peter, op. 56a; Hymn of St. Columba; Antiphon, op. 56b. See no. 744
Songs: Hymn to St. Cecilia, op. 27. See no. 4005
Songs: Hymn to the virgin. See no. 3619. See no. 3685
Suite, violoncello, no, 3, op. 87. See no. 1016
Te Deum, C major. See no. 3614
1029 Temporal variations. GRABET: Sonata, oboe, op. 52, G minor. RONTGEN: Sonata, oboe, no. 1. RUBBRA: Duo, op. 156. Sonata, oboe, op. 100, C minor. Peter Bree, ob, cor anglais; Paul Komen, pno. CRCI/TOL 180550
+-Gr 11-81 p719
1030 Young person's guide to the orchestra, op. 34. PROKOFIEV: Peter and the wolf, op. 67. Sean Connery, narrator; RPO; Antal Dorati. Contour CC 7519 Tape (c) CCT 7519
+Gr 8-81 p316
1031 Young persons' guide to the orchestra, op. 34. PROKOFIEV: Peter and the wolf, op. 67. SAINT-SAENS: Carnival des animaux. Michael Flanders, narrator; Hephizbah Menuhin, Abbey Simon, pno; PhO, Royal Liverpool Orchestra; Efrem Kurtz, Charles Groves. HMV ESD 7114 Tape (c) TC ESD 7114 (From ASD 3417, 299)
++Gr 9-81 p382 +-HFN 9-81 p89

BRIXI, Franz Xavier
1032 Concerto, organ, no. 2, G major. LINEK: Concerto, organ, C major.

STAMITZ: Concerto, organ, no. 6, F major. Alena Vesela, org; Bohuslav Martinu Chamber Orchestra; Frantisek Jilek. SDG 610706
/-HFN 5-81 p89

BROADWOOD
Songs: The keys of heaven. See no. 3650

BROCHUS, Nicolo
Tienalora. See no. 3661

BRONSART, Ingeborg von
Jery und Bately: Lied and duet. See no. 3814

BROUWER, Leo
Concerto, guitar. See no. 73
Elogio de la danza. See no. 383
La espiral eterna. See no. 328
Etudes simples. See no. 4108
Micro piezas. See no. 3879

BROWN, Christopher
Laudate dominum. See no. 3621

BROWN, Richard
We cats when assembled. See no. 4093

BROWNE, John

1033 Salve regina. CORNYSH: Ave Maria. LAMBE: Nesciens mater; Stella caeli. WILKINSON: Salve regina. The Sixteen; Harry Christophers. Meridian E 77039
+-Gr 11-81 p748

BRUBECK, Dave

1034 La fiesta de la posada. Phyllis Bryn-Julson, s; Gene Tucker, t; Jake Gardner, bar; John Stephens, bs; Dave Brubeck, pno; Dale Warland Singers, St. Paul Chamber Orchestra, Edith Norberg's Carillon Choristers; Dennis Russell Davies. CBS 73903 Tape (c) 40-73903 (also CBC IM 36662 Tape (c) HMT 36662)
+FF 3/4-81 p95 +HFN 1-81 p107
+Gr 8-80 p276 ++HFN 6-81 p87 tape
+HFN 4-80 p103 +-RR 5-80 p93

BRUCH, Max

1035 Adagio appassionata, op. 57. Concerto, violin, no. 3, op. 58, D minor. Romance, op. 42. Salvatore Accardo, vln; Leipzig Gewandhaus Orchestra; Kurt Masur. Philips 9500 589 Tape (c) 7300 711 (From 6768 065)
+ARG 1-80 p24 +HFN 9-80 p115
+Audio 2-80 p42 +MT 2-81 p111
++FF 3/4-80 p71 ++RR 5-80 p57
++Gr 5-80 p1659 ++SFC 11-18-79 p47
++HF 4-80 p80 ++St 2-80 p122
+HFN 5-80 p135

1036 Concerto, clarinet and viola, op. 88. E minor. CRUSELL: Introduction and variations on a Swedish air, op. 12. MENDELSSOHN: Concert pieces, clarinet and basset horn, op. 113, F minor; op. 114, D minor. Thea King, clt; Georgina Dobree, basset hn; Nobuko Imai, vla; LSO; Alun Francis. Hyperion A 66022
++Gr 11-81 p713 +HFN 11-81 p100

1037 Concerto, violin, no. 1, op. 26, G minor. MENDELSSOHN: Concerto, violin, op. 64, E minor. Shlomo Mintz, vln; CSO; Claudio Abbado. DG 2531 304 Tape (c) 3301 304
+-ARG 11-81 p28 +MUM 9/10-81 p32

+FF 5/6-81 p105 +NR 5-81 p7
+Gr 4-81 p1314 +SR 11-81 p62
+Gr 6-81 p94 +St 9-81 p92
+HFN 4-81 p68 +-ST 5-81 p45
+HFN 4-81 p81 tape +STL 2-8-81 p40

1038 Concerto, violin, no. 1, op. 26, G minor. MENDELSSOHN: Concerto, violin, op. 64, E minor. Anne-Sophie Mutter, vln; BPhO; Herbert von Karajan. DG 2532 016 Tape (c) 3302 016
+Gr 11-81 p686 +-HFN 11-81 p91

1039 Concerto, violin, no. 1, op. 26, G minor. MENDELSSOHN: Concerto, violin, op. 64, E minor. Leonid Kogan, vln; Berlin Radio Orchestra; Lorin Maazel. Eurodisc 88 466
+-NR 12-81 p6

1040 Concerto, violin, no. 1, op. 26, G minor. BEETHOVEN: Romance, no. 2, op. 50, F major. Vera Predescu, vln; Pro Musica Orchestra; Jon Conta. Intercord INT 120935
-HFN 12-81 p93

1041 Concerto, violin, no. 1, op. 26, G minor. SIBELIUS: Concerto, violin, op. 47, D minor. Shizuka Ishikawa, vln; Brno State Philharmonic Orchestra; Jiri Belohlavek. Supraphon 110 2289
/-FF 5/6-81 p148 +NR 3-81 p2
+HF 7-81 p68

Concerto, violin, no. 1, op. 26, G minor. See no. 242. See no. 896

Concerto, violin, no. 3, op. 58, D minor. See no. 1035

1042 In memoriam, op. 65. Serenade, op. 75. Salvatore Accardo, vln; Leipzig Gewandhaus Orchestra; Kurt Masur. Philips 9500 590 Tape (c) 7300 712 (From 6768 065)
+ARG 7/8-80 p18 +MT 2-81 p111
+FF 5/6-80 p62 +NR 4-80 p15
+Gr 10-80 p496 +NYT 7-6-80 pD15
+HF 4-80 p80 ++RR 3-80 p48
++HFN 3-80 p105 ++SFC 1-20-80 p47
+HFN 6-80 p119 tape

Kol Nidrei, op. 47. See no. 3

1043 Konzertstuck, op. 84. Scottish fantasia, op. 46. Salvatore Accardo, vln; Leipzig Gewandhaus Orchestra; Kurt Masur. Philips 9500 423 Tape (c) 7300 641
+-ARG 8-79 p16 +MT 3-81 p111
+FF 11/12-79 p53 +NR 10-79 p12
+HF 8-79 p87 ++RR 3-80 p48
++HFN 3-80 p105 +SFC 7-29-79 p49
+HFN 8-80 p109 tape ++St 9-79 p93
+MJ 7/8-79 p57

Romance, op. 42. See no. 1035

1044 Scottish fantasia, op. 46. WIENIAWSKI: Concerto, violin, no. 1, op. 14, F sharp minor. Michael Rabin, vln; PhO; Adrian Boult. Seraphim 60342
+ARG 3-81 p21

Scottish fantasia, op. 46. See no. 1043

Serenade, op. 75. See no. 1042

Songs: Lasst uns das Kindlein wiegen. See no. 3963

BRUCKNER, Anton

Helgoland, op. 150. See no. 1061

1045 Mass, no. 0, C major. Psalm, no. 146, A major. Ursula Wendt, s;

Ingeborg Russ, alto; Frieder Stricker, t; Sigmund Nimsgern, bs; Hans Sachs Chor im Verband Merkur and Lehrergesangverein Nurnberg; Nurnberg Symphony Orchestra; Wolfgang Riedelbauch. Colosseum SM 548
+FF 11/12-81 p129

Psalm, no. 146, A major. See no. 1045

Psalm, no. 150. See no. 1061

1046 Quintet, strings, F major. WOLF: Italian serenade, G major. Melos Quartet; Enrique Santiago, vla. Intercord 160 806
+HFN 12-81 p93

Songs: Ave Maria. See no. 3634. See no. 3963

Songs (motets): Locus iste. See no. 3619. See no. 3895

Songs (motets): Tota pulchra es; Virga Jesse. See no. 3638

1047 Symphonies, nos. 0-9. CSO; Daniel Barenboim. DG 2740 253 (12) (From 2531 319, 2530 336, 2707 113, 2531 043, 2707 116, 2741 007, 2530 639, nos. 1-3 new)
+-Gr 10-81 p542

1048 Symphony, no. 0, D minor. CSO; Daniel Barenboim. DG 2531 319
+FF 5/6-81 p68
+-Gr 3-81 p1186
+HFN 4-81 p68
++NR 7-81 p2
+SFC 4-12-81 p21
++St 6-81 p113
+-ST 9-81 p351

1049 Symphony, no. 3, D minor. BPhO; Herbert von Karajan. DG 2532 007 Tape (c) 3302 007
+FF 11/12-81 p129
+-Gr 7-81 p152
+-Gr 8-81 p324 tape
+HFN 8-81 p83
++HFN 8-81 p92 tape
+SFC 12-13-81 p18

1050 Symphony, no. 3, D minor. Dresden State Orchestra; Eugen Jochum. HMV ASD 4009
+-Gr 6-81 p36
+HFN 7-81 p71

1051 Symphony, no. 4, E flat major. CSO; Georg Solti. Decca SXDL 7538 Tape (c) KSXDC 7538 (also London LDR 71038)
++Gr 8-81 p264
+Gr 11-81 p783
+HFN 9-81 p79

1052 Symphony, no. 4, E flat major. COA; Bernard Haitink. Philips 6527 101 Tape (c) 7311 101 (From SAL 3617)
-FF 11/12-81 p130
++Gr 11-81 p686
+HFN 12-81 p109

Symphony, no. 4, E flat major. See no. 3791

1053 Symphony, no. 5, B flat major. CSO; Georg Solti. Decca D221D2 (2) Tape (c) K221K2 (also London LDR 10031)
+-ARG 10-81 p19
++FF 7/8-81 p83
+-Gr 2-81 p1082
+HFN 1-81 p91
+-NR 5-81 p4
++SFC 4-12-81 p21
+-St 9-81 p92
+-ST 8-81 p275

Symphony, no. 5, B flat major. See no. 3791

1054 Symphony, no. 6, A major. Dresden Staatskapelle; Eugen Jochum. Angel SZ 37695 (also HMV ASD 4080)
++FF 11/12-81 p130
+Gr 10-81 p546
+HFN 12-81 p93
++NR 8-81 p5
+SFC 8-9-81 p18

1055 Symphony, no. 6, A major. CSO; Georg Solti. Decca SXL 6946 Tape (c) KSXC 6946 (also London CS 7173 Tape (c) CS 5-7173)
+ARG 1-81 p24
+-FF 1/2-81 p96
+-HFN 5-80 p118
++RR 6-80 p45

+Gr 5-80 p1659 ++SFC 8-17-80 p36
+-HF 6-81 p70 tape +St 12-80 p119
+-HF 12-80 p72

1056 Symphony, no. 6, A major. BPhO; Herbert von Karajan. DG 2531 295 Tape (c) 3301 295
-FF 5/6-81 p68 +HFN 12-80 p159 tape
+-Gr 11-80 p665 ++NR 4-81 p4
+-HF 6-81 p70 tape +SR 5-81 p96
+HFN 11-80 p116 +-ST 5-81 p47

1057 Symphony, no. 6, A major. BRSO; Eugen Jochum. DG 2535 415 Tape (c) 3335 415 (From SKL 929/39)
+Gr 3-81 p1186 +HFN 4-81 p94
+HFN 11-80 p131 tape

1058 Symphony, no. 6, A major. NPhO; Otto Klemeperer. HMV SXLP 30448 Tape (c) TC SXLP 30448 (From Columbia SAX 2582)
+Gr 3-81 p1186 +-HFN 3-81 p94

1059 Symphony, no. 7, E major. Dresden State Orchestra; Eugen Jochum. Angel SZB 3892 (2) (also HMV SLS 5194)
+ARG 2-81 p13 +HFN 4-81 p68
++Gr 3-81 p1186 +NR 10-80 p4
++HF 12-80 p74 +-St 12-80 p119

1060 Symphony, no. 7, E major. Dresden Staatskapelle; Herbert Blomstedt. Denon OB 7375/6 (2)
+FF 11/12-81 p130

1061 Symphony, no. 7, E major. Helgoland, op. 150. Psalm, no. 150. Ruth Welting, s; CSO and Chorus; Daniel Barenboim. DG 2707 116 (2)
+Audio 8-81 p65 +HFN 9-80 p100
+-FF 3/4-81 p95 +NYT 12-14-80 pD38
+-Gr 9-80 p332

1062 Symphony, no. 7, E major (ed. Haas). Cologne Radio Symphony Orchestra; Gunter Wand. Harmonia Mundi 153 99877/8 (2)
+-HFN 8-81 p83

1063 Symphony, no. 7, E major. Cincinnati Symphony Orchestra; Max Rudolf. Westminster MCA 1412 (From Decca DL 710 139)
-ARG 2-81 p13 -HF 12-80 p74
-FF 11/12-80 p90

Symphony, no. 7, E major. See no. 3781

1064 Symphony, no. 8, C minor. BPhO; Eugen Jochum. DG 2726 077 (2) Tape (c) 3372 077 (From SLPM 138918/9)
+FF 7/8-79 p42 +-MJ 7/8-79 p58
+Gr 1-78 p1255 +NYT 8-5-79 pD19
+HF 7-80 p82 +-RR 1-78 p42
+HFN 1-81 p109 tape ++SFC 4-29-79 p53

1065 Symphony, no. 8, C minor. Te deum, C major. Jessye Norman, s; Yvonne Minton, ms; David Rendall, t; Samuel Ramey, bs; CSO and Chorus; Daniel Barenboim. DG 2741 007 (2) Tape (c) 3382 007
+Gr 10-81 p542 +HFN 12-81 p112 tape
+HFN 11-81 p91

1066 Symphony, no. 8, C minor. Cologne Radio Orchestra; Gunter Wand. Harmonia Mundi 1C 153 99853/4 (2)
+-FF 9/10-80 p93 +-HFN 12-81 p93

Symphony, no. 8, C minor. See no. 693

Symphony, no. 8, C minor: Finale. See no. 3452

1067 Symphony, no. 9, D minor (original version). Munich Philharmonic

Orchestra; Sigmund von Hausegger. Past Masters PM 13
+ARG 9-78 p14 +FF 11/12-81 p336
+-FF 11/12-78 p40 -HF 9-79 p114

Te Deum, C major. See no. 1065

BRUHNS, Nicolaus

Toccata, G major. See no. 3720

BRULE, Gace

Biaus m'est estez. See no. 4086

BRUMEL, Anton

Cogitavit...Defecerunt. See no. 3909

1068 Songs: Ave ancilla trinitatis; Mater patris et filia; O domine Jesu Christe; Quae est ista; Sub tuum Praesidium. JOSQUIN DEPRES: Absalom fili mi; Alma redemptoris mater; Domine ne in furore. Harvard Glee Club; F. John Adams. Musical Heritage Society MHS 3558
+FF 9/10-81 p226

Songs: Noe noe; Tandernac. See no. 3777

BRUNA, Pablo

Tiento lleno por Cesolfami. See no. 3958

BRUYNEL, Ton

1069 Phases. Serene. Soft song. Toccare. Translucent II. Utrecht Symphony Orchestra; Huub Kerstens, Paul Hupperts; Frank van Koten, ob; Ton Bruynel, pno; Jorg Caryevschi, flt. Composers Voice VC 8003
+FF 7/8-81 p85

Serene, See no. 1069

Soft song. See no. 1069

Toccare. See no. 1069

Translucent II. See no. 1069

BUCHNER, Hans

Christ ist erstanden. See no. 3960

Sancta Maria won unss bey. See no. 3960

BUCHWIESER

Canzonettas: Cavatina, no. 2. See no. 3907

BUCK, Dudley

Fugue "Hail Columbia". See no. 3950

Grande sonata, op. 22, E flat major: Finale. See no. 3950

On the coast. See no. 3950

BULL, John

Dallying alman. See no. 1070

Duchess of Brunswick's toy. See no. 1070

Duke of Brunswick's alman. See no. 1070

Fantasia. See no. 3926

Fantastic pavan and galliard. See no. 1070

In nomine. See no. 3926. See no. 4092

Italian ground. See no. 1070

The king's hunt. See no. 1070. See no. 3734

Lord Lumley's pavan and galliard. See no. 1070. See no. 4090

My choice. See no. 1070

My grief. See no. 3734

My jewel. See no. 1070

My self. See no. 1070. See no. 3734

Prelude, alman, coranto "Joyeuse" and Coranto "A round". See no. 1070

Prelude and fantasia. See no. 4090

The prince's galliard. See no. 4090
Salve regina. See no. 3625
Ut re mi fa sol la. See no. 1070
Why ask you. See no. 1070

1070 Works, selections: Dallying alman. Duchess of Brunswick's toy. Duke of Brunswick's alman. Fantastic pavan and galliard. Italian ground. The king's hunt. Lord Lumley's pavan and galliard. My choice. My jewel. My self. Prelude, alman, coranto "Joyeuse" and Coranto "A round". Ut re mi fa sol la. Why ask you. John Payne, hpd. Musical Heritage Society MHS 4092
+FF 5/6-81 p70

BULL, Ole

1071 Adagio religioso. Concerto, violin, E minor: Adagio. Et Saeterbesog (Visit to a summer farm): In lonely moments. Fantasy and variations on a theme by Bellini. Nocturne. Polacca guerriera. Arve Tellefsen, vln; Bergen Symphony Orchestra; Karsten Andersen. Norsk Kulturrads NFK 30041
+-FF 7/8-81 p86 +HFN 8-81 p83
+Gr 8-81 p317

Concerto, violin, E minor: Adagio. See no. 1071
Et Saeterbesog (Visit to a summer farm): In lonely moments. See no. 1071
Fantasy and variations on a theme by Bellini. See no. 1071
Nocturne. See no. 1071
Polacca guerriera. See no. 1071

BULLER, John

1072 Proenca. Sarah Walker, ms; Timothy Walker, electric gtr; BBC Symphony Orchestra; Mark Elder. Unicorn UNS 266
++Gr 12-81 p917 +HFN 11-81 p91

BULLOCK, Ernest

Give us the wings of faith. See no. 3619

BUNGER, Richard

Mirrors, piano and tape recordist. See no. 3915

BURKHARD, Willy

Songs: Die VErkundigung Mariae, op. 51. See no. 3963

BURNEY, Charles

1073 The cunning man. Jennifer Paterson, s; David Ripley, bar; Charles Walker, t; Friends of Dr. Burney; Charlotte Kaufman. AFKA SK 285
+FF 3/4-81 p35

BUSATTI, Cherubino

Surrexit pastor bonus. See no. 3853

BUSNOIS, Antoine

Songs: Est il mercy de quoy l'on puest finer; J'ay moins de bien. See no. 3948
Spinacino: Je ne fay plus. See no. 3945

BUSONI, Ferruccio

1074 Concerto, piano, op. 39. Elegie, no. 4. Sonatina, no. 6. Variations on a Chopin prelude, op. 22. John Ogdon, pno; RPO and Chorus; Daniel Revenaugh. HMV SXDW 3053 (2) Tape (c) TC 2-SXDW 3053 (From ASD 2336/7, 434)
+Gr 8-81 p267 +HFN 8-81 p91

Elegie, no. 4. See no. 1074
Elegie: Turandot's Frauengemach. See no. 589

Overture to a comedy. See no. 80

1075 Sonatina, no. 6. SZYMANOWSKI: Variations on a Polish folk tune, op. 10. TOCH: Burlesken, op. 31. WEBER: Aufforderung zum Tanz, op. 65. Evelinde Trenkner, pno. Orion ORS 80382
+-CL 2-81 p13 +NR 11-80 p10
+-FF 5/6-81 p204

Sonatina, no. 6. See no. 1074

Variations on a Chopin prelude, op. 22. See no. 1074

BUSTAMANTE, F.

1076 Misionera (arr.). MOREL: Danza. Malambo. MORES: Danza brasilera. Milonga. ZALDIVAR: Carnavalito. Jorge Morel, gtr. GMR 1002
++GTR Fall 1981 p27

BUTTERWORTH, George

The banks of green willow: Idyll. See no. 467

English idylls, nos. 1, 2. See no. 3856

1077 Love blows as the wind blows. ELGAR: Pleading op. 48, no. 1. Song cycle, op. 59. Songs, op. 60. VAUGHAN WILLIAMS: On Wenlock edge (orch. composer). Robert tear, t; Birmingham Symphony Orchestra; Vernon Handley. HMV ASD 3896 Tape (c) TC ASD 3896
+FF 1/2-81 p202 +HFN 11-80 p123
+Gr 9-80 p380 +HFN 12-80 p159 tape
+Gr 1-81 p1001 tape +-MT 6-81 p392

A Shropshire lad. See no. 467

A Shropshire lad: Loveliest of trees; When I was one and twenty; Look not in my eyes; Think no more lad; The lads in their hundreds; Is my team ploughing. See no. 3893

A Shropshire lad: Songs. See no. 4057

BUXTEHUDE, Dietrich

1078 Cantatas: Ich sprach in meinem Herzen; O clemens o mitis O coelestis pater; O Gottes stadt. La capricciosa. Prelude and fugue, no. 15, F major. Trio sonata, op. 2, no. 4, C minor. Gabor Lehotka, org; Peter Komlos, vln; Geza Nemeth, vla; Janos Sebestyen, hpd.; Margit Laszlo, s; Liszt Ferenc Chamber Orchestra; Frigyes Sandor. Budapest FX 12296
+FF 11/12-81 p132 ++HFN 5-81 p79

1079 Cantatas: Herr ich lasse dich nicht; Ich suchte des Nachts; Mein Herz ist bereit; O Gottes Stadt. Helen Donath, s; Theo Altmeyer, t; Jakob Stampfli, bs; Stuttgart Bach Collegium; Helmuth Rilling. Cantate 658 214
+-Gr 1-81 p972 +-HFN 10-80 p102

1080 Cantatas: Hertlich lieb hab ich Dich, o Herr; Jesu meine Freude; Wachet auf, ruft uns die Stimme. Herrad Wehrung, Gundula Bernat-Klein, s; Frauke Haasemann, con; Friedreich Melzer, c-t; Johannes Hoefflin, t; Wilhelm Pommerien, bs; Westphalian Choral Ensemble; South West German Chamber Orchestra; Wilhelm Ehmann. Nonesuch H 71332 (also Cantate 658219)
+ARG 3-77 p34 +NR 4-77 p7
+-HF 4-77 p97 +HFN 1-81 p92
+-St 3-77 p127

Canzonas, G major, D minor. See no. 1084

1081 Canzonettas, G major, E minor. Chorales: Gelobet seist du Jesu Christ; Gott der Vater wohn uns bei; Komm Heiliger Geist Herre Gott; Vater unser in Himmelreich. Preludes, C major, G minor, E minor. Prelude, fugue and chaconne, F major. Toccata, F

major. Verset on the chorale "Vater unser im Himmelreich". Bernard Lagace, org. Calliope CAL 1731 Tape (c) CAL 4731
+Gr 8-80 p241 +MT 3-81 p195
Canzonettas, G minor, E minor, G major, C major. See no. 1084
La capricciosa. See no. 1078
Chaconnes, E major, C minor. See no. 1084
Choral fantasias: Gelobet seist du Jesu Christ; Wie schon leuchtet der Morgenstern. See no. 1084
1082 Choral partita, Ach Gott und Herr. Magnificat primi tono. Chorale prelude, Nun bitten wir den Heilgen Gott. Prelude and fugue, no. 20, D minor: Toccata. MENDELSSOHN: Sonata, organ, op. 65, no. 2, C minor. BAUSZNERN: Veni creator spiritus. Gunter Maurischat, org. Pape 5
+NR 2-81 p13
Choral partita, Auf meinen lieben Gott. See no. 1084
Chorale preludes: Ach Gott und Herr; Ach Herr mich armen sunder; Christ unser Herr zum Jordan kam; Daniet dem Herrn; Der Tag der ist so freudenreich; Durch Adams Fall ist ganz verderbt; Ein feste Burg ist unser Gott; Erhalt uns Herr bei deinem Wort; Es spricht der Unweisen Mund; Est ist das Heil uns kommen her; Gelobet seist du Jesu Christ; Gott der Vater wohn uns bei; Herr Christ der einig Gottes Sohn; Herr Jesu Christ ich weiss gar wohl; Ich dank dir lieber Herre; Ich dank dir schon durch deinen Sohn; Ich ruf zu dir; In dulci jubilo; Jesus Christus unser Heiland; Komm heiliger Geist Herre Gott; Kommt her zu mir spricht Gottes Sohn; Lobt Gott ihr Christen allzugleich; Mensch willt du leben seliglich; Mit Fried und Freud fahr ich dahin; Nimm von uns; Nimm von uns Herr du treuer Gott; Nun bitten wir den heil'gen Geist; Nun freut euch lieben Christen g'mein; Nun komm der einig Gottes Sohn; Nun komm der Heiden Heiland; Nun lob mein Seel den Herren; Puer natus in Bethlehem; Vater unser im Himmelreich; Von Gott will ich nicht lassen; War Gott nicht mit uns diese Zeit; Wir danken dir Herr Jesu Christ. See no. 1084
Chorale preludes; Gelobet seist du Jesu Christ; Gott der Vater wohn uns bei; Komm Heiliger Geist Herre Gott; Vater unser im Himmelreich. See no. 1081
Chorale preludes: Nun bitten wir den heiligen Gott. See no. 1082
1083 Chorale preludes, Nun komm der Heiden Heiland. Fugue, C major. Magnificat primi toni. Prelude and fugue, G minor. Prelude, fugue and chaconne, C major. JACKSON: Archbishop's fanfare. Fanfare, organ. Pagaent. Diversion for mixtures. Toccata, B minor. Toccata prelude, Wachet auf. Graham Matthews, org. Vista VPS 1087
+Gr 12-81 p898
Erschienen ist der herrlich Tag. See no. 3905
Fugue, C major. See no. 1083
Fugues, C major, B flat major. See no. 1084
Jubilate domino. See no. 124
Magnificat. See no. 3921
Magnificat primi toni. See no. 1082. See no. 1083. See no. 1084
Mensch wilt du leben seliglich. See no. 3720
Muss der Tod denn nun doch trennen, aria. See no. 124
1084 Organ works: Canzonas, G major (3), D minor. Canzonettas, E minor, G minor, G major, C major. Chaconnes, C minor, E minor. Chor-

al fantasias: Gelobet seist du Jesu Christ; Wie schon leuchtet der Morgenstern. Choral partita, Auf meinen lieben Gott. Chorale preludes: Acht Gott und Herr; Ach Herr mich armen sunder; Christ unser Herr zum Jordan kam; Daniet dem Herrn; Der Tag der ist so freudenreich; Durch Adams Fall ist ganz verderbt; Ein feste Burg ist unser Gott; Erhalt uns Herr bei deinem Wort; Es spricht der Unweisen Mund; Est ist das Heil uns kommen her; Gelobet seist du Jesu Christ; Gott der Vater wohn uns bei; Herr Christ der einig Gottes Sohn; Herr Jesu Christ ich weiss gar wohl; Ich dank dir lieber Herre; Ich dank dir schon durch deinen Sohn; Ich ruf zu dir; In dulci jubilo; Jesus Christus unser Heiland; Komm heiliger Geist Herre Gott (2); Kommt her zu mir spricht Gottes Sohn; Lobt Gott ihr Christen allzugleich; Mensch willt du leben seliglich; Mit Fried und Freud fahr ich dahin; Nimm von uns; Nimm von uns Herr du treuer Gott; Nun bitten wir den heil'gen Geist (2); Nun freut euch lieben Christen g'mein; Nun komm der einig Gottes Sohn; Nun komm der Heiden Heiland; Nun lob mein Seel den Herren; Puer natus in Bethelehem; Vater unser im Himmelreich; Von Gott will ich nicht lassen (2); War Gott nicht mit uns diese Zeit; Wir danken dir Herr Jesu Christ. Fugues, C major, B flat major. Magnificat primi toni (3). Passacaglia, D minor. Preludes and fugues (19). Prelude, fugue and chaconne, C major. Te deum laudamus. Toccatas and fugues, D minor, F major (2). Lionel Rogg, org. EMI 1C 137 16351/8 (8)
+Gr 12-81 p898

Passacaglia, D minor. See no. 1084
Prelude, A minor. See no. 3812
Preludes, C major, G minor, E minor. See no. 1081
Preludes and fugues (19). See no. 1084
Prelude and fugue, G minor. See no. 1083
Prelude and fugue, G minor. See no. 3992
Prelude and fugue, no. 15, F major. See no. 1078
Prelude and fugue, op. 20, D minor: Toccata. See no. 1082
Prelude and fugue, no. 21, G minor. See no. 249
Prelude and fugue, no. 22, G minor. See no. 4087
Prelude, fugue and chaconne, C major. See no. 1083. See no. 1084
Prelude, fugue and chaconne, F major. See no. 1081
Prelude on "Ach wir armen Sunder". See no. 4117
Sonatas, op. 1, nos. 2-4. See no. 3783
Sonata, op. 1, no. 5, C major. See no. 3833
Suite, E minor. See no. 312
Te deum laudamus. See no. 1084
Toccata, D major. See no. 3720
Toccata, F major. See no. 1081
Toccata and fugue, F major. See no. 3673
Toccatas and fugues, F major, D minor. See no. 1084
Trio sonata, op. 2, no. 4, C minor. See no. 1078
Verset on chorale "Vater unser im Himmelreich". See no. 1081
Wie schon leuchtet der Morgenstern. See no. 4088

BUZZI-PECCIA, Arturo
Lolita. See no. 3967. See no. 3995. See no. 4046
El morenito. See no. 4083

BYRD, William
Ave verum corpus. See no. 4061

The battel. See no. 3663
The bells. See no. 3732
Carmans whistle. See no. 3734
Cogitavit dominus. See no. 3909
Coranto. See no. 3926
Exalt thyself O God, anthem. See no. 42
Fantasia, C major. See no. 3625
Galliard. See no. 3926
Laudibus in sanctis. See no. 3621
Lord Willoughby's welcome home. See no. 3734

1085 Mass, 4 voices. Mass, 5 voices. Christ Church Cathedral Choir; Simon Preston. Argo ZRG 858 Tape (c) KZRC 858
+-Gr 4-77 p1582 +-MT 10-77 p825
+Gr 12-81 p944 tape +NR 8-77 p8
+-HF 11-77 p138 tape +RR 3-77 p89
+HFN 3-77 p101 ++RR 5-77 p90 tape
++HFN 5-77 p138 tape +RR 1-78 p84 tape

Mass, 5 voices. See no. 1085

1086 Motets: Gaudeamus omnes; Beati mundo corde; Iustorum animae; Non vos relinquam orphanos; Beata es Virgo Maria; Visita quaesumus Domine; Salve sancta parens; Confirma hoc Deus; Senex puerum portabat; Tribulationes civitatum. William Byrd Choir; Gavin Turner. Philips 9502 030
++ARG 6-81 p20 +-HFN 4-81 p68
++FF 3/4-81 096 +NR 1-81 p7
+-Gr 7-81 p180 ++STL 5-10-81 p41
++HF 5-81 p55

1087 My Lady Nevells booke: The fourth pavan and galliard; Qui passe; The battell; Sellinger's round; Monsieur's alman; Hugh Ashton's ground; A galliard's gigge; The second ground; The fifth pavan and galliard; The carman's whistle; A voluntary. Christopher Hogwood, virginals, hpd, org. L'Oiseau-Lyre DSLO 566
+FF 3/4-81 p97 ++MT 4-81 p245
++HFN 5-80 p118 +RR 5-80 p84

Non vos relinquam orphanos. See no. 3636
Pavan. See no. 3926
Psallite domino. See no. 4061
The queenes alman. See no. 3732

1088 Songs: Aspice domine; Attollite portas; Emendemus in melius; Libera me; Laudate pueri; Memento homo; O lux beata trinitas; Peccantem me quotidie; Siderum rector. Deller Consort; Mark Deller. Harmonia Mundi HM 1053
+Gr 7-81 p180 +HFN 5-81 p79

Songs: Come woeful Orpheus. See no. 4085
Songs: From virgin's womb this day did spring; Laudibus in sanctis. See no. 3616
Songs: Justorum animae. See no. 3632
Songs: Laetentur coeli; Lullaby, my sweet little baby. See no. 3685
Songs: Sacerdotes domini. See no. 3634. See no. 3822
Songs: Sing joyfully unto God. See no. 3620. See no. 4107
La volta. See no. 3807
Watkin's ale. See no. 3734
The woods so wild. See no. 3883

CABANILLES, Juan
Batalla imperial. See no. 4098
Batalla imperial del 5th tono. See no. 3958
CABEZON, Antonio de
Ave maris stella. See no. 3676
Ay joly bois. See no. 1090
Ayme que vouldra. See no. 1090
1089 Coleccion de la musica antiqua espanola, vols. 24-31, obras completas. Antonio Baciero, keyboard. Sra. Halte, Union Musical Espanola, Carrera San Jeronima 26, Madrid, 14
+MU 3-81 p10
Diferencias sobre el canto de La dama le demanda. See no. 1090
Diferencias sobre el canto Llano del caballero. See no. 3778. See no. 4094
Diferencias sobre la Gallarda milanesa. See no. 1090. See no. 3778
Fabordones. See no. 1090
Magnificat: Versos. See no. 1090
Pavana con su glosa. See no. 3778
Pavana italiana. See no. 1090. See no. 3778
Songs: Un gay bergier; Pour un plaisir. See no. 3835
Susanne en jour. See no. 1090
Tientos, nos. 2 and 3. See no. 1090
Tiento de 1 quinto tono. See no. 4098
Ultimi miei sospiri. See no. 1090
Versos in 7 ton. See no. 1090
1090 Works, selections: Ay joly bois. Ayme que vouldra. Diferencias sobre el canto de La dama le demanda. Diferencias sobre el Gallarda milanesa. Fabordones. Pavana italiana. Susanne en jour. Tientos, nos. 2 and 3. Ultimi miei sospiri. Versos in 7 ton. Magnificat: Versos. Gertrud Mersiovsky, org. Harmonia Mundi 065 99678
+-HFN 1-81 p105 +-RR 7-80 p77
+MT 3-81 p196
CACCINI, Francesca
La liberazione di Ruggiero dall'Isola d'Alcina, excerpts. See no. 3814
CACCINI, Giulio
Songs: Amarilli mia bella; Dovro dunque morire. See no. 3946
Songs: Amarilli mia bella. See no. 3692
Songs: Nell amoroso ciel dei vostro volto. See no. 3630
CADMAN, Charles
At dawning, op. 29, no. 1. See no. 4033
From the land of the sky blue water. See no. 4076
A mad empress remembers. See no. 1495
CAGE, John
Bacchanal. See no. 3915
Waltzes for the five boroughs (49). See no. 3942
CAHN, Bill
The birds. See no. 3931
CAJKOVSKIJ
Panna Orleanska: Prasite vy chalmy palja radnyje. See no. 4080
CALACE, Raffaele
Prelude, no. 2, op. 49. See no. 3872

CALDARA, Antonio
1091 Vicino a un rivoletto. HANDEL: Mi palpita il cor. PORPORA: Or che una nube ingrata. Rene Jacobs, c-t; Sigiswald Kuijken, vln; Anner Bylsma, vlc; Barthold Kuijken, flt; Gustav Leonhardt, hpd. ABC AY 67029 (also RCA RL 3-0417)
+-FF 11/12-78 p135 +-NR 2-79 p12
+-Gr 11-81 p747
CALESTANI, Vincenzo
Songs: Damigella tutta bella. See no. 3692
CALLAHAN, Charles
Aria. See no. 3806
CALVERT
Challenge. See no. 3955
CALVERT, Morley
Introduction, elegy and caprice. See no. 3716
Suite from the Monteregian Hills. See no. 3671
CALVI, Carlo
La bertazzina. See no. 3938
CAMIDGE, Matthew
Gavotte, G minor. See no. 3627
CAMILLERI, Charles
1092 The flower and the wind. Noospheres. Stone island within. Christine Barker, s; Kyla Crowcroft, pno; Judith Hall, flt; Lesley Shrigley-Jones, vlc; Gregory Knowles, per. Bedivere BVR 303
+HFN 9-81 p79
Noospheres. See no. 1092
Stone island within. See no. 1092
CAMPBELL, Sidney
Sing we merrily unto God. See no. 3633
CAMPIAN, Thomas
Songs: If thou long'st so much to learn; Shall I come sweet love. See no. 3871
Songs: Move now; Now hath Flora; Woo her. See no. 3876
Songs: Never weather-beaten sail; Jack and Jone; A secret love. See no. 4085
Songs: L'ultima speme. See no. 3758
CAMPRA, Andre
1093 Requiem mass. Judith Nelson, Dinah Harris, s; Jean-Claude Orliac, Wynford Evans, t; Stephen Roberts, bs; Monteverdi Choir; English Baroque Soloists; John Eliot Gardiner. Erato STU 71310 Tape (c) MCE 71310
+Gr 10-80 p524 +-HFN 12-80 p135
++Gr 12-81 p945 tape
1094 Tancrede, excerpts. Catherine Dussaut, s; Jacques Bona, t; Armand Arapian, bar; Provence Instrumental Ensemble; Clement Zaffini. Pierre Verany PV 1811
-FF 9/10-81 p93
CANNABICH, Christian
Sinfonia, B flat major. See no. 3782
Sinfonia concertante, C major. See no. 3782
CANONICO
Aire de Joropa. See no. 4108
CANTELOUBE, Joseph
1095 Songs from the Auvergne, excerpts. Folk songs: Fare thee well;

Gentle Johnny my jingalo; Sweet Betty from Pike; Turtle dove; Next market day; The riddle song; The zebra dun; My lagan love; Molly Malone. Susan Reed, s; Chamber Group. CBS 61359 Tape (c) 40-61359

+HFN 9-81 p93 tape +STL 9-13-81 p41

Songs from the Auvergne: Bailero. See no. 3642

CAPIROLA, Vincenzo

Balletto. See no. 3661

Padoana. See no. 3661

CAPLET, Andre

Ecoute. See no. 3953

1096 Epiphanie. LALO: Concerto, violoncello, D minor. Frederic Lodeon, vlc; PhO; Charles Dutoit. Erato STU 71368

+Gr 3-81 p1192 +-MUM 3/4-81 p32

Un tas de petites choses. See no. 3665

CAPUA, Eduardo de

Songs: I te vurria vasa. See no. 3718

Songs: Mari Mari. See no. 4045

Songs: Mari Mari; I te vurria vasa; O sole mio. See no. 3641

Songs: O sole mio. See no. 3839. See no. 4032

CARA, Marchetto

Per fuggir d'amor le punte. See no. 3661

Poiche in van. See no. 3661

CARDILLO

Core 'ngrato. See no. 3641. See no. 3838. See no. 3839. See no. 3997

CAREY

Sally in the alley. See no. 3972

CARISSIMI, Giacomo

Beatus vir. See no. 3637

1097 Cantatas: Amor mio che cosa e questo; Deh memoria; In un mar di pensieri; Lamento della Maria Stuarda; Suonera l'ultimo tromba. Elisabeth Speiser, s; Hans Ludwig Hirsch, hpd and org. Jecklin 5004

+-FF 3/4-81 p97

1098 Cantatas: Amor mio che cosa e questo; Apritevi inferni; Bel tempo per me se n'ando; Deh memoria; In un mar di pensieri; No no mio core; Suonera l'ultima tromba; V'intendo v'intendo occhi. Martyn Hill, t; Trevor Jones, vla da gamba; Robert Spencer, lt; Christopher Hogwood, hpd, org. L'Oiseau-Lyre DSLO 547

+FF 1/2-81 p97 +MT 8-80 p504
+Gr 9-79 p495 +RR 9-79 p116
+HFN 9-79 p105 ++St 5-81 p72

CARLETON, Nicholas

Praeludium. See no. 3676

CAROLS FOR BRASS. See no. 3922

CARON, Philippe

Cent mille escus. See no. 3948

CAROSO, Fabricio

Canario. See no. 4097

Gagliarda. See no. 4097

Nido d'amore. See no. 4097

Rotto. See no. 4097

Spagnoletta nuovo al modo di madrigalia. See no. 4097

CARR, Richard
1099 Division upon an Italian ground. PARCHAM: Solo, G major. PEPUSCH: Sonata, recorder, no. 4, F major. VAN EYCK: Doen Daphne. Engels Nachtegaeltje. Pavane lachrymae. Frans Bruggen, rec; Nikolaus Harnoncourt, vla da gamba; Anner Bylsma, vlc; Gustav Leonhardt, hpd. Telefunken 6-42050 Tape (c) 4-42050
-FF 1/2-80 p170 +Gr 10-81 p579
CARTER, Andrew
Songs: A maiden most gentle. See no. 3634
CARTER, Elliott
Elegy. See no. 377
1100 A mirror on which to dwell. Symphony of three orchestras. Speculum Musicae, NYP; Pierre Boulez. Columbia M 35171 Tape (c) MT 35171
++ARG 3-81 p24 +-NR 1-81 p1
+FF 1/2-81 p98 +NYT 9-28-80 pD31
+HF 8-81 p55 +St 4-80 p103
+-MUM 9/10-81 p31
1101 Quintet, woodwinds. CHERNEY: Notturno. HEIDEN: Sinfonia, woodwind quintet. REA: Reception and offering music. York Winds; Tom Plaunt, pno; Russell Hartenberger, perc. Melbourne SMLP 4040
+-MUM 3/4-81 p31
Symphony of three orchestras. See no. 1100
CASALS, Pablo
O vos omnes. See no. 3660
CASANOVAS, Narciso
Sonata, organ, no. 5. See no. 4088
CASANOVES
Songs: Amicus meus; Caligaverunt; Tenebrae factae sunt. See no. 2155
CASSADO, Gaspar
1102 Suite, solo violoncello. CHOPIN: Sonata, violoncello and piano, op. 65, G minor. SCHUBERT: Sonatina, violin and piano, no. 1, op. 137, D 384, D major. Janos Starker, vlc; Shigeo Neriki, pno. Denon OX 7171
+Audio 9-81 p82 +FF 9/10-80 p94
CASTELLO, Dario
Sonata. See no. 3937
1103 Sonate concertate in stil moderno, 1st libro: Sonata sesta a 2. Sonate concertate in stil moderno, 2nd libro: Sonata decima terza a 4; Sonata decima quarta a 4. MARINI: Affetti musicali, op. 1: Sinfonia a 2; Sinfonia La Orlandina; Corente a 3; Brando a 2; Aria a 3. Sonate, op. 8: Sonata seconda a 2; Sonata terza per sonar variato. PICCHI: Canzoni, nos. 3, 12. Toccata. SELMA Y SALAVERDE: Canzona a due 11. Festiva i colli passaggiato a 2. Concerto Castello Ensemble. Harmonia Mundi 1C 065 99917
+Gr 11-81 p719 +FF 11/12-81 p221
Sonate concertate in stil moderno, 2nd libro: Sonata decima terza a 4; Sonata decima quarta a 4. See no. 1103
CASTELNUOVO-TEDESCO, Mario
1104 Alghe. Alt Wien. Piedigrotta. La sirenette e il pesce turchino. Michael McFrederick, pno. Orion ORS 80370
+ARG 3-81 p25 +FF 9/10-80 p97

-CL 3-81 p13 +NR 10-80 p14
Alt Wien. See no. 1104
1105 Concerto, guitar, op. 99, D major. RODRIGO: Concierto de Aranjuez. Siegfried Behrend, gtr; BPhO; Reinhard Peters. Contour CC 7510 Tape (c) CCT 7510
++Gr 8-81 p316 +-HFN 8-81 p91
Concerto, guitar, op. 99, D major. See no. 3712
Piedigrotta. See no. 1104
La sirenette e il pesce turchino. See no. 1104
CASTEREDE, Jacques
Sonatine. See no. 3742
CATALANI, Alfredo
Loreley: Da che tutta. See no. 4041
Loreley: Nel verde maggio. See no. 4045
La Wally: Ebben ne andro lontana. See no. 3711. See no. 4041
La Wally: T'amo ben mio. See no. 4034
CATS, Jacob
Cadence 1. See no. 3728
CAVALLI, Francesco
Canzon a 3. See no. 3808
1106 Egisto. Lilian Sukis, Hildegard Heichele, s; Trudeliese Schmidt, ms; Rudiger Wohlers, Heiner Hopfner, t; Kehko Kawata, alto; Nikolaus Hillebrand, bs; Bavarian State Orchestra Chamber Ensemble; Hans Ludwig Hirsch. Eurodisc 87 120 (2)
+-HF 12-74 p102 +-HFN 12-81 p93
1107 Ercole amante. Colette Alliot-Lugaz, Marilyn Hill-Smith, Yvonne Minton, ms; Ulrik Cold, John Tomlinson, bs; English Bach Festival Orchestra; Michel Corboz. Erato STU 71328 (3)
+/Gr 10-80 p533 +STL 11-9-80 p40
+HFN 1-81 p92 +STL 12-14-80 p38
+MT 4-81 p245
CAVENDISH, Michael
Songs: Come gentle swains. See no. 3876
CELEBRATION OF THE FEAST OF ST. IVAN OF RILA. See no. 3773
CELIBIDACHE, Sergiu
1108 Der Taschengarten (The pocket garden). Stuttgart Radio Orchestra; Sergiu Celibidache. Intercord INT 160 832
*FF 3/4-81 p98 +HFN 12-81 p94
+HF 5-81 p55
CELLI, Joseph
1109 S for J. Sky. GOLDSTEIN: A summoning of focus. SCHWARTZ: Extended oboe. STOCKHAUSEN: Spiral. Joseph Celli, ob; Various electronics. Organic Oboe Records 1
+-ARG 2-80 p52 +FF 9/10-81 p266
Sky. See no. 1109
CELLIER, Alexandre
1110 Theme and variations on Psalm, no. 149. HOLMBOE: Triade, op. 123. WERNER: Duo, op. 53. WEINER: Fantasy, no. 1, op. 57. Edward Tarr, tpt; Elizabeth Westenholz, org. BIS LP 151
+FF 5/6-81 p212 +HFN 1-81 p107
+HF 3-81 p77
CEREROLS, Juan
1111 Vesperae beatae mariae virginis. Montserrat Escolania and Capella; Ars Musicae of Barcelona; Ireneu Segarra. Schwann Musica Sacra AMS 3526
+FF 5/6-81 p70

CERNOHORSKY, Bohuslav
Fuga moderato. See no. 3826
Fugue, C minor. See no. 3962
CERTON, Pierre
La la la je ne l'oise dire. See no. 4114
CHABRIER, Emmanuel
Cortege burlesque. See no. 3665
1112 Espana. FALLA: El sombrero de tres picos: Introduction; Dance of the miller's wife; Corregidor; Miller's wife; The grapes; The neighbours; Miller's dance; Final dance. RIMSKY-KORSAKOV: Capriccio espagnol, op. 34. LAPO; Jesus Lopez-Cobos. Decca SXL 6956 Tape (c) KSXC 6956
+-Gr 3-81 p1192 +-HFN 3-81 p94
1113 Espana. DEBUSSY: Prelude a l'apres-midi d'un faune. IBERT: Escales. RAVEL: La valse. Tokyo Metropolitan Orchestra; Jean Fournet. Denon OX 7213
+FF 11/12-81 p296
1114 Espana. FALLA: El sombrero de tres picos: Suites, nos. 1 and 2. RAVEL: Rapsodie espagnole. PO; Riccardo Muti. HMV ASD 3902 Tape (c) TC ASD 3902 (also Angel DS 37742 Tape (c) 4ZS 37742)
+-FF 3/4-81 p234 +-HFN 5-81 p85
++Gr 12-80 p831 ++NR 3-81 p4
+-HFN 3-81 p93 +ST 6-81 p122
+-HFN 4-81 p81 tape
1115 Espana. DUKAS: The sorcerer's apprentice. DEBUSSY: Nocturnes: Fetes. Prelude to the afternoon of a faun. PH; Zoltan Rozsnyai. M & K RT 202 Tape (c) EC 7012
+ARG 5-80 p45 +-HF 8-81 p69 tape
/FF 9/10-80 p38
Espana. See no. 21. See no. 752
Espana: Rhapsody. See no. 4121
1116 Gwendoline. Ana Maria Miranda, Claude Meloni, Peyo Garazzi, Bernard Angot, Jose Etchebarne, soloists; Radio France Choeurs; Orchestre National de France; Henri Gallois. MRF Records MRF 150-5 (2)
++FF 1/2-81 p99
Souvenirs de Munich. See no. 3665
CHAMBONNIERES, Jacques
Chaconne, F major. See no. 3916
Pieces de clavecin. See no. 58
Rondeau. See no. 3916
CHAMINADE, Cecile
1117 Arabesque, op. 61, G minor. Etudes, op. 35, nos. 1-3, 5-6. Piece in the old style, op. 74, E minor. Sonata, piano, no. 21, C minor. Songs without words, op. 76, nos. 3, 5. Danielle Laval, pno. EMI Pathe Marconi 2C 069 16410
+FF 5/6-81 p71
Caprice espagnole. See no. 3814
1118 Concertino, flute, op. 107. FAURE: Fantaisie, flute (orch. Galway). IBERT: Concerto, flute. POULENC: Concerto, flute (orch. Berkeley). James Galway, flt; RPO; Charles Dutoit. RCA RL 2-5109 Tape (c) RK 2-5109 (also RCA ARL 1-3777 Tape (c) ARK 1-3777)
++FF 3/4-81 p231 +MT 9-78 p770
+Gr 10-77 p648 ++NR 1-81 p2

++Gr 1-78 p1302 tape +RR 10-77 p47
+HFN 2-78 p109 +RR 8-78 p102 tape
+HFN 5-78 p147 tape ++St 4-81 p108

Concertstuck, piano, op. 40. See no. 61
Etudes, op. 35, nos. 1-3, 5-6. See no. 1117
Piece in the old style, op. 74, E minor. see no. 1117

1119 Sonata, piano, op. 21, C minor. GAINSBORG: Lullaby. MARTINEZ: Sonata, piano, A major. SCHUMANN, C.: Impromptu. Piece fugitive, op. 15, no. 1. Prelude and fugue, op. 16. Scherzo, op. 14, C minor. Nancy Fierro, pno. Pelican LP 2017
+FF 9/10-81 p235

Sonata, piano, op. 21, C minor. See no. 1117
Songs: Berceuse. See no. 3758
Songs: The little silver ring. See no. 3967. See no. 4043
Songs without words, op. 76, nos. 3, 5. See no. 1117

CHAN HAO HO, KANG CHEN
Concerto, violin. See no. 3857

CHAN PUI FAN
Cantonese scenes. See no. 3861
CHANTS A LA VIERGE. See no. 3825

CHAPI Y LORENTE, Ruperto
La chavala: Cancion de la gitana. See no. 3642
Las hijas del Zebedeo: Carceleras. See no. 3642
El milagro de la virgin: Flores purisimas. See no. 4036
La patria chica: Cancion de pastora. See no. 3642
Serenata morisca. See no. 3886

CHARPENTIER, Gustave
Louise: Depuis le jour. See no. 3604. See no. 3713. See no. 3844. See no. 4038

CHARPENTIER, Marc-Antoine
Carols (3). See no. 1122

1120 David et Jonathas. Colette Alliot-Lugaz, s; Paul Esswood, Rene Jacobs, alto; Antoine David, t; Philippe Huttenlocher, bar; Roger Soyer, bs; Lyons Opera Chorus Members; English Bach Festival Orchestra; Michel Corboz. Erato STU 71435 (3)
+Gr 10-81 p598 +HFN 12-81 p94

Dialogus inter Christum et peccatores. See no. 1127

1121 In nativitatem Domini: Nuit. Salve regina. Seniores populi. Te deum, D major. Tenebrae factae sunt. Elsa Saque, Joana Silva, s; John Williams, c-t; Fernando Serafim, t; Philippe Huttenlocher, bar; Jose Oliveira Lopes, bs; Antoine Silbertin-Blanc, org; Gulbenkian Foundation Orchestra and Chorus; Michel Corboz. Erato STU 71002 (also Musical Heritage Society MHS 3986)
+FF 7/8-79 p43 +MU 6-81 p14
+HF 3-79 p92

1122 Magnificat. Te deum. Carols (3). Pro Cantione Antiqua Soloists; Collegiate Church of St. Mary Choir; La Grande Ecurie et la Chambre de Roy; Jean-Claude Malgoire. CBS 76891
+-Gr 1-81 p972 +RR 6-80 p83
+HFN 6-80 p106 ++STL 5-11-80 p39

1123 Magnificat. Pastorale sur la naissance de notre Seigneur Jesus Christ. Les Arts Florissants Vocal and Instrumental Ensemble; William Christie. Harmonia Mundi HM 1082 Tape (c) HM 40-1082
++Gr 12-81 p917 +STL 11-8-81 p40
+HFN 12-81 p94

1124 Messe de minuit. Martha Angelici, Edith Selig, s; Andre Meurant, c-t; Jean-Jacques Lesueur, t; Georges Abdoun, bs; Anne-Marie Beckensteiner, Maurice Durufle, org; Chorale des Jeunesses Musicales de France; Jean-Francois Paillard Orchestra; Louis Martini. Erato STU 70083 (also Musical Heritage Society MHS 532)
+MU 9-81 p14 ++St 7-78 p90

1125 Messe de minuet. Sonata a 6. Boston Camerata; Joel Cohen. Telefunken 6-42630
+STL 12-13-81 p39

1126 Messe de morts, G minor, D minor. Bernadette Degelin, Anne Verkinderen, s; David James, c-t; Jan Caals, t; Kurt Widmer, bs; Westvlaams Vocal Ensemble; Musica Polyphonica; Louis Devos. Musical Heritage Society MHS 4350
+FF 7/8-81 p88

1127 Missa Assumpta est Maria. Dialogus inter Christum et peccatores. English Bach Festival Soloists; Orchestra and Chorus. Erato STU 71281
+Gr 1-81 p977 +HFN 12-80 p135

Pastorale sur la naissance de notre Seigneur Jesus Christ. See no. 1123
Salve regina. See no. 1121
Seniores populi. See no. 1121
Sonata a 6. See no. 1125
Te deum. See no. 1122
Te deum, D major. See no. 1121
Tenebrae factae sunt. See no. 1121

CHATMAN, Stephen

1128 Hesitation. On the contrary. HUDSON: Fantasy/refrain. MORGAN: Trio, flute, violoncello and harpsichord. Robert Onofrey, clt; John Loban, Linda Quan, vln; Maura Chatman, celeste; Carole Morgan, flt; Barbara Haffner, Andre Emelianoff, vlc; Lambert Orkis, hpd; John Graham, vla; Eastman Musica Nova; Sydney Hodkinson. CRI SD 414
+ARG 2-81 p46 +-HF 10-80 p72
+FF 9/10-81 p297 ++NR 10-80 p6

On the contrary. See no. 1128
Whisper baby. See no. 464

CHAUMONT, Lambert

Suite sur 13 2nd ton. See no. 92

CHAUSSON, Ernest

1129 Concerto, violin and piano, op. 21. FAURE: Dolly suite, op. 56: Berceuse. Alfred Cortot, pno; Jacques Thibaud, vlc; Ensemble. EMI 2C 051 03719
+Gr 7-81 p192

1130 Poeme, op. 25, E major. PAGANINI: Cantabile, op. 17, D major. Caprices, op. 1, nos. 1-3, 5, 9, 11, 17, 20, 24 (arr. Schumann). Concerto, violin, no. 2, op. 7, B minor: La campanella (arr. Kreisler). Moses, op. 24. Perpetual motion, op. 11. RAVEL: Tzigane. SAINT-SAENS: Havanaise, op. 83. Introduction and rondo capriccioso, op. 28. Igor Oistrakh, vln; Natalia Zertsalova, pno; MRSO; Gennady Roszhdestvensky. Musical Heritage Society MHS 824311 (2)
+FF 9/10-81 p259

1131 Poeme, op. 25, E major. MILHAUD: Le boeuf sur le toit. VIEUX-

TEMPS: Fantasia appassionata, op. 35. Gidon Kremer, vln; LSO; Riccardo Chailly. Philips 9500 930 Tape(c) 7300 930
+Gr 8-81 p267 ++HFN 9-81 p87
Poeme, op. 25. See no. 564. See no. 3841
Soir de fete, op. 23. See no. 1132
1132 Symphony, op. 20, B flat major. Soir de fete, op. 32. Toulouse Capitole Orchestra; Michel Plasson. Pathe Marconi C 069 14086 (also Seraphim S 60310)
++FF 11-77 p15 ++SFC 8-27-78 p54
+Gr 3-81 p1192 +-St 1-79 p95
+NR 11-78 p3
CHAVEZ Y RAMIREZ, Carlos
Caballos de vapor: Danza agil; Tango of the sirens. See no. 3880
Daughter of Colchis. See no. 776
1133 Sinfonia india. JIMENEZ MABARAK: Balada del venado y la luna. MONCAYO GARCIA: Huapango. REVUELTAS: Sensemaya. Mexico Philharmonic Orchestra; Fernando Lozano. Oriane UM 3551 Tape (c) UKM 3551
+Gr 9-81 p396
1134 Sinfonia india. GALINDO: Sones de Mariachi. HALFFTER: Don Lindo de Almeria. MONCAYO GARCIA: Huapango. National Symphony Orchestra of Mexico; Kenneth Klein. Unicorn RHS 365 Tape (c) UKC 365
+-FF 5/6-80 p69 +-RR 11-79 p74
++Gr 1-80 p1162 ++SFC 5-11-80 p35
+HFN 3-81 p97 tape +St 9-80 p87
CHAYNES, Charles
1135 For a black world. Christiane Eda Pierre, s; NPhO; Gilbert Amy. Calliope CAL 1857
+FF 5/6-81 p71
Implusions. See no. 3742
CHEBOTARIAN
Prelude. See no. 3917
CHEDEVILLE, Nicolas
1136 Le printems ou les saisons amusantes. STAMITZ: Concerto, viola d'amore, no. 1, D major. TELEMANN: Concerto, oboe d'amore, A major. Suite, sopranino recorder. Jean-Philippe Vasseur, vla d'amore; Michele Fromenteau, hurdy gurdy; Michel Sanvoisin, rec; Jacques Vandeville, ob d'amore; Grenoble Ensemble Instrumental; Stephane Cardon. Arion ARN 38525 (also Musical Heritage Society MHS 4262)
++FF 9/10-81 p271 +RR 5-80 p58
CHENOWETH
Candles. See no. 4068
CHERNEY, Brian
Notturno. See no. 1101
CHERUBINI, Luigi
Anacreon: Overture. See no. 985. See no. 3644. See no. 3792
Ave Maria. See no. 3790
1137 Medea. Maria Callas, s; Teresa Berganza, ms; Jon Vickers, t; Nicola Zaccaria, bs; Orchestra and Chorus; Nicola Rescigno. Historical Recordings HRE 358/2 (2)
+-NR 9-81 p9
Medea: Dei tuoi figli. See no. 4014
1138 Requiem, C minor. ORTF Symphony Orchestra and Chorus; Lamberto

Gardelli. Philips 9500 715 Tape (c) 7300 805
-ARG 6-81 p21
-Audio 3-81 p60
*FF 1/2-81 p99
/Gr 2-81 p1108
/-HFN 3-81 p86
+-HFN 4-81 p81 tape
+NR 11-80 p6
+NYT 5-31-81 pD23

1139 Requiem, D minor. Brassus Chorale, Lausanne Pro Arte Chorus; OSR and Chorus; Horst Stein. Decca SXDL 7518 (also London LDR 10034)
+FF 7/8-81 p89
+Gr 11-80 p717
+HFN 11-80 p116
+NYT 5-31-81 pD23
+St 8-81 p92

1140 Requiem, D minor. CPhO and Chorus; Igor Markevitch. DG 2535 404 Tape (c) 3335 404
+FF 9/10-80 p102
+NYT 5-31-81 pD23
++St 11-80 p84

1141 Requiem, D minor. Ambrosian Singers; NPhO; Riccardo Muti. HMV ASD 3073 (Q) SQ 4 ASD 3073 Tape (c) TC ASD 3073 (also Angel S 37096)
+Gr 5-75 p200 Quad
+Gr 2-78 p1447
+Gr 4-78 p1779 tape
++HF 12-75 p90
+HFN 9-75 p97
+MT 11-75 p977
+MT 6-78 p514
+NR 8-75 p8
++NYT 9-21-75 pD18
+NYT 5-31-81 pD23
+ON 1-17-76 p32
+RR 4-75 p58
+RR 3-78 p61
++SFC 10-19-75 p33

Sonatas, horn, nos. 1 and 2. See no. 3655
Sonata, horn, no. 2, F major. See no. 575
Sonata, horn and piano, no. 1, E flat major. See no. 575

CHIEN HUA CHEN
Adagio, klavier. See no. 3860

CHIH HUNG KUO
Sinkiang dance. See no. 3860

CHIN YE CHU
Prelude. See no. 3860

CHIRBURY, Robert
Agnus Dei. See no. 4085

CHOPIN, Frederic

1142 Allegro de concert, op. 46, A major. Ballades, nos. 1-4. Introduction and variations, op. 12, B flat major. Hamish Milne, pno. CRD CRD 1060 Tape (c) CRDC 4060
+Gr 7-81 p175
+HFN 7-81 p72
+HFN 9-81 p93 tape

Allegro de concerto, op. 46, A major. See no. 1178

1143 Andante spianato and grande polonaise, op. 22, E flat major. Polonaises, opp. 26, 40, 44, 53. Polonaise-fantaisie, op. 61, A flat major. Scherzi, nos. 1-4, opp. 20, 31, 39, 54. Artur Rubinstein, pno. Da Capo 1C 187 53057/8 (2)
+-FF 5/6-81 p72

1144 Andante spianato and grande polonaise, op. 22, E flat major. Concerto, piano, no. 2, op. 21, F major. Krystian Zimerman, pno; LAPO; Carlo Maria Giulini. DG 2531 126 Tape (c) 3301 126
-FF 5/6-81 p71
+Gr 10-80 p496
+HF 5-81 p56
+HFN 10-80 p103
+-HFN 10-80 p117 tape
-NR 3-81 p5
+SR 11-81 p62
+-St 5-81 p72

1145 Andante spianato and grande polonaise, op. 22, E flat major. Concerto, piano, no. 1, op. 11, E minor. Bella Davidovich, pno; LSO; Neville Marriner. Philips 9500 889 Tape (c) 7300 889
+-FF 9/10-81 p93 +HFN 9-81 p79
+-Gr 8-81 p382 +St 12-81 p114

Andante spianato and grande polonaise, op. 22, E flat major. See no. 1177

1146 Ballades, nos. 1-4, opp. 23, 38, 47, 52. Nicolai Petrov, pno. Classics for Pleasure CFP 40346
+-Gr 2-81 p1101 -HFN 2-81 p86

1147 Ballades, nos. 1-4, opp. 23, 38, 47, 52. Barcarolle, op. 60, F sharp majro. Abbey Simon, pno. Turnabout TV 34763 Tape (c) CT 2279
+-ARG 6-81 p22 +SFC 1-4-81 p18
+FF 3/4-81 p99

Ballades, nos. 1-4, opp. 23, 38, 47, 52. See no. 1142. See no. 1177. See no. 1178

1148 Ballade, no. 1, op. 23, G major. Barcarolle, op. 60, F sharp major. Etude, C sharp major. Mazurkas (5). Ivan Moravec, pno. Connoisseur Tape (c) In Sync C 4007
+Audio 12-79 p121 tape +St 1-81 p90 tape

Ballade, no. 1, op. 23, G minor. See no. 1170. See no. 3869

Ballade, no. 3, op. 47, A flat major. See no. 1172. See no. 1179

1149 Ballade, no. 4, op. 52, F minor. Etudes, op. 10, nos. 4, 8, 12. Nocturne, op. 27, no. 2, D flat major. Sonata, piano, no. 2, op. 35, B flat minor. Cecile Ousset, pno. Cambridge CAM 1 Tape (c) CAMC 1
+Gr 8-81 p292 +-HFN 8-81 p83

Ballade, no. 4, op. 52, F minor. See no. 1176

1150 Barcarolle, op. 60, F sharp major. Fantaisie-Impromptu, op. 66, C sharp minor. Impromptus, nos. 1-3, opp. 29, 36, 51. Waltzes, nos. 15-19. Claudio Arrau, pno. Philips 9500 963 Tape (c) 7300 963
+Gr 11-81 p722 +-HFN 11-81 p91

Barcarolle, op. 60, F sharp major. See no. 1147. See no. 1148. See no. 1169. See no. 1177. See no. 1178. See no. 3749

Berceuse, op. 57, D flat major. See no. 1168. See no. 1169. See no. 1175. See no. 1178. See no. 1179

Bolero, op. 19, C major. See no. 1177. See no. 1178

Cantabile, B flat major. See no. 1178

Chants polonaise, op. 74: Spring; The ring. See no. 1182

1151 Concerto, piano, no. 1, op. 11, E minor. Murray Perahia, pno; NYP; Zubin Mehta. CBS M 35893 Tape (c) MT 35893 (also CBS 76970 Tape (c) 40-76970)
+ARG 7-81 p14 +HFN 7-81 p71
+-FF 3/4-81 p100 ++NR 6-81 p7
+-Gr 6-81 p36 +OV 12-81 p38
+-HF 5-81 p56

1152 Concerto, piano, no. 1, op. 11, E minor. Emanuel Ax, pno; PO; Eugene Ormandy. RCA ATC 1-4097
+-NR 11-81 p5

Concerto, piano, no. 1, op. 11, E minor. See no. 1145. See no. 1177. See no. 3749

1153 Concerto, piano, no. 2, op. 21, F minor. SCHUMANN: Concerto, piano, op. 54, A minor. Fou Ts'ong, pno; LSO; Peter Maag. Westminster MCA 1415 Tape (c) 1415 (From WST 17040)

+-FF 1/2-81 p100 +SFC 1-4-81 p18
+-HF 4-81 p86

Concerto, piano, no. 2, op. 21, F minor. See no. 1144. See no. 1177. See no. 4017

Contredanse, G flat major. See no. 1171. See no. 1178

Ecossaises, op. 72 (3). See no. 1177. See no. 1178. See no. 1181

Eccosaises, op. 72, no. 3, B flat major. See no. 1173

Etude, C sharp minor. See no. 1148

1154 Etudes, opp. 10 and 25. Wilhelm Backhaus, pno. Bruno Walter Society IGI 286
+CL 5/6-81 p9 +NR 4-77 p14
+-HF 6-78 p90

1155 Etudes, opp. 10 and 25. Polonaise, opp. 26, 40, 44, 53, 61. Preludes, op. 28, nos. 1-24. Maurizio Pollini, pno. DG 2740 230 (3) (From 2530 291, 2530 550, 2530 659)
++FF 11/12-81 p133 +NYT 4-26-81 pD23
+Gr 8-80 p241 ++SFC 5-10-81 p18
+HFN 10-80 p113 +STL 9-14-80 p40
+-NR 6-81 p15

1156 Etudes, opp. 10 and 25. Francois-Rene Duchable, pno. Erato STU 71406
+HFN 8-81 p83

1157 Etudes, opp. 10 and 25. Nikita Magaloff. Philips 6570 016 Tape (c) 7310 016
+-HFN 3-81 p95 +HFN 5-81 p93 tape

1158 Etudes, opp. 10 and 25. Alfred Cortot, pno. World Records SH 326 Tape (c) TC SH 326
+FF 1/2-81 p100 +Gr 9-80 p413 tape

Etudes, opp. 10 and 25. See no. 1178. See no. 1182

Etudes, op. 10. See no. 1177

Etudes, op. 10, nos. 3-5, 12. See no. 1170

Etudes, op. 10, no. 3, E major. See no. 1168

Etudes, op. 10, nos. 4, 8, 12. See no. 1149

Etudes, op. 10, nos. 5, 7, 12. See no. 1175

1159 Etudes, op. 10, no. 8, F major. Etudes, op. 25, no. 2, F minor. Souvenir de Paganini, A major. MENDELSSOHN: Etudes, op. 104 (3). SCHUMANN: Etude in form freier Varitionen uber ein Beethovensches Thema. WEBER: Variations, op. 9, F major. Marian Freidman, pno. Jecklin 557
+-Gr 4-81 p1351

Etudes, op. 10, no. 8, F major. See no. 1176

Etudes, op. 10, nos. 8, 10. See no. 1174

1160 Etudes, op. 10, no. 10, A flat major. Polonaise-Fantaisie, op. 61, A flat major. LISZT: Sonata, piano, S 178, B minor. Diana Kacso, pno. DG 2535 008
+-FF 11/12-81 p187 -NR 8-81 p12
-HF 6-81 p52 +-NYT 4-26-81 pD23
+-HFN 10-80 p103

Etudes, op. 10, no. 2, C minor. Eee no. 1003

Etudes, op. 25. See no. 1177

Etudes, op. 25, no. 1, A flat major. See no. 1003

Etudes, op. 25, no. 2, F minor. See no. 1159

Etudes, op. 25, no. 5, E minor. See no. 1176

Etudes, op. 25, no. 6, G sharp minor. See no. 1174

Etudes, op. 25, nos. 6, 9. See no. 1175
Etudes, op. posth., nos. 25 and 26. See no. 3857

1161 Fantasie, op. 49, F minor. SCHUMANN: Kinderscenen, op. 15. James Boyk, pno. Performance Recordings PR 2
-FF 3/4-81 p229

1162 Fantasie, op. 49, F minor. Scherzo, no. 2, op. 31, B flat minor. SCHUMANN: Carnival, op. 9. SMETANA: Reves. Esquisses. Frantisek Rauch, pno. Supraphon 111 2741/2 (2)
+ARG 2-81 p50 +NR 8-80 p13
-FF 9/10-80 p201

Fantasie, op. 49, F minor. See no. 1169. See no. 1172. See no. 1177. See no. 1178
Fantasie-Impromptu, op. 66, C sharp minor. See no. 1150. See no. 1179. See no. 1181
Feuille d'album, E major. See no. 1178
Fugue, A minor. See no. 1178
Funeral march, op. 72, no. 2, C minor. See no. 1169. See no. 1171. See no. 1178
Impromptus, nos. 1-3, opp. 29, 36, 51. See no. 1150. See no. 1178
Impromptus, nos. 1-4, opp. 29, 36, 51, 66. See no. 1177
Impromptus, no. 1, op. 29, A flat major. See no. 1179
Impromptus, no. 2, op. 36, F sharp major. See no. 1175. See no. 3866
Impromptus, no. 3, op. 51, G flat major. See no. 1180
Introduction and polonaise, op. 3, C major. See no. 3667
Introduction and rondo, op. 16. See no. 1170
Introduction and variations, op. 12, B flat major. See no. 1142
Largo, E flat major. See no. 1178
Mazurkas, B flat major, G major. See no. 1171
Mazurkas, D major, G major, B flat major (2), C major, A flat major. See no. 1178
Mazurkas (5). See no. 1148
Mazurkas, nos. 1-51. See no. 1178

1163 Mazurkas, opp. 6-7, 17, 24, 30, 33, 41, 50, 56, 63, 67-69. Mazurka, op. posth., A minor. Artur Rubinstein, pno. DaCapo 1C 153 01170/1 (2)
+FF 5/6-81 p72

Mazurkas, op. 6, nos. 1-2, op. 7, nos. 5-7; op. 24, nos. 14-15, 17; op. 33, nos 22, 24; op. 41, no. 29; op. 50, no. 31; op. 56, nos. 34-35; op. 59, nos. 36-37; op. posth., no. 51. See no. 1177
Mazurkas, op. 7, nos. 1-3. See no. 1175
Mazurkas, op. 7, no. 3, F minor. See no. 1170
Mazurkas, op. 17, no. 4, A minor. See no. 1004. See no. 1170
Mazurkas, op. 24, no. 4, B flat minor. See no. 1175
Mazurkas, op. 30, no. 3, D flat major. See no. 1170
Mazurkas, op. 33, no. 2, D major. See no. 1170. See no. 3969
Mazurkas, op. 33, nos. 2, 4. See no. 1175
Mazurkas, op. 41, no. 1. See no. 1175
Mazurkas, op. 41, no. 2, B major. See no. 1170
Mazurkas, op. 50 (3). See no. 1172
Mazurkas, op. 50, no. 2, A flat major. See no. 1175
Mazurkas, op. 50, no. 3, C sharp minor. See no. 1170. See no. 3749
Mazurkas, op. 56, nos. 1, 2. See no. 1176

Mazurkas, op. 56, no. 2, C major. See no. 3806
Mazurkas, op. 59, no. 3, F sharp minor. See no. 1170
Mazurkas, op. 63, no. 3, C sharp minor. See no. 1175
Mazurkas, op. 67, nos. 3-4. See no. 1175
Mazurkas, op. 68, no. 2, A minor. See no. 1171. See no. 1175
Mazurkas, op. 68, no. 4, F minor. See no. 1168
Mazurkas, op. posth., A minor. See no. 1163
Mazurka, a Emile Gailliard, A minor. See no. 1172
A month in the country: Alla polacca; Andantino; Largo non troppo; Presto, lento quasi adagio, molto piu mosso. See no. 3840
Nocturnes, complete. See no. 1178

1164 Nocturnes (19). Ivan Moravec, pno. Connoisseur CS 1065/1165 (2) Tape (c) In Sync C 4025/6
+Gr 8-81 p324 tape +RR 2-75 p51
+NR 9-80 p2 +St 1-81 p90 tape

1165 Nocturnes (21). Arthur Lima, pno. Arabesque 6502 (3)
+-FF 11/12-81 p135

Nocturnes, nos. 1-31. See no. 1177

1166 Nocturnes, opp. 9, 15, 27, 32, 37, 48, 55, 62, 72. Artur Rubinstein, pno. EMI Electrola 1C 187 00162/3 (2)
+-FF 5/6-81 p72

1167 Nocturnes, op. 9, no. 2, E flat major. PUCCINI: Tosca: Non io sospiro...Vissi d'arte;...Amara sol per te; ...trionfal di nova speme. ROSSINI: Stabat mater: Inflammatus. VERDI: Aida: Ahime di guerra fremere;...Fu la sorte...Ebben qual nuovo fremito...Pieta ti prenda...La tra foreste vergine;...Morir si pur e bella...O terra addio. La forza del destino: La vergine degli angeli. Elena Zobinska-Ruszkowska, s; Egidio Cunego, Carlo Barrera, t. Rubini GV 566
+-ARG 11-81 p10

Nocturnes, op. 9, no. 2, E flat major. See no. 3764
Nocturnes, op. 15, no. 1, F major. See no. 4018
Nocturnes, op. 15, no. 2, F sharp major. See no. 1180
Nocturnes, op. 27, no. 2, D flat major. See no. 1003. See no. 1149. See no. 1180. See no. 3749. See no. 4018
Nocturnes, op. 32, no. 1, B major. See no. 3723
Nocturnes, op. 48 (2). See no. 1172
Nocturnes, op. 48, no. 1, C minor. See no. 1179
Nocturnes, op. 48, no. 2, F sharp minor. See no. 1180
Nocturnes, op. 55, no. 1, F minor. See no. 1170
Nocturnes, op. 55, no. 2, E flat major. See no. 1174. See no. 1175
Nocturnes, op. 62, no. 1, B major. See no. 1176. See no. 3866
Nocturnes, op. 72, E minor. See no. 1171. See no. 3697. See no. 3764
Nocturnes, op. posth., C sharp minor. See no. 3841
Nouvelles etudes (3). See no. 1169. See no. 1177. See no. 1178
Nouvelles etudes, no. 1, F minor. See no. 3920

1168 Piano works: Berceuse, op. 57, D flat major. Etudes, op. 10, no. 3, E major. Mazurkas, op. 68, no. 4, F minor. Polonaise, op. 40, no. 1, A major; op. 53, A flat major. Preludes, op. 28, nos. 7, 15. Scherzo, no. 2, op. 31, B flat minor. Waltzes, op. 34, no. 1, A flat major; op. posth., A minor. VALLIER: Witches ride. VERNE (trans. Vallier): H. M. Queen Elizabeth's march. John Vallier, pno. Argem ARG 001
/Gr 4-81 p1345

1169 Piano works: Barcarolle, op. 60, F sharp major. Berceuse, op. 57, D flat major. Fantasia, op. 49, F minor. Funeral march, op. 72, no. 2, C minor. Nouvelles etudes, op. posth. (3). Polonaise-Fantasie, op. 61, A flat major. Fou Ts'ong, pno. CBS 61166 Tape (c) 40-61166 (From 61957, 61866)

+Gr 9-81 p411
+HFN 12-81 p112 tape

1170 Piano works: Ballade, no. 1, op. 23, G minor. Etudes, op. 10, no, 3, E major; no. 4, C sharp minor; no. 5, G flat major; no. 12, C minor. Introduction and rondo, op. 16. Mazurkas, op. 7, no. 3, F minor; op. 17, no. 4, A minor; op. 30, no. 3, D flat major; op. 33, no. 2, D major; op. 41, no. 2, E minor; op. 50, no. 3, C sharp minor; op. 59, no. 3, F sharp minor. Nocturne, op. 55, no. 1, F minor. Polonaise-Fantaisie, op. 61, A flat major. Prelude, op. 28, no. 6, B minor. Sonata, no. 2, op. 35, B flat minor. Waltz, op. 34, no. 2, A minor; op. 64, no. 2, C sharp minor. Vladimir Horowitz, pno. CBS 79340 (3)

+Gr 12-81 p903

1171 Piano works: Contredanse, G flat major. Funeral march, op. 72, no. 2, C minor. Mazurkas, op. 68, no. 2, A minor; B flat major; G major. Nocturne, op. 72, E minor. Polonaise, op. 71, no. 2, B flat major. Rondo, op. 73, C major. Sonata, piano, no. 1, op. 4, C minor. Waltzes, op. posth., A flat major, E flat major. Vladimir Ashkenazy, pno. Decca SXL 6911 Tape (c) KSXC 6911 (also London CS 7135)

+FF 3/4-81 p101
+Gr 11-80 p703
+Gr 4-81 p3176 tape
+HFN 11-80 p117
++NR 1-81 p14
+NYT 4-26-81 pD23
+STL 1-11-81 p38

1172 Piano works: Ballades, no. 3, op. 47, A flat major. Fantaisie, op. 49, F minor. Mazurkas, op. 50 (3). Mazurka, a Emile Gaillaird, A minor. Nocturnes, op. 48 (2). Prelude, op. 45, C sharp minor. Tarantelle, op. 43, A flat major. Vladimir Ashkenazy, pno. Decca SXL 6922 Tape (c) KSXC 6922 (also London CS 7150)

+CL 2-81 p12
+FF 11/12-80 p93
+Gr 5-80 p1693
+Gr 1-81 p1001 tape
++HFN 5-80 p119
+NYT 4-26-81 pD23
++RR 6-80 p74

1173 Piano works: Ecossaises, op. 72, no. 3, B flat major. Variations on a German air, op. posth. Polonaises, op. 71, no. 1, D minor; op. posth., G minor, A flat major, B flat major, G sharp minor, B flat minor. Rondo, op. 1, C minor. Rondo, op. 5, F major. Vladimir Ashkenazy, pno. Decca SXL 6981 Tape (c) KSXC 6981

++Gr 12-81 p898

1174 Piano works: Etudes, op. 10, nos. 8, 10. Etude, op. 25, no. 6, G sharp minor. Nocturne, op. 55, no. 2, E flat major. Prelude, op. 45, C sharp minor. Scherzo, no, 3, op. 39, C sharp minor. Sonata, no. 2, op. 35, B flat minor. Ivo Pogorelich, pno. DG 2531 346 Tape (c) 3301 346

++CL 12-81 p10
+FF 11/12-81 p138
++Gr 7-81 p175
++Gr 9-81 p460 tape
+-HF 8-81 p66
+HFN 9-81 p93 tape
+-MT 11-81 p754
-MUM 11/12-81 p31
+SR 11-81 p62
/-St 9-81 p86

+HFN 7-81 p71 +STL 6-14-81 p40

1175 Piano works: Etudes, op. 10, nos, 5, 7, 12. Etudes, op. 25, nos. 6, 9. Impromptu, no. 2, op. 36, F sharp major. Mazurkas, op. 7, nos. 1-3; op. 24, no. 4; op. 33, nos. 2, 4; op. 41, no. 1; op. 50, no. 2; op. 63, no. 3; op. 67, nos. 3-4; op. 68, no. 2. Nocturne, op. 55, no. 2, E flat major. Polonaise, op. 53, A flat major. Prelude, op. 28, no. 19, E flat major. Waltz, op. 34, no. 2, A minor. Ignaz Friedman, pno. Encore E 303

+FF 11/12-81 p134

1176 Piano works: Ballade, no. 4, op. 52, F minor. Etude, op. 10, no. 8, F major. Etude, op. 25, no. 5, E minor. Mazurkas, op. 56, nos. 1 and 2. Nocturne, op. 62, no. 1, B major. Jeffrey Swann, pno. Muza SX 0686 (also Stolat SZM 0108)

++CL 10-79 p38 *NYT 7-27-81 pD23
+/FF 11/12-81 p211

1177 Piano works: Andante spianato and grande polonaise, op. 22, E flat major. Ballades, nos. 1-4, opp. 23, 38, 47, 52. Berceuse, op. 57, D flat major. Barcarolle, op. 60, F sharp major. Bolero, op. 19, C major. Concerto, piano, no. 1, op. 11, E minor. Concerto, piano, no. 2, op. 21, F minor. Ecoccaises, op. 72 (3). Etudes, op. 10. Etudes, op. 25. Fantasia, op. 49, F minor. Impromptus, nos. 1-4, opp. 29, 36, 51, 66. Mazurkas, op. 6, nos. 1-2, op. 7, nos. 5-7; op. 24, nos. 14-15, 17; op. 33, nos. 22, 24; op. 41, no. 29; op. 50, no. 31; op. 56, nos. 34-35; op. 59, nos. 36-37; op. posth., no. 51. Nocturnes, nos. 1-31. Nouvelles etudes. Polonaise, opp. 26, 40, 44, 53, 61, 71, op. posth. Preludes, op. 28, nos. 1-24. Prelude, op. 45, C sharp minor. Prelude, op. posth., A flat major. Rondo, op. 1, C major. Rondo, op. 5, F sharp major. Scherzi, nos. 1-4, opp. 20, 31, 39, 54. Sonatas, piano, nos. 1-3. Souvenir de Paganini, A major. Tarantelle, op. 43, A flat major. Variations on a waltz from Bellini's "I puritani". Waltzes (19). Adam Harasiewicz, pno; VSO; Heinrich Hollreiser. Philips 6747 017 (14)

+FF 11/12-81 p132

1178 Piano works: Allegro de concert, op. 46, A major. Ballades, nos. 1-4, opp. 23, 38, 47, 52. Barcarolle, op. 60, F sharp major. Berceuse, op. 57, D flat major. Bolero, op. 19, C major. Cantabile, B flat major. Contredanse, G flat major. Ecossaise, op. 72 (3). Etudes, opp. 10 and 25. Fantasie, op. 49, F minor. Feuille d'album, E major. Fugue, A minor. Impromptus, nos. 1-3. Funeral march, op. 72, no. 2, C minor. Mazurkas, nos. 1-51. Mazurkas, G major, B flat major, D major, B flat major, C major, A flat major. Nocturnes, complete. Nouvelles etudes (3). Polonaises, complete. Rondos, op. 1, C major; op. 5, F major; op. 16, E flat major; op. 73, C major. Scherzi, nos. 1-4, opp. 20, 31, 39, 54. Sonatas, piano, nos. 1-3. Souvenir de Paganini, A major. Tarantelle, op. 43, A flat major. Variations, op. 12, B flat major. Variations sur un air national allemand. Variations sur un air national de Moore. Variations sur la marche des Puritans de Bellini. Waltzes complete. Preludes, complete. Nikita Magaloff, Michel Dalberto, pno. Philips 6768 067 (16) (Some reissues from 6580 199, 6580 198, 6580 117, 6580 119, 6580, 024, 6590 173, 6580 118)

+-Gr 11-79 p874 +-HFN 3-81 p95
+-HFN 10-79 p151 +-RR 10-79 p46

1179 Piano works: Berceuse, op. 57, D flat major. Ballade, no. 3, op. 47, A flat major. Fantasie-Impromptu, op. 66, C sharp minor. Impromptu, no. 1, op. 29, A flat major. Nocturne, op. 48, no. 1, C minor. Polonaise, op. 53, A flat major. Scherzo, no. 2, op. 31, B flat minor. Waltz, op. 64, no. 2, C sharp minor. GERSHWIN (trans. Wild): Grand fantasy on airs from "Porgy and Bess". Virtuoso etudes on popular songs (7). LISZT: Etudes de concert, S 145: Gnomenreigen. Harmonies poetiques et religieuses, S 173: Funerailles. Annees de pelerinage, 3rd year, S 163: Les jeux d'eau a la Villa d'Este. Hungarian rhapsody, no. 4, S 244, E flat major. Sonata, piano, S 178, B minor. Earl Wild, pno. Quintessence 3PC 3704
+-FF 9/10-81 p232

1180 Piano works: Impromptu, no. 3, op. 51, G flat major. Nocturne, op. 15, no. 2, F sharp major. Nocturne, op. 27, no. 2, D flat major. Nocturne, op. 48, no. 2, F sharp minor. Polonaise-Fantaisie, op. 61, A flat major. Waltz, op. 34, no. 3, F major. Waltz, op. 64, no. 1, D flat major. Waltz, op. 70, no. 1, G flat major. Peter Serkin, pno. RCA ATC 1-4036
+-FF 11/12-81 p137 +-NR 9-81 p14
+-MUM 11/12-81 p31

1181 Piano works: Ecossaise, no. 1, op. 72, no. 3. Fantaisie-Impromptu, op. 66, C sharp minor. Waltzes, op. 34, nos. 2-3; op. 64, nos. 1, 3. Raoul Koczalski, pno; BPhO; Sergiu Celibidache. Rococo 2095
+NR 3-81 p5

1182 Piano works: Etudes, opp. 10 and 25. Preludes, op. 28, nos. 1-24. Prelude, op. 45, C sharp minor. Chants polonaise, op. 74: Spring; The ring. Alfred Cortot, pno. World Records SH 326/7 (2) (From HMV DB 2027/9, 2308/10, 2015/8, 2108, DA 1682)
+Gr 3-80 p1417 +RR 6-80 p75
+HFN 7-80 p106 +STL 7-13-80 p38
+MT 1-81 p33

Polonaise, complete. See no. 1178

1183 Polonaise, opp. 26, 40, 44, 53. Lazar Berman, pno. DG 2531 094 Tape (c) 3301 094
+-CL 7/8-80 p8 +-MT 9-80 p566
+FF 7/8-80 p71 +-NR 5-80 p13
+-Gr 12-79 p1028 +-NYT 4-6-80 pD22
+HF 4-81 p90 +-RR 1-80 p98
+HFN 2-80 p91 +St 6-80 p111

Polonaise, opp. 26, 40, 44, 53. See no. 1143

1184 Polonaise, opp. 26, 40, 44, 53, 61. Nikita Magaloff, pno. Philips 6570 137 Tape (c) 7310 137 (From 6768 067)
-Gr 3-80 p1417 +HFN 6-81 p85

Polonaise, opp. 26, 40, 44, 53, 61. See no. 1155

Polonaise, opp. 26, 40, 44, 53, 61, 71, op. posth., See no. 1177

Polonaise, op. 3, C major. See no. 1197

Polonaise, op. 40, no. 1, A major. See no. 1003. See no. 1168. See no. 1170

Polonaise, op. 44, F sharp minor. See no. 1170

Polonaise, op. 53, A flat major. See no. 1168. See no. 1170. See no. 1175. See no. 1179

Polonaise, op. 71, no. 1, D minor; op. posth., G minor, A flat major, B flat major, G sharp minor, B flat minor. See no. 1173
Polonaise, op. 71, no. 2, B flat major. See no. 1171
Polonaise-Fantaisie, op. 61, A flat major. See no. 1143. See no. 1160. See no. 1169. See no. 1170. See no. 1180
1185 Preludes, complete. Christoph Eschenbach, pno. Contour CC 7511 Tape (c) CCT 7511
+Gr 8-81 p316
Preludes, complete. See no. 1178
1186 Preludes, op. 18, nos. 1-24; op. 45, C sharp minor; op. posth., A flat major. Fou Ts'ong, pno. CBS 61944 Tape (c) 40-61944
+Gr 11-80 p703 +HFN 12-80 p159
+Gr 2-81 p1122 tape
1187 Preludes, op. 28, nos. 1-24. Ivan Moravec, pno. Connoisseur Society Tape (c) InSync 4051
++St 1-81 p90 tape
1188 Preludes, op. 28, nos. 1-24; op. 45, C sharp minor; op. posth., A flat major. Claudio Arrau, pno. Philips 6527 091 Tape (c) 7311 091 (From 6500 622)
+Gr 5-81 p1498 +-HFN 5-81 p91
+Gr 7-81 p196 tape +-HFN 7-81 p81 tape
1189 Preludes, op. 28, nos. 1-24. Bella Davidovich, pno. Philips 9500 666 Tape (c) 7300 764
+CL 10-79 p37 +NR 1-80 p14
-FF 3/4-80 p76 +-NYT 4-6-80 pD22
+Gr 2-81 p1101 -SFC 10-28-79 p53
+-HF 1-80 p73
Preludes, op. 28, nos. 1-24. See no. 1155. See no. 1177. See no. 1182
Preludes, op. 28, no. 6, B minor. See no. 1170
Preludes, op. 28, no. 7, A major. See no. 3886
Preludes, op. 28, nos. 7, 15. See no. 1168
Preludes, op. 28, no. 17, A flat major. See no. 1003
Preludes, op. 28, no. 19, E flat major. See no. 1175
Preludes, op. 45, C sharp minor. See no. 1172. See no. 1174. See no. 1177. See no. 1182. See no. 1186. See no. 1188
Preludes op. posth., A flat major. See no. 1177. See no. 1186. See no. 1188
1190 Rondos, op. 1, C minor; op. 16, E flat major; op. 73, C major. Rondos, op. 5, F major. Variations, op. 12, B flat major. Danielle Laval, Teresa Llacuna, pno. Pathe C 069 16384
+FF 11/12-81 p137
Rondos, op. 1, C minor. See no. 1173. See no. 1177. See no. 1178
Rondos, op. 5, F major. See no. 1173. See no. 1177. See no. 1178. See no. 1190
Rondos, op. 16, E flat major. See no. 1178. See no. 1190
Rondos, op. 73, C major. See no. 1171. See no. 1178. See no. 1190
1191 Scherzi, nos. 1-4, opp. 20, 31, 39, 54. Sviatoslav Richter, pno. CBS M 36681 Tape (c) MT 36681
++FF 11/12-81 p137 +-NR 8-81 p12
+HF 11-81 p103 tape
1192 Scherzi, nos. 1-4, opp. 20, 31, 39, 54. Tamas Vasary, pno. DG 2535 285 Tape (c) 3335 285 (From SLPEM 136451)

+-FF 9/10-81 p94 +-NYT 4-26-81 pD23
+-Gr 6-79 p79 +-RR 6-79 p104
+-HFN 6-79 p117

1193 Scherzi, nos. 1-4, opp. 20, 31, 39, 54. Shura Cherkassky, pno. Tudor 73024
+-Gr 4-81 p1345 +-HFN 2-81 p86

Scherzi, nos. 1-4, opp. 20, 31, 39, 54. See no. 1143. See no. 1177. See no. 1178

Scherzo, no. 2, op. 31, B flat minor. See no. 1162. See no. 1168. See no. 1179

Scherzo, no. 3, op. 39, C sharp minor. See no. 1174

Sonatas, piano, nos. 1-3. See no. 1177. See no. 1178

Sonata, piano, no. 1, op. 4, C minor. See no. 1171

1194 Sonata, piano, no. 2, op. 35, B flat minor. Sonata, piano, no. 3, op. 58, B minor. Henri Barda, pno. Calliope CAL 1680
+Gr 8-81 p292 +HFN 8-81 p83

1195 Sonata, piano, no. 2, op. 35, B flat minor. Sonata, piano, no. 3, op. 58, B minor. Fou Ts'ong, pno. CBS 61149 (From 61857, 61866)
+-Gr 9-81 p411 +HFN 9-81 p90

1196 Sonata, piano, no. 2, op. 35, B flat minor. Sonata, piano, no. 3, op. 58, B minor. Martha Argerich, pno. DG 2531 289 Tape (c) 3301 289 (From 2530 530, 139317)
+CL 3-81 p10 +HFN 10-80 p117 tape
+Gr 10-80 p518 +NR 4-81 p12
+-HFN 10-80 p113 +SR 11-81 p62

Sonata, piano, no. 2, op. 35, B flat minor. See no. 20. See no. 1149. See no. 1170. See no. 1174. See no. 3697

Sonata, piano, no. 3, op. 58, B minor. See no. 1194. See no. 1195. See no. 1196. See no. 3749

1197 Sonata, violoncello and piano, op. 65, G minor. Polonaise, op. 3, C major. SCHUMANN: Adagio and allegro, op. 70, A flat major. Martha Argerich, pno; Mstislav Rostropovich, vlc. DG 2531 201 Tape (c) 3301 201
+ARG 9-81 p18 +-MT 10-81 p677
++CL 9-81 p18 +MUM 9/10-81 p31
+-FF 7/8-81 p89 ++NR 5-81 p11
++Gr 2-81 p1095 +SR 10-81 p86
++HF 8-81 p58 ++St 7-81 p78
++HFN 3-81 p87 ++STL 3-8-81 p38
+HFN 3-81 p97 tape

1198 Sonata, violoncello and piano, op. 65, G minor. GRIEG: Sonata, violoncello and piano, op. 36, A minor. Roger Drinkall, vlc; Rene Lozano, pno. Orion ORS 80387
+-FF 7/8-81 p89 +St 7-81 p79
+NR 1-81 p5

1199 Sonata, violoncello and piano, op. 65, G minor. STRAUSS, R.: Sonata, violoncello and piano, op. 6, F major. Clark Shuldmann. Spectrum Tape (c) SC 233
*HF 9-81 p46 tape

Sonata, violoncello and piano, op. 65, G minor. See no. 1102

Souvenir de Paganini, A major. See no. 1159. See no. 1177. See no. 1178

Tarantella, op. 43, A flat major. See no. 1172. See no. 1177. See no. 1178

Variations, op. 12, B flat major. See no. 1178. See no. 1190
Variations on a German air, op. posth. See no. 1173
Variations on a waltz from Bellini's "I puritani". See no. 1177
Variations sur la marche des Puritans de Bellini. See no. 1178
Variations sur un air national allemand. See no. 1178
Variations sur un air national de Moore. See no. 1178
1200 Waltzes. Alfred Cortot, pno. World Records SH 383
-FF 11/12-81 p139
Waltzes, complete. See no. 1178
Waltzes (13). See no. 298
Waltzes (14). See no. 3749
Waltzes (19). See no. 1177
1201 Waltzes, nos. 1-14. Leonard Pennario, pno. Angel DS 37332
+-FF 3/4-81 p102 +SFC 12-21-80 p22
+-NR 4-81 p12 +St 7-81 p79
-MUM 3/4-81 p32
1202 Waltzes, nos. 1-14. Arthur Moreira-Lima, pno. Denon OX 7084
+-HFN 5-81 p80
1203 Waltzes, nos. 1-14. Claudio Arrau, pno. Philips 9500 739 Tape (c) 7300 824
+-CL 3-81 p12 +-HFN 10-80 p103
+-FF 3/4-81 p102 +NR 4-81 p12
+Gr 9-80 p375 +-SFC 1-4-81 p18
+-Gr 1-81 p1001 tape +St 7-81 p79
Waltzes, nos. 15-19. See no. 1150
Waltzes, op. 34, no. 1, A flat major; op. posth., A minor. See no. 1168
Waltzes, op. 34, nos. 2-3. See no. 1181
Waltzes, op. 34, no. 2, A minor. See no. 1170. See no. 1175
Waltzes, op. 34, no. 3, F major. See no. 1180
Waltzes, op. 42, A flat major. See no. 3993
Waltzes, op. 64, nos. 1, 3. See no. 1181
Waltzes, op. 64, no. 1, D flat major. See no. 1180
Waltzes, op. 64, no. 2, C sharp minor. See no. 1170. See no. 1179
Waltzes, op. 70, no. 1, G flat major. See no. 1180
Waltzes, op. posth., E flat major, A flat major. See no. 1171
Waltz brillante, E flat major. See no. 20

CHORBAJIAN, John
Songs: Bitter for sweet. See no. 3951

CHOVI
Pepite greus. See no. 3981
CHRIST IN THE HOLY LAND. See no. 3780

CHRISTIAN, Bobby
1204 Mt. Fugiyama suite. ISHII: Dipol. Kio-oo. Orchestra, Japanese Youth Symphony Orchestra; Bobby Christian, Toru Misago. Aries LP 1620
+-FF 1/2-81 p100
CHRISTMAS CAROLS. See no. 3672. See no. 3887
CHRISTMAS FROM ST. ANNE'S CATHEDRAL. See no. 3635
CHRISTMAS MUSIC. See no. 3705. See no. 3899
CHRISTMAS SERVICE OF LESSONS AND CAROLS. See no. 3628
CHRISTMAS SONGS. See no. 3802. See no. 4109
CHRISTMAS WITH PLACIDO DOMINGO. See no. 3708
CHRISTMAS WITH RENATA SCOTTO. See no. 4004
CHRISTMAS WITH THE KING's SINGERS. See no. 3900

CHU WEI
1205 Heroes monument. LI HUAN-CHICH: Spring festival overture. MAK'O CHANG LAO: The white haired girl: Suite. Tokyo Philharmonic Orchestra; Kek-Tjing Lim. Hong Kong HK 24 0024
+-FF 1/2-81 p231
CHUKHADJIAN, Tigran
Impromptus. See no. 3912
CHUN WAI YEUNG
The peacock. See no. 3860
CICONIA, Johannes
1206 Songs (madrigals and ballads): Aler m'en veus; Caciando un giorno; Che vole amar; Con lagreme; Credo; Gloria; O beatum incendium; O Padua; Poy che morir; Regina gloriosa; Una pantera. Clemencic Consort; Rene Clemencic. Harmonia Mundi (France) HM 10068
+FF 5/6-81 p75 +Gr 4-81 p1352
CILEA, Francesco
Adriana Lecouvreur: Io son l'umile ancella. See no. 3713. See no. 3751. See no. 3752
Adriana Lecouvreur: Io son l'umile ancella; Poveri fiori. See no. 3711. See no. 4041
Adriana Lecouvreur: La dolcissima effigie. See no. 3707. See no. 3750
Adriana Lecouvreur: La dolcissima effigie; L'anima ho stanca. See no. 3757. See no. 3839
Adriana Lecouvreur: L'anima ho stanca. See no. 4032
Adriana Lecouvreur: Prelude, Act 4. See no. 4081
L'Arlesiana: E la solita storia. See no. 3843. See no. 3982. See no. 4022
L'Arlesiana: Lamento di Federico. See no. 4054
Songs: Lontananza. See no. 4032
CIMA, Andrea
Canzona. See no. 3808
La novella. See no. 3808
CIMARA
Songs: Stornello. See no. 3758
CIMAROSA, Domenico
Concertante, 2 flutes, G major. See no. 4008
1207 Il matrimonio segreto: Cara cara; Io ti lascio. MASSENET: Manon: Act 2. Werther, excerpts (3). MOZART: Don Giovanni, K 527: Duet, Act 1; Il mio tesoro. Bidu Sayao, s; Rosa Ponselle, con; Tito Schipa, t; Alda Noni; Orchestras and conductors. MDP Records 024
+5/6-80 p176 +-FF 9/10-81 p214
1208 Sonatas, guitar, D minor, A major, B minor (trans. Bream). PAGANINI: Sonatas, violin and guitar, op. 3, nos. 1, 6 (arr. Barrueco). GIULIANI: Sonata, guitar, op. 150, A major. Variations sur les Folies d'Espagne, op. 45. SCARLATTI: Sonatas, harpsichord, K 490/L 206, D major; K 292/L 24, E minor; K 380/L 23, E major; K 208/L 238, A major; K 209/L 428, A major (trans. Barrueco). Manuel Barrueco, gtr. Turnabout TV 34770
+ARG 12-81 p40 +NR 7-81 p16
Sonatas, guitar, C sharp minor, A major. See no. 4001
1209 Sonatas, piano, nos. 1-3, 5, 7, 9, 13-15, 19-21, 26-27, 30-32, 42-44, 46-47, 50, 57, 66-68, 73-74, 76, 78. Donatella Failoni, pno. Hungaroton SLPX 12176

+Gr 7-81 p175 +-NR 11-81 p13
+-HFN 6-81 p71

CIOFFI

Na sera e maggio. See no. 3641

CIRRI, Giovanni

1210 Sonatas, violoncello, op. 16. Rama Jucker, vlc; Caspar Guyer, hpd. Accord ACC 140 029
+HFN 12-81 p94

CLARK, Robert Keyes

Concerto, clarinet and chamber orchestra. See no. 1009

CLARKE, Jeremiah

Trumpet voluntary. See no. 3629. See no. 3959

1211 Voluntary, D major (Prince of Denmark's march). HAYDN: Concerto, trumpet, E flat major. PURCELL: Sonata, trumpet, D major. Trumpet tune and air, D major. Voluntary, 2 trumpets, C major. VIVALDI: Concerto, 2 trumpets, C major. Roger Voisin, tpt; Orchestra; Harry Dickson. Westminster MCA 1417 (From Kapp KS 3380)
+FF 3/4-81 p235 +NR 11-80 p5

CLARKE, Rebecca

Sonata, viola. See no. 1023

1212 Trio, violin, violoncello and piano. HOOVER: Trio, violin, violoncello and piano. Suzanne Ornstein, vln; James Kreger, vlc; Virginia Eskin, pno; Rogeri Trio. Leonarda LPI 103
+ARG 2-81 p42 +NYT 6-21-81 pD23
+FF 9/10-80 p104 +-NR 8-80 p10

CLAY, Frederic

I'll sing three songs of Araby. See no. 4046

CLEMENCIC, Rene

Chronos, no. 2. See no. 1213

1213 Maraviglia, no. 3. Chronos, no. 2. Sesostris. Clemencic Consort. Scorpios SC 1094013
+HFN 1-81 p92 *RR 8-80 p39

Sesostris. See no. 1213

CLEMENS NON PAPA

Iuvons beau lieu. See no. 3677

CLEMENTI, Muzio

Montferrin, op. 49. See no. 1216

1214 Sonatas, piano, op. 3, no. 2, E flat major; op. 6, no. 1, C major; op. 14, no. 1, C major. Genevieve Chinn, Allen Brings, pno. Orion ORS 80395
+ARG 10-81 p20 ++NR 6-81 p14
+FF 7/8-81 p90

1215 Sonatas, piano, op. 13, no. 6, F minor; op. 24, no. 2, B flat major; op. 25, no. 5, F sharp minor; op. 37, no. 2, G major. Jos van Immerseel, pno. Chandos Accent 7911
+-FF 1/2-81 p101 +-MT 6-81 p389
+HFN 6-80 p101 +RR 6-80 p31

1216 Sonatas, piano, op. 14, no. 3, F minor; op. 26, no. 2, F sharp minor; op. 31, no. 1, A major. Montferrine, op. 49 (3). Luciano Sgrizzi, pno. Abbey Alpha DB 195
+FF 11/12-80 p94 +HFN 12-80 p135
+Gr 12-80 p848 -MT 6-81 p389

1217 Sonata, piano, op. 14, no. 3. Sonata, piano, op. 34, no. 2, G minor. Sonata, piano, op. 26, no. 2, F sharp minor. Vladimir

Horowitz, pno. RCA ARM 1-3689 Tape (c) ARK 1-3689 (From LM 1902)
+HF 2-81 p81 tape +-HF 5-81 p57

Sonata, piano, op. 24, no. 2, B flat major. See no. 1215

Sonata, piano, op. 25, no. 5, F sharp minor. See no. 1215

1218 Sonata, piano, op. 26, no. 2, F sharp minor. Sonata, piano, op. 36, no. 2, C major. LISZT: Annees de pelerinage, 2nd year, S 161: Apres une lecture du Dante; Sonetto del Petrarca. Laszlo Simon, pno. BIS LP 154
+-FF 3/4-81 p147 +-HFN 12-80 p137

Sonata, piano, op. 26, no. 2, F sharp minor. See no. 1217

Sonata, piano, op. 34, no. 2, G minor. See no. 1217

Sonata, piano, op. 36, no. 2, G major. See no. 1218

Sonata, piano, op. 37, no. 2, G major. See no. 1215

Sonata, piano, op. 40, no. 2, B minor. See no. 3697

1219 Symphonies (4) (ed. Spada). PhO; Claudio Scimone. Erato STU 71174 (2) (also Musical Heritage Society Tape (c) MHC 6150/1)
++ARG 2-81 p14 ++HF 11-80 p88 tape
+FF 1/2-81 p101 +HFN 3-79 p123
++Gr 2-79 p1415 +RR 2-79 p20
+HF 5-79 p73

CLERAMBAULT, Louis

1220 Medee. Orphee. Rachel Yakar, s; Reinhard Goebel, vln; Wilbert Hazelzet, flt; Charles Medlam, vla da gamba; Alan Curtis, hpd. DG 2533 442
+FF 3/4-81 p102 +-NR 3-81 p12
+Gr 8-80 p248 +RR 8-80 p80
+HFN 8-80 p95 ++St 4-81 p104
+-MT 12-81 p827

Orphee. See no. 1220

1221 Suites, C major, C minor. JACQUET DE LA GUERRE: Suite, D minor. Kenneth Gilbert, hpd. Argo ZK 64
+Gr 7-80 p153 ++RR 7-80 p79
++HFN 7-80 p106 +STL 9-14-80 p40
+MT 3-81 p184

Suite du 2ieme ton. See no. 310

CLEVE, Halfdan

1222 Concerto, piano, no. 4, op. 12, A minor. Etude, op. 17, no. 2, F sharp major. Sonata, piano, op. 19, D minor. Waves of spring, op. 13, no. 1, D flat major. Einar Steen-Nokleberg, pno; NSO; Roy Wales. NKF 30038
+-FF 5/6-81 p78 +HFN 9-81 p79
+Gr 8-81 p317

Etude, op. 17, no. 2, F sharp major. See no. 1222

Sonata, piano, op. 19, D minor. See no. 1222

Waves of spring, op. 13, no. 1, D flat major. See no. 1222

CLEWING, Carl

Alle Tag ist kein Sonntag. See no. 4083

COATES, Eric

1223 Cinderella phantasy. London again suite. London suite. Three bears phantasy. Royal Liverpool Orchestra; Charles Groves. Arabesque 8036 Tape (c) 9036
+ARG 6-81 p23 ++NR 2-81 p6
++FF 3/4-81 p103

London again suite. See no. 1223

London suite. See no. 1223
Songs: Bird songs of eventide. See no. 4043
Songs: I heard you singing. See no. 4033
Songs: Orpheus with his lute; Tell me where is fancy bred. See no. 3878
Three bears phantasy. See no. 1223

COCCIA
Per la patria: Bella Italia. See no. 4024

COCIUBEI
Ditele. See no. 4027

COGAN, Robert
1224 Utterances. DeLIO: Serenade. ESCOT: Neyrac lux. KORDE: Constellations. Harry Chambers, gtr; Michael Dewart, pno; Joan Heller, voice; Boston Saxophone Quartet. Spectrum SR 128
-FF 9/10-81 p296

COHAN, George
Over there. See no. 4036

COLEMAN, Edward
The glories of our birth and state. See no. 4093

COLERIDGE-TAYLOR, Samuel
Quintet, clarinet, op. 15, F sharp minor. See no. 807

COLOMBIER, Michel
Sextet, op. 335. See no. 3796

COLOMER
Menuet. See no. 4019

COMPERE, Loyset
Motets: O vos omnes. See no. 3906
Virgo celesti. See no. 3945

CONRADI, Johann
1225 Suite, A minor. DUFAUT: Suite, G minor. GALLOT: Suite, D minor. REUSNER: Suite, A minor. Michael Schaffer, lt; Musical Heritage Society MHS 4199 (also RCA RL 3-0344)
+FF 9/10-81 p255 +-HFN 8-81 p91
+Gr 7-81 p176

CONSTANTEN, Tom
Dejavalse. See no. 3942

CONTINELLO-ALOGON
Lo Tedya Milhama. See no. 3897

COOKE, Arnold
Rondo, B flat major. See no. 3731

COOKE, John
Alma proles. See no. 4085

COPLAND, Aaron
1226 Appalachian spring. Music for movies. London Sinfonietta; Elgar Howarth. Argo ZRG 935
++Gr 11-81 p686 +HFN 11-81 p91
1227 Appalachian spring (original version). Columbia Chamber Orchestra; Aaron Copland. CBS 61894 Tape (c) 40-61894 (also Columbia M 32726 Tape (c) MT 32726 (ct) MA 32726)
+Gr 6-80 p43 +HFN 6-80 p106
+Gr 9-80 p413 tape +HFN 9-80 p115 tape
+Gr 6-81 p93 tape +RR 7-80 p53
1228 Appalachian spring: Suite. El salon Mexico. NYP; Leonard Bernstein. Columbia MS 7521 Tape (c) 16-11-0138 (also CBS 61431 Tape (c) 40-61431)

+Gr 4-81 p1378 +HFN 6-81 p87 tape
+Gr 7-81 p196 tape

1229 Billy the kid. Rodeo: Four dance episodes. NYP; Leonard Bernstein. CBS MY 36727 (From MS 6175, M 31823)
+-FF 9/10-81 p94

1230 Billy the kid. Statements. LSO; Aaron Copland. Edition 43015 Everest Tape (c) 3015
+FF 11/12-81 p140 +HF 10-81 p91 tape

1231 Billy the kid. Fanfare for the common man. Rodeo. Dallas Symphony Orchestra; Donald Johanos. Turnabout TV 34169 dbs SS 3007 Tape (c) CT 2201
+Audio 12-81 p66

Concerto, piano. See no. 1237

1232 Dance symphony. Short symphony. LSO; Aaron Copland. CBS 61997 Tape (c) 40-61997 (From 72731, MS 7223)
+Gr 2-81 p1082 +HFN 3-81 p97 tape
+Gr 11-81 p783 tape

Danzon cubano. See no. 1237

Down a country lane. See no. 1234

Early blues. See no. 1237

1233 Emblems. HANSON: Young composer's guide to the six-tone scale. SCHWANTNER: ...Amid the mountains rising nowhere. Eastman Wind Ensemble; Donald Hunsberger. Mercury SRI 75132
+ARG 1-81 p50 +NYT 9-28-80 pD31
+FF 1/2-81 p118 ++SFC 8-3-80 p33
+NR 12-80 p11

Fanfare for the common man. See no. 1231. See no. 3660. See no. 3745

Fantasy. See no. 1234

In the evening air. See no. 1234

Midsummer nocturne. See no. 1234

Music for movies. See no. 1226

Night thoughts. See no. 1234

Nocturne, violin and piano. See no. 1237

Old American songs. See no. 3842

Our town. See no. 1235

Our town: Suite. See no. 2137

Outdoor overture. See no. 1235

Passacaglia. See no. 1234

Piano blues (4). See no. 844. See no. 1234

Piano blues, nos. 1, 4. See no. 1237

1234 Piano works: Down a country lane. Fantasy, piano. In evening air. Midsummer nocturne. Night thoughts(Homage to Ives). Piano blues (4). Passacaglia. Scherzo humoristique: The cat and the mouse. Sonata, piano. Sunday afternoon music. Variations, piano. The young pioneers. Leo Smit, pno. Columbia M2 35901 (2) (also CBS 79234)
+ARG 7/8-80 p20 +HFN 7-81 p72
+FF 7/8-80 p72 +NR 4-80 p13
+Gr 6-81 p58 +NYT 9-28-80 pD31
+HF 5-80 p67 ++St 4-80 p87

1235 Pieces, string orchestra (2). Outdoor overture. Our town. Quiet city. LSO; Aaron Copland. CBS 61728 Tape (c) 40-61728 (From 72809)
++Gr 8-81 p267 +HFN 9-81 p89

++Gr 10-81 p614 tape +HFN 9-81 p93 tape
Quiet city. See no. 1235
The red pony. See no. 1027
The red pony: Morning on the ranch. See no. 4105
Rodeo. See no. 1231
Rodeo: Four dance episodes. See no. 1229
Rodeo: Hoe down. See no. 1237. See no. 3847
El salon Mexico. See no. 1228
Scherzo humoristique: The cat and the mouse. See no. 1234
Serenade, ukelele. See no. 1237
Short symphony. See no. 2132
Sonata, piano. See no. 1234
Statements. See no. 1230
Sunday afternoon music. See no. 1234
Variations, piano. See no. 1234

1036 Vitebsk. MANZIARLY: Trilogue. TCHEREPNIN: Trio, op. 34, D major. TURINA: Trio, piano, no. 2, op. 74, B minor. Brian Hanly, vln; David Tomatz, vlc; Werner Rose, pno. Laurel LR 109
+ARG 2-81 p47 ++NR 4-80 p7
++Audio 12-80 p88 ++SFC 5-4-80 p42
+FF 9/10-80 p227 ++St 1-81 p88

1237 Works, selections: Concerto, piano. Danzon cubano. Early blues. Nocturne, violin and piano. Our town: Suite. Piano blues, nos. 1, 4. Rodeo: Hoe down. Serenade, ukelele. Leo Smit, Aaron Copland, Annette Kaufman, pno; Louis Kaufman, vln; Rome Radio Orchestra; Aaron Copland. Varese VC 81098
+FF 5/6-81 p78 +St 7-81 p80

The young pioneers. See no. 1234

COPRARIO, John (John Coperario, John Cooper)
Al primo giorno. See no. 3762

1238 Almaines, nos. 1-5. Coranto. Fantasias, nos. 1-10. Jordi Savall, Christophe Coin, Sergi Casademunt, viol and lyra. Astree AS 54
+FF 3/4-81 p103 +HFN 9-81 p80
+-Gr 4-81 p1334

Coranto. See no. 1238
Fancie a 5. See no. 3762
Fantasias, nos. 1-3. See no. 1239
Fantasias, nos. 1-10. See no. 1238

1239 Fantasias, no. 5: Almain; Galliard. Fantasias, nos. 1-3. Fantasia, no. 8: Almain: Galliard. Funeral teares (song cycle). Consort of Musicke; Anthony Rooley. L'Oiseau-Lyre DSLO 576
+-Gr 6-81 p69 +HFN 6-81 p71

Fantasias, no. 8: Almain; Galliard. See no. 1239
Fantasias a 4, a 5, a 6. See no. 4092
Funeral teares. See no. 1239
Songs: Go happy man; Come ashore; While dancing rests. See no. 3876

CORBEIL, Pierre de

1240 Feast of fools. Guillaume Dufay Vocal and Instrumental Ensemble; Arsene Bedois. Musical Heritage Society MHS 4292
+FF 5/6-81 p78

CORBETTA, Francisco
Chiacconi. See no. 3937
La guitarre royalle: Suite, A minor. See no. 312

Preludio. See no. 3937
Sarabanda. See no. 3937
Sinfonia. See no. 3937. See no. 4097
Sinfonia a 2. See no. 4097

CORELLI, Arcangelo
Concerto, oboe: Prelude-gavotte. See no. 3617
1241 Concerto grosso, op. 6, no. 8, G minor. LOCATELLI: Concerto grosso, op. 1, no. 8, F minor. MANFREDINI: Concerto grosso, op. 3, no. 12, C major. TORELLI: Concerto grosso, op. 8, no. 6, G minor. I Musici. Philips 6570 179 Tape (c) 7310 179 (From 6580 121)
+Gr 11-80 p683 +-HFN 3-81 p97 tape
+HFN 11-80 p129
Concerto grosso, op. 6, no. 8, G minor. See no. 3719
La folie d'Espagne. See no. 3853
1242 Sonatas, op. 5 (12). Yehudi Menuhin, vln; George Malcolm, hpd; Robert Donington, vla da gamba. EMI Electrola 1C 151 03767/8 (2)
+FF 3/4-81 p104 +Gr 10-81 p573
1243 Sonatas, op. 5, nos. 1-6. Hans-Martin Linde, rec; Rudolf Scheidegger, hpd; Michael Jappe, vla da gamba. EMI 1C 065 45712
++FF 11/12-81 p104 ++Gr 10-81 p568
Sonata, op. 5, no. 4, F major. See no. 4056

CORIGLIANO, John
Concerto, clarinet. See no. 376
1244 Elegy. Tournaments overture. MARTINU: Concerto, oboe. Marion Gibson, ob; Louisville Orchestra; Sidney Harth. Louisville LS 771
+-FF 3/4-81 p150 +NR 3-81 p5
+HF 4-81 p77 ++SFC 1-25-81 p17
Tournaments overture. See no. 1244

CORNAGO, Juan
Songs: Gentil dama non se gana. See no. 4063
Songs: Que es mi vida preguntais. See no. 3642

CORNELIUS, Peter
Songs: Weihnachtslieder, op. 8. See no. 3702

CORNYSHE, William
1245 Ave Maria mater dei. LAMBE: Magnificat. TALLIS: Salvator mundi domine. WHITE: Lamentations of Jeremiah. The Scholars. Arion ARN 31939
+Gr 6-81 p75
Ave Maria. See no. 1033
Fa la sol. See no. 4092
Songs: Ah Robin. See no. 3670

CORREA DE ARAUXO, Francisco
Tiento, no. 5. See no. 4098
1246 Tientos, nos. 10, 15-16, 28, 34, 37, 47, 52, 54. Gertrud Mersiovsky, org. Harmonia Mundi 065 99679
+HFN 1-81 p105 +RR 7-80 p77
+MT 3-81 p196
Tiento de baxon del 5th tono. See no. 3958

CORRETTE, Michel
1247 Concerto, hurdy gurdy, C major. HANDEL: Concerto, harp, F major. HASSE: Concerto, mandolin, G major. SCHROTER: Concerto, fortepiano, F major. Annie Challan, hp; Michelle Fromenteau, hurdy gurdy; Elisabeth Maitre, mandolin; Jean Ver Hasselt, forte-

piano; Chamber Orchestra; Roger Cotte. Arion ARN 30S 152 (also Musical Heritage Society MHS 4175)
+FF 3/4-81 p235 ++RR 9-79 p87
+-Gr 4-73 p1884 +-RR 3-73 p47
Livre de orgue, no. 3: Suite, D minor. See no. 3812
Magnificat du 3 and 4 ton. See no. 4112
Vous qui desirez sans fin. See no. 4088

COSTA
Songs: Napulitanata; Tu sei morta nella vita mia; Oili oila; Era de maggio. See no. 4032

COSTANZI, Giovanni
Eupatra: Lusinga la speme. See no. 3756

COSTE, Napoleon
Adagio et menuet, op. 50. See no. 1248
Andante et polonaise, op. 44. See no. 1248
Marche et scherzo, op. 33. See no. 1248
Le montagnard, op. 34. See no. 1248
Rondo, op. 40. See no. 1248
La source du Lyson, op. 47. See no. 1248

1248 Works, selections: Adagio et menuet, op. 50. Andante et polonaise, op. 44. Le montagnard, op. 34. Marche et scherzo, op. 33. Rondo, op. 40. La source du Lyson, op. 47. Simon Wynberg, gtr; John Anderson, ob. Chandos ABR 1031 Tape (c) ABT 1031
+Gr 9-81 p401 +HFN 10-81 p95 tape
+-HFN 8-81 p83

COTTRAU, Teodoro
Addio a Napoli. See no. 4036
Fenesta che lucive. See no. 4032

COUPERIN, Francois

1249 L'Art de toucher le clavecin: Prelude, no. 3. Pieces de clavecin, Bk I, Ordre no. 1. Blandine Verlet, hpd. Astree AS 21
++Gr 7-81 p175 ++STL 2-8-81 p40
Concerts royaux, no. 3, A major. See no. 839
Concerts royaux, no. 4. See no. 3807
Harlequin in the street: Allegro. See no. 3840
Livres de clavecin, Bk I, Order no. 1. See no. 1249

1250 Livres de clavecin, Bk I, Ordre no. 2. Blandine Verlet, hpd. Astree AS 22
+FF 3/4-81 p105

1251 Livres de clavecin, Bk I, Ordre no. 5. Blandine Verlet, hpd. Astree AS 24
+FF 3/4-81 p105
Livres de clavecin, Bk II, Ordre no. 6: Les barricades mysterieuses. See no. 3643

1252 Livres de clavecin, Bk III, Ordres nos. 14, 19. Blandine Verlet, hpd. Astree AS 29
+FF 3/4-81 p105
Livres de clavecin, Bk III, Ordre no. 14: Le rossignol vainqueur. See no. 4095

1253 Livres de clavecin, Bk III, Ordre no. 17. RAMEAU: Suite, E major. Robert Edward Smith, hpd. Towerhill T 1006
+FF 3/4-81 p174
Livres de clavecin, Bk IV, Ordre no. 23. See no. 371

1254 Messe pour les couvents. Michel Chapuis, org. Astree AS 35 (also Harmonia Mundi HMF 715)
+FF 7/8-81 p90

Messe pour les couvents: Elevation. See no. 3674
Messe pour les couvents: Movements. See no. 3811
1255 Messe pour les paroisses. Michel Chapuis, org. Astree AS 34 (also Harmonia Mundi HMF 714)
+FF 7/8-81 p90
Messe pour les paroisses, excerpts. See no. 309
Piece de clavecin, G minor. See no. 3763
Pieces en concert. See no. 102
Prelude, harpsichord, G minor. See no. 4067
Recit de tierce en taille. See no. 3674
Sonata, B flat major. See no. 3763

COUPERIN, Louis
Allemande. See no. 1257
Allemande, G minor. See no. 1256
Bransle de Basque. See no. 1256. See no. 1257
Les carillons de Paris. See no. 1256
Chaconne. See no. 3746
Chaconne, D major. See no. 4088
Chaconne, D minor. See no. 1257
Chaconne, F major. See no. 4115
Chaconnes, F major, D minor, G minor, C minor. See no. 1256
Duo, G minor. See no. 1256
Fantaisies (2). See no. 1257
Fantaisie, G minor. See no. 1256
Gavotte and double. See no. 1256
1256 Organ works: Allemande, G minor. Bransle de Basque. Les carillons de Paris. Chaconnes, F major, D minor, G minor, C minor. Duo, G minor. Fantasia, G minor. Gavotte and double. Passacaille, G minor. Pastoral. Pavan, F sharp minor. Rigadoon and double. Sarabandes, D major, F major, D minor. Georges Delvalee, org. Arion ARN 38582
-Gr 6-81 p58
1257 Organ works: Allemande. Branle de Basque. Chaconne, D minor. Fantaisies (2). Passacaille. Sarabande en canon. GEOFFROY: Lucis creator. La marche. L'ouverture d'Isis. Offerte grave. Menuets: Kyrie. Andre Isoir, org. Musical Heritage Society MHS 4202
+FF 3/4-81 p118 +MU 4-81 p21
Passacaille. See no. 1257
Passacaille, C major. See no. 3916
Passacaille, G minor. See no. 1256
Pastoral. See no. 1256
Pavane. See no. 1259
1258 Pavane, F sharp minor. Suites, A minor, C major, F major. Gustav Leonhardt, hpd. Harmonia Mundi 1C 065 99871
+Gr 10-80 p518 ++MT 7-81 p481
++HFN 9-80 p101
Pavane, F sharp minor. See no. 1256
La Piemontaise, A minor. See no. 1259. See no. 3916
Rigadoon and double. See no. 1256
Sarabandes, D major, F major, D minor. See no. 1256
Sarabande en canon. See no. 1257
Suites, A minor, C major, F major. See no. 1258
1259 Suites, harpsichord, D minor, C major, F major. La Piemontaise, A minor. Pavane. Blandine Verlet, hpd. Astree Valois MB 314
+FF 7/8-81 p91

Tombeau de M. Blancrocher. See no. 785

COWELL, Henry

1260 Hymn and fuguing tune, no. 16. Sonata, violin and piano. Suite, violin and piano. David Sackson, vln; Dwight Peltzer, pno. Folkways FSS 37450
+-FF 7/8-81 p91 +-NR 7-81 p6

Sonata, violin and piano. See no. 1260

Suite, violin and piano. See no. 1260

CRAWFORD, Paul

Quartet, strings. See no. 442

CRECQUILLON, Thomas

1261 Lute settings (Ochsenkhun): Pour ung plaisir. Un gay bergiere. Organ settings (Cabezon): Pour un plaisir. Prenes peitie. Ye preus en grey. Motets: Factus est repente de celo sonus; Servus tuus ego sum; Virgo gloriosa. Songs: Au monde n'est plus grant solas; Dedans Tournay; Fortune hellas que te peult profiter; Grant heur seroit; Je ne fais riens que plaindre et souspirer; Quand me convient; Si des haulx cieulx; Un gay bergier. Songs with lute settings (Phalese): A vous en est; Ung triste coeur. Per Cantar E Sonar Ensemble; Stephane Caillat Vocal Ensemble; Terence Waterhouse, lt; Jean Boyer, org. Musical Heritage Society MHS 4205
+FF 1/2-81 p103

Pour ung plaisir. See no. 1261

Prenes pietie. See no. 1261

Songs: Au monde n'est plus grant solas; Dedans Tournay; Fortune helas que te peult profiter; Grant heur seroit; Je ne fais riens que plaindre et souspirer; Quand me convient; Si des haulz cieulx; Un gay bergier. See no. 1261

Songs (motets): Factus est repente de celo sonus; Servus tuus ego sum; Virgo gloriosa. See no. 1261

Songs with lute settings: A vous en est; Un triste coeur. See no. 1261

Toutes les nuictz. See no. 3766

Un gay bergiere. See no. 1261

Ye preus en grey. See no. 1261

CRESCENZO, de

Tarantella sincera. See no. 3997

CRESHEVSKY, Noah

1262 Broadcast. Great performances. HOWE: Studies in timbre, no. 3. Canons 4. Opus One no. 47
+CMJ Fall 1981 p82

Great performances. See no. 1262

CRESPO, Enrique

American suite, no. 1: Ragtime; Son de Mexico. See no. 3671

CRESTON, Paul

Choric dances, op. 17a. See no. 809

1263 Fantasy. DEFAYE: Danses (2). HINDEMITH: Sonata, trombone and piano. PRYOR: Air varie. John Kitzman, trom; Janice Kay Hodges, pno. Crystal S 386
+NR 12-81 p11

Sonata, saxophone and piano. See no. 3819

1264 Symphony, no. 2, op. 35: Intermezzo and dance. SMETANA: Ma Vlast: Vltava. TCHAIKOVSKY: Meditation, op. 42. WAGNER: Gotterdammerung: Dawn and Siegfried's Rhine journey. Isaac

Stern, vln; National Symphony Orchestra; Hans Kindler, Howard Mitchell, Antal Dorati, Mstislav Rostropovich. Richardson Records RRS 11 (From Victor M 921, Westminster 5272, London 6970, Columbia M 35126)
+-FF 7/8-81 p232

CROCE, Giovanni
Cantate domino. See no. 4060

CROFT, William
1265 Courtship a la mode: Overture and ayres. The funeral: Overture and ayres. Songs: Ah how sweet are the cooling breeze and blooming trees; Lost is my love; Musicus apparatus academicus: With noise of cannon; The wanton Celia. David Thomas, bs; Parley of Instruments. Meridian E 77038
+Gr 6-81 p69 ++HFN 5-81 p80
The funeral: Overture and ayres. See no. 1265
Lords of the world above. See nol 3895
Sonata, harpsichord, no. 3, C minor. See no. 3732
Songs: Ah how sweet are the cooling breeze and blooming trees; Lost is my love; Musicus apparatus academicus: With noise of cannon; The wanton Celia. See no. 1265

CROSSE, Gordon
1266 Dreamsongs, op. 43. Elegy, op. 1. Symphony, no. 1, op. 13a. Scottish Chamber Orchestra; Roderick Brydon. Oxford University Press OUP 203
+Gr 3-81 p1192 +Te 6-81 p49
+HFN 4-81 p68
Elegy, op. 1. See no. 1266
Symphony, no. 1, op. 13a. See no. 1266

CRUMB, George
1267 Variazioni. HODKINSON: Fresco. Louisville Orchestra; David Gilbert. Louisville LS 774
+FF 11/12-81 p141 +NR 9-81 p2

CRUSELL, Bernhard
Divertimento, op. 9. See no. 11
Introduction and variations on a Swedish air, op. 12. See no. 1036
Symphony concertante, no. 3, B flat major. See no. 3794

CSABA
Variations, orchestra. See no. 12

CUI, Cesar
Causerie, op. 40. See no. 3952
Perpetual motion. See no. 3736

CUNNINGHAM, Michael
1268 Trio, piano, no. 3. LAMB: Barefoot dances (6). LOEILLET: Trio. SMITH: Mood music 2. Eugene Rousseau, Dennis Bamber, sax; Wallace Hornibrook, pno. Crystal Records S 156
+/ARG 9-81 p38 +NR 7-81 p5
+FF 9/10-81 p269

CURTIS, E. de
Songs: Autunno; Senza nisciuno; Torna a Surrineto; Tu ca nun chaigne; Voce e notte. See no. 3641
Songs: Canta pe me. See no. 3997
Songs: Carme. See no. 3967
Songs: Carmela; A surrentina. Seeno. 4032
Songs: Torna a Surriento. See no. 3759. See no. 3885

Songs: Tu ca nun chiagne. See no. 3839
Songs: Tu ca non chiagne; Senza nisciuno; Canta pe'me. See no 4036
Songs: Voce e notte. See no. 3843

CYR, Gordon
Tabb songs. See no. 1269
1269 Tetramusic. Tabb songs. MOSS: Hear this touch. WILSON: Sappho. Phyllis Bryn-Julson, Ruth Drucker, s; Arno Drucker, pno; Towson Chamber Players; John Stephens. Orion ORS 83074
+-ARG 3-81 p55 *NR 2-81 p12
+-FF 9/10-81 p297

CZERNIK
Chi sa. See no. 4083

CZERNY, Karl
1270 Les charmes de l'Amitie, op. 55. Valses di bravura, op. 35. Variationen uber einen beliebten Wiener Walzer, op. 12. Variations sur un motif de l'opera "La sonnambule de Bellini", op. 333. Vivien Harvey Slater, pno. Musical Heritage Society MHS 4251
+FF 5/6-81 p79
Valses di bravura, op. 35. See no. 1270
Variationen uber einen beliebten Wiener Walzer, op. 12. See no. 1270
Variations sur un motif de l'opera "La sonnambule de Bellini", op. 333. See no. 1270

DAHL, Ingolf
1271 Music, brass instruments. LINN: Quintet, brass instruments. MICHALSKY: Fantasia alla marcia. Fantasia sopra M. F. V. PLOG: Sierra scenes. Fine Arts Brass Quintet; Barbara Bing-Storm, s. Crystal S 205
+NR 3-81 p7

DALAYRAC, Nicolas-Marie
Nina ou la folle par amour: Quand le bien-aime reviendra. See no. 3758

DALE, Benjamin
Romance. See no. 3971

DALLA CASA
Ancor che col partire. See no. 3766

DALLAPICCOLA, Luigi
1272 Rencesvals. HUSA: Moravian songs (12). VAUGHAN WILLIAMS: Poems by Fredegond Shove (4). WEBERN: Songs (Richard Dehmel) (5). David Pelton, t; Stephen Martorella, pno. Redwood Records ES 12
+FF 1/2-81 p217 +NR 1-81 p11
1273 Songs: Canti (5); Divertimento in quattro esercizi; Liriche de Antonio Machado; Rencesvals. Anna Carol Dudley, s; Tom Buckner, t; Instrumental accompaniments; Robert Hughes. 1750 Arch S 1782
+-FF 1/2-81 p103 +-St 2-81 p104
+NR 10-80 p11

DALZA, Joanambrosio
Passa e mezzo. See no. 3692
Pavana alla venetiana. See no. 3692
Pavana and piva Ferrarese. See no. 3945
Piva. See no. 3661

Piva. See no. 3692
Songs: Dame acogida en tu hato; Enfermo estaba Antioco. See no. 4063

DAMASE, Jean-Michel
Pavane variee. See no. 3986

DAMETT, Thomas
Salve porta paradisi. See no. 4085

DAMMONIS, Innocentius
Songs: Amor Jesu divino; Jesu dulcis memoria; O gloriosa vergine Maria; Tutti debiam cantare. See no. 4011

1274 Stabat mater. STEFFANI: Stabat mater. ANON.: Stabat mater. Kurt Equiluz, Rudolf Resch, t; Nikolaus Simkowski, bs; Wiener Sangerknaben, Chorus Viennensis, VCM, Capella Antiqua Munich; Nikolas Harnoncourt, Konrad Ruhland. Musical Heritage Society MHS 4125 (also Disco Center 3501) (From Barenreiter 078 644)
+FF 5/6-81 p124

DANDRIEU, Jean
Allons voir de divin Gage. See no. 3894
Armes amours. See no. 2094. See no. 3846
Magnificat. See no. 3921
Michau qui causoit de grand bruit. See no. 3950
Noel de Saintonge. See no. 3921
Danses anciennes de Hongrie et de Transylvanie. See no. 3827

DANYEL, John
1275 Lute songs, 1606. Consort of Musicke. L'Oiseau-Lyre DSLO 568
+Gr 4-81 p1352 +HFN 3-81 p87
Songs: Eyes look no more. See no. 3871

DANZI, Franz
1276 Concerto, horn, E major. HAYDN: Concerto, horn, no. 3, D major. ROSETTI: Concerto, horn, D minor. Hermann Baumann, hn; Concerto Amsterdam. Telefunken 6-41288 Tape (c) 4-41288
+Gr 9-81 p460 tape +HFN 3-81 p95
Latin vesper psalms. See no. 3908
1277 Quintet, op. 41, D minor. SPOHR: Quintet, op. 52, C minor. Wolfgang Sawallisch, pno; Munich Residenz Quintet. Claves D 8101
+Gr 6-81 p48
Sonata, horn and piano, op. 28, E flat major. See no. 575
Symphony concertante, op. 41, B major. See no. 3794
Trio, op. 23, F major. See no. 7

DAQUIN, Louis-Claude
Le coucou. See no. 3643
Noel, no. 10. See no. 3806
Noel Suisse. See no. 3735. See no. 3894

DARGOMYZHSKY, Alexander
Russalka: Miller's aria. See no. 3854
Russalka: Unwillingly to these sad shores...Everything here reminds me. See no. 4030
The stone guest. See no. 3854

DARKE, Harold
In the bleak midwinter. See no. 3809
Songs: Creed; Gloria. See no. 3632

DASER, Ludwig
Benedictus Dominus. See no. 3675
Dominus regit me. See no. 3675

DAVEY
The Bay of Biscay. See no. 4046
DAVID, Felicien
Le desert: Chant du muezzin. See no. 4051
La perle du Bresil: Charmant oiseau. See no. 4026. See no. 4040
DAVID, Ferdinand
Songs: Les hirondelles. See no. 3758
DAVID, Johann
Chaconne, A minor. See no. 179
DAVIDOV, Karl
Che felicita. See no. 4027
DAVIDOVSKY, Mario
Pennplay. See no. 3933
DAVIES, Henry Walford
Madgalen at Michael's gate. See no. 3621
Solemn melody. See no. 3806
Songs: Close thine eyes. See no. 3721
Songs: God be in my head. See no. 3852
DAVIS, Thomas
A nation once again. See no. 4046
DAWSON
Songs: Good news; Hymn settings: Amazing grace; At the river; Copland; Furnival. See no. 3810
DEBUSSY, Claude
Arabesques (2). See no. 1306. See no. 1310
1278 Arabesques, nos. 1 and 2. La plus que lente. Estampes: Jardins sous la pluie. MILHAUD: Concerto, piano, no. 1, op. 127. Autumne: Alfama. Saudades do Brasil: Paysandu. RAVEL: Concerto, piano, G major. Marguerite Long, pno; Symphony Orchestra; Darius Milhaud, Maurice Ravel. EMI 2C 015 16349
+Gr 7-81 p192
Arabesques no. 1. See no. 1308
Arabesques, no. 2. See no. 4019
Ballade. See no. 1310
1279 Berceuse heroique. Children's corner suite: Golliwog's cake walk. Preludes, Bk 1: La fille aux cheveux de lin. Le petit negre. Petite suite: Ballet. GOUNOD: Petite symphony, B flat major. SATIE: Gymnopedies (3). (all arranged by Brian Raby). Welsh Brass Consort; Gyorgy Fischer. Nimbus 45006
+FF 7/8-81 p222 +-HFN 6-81 p82
+Gr 1-81 p959
Chansons de Charles d'Orleans (3). See no. 951
Chansons de Charles d'Orleans: Dieu qu'il la fait bon regarder; Quant j'ai ouy le tambourin; Yver vous n'estes qu'un villian. See no. 4005
1280 Children's corner suite. Preludes (5). Suite bergamasque: Clair de lune. Ivan Moravec, pno. Connoisseur Society Tape (c) In Sync 4049
++St 1-81 p90 tape
1281 Children's corner suite. Preludes, Bk 1. Pascal Roge, pno. Decca SXL 6928 Tape (c) KSXC 6928
+Gr 4-81 p1345 ++HFN 4-81 p69
+Gr 6-81 p94 tape
1282 Children's corner suite. Suite bergamasque: Clair de lune. RAVEL: Ma mere l'oye (5 movement version). Pavane pour une

infante defunte. Keiko Nosaka; Ensemble of Twenty-string Kotos; Miki. Denon OX 7155
+HFN 6-81 p73

1283 Children's corner suite. Images, Bk I and II. Claude Helffer, pno. Harmonia Mundi HM 954
+-FF 11/12-81 p143

Children's corner suite. See no. 1308. See no. 1310. See no. 3680

Children's corner suite: Golliwog's cake walk. See no. 1279. See no. 3645

1284 Children's corner suite: The snow is dancing; Golliwog's cake walk. L'Isle joyeuse. Images, Bk I. Aki Takahashi, pno. Toshiba EMI EWLF 98011
*FF 7/8-81 p93

Danse. See no. 1307

Danse bohemienne. See no. 1308. See no. 1310

1285 Danses sacree et profane. Images. Vera Badings, hp; COA; Bernard Haitink. Philips 9500 509 Tape (c) 7300 669 (r) G 9500 509
+ARG 9-79 p22
+Gr 2-79 p1416
+Gr 6-79 p109 tape
+-HF 11-79 p92
+HF 6-81 p70
++HFN 2-79 p103
++HFN 4-79 p134 tape
+MT 8-79 p656
+RR 2-79 p62
+RR 8-79 p128 tape
+St 10-79 p136

Danses sacree et profane. See no. 1324

D'un cahier d'esquisses. See no. 1307

En blanc et noir. See no. 449

Epigraphes antiques (6). See no. 3665

1286 Estampes. L'Isle joyeuse. Masques. Suite bergamasque. Jeremy Menuhin, pno. Ades 14025
+-Gr 8-81 p295
+-HFN 9-81 p80

1287 Estampes. Images. Preludes, Bks I and II. Walter Gieseking, pno. HMV RLS 752 (2) Tape (c) TC RLS 752 (From Columbia 33CX 1098, 33CS 1304, 33CS 1137)
+Gr 12-80 p889 tape
+Gr 9-80 p375
+-HFN 1-81 p109 tape

1288 Estampes. Images. Claudio Arrau, pno. Philips 9500 965 Tape (c) 7300 965
++Gr 11-81 p722
+HFN 11-81 p93

1289 Estampes: Jardins sous la pluie. Pour le piano. Preludes, Bk II: La puerta del vino; Ondine; Feuilles mortes. RAVEL: Sonatine. Ivan Moravec, pno. Connoisseur Society CS 2010 Tape (c) InSync C 4013
+Audio 12-79 p121 tape
+HF 2-80 p102 tape
+RR 2-75 p55
+St 1-81 p90 tape

1290 Estampes: Jardins sous la pluie. Images: Reflets dans l'eau; Poissons d'or. Preludes, Bk I: La catedrale engloutie. Preludes, Bk II: Ondine. GRIFFES: Roman sketches, op. 7: The fountain of Acqua Paola. LISZT: Annees de pelerinage, 3rd year, S 163: Les jeux d'eau a la Villa d'Este. RAVEL: Jeux d'eau. Gaspard de nuit: Ondine. Carol Rosenberger, pno. Delos D/DMS 3006
+Audio 9-81 p83
+HF 8-80 p70
/-HFN 4-80 p116
+-NR 4-80 p14
+-RR 4-80 p104
++St 7-80 p88

Estampes: Jardins sous la pluie. See no. 1278
1291 Etudes, Bks I and II. Theodore Paraskivesco, pno. Calliope CAL 1836
+-FF 9/10-81 p94 +-HFN 10-81 p86
+Gr 3-81 p1214
1292 Etudes, Bks I and II. Anne Queffelec, pno. Erato STU 71384
+Gr 8-81 p295 +HFN 10-81 p86
Etudes: Pour les arpeges composes. See no. 1309
Etudes retrouvee. See no. 1309
1293 Fantaisie, piano. Rhapsody, clarinet. Rhapsody, saxophone (comp. and orch. Roger-Ducasse). Antony Morf, clt; Claude Delangle, sax; Anne Queffelec, pno; Monte Carlo Opera Orchestra; Armin Jordan. Erato STU 71400
+-Gr 8-81 p267 +HFN 10-81 p86
1294 Fantaisie, piano. DELIUS: Concerto, piano, C minor. Jean-Rodolphe Kars, pno; LSO; Alexander Gibson. London STS 15503 (From CS 6657)
+FF 5/6-81 p81
Hommage a Joseph Haydn. See no. 1310
Images. See no. 1285. See no. 1287. See no. 1288. See no. 1307. See no. 1324
Images, Bks I and II. See no. 1283. See no. 1309
Images, Bk I. See no. 1248
Images: Cloches a travers les feuilles; Reflets dans l'eau. See no. 1308
1295 Images: Reflets dans l'eau. Preludes, Bk I: La fille aux cheveux de lin. Preludes, Bk II: Feux d'artifice; Bruyeres. PROKOFIEV: Sonata, piano, no. 3, op. 38, A minor. RACHMANINOFF: Prelude, op. 3, no. 2, C sharp minor. SCRIABIN: Etude, op. 2, no. 1, C sharp minor. Poem, op. 32, no. 1, F sharp minor. Sonata, piano, no. 9, op. 68, F minor. Ruth Laredo, pno. Connoisseur Society Tape (c) InSync 4060
++Audio 7-81 p64 tape +HF 4-81 p93 tape
+-CL 5/6-81 p8 tape +St 4-81 p110 tape
Images: Reflets dans l'eau; Hommage a Rameau; Mouvement. See no. 913
Images: Reflets dans l'eau; Poisson d'or. See no. 1290
Images oubliees. See no. 1309
1296 Images pour orchestra. Prelude a l'apres-midi d'un faune. LSO; Andre Previn. HMV ASD 3804 Tape (c) TC ASD 3804 (also Angel DS 37674)
+-FF 9/10-80 p106 +-MT 2-81 p111
++Gr 12-79 p1008 +-MUM 10-80 p34
++Gr 3-80 p1446 tape ++NR 4-80 p2
+Gr 8-81 p324 tape +RR 1-80 p70
+-HF 8-80 p79 +SFC 3-23-80 p35
+HFN 12-79 p159 ++St 6-80 p116
+HFN 2-80 p107 tape +STL 12-2-79 p37
1297 Images pour orchestra: Iberia. RIMSKY-KORSAKOV: Capriccio espagnol, op. 34, TURINA: Danzas fantasticas, op. 22: Orgia. Dallas Symphony Orchestra; Eduardo Mata. Telarc DG 10055
++SFC 11-1-81 p18
L'isle joyeuse. See no. 1248. See no. 1286. See no. 1306. See no. 1307
1298 Jeux. Nocturnes (3). COA; Bernard Haitink. Philips 9500 674

Tape (c) 7300 769
++ARG 4-81 p21
+FF 1/2-81 p105
++Gr 11-80 p665
++Gr 3-81 p1171
+Gr 1-81 p1001 tape
+-HF 3-81 p66
++HFN 11-80 p117
++HFN 1-81 p109 tape
++NR 12-80 p2
+SFC 10-26-80 p20
++St 2-81 p104

Jeux. See no. 1324

Marche ecossaise. See no. 1324

1299 Le martyre de Saint Sebastien. La mer. PhO; Guido Cantelli. World Records SH 374 (From HMV ALP 1228)
++Gr 3-81 p1192
+-HFN 6-81 p85

Le martyre de Saint Sebastien: Fanfare. See no. 3624

Masques. See no. 1286. See no. 1307

Mazurka. See no. 1310

1300 La mer. RAVEL: Daphnis and Chloe: Suite, no. 2. LSO; Charles Mackerras. Centaur CRC 1007
+FF 5/6-81 p79
+-Gr 6-81 p36
+HF 7-81 p66
+-HFN 6-81 p71
-NR 8-81 p5

1301 La mer. RAVEL: Ma mere l'oye. Rapsodie espagnole. LAPO; Carlo Maria Giulini. DG 2531 264 Tape (c) 3301 264
+-FF 1/2-81 p169
+-Gr 6-80 p32
+-HF 3-81 p66
+HFN 6-80 p106
+HFN 8-80 p109 tape
++RR 6-80 p46
+SR 1-81 p92
++STL 5-11-80 p39

1302 La mer. Nocturnes. Strasbourg Philharmonic Orchestra; Alain Lombard. Erato STU 71158
+-HFN 8-81 p83

1303 La mer. Prelude a l'apres-midi d'un faune. RAVEL: Bolero. BPhO; Herbert von Karajan. Mobile Fidelity Sound Lab MFSL 1-1513 (From Angel S 37438)
+ARG 10-81 p36
+-FF 7/8-81 p93
+NR 5-81 p5
+-SFC 4-5-81 p18

La mer. See no. 1299. See no. 1324

Morceau de concours. See no. 1309

Nocturnes. See no. 1298. See no. 1302. See no. 1306. See no. 1310. See no. 1324

Nocturnes, D major. See no. 1308

Ncoturnes: Fetes. See no. 1115

1304 Pelleas et Melisande. Frederica von Stade, Christine Barbaux, s; Nadine Denize, con; Richard Stilwell, Jose van Dam, bar; Ruggero Raimondi, Pascal Thomas, bs; German Opera Chorus; BPhO; Herbert von Karajan. HMV SLS 5172 (3) Tape (c) TC SLS 5172 (also Angel SZX 3885)
+ARG 7/8-80 p22
++FF 5/6-80 p72
+Gr 12-79 p1040
+-HF 4-80 p84
++HFN 4-80 p121 tape
++HFN 2-80 p91
+-MT 5-81 p317
++NR 3-80 p12
+NYT 12-23-79 pD28
+ON 3-15-80 p45
+Op 5-80 p471
++RR 1-80 p56
+-SFC 1-6-80 p43
+SR 7-81 p90
++St 3-80 p100
+-STL 2-10-80 p40

Le petit negre. See no. 1279. See no. 1306. See no. 1310

Petite piece. See no. 3738

Petite piece, clarinet and piano. See no. 1323. See no. 3793
1305 Petite suite (orch. Busser). EGK: French suite after Rameau. MASSENET: Espada. ROUSSEL: Petite suite. BRSO, Paris Opera Orchestra, Leipzig Gewandhaus Orchestra; Sergiu Celibidache, Georges Sebastian, Werner Egk. Varese VC 81110 (From Urania UR 5006, 8013, 7022)
+-ARG 4-81 p41 +HF 5-81 p55
+-FF 1/2-81 p160
Petite suite: Ballet. See no. 1279
1306 Piano works: Arabesques (2). L'Isle joyeuse. Nocturne. La plus que lente. Le petit negre. Suite bergamasque. Theodore Paraskivesco, pno. Calliope CAL 1835
+FF 3/4-81 p106
1307 Piano works: Danse. D'un cahier d'esquisses. Images. L'Isle joyeuse. Masques. Pascal Roge, pno. Decca SXL 6957 Tape (c) KSXC 6957
+Gr 2-81 p1104 +HFN 2-81 p87
+-Gr 6-81 p94
1308 Piano works: Arabesque, no. 1. Children's corner suite. Danse bohemienne. Images: Reflets dans l'eau; Cloches a travers les feuilles. Nocturne, D major. Preludes, Bk I: La fille aux cheveux de lin; La catedrale engloutie. Suite bergamasque: Clair de lune. Jorg Demus, pno. Eurodisc 25019
-FF 11/12-81 p142
1309 Piano works: Images, Bk I and II. Images oubliees. Etudes retrouvee. Morceau de concours. Etudes: Pour les arpeges composes. Roy Howat, pno. Nimbus 2122
+-Gr 1-81 p967 +MT 3-81 p183
+-HFN 9-80 p101 +RR 8-80 p70
1310 Piano works: Arabesques (2). Ballade. Children's corner suite. Danse bohemienne. Mazurka. Nocturne. Hommage a Joseph Haydn. Le petit negre. Tarantelle styrienne. Valse romantique. Livia Rev, pno. Saga SAGA 5480
+-Gr 5-81 p1498 +-HFN 6-81 p71
La plus que lente. See no. 17. See no. 1278. See no. 1306
1311 Pour le piano. HAYDN: Andante and variations, F minor. SCHUMANN: Fantasia, op. 17, C major. Rudolph Buchbinder, pno. Everest 3479
-FF 9/10-81 p234 -NR 2-81 p14
Pour le piano. See no. 1289
Preludes (5). See no. 1280
1312 Preludes, Bk I and II. Ernest Ulmer, pno. Protone PR 151/2 (2)
+-FF 11/12-80 p98 +-St 4-81 p103
++HF 8-80 p71
Preludes, Bk I and II. See no. 1287
1313 Preludes, Bk I. Claudio Arrau, pno. Philips 9500 676 Tape (c) 7300 771
++FF 1/2-81 p104 +HFN 12-80 p159 tape
++Gr 10-80 p518 ++NR 11-80 p9
+Gr 1-81 p1001 tape ++SFC 9-21-80 p21
++FF 6-81 p58 ++St 12-80 p120
+HFN 11-80 p117 +STL 11-9-80 p40
Preludes, Bk I. See no. 1281
Preludes, Bk I: La catedrale engloutie. See no. 1290
Preludes, Bk I: La fille aux cheveux de lin. See no. 1279. See no. 1295. See no. 3730. See no. 4003

Preludes, Bk I: La fille aux cheveux de lin; La catedrale engloutie. See no. 1308

1314 Preludes, Bk II. Claudio Arrau, pno. Philips 9500 747 Tape (c) 7300 832
+FF 11/12-81 p143 +HFN 6-81 p71
+Gr 6-81 p58 +-HFN 9-81 p93 tape
++Gr 9-81 p460 tape ++St 10-81 p124

Preludes, Bk II: Feux d'artifice; Bruyeres. See no. 1295

Preludes, Bk II: Ondine. See no. 1290

Preludes, Bk II: La puerta del vino; Ondine; Feuilles mortes. See no. 1289

Prelude a l'apres-midi d'un faune. See no. 1113. See no. 1115. See no. 1296. See no. 1303. See no. 1324. See no. 3709. See no. 4121

Printemps. See no. 4122

1315 Quartet, strings, G minor. RAVEL: Quartet, strings, F major. Capet Quartet. EMI 2C 051 16419
+-Gr 7-81 p192

Reverie. See no. 4003. See no. 4007

Rhapsody, clarinet. See no. 1293. See no. 1323. See no. 1324. See no. 3738. See no. 3793

Rhapsody, saxophone. See no. 1293

1316 Sonata, flute, viola and harp. Sonata, violin and piano. Sonata, violoncello and piano, D minor. Syrinx. Boston Symphony Chamber Players. DG 2535 455 Tape (c) 3335 455 (From 2530 049) (also DG 2733 007)
+-Gr 4-81 p1334 +-HFN 8-81 p92 tape
+HFN 5-81 p91

1317 Sonata, flute, viola and harp. Syrinx. DEVIENNE: Duo, flute and viola, no. 3, FAURE: Impromptu, op. 86. RAVEL: Sonatine en trio (arr. Salzedo). Orpheus Trio. Vanguard VA 25002
++NR 7-81 p6 +SFC 4-5-81 p18
+NYT 9-27-81 pD24 +St 8-81 p106

Sonata, flute, viola and harp. See no. 1323

Sonata, flute, viola and harp, no. 2. See no. 851

Sonata, violin and piano. See no. 1316. See no. 1323

1318 Sonata, violin and piano, G minor. FRANCK: Sonata, violin and piano, A major. Kyung Wha Chung, vln; Radu Lupu, pno. London CS 7171 (also Decca SXL 6944 Tape (c) KSXC 6944)
++FF 1/2-81 p111 +HFN 9-80 p101
+Gr 9-80 p359 ++St 12-80 p124
+Gr 12-80 p889 tape ++ST 6-81 p733

1319 Sonata, violin and piano, G minor. PROKOFIEV: Songs without words, op. 35 (5). RAVEL: Sonata, violin, G major. YSAYE: Sonata, solo violin, no. 3, op. 27, D minor. David Oistrakh, vln; Frida Bauer, pno. Philips 6570 206 Tape (c) 7310 206
+-FF 1/2-81 p171 +HFN 11-81 p105
+Gr 12-81 p897

1320 Sonata, violin and piano, G minor. FRANCK: Sonata, violin and piano, A major. Ivry Gitlis, vln; Martha Argerich, pno. Ricordi RCL 27018
+-FF 11/12-81 p165

Sonata, violin and piano, G minor. See no. 3841

Sonata, violoncello and piano, D minor. See no. 1316. See no. 1323

1321 Songs: La damoiselle elui; Ballades de Francois Villon (3); Invocation; Salut printemps. Barbara Hendricks, s; Jocelyne Taillon, ms; Dietrich Fischer-Dieskau, bar; Leonard Pezzino, t; L'Orchestre and Chorus de Paris; Daniel Barenboim. DG 2531 263
+-FF 1/2-81 p104 +-NR 11-80 p7
+Gr 8-80 p248 +NYT 12-14-80 pD38
+-HF 3-81 p69 +NYT 9-21-80 pD22
+-HFN 9-80 p101 +RR 8-80 p81

1322 Songs: Aimons-nous et dormons; Angelus; Apparition; Ariettes oubliees; Ballades de Francois Villon (3); Beau soir; La belle au bois dormant; Chanson de Bilitis; Chanson de France: Rondel; Le temps a laissee son manteau; Rondel: Pour ce que plaisance est monte; Claire de lune; Dans le jardin; Fetes galantes, Set 1 and 2; Fleur des bles; Jane; Mandoline; Melodies (3); Noel des enfants qui n'ont plus de maison; Nuit d'etoiles; Pantomime; Paysage sentimental; Pierrot; Poemes de Charles Baudelaire (5); Poemes de Stephane Mallarme (3); Le promenoir des deux amants; Proses lyriques; Romances: Romance, Les cloches; Rondeau; Rondel chinois; Voici que le printemps; Zephyr. Elly Ameling, Michele Command, Mady Mesple, s; Frederica von Stade, ms; Gerard Souzay, bar; Dalton Baldwin, pno. Pathe Marconi 2C 16371/4 (4)
++FF 9/10-81 p95 +-HFN 12-80 p137
+Gr 12-80 p860

Songs: Ballade des femmes de Paris; C'est l'extase langoureuse. See no. 3823
Songs: Le faune; Je tremble en voyant ton visage. See no. 3653
Songs: Mandoline. See no. 4076
Suite bergamasque. See no. 1286. See no. 1306
Suite bergamasque: Clair de lune. See no. 1280. See no. 1282. See no. 1308. See no. 3764. See no. 3816. See no. 3820
Suite bergamasque: Passepied. See no. 4003
Syrinx. See no. 1316. See no. 1317. See no. 1323. See no. 3668. See no. 3914. See no. 3928
Tarantelle styrienne. See no. 1310
Valse romantique. See no. 1310

1323 Works, selections: Petite piece, clarinet and piano. Rhapsody, clarinet and piano. Sonata, flute, viola and harp. Sonata, violin and piano. Sonata, violoncello and piano, D minor. Syrinx. Athena Ensemble. Chandos ABR 1036 Tape (c) ABT 1036
+Gr 11-81 p714 ++STL 11-8-81 p40
+HFN 11-81 p93

1324 Works, selections: Danses sacree et profane. Jeux. Images. Marche ecossaise. La mer. Nocturnes. Prelude a l'apres-midi d' un faune. Rhapsody, clarinet and paino. George Pieterson, clt; Vera Badings, hp; COA; Bernard Haitink. Philips 6769 284 (3) (From 9500 359, 9500 509, 9500 674)
+Gr 10-81 p546 ++HFN 11-81 p103

DECAUX, Abel-Marie
Clairs de lune. See no. 1019

DECSENYI, Janos
1325 Comments on Marcus Aurelius. Csontvary pictures, excerpts. Variations, piano. Liszt Ferenc Chamber Orchestra, Budapest Symphony Orchestra; Adam Fellegi, pno; Peter Gazda, Geza Oberfrank, Janos Sandor. Hungaroton SLPX 12122
+FF 5/6-81 p80 -NR 5-81 p2

Csontvary pictures, excerpts. See no. 1325
Variations, piano. See no. 1325

DEDLER, Rochus

1326 Symphony, D major. MOZART: Symphony, K 19a. TOESCHI: Symphony, D major. Convivium Musicum, Munich; Erich Keller. Musica Bavarica MB 70702
+ARG 12-81 p48 +-St 11-81 p82

DEFAYE, Jean-Michel

Danses (2). See no. 1263. See no. 3742

DE LARA

Partir c'est mourir un peu. See no. 4026

DEL BORGO, Elliot

Canto. See no. 3819

DELERUE, Georges

Adagio. See no. 4007

DELIBES, Leo

Coppelia: Csardas. See no. 3863
Good morning Sue. See no. 4039
Lakme: Air des clochettes; Blanche Dourga; D'ou viens tu...C'est la Dieu; Les filles de Cadiz. See no. 3649
Lakme: Ou va la jeune indoue. See no. 4040
Lakme: Vieni al contenot profondo. See no. 3967

1327 Naila waltz (arr. Dohnanyi). DOHNANYI: Rhapsodies, op. 11 (4). STRAUSS: Schatz waltz (arr. Dohnanyi). Miklos Schwalb, pno. AFKA SK 4636
+-FF 3/4-81 p35

Songs: Les filles de Cadiz. See no. 3758

DeLIO, Thomas

Serenade. See no. 1224

DeLISLE, Rouget

La Marsellaise. See no. 3699

DELIUS, Frederick

1328 Air and dance. ELGAR: Serenade, op. 20, E minor. VAUGHAN WILLIAMS: Concerto grosso. WARLOCK: Serenade for the 10th birthday of Delius. Gerald Jarvis, vln; Bournemouth Symphony Orchestra; Norman Del Mar. HMV ESD 7088 Tape (c) TC ESD 7088 (From ASD 2531)
+FF 1/2-81 p230 +HFN 9-80 p115
+Gr 8-80 p234

1329 Appalachia. Sea drift. John Shirley-Quirk, bar; London Symphony Chorus; RPO; Richard Hickox. Argo ZRG 934 Tape (c) KZRC 934
++Gr 7-81 p182 +STL 10-11-81 p41
+HFN 7-81 p72

1330 Appalachia. Brigg Fair. Alun Jenkins, bar; Ambrosian Singers; Halle Orchestra; John Barbirolli. HMV Tape (c) TC ESD 7099
+Gr 6-81 p81 p93 tape +STL 4-12-81 p40

Aquarelles (2). See no. 1338
Brigg Fair. See no. 1330
La Calinda. See no. 1338
Caprice and elegy. See no. 1338
Concerto, piano, C minor. See no. 1294
Fantastic dance. See no. 1338

1331 Hassan: Serenade (arr. Beacham).* WALTON (Bach): The wise virgins: Ballet suite. VAUGHAN WILLIAMS: The lark ascending.* WARLOCK: Serenade, strings.* Rafael Druian, vln; Martha Dalton,

hp; Cleveland Sinfonietta, CO; Louis Lane. CBS 61433 Tape (c) 40-61433 (*From Columbia SCX 3525)
+-Gr 3-81 p1208 +-HFN 3-81 p94
Irmelin. See no. 468
Irmelin: Prelude. See no. 1338
1332 The magic fountain. Katherine Pring, ms; John Mitchinson, t; Norman Welsby, bar; Richard Angas, Francis Thomas, bs; BBC Singers; BBC Concert Orchestra; Norman Del Mar. BBC Artium BBC 2001 (2) (also Arabesque 8121 Tape (c) 9121)
+-ARG 9-81 p46 +NR 5-81 p11
+Gr 8-80 p265 /ON 4-11-81 p52
+HF 7-81 p55 +SFC 5-3-81 p22
+HF 11-81 p103 tape +St 7-81 p84
+-MT 6-81 p389
On hearing the first cuckoo in spring. See no. 3666. See no. 4122
1333 Quartet, strings. SIBELIUS: Quartet, strings, op. 56, D minor. Fitzwilliam Quartet. L'Oiseau-Lyre DSLO 47
+Gr 1-81 p959 +ST 8-81 p276
+HFN 1-81 p92 +STL 2-8-81 p40
++MT 10-81 p678
Romance. See no. 3667
Sea drift. See no. 1329
1334 Sonatas, violin and piano, nos. 1-3. Yehudi Menuhin, vln; Eric Fenby, pno. HMV ASD 3864
+FF 1/2-81 p106 +MT 12-80 p785
+Gr 6-80 p44 +RR 6-80 p76
/HFN 6-80 p106 ++ST 9-80 p344
1335 Sonatas, violin and piano, nos. 1-3. Derry Dean, vln; Eleanor Hancock, pno. Sine Qua Non SA 2037 Tape (c) 2037
+ARG 5-81 p16
A song of summer. See no. 468. See no. 1338
1336 Songs: The birds story; Hidden love; The homeward way; The nightingale; Twilight fancies; Young Venevil. GURNEY: All night under the moon; Bread and cherries; Brown is my love; The cloths of heaven; Desire in spring; Down by the salley gardens; An epitaph; The fields are full; The folly of being comforted; Severn meadows; The singer; Snow. VAUGHAN WILLIAMS: A clear midnight; Four nights; How can the tree but wither; Joy shipmate joy; Motion and stillness; The new ghost; Nocturne; Twilight people; The water mill. WARLOCK: After two years; Away to Twiver; Balulalow; The frostbound wood; Jillian of Berry; My own country; Passing by; Pretty ring time; Rest sweet numphs; Sleep; Sweet and twenty; Yarmouth fair. Ian Partridge, t; Jennifer Partridge, pno. Oxford University Press OUP 155/6 (2) (also Peters International PLE 136/7)
+ARG 11-81 p44 +St 10-81 p132
+Gr 1-81 p982
Songs: Cynara; Idyll; A late lark; Songs of farewell. See no. 1338
Songs: Songs of sunset. See no. 372
1337 To be sung on a summer night on the water. HADLEY: The hills. Felicity Palmer, s; Robert Tear, t; Robert Lloyd, bs; Cambridge King's College Choir, Cambridge University Musical Society Chorus; LPO; Philip Ledger HMV SQ SAN 393

+ARG 2-81 p38
+Gr 6-76 p71
+-HFN 7-76 p85
+-MT 9-76 p746
+RR 7-76 p75

A village Romeo and Juliet: Walk into paradise garden. See no. 468

1338 Works, selections: Aquarelles (2) (arr. Fenby). La Calinda (arr. Fenby). Caprice and elegy. Fantastic dance. Irmelin: Prelude. A song of summer. Songs: Cynara; Idyll; A late lark; Songs of farewell. Felicity Lott, s; Anthony Rolfe Johnson, t; Thomas Allen, bar; Julian Lloyd Webber, vlc; RPO; Eric Fenby. Unicorn UHJI DKP 9008/9 (2)

++Gr 10-81 p546
++HFN 10-81 p86
++STL 10-11-81 p41

DELLO JOIO, Norman

Variants from a medieval tune. See no. 3817

DEL TREDICI, David

1339 Final Alice. Barbara Hendricks, s; CSO; George Solti. London LDR 71018 (also Decca SXDC 7516)

++FF 11/12-81 p144
+Gr 8-81 p306
+HFN 6-81 p79
+NR 12-81 p14
++ON 12-19-81 p44
++SFC 8-23-81 p18
++St 11-81 p82

de MARS, James

Premonitions of Christopher Columbus. See no. 868

DEMESSIEUX, Jeanne

1340 Repons pour le Temps de Paques. DURUFLE: Prelude et fugue sur le nom d'Alain, op. 7. FRANCK: Chorale, no. 1, E major. LITAIZE: Variations sur un Noel Angevin. Anita Werling, org. Central Congregational Church, Galesburg, Il.

+MU 5-81 p23

DENISOV, Edison

1341 Signes en blanc. Sonata, violin and piano. Trio, piano. Jean-Pierre Armengaud, pno; Devy Erlih, vln; Alain Meunier, vlc. Chant du Monde LDX 78685

+HFN 5-81 p80

Sonata, violin and piano. See no. 1341

Trio, piano. See no. 1341

DENNIS, Robert

Of a rose. See no. 3911

DENZA, Luigi

Songs: Culto; Occhi di fata. See no. 4024

Songs: Funiculi funicula. See no. 3759. See no. 4045. See no. 4083

Songs: Occhi di fata. See no. 4031. See no. 4032

DERING, Richard

Factum est silentium. See no. 3616

Songs: Contristatus est Rex David; Quem vidistis pastores. See no. 3620

Songs: Duo seraphim; Gaudent in coelis. See no. 3636

DESENCLOS

Quartet, saxophones. See no. 3737

DESTOUCHES, Andre Cardinal

1342 Suite des elements, no. 1. REBEL: Les elements. Academy of Ancient Music; Christopher Hogwood, hpd and cond. L'Oiseau-Lyre DSLO 562

+FF 3/4-81 p176 +MT 7-81 p482
+Gr 9-80 p332 ++NR 2-81 p2
+-HF 5-81 p61 ++St 3-81 p94
+HFN 9-80 p101

DEVIENNE, Francois

1343 Concerto, flute, no. 7, E minor. Symphonie concertante, op. 76, G major. Aurele Nicolet, Christiane Nicolet, flt; Netherlands Chamber Orchestra; Antonio Ros-Marba. Philips 9500 773
+FF 9/10-81 p96 ++NR 9-81 p4

Duo, flute and viola, no. 3, See no. 1317

Symphonie concdrtante, op. 76, G major. See no. 1343

DIA, Comtesse de

A chanter m'er de so qu'eu no volria. See no. 4086

DIABELLI, Anton

1344 Sonatinas, op. 151, nos. 1-3. DUSSEK: Sonatinas, op. 20, nos. 1, 4. HAYDN: Sonata, piano, no. 48, C major. MOZART: Sonata, piano, no. 15, K 545, C major. Hans Kann, pno. Musical Heritage Society MHS 4207
-FF 9/10-81 p239

DIAMOND, David

Rounds. See no. 377

DICKINSON, Peter

1345 Surrealist landscape. HARVEY: Correspondances. LUTYENS: Steven Smith songs. PANUFNIK: Dreamscape. Meriel Dickinson, s; Peter Dickinson, pno. Unicorn UNS 268
+Gr 4-81 p1356 ++HFN 5-81 p84

DIEMER, Emma

Youth overture. See no. 3880

DIEPENBROCK

Songs: Berceuse. See no. 3702

DIEUPART, Charles

Sonata, A major. See no. 4095

DiGIACOMO, Frank

1346 Beauty and the beast. Christine Klemperer, s; Gayle Ross, s; Donna Miller, ms; William Black, Richard McCullough, bar; Orchestra and Chorus; Gary Sheldon. 20th Century CEJS 101/3 (3)
+NR 9-81 p11

DINICU, Dimitri

Hora staccato. See no. 3693. See no. 3841. See no. 4066

DIRKSEN

Rejoice ye pure in heart. See no. 3810

DIRKSEN, Richard

Welcome all wonders, excerpt. See no. 3818

DISTLER, Hugo

1347 Ach wie fluchtig ach wie nichtig. Das alte Jahr vergangen ist. Mit Freuden zart. Sonata, organ, op. 18, no. 2. Partitas: Christ der du bist der helle Tag; Christe du Lamm Gottes; Jesus Christus unser Heiland; Nun komm der Heiden Heiland; Wachet auf ruft uns die Stimme. Spielstucke, op. 18, nos. 1-31. Wie schon leuchtet der Morgenstern (2 settings). FRESCOBALDI: Canzon per sonar. PACHELBEL: Fantasie, G major. PRAETORIUS: O lux beata trinitas. Arno Schonstedt, Hugo Distler, org. Pape 1001 (4)
+FF 11/12-81 p146

Das alte Jahr vergangen ist. See no. 1347

Choral motet, op. 12: Singet frisch und wohlgemut. See no. 3963
1348 Choralpassion, op. 7. Paul Muhlschlegel, Theo Diegritz, t; Gerhard Hess, Peter Jank, bar; Bruch Abel, Gunther Trag, bs; St. Lorenz Chamber Choir; Hermann Harrassowitz. Motette M 5001
+ARG 10-81 p22 +FF 1/2-81 p107
1349 Der Jahrkreis, op. 5, excerpts. Variation, organ, op. 8. Westphalian Kantorei; Arno Schonstedt, org; Wilhelm Ehmann. Musical Heritage Society MHS 3655
+MU 10-81 p8
Mit Freuden zart. See no. 1347
Nun komm der Heiden Heiland, partita. See no. 182
Partitas: Christ der du bist der helle Tag; Christe du Lamm Gottes; Jesus Christus unser Heiland; Nun komm der Heiden Heiland; Wachet auf ruft uns die Stimme. See no. 1347
Spielstucke, op. 18, nos. 1-31. See no. 1347
Sonata, organ, op. 18, no. 2. See no. 1347
Variations, organ, op. 8. See no. 1349
Wie schon leuchtet der Morgenstern. See no. 1347

DITTERSDORF, Carl Ditters von
Concerto, harp, A major: Rondeau and allegretto. See no. 164
Concerto, harp, op. 4, no. 6, B flat major. See no. 836
DIVINE ORTHODOX LITURGY. See no. 3724

DLUGORAJ, Adalbert
Fantasia. See no. 4016
Finales (2). See no. 4016
Vilanellas, nos. 1 and 2. See no. 4016

DODGSON, Stephen
1350 Concerto, guitar. Duo concertante, harpsichord and guitar. Partita, no. 1. John Williams, gtr; Rafael Puyana, hpd; ECO; Charles Groves. CBS 61841 Tape (c) 40-61841 (From 72661, 72948, 72348)
++Gr 1-80 p1145 +HFN 3-80 p107 tape
+Gr 2-81 p1122 tape ++RR 2-80 p74
+HFN 2-80 p105
Duo concertante, harpsichord and guitar. See no. 1350
Partita, no. 1. See no. 1350

DOHNANYI, Ernst von
Aria, flute and piano, op. 48, no. 1. See no. 3923
Cascades, op. 41, no. 4. See no. 3866
Humoresque, op. 17, no. 1. See no. 3866
Passacaglia, op. 48, no. 2. See no. 3923
Pastorale. See no. 3866
Postludium, op. 13, no. 10. See no. 3920
1351 Quintet, piano, no. 2, op. 26, E minor. Serenade, op. 10, C major. Carol Lieberman, Ronan Lefkowitz, vln; Marcus Thompson, vla; David Fink, vlc; Andrew Wolf; pno. AFKA SK 290
+FF 5/6-81 p81
Rhapsodies, op. 11. See no. 1327
Rhapsody, op. 11, no. 2, F sharp minor. See no. 3866
1352 Ruralia Hungarica, op. 32. Variations on a nursery song, op. 25. Istvan Lantos, pno; Budapest Symphony Orchestra; Gyorgy Lehel. Hungaroton SLPX 12149
+FF 3/4-81 p106 +NR 4-81 p1
+Gr 11-80 p665 ++SFC 2-8-81 p21
1353 Ruralia hungarica, op. 32. Winterreigen, op. 13. Timothy Lowe,

pno. Vivace VV 5001
/Gr 8-81 p295 +-HFN 12-81 p94
Serenade, op. 10, C major. See no. 1351
1354 Sonata, violoncello and piano, op. 8, B flat major. WEILL: Sonata, violoncello and piano. Jerry Grossman, vlc; Diana Walsh, pno. Nonesuch D 79016 Tape (c) D1 79016
+FF 11/12-81 p280 ++NYT 9-13-81 pD41
+HF 12-81 p93 tape
Variations on a nursery song, op. 25. See no. 1352
Winterreigen, op. 13. See no. 1353

DOMPIERRE, Francois
1355 Concerto, piano. Harmonica flash. Edith Boivin-Beluse, pno; Claude Garden, harm; Montreal Symphony Orchestra; Charles Dutoit. DG 2531 265
+FF 11/12-81 p147 +-HFN 11-80 p117
+Gr 8-80 p215 +MUM 7/8-80 p30
Harmonica flash. See no. 1355

DONATI
In te Domine speravi. See no. 3853

DONATO DA FIRENZE
Come in sul fonte. See no. 4102

DONAUDY, Stefano
Songs: Luoghi sereni e cari. See no. 4043
Songs: O del mio amato ben; Luoghi sereni e cari. See no. 3967

DONIZETTI, Gaetano
1356 Anna Bolena. Renata Scotto, s; Tatiana Troyanos, ms; Umberto Grilli, Piero de Palma, t; Ezio Flagello, bs-bar; Nicola Zaccaria, bs; Orchestra and Chorus; Fernando Previtali. Historical Recordings HRE 348/3 (3)
+-NR 9-81 p10
1357 L'Assedio di Calais: Danza militare; Ballabile. Don Sebastiano: Passo a tre; Passo a due; Ballabile di Schiavi. La favorita: Introduzione delle danze; Passo a tre; Passo a sei; Finale delle danze. Les martyrs: Airs de danse, nos. 1-3. PhO; Antonio de Almeida. Philips 9500 673 Tape (c) 7300 768
+ARG 12-80 p24 /+HFN 10-80 p117
+-FF 11/12-80 p100 /MT 3-81 p183
+/Gr 9-80 p334 /NR 10-80 p3
+Gr 10-80 p548 tape ++SFC 8-10-80 p29
+-HFN 9-80 p101
Belisario: O si tremenda. See no. 1359
1358 Don Pasquale. Lucia Popp, s; Francisco Araiza, t; Bernd Weikl, bar; Evgeny Nesterenko, Peter Lika, bs; Bavarian Radio Chorus; Munich Radio Orchestra; Heinz Wallberg. Eurodisc 300 832-435 (2)
+NR 12-81 p10 +SFC 12-13-81 p18
Don Pasquale: Com'e gentile; Cerchero lontano. See no. 4035
Don Pasquale: Com'e gentile; Tornami a dir. See no. 4047
Don Pasquale: Overture. See no. 1373
Don Pasquale: Quel guardo il cavaliere. See no. 3748
Don Pasquale: Quel guardo il cavaliere...So anch'io la virtu magica. See no. 4081
Don Pasquale: Quel guardo il cavaliere...So anch'io la virtu magica; Pronto io son; Tornami a dir che m'ami. See no. 3640
Don Sebastiano: Deserto in terra. See no. 3995. See no. 4053. See no. 4075

Don Sebastiano: O Lisbona. See no. 1359
Don Sebastiano: Passo a tre; Passo a due; Ballabile di Schiavi. See no. 1357

1359 Il duca d'Alba. Arias: Belisario: O si tremenda. Don Sebastiano: O Lisbonne. La favorita: Ange si pur; O mon Fernando. La fille du regiment: Salut a la France; Au bruit de la guerre. Linda di Chamounix: Ah del destin. Lucrezia Borgia: Il segreto per esser felici. Poliuto: Al suon dell'arpa. Marina Krilovici, Ottavio Garaventa, Silvano Carroli, Pali Marinov, Frangiskos Voutsinos, Pierre Lanne; Agustarello Affre, Eugenia Mantelli, Apollo Granforte, Rosina Storchio, Ida Rappini, Antonio Paoli, Honoria Popovici, Alfred Piccaver, Lisa Landouzy, soloists; Brussels Theatre de la Monnaie Orchestra and Chorus; Oliviero de Fabritiius. MRF Records MRF 170 (3)
+FF 11/12-81 p148

1360 Il duca d'Alba. Caterina Mancini, s; Amadeo Berdini, Aldo Bertocci; Giangiacomo Guelfi, bar; Dario Caselli, bs; RAI Rome Orchestra and Chorus; Fernando Previtali. Voce 33 (3)
+-FF 7/8-81 p93

1361 Il duca d'Alba: Angelo casto e bel. FLOTOW: Martha: M'appari. GOLDMARK: Die Konigin von Saba: Magische tone. VERDI: Aida: Celeste Aida;...Gia i sacerdoti;...Misero appien;...La fatal pietra;...O terra addio. Otello: Ora e per sempre addio. Rigoletto: Questa o quella; Parmi veder le lagrime; La donna e mobile; Quartet. Enrico Caruso, t; Bessie Abbott, Johanna Gadski, s; Louise Homer, con; Antonio Scotti, bar. Rubini GV 536
+ARG 11-81 p10

L'Elisir d'amore: Duet, Act 1. See no. 4081
L'Elisir d'amore: Ecco il magico liquore...Obbligato obbligato. See no. 4032

1362 L'Elisir d'amore: Prendi per me sei libero. La fille du regiment: Il faut partir. Lucrezia Borgia: Tranquillo ei posa...Com'e bello. ROSSINI: La cenerentola: Nacqui all'affanno...Non piu mesta. Guillaume Tell: Ils s'eloignent...Sombre foret. Semiramide: Bel raggio. Maria Callas, s; OSCCP; Nicola Rescigno. HMV ASD 3984 Tape (c) TC ASD 3984 (From SAX 2564)
+Gr 4-81 p1361 +-Op 8-81 p823
+HFN 5-81 p93

L'Elisir d'amore: Quanto e bella. See no. 3965
L'Elisir d'amore: Quanto e bella; Adina credimi; Una furtiva lagrima. See no. 4035

1363 L'Elisir d'amore: Una furtiva lagrima. MOZART: Cosi fan tutte, K 588: Un aura amorosa. Die Entfuhrung aus dem Serail, K 384: Hier soll ich dich denn sehen; Constance O wie Angslicht; Ich baue ganz. Die Zauberflote, K 620: Die Bildnis. Songs: Per pieta, K 420. PUCCINI: Tosca: Recondita armonia; E lucevan le stelle. TCHAIKOVSKY: Eugen Onegin: Faint echo of my youth. Anton Dermota, t. Preiser PR 135003
+Gr 1-81 p998

L'Elisir d'amore: Una furtiva lagrima. See no. 3751. See no. 3759. See no. 3769. See no. 3836. See no. 3843. See no. 3967. See no. 3972. See no. 3997. See no. 4075
L'Elisir d'amore: Una furtiva lagrima; Venti scudi. See no. 3707
L'Elisir d'amore: Una parola...Chiedi all'aura. See no. 3754

L'Elisir d'amore: Venti scudi. See no. 4048
Etude, no. 1, solo clarinet. See no. 3669
La favorita: A tanto amour; Vien Leonora. See no. 4034
La favorita: Ah l'alto ardor. See no. 4031
La favorita: Ange si pur; O mon Fernando. See no. 1359
La favorita: Introduzione delle danze; Passo a tre; Passo a sei; Finale delle danze. Seeno. 1357
La favorita: Non sai tu; Splendon piu belle. See no. 3968
La favorita: O mio Fernando. See no. 3970
La favorita: Spirto gentil. See no. 3657. See no. 3759. See no. 3885. See no. 3967. See no. 3995. See no. 4075
La favorita: Una vergine un angel di Dio. See no. 4032

1364 La fille du regiment. Mirella Freni, s; Anna di Stasia, ms; Alfredo Kraus, t; Vladimiro Ganzarolli, bs; Orchestra and Chorus; Nino Sanzogno. Historical Recordings HRE 288 (2)
+FF 1/2-81 p107

La fille du regiment: Convien partir. See no. 3754
La fille du regiment: Il faut partir. See no. 1362
La fille du regiment: O mes amis...Pour mon ame. See no. 3759. See no. 3885
La fille du regiment: Per viver vicino a Maria. See no. 3967
La fille du regiment: Salut a la France; Au bruit de la guerre. See no. 1359
Gemma di Vergy: Eccomi sola alfine. See no. 3713

1365 Linda di Chamounix: Ah tardai troppo...O luce di quest'anima. Lucia di Lammermoor: Il dolce suono mi corpi sua voce...Ardon gl'incensi; Ancor non giunse...Regnava nel silenzio. VERDI: Ernani: Surta e la notte...Ernani Ernani involami. I vespri siciliani: Merce diletti amiche. Joan Sutherland, Nadine Sautereau, s; Paris Opera Chorus; OSCCP; Nello Santi. Decca JB 97 Tape (c) KJBC 97 (From SXL 2159)
++Gr 7-81 p192 +HFN 6-81 p88

Linda di Chamounix: Ah del destin. See no. 1359
Linda di Chamounix: Overture. See no. 1373

1366 Lucia di Lammermoor. Joan Sutherland, s; Margreta Elkins, ms; Kenneth McDonald, Joao Gibin, Robert Bowman, t; John Shaw, bar; Joseph Rouleau, bs; ROHO and Chorus; Tullio Serafin. Historical Recordings HRE 342 (2)
+FF 5/6-81 p82

1367 Lucia di Lammermoor. Maria Callas, s; Giuseppe de Stefano, t; Rolando Panerai, bar; Nicola Zaccaria, bs; BRSO; Herbert von Karajan. Movimento Musica 02001
+-HFN 12-81 p94

1368 Lucia di Lammermoor. Anna Moffo, s; Carlo Bergonzi, t; Mario Sereni, bar; Ezio Flagello, bs; RCA Italiana Opera Orchestra and Chorus; Georges Pretre. RCA AGL 3-3971 (3)
-FF 9/10-81 p96

Lucia di Lammermoor: Chi mi frena. See no. 3995
Lucia di Lammermoor: Cruda funesta smania. See no. 4034
Lucia di Lammermoor: Dalle stanze. See no. 3968
Lucia di Lammermoor: Fra poco a me ricovero. See no. 3839
Lucia di Lammermoor: Fra poco a me; Tu che a dio. See no. 3967. See no. 4037
Lucia di Lammermoor: Hai tradito il ciel. See no. 3944
Lucia di Lammermoor: Il dolce suono mi corpi sua voce...Ardon gl'

incensi; Ancor non giunse...Regnava nel silenzio. See no. 1365
Lucia di Lammermoor: Io di te memoria viva...Verrano a te. See no. 3843
Lucia di Lammermoor: O giusto cielo...Il dolce suono. See no. 3649
1369 Lucia di Lammermoor: Quando rapito in estasi...Verranno a te; Che mi frena in tal momento...Maledetto sia l'istante...Eccola... Il dolce suono; Tombi degl' avi miei...Tu che a Dio spiegasti l'ali. Montserrat Caballe, s; Ann Murray, ms; Jose Carreras, Claes Ahnsjo, Vincenzo Bello, t; Vincenzo Sardinero, bar; Samuel Ramey, bs; Ambrosian Opera Chorus; NPhO; Jesus Lopez Cobos. Philips 6570 155 Tape (c) 7310 155 (From 6703 080)
+-Gr 1-81 p986 +HFN 10-81 p95
+HFN 9-81 p93 tape
Lucia di Lammermoor: Scena della pazzia. See no. 4021
Lucia di Lammermoor: Sparsa e di rose...Il dolce suono...Spargi d'amaro pianto. See no. 3850
Lucia di Lammermoor: Sulla tomba. See no. 4023
Lucia di Lammermoor: Tombe degli avi miei. See no. 3769
Lucia di Lammermoor: Tombe degli avi miei; Giusto cielo rispondente; Tu che a Dio. See no.3965
Lucia di Lammermoor: Tombe degli...Fra poco; Tu che a Dio. See no. 4045
Lucia di Lammermoor: Tombe degli avi miei...Fra poco a me ricovero. See no. 3750
Lucrezia Borgia: Brindisi. See no. 4039
Lucrezia Borgia: Il segreto per esser felici. See no. 1359. See no. 3650
Lucrezia Borgia: Tranquillo ei posa...Com'e bello. See no. 1362
Maria di Rohan: Overture. See no. 1373
1370 Maria Padilla. Janet Price, s; Margreta Elkins, ms; Gunnar Drago, Ian Caley, t; Christian du Plessis, bar; Opera Rara Chorus; Bournemouth Sinfonietta; Kenneth Montgomery. BJRS 135/3 (3)
+NR 9-81 p10
1371 Maria Padilla. Lois McDonall, Della Jone, Christian du Plessis, Graham Clark, soloists; Geoffrey Mitchell Choir; LSO; Alun Francis. Opera Rara OR 6 (3)
+-FF 11/12-81 p149 +OC Fall 1981 p51
+Gr 6-81 p82 +-ON 5-81 p44
+-MT 9-81 p607 +Op 7-81 p717
Marin Faliero: Les martyrs. See no. 1373
Les martyrs: Airs de danse, nos. 1-3. See no. 1357
1372 Miserere, D minor. Julia Paszthy, s; Zsolt Bende, bar; Slovak Philharmonic Orchestra and Chorus; Jozsef Maklari. Hungaroton SLPX 12147
+ARG 9-81 p18 -HFN 12-80 p137
+FF 3/4-81 p107 +NR 3-81 p11
+Gr 11-80 p717
1373 Overtures: Don Pasquale. Linda di Chamounix. Marin Faliero: Les martyrs. Maria di Rohan. Monte Carlo Opera Orchestra; Claudio Scimone. Erato STU 71211 (also Musical Heritage Society MHS 4225)
+ARG 6-81 p25 +-Gr 1-80 p1145
-FF 1/2-81 p108
Poliuto: Al suon dell'arpa. See no. 1359
1374 Poliuto: Questo pianto...Ah fuggi da morte. Roberto Devereux:

Tutto e silenzio. PUCCINI: Madama Butterfly: Bimba bimba non piangere. VERDI: I Lombardi: Dove sola m'inoltro...Per dirupi e per foreste. Katia Ricciarelli, s; Jose Carreras, t; Linda Finnie, ms; Ambrosian Opera Chorus; LSO; Lamberto Gardelli. Philips 9500 750 Tape (c) 7300 835

+-ARG 9-81 p43
+Gr 11-80 p735
+FF 7/8-81 p206
++Gr 4-81 p1376 tape
+HFN 11-80 p125
+NR 6-81 p9
+NYT 4-5-81 pD33
+-ON 3-28-81 p36
+Op 3-81 p312
+SFC 5-24-81 p19
++St 7-81 p90

1375 Quartets, strings, nos. 1-6. Amati Quartet. Dischi Ricordi ARCL 327 002 (3)

-FF 11/12-81 p151
-Gr 11-80 p691
+-SFC 8-30-81 p18

1376 Requiem. Viorica Cortez, s; Luciano Pavarotti, t; Renato Bruson, bar; Paolo Washington, bs; Verona Arena Ente Lirico Orchestra and Chorus; Gerhard Fackler. Decca SDD 566 (From CIME 25010)

-Gr 4-81 p1352
+-HFN 3-81 p87

Roberto Devereux: E Sara...Vivi ingrato...Quel sangue versato. See no. 4014

Roberto Devereux: Tutto e silenzio. See no. 1374

1377 Sonata, flute and piano, G minor. HOVHANESS: The garden of Adonis, op. 245. KRUMPHOLZ: Sonata, flute and harp, F major. SPOHR: Sonata, harp and flute, op. 113, E flat major. Robert Aitken, flt; Erica Goodman, hp. BIS LP 143

+FF 9/10-81 p264
+HFN 5-81 p87
+MUM 7/8-81 p34
++NR 5-81 p10

1378 Songs and arias: Amore e morte; L'amor funesto; Le dernier chant du troubador; Malvina; Il rinnegato. ROSSINI: Songs and arias: A me innocente e misero; Alle voci della gloria; Mi lagnero tacendo. L'Inganno Felice: Una voce m'ha colpito. Luis Giron May, bar; Mary Ann Bulla, pno. Centaur CRC 1003

+-ARG 7/8-81 p29
+FF 3/4-81 p183

Songs: A mezzanotte; J'attends toujours; Il sospiro. See no. 3758

Songs: Il sospiro; Le crepuscule. See no. 3838

Sons: La conocchia; La tradimiento; Me voglia fa'na casa. See no. 3718

La Zingara: Fra l'erbe cosparse. See no. 3649

DONNER, Henrik

Songs: En liten konstnar; Etude for sommarvind. See no. 3805

DOPPLER, Albert Franz

L'Oiseau des bois, op. 21. See no. 4065

DORNEL, Louis Antoine

Sonate en quatuor, D minor. See no. 3631

DOWLAND, John

Can she excuse. See no. 3734

Captain Digorie piper his pavan and galliard. See no. 1380

Dowland's first galliard. See no. 4015

Earle of Derby his galliard. See no. 4015

Earle of Essex galliard. See no. 3883. See no. 4015

Fantasia. See no. 3883. See no. 3937. See no. 4016

Farewell. See no. 3883

Fortune my foe. See no. 138

Frogg galliard. See no. 4015
Lachrimae. See no. 1380
Lachrimae antiquae. See no. 4015
Lachrimae pavan. See no. 3883
Lachrimae verae. See no. 4015
Lady Hunsdon's almain. See no. 1380
Lady Rich galliard. See no. 4015
Lord d'Lisle galliard. See no. 4015
Melancholie galliard. See no. 4015
Mistress Winter's jump. See no. 1380
Mrs. Vaux's gigge. See no. 4015
Mrs. White's nothinge. See no. 3973
My Lady Hunsdon's puffe. See no. 3973. See no. 4015
Queen Elizabeth her galliard. See no. 3807. See no. 3883. See no. 4016
Semper Dowland semper dolens. See no. 4015
Shoemaker's wife, a toy. See no. 1380. See no. 4015
Sir George Whitehead his almain. See no. 1380
Sir Henry Gifford's almain. See no. 4015.
Sir Henry Guilford his almain. See no. 1380
Sir Henry Umpton's funeral. See no. 1380
Sir John Smith's almain. See no. 1380. See no. 3883. See no. 4015. See no. 4059
Sir John Souche's galliard. See no. 138
Sir Thomas Collier his galliard. See no. 1380

1379 Songs (A pilgrims solace): Cease these false sports; Disdain me still; From silent night; Go nightly cares; If that a sinner's sighs; In this trembling shadow cast; Lasso vita mia; Love those beams that breed; My heart and tongue were twins; Shall I strive with words to move; Stay time awhile thy flying; Sweet stay awhile; Tell me true love; Thou mighty God; To ask for all thy love; Up merry mates; Welcome black night; Were every thought an eye; When David's life; When the poor cripple; Where sin sore wounding. Consort of Musicke; Anthony Rooley. L'Oiseau-Lyre DSLO 585/6 (2)
+FF 9/10-81 p97 +HFN 1-81 p92
++Gr 1-81 p977 ++St 12-81 p116

Songs: A shepherd in the shade. See no. 3677
Songs: Come away come sweet love; Fine knacks for ladies; Flow my tears; Humour say what mak'st thou there; In darkness let me dwell; Now o now I needs must part; What time's eldest son old age. See no. 3871
Songs: Far from triumphing court; Lady if you so spite me; In darkness let me dwell. See no. 3946
Songs: Fine knacks for ladies; I must complain; Mr. Dowland's midnight; Now oh now I needs must part; A shepherd in a shade; Sweet stay awhile; Where sin sore wounding. See no. 4085
Songs: Welcome black night. See no. 3876
Susanna galliard. See no. 1380
Volta. See no. 3762
What if I never speed. See no. 4059

1380 Works, selections: Captain Digorie Piper his pavan and galliard. Fortune my foe. Lachrimae. Lady Hunsdon's almain. Sir John Souche's galliard. Mistress Winter's jump. The shoemaker's wife, a toy. Sir George Whitehead his almain. Sir Henry

Guilford his almain. Sir Henry Umpton's funeral. Sir John Smith's almain. Sir Thomas Collier his galliard. Susanna galliard. Extempore String Ensemble; George Weigand. Hyperion A 66010

++Gr 8-81 p284 ++HFN 7-81 p72

DOWNEY, John

The edge of space. See no. 57

DRAGANSKI, Donald

The bestiary: Weathervane cock; Fish and the river; Fish eggs; Ic ane geseah idese sittan; Book worm. See no. 3953

DRAGHI, Giovanni

Ground, C minor. See no. 3733. See no. 4103

DRAGONETTI, Domenico

1381 Concerto double bass, A major (instr. Schuller). KOUSSEVITZKY: Concerto, double bass, op. 3. PAGANINI: Variations on a theme from Rossini's "Moses in Egypt" (arr. Karr). Gary Karr, double bs; BRSO: Uros Lajovic. Schwann VMS 2063

+ARG 4-81 p55

DRING, Madeleine

1382 Dances (3). For the New Year march. Italian dance. Jig. Moto perpetuo. Sarabande. Tango. Tarantelle. Valse francaise. Waltz finale. West Indian dance. WIB waltz. Leigh Kaplan, Robin Paterson, pno; Louise Di Tullio, flt. Cambria C 1015

+FF 9/10-81 p97 /-NR 9-81 p13

For the New Year march. See no. 1382

Italian dance. See no. 1382

Jig. See no. 1382

Moto perpetuo. See no. 1382

Sarabande. See no. 1382

Tango. See no. 1382

Tarantelle. See no. 1382

Valse francaise. See no. 1382

Waltz finale. See no. 1382

West Indian dance. See no. 1382

WIB waltz. See no. 1382

DRISCHNER, Max

Chorale partita on "Praise to the Lord the almighty". See no. 3822

DROZIN, Garth

1383 Systemics. HELLER: John Barleycorn. John Barleycorn variations. PELLMAN: Horizon. Steven Mauk, sax; Cornell Symphonic Band and Chamber Singers; Cornell Chorus and Clarinet Ensemble, Cornell Wind Ensemble; Duane Heller, Garth Drozin. Cornell CUWE 26

/FF 1/2-81 p233 +NR 9-81 p8

DUARTE, John

Variations on a Catalan folksong, op. 25. See no. 3870

DUBOIS, Francis Theodore

Pieces nouvelles: Noel. See no. 3894

Toccata, G major. See no. 3799. See no. 4112

DUBROVAY, Laszlo

Duets, violin and percussion. See no. 3865

1384 Interferences, no. 1. Music, 2 cimbaloms. KAROLYI: Rondo, 2 cimbaloms. PETROVICS: Movement in ragtime. Nocturne. SZOKOLAY: Playing with intervals. Ilona Szeverenyi, Tunde Enzsol, cimb. Hungaroton SLPX 12064

++FF 3/4-81 p230 +NR 4-81 p15

1385 Matuziada, nos. 1-5. Istvan Matuz, flt. Hungaroton SLPX 12228 (also 11920)

+FF 3/4-81 p108 -NR 4-81 p15

Music, 2 cimbaloms. See no. 1384

DUESENBERRY, John

1386 Moduletude. Movements, tape and prepared piano (4). Phrase. Variations, 2 interludes. Electronic Music Studio, University of Mass.; Experimental Music Studio, MIT; Boston School of Electronic Music; Engineered by Michael Gilbert, John Duesenberry. Opus One 60

+CMJ Winter 1981 p80 +NR 7-81 p15

Movements, tape and prepared piano. See no. 1386

Phrase. See no. 1386

Variations, 2 interludes. See no. 1386

DUFAUT (Dufault), Francois

1387 Pavane, E minor. Suites, A minor, C major, C minor, G minor. Hopkinson Smith, lt. Telefunken 6-42328 Tape (c) 4-42328 (also Astree AS 15)

+-ARG 2-80 p51 +HF 2-80 p102 tape
+FF 1/2-80 p170 ++HFN 2-80 p92
+FF 7/8-81 p153

Suite, G minor. See no. 1225

Suites, A minor, C major, C minor, G minor. See no. 1387

DUFAY, Guillaume

Ce moys de may lamentatio sanctae matris ecclesiae Constantinopolitanae. See no. 3853

Donnez l'assault. See no. 3896

1388 Motets: Supremum est mortalibus; Flos forum; Ave virgo quae de caelis; Vasilissa ergo gaude; Alma redemptoris mater (II). DUNSTABLE: Motets: Beata mater; Preco proheminencie; Salve regina misericordie; Veni sancti spiritus. Pro Cantione Antiqua, Hamburg Wind Ensemble Members; Bruno Turner. DG 2533 291

++FF 9/10-81 p336 ++HFN 8-75 p75
++Gr 8-75 p352 +NR 3-76 p6
++HF 3-76 p81 ++St 1-76 p103

Se la face ay pale, mass: Sanctus. See no. 3853

1389 Songs (complete secular music). Medieval Ensemble, London; Peter and Timothy Davies. L'Oiseau-Lyre D237D6 (6)

+Gr 12-81 p918

Songs: Dona gentile; Le serviteur hault guerdonne; Vostre bruit et vostre grant fame. See no. 3948

DUISBERG, Robert

Airs and divisions. See no. 3739

Relativity's rainbow. See no. 3739

DUKAS, Paul

1390 L'Apprenti sorcier. MUSSORGSKY: Night on the bare mountain. SAINT-SAENS: Danse macabre, op. 40. STRAUSS, R.: Till Eulenspiegels lustige Streiche, op. 28. David Nadien, vln; NYP; Leonard Bernstein. CBS 61976 Tape (c) 40-61976 (From 72740)

+Gr 9-80 p414 +-HFN 10-80 p115
+-Gr 2-81 p1122 tape

1391 L'Apprenti sorcier. OFFENBACH: Gaite parisienne, excerpts (arr. Rosenthal). SAINT-SAENS: Danse macabre, op. 40. French National Orchestra; Lorin Maazel. CBS 76909 Tape (c) 40-76909 (also

CBS M 35843)
+Gr 10-80 p496 +-NR 11-81 p2
+-HFN 10-80 p111 ++SFC 9-13-81 p17
+-HFN 12-80 p159 tape

1392 L'Apprenti sorcier. ROSSINI: La boutique fantasque: Suite. SAINT-SAENS: Danse macabre, op. 40. Scottish National Orchestra; Alexander Gibson. Chandos CBR 1003 Tape (c) CBBT 1003 (From Music for Pleasure CFP 57012)
+FF 9/10-81 p288 +HFN 4-81 p80
+Gr 4-81 p1377 +-HFN 5-81 p93 tape

L'Apprenti sorcier. See no. 746. See no. 1115
La peri: Fanfare. See no. 3624
Villanelle. See no. 561

DUMONT, Henri

1393 Allemande. Preludes, nos. 1, 5. Symphonia. Symphonie, nos. 5, 23, 28. Motets: Domine non secundum; In lectulu meo; O aeterne misericors Deus; O fideles; Panis angelicus; Regina divina. Rene Jacobs, alto; Janine Rubinlicht, Anne Maria Hess, vln; Jerome Lejeune, bs viol; Ku Ebbinge, bsn; Johann Huys, org, hpd; Joseph Wolteche, org. Alpha MBM 21
+-Gr 2-81 p1110 +-HFN 11/12-81 p105
+HFN 4-81 p72

Motets: Domine non secundum; In lectulu meo; O aeterne misericors Deus; O fideles; Panis angelicus; Regina divina. See no. 1393
Pavane, D minor. See no. 3916
Preludes, nos. 1, 5. See no. 1393
Symphonia. See no. 1393
Symphonie, nos. 5, 23, 28. See no. 1393

DUNHILL, Thomas

Cornucopia. See no. 3731

DUNSTABLE, John

Motets: Beata mater; Preco proheminencie; Salve regina misericordie; Veni sancti spiritus. See no. 1388
Songs: Albanus roseo rutilat; Crux fidelis O crux gloriosa; Guado virgo. See no. 4085
Songs: O rosa bella. See no. 3948
Songs: Veni sancte spiritus. See no. 3845
Specialis virgo. See no. 3896
Veni sancte/Veni creator spiritus. See no. 4101

DUPARC, Henri

1394 Songs: Chanson triste, op. 2; Elegie; Extase; Le galop; L'invitation au voyage; Lamento; Le manoir de Rosamonde; Phydile; Serenade florentine; Soupir; Testament; La vague et la cloche; La vie anterieure. Ruud van der Meer, bar; Rudolf Jansen, pno. Musical Heritage Society MHS 4228
+-FF 9/10-81 p98

1395 Songs: Chanson triste; Extase; Phidyle; Testament. FAURE: Songs: Adieu, op. 21, no. 3; Apres un reve, op. 7, no. 1; Barcarolle, op. 7, no. 3; Clair de lune, op. 46, no. 2; Chanson d'amour, op. 27, no. 1; En priere; Nell, op. 18, no. 1; Poeme d'un jour, op. 21; Le secret, op. 23, no. 3. Ian Partridge, t; Jennifer Partridge, pno. Pearl SHE 526
++Gr 2-76 p1364 +-RR 3-76 p67
++HFN 1-81 p92 +STL 1-11-76 p36

1396 Songs: Au pays ou se fait la guerre; Elegie; Extase; Chanson triste; L'invitation au voyage; Lamento; Le manoir de Rosamonde;

Phidyle; Serenade florentine; Soupir; Testament; La vague et la cloche; La vie anterieure. Danielle Galland, s; Bernard Kruysen, bar; Noel Lee, pno. Telefunken AS 6-42113 (also Valois MB 312)
-FF 9/10-81 p98 +RR 5-77 p80
+FF 3/4-80 p82 ++St 6-80 p113
+Gr 5-77 p1718
Songs: Chanson triste, op. 2, no. 2. See no. 4038
Songs: L'invitation au voyage. See no. 3642
Songs: Phidyle. See no. 3823
DUPHLY, Jacques
La felix. See no. 371
La de belomere. See no. 371
La vanlo. See no. 371
DUPRE, Mardel
Placare. See no. 3901
Poeme heroique. See no. 3746
Prelude and fugue, G minor. See no. 3744
Prelude and fugue, op. 7, no. 1, B major. See no. 3811. See no. 3822
Variations sur un Noel, op. 20. See no. 3894. See no. 4120
Vepres du commun des fetes de la Sainte Vierge, op. 18: Antiphon; Magnificat, nos. 1 and 6. See no. 185
DURANTE, Francisco
Concerto, strings, F minor. See no. 3980
DUREY, Louis
Songs: La boule de neige; La metempsychose; La grenade. See no. 3687
DURON, Sebastian
Gaitilla de mano izquierda. See no. 4098
DURUFLE, Maurice
1397 Mass, op. 11. LANGLAIS: Mass "Salve Regina". Stephen Roberts, bar; Richard Hickox Singers, Wooburn Singers; Philip Jones Brass Ensemble; Ian Watson, Alastair Ross, org; Richard Hickox. Argo ZRG 938
+Gr 11-81 p733 +HFN 11-81 p93
1398 Motets on Gregorian themes, op. 10. HOWELLS: Here is the little door; Long long ago. VICTORIA: The lamentations of Jeremiah for holy Saturday: Lessons, 1-3. Exon Singers; Christopher Tolley. Alpha APS 309
+Gr 10-80 p527 +-MT 3-81 p197
+HFN 10-80 p110 ++NR 3-81 p10
Motets: Ubi caritas. See no. 3634. See no. 4060. See no. 4061
Prelude and fugue sur le nome d'Alain, op. 7. See no. 1340
Requiem, op. 9: Pie Jesu. See no. 3713
Suite, op. 2, no. 5: Prelude. See no. 3822
Suite, op. 5: Toccata. See no. 4118
Variations on "Veni creator", op. 4. See no. 3673. See no. 3674
DUSSEK, Johann
Sonatina. See no. 3816
Sonatinas, op. 20, nos. 1, 4. See no. 1344
DUTILLEUX, Henri
1399 Sarabande et cortege. MOSCHELES: Grand duo concertante, piano and bassoon. SAINT-SAENS: Sonata, bassoon and piano, op. 168, G major. TCHAIKOVSKY: Nocturne, op. 19, no. 4. Eberhard Busch-

mann, bsn; Monica von Saalfeld, pno. Da Camera SM 92920
-FF 3/4-80 p188 +-HFN 11-81 p100

1400 Sonatine, flute and piano. IBERT: Jeux. JOLIVET: Sonata, flute and piano. ROUSSEL: Joueuers de flute, op. 27. Gunther Pohl, flt; Wilfried Kassebaum, pno. Musicaphon BM SL 1920
++FF 5/6-81 p209 +RR 8-80 p74
+HFN 1-81 p105

1401 Symphony, no. 1. Lille Philharmonic Orchestra; Jean-Claude Casadesus. Calliope CAL 1861
+Gr 5-80 p1660 +MT 1-81 p33
+HFN 11-78 p168 +RR 6-80 p47
+HFN 8-80 p97

DVORACEK
Music. See no. 803

DVORAK, Anton

1402 Armida. Montserrat Caballe, Theodore Schlott, Jacob Engels, Fritz Bramboeck, Elfego Esparza, Kurt Ruesche, Alfred Scheibner, Georg Koch, Marcus Platzer, soloists; Bremen City Theater Orchestra and Chorus; Alexander Albrecht. Voce 2 (2)
+FF 1/2-81 p108

1403 Carnival overture, op. 92. Concerto, violin, op. 53, A minor. Concerto, violoncello, op. 104, B minor. Romance, op. 11, F minor. Mstislav Rostropovitch, vlc; Josef Suk, vln; CPhO; Vaclav Talich, Karel Ancerl. Quintessence 2PMC 2711 (2) Tape (c) 2P4C 2711
+FF 3/4-81 p108 +HF 10-81 p91 tape

Carnival overture, op. 92. See no. 1438. See no. 3717

1404 Concerto, piano, op. 33, G minor. Radoslav Kvapil, pno; Brno Philharmonic Orchestra; Frantisek Jilek. Supraphon 110 2373
+-ARG 6-81 p25 +-HFN 10-80 p103
+-FF 3/4-81 p109 +-NR 1-81 p5
+Gr 10-80 p496

1405 Concerto, violin, op. 53, A minor.* TCHAIKOVSKY: Concerto, violin, op. 35, D major. Hermann Krebbers, Ulf Hoelscher, vln; Amsterdam Philharmonic Orchestra, NPhO; Anton Kersjes, Okko Kamu. Classics for Pleasure CFP 40349 Tape (c) TC CFP 40349 (*From HMV SXLP 30170)
+-Gr 4-81 p1316 +-HFN 5-81 p93 tape
+-HFN 4-81 p80

1406 Concerto, violin, op. 53, A minor. Romance, op. 11, F minor. Salvatore Accardo, vln; COA; Colin Davis. Philips 9500 406 Tape (c) 7300 614
+ARG 5-81 p17 +HFN 4-81 p81 tape
+FF 3/4-81 p109 +NR 5-81 p7
++Gr 2-81 p1082 +St 4-81 p104
+HF 3-81 p69 +-ST 6-81 p123
++HFN 2-81 p87

1407 Concerto, violin, op. 53, A minor. Romance, op. 11, F minor. Josef Suk, vln; CPhO; Karel Ancerl. Quintessence PMC 7112 Tape (c) P4C 7112 (From Artia ALP 193) (also Supraphon 410 2423)
+-FF 9/10-79 p79 +HF 3-81 p69
+Gr 7-80 p136 ++SFC 7-1-79 p44

1408 Concerto, violin, op. 53, A minot. TCHAIKOVSKY: Concerto, violin, op. 35, D major. Nathan Milstein, vln; Minneapolis Symphony Orchestra, BSO; Antal Dorati, Charles Munch. RCA Musique GM 43275 (From RCA LM 1147, 1760)

+FF 5/6-81 p83

1409 Concerto, violin, op. 53, A minor. Romance, op. 11, F minor. Josef Suk, vln; CPhO; Vaclav Neumann. Supraphon 410 2423 (also Pro Arte PAL 1002)
+FF 9/10-80 p111
++FF 11/12-81 p152
+HF 3-81 p69
+-HFN 8-80 p97
++NR 8-80 p6
+RR 7-80 p55
++St 4-81 p104

Concerto, violin, op. 53, A minor. See no. 1403

1410 Concerto, violoncello, op. 104, B minor. TCHAIKOVSKY: Variations on a Rococo theme, op. 33. Robert Cohen, vlc; LPO; Zdenek Macal. Classics for Pleasure CFP 40361 Tape (c) TC CFP 40361
+-Gr 11-81 p686
+-HFN 11-81 p94
+-HFN 12-81 p112 tape

1411 Concerto, violoncello, op. 104, B minor. Silent woods, op. 68. Heinrich Schiff, vlc; COA; Colin Davis. Philips 6514 071 Tape (c) 3337 071
+-Gr 11-81 p686
+HFN 11-81 p94

1412 Concerto, violoncello, op. 104, B minor. Gregor Piatigorsky, vlc; BSO; Charles Munch. RCA AGL 1-3878
+FF 7/8-81 p95

Concerto, violoncello, op. 104, B minor. See no. 1403
Czech suite, op. 39. See no. 1458
The golden spinning wheel, op. 109. See no. 4122
Humoresque, op. 101. See no. 4066
Humoresque, op. 101, no. 7, G flat major. See no. 3662. See no. 3686. See no. 4083
Husitska overture, op. 67. See no. 1432. See no. 1434
In nature's realm, op. 91. See no. 1435

1413 The Jacobin. Marcela Machotkova, Daniela Sounova, s; Ivana Mixova, ms; Vilem Pribyl, Beno Blachut, t; Vaclav Zitek, Rene Tucek, bar; Karel Berman, bs-bar; Karel Prusa, bs; Brno Philharmonic Orchestra; Kantilena Childrens Chorus, Kuhn Chorus; Jiri Pinkas. Supraphon 110 2481/3 (also Pro Arte PAL 3000 Tape (c) 3PAC 3000)
++ARG 10-80 p12
++FF 9/10-80 p112
+FF 11/12-81 p153
+-Gr 2-80 p1293
+HF 12-80 p75
+HF 12-81 p93 tape
+-HFN 1-80 p105
+MT 9-80 p566
+NR 8-80 p11
+NYT 8-23-81 pD19
+-ON 10-81 p52
+Op 1-80 p63
+RR 1-80 p57
++SFC 8-24-80 p36
+SFC 12-13-81 p18
+SR 9-80 p96
+St 10-80 p112

1414 My home overture, op. 62. Scherzo capriccioso, op. 66, D flat major. Bavarian Radio Symphony Orchestra; Rafael Kubelik. DG 2726 122 (2) (From 2530 446, 2530 593)
+Gr 8-81 p270
+HFN 8-81 p91

Nocturne, op. 40, B major. See no. 1458. See no. 3851
Polonaise, E flat major. See no. 1458
Polka, op. 53a, no. 1, B flat major. See no. 1458
Prague waltzes. See no. 1458

1415 Quartet, piano, no. 1, op. 23, D major. Quartet, piano, no. 2, op. 87, E flat major. Rudolf Firkusny, pno; Juilliard Quartet. CBS 79218 (2) (also CBS MG 35913)

++FF 3/4-81 p110 +NYT 8-23-81 pD19
+-Gr 6-79 p66 +RR 7-79 p75
+HFN 6-79 p107 +SFC 1-11-81 p17
+MT 12-79 p1007 ++St 5-81 p56
++NR 4-81 p6 +STL 12-2-79 p37

Quartet, piano, no. 2, op. 87, E flat major. See no. 1415

1416 Quartet, strings, no. 12, op. 96, F major. MENDELSSOHN: Quartet, strings, no. 1, op. 12, E flat major. Orlando Quartet. Philips 9500 995 Tape (c) 7300 995
+-FF 11/12-81 p153 +HFN 10-81 p95 tape
+Gr 7-81 p167 +-ST 11-81 p510
+HFN 7-81 p72

1417 Quartet, strings, no. 12, op. 96, F major. HAYDN: Quartet, strings, op. 64, no. 5, D major. SCHUBERT: Quartet, strings, no. 12, D 703, C minor. Panocha Quartet. Quintessence PMC 7183
+-FF 7/8-81 p95

Quartet, strings, no. 12, op. 96, F major. See no. 859

1418 Quartet, strings, no. 13, op. 106, G major. Guarneri Quartet. RCA ARL 1-4051
-FF 11/12-81 p154 +-NYT 8-23-81 pD19
+-NR 9-81 p5

1419 Quintet, piano, op. 81, A major. SCHUBERT: Quartet, strings, no. 12, D 703, C minor. Clifford Curzon, pno; Vienna Philharmonic Quartet. London STS 11525
+FF 3/4-81 p112

1420 Quintet, strings, op. 77, G major. Waltzes, op. 54, nos. 1, 4. Sequoia String Quartet; Julius Levine, bs. Nonesuch D 79012
+-FF 11/12-81 p155

1421 Requiem, op. 89. Teresa Zylis-Gara, s; Stefania Toczynska, con; Peter Dvorsky, t; Leonard Mroz, bs; French Radio New Philharmonic Orchestra and Chorus; Armin Jordan. Erato STU 71430 (2)
/-Gr 10-81 p593 +HFN 11-81 p94

Romance, op. 11, F minor. See no. 1403. See no. 1406. See no. 1407. See no. 1409

1422 Romantic pieces, op. 75. Rondo, op. 94, G minor. Trios, piano, nos. 1-4. Cohen Trio. CRD 1086/8 (3)
+-Gr 2-81 p1096 +MT 7-81 p481
+-HFN 2-81 p87 +-HFN 11-81 p105 tape

1423 Rondo, op. 94, G minor. Silent woods, op. 68, no. 5. GLAZUNOV: Chant du menestrel, op. 71. Serenade espagnole, op. 20, no. 1: Melodia. RIMSKY-KORSAKOV: Serenade, op. 37. TCHAIKOVSKY: Quartet, strings, no. 1, op. 11, D major: Andante cantabile. Nocturne, op. 19, no. 4. Pezzo capriccioso, op. 62. David Geringas, vlc; BRSO; Lawrence Foster. Eurodisc 201867
+Gr 12-81 p895

Rondo, op. 94, G minor. See no. 1422. See no. 3686

Rusalka: Cury mury fuk. See no. 4080

Scherzo capriccioso, op. 66, D flat major. See no. 1414. See no. 1442. See no. 1445

1424 Serenade, op. 22, E major. TCHAIKOVSKY: Serenade, op. 48, C major. St. John's Smith Square Orchestra; John Lubbock. ASV CDCA 505 Tape (c) ZCDCA 505
+Gr 5-81 p1472 +HFN 4-81 p71
+Gr 7-81 p196 tape +HFN 6-81 p87 tape

1425 Serenade, op. 22, E major. Symphonic variations, op. 78. LPO;

Zdenek Macal. Classics for Pleasure CFP 40345
+Gr 1-81 p948 +HFN 1-81 p92

1426 Serenade, op. 22, E major. TCHAIKOVSKY: Serenade, op. 48, C major. Sofia Chamber Orchestra; Vassil Kasandjiev. Denon OX 7078
+HFN 5-81 p80

1427 Serenade, op. 22, E major. TCHAIKOVSKY: Serenade, op. 48, C major. BPhO; Herbert von Karajan. DG 2532 012 Tape (c) 3302 012
+Gr 10-81 p551 ++HFN 10-81 p87
+Gr 11-81 p783 tape +HFN 11-81 p105 tape

1428 Serenade, op. 44, D minor. KROMMER: Nonet, op. 79. Czech Philharmonic Wind Ensemble. Panton 110 693
+Gr 10-81 p551 +-HFN 9-81 p80

1429 Serenade, op. 44, D minor. GOUNOD: Petite symphonie, B flat major. SCHUBERT: Minuet and finale, D 72, F major. NWE; Edo de Waart. Philips 6570 205 Tape (c) 7310 205 (From 6500 163)
++ARG 9-81 p37 +HFN 3-81 p97
+FF 9/10-81 p280 +HFN 5-81 p93 tape
+Gr 3-81 p1192 ++NR 4-81 p14
+Gr 7-81 p196 tape ++SFC 3-8-81 p18

Serenade, op. 44, D minor. See no. 935

Silent woods, op. 68. See no. 1411. See no. 1423. See no. 3686

1430 Slavonic dances, op. 46, nos. 1-8. Slavonic dances, op. 72, nos. 1-8. Alfons and Aloys Kontarsky, pno. DG 2531 349
+HFN 12-81 p94

1431 Slavonic dances, op. 46, nos. 1-8. Slavonic dances, op. 72, nos. 1-8. CPhO; Zdenek Kosler. Supraphon 110 2981/2 (2)
+-Gr 7-81 p270 +-NR 9-81 p3
+-HFN 8-81 p84

Slavonic dances, op. 46, no. 8, G minor. See no. 1444. See no. 3858

Slavonic dances, op. 72. See no. 1414

Slavonic dances, op. 72, nos. 1-8. See no. 1430. See no. 1431

Slavonic dances, op. 27, no. 2, E minor. See no. 4106

Songs: Als die alte Mutter. See no. 3703

Songs: Biblical songs, op. 99. See no. 3650

Songs: Folk songs, op. 73 (4); Gypsy songs, op. 55. See no. 954

Songs: Gypsy songs, op. 55: Als die alte Mutter. See no. 3753

Songs, op. 55: Songs my mother taught me. See no. 3686. See no. 3823. See no. 3847. See no. 3969. See no. 4106

Symphonic variations, op. 78. See no. 1425

1432 Symphonies, nos. 1-3. Husitska overture, op. 67. LSO; Istvan Kertesz. Vox SVBX 5137 (30
+-FF 11/12-81 p155 +SFC 7-26-81 p19

1433 Symphonies, nos. 1-9. BPhO. Rafael Kubelik. DG 2720 066 (9)
+FF 3/4-81 p112 ++RR 10-73 p62
+Gr 10-73 p681 ++SFC 12-7-80 p33
+HF 2-74 p82

1434 Symphonies, nos. 1-9. Husitska overture, op. 67. LSO; Witold Rowicki. Philips 6770 045 (7) (From 6500 122, 6500 123, 6500 286, 6500 124, 6500 287, SAL 3631, 3570, 3761, 3762)
+Gr 4-81 p1314 +HFN 5-81 p89

1435 Symphony, no. 4, op. 13, D minor. In nature's realm overture, op. 91. LSO; Istvan Kertesz. Decca JB 113 Tape (c) KJBC 113 (From SXL 6257)
+Gr 11-81 p689

1436 Symphony, no. 6, op. 60, D major. LPO; Mstislav Rostropovich. Angel SZ 37716
+/FF 11/12-81 p157
+-NR 8-81 p5
+NYT 8-23-81 pD19
+St 11-81 p84

1437 Symphony, no. 6, op. 60, D major. Symphony, no. 7, op. 70, D minor. Slovak Philharmonic Orchestra; Zdenek Kosler. Musical Heritage Society MHS 824332
++ARG 11-81 p22
/-FF 9/10-81 p99

1438 Symphonies, nos. 7*-9. Carnival overture, op. 92. PhO; Andrew Davis. CBS 79342 (3) (From 76893, 76817, *new)
+Gr 12-81 p884
+-HFN 12-81 p94

1439 Symphony, no. 7, op. 70, D minor. PhO; Andrew Davis. CBS M 36684 Tape (c) MT 36684
+-FF 7/8-81 p95
++NR 7-81 p2
++SFC 4-12-81 p21

1440 Symphony, no. 7, op. 70, D minor. CPhO; Zdenek Kosler. Quintessence PMC 7126 (From Supraphon SUA 50647, Crossroads 2216098)
+ARG 4-80 p22
+Audio 6-81 p18
+-FF 3/4-80 p83
+-SFC 11-4-79 p40

1441 Symphony, no. 7, op. 70, D minor. PO; Eugene Ormandy. RCA ARL 1-3555 Tape (c) ARK 1-3555
+ARG 10-80 p42
-FF 11/12-80 p106
+-Gr 3-81 p1192
+-Gr 6-81 p93
++HF 11-80 p61
+HFN 4-81 p69
+HFN 6-81 p87 tape
+NR 7-80 p4
++SFC 7-20-80 p34
++St 11-80 p84

Symphony, no. 7, op. 70, D minor. See no. 1347

1442 Symphony, no. 8, op. 88, G major. Scherzo capriccioso, op. 66, D flat major. LPO; Mstislav Rostropovich. Angel SZ 37718 (also HMV ASD 4058 Tape (c) TC ASD 4058)
-FF 9/10-81 p100
+-Gr 8-81 p270
+-HFN 8-81 p84
-NR 8-81 p6
+NYT 8-23-81 pD19
+St 11-81 p84

1443 Symphony, no. 8, op. 88, G major. The water goblin, op. 107. LSO; Istvan Kertesz. Decca JB 117 Tape (c) KJBC 117 (From SXL 6044, 6543)
+Gr 9-81 p383
+HFN 9-81 p89

1444 Symphony, no. 8, op. 88, G major. Slavonic dances, op. 46, no. 8, G minor. BPhO; Herbert von Karajan. HMV ASD 3775 Tape (c) TC ASD 3775 (also Angel SZ 37686 Tape (c) 4ZS 37686)
+-ARG 12-80 p26
+-FF 9/10-80 p113
+-Gr 5-80 p1660
+-HF 11-80 p62
++HFN 5-80 p121
+HFN 9-80 p116 tape
+NR 8-80 p4
++RR 6-80 p47
++SFC 7-20-80 p34
+-St 1-81 p78

1445 Symphony, no. 8, op. 88, G major. Scherzo capriccioso, op. 66, D flat major. LSO; Istvan Kertesz. London STS 15526
*FF 3/4-81 p112

1446 Symphony, no. 8, op. 88, G major. Sydney Symphony Orchestra; Jose Serebrier. RCA ARL 1-3550 Tape (c) ARK 1-3550
-ARG 12-80 p26
-FF 9/10-80 p113
-HF 11-80 p62
++NR 7-80 p2
+St 1-81 p78

1147 Symphony, no. 9, op. 95, E minor. MOZART: Symphony, no. 33, K 319, B flat major. Berlin State Opera Orchestra, West German Radio

Orchestra; Erich Kleiber. Bruno Walter Society RR 398
-FF 7/8-81 p96 +-NR 4-81 p2

1448 Symphony, no. 9, op. 95, E minor. Toronto Symphony Orchestra; Andrew Davis. CBS SM 5007
+MUM 11/12-81 p36

1449 Symphony, no. 9, op. 95, E minor. PhO; Andrew Davis. CBS M 35834 Tape (c) MT 35834 (also CBS 76817 Tape (c) 40-76817)
-FF 3/4-81 p113 +HFN 4-81 p81 tape
+Gr 2-81 p1088 +SFC 1-18-81 p21
+HFN 2-81 p87 +-St 9-81 p92
+HFN 3-81 p97 tape /ST 6-81 p123

1450 Symphony, no. 9, op. 95, E minor. COA; Colin Davis. Philips 9500 511 Tape (c) 7300 671 (r) G 9500 511
+Audio 6-79 p132 +HFN 4-79 p134 tape
++FF 1/2-79 p46 +-NR 12-78 p4
++Gr 2-79 p1421 +RR 2-79 p61
+-HF 3-80 p78 +RR 4-79 p124 tape
+-HF 8-81 p69 tape +-SFC 10-8-78 p46
+HFN 3-79 p123 +St 1-79 p98

1451 Symphony, no. 9, op. 95, E minor. CPhO; Vaclav Neumann. Pro Arte PAL 1003
+FF 11/12-81 p152

1452 Symphony, no. 9, op. 95, E minor. St. Louis Symphony Orchestra; Leonard Slatkin. Telarc DG 10053
+FF 5/6-81 p83 +NR 5-81 p2
+Gr 4-81 p1316 +SFC 4-5-81 p18
+HFN 6-81 p73 +St 9-81 p92

1453 Symphony, no. 9, op. 95, E minor. LPO; Enrique Batiz. Varese VCDM 1000.190
+-FF 11/12-81 p157

Symphony, no. 9, op. 95, E minor: Heimatlied. See no. 4083
Symphony, no. 9, op. 95, E minor: Largo. See no. 4106
Terzetto, op. 74: Scherzo. See no. 3662

1454 Trios, piano, nos. 1-4, opp. 21, 26, 65, 90. Beaux Arts Trio. Philips 6770 007 (2) Tape (c) 7650 007 (From SAL 3627, 3628)
+Gr 5-81 p1486

1455 Trios, piano, nos. 1-4, opp. 21, 26, 65, 90. Suk Trio. Supraphon 410 2621/3 (3)
+FF 9/10-81 p101 +-MT 7-81 p481
+Gr 1-81 p960 ++SFC 5-10-81 p18
+HFN 1-81 p92 ++NR 6-81 p5
++NYT 6-21-81 pD23

Trios, piano, nos. 1-4, opp. 21, 26, 65, 90. See no. 1422

1456 Trio, piano, no. 3, op. 65, F minor. Raphael Trio. Sonar SD 180 (also Nonesuch H 71397)
-ARG 12-81 p16 +NYT 6-21-81 pD23
-FF 9/10-81 p101 +SFC 5-31-81 p22
+-FF 7/8-80 p82 ++St 2-80 p121
++NR 12-80 p7

1457 Trio, piano, no. 4, op. 90, E minor. MENDELSSOHN: Trio, piano, no. 1, op. 49, D minor. Beaux Arts Trio. Pearl SHE 553
+Gr 9-80 p359 +HFN 1-81 p93

Trio, piano, no. 4, op. 90, E minor. See no. 823
Waltzes, op. 54 (2). See no. 835
Waltzes, op. 54, nos. 1, 4. See no. 1420

The water goblin, op. 107. See no. 1443
1458 Works, selections: Czech suite, op. 39. Nocturne, op. 40, B major. Polonaise, E flat major. Polka, op. 53a, no. 1, B flat major. Prague waltzes. Detroit Symphony Orchestra; Antal Dorati. Decca SXDL 7522 Tape (c) KSXDC 7522
+Gr 8-81 p267 +HFN 7-81 p72
+Gr 9-81 p460 tape

DYSON, Goerge
Songs: Lauds; Poet's humn; Praise. See no. 3633

EAST, Michael
Magnificat: Nunc dimittis. See no. 42
Songs: Hence stars; You meaner beauties. See no. 3876
Songs: O Lord of whom I do depend; When Israel came out of Egypt; When David heard that Absalom was slain. See no. 42
Songs: When David heard that Absalom was slain. See no. 3620
EASTER ON MOUNT ATHOS. See no. 3770. See no. 3771

EASTWOOD, Tom
Ballade phantasy. See no. 3870

EATON, John
1459 Danton and Robespierre. Edith Vanerette, Nelda Nelson, Mary Shearer, s; Debra Dominiak, Diane Coloton, ms; Paula Redd, alto; James Anderson, Randy Hansen, Gran Wilson, t; Tim Noble, bar; William Parcher, bs-bar; Kevin Langan, bs; Indiana University Opera Theater Orchestra and Chorus; Thomas Baldner. CRI IUS 421 (3)
+-ARG 10-80 p14 +NYT 2-24-80 pD20
++FF 7/8-80 p83 +ON 1-10-81 p29
+HF 7-80 p67 +SR 9-80 p96
+NR 7-80 p9

EBEN, Petr
Sonntagsmusik: Moto ostinato. See no. 3786

EBERLIN, Johann
Toccata and fugue tertia. See no. 3622
Toccata e fuga tertia. See no. 4012
Toccata sexta. See no. 3622. See no. 4012

ECCARD, Johann
Songs: Over the mountains Mary goes; Von der Geburt Christi. See no. 3775

ECCLES, Henry
Sonata, G minor. See no. 3819
Sonata, horn, G minor. See no. 3731
Sonata, viola, G minor. See no. 1023

ECCLES, John
Songs: So well Corinna likes the joy; My man John. See no. 4058

ECKHARDT-GRAMATTE, Sophie-Carmen
1460 Concerto, solo violin, A minor. BACH: Partita, violin, no. 2, S 1004, D minor: Chaconne. Sophie-Carmen Eckhardt-Gramatte, vln. Masters of the Bow MB 1031
+FF 3/4-81 p113 ++MUM 2-81 p31

EDLUND, Lars
1461 Missa Sancti Nicolai. NAUMANN: Vita vinum est. Swedish Radio Choir, Stockholm Cathedral Choir; Eric Ericson, Gustaf Sjokvist. Caprice CAP 3025
+FF 9/10-81 p222 ++NR 7-81 p9

EDMUNDSON, Garth
Vom Himmel hoch toccata. See no. 3894

EGGEN, Arne
Ciaconna, G minor. See no. 2880
EGK, Werner
French suite after Rameau. See no. 1305
ELGAR, Edward
The apostles, op. 49: The spirit of the Lord. See no. 3875
Ave verum corpus, op. 2, no. 1. See no. 3619
Bavarian dances, op. 27, no. 2. See no. 1482
Beau Brummel: Minuet. See no. 1482
Chanson de matin, op. 15, no. 2. See no. 1482
Civic fanfare. See no. 4006
1462 Cockaigne overture, op. 40. Enigma variations, op. 36. LSO; Colin Davis. Philips 6570 188 Tape (c) 7310 188 (From SAL 3516)
+FF 9/10-80 p114 +HFN 12-80 p153
+-Gr 12-80 p832 +HFN 1-81 p109 tape
1463 Concerto, violoncello, op. 85, E minor. WALTON: Concerto, violoncello. Ralph Kirschbaum, vlc; Scottish National Orchestra; Alexander Gibson. Chandos ABR 1007
+FF 3/4-81 p115 +-HFN 7-81 p72
++HF 9-80 p87 -RR 2-80 p52
+-HFN 2-80 p92 ++St 8-80 p93
1464 Concerto, violoncello, op. 85, E minor. Elegy, op. 58. In the south overture, op. 50. Robert Cohen, vlc; LPO; Norman Del Mar. Classics for Pleasure CFP 40342 Tape (c) TC CFP 40342
+Gr 12-80 p831 +ST 5-81 p47
+HFN 1-81 p93
1465 Concerto, violoncello, op. 85, E minor. TCHAIKOVSKY: Variations on a Rococo theme, op. 33. Pezzo capriccioso, op. 62. Lynn Harrell, vlc; CO; Lorin Maazel. London CS 7195 (also Decca SXL 6965 Tape (c) KSXC 6965)
-FF 11/12-81 p158 +-HFN 7-81 p72
+Gr 7-81 p152 +NR 12-81 p5
Coronation ode, op. 44: Land of hope and glory. See no. 3650
Dream children, op. 43, nos. 1 and 2. See no. 1482
Dream of Gerontius, op. 38: Softy and gently. See no. 3650
1466 Elegy, op. 58. Froissart overture, op. 19. Pomp and circumstance marches, op. 39. Sospiri, op. 70. PhO, NPhO; John Barbirolli. HMV SXLP 30456 Tape (c) TC SXLP 30456 (From ASD 2292)
+Gr 4-81 p1316 +-HFN 5-81 p91
Elegy, op. 58. See no. 1464
1467 Enigma variations, op. 36. MUSSORGSKY: Pictures at an exhibition. LAPO; Zubin Mehta. Decca JB 106 Tape (c) KJBC 106 (From SXL 6592, 6328)
+Gr 11-81 p689
Enigma variations, op. 36. See no. 1462. See no. 3817
Enigma variations, op. 36: Nimrod. See no. 3617. See no. 3721. See no. 3930
1468 Falstaff, op. 68, C minor. In the south overture, op. 50. LPO; Georg Solti. Decca SXL 6963 Tape (c) KSXC 6963 (also London 7193 Tape (c) CS5-7193)
+ARG 7/8-81 p15 +HF 6-81 p70 tape
+-FF 3/4-81 p115 +HFN 10-80 p103
+-Gr 11-80 p665 +MT 6-81 p389
+Gr 12-80 p889 tape ++SFC 2-8-81 p21
+-HF 5-81 p58 +ST 2-81 p734

Froissart overture, op. 19. See no. 1466

1469 In the south overture, op. 50. Sea pictures, op. 37. Yvonne Minton, ms; LPO; Daniel Barenboim. CBS 76579 Tape (c) 40-76579 (also Columbia M 35880 Tape (c) 35880)
+-FF 11/12-80 p110
+-Gr 8-77 p328
+-Gr 1-78 p1307 tape
+-HF 5-81 p58
+HFN 9-77 p141
+HFN 12-77 p187 tape
+MT 12-77 p1014
+NR 12-80 p2
+-NYT 12-14-80 pD38
+RR 9-77 p87
+-RR 12-77 p1145 tape
+RR 12-77 p94 tape

In the south overture, op. 50. See no. 1464. See no. 1468. See no. 3617

Introduction and allegro, op. 47. See no. 374

1470 King Arthur: The king and Sir Bedivere; Elaine asleep; The banqueting hall at Westminster; The queen's tower at night; Battle scene; Arthur's passage to Avalon. The starlight express, op. 78: O children open your arms to me; There's a fairy; I'm everywhere; O stars shine brightly; We shall meet the morning spiders; My old tunes are rather broken; Dandelions daffodils; Finale. Cynthia Glover, s; John Lawrenson, bar; Bournemouth Sinfonietta; George Hurst. Chandos CBR 1001 Tape (c) CBT 1001 (From Polydor 2383 224)
+Gr 5-81 p1504
+-HFN 5-81 p93 tape
+-HFN 5-81 p93

1471 The light of life, op. 29. Margaret Marshall, s; Helen Watts, con; Robin Leggate, t; John Shirley-Quirk, bar; Liverpool Orchestra and Chorus; Charles Groves. HMV ASD 3952 Tape (c) TC ASD 3952
+Gr 4-81 p1352
+HFN 4-81 p71
+STL 5-10-81 p41

Nursery suite, no. 2. See no. 1482

1472 Pomp and circumstance marches, op. 59. Sea pictures, op. 37. LPO; Bernadette Greevy, con; Vernon Handley. Classics for Pleasure CFP 40363 Tape (c) TC CFP 40363
+Gr 11-81 p689
+HFN 11-81 p94
+HFN 12-81 p112 tape

Pomp and circumstance marches, op. 39. See no. 1466

Pomp and circumstance marches, op. 39, no. 1, D major. See no. 3699

Pomp and circumstance marches, op. 39, no. 4, G major. See no. 3976

Salut d'amour, op. 12. See no. 1482. See no. 3667

Sea pictures, op. 37. See no. 756. See no. 1469. See no. 1472

Sea pictures, op. 37: Where corals lie. See no. 3650

Serenade, op. 20, E minor. See no. 1328

1473 Sonata, violin and piano, op. 82, E minor. MESSIAEN: Theme and variations. WALTON: Pieces, violin and piano (2). Michael Davis, vln; Rosemary Platt, pno. Orion ORS 79360
+FF 9/10-80 p117
+NR 8-80 p8
+St 1-81 p82

1474 Songs: Ave verum corpus; Ecce sacerdos magnus; Psalm, op. 48. LISZT: Via Crucis, S 63. Stephen Connolly, treble; Donald Holmes, bar; John Wheeler, bs; Tom Corfield, Francis Jackson, org; Leeds Parish Church Choir; Simon Lindley. Abbey LPB 813
+Gr 3-80 p1427
+HFN 11-80 p117
+-MT 3-81 p196

1475 Songs: From the Bavarian highlands, op. 27. Songs, op. 18: O happy eyes; Love; My love dwelt in a northern land. Partsongs, op. 26: The snow; Fly singing bird. Spanish serenade, op. 23: The prince of sleep. Donald Hunt Singers; Keith Swallow, pno; Jeremy Ballard, Paul Smith, vln. Abbey ABY 821
+-Gr 6-81 p69 +-HFN 8-81 p84

1476 Songs: Angelus; Ave Maria; Fear not O land; Go song of mine; I sing the birth; Psalm, no. 29, Give unto the Lord; Psalm, no. 48, Great is the Lord; O salutaris hostia; O hearken thou; They are at rest. Worcester Cathedral Choir; Paul Trepte, David Hill, org. Abbey ABY 822
+Gr 8-81 p302 +HFN 8-81 p84

1477 Songs: From the Bavarian Highlands, op. 27. VAUGHAN WILLIAMS: In Windsor forest. Helen Field, s; Bournemouth Sinfonietta; Bournemouth Symphony Chorus; Norman Del Mar. HMV ASD 4061 Tape (c) TCC ASD 4061
+Gr 9-81 p421 +HFN 10-81 p87

1478 Songs: Credo, E minor; Death on the hills, op. 72; Evening scene; How calmly the evening; Good morrow; Lo Christ the Lord is born; Love, op. 18, no. 2; O happy eyes, op. 18, no. 1; O mightiest of the mighty; Serenade, op. 73, no. 2; To her beneath whose steadfast star; Weary wind of the west; Windlass song. Philharmonic Chamber Choir; Keith Beniston, org; David Temple. Meridian E 77040
+Gr 11-81 p733 +HFN 10-81 p87

Songs: Ave verum. See no. 3822

Songs: Pleading, op. 48, no. 1; Song cycle, op. 59; Songs, op. 60. See no. 1077

Songs: The shower, op. 71, no. 1. See no. 4005

Songs: Violet. See no. 4033

Sospiri, op. 70. See no. 1466

1479 The starlight express, op. 78. Valerie Masterson, s; Derek Hammond-Stroud, bar; LPO; Vernon Handley. HMV ESDW 711 (2) Tape (c) TC ESDW 711 (From SLS 5036)
++Gr 11-81 p733 ++HFN 11-81 p105

The starlight express, op. 78: O children open your arms to me; There's a fairy; I'm everywhere; O stars shine brightly; We shall meet the morning spiders; My old tunes are rather broken; Dandelions daffodils; Finale. See no. 1470

The starlight express, op. 78: To the children; My old tunes. See no. 1482

1480 Symphony, no. 1, op. 55, A flat major. LPO; Vernon Handley. Classics for Pleasure CFP 40331 Tape (c) CT 40331
+Gr 6-80 p32 +HFN 5-81 p93 tape
+-HFN 5-80 p121 +RR 6-80 p48

1481 Symphony, no. 2, op. 63, E flat major. LPO; Vernon Handley. Classics for Pleasure CFP 40350 Tape (c) TC CFP 40350
++Gr 7-81 p152 +HFN 10-81 p95 tape
+-HFN 9-81 p80 ++STL 9-13-81 p41

The wand of youth, op. 1: Suite; Serenade; Sun dance; The tame bear. See no. 1482

1482 Works, selections: Bavarian dances, op. 27, no. 2 (Lullaby). Beau Brummel: Minuet. Chanson de matin, op. 15, no. 2. Dream children, op. 43, nos. 1 and 2. Nursery suite, no. 2. Salut d'amour, op. 12. The starlight express, op. 78: To the children; My old tunes. The wand of youth, op. 1: Suite; Serenade; Sun dance; The tame bear. RPO; Frederick Harvey, bar; Lawrence Collingwood. HMV ESD 7068 Tape (c) TC ESD 7068 (From CSD 1555)

+FF 3/4-81 p116
+Gr 3-79 p1562
+Gr 6-79 p109 tape
++HFN 4-79 p131
+HFN 5-79 p134 tape
+RR 3-79 p68

ELIAS, Manuel de Santo

Minuet, D major. See no. 4115

ELIASSON, Anders

Disegno. See no. 3690

ELLIOTT

Hybrius the Cretan. See no. 4074

ELLIS

Coronation Scot. See no. 3956

ELLSTEIN

V'liyerushalayim Ir'cha. See no. 3897

ELMAS, Stepan

Nocturne. See no. 3912

ELVEY, George

Psalm, no. 84, How lovely are thy dwellings. See no. 3895

EMMETT, Daniel

Dixie. See no. 4026

ENCINA, Juan del

Songs: Amor con fortuna contrefacon de Halcon que se atreve. See no. 3828

Songs: Ay triste que vengo. See no. 4063

ENDLER, Johann Samuel

1483 Concerto, trumpet, F major. MOLTER: Concerto, trumpet, no. 2, D major. NERUDA: Concerto, trumpet, E flat major. TELEMANN: Concerto, trumpet, D major. Wolfgang Basch, tpt; German Bach Soloists; Helmut Winschermann. Pro Arte PAD 100 Tape (c) PCD 100

+/ARG 10-81 p48
+FF 7/8-81 p184
+MUM 9/10-81 p37 tape
+SFC 4-26-81 p18
++St 9-81 p103

ENESCO, Georges

Cantabile et presto. See no. 3914. See no. 3928

1484 Rumanian rhapsody, op. 11, no. 1, A major. LISZT: Hungarian rhapsody, no. 2, S 244, C sharp minor. SMETANA: The bartered bride: Overture. Ma Vlast: The Moldau. RCA Symphony Orchestra; Leopold Stokowski. RCA AGL 1-3880 (also RCA GL 4-2068) (From LSC 2471)

-FF 9/10-81 p288

Rumanian rhapsody, op. 11, no. 1, A major. See no. 750

1485 Sonata, piano, no. 1, op. 24, F sharp minor. Suite, piano, no. 2, op. 10, D major. Theodor Parashivesco, pno. Metropole 2599 022

+Gr 12-81 p896

Sonata, piano, no. 3, op. 24, D major. See no. 3749

Sonata, violin and piano, no. 3, op. 25, A minor. See no. 813

1486 Songs, op. 15 (7). ROUSSEL: Songs: Adieu; A flower given to my daughter; Jazz dans la nuit; Light; Melodies, op. 20 (2); Odes anacreontiques, nos. 1, 5; Odelette; Poemes chinois, op. 12 (2); Poemes chinois, op. 35 (2). Yolanda Marcoulescou, s; Katja Phillabaum, pno. Orion ORS 75184 (also Saga 5416)

++Gr 5-76 p1788 +NYT 6-8-75 pD19
+Gr 9-81 p427 +ON 7-77 p29
++HF 10-75 p78 +RR 4-76 p70
+-MT 8-76 p660 +-St 5-76 p114
+NR 7-75 p12

Suite, piano, no. 2, op. 10, D major. See no. 1485

ENGLUND, Einar

Passacaglia. See no. 3804

ENRIQUE

Mi querer tanto vos quiere. See no. 4063

ERB, Donald

1487 Autumn music. Christmas music. Concerto trombone. Spatial fanfare. Stuart Dempster, trom; Louisville Orchestra; Louis Lane. Louisville LL 772
++FF 7/8-81 p97 *NR 5-81 p5

Christmas music. See no. 1487

Concerto, trombone. See no. 1487

Spatial fanfare. See no. 1487

ERBACH, Christian

Ricercare secundi toni. See no. 4094

ERKEL, Ferenc

Festival overture. See no. 3863

Hunyadi Laszlo, excerpt. See no. 4076

Hunyadi Laszlo: Palotas dance. See no. 3863

ESCOT, Pozzi

Neyrac lux. See no. 1224

ETIENNE DE MEAUX

Trop est mes maris jalos. See no. 4086

EUROPE, James

Castles half and half. See no. 4104

EVETT, Robert

Billy in the Darbies. See no. 3932

EWALD, Victor

Quintet, no. 3, op. 7. See no. 3662

EWING, Alexander

Jerusalem the golden. See no. 4107

EYBLER, Joseph

Omnes de Saba venient. See no. 3999

FACOLI, Marco

Aria della comedia nuovo. See no. 3676

Hor ch'io son gionto quivi. See no. 3676

Padoana terza dita la finetta. See no. 3676

S'io m'accorgo ben mio. See no. 3676

FALL, Leo

1488 Die Kaiserin, excerpts. Die Rose von Stambul, excerpts. Anny Schlemm, Gretel Hartung, Gretl Schorg, s; Franz Fehringer, Willy Hofmann, Fritz Wunderlich, t; Willy Schneider, bs-bar; Koln Radio Orchestra and Chorus; Franz Marszalek. RCA VL 30407
+FF 3/4-81 p116

Die Kaiserin, excerpts. See no. 3975

Die Rose von Stambul, excerpts. iee no. 1488

FALLA, Manuel de

El amor brujo. See no. 21. See no. 759

El amor brujo: Air. See no. 3713

El amor brujo: Cancion de amor dolido; Cancion de fuego fatua; Danza del jungo de amor. See no. 4038

El amor brujo: El circulo magico; Cancion del fuego fatuo. See no. 18

1489 Concerto, harpsichord. Psyche. El retablo de Maese Pedro. Jennifer Smith, s; Alexander Oliver, t; Peter Knapp, bar; John Constable, hpd; London Sinfonietta; Simon Rattle. Argo ZRG 921
+Gr 5-81 p1510 ++HFN 6-81 p73

Homenaje a Debussy. See no. 3870
Piezas espanolas: Andaluza. See no. 3857
Psyche. See no. 1489
El retablo de Maese Pedro. See no. 1489
El sombrero de tres picos: Danza del Corregidor; Danza del molinero. See no. 3727
El sombrero de tres picos: Danza del molinero. See no. 18
El sombrero de tres picos: Introduction; Dance of the miller's wife; Corregidor; Miller's wife; The grapes; The neighbours; Miller's dance; Final dance. See no. 1112
El sombrero de tres picos: Suites, nos. 1 and 2. See no. 1114
Songs: Oracion de las madres que tienen a sus hijos en brazos; Tus ojillos negros. See no. 3889
Spanish popular songs (7). See no. 4119

1490 Spanish popular songs: Suite. STRAVINSKY: Divertimento (arr. Stravinsky, Dushkin). WEINER: Sonata, violin and piano, no. 2, op. 11, F sharp minor. Leila Rasonyi, vln; Gyorgy Miklos, pno. Hungaroton SLPX 12225
+FF 9/10-81 p259

1491 Suite populaire espagnole (arr. Kochanski). GRANADOS: Spanish dance, op. 37: Andaluza (arr. Kreisler). HALFFTER: Danza de la gitana (arr. Heifetz). SARASATE: Caprice basque, op. 24. Spanish dances, nos. 1 and 2, op. 21; no. 5, op. 23; no. 8, op. 26. Itzhak Perlman, vln; Samuel Sanders, pno. Angel SZ 37590 Tape (c) 4ZS 37590 (also HMV ASD 3910 Tape (c) TC ASD 3910)
+-FF 9/10-80 p284 +NR 10-80 p8
+Gr 10-80 p512 +NYT 7-6-80 pD15
+-HFN 10-80 p112 ++St 10-80 p120
+HFN 12-80 p159 tape +ST 2-81 p734

Suite populaire espagnole. See no. 3686

1492 La vida breve: Dance, no. 1. PROKOFIEV: Love for three oranges, op. 33: Suite. RAVEL: La valse. LPO; Walter Susskind. Crystal Clear CCS 7006
+-ARG 6-79 p51 -HFN 5-81 p89
+Audio 4-79 p84 +NR 2-79 p5
+-FF 5/6-79 p10 +-RR 3-79 p81
+HF 6-79 p94 -SFC 6-3-79 p49

La vida breve: Danse espagnole. See no. 3841
La vida breve: Vivan los que rien, Alli esta riyendo. See no. 3642 See no. 3755

FALVO, Rudolfo
Dicitencello vuie. See no. 3641

FARINA, Carlo
Pavane. See no. 3719. See no. 3938

1493 Sonata, violin, G minor. MONTEVERDI: Il combattimento di Tancredi e Clorinda. Lamento d'Arianna. Lamento d'Olimpia. Nigel Rogers, t; Patrizia Kwella, s; David Thomas, bar; Carolyn Watkinson, alto; Reinhard Goebel, vln; Musica Antiqua Koln. DG 2533 460
+Gr 12-81 p923 +HFN 12-81 p97

FARKAS, Ferenc
1494 Canephorae. HINDEMITH: Sontas, organ, nos. 1-3. Sebestyen Pecsi, org. Hungaroton SLPX 12137
+-Gr 7-81 p176 +NR 9-81 p15
-HFN 6-81 p73
FARMER, John
Songs: A little pretty bonny lass. See no. 3845
FARNABY, Giles
Fancies toyes and reames: The old spagnoletta; His rest; Tell me Daphne; A toye; His dreame; The new Sa-Hoo. See no. 3798
Fantasias, nos. 10, 27. See no. 4084
Farmer's pavan. See no. 4084
The flatt pavan. See no. 4084
Lachrymae pavan. See no. 4084
Loath to depart. See no. 3734. See no. 3926
Mal Sims. See no. 4084
Meridian alman. See no. 4084
Muscadin. See no. 3734. See no. 4084
The old spagnoletta. See no. 4084
Praeludium. See no. 4084
Rosasolis. See no. 4084
Tell me Daphne. See no. 4084
Tower hill. See no. 4084
A toye. See no. 3926. See no. 4084
Up tails all. See no. 4084
Why aske you. See no. 4084
FARNHAM
Toccata on "O filii et filiae". See no. 3821
FARRANT, Richard
Call to remembrance. See no. 3614
FARRAR, Ernest
Sons: O mistress mine. See no. 3874
FARRENC, Louise
Quintet: Scherzo. See no. 3814
Trio, op. 45, E minor. See no. 3884
FARWELL, Arthur
1495 Land of Luthany. Sonata, violoncello and piano. CADMAN: A mad empress remembers. Douglas Moore, vlc; Paul Ennis-Dwyer, pno. Musical Heritage Society MHS 4348
++FF 11/12-81 p159 ++St 12-81 p79
Sonata, violoncello and piano. See no. 1495
Wa-Wan choral. See no. 4104
FAURE, Gabriel
Andante, op. 75, F flat major. See no. 1509
Apres un reve, op. 7,, no. 1. See no. 3667. See no. 3686. See no. 4113
Ballade, op. 19, F sharp major. See no. 1510
Berdeuse, op. 16, D major. See no. 1509. See no. 1510
1496 La bonne chanson, op. 61. Trio, piano, op. 120, D minor. Sarah Walker, ms; Nash Ensemble; Ian Brown, pno; Marcia Crayford, vln; Christopher van Kampen, vlc. CRD CRD 1089 Tape (c) CRDC 4089
+Gr 4-81 p1355 +-HFN 4-81 p71
+Gr 9-81 p460 tape +HFN 9-81 p93 tape
Caligula, op. 52: Incidental music. See no. 1510
Cantique de Jean Racine, op. 11. See no. 3796

Les Djinns, op. 12. See no. 1510

1497 Dolly suite, op. 56. FRANCK: Prelude, chorale and fugue. MENDELSSOHN: Allegro brillant, op. 92, A major. Cyril Smith, Phyllis Sellick, pno. Nimbus 2120
+Gr 1-81 p970 +RR 8-80 p69

Dolly suite, op. 56. See no. 3665

Dolly suite, op. 56: Berceuse. See no. 1129. S-e no. 3666

Elegie, op. 24, C minor. See no. 1509. See no. 1510

Fantaisie, flute. See no. 1118

Fantaisie, op. 79, C major. See no. 1509. See no. 3668. See no. 3914. See no. 3928

Fantaisie, op. 111, G major. See no. 1510

Impromptu, op. 86. See no. 1317

Masques et bergamasques, op. 112: Overture. See no. 3666

Masques et bergamasques, op. 112: Suite. See no. 1510

Messe basse. See no. 3924

Morceau de concours, F major. See no. 1509. See no. 3914. See no. 3928

Morceau de lecture a vue, A major. See no. 1509

Motet: Maria mater gratiae, op. 47, no. 2. See no. 3924

1498 Nocturnes, nos. 1-13. Theme and variations, op. 73, C sharp minor. Jean-Philippe Collard, pno. EMI 2C 069 12575/6 (2)
+Gr 6-81 p60

Papillon, op. 77, A major. See no. 1509

1499 Pavane, op. 50. RAVEL: Introduction and allegro. Pavane pour une infante defunte. Le tombeau de Couperin. SATIE: Gymnopedies (2) (orch. Debussy). William Bennett, flt; David Theodore, ob; Tom Kelly, clt; James Brown, hn; John Wilbraham, tpt; David Watkins, hp; National Philharmonic Orchestra; Charles Gerhardt. RCA ARL 1-2783 Tape (c) ARK 1-2783 (also RL 2-5094)
+-FF 9/10-78 p96 +NYT 9-27-81 pD24
+-Gr 2-78 p1419 +-RR 2-78 p58
++HFN 4-78 p114 ++SFC 8-27-78 p54
+NR 9-78 p2

Pavane, op. 50. See no. 3851. See no. 4082

1500 Pelleas et Melisande, op. 80. SCHOENBERG: Pelleas und Melisande, op. 5. SIBELIUS: Pelleas et Melisande, op. 46. Rotterdam Philharmonic Orchestra; David Zinman. Philips 6769 045 (2)
+-FF 5/6-81 p137 +NR 3-81 p2
+-Gr 2-81 p1088 +SFC 12-9-80 p33
+HFN 2-81 p95 ++St 4-81 p104

Pelleas et Melisande, op. 80: Incidental music. See no. 1510

Pelleas et Melisande, op. 80: Sicilienne. See no. 3645

1501 Penelope. Regine Crespin, s; Raoul Jabin, t; Christiane Gayraud, con; Andre Vessieres, bs; Joseph Peyron, t; RTF Orchestra and Chorus; D. E. Inghelbrecht. Discoreale DR 10012/14 (3)
+-Gr 10-81 p598 +-Te 6-81 p52

1502 Penelope. Jessye Norman, Colette Alliot-Lugaz, s; Jocelyne Taillon, ms; Alain Vanzo, Jean Dupouy, t; Paul Guigue, bar; Jose van Dam, bs; Jean Laforge Vocal Ensemble; Monte Carlo Philharmonic Orchestra; Charles Dutoit. Erato STU 71386 (3)
+Gr 10-81 p598 +STL 10-11-81 p41

Penelope: Prelude. See no. 1510

1503 Quartet, piano, no. 1, op. 15, C minor. Quartet, piano, no. 2, op. 45, G minor. Marguerite Long, pno; Jacques Thibaud, vln;

Maurice Vieux, vla; Pierre Fournier, vlc; Pasquier Trio. EMI 2C 051 12815
+-Gr 7-81 p192

Quartet, piano, no. 1, op. 15, C minor. See no. 1509

Quartet, piano, no. 2, op. 45, G minor. See no. 1503. See no. 1509

Quartet, strings, op. 121, E minor. See no. 1509

Quintet, piano, no. 1, op. 89, D minor. See no. 1509

Quintet, piano, no. 2, op. 115, C minor. See no. 1509

1504 Requiem, op. 48. Doda Conrad, bar; Maurice Durufle, org; Orchestra; Nadia Boulanger. EMI 2C 051 16359
-Gr 6-81 p84

1505 Requiem, op. 48. Martina Arroyo, s; Hermann Prey, bar; Robert Arnold, org; Musica Aeterna Orchestra and Chorus; Frederic Waldman. Westminster MCA 1411 (From Decca)
+-ARG 1-81 p26 -FF 11/12-80 p111

Romance, op. 28, B flat major. See no. 1509

Romance, op. 69, A major. See no. 1509

Serenade, op. 98, B minor. See no. 1509

Shylock suite, op. 57: Incidental music. See no. 1510

Sicilienne, op. 78, G minor. See no. 1509

1506 Sonata, violin and piano, no. 1, op. 13, A major. Sonata, violin and piano, no. 2, op. 108, E minor. Pierre Amoyal, vln; Anne Queffelec, pno. Erato STU 71195
+-Gr 10-79 p667 +-MT 4-80 p251
+-Gr 5-81 p1486 +RR 11-79 p123
+HFN 11-79 p139

Sonata, violin and piano, no. 1, op. 13, A major. See no. 1509

Sonata, violin and piano, no. 2, op. 108, E minor. See no. 1506. See no. 1509

Sonata, violoncello and piano, no. 1, op. 109, D minor. See no. 1509

Sonata, violoncello and piano, no. 2, op. 117, G minor. See no. 1509

1507 Songs: L'Absent, op. 5, no. 3; Accompangement, op. 85, no. 3; Apres un reve, op. 7, no. 1; Arpege, op. 76, no. 2; Au bord de l'eau, op. 8, no. 1; Au cimetiere, op. 51, no. 2; Aubade, op. 6, no. 1; Aurore; Aurore, op. 39, no. 1; Automne, op. 18, no. 3; Barcarolle, op. 7, no. 3; Les berceaux, op. 23, no. 1; La bonne chanson, op. 61; C'est la paix, op. 114; Chanson d'amour, op. 27, no. 1; La chanson d'Eve, op. 95; Chanson du pecheur, op. 4, no. 1; Chanson de Shylock, op. 57; Chant d'automne, op. 5, no. 1; Claire de lune, op. 46, no. 2; Dans le foret de Septembre, op. 85, no. 1; Dans les ruines d'une abbaye, op. 2, no. 1; Le don silencieux, op. 92; En priere; La fee aux chansons, op. 27, no. 2; Fleur jetee, op. 39, no. 2; Le fleur qui va sur l'eau, op. 85, no. 2; L'horizon chimerique, op. 118; Hymne, op. 7, no. 2; Ici-bas, op. 8, no. 3; Le jardin clos, op. 106; Larmes, op. 51, no. 1; Lydia, op. 4, no. 2; Les matelots, op. 2, no. 2; Melisande's song, op. posth.; Melodies, op. 58; Mirages, op. 113; Mai, op. 1, no. 2; Nocturne, op. 43, no. 2; Nell, op. 18, no. 1; Noel, op. 43, no. 1; Notre amour, op. 23, no. 2; Le papillon et la fleur, op. 1, no. 1; Le pays des reves, op. 39, no. 3; Pleurs d'or, op. 72; Poeme d'un jour, op. 21; Le plus doux chemin, op. 87, no. 1; Puisqui ici-bas toute ame, op. 10, no. 1; Les presents, op. 46, no. 1; Prison, op. 83, no. 1; La rancor, op. 8, no. 2; Le parfum imperissable, op. 76, no. 1; Le ramier, op. 87, no. 2; Reve d'amour, op. 5, no. 2; La rose, op. 51, no. 4; Les roses d'Ispahan, op. 39, no. 4; Le secret, op. 23, no. 3; Seule, op. 3, no. 1; Serenade Toscane, op. 3, no. 2; Serenade du bourgeois gentilhomme, op. posth.; Soir, op. 82, no. 2; Spleen, op. 51, no. 3; Sylvie, op. 6, no. 3; Tarantelle, op. 10, no. 2; Tristesse op. 6, no. 2; Vocalise; Le voyageuer, op. 18, no. 2. Elly Ameling, s; Gerard Souzay, bar; Dalton Baldwin, pno. Connoisseur Society CS 2127/8 (4) (also EMI 2C 16512831/5. From HMV HQS 1258)

+ARG 6-77 p5
+Gr 11-81 p737
+HF 8-77 p80
++MJ 5-77 p33
++NR 4-77 p11
+ON 7-77 p29
+RR 2-77 p25
+SFC 2-27-77 p42
++St 8-77 p120

Songs: Adieu, op. 21, no. 3,; Apres un reve, op. 7, no. 1; Barcarolle, op. 7, no. 3; Clair de lune, op. 46, no. 2; Chanson d'amour, op. 27, no. 1; En priere; Nell, op. 18, no. 1; Poeme d'un jour, op. 21; Le secret, op. 23, no. 3. See no. 1395

Songs: Apres un reve, op. 7, no. 1; Toujours, op. 21, no. 2. See no. 3838

Songs: Clair de lune, op. 46, no. 2. See no. 3642

Songs: Le papillon et la fleur. See no. 3758

Songs: Les rameaux. See no. 3688

Souvenirs de Bayreuth. See no. 3665

Tantum ergo, op. 65, no. 2. See no. 3619

Theme and variations, op. 73, C sharp minor. See no. 1498

1508 Trio, piano, op. 120, D minor. SAINT-SAENS: Trio, piano, no. 1, op. 18, F major. Jerome Lowenthal, pno; Christiaan Bor, vln; Jeffrey Solow, vlc. Pelican LP 2015

+FF 5/6-81 p136

Trio, piano, op. 120, D minor. See no. 1496. See no. 1509

1509 Works, selections: Andante, op. 75, B flat major. Berceuse, op. 16, D major. Elegie, op. 24, C minor. Fantaisie, op. 79, C major. Morceau de concours, F major. Morceau de lecture a vue, A major. Papillon, op. 77, A major. Quartets, piano, no. 1, op. 15, C major; no. 2, op. 45, G minor. Quartet, strings, op. 121, E minor. Quintets, piano, no. 1, op. 89, D minor; no. 2, op. 115, C minor. Romance, op. 28, B flat major. Romance, op. 69, A major. Serenade, op. 98, B minor. Sicilienne, op. 78, G minor. Sonatas, violin, no. 1, op. 13, A major; no. 2, op. 108, E minor. Sonatas, violoncello and piano, no. 1, op. 109, D major; no. 2, op. 117, G minor. Trio, piano, op. 120, D minor. Augustin Dumay, Jacques Ghestem, vln; Bruno Pasquier, Gerard Causse, vla; Frederic Lodeon, Pierre Penasson, vlc; Michel Debost, flt; Jean-Philippe Collard, pno; Parrenin Quartet. EMI 2C 165 16331/6 (6)

+Gr 6-81 p48
+SFC 12-9-80 p33

1510 Works, selections: Ballade, op. 19, F sharp major. Berceuse, op. 16, D major. Caligula, op. 52: Incidental music. Les Djinns, op. 12. Elegie, op. 24, C minor. Fantaisie, op. 111, G major. Masques et bergamasques, op. 112: Suite. Pelleas et Melisande, op. 80: Incidental music. Penelope: Prelude. Shylock, op. 57: Incidental music. Frederica von Stade, s; Nicolai Gedda, t;

Alex Bourbon Vocal Ensemble; Jean-Philippe Collard, pno; Paul Tortelier, vlc; Yan Pascal Tortelier, vln; Toulouse Capitole Orchestra; Michel Plasson. HMV SLS 5219 (3)
+Gr 12-81 p885 +STL 12-13-81 p39

FAURE, Jean-Baptiste
Crucifix. See no. 3997. See no. 3999
Crucifix; The palms. See no. 3967

FAYRFAX, Robert
Songs: I love, loved. See no. 3945

FELCIANO, Richard
Two hearts. See no. 3942

FELDMAYER, Johann
1511 Concerto, 2 horns, F major. FIALA: Concerto, 2 horns, E flat major. TELEMANN: Suite, orchestra, no. 63, F major. WITT: Concertino, 2 horns, E flat major. Ab Koster, Jan Schroder, hn; Deutsche Bachsolisten; Helmut Winschermann. Musical Heritage Society MHS 4356 (also RCA RL 3-0419)
+ARG 12-81 p40

FELIX
Die Katzchen: Unter dem Lindenbaum. See no. 4083

FENNELLY, Brian
1512 Quartet, strings, in 2 movements. Tesserae VII. KRAFT: Quartet, strings, no. 2. Antiphonies, piano and tape. Murray Colosimo, clt; Genevieve Chinn, Allen Brings, pno; Audubon Quartet. Orion ORS 80398
+ARG 9-81 p23 +NR 7-81 p6
+FF 7/8-81 p102

1513 Scintilla prisca. GHEZZO: Aphorisms. GILBERT: Suonare. SAYLOR: Psalms (4). Constance Beavon, ms; Irene Simonsen, flt; Jack Kreiselman, clt; Roger Boardman, Brian Fennelly, pno; David Moore, vlc. Orion ORS 80368
+-ARG 2-81 p45 +-NR 7-80 p15
+-FF 11/12-80 p221

Tesserae VII. See no. 1512

FENNIMORE, Joseph
Titles waltz: After Max Steiner. See no. 3942

FERGUSON, Barry
Songs: Death and darkness get you packing; Psalm, no. 137, verses, nos. 1-6; Reverie. See no. 3615

FERGUSON, Howard
1514 Short pieces, op. 6 (4). FINZI: Bagatelles, op. 23 (5). HURLESTONE: Characteristic pieces (4). STANFORD: Sonata, clarinet and piano, op. 129. Thea King, Clifford Benson. Hyperion A 66014
+Gr 6-81 p55 ++MT 10-81 p677
+HFN 6-81 p82

FERNANDEZ DE HUETE, Diego
Cancion francesa, Monsieur de la boleta. See no. 3778
Cancion italiana con diferencias. See no. 3778

FERNSTROM, John
Quintet, winds, op. 59. See no. 781

FERRABOSCO, Alfonso I
Four note pavan. See no. 4092
Pavan. See no. 4016

FERRABOSCO, Alfonso II
Almayne. See no. 3762

Dovehouse pavan. See no. 3762
Pavan, no. 4. See no. 3719
Songs: Tell me o love. See no. 3871
Spanish pavane. See no. 3937

FESCH, Willem de
Concerto, oboe, op. 3, no. 2, B flat major. See no. 3978

FESTA, Constanzo
Quis dabit oculis nostris. See no. 3777

FIALA, Josef
Concerto, 2 horns, E flat major. See no. 1511
Divertimento pastorale, B flat major. See no. 4078

1515 Quartet, oboe, F major. STAMITZ: Quartet, oboe, op. 8, no. 4, E flat major. VANHAL: Sonata, flute and violin, op. 3, G major. VRANICKY: Quartet, flute, no. 3, F major. Musica da Camera Prague. Supraphon 111 2470 (also Barenreiter BM 4118)
+FF 9/10-81 p274

FIBICH, Zdenek
Poeme, op. 41, no. 6. See no. 3693

FIELD, John
1516 Nocturnes, nos. 1-18. Veronica McSwiney, pno. Claddagh CSM 50/1
+Gr 6-74 p79 -RR 4-74 p67
+Gr 9-81 p412

FILTZ, Anton
Concerto, violoncello, G major. See no. 3782

FINCK, Heinrich
Greiner Zanner. See no. 3671
Greiner Zanner; Ich stund an einem morgen; Ich wird erlost; Der Ludel und der Hensel. See no. 3862
Instrumental pieces (3). See no. 3862

FINE, Irving
Serious song: A lament for string orchestra. See no. 377

FINEGAN, Bill
Arrangements of Moonlight sonata; Tchaikovsky's piano concerto; Midnight sleighride; Azure-te; Rain; Nina never knew; When hearts are young. See no. 2023
Doddletown fifers. See no. 2023

FINGER, Gottfried
Division on a ground. See no. 3927

FINNEY, Ross Lee
Trio, piano, no. 2. See no. 845

FINZI, Gerald
Bagatelles, op. 23. See no. 1514

1517 Concerto, clarinet, op. 31. STANFORD: Concerto, clarinet, op. 80, A minor. Thea King, clt; PhO; Alun Francis. Hyperion A 66001 Tape (c) KA 66001
+Gr 11-80 p666 ++HFN 6-81 p87 tape
+Gr 11-81 p783 tape +MT 2-81 p113
++HFN 11-80 p117

1518 Songs (choral): All this night, op. 33. Elegies, op. 5 (3). God is gone up, op. 27, no. 2. Lo the full final sacrifice. Magnificat, op. 36. Partsongs, op. 17 (7). Exultate Singers; Timothy Farrell, org; Garrett O'Brien. L'Oiseau-Lyre DSLO 32 (also Musical Heritage Society MHS 4320)
+-FF 11/12-81 p160 +-HFN 9-80 p104
+Gr 8-80 p251 +MT 6-81 p389

Songs: Let us garlands bring, op. 18; Love's labour's lost, op. 28; Riddle song; Sigh no more ladies. See no. 3878
Songs: Oh fair to see, op. 13b; To a poet, op. 13a. See no. 3874

FIOCCO, Joseph-Hector
1519 Pieces de clavecin: Suites, nos. 1 and 2. Jos van Immerseel, hpd. Monumenta Belgicae Musicae MBM 26
*/FF 3/4-81 p117

FISCHER, Johann Caspar
Christ ist erstanden. See no. 3961
1520 Journal du printemps: Suites, nos. 1, 3, 6, 8. Heidelberg Chamber Orchestra; Da Camera SM 91014
/-HFN 12-81 p94
Musicalisches Blumenbuschlein: Suite, no. 6, D major. See no. 4087
Preludes and fugues, B minor, D major, E flat major, C minor. See no. 4012. See no. 3622

FISCHER, L.
Amoroso. See no. 3693

FISER, Lubos
1521 Sonata, piano, no. 4. KILLMAYER: An John Field. SCRIABIN: Etudes, op. 65, nos. 1-3. Sonata, piano, no. 10, op. 70, C major. Volker Banfield, pno. Wergo 60081
++FF 9/10-80 p141 +NR 2-81 p14
+MUM 12-80 p34

FISSINGER, Alfred
Suite, marimba. See no. 3678
FITZWILLIAM VIRGINAL BOOK: Pieces. See no. 3926
FLAMENCO. See no. 3743

FLETCHER, Percy
Festival toccata. See no. 3930

FLEURY, Andre
Variations sur un noel bourguignon. See no. 310
FLOATING PETALS...Wild geese...The moon on high: Music of the Chinese pipa. See no. 3939

FLORENCE, Paulo
1522 Sonata fantasia. GUARNIERI: Canto, no. 1. Sonata, violin and piano, no. 4. SANTORO: Sonata, solo violin. Oscar Borgerth, vln; Ilara Gomes Grosso, pno. Promemus MMB 79008
+-FF 5/6-81 p208

FLOTOW, Friedrich von
1523 Alessandro Stradella. Helen Donath, s; Werner Hollweg, t; Richard Kogel, bs; Alexander Malta, Ferry Gruber, bar; Bayerischer Rundfunk Orchestra and Chorus; Heinz Wallberg. Voce 24 (2)
+-ARG 5-81 p45 +FF 11/12-81 p161
1524 Martha. Anneliese Rothenberger, s; Brigitte Fassbaender, ms; Nicolai Gedda, t; Hermann Prey, Dieter Weller, bar; Hans Georg Knoblich, bs; Bavarian State Opera Orchestra and Chorus; Robert Heger. EMI 1C 197 30241/3 (3) (From SLS 944/3)
+Gr 10-81 p603
1525 Martha. Lucia Popp, s; Doris Soffel, ms; Siegfried Jerusalem, t; Karl Ridderbusch, bar; Siegmund Nimsgern, bs; Bavarian Radio Chorus; Munich Radio Orchestra; Heinz Walburg. Eurodisc 25422 (3)
+-FF 9/10-79 p83 +ON 10-79 p67
+FF 11/12-81 p162 +ON 10-81 p52
+NYT 7-26-81 pD23

Martha: Ach so fromm ach so traut. See no. 3800. See no. 3966
Martha: Canzone del porter. See no. 4025
Martha: M'appari. See no. 1361. See no. 3995. See no. 4022
Martha: Qui sola vergin rose. See no. 4040
Martha: Siam giunti o giovinette; Questo cameo e per voi; Che vuol dir cio; Presto presto andiam; T'ho raggiunto sciagurata. See no. 3997
Martha: Solo profugo reietto. See no. 3996. See no. 4048

FOLEY, David
Pieces for Saturday afternoon (4). See no. 1009

FONTANA, Giovanni
Madonna mia pieta. See no. 3766

FONTEI, Nicolo
Fortunato cantore. See no. 3947

FOOTE, Arthur
A night piece. See no. 469

FORBES, Sebastian
Capriccio. See no. 3625

FORD, Thomas
1526 The baggepipes. Musicke of sundrie kindes: Why not here. Pavan and galliard. JENKINS: Fantasias, G minor, D minor. LOCKE: Duos, C major, C minor. SIMPSON, C.: Divisions on a ground, G major, F major, E minor. Wieland and Sigiswald Kuijken, bs viols, vln; Robert Kohnen, hpd. Accent ACC 8014
+FF 3/4-81 p227 +HFN 11-80 p127
+-Gr 11-80 p697
Musicke of sundrie kindes: Why not here. See no. 1526
Pavan and galliard. See no. 1526
A prayer to our lady. See no. 3852
Songs: Since first I saw your face. See no. 3967
Songs: Since first I saw your face; There is a lady. See no. 4085

FOREST
Qualis est dilectus. See no. 4085

FORSTER, Christoph
1527 Concerto, horn, E flat major. TELEMANN: Concerto, 2 horns, E flat major. Suite, 2 horns, F major. Adam Friedrich, Albert Brunner, hn; Zsuzsa Pertis, hpd; Maria Frank, vlc; Liszt Chamber Orchestra; Janos Rolla. Hungaroton SLPX 12118
+FF 5/6-81 p171 ++NR 2-81 p6

FORSTER, Georg
Vitrum nostrum gloriosum. See no. 3945

FORSTER, Joseph
1528 Cyrano de Bergerac, op. 55. CPhO; Vaclav Smetacek. Supraphon 110 2456
+ARG 4-81 p22 +-HFN 10-80 p103
++FF 1/2-81 p109 +NR 1-81 p1
+-Gr 10-80 p496 +St 6-81 p113
1529 Sonata, violin and piano, op. 117. JANACEK: Dumka, C minor. Romance, E major. Sonata, violin and piano. NEDBAL: Sonata, violin and piano, op. 9, B minor. NOVAK: Sonata, violin and piano, D minor. Josef Suk, vln; Jan Panenka, pno. Supraphon 111 2341/2 (2)
+FF 9/10-81 p257 +NR 4-80 p7
+Gr 8-80 p239 ++RR 7-80 p82
+HFN 7-80 0113 +SFC 1-27-80 p44
+MT 10-81 p680 ++St 4-80 p87

FOSCARINI, Giovanni
Sinfonias, nos. 1-2. See no. 4097
FOSS, Lukas
1530 Curriculum vitae. Music for six. Quartet, strings, no. 3. Columbia Quartet; University of Buffalo Percussion Ensemble; Guy Klucevsek, accord. CRI SD 413
*ARG 6-81 p26 +HF 4-81 p77
+FF 3/4-81 p117 +NR 1-81 p6
Music for six. See no. 1530
Quartet, strings, no. 3. See no. 1530
Thirteen ways of looking at a blackbird. See no. 2265
FOSSA, Johann de
Missa super theutonicam cantionem. See no. 3675
FOSTER, Stephen
A Stephen Foster treasury. See no. 4000
FOUGSTEDT, Nils-Eric
Songs: Det gar en liten speleman; Marsbjorkar; Naktergalen. See no. 3805
FRANCAIX, Jean
Impromptus, flute and bassoon (7). See no. 78
1531 Quintet, woodwinds. HINDEMITH: Kleine Kammermusik, op. 24, no. 2. SEIBER: Permutazioni a cinque. Taffanel Wind Quintet. Denon OX 7217
+FF 11/12-81 p295
Quintet, woodwinds. See no. 3934
Serenade. See no. 3788
FRANCHETTI, Alberto
Germania: Studenti udite; Ah vieni qui...No non chiuder gli occhi vaghi. See no. 3996
FRANCHOMME, August
Valse de Chopin. See no. 3789
FRANCISQUE (Franciscus), Antoine
Bransles. See no. 3643
Courante. See no. 3643
Pavane. See no. 3643
FRANCK
Courante-Gagliarda. See no. 4071
Intrada. See no. 4071
FRANCK, Andrew
1532 Arcadia. Sonata da camera. OLAN: Composition, clarinet and tape. Sonata, violin and piano. Robert Miller, pno; Linda Quan, Rolf Schulte, vln; Paul Dunkel, flt; Laura Flax, clt. CRI SD 491
+ARG 11-80 p51 +NR 7-80 p6
+FF 9/10-81 p296
Sonata da camera. See no. 1532
FRANCK, Cesar
Cantabile. See no. 833. See no. 1537. See no. 1538. See no. 1540
Chant de la Creuse: Un vieux Noel. See no. 1539
Chorales (3). See no. 1538
1533 Chorales, nos. 1-3. Piece heroique. Frederick Swann, org. Gothic 8787 9801
++ARG 2-79 p16 +NR 1-81 p12
+FF 9/10-79 p84 +St 4-79 p136
+MU 5-79 p8

Chorales, nos. 1-3. See no. 1537. See no. 1540
1534 Chorales, no. 1, E major. Priere, op. 20, C sharp minor. LISZT: Ad nos ad salutarem undam, S 259. Jane Parker-Smith, org. HMV ASD 3994 Tape (c) TC ASD 3994 (also Angel DS 37748)
+-Gr 3-81 p1214 +-HF 11-81 p87
+Gr 7-81 p196 tape +-HFN 3-81 p87
Chorales, no. 1, E major. See no. 1340. See no. 2028
Chorales, no. 3, A minor. See no. 1539
1535 Les djinns. Prelude, chorale and fugue. Symphonic variations. Kerstin Aberg, pno; Gothenburg Symphony Orchestra; Okko Kamu. BIS LP 137
+-ARG 6-81 p27 +-HFN 3-81 p87
-FF 3/4-81 p118 ++St 4-81 p71
+-Gr 1-81 p948
1536 Les djinns. Symphonic variations. GRIEG: Concerto, piano, op. 16, A minor. Cristina Ortiz, pno; PhO; Vladimir Ashkenazy. HMV ASD 3960 Tape (c) TC ASD 3960
+-FF 7/8-81 p104 ++HFN 11-80 p120
+Gr 11-80 p666 +HFN 12-80 p159
Elevation, A major. See no. 1539
Fantasia, A major. See no. 185. See no. 1537. See no. 1538. See no. 1540
Fantasia, op. 16, C major. See no. 1537. See no. 1538. See no. 1540
Final, op. 21, B flat major. See no. 1537. See no. 1538. See no. 1540. See no. 4069
Grande piece symphonique, op. 17. See no. 1537. See no. 1538. See no. 1540
Interlude symphonique de redemption. See no. 1537
Offertory, E flat major. See no. 1539
1537 Organ works: Chorales, nos. 1-3. Cantabile. Fantasia, A major. Fantasia, op. 16, C major. Final, op. 21, B flat major. Grande piece symphonique, op. 17. Interlude symphonique de redemption (trans. Dupre). Piece heroique. Priere, op. 20. Pastorale, op. 19, E major. Prelude, fugue et variation, op. 18. Graham Steed, org. Decca D165D3 (3) (also L'Oiseau-Lyre D165D3)
+FF 11/12-81 p164 +-HFN 12-80 p137
+-Gr 12-80 p854 +SFC 12-13-81 p18
-HF 11-81 p87 ++St 10-81 p72
1538 Organ works: Cantabile. Chorales (3). Fantasias, op. 16, C major; A major. Final, op. 21, B flat major. Grande piece symphonique, op. 17. Pastorale, op. 19. Piece heroique. Prelude, fugue et variation, op. 18, B minor. Priere, op. 20. Marie-Clair Alain, org. Erato STU 71035/7 (3)
++Gr 4-81 p1345 +MU 3-81 p12
1539 Organ works: Chant de la Creuse: Un vieux Noel. Chorale, no. 3, A minor. Elevation, A major. Offertory, E flat major. Piece heroique. Poco allegretto, D major. Prelude, fugue et variation, B minor. Ferenc Gergely, org. Hungaroton SLPX 12192
+NR 11-81 p14
1540 Organ works: Cantabile. Chorales, nos. 1-3. Fantasia, A major. Fantasia, op. 16, C major. Final, op. 21, B flat major. Grande piece symphonique, op. 17. Piece heroique. Prelude, fugue et variation, op. 18. Pastorale, op. 19, E major.

Priere, op. 20. Gunther Kaunzinger, org. Solist 1178/80 (3)
+FF 11/12-81 p164

Panis Angelicus. See no. 3759. See no. 3924. See no. 3999. See no. 4054

Pastorale, op. 19, E major. See no. 1537. See no. 1538. See no. 1540

Piece heroique. See no. 833. See no. 1533. See no. 1537. See no. 1538. See no. 1539. See no. 1540. See no. 3660. See no. 3744. See no. 4111

Poco allegretto, D major. See no. 1539

Prelude, chorale et fugue. See no. 300. See no. 914. See no. 1497. See no. 1535

Prelude, fugue et variation. See no. 3950

Prelude, fugue et variation, op. 18, B minor. See no. 1537. See no. 1538. See no. 1539. See no. 1540

Priere, op. 20, C sharp minor. See no. 1534. See no. 1537. See no. 1538. See no. 1540. See no. 2028

Psalm, no. 150. See no. 4060. See no. 4107

1541 Quartet, strings, D major. Fitzwilliam Quartet. L'Oiseau-Lyre DSLO 46
+Gr 5-80 p1679 ++ST 3-81 p820
++HFN 5-80 p121 ++STL 6-8-80 p38
++RR 5-80 p76

1542 Sonata, violin and piano, A major (trans.). GRIEG: Sonata, violoncello, op. 36, A minor. Robert Cohen, vlc; Roger Vignoles, pno. CRD CRD 1091 Tape (c) CRDC 4091
+-Gr 8-81 p284 +HFN 8-81 p84
+Gr 10-81 p614 tape +HFN 10-81 p95 tape

1543 Sonata, violin and piano, A major. SZYMANOWSKI: Mythes, op. 30. King Roger: Roxanna's song. Kaja Danczowska, vln; Krystian Zimerman, pno. DG 2531 330 Tape (c) 3301 330
++GR 6-81 p50 +SFC 9-27-81 p18
++Gr 9-81 p460 tape +SR 11-81 p62
+HFN 8-81 p84 +-St 11-81 p94
+HFN 9-81 p93 tape +ST 11-81 p511

1544 Sonata, violin and piano, A major (trans.). SCHUMANN: Fantasiestucke, op. 73 (trans.). Stucke im Volkston, op. 102. Alexander Michejew, vlc; Geoffrey Parsons, pno. Nimbus 2121
+Gr 8-81 p284 +-HFN 10-81 p87

1545 Sonata, violin and piano, A major. GRIEG: Sonata, violin and piano, no. 3, op. 45, C minor. Arthur Grumiaux, vln; Gyorgy Sebok, pno. Philips 9500 568
+-ARG 2-80 p27 ++HFN 10-80 p103
+-FF 9/10-80 p120 +NR 1-80 p5
+FU 2-80 p45 ++ST 6-81 p121
+-Gr 10-80 p511

Sonata, violin and piano, A major. See no. 1318. See no. 1320

Songs: Domine non secundum. See no. 3809

Songs: La procession; Panis angelicus. See no. 3967

1546 Symphonic variations. TCHAIKOVSKY: Concerto, piano, no. 1, op. 23, B flat minor. John Ogdon, pno; PhO; John Barbirolli. Arabesque 8012 Tape (c) 9012 dbx 3020
+-FF 1/2-81 p199 +-FF 9/10-81 p186 dbx

1547 Symphonic variations. Symphony, D minor. Sylvia Kersenbaum, pno; Bournemouth Symphony Orchestra; Paavo Berglund. Classics for

Pleasure CFP 40347 Tape (c) TC CFP 40347 (From HMV ASD 3308)
+Gr 4-81 p1316 /-HFN 5-81 p93 tape
/-HFN 4-81 p80

1548 Symphonic variations. Symphony, D minor. COA, LPO; Willem Mengelverg, Walter Gieseking. Past Masters PM 34
+FF 7/8-81 p100

1549 Symphonic variations. MENDELSSOHN: Hebrides overture, op. 26. PROKOFIEV: Scythian suite, op. 20. Takahiro Sonada, pno; Orchestra; Sergiu Celibidache. Rococo 2136
+NR 3-81 p1

Symphonic variations. See no. 1535. See no. 1536

1550 Symphony, D minor. Paris Philharmonic Society Orchestra; Roger Desormiere. Chant du Monde LDX 78695
-HFN 4-81 p71

Symphony, D minor. See no. 1547. See no. 1548

FRANCO, Hernando

Salve regina. See no. 3911

FRANZ, Robert

Widmung, op. 14, no. 1. See no. 3967

FRANZL

Quartet, op. 9, no. 2: Andante con moto. See no. 3907

FREDERICK II, King

Sonata, flute, B minor. See no. 3807

Sonata, flute, no. 17, A major. See no. 111

1551 Symphonies, nos. 1-4. Munich Pro Arte Orchestra; Kurt Redel. Philips 9502 057 Tape (c) 7313 057
+FF 7/8-81 p101 +HFN 12-81 p95
+HF 7-81 p56 +NR 5-81 p4

Symphony, D major. See no. 123

FREEDMAN

Hoko Hoki. See no. 3956

FREIERE, Osman

Ay ay ay. See no. 3983

FRESCOBALDI, Girolamo

Aria detta "La frescobalda". See no. 3630. See no. 4001

Aria with variations. See no. 3619

Ave maris stella. See no. 4088

La bernadina. See no. 3927

Canzon per sonar. See no. 1347

Capriccio sopra l'Aria di Ruggiero. See no. 3692

Corrente. See no. 3881

La donatina. See no. 3927

Fugue. See no. 4071

Songs: Maddalena alla Croce. See no. 3947

Toccata. See no. 170

Toccatas, nos. 2, 3. See no. 3630

FREUNDT, Cornelius

Songs: Wie schon singt uns der Engel Schar. See no. 3775. See no. 3963

FRIED, Alexej

1552 Concerto, clarinet, no. 2. Guernica. GLAZUNOV: Concerto, saxophone, op. 109, E flat major. Felix Slovacek, clt, sax; PSO, Kocian Quartet; Vladimir Valek. Supraphon 110 2750
+HFN 8-81 p84 +NR 9-81 p4

Guernica. See no. 1552

FRIEDMAN, Ignaz
Viennese dance, no. 3. See no. 3920
FROBERGER, Johann
Capriccio, no. 8. See no. 3688. See no. 4012
Ricercare, no. 1. See no. 3622. See no. 4012
Suite, G major. See no. 3877
Toccata, no. 6. See no. 4117
Tombeau. See no. 4071
FRUMERIE, Gunnar de
Aria, op. 77. See no. 3681
1553 Musica per nove, op. 75. Puck, op. 28, no. 1. Trio, piano, no. 2, op. 45. Esther Bodin, Kerstin Hindart, pno; Mircea Saulesco, Bernt Lysell, vln; Leo Winland, Ake Olofsson, vlc; Torlief Lannerholm, ob; Ulf Nilsson, clt; Tore Ronneback, bsn; Mark Schrello, tpt; Gideon Roehr, vla; Thorsten Sjogren, double bs. Caprice CAP 1170
++ARG 2-81 p39 +NR 12-80 p7
+FF 11/12-80 p112
Puck, op. 28, no. 1. See no. 1553
Symphonic variations. See no. 862
Trio, piano, no. 2, op. 45. See no. 1553
FRYE, Walter
Tout a par moy. See no. 3948
FUCHS, Robert
Fantasia, op. 91, E minor. See no. 877
Songs: O freudenreicher Tag. See no. 3963
FUCITO
Scordame. See no. 4036
FUENLLANA
Songs: De antequera salio el Moro; De los diamos vengo madre; Duelete de mi senora. See no. 4063
FULLER, Wesley
1554 Time into pieces. MORRILL: Fantasy quintet. No. SULLIVAN: Luckeystone. Dwight Peltzer, pno; David Glick, clt; Washington University Chamber Singers; Colgate Computer Music Studio; Orland Johnson. Redwood Records ES 13
+CMJ Winter 1981 p82 *NR 2-81 p15
+-FF 5/6-81 p222
FURSTENEAU, Anton
Rondo brillant, op. 38. See no. 4065
FURSTENAU, Casper
1555 Pieces, flute and guitar, op. 35, nos. 5-7, 12. MOZART: Sonata, piano, no. 11, K 331, A major (arr. Traeg). PRAGER: Introduction, theme and variations, op. 12. SCHUBERT: Tanze, op. 9, D 365 (arr. Diabelli). Hans-Martin Linde, flt; Konrad Ragossnig, gtr. Seraphim S 60347 (also EMI 065 45386)
+NR 5-81 p10
FURTWANGLER, Wilhelm
Symphony, no. 2, E minor. See no. 3781
FUX, Johann
Gli ossequi della notte: Caro mio ben. See no. 3813
Parthie, G minor. See no. 4084
1556 Partita, harpsichord, A major. Partita, 2 violins, G minor. Sinfonia, F major. Suite, G major. Jorg-Wolfgang Jahn, Gudrun Hehrmann, vln; Jurgen Wolf, vlc; Manfred Peters, rec; Adolf

Meidhof, ob; Ernst Prappacher, bsn; Marga Scheurich, Hans Schmidt, hpd. Musical Heritage Society MHS 4046 (also Da Camera SM 192802. Impromptu 192802, CMS/Oryx 1717)
+/AR 5-81 p23 /FF 1/2-80 p85
Partita, 2 violins, G minor. See no. 1556
Sinfonia, F major. See no. 1556. See no. 3631
Sonata, organ, no. 5. See no. 4012
Sonata quinta. See no. 3622
Suite, G major. See no. 1556
GABRIEL
No soy yo quien la descubre. See no. 4063
GABRIEL-MARIE
La cinquantaine. See no. 4066
GABRIELI
Ecco l'aurora. See no. 3692
GABRIELI, Andrea
Intonatione del primo tono. See no. 3808
Ricercar. See no. 3845
Ricercar del sesto tuono. See no. 3762
GABRIELI, Domenico
Canon. See no. 63
GABRIELI, Giovanni
Benedixisti domine. See no. 3775
Canzoni, nos. 1, 2, 28. See no. 3936
Canzoni, no. 3. See no. 3898
Canzoni, nos. 5, 6. See no. 4072
Canzona per sonare, no. 2. See no. 4002
Canzona per sonare, nos. 4, 5. See no. 3762
Canzona per sonare "La spiritata". See no. 3762
Canzona primi toni, septimi toni. See no. 3936
1557 Compositions, brass instruments. PEZEL: Compositions for brass instruments. Prague Brass Soloists; Frantisek Vajnar. Supraphon 411 2614
++NR 7-81 p7
Fuga del non tono. See no. 3808
In ecclesiis, motet. See no. 3845
Intonatione del primo tono. See no. 3808
Sonata con tre violini. See no. 3808
GABUNIYA, Nodar
Elegy. See no. 88
GADE, Niels
Fantasy pieces. See no. 3738
GAGNEBIN, Henri
Dialogue et passacaille. See no. 379
Toccata, no. 3. See no. 379
GAINSBORG, Lolita Cabrera
Lullaby. See no. 1119
GALAS
Lake Como. See no. 3645
GALILEI, Vincenzo
Anchor che chol partire. See no. 4010
Studies, guitar (6). See no. 381
GALINDO, Dimas Blas
Sones de Mariachi. See no. 1134
GALLES, Jose
Sonata, guitar, E minor. See no. 3879

GALLOT, Jacques
Suite, D minor. See no. 1225
GALUPPI, Baldassare
Aria amorosa. See no. 3971
Concerta a 4, no. 2, G major. See no. 3980
GAMBARDELLA
Nun me guardate chiu. See no. 4032
O Marenariello. See no. 3641. See no. 3843
GARDANE, Antonio
Anchor che col partire. See no. 4010
GARDINER, Henry Balfour
Shepherd Fennel's dance. See no. 3652
GARDNER, John
Songs: Fight the good fight; Tomorrow shall be my dancing day. See no. 3618
GARDNER, Johann von
Songs (anthems): Antiphon stepjenny; Cherubikon; Dostojno jest; Sedalen woskressen. See no. 1946
GARDONYI, Zsolt
Hommage a Marcel Dupre. See no. 200
GARSI DA PARME, Santino
La Lisfeltina. See no. 3938
GASPARINI, Francesco
Prelude, recorder. See no. 3949
GASSMANN, Florian
1558 Quartet, strings, no. 3, E minor. HAYDN: Divertimento, no. 3, A major. MONN: Quartet, strings, no. 1, B flat major. WAGENSEIL: Concerto, trombone, E flat major. VCM; Nikolaus Harnoncourt. Telefunken 6-41199 Tape (c) 4-41199 (From SAWT 9475)
+Gr 6-81 p55 +HFN 3-81 p97
GAUBERT, Philippe
Sonata, flute and piano, no. 1, A major. See no. 3914
Sonata, flute and piano, no. 1, A major. See no. 3928
GAULTIER, Denis
Corante. See no. 3927
Narcisse. See no. 4097
Prelude. See no. 3927
1559 La rhetorique des dieux: Suites, nos. 1-2, 12. Hopkinson Smith, lt; Telefunken AW 6-42122 (also Astree AS 6)
+FF 7/8-81 p153 +HFN 1-78 p123
++Gr 12-77 p1117 ++RR 12-77 p61
Sarabande. See no. 4097
GAULTIER, Ennemond
Canaries. See no. 3927. See no. 4097
L'Immortelle. See no. 4097
Les larmes de Boisset. See no. 4097
Tombeau de Mezangeau. See no. 3927
GAUTIER DE CHATILLON
Ver pacis apperit. See no. 4009
GAUTIER DE COINCY
1560 Les miracles de Notre-Dame. Ensemble Guillaume de Machaut. Arion ARN 38347
+FF 7/8-81 p48 +RR 3-80 p32
GAVEAUX, Pierre
Le tromperer trompee: Polacca. See no. 3954

GAY, John
1561 The beggar's opera (arr. Bonynge, Gamley). Kiri Te Kanawa, Joan Sutherland, s; Angela Lansbury, ms; Regina Resnik, con; Anthony Rolfe Johnson, Graham Clark, t; James Morris, Alfred Marks, bar; London Voices; National Philharmonic Orchestra; Richard Bonynge. Decca D252D2 (2) Tape (c) K252K22
+Gr 12-81 p929
1562 The beggar's opera (arr. Austin). Sylvia Nelis, s; Violet Marquesita, s; Kathleen Hilliard, ms; Nellie Walker, con; Frederic Austin, bar; Alfred Heather, t; Frederick Ranalow, bar; Hammersmith Lyric Theatre Orchestra and Chorus; Frederic Austin. EMI WRC RTRM 501
+FF 9/10-81 p102 +HFN 12-80 p140
+Gr 1-81 p994 +ON 8-81 p36
GAZAROSSIAN
Prelude. See no. 3913
GEDDES, John Maxwell
Callandish IV. See no. 4062
GEEHL, Henry
For you alone. See no. 3996. See no. 4033
GEHYN, Matthias van den
Prelude and fugue, G minor. See no. 183
GEISER, Walther
Sonatina, flute, op. 33h. See no. 235
GELALIAN
Andantino. See no. 3913
GELBRUN, Artur
Miniature. See no. 3739
GEMINIANI, Francesco
Concerti grossi, op. 2, no. 4, D major. See no. 3631
1563 Sonatas, guitar, nos. 1-4, 6, 10. Laszlo Karper, gtr; Ede Banda, vlc; Janos Sebestyen, hpd. Hungaroton SLPX 12013
+ARG 4-80 p23 +HFN 2-81 p89
+FF 3/4-80 p87 ++NR 4-80 p8
+-Gr 4-81 p1334
GENA, Peter
Valse. See no. 3942
GENET, Elzear
Omnis populus ejus. See no. 3909
GENZMER, Harald
1564 Concerto, organ and percussion. Symphonic concerto, organ. Trio partita, organ, F major. Edgar Krapp, org; Hermann Gschwendtner, perc. Wergo WER 60082
+FF 7/8-81 p101 +NR 1-81 p13
1565 Symphonic concerto, organ. HINDEMITH: Chamber music, no. 7, op. 46, no. 2. MARTIN: Passacaglia. PEETERS: Konzertstuck, op. 52a. Edgar Krapp, org; Bochum Symphony Orchestra; Othmar Maga. Da Camera SM 93276
+FF 9/10-81 p252
Symphonic concerto, organ. See no. 1564
Trio partita, organ, F major. See no. 1564
GEOFFROY, Nicholas
Lucis creator. See no. 1257
La marche. See no. 1257
Menuets: Kyrie. See no. 1257
Offerte grave. See no. 1257

L'ouverture d'Isis. See no. 1257
GEOGHEGAN, Thomas
Duos, guitar, nos. 1 and 2. See no. 765
Spanish folk songs (arr.). See no. 765
GERLE
Ach Elslein liebes Elselein. See no. 3676
GERMAN, Edward
Have you news of my boy Jack. See no. 4122
My bonnie lass. See no. 3618
The president. See no. 3955
GERMANI, Fernando
Toccata. See no. 4110
GERSHWIN, George
1566 An American in Paris. Rhapsody in blue. George Gershwin, pno; Columbia Jazz Band, NYP; Michael Tilson Thomas. CBS 44205 (From M 34205)
+FF 9/10-81 p103 ++NR 8-81 p13
1567 An American in Paris. Rhapsody in blue. Pittsburgh Symphony Orchestra; Jesus Maria Sanroma, pno; William Steinberg. Everest Tape (c) 3067
+HF 10-81 p91 tape
1568 An American in Paris. Rhapsody in blue. Earl Wild, pno; Boston Pops Orchestra; Arthur Fiedler. RCA AGL 1-3649 (From LSC 2367)
++FF 9/10-81 p103
1569 An American in Paris. Cuban overture. Porgy and Bess: Suite. Dallas Symphony Orchestra; Eduardo Mata. RCA ATC 1-4149
++SFC 11-29-81 p18
1570 An American in Paris. Rhapsody in blue. Eugene List, pno. Cincinnati Symphony Orchestra; Erich Kunzel. Telarc DG 10058
+-FF 9/10-81 p103 +-HFN 10-81 p87
+-Gr 10-81 p551 +NR 8-81 p12
+-HF 9-81 p71
An American in Paris. See no. 1577. See no. 1578
1571 Concerto, piano, F major. Rhapsody in blue. Katia and Marielle Labeque, pno. Philips 9500 917 Tape (c) 7300 917
+-FF 9/10-81 p103 +NR 9-81 p14
+Gr 6-81 p60 +-St 9-81 p93
+-HF 9-81 p71 +STL 7-12-81 p40
+HFN 6-81 p73
Concerto, piano, F major. See no. 1577. See no. 1578
1572 Cuban overture (arr. McBride). Porgy and Bess, symphonic picture (arr. Russell Bennett). Rhapsody, no. 2. Cristina Ortiz, pno; LSO; Andre Previn. HMV ASD 3982 Tape (c) ASD 3982
+Gr 7-81 p152 +HFN 7-81 p73
+Gr 8-81 p324 tape +HFN 10-81 p95 tape
Cuban overture. See no. 1569. See no. 1578
Funny face: Overture. See no. 1577
1573 George Gershwin's songbook: Clap yo hands. Do do do. Do it again. Fascinating rhythm. I got rhythm. I'll build a stairway to paradise. Impromptu in two keys. Liza. The man I love. Merry Andrew. My one and only. Nobody but you. Oh lady be good. Porgy and Bess: Jazzbo Brown blues. Preludes, nos. 1-3. Promenade. Rialto ripples. 'S wonderful. Somebody loves me. Strike up the band. Swanee. Sweet and low-down. Three-quarter blues. That certain feeling. Waltzes, C major (2). Who cares.

Richard Rodney Bennett, pno. HMV EMD 5538 Tape (c) TC EMD 5538
+-Gr 8-81 p295 +HFN 8-81 p84
Girl crazy: Overture. See no. 1575. See no. 1577
Grand fantasy on airs from "Porgy and Bess". See no. 1179
Let 'em eat cake: Overture. See no. 1577
Of thee I sing: Overture. See no. 1577
Oh Kay: Overture. See no. 1577

1574 Porgy and Bess: Introduction; Summertime; A woman is a sometime thing; Gone gone gone; I got plenty of nuttin'; Bess you is my woman; It ain't necessarily so; What you want wid Bess; I loves you Porgy; There's a boat dat's leavin' soon for New York; Oh Bess oh where's my Bess; Oh Lawd I'm on my way. Leontyne Price, s; William Warfield, bar; Orchestra and Chorus; Skitch Henderson. RCA AGL 1-3654 Tape (c) GK 1-3654 (From LSC 2679, SB 6552)
+FF 9/10-81 p102 +Gr 10-81 p603

1575 Porgy and Bess: Introduction; Summertime; A woman is a sometime thing; My man's gone now; I got plenty o nuttin; Bess you is my woman now; Oh I can't sit down; It ain't necessarily so; I loves you Porgy; There's a boat dat's leavin soon for New York; Oh Lawd I'm on my way; Finale. Girl Crazy: Overture. Benjamin Matthews, bs-bar; Claudia Lindsey, s; Slovak Philharmonic Orchestra; Ettore Stratta. Moss Music Group MMG D 103
-FF 9/10-81 p102 +NR 6-81 p12
Porgy and Bess: Suite. See no. 778. See no. 1569
Porgy and Bess, symphonic picture. See no. 1572. See no. 1577. See no. 1578
Preludes, nos. 1-3. See no. 1578
Preludes, no. 2. See no. 3697
Rhapsody, no. 2. See no. 1572. See no. 1578
Rhapsody in blue. See no. 43. See no. 1566. See no. 1567. See no. 1568. See no. 1570. See no. 1571. See no. 1577. See no. 1578

1576 Songs: But not for me; Blue Monday: Has anyone seen Joe; Embraceable you; I got rhythm; The man I love; Nice work if you can get it; Porgy and Bess: Summertime; I loves you Porgy; They can't take that away from me. Barbara Hendricks, vocals; Katia and Marielle Labeque, pno. Philips 9500 987 Tape (c) 7300 987
+Gr 12-81 p918
Songs: By Strauss. See no. 3703
Songs: The man I love; Bidin' my time; I've got a crush on you; Aren't you kind of glad we did; Looking for a boy; He loves and she loves. See no. 1578
Strike up the band. See no. 3976
Strike up the band: Overture. See no. 1577
Variations on "I got rhythm". See no. 1578
Virtuoso etudes on popular songs. See no. 1179

1577 Works, selections: An American in Paris. Concerto, piano, F major. Funny face: Overture. Girl crazy: Overture. Let 'em eat cake: Overture. Of thee I sing: Overture. Oh Kay: Overture. Porgy and Bess: Symphonic picture (arr. Russell Bennett). Rhapsody in blue (orig. version). Strike up the band: Overture. George Gershwin, Philippe Entremont, pno; Columbia Jazz Band, NYP,

Buffalo Philharmonic Orchestra, PO; Michael Tilson Thomas, Eugene Ormandy. CBS 79329 (3) Tape (c) 40-79329 (From 76509, 76632, 61240, 61109)
+Gr 2-81 p1088 +HFN 3-81 p95
+-Gr 6-81 p93 tape ++HFN 4-81 p81 tape
+Gr 7-81 p196 tape

1578 Works, selections: An American in Paris (rev. Campbell-Watson). Concerto, piano, F major. Cuban overture. Porgy and Bess, symphonic picture (arr. Russell Bennett). Preludes, nos. 1-3. Rhapsody, no. 2 (arr. McBride). Rhapsody in blue. Songs: The man I love; Bidin' my time; I've got a crush on you; Aren't you kind of glad we did; Looking for a boy; He loves and she loves. Variation on "I got rhythm" (rev. Schoenfeld). Werner Haas, pno; Sarah Vaughan, singer; Monte Carlo Opera Orchestra, Hal Mooney Orchestra; Edo de Waart, Eliahu Inbal, Hal Mooney. Philips 6747 062 (3) (From 6500 118, 6500 290, Mercury CMS 18011, CMS 18012)
+-Gr 6-81 p36 +-HFN 6-81 p85

GERSTER, Robert
Cantata, flute, oboe, clarinet and bassoon. See no. 78

GESUALDO, Carlo
Motets: Ave regina coelorum; Ave dulcissima Maria. See no. 3906

1579 Responsoria: Sabbato sancto. Deller Consort; Alfred Deller. Musical Heritage Society MHS 4132
+-FF 5/6-81 p84 +HF 12-80 p79

GHENT, Emmanuel
Entelechy. See no. 90

GHERARDELLO DE FLORENTIA

1580 De poni amor; I' vo' bene; Donna l'altrui mirar; Per non far lieto. LAURENTIUS MASII DE FLORENTIA: Non so qual i' mi voglia; Sento d'amor la fiamma; Non vedi tu amor; Non perch' i' speri. LANDINI: Angelica belta; Io son un pellegrin. ANON.: Amor mi fa cantar; Che ti cova; Donna tu pur in vecchi; Per tropo fede; Lucente Stella. Esther Lamandier, singer, positiv organ, hp, vielle and lt. Astree AS 56
+Gr 1-81 p985 +HFN 4-81 p77
++HF 9-81 p80 ++St 7-81 p89

GHEZZO, Dinu
Aphorisms. See no. 1513

GHISELIN, Johannes
La spagna a 4. See no. 3661

GHORGHANIAN, Guenarios
Bayati. See no. 3912

GIAMPIERI, Alamiro
Variations on "The carnival of Venice". See no. 3714

GIANELLA, Luigi

1581 Concerto, flute, no. 1, D minor. Concerto lugubre, C minor (attrib.). Concerto, flute, no. 3, C major. Jean-Pierre Rampal, flt; I Solisti Veneti; Claudio Scimone. Erato STU 70849 (also Musical Heritage Society MHS 4221)
++FF 1/2-81 p112 +RR 9-79 p89
+HFN 4-80 p104

Concerto, flute, no. 3, C major. See no. 1581
Concerto lugubre, C minor. See no. 1581

GIANNINI
Praeludium and allegro. See no. 3817
Variations and fugue. See no. 3817
GIBBONS, Ellis
Songs: Long live Oriana. See no. 3876
GIBBONS, Orlando
The fairest nymph. See no. 3734
Fancy, A major. See no. 4088
Fantasia, A minor. See no. 4090
1582 Fantasias, 3 parts, nos. 1-10, 12, 14-15. In nomine a 4. Jordi Savall, Christophe Coin, Sergei Casademunt, viols; Johannes Sonnleitner, org. Astree AS 43
+FF 9/10-80 p122 +HFN 4-81 p71
+Gr 5-80 p1678 ++RR 6-80 p78
Ground, A minor. See no. 4090
In nomine a 4. See no. 1582
The king's juell. See no. 4088
Lord of Salisbury's pavan and galliard. See no. 3734
Pavan. See no. 3926
1583 Songs (choral): Almighty and everlasting God; Blessed are all they; Glorious and powerful God; Lord grant grace; O father; O Lord how do my woes increase; O Lord I lift my heart; Preces and psalm, no. 145; Sing unto the Lord; This is the record of John; We praise thee. Clerkes of Oxenford; David Wulstan. Calliope CAL 1612 (also Nonesuch H 71391)
+ARG 10-81 p22 +FU 11-79 p46
++FF 7/8-81 p102 +NR 8-81 p10
Songs: Hosanna to the son of David. See no. 3621
Songs: The secret sins. See no. 3616
Songs: This is the record of John. See no. 3636
The woods so wild. See no. 3734
GIBBS, Cecil Armstrong
Fancy dress: Dusk. See no. 3652
When I was one and twenty. See no. 3893
GIBBS, D.
I heard a maiden softly sing. See no. 3685
GIBBS, Thomas
The Lord Monck's march. See no. 3733. See no. 4103
GIBSON, Robert
Quintet, winds. See no. 3815
GIGOUT, Eugene
Grand choeur dialogue. See no. 3745. See no. 3821. See no. 4069
Toccata. See no. 3744
Toccata, B minor. See no. 3799
GILBERT, John
Suonare. See no. 1513
GILBERT, Michael
1584 The call. Gibex 002
+FF 9/10-81 p105
GILBERT, Pia
Interrupted suite. See no. 850
Transmutations. See no. 850
GILES, Thomas
Triumph now. See no. 3876
GILL Harry
In memoriam. See no. 3874

GILLEBERT DE BERNEVILLE
De moi doleros vos chant. See no. 4086
GILLES, Jean
1585 Requiem. Anne-Marie Rodde, s; Jean Nirouet, alto; Martyn Hill, t; Ulrich Studer, Peter Kooy, bs; Ghent Collegium Vocale; Cologne Musica Antiqua; Philippe Herreweghe. DG 2533 461
+-Gr 12-81 p923 +STL 11-8-81 p40
+HFN 12-81 p95
GINASTERA, Alberto
Danza de la moza donosa. See no. 3789
The lamentations of Jeremiah. See no. 3925
Pampeana, no. 2. See no. 949
1586 Quartet, strings, no. 1, op. 20. PROTO: Quartet, strings, no. 1, B minor. Blair Quartet. QCA/Red Mark RM 3105
+ARG 1-81 p26 ++St 11-80 p88
+IN 11-81 p96 +ST 5-81 p43
+-NR 8-80 p8
Sonata, piano. See no. 3723
GIORDANI, Giuseppe
Songs: Caro mio ben. See no. 3756. See no. 3836. See no. 3970
GIORDANO, Umberto
1587 Andrea Chenier. Renata Tebaldi, s; Gilda Cossio, Guadalupe Salarzano, ms; Richard Tucker, t; Ettore Bastianini, bar; Orchestra and Chorus; Oliviero de Fabritiius. Historical Recordings HRE 350 (2)
+FF 11/12-81 p165
Andrea Chenier: Colpito qui mi avete. See no. 3944
Andrea Chenier: Colpito qu m'avete...Un di all'azzurro spazio; Come un bel di di maggio; Si fui soldato. See no. 3757
Andrea Chenier: Colpito que m'avete...Un di all'azzurro spazio; Credo a una possanza arcana; Si fui soldato; Come un bel di di maggio. See no. 3646
Andrea Chenier: Improviso. See no. 3838
Andrea Chenier: Improviso; Credi al destino; Su fui soldato; Come un bel di. See no. 3839
1588 Andrea Chenier: La mamma morta. PUCCINI: Manon Lescaut: Sola perduta abbandonata. Tosca: Scene, Act 2 including Vissi d' arte. VERDI: Aida: Ritorna vincitor. Don Carlo: Tu che la vanita. La forza del destino: Madre pietosa vergine; Pace pace o mio dio. Eva Marton, s; Various orchestras and conductors. Legendary Recordings LR 130
+-FF 9/10-81 p208
Andrea Chenier: La mamma morta. See no. 3623
Andrea Chenier: Son sessant'anni; Nemico della patria. See no. 3751
Andrea Chenier: Un di all'azzuro spazio. See no. 3750. See no. 3982. See no. 3995
Fedora: Amor ti vieta. See no. 3750. See no. 3757
Fedora: Amor ti vieta; Mia madre la mia vecchia madre; Vedi io piangi. See no. 4032
Fedora: Vedi io piango. See no. 3944
Marcella: Dolce notte misteriosa. See no. 3836
Marcella: O santa liberta. See no. 4027
GIOVANNI DA CASCIA
De' come dolcemente. See no. 4102

GIOVANNINI
Morocco. See no. 3820
GIULIANI, Mauro
1589 Concerto, guitar, op. 30, A major. HAYDN: Quartet, strings, op. 2, no. 2, E major (arr. Karl Scheit). Vladimir Mikula, gtr; Ostrava Janacek Chamber Orchestra; Jiri Pinkas. Supraphon 110 2700 (also Barenreiter BM 1415)
-FF 11/12-81 p177 +NR 6-81 p7
Concerto, guitar, op. 30, A major. See no. 74. See no. 3712
Grand overture, op. 61. See no. 383. See no. 1590
1590 Sonata, guitar, op. 15, C major. Grande overture, op. 61. SOR: Etude, op. 6, no. 11, E minor. Etudes, op. 29, nos. 12, 23. Fantasia, op. 7, C minor. Robert Secrist, gtr. Musical Heritage Society MHS 4285 Tape (c) MHC 6285
-FF 9/10-81 p252 +St 8-81 p102
1591 Sonata, guitar, op. 15, C major. Variations, op. 9. MERTZ: Fantaisie hongroise, op. 65, no. 1. Kindermarchen, op. 13, no. 8. Liebeslied, op. 13, no. 4b. Polacca, op. 5, no. 3. Romanze, op. 13, no. 1b. Tarantelle, op. 13, no. 6. David Leisner, gtr. Titanic TI 46
+ARG 11-81 p36 +-St 8-81 p102
+-FF 9/10-81 p136
Sonata, guitar, op. 150, A major. See no. 1208
Sonata, violin and guitar, op. 25, E minor. See no. 381
Variations, op. 9. See no. 1591
Variations on a theme by Handel, op. 107. See no. 4108
Variations sur les Folies d'Espagne, op. 45. See no. 1208
GIUSTINI DI PISTOIA, Lodovico
1592 Sonatas, piano, nos. 1-2, 4-5, 7, 9-10. Miczyslaw Horszowski, fortepiano. Titanic TI 78/9
+AR 8-81 p78 +HF 2-81 p62
++FF 1/2-81 p112
GLANTZ-KRAUSS
Sim Shalom. See no. 3897
GLASS, Philip
1593 Dances, nos. 1 and 3. Philip Glass Ensemble. Tomato TOM 8029
+FF 11/12-80 p113 ++St 3-81 p84
Modern love waltz. See no. 3942
GLAZUNOV, Alexander
1594 Ballade, op. 78. Cortege solennel, op. 50. The Kremlin, op. 30. BORODIN: Prince Igor: Overture (arr. Glazunov). Nurnberg Symphony Orchestra; Heinz Feudenthal. Colosseum SM 590
+-FF 9/10-81 p105
Chant du menestral, op. 71. See no. 1423
Concerto, saxophone, op. 109, E flat major. See no. 1552. See no. 1600
Cortege solennel, op. 50. See no. 1594
1595 In memory of Gogol, op. 87. The Kremlin, op. 30. Stenka Razin, op. 13. Bamberg Symphony Orchestra; Aldo Ceccato. RCA RL 3-0323 (also Arabesque 8091 Tape (c) 9091)
++FF 9/10-80 p124 +NR 11-81 p3
+-HF 12-81 p70 +SFC 10-11-81 p19
In modo religioso, op. 38. See no. 3662
The Kremlin, op. 30. See no. 1594. See no. 1595
Quartet, saxophone, op. 109, B flat major. See no. 3737
1596 The seasons, op. 67. MRSO; Boris Khaikin. Musical Heritage Soci-

ety MHS 4201 (also Angel Melodiya SR 40088)
+FF 1/2-81 p113

1597 The seasons, op. 67. Symphony, no. 1, op. 5, E major. Symphony Orchestra; Soviet State Symphony Orchestra; Alexander Glazunov, Konstantin Ivanov. Pearl GEMM 195
+-HFN 8-81 p84

1598 The seasons, op. 67. MRSO; Boris Khaikin. Quintessence PMC 7172 (From Angel)
+FF 3/4-81 p122

Serenade espagnole, op. 20, no. 1: Melodia. See no. 1423

Stenka Razin, op. 13. See no. 1595

Symphony, no. 1, op. 5, E major. See no. 1597

1599 Symphony, no. 3, op. 33, D major. MRSO; Valdimir Fedoseyev. HMV ASD 3993
+Gr 4-81 p136 +-HFN 5-81 p80

1600 Symphony, no. 4, op. 48, E flat major. Concerto, saxophone, op. 109, E flat major. Kansas City Philharmonic Orchestra, New York Studio Orchestra; Vincent Abato, sax; Hans Schwieger, Cedric Henderson. Varese VC 81111
+FF 5/6-81 p85

GLEISSNER, Franz

Sinfonia, op. 2, no. 4. See no. 3908

GLIERE, Reinhold

Intermezzo and tarantella, op. 9, nos. 1 and 2. See no. 863

Prelude and scherzo, op. 32, nos. 1 and 2. See no. 863

1601 The red poppy, op. 70: Ballet suite. RIMSKY-KORSAKOV: The legend of Sadko, op. 5. SHOSTAKOVICH: Age of gold, op. 22. Seattle Symphony Orchestra; Milton Katims. Turnabout TV 34644 Tape (c) Vox CT 2224
+Audio 7-77 p103 +NR 6-77 p2
+HF 4-81 p93 tape +SFC 4-10-77 p30
+MJ 5-77 p32

GLINKA, Mikhail

Ivan Sussanin: Brother in the snowstorm. See no. 4030

1602 A life for the Tsar. Teresa Stich-Randall, s; Mela Bugarinovich, con; Nicolai Gedda, t; Boris Christoff, bs; Belgrade Opera Chorus; Lamoureux Orchestra; Igor Markevitch. EMI 2C 163 73011/3 (3) (From HMV ALP 1613/5)
+-Gr 9-81 p428 +-Gr 12-81 p934

1603 A life for the Tsar: Dances (3). Prince Kholmsky: Overture; Entr'actes. Souvenir of a summer night in Madrid, overture no. 2. Bamberg Symphony Orchestra; Aldo Ceccato. Arabesque AR 8072 Tape (c) 9072
+-FF 1/2-81 p113 +St 1-81 p82
++SFC 2-22-81 p18

A life for the Tsar: They guess the truth. See no. 4064

Prince Kholmsky: Overture; Entr'actes. See no. 1603

Souvenir of a summer night in Madrid, overture, no. 2. See no. 1603

GLUCK, Christoph

Alceste: Divinites du Styx. See no. 3989

Alceste: Overture. See no. 3792

1604 Der betrogene Kadi. Anneliese Rothenberger, Helen Donath, Regina Marheineke, s; Nicolai Gedda, t; Klaus Hirte, bar; Walter Berry, bs; Bavarian State Opera Orchestra; Otmar Suitner. EMI 1C 065 28834

+FF 7/8-81 p102

1605 Le cinesi: Sinfonia. La rencontre imprevue: Overture. Iphigenie en Tauride: Ballet music; Scythian dance. HAYDN, M.: Zaire: Incidental music. Turkish march. MOZART: Die Entfuhrung aus dem Serail, K 384: Overture; March of the Janissaries. Collegium Aureum; Franzjosef Maier. Harmonia Mundi 1C 065 99897
++Gr 10-81 p567 +HFN 8-81 p89

1606 Iphigenie en Tauride (R. Strauss version). Montserrat Caballe, s; Jean Cox, Raymond Wolandsky, Paul Schoeffler; Sao Carlos Teatro Nacional Orchestra and Chorus; Antonio de Almeida. Voce 31 (2)
+-FF 9/10-81 p106 +-FF 11/12-81 p167

Iphigenie en Tauride: Ballet music; Schythian dance. See no 1605

Iphigenie en Tauride: Nur einen Wunsch nur ein verlangen. See no. 3800

Iphigenia in Aulis: Overture. See no.3792

1607 Orfeo ed Euridice. Erna Berger, Rita Streich, s; Margarete Klose, alto; Berlin State Opera Orchestra; Arthur Rother. Acanta FA 22140 (3)
+HFN 2-81 p87

1608 Orfeo ed Euridice. Teresa Stich-Randall, Hanny Steffek, s; Maureen Forrester, con; VSOO and Choir; Charles Mackerras. Bach Guild HM 66/7 (2) (Reissue)
+ARG 10-79 p11 +-MUM 5/6-81 p30
+FF 11/12-79 p74 +NYT 8-5-79 pD19

1609 Orfeo ed Euridice. Julia Hamari, Veronika Kincses, Maria Zempleni, s; HSOO and Chamber Chorus; Ervin Lukacs. Hungaroton SLPX 12100/1 (2)
++FF 7/8-81 p103 +HFN 1-81 p93
+-Gr 12-80 p872 +NR 3-81 p12
/HF 7-81 p59 +St 7-81 p80

1610 Orfeo ed Euridice. MOZART: La clemenza di Tito, K 621: Ah perdona al primo affetto; Saltro che lacrime. Sena Jurinac, Graziella Sciutti, s; Giulietta Simionato, ms; Giorgio Marelli, t; Salzburg Festival Orchestra and Chorus, Piccola Scala Orchestra; Herbert von Karajan, Nino Sanzogno. Legendary Recordings LR 132 (2)
+FF 5/6-81 p86

1611 Orfeo ed Euridice. Suzanne Danco, Pierette Alarie, s; Leopold Simoneau, t; Lamoureux Concerts Orchestra; Roger Blanchard Vocal Ensemble; Hans Rosbaud. Philips 6770 033 (From ABL 3359/60)
++Gr 10-81 p603 +MUM 11/12-81 p31
+-HFN 11-81 p105

Orfeo ed Euridice: Ballet music. See no. 361

Orfeo ed Euridice: Dance of the blessed psirits. See no. 335. See no. 3695

1612 Orfeo ed Euridice: Dance of the furies; Dance of the blessed spirits. HANDEL: Berenice: Oveture, minuet and gigue. Solomon: Arrival of the Queen of Sheba. Water music: Air and hornpipe. PACHELBEL: Canon and gigue, D major. VIVALDI: Concerto, op. 3, no. 10, B minor. Concerto, 2 trumpets, RV 537, C major. Academy of Ancient Music; Christopher Hogwood. L'Oiseau-Lyre DSLO 594 Tape (c) KDSLC 594
+Gr 12-81 p897

Orfeo ed Euridice: Melodie. See no. 3841. See no. 3920. See no. 3993

Orfeo ed Euridice: Recitative; Che faro senza Euridice. See no. 3654
Orfeo ed Euridice: Reigen seliger Geister. See no. 3881
Orfeo ed Euridice: Sposa Euridice...Che faro senza Euridice. See no. 3650
Paride ed Elena: Gavotte. See no. 3881
Paride ed Elena: O del mio dolce ardor. See no. 3718. See no. 3836
La rencontre imprevue: Einmen Bach der flieset. See no. 3844
La rencontre imprevue: Overture. See no. 1605
Songs: Die fruhen Graber; Die Sommernacht; Der Jungling. See no. 3985

GNATTALI, Radames
Concerto, guitar, no. 4. See no. 55

GODARD, Benjamin
Idylle. See no. 3820
Jocelyn: Beneath the quivering leaves. See no. 3967
Songs: Embarquez-vous. See no. 4025
La vivandiere: Viens avec nous petit. See no. 4026

GOETZ, Hermann
The taming of the shrew: Die Kraft versagt. See no. 3989

GOEURY, Carlo
Entrada, C major. See no. 4115

GOLDMAN
March on the Hudson. See no. 3817

GOLDMARK, Karl

1613 Die Konigin von Saba. Veronika Kincses, Magda Kalmar, s; Klara Takacs, ms; Siegfried Jerusalem, t; Sandor Solyom Nagy, Lajos Miller, bar; Jozsef Gregor, Laszlo Polgar, bs; HSOO and Chorus; Adam Fischer. Hungaroton SLPX 12179/82 (4)
+-ARG 6-81 p49 +-OC Fall 1981 p51
+-FF 3/4-81 p122 ++SFC 1-11-81 p17
+Gr 2-81 p1114 +SR 9-81 p52
++HF 4-81 p71 +St 3-81 p84
++HFN 2-81 p89 /+STL 2-8-81 p40

Die Konigin von Saba: Magische Tone. See no. 1361. See no. 3996. See no. 4075

1614 Symphony, no. 1, op. 26, E flat major. LAPO; Jesus Lopez-Cobos. Decca SXDL 7528 Tape (c) KSXDC 7528 (also London LDR 71030)
+/FF 11/12-81 p168 +HFN 5-81 p80
+Gr 5-81 p1474 /ST 10-81 p429

1615 Symphony, no. 1, op. 26, E flat major. Pittsburgh Symphony Orchestra; Andre Previn. HMV ASD 3891 Tape (c) TC ASD 3891 (also Angel SZ 37662 Tape (c) 4ZS 37662)
+ARG 1-81 p27 +MT 12-80 p785
++FF 11/12-80 p115 ++NR 11-80 p3
+Gr 8-80 p216 +NYT 9-7-80 pD29
+HF 1-81 p70 ++RR 8-80 p42
+HFN 9-80 p104 +St 12-80 p124
+HFN 12-80 p159 tape

GOLDMARK, Rubin
Trio, piano, op. 1, D minor. See no. 715

GOLDSTEIN, Malcolm

1616 Soundings. Malcolm Goldstein, vln. MG Records MG 1
-FF 1/2-81 p114

A summoning of focus. See no. 1109
GOLUB-FRUG
Der Becher. See no. 3897
GOMES, Antonio
Fosca: Intenditi con Dio. See no. 3982
Il Guarany: Sento una forza indomita. See no. 4048
Lo schiavo: L'importuna insistenza; Quando nascesti tu. See no. 3997
Salvator Rosa: Mia piccirella. See no. 4053. See no. 4076
GOODHART
A fairy went a-marketing. See no. 3650
GOODWIN
Where eagles dare. See no. 3956
GOOSSENS, Eugene
Kaleidoscope, op. 18. See no. 4055
1617 Symphony, no. 1, op. 58. Adelaide Symphony Orchestra; David Measham. Unicorn KP 8000
+-FF 1/2-81 p115 ++HFN 11-80 p105
++Gr 11-80 p666 +ST 3-81 p819
GORDON, Gavin
The rake's progress: Sarabande and orgy. See no. 3840
GORING, Thomas
Ma voisine. See no. 4026
GORNER, Johann
Das Heidelberger Fass. See no. 3985
GOSS, John
Praise my soul the king of heaven. See no. 4061
Psalms, nos. 127, 128. See no. 3824
GOSSEC, Francois-Joseph
Gavotte. See no. 3695
GOSSWIN, Antoine
Am Abend spat lieb Breuderlein. See no. 3675
GOTTLIEB, Jack
Downtown blues for uptown halls. See no. 3957
GOULD
The curfew. See no. 4074
GOULD, Glenn
A Glenn Gould fantasy. See no. 3698
1618 The idea of north. The latecomers. Canadian Broadcasting Corporation unnumbered.
+FF 9/10-81 p106
The latecomers. See no. 1618
So you want to write a fugue. See no. 3698
GOULD, Morton
1619 Amercan ballads. Cheers, celebration march. Fanfare for freedom. Symphony, band. University of Florida Symphony Band; Morton Gould. Golden Crest ATH 5067
+ARG 4-81 p22 *NR 7-81 p14
American ballads. See no. 1619
American salute. See no. 3817
Cheers, celebration march. See no. 1619
Fanfare for freedom. See no. 1619
Folk suite. See no. 3817
1620 Foster gallery. Spirituals for orchestra. LPO; Morton Gould Crystal Clear CCS 7005

++ARG 6-79 p51
+Audio 4-79 p84
+FF 5/6-79 p10
+HF 6-79 p94
+HFN 1-79 p73
++HFN 6-81 p73
+NR 2-79 p5
+RR 3-79 p72
++St 7-79 p96

St. Lawrence suite. See no. 3817
Spirituals for orchestra. See no. 1620
Symphony, band. See no. 1619
Windjammer: Main theme. See no. 4105

GOUNOD, Charles
Biondina. See no. 1628

1621 Faust. Renata Scotto, Milena dal Piva, s; Anna di Stasio, ms; Alfredo Kraus, t; Lorenzo Saccomani, bar; Nicolai Ghiaurov, bs; Orchestra and Chorus; Paul Ethuin. Historical Recordings HRE 345 (3)
+FF 9/10-81 p109
+-NR 11-81 p11

1622 Faust. Mirella Freni, Michele Command, s; Jocelyne Taillon, ms; Placido Domingo, t; Marc Vento, bs; Thomas Allen, bar; Nicolai Ghiaurov, bs; Paris Opera Orchestra and Chorus; Georges Pretre. HMV SLS 5170 (4) Tape (c) TC SLS 5170 (also Angel SZ DX 3868 Tape (c) 4Z4X 3868)
++ARG 1-80 p31
+FF 1/2-80 p88
+FU 2-80 p45
+Gr 9-79 p508
+-HF 1-80 p79
+HFN 10-79 p153
+HFN 12-79 p185 tape
+HFN 2-80 p107 tape
+NYT 9-30-79 pD22
+OC Fall 1981 p52
+ON 3-15-80 p45
+Op 12-79 p1168
+RR 9-79 p48
+RR 6-80 p94 tape
++SFC 9-23-79 p37
+St 12-79 p142

1623 Faust. Renata Scotto, s; Orchestra and Chorus Radiotelevisione Italiana di Torino; La Rosa Parodi. Movimento Musica 03 003 (3)
+-HFN 12-81 p95

Faust: Ah je ris de me voir si belle; Il maime il m'aime que trouble en mon coeur. See no. 3837
Faust: Air des bijoux. See no. 4042
Faust: Ballet music. See no. 752
Faust: Dio possente. See no. 4031
Faust: Il etait un Roi de Thule; Air des Bijoux. See no. 4038
Faust: Il se fait tard. See no. 3849
Faust: Jewel song. See no. 3642
Faust: Le veau d'or. See no. 4029
Faust: Le veau d'or; Ebben che te pare...Io voglio il piacer. See no. 3968
Faust: O merveille. See no. 4048
Faust: O santa medaglia; Vous qui faites l'endormie; Le veau d'or. See no. 3751
Faust: Quel trouble inconnu...Salut demeure. See no. 842
Faust: Recitative and cavatina. See no. 4022
Faust: Salut demeure chaste et pure. See no. 3752. See no. 3759. See no. 3972. See no. 3995
Faust: Salve dimora casta e pura; Alerte alerte. See no. 3967
Faust: Salve dimora; Tardi si fa. See no. 4047
Faust: Seigneur Dieu que vois-je; Eh quoi toujours seule; Il se fait tard...Eternelle o nuit d'amour; O merveille; Que voulez-vous messieurs; Mon coeur est penetre d'epouvante;

Attends; Voice la rue; Alerte ou vous etes perdus. See no. 3996
Faust: Serenade; Le veau d'or. See no. 4025
Faust: Soldiers chorus. See no. 3721
Faust: Tardi si fa; Salve dimora casta e pura; Tardi si fa. See no. 4032
Faust: The calf of gold. See no. 4074
Le medecin malgre lui. See no. 1627

1624 Mireille. Mirella Freni, Christine Barbaux, Michele Command, s; Jane Rhodes, ms; Alain Vanzo, t; Jose van Dam, bar; Gabriel Bacquier, Marc Vento, bs-bar; Jean-Jacques Cubaynes, bs; Toulouse Capitole Orchestra and Chorus; Michel Plasson. HMV SLS 5203 (3) (also Angel SX 3095, also HMV C167 73021-3)
+FF 3/4-81 p127 +NR 2-81 p11
+Gr 12-80 p872 +ON 2-28-81 p36
+HF 6-81 p55 +Op 2-81 p160
+HFN 12-80 p140 +SFC 1-11-81 p17
-MT 12-81 p827 ++St 4-81 p104
+MUM 5/6-81 p30

Mireille: Anges du paradis. See no. 4049
Mireille: Mon coeur ne peut changer. See no. 4044
Mireille: Valse. See no. 4040

1625 Petite symphonie, B flat major. d'INDY: Chansons et danses, op. 50. Maurice Bourgue Wind Ensemble. Nonesuch H 71382 (From Calliope)
+ARG 1-81 p28 ++SFC 8-10-80 p29
++FF 9/10-80 p124 +St 10-80 p113

Petite symphonie, B flat major. See no. 1279. See no. 1429
Petite symphonie, B flat major: 1st movement. See no. 3617
Philemon and Baucis: Aux bruit des lourds. See no. 4029
Reine de Saba: Faibless de la race humaine...Inspirez-moi race divine. See no. 3689

1626 Romeo et Juliette. Mirella Freni, Elaine Lublin, s; Michele Vilma, ms; Franco Corelli, Robert Cardona, Maurice Auzeville, t; Henri Gui, Yves Bisson, Christos Grigoriou, Claude Cales, bar; Xavier Depraz, Pierre Thau, bs; French National Opera Theatre Orchestra and Chorus; Alain Lombard. EMI CAN 235/7 (3) (From SAN 235/7)
+Gr 2-81 p1114

Romeo et Juliette: Ah leve toi soleil. See no. 3836. See no. 3838
Romeo et Juliette: Allons jeunes gens. See no. 4025
Romeo et Juliette: Deh sorgi il luce in ciel. See no. 4032
Romeo et Juliette: Depuis hier je cherche en vain. See no. 3710
Romeo et Juliette: Duo de la chambre; Duo final. See no. 4051
Romeo et Juliette: L'amour; Oui son ardeur; Ah leve toi soleil. See no. 3646
Romeo et Juliette: Salut tombeau. See no. 4050

1627 Sapho. Le medecin malgre lui. Soloists; French Radio Chorus; NPhO; Orchestra; Sylvain Cambreling, Jean-Claude Hartemann. MRF Records MRF 157 (3)
+FF 3/4-81 p129

Sapho: O ma lyre immortelle. See no. 4039
Sonata, piano, E flat major: 1st movement. See no. 3665

1628 Songs: Biondina. Au rossignol; Aubade; Medge; O ma belle rebelle; Premier jour de Mai; Solitude; Le soir. Jacques Herbil-

lon, bar; Odette Chaynes-Decaux, pno. Calliope CAL 1851
+FF 9/10-81 p109 +-NR 9-81 p12

Songs: Au printemps; Chanson de Florian. See no. 3758
Songs: Ave Maria; O divien redeemer. See no. 4042
Songs: Barcarolle; Serenade. See no. 4026
Songs: Le soir. See no. 4031

1629 Symphony, no. 1, D major. Symphony, no. 2, E flat major. Toulouse Capitole Theatre Orchestra; Michel Plasson. Angel SZ 37726 Tape (c) 4ZS 37726 (also HMV ESD 7093 Tape (c) TC ESD 7093)
+-ARG 9-80 p27
+FF 7/8-80 p88
+FF 9/10-81 p110
+Gr 8-80 p221
-HF 7-80 p68
+-HFN 9-80 p104
+MT 2-81 p111
++NR 5-80 p2
++RR 8-80 p42
+SFC 5-25-80 p41
+-STL 9-14-80 p40

Symphony, no. 2, E flat major. See no. 1629

GOWERS, Patrick

1630 Chamber concerto, guitar. Rhapsody, guitar, electric guitars and electric organ. John Williams, gtr; John Scott, sax, flt; Patrick Halling, vln; Stephen Shingles, vla; Denis Vigay, vlc; Herbie Flowers, bs guitar; Patrick Gowers, org; Tristan Fry, drum; Godfrey Salmon. CBS 61790 Tape (c) 40-61790 (From 72979, 73350) (also CBS M 35866 Tape (c) MT 35866)
+-ARG 3-81 p26
+FF 9/10-80 p125
+-Gr 10-77 p628
+HFN 9-77 p151
+HFN 10-77 p169 tape
+-RR 8-77 p67
+-RR 11-77 p119
+-St 11-80 p86

Rhapsody, guitar, electric guitars and electric organ. See no. 1630
Toccata. See no. 4120

GRABET, Martin

Sonata, oboe, op. 52, G minor. See no. 1029

GRAINGER, Percy

Country gardens. See no. 3652
Handel in the Strand. See no. 3652
Irish tune from County Derry. See no. 4082
Lincolnshire posy. See no. 69
Londonderry air. See no. 3652
Mock Morris. See no. 3652
Molly on the shore. See no. 1021. See no. 3652
Over the hills and far away. See no. 75
Shepherd's hey. See no. 69. See no. 1021. See no. 3652
Songs: The jolly-sailor song; Six dukes went a'fishing. See no. 3842

GRANADOS, Enrique

A la pradera. See no. 1633
Barcarola, op. 45. See no. 1633
Bocetos. See no. 1633
Cuentos de la juventud, op. 1. See no. 1633
Danzas espanolas, op. 37: Andaluza. See no. 1491. See no. 3727
Danzas espanolas, op. 37: Villanesca. See no. 18
Danzas espanolas, op. 37: Villanesca; Asturiana; Mazurca. See no. 21
Danza lenta. See no. 765
Elisenda. See no. 1633

Escenas poeticas. See no. 1631
Estudio, op. posth. See no. 1633
Estudios expresivos (6). See no. 1633

1631 Goyescas. Escenas poeticas. Libro de horas. Thomas Rajna, pno. CRD CRD 1001/2 Tape (c) CRD 4001/2
++Gr 5-74 p2045 ++RR 4-74 p67
+HFN 10-81 p95 tape

1632 Goyescas, nos. 1-7. Joaquin Achucarro, pno. RCA RL 3-5301 Tape (c) RK 3-5301
+Gr 4-81 p1345 ++STL 2-8-81 p40
+HFN 4-81 p81 tape

Goyescas: Intermezzo. See no. 3686. See no. 3787. See no. 3879
Goyescas: The maiden and the nightingale. See no. 1003
Goyescas: La maja y el ruisenor. See no. 3642. See no. 3755
Impromptus, op. 39. See no. 1633
Libro de horas. See no. 1631
Marche militaire. See no. 1633
Mazurka, op. 2. See no. 1633
Mosque y arabe. See no. 1633
Paisaje, op. 35. See no. 1633
Pequena suite. See no. 1633

1633 Piano works: A la pradera. Barcarola, op. 45. Bocetos. Cuentos de la juventud, op. 1. Elisenda. Estudio, op. posth. Estudios expresivos (6). Impromptus, op. 39. Marche militaires (2). Mosque y arabe. Mazurka, op. 2. Paisaje, op. 35. Pequena suite. Sardana. Los soldados de carton. Thomas Rajna, pno. CRD CRD 1036/7 (2) Tape (c) 4036/7
+Gr 5-78 p1898 ++HFN 3-81 p97 tape
+Gr 4-81 p1376 tape +HFN 9-81 p93 tape
+HFN 5-78 p129 +RR 5-78 p49

Sardana. See no. 1633
Los soldados de carton. See no. 1633
Tonadillas: La maja dolorosa. See no. 3642. See no. 3889
Tonadillas: El majo discreto. See no. 3703
Valses poeticas. See no. 4108

GRANATA, Battista
Sinfonia a due. See no. 4097

GRANDI, Alessandro
O intemerata. See no. 3808
Songs: Spine care e soavi. See no. 3947

GRANIER
Hosanna. See no. 3688

GRAUN, Carl
Sonata, F major. See no. 111
Trio sonata, F major. See no. 123

GRAUNKE, Kurt

1634 Air, harp and orchestra. Sinfonische Tanze (2). Symphony, no. 3. Geraldine Graunke, hp; Christian Fink, vln; Symphonie Orchestre Graunke; Kurt Graunke. Sedina ES 902
-FF 9/10-81 p111

Sinfonische Tanze (2). See no. 1634
Symphony, no. 3. See no. 1634

GRAVES, Mel
Cave dwellers. See no. 1635
Coral reef. See no. 1635

Energy fields. See no. 1635
Ladder to the moon. See no. 1635
Sky above the clouds. See no. 1635
Watercourse. See no. 1635

1635 Works, selections: Cave dwellers. Coral reef. Energy fields. Ladder to the moon. Sky above clouds. Watercourse. Mel Graves, bs and perc; George Marsh, perc; Julie Feves, bsn; Andy Narrell, steel drums. 1750 Arch S 1780
+FF 5/6-81 p87 +NR 4-81 p7

GREATEST HITS FOR CHRISTMAS. See no. 3706

GREEN, George

1636 Triptych. KENNAN: Sonata, trumpet and piano. STEVENS: Sonata, trumpet and piano. Marice Stith, tpt; Malcolm Bilson, pno. Redwoods Records ES 7
+FF 1/2-81 p225

GREENE, Maurice

Lord let me know mine end. See no. 3824
Overture, D major. See no. 3733. See no. 4103

GREENWALD

1637 Duration. SEMEGEN: Spectra. TODD: Satan's sermon. Variations on a bagatelle. WELLS: Electronic music. Realized at Dartmouth College, SUNY, Ohio State University, Calif. Institute of the Arts. CRI SD 443
+-NR 7-81 p15

GREFINGER, Wolfgang

Sons: Ach Gott; Ich stel leicht ab; Wol kumbt der mey. See no. 3862

GREGORIAN CHANTS. See no. 3776. See no. 3784. See no. 3803. See no. 3830. See no. 4013. See no. 4070. See no. 4089
GREGORIAN CHANTS: Easter. See no. 3864
GREGORIAN CHANTS: Hungarian saints. See no. 3868
GREGORIAN CHANTS: Kergonan Abbey. See no. 3664
GREGORIAN CHANTS: Messe et office de Sainte Cecile. See no. 3882
GREGORIAN CHANTS: Prague Easter play. See no. 3977
GREGORIAN CHANTS: Proper for the Feast of the Assumption. See no. 2095
GREGORIAN CHANTS: Proper of the third Mass of Christmas. See no. 3994
GREGORIAN CHANTS: Saint Benoit. See no. 4073
GREGORIAN CHANTS: Vir Dei benedictus. See no. 3834

GREGSON, Edward

Connotations. See no. 3716
Swedish march. See no. 3955

GRESSEL, Joel

1638 Crossings. P-vibes. HOFFMANN: In memoriam patris. VERCOE: Synapse. WINHAM: N.P. CRI SD 393
++CMJ Spring 1981 p77

P-vibes. See no. 1638

GRETCHANINOV, Alexander

Dobrynia Nikitich: Flowers are blooming; Alecha's aria. See no. 4028

GRETRY, Andre

1639 L'amant jaloux. Richard Coeur-de-Lion. Mady Mesple, Daniele Perriers, s; Charles Burles, Bruce Brewer, t; Michel Trempont, bar; Jules Bastin, bs; IMFP Chorus; Belgian Radio and Tele-

vision Chamber Orchestra; Edgard Doneux. EMI Pathe 2C 167 16236-8 (3)
+-Gr 3-81 p1233

1640 Lucile. Andree Francois, Claudine Granger, s; Jose Razador, Louis Mathieu, t; Jean Segani, Guy Fontagnere, bar; Walloon Opera Orchestra and Chorus; Roger Rossel. Alpha Belgicae Musicae MBM 28
+FF 1/2-81 p116 /-Gr 1-81 p988

Richard Coeur-de-Lion. See no. 1639

1641 Zemire et Azor. Mady Mesple, s; Suzanne Simonka, Sabine Louis; Roland Bufkens, Jean van Gorp; Belgium Radio Television Orchestra and Chorus; Edgard Doneux. Arabesque 8060-2 (2)
+SFC 9-20-81 p18

Zemire et Azor: Air de ballet. See no. 4121

GREVER

Jurame. See no. 3893

GRIEG, Edvard

1642 Albumblatter, op. 28. Ballade, op. 24, G minor. Scenes from peasant life, op. 19. Eva Knardahl, pno. BIS LP 110
+FF 7/8-79 p54 +-RR 3-80 p81
+Gr 8-80 p242 +SR 9-81 p52
+HF 8-81 p51 ++St 11-79 p86
++NR 5-79 p12

Ballade, op. 24, G minor. See no. 1642

1643 Concerto, piano, op. 16, A minor. Norwegian dances, op. 35. Kjell Ingebretsen, Eva Knardahl, pno; RPO; Kjell Ingebretsen. BIS LP 115
+Gr 8-80 p247 +NR 3-80 p13
+HF 8-81 p51 +-RR 3-80 p55
+-HFN 3-80 p89 +SR 9-81 p52

1644 Concerto, piano, op. 16, A minor. SCHUMANN: Concerto, piano, op. 54, A minor. Julius Katchen, pno; Israel Philharmonic Orchestra; Istvan Kertesz. Contour CC 7506 Tape (c) CCT 7506
*Gr 8-81 p316

1645 Concerto, piano, op. 16, A minor. SCHUMANN: Concerto, piano, op. 54, A minor. Claudio Arrau, pno; COA; Christoph von Dohnanyi. Philips 6570 170 Tape (c) 7310 170
-HFN 2-81 p97 /HFN 5-81 p93 tape

Concerto, piano, op. 16, A minor. See no. 213. See no. 1536. See no. 3749. See no. 4017

1646 Elegiac melodies, op. 34. NIELSEN: Little suite, op. 1, A minor. SIBELIUS: Rakastava, op. 14. Kuolema, op. 44: Valse triste. WIREN: Serenade, op. 11. AMF: Neville Marriner. Argo ZRG 877 Tape (c) KZRC 877
+-FF 1/2-81 p230 +MUM 3/4-81 p32
++Gr 4-80 p1567 +RR 4-80 p80
++HFN 4-80 p113

Elegiac melodies, op. 34. See no. 1657. See no. 3851

1647 Elegaic melodies, op. 34: Heart's wound; Last spring. MAHLER: Symphony, no. 5, C sharp minor: Adagietto. MOZART: Serenade, no. 13, K 525, G major. TCHAIKOVSKY: Serenade, op. 48, C major. COA; Willem Mengelberg. Past Masters PM 35
+FF 9/10-81 p292

Elegiac melodies, op. 34: Heart's wounds; The last spring. See no. 3317

Funeral march for Rikard Nordraak. See no. 1657

1648 Haugtussa, op. 67. Poems by Vilhelm Krag, op. 60. Ellen Westberg Andersen, s; Jens Harald Bratlie, pno. Simax PS 1011
+-Gr 1-81 p977 +HFN 10-80 p105

1649 Holberg suite, op. 40. Lyric pieces, op. 54. Sigurd Jorsalfar, op. 56: Suite. ECO; Raymond Leppard. Philips 9500 748 Tape (c) 7300 833
+FF 3/4-81 p130 +-HFN 1-81 p93
/Gr 12-80 p832 +NR 2-81 p6

Holberg suite, op. 40. See no. 1660. See no. 3317

Humoresques, op. 6. See no. 1657

1650 Improvisations on Norwegian folk songs, op. 29. Norwegian mountain melodies, op. 112. Norwegian songs and dances, op. 17. Eva Knardahl, pno. BIS LP 109
+FF 7/8-79 p54 ++NR 5-79 p12
+Gr 8-80 p247 +-RR 3-80 p81
+HF 8-81 p50 +SR 9-81 p52

1651 Lyric pieces, opp. 12, 38, 43, 47, 54, 57, 62, 65, 68, 71. Eva Knardahl, pno. BIS LP 104/7 (4)
+FF 9/10-78 p54 +RR 7-79 p91
+Gr 8-80 p247 +SFC 4-23-78 p49
+HF 8-81 p50 +SR 9-81 p52
+-HFN 7-79 p105 ++St 8-78 p91
++RR 6-78 p78

Lyric pieces, op. 12: Arietta; Feuille d'album. See no. 20

Lyric pieces, op. 43: Erotik. See no. 213

Lyric pieces, op. 43: To the spring. See no. 20

Lyric pieces, op. 54. See no. 1649

Lyric pieces, op. 54: March of the dwarfs. See no. 3699

1652 Lyric pieces, op. 65: Wedding day at Troldhaugen. Peer Gynt, op. 46: Suite, no. 1. Sigurd Jorsalfar, op. 56: Hommage march. SIBELIUS: Finlandia, op. 26. Legends, op. 22: Swan of Tuonela. Kuolema, op. 44: Valse triste. Gerhard Stempnik, English hn; Nordmark Symphony Orchestra, Bamberg Symphony Orchestra, BPhO; Heinrich Stein, Richard Krauss, Herbert von Karajan. DG 2535 635-10 Tape (c) 3335 635
+-FF 11/12-81 p169 +HFN 10-80 p117 tape

Melodies, op. 53. See no. 1658

Moods, op. 73. See no. 1654. See no. 1657

Nordic melodies, op. 63. See no. 1658

Norwegian bridal procession, op. 19, no. 2. See no. 20

Norwegian dances, op. 35. See no. 1643

Norwegian folk melodies, op. 66. See no. 1657

Norwegian mountain melodies, op. 112. See no. 1650

1653 Norwegian peasant dances, op. 72. Eva Knardahl, pno. BIS LP 114
+Gr 8-80 p247 +-NR 7-80 p12
+Gr 3-81 p1237 +RR 7-80 p79
+HF 8-81 p50 +SR 9-81 p52
+-HFN 8-80 p97 ++St 6-80 p112

1654 Norwegian peasant dances, op. 72. Moods, op. 73. John McCabe, pno. RCA GL 2-5329 Tape (c) GK 2-5329
+Gr 8-81 p295 +-HFN 8-81 p92 tape

Norwegian songs and dances, op. 17. See no. 1650

Olav Trygvason, op. 50. See no. 1658

Papillon. See no. 20

Peer Gynt, op. 23: Solveig's song. See no. 4042

1655 Peer Gynt, op. 46: Suite, no. 1. Peer Gynt, op. 55: Suite, no. 2. Sigurd Jorsalfar, op. 56: Incidental music. Eva Knardahl, pno. BIS 116
+Gr 3-81 p1237 +RR 7-80 p79
+HF 8-81 p51 +SR 9-81 p52
+-HFN 8-80 p97

1656 Peer Gynt, op. 46: Suite, no. 1. Peer Gynt, op. 55: Suite, no. 2. SIBELIUS: Finlandia, op. 26. Legends, op. 22: Swan of Tuonela. Kuolema, op. 44: Valse triste. NYP; Leonard Bernstein. CBS MY 36718
+-FF 11/12-81 p168

Peer Gynt, op. 46: Suite, no. 1. See no. 1652
Peer Gynt, op. 46: Suite, no. 1: Morning. See no. 3666
Peer Gynt, op. 55: Suite, no. 2. See no. 1655. See no. 1656

1657 Piano works: Elegiac melodies, op. 34 (2). Funeral march for Rikard Nordraak. Humoresques, op. 6. Moods, op. 73. Norwegian folk melodies, op. 66 (19). Pieces, piano, op. 1 (4). Poetic tone pictures, op. 3. Songs, opp. 41 and 52 (arr. for piano). Eva Knardahl, pno. BIS LP 111/3
+FF 11/12-79 p77 +-RR 3-80 p81
+Gr 8-80 p247 +SR 9-81 p52
+HF 8-81 p50 +St 1-80 p95

1658 Piano works: Melodies, op. 53 (22. Nordic melodies, op. 63 (2). Pieces,piano, op. posth. (3). Olav Trygvason, op. 50. Waltz-caprices, op. 37. Eva Knardahl, pno. BIS LP 117
++FF 3/4-81 p130 +HFN 5-81 p80
+Gr 8-81 p317 +NR 9-81 p14
+HF 8-81 p50 +SR 9-81 p52

Pieces, piano, op. 1 (4). See no. 1657
Pieces, piano, op. posth. See no. 1658
Poems by Vilhelm Krag, op. 60. See no. 1648

1659 Poetic tone pictures, op. 3. Songs, opp. 41 and 52 (arr. for piano). Eva Knardahl, pno. BIS LP 112
+FF 11/12-79 p77 +SR 9-81 p52
+Gr 8-80 p247 +St 1-80 p95
+HF 8-81 p51

Poetic tone pictures, op. 3. See no. 1657
Scenes from peasant life, op. 19. See no. 1642
Sigurd Jorsalfar, op. 56: Hommage march. See no. 1652
Sigurd Jorsalfar, op. 56: Incidental music. See no. 1655
Sigurd Jorsalfar, op. 56: Suite. See no. 1649

1660 Sonata, piano, op. 7, E minor. Holberg suite, op. 40. Eva Knardahl, pno. BIS LP 108
+FF 7/8-79 p55 +-HFN 7-79 p105
+Gr 8-80 p247 +RR 7-79 p91
+HF 8-81 p50 +SR 9-81 p52

Sonata, violin and piano, no. 3, op. 45, C minor. See no. 1545
Sonata, violoncello and piano, op. 36, A minor. See no. 1198. See no. 1542
Songs, opp. 41 and 52 (arr. for piano). See no. 1657. See no. 1659
Songs: Ein Schwan, op. 25, no. 2. See no. 952
Songs: Hvad est du dog skjon; I himmelen. See no. 3991
Songs: I love thee. See no. 3839

Songs: Last spring. See no. 3966
Songs: Thanks for advice. See no. 3823
1661 Symphony, C minor. Bergen Symphony Orchestra; Karsten Andersen. London LDR 71037 (also Decca SXDL 7537 Tape (c) KSXDC 7537)
+FF 11/12-81 p169
+Gr 6-81 p38
+Gr 9-81 p460 tape
+HFN 7-81 p73
+MT 11-81 p754
*NYT 10-18-81 pD21
+SFC 8-30-81 p18
+St 10-81 p124
+ST 12-81 p589
Waltz-caprices, op. 37. See no. 1658
GRIFFES, Charles
Roman sketches, op. 7. See no. 3952
Roman sketches, op. 7: The fountain of Acqua Paola. See no. 1290
Songs: An old song resung; Das ist ein Brausen und Heulen; Des Muden Abendlied; The first snowfall; Wo ich bin mich rings Umdunkelt; Zwei Konige. See no. 3932
GRIGNY, Nicolas de
1662 Les hymnes. Michel Chapuis, org. Astree AS 9
+FF 7/8-81 p90
1663 Live d'orgue: Mass; Hymns: Veni creator; Pange lingua; Verbum supernum; Ave maris stella; A solis ortus. Marie-Claire Alain, org; Guillaume Bony Choir; Jean Teixeira. Erato STU 71380 (2)
+-Gr 10-80 p527
+HFN 1-81 p93
+-MU 9-81 p12
1664 La messe. Michel Chapuis, org. Astree AS 8
+FF 7/8-81 p90
1665 La messe. LEBEGUE: Elevation, G major. Symphonie sur le bemol fa. Suite du deuxieme ton. Andre Isoir, org. Calliope CAL 1910/11 (2)
+Gr 10-75 p657
+MU 9-81 p12
GRIMES, David
All wounds. See no. 1666
GRIMES, David and David Jaeger, Larry Lake, James Montgomery
1666 Chaconne a son gout. GRIMES: All wounds. Canadian Electronic Ensemble; Billie Bridgman, s; Karen Kieser, pno. Centrediscs CMC 1
+MUM 9/10-81 p31
GROFE, Ferde
1667 Grand Canyon suite. PO; Eugene Ormandy. CBS HM 40446 Tape (c) MT 30446
+FF 9/10-81 p111
++NR 6-81 p3
+SFC 12-27-81 p18
1668 Grand Canyon suite. Andre Kostelanetz Orchestra; Andre Kostelanetz. CBS 61835 Tape (c) 40-61835
+-Gr 7-81 p195
+-HFN 7-81 p79
+-HFN 8-81 p92 tape
GROSSI, Carlo
1669 Cantata ebraica in dialogo. ROSSI: Les cantiques de Solomon. SALADIN: Canticum Hebraicum. Boston Camerata; Joel Cohen. Harmonia Mundi HM 1021
++ARG 11-80 p51
+Audio 12-81 p26
+FF 7/8-80 p180
+Gr 10-80 p527
+HFN 5-80 p129
++NR 6-80 p6
+NYT 8-10-80 pD17
+RR 6-80 p85
++St 9-80 p85

GROVEN, Eivind
Sun mood. See no. 3683
GRUBER, Franz
Stille Nacht heilige Nacht. See no. 3775
GUAMI, Gioseffo
La brillantina. See no. 3945
Canzona, no. 25. See no. 3936
GUARNIERI, Camargo
Canto, no. 1. See no. 1522
Sonata, violin and piano, no. 4. See no. 1522
Suite Vila Rica. See no. 3880
GUASTAVINO, Carlos
La presencias, no. 6. See no. 828
La rosa y el sauce. See no. 3703
GUBAIDULINA, Sofia
Concerto, bassoon and low strings. See no. 838
GUEDRON, Pierre
Songs: Ce penser qui sans fin tirannise ma vie; Si le parler et le silence; Vous que le bonheur rappelle. See no. 3946
GUERRERO, Jacinto
El huesped de Sevillano: Canto a la Espada. See no. 3888
GUGLIELMI, Pietro
Gratias agimus. See no. 3790
GUIDE, Richard de
1670 Characters of the trombone, suite. NILSSON: Concertino, trombone and organ. VIVALDI: Sonata, trombone, no. 1. WEBER: Romanze appassionata. Christer Torge, trom; Hans Fagius, org. BIS LP 138
+FF 9/10-81 p270 +NR 5-81 p10
+HFN 6-81 p83
GUIDO OF AREZZO
Ut queant laxis resonare. See no. 4009
GUILAIN, Jean
Pieces d'orgue pour le Magnificat sur les huit tons differens de l'Eglise: Suite, G minor. See no. 3812
GUILLOU, Jean
Improvisations. See no. 1671
1671 Improvisation on "The old hundredth". Improvisations. Improvisations on 3 themes. Toccata. Jean Guillou, org. Festivo SBO 502
+*Gr 2-81 p1104
Improvisations on 3 themes. See no. 1671
Toccata. See no. 1671
GUILMANT, Felix Alexandre
Introduction et variations sur un ancien Noel polonais. See no. 3894
Marche funebre et chant seraphique. See no. 4112
Noel Brabancon. See no. 3894
Offertoire sur des Noels. See no. 3894
1672 Sonatas, organ, nos. 1-8. Feike Asma, org. Cantilena FAG 4001/5
++Gr 10-81 p582
GUIOT DE DIJON
Chanterai por mon coraige. See no. 4086
GUIRAUT DE BORNELH
Le chansonet e vil. See no. 4086

GUMPELZHAIMER, Adam
Sacred songs (3). See no. 4071
Vom Himmel hoch. See no. 3775
GUO QUAN LI
Singing the night among fishing boats. See no. 3859
GURNEY, Ivor
1673 Ludlow and teme. VAUGHAN WILLIAMS: On Wenlock edge. Martyn Hill, t; Graham Johnson, pno; Coull Quartet. Hyperion A 66013
+Gr 6-81 p70 +STL 6-14-81 p40
/HFN 7-81 p73
Songs: All night under the moon; Bread and cherries; Brown is my love; The cloths of heaven; Desire in spring; Down by the salley gardens; An epitaph; The fields are full; The folly of being comforted; Severn meadows; The singer; Snow. See no. 1336
Songs: Down by the salley gardens; Hawk and buckle; Sleep. See no. 3874
Songs: Under the greenwood tree. See no. 3878
The western playland: Reveille; Loveliest of trees; Golden friends; Twice a week; The aspens; Is my team ploughing; The far country; March. See no. 3893
GWILT, David
Sonatina. See no. 3731
HABA, Alois
1674 Nonet, no. 4, op. 94. HALVELKA: Nonet. KREJCI: Nonet divertimento. TAUSINGER: Nonet of Hukvaldy. Czech Nonet. Supraphon 111 2545
++FF 9/10-81 p279 +NR 8-81 p9
HADLEY, Patrick
The hills. See no. 1337
HAGEMAN
Christ went up into the hills alone. See no. 3967
HAHN, Reynaldo
Songs: Aimons-nous. See no. 3758
Songs: Dernier voeu; L'heure exquise. See no. 4026
Songs: Le rossignol des lilas. See no. 3642. See no. 3703
Songs: Si mes vers avaient des ailes. See no. 3653
HAIEFF, Alexei
1675 Sonata, violoncello and piano. ORNSTEIN: Preludes (6). Italo Babini, vlc; Elizabeth Sawyer Parisot, pno. Serenus SRS 12090
+FF 11/12-81 p214 +NR 6-81 p6
++HF 10-81 p84 +St 8-81 p96
HALES, Robert
Songs: O eyes leave off your weeping. See no. 3946
HALEVY, Jacques
1676 La juive: Dieu que ma voix tremblante; Rachel quand du Seigneur. MEYERBEER: L'Africaine: O paradiso; Combien tu m'es chere; Erreur fatal. Dinorah: Les bles sont beaux a faucher. Les Huguenots: Plus blanche que la blanche hermine. Le Prophete: Roi du ciel; Pour Bertha moi je souspire. REYER: Sigurd: Prince du Rhin; J'ai garde mon ame ingenue; Oui Sigurd est vainqueur; Esprits gardiens; Un souvenir poignant. Cesar Vezzani, t; Various orchestras and conductors. EMI 2C 051 16367
+ARSC Vol 12, nos. 1-2 1980 p101 +Gr 6-81 p84

La juive: Loin de son amie. See no. 4051
La juive: Rachel quand du Seigneur. See no. 3769. See no. 4053. See no. 4081
La juive: Se oppressi ognor; Voi che del Dio vivante. See no. 3968

HALFFTER, Cristobal
Introduction, fugue and finale. See no. 4072

HALFFTER, Ernesto
Danza de la gitana. See no. 1491. See no. 3847

HALFFTER, Rodolfo
Don Lindo de Almeria. See no. 1134

HALLNAS, Hilding
Epitaph for strings. See no. 4072

HALVELKA, Svatopluk
Nonet. See no. 1674

HALVORSEN, Johan
1677 Air norvegien, E minor. Norwegian dances. Terje Tonnesen, vln; Oslo Philharmonic Orchestra; Karsten Andersen. NFK 30032
+Gr 8-81 p317 +HFN 9-81 p80
Norwegian dances. See no. 1677
1678 Norwegian rhapsodies, nos. 1-2. Suite ancienne, op. 31. Bergen Symphony Orchestra; Karsten Andersen. Norway NFK 30030
+FF 7/8-81 p105 +Gr 1-80 p1167
Suite ancienne, op. 31. See no. 1678
1679 Symphony, no. 2, C minor. Oslo Philharmonic Orchestra; Karsten Andersen. NK 30031 Tape (c) IMS NKF 30031
+-Gr 8-81 p317 +-HFN 9-81 p80

HAMBLEN
Tick tick tock. See no. 4043

HAMMERSCHMIDT, Andreas
Songs: Der Verfuhrer. See no. 3985

HANDEL, Georg Friedrich
1680 Acis and Galatea. Norma Burrowes, s; Anthony Rolfe Johnson, Martyn Hill, Paul Elliot, t; Willard White, bs; English Baroque Soloists; Nicholas Kramer, hpd; John Eliot Gardiner. DG 2708 038 (2) Tape (c) 3375 004
++ARG 4-79 p22 ++NR 1-79 p12
+FF 7/8-79 p56 +-NYT 5-20-79 pD26
+Gr 9-78 p523 +OC Fall 1981 p52
+Gr 12-78 p1178 tape +-ON 3-31-79 p40
+-HF 4-79 p84 +RR 10-78 p43
+-HF 7-79 p157 tape +RR 12-78 p114 tape
+HFN 10-78 p125 +-SFC 1-28-79 p43
++MJ 2-79 p47 +-St 3-79 p89
+-MT 4-79 p313
Acis and Galatea: O ruddier than the cherry. See no. 3853
Air, A major. See no. 1708
Air, B flat major. See no. 1709
Air, wind band, F major. See no. 1727
Air and variations. See no. 3764
Air with variations, B flat major. See no. 1004. See no. 1709
1681 Alceste: Incidental music. Judith Nelson, Emma Kirkby, s; Margaret Cable, ms; Paul Elliot, t; David Thomas, bs; Academy of Ancient Music; Christopher Hogwood. L'Oiseau-Lyre DSLO 581 Tape (c) KDSLC 581
+Gr 12-80 p860 +MT 9-81 p607
+HFN 1-81 p93 ++STL 1-11-81 p38

Alcina: Ballet music. See no. 1738
Alcina: Verdi prati. See no. 3629
Alessandro: Ne trionfi d'Alessandro...Lusinghe piu care. See no. 3650

1682 Alexander's feast. Helen Donath, Sally Burgess, s; Robert Tear, t; Thomas Allen, bar; King's College Chapel Choir; ECO; Philip Ledger. HMV SLS 5168 (2) Tape (c) TC SLS 5168 (also Angel SZB 3874)
+-ARG 5-80 p23
++FF 5/6-80 p86
+Gr 10-79 p689
+-HF 4-80 p90
+HFN 11-79 p139
+HFN 2-80 p107 tape
+Gr 12-81 p945 tape
+MT 6-80 p382
+NR 3-80 p11
+NYT 1-20-80 pD22
+RR 10-79 p135
+St 5-80 p83
+STL 12-2-79 p37

1683 Alexander's feast. Overture, D major. Royal fireworks music. AMF; Neville Marriner. Philips 9500 768 Tape (c) 7300 843
+ARG 5-81 p18
+FF 1/2-81 p118
+Gr 11-81 p689
+HFN 12-81 p95
+NR 12-80 p2

Alexander's feast. See no. 1696
Alexander's feast: Behold a ghastly band...Revenge Timotheus cries. See no. 4074
Allegro, F major. See no. 1733

1684 L'Allegro, il penseroso ed il moderato: Pts 1 and 2. Payrizia Kwella, Marie McLaughlin, Jennifer Smith, s; Michael Ginn, treble; Maldwyn Davies, Martyn Hill, t; Stephen Varcoe, bs; Monteverdi Choir, English Baroque Soloists; John Eliot Gardiner. Erato STU 71325 (2)
++Gr 11-80 p718
++Gr 3-81 p1170
++HFN 1-81 p95
++MUM 2-81 p31

1685 Ariodante. Edith Mathis, Norma Burrowes, s; Janet Baker, ms; James Bowman, c-t; David Rendall, t; Samuel Ramey, bs; Alexander Oliver, t; London Voices; ECO; Raymond Leppard. Philips 6769 025 (4) Tape (c) 7699 112
+-ARG 10-80 p16
+FF 7/8-80 p93
+-Gr 12-80 p889 tape
+-Gr 9-80 p391
+HFN 9-80 p104
+HFN 11-80 p131 tape
+HF 8-80 p72
+-MT 1-81 p33
+NR 6-80 p10
++NYT 4-20-80 pD24
+-ON 11-1-80 p44
+-Op 10-80 p1013
++SFC 4-20-80 p34
++St 7-80 p71

Ariodante: Ballet music. See no. 1738
Arminio: Overture. See no. 1723
Atalanta: Come my beloved. See no. 3967
Aylesford pieces: Gavotte and passepied. See no. 3881
Aylesford pieces: Minuet, G minor. See no. 361

1686 Belshazzar. Felicity Palmer, s; Maureen Lehane, con; Paul Esswood, c-t; Robert Tear, Thomas Sunnegaardh, t; Peter van der Bilt, Staffan Sandlund, bs; Stockholm Chamber Chorus; VCM; Nikolaus Harnoncourt. Telefunken 6-35326 (4) Tape (c) 4-35326
+Gr 2-77 p1311
+-HF 1-78 p95
+HF 5-79 p103 tape
++HFN 1-77 p109
+-MT 11-77 p923
+NR 9-77 p9
+RR 1-77 p80; 1-78 p14
+SR 12-81 p64
++SFC 6-26-77 p46
++St 9-77 p134

Belshazzar: Sinfonia. See no. 1723
Berenice: Minuet. See no. 336

1687 Berenice: Overture. Concerto a due cori, no. 3, F major. Royal fireworks music. NYP, Philharmonia Chamber Orchestra; Pierre Boulez. Columbia M 35833 Tape (c) MT 35833 (also CBS 76834 Tape (c) 40-76834)
+-ARG 1-81 p29
+FF 11/12-80 p119
+-Gr 7-80 p141
+HF 7-80 p68
+HFN 7-80 p107
+HFN 9-80 p116 tape
+-HFN 10-80 p117 tape
+-MT 3-81 p183
+RR 7-80 p57

Berenice: Overture. See no. 1738
Berenice: Overture, minuet and gigue. See no. 1612

1688 Blessed are they that consider the poor. Ode for Queen Anne's birthday. Judith Nelson, Emma Kirkby, s; Shirley Minty, con; James Bowman, c-t; Martyn Hill, t; David Thomas, bs; Christ Church Cathedral Choir; Academy of Ancient Music; Simon Preston. L'Oiseau-Lyre DSLO 541 Tape (c) KDSLO 541
+FF 9/10-79 p93
+Gr 12-78 p1142
++Gr 12-81 p945 tape
+HFN 12-78 p155
+RR 12-78 p105
+-St 6-79 p128

1689 Cantatas: Il gelsomino; Mi palpita il cor. SCARLATTI, D.: Sonatas, harpsichord, K 87, 238, 239, 401. TELEMANN: Sonata, viola da gamba, D major. Penelope Jensen, s; James Caldwell, ob; Catharine Meints, vlc, vla da gamba; Doris Ornstein, hpd and cond. Gasparo GS 213
+NR 11-81 p4

1690 Cantatas: Nell' Africane selve; Nella stagion che di viol e rose. Duets: No di vol non vuo fidarmi; Quel fior che all' alba ride; Se tu non lasci amore; Tacete ohime tacete. Emma Kirkby, Judith Nelson, s; David Thomas, bs; Susan Sheppard, vlc; Christopher Hogwood, hpd. L'Oiseau-Lyre DSLO 580
++Gr 7-81 p182
+HFN 7-81 p73

Capriccio, F major. See no. 1708
Capriccio, G minor. See no. 1708

1691 Chaconne, G major. Minuet, G minor. Suites, harpsichord, B flat major, G minor, D minor, E minor. Robert Woolley, hpd. Saga 5476
+Gr 11-80 p703
+HFN 11-80 p105
+MT 2-81 p111

Concerto, harp, F major. See no. 1247
Concerto, harp, op. 4, no. 5, F major. See no. 4008. See no. 216
Concerto, harp, op. 4, no. 6, B flat major. See no. 164
Concerto, harpsichord, G major. See no. 1709
Concerto, 2 horns, F major. See no. 384
Concerti, oboe, nos. 1-3. See no. 1738
Concerto, oboe, no. 3, G minor. See no. 227
Concerti, organ (6). See no. 1738
Concerto, organ, no. 6, B flat major. See no. 3980
Concerto, organ, op. 4, no. 1, G major: Finale. See no. 3930
Concerto, organ, op. 7, no. 13, F major. See no. 4091

1692 Concerti, organ, op. 7, nos. 14-16. Daniel Chorzempa, org; Concerto Amsterdam; Jaap Schroder. Philips 9502 007 (From 6700 009)
+Gr 8-81 p270
++HFN 9-81 p90

1693 Concerto, recorder, F major. SAMMARTINI: Concerto, recorder, F major. TELEMANN: Concerto, recorder, C major. VIVALDI: Concerto, recorder, RV 443, C major. Michala Petri, rec; AMF; Iona Brown. Philips 9500 714 Tape (c) 7300 808
++ARG 3-81 p55 +HF 4-81 p93 tape
+FF 3/4-81 p235 ++HFN 11-80 p127
+Gr 11-80 p683 ++NR 11-80 p4
+Gr 4-81 p1376 +St 1-81 p88

1694 Concerti, recorder, G major, F major. TELEMANN: Concerto, recorder, C major. VIVALDI: Concerto, recorder, RV 445, C major. Bernard Krainis, rec; London Strings; Neville Marriner. Quintessence PMC 7146 (From Mercury SR 90443)
+ARG 11-80 p39 +/St 1-81 p88
+FF 9/10-80 p278

1695 Concerti a due cori, nos. 1-3. AMF; Neville Marriner. Philips 9500 756 Tape (c) 7300 837
+ARG 11-81 p23 ++St 9-81 p103
++NR 7-81 p4

Concerto a due cori, no. 3, F major. See no. 1687

1696 Concerti grossi, op. 3. Alexander's feast. BBS; Helmut Winschermann. Arabesque 8089 (2)
+NR 12-81 p4 +-NYT 12-20-81 pD21

1697 Concerti grossi, op. 3. Northern Sinfonia; George Malcolm. ASV ACM 2004 Tape (c) ZCACM 2004 (From Enigma VAR 1045)
+Gr 4-81 p1316 +-HFN 4-81 p80
+Gr 7-81 p196 tape +HFN 6-81 p87 tape

1698 Concerti grossi, op. 3. English Baroque Soloists; John Eliot Gardiner. Erato STU 71367
+-Gr 10-81 p551 +NYT 12-20-81 pD21

1699 Concerti, grossi, op. 3. ECO; Raymond Leppard. Philips 9502 006 Tape (c) 7313 006 (From 6700 050)
+Gr 3-81 p1194 ++HFN 7-81 p81 tape

1700 Concerti grossi, op. 3. Smithsonian Chamber Players; James Weaver. Smithsonian Collection N 023 (2)
++FF 11/12-81 p171

Concerti grossi, op. 3. See no. 1738

1701 Concerti grossi, op. 6 (12). Emanuel Hurwitz, Raymond Keenlyside, vln; Keith Harvey, vlc; Raymond Leppard, Leslie Pearson, hpd; ECO; Raymond Leppard. Philips 6768 164 (3) Tape (c) 7699 157
++FF 3/4-81 p131 ++NR 1-81 p3

Concerti grossi, op. 6. See no. 1738

1702 Coronation anthems: The king shall rejoice. My heart is inditing. Let thy hand be strengthened. Zadok the priest. King's College Chamber Choir; ECO; David Willcocks. Argo ZRG 5369 Tape (c) KZRC 5369
+Gr 9-78 p566 tape +-HFN 7-78 p111 tape
+Gr 12-81 p945 tape +RR 6-78 p94 tape

1703 Crudel tiranno amor. Giulio Cesare: E pur cosi in un giorno... Piangero la sorta mia. Silete venti. Elly Ameling, s; ECO; Raymond Leppard. Philips 6570 113 Tape (c) 7310 113 (From 6500 009)
+ARG 3-79 p13 +HFN 9-81 p90
+Gr 9-81 p421 ++NR 2-79 p12

Deidamia: Overture. See no. 1723

1704 Dettingen Te deum. Philippe Huttenlocher, bs; Vocal Ensemble "A

Coeur Joie"; Jean-Francois Paillard Chamber Orchestra; Jean-Francois Paillard. Musical Heritage Society MHS 4304 (also RCA ZL 30559)
+FF 7/8-81 p105

1705 Dixit dominus. Teresa Zylis-Gara, s; Janet Baker, ms; Martin Lane, alto; Robert Tear, t; John Shirley-Quirk, bar; John Langdon, or; Andrew Davis hpd; King's College Choir; ECO; David Willcocks. HMV SXLP 30444 Tape (c) TC SXLP 30444 (From ASD 2262)
+Gr 10-80 p527 +HFN 11-80 p129
+Gr 12-81 p945 tape +HFN 12-80 p159 tape

Fantasia, C major. See no. 1709
Faramondo: Overture. See no. 1723
Fugue, A minor. See no. 1709
Gavotte, B flat major. See no. 4115
Giulio Cesare: E pur cosi in un giorno...Piangero la sorte mia. See no. 1703
Giulio Cesare: Overture; Minuet, Act 1. See no. 1723

1706 Giulio Cesare: Silete venti; Crudel tiranno amor; E pur cosi in giorno...Piangero la sorte mia. Elly Ameling, s; ECO; Raymond Leppard. Philips 6570 113
+Op 11-81 p1152

1707 Giulio Cesare: Tu la mia stella sei; Va tacito e nascosto; Priva son d'ogni conforto; Si spietata il tuo rigore; V'adoro pupille; Venere bella; Se pieta di me non senti; Da tempeste il legno infranto; Aure deh per pieta; Piangero la sorte mia; Sperai ne m'ingannai. Joan Sutherland, s; Marilyn Horne, Margreta Elkins, ms; Monica Sinclair, con; Richard Conrad; NSO; Richard Bonynge. Decca SDD 574 (From SXL 6116)
+-Gr 1-81 p988 +-Op 6-81 p652

1708 Harpsichord works: Air, A major. Capriccio, F major. Capriccio, G minor. Prelude, allemande and courante, C minor. Prelude and allegro, G minor. Sonata, C major. Sonatina, A minor. Suites, D minor, E minor, G minor, G major, B flat major. Luciano Sgirzzi, hpd. Erato ERA 9068/9 (also Musical Heritage Society MHS 4183/4)
/Gr 7-73 p215 +RR 7-73 p71
+HF 2-81 p64

1709 Harpsichord works: Air con variazioni, B flat major. Air, B flat major. Concerto, harpsichord, G major. Fantasia, C major. Fugue, A minor. Prelude and allegro, G minor. Sonatas, C major, G minor. Suites, G major, D minor, F major, B flat major. Zuzana Ruzickova, hpd. Supraphon 111 2491/2 (2)
+ARG 2-81 p18 +-HFN 12-80 p140
-Gr 10-80 p518 +NR 10-80 p14
+-HF 2-81 p64

1710 Israel in Egypt. Jean Knibbs, Marilyn Troth, Daryl Greene, Elisabeth Priday, s; Christopher Royall, Ashley Stafford, Brian Gordon, Julian Clarkson, c-t; Paul Elliott, William Kendall, t; Stephen Varcoe, Charles Stewart, bs; Marilyn Sansom, vlc; Malcolm Hicks, org; Alastair Ross, hpd; Monteverdi Orchestra and Choir; John Eliot Gardiner. Erato STU 71245 (2) (also Musical Heritage Society 824273 Tape (c) 284273)
+-ARG 7/8-81 p16 +-HF 1-81 p71
+FF 9/10-81 p112 +RR 2-80 p88
+Gr 1-80 p1187 ++St 6-81 p114

Israel in Egypt: But as for his people; Moses and the children of Israel; The Lord is a man of war. See no. 4122

1711 Jeptha. Margaret Marshall, Emma Kirkby, s; Alfreda Hodgson, con; Paul Esswood, c-t; Anthony Rolfe Johnson, t; Christopher Keyte, bs; Southend Boys Choir; AMF and Chorus; Neville Marriner. Argo D181D4 (4) Tape (c) K181K44
+FF 1/2-81 p116
+Gr 2-80 p1287
+Gr 12-81 p945 tape
+-HF 1-81 p71
+HFN 1-80 p119
+RR 1-80 p107
+St 2-81 p105

1712 Judas Maccabaeus. Felicity Palmer, s; Janet Baker, ms; Paul Esswood, c-t; Ryland Davies, t; John Shirley-Quirk, bar; Christopher Keyte, bs; Wandsworth School Choir; ECO; Charles Mackerras. DG 2723 050 (3) Tape (c) 3376 011 (also DG 2710 021 Tape (c) 3376 021)
+ARG 1-78 p23
++FF 3/4-78 p38
++Gr 9-77 p467
++Gr 11-77 p900 tape
+Gr 12-81 p945 tape
++HFN 11-77 p163
+MJ 2-79 p43
+MT 3-78 p243
+NR 1-78 p10
++RR 9-77 p88
++RR 1-78 p14
+St 2-78 p146

Judas Maccabaeus: Overture. See no. 1723
Judas Maccabaeus: See the conquering here comes. See no. 3930
The king shall rejoice. See no. 1702

1713 Lesson, B flat major. Suite, harpsichord, no. 7, G minor. SCARLATTI: Sonatas, harpsichord, K 501-502, 490-492, 441-442. Mark Kroll, hpd. Titanic TI 49
+AR 11-81 p133
+-ARG 11-81 p24
+-FF 5/6-81 p87

1714 Lesson, no. 1, B flat major (omits final minuet). Lesson, no. 3, G major: Chaconne and variations. Suite, harpsichord, no. 9, G minor. Suite, harpsichord, no. 41, G major. Christopher Wood, hpd. Musical Heritage Society MHS 4227
-FF 1/2-81 p118

Lesson, no. 3, G major: Chaconne and variations. See no. 1714
Let thy hand be strengthened. See no. 1702

1715 Messiah. James Bowman, c-t; Robert Tear, t; Benjamin Luxon, bar; Boys of King's College Choir, soprano solos; King's College Choir; AMF; David Willcocks. Arabesque 8030-3 (3)
+ARG 2-81 p17
+FF 11/12-80 p118
-NR 1-81 p7
+SFC 12-14-80 p20

1716 Messiah. Elly Ameling, s; Anna Reynolds, con; Philip Langridge, t; Gwynne Howell, bs; AMF; Neville Marriner. Argo D18D3 (3) Tape (c) K18K32 (r) V D18D3
+ARG 3-77 p19
+Audio 6-77 p133
++Audio 9-79 p97 tape
+Audio 11-79 p130 tape
+FF 11/12-79 p18 tape
+Gr 11-76 p852
+-Gr 1-77 p1183 tape
+-HF 4-77 p103
+HF 6-79 p96 tape
++HFN 11-76 p160
++HFN 1-77 p123 tape
+MM 2-77 p33
+-MT 3-77 p216
+NYT 2-15-81 pD21 tape
+-RR 11-76 p95
+RR 1-77 p90 tape
++St 4-77 p119

1717 Messiah. Elizabeth Harwood, s; Janet Baker, ms; Paul Esswood, c-t; Robert Tear, t; Raimund Herincx, bar; Ambrosian Singers;

ECO; Charles Mackerras. HMV SLS 774 Tape (c) TC SLS 774 (also Angel S 3705)

+-ARG 12-76 p6 +HFN 1-76 p125 tape
+Gr 12-76 p1066 tape ++RR 1-76 p66 tape
+Gr 12-81 p945 tape +SR 12-81 p64

1718 Messiah. Judith Nelson, Emma Kirkby, s; Carolyn Watkinson, con; Paul Elliott, t; David Thomas, bs; Christ Church Cathedral Choir; Academy of Ancient Music; Christopher Hogwood. L'Oiseau-Lyre D189D3 (3) Tape (c) K189K33

+FF 3/4-81 p131 +MT 10-80 p634
++Gr 4-80 p1575 +NYT 10-19-80 pD24
++Gr 9-80 p413 tape ++RR 4-80 p111
+Gr 1-81 p1001 tape +-SFC 12-14-80 p20
+Gr 12-81 p945 tape +SR 12-81 p64
+HF 4-81 p78 +St 3-81 p74
++HFN 4-80 p99

1719 Messiah. Smithsonian Chamber Players; American Boychoir, Norman Scribner Chorus; James Weaver. Smithsonian Institution Collection NO 25

+-NYT 12-20-81 pD21 +-SFC 12-20-81 p18

1720 Messiah. Margaret Price, s; Yvonne Minton, con; Alexander Young, t; Justino Diaz, bs; Amor Artis Chorale; ECO; Johannes Somary. Vanguard C 10090/2 Tape (c) ZCVX 10092, CA 410090/2

+ARG 12-76 p6 +NR 5-71 p9
+Gr 11-71 p870 +ON 4-17-71 p34
+-HF 3-71 p58 +RR 3-75 p74 tape
+HF 5-81 p53 tape ++SFC 3-28-71 p20

Messiah: Alleluia. See no. 3796

1721 Messiah: Comfort ye my people; Ev'ry valley shall be exalted; And the glory of the Lord; But how may abide the day of his coming; Behold a virgin shall conceive; O thou that tellest good tidings; For unto us a child is born; Rejoice greatly; O daughter of Zion; Why do the nations so furiously rage together; Let us break their bonds asunder; Hallelujah; I know that my redeemer liveth; Behold I tell you a mystery; The trumpet shall sound; Worthy is the lamb that was slain. Emma Kirkby, Judith Nelson, s; Carolyn Watkinson, con; Paul Elliott, t; David Thomas, bs; Christ Church Cathedral Choir; Academy of Ancient Music; Christopher Hogwood. L'Oiseau-Lyre DSLO 592 Tape (c) KDSLC 592 (From D189D3)

+Gr 10-81 p593 ++HFN 11-81 p105

Messiah: Hallelujah chorus. See no. 3700
Messiah: He was despised. See no. 3970
Messiah: The trumpet shall sound. See no. 159
Messiah: Why do the nations; The trumpet shall sound. See no. 4077
Mi palpita il cor. See no. 1091
Minuet, E minor. See no. 1733
Minuet, G minor. See no. 1691
Movements, D minor. See no. 1733
My heart is inditing. See no. 1702
Ode for Queen Anne's birthday. See no. 1688

1722 Ode for St. Cecilia's day. Jill Gomez, s; Robert Tear, t; King's College Chapel Choir; Philip Ledger. ASV DCA 512

+STL 12-13-81 p39

The origin of design: Ballet suite. See no. 4122

Overture, D major. See no. 1683

1723 Overtures: Arminio. Belshazzar: Sinfonia. Deidamia. Faramondo. Giulio Cesare: Overture; Minuet, Act 1. Judas Maccabaeus. Radamisto. Scipio. Semele: Sinfonia, Act 1. ECO; Richard Bonynge. London STS 15532

+FF 1/2-81 p117

1724 Partenope. Krisztina Laky, s; Helga Muller Molinari, con; Rene Jacobs, John Skinner, c-t; Martyn Hill, t; Stephen Varcoe, bar; La Petite Bande; Sigiswald Kuijken. Harmonia Mundi 1C 159 99855/8 (4)

+ARG 3-81 p28
+FF 9/10-80 p127
+Gr 12-79 p1047
+HFN 12-79 p161
+MT 4-80 p251
+NYT 4-20-80 pD24
+ON 11-1-80 p44
+RR 12-70 p18
+STL 12-2-79 p37

Il pastor Fido: Ballet music. See no. 1738

Il pastor Fido: Caro amor. See no. 3657

Prelude, allemande and courante, C minor. See no. 1708

Prelude and allegro, G minor. See no. 1708. See no. 1709

1725 Psalms: Laudate pueri, D major; Nisi dominus; Salve regina. Deller Consort, King's Music; Mark Deller. Harmonia Mundi HM 1054 Tape (c) 1054

++ARG 9-81 p53
+Gr 12-80 p865
+-MT 5-81 p317

Radamisto: Overture. See no. 1723

La rejouissance. See no. 3663

Rigadoon. See no. 3959

Rinaldo: Lascia ch'io pianga. See no. 3713

1726 Rodelinda. Joan Sutherland, Patricia Kern, s; Janet Baker, Margreta Elkins, ms; Alfred Hallett, t; Raimond Herincx, bar; Sadlers Wells Orchestra and Chorus; Charles Farncombe. Historial Recordings HRE 355/3 (3)

+-NR 12-81 p8

1727 Royal fireworks music. Airs, wind band, F major (2). Sonata, flute, no. 1, A minor (attrib.). Stephen Preston, flt; Anthony Pleath, vlc; Academy of Ancient Music; Christopher Hogwood. L'Oiseau-Lyre DSLO 548 Tape (c) KDSLC 548

+Gr 9-81 p383
+HFN 9-81 p80

1728 Royal fireworks, music. Water music: Suite, no. 1. ECO; Raymond Leppard. Philips 6527 047 Tape (c) 7311 047 (From 6500 047, 6500 369)

+Gr 4-81 p1316
+HFN 4-81 p80
+HFN 7-81 p81 tape

Royal fireworks music. See no. 247. See no. 1683. See no. 1687. See no. 1738

1729 Samson. Norma Burrowes, Felicity Lott, s; Janet Baker, ms; Helen Watts, alto; Robert Tear, Philip Langridge, Alexander Oliver, t; John Shirley-Quirk, bar; Benjamin Luxon, bs-bar; London Voices; ECO; Raymond Leppard. RCA ARL 4-3635 (4) Tape (c) ARK 3-3635 (also Erato STU 71240)

++ARG 2-81 p15
+Audio 6-81 p18
+FF 3/4-81 p133
+Gr 9-80 p392
-HF 1-81 p72
+HF 7-81 p71 tape
+NR 10-80 p9
++SFC 11-23-80 p21
+St 12-80 p124

Samson: Let the bright seraphim. See no. 159
Sarabande. See no. 3816
1730 Saul. Sally Burgess, Margaret Marshall, s; Paul Esswood, alto; Robert Tear, Charles Daniels, Martyn Hill, Christopher Gillett, t; Thomas Allen, Gareth Morrell, bar; Matthew Best, bs; King's College Choir; Thomas Trotter, hpd; Adrian Partington, org; Robert Spencer, theorbo; Thelma Owen, hp; ECO; Philip Ledger. HMV SLS 5220 (3) Tape (c) TCC SLS 5220
+-Gr 11-81 p753 +-HFN 12-81 p95
Scipio: Hear me ye winds and waves. See no. 4074
Scipio: Oveture. See no. 1723
Semele: O sleep why dost thou leave me. See no. 3967
Semele: Sinfonia, Act 1. See no. 1723
1731 Serse (Xerxes). Barbara Hendricks, Anne-Marie Rodde, s; Carolyn Watkinson, Ortrun Wenkel, con; Paul Esswood, c-t; Ulrik Cold, Ulrich Studer, bs; Jean Bridier Vocal Ensemble; La Grande Ecurie et la Chambre du Roy; Jean-Claude Malgoire. CBS 79325 (3)
+-Gr 10-79 p698 +-MT 3-80 p180
+FF 11/12-81 p172 +-Op 11-79 p1070
+-HFN 10-79 p153 ++RR 10-79 p56
Serse: Largo. See no. 3645
Serse: Ombra mai fu. See no. 3753. See no. 3838. See no. 3999
Serse: Va godendo. See no. 4027
Silete venti. See no. 1703
Sing unto God; Hallelujah amen. See no. 4060
Solomon: Arrival of the Queen of Sheba. See no. 336. See no. 1612. See no. 1738. See no. 4122
Sonata, flute, A major. See no. 1733
Sonata, flute, no. 1, A minor. See no. 1727
Sonatas, flute, op. 1, nos. 1-2, 4-5, 7-9, 11. See no. 1733
Sonata, flute (oboe), op. 1, no. 6, G minor. See no. 317. See no. 840
Sonata, flute, no. 1, op. 11, F major. See no. 235
Sonata, harpsichord, C major. See no. 1708
Sonatas, harpsichord, C major, G minor. See no. 1709
1732 Sonatas, 2 oboes and harpsichord, nos. 1-6. Heinz Holliger, Maurice Bourgue, ob; Christiane Jaccottet, hpd; Manfred Sax, bsn. Philips 9500 671 Tape (c) 7300 766
+ARG 3-81 p27 ++HFN 5-81 p80
+FF 9/10-80 p128 ++NR 10-80 p8
++Gr 5-81 p1488
1733 Sonatas, recorder, nos. 1, 3, 5. Sonata, flute, A minor. Sonata, flute, op. 1, nos. 1-2, 4-5, 7-9, 11. Allegro, F major. Minuet, E minor. Movements, D minor (2). Frans Bruggen, flt; rec; Anner Bylsma, vlc; Bob van Asperen, hpd. RCA AR 3-0408 (3)
+HFN 8-81 p84 +SR 10-81 p96
Sonatas, recorder, op. 1, no. 4, A minor; D minor. See no. 151
1734 Sonatas, violin and harpsichord, op. 1, nos. 3, 10, 12. Susanne Lautenbacher, vln; Hugo Ruf, hpd; Johannes Koch, vla da gamba. Musicaphon BM 30 SL 3010
+-HFN 12-80 p140 +RR 7-80 p80
+-HFN 1-81 p95
Sonata, violin and harpsichord, op. 1, no. 12, F major. See no. 29

1735 Sonatas, violin and harpsichord, no. 4, D major; no. 6, E major. TARTINI: Sonata, violin and harpsichord, no. 10, G minor. VERACINI: Sonata, violin, E minor. Eszter Perenyi, vln; Gyula Kiss, pno. Hungaroton SLPX 11975
+-FF 9/10-81 p256 ++NR 5-81 p9

Sonata, violin and harpsichord, no. 6, E major. See no. 1735
Sonatina, A minor. See no. 1708
Songs (German arias): Die ihr aus dunkeln Gruften; Kunst'ger Zeiten eitler Kummer. See no. 3985
Sosarme: Rendi'l sereno. See no. 3650
Suite, harpsichord, D minor, E minor, G minor, G major, B flat major. See no. 1708
Suites, harpsichord, D minor, G minor, E minor, B flat major. See no. 1691
Suites, harpsichord, G major, D minor, F major, B flat major. See no. 1709
Suite, harpsichord, no. 2, D minor. See no. 4087
Suite, harpsichord, no. 5, E major. See no. 3732
Suite, harpsichord, no. 7, G minor. See no. 1713
Suite, harpsichord, no. 9, G minor. See no. 1714
Suite, harpsichord, no. 41, G major. See no. 1714
Il trionfo del tempo e del disinganno: Sonata. See no. 1738

1736 Water music. Los Angeles Chamber Orchestra; Gerard Schwarz. Delos DMS 3010
+Gr 12-81 p885 +NYT 12-20-81 pD21
+-HFN 12-81 p95 ++SFC 11-22-81 p18
+NR 12-81 p4

1737 Water music. Prague Chamber Orchestra; Charles Mackerras. Supraphon 110 2629
+FF 3/4-81 p135 +NR 2-81 p5

Water music. See no. 1738
Water music: Air and hornpipe. See no. 336. See no. 1612
Water music: Suite. See no. 170. See no. 1747. See no. 3796. See no. 3817.
Water music: Suite, no. 1. See no. 1728
Water music: Suite: Allegro; Andante espressivo; Allegro deciso. See no. 164

1738 Works, selections: Alcina: Ballet music. Ariodante: Ballet music. Concerti, oboe (3). Concerti, organ (16). Concerti grossi, op. 3 (6). Concerti grossi, op. 6 (12). Berenice: Overture. Il pastor Fido: Ballet music. Royal fireworks music. Solomon: Arrival of the Queen of Sheba. Il trionfo del tempo e del disinganno: Sonata. Water music. Various soloists; AMF; Neville Marriner. Telefunken 6-35381 (11)
+FF 11/12-81 p170

Zakok the priest. See no. 1702

HANDY, William
St. Louis blues march. See no. 3976

HANLON, Kevin

1739 Variations. KORTE: Symmetrics. MCLEAN: Dimension III and IV. Albert Regni, sax; University of Texas Percussion Ensemble; George Frock; Electronic tape and tape recorders. CRI SD 431
+FF 5/6-81 p223 +NR 2-81 p15

HANSON, Howard
Young composer's guide to the six-tone scale. See no. 1233

HARBISON, John

1740 Concerto, piano. STOCK: Inner space. American Composers Orchestra; Gunther Schuller. CRI SD 440
+NR 8-81 p4 +St 12-81 p116
+NYT 6-7-81 pD26

1741 Quintet. ROCHBERG: Slow fires of autumn. Aulos Wind Quintet; Carol Wincenc, flt; Nancy Allen, hp. CRI SD 436
++FF 1/2-81 p120 ++NR 11-80 p6
++ARG 4-81 p24 *NYT 9-27-81 pD24

HARRIS, Roy

Cimarron. See no. 1742

1742 Concerto, piano. Cimarron. Symphony, band. Johana Harris, pno; UCLA Wind Ensemble, International String Congress Orchestra, 1960; James Westbrook, Roy Harris. Varese VC 81100
+-ARG 1-81 p30 +NYT 9-28-81 pD31
++FF 7/8-80 p95 +RR 6-80 p49
++Gr 5-80 p1660 +-St 2-81 p105
+HFN 5-80 p121

1743 Quartet, strings, no. 3. Quintet, piano. Johana Harris, pno; Blair Quartet. Varese VC 81123
+Gr 10-81 p573 +HFN 10-81 p87
++FF 11/12-81 p173

Quintet, piano. See no. 1743

Symphony, band. See no. 1742

HARRIS, William

Benedicite, A major. See no. 3637

King of glory, king of peace. See no. 3632

Songs: Almighty and most merciful father; I was glad when they said unto me; Come down O lord divine; King of glory king of peace. See no. 42

HARRISON, Lou

1744 Concerto, violin and percussion. LINN: Concertino, violin and wind octet. Eudice Shapire, vln; Los Angeles Percussion Ensemble; Crystal Chamber Players; William Kraft. Crystal S 853
+-HF 12-72 p82 ++SFC 8-13-72 p30
++LJ 2-73 p43 +-St 2-73 p122
++NR 10-72 p5 +St 4-81 p105

May rain. See no. 3915

A waltz for Evelyn Hinrichsen. See no. 3942

HARTMANN, Johann Peter

Prelude, G minor. See no. 3681

HARTMANN, Karl

Gesangsszene. See no. 1745

1745 Symphonies, nos. 1-8. Gesangsszene. Doris Soffel, alto; Dietrich Fischer-Dieskau, bar; Bavarian Radio Orchestra; Fritz Rieger, Rafael Kubelik, Ferdinand Leitner, Zdenek Macal. Wergo WER 60086 (5)
+Gr 6-81 p38 +Te 9-81 p59
+HFN 6-81 p73

HARTY, Hamilton

1746 A comedy overture. An Irish symphony. Ulster Orchestra; Bryden Thomson. Chandos ABRD 1027 Tape (c) ABT 1027
+FF 9/10-81 p113 +HFN 6-81 p74
+Gr 6-81 p38 +HFN 7-81 p81 tape
+Gr 7-81 p196 tape

1747 Concerto, violin. John Field suite. Londonderry air. Variations on a Dublin air. HANDEL (arr. Harty): Water music: Suite. Ralph Holmes, vln; Ulster Orchestra; Bryden Thomson. Chandos BDR 2001 (2) Tape (c) DBT 2001
++FF 11/12-81 p173 +HFN 1-80 p93
+Gr 1-80 p1151 ++FF 1/2-81 p120
An Irish symphony. See no. 1746
John Field suite. See no. 467. See no. 1747
Londonderry air. See no. 1747
Variations on a Dublin air. See no. 1747
HARVEY, Jonathan
Correspondances. See no. 1345
HARWOOD, Basil
O how glorious is the kingdom. See no. 3636
HASSE, Johann
1748 Concerto, mandolin, G major. HOFFMANN: Concerto, mandolin, D major. HUMMEL: Concerto, mandolin, G major. Takashi Ochi, mand; Paul Kuentz Chamber Orchestra; Paul Kuentz. Philips 6527 098 Tape (c) 7311 098
++FF 11/12-81 p292
Concerto, mandolin, G major. See no. 1247
1749 Venetian ballads. Ana Maria Miranda, s; Carlo Gaifa, t; Hans Ludwig Hirsch, hpd. Jecklin 5003
+FF 3/4-81 p98
HASSLER, Hans
Cantata domino. See no. 4071
Domine Deus. See no. 4071
Verbum caro factum est. See no. 3775
HATTON, John
The enchantress. See no. 3650
Simon the cellerer. See no. 4077
HAUFRECHT, Herbert
1750 Symphony, brass and timpani. HUSA: Landscapes. MOURANT: Aria for orchestra. Western Brass Quintet, New York Brass Ensemble Society, Hamburg Symphony Orchestra; Simon Karasick, Frederick Balazs. CRI SD 192
+ARG 8-79 p50 +-FF 7/8-81 p221
+-Audio 9-79 p98 +NR 4-79 p7
HAVEL, Vaclav
Allegro and pastorella, B flat major. See no. 4078
HAWES, Jack
Magnificat, D major. See no. 3637
HAWKINS, John
1751 Etudes, 2 pianos. HUNT: Merkabah. MATHER: In memoriam Alexandre Uninsky. Fantasy. Bruce Mather, Pierrette LePage, pno. Radio Canada RCI 464
+FF 9/10-81 p240
HAYDN, Josef
1752 Acide ed Galatea: Tergi i vezzosi rai. Il disertore: Un cor si tenero. La sucola de gelosi: Dice benissimo. La vera costanza: Spann deine lange Ohren. MOZART: La finta giardiniera, K 196: Nach der weischen art. Le nozze di Figaro, K 492: Hai gia cinta la causa...Vedro mentr'is sospiro. Arias: Ich mochte wohl der Kaiser sein, K 539; Cosi dunque tradisci...Aspri rimorsi atroci, K 432; Manner suchen stets zu naschen (arr. Furst);

Mentre ti lascio, K 513; Un bacio di mano, K 541. Dietrich Fischer-Dieskau, bar; Vienna Haydn Orchestra; Reinhard Peters. Decca JB 100 Tape (c) KJBC 100 (From SXL 6490)
+Gr 2-81 p1114 +Gr 2-81 p1122 tape
Acide e Galatea: Tergi i vezzosi rai. See no. 1765
Andante and variations, F minor. See no. 1311
Andantino and minuet, C minor. See no. 4096
1753 Arias: D'una sposa meschinella; Chi vive amante; Infelice sventurata; Solo e pensos; Son pietosa son bonina; Sono Alcina e sono ancora; Vada adagio Signorina. Cantata: Misera noi miserá patria. Edith Mathis, s; Lausanne Chamber Orchestra; Armin Jordin. Philips 9500 929
++FF 11/12-81 p173 +NYT 9-27-81 pD24
Awake the harp. See no. 3700
La Circe: Lavatevi presto. See no. 1765
1754 Concerto, flute, D major. Concerto, harpsichord, no. 9, G major. Concerto, violin, no. 1, C major. Concerto, violoncello, no. 1, C major. Christian Larde, flt; Huguette Dreyfus, hpd; Michel Renard, vlc; Monique Frasca-Colombier, vln; Paul Kuentz Chamber Orchestra; Paul Kuentz. Tudor RUD 75001 (2)
+Gr 7-81 p154
Concerto, harpsichord, no. 6, F major. See no. 1757
Concerto, harpsichord, no. 9, D major. See no. 1754
Concerto, horn, no. 3, D major. See no. 1276
1755 Concerto, oboe, A major. MARCELLO, A.: Concerto, oboe, D minor. VIVALDI: Concerto, oboe, RV 461, A minor. Derek Wickens, ob; RPO; Elgar Howarth. ASV ACA 1003 Tape (c) ZCACA 1003
+Gr 5-81 p1485 +-HFN 4-81 p79
+-HFN 6-81 p87 tape
Concerto, organ, F major. See no. 37
Concerto, piano, D major. See no. 228
Concerto, trumpet, E flat major. See no. 336. See no. 784. See no. 1211
Concerto, trumpet, E flat major: Finale. See no. 3695
1756 Concerto, violin, F major. Dovertimento, G major. Pina Carmirelli, vln; Maria Teresa Garatti, hpd; I Musici. Philips 9500 602 Tape (c) 7300 724
+Gr 3-81 p1194 +-ST 8-81 p275
+HFN 4-81 p71
1757 Concerti, violin, nos. 1, 3-4. Concerto, harpsichord, no. 6, F major. Sinfonia concertante, op. 84, B flat major. Salvatore Accardo, vln; Heinrich Schiff, vlc; Neil Black, ob; Graham Sheen, bsn; Bruno Canino, hpd; ECO; Salvatore Accardo. Philips 6769 059 (2) Tape (c) 7654 059
+FF 11/12-81 p174 +-NYT 9-27-81 pD24
++Gr 10-81 p552 ++SFC 12-20-81 p18
+HFN 10-81 p87 +STL 11-8-81 p40
Concerto, violin, no. 1, C major. See no. 1754
1758 Concerti, violoncello, C major, D major. Yo Yo Ma, vlc; ECO; Jose Luis Garcia. CBS 36674 Tape (c) 36674 (also CBS 76978)
-FF 7/8-81 p106 +SFC 3-8-81 p19
+Gr 7-81 p152 +St 8-81 p92
+HFN 7-81 p73 +-ST 10-81 p431
++NYT 5-24-81 pD21 +STL 7-12-81 p40
1759 Concerto, violoncello, no. 1, C major. Concerto, violoncello, no.

2, op. 101, D major. Miklos Perenyi, vlc; Liszt Chamber Orchestra; Janos Rolla. Hungaroton SLPX 12121
+ARG 6-81 p27 ++NR 2-81 p6
+FF 5/6-81 p87

Concerto, violoncello, no. 1, C major. See no. 1754

Concerto, violoncello, no. 2, op. 101, D major. See no. 819. See no. 1759

Contradanse. See no. 1830

Contradanses with quadrille. See no. 1831

Deutsche Tanze, nos. 1-6. See no. 1831

Il disertore: Un cor si tenero. See no. 1752

Divertimento, B flat major. See no. 471

Divertimento, G major. See no. 1756

Divertimento, no, 3, A major. See no. 1558

1760 Divertimenti, nos. 4, 7-9, 13. Janos Sebestyen, hpd; Vilmos Tatrai, Gyorgy Konrad, vln; Ede Banda, vlc. Budapest FX 12300
*FF 9/10-81 p113 +HFN 4-81 p80

Divertimento, no. 5, D major. See no. 1831

1761 Divertimenti, winds, E flat major (3), G major (2), C major, F major (3), D major (3), B flat major. Parthia, B flat major, E flat major (2). Suite, E flat major. Consortium Classicum. Telefunken 6-35473 (4)
++FF 1/2-81 p123

Fantasia, C major. See no. 205

1762 La fedelta premiata. Julia Paszthy, Veronika Kincses, Maria Zempleni, Ilona Tokody, s; Attila Fulop, Istvan Rozsos, t; Gabor Vaghelyi, Jozsef Gregor, bs; Ferenc Liszt Academy Chamber Orchestra and Chorus; Frigyes Sandor. Hungaroton SLPX 11854/7 (4)
+ARG 8-78 p12 +-HFN 1-81 p95
+FF 3/4-79 p59 +NR 9-78 p12
+Gr 9-78 p537 +NYT 11-19-78 pD21

1763 La fedelta premiata. Ileana Cotrubas, Kari Lovaas, s; Frederica von Stade, ms; Lucia Valentini, con; Tonny Landy, Luigi Alva, t; Alan Titus, Maurizio Mazzieri, bar; OSR Chorus; Lausanne Chamber Orchestra; Antal Dorati. Philips 6707 028 (also 9500 072/5)
+Gr 9-76 p466 +OC 12-77 p49
+HF 6-76 p68 +-ON 9-76 p70
+HFN 9-76 p122 +RR 9-76 p19
+MJ 10-76 p24 +SR 9-18-76 p50
++MT 4-77 p307 +SR 2-81 p90
++NR 5-76 p11 ++St 8-76 p94

I finti eredi: Se tu mi sprezzi ingrata. See no. 1765

Ifigenia in Tauride: Ah tu non senti amico...Qual destra omicida. See no. 1765

1764 L'Incontro improviso. Linda Zoghby, Margaret Marshall, s; Della Jones, ms; Claes Ahnsjo, t; Domenico Trimarchi, Benjamin Luxon, bar; Lausanne Chamber Orchestra; Antal Dorati. Philips 6769 040 (3) (also Philips 9500 705/7)
+ARG 6-81 p52 +MUM 3/4-81 p32
+FF 3/4-81 p136 +NR 1-81 p10
+Gr 9-80 p392 +Op 10-80 p1013
++HF 2-81 p64 ++St 2-81 p105
+HFN 9-80 p105 ++STL 9-14-80 p40
+-MT 3-81 p183

1765 L'infedelta delusa. Arias: Acide e Galatea: Tergi i vezzosi rai. La Circe: Lavatevi presto. I finti eredi: Se tu mi sprezzi ingrata. Ifigenia in Tauride: Ah tu non senti amico...Qual destra omicida. Edith Mathis, Barbara Hendricks, s; Claes Ahnsjo, Aldo Baldin, t; Michael Devlin, bs; Lausanne Chamber Orchestra; Antal Dorati. Philips 6769 061 (3) Tape (c) 7654 061

+FF 11/12-81 p175
+Gr 8-81 p309
+HFN 8-81 p84
+NYT 9-27-81 pD24
+Op 12-81 p1262
+SFC 9-20-81 p18
+STL 9-13-81 p41

1766 Die Jahreszeiten. Edda Moser, s; Eric Tappy, t; Philippe Huttenlocher, bs; OSR Choirs, Lausanne Pro Arte; Lausanne Chamber Orchestra; Armin Jordan. Erato STU 71292 (3)

+FF 5/6-81 p88

1767 Die Jahreszeiten. Edith Mathis, s; Siegfried Jerusalem, t; Dietrich Fischer-Dieskau, bar; AMF and Chorus; Nicholas Kramer, fortepiano; Denis Vigay, vlc; Raymund Koster, double bass; Neville Marriner. Philips 6769 068 (3) Tape (c) 7654 068

++Gr 11-81 p737
++HFN 12-81 p95

1768 Die Jahreszeiten. Heather Harper, s; Ryland Davies, t; John Shirley-Quirk, bar; BBC Symphony Orchestra and Chorus; Maurits Sillem, fortepiano; Colin Davis. Philips 6770 035 (3) Tape (c) 7650 035 (From SAL 3689-3700)

++FF 1/2-81 p126
+Gr 11-80 p718
++Gr 2-81 p1122 tape
+HFN 11-80 p129

Die Jahreszeiten: Air du laboureur. See no. 4029

Die Jahreszeiten: Landler. See no. 1831

1769 Mass, no. 2, E flat major. Judith Nelson, s; Carolyn Watkinson, con; Martyn Hill, t; David Thomas, bs; Christ Church Cathedral Choir; Academy of Ancient Music; Simon Preston. L'Oiseau-Lyre DSLO 563 Tape (c) KDSLC 563

+FF 1/2-81 p125
+Gr 11-79 p892
+HF 3-81 p72
+HFN 12-79 p161
++MT 8-80 p504
+NYT 5-24-81 pD21
+RR 12-79 p11

1770 Mass, no. 3, C major. Mass, no. 14, G major. Judith Nelson, s; Margaret Cable, ms; Martyn Hill, t; David Thomas, bs; Christ Church Cathedral Choir; Academy of Ancient Music; Simon Preston. L'Oiseau-Lyre DSLO 583/4 (2)

+Gr 3-81 p1218
+HFN 4-81 p71
+STL 2-8-81 p40

1771 Mass, no. 6, C major. Rotraud Hansmann, s; Christine West Robbins, con; Darrell Parsons, t; Leopold Spitzer, bs; St. Augustine Orchestra and Choir, Vienna; Friedrich Wolf, Philips 6598 540

+-Gr 1-81 p978
+HFN 1-81 p95

1772 Mass, no. 10, B flat major. Lucia Popp, s; Rosalind Elias, ms; Robert Tear, t; Paul Hudson, bar; LSO and Chorus; Leonard Bernstein. CBS IM 35839 Tape (c) HMT 35839

/-FF 3/4-81 p137
+Gr 5-81 p1504
+-HF 3-81 p69
+HF 4-81 p93 tape
+-HFN 5-81 p80
+-HFN 8-81 p92 tape
+-NYT 5-24-81 pD21
++St 3-81 p91
++STL 4-12-81 p40

1773 Mass, no. 10, B flat major. Elisabeth Speiser, s; Maureen Lehane,

con; Theo Altmeyer, t; Wolfgang Schone, bs; Tolzer Knabenchor; Collegium Aureum; Franzjosef Maier. Quintessence PMC 7166 (From Harmonia Munid 065 99693)
/FF 3/4-81 p137

1774 Mass, no. 11, D minor. Krisztina Laki, s; Ria Bollen, alto; Heinz Hopfner, t; Gunter Reich, bs; Stuttgart Chamber Choir; Wurttemberg Chamber Orchestra; Frieder Bernius. Intercord INT 160 826
+-HFN 9-81 p80

Mass, no. 14, G major. See no. 1770

Minuet da ballo, nos. 1-6. See no. 1831

Misera noi misera patria, cantata. See no. 1753

1775 Nocturnes (8). Haydn Ensemble Tokyo; Makoto Ohmiya. Barenreiter Musicaphon BM 30 SL 1404/5
+AR 5-81 p23

1776 Orlando Paladino. Arleen Auger, Elly Ameling, s; Gwendolyn Killebrew, ms; George Shirley, Claes Ahnsjo, t; Benjamin Luxon, Domenico Trimarchi, bar; Maurizio Mazzieri, bs; Lausanne Chamber Orchestra; Antal Dorati. Philips 6707 029 (4)
+ARG 11-77 p16
+Gr 9-77 p481
++HF 12-77 p107
+HFN 9-77 p144
++MJ 11-77 p28
+MT 2-78 p145
+NR 12-77 p9
+OC Winter 1978 p46
+ON 1-21-78 p33
+RR 9-77 p39
++SFC 8-28-77 p46
+SR 2-81 p90
++St 1-78 p79

Parthia, B flat major, E flat major. See no. 1761

Pieces, musical clock (3). See no. 4111

Pieces, musical clock: Auswahl. See no. 519

Pieces, musical clock: March. See no. 3959

Pieces, musical clock: Minuet, C major; Andante, C major; Allegretto, G major; Marcia, D major; Andante and allegro, E major; Fugue, C major; Allegro, C major. See no. 471

1777 Quartet, strings, op. 2, no. 2, E major. STRAUBE: Sonatas, nos. 1-3. John Williams, gtr; Alan Loveday, vln; Cecil Aronowitz, vla; Amaryllis Fleming, vlc; Rafael Puyana, hpd; Jordi Savall, vla da gamba. CBS 61842 Tape (c) 40-61842 (From 72678, 72948)
+Gr 1-81 p960
+HFN 1-81 p107
++HFN 3-81 p97 tape

Quartet, strings, op. 2, no. 2, E major. See no. 1589

Quartet, strings, op. 3, no. 5, F major: Andante cantabile. See no. 3695. See no. 4066

Quartet, strings, op. 3, no. 5, F major: Presto and andante cantabile. See no. 543

1778 Quartet, strings, op. 20, no. 2, C major. Quartet, strings, op. 20, no. 4, D major. Esterhazy Quartet. ABC L 67011 (also Pro Arte PAL 1018 Tape (c) PAC 1018)
+FF 11/12-81 p177
+HF 9-81 p46 tape
++IN 12-77 p28
+-MJ 2-77 p30
-MUM 11/12-81 p32
++NR 3-77 p8
++PRO 5-77 p25
-SFC 12-12-76 p55
+St 5-77 p54

1779 Quartet, strings, op. 20, no. 4, D major. Quartet, strings, op. 33, no. 3, C major. Quartet, strings, op. 76, no. 3, C major. Quartet, strings, op. 76, no. 4, B flat major. Melos Quartet. Intercord 180 802 (2)
+HFN 12-81 p95

1780 Quartet, strings, op. 20, no. 4, D major. Quartet, strings, op. 74, no. 3, G minor. Guarneri Quartet. RCA ARL 1-3485 Tape (c) ARK 1-3485
+-ARG 12-80 p33 +HF 4-81 p72
+-FF 9/10-81 p113 ++NR 7-80 p7
+Gr 3-81 p1210 +St 10-80 p114

Quartet, strings, op. 20, no. 4, D major. See no. 1778

Quartet, strings, op. 20, no. 4, D major: Un poco adagio. See no. 543

1781 Quartet, strings, op. 20, no. 5, F minor. Quartet, strings, op. 76, no. 2, D minor. Esterhazy Quartet. Telefunken 6-42354
++ARG 9-81 p22 +FF 3/4-81 p138

1782 Quartet, strings, op. 33, no. 2, E flat major. Quartet, strings, op. 76, no. 3, C major. Quartetto Italiano. Quintessence PMC 7170
+-FF 3/4-81 p138

1783 Quartet, strings, op. 33, no. 3, C major. Quartet, strings, op. 64, no. 5, D major. Smetana Quartet. Denon OX 7212
+FF 11/12-81 p178

Quartet, strings, op. 33, no. 3, C major. See no. 1779

1784 Quartet, strings, op. 50, nos. 1-6. Tatrai Quartet. Hungaroton LSPX 11934/6 (3)
++FF 3/4-81 p139 +NR 1-81 p6

1785 Quartet, strings, op. 50, no. 1, B flat major. Quartet, strings, op. 50, no. 2, C major. Tokyo String Quartet. DG 2535 464 Tape (c) 3335 464 (From 2530 444)
+-Gr 10-81 p573 ++STL 11-8-81 p40

Quartet, strings, op. 50, no. 2, C major. See no. 1785

1786 Quartets, strings, op. 51;* op. 54, nos. 1-3;* op. 55, nos. 1-3; op. 64, nos. 1-6;* op. 71, nos. 1-3; op. 74, nos. 1-3;* op. 76, nos. 1-6;* op. 77, nos. 1-2;* op. 103. Amadeus Quartet. DG 2740 250 (14) (*From 2530 213, 2530 302, 2530 090, 2530 089, 139191, 2530 089, 2530 072, 138980)
+-Gr 11-81 p714

1787 Quartet, strings, op. 54, nos. 1-2. Orlando Quartet. Philips 9500 996 Tape (c) 7300 996
++Gr 10-81 p573 ++HFN 10-81 p89

1788 Quartet, strings, op. 64, no. 5, D major. SCHUMANN: Quintet, piano, op. 44, E flat major. Kazuko Nagatomi, pno; Berlin Quartet. Denon OX 7073
+-HFN 6-81 p74

Quartet, strings, op. 64, no. 5, D major. See no. 1417. See no. 1783

Quartet, strings, op. 71, no. 3, E flat major. See no. 1830

Quartet, strings, op. 74, no. 3, G minor. See no. 1780

1789 Quartet, strings, op. 76, no. 2, D minor. Quartet, strings, op. 76, no. 4, B flat major. Collegium Aureum Quartet. Harmonia Mundi C 065 99912
+FF 11/12-81 p177 +-HFN 9-81 p80

1790 Quartet, strings, op. 76, no. 2, D minor. VRANICKY: Quartet, strings, D major. Suk Quartet. Sarastro SAR 7703
+FF 1/2-81 p126

Quartet, strings, op. 76, no. 2, D minor. See no. 1781

1791 Quartet, strings, op. 76, no. 3, C major. Quartet, strings, op. 76, no. 5, D major. Collegium Aureum Quartet. Harmonia Mundi 1C 065 99876

+-Gr 2-81 p1096 +STL 1-11-81 p38
+-HFN 1-81 p96

Quartet, strings, op. 76, no. 3, C major. See no. 1779. See no. 1782

Quartet, strings, op. 76, no. 4, B flat major. See no. 1779. See no. 1789

Quartet, strings, op. 76, no. 5, D major. See no. 1791

Quartet, strings, op. 103, B flat major: Minuet. See no. 549

1792 Il ritorno di Tobia. Barbara Hendricks, Linda Zoghby, Della Jones, s; Philip Langridge, t; Benjamin Luxon, bar; Brighton Festival Chorus; RPO; Antal Dorati. Decca D216D4 (4) Tape (c) K216K44 (also London 1445 Tape (c) 4-1445)
++FF 7/8-81 p108 +HFN 3-81 p87
+Gr 2-81 p1108 +NYT 5-24-81 pD21
++Gr 7-81 p196 tape ++St 7-81 p81
+HF 8-81 p59 ++STL 1-11-81 p38

Salve regina, G minor. See no. 1796

1793 Die Schopfung. Elisabeth Grummer, s; Joseph Traxel, t; Gottlob Frick, bs; St. Hedwig's Cathedral Choir; BeSO; Karl Forster. Pathe 2C 181 29144/5 (2)
++FF 11/12-81 p174

1794 Die Schopfung. Edith Mathis, s; Catherine Denly, ms; Aldo Baldin, t; Dietrich Fischer-Dieskau, bar; Nicholas Kramer, hpd; AMF and Chorus; Neville Marriner. Philips 6769 047 (2) Tape (c) 7699 154
++ARG 11-81 p52 ++HFN 1-81 p95
++FF 7/8-81 p107 ++MT 10-81 p677
+Gr 1-81 p978 +-NR 6-81 p8
+Gr 7-81 p196 tape ++NYT 5-24-81 pD21
+HF 12-81 p93 tape

Die Schopfung: Now heaven in fullest glory. See no. 4077

La scuola de gelosi: Dice benissimo. See no. 1752

1795 The seven last words of Christ, op. 71. Quatuor Danois. Astree MB 313
/FF 11/12-81 p178

1796 The seven last words of Christ. Salve regina, G minor. Veronika Kincses, s; Klara Takacs, con; Gyorgy Korondy, t; Jozsef Gregor, bs; Issvan Lantos, org; Budapest Chorus; Hungarian State Symphony Orchestra; Janos Ferencsik. Hungaroton SLPX 12199/200(2)
++FF 5/6-81 p89 +-HFN 1-81 p95
/GR 12-80 p865 +NR 3-81 p9
+-HF 5-81 p58 +-St 8-81 p95

Sinfonia concertante, op. 84, B flat major. See no. 1757. See no. 1812

Sonata, piano, E flat major. See no. 3952

1797 Sonatas, piano, nos. 20, 23, 26, 32, 34, 43, 46. Malcolm Bilson, fortepiano. Titanic TI 51/2 Tape (c) Advent E 1068 (Nos 20, 23, 32, 43)
+AR 8-81 p78 +HF 1-81 p61
+FF 1/2-81 p123 +NYT 10-19-80 pD24
+HF 8-79 p53 +St 1-81 p84

1798 Sonatas, piano, no. 20, C minor. Sonata, piano, no. 49, E flat major. Alfred Brendel, pno. Philips 9500 774 Tape (c) 7300 862
++CL 12-81 p44 ++NR 6-81 p13

+FF 5/6-81 p90 +NYT 5-24-81 pD21
++Gr 8-81 p295 ++SFC 4-12-81 p21
+HFN 8-81 p85 ++St 9-81 p94

Sonata, piano, no. 33, C minor. See no. 3723
Sonata, piano, no. 42, D major. See no. 53
Sonata, piano, no. 48, C major. See no. 1344
Sonata, piano, no. 49, E flat major. See no. 1798

1799 Sonatas, piano, nos. 60-62. Paul Badura-Skoda, pianoforte. Astree AS 83
++FF 11/12-81 p179 +HFN 10-81 p89
++Gr 9-81 p412

1800 Songs: Abschiedslied; Als einst mit Weibes Schonheit; An Iris; An Thyrsis; Auch die sprodeste der Schonen; Auf meines Vaters Grab; Bald wehen uns des Fruhlings Lufte; Beim Schmerz der dieses Herz durchwuhlet; Content; Cupido; Das Leben ist ein Traum; Das strickende Madchen; Der Gleichsinn; Der erste Kuss; Der Schlaue und dienstfertige Pudel; Despair; Die Landlust; Die Verlassene; Die zu spate Ankuft der Mutter; Eine sehr Bewohnliche Geschichte; Fidelity; Gegenliebe; Geistliches Lied; Gott erhalte den Kaiser; Jeder meint der Gegenstand; Lachet nicht Madchen; The lady's looking glass; Lob der Faulheit; Liebeslied; The mermaid's song; Minna; A pastoral song; Piercing eyes; Pleasing pain; Pensi a me si fido amante; O liebes Madchen hore mich; O tuneful voice; O fliess ja wallend fliess in Zahren; Recollection; The sailor's song; She never told her love; The spirit's song; Sympathy; Trachten will ich nicht auf Erden; Trost unglucklicher Liebe; Un tetto umil; The wanderer; Zufriedenheit. Elly Ameling, s; Jorg Demus, pno. Philips 6769 064 (3)
+Gr 12-81 p923

Songs: Schottische und Walisische Lieder. See no. 640
Songs: The lady's looking glass; Lord Cathcart's welcome home; My mother bids me bind my hair; The mermaid's song; The white cockade; Will ye go on to Flanders; The birks of Abergeldie; The flowers of Edinburgh; Up in the morning early. See no. 1830
Suite, E flat major. See no. 1761

1801 Symphonies, nos. 1-2, 4, 10, 15, 18, 37. L'Estro Armonico; Derek Solomons. Saga HAYDN 1
+Gr 4-81 p1316 +MT 8-8. p539
+HFN 4-81 p71 +STL 4-12-81 p40

1802 Symphonies, nos. 17, 27, 45. Baden Baden Ensemble 13; Manfred Reichert. Harmonia Mundi 1C 065 99900
+Gr 10-81 p551

1803 Symphony, no. 31, D major. Symphony, no. 73, D major. AMF; Neville Marriner. Philips 9500 518 Tape (c) 7300 674
++ARG 5-80 p25 +HFN 9-79 p123 tape
+Audio 12-79 p101 +NYT 2-3-80 pD22
+Gr 7-79 p199 +ON 3-80 p4
+Gr 9-79 p534 tape +RR 7-79 p57
+HF 6-81 p69 ++SFC 8-31-80 p31
+HFN 7-79 p105 +St 3-80 p95

1804 Symphony, no. 40, F major. Symphonies, nos. 93-98, RPO; Thomas Beecham. Arabesque 8024/3 (3) Tape (c) 9024/3 (From Capitol GCR 7127)
++ARG 7/8-81 p17 +NR 12-80 p4

+-FF 3/4-81 p140 +NYT 5-24-81 pD21
+HF 5-81 p53 tape +SFC 3-1-81 p19
++HF 6-81 p58

Symphony, no. 40, F major. See no. 4122

1805 Symphony, no. 45, F sharp minor. Symphony, no. 48, C major. Symphony, no. 88, G major. Symphony, no. 92, G major. Stuttgart Chamber Orchestra; Karl Munchinger. Intercord INT 180 836 (2)
+-FF 7/8-81 p110 +-NYT 3-29-81 pD31
+HFN 12-81 p95

1806 Symphony, no. 46, B major. Symphony, no. 48, G major. ECO; Daniel Barenboim. DG 2531 324 Tape (c) 3301 324
++FF 11/12-81 p179 +HFN 8-81 p85
+-Gr 8-81 p270 +HFN 9-81 p93 tape

Symphony, no. 47, G major. See no. 1806
Symphony, no. 48, C major. See no. 1805
Symphony, no. 73, D major. See no. 1803

1807 Symphonies, nos. 82-87. BPhO; Herbert von Karajan. DG 2741 005 (3) Tape (c) 3382 005
+-Gr 9-81 p383 +-HFN 11-81 p105 tape
+-HFN 10-81 p87

1808 Symphonies, nos. 82-87. BeSO; Kurt Sanderling. Eurodisc 85961 (3)
+-FF 11/12-81 p179 +-NYT 7-26-81 pD23
+-HF 6-74 p84

1809 Symphony, no. 82, C major. Symphony, no. 83, G minor. Collegium Aureum; Franzjosef Maier. Harmonia Mundi 1C 065 99762 (also Pro Arte PAL 1001 Tape (c) PAC 1001)
+FF 7/8-81 p111 +-RR 4-80 p64
/Gr 5-80 p1665 ++SFC 5-31-81 p22
+HF 8-81 p60 +St 8-81 p95
+-HFN 3-80 p91

1810 Symphony, no. 82, C major. Symphony, no. 83, G minor. AMF; Neville Marriner. Philips 9500 519 Tape (c) 7300 675
++ARG 2-80 p33 +HFN 2-80 p88
+FF 1/2-80 p93 ++NR 1-80 p3
++Gr 5-79 p1894 +NYT 2-3-80 pD22
+HF 6-81 p69 +RR 5-79 p58
+HFN 5-79 p123 +-RR 9-79 p134 tape
+HFN 7-79 p119 tape

Symphony, no. 83, G minor. See no. 1809. See no. 1810

1811 Symphony, no. 86, D major. Symphony, no. 98, B flat major. COA; Colin Davis. Philips 9500 678 Tape (c) 7300 773
++ARG 3-81 p29 +HF 6-81 p69 tape
++FF 1/2-81 p127 +HFN 12-80 p140
++Gr 12-80 p832 +HFN 3-81 p97 tape
+Gr 4-81 p1376 tape +-NR 12-80 p3
+HF 6-81 p58 ++St 12-80 p126

1812 Symphonies, nos. 88-92. Sinfonia concertante, op. 84, B flat major. Naples Orchestra; Denis Vaughan. Arabesque 8048 (3) Tape (c) 9048 (From RCA LSC 6805)
+ARG 9-81 p20 +SFC 5-31-81 p22
/NR 6-81 p4

Symphony, no. 88, G major. See no. 1805. See no. 3781

1813 Symphony, no. 92, G major. Symphony, no. 104, D major. AMF; Neville Marriner. Philips 9500 304 Tape (c) 7300 593 (r) G 9500 304

+Audio 4-79 p81
+-Gr 11-78 p878
+Gr 2-79 p1472 tape
+HF 2-81 p81 tape
+-HFN 10-78 p125
+-HFN 12-78 p171 tape
++MJ 12-78 p45
+-NR 9-78 p3
+-RR 10-78 p71
+-RR 5-79 p109 tape
+SFC 6-25-78 p61

1814 Symphony, no. 92, G major. Symphony, no. 103, E flat major. MOZART: Symphony, no. 25, K 183, G minor. Symphony, no. 29, K 201, A major. BRSO; Lorin Maazel. Quintesence 2PMC 2709 (2) (from PMC 7149/57)
-FF 3/4-81 p166
+-HF 6-81 p58

1815 Symphony, no. 92, G major. Symphony, no. 103, E flat major. BRSO; Lorin Maazel. Quintessence PMC 7157 Tape (c) 7157
+-ARG 9-81 p21
-FF 11/12-80 p121

Symphony, no. 92, G major. See no. 1805

Symphonies, nos. 93-98. See no. 1804

1816 Symphonies, nos. 93-104. LPO; Eugen Jochum. DG 2720 091 (6) (From 2720 064)
+FF 9/10-81 p114

Symphony, no. 93, D major. See no. 652

1817 Symphony, no. 94, G major. Symphony, no. 103, E flat major. Collegium Aureum. Harmonia Mundi 1C 065 99873 (also Pro Arte PAL 1005 Tape (c) PAC 1005)
+FF 11/12-80 p122
+FF 7/8-81 p111
/Gr 2-81 p1088
+HF 8-81 p60
+-HFN 1-81 p95
+MUM 7/8-81 p35
+-ST 6-81 p124

1818 Symphony, no. 94, G major. Symphony, no. 103, E flat major. Collegium Aureum; Franzjosef Maier. Pro Arte PAL 1005 Tape (c) PAC 1005
++St 8-81 p95

Symphony, no. 94, G major. See no. 1830

Symphony, no. 98, B flat major. See no. 1811

Symphony, no. 99, E flat major. See no. 652

1819 Symphony, no. 100, G major. Mostly Mozart Orchestra; Johannes Somary. Vanguard VS 25000
+ARG 1-81 p32
+Audio 3-81 p66
+FF 11/12-80 p122
+-NR 8-80 p4
+SR 1-81 p92
+St 10-80 p116

1820 Symphony, no. 100, G major. Symphony, no. 103, E flat major. Mostly Mozart Orchestra; Johannes Somary. Vanguard VA 25007
+FF 7/8-81 p111
+NR 5-81 p6
+St 9-81 p94

1821 Symphony, no. 101, D major. Symphony, no. 102, B flat major. COA; Colin Davis. Philips 9500 679 Tape (c) 7300 774
++FF 1/2-81 p127
++Gr 7-81 p154
++Gr 10-81 p614 tape
+HF 6-81 p58
+HFN 8-81 p85
+HFN 10-81 p95 tape
++NR 12-80 p2
++St 1-81 p85

Symphony, no. 102, B flat major. See no. 1821

Symphony, no. 103, E flat major. See no. 1814. See no. 1815. See no. 1817. See no. 1818. See no. 1820

Symphony, no. 104, D major. See no. 652. See no. 1813

1822 Trios, baryton, D major (2), D minor, C major, B minor. Baryton Trio. DG 2533 405 Tape (c) 3310 405

+ARG 7-79 p34 ++NR 7-79 p10
++FF 9/10-79 p94 ++RR 5-79 p76
+Gr 4-79 p1735 +SFC 7-15-79 p47
+-HF 4-80 p138 tape +ST 1-81 p649
+HFN 4-79 p123

1823 Trios, baryton, nos. 63-64, 82, 87, 88, 107, 110. Esterhazy Baryton Trio. HMV SQS 1424
++FF 1/2 - 81 p121 +MT 8-81 p540
++Gr 9-80 p359 +ST 1-81 p649
+HFN 10-80 p105

1824 Trios, baryton, nos. 87, 97, 101, 111. John Hsu, baryton; David Miller, vla; Fortunato Arico, vlc. Musical Heritage Society MHS 4354
+FF 11/12-81 p180 +MUM 9/10-81 p31

1825 Trios, flute (3). Paul Badura Skoda, pno; Amphion Quartet. Spectrum Tape (c) SC 205
*HF 9-81 p46 tape

Trio, 2 flutes and violoncello, no. 2, G major: Allegro, O tuneful voice. See no. 1830

1826 Trios, piano, G major (2), D major, D minor. Mozartean Players. Arabesque 8123-2 (2) Tape (c) 9123-2
+HF 7-81 p60 ++St 6-81 p115
+-NR 5-81 p8

1827 Trios, piano, nos. 1, 6, 37, 39. Beaux Arts Trio. Philips 9500 657 (From 6768 077)
+FF 3/4-80 p99 +NYT 2-3-80 pD22
+Gr 1-81 p960 +-RR 4-80 p85
++HFN 4-80 p119 ++SFC 12-23-79 p40
+-NR 2-80 p7

1828 Trios, piano, no. 1, C major; no. 41, G major. Beaux Arts Trio. Philips 9500 658 (From 6768 077)
++FF 7/8-80 p99 ++NR 5-80 p7
+Gr 1-81 p960 ++SFC 8-31-80 p31
+HFN 12-80 p153

1829 Trio, piano, no. 16, D major. Trio, piano, no. 27, C major. Emil Gilels, pno; Leonid Kogan, vln; Mstislav Rostropovitch, vlc. Saga STXID 5311 (Reissue)
++FF 9/10-81 p115 +-RR 5-73 p75
+-HFN 7-80 p117 ++RR 7-80 p72

Trio, piano, no. 18, A major. See no. 1830
Trio, piano, no. 27, C major. See no. 715. See no. 1829
Variations, F minor. See no. 717
La vera costanza: Spann deine lange Ohren. See no. 1752

1830 Works, selections: Country dance. Quartet, strings, op. 71, no. 3, E flat major. Songs: The lady's looking glass; Lord Cathcart's welcome home; My mother bids me bind my hair; The mermaid's song; The white cockade; Will ye go on to Flanders; The Birks of Abergeldie; The flowers of Edinburgh; Up in the morning early. Symphony, no. 94, G major (arr. Salomon). Trio, piano, no. 18, A major. Trio, 2 flutes and violoncello, no. 2, G major: Allegro, O tuneful voice. Academy of Ancient Music. Folio Society FS 1005/6 (2)
+Gr 1-81 p977 +HFN 10-80 p140

1831 Works, selections: Contredanses with quadrille. Deutsche Tanze, nos. 1-6. Divertimento, no. D5, D major. Die Jahreszeiten:

Landler. Minuet da ballo, nos. 1-6. Zingarese, nos. 1-8. Ensemble Bella Musica Vienna; Michael Dittrich. Harmonia Mundi HM 1057
+FF 9/10-81 p115 +-HFN 8-81 p85
+Gr 8-81 p270
Zingarese, nos. 1-8. See no. 1831
HAYDN, Michael
1832 Concerto, horn, D major. STAMITZ: Concerto, horn, E major. TEYBER: Concerto, horn, E flat major. Hermann Baumann, hn; PH; Yoav Talmi. Telefunken 6-42418
+-FF 11/12-80 p214 ++NR 2-81 p6
Divertimento. See no. 125
1833 Graduale in festo SS Innocentium die Dominica. Graduale in festo SS Innocentium extra Dominica. Vesperae in festo SS Innocentium. Krisztina Laki, Adrienne Csengery, s; Zsuzsa Nemeth, alto; Gyor Girls Choir; Gyor Philharmonic Orchestra; Miklos Szabo. Budapest FX 12301 (From Hungaroton SLPX 11531)
++FF 9/10-81 p116 +-HFN 4-81 p81
+Gr 8-81 p302
Graduale in festo SS Innocentium extra Dominica. See no. 1833
Polonaise, C major. See no. 4096
Quartet, P 115, C major. See no. 125
Turkish march. See no. 1605
Vesperae in festo SS Innocentium. See no. 1833
Zaire: Incidental music. See no. 1605
HAYNE
Loving shepherd of thy sheep. See no. 3618
HEATH, John
Verse service: Magnificat. See no. 3615
HEIDEN, Bernard
1834 Quintet, horn and string quartet. MOZART: Quintet, horn, K 407, E flat major. Mason Jones, Fr hn; Philarte Quartet. Gasparo GS 207
/-ARG 4-81 p30 ++IN 7-81 p29
+-FF 11/12-80 p140 +NR 8-80 p10
Sinfonia, woodwind quintet. See no. 1101
HELLER, Duane
John Barleycorn. See no. 1383
John Barleycorn variations. See no. 1383
HELPS, Robert
1835 Symphony, no. 1.* THOMSON: Symphony, no. 3, New Hampshire Symphony Orchestra, Columbia Symphony Orchestra; James Bolle, Zoltan Rozsnyai. CRI SD 411 (*From Columbia MS 6801)
+ARG 1-81 p43
Valse mirage. See no. 3942
HELSTED, Eduard
1836 Flower festival at Genzano: Pas de deux. LOVENSKJOLD: La sylphide. PAULLI: The Kermesse in Bruges: Slovanka; Pas de deux. Copenhagen Philharmonic Orchestra; Ole Schmidt. EMI 6C 165 39262/3 (2)
+-FF 9/10-81 p292 +RR 7-80 p53
+-Gr 8-80 p221
HEMBERG, Eskil
Epitaffio per organo, op. 34. See no. 3992

HENDERSON, William

1837 The heart has its own memory. Quintet, brass instruments. Songs: Love's answer; Valentine songs; Take o take; Live with me and be my love; How should I your true love know. Suite, harp and flute. Thematic encounters. Kathleen Riggs, s; Modern Brass Quintet; Barbara Poper, pno; Nils Oliver, vlc; Anton Sen, vln; Dorothy Ashby, hp; Cheryl Grant, flt. Orion ORS 80399
+ARG 10-81 p24 +NR 7-81 p5
+FF 7/8-81 p113

Quintet, brass instruments. See no. 1837

Songs: Love's answer; Valentine songs; Take o take; Live with me and be my love; How should I your true love know. See no. 1837

Suite, harp and flute. See no. 1837

Thematic encounters. See no. 1837

HENNAGIN, Michael

Songs: Crossing the Han River; Walking on the green grass. See no. 3951

HENRY VIII, King

Consorts IV, XII. See no. 4092

1838 Songs: Adew madam et ma mastres; Alac alac what shall I do; Alas what shall I do for love; En vray amoure; Gentil prince de Renom; Helas madam; If love now reynyd; Lusti youth shuld us ensue; O my hart; Pastyme with good companye; Taunder naken; The tyme of youthe; Without dyscord; Whoso what wyll all feattes optayne; Whoso that will for grace sew; Thow that men do call it dotage; Consort II-XVI, XXII-XXIII. St. George Canzona. Desto DC 7187 (From Oryx EXP 57, Musical Heritage Society MHS 1530)
+-ARG 2-81 p48

Songs: En vray amoure. See no. 4092

Songs: If love now reigned. See no. 4092

Songs: Pastime with good company. See no. 3853

HENSEL

Young Dietrich. See no. 4077

HENZE, Hans Werner

Kammermusik, 1958: Tentos (3). See no. 3870

HEPPENER, Robert

Canzona. See no. 3729

HERBECK, Johann Ritter von

Pueri concinite. See no. 3999

HERBERT, Victor

Eileen: Thine alone. See no. 3640

Mlle. Modiste: Kiss me again. See no. 4042

Natoma: No country can my own outvie. See no. 3967

Naughty Marietta: Italian street song; Ah sweet mystery of life. See no. 3640

Sweethearts: Sweethearts. See no. 3640

HERITTE-VIARDOT, Louise

Quartet: Serenade. See no. 3814

HERMANN DE MONCH VON SALZBURG

Das Taghorn. See no. 3896

HEROLD, Louis

Pre aux clercs: Enfin me voila donc dans cette ville. See no. 4051

Zampa: Perche tremar. See no. 4024

HERVE (Ronger, Florimond)

Mam'zelle Nitouche: Couplets de l'inspecteur. See no. 4051

HEUBERGER, Richard

Der Opernball: Overture. See no. 3964

HEWITT-JONES, Tony

Fanfare. See no. 3822

HILDACH

Der Lenz. See no. 3988

HILLER, Lejaren

1839 A portfolio for diverse performers. MASLANKA: Pieces, clarinet and piano (3). YTTREHUS: Quintet. Philip Rehfeldt, clt; Barney Childs, pno; Gregg Smith Singers; Speculum Musicae Members; Gregg Smith. CRI SD 438
+-NR 8-81 p7

HILLER, Wilfried

Muspilli. See no. 4119

HINDEMITH, Paul

Chamber music, no. 7, op. 46, no. 2. See no. 1565

1840 Concert music, piano, brass and harps, op. 49. Concerto music, strings and brass, op. 50. Morgenmusik. Philip Jones Ensemble; Paul Crossley, pno; Elgar Howarth. Argo ZRDL 1000
+Gr 11-81 p690 ++STL 11-8-81 p40
+HFN 11-81 p94

Concert music, strings and brass, op. 50. See no. 1840

1841 Concerto, violoncello. PIZZETTI: Concerto, violoncello, C major. Enrico Mainardi, vlc; Orchestra; Carlo Maria Giulini, Carlo Zecchi. Rococo 2091
/NR 3-81 p5

Four temperaments: Theme and variations. See no. 4020

1842 In einer Nacht, op. 15. Tanzstucke, op. 19. Suite, op. 26. Hans Petermandl, pno. Supraphon 111 2476
+ARG 6-81 p28 +-NR 1-81 p14
++FF 3/4-81 p141 +SFC 6-14-81 p18
++HF 5-81 p59

1843 Kleine Kammermusik, op. 24, no. 1; op. 36, nos. 2-5; op. 46, nos. 6-7. Maria Bermann, pno; Martin Ostertag, vlc; Wolfgang Hock, vln; Ulrich Koch, vla, vla d'amore; Maria Schuster, org; Ensemble 13 Baden Baden; Manfred Reichert. Harmonia Mundi 1C 99721/3 (3)
+FF 5/6-81 p90 +-HFN 3-79 p124
+Gr 5-79 p1906 +RR 4-79 p84

Kleine Kammermusik, op. 24, no. 2. See no. 1531

1844 Mathis der Maler symphony (arr. for piano). Sonata, piano, 4 hands. Karl-Heinz and Michael Schluter, pno. Da Camera SM 93153
+FF 11/12-81 p181

Morgenmusik. See no. 1840

Morgenmusik: Acht Stucke. See no. 835

1845 Nobilissima visione: Meditation. Sonata, solo viola, op. 11, no. 5. Sonata, solo viola, op. 25, no. 1. Sonata, viola and piano, op. 11, no. 4. Karel Spelina, Josef Kodousek, vla; Karel Friesl, Jan Novotny, pno. Supraphon 111 2271/2 (2)
+-FF 9/10-81 p116 +NR 4-80 p7
+Gr 6-80 p44 +RR 7-80 p80
+HFN 7-80 p107 +ST 5-81 p43

Der Schwanendreher. See no. 402
1846 Sonata, clarinet and piano. POULENC: Sonata, clarinet and bassoon. Sonata, clarinet and piano. Thomas Kelly, clt; Martin Gatt, bsn; Leslie Pearson, pno. Merlin MRF 80701
+FF 5/6-81 p129 +-HFN 8-81 p85
+-Gr 6-81 p50 +St 5-81 p88
1847 Sonatas, organ (3). Elisabeth Ullmann, org. Telefunken 6-42575
++FF 1/2-81 p129 ++St 5-81 p76
++HF 5-81 p59
Sonatas, organ, nos. 1-3. See no. 1494
Sonata, organ, no. 3. See no. 235
Sonata, piano, 4 hands. See no. 1844
Sonata, trombone and piano. See no. 1263
Sonata, trumpet and piano. See no. 43
Sonata, solo viola, op. 11, no. 5. See no. 1845
Sonata, solo viola, op. 25, no. 1. See no. 1845
Sonata, viola and piano, op. 11, no. 4. See no. 1845
Sonata, violoncello and piano, op. 11, no. 3. See no. 1848
1848 Sonata, solo violoncello, op. 25, no. 3. Sonata, violoncello and piano, op. 11, no. 3. Variations on "A frog he went a-courting". Nancy Donaruma, vlc; Zita Carno, pno. Musical Heritage Society MHS 4306
++FF 5/6-81 p93
Suite, op. 26. See no. 1842
1849 Symphonic metamorphoses on themes by Weber. SCHOENBERG: Verklarte Nacht, op. 4. CPhO; Gaetano Delogu, Vaclav Neumann. Quintessence PMC 7177
+FF 9/10-81 p117
Symphonic metamorphoses on themes by Weber. See no. 2556
Tanzstucke, op. 19. See no. 1842
Variations on "A frog he went a-courting". See no. 1848

HIROTA
Shikararete. See no. 3696

HODDINOTT, Alun
1850 Symphony, no. 2, op. 29. Variants for orchestra, op. 47. LSO; Norman Del Mar. Oriel ORM 1003 (From Pye TPLS 13013)
+Gr 3-81 p1194
Variants for orchestra, op. 47. See no. 1850

HODKINSON, Sydney
Dance variations on a Chopin fragment. See no. 8
1851 The edge of the olde one. PERSICHETTI: Concerto, English horn, op. 137. Thomas Stacy, hn; New York String Orchestra, Eastman Musica Nova; Vincent Persichetti, Paul Phillips. Grenadilla GS 1048
+ARG 3-81 p38 +HF 11-80 p72
+-FF 9/10-80 p178 +-NR 7-80 p4
Fresco. See no. 1267
November voices. See no. 461

HOFFERT, Paul
1852 Concerto, contemporary violin. STRAVINSKY: L'Histoire du soldat. Stephen Staryk, vln; Orchestra; Paul Hoffert. UltraFi ULDD 12
+Gr 3-81 p1194 +HFN 1-81 p101

HOFFMANN, Johann
Concerto, mandolin, D major. See no. 1748

HOFFMANN, Richard
In memoriam patris. See no. 1638
HOFFMEISTER, Franz Anton
1853 Concerto, flute, D major. ALBRECHTSBERGER: Partita, harp, F major. Janos Szebenyi, flt; Anna Lelkes, hp; Gyor Philharmonic Orchestra; Janos Sandor. Budapest FX 12299 (From Hungaroton SLPX 11454)
/FF 9/10-81 p118 +-Gr 6-81 p33
Concerto, flute, D major. See no. 38
Concerto, flute, no. 6, D major. See no. 95
Symphonie concertante, E flat major, B flat major. See no. 3794
HOFHAIMER, Paul
Recordare. See no. 4094
Songs: Carmen in re; Carmen magistri Pauli; Cupido; Der Hundt; Man hat bisher; Greiner zanner; Nach willen dein. See no. 3862
Songs: Herzliestes pild; Maecenas atavis; Ohn freud. See no. 3896
Tandernaken. See no. 3777
HOIBY, Lee
Summer and smoke: Anatomy lesson and scene. See no. 3932
HOLBORNE, Anthony 1854
Almayne. See no. 1854
As it fell upon holy eve. See no. 1854. See no. 4092
The choise. See no. 4092
Dances (5). See no. 3853
Ecce quam bonum. See no. 1854
Faerie round. See no. 4092
The funerals. See no. 1854
Galliard. See no. 4002
Galliards (3). See no. 1854
Galliards, nos. 1 and 2. See no. 3798
Galliard "Lullabie". See no. 4092
Heigh ho holiday. See no. 1854
Heres paternus. See no. 1854
The honeysuckle. See no. 1854. See no. 4002
The image of melancholly. See no. 1854
Infernum. See no. 1854
Muylinda. See no. 1854. See no. 4002
Night watch. See no. 4002
Paradizo. See no. 1854
Pavan. See no. 1854. See no. 4002. See no. 4092
Pavana ploravit. See no. 1854
Sic semper soleo. See no. 1854
The sighes. See no. 1854
Songs: My heavie sprite oppress'd with sorrow's might. See no. 3946
Suite of Elizabethan dances: The honie-suckle; Wanton; The fruit of love; The choise; The fairie-round. See no. 3798
The widowes myte. See no. 3762
1854 Works, selections: Almayne. As it fell on holy eve. Ecce quam bonum. The funerals. Galliards (3). Heres paternus. Heigh ho holiday. The honey-suckle. The iamge of melancholly. Infernum. Muylinda. Paradizo. Pavan. Pavana ploravit. Sic semper soleo. The sighes. Consorte of Musicke, Guildhall Waits; Anthony Rooley, Trevor Jones. L'Oiseau-Lyre DSLO 569
+FF 3/4-81 p142 +HFN 9-80 p105
+-Gr 10-80 p511

HOLDRIDGE, Lee
1855 Concerto, violin, no. 2. Lazarus and his beloved. Glenn Dicterow, LSO; Lee Holdridge. Varese VCDM 100040
+Gr 10-81 p552 +HFN 10-81 p88
Lazarus and his beloved. See no. 1855
HOLLER
1856 Fantasie, op. 49. KAMINSKI: Canzone. REGER: Romanze. RHEINBERGER: Suite, op. 150: Gigue; Theme and variations. Suite, op. 166, C major. Josef Sepsei, vln; Rolf Schonstedt, org. Impromptu SM 192921
+-FF 9/10-81 p259
HOLLIGER, Heinz
1857 Chaconne. Die Jahreszeiten. Quartet, strings. Bern String Quartet; Schola Cantorum Stuttgart; Clytus Gottwald; Walter Grimmer, vlc. Wergo WER 60084
-FF 9/10-81 p118 ++Gr 8-81 p284
Die Jahreszeiten. See no. 1857
Quartet, strings. See no. 1857
HOLMBOE, Vagn
Triade, op. 123. See no. 1110
HOLST, Gustav
1858 Brook green. Somerset rhapsody, op. 21. VAUGHAN WILLIAMS: The wasps. Bournemouth Sinfonietta; Norman Del Mar. HMV ASD 3953 Tape (c) TC ASD 3953
+Gr 2-81 p1091 +-HFN 4-81 p72
Christmas day. See no. 3818
1859 Hammersmith, op. 52. Suite no. 1, op. 28, no. 1, E flat major. Suite, no. 2, op. 28, no. 2, F major. VAUGHAN WILLIAMS: English folk song suite. Toccata marziale. London Wind Orchestra; Denis Wick. Enigma K 53565 (also Nonesuch N 78002, also ASV ACA 1002 Tape (c) ZCACA 1002)
+ARG 4-81 p25 +Gr 6-81 p38
/-Audio 12-81 p24 ++SFC 9-21-80 p21
+FF 1/2-81 p129 +-St 1-81 p89
+-Gr 12-78 p1117
1860 The planets, op. 32. PhO; Ambrosian Singers; Simon Rattle. Angel DS 37817 (also HMV ASD 4047 Tape (c) TCC ASD 4047)
++FF 7/8-81 p114 +HFN 7-81 p73
+-Gr 7-81 p154 +HFN 10-81 p95 tape
+Gr 8-81 p324 tape +MUM 11/12-81 p32
1861 The planets, op. 32. Vancouver Cantata Singers; Vancouver Symphony Orchestra; Kazuyoshi Akiyama. CBS SM 5002
+-MUM 7/8-81 p32
1862 The planets, op. 32. NYP; Leonard Bernstein. CBS MY 37226
-NR 11-81 p3
1863 The planets, op. 32. Scottish National Orchestra and Chorus; Alexander Gibson. Chandos ABRD 1010 Tape (c) ABTD 1010
++ARG 5-81 p55 ++HF 2-81 p67
+FF 7/8-81 p114 ++HFN 11-80 p120
+Gr 11-80 p671 +HFN 1-81 p109 tape
+Gr 2-81 p1122 tape ++St 4-81 p106
1864 The planets, op. 32. LPO and Chorus; Bernard Hermann. Contour CC 7518 Tape (c) CCT 7518
-Gr 8-81 p316
1865 The planets, op. 32. BPhO; Herbert von Karajan. DG 2532 019

+Gr 9-81 p386
+Gr 11-81 p783 tape
+-HF 11-81 p80
+HFN 9-81 p80
++HFN 11-81 p105 tape
++SFC 11-1-81 p18
+-St 12-81 p116
+STL 9-13-81 p41

1866 The planets, op. 32. LPO and Chorus; Georg Solti. Mobile Fidelity MFSL 1-510 (From London CS 7110)
+-HF 11-81 p80
+NR 9-81 p3
+SFC 8-9-81 p18

1867 The planets, op. 32. Ambrosian Singers; COA; Neville Marriner. Philips 9500 425 Tape (c) 7300 643 (r) G 9500 425
++ARG 2-79 p18
++FF 1/2-79 p57
+Gr 8-78 p331
+-Gr 11-78 p963 tape
+HF 2-79 p76
++HF 11-80 p88
+-HFN 8-78 p103
+HFN 10-78 p139 tape
+MJ 12-78 p45
+-NR 10-78 p2
+NYT 2-15-81 pD21 tape
+RR 8-78 p59
+RR 11-78 p113 tape
+SFC 7-16-78 p50

1868 The planets, op. 32. New England Conservatory Chorus; BSO; Seiji Ozawa. Philips 9500 782 Tape (c) 7300 856
+-HF 11-81 p80
+-HFN 6-81 p74
+-HFN 9-81 p93 tape
+-MUM 11/12-81 p32
+NR 8-81 p5
+-SFC 8-16-81 p19
+St 12-81 p116

1869 The planets, op. 32. Mendelssohn Club Chorus, Women's Voices; PO; Eugene Ormandy. RCA AGL 1-3885 Tape (c) GK 1-3885 (From RL 1-1797)
+-FF 7/8-81 p114
+Gr 8-81 p274
+-HFN 8-81 p92 tape

1870 The planets, op. 32. St. Louis Symphony Orchestra; Walter Susskind. Vox Turnabout (Q) QTVS 34598 DBS SS 3002 Tape (c) KTVC 34598
+Audio 12-81 p67
-Gr 4-77 p1549
+-HF 4-76 p111
+-HFN 12-76 p155 tape
+HFN 2-77 p121
++NR 12-75 p3
+-RR 2-77 p47
+-RR 2-77 p97 tape
++SFC 11-16-75 p32

The planets, op. 32: Venus; Mercury. See no. 4003
Somerset rhapsody, op. 21. See no. 1858
Suite, no. 1, op. 28, E flat major. See no. 247. See no. 1859
Suite, no. 2, op. 28, F major. See no. 247. See no. 1859

HOLZBAUER, Ignaz
Sinfonia, op. 4, no. 3, E flat major. See no. 3782

HOMILIUS, Gottfried August
1871 Chorales: Straf mich nicht in deinem Zorn; Wer nur den lieben Gott; Schmucke dick o liebe Seele; Mien Gott das Herz bring ich dir; Dies sind die heiligen zehn Gebote; Wer nur den lieben Gott lasst walten; Mache dich mein Geist bereit; Christ lag in Todesbanden; Hilft Herr Jesu lass gelingen; Wir Christenleute; Sei Lob und Ehr dem hochsten Gut; Erbarm dich mein o Herr Gott; Christ lag in Todesbanden; O Grosser Gott du reines Wesen; Wo soll ich fliehen hin. Trio, G major. Georges Guillard, org. Arion ARN 38552
+Gr 6-81 p60

Trio, G major. See no. 1871

HONEGGER, Arthur
1872 Concertino, piano. POULENC: Aubade. ROUSSEL: Concerto, piano, op. 36, G major. Boris Krajny, pno; PCO; Stanislav Macura. Supraphon 410 2705
+-FF 9/10-81 p244 +-NR 6-81 p7
+-Gr 10-81 p552 +SFC 8-23-81 p18
+HFN 8-81 p90
1873 Concerto, violoncello. SHOSTAKOVICH: Concerto, violoncello, no. 1, op. 107, E flat major. Milos Sadlo, vlc; CPhO; Vaclav Neumann, Karel Ancerl. Supraphon 110 0604
+Gr 3-81 p1194 +-HFN 3-81 p95
1874 Concerto da camera. STRAUSS, R.: Duet-concertino. Los Angeles Chamber Orchestra; Gerard Schwarz. Nonesuch D 79018
+SFC 10-4-81 p17
Danse de la chevre. See no. 3914. See no. 3928. See no. 3934
1875 La danse des morts. Jean Davy, narrator; Claudine Collart, s; Anne Seghers, alto; Michel Piquemal, bar; Roland de Lassus Vocal Ensemble; Youth Orchestra Douau and Hauts-de-France; Henri Vachey. Calliope CAL 1855
+FF 9/10-81 p119 ++NR 9-81 p12
1876 Pacific 231. IBERT: Divertissement. POULENC: Les biches: Suite. SATIE (orch. Debussy): Gymnopiedies. Birmingham Symphony Orchestra; Louis Fremaux. Arabesque 8035
+-FF 5/6-81 p218 +SFC 2-8-81 p21
+NR 1-81 p2
Pacific 231. See no. 1878. See no. 4003
1877 Poemes (4). SATIE: La diva de l'empire; Dapheneo; Le chapelier; Je te veux; La statue de bronze; Tendrement. SCHMITT: Chants, op. 98 (3); Poemes de Ronsard, op. 100 (4). Yolanda Marcoulescou, s; Katja Phillabum, pno. Orion ORS 76240
+ARG 4-77 p30 +NR 4-77 p12
+Gr 9-81 p427 ++NYT 6-5-77 pD19
+HF 4-77 p116 +ON 7-77 p29
Sonata, solo violin. See no. 450
Songs: Les cloches; Clotilde; Le delphinium. See no. 3687
1878 Symphonies, nos. 1-5. Pacific 231. Toulouse Capitole Orchestre; Michel Plasson. EMI/La Vox de Son Maitre 2C 1-7 16327/9 (3)
++FF 5/6-81 p93 ++STL 3-8-81 p38
+Gr 2-81 p1091

HOOVER, Katherine
Divertimento. See no. 469
On the betrothal of Princess Isabelle of France, aged six. See no. 3884
Trio, violin, violoncello and piano. See no. 1212

HOROVITZ, Joseph
Majorcan pieces (2). See no. 3715

HORSLEY, William
There is a green hill far away. See no. 4107

HOSKINS, William
1879 Eastern reflections. Galactic fantasy. Moog synthesizer. Spectrum SR 106
+-FF 3/4-81 p30
Galactic fantasy. See no. 1879

HOTTETERRE, Jacques
Bourree d'Achille. See no. 151

1880 Suite, op. 2, no. 2, F major. MORLEY: Introduction, nos. 3, 5-6. La sampogna. Il torello. TELEMANN: Sonata, recorder, op. 5, no. 6, A minor/A major. Sonata, recorder, Anh 1, no. 5, A major/C major. VAN EYCK: Amarilli mia bella. Blyndschap van mijn vliedt. O slaep o zoete slaep. Kees Boeke, Walter van Hauwe, rec. Telefunken 6-42522
+AR 11-81 p135 +FF 9/10-81 p262
Suite, op. 2: Ecos pour la flute traversiere, B major. See no. 151
Trio sonata, op. 3, C major. See no. 151
HOVHANESS, Alan
Achtamar. See no. 3913
Farewell to the mountains. See no. 3913
The garden of Adonis. See no. 1377
Mystic flute. See no. 3913
Prayer of St. Gregory. See no. 3629. See no. 3740
Sharagan and fugue, op. 58. See no. 835
Vanadour. See no. 3913
HOVLAND, Egil
1881 Four interludes to "Missa vigilate", op. 67 (4). Suite, organ, no. 2, op. 79. Kjell Johnsen, org. Polyhymnia PRC 7811
+FF 9/10-81 p120
Og ordet ble kjod. See no. 3618
Suite, organ, no. 2, op. 79. See no. 1881
HOWARD, Leslie
Ramble on a Russian theme. See no. 3872
HOWE, Hubert
Canons 4. See no. 1262
1882 Improvisation on the overtone series. VIOLETTE: Black tea. Piece, piano, no. 2. Opus One 53
+CMJ Fall 1981 p82
Studies in timbre, no. 3. See no. 1262
HOWELLS, Herbert
Gloucester service: Magnificat. See no. 3619
Jubilate Deo. See no. 3620
Master Tallis' testament. See no. 3625
1883 Partita. Sonata, organ, no. 2. Graham Barber, org. Vista VPS 1099
+Gr 11-81 p722
Rhapsody, op. 17, no. 3, C sharp minor. See no. 3875
Siciliano for a high ceremony. See no. 4118
Sonata, organ, no. 2. See no. 1883
1884 Songs: Come sing and dance; The dunce; King David; Lady Caroline; Merry Margaret; Miss T; On the merry first of May; The three cherry trees. ORR: Along the field; Bahnhofstrasse; Farewell to barn and stack and tree; In valleys green and still; Is my team ploughing; The lads in their hundreds; When I watch the living meet; When smoke stood up from Ludlow; With rue my heart is laden; While summer on is stealing. Philip Langridge, t; Bruce Ogston, bar; Eric Parkin, pno. Unicorn RHS 369
++FF 1/2-81 p162 +HFN 11-80 p120
+-Gr 12-80 p866 +MT 6-81 p389
Songs: A spotless rose. See no. 3809
Songs: All my hope on God is founded. See no. 3619
Songs: Here is the little door; Long long ago. See no. 1398
Songs: I love all beauteous things. See no. 3875

Songs: Like as the hart desireth the waterbrooks. See no. 3633

HOWETT, Gregory

Fantasia. See no. 4016

HOYOUL, Balduin

Anchor che col partire. See no. 4010

Wenn mein Stuendlein vorhanden ist. See no. 3675

HRABOVSKY, Leonid

1885 Trio, violin, contrabass and piano. KOSENKO: Pieces, violin and piano, op. 4. LYATOSHINSKY: Sonata, violin and piano, op. 19. STANKOVYCH: Triptych "In the highlands". Eugene Gratovich, vln; Virko Baley, pno; Bertram Turetzky, contrabass. Orion ORS 79331

++St 9-81 p102

HSAN-TE TING

1886 "Long March" symphony. Nagoya Philharmonic Orchestra; Kek-Tjiang Lim. Hong Kong HK 1004

+FF 1/2-81 p231

HUANG HU WEI

Szechuan suite. See no. 3861

HUANG TSEN JUNG

North Shansi scenes. See no. 3861

HUBER, Paul

Symphonic music. See no. 3716

HUDSON, Joseph

Fantasy/refrain. See no. 1128

HUE, George

Fantasy, flute and piano. See no. 3923

HUGHES

Royal Doulton march. See no. 3721

HU KUANG HSIN

1887 Ka ta mei ling. LIU TING HO: Night party. Sum che tak ma. SHAN TE-TING: Sinkiang dance, no. 2. YUEN MAO: Dance of the Tao people. Nagoya Philharmonic Orchestra; Kek-Tjiang Lim. Hong Kong HK 1002

+-FF 1/2-81 p231

HULLAH, John Pike

Three fishers went sailing. See no. 3650

HUME, Tobias

Songs: Tobacco tobacco. See no. 3871

HUMFREY, Pelham

Hymn to God the father. See no. 3614

O Lord my god. See no. 815

HUMMEL, Johann

Concerto, mandolin, G major. See no. 1748

Concerto, trumpet, E flat major. See no. 32. See no. 784

Partita, E flat major. See no. 519

1888 Septet, op. 114, C major. KREUTZER, C.: Septet, op. 62, E flat major. Nash Ensemble. CRD CRD 1090 Tape (c) CRDC 4090

+Gr 7-81 p167 ++HFN 10-81 p95 tape

+HFN 7-81 p73

1889 Serenatas (2). Consortium Classicum. Musical Heritage Society MHS 4195

/FF 3/4-81 p143

1890 Sonata, piano, op. 38, C major. Sonata, piano, op. 81, F sharp minor. Phyllis Moss, pno. Orion ORS 81409

++FF 11/12-81 p181

Sonata, piano, op. 81, F sharp minor. See no. 1890

HUMPERDINCK, Engelbert

1891 Hansel und Gretel: Ach wir armen armen Leute. Konigskinder: Verdorben gestorben. LORTZING: Zar und Zimmermann: Auf Gesellen greift zur Axt...Sonst spielt ich mit zepter. MOZART: Don Giovanni, K 527: La ci darem la mano. Le nozze di Figaro, K 492: Non piu andrai...Hai gia vinta la causa...Vedro mentr'io sospiro. Die Zauberflote, K 620: Bei Mannern. WAGNER: Tannhauser: Als du in kuhnem Sange...Blick ich umher...Wohl wusst ich hier; Wie Todesahnung...O du mein holder Abendstern. Gerhard Husch, bar; Berlin State Opera Orchestra; Hans Udo Muller. Arabesque 8022 Tape (c) 9022

+ARG 11-80 p47 +HF 2-81 p81 tape
+-FF 11/12-80 p197 +MUM 12-80 p35

Hansel und Gretel: Der kleine Sandman; Children's prayer. See no. 3713

Hansel und Gretel: Gesenbinderlied. See no. 3639

Hansel und Gretel: Overture. See no. 3644

1892 Hansel und Gretel: Oveture; Witch's ride; Dream pantomime; The gingerbread house; Finale. Lucia Popp, Norma Burrowes, Edita Gruberova, s; Brigitte Fassbaender, Julia Hamari, ms; Walter Berry, bar; Vienna Boys Choir; VPO; Georg Solti. Decca SET 633 (From D131D2)

+-Gr 12-80 p876 +Op 8-81 p824
+HFN 12-80 p153

Hansel und Gretel: Suse liebe Suse...Bruderchen komm tanz mit mir; Dance duet; Der kleine Sandmann bin ich; Sandman's song; Abends will ich schlafen geh'n; Evening prayer. See no. 3844

1893 Konigskinder. Helen Donath, s; Hanna Schwarz, Heidrun Ankersen, ms; Adolf Dallapozza, Gerhard Unger, t; Hermann Prey, bar; Karl Ridderbusch, Gunter Wewel, bs; Bavarian Radio Chorus, Tolzer Childrens Choir; Munich Radio Orchestra; Heinz Wallberg. Arabesque 8061 (3)

+NR 12-81 p7 ++SFC 10-4-81 p17

Konigskinder: Verdorben gestorben. See no. 1891. See no. 3639

HUNT, Jerry

1894 Cantegral segments 17 and 18. Haramand plane. Transform (stream). Transphalba. Volta. Irida 0032

+CMJ Fall 1981 p86

Haramand plane. See no. 1894

Transform (stream). See no. 1894

Transphalba. See no. 1894

Volta. See no. 1894

HUNT, Oliver

The barber of Baghdad. See no. 4108

HUNT, Richard

Merkabah. See no. 1751

HURFORD, Peter

Fanfare on "Old 100th". See no. 3959

HURLESTONE, William

Characteristic pieces. See no. 1514

HUSA, Karel

Landscapes. See no. 1750

1895 Little pieces: Coda; Danza; Notturno; Theme and variations. MAULDIN: Petroglyph. ROBB: Symphony, no. 1: Elegy. Albuquer-

que Chamber Orchestra; David Oberg. Opus One 51
+ARG 11-81 p48

Moravian songs. See no. 1272

HYMNS OF THE RUSSIAN ORTHODOX CHURCH. See no. 3990

IANNACCONE, Anthony

1896 After a gentle rain. Antiphonies. Of fire and ice. Scherzo. Eastern Michigan University Symphonic Band; Max Plant. Golden Crest ATH 5072
+-ARG 4-81 p26 *NR 7-81 p14
/FF 1/2-81 p130

Antiphonies. See no. 1896

Of fire and ice. See no. 1896

Parodies. See no. 3815

Scherzo. See no. 1896

1897 Trio, flute, clarinet and piano. VAN DE VATE: Music, viola, percussion and piano. Rodney Hill, flt; Armand Abramson, clt; Elaine Jacobson, pno; Maxine Karen Johnson, vla; William Wiley, perc; Evelyn Zuckerman, pno. Orion ORS 80386
+ARG 6-81 p45 +FF 1/2-81 p130
+Audio 10-81 p32 /NR 4-81 p7

IBERT, Jacques

Aria. See no. 3819. See no. 3953

Bacchanale. See no. 751

Concerto, flute. See no. 1118

Divertissement. See no. 751. See no. 1876

Escales. See no. 1113

Histoires. See no. 1898

Impromptu. See no. 3741

Jeux. See no. 1400

Little white donkey. See no. 3952

Petite suite en quinze images. See no. 1898

1898 Piano works: Histoires. Petite suite en quinze images. Les rencontres. Toccata sur le nom d'Albert Houssel. Le vent dans les ruines. Francois Gobet, pno. Metropole 2599 016
+Gr 8-81 p296

Piece, flute. See no. 3668

Piece, solo flute. See no. 3923

Pieces breves. See no. 3934

Les rencontres. See no. 1898

Steles orientees: Mon amant a la vertus dans l'eau; On me dit. See no. 3953

Toccata sur le nom d'Albert Roussel. See no. 1898

Le vent dans les ruines. See no. 1898

IMPROVISATIONS ON "SERDECZNA MATKO", "MARIA BREIT DEN MANTEL AUS". See no. 3904

INDIA, Sigismondo d'

Songs: Alla guerra d'amore; La mia filli crudel; La virtu. See no. 3947

Songs: O primavera gioventu dell'anno; Vostro fui vostro son e saro vostro. See no. 3630

d'INDY, Vincent

Chansons det danses, op. 50. See no. 1625

1899 La foret enchantee, op. 8. Istar, op. 42. Jour d'ete a la Montagne, op. 61. Tableaux de voyage, op. 36. Orchestre Philharmonique des Pays de Loire; Pierre Dervaux. Pathe Marconi C 069 16301 (also Arabesque 8097-2 Tape (c) 9097-2)

+ARG 9-80 p45 +HFN 4-81 p72
+ARG 12-81 p15 +NR 8-81 p2
+Gr 1-81 p948 +SFC 8-16-81 p19
+-HF 11-81 p83 ++St 11-81 p88

Istar, op. 42. See no. 1899
Jour d'ete a la Montagne, op. 61. See no. 1899
Tableaux de voyage, op. 36. See no. 1899

IPPOLITOV-IVANOV, Mikhail
Caucasian sketches, op. 10: Procession of the Sardar. See no. 3699

IRELAND, John
Aubade. See no. 4055

1900 Epic march. The overlanders (arr. Mackerras). VAUGHAN WILLIAMS: On Wenlock edge (orch. composer). Gerald English, t; West Australian Symphony Orchestra; David Measham. Unicorn KP 8001
+FF 3/4-81 p214 +-HFN 11-80 p123
+Gr 11-80 p723

A London overture. See no. 468
The overlanders. See no. 1900
Sonata, violoncello and piano, G minor. See no. 1016
Songs: I have twelve oxen; Love and friendship; My fair; The sally gardens; Sea fever. See no. 4057
Songs: The boys are up in the woods all day. See no. 3893
Songs: The holy boy. See no. 3856
IRISH MELODIES. See no. 3658

ISAAC, Heinrich
Choruses (2). See no. 3720
Herr Gott lass dich erbarmen. See no. 3960
Innsbruck ad equalis. See no. 3960
Innsbruck ich muss dich lassen. See no. 396. See no. 3720
La la ho ho. See no. 3945
Songs: A la bataglia; An buos; Carmen in fa; Fortuna in mi; Imperii proceres; Innsbruck ich muss dich lassen; J'ay pris amours; La morra; San Sancti spiritus assit nobis gratia. See no. 3777
Songs: Intradas (2); Carmen; J'ai pris amour; O Venus bant. See no. 3896

ISHAM (Isum), John
Celia learning. See no. 4093

ISHII, Maki
Dipol. See no. 1204
Kio-oo. See no. 1204

ISRAEL, Brian
Concerto, piano and wind ensemble. See no. 75

IVES, Charles Edward
A Christmas carol. See no. 3911

1901 Sonata, piano, no. 2. Yvar Mikhashoff, pno; Josef Jelinek, flt. Spectrum SR 120
/FF 9/10-81 p121

1902 Sonata, piano, no. 2. Herbert Henck, pno. Wergo WER 60080
-FF 1/2-81 p131 +RR 6-79 p106

1903 Symphony, no. 4. John Alldis Choir; LPO; Jose Serebrier. RCA AGL 1-3787
+FF 7/8-81 p116

IVES, Charles Grayston
Listen sweet dove. See no. 3637

O sing joyfully. See no. 3636

IVES, Simon

Ayre. See no. 3807

Coranto. See no. 3807

Pavan. See no. 3807

The virgin: Fancy. See no. 3807

JACKSON, Francis

Archbishop's fanfare. See no. 1083. See no. 3959

Diversion for mixtures. See no. 1083

Fanfare, organ. See no. 1083

Magnificat and nun dimittis, G major. See no. 3632

Pagaent. See no. 1083

Toccata, D minor. See no. 1083

Toccata prelude, Wachet auf. See no. 1083

JACKSON, Nicholas

Magnificat and nunc dimittis (St. David's service). See no. 3614

JACOB, Gordon

Concerto, bassoon. See no. 57

Music for a festival: Interludes for trumpets and trombones, Intrada; Round of seven parts; Interlude; Saraband; Madrigal. See no. 4006

1904 Quintet, clarinet. SOMERVELL: Quintet, clarinet. Thea King, clt; Aeolian Quartet. Hyperion A 66011

++FF 9/10-81 p179 +HFN 3-81 p87
++Gr 3-81 p1210 +-MT 10-81 p679

Songs: Of all the birds that I do know; Flow my tears; He who comes here. See no. 3954

JACOPO DA BOLOGNA

I'Sent'za. See no. 402

Vola el bel sparver. See no. 4102

JACQUES

When Christ was born. See no. 3921

JACQUES DE CAMBRAI

Retrowange novelle. See no. 4086

JACQUET DE LA GUERRE, Elizabeth

Jacob et Rachel: Air. See no. 3814

Suite, D minor. See no. 1221

Susanne: Recitative and air. See no. 3814

JAGER, Robert

1905 A child's garden of verses. Concerto, alto saxophone, no. 2. Japanese prints. March "Dramatic". Pastorale and country dance. Preamble. Nicholas Brightman, sax; Donna Woofter, s; Asbury College Concert Band; Joseph Parker. Golden Crest ATH 5068

+ARG 6-81 p30 -NR 7-81 p14

Concerto, alto saxophone, no. 2. See no. 1905

Japanese prints. See no. 1905

March "Dramatic". See no. 1905

Pastorale and country dance. See no. 1905

Preamble. See no. 1905

JAMES, Ifor

Merry-go-round. See no. 3986

Phoenix. See no. 3986

JANACEK, Leos

Capriccio. See no. 1924

Concertino. See no. 1924

1906 The cunning little vixen. Helena Tattermuschova, s; Eva Zikmundova, ms; Jaroslava Prochazkova, con; Jan Hlavsa; Rudolf Vonasek, t; Zdenek Kroupa, bar; Dalibor Jedlicka, Jozef Heriban, bs; Prague National Theatre Orchestra and Chorus; Bohumil Gregor. Supraphon 112 1181/2 (2)
+-Gr 12-72 p1199
+HFN 12-72 p2441
++NR 11-73 p9
+ON 12-2-78 p68
+Op 12-72 p1094
+RR 12-72 p40
+SFC 7-22-73 p29
+SR 4-81 p90
+STL 12-10-72 p35

1907 The diary of the young man who disappeared. Clara Wirz, con; Peter Keller, t; Lucerne Singers; Hansruedi Willisegger. Accord ACC 140007
+-Gr 5-81 p1504
+HFN 12-81 p96

1908 The diary of a young man who disappeared. Libuse Marova, con; Vilem Pribyl, t; Kuhn Female Choir; Josef Palenicek, pno. Supraphon 112 2414
++ARG 1-81 p33
++FF 3/4-81 p143
+Gr 8-80 p251
+HF 10-80 p68
++HFN 7-80 p107
+NR 10-80 p11
+NYT 7-5-81 pD17
+RR 7-80 p88
+SFC 1-25-81 p17
++St 1-81 p85

Dumka, C minor. See no. 1529. See no. 1924

Fairy tale. See no. 1924

1909 Fate. Magdalena Hajossyova, s; Jarmila Palivcova, ms; Vilem Pribyl, t; Brno State Theatre Opera Orchestra and Chorus; Frantisek Jilek. Supraphon SUP 112 2011/2 (2)
+ARG 10-80 p18
+-FF 9/10-80 p139
+Gr 3-80 p1437
+-HF 10-80 p66
+HFN 1-80 p106
+-MT 9-81 p608
+NR 8-80 p10
+ON 3-14-81 p44
+RR 2-80 p38
++SFC 9-21-80 p21
+-St 3-81 p85
+STL 12-2-79 p37

1910 From the house of the dead. Jaroslava Janska, s; Eva Zikmundova, ms; Jiri Zahradnicek, Vladimir Krejcik, Beno Blachut, Ivo Zidek, t; Dalibor Jedlicka, bar; Antonin Svorc, bs-bar; Richard Novak, bs; VSOO Chorus; VPO; Charles Mackerras. Decca D224D2 Tape (c) K224K22 (also London LDR 10036)
++FF 5/6-81 p95
++Gr 11-80 p731
++Gr 3-81 p1172
++HF 7-81 p60
++HFN 11-80 p120
++MT 9-81 p607
++MUM 9/10-81 p32
+NYT 7-5-81 pD17
+-ON 3-14-81 p44
+Op 3-81 p272
++SFC 1-25-81 p17
+SR 4-81 p90
+St 6-81 p118

1911 Glagolitic mass. Gabriela Benackova, s; Vera Soukupova, con; Frantisek Livora, t; Karel Prusa, bs; Jan Hora, org; CPhO; and Chorus; Vaclav Neumann. Panton 110 720
/Gr 10-81 p593
+HFN 9-81 p81

1912 Glagolitic mass. Gabriela Benackova-Capova, s; Eva Randova, con; Vilem Pribyl, t; Sergej Kopcak, bs; Czech Philharmonic Chorus; Brno Philharmonic Orchestra; Frantisek Jilek. Supraphon 112 2698
+FF 9/10-81 p123
-Gr 8-81 p302
+NR 7-81 p8
+NYT 7-5-81 pD17

+-HFN 8-81 p85 ++St 8-81 p68

In the mists. See no. 1924

1913 Jenufa. Nadezda Kniplova, Gabriela Benackova, s; Anna Barova, con; Vilem Pribyl, Vladimir Krejcik, t; Karel Berman, bar; Vaclav Halir, bs; Brno Opera Orchestra and Chorus; Frantisek Jilek. Supraphon SUP 116 2751/2 (2)

-ARG 12-81 p42 +NR 8-81 p10
+Gr 1-81 p988 +-NYT 7-5-81 pD17
+HFN 1-81 p96 +-St 11-81 p88
+-MT 12-81 p827 +STL 1-11-81 p38

Lachian dances, no. 1. See no. 3964

1914 The Makropoulos affair. Elisabeth Soderstrom, s; Anna Czakova, ms; Petr Dvorsky, Vladimir Krejcik, Beno Blachut, Zdenek Svehla, t; Vaclav Zitek, bar; Dalibor Jedlicka, bs; Vienna State Opera Chorus; VPO; Charles Mackerras. Decca D144D2 (2) Tape (c) K144 K22 (also London OSA 12116 Tape (c) OSA 5-12116)

+ARG 5-80 p26 +OC Spring 1981 p51
+FF 3/4-80 p107 +ON 3-8-80 p29
++Gr 10-79 p703 +Op 3-80 p270
*Gr 2-80 p1302 tape +RR 10-79 p59
+HF 5-80 p75 +RR 6-80 p94 tape
+HF 8-80 p87 tape ++SFC 1-27-80 p44
++HFN 10-79 p157 +-St 4-80 p126
++MT 4-80 p252 +STL 12-2-79 p37
++NYT 12-16-79 pD21

1915 Mladi. March of the blue-throats. POULENC: Sextet, piano and winds. Sonata, flute. Jan Latham Koenig, pno; Judith Hall, flt; Koenig Ensemble. Bedivere BVR 304

+Gr 10-81 p573

Mladi. See no. 1924

On an overgrown path. See no. 1924

Presto, E minor. See no. 1924

Quartets, strings, nos. 1 and 2. See no. 1924

1916 Quartet, strings, no. 1. Quartet, strings, no. 2. Smetana Quartet. Denon OX 7192

+FF 5/6-81 p96

1917 Quartet, strings, no. 1. Quartet, strings, no. 2. Medici Quartet. HMV HQS 1433

+Gr 2-81 p1096 ++ST 7-81 p206
++HFN 2-81 p89 +STL 2-8-81 p40

1918 Quartet, strings, no. 2. SMETANA: Quartet, strings, no. 1, E minor. Melos Quartet. Intercord 29728-3

+HFN 12-81 p96

Quartet, strings, no. 2. See no. 422. See no. 1916. See no. 1917

Recollection. See no. 1924

Romance, E major. See no. 1529

Romance, E minor. See no. 1924

1919 Sinfonietta, op. 60. Taras Bulba. VPO; Charles Mackerras. London LDR 71021 Tape (c) LDR 5-71021 (also Decca SXDL 7519 Tape (c) KSDC 7519)

++FF 11/12-81 p182 ++HFN 7-81 p74
+Gr 7-81 p154 ++NR 12-81 p2
+Gr 8-81 p324 tape +SFC 12-13-81 p18
+HF 11-81 p103 tape ++St 11-81 p75

1920 Sinfonietta, op. 60. Taras Bulba. Brno State Philharmonic Orch-

estra; Jiri Belohlavek. Panton 110 728
+Gr 11-81 p690 +-HFN 9-81 p81

1921 Sinfonietta, op. 60. Taras Bulba. Rotterdam Philharmonic Orchestra; David Zinman. Philips 9500 874 Tape (c) 7300 874
+FF 7/8-81 p116 +-NYT 7-5-81 pD17
+-NR 5-81 p5 +-St 6-81 p119

1922 Sinfonietta, op. 60. Taras Bulba. CPhO; Karel Ancerl. Quintessence PMC 7184
+FF 7/8-81 p116

Sinfonietta, op. 60: Allegretto. See no. 3660

Sonata, piano, See no. 1924

Sonata, violin and piano. See no. 1529. See no. 1924

1923 Songs: Czech legion; The evening witch; Leave taking; Marycka Magdonova; Our birch tree; Schoolmaster Halfar; Seventy thousand; The soldier's lot; The wandering madman. Moravian Teachers Choir; Antonin Tucapsky. Supraphon 112 0878
+Gr 5-81 p1504

Taras Bulba. See no. 1919. See no. 1920. See no. 1921. See no. 1922

Theme and variations. See no. 1924

1924 Works, selections: Capriccio. Concertino. Dumka, C minor. Fairy tale. In the mists. Mladi. On an overgrown path. Presto, E minor. Recollection. Romance, E minor. Quartets, strings, nos. 1 and 2. Sonata, piano. Sonata, violin and piano. Theme and variations. Youth Suite. Paul Crossley, pno; Kenneth Sillito, vln; Christopher Van Kampen, vlc; Gabrieli Quartet, London Sinfonietta Orchestra and Chorus; David Atherton. Decca D223D5 (5)
+-FF 9/10-81 p122 +NYT 7-5-81 pD17
++Gr 4-81 p1334 ++STL 3-8-81 p38
+HFN 7-81 p74

Youth suite. See no. 1924

JANEQUIN, Clement

1925 Songs: Aller my fault sur la verdure; Aria della battaglia; Le chant des oyseaux; Le chant du rossignol; Chantons sonnons trompettes; Les cries de Paris; La jalousie; La guerre "La bataille de Marignan". Pro Arte Antiqua Ensemble; Hanns Kann, hpd; Leo Witoszynskyj, vihuela. Harmonia Mundi (France) HM 10070
+FF 5/6-81 p97

Songs: Le chant des oyseaux; Au joli jeu. See no. 3677

JANSSEN, Guus

Toonen. See no. 3943

JARRETT, Keith

1926 The celestial hawk. Keith Jarrett, pno; Syracuse Symphony Orchestra; Christopher Keene. ECM Records 1-1175 Tape (c) MSE 1175
+FF 5/6-81 p97

JAVALOYES

El abanico. See no. 3981

JEFFRIES, George

1927 Songs (anthems and devotional songs): Ecce dilectus meus; Hei mihi Domine; Heu me miseram; In the midst of life; Jubilate Deo; A musick strange; O Deus meus; O domine Deus; O quam suave; Timor et tremor; Whisper it easily. Yvonne Seymour, Carol Smith, s; Joseph Cornwell, Paul Elliott, Richard Morton, t; Stephen Varcoe, bar; Peter Seymour, org; Mark Caudle, bs viol; University

of East Anglia Singers; Peter Aston. University of East Anglia UEA 80031
+Gr 2-81 p1108

JENCKS, Gardner

1928 Sonata, piano, op. 8, no. 2. Sonata, piano, op. 10, no. 3. Sonata, piano. op, 80, no. 8a. Sonata, piano, op. 118, no. 12. Marcia Mikulak, pno. 1750 Arch S 1781
+NR 11-81 p13

Sonata, piano, op. 10, no. 3. See no. 1928
Sonata, piano, op. 80, no. 8a. See no. 1928
Sonata, piano, op. 118, no. 12. See no. 1928

JENEY, Zoltan

1929 End game. A hundred years average. Impho 102/6. Orpheus garden. New Music Studio Budapest Members; Sandor Papp, vla; Zoltan Kocsis, pno; Zoltan Jeney. Hungaroton SLPX 12059
-FF 1/2-81 p132

A hundred years average. See no. 1929
Impho 102/6. See no. 1929
Orpheus garden. See no. 1929

JENKINS, John

Fantasias, G minor, D minor. See no. 1526
Newark siege fantasia. See no. 3663

JENNEFELT, Thomas

1930 Warning to the rich. MELLNAS: Bossa buffa. SANDSTROM: A cradle song/The Tyger. WERLE: Trees. Stockholm Chamber Choir, Swedish Radio Choir, Bromma Chamber Choir; Eric Ericson, Bo Johansson. Caprice CAP 3024
+FF 9/10-81 p222 +NR 7-81 p9

JEPPESEN, Knud

Little trio, D minor. See no. 3683

JERSILD, Jorgen

1931 Trois pieces en concert. NIELSEN: Suite, op. 45. OLSEN: Inventions, op. 38. Lis Smed Christensen, pno. Simax PN 2001
+Gr 11-81 p764

JEUNE, Claude le

Fiere cruelle. See no. 3945

JIAN CHEN

Song of the five fingers mountain. See no. 3859

JIMENEZ MABARAK, Carlos

Balada del venado y la luna. See no. 1133

JOACHIM, Joseph

Hebrew melodies, op. 9, nos. 1 and 3. See no. 2851

JOHNSEN, Hinrich Philip

1932 Church music for Easter day 1757. Odes, nos. 3, 7, 9, 11, 17. Trio sonata, no. 10, D major. Margareta Ljunggren, s; Stig Benston, Ulf Rosenberg, flt; Lars Brolin, Predrag Novovic, vln; Karl Goran Ehntorp, org; Eva Nordenfelt, hpd; Lennart Skold, vlc. Proprius PROP 7805
+FF 1/2-81 p133

Odes, nos. 3, 7, 9, 11, 17. See no. 1932
Trio sonata, no. 10, D major. See no. 1932

JOHNSON, Edward

Eliza is the fairest queen. See no. 3807

JOHNSON, James

1933 Carolina shout. Eccentricity. Modernistic. Mule-walk stomp.

Snowy morning blues. JOPLIN (Marshall): Lily queen. Swipesy cakewalk. JOPLIN (Hayden): Felicity rag. Something doing. Sunflower slow rag. William Albright, William Bolcom, pno. Musicmasters MM 20002 Tape (c) MM 40002 (From Musical Heritage Society MHS 4022)
+HF 8-81 p65 +NYT 4-12-81 pD28
Eccentricity. See no. 1933
Modernistic. See no. 1933
Mule-walk stomp. See no. 1933
Snowy morning blues. See no. 1933

JOHNSON, John
Chi passa. See no. 4059
Quadrone pavene. See no. 4059

JOLIVET, Andre

1934 Arioso barocco. Hymne a l'univers. Mandala. Songs: Hymne a Saint-Andre. Dany Barraud, s; Rene Perinelli, tpt; Daniel Roth, org. Arion ARN 38530
+HFN 2-81 p89 +RR 7-80 p88
Fanfares pour Britannicus. See no. 3624
Hymne a l'univers. See no. 1934
Mandala. See no. 1934
Sonata, flute and piano. See no. 1400
Songs: Hymne a Saint-Andre. See no. 1934

JONES
Songs: Morte Christe. See no. 3721

JONES, Daniel

1935 Symphony, no. 6. MATHIAS: Symphony, no. 1. RPO; Charles Groves. Oriel ORM 1004 (From Pye TPLS 13023)
+Gr 2-81 p1091

JONES, Robert
Songs: Now what is love. See no. 3871
Thinkst thou Kate. See no. 4085

JONGEN, Joseph
Chant de Mai, op. 53. See no. 3619

1936 Priere, op. 37, no. 3. LANGLAIS: Suite medievale. PEETERS: Passacaglia and fugue, op. 42. TOURNEMIRE: Pater dimite illis nesciunt enim quid faciunt, op. 67, no. 1. Alan Wicks, org. Wealden WS 200 Tape (c) WS 200
+Gr 1-81 p972
Symphonie concertante: Toccata. See no. 3744

JOPLIN, Scott
Bethena. See no. 4104
The cascades. See no. 3737
Easy winners. See no. 1937
The entertainer. See no. 1937
Felicity rag. See no. 1933
Gladiolus rag. See no. 1937
Heliotrope bouquet. See no. 1937
Lily queen. See no. 1933
Magnetic rag. See no. 1937
Maple leaf rag. See no. 1937
Paragon rag. See no. 778. See no. 1937

1937 Piano works: Easy winners. The entertainer. Gladiolus rag. Heliotrope bouquet. Magnetic rag. Maple leaf rag. Paragon rag. Pineappe rag. Solace. Joshua Rifkin, pno. Angel DS

37331 Tape (c) 4ZS 37331
+ARG 3-81 p30 +NR 9-80 p11

1938 Pineapple rag (Krasicky). RUSSO: Essay, band, no. 1. Variations on a yank. Winchester overture. WILDING-WHITE: Band music. Cornell University Wind Ensemble; Marice Stith. Cornell CUWE 28
/FF 1/2-81 p233

Pineappe rag. See no. 1937
Solace. See no. 1937. See no. 4104
Something doing. See no. 1933
Sunflower slow rag. See no. 1933
Swipesy cakewalk. See no. 1933

JOSEFFY, Rafael
At the spring. See no. 3920

JOSEPHS, Wilfrid
Song of freedom. See no. 4007

JOSQUIN DES PRES

1939 Benedicta es. PALESTRINA: Missa Benedicta es. Tallis Scholars; Peter Phillips. Gimell GAMUT 1585-01
-Gr 11-81 p738 ++NR 11-81 p8
+Gr 12-81 p945 tape +STL 9-13-81 p41
+HFN 9-81 p84

Fortuna d'un gran tempo. See no. 3661
Motets: Ave Maria. See no. 3906
Royal fanfare. See no. 4002
Scaramella. See no. 3661
Songs: Absalon fili mi; Alma redemptoris mater; Domine ne in furore. See no. 1068
Songs: Comment peult. See no. 3777
Songs: El grillo; Inviolata integra et casta es Maria; Scaramella. See no. 3853

JOUBERT, John
O Lord the maker of all things. See no. 3633

JUDE
The mighty deep. See no. 4074

JUDENKUNIG, Hans
Rosina. See no. 3661

JUDGE (Williams)
It's a long way to Tipperary. See no. 3967

JULLICH, Michael
Improvisation music. See no. 2007

JUON, Paul
Litaniae, op. 70. See no. 810

KABALEVSKY, Dimitri

1940 Sonata, violoncello and piano, op. 71, B flat major. LOCATELLI: Sonata, violoncello and piano, D major. (arr. from Sonatas, violin, op. 12, nos. 6, 12). Antony Cooke, vlc; Armin Watkins, pno. Golden Crest RE 7093
+-ARG 7/8-81 p21

KADOSA, Pal

1941 Concerto, violin, no. 1, op. 19. Concerto, violin, no. 2, op. 32. Maria Balint, Denes Kovacs, vln; Budapest Symphony Orchestra; Gyorgy Lehel, Tamas Breitner. Hungaroton SLPX 12313
+FF 11/12-81 p182 +-HFN 10-81 p89

Concerto, violin, no. 2, op. 32. See no. 1941

KALAJIAN
Songs: See no. 3913
KALLIWODA, Johann
Introduction and rond, F minor/F major. See no. 3655
KALMAN, Emmerich
1942 Die Csardasfurstin. Annelies Rothenberger, Olivera Miljakovic, s; Nicolai Gedda, Willi Brokmeier, t; Wolfgang Annheisser, bar; Bavarian State Opera Chorus; Graunke Symphony Orchestra; Willi Mattes. EMI 1C 157 29066/7(2) Tape (c) 1C 289 29066/7 (also Odeon 29066/7)
+Gr 9-81 p451 ++St 1-73 p108
+-HF 12-73 p91
Die Csardasfurstin, excerpts. See no. 3975
1943 Grafin Maritza. Anneliese Rothenberger, Olivera Miljakovic, Edda Moser, s; Willi Brokmeier, Nicolai Gedda, t; Kurt Bohme, bs; Bavarian State Opera Chorus; Graunke Symphony Orchestra; Willi Mattes. EMI 1C 157 29068/9 (2)
-Gr 4-81 p1377
Kom Zigany. See no. 3823
KALMAR, Laszlo
Anera. See no. 3865
KALNIN, Alfred
Pastorale, no. 2, G major. See no. 3910
KAMINSKI
Canzone. See no. 1856
KAPELLER
Ich hab' a mal a Rauscherl g'habt. See no. 4083
KAPSBERGER, Johann
1944 Canzone, no. 1. Corrente, no. 12. Gagliardi, nos. 1-2, 4, 7. Toccatas, nos. 1-2, 4-5, 7. PICCININI: Correnti, nos. 5, 6, 10. Gagliarda, no. 3. Partite variate sopra la folia aria romanesca. Passacaglia. Ricercar, no. 1. Toccatas, nos. 2, 8, 11-13. Konrad Junghanel, lt, arch-lute, chitarrone. Accent ACC 8016
-FF 7/8-81 p217 +HFN 1-81 p105
+Gr 1-81 p972
Corrente, no. 12. See no. 1944
Gagliardi, nos. 1-2, 4, 7. See no. 1944
Songs: Io amo io ardo io moro; Io mi parto cor mio; O cor sempre dolente. See no. 3630
Toccata. See no. 3937
Toccatas, nos. 1-2, 4-5, 7. See no. 1944
KARAMANUK
Admiration. See no. 3913
KARG-ELERT, Sigfried
Abide O dearest Jesus. See no. 3821
Ach bleib mit deiner Gnade, op. 65, no. 1. See no. 3806
Chorale improvisation, op. 65: Herzlich tut mich verlangen. See no. 3950
1945 Fantasie, canzona, passacaglia and fugue, op. 85, no. 2. Kaleidoscope, op. 144. Three impressions, op. 72: Claire de lune; La nuit. Graham Barber, org. Vista VPS 1078
+-Gr 7-81 p176
Kaleidoscope, op. 144. See no. 1945
Pastels from the Lake of Constance, op. 96: Pastel. See no. 185

Rondo alla campanella, op. 156. See no. 185
Three impressions, op. 72: Clair de lune; La nuit. See no. 1945
Triptych, op. 141: Legend. See no. 4116
Valse mignonne, op. 142, no. 2. See no. 4110

KAROLYI, Pal
Rondo, 2 cimbaloms. See no. 1384

KASCHEVAROV
Tranquility. See no. 4028. See no. 4030

KASTALSKIJ, Alexander
1946 Russian nuptial mass. GARDNER: Antiphon Stepjenny; Cherubikon; Dostojno jest; Sedalen woskressen. Ramons-Chor for Easter Church Liturgy; Winfried Pentek. Schwann Musica Sacra AMS 3530
+FF 7/8-81 p117

KAUFMANN, Armin
Burletta. See no. 3872
Mitoka dragomirna. See no. 3872

KAZACHANKO
Pan Sotnik: Peter's aria. See no. 4028

KEE, Piet
Gedenck-Clanck '76. See no. 184

KEEL, Frederick
Salt water ballads: Trade winds. See no. 4057

KELLEWAY, Roger
Dance of the ocean breeze. See no. 3736
1947 Morning song. Westwood song. TACKETT: The yellow bird. Roger Bobo, tuba; Roger Kellaway, pno; Fred Tackett, gr; Ralph Grierson, pno; Skip Mosher, bs; Ray Rich, drums. Crystal S 396
+FF 9/10-81 p270 +NR 4-81 p15
Sonoro. See no. 3736
Westwood song. See no. 1974

KELLY
Te deum. See no. 3875

KENNAN, Kent
Sonata, trumpet and piano. See no. 1636

KERCKHOVEN, Abraham van den
Fantasias, D minor, C minor, G major, E minor, F major. See no. 1948
Fugues, A minor, C major. See no. 1948
1948 Organ works: Fantasias, D minor, C minor, G major, E minor, F major. Fugues, A minor, C major. Prelude and fugue, G major. Versus, no. 5, B major. Versus, no. 7, E major. Jozef Sluys, org. Zephyr ZO 3
+-Gr 7-80 p153 +MT 3-81 p197
Prelude and fugue, G major. See no. 1948
Versus, no. 5, B major; no. 7, E major. See no. 1948

KERLL, Johann
Canzona, G minor. See no. 3622. See no. 4012
Canzona, no. 1, D minor. See no. 4084
Ciacona, C major. See no. 3832. See no. 4084
Passacaglia, D minor. See no. 3902
Toccatas, nos. 1-3. See no. 4084
Toccata con durezza e ligature. See no. 3622. See no. 4012

KESSLER, Minuetta
1949 Ballet sonatina. Fantasy, oboe and piano. Sonata, clarinet and piano. Sonata concertante, violin and piano. Marylou Speaker,

vln; William Wrzesian, clt; Patricia Morehead, ob; Minuetta Kessler, pno. AFKA SK 288
*+FF 3/4-81 p34
Fantasy, oboe and piano. See no. 1949
Sonata, clarinet and piano. See no. 1949
Sonata concertante, violin and piano. See no. 1949
KETTING, Piet
Trio, flute, clarinet and bassoon. See no. 78
KEURIS, Tristan
Quartet, saxophone. See no. 3729
KHACHATURIAN, Aram
The battle of Stalingrad. See no. 3891
1950 Concerto, piano. Leonard Pennario, pno; Concert Arts Orchestra; Felix Slatkin. Seraphim S 60352
+FF 7/8-81 p117 +NR 4-81 p6
1951 Concerto, piano. Dance suite: Allegretto, Largo, Presto. Mirka Pokorna, pno; Prague Symphony Orchestra; Valdimir Valek. Supraphon 110 2778
+FF 11/12-81 p183 -NR 12-81 p5
1952 Concerto, violin. Wanda Wilkomirska, vln; Warsaw National Philharmonic Orchestra; Witold Rowicki. Stolat SZM 0140
+FF 11/12-81 p183 *NYT 7-26-81 pD23
1953 Concerto, violin, D minor. David Oistrakh, vln; MRSO; Aram Khachaturian. Musical Heritage Society MHS 4340
+-ARG 11-81 p25 +FF 9/10-81 p124
Dance. See no. 3917
Dance suite: Allegretto, Largo, Presto. See no. 1951
Gayaneh: Lezghinka. See no. 3891
Gayaneh: Sabre dance. See no. 3645
Poem. See no. 3917
Sonatina. See no. 3917
1954 Symphony, no. 3, RIMSKY-KORSAKOV: Russian Easter festival overture, op. 36. RACHMANINOFF: Vocalise, op. 34, no. 14. Anna Moffo, s; CSO, American Symphony Orchestra; Leopold Stokowski. RCA GL 4-2923 Tape (c) GK 4-2923 (From SB 6804)
+Gr 8-80 p222 +HFN 10-80 p117 tape
+Gr 9-80 p413 tape +-HFN 1-81 p109 tape
+HFN 8-80 p107 +-RR 8-80 p46
Toccata. See no. 3917
Valse caprice. See no. 3917
KHANDOSHKIN, Ivan
Sentimental aria. See no. 3693
KIENZL, Wilhelm
Der Evangelimann: Selig sind die Verfolgung leiden. See no. 3747. See no. 3999
Der Kuhreigen: Lug Dursel lug. See no. 3747
KILLMAYER, Wilhelm
An John Field. See no. 1521
KING
The huntress. See no. 3817
Songs of praise the angels sang. See no. 4107
KINLOCH, William
Konloch his fantassie. See no. 4101
KIRCHNER, Leon
1955 Trio, piano. VILLA-LOBOS: Trio, piano, no. 2. Philadelphia Trio.

Centaur CRC 1004
+ARG 1-81 p44 +NR 9-81 p7

KITTEL, Caspar
Songs: Coridon der gieng betrubet; Jetz und kompt die Nacht herbey. See no. 24

KLEBER, Leonard
Die Brunnlein die da fliessen. See no. 3676
Zucht Ehr und Lob. See no. 3676

KLEINKNECHT, Jakob
Sonata, flute and oboe, C minor. See no. 112

KLEMETTI
Songs: Angelus emittitur; Ave maris stella. See no. 3991

KLEPPER
1956 Symphony, no. 1. Impressions of Resita, symphonic triptych. Timisoara Symphony Orchestra; Remus Georgescu. Electrecord ST ECE 01502
+/FF 5/6-81 p219
Impressions of Resita, symphonic triptych. See no. 1956

KLUGE, Manfred
1957 Choralvorspiele, nos. 1-9. Vater unser im Himmelreich. Uwe Grosse, org. Pape 8
-FF 11/12-81 p184 -NR 4-81 p14
Vater unser im Himmelreich. See no. 200. See no. 1957

KLUGHARDT, August
Quintet, winds, op. 79. See no. 742

KNAPP
Open the gates. See no. 4100

KNIPPER, Lev
Cavalry of the Steppes. See no. 3721

KOCH, Erland von
Monologue, no. 1. See no. 3679

KODALY, Zoltan
Children's dances. See no. 1960
1958 Concerto, orchestra. Hary Janos, op. 15: Suite. Budapest Philharmonic Orchestra; Janos Ferencsik. Hungaroton SLPX 12190
+FF 7/8-81 p118 +St 7-81 p83
+NR 4-81 p1
Dances of Marosszek. See no. 1960
1959 Duo, violin and violoncello, op. 7. Sonata, violoncello and piano, op. 4. Sonatina, violoncello and piano. Elemer Lavotha, vlc; Nils-Erik Sparf, vln; Kerstin Aberg, pno. BIS LP 172
++FF 9/10-81 p124 +HFN 9-81 p81
+Gr 9-81 p402 +NR 8-81 p8
Duo, violin and violoncello, op. 7. See no. 569
Hary Janos, op. 15: Suite. See no. 1958
Little canons on the black keys. See no. 1960
Meditation sur un motif de Claude Debussy. See no. 1960
1960 Piano works: Children's dances. Dances of Marosszek. Little canons on black keys (24). Meditation sur un motif de Claude Debussy. Pieces, op. 3 (9). Pieces, op. 11 (7). Valsette. Kornel Zempleni, pno. Hungaroton SLPX 11913/4 (2)
++Gr 5-81 p1498 +HFN 3-81 p97
Pieces, piano, op. 3 (9). See no. 1960
Pieces, piano, op. 11 (7). See no. 1960
Sonata, violoncello and piano, op. 4. See no. 1959
Sonatina, solo violoncello. See no. 1959

Songs: Evening song; Evening; Norwegian girls; Szekely lament; Te deum of Sandor Sik; Those who are always late. See no. 380
Valsette. See no. 1960

KOHAUT, Karl

1961 Concerto, lute, D major. Concerto, lute, F major. VIVALDI: Concerto, lute, RV 93, D major. Concerto, viola d'amore, RV 540, D minor. Anthony Bailes, lt; Wim Ten Have, vla d'amore; Troels Svendsen, Janneke van der Meer, vln; Wiel Peters, vla; Richte van der Meer, vlc; Jakob Lindberg, theorbo. EMI 1C 065 43046
+-FF 11/12-81 p273

Concerto. lute, F major. See no. 1961

KOHN, Karl

Castles and kings. See no. 3880

KOHOUTEK, Ctirad

1962 Fesivals of light. KUBIK, L.: Tribute to Mayakovsky. Vaclav Halir, bs; Alena Vesela, org; Brno Philharmonic Orchestra; Jiri Belohlavek, Otakar Trhlik. Supraphon 110 2487
+-FF 3/4-81 p145 +NR 2-81 p3

KOKKONEN, Joonas

Lux aeterna. See no. 3804

1963 Symphony, no. 3. SIBELIUS: Tapiola, op. 112. Finnish Radio Orchestra; Paavo Berglund. Finlandia FA 311 (From Decca SXL 6432)
+ARG 9-80 p43 +HFN 11-80 p129
+FF 7/8-80 p101 +NR 11-80 p4
+Gr 1-81 p998

KOMITAS

Dances. See no. 3912

KORDE, Shirish

Constallations. See no. 1224

KORNGOLD, Wolfgang Erich

1964 Schauspiel overture, op. 4. WEILL: Der Silbersee: Suite. MIT Symphony Orchestra; David Epstein. Turanbout TV 34760 Tape (c) CT 2315
+-Gr 11-81 p690 +-HFN 11-81 p94
+-HF 2-81 p57

Die tote Stadt: Gluck dass mir verblieb. See no. 3800

1965 Violanta. Eva Marton, Getraut Stocklass, s; Ruth Hesse, ms; Siegfried Jerusalem, Horst Laubenthal, Manfred Schmidt, Heinrich Weber, t; Walter Berry, Paul Hansen, bs; Bavarian Radio Chorus; Munich Radio Orchestra; Marek Janowski. CBS 79229 (2) (also CBS M2 35909)
+FF 7/8-81 p119 +-ON 8-81 p36
+Gr 12-80 p876 +Op 1-81 p55
+-HFN 12-80 p141 +SFC 5-3-81 p22
++MT 5-81 p318 +-St 7-81 p83
+NR 6-81 p10 +STL 12-14-80 p38

KORTE, Karl

Symmetrics. See no. 1739

KOSA, Gabor

Two. See no. 3865

KOSA, Gyorgy

Divertimento. See no. 3865

KOSENKO, Victor

Pieces, violin and piano, op. 4. See no. 1885

KOSINS
Love letters. See no. 3820
KOSTIAINEN, Pekka
1966 Fantasia. Mass, organ. SIBELIUS: Pieces, op. 111: Funeral; Intrada. Masonic ritual music, op. 113: Hymn; Marche funebre. Matti Vainio, org. Finlandia FA 318
+FF 11/12-80 p210 +-HFN 12-80 p151
*Gr 1-81 p972
Mass, organ. See no. 1966
KOTTER, Johannes
Prelude, D major. See no. 3960
Salve regina. See no. 4094
KOUSSEVITZKY, Serge
Concerto, double bass, op. 3. See no. 1381
KOX, Hans
Dorian Gray suite. See no. 3943
KOZELUCH, Leopold Anton
Symphony concertante, E flat major. See no. 3794
KRAFT, Leo
Antiphonies, piano and tape. See no. 1512
Quartet, strings, no. 2. See no. 1512
Sestina. See no. 1010
KRAMER, A. Walter
Songs: The last hour; Swans. See no. 3967
KRAPF
Fantasy on Psalm CL. See no. 3786
KRAUSS
Yehi Ratzon. See no. 3897
KRAUZE, Zygmunt
Music box waltz. See no. 3942
KREBS, Johann
Ach Gott erhor mein Seufzen. See no. 183
Chorale preludes: Allein Gott in der Hoh sei Ehr; Von Gott will ich nicht lassen; Jesu meine Freude. See no. 3735
Jesu meine Freude. See no. 3622
Jesus meine Zuversicht. See no. 3622
Klavierubung: Praeambulum sopra "Jesu meine Freude". See no. 4012
Trio, C minor. See no. 183
Von Gott will ich nicht lassen. See no. 183. See no. 3622
Wachet auf ruft uns die Stimme. See no. 3629
KREISLER, Fritz
Allegretto in the style of Boccherini. See no. 1972
Arrangements; Frasquita serenade (Lehar); Serenade espagnole (Chaminade); Melody, op. 16, no. 2 (Paderewski); Andante cantabile; Chant sans paroles, op. 2, no. 3 (Tchaikovsky); Slavonic dance, no. 1, G minor (Dvorak); Caprice, op. 20 (Paganini); Molly on the shore (Grainger). See no. 1971
Aubade provencale. See no. 1971
Aucassin et Nicolette. See no. 1968
Berceuse romantique, op. 9. See no. 1968
Canzonetta. See no. 1972
Caprice, E flat major (Wieniawski). See no. 1970
Caprice Viennois, op. 2. See no. 1970. See no. 1972. See no. 4007
Cavatina. See no. 1972

Chanson Louis XIII and pavane (Couperin). See no. 1972
Danza espanola (Granados). See no. 1970
Episode. See no. 1968
French song. See no. 1968
La gitana. See no. 1970. See no. 1972
Humoresque (Dvorak). See no. 1969
Humoresuqe, op. 10, no. 2 (Tchaikovsky). See no. 1969
Larghetto (Weber). See no. 1970

1967 Liebesfreud. Liebesleid (arr. Rachmaninoff). RACHMANINOFF: Etudes tableaux, op. 39, nos. 3, 5, 9. Preludes, op. 3, no. 2, C sharp minor; op. 23, nos. 6-7; op. 32, nos. 2, 5, 10-12. Jeffrey Siegel, pno. Denon OX 7189
+-St 6-81 p122

Liebesfreud. See no. 1968. See no. 1970. See no. 1972. See no. 3872
Liebesleid. See no. 1967. See no. 1968. See no. 1970. See no. 1972. See no. 3872
Madrigal. See no. 1972
Marche miniature Viennoise. See no. 3693
Minuet (Porpora). See no. 1971
Polichinelle. See no. 1968. See no. 1970. See no. 1972
Praeludium and allegro, in the style of Pugnani. See no. 1972
La precieuse (Couperin). See no. 1970. See no. 1971
Quartet, strings, no. 1, op. 11, D major: Andante cantabile. See no. 1969
Recitative and scherzo caprice, op. 6. See no. 1968. See no. 1970. See no. 1972
Romance. See no. 1972
Romance, op. 4. See no. 1968
Rondino on a theme by Beethoven. See no. 1968. See no. 1970. See no. 1972
Scherzo. See no. 1971. See no. 3969
Schon Rosmarin. See no. 1968. See no. 1972. See no. 3872. See no. 4066
Serenade espagnole (Glazunov). See no. 1970
Sicilienne et rigaudon (Francoeur). See no. 1971
Slavonic dances, nos. 1-3; op. 46, no. 2; op. 72, nos. 2, 8. See no. 1969
Slavonic dance, op. 72, no. 2, E minor (Dvorak). See no. 1970
Sonatina, op. 100, G major: 2nd movement. See no. 1969
Songs my mother taught me. See no. 1969
Songs without words, op. 2, no. 3. See no. 1969
Souvenir d'un lieu cher, op. 42: Scherzo. See no. 1969
Symphony, no. 9, op. 95, E minor: Largo. See no. 1969
Syncopation. See no. 1970. See no. 1971
Tambourin Chinois, op. 3. See no. 1968. See no. 1970
Tango, op. 162, no. 2 (Albeniz). See no. 1970
Toy soldier's march. See no. 1968. See no. 1971. See no. 1972

1968 Works, selections: Aucassin et Nicolette. Berceuse romantique, op. 9. Episode. French song. Liebesleid. Liebesfreud. Polichinelle. Recitative and scherzo caprice. Romance, op. 4. Rondino on a theme by Beethoven. Schon Rosmarin. Tambourin Chinois, op. 3. Toy soldier's march. Takako Nishizaki, vln; Monique Duphil, pno. Camerata CMT 1501
++St 9-81 p94

1969 Works, selections: Humoresque (Dvorak). Slavonic dances, nos. 1-3; op. 46, no. 2; op. 72, nos. 2, 8. Sonatina, op. 100, G major: 2nd movement. Songs my mother taught me. Symphony, no. 9, op. 95, E minor: Largo. Humoresque, op. 10, no. 2 (Tchaikovsky). Qaurtet, strings, no. 1, op. 11, D major: Andante cantabile. Souvenir d'un lieu cher, op. 42: Scherzo. Song without words, op. 2, no. 3. Takako Nishizaki, vln; Michael Ponti, pno. Camerata CMTX 1502

+-FF 9/10-81 p125

1970 Works, selections: Caprice Viennois, op. 2. La gitana. Liebesfreud. Liebesleid. Polichinelle. La precieuse (after Couperin). Recitative and scherzo caprice, op. 6. Rondino on a theme by Beethoven. Syncopation. Tambourin Chinois, op. 3. Zigeunercapriccio. Arrangements: Tango, op. 162, no. 2 (Albeniz). Larghetto (Weber). Caprice, E flat major (Wieniawski). Slavonic dance, op. 72, no. 2, E minor (Dvorak). Serenade espagnole (Glazunov). Danza espanola (Granados). Shlomo Mintz, vln; Clifford Benson, pno. DG 2531 305 Tape (c) 3301 305

+Gr 4-81 p1339
+HFN 3-81 p97 tape
+HFN 4-81 p72
+MUM 9/10-81 p32
+-SR 11-81 p62
+ST 5-81 p45

1971 Works, selections: Aubade provencale. Menuet (Porpora). La precieuse (Couperin). Scherzo (Dittersdorf). Siciliano and rigaudon (Francoeur). Syncopation. Toy soldiers march. Arrangements: Frasquita serenade (Lehar); Serenade espagnole (Chaminade); Melody, op. 16, no. 2 (Paderewski); Andante cantabile; Chant sans paroles, op. 2, no. 3 (Tchaikovsky); Slavonic dance, no. 1, G minor (Dvorak); Caprice, no. 20, (Paganini); Molly on the shore (Grainger). Itzhak Perlman, vln; Samuel Sanders, pno. HMV ASD 3980 Tape (c) TC ASD 3980 (also Angel SZ 37630 Tape (c) 4ZS 37630)

+FF 9/10-81 p125
+Gr 3-81 p1210
+HFN 3-81 p87
+NR 5-81 p15
++St 9-81 p94

1972 Works, selections: Allegretto (Boccherini). Canzonetta. Caprice Viennois, op. 2. Cavatina. Chanson Luis XIII and pavane (Couperin). La gitana. Liebesfreud. Liebesleid. Madrigal. Polichinelle. Praeludium and allegro (Pugnani). Recitative and scherzo caprice, op. 6. Romance. Rondino on a theme by Beethoven. Schon Rosmarin. Toy soldiers march. Miklos Szenthelyi, vln; Judit Szenthelyi, pno. Hungaroton SLPX 12141

+ARG 2-81 p19
+FF 9/10-80 p143
++NR 7-80 p13
++SFC 7-27-80 p34
+St 10-80 p128

Zigeuner capriccio. See no. 1970

KERJCI, Isa

Nonet divertimento. See no. 1674

KRENEK, Ernst

Quintina, op. 191. See no. 1975

KRENEK, Ernst

1973 Lamentatio Jeremiae prophetae, op. 93. NCRV Vocal Ensemble; Marinus Voorberg. Musicaphon BM 30 L 1303/4 (2)

+-HFN 1-81 p96

1974 Songs: Songs, op. 30a (3); Songs, op. 112 (4); Zeitlieder, op. 125 (2). NORDENSTROM: Zeit XXIV. Neva Pilgrim, s; Dennis

Helmrich, pno; Madison Quartet; William Nichols, clt. Orion ORS 79348

+-ARG 2-80 p38 +NR 4-80 p12
+Gr 6-81 p70 ++RR 1/2-80 p101

1975 They knew what they wanted, op. 227. Quintina, op. 191. Rheda Becker, narrator; Constance Navratil, s; James Ostryniec, ob; Paul Hoffmann, pno; Carol Winterbourne, flt; Carrie Holzman, vla; John Kneubuhl, gtr; Fred Lee, vibraphone; Joseph Kucera, Sue Hopkins, Mark Goldstein, perc; Ernst Krenek. Orion ORS 80380

+-ARG 5-81 p21 -NR 12-80 p11
+FF 1/2-81 p133

KREUTZER, Conradin

Septet, op. 62, E flat major. See no. 1888

KRIEGER, Adam

Der Rheinsche Wein. See no. 3985

KROKTOV

The poet: Aria of Luiidy. See no. 4030

KROL, Bernhold

Linzer Harmoniemusik, op. 67. See no. 519

KROMMER, Franz

Nonet, op. 79. See no. 1428

1976 Quartet, clarinet, op. 82, D major. WEBER: Quintet, clarinet, op. 34, B flat major. Alan Hacker, clt; Music Party. L'Oiseau-Lyre DSLO 553

+Gr 1-81 p960 +HFN 1-81 p96

1977 Quintet, clarinet, op. 95, B flat major. MOZART: Quintet, clarinet, K 581, A major. Georgina Dobree, clt; Alberni Quartet. Chantry CHT 006

+MT 10-81 p677

KRUMPHOLZ, Johann

Sonata, flute and harp, F major. See no. 1377

KUBIK, Gail

Prayer and toccata, organ and 2 pianos. See no. 1978

1978 Symphony, 2 pianos. Prayer and toccata, organ and 2 pianos. Leonid Hambro, Chet Swiatkowski, pno; Leonard Raver, org. Orion ORS 80372

+ARG 7/8-81 p21 +NR 1-81 p13
+FF 3/4-81 p144

KUBIK, Ladislav

Tribute to Mayakovsky. See no. 1962

KUCHAR, Jan

Fantasia, D minor. See no. 3962

KUHLAU, Friedrich

Le colporteur, op. 98. See no. 3682

KUHNAU, Johann

The battle between David and Goliath. See no. 3663
Der Gerechte kommt um. See no. 262

KUHNEL, August

Sonata, 2 viola da gamba, E minor. See no. 3833

KUMMER, Gaspard

Divertissement, op. 13. See no. 4065

KUNST, Jos

Exterieur. See no. 3728

KUPFERMAN, Meyer
Illusions. See no. 1980
1979 Infinities 15. PERSICHETTI: Concerto, piano, 4 hands. STARER: Fantasia concertante. Jean and Kenneth Wentworth, pno. Grenadilla GS 1050
+ARG 4-81 p44 ++NR 10-80 p14
+-FF 9/10-80 p178
1980 Infinities 19. Illusions. Sensations. NIEMANN: Meditation on "Paradise regained". Rohan de Saram, vlc; Yitkin Seow, pno; Ronald Roseman, ob; Gilbert Kalish, pno. Serenus SRS 12092
+-FF 11/12-81 p212
Second thoughts. See no. 1010
Sensations. See no. 1980
Short suite. See no. 1010
KUUSISTO, Taneli
Ramus virens olivarum, op. 55, no. 1. See no. 3804
KVANDAL, Johan
1981 Fantasies on 3 country dances, op. 31. MONRAD-JOHANSEN: Suite, no. 2, op. 9. SOMMERFELDT: Sonatina, no. 3, op. 14. Kjell Baekkelund, pno. Philips 6507 012
+FF 7/8-81 p159
Introduction and allegro, op. 30. See no. 3683
LA BARBARA, Joan
1982 Austum signal. Klee alee. q-/-uatre petites betes. Shadow song. Wizard Records RVW 2279
+FF 3/4-81 p146
Klee alee. See no. 1982
q-/-uatre petites betes. See no. 1982
Shadow song. See no. 1982
LACALLE, Jose
Amapola. See no. 3983
LACHNER, Franz
Elegy, op. 160. See no. 3788
LAI
A man and a woman. See no. 3816
LALO, Edouard
1983 Concerto, violoncello, D minor. SAINT-SAENS: Concerto, violoncello, no. 1, op. 33, A minor. Yo Yo Ma, vlc; Orchestra National de France; Lorin Maazel. CBS IM 35848 Taep (c) HMT 35848
+ARG 7/8-81 p22 +-HFN 5-81 p81
+Audio 4-81 p59 +MUM 5/6-81 p31
+FF 1/2-81 p134 ++St 2-81 p108
+Gr 5-81 p1474 +ST 9-81 p351
+HF 1-81 p73
Concerto, violoncello, D mionr. See no. 1096
Le Roi d'Ys: Le salut nous est promis; Vainement. See no. 4049
Le Roi d'Ys: Overture. See no. 3817
Songs: L'esclave. See no. 3758
1984 Symphonie espagnole, op. 21, D minor. SAINT-SAENS: Havanaise, op. 83. Introduction and rondo capriccioso, op. 28. Yehudi Menuhin, vln; PhO; Eugene Goossens. Classics for Pleasure CFP 40364 Tape (c) TC CFP 40364 (From ASD 290)
++Gr 9-81 p386 +HFN 12-81 p112 tape
+-HFN 9-81 p90
1985 Symphonie espagnole, op. 21, D minor. SAINT-SAENS: Concerto,

violin, no. 1, op. 20, A major. Kyung Wha Chung, vln; Montreal Symphony Orchestra; Charles Dutoit. Decca SXDL 7527 Tape (c) KSXDC 7527 (also London LDR 71029)
+-Gr 6-81 p40 +HFN 6-81 p74
+Gr 9-81 p460 tape ++SFC 12-13-81 p18

1986 Symphonie espagnole, op. 21, D minor. SAINT-SAENS: Introduction and rondo capriccioso, op. 28. Havanaise, op. 83. Arthur Grumiaux, vln; Lamoureux Concerts Orchestra; Manuel Rosenthal. Philips 6570 192 Tape (c) 7310 192
+FF 9/10-80 p144 +-HFN 2-81 p97
+Gr 2-81 p1091 +HFN 5-81 p93 tape

1987 Trio, no. 1, op. 7, C minor. SAINT-SAENS: Trio, piano, no. 1, op. 18, F major. Caecilian Trio. Turnabout TVC 37002 Tape (c) CT 7002
+FF 9/10-79 p130 +NYT 6-21-81 pD23
+HF 11-79 p100 ++SFC 6-17-79 p41
+HF 1-80 p91 tape

LAMA
Silenzio cantatore. See no. 3641

LAMB
Barefoot dances. See no. 1268

LAMBE, Walter
Magnificat. See no. 1245
Nesciens mater; Stella caeli. See no. 1033

LAMBERT, Constant
Horoscope: Valse of the Gemini. See no. 3840

LANCHBERRY, John
Tales of Beatrix Potter: The mouse waltz. See no. 3840

LANDGRAVE DE HESSE
Pavan. See no. 4016

LANDINI, Francesco
Caro signor pales. See no. 4102
Donna i prego. See no. 4102
In somm' alteca. See no. 4102
Ochi dolenti mie. See no. 4102
Songs: Angelica belta; Io son un pellegrin. See no. 1580

LANG, Craig
Tuba tune, op. 15, D major. See no. 3619

LANG, Istvan
1988 Concerto, violin. Quintet, winds, no. 3. Preludes for a postlude (2). Gyorgy Pauk, vln; Hungarian Wind Quartet; Gabor Janota, bsn; Kodaly Quartet Members, Budapest Philharmonic Orchestra Members; Gyorgy Lehel. Hungaroton SLPX 12051
+-Te 9-81 p61
Preludes for a postlude. See no. 1988
Quintet, winds, no. 3. See no. 1988

LANG, Josephine
1989 Songs: Der Winter; Fruhzeitiger Fruhling; O sehntest due dich so nach mir; Wie glanzt so hell dein Auge; Wie wenn die Sohn aufgeht. MENDELSSOHN-HENSEL: Die Nonne; Du bist die Ruh; Im Herbste; Nachtanderer; Rosenkranz; Vorwurf. SCHUMANN, C.: Das ist ein Tag der klingen mag; Die stille Lotosblume; Er ist gekommen in Sturm und Regen; Liebst du um Schonheit; Ich stand in dunkeln Traumen; Warum willst du And're fragen; Was weinst du Blumlein. VIARDOT-GARCIA: Das Voglein; Des Nachts; Die

Beschworung. Katherine Giesinski, s; John Ostendorf, bs-bar; Rudolph Palmer, pno. Leonarda LPI 107
+NR 12-81 p12
Songs: Sie liebt mich. See no. 3814
LANGLAIS, Jean
Chorale preludes: Aus tiefer Not schrei ich zu dir; Ein feste Burg ist unser Gott. See no. 3740
1990 Incantation pour un jour saint, op. 46. Paraphrases gregoriennes, op. 5. REGER: Fantasia on "Wachet auf ruft uns die Stimme", op. 52, no. 2. Pieces, organ, op. 59: Benedictus; Toccata. John Obetz, org. Lyrichord LLST 7353
+HF 11-81 p87 +-NR 11-81 p14
Kyrie (orbis factor). See no. 3901
Kyrie Dieu pere eternel. See no. 3901
Mass "Salve regina". See no. 1397
Mon ame cherche un fin paisible. See no. 3901
Notre Dieu est une puissante fortress. See no. 3901
Paraphrases gregoriennes, op. 5. See no. 1990
Salve regina. See no. 3614
Suite medievale. See no. 1936
Te deum. See no. 3821
LANIER, Nicholas
Songs: Bring away; Mark how the blushful morn. See no. 3876
Songs: Mark how the blushful morn. See no. 3807
Songs: Tho I am young. See no. 4058
LANNER, Joseph
Amazonen, op. 148. See no. 1991
Bankett Polonaise, op. 135. See no. 1991
Dampf Walzer, op. 94. See no. 1991
Favorit Polka, op. 201. See no. 1991
Hans Jorgel Polka, op. 194. See no. 1991
Hofballtanze, op. 161. See no. 3169
Die Humoristiker, op. 92. See no. 1991
Kronungs Walzer, op. 133. See no. 1991
Die Neapolitaner, op. 107. See no. 1991
Die Osmanen, op. 146. See no. 1991
Pest Waltz, op. 93. See no. 3863
Roccoco Walzer, op. 136. See no. 1991
Die Schonbrunner, op. 200. See no. 3169
Tarantel, op. 125. See no. 1991
1991 Works, selections: Amazonen, op. 148. Bankett Polonaise, op. 135. Dampfwalzer, op. 94. Favorit Polka, op. 201. Hans Jorgel Polka, op. 194. Dei Humoristiker, op. 92. Die Neapolitaner, op. 107. Kronungs Walzer, op. 133. Die Osmanen, op. 146. Tarantel, op. 125. Roccoco Walzer, op. 136. Die Zapfenstreich, op. 108. Vienna Chamber Orchestra, String Trio; Paul Angerer. Intercord INT 180 818 (2)
++HFN 11-81 p100
Der Zapfenstreich, op. 108. See no. 1991
LAPPI, Pietro
La negrona. See no. 3936
LARA, Agustin
Granada. See no. 3838
LARCHET
Padraic the fiddler. See no. 3967

LARSSON, Lars-Erik

1992 Barococo, op. 64. Concertino, trumpet, op. 45, no. 6. Lyrisk fantasi, op. 54. Pastoral. Urban Eriksson, tpt; Unga Musiker; Sven Verde. Artemis ARTE 7105
+FF 3/4-81 p146

Concertino, op. 45, no. 6. See no. 1992
Divertimento. See no. 862
Lyrisk fantasi, op. 54. See no. 1992
Pastoral. See no. 1992
Pastoral suite, op. 19. See no. 79
Quartet, strings, no, 3, op. 65. See no. 923
A winter's tale, op. 18. See no. 9
A winter's tale, op. 18: Vignettes. See no. 79

LASSUS, Roland de

A voi Guglielmo. See no. 3675
Am Abend spat beim buehlen Wein. See no. 3675

1993 Bell Amfitrit altera mass. Psalmi poenitentalis VII. Christ Church Cathedral Choir; Simon Preston. Argo ZRG 735
+AR 8-81 p76 *NR 2-75 p7
+Gr 8-74 p382 +RR 7-74 p75
+MQ 1-76 p144 ++St 2-76 p106

Bicinium. See no. 3675
Bonjour mon coeur. See no. 3766. See no. 4114
Die fasstnacht ist ein schoene Zeit. See no. 3675
Im Mayen hoert man die hanen krayen. See no. 3675
Kombt her zu mir spricht gottes son. See no. 3675

1994 Lagrime de San Pietro. Psalmus poenitentialis, no. 2. Motets: Timor et tremor; Pronuba Juno; Cum rides mihi. Liszt Chamber Choir; Istvan Parkai. Hungaroton SLPX 12081/2 (2)
+-AR 8-81 p77 +-HFN 1-81 p96
+FF 3/4-81 p146 ++NR 2-81 p9
+-Gr 11-80 p723

Magnificat sexti toni. See no. 3675
Matona mia cara. See no. 3675
Missa sexta, 8 voices. See no. 3675

1995 Motets: Ave regina caelorum; Salve regina; O mors quam amara est. Psalmi poenitentialies: Miserere mei Deus; Domine, ne in furore tuo. Roderick Skeaping, Trevor Jones, viol; Pro Cantione Antiqua, Early Music Wind Ensemble; Bruno Turner. DG 2533 290
+-AR 8-81 p76 +HFN 11-75 p155
+Gr 10-75 p699 +RR 10-75 p85
+-HF 5-76 p86 ++St 2-76 p106

Motets: Justorum animae. See no. 3906

1996 Motets: Lauda Sion salvatorem; Musica Dei donum. Puisque j'ay perdu, mass. Pro Cantione Antiqua; Bruno Turner. Harmonia Mundi 1C 065 99741 (also BASF EA 226174)
+-AR 8-81 p76 +FF 3/4-80 p111

Motets: Timor et remor; Pronumba Juno; Cum rides mihi. See no. 1994
La nuict froide et sombre. See no. 3675
La nuit froide et sombre. See no. 3766
O fugace dolcezza. See no. 3675

1997 Psalmi poenitentialis. CPhO; Josef Veselka. Supraphon 112 2531/2 (2)
++NR 6-81 p8

Psalmus poenitentalis, no. 2. See no. 1994.
Psalmus poenitentalis, no. 7. See no. 1993
Psalmus poenitentialis: Miserere mei Deus; Domine ne in furore tuo. See no. 1995
Puisque j'ay perdu, mass. See no. 1996
Schaff mir doch Recht in Sachen mein. See no. 3675

1998 Songs: Alma redemptoris mater; Omnes de Saba venient; Psalmus poenitentalis V: Domine exaudi orationem meam; Tui sunt coeli; Salve regina. Christ Church Cathedral Choir; Simon Preston. Argo ZRG 795
+AR 8-81 p76
+Gr 9-76 p454
+HF 3-78 p101
+HFN 7-76 p89
+MT 1-77 p45
+MT 2-77 p133
+-NR 7-77 p8
++RR 7-76 p76

1999 Songs: Alma Deus; Alma redemptoris mater; Aurora lucis; Ave Maria; Benedic domine; Bone Jesu; Dic mihi; Domine convertere; Inclina domine; Jam lucis; Laudabit; Laudate dominum; Omnes de Saba; Regina caeli; Salve regina. Knabenchor Hannover, Collegium Vocale; Hesperion XX; Philippe Herreweghe, Jordi Savall. Astree AS 57
+-FF 3/4-81 p146

2000 Songs (madrigals and motets): Al dolce suon; Ben convenne; Bestia curvafia pulices; Beati pauperes; Da pacem domine; Domine quando veneris; Gloria patri et filio; Lucescit jam o socii; Ove d'altra montagna; Praesidium sara; Spent e d'amor; Voir est beaucoup. Alsfeld Vocal Ensemble; Wolfgang Helbich. Telefunken 6-42632 Tape (c) 4-42632
+FF 11/12-81 p184
+-Gr 7-81 p182
+OV 12-81 p36
++SFC 11-29-81 p18
+St 12-81 p116

Songs: Fuyons tous d'amour; Quand mon mari. See no. 3845
Stabat mater. See no. 3638
Susanne un jour. See no. 4090
Sybilla Europea. See no. 3675
Der Tag ist so freudenreich. See no. 3675
Timor Domini principium. See no. 3675
Timor et tremor Exaudi Deus. See no. 3675
Vedi l'aurora. See no. 3675

LAURENTIUS MASII DE FLORENTIA
Songs: No so qual i' mi voglia; Sento d'amor la fiamma; Non vedi tu amor; Non perch' i' speri. See no. 1580

LAURIDSEN, Morten
Be still my soul be still. See no. 3954

LAURO, Antonio
Angostura. See no. 3929
Carora. See no. 3929
El marabino, El totumo de Guarenas. See no. 3929
El nino. See no. 3929
Seis por derecho. See no. 3929
Vals criollo. See no. 3727
Venezuelan waltzes. See no. 4108

LAWES, William
Alman. See no. 4097

2001 Consort, no. 10, G minor. Sonata, no. 8, D major. Suite, no. 2,

D minor. Songs: Beauty in eclipse; Cupids weary of the court; Gather your rosebuds; Justitiae sacrum; O my Clarissa; When man for sin. Rene Jacobs, alto; Sigiswald Kuijken, Lucy van Dael, baroque violin; Wieland Kuijken, Gustav Leonhardt, vla da gamba, org; Edward Witsenburg, hp; Toyohiko Satoh, theorbo, lt; Gustav Leonhardt. RCA RL 3-0375
+-Gr 11-81 p737

Corant. See no. 4097

2002 Sett, 3 lyra viols. Setts, 2 violins, 2 bass viols, 2 theorbos, nos. 1, 7, 8. Consort of Musicke; Anthony Rooley. L'Oiseau-Lyre DSLO 573
++Gr 12-80 p846 +MT 11-81 p754
+HFN 12-80 p141 +STL 1-11-81 p38

Setts, 2 violins, 2 bass viols, 2 theorbos, nos. 1, 7-8. See no. 2002

2003 Setts, no. 2, A minor; no. 3, F major, C minor; no. 4, B flat major. Consort of Musicke. L'Oiseau-Lyre DSLO 560
+Gr 4-81 p1339 +MT 11-81 p754

Sonata, no. 8, D major. See no. 2001

Songs: Beauty in eclipse; Cupids weary of the court; Gather your rosebuds; Justitiae sacrum; O my Clarissa; When man for sin. See no. 2001

Suite, no. 2, D minor. See no. 2001

LAZAROF, Henri

Concerto, orchestra. See no. 462

LEBEGUE, Nicolas

Elevation, G major. See no. 1665

Suite du deuxieme ton. See no. 1665

Symphonie sur le bemol fa. See no. 1665

LEBRUN, Ludwig

Concerto, oboe, D minor. See no. 3782

LECHNER, Leonhard

Allein zu dir Herr Jesus Christ. See no. 3675

Nach meiner Lieb viel hundert Knaben trachten. See no. 3675

Songs (choral): Nun schein du Glanz der Herrlichkeit; O Tod du bist ein bitter Gallen. See no. 3720

LECLAIR, Jean-Marie

2004 Concerti, op. 7, nos. 1-6. Concerti, op. 10, nos. 1-6. Gerard Jarry, vln; Christian Larde, flt; Jean-Francois Paillard Chamber Orchestra; Jean-Francois Paillard. Musical Heritage Society MHS 834308 (3) (also RCA ZL 3-0692)
++FF 7/8-81 p121

Concerti, op. 10, nos. 1-6. See no. 2004

Forlane and tambourin, op. 8, F major. See no. 3867

2005 Sonatas, flute, op. 1. Christian Larde, flt; Huguette Dreyfus, hpd; Jean Lamy, vla da gamba. Musical Heritage Society MHS 1673/4
+-AR 5-81 p23

Sonatas, flute, op. 2, no. 8, D major. See no. 839

LEDUC, Simon

Sonatas, violin and harpsichord, op. 1, no. 1, D major; op. 4, nos. 1 and 4. See no. 120

2006 Symphonies (3). Orchestra de Chambre de Versailles. Arion ARN 38577
+STL 6-14-81 p40

LEES, Benjamin
Concerto, string quartet. See no. 3079
LEEUW, Ton de
2007 Mildare. JULLICH: Improvisation music. STOCKHAUSEN: Zyklus. Michael Jullich, per. Moers 01068
+HFN 1-81 p104
LeFANU, Nocola
2008 But stars remaining. Deva. The same day dawns. Jane Manning, s; Christopher van Kampen, vlc; Nash Ensemble; Nicola LeFanu. Chandos ABR 1017 Tape (c) ABT 1017
+FF 9/10-81 p127
+Gr 4-81 p1339
+-HFN 4-81 p72
+HFN 4-81 p81 tape
*MT 6-81 p390
Deva. See no. 2008
The same day dawns. See no. 2008
LEFEBVRE, Claude
D'un arbre de nuit. See no. 866
Etwas Weiter. See no. 866
Suite, op. 57. See no. 4019
LEFEVRE
Suites faciles: Allemande de Mr. le Fevre; Passecaille de Mr. le Fevre. See no. 3927
LEGRAND
Brain's song. See no. 3820
Pastorales. See no. 3705
LEGRENZI, Giovanni
La pezzoli, op. 4, no. 6. See no. 3808
LEHAR, Franz
2009 Friederike. Helen Donath, Gabriele Fuchs, Martin Finke, Adolf Dallapozza, soloists; Munich Radio Orchestra and Chorus; Heinz Wallberg. HMV SLS 5230 (also EMI 1C 157 30997/8)
+FF 11/12-81 p184
++Gr 8-81 p310
+HFN 8-81 p85
+ON 9-81 p60
+Op 11-81 p1151
+STL 9-13-81 p41
Giuditta: Du bist meine Sonne; Freunde das Leben ist lebenswert. See no. 3648
Giuditta: Meine Lippen sie Kussen so heiss. See no. 3837
Gold und Silber, op. 79. See no. 4083
2010 Das land des Lachelns, excerpts. Die lustige Witwe, excerpts. OFFENBACH: La belle Helene, excerpts. Orfee au Enfers, excerpts. La vie parisienne, excerpts. STRAUSS, J.: Die Fledermaus, op. 363, excerpts. Die Zigeunerbaron, op. 420, excerpts. Soloists; Sadler's Wells Orchestra and Chorus; Vilem Tauskay, William Reid, John Matheson, Alexander Faris. HMV ESDW 712 (2) Tape (c) TC ESDW 712
+FF 9/10-81 p219
+Gr 6-81 p93 tape
+Gr 1-81 p1005
+Op 6-81 p650
Das land des Lachelns: Da kommt Lisa...Ich danke fur die Huldigung ...Flirten bisschen flirten; Guten Abend, Hoheit...Bei einem Tee en daux. See no. 3844
2011 Die lustige Witwe. Helen Donath, Edda Moser, s; Siegfried Jerusalem, Norbert Orth, Friedrich Lenz, t; Benno Kusche, Hermann Prey, bar; Bavarian Radio Chorus; Munich Radio Orchestra; Heinz Wallberg. HMV SLS 5202 Tape (c) TC SLS 5202 (also Angel SZBX 3906)

+FF 7/8-81 p122 +NR 4-81 p10
+Gr 10-80 p534 +-ON 4-4-81 p28
+HFN 2-81 p89 +-Op 1-81 p55

Die lustige Witwe, excerpts. See no. 2010

Die lustige Witwe: Frau Glawari darf keinen...Bitte meine Herr'n; Nun lasst uns aber daheim...Vilja o Vilja; Heia Madel auf geschaut...Dummer dummer Reitersmann. See no. 3844

Die lustige Witwe: Vilja; Waltz. See no. 3640

Paganini, excerpts. See no. 3975

2012 Der Zarewitsch. Lucia Popp, Elfriede Hobarth, s; Rene Kollo, Norbert Orth, Hartmut Brosius, t; Ivan Rebroff, bs; Bavarian Radio Chorus; Munich Radio Orchestra; Heinz Wallberg. Eurodisc 301 291 (2) Tape (c) 501 291
+Gr 12-81 p940 +HFN 12-81 p96

LEHMANN, Liza

The birth of the flowers. See no. 3650

Myself when young. See no. 4074

LEIGH, Walter

Concertino. See no. 3856

LEIGHTON, Kenneth

Lully lulla thou little tiny child. See no. 3685

Songs: Paean. See no. 3875

LEKEU, Guillaume

2013 Adagio, op. 3. MATTON: Mouvement symphonique, no. 1. MILHAUD: Suite provencale, op. 152a. Quebec Symphony Orchestra; James De Preist. Radio Canada International RCI 454
+FF 5/6-81 p218

2014 Sonata, violin and piano, G major. WUORINEN: Pieces, violin and piano (6). John Ferrell, vln; James Avery, pno. Orion ORS 80381
+St 12-81 p118

2015 Sonata, violin and piano, G major. VIEUXTEMPS: Ballade et polonaise, op. 38. YSAYE: Reve d'enfant, op. 14. Arthur Grumiaux, vln; Dinorah Varsi, pno. Philips FH 30
+FF 7/8-81 p218

LEMBA, Arthur

Estonian cradle song. See no. 3678

LEMMENS, Jaak-Nicolaas

Cantabile, B minor. See no. 2016

Creator alma siderum. See no. 2016

Invocation, F minor. See no. 3902

2016 Organ works: Cantabile, B minor. Creator alma siderum. Pater superni. Pastorale, F major. Prelude a cinque, E flat major. Priere, E major. Sonate pascale. Sonate pontificale: Fanfare. Jozef Sluys, org. Zephyr ZO 4
+-Gr 7-80 p153 +MT 3-81 p197

Pastorale, F major. See no. 2016

Pater superni. See no. 2016

Prelude a cinque, E flat major. See no. 2016

Priere, E major. See no. 2016

Sonate pascale. See no. 2016

Sonate pontificale. See no. 4111

Sonate pontificale: Fanfare. See no. 2016

LENDVAY, Kamillo

2017 The respectful prostitute. Julia Paszthy, s; Denes Gulyas, t;

Laszlo Polgar, bs; Istvan Gati, bar; Janos Csanyi, Tamas Kertesz, t; Budapest Symphony Orchestra Members; Tamas Breitner. Hungaroton SLPX 12132
+ARG 12-79 p43 +NR 12-79 p10
+FF 1/2-80 p103 +SFC 12-16-79 p60
+-HFN 2-81 p89

LEONCAVALLO, Ruggiero
La boheme: Musette; O gioia della mia dimora; Io non ho che una povera stanzetta; Testa dorata. See no. 3997
La boheme: Questa e Mimi. See no. 4023
La boheme: Testa adorata. See no. 3982
Lady Chatterton: Tu sola mi rimani. See no. 3838
I Pagliacci, excerpts. See no. 4077
I Pagliacci: Balatella. See no. 4042
I Pagliacci: Balatella; Non mi tentar. See no. 3837
I Pagliacci: E fra quest'ansie...Decido il mio destino. See no. 3849
I Pagliacci: Intermezzo. See no. 3787
I Pagliacci: O Columbina. See no. 3972. See no. 4023. See no. 4054
I Pagliacci: No Pagliaccio non son. See no. 3996
I Pagliacci: No Pagliaccio non son; Vesti la giubba. See no. 4053
2018 I Pagliacci: Qual fiamma avea nel guardo. PUCCINI: La boheme: Si mi chiamano Mimi; O soave fanciulla; Donde lieta usci. Madama Butterfly: Love duet, Act 1; Un bel di; Con onor muore. Turandot: Signore ascolta; Tu che di gel sei cinta. VERDI: Nabucco: Anch'io dischiuso...Salgo gia del trono. Renata Scotto, s; Carlo Bergonzi, Alfredo Kraus, t; Robert Lloyd, bs; Various orchestras; Riccardo Muti, John Barbirolli, Francesco Molinari-Pradelli, James Levine. Angel SZ 37819 Tape (c) 4XS 37819
+-FF 9/10-81 p207 +St 10-81 p139
+-NR 6-81 p9
I Pagliacci: Recitar...Vesti la giubba. See no. 3646. See no. 3750. See no. 3995. See no. 4035
I Pagliacci: Si puo. See no. 4079
I Pagliacci: Un tal gioco; Vesti la giubba; Non Pagliaccio non son. See no. 3839
I Pagliacci: Vesti la giubba. See no. 3759. See no. 3982. See no. 3987
Songs: Lasciata amar; Mattinata. See no. 4036
Songs: Mattinata. See no. 3759. See no. 3885
Songs: Serenata francese. See no. 3758
Zaza: O mio piccolo tavolo. See no. 3982
I Zingari: Principe Radu io son. See no. 3982

LEONINUS (12th century France)
Viderunt omnes. See no. 3779

LEONTOVYCH, Mykola
Ukrainian folktunes. See no. 3662

LEOPARDI
L'infinito. See no. 4027

LE ROUX, Gaspard
2019 Pieces de clavecin: Suites, nos. 2-3, 5-6. William Christie, Arthur Haas, hpd. Harmonia Mundi HM 399 (also Musical Heritage Society MHS 4344)
+FF 1/2-80 p137 +HFN 1-79 p121

++FF 9/10-81 p164 +RR 11-78 p92
++Gr 10-78 p711

LEROUX, Xavier
Le nil. See no. 3967
LESCUREL, Jehan de
A vous douce debonaire. See no. 3846
LEVITZKI
Arabesque valsante, op. 6. See no. 3920
LEWIS, Robert Hall
2020 Duet, violin and piano. WEBERN: Pieces, violin and piano, op. 7 (4). WEINER: Sonata, violin and piano, no. 2, op. 11, F sharp minor. Robert Gerle, vln; Marilyn Neeley, pno. Grenadilla GS 1055
+NR 11-81 p7
LEWKOVITCH, Bernhard
Songs: Cantabo domino; O bone Jesu. See no. 3991
LIADOV, Anatol
2021 The enchanted lake, op. 62. RIMSKY-KORSAKOV: Russian Easter festival overture, op. 36. STRAVINSKY: L'Oiseau de feu: Suite. USSR State Academic Orchestra; Dimitri Kitaenko. CBS 36696
+-FF 7/8-81 p228 +-NR 6-81 p4
Musical snuff box, op. 32. See no. 3723
Russian folksongs, op. 58. See no. 3333
LIDDLE, Samuel
How lovely are thy dwellings; The Lord is my shepherd; Abide with me. See no. 3852
LIDHOLM, Ingvar
2022 Greetings from an old world. Kontakion. Music for strings. Swedish Radio Orchestra, Polish Chamber Orchestra; Leif Segerstam, Jerzy Maksymiuk. Caprice CAP 1167
+FF 1/2-81 p135
Kontakion. See no. 2022
Kort ar rosornas tid. See no. 3691
Music for strings. See no. 2022
Sonata, solo flute. See no. 3679
LIDL, Anton
Trio, violin, violoncello and viola da gamba, E major. See no. 3813
LIDON, Jose
Sonata con trompeta real. See no.3619
Sonata de primo tono. See no. 3806
LIEBERMANN, Rolf
2023 Concerto, jazz band and symphony orchestra. SAUTER-FINEGAN: Doddletown fifers. Arrangements of Moonlight sonata; Tchaikovsky piano concerto; Midnight sleighride; Azure-te (Paris blues); Rain; Nina never knew; When hearts are young. CSO; Fritz Reiner, Sauter-Finegan Orchestra. RCA AGL 1-3822
+FF 9/10-81 p127
LIGETI, Gyorgy
2024 Bagatelles, wind quintet (6). Pieces, wind quintet (10). NILSSON: Deja-vu. Deja connu. Deja connu deja entendu. Stockholm Wind Quintet. Caprice CAP 1150
+FF 9/10-81 p151 +-NR 8-81 p8
2025 Continuum. Lontano. Requiem. Liliana Poli, s; Barbro Ericson, ms; Antoinette Vischer, hpd; Bavarian Radio Choir; Hesse Radio Symphony Orchestra, South West German Radio Orchestra; Michael

Gielen, Bernest Bour. Wergo WER 60045
+Gr 10-81 p553

2026 Le grand macabre: Scenes and interludes. Inga Nielsen, s; Olive Fredericks, ms; Peter Haage, t; Dieter Weller, bar; Danish Radio Orchestra and Chorus; Elgar Howarth. Wergo WER 60085
++FF 11/12-81 p185
+Gr 7-81 p191
+HFN 6-81 p74
*STL 6-14-81 p40
+Te 3-81 p27

Lontano. See no. 2025

2027 Pieces, 2 pianos. ZIMMERMANN: Monologue. Perspectives. Alfons and Aloys Kontarsky, pno. DG 2531 102
++CL 3-81 p10
++FF 1/2-81 p135
+Gr 9-80 p376
++HF 3-81 p56
+-HFN 11-80 p120
+MT 1-81 p34
+NR 2-81 p14
+STL 8-10-80 p30

Pieces, wind quintet. See no. 2024

Requiem. See no. 2025

LI HUAN-CHIH

Spring festival overture. See no. 1205

LINCKE, Joseph

Lysystrata: Glow worm idyll. See no. 4083

LINDBERG, Oskar

Pingst. See no. 3991

LINDE, Bo

Prelude and finale, op. 16. See no. 48

LINDPAINTNER, Peter von

Fantasy, variations and rondo, op. 49. See no. 3907

LINEK, Jiri (George)

Concerto, organ, C major. See no. 1032

Concerto, organ, D major. See no. 3826

Fanfares, nos. 1-3, 5-6, 13-14. See no. 3826

LINN, Robert

Concertino, violin and wind octet. See no. 1744

Quintet, brass instruments. See no. 1271

LIONCOURT, Guy de

Quid retribuam Domino. See no. 3637

LISZT, Franz

Ab irato, S 143. See no. 2048

2028 Ad nos ad salutarem undam, S 259. FRANCK: Chorale, no. 1, E major. Priere, op. 20. Jane Parker-Smith, org. Angel DS 37748
-FF 5/6-81 p98

2029 Ad nos ad salutarem undam, S 259. Prelude and fugue on the name B-A-C-H, S 260. Variations on Bach's "Weinen, Klagen, Sorgen, Zagen", S 673. Jennifer Bate, org. ASV ACM 2008 (From Enigma VAR 1051)
+Gr 6-81 p60

2030 Ad nos ad salutarem undam, S 259. Prelude and fugue on the name B-A-C-H, S 260. Variations on Bach's "Weinen, Klagen, Sorgen, Zagen", S 673. Hans Fagius, org. BIS LP 170
+ARG 12-81 p18
+FF 9/10-81 p130
+Gr 11-81 p724
+-HFN 6-81 p83
++NR 8-81 p13

2031 Ad nos ad salutarem undam, S 259. REGER: Pieces, organ, op. 80: Prelude, E minor. Pieces, organ, op. 129: Prelude and fugue, B minor. Gottfried Miller, org. Motette M 1017
+-FF 1/2-81 p222

Ad nos ad salutarem undam, S 259. See no. 1534
Am Grabe Richard Wagners, S 203. See no. 2060
2032 Annees de pelerinage, 1st year, S 160; 2nd year, S 161; 3rd year, S 163. Lazar Berman, pno. DG 2531 257/9 (3)
++ARG 3-81 p31
+-FF 1/2-81 p137
+CL 1-81 p12
Annees de pelerinage, 1st year, S 160: Les cloches de Geneve; Vallee d'Obermann. See no. 2041
2033 Annees de pelerinage, 2nd year, S 161: Apres une lecture du Dante. Paraphrases: Verdi: Rigoletto: Quartet. Sonata, piano, S 178, B minor. Daniel Barenboim, pno. DG 2531 271 Tape (c) 3301 271
+-ARG 9-81 p25
-CL 12-81 p10
++FF 7/8-81 p123
+-Gr 8-81 p296
+HFN 8-81 p85
+HFN 9-81 p93 tape
++NR 5-81 p14
+-NYT 4-26-81 pD23
+St 5-81 p76
+STL 9-13-81 p41
Annees de pelerinage, 2nd year, S 161: Apres une lecture du Dante; Sonetto del Petrarca. See no. 1218
2034 Annees de pelerinage, 2nd year, S 161: Petrarch sonnets, nos. 47, 104, 123. Consolations, S 172 (6). Liebestraume, S 541 (3). Daniel Barenboim, pno. DG 2531 318 Tape (c) 3301 318
+ARG 9-81 p24
-CL 12-81 p44
++FF 7/8-81 p123
+Gr 3-81 p1214
+HFN 4-81 p72
+HFN 4-81 p81 tape
+NR 5-81 p14
+NYT 4-26-81 pD23
+St 5-81 p76
Annees de pelerinage, 2nd year, S 161: Sonetto del Petrarca. See no. 3749
Annees de pelerinage, 2nd year, S 161: Sposalizio; Supplement, S 162. See no. 3723
2035 Annees de pelerinage, 2nd year, S 162: Venezia e Napoli. Harmonies poetieques et religieuses, S 173: Funerailles; Invocation. Legendes, S 175. Aldo Ciccolini, pno. Seraphim S 60343
+CL 1-81 p12
+FF 9/10-80 p145
+NR 5-80 p11
Annees de pelerinage, 2nd year, S 162: Venezia e Napoli. See no. 3869. See no. 3964
Annees de pelerinage, 3rd year, S 163: Aux cypres de la Villa d' Este; Les jeux d'eau a la Villa d'Este; Sunt lacrymae rerum. See no. 2063
2036 Annees de pelerinage, 3rd year, S 163: Les jeux d'eau a la Villa d'Este. Mephisto waltz, no. 1, S 514. Harmonies poetiques et religieuses, S 173: Funerailles. Les preludes, S 97. Stefan Ferrier, Randall Moselle, pno. Orion ORS 80396
+-FF 7/8-81 p124
-NR 4-81 p12
Annees de pelerinage, 3rd year, S 163: Les jeux d'eau a la Villa d'Este. See no. 1179. See no. 1290. See no. 3723
2037 Apparitions, nos. 1 and 2, S 185. Mephisto waltzes, nos. 1-4, S 514. Paraphrases: Chopin: Meine Freuden, S 480. Joseph Banowetz, pno. Orion ORS 80385
+-CL 9-81 p18
+FF 7/8-81 p122
+NR 4-81 p12
Apparitions: Consolation; Galop. See no. 3840
2038 Bagatelle without tonality. Harmonies poetiques et religieuses: Benediction de Dieu dans la solitude. Mephisto polka. Mephisto waltzes, nos. 1-4, S 514. Cyprien Katsaris, pno. Tele-

funken 6-42829 Tape (c) 4-42829
++FF 11/12-81 p186
Bagatelle sans tonality. See no. 2060. See no. 2062
Balcsillagzat. See no. 2062
Ce qu'on entend sur la montage, G 95. See no. 2073
2039 Christus: Annunciation; Les beatitudes; Ride into Jerusalem; Easter hymns; Resurrexit. Eva Andor, s; Zsuzsa Nemeth, ms; Josef Reti, t; Sandor Solyom Nagy, bar; Jozsef Gregor, bs; Sandor Margittay, org; Budapest Chorus; Budapest Kodaly Zoltan Girls' Choir; HSO; Miklos Forrai. Budapest FX 12302
+-FF 11/12-81 p186 +-HFN 6-81 p87
+-NR 11-81 p8
2040 Concerto, piano, no. 1, S 124, E flat major. Concerto, piano, no. 2, S 125, A major. Sviatoslav Richter, pno; LSO; Kyril Kondrashin. Bruno Walter Society RR 489
+-FF 11/12-81 p186
2041 Concerto, piano, no. 1, S 124, E flat major. Annees de pelerinage, 1st year, S 160: Vallee d'Obermann. Nicholas Zumbro, pno; RPO; Paul Freeman. Musical Heritage Society MHS 4359
/-FF 9/10-81 p129
2042 Concerto, piano, no. 1, S 124, E flat major. Hungarian rhapsody, no. 6, S 244, D flat major. Byron Janis, pno; MPO; Kyril Kondrashin. Philips (Japanese) FH 1
+FF 3/4-81 p148
2043 Concerto, piano, no. 1, S 124, E flat major. Concerto, piano, no. 2, S 125, A major. Byron Janis, pno; MPO; Kyril Kondrashin; MRSO; Gennady Rozhdestvensky. Philips 6527 048 Tape (c) 7311 048 (From SFM 23004)
+-Gr 4-81 p1318 +-HFN 7-81 p81 tape
+-HFN 5-81 p91
2044 Concerto, piano, no. 1, S 124, E flat major. Concerto, piano, no. 2, S 125, A major. Claudio Arrau, pno; LSO; Colin Davis. Philips 9500 780 Tape (c) 7300 854
++Gr 9-81 p386 +SFC 12-13-81 p18
+HFN 9-81 p81
2045 Concerto, piano, no. 1, S 124, E flat major. Concerto, piano, no. 2, S 125, A major. Jorge Bolet, pno; Rochester Philharmonic Orchestra; David Zinman. Vox VCL 9001 Tape (c) VCS 9001
+FF 9/10-81 p128 +NR 7-81 p4
+HF 11-81 p103 tape +SFC 6-14-81 p18
+HFN 10-81 p89 +St 10-81 p126
Concerto, piano, no. 1, S 124, E flat major. See no. 2061
Concerto, piano, no. 2, S 125, A major. See no. 2040. See no. 2043. See no. 2044. See no. 2045. See no. 2061
Consolations, S 172. See no. 2034
2046 Consolation, no. 3, S 172, D flat major. Mephisto waltz, no. 1, S 514. RACHMANINOFF: Barcarolle, op. 10, no. 3, G minor. Humoresque, op. 10, no. 5, G major. SCHUMANN: Humoreske, op. 20, B flat major. Vladimir Horowitz, pno. RCA ARL 1-3433 Tape (c) ARK 1-3433
+-ARG 6-80 p50 +-HFN 11-80 p131 tape
+CL 12-79 p10 +MT 2-81 p112
++FF 1/2-80 p208 ++NR 1-80 p14
++Gr 4-80 p1571 +-RR 5-80 p90
++HF 1-80 p63 +-SFC 10-28-79 p53
++HF 2-80 p102 tape +-St 2-80 p133

+-HFN 4-80 p116 +STL 6-8-80 p38

Consolation, no. 3, S 172, D flat major. See no. 3866

Csardas macabre, S 224. See no. 2062. See no. 2063

Csardas obstine, S 225. See no. 2060. See no. 2062. See no. 3869

Dante symphony, S 109. See no. 2073

Duo, violin and piano, S 127. See no. 2050

En reve, S 207. See no. 2060. See no. 2062

2047 Episodes from Lenau's "Faust". A Faust symphony, S 108. Gyorgy Korondy, t; Hungarian People's Army Male Chorus; HSO; Janos Ferencsik. Hungaroton SLPX 12022/3 (2) Tape (c) MK 12022/3

+ARG 10-80 p43 +HFN 2-81 p89
+-FF 7/8-80 p104 ++NR 4-80 p2
+HF 7-80 p70 +SFC 2-3-80 p45
+HF 10-80 p98 tape

Episodes from Leanu's "Faust": Der Nachtliche Zug; Mephisto waltz, no. 1. See no. 2074

Epithalam, S 129. See no. 2050

Etude de concert, S 144: Un sospiro. See no. 2048

Etudes de concert, S 145: Gnomenreigen. See no. 1179

Etudes de concert, S 145: Waldesrauschen; Gnomenreigen. See no. 2048. See no. 3993

2048 Etudes d'execution transcendente, S 139. Etudes de concerto, no. 3, S 144: Un sospiro. Etudes de concert, nos. 1-2, S 145: Waldesrauschen, Gnomenreigen. Ab irato, S 143. Roman Rudnytsky, pno. Muza SXL 0940-0941

+-CL 10-81 p8

Etudes d'execution transcendente, S 139: Ricordanza. See no. 4018

Etudes d'execution transcendente d'apres Paganini, S 140: La campanella. See no. 4018

2049 Fantasia and fugue on the name B-A-C-H, S 529. Orpheus, S 98. Prelude and fugue on the name B-A-C-H, S 260. Prometheus, S 99. Jean Guillou, org.(trans. Guillou). Festivo F 504

+Gr 12-81 p903

Faust symphony, S 108. See no. 2047. See no. 2074

Festklange, S 101. See no. 2073

2050 Grand duo concertante, S 128. Duo, violin and piano, S 127. Epithalam, S 129. Romance oubliee, S 132. Jean-Jacques Kantorow, vln; Henri Barda, pno. Arion ARN 38466 (also Musical Heritage Society MHS 4211)

++Gr 8-80 p239 +RR 7-80 p80
+HFN 8-80 p19 ++St 1-81 p85

Hamlet, S 104. See no. 2074

Harmonies poetiques et religieuses, S 173: Ave Maria. See no. 2060

Harmonies poetiques et religieuses, S 173: Benediction de Dieu dans la solitude. See no. 2038

Harmonies poetiques et religieuses, S 173: Funerailles. See no. 1179. See no. 2036

Harmonies poetiques et religieuses, S 173: Funerailles; Invocation. See no. 2035

Heroide funebre, S 102. See no. 2074

Historic Hungarian portraits. See no. 2062

Hungaria, S 103. See no. 2074

2051 Hungarian coronation mass, S 11. Iren Szecsody, s; Magda Tiszay, con; Jozsef Simandy, t; Andras Farago, bs; Budapest Choir; Budapest State Orchestra; Janos Ferencsik. Budapest FX 12293

+FF 9/10-81 p129

2052 Hungarian coronation mass, S 11. Veronika Kincses, s; Klara Takacs, alto; Denes Gulyas, t; Laszlo Polgar, bs; HRT Chorus; Budapest Symphony Orchestra; Gyorgy Lehel. Hungaroton SLPX 12148
+-FF 5/6-81 p98 +HFN 1-81 p96
+-HF 12-81 p72

2053 Hungarian fantasia, S 123. Malediction, S 121. Paraphrases (transcriptions): Beethoven: Fantasy on "Ruins of Athens", S 649. Totentanz, S 126. Michel Beroff, pno; Leipzig Gewandhaus Orchestra; Kurt Masur. Angel SZ 37761
+-FF 3/4-81 p148 +NR 7-81 p1

Hungarian fantasia, S 123. See no. 909. See no. 2061

2054 Hungarian rhapsodies, S 244 (19). Louis Kentner, pno. Vox SVBX 5452 Tape (c) CBS 5452 (also Turnabout TV 34266)
+Gr 4-71 p1640 +HF 5-81 p53 tape

Hungarian rhapsody, no. 2, S 244, G sharp minor. See no. 1484

2055 Hungarian rhapsodies, nos. 2, 4, S 244. Mazeppa. Les preludes, S 97. BPhO; Herbert von Karajan. DG 2535 110 Tape (c) 3335 110
++FF 7/8-81 p124

2056 Hungarian rhapsodies, nos. 2, 6, 11-15, S 244. Solomon, Ignaz Friedman, Mischa Levitzki, Alfred Cortot, Gina Bachauer, Ferruccio Busoni, Mark Hambourg, pno. Arabesque AR 8011 Tape (c) 9011 (From various Columbia and HMV originals)
+ARG 2-81 p20 +NR 10-80 p12
+-FF 11/12-80 p128 ++St 11-80 p92
+HF 12-80 p81

Hungarian rhapsody, no. 4, S 244, E flat major. See no. 909. See no. 1179
Hungarian rhapsody, no. 5, S 244, E minor. See no. 909
Hungarian rhapsody, no. 6, S 244, D flat major. See no. 2042
Hungarian rhapsody, no. 11, S 244, A minor. See no. 3723
Hunnenschlacht, S 105. See no. 2073
Die Ideale, S 106. See no. 2073
Legends, S 175. See no. 2035
Liebestraume, S 541. See no. 2034
Liebestraum, no. 3, S 541, A flat major. See no. 3645
La lugubre gondola, S 200. See no. 2060. See no. 2062. See no. 3693
Malediction, S 121. See no. 2053. See no. 2061
Mazeppa. See no. 2055
Mazeppa, S 100. See no. 2074
Mephisto polka. See no. 2038
Mephisto waltz. See no. 89
Mephisto waltzes, nos. 1-4, S 514. See no. 2037. See no. 2038
Mephisto waltz, no. 1, S 514. See no. 2036. See no. 2046
Mephisto waltz, no. 2, S 111. See no. 2074
Mephisto waltz, no. 3, S 216. See no. 2062
Mephisto waltz, no. 4. See no. 2062

2057 Missa coronationalis. Veronika Kincses, s; Klara Takacs, con; Denes Gulyas, t; Laszlo Polgar, bs; HRT Chorus; Budapest Symphony Orchestra; Gyorgy Lehel. Hungaroton SLPX 12148
+-FF 5/6-81 p98 +NR 3-81 p11
+-HF 12-81 p72 ++SFC 3-15-81 p18
+HFN 1-81 p96

Mosonyi's Grabgeleit, S 194. See no. 2063
Nuages gris, S 199. See no. 2060. See no. 2062
Orpheus, S 98. See no. 2049. See no. 2073. See no. 4069

2058 Paraphrases (transcriptions): Auf dem Wasser zu Singen, S 558; Ave Maria; Die Forelle, S 563; Der Erlkonig, S 558; Du bist die Ruh, S 558; Fruhlingsglaube, S 558; Gretchen am Spinnrade, S 558; Horch horch die Lerche, S 558; Wohin, S 565. Antonio Barbosa, pno. Connoisseur Society Tape (c) InSync 4058
++Audio 10-81 p26 +HF 4-81 p93 tape
++CL 4-81 p14 +St 4-81 p110 tape

2059 Paraphrases: Mendelssohn: A midsummer night's dream: Wedding march; Elfin chorus. Gounod: Faust: Waltz. Beethoven: Adelaide, S 466. Mephisto waltz (arr. Busoni). Mozart: Marriage of Figaro: Fantasie. Egon Patri, pno. Westminster MCA 1414 Tape (c) 1414
+-CL 2-81 p13 +SFC 1-18-81 p21
+FF 1/2-81 p138

Paraphrases (transcriptions): Beethoven: Fantasy on "Ruins of Athens", S 649. See no. 2053
Paraphrases (reminiscences): Beethoven: Fantasy on themes from "Ruins of Athens", S 122. Berlioz: Fantaisie symphonique on themes from "Lelio", S 120. Schubert: Fantasy on Wanderer, S 366, C major. Weber: Polonaise brillante on Polacca brillante, S 367, E major. See no. 2061
Paraphrases: Chopin: Meine Freuden, S 480. See no. 2037
Paraphrases: Chopin: My jous; The maiden's wish. See no. 3993
Paraphrases: Mozart's "Le nozze di Figaro". See no. 589
Paraphrases: Schubert: Ave Maria; Der Erlkonig; Die junge Nonne; Der Leiermann; Tauschung; Wohin. See no. 3041
Paraphrases: Verdi: Rigoletto. See no. 3920
Paraphrases: Verdi: Rigoletto: Quartet. See no. 2033

2060 Piano works: Bagatelle sans tonality. Am Grabe Richard Wagners, S 203. Csardas obstinee, S 225. En reve, S 207. Harmonies poetiques et religieuses, S 173: Ave Maria. La lugubre gondola, nos. 1 and 2, S 200. Nuages gris, S 199. Sonata, piano, B minor, S 178. Michael Rudy, pno. Calliope CAL 1685
+FF 7/8-81 p125 +-HFN 4-81 p72
+Gr 4-81 p1346

2061 Piano works: Concerto, piano, no. 1, S 124, E flat major. Concerto, piano, no. 2, S 125, A major. Hungarian fantasia, S 123. Malediction, S 121. Totentanz, S 126. Paraphrases (reminiscences): Beethoven: Fantasy on themes from "Ruins of Athens", S 122. Berlioz: Fantaisie symphonique on themes from "Lelio", S 120. Schubert: Fantasy on Wanderer, S 366, C major. Weber: Polonaise brillante on Polacca brillante, S 367, E major. Michel Beroff, pno; Leipzig Gewandhaus Orchestra; Kurt Masur. HMV SLS 5207 (3)
+-FF 7/8-81 p125 ++SFC 1-18-81 p21
+Gr 1-81 p951 +-STL 1-11-81 p38
+HFN 1-81 p96

2062 Piano works: Bagatelle without tonality. Balcsillagzat. Csardas, S 225. Csardas macabre, S 224. En reve, S 207. Historic Hungarian portraits. La lugubre gondola, S 200. Mephisto waltz, no. 3, S 216. Mephisto waltz, no. 4. Nuages gris, S 199. Preludio funebre. R. W.: Venezia, G 201. Schlaflos, Frage und Antwort. Schwanengesang, S 560: Abschied. Valse oubliee,

no. 4. Erno Szegedi, pno. Hungaroton SLPX 11976/7 (2)
+ARG 1-79 p16 +HFN 2-81 p90
+-FF 1/2-79 p73 +-NR 10-78 p14

2063 Piano works: Annees de pelerinage, 3rd year, S 163: Aux cypres de la Villa d'Este; Les jeux d'eau a la Villa d'Este; Sunt lacrymae rerum. Csardas macabre, S 244. Mosonyi's Grabgeleit, S 194. Schlaflos, Frage und Antwort. Valse oubliee, no. 1, S 215, F sharp minor: Unstern Sinistre-Disastro. Weihnachtsbaum, S 186: Schlummerlied. Alfred Brendel, pno. Philips 9500 775 Tape (c) 7300 863
+ARG 12-81 p17 ++HFN 9-81 p93 tape
+-CL 12-81 p11 ++NR 6-81 p14
+-FF 5/6-81 p98 ++NYT 4-26-81 pD23
++Gr 5-81 p1498 ++SFC 4-12-81 p21
+HFN 5-81 p81 +STL 6-14-81 p40

2064 Les preludes, S 97. Tasso lamento e trionfo, S 96. RIMSKY-KORSAKOV: May night. PhO; Constantin Silvestri. HMV SXLP 30447 Tape (c) TC SXLP 30447 (From ALP 1648, ASD 338)
+FF 7/8-81 p125 +-HFN 11-80 p129
+Gr 1-81 p1002

Les preludes, S 97. See no. 749. See no. 2036. See no. 2055. See no. 2073. See no. 3792

Prelude and fugue on the name B-A-C-H, S 260. See no. 246. See no. 2029. See no. 2030. See no. 2049. See no. 3786. See no. 3902. See no. 3930

Preludio funebre. See no. 2062

Prometheus, S 99. See no. 2049. See no. 2074

Rapsodie espagnole, S 254. See no. 3697

Richard Wagner: Venezia, S 201. See no. 2062

Romance oubliee, S 132. See no. 2050

Schlaflos, Frage und Antwort. See no. 2062. See no. 2063

Schwanengesang, S 560: Abschied. See no. 2062

2065 Sonata, piano, S 178, B minor. SCHUMANN: Fantasia, op. 17, C major. Dag Achatz, pno. BIS LP 144
+ARG 2-81 p29 +HFN 8-80 p98
+-FF 11/12-80 p172 +-RR 7-80 p84

Sonata, piano, G 178, B minor. See no. 1160. See no. 1179. See no. 2033. See no. 2060

2066 Songs: Der du von dem Himmel bist, S 279; Die drei Zigeuner, S 320; Es muss ein Wunderbares sein, S 314; Die Loreley, S 273; Oh quand je dors, S 282; Sonetti di Petrarca, S 270: Benedetto sia il giorno; I vidi in terra angelici costumi; Uber allen Gipfeln ist Ruh, S 306, Wer nie sein Brot mit Tranen ass, S 297. Sylvia Lindenstrand, ms; Janos Solyom, pno. Artemis ARTE 7111
+Gr 5-81 p1504

2067 Songs: Der Alpenjager, S 292, no. 3; Anfants wollt ich fast verzagen, S 311; Angiolin dal biondo crin, S 269; Blume und Duft, S 324; Comment disaient-ils, S 276; Des Tages laute Stimmen schweigen, S 337; Die drei Zigeuner, S 320; Du bist wie eine Blume, S 287; Der du von dem Himmel bist, S 278; Enfant si j'etais roi, S 283; Es muss ein Wunderbares sein, S 314; Es rauschen die Winde, S 294; Ein Fichtenbaum steht einsam, S 309; Der Fischerknabe, S 292, no. 1; Gastibelza, S 286; Gestorben war ich, S 308; Der Hirt, S 292, no. 2; Hohe Liebe, S 307; Ich mochte hingehn, S 296; Ihr Glocken von Marling, S 328; Im Rhein im schonen Strome, S 272; In Liebeslust, S 318; J'ai perdu ma force et ma vie, S 327; Kling leise mein Lied, S 301; La tombe et la rose, S 285; Lasst mich ruhen, S 317; Le vieux vagabond, S 304; Die Lorelei, S 273, no. 1; Morgens steh ich auf und frage, S 290; O lieb so lang du lieben kannst, S 298; Oh quand je dors, S 282; Schwebe schwebe blaues Auge, S 305; S'il est un charmant gazon, S 284; Die stille Wasserrose, S 321; Tre sonetti de Petraraca, S 270: Pace non trovo, Benedetto sia'l gorno, I vidi in terra angelici costume; Der traurige Monch, S 348; Uber allen Gipfeln ist Ruh, S 306; Die Vatergruft, S 281; Vergiftet sind meine Lieder, S 289; Wer nie sein Brot mit Tranen ass, S 297; Wie singt die Lerche schon, S 312; Wieder mocht ich dir begegnen, S 322. Dietrich Fischer-Dieskau, bar; Daniel Barenboim, pno. DG 2740 254 (4)

++Gr 10-81 p593 +HFN 11-81 p95

2068 Songs: Anfangs wollt ich fast verzagen, S 311; Wer nie sein Brot mit Tranen ass, S 297; Blume und Duft, S 324; Der du von dem Himmel bist, S 279; Drei Sonette von Petrarca, S 270; Die drei Zigeuner, S 320; Es muss ein Wunderbares sein, S 314; Ein Fichtenbaum steht einsam, S 309; Die Fischerstochter, S 325; Lasst mich ruhen, S 317; Morgens steh ich auf und frage, S 290; Nimm einen Strahl der Sonne, S 310; Uber allen Gipfeln ist Ruh, S 306; Die Vatergruft. Hermann Prey, bar; Alexis Weissenberg, pno. EMI 1C 065 30845

++FF 1/2-81 p137 +HFN 11-80 p120
+Gr 10-80 p528 +STL 1-11-81 p38

2069 Songs: Der du von dem Himmel bist, S 279; Die drei Zigeuner, S 320; Du bist wie eine Blume, S 287; Es war ein Konig in Thule, S 278; Fischerstochter, S 325; Freudvoll und Leidvoll, S 280; Im Rhein im schonen Strome; Die Lorelei, S 273; S'il est un charmant gazon, S 284; Uber allen Gipfeln ist Ruh, S 306; Die Vatergruft, S 281; Das Veilchen, S 316, no. 1. Janet Baker, ms; Geoffrey Parsons, pno. HMV ASD 3965 Tape (c) TC ASD 3965 (also Angel ASD 3906 Tape (c) TC ASD 3906)

+-FF 9/10-81 p130 +HFN 2-81 p89
+Gr 11-80 p723 +-STL 1-11-81 p38
+-Gr 2-81 p1122 tape

Songs: Ave Maria, S 20; Salve regina, S 66. See no. 3638

Songs: Die drei Zigeuner, S 320; Es muss ein Wunderbares sein, S 314; Es war ein Konig in Thule, S 278; Kling leise mein Lied, S 301; Die Loreley, S 273; Ne brany menya moy drug; Enfant si j'etais roi, S 283; Vergiftet sind meine Lieder, S 289. See no. 454

Songs: Es muss ein Wunderbares sein, S 314. See no. 3703. See no. 3966

Songs: Es war ein Konig in Thule, S 278; Mignon's Lied. See no. 465

Tarantelle. See no. 3964

Tasso, lamento e trionfo, S 96. See no. 747. See no. 2064. See no. 2073

2070 Totentanz, S 126. STENHAMMER: Concerto, piano, no. 2, op. 23, D minor. Janos Solyom, pno; Munich Philharmonic Orchestra; Stig Westerberg. EMI 4E 063 343284

+FF 3/4-78 p74 +Gr 8-81 p274

Totentanz, S 126. See no. 2053. See no. 2061

Trauervorspiel und Trauermarsch, S 206. See no. 3697

Valse oubliee, no. 1, S 215, F sharp minor: Unstern Sinistre-Disastro. See no. 2063
Valse oublee, no. 4. See no. 2062
2071 Variations on Bach's "Weinen, Klagen, Sorgen, Zagen", S 673. RITTER: Sonata, organ, no. 3, A minor. Ulrich Bremsteller, org. Pape 7
+NR 2-81 p13
Variations on Bach's "Weinen, Klagen, Sorgen, Zagen", S 673. See no. 2029. See no. 2030
Via crucis, S 53. See no. 1474
Von der Wiege bis zum Grabe, S 107. See no. 2073
2072 Weihnachtsbaum, S 186. Rhondda Gillespie, pno. Chandos ABR 1006 Tape (c) ABT 1006
++FF 3/4-81 p149 +HFN 2-80 p95
+Gr 2-80 p1281 +RR 2-80 p77
+Gr 8-80 p275 tape +RR 8-80 p95 tape
Weihnachtsbaum, S 186: Schlummerlied. See no. 2063
2073 Works, selections: Ce qu'on entend su la montagne, S 95. Dante symphony, S 109. Festklange, S 101. Hunnenschlacht, S 105. Die Ideale, S 106. Orpheus, S 98. Les preludes, S 97. Tasso lamento e trionfo, S 96. Von der Wiege bis zum Grabe, S 107. Volker Arndt, treble; St. Thomas Church Choir, Leipzig; Mathias Eisenberg, org; Leipzig Gewandhaus Orchestra; Kurt Masur. HMV SLS 5235 (4)
+Gr 11-81 p690 +HFN 11-81 p94
2074 Works, selections: Episodes from Lenau's "Faust", S 110: Der nachtliche Zug; Mephisto waltz, no. 1. A Faust symphony, S 108. Hamlet, S 104. Hungaria, S 103. Heroide funebre, S 102. Mazeppa, S 100. Mephisto waltz, no. 2, S 111. Prometheus, S 99. Klaus Konig, t; Leipzig Radio Chorus Male Members; Walter Heinz Bernstein, org; Leipzig Gewandhaus Orchestra; Kurt Masur. HMV SLS 5236
+Gr 11-81 p690 +HFN 11-81 p94

LITAIZE, Gaston
2075 Pieces, organ: Lied; Toccata. Prelude et danse fugue. Zint Marte os all we'r op Rett. Gaston Litaize, org. Motette M 1043
+FF 9/10-81 p247
Prelude et danse fugue. See no. 2075
Stucke, organ: Prelude et danse fugue. See no. 4069
Variations sur un Noel Angevin. See no. 1340
Zint Marte os all we'r op Rett. See no. 2075

LITHGOW
Invercargill. See no. 3955

LIU TING HO
Night party. See no. 1887
Sum che tak ma. See no. 1887

LLOBET, Miguel
Scherzo. See no. 3886
Vals. See no. 3886

LLOYD, C. H.
Allegretto. See no. 4112

LOCATELLI, Pietro
2076 Concerto, violin, op. 3, no. 1, D major. TORELLI: Concerti, trumpet, nos. 1 and 2. VIVALDI: Concerto, op. 10, no. 5, G minor. Concerto, 2 horns, P 321. Frans Bruggen, Jaap Schroder, vln;

Frans Bruggen, rec; Maurice Andre, tpt; Hermann Baumann, Adriaan van Woudenberg, hn; Concerto Amsterdam. Telefunken QC 6-41217 Tape (C) 4-41217
+Gr 9-81 p460 tape +HFN 3-81 p95
Concerto grosso, op. 1, no. 8, F minor. See no. 1241
Concerto grosso, op. 1, no. 11. See no. 3980
Sonata, violoncello and piano, D major. See no. 1940

LOCKE, Matthew
Duos, C major, C minor. See no. 1526
How doth the city sit solitary. See no. 815
Music for His Majesty's sackbuts and cornetts. See no. 3936
Suite, no. 4, D major. See no. 3733. See no. 4103

LOCKWOOD, Anna
2077 Glass world. Anna Lockwood, glass objects. Tangent TGS 104
+St 3-81 p86

LOEB, David
2078 Fantasia e due scherzi. Sonata, viola da gamba. SCHAFFRATH: Duetto, 2 bass viols, D minor. SCHENCK: Le nymphe de Rheno: Sonata, 2 viols, op. 8, no. 10, G major. August Wenzinger, Hannelore Muller, vla da gamba. Gasparo GS 210
+-FF 5/6-81 p208 ++NR 10-80 p7
++IN 11-81 p96
Sonata, viola da gamba. See no. 2078

LOEILLET, Jean-Baptiste
Sonata, op. 2, G minor. See no. 4095
Toccata. See no. 3643
Trio. See no. 1268

LOEWE, Carl
Quem pastores laudavere. See no. 3775
2079 Songs: Abendstunde; Abschied; Die Blume der Ergebung; Fruhling; Fruhlingsankunft; Liebesliedchen; Marz; O susse Mutter; Sonnenlicht. REGER: Wiegenlied, op. 97, no. 2. WEBER: Duets, op. 31 (3). Elisabeth Schwarzkopf, Lea Piltti, s; Michael Raucheisen, pno. Burno Walter Society IGI 385
++FF 9/10-81 p210 +NR 6-81 p11
2080 Songs: Archibald Douglas, op. 128; Heinrich der Vogler, op. 56, no. 1; Kleiner Haushalt, op. 71; Der Nock, op. 29, no. 2; Prinz Eugen der edle Ritter, op. 92; Susses Begrabnis, op. 62, no. 4; Tom der Reimer, op. 135; Die Uhr, op. 123, no. 3. Barry McDaniel, bar; Otto von Rohr, bs; Hermann Reutter, pno. Intercord INT 120 820
+HFN 12-81 p96
2081 Songs: Graf Eberstein, op. 9, no. 5; Harald, op. 45, no. 1. SCHUBERT: Songs: Erlkonig, D 328; Lodas Gespenst; Der Zwerg, D 771. SCHUMANN: Songs: Die Beiden Greandiere, op. 49, no. 1; Die Fiendlichen Bruder, op. 49, no. 2; Belsazar, op. 57; Der Soldat; Die Wandelnde Glocke, op. 79, no. 17. Werner Hollweg, t; Roman Ortner, pno. Telefunken 6-42620
++St 9-81 p101
Songs: Die wandelnde Glocke. See no. 952
Songs: Tom der Reimer, op. 135. See no. 3988

LOFFELHOLTZ, Christoph
Es het ein Baur sein freylein vorlohren. See no. 3676
Die kleine Schacht. See no. 3676

LOOSEMORE
O Lord increase our faith. See no. 4107
LOPE
Gallito. See no. 3981
Gerona. See no. 3981
LOPEZ BUCHARDO, Carlos
Bailecito. See no. 3789
LORTZING, Gustav
Undine, excerpts. See no. 3975
Undine: Vater, Mutter, Schwestern, Bruder. See no. 3966
Der Waffenschmied, excerpts. See no. 3975
2082 Der Wildschutz. Anneliese Rothenberger, s; Gertrud Vordemfelde, ms; Gisela Litz, con; Fritz Wunderlich, t; Hermann Prey, bar; Fritz Ollendorff, bs; Children's Choir; Bavarian State Opera Orchestra and Chorus; Robert Heger. EMI 1C 149 28534/6 (3)
+Gr 1-81 p988 +HFN 1-81 p96
Der Wildschutz, excerpts. See no. 3975
2083 Zar und Zimmermann. Lucia Popp, s; Werner Krenn, Adalbert Kraus, t; Hermann Prey, Karl Ridderbusch, bs; Bavarian Radio Orchestra; Heinz Wallberg. Columbia M2 35904 (2) (also Acanta JB 22424)
+ARG 3-81 p33 +HFN 9-80 p105
+FF 11/12-80 p130 +NYT 6-1-80 pD20
+Gr 10-80 p534 +ON 12-20-80 p52
Zar und Zimmermann, excerpts. See no. 3975
Zar und Zimmermann: Auf Gesellen greift zur Axt...Sonst spielt ich mit zepter. See no. 1891
LOTTI, Antonio
Songs: Pur dicesti. See no. 3756. See no. 3967
LOVENSKJOLD, Hermann
La sylphide. See no. 1836
LOVREGLIO (19th century Italy)
Concert fantasia on Verdi's "La traviata". See no. 3714
LOW
A Din-Toire mit Gott. See no. 3897
LUBECK, Vincenz
Prelude, G minor. See no. 3903
Prelude and fugue, C minor. See no. 3960
LUBLIN, Jan van
Chorea. See no. 4071
Dances. See no. 3862
Mon mary. See no. 3862
Tabulatur: De profundis. See no. 3960
LUCIUK, Julius
Lirica di timbre. See no. 4072
LUENING, Otto
2084 Short sonatas, piano, nos. 1-3, 5-7. Dwight Pelzer, pno. Serenus SRS 12091
+ARG 11-81 p25 *NR 7-81 p13
/HF 9-81 p73 +St 12-81 p118

LUKAS, Zdenek
2085 Concerto, bassoon. MATEJ: Concerto, flute and harpsichord. Frantisek Herman, bsn; Frantisek Cech, flt; Czechoslovak Radio Orchestra, Dvorak Chamber Orchestra; Petr Vronsky, Vladimir Valek. Panton 8110 0006
+FF 9/10-81 p266

LULLY, Jean
Amadis de Gaule: Amour que veux-tu. See no. 4026
Le divertissement de Chambord. See no. 3978
2086 Te deum. Jennifer Smith, Francine Bessac, s; Zeger Vandersteene, c-t; Louis Devos, t; Philippe Huttenlocher, bs; A Coeur Joi Vocal Ensemble of Valence; Jean-Francois Paillard Chamber Orchestra; Jean-Francois Paillard. Erato STU 70927 Tape (c) MCE 70927 (also Musical Heritage Society MHS 4145)
+FF 9/10-80 p149 +-HF 3-79 p92
-Gr 6-76 p71 ++MU 10-80 p10
+Gr 12-81 p945 tape -RR 6-76 p79
LUNA Y CARNE, Pablo
La mancha: El pan el queso el vino; En el fondo de la nina. See no. 3836
La picara molinera: Paxarin tu que vuelas. See no. 3888
Songs: En el fondo de la nina; En toda la quintana. See no. 3838
LUNDBORG, Erik
Soundsoup. See no. 3933
LUNDE, Lawson
2087 Sonata, saxophone and piano, no. 1. PERSICHETTI: Parable XI. STEIN: Quintet, saxophone and string quartet. Brian Minor, sax; Lawson Lunde, pno; Chicago Symphony Quartet. Crystal S 151
+ARG 5-81 p40 +NR 2-81 p7
+-FF 5/6-81 p211
LUNDQUIST, Torbjorn
2088 Symphony, no. 3. Stockholm Philharmonic Orchestra; Peter Maag. Artemis 50 104
++FF 7/8-79 p65 +FF 5/6-81 p99
LUPO, Thomas
Fantasia a 5. See no. 4092
Songs: Shows and nightly revels; Time that leads. See no. 3876
LUSHER
Concert variations. See no. 3956
LUTHER, Martin
A mighty fortress is our God. See no. 3999
LUTOSLAWSKI, Witold
Dance preludes. See no. 3738. See no. 3793
Mi-Parti. See no. 369
2089 Quartet, strings. PENDERECKI: Quartet, strings, no. 1. SZYMANOWSKI: Quartet, strings, no. 2. Warsaw Quartet. Da Camera Magna SM 92418
+FF 5/6-81 p99 +STL 6-14-81 p40
LUYTENS, Elisabeth
Steven Smith songs. See no. 1345
LUZZASCHI, Luzzasco
Quivi sospire. See no. 3692
Songs: Ch'io non t'ami; Aura soave; O primavera. See no. 3835
LYATOSHINSKY, Boris
Sonata, violin and piano, op. 19. See no. 1885
LYMBURGIA, Johannes de
Recordare frater pie. See no. 4011
LYNE, Peter
There was a naughty boy. See no. 3691
MACDONALD
2090 Ad cenam Agni providi. Songs: Veni creator; Pange lingua. PALE-

STRINA: Domine quando veneris, motet. Compline. Ruth Saye, s; Robert Horvath, treb; Philip Rock, cantor; Academy of English Plainchant; Peter Macdonald, org. Gamut RR 180
+-Gr 3-81 p1224
Songs: Veni creator; Pange lingua. See no. 2090
MACDONALD, Robert
Lourdes hymn (arr.). See no. 3822
Salve regina coelitum (arr.). See no. 3822
MACDOWELL, Edward
Sonata, piano, no. 1, op. 45, G minor. See no. 808
MACGREGOR, Laurie
2091 Intrustion of the hunter. READ: Los dioses aztecas, op. 107. Paul Price Percussion Ensemble, New Jersey Percussion Ensemble; Paul Price, Raymond des Roches. CRI SD 444
+-NR 7-81 p15
MACHA, Otmar
2092 Sinfonietta. OSTRCIL: Suite, op. 14, D minor. CPhO, Czech Radio Orchestra; Jaroslav Krombholc, Vaclav Neumann. Panton 110 0066
+FF 3/4-81 p169 +-HFN 9-81 p81
+Gr 10-81 p552
MACHAUT, Guillaume de
Hoquetus David. See no. 3779
Lasse: Se j'aim mon loyal ami; Pour quoy. See no. 3779
2093 Messe de Nostre Dame. ANON. (14th c.): Messe de Tournai. Dufay Vocal Ensemble, Les Saqueboutiers; Arsene Bedois. Erato STU 71303
+FF 11/12-81 p187 +-Gr 3-81 p1217
2094 Messe de Nostre Dame. Songs (motets): Christe qui lux; Fons tocius superbie; Felix virgo. DANDRIEU: Armes amours. Seminaire Europeen de Musique Ancienne; Bernard Gagnepain. Erato EFM 18041
-FF 11/12-81 p187
2095 Messe de Nostre Dame. GREGORIAN CHANT: Proper for the Feast of the Assumption. London Ambrosian Singers, Les Menestrels of Vienna; John McCarthy. Harmonia Mundi HM 10071 (From Tudor ELY 0430)
+FF 1/2-81 p138
2096 Messe de Nostre Dame. Songs: Christe qui lux; Dame se vous n'avez; Dix et sept; Doulz viaire; Longuement; Nes que on porroit; Ploures dames; Quant Theseus; Sans cuer dolens; Se pour ce muir; Tels rit au main; Tres donne et belle. ADAM DE LA HALLE: Fines amourettes. ANON.: Works (6). Rene Jacobs, c-t; Les Menestrels Ensemble, Mozartsangerkanben, Vienna. Mirror Music 00006-9 (4)
+FF 11/12-81 p187
Songs: Amours me fait desirer; Dame se vous m'estes; De bon espoir; Puis que la douce; De toutes flours; Douce dame jolie; Hareu hareu helas ou sera pris confors; Ma fin est mon commencement; Mes esperis se combat; Phyton le merveilleus serpent; Quant j'ay l'espart; Quant je sui mis; Quant Theseus ne quier veoir; Trop plus est belle-Biaute paree Je ne su; Se je souspir. See no. 3846
Songs (motets): Christe qui lux; Fons tocius superbie; Felix virgo. See no. 2904
Songs: Christe que lux; Dame se vous n'avez; Dix et sept; Doulz viaire; Longuement; Nes que on porroit; Ploures dames; Quant Theseus; Sans cuer dolens; Se pour ce muir Tels rit au main;

Tres donne et belle. See no. 2096
Songs (motets): Christe qui lux; Veni creator spiritus. See no. 3779
Songs: Douce dame jolie. See no. 3853
MACMURROUGH
Aileen Aroon. See no. 4046
MACPHERSON, Charles
A little organ book: Andante, G major. See no. 3824
MACQUE, Jean de
Gagliarden, nos. 1 and 2. See no. 3832
MADERNA, Bruno
2097 Aura. Biogramma. Quadrivium. North German Radio Orchestra; Giuseppe Sinopoli. DG 2531 272
++FF 1/2-81 p139 +HFN 11-80 p120
+Gr 9-80 p334 ++NR 12-80 p3
+HF 3-81 p56
Biogramma. See no. 2097
Quadrivium. See no. 2097
MADETOJA, Leevi
Comedy overture. See no. 2098
2098 Symphony, no. 3. Comedy overture. Helsinki Philharmonic Orchestra; Jorma Panula. Finnlevy SFX 20 (also FA 307)
/FF 11-77 p35 +NR 11-80 p4
+FF 5/6-80 p99 +-RR 7-76 p54
+Gr 1-81 p998 +RR 11-78 p28
+HFN 10-80 p106
Songs: Solta somer. See no. 3805
MAGNARD, Alberic
2099 Sonata, violoncello and piano. POULENC: Sonata, violoncello and piano. Mark Drobinsky, vlc; Alexander Rabinovitch, pno. Calliope CAL 1852
+FF 9/10-81 p131 +HFN 9-81 p81
MAHLER, Gustav
2100 Kindertotenlieder. Lieder eines fahrenden Gesellen. Klara Takacs, ms; Sandor Solyom Nagy, bar; Budapest Symphony Orchestra; Gyorgy Lehel. Hungaroton SLPX 12044
++FF 9/10-81 p131 +-HFN 6-81 p75
+Gr 7-81 p182 ++NR 9-81 p13
Kindertotenlieder. See no. 2138
2101 Des Knaben Wunderhorn. Lieder eines fahrenden Gesellen. Lieder und Gesange aus der Jugendzeit. Ruckert Lieder. Dietrich Fischer-Dieskau, bar; Daniel Barenboim. HMV SLS 5172 (3) (also EMI 1C 165 03446/8)
+-FF 1/2-81 p142 +NYT 9-21-80 pD22
+Gr 6-80 p54 ++RR 8-80 p83
+HFN 6-80 p107 ++STL 7-13-80 p38
++MT 12-80 p786
2102 Des Knaben Wunderhorn. Eva Andor, s; Istvan Gati, bar; Budapest Symphony Orchestra; Gyorgy Lehel. Hungaroton SLPX 12043
-FF 5/6-81 p100 ++NR 3-81 p12
-HFN 2-81 p90
2103 Des Knaben Wunderhorn. Jessye Norman, s; John Shirley-Quirk, bar; COA; Bernard Haitink. Philips 9500 316 Tape (c) 7300 572 (r) G 9500 316
++ARG 11-77 p21 ++HFN 4-78 p131 tape

+Audio 6-78 p127 ++HFN 6-78 p139 tape
+Gr 11-77 p874 +MJ 5-78 p29
++Gr 2-78 p1473 tape +NR 12-77 p10
+HF 12-77 p94 +RR 11-77 p106
+HF 8-81 p69 tape ++RR 1-78 p86 tape
++HFN 11-77 p172 +St 1-78 p92
++HFN 1-78 p139 tape

2104 Des Knaben Wunderhorn: Wer hat dies Liedlein erdacht; Rheinlegendchen. Lieder eines fahrenden Gesellen. Ruckert Lieder. Frederica von Stade, ms; LPO; Andrew Davis. CBS 76828 (also CBS M 35863 Tape (c) MT 35863)
+-ARG 1-81 p34 +HFN 11-79 p141
+-Gr 11-79 p892 +RR 12-79 p112

2105 Das Lied von der Erde. Nan Merriman, alto; Ernst Hafliger, t; COA; Eduard van Beinum. Philips 6570 193 Tape (c) 7310 193 (From A00410-1L, Epic SC 6023)
+ARG 12-80 p36 +HF 10-80 p82
+FF 9/10-80 p149 +-HFN 2-81 p97
+Gr 1-81 p978 +-HFN 4-81 p81 tape

2106 Das Lied von der Erde. Maureen Forrester, con; Richard Lewis, t; CSO; Fritz Reiner. RCA Musique GL 43272 (From VICS 1390)
+-FF 5/6-81 p101

Das Lied von der Erde: Von der Schonheit; Der Abschied. See no. 2117

2107 Lieder eines fahrenden Gesellen. STRAUSS, R.: Liebeshymnus, op. 32, no. 3; Verfuhrung, op. 33, no. 1; Waldseligkeit, op. 49, no. 1; Winterliebe, op. 48, no. 4. WOLF: Anakreons Grab; Bedeckt mich mit Blumen; Im Fruhling; Mogen alle Bosen zungen; Die Zigeunerin. Elisabeth Schwarzkopf, s; Peter Anders, t; Dietrich Fischer-Dieskau, bar; Wilhelm Furtwangler, pno; VPO, BPhO; Wilhelm Furtwangler. Bruno Walter Society IGI 382
+NR 6-81 p11

Lieder eines fahrenden Gesellen. See no. 2100. See no. 2101. See no. 2104. See no. 2130

2108 Lieder und Gesange aus der Jugendzeit. Hanna Schaer, con; Christian Ivaldi, pno. Musical Heritage Society MHS 4367
+-ARG 11-81 p27 +FF 9/10-81 p132

Lieder und Gesange aus der Jugendzeit. See no. 2101

2109 Quartet, piano, A minor. SCHUMANN: Quintet, piano, op. 44, E flat major. Quintetto Italiano. Dischi Ricordi RCL 27014
+-FF 11/12-81 p189 +-Gr 11-79 p862

Ruckert Lieder. See no. 2101. See no. 2104. See no. 2129

2110 Symphonies, nos. 1-9. LSO, COA, CSO; Georg Solti. Decca 6-35230 (15)
+FF 11/12-81 p190

2111 Symphony, no. 1, D major. Orchestre Nationale de France; Lorin Maazel. CBS 35886 Tape (c) MT 35886
+FF 5/6-81 p100 +-NYT 5-10-81 pD29
+-HF 11-81 p71

2112 Symphony, no. 1, D major. Bavarian Radio Orchestra; Rafael Kubelik. DG 2535 172 Tape (c) 3335 172
+ARG 3-81 p35 +RR 9-76 p94 tape
+FF 1/2-81 p141

2113 Symphony, no. 1, D major. RPO; Carlos Paita. Lodia LOD 776 Tape (c) LOC 776 (From Decca PFS 4402)

++HFN 6-81 p85 +HFN 6-81 p87 tape

2114 Symphony, no. 1, D major. COA; Bernard Haitink. Philips 6527 062 Tape (c) 7311 062 (From 835127)
+-Gr 6-81 p40 +HFN 11-81 p105 tape

2115 Symphony, no. 1, D major. St. Louis Symphony Orchestra; Leonard Slatkin. Telarc DG 10066
++NR 12-81 p5

2116 Symphony, no. 1, D major. LSO; Jascha Horenstein. Unicorn RHS 301 Tape (r) F 0301
+HFN 10-78 p137 ++RR 10-78 p76
+NYT 2-15-81 pD21 tape

2117 Symphony, no. 2, C minor. Das Lied von der Erde: Von der Schonheit; Der Abschied. Jo Vincent, s; Kathleen Ferrier, con; COA; Orchestra; Otto Klemperer, Bruno Walter. Bruno Walter Society IGI 374 (2)
+FF 7/8-81 p126 +NR 4-81 p5

2118 Symphony, no. 2, C minor. MOZART: Symphony, no. 25, K 183, G minor. Maria Cebotari, s; Rosette Anday, con; VPO; Bruno Walter. Bruno Walter Society BWS 367 (2)
+-FF 7/8-81 p126 +NR 4-81 p5

2119 Symphony, no. 2, C minor. Edith Mathis, s; Norma Proctor, con; Bavarian Radio Orchestra and Chorus; Rafael Kubelik. DG 2726 062 (2) Tape (c) 3372 062 (From 139332/3)
+FF 9/10-80 p150 +HFN 1-81 p109 tape
+-Gr 3-77 p1396 +-RR 3-77 p50
+HFN 8-77 p93

2120 Symphony, no. 2, C minor. Isobel Buchanan, s; Mira Zakai, con; CSO and Chorus; Georg Solti. London LDR 72006 (2) Tape (c) LDR 5 72006 (also Decca D229D2 Tape (c) K229K22)
++FF 9/10-81 p132 ++HFN 6-81 p74
+Gr 6-81 p40 +NYT 9-20-81 pD29
++Gr 8-81 p324 tape +SFC 6-14-81 p19
+-HF 11-81 p71 +St 10-81 p126
+HF 11-81 p103 tape +STL 6-14-81 p40

Symphony, no. 2, C minor: Finale. See no. 3818

2121 Symphony, no. 3, D minor. Ortrun Wenkel, con; Southend Boys Choir; LPO and Chorus; Klaus Tennstedt. HMV SLS 5195 (2) Tape (c) TC SLS 5195 (also Angel DS 3902 Tape (c) 4Z2S 3902)
+FF 7/8-81 p127 +HF 11-81 p71
+Gr 11-80 p671 ++HFN 1-81 p97
+Gr 2-81 p1122 tape +MUM 7/8-81 p36
++Gr 6-81 p93 tape +NYT 5-10-81 pD29

2122 Symphony, no. 3, D minor. Norma Procter, con; Wandsworth Boys School Choir; Ambrosian Singers; LSO; Jascha Horenstein. Unicorn UN 2-75004 Tape (r) N 302 (From ZCUN 302/3)
+FF 3/4-79 p76 +NR 6-79 p5
+HF 11-80 p88 tape +NYT 2-15-81 pD21 tape
+MUM 7/8-81 p36 ++SFC 4-15-79 p41

2123 Symphony, no. 4, G major. Judith Raskin, s; CO; Georg Szell. CBS MY 37225 (From Columbia MS 6833)
+FF 11/12-81 p192

2124 Symphony, no. 4, G major. Margaret Marshall, s; Scottish National Orchestra; Alexander Gibson. Chandos ABRD 1025 Tape (c) ABTD 1025 (also Digitech DIGI 111 Tape (c) SCR 111)
++FF 9/10-81 p133 -HF 11-81 p71

+-Gr 5-81 p1476 ++HFN 5-81 p81
+Gr 9-81 p460 tape ++HFN 7-81 p83 tape

2125 Symphony, no. 4, G major. Edith Mathis, s; BPhO; Herbert von Karajan. DG 2531 205 Tape (c) 3301 205
+-ARG 5-80 p10 +-NR 6-80 p4
+FF 5/6-80 p100 ++NYT 5-10-81 pD29
++Gr 11-79 p827 ++RR 1-80 p77
+HF 4-80 p71 ++SFC 2-3-80 p45
+HF 7-80 p82 tape ++St 5-80 p83
++HFN 12-79 p163

2126 Symphony, no. 4, G major. Elsie Morison, s; Bavarian Radio Orchestra; Rafael Kubelik. DG 2535 119 (From 139339) (also DG 139339 Tape (c) 923 082, Tape (c) 3335 119)
+-FF 7/8-81 p128 +RR 7-75 p26
+-Gr 8-75 p325 +St 9-81 p95
+HFN 8-75 p89

2127 Symphony, no. 4, G major. Heather Harper, s; BRSO; Lorin Maazel. Pearl SHE 552
+-Gr 4-81 p1318 +-HFN 1-81 p107

2128 Symphony, no. 4, G major. Elisabeth Schwarzkopf, s; PhO; Otto Klemperer. Seraphim S 60359 (From Angel S 35829)
/FF 11/12-81 p191

2129 Symphony, no. 5, C sharp minor. Ruckert Lieder. CSO; Hanna Schwarz, ms; Claudio Abbado. DG 2707 128 (2) Tape (c) 3370 128
-Gr 10-81 p557 +-HFN 11-81 p95

2130 Symphony, no. 5, C sharp minor. Lieder eines fahrenden Gesellen. Dietrich Fischer-Dieskau, bar; Bavarian Radio Orchestra; Rafael Kubelik. DG 2726 064 (2) Tape (c) 3372 064 (From 2720 033)
+-Gr 3-77 p1396 +HFN 1-81 p109 tape
+HFN 4-78 p127 +RR 3-77 p50

2131 Symphony, no. 5, C sharp minor. STRAUSS, R.: Tod und Verklarung, op. 24. NYP; Dimitri Mitropoulos. New York Philharmonic 881/2
++FF 11/12-81 p192 ++HF 11-81 p71

Symphony, no. 5, C sharp minor: Adagietto. See no. 1647. See no. 2138

2132 Symphony, no. 6, A minor. CSO; Claudio Abbado. DG 2707 117 (2) Tape (c) 3370 031
+-FF 1/2-81 p142 +HFN 11-80 p120
++Gr 11-80 p672 +HFN 1-81 p109 tape
+HF 4-81 p80 +-NR 2-81 p4
+HF 11-81 p103 tape ++STL 11-9-80 p40

2133 Symphony, no. 6, A minor. SCHOENBERG: Variations, op. 31. Symphony Orchestra; Hans Rosbaud. Rococo 2078 (2)
+-NR 4-81 p4

2134 Symphony, no. 6, A minor. Symphony, no. 10, F sharp major: Adagio. CPhO; Vaclav Neumann. Supraphon 410 3141/2 (2)
+HF 11-81 p71 ++SFC 9-27-81 p18
+-NR 9-81 p3

2135 Symphony, no. 7, B minor. LPO; Klaus Tennstedt. HMV SLS 5238 (2) Tape (c) TCC SLS 5238 (also Angel DS 3908)
+-Gr 12-81 p885

2136 Symphony, no. 8, E flat major. Symphony, no. 10, F sharp major: Adagio. Martina Arroyo, Erna Spoorenberg, s; Julia Hamari, Norma Procter, con; Donald Grobe, t; Dietrich Fischer-Dieskau, bar; Franz Crass, bs; Bavarian Radio, NDR Radio and WDR Radio

Choruses; Regensburg Cathedral Boys Choir, Munich Motet Choir Women's Chorus; Eberhard Kraus, org; Bavarian Radio Orchestra; Rafael Kubelik. DG 2726 053 Tape (c) 3372 053 (From 2707 062, 2707 037)

+-FF 9/10-80 p152
+Gr 8-75 p465
+-HF 7-80 p82 tape
+HFN 8-75 p89
+HFN 1-81 p109 tape
+NYT 8-5-79 pD19
+-RR 7-75 p39

2137 Symphony, no. 8, E flat major. Faye Robinson, Judith Blegen, Deborah Sasson, s; Florence Quivar, Lorna Myers, alto; Kenneth Riegel, t; Benjamin Luxon, bar; Gwynne Howell, bs; Tanglewood Festival Chorus, Boston Boys Choir; BSO; Seiji Ozawa. Philips 6769 069 (2)

+-HFN 11-81 p95
+SFC 11-1-81 p18
+St 12-81 p124

2138 Symphony, no. 8, D major.* Kindertotenlieder.* Symphony, no. 5, C sharp minor: Adagietto. Kathleen Ferrier, alto; VPO; Bruno Walter. DaCapo 1C 174 01402/3 (2) (*From Turnabout THS 65008/9, Odyssey 32260016, Seraphim 60203)

+FF 3/4-81 p149

2139 Symphony, no. 9, D major. BPhO; Herbert von Karajan. DG 2707 125 (2) Tape (c) 3370 038

+FF 9/10-81 p134
++Gr 5-81 p1474
++HF 11-81 p71
+HFN 6-81 p74
+HFN 7-81 p81 tape
++NYT 9-20-81 pD29
+-SFC 7-12-81 p18
++St 10-81 p122
+STL 6-14-81 p40

2140 Symphony, no. 9, D major. LPO; Klaus Tennstedt. HMV SLS 5188 (2) Tape (c) TC SLS 5188 (also Angel SZ 3899 Tape (c) 4Z2S 3899)

+ARG 11-80 p24
+-FF 9/10-80 p153
+Gr 3-80 p1391
+Gr 7-80 p166 tape
++HF 10-80 p80
+HFN 3-80 p93
+HFN 8-80 p109 tape
+MUM 11/12-80 p34
++NR 9-80 p3
+NYT 5-10-81 pD29
+RR 4-80 p66
++SFC 6-8-80 p36
++St 10-80 p110
++STL 4-13-80 p39

2141 Symphony, no. 10, F sharp major (performing edition by Deryck Cooke). PO; Eugene Ormandy. CBS 61447 Tape (c) 40-61447 (also Columbia M 25735, Columbai D3S 774)

+ARG 10-81 p28
+-HFN 12-75 p173
+HF 4-71 p67
+-RR 12-75 p99 tape
+-St 10-76 p80

2142 Symphony, no. 10, F sharp major. (rev. ed. Deryck Cooke). Bournemouth Symphony Orchestra; Simon Rattle. HMV SLS 5206 (2) Tape (c) TC SLS 5206 (also Angel D5B 3909)

+-ARG 10-81 p28
+FF 7/8-81 p128
+Gr 12-80 p832
+HF 10-81 p109
++HFN 2-81 p90
+MT 6-81 p390
+MUM 7/8-81 p37
+NYT 5-10-81 pD23
++St 7-81 p86

2143 Symphony, no. 10, F sharp minor. (rev. ed. Deryck Cooke). NPhO; Wyn Morris. Philips 6700 067 (2)

+ARG 10-81 p28
+Gr 3-74 p1700
+HF 5-74 p74
+NYT 2-10-74 pD26
+-RR 3-74 p40
+SFC 1-13-74 p20

+HFN 3-74 p109 +St 5-74 p103
+NR 2-74 p3 ++St 10-76 p80

2144 Symphony, no. 10, F sharp major. PO; James Levine. RCA CTC 2-3726 (2) Tape (c) CTK 2-3726 (also RL 1-3726 Tape (c) RK 1-3726)

++ARG 10-81 p25 +-HFN 9-81 p81
++FF 7/8-81 p128 +MUM 7/8-81 p37
+-Gr 7-81 p156 +NYT 5-10-81 pD23
+HF 8-81 p69 ++St 7-81 p86
+-HF 10-81 p109

Symphony, no. 10, F sharp major: Adagio. See no. 2134. See no. 2136

MAILLART, Louis-Amie

Les Dragons de Villars; Duo de Rose et Sylvain. See no. 4051

MAINERIO, Giorgio

Primo libro de balli, 1578: Dances. See no. 3853

MAINGUENEAU

Mon coeur est un oiseau. See no. 4051

MAK'O CHANG LAO

The white haired girl: Suite. See no. 1205

MALATS, Joaquin

Serenata espanola. See no. 3727

MALDERE, Pierre van

2145 Symphonies, no. 1, op. 5, D major; A major, D major, E flat major. Liege Soloists. DG 2547 052 Tape (c) 3347 052 (From SAPM 198 379)

+Gr 4-81 p1315 +-HFN 7-81 p83 tape
+Gr 9-81 p460 tape

MALDEREN

Le tango du reve. See no. 4051

MALIBRAN, Maria

Le reveil d'un beau jour. See no. 3814

MALIPIERO, Gian-Francesco

Dialogue, no. 4. See no. 561
Serenade, bassoon. See no. 838
Sonata, piano trio. See no. 810

MALOTTE, Albert

The Lord's prayer. See no. 3700. See no. 4100

MANAS, Edgar

Petite suite. See no. 3912

MANCINUS, Thomas

Anchor che col partire. See no. 4010

MANFREDINI, Francesco

Concerto grosso, op. 3, no. 12, C major. See no. 1241

MANSURIAN

Short suite. See no. 3917

MANTUANUS

Lirum bililirum. See no. 3692

MANZ, Paul

Blessed Jesus at thy word. See no. 3673
God of grace. See no. 3806
Improvisations on St. Anne. See no. 3673

MANZIARLY, Marcelle de

Trilogue. See no. 1236

MARAIS, Marin

Le basque. See no. 561. See no. 989. See no. 3986

2146 Folies d'Espagne. Suite, B minor. Les voix humaines. Jordi Savall, vla da gamba; Anne Gallet, hpd; Hopkinson Smith, theorbo and Baroque gtr. Astre AS 4
+FF 5/6-81 p101

Suite, B minor. See no. 2146

2147 Suite d'un Gout etrangere. Jordi Savall, vla da gamba; Ton Koopman, hpd; Hopkinson Smith, theorbo and Baroque gtr. Astree AS 13
+FF 5/6-81 p101

Les voix humaines. See no. 2146

MARCELLO, Alessandro

2148 Concerto, oboe, D minor. PLATTI: Concerto, oboe, G major. VIVALDI: Concerti, oboe, RV 447, C major; RV 457, F major. Bruce Haynes, ob; Baroque Orchestra; Frans Bruggen. RCA RL 3-0371
+Gr 7-81 p164 +-HFN 8-81 p89

Concerto, oboe, D minor. See no. 3808

2149 Concerti, 2 oboes, nos. 1-6. Heinz Holliger, Louise Pellerin, ob; Camerata Bern; Thomas Furi. DG 2533 462
+HFN 12-81 p96

MARCELLO, Benedetto

Concerto, oboe, D minor. See no. 1755

2150 Psalm, no. 50. Rene Jacobs, c-t; Guy de Mey, t; Kurt Widmer, bs; Schola Cantorum Basiliensis. Harmonia Mundi (Germany) 1C 065 99899
+FF 5/6-81 p103 +HFN 8-81 p85
+-Gr 7-81 p185

Sonata, flute, F major. See no. 3820

2151 Sonatas, harpsichord, F major, D minor, D major, C minor. Hans Ludwig Hirsch, hpd. Jecklin 5001
+FF 3/4-81 p149

2152 Sonatas, harpsichord, G major, D minor, F major, A major. Judith Norell, hpd. Musical Heritage Society MHS 4297
+FF 9/10-81 p58

Sonata, recorder, op. 2, no. 2, D minor. See no. 4056

2153 Sonatas, violoncello, nos. 1-6. Anthony Pleeth, Richard Webb, vlc; Christopher Hogwood, hpd. L'Oiseau-Lyre DSLO 546
+Gr 7-80 p148 +RR 8-80 p72
+HFN 7-90 p107 +ST 5-81 p46
+MT 12-80 p786

Songs: Quella fiamma che m'accende. See no. 3756

MARCHETTI, Filippo

Ruy Blas: O dolce volutta. See no. 4035

MARINI, Biagio

Affetti musicali, op. 1: Sinfonia a 2; Sinfonia "La Orlandina"; Corente a 3; Brando a 2; Aria a 3. See no. 1103

Sonate, op. 8: Sonata seconda a 2; Sonata terza per sonar variato. See no. 1103

Sonata a tre, op. 22. See no. 3808

MARIO

Santa Lucia luntana. See no. 3641

MARKOPOULOS

Who pays the ferryman. See no. 3956

MARQUINA
Espana cani. See no. 3981
MARSHALL, Charles
Songs: A child's song; When shadows gather. See no. 4046
Songs: I hear you calling me; When shadows gather. See no. 3967
MARSHALL, Ingram
2154 Fragility cycles. Ingram Marshall, gambuh and electronics. IBU Records 101
+FF 1/2-81 p143
MARTI
2155 Magnificat. CASANOVES: Amicus meus; Caligaverunt; Tenebrae factae sunt. Maria del Carmen Bustamante, s; Montserrat Martorell de Cornudella, alto; Jose Louis Ochoa de Olza, bs; Montserrat Torrent, org; Chorale Sant Jorde; Chamber Orchestra; Orion Martorell. Harmonia Mundi B 10023
++FF 11/12-81 p193
MARTIN, Easthope
The holy child. See no. 3852. See no. 3967
MARTIN, Frank
Clair de lune. See no. 2157
Esquisse. See no. 2157
Etude rythmique. See no. 2157
Fantaisie sur des rythmes flamenco. See no. 2157
2156 Passacaglia. NIELSEN: Commotio, op. 58. SCHOENBERG: Variations on a recitative, op. 40. Ivor Bolton, org. Wealden WS 195
+Gr 9-81 p412
Passacaglia. See no. 1565
2157 Piano works: Clair de lune. Esquisse. Etude rythmique. Fantaisie sur des rythmes flamenco. Quatre pieces breves pour piano: Guitare. Rebecca la Brecque, pno. Opus One 686
++St 12-81 p138
Quatre pieces breves pour piano: Guitare. See no. 2157
Sonata da chiese. See no. 3681. See no. 4113
MARTIN, Richard
Songs: Change thy mind since she doth change. See no. 3946
MARTIN CODAX
Cantigas de amigo. See no. 44
MARTIN Y COLL, Antonio
Entrada y tres canciones de clarin. See no. 3958
MARTINEZ, Marianne
Sonata, piano, A major. See no. 1119
MARTINI
Toccata. See no. 4100
MARTINI, Giovanni Battista
Allegro. See no. 3971
Largo, E major. See no. 3905
MARTINI IL TEDESCO, Johann
Songs: Plaisir d'amour. See no. 3718. See no. 3970
MARTINU, Bohuslav
2158 Arabeskes (7). Nocturnes (4). Variations on a theme by Rossini. Philippe Muller, vlc; Ralf Gothoni, pno. Da Camera Magna SM 93719
+ST 10-81 p432
Ariadne: Ariadne's final aria. See no. 2173
Borova. See no. 2162

Bouquet of flowers. See no. 2173
2159 Butterflies and birds of paradise. Czech danses (3). Madrigal sonata, flute, violin and piano. Les ritournelles. Boris Krajny, Jiri Holena, Eva Kramska, pno; Eva Dostalova, flt; Maria Motulkova, vln. Panton 110 446
+Gr 4-76 p1623 +HFN 9-81 p89
+Gr 10-81 p573 ++RR 1-76 p51
2160 Concertino, violoncello, winds, piano and percussion. Sonata da camera, violoncello and chamber orchestra. ROUSSEL: Concertino, violoncello and orchestra, op. 57. Sasa Vectomov, vlc; Prague Chamber Soloists, Collegium Musicum Pragense, Prague Radio Symphony Orchestra; Eduard Fischer, Frantisek Vajnar. Supraphon 110 2084
+ARG 9-78 p41 +-HFN 7-78 p97
+FF 9/10-78 p72 +-HFN 3-81 p97
+-Gr 8-78 p332 +NR 7-78 p4
+-Gr 3-81 p1198 +-RR 6-78 p50
Concerto, oboe. See no. 1244
2161 Concerto, piano, no. 5, B flat major. Concerto, 2 pianos. Ales Bilek, Vera Lejskova, Vlastimil Lejsek, pno; PSO, Brno Philharmonic orchestra; Jindrich Rohan, Jiri Waldhans. Supraphon 110 2338 (also Pro Arte PAL 1034)
+ARG 3-81 p36 +NR 9-80 p5
+-FF 11/12-80 p132 +SFC 9-13-81 p17
+FF 7/8-81 p131 +SFC 10-11-81 p19
+FF 11/12-81 p194
Comcerto, piano, timpani and 2 strings orchestras. See no. 2173
Concerto, 2 pianos. See no. 2161
Concerto, viola. See no. 2173
Czech dances (3). See no. 2159
2162 Etudes and polkas. Borova. Josef Hala, pno. Supraphon 111 1104
+Gr 7-74 p338 +HFN 3-81 p97
+Gr 3-81 p1214 ++NR 4-74 p11
++HF 5-74 p85 +RR 2-74 p48
+HFN 2-74 p338 +SFC 12-8-74 p36
2163 Greek passion (sung in English). Helen Field, Rita Cullis, s; Catherine Savory, ms; John Mitchinson, Jeffrey Lawton, t; Phillip Joll, bar; John Tomlinson, bs; Kuhn Children's Chorus, CPhO Chorus; Brno State Philharmonic Orchestra; Charles Mackerras. Supraphon 116 3611/2 (2) Tape (c) KSUP 116 3611/2
+Gr 12-81 p929 +HFN 12-81 p96
Greek passion; Katharina's and Manolio's meeting. See no. 2173
Inventions. See no. 2167
2164 Madrigals, violin and viola (3). Quartet, piano. Quatuor Elyseen; Pina Carmirelli, vln; Philipp Naegele, vla. Da Camera SM 92417
+-FF 11/12-81 p194
Madrigal sonata, flute, violin and piano. See no. 2159
Nocturnes. See no. 2158
Parables. See no. 2173
Pieces breves. See no. 2172
Quartet, piano. See no. 2164
2165 Quartet, strings, no. 5. Quartet, strings, no. 7. Panocha Quartet. Supraphon 111 2675
+Gr 12-81 p897 +HFN 12-81 p96
Quartet, strings, no. 7. See no. 2165. See no. 2173

Les ritournelles. See no. 2159
Sinfonietta La Jolla. See no. 2170
Sonata, flute. See no. 2173
Sonata, piano. See no. 2173

2166 Sonata, violin and piano, no. 1. Sonata, violin and piano, no. 2. Sonatina, 2 violins and piano. Pina Carmirelli, vln; Philipp Naegele, vln and vla; Ralf Gothoni, pno. Da Camera SM 92209
+-FF 11/12-81 p194

Sonata, violin and piano, no. 2. See no. 2166
Sonata da camera, violoncello and chamber orchestra. See no. 2160
Sonatina. See no. 43
Sonatina, 2 violins and piano. See no. 2166

2167 Symphony, no. 1. Inventions. CPhO; Vaclav Neumann. Supraphon 410 2166
++ARG 6-79 p27
++FF 9/10-79 p106
++Gr 5-80 p1666
+HF 9-79 p106
+HF 12-81 p93 tape
+-HFN 1-80 p107
+MT 4-81 p246
++NR 7-79 p5
+RR 1-80 p78
+SR 9-81 p52
+STL 12-2-79 p37

2168 Symphony, no. 2. Symphony, no. 6. CPhO; Vaclav Neumann. Supraphon 410 2096
+ARG 1-81 p34
+MT 4-81 p246
+SR 9-81 p52

2169 Symphonies, nos. 3-5. CPhO; Vaclav Neumann. Supraphon SUP 410 2771/2
++Gr 5-80 p1666
+-HFN 1-80 p107
+MT 10-80 p635
++NR 6-81 p3
+RR 1-80 p78
++SFC 12-13-81 p18
+STL 12-2-79 p37

2170 Symphony, no. 4. Sinfonietta La Jolla. Royal Liverpool Orchestra; Walter Weller. HMV ASD 3888 Tape (c) TC ASD 3888
+FF 1/2-81 p144
+Gr 7-80 p141
+HFN 6-80 p107
+HFN 9-80 p116
+MT 2-81 p112
+RR 8-80 p48
+SR 9-81 p52

Symphony, no. 4. See no. 2173

2171 Symphony, no. 6. PISTON: Symphony, no. 6. BSO; Charles Munch. RCA AGL 1-3794 Tape (c) AGK 1-3794
++FF 3/4-81 p150
+-NR 3-81 p4
++SFC 1-25-81 p17

Symphony, no. 6. See no. 2168

2172 Trio, piano, violin and violoncello, D minor. Pieces breves (6). SHOSTAKOVICH: Trio, piano, op. 67, E minor. Trio Rouvier. Da Camera SM 92110
+HFN 12-81 p97

Variatons on a theme by Rossini. See no. 2158

2173 Works, selections: Ariadne: Ariadne's final aria. Concerto, piano, timpani and 2 string orchestras. Concerto, viola. Greek passion: Katharina's and Manolio's meeting. Bouquet of flowers. Parables. Quartet, strings, no. 7. Sonata, flute. Sonata, piano. Symphony, no. 4. Nadja Sormova, Alena Mikova, s; Libuse Marova, con; Miroslav Svejda, Ivo Zidek, t; Richard Novak, bs; Josef Ruzicka, Jaroslav Saroun, Frantisek Maly, Josef Hala, pno; Jaroslav Tvrzky, harmonium; Jiri Valek, flt;

Lubomir Maly, vla; Prague Philharmonic Choir, Kuhn Children's Choir; CPhO, Czech Radio Orchestra, PSO, Talich Quartet, Prague National Theatre Orchestra; Libor Pesek, Stanislav Macura, Zdenek Kosler, Jiri Belohlavek, Vaclav Smetacek, Vaclav Neumann. Panton 8116-0021/25 (5)

+-Gr 3-81 p1194 +-HFN 3-81 p89

MARX, Josef

Songs: Der bescheidene Schafer; Hat dich die Liebe beruhrt; Und gestern hat er mir Rosen gebracht; Valse de Chopin; Windrader. See no. 958

MASCAGNI, Pietro

L'Amico Fritz: Ed anche Beppe...O amore. See no. 3843. See no. 3892

L'Amico Fritz: Intermezzo. See no. 3644. See no. 3787

L'Amico Fritz: Suzel buon di. See no. 3754. See no. 3849

Cavalleria rusticaca: Addio alla madre. See no. 3944

Cavalleria rusticana: Ave Maria. See no. 3967

Cavalleria rusticana: Mamma quel vino e generoso. See no. 3646. See no. 3750

Cavalleria rusticana: O Lola ch' hai di latti. See no. 4032. See no. 4054

Cavalleria rusticana; Siciliana. See no. 3657. See no. 3996. See no. 4037

Cavalleria rusticana: Siciliana; Addio alla madre; Brindisi. See no. 3839

Cavalleria rusticana: Voi lo sapete. See no. 3623. See no. 3647. See no. 4026. See no. 4080

Iris: Apri la tua finestra. See no. 3757. See no. 4037

Iris: Oh come al tuo sottice corpo. See no. 3843

Iris: Un di al tempio. See no. 3711

Lodoletta: Ah il suo nome; Flammen perdonami. See no. 3711

Serenata. See no. 3987

Songs: La tua stella. See no. 3758

MASCHERONI, Eduardo

Eternamente. See no. 3997

MASEK, Vaclav

Partita, D major. See no. 4078

MASLANKA, David

Pieces, clarinet and piano. See no. 1839

MASSENET, Jules

L'Annee passee. See no. 3665

L'Annee passee, Bks 1-4. See no. 2180

Berceuse (2). See no. 2180

Cendrillon; ah que mes soeurs sont heureuses. See no. 3713

Cendrillon: Enfin je suis ici. See no. 3710

Le Cid: A St. Jacques de Compostelle; Priere et vision de St. Jacques. See no. 4051

2174 Le Cid: Ballet music. Suite, orchestra: Scenes pittoresques. La vierge: The last sleep of the virgin. Birmingham Symphony Orchestra; Vivian Dunn, Louis Fremaux. Kalvier KS 522 (also DBX GS 2011)

+ARG 5-80 p45 +-NR 12-73 p4
+-Audio 4-81 p61 +St 5-74 p104
-HF 7-74 p113

Le Cid: O noble lame etincelante; O souverain o juge o pere. See no. 3688. See no. 3707

Le Cid: O souverain o juge o pere. See no. 3839. See no. 4053
2175 Cigale. Valse tres lente. National Philharmonic Orchestra; Richard Bonynge. London CS 7163 (also Decca SXL 6932)
++ARG 4-81 p28 ++HFN 9-80 p105
+FF 1/2-81 p144 +NYT 10-12-80 pD28
+Gr 10-80 p498 +SFC 10-26-80 p20
++HF 1-81 p74 ++St 6-81 p119
Concerto, piano, E flatmajor. See no. 2180
Danses (6). See no. 2180
Devant la Madone. See no. 2180
2176 Don Quichotte: Interludes, nos. 1 and 2. Suites, orchestra, nos. 3-4, 6-7. La vierge: Le dernier sommeil de la vierge. Monte Carlo Opera Orchestra; John Eliot Gardiner. Musical Heritage Society MHS 4212/3 (2)
+HF 1-81 p74 +St 12-80 p134
Duo, D major. See no. 4096
Eau courante. See no. 2180
Eau dormante. See no. 2180
Espada. See no. 1305
Griselidis: Je suis l'oiseau. See no. 4051
Griselidis: Voir Griselidis...Je suis l'oiseau. See no. 4049
Herodiade: Il est doux il est bon. See no. 4038
Herodiade: Jean je te revois. See no. 3689
Herodiade: Ne pouvant reprimer. See no. 4050
Herodiade: Ne pouvant reprimer...Adieu donc vains objets. See no. 3688
Improvisations (7). See no. 2180
2177 Le jongleur de Notre Dame. Alain Vanzo, Tibere Raffali, t; Marc Vento, Jules Bastin, bs; Jean-Marie Fremeau, Michel Carey, bar; Monte Carlo Opera Orchestra and Chorus; Roger Boutry. Angel SBLX 3877 (2) Tape (c) 4X2X 3877 (also EMI 2C 167 16275/6)
+ARG 8-79 p24 +NR 5-79 p9
+FF 7/8-79 p70 +NYT 5-6-79 pD21
+-Gr 9-80 p397 +ON 6-79 p44
+HF 6-79 p84 +Op 1-81 p54
+HF 9-79 p131 tape ++SFC 3-18-79 p44
+HFN 11-80 p121 ++St 7-79 p100
Le jongleur de Notre Dame: Il fait beau voir; Mon beau seigneur. See no. 4049
2178 Manon. Mirella Freni, s; Luciano Pavarotti, Franco Ricciardi, t; Giuseppe Morresi, bar; Wladimiro Ganzarolli, Antonio Zerbini, bs; Orchestra and Chorus; Peter Maag. Historical Recordings HRE 332 (3)
+FF 5/6-81 p103
Manon: Act 2. See no. 1207
Manon: Adieu notre petite table. See no. 3642
Manon: Ah dispar vision; Oh dolce incanto...Chiudo gli occhi. See no. 3843
Manon: Chiudo gli occhi. See no. 3967. See no. 4032
Manon: En fermant les yeux; Ah fuyez douce image. See no. 4033
Manon: Il sogno. See no. 4053. See no. 4054
Manon: Je suis seul...Ah fuyez douce image. See no. 3997
Manon: Je suis encore toute entourdie; Voyons Manon; Duo de la lettre; Adieu notre petite table; Je marche sur tous les chemins; Gavotte. See no. 4044

Manon: Le reve; Au fuyez douce image. See no. 4051
Manon: Toi vous...N'est-ce plus ma main que cette main presse. See no. 4081
Marches (3). See no. 2180
Musique pour bercer les petits enfants. See no. 2180
2179 La navarraise. Marilyn Horne, ms; Placido Domingo, Ryland Davies, Leslie Fyson, t; Sherrill Milnes, Gabriel Bacquier, bar; Nicolas Zaccaria, bs; Ambrosian Opera Chorus; LSO; Henry Lewis. RCA AGL 1-3793
+FF 9/10-81 p134
Papillons blancs. See no. 2180
Papillons noirs. iee no. 2180
2180 Piano works: L'Annee passee, Bks 1-4. Berceuse (2). Concerto, piano, E flat major. Danses (6). Devant la Madone. Eau courante. Eau dormante. Improvisations (7). Marches (3). Musique pour bercer les petits enfants. Papillons blancs. Papillons noirs. Pieces de genre, op. 10. Suite, orchestra, no. 1, op. 11. Toccata. Valse folle. Valse tres lente. La vierge: Danse galilienne. Aldo Ciccolini, pno; Monte Carlo Opera Orchestra; Sylvain Cambreling. Pathe Marconi 2C 167 73005/7 (3)
++FF 5/6-81 p105
+Gr 12-80 p835
+HFN 1-81 p97
Pieces de genre, op. 10. See no. 2180
2181 Le Roi de Lahore. Joan Sutherland, Huguette Tourangeau, s; Sherrill Milnes, bar; James Morris, Nicolai Ghiaurov, bs; Louis Lima, t; London Voices; National Philharmonic Orchestra; Richard Bonynge. London 3RLD 10025 (3) Tape (C) LDR 5 10025 (also Decca D210D3 Tape (c) K210K3)
+-ARG 7/8-81 p46
+-FF 3/4-81 p152
+Gr 11-80 p732
+Gr 1-81 p1001 tape
+HF 1-81 p74
+HFN 11-80 p121
+-NYT 10-12-80 pD28
+ON 1-10-81 p29
+SFC 10-12-80 p21
+St 3-81 p86
2182 Sapho. Renee Doria, Elya Waisman, s; Gisele Ory, ms; Gines Sirera, Christian Baudean, t; Rene Gamboa, bar; Jacques Doumene, bs; Paris Radio Orchestra; Roger Boutry. Peters PLE 129/31 (3) (also HMV 2C 167 16203/5)
-ARG 5-80 p28
/HF 5/6-80 p102
+-Gr 9-81 p428
-HF 4-80 p67
+HFN 10-80 p106
-NYT 12-16-79 pD21
+ON 6-90 p45
+-Op 1-81 p54
+-SFC 1-6-80 p43
+-St 4-80 p134
Sapho: Pendant un an je fus ta femme. See no. 4026
Songs: Elegie; Ouvre tes yeux bleus. See no. 3838
Songs: Pensee d'automne; Puisqu'elle a pris ma vie; Oh si les fleurs avaient des yeux. See no. 3758
Songs: Si tu veux Mignonne. See no. 4029
Suite, orchestra, no. 1, op. 11. See no. 2180. See no. 3665
Suites, orchestra, nos. 3-4, 6-7. See no. 2176
Suite, orchestra: Scenes pittoresques. See no. 796. See no. 2174
Thais: Air du Miroir. See no. 4044
Thais: Dis-moi que je suis belle; Death of Thais. See no. 3640
Thais: Meditation. See no. 3626. See no. 3644. See no. 3817
Toccata. See no. 2180
Valse folle. See no. 2180

Valse tres lente. See no. 2175. See no. 2180
La vierge: Danse galileenne. See no. 2180
La vierge: Le dernier sommeil de la vierge. See no. 2174. See no. 2176. See no. 4122
2183 Werther. Frederica von Stade, Isobel Buchanan, s; Jose Carreras, Paul Crook, t; Thomas Allen, bar; Robert Lloyd, bs; ROHO and Chorus; Colin Davis. Philips 6769 051 (3) Tape (c) 7654 051
++Gr 10-81 p603 +Op 10-81 p1040
+HFN 10-81 p89 +SFC 10-25-81 p21
+ON 12-5-81 p60
Werther, excerpts. See no. 1207
Werther: Air des lettres. See no. 3642
Werther: Ah non mi ridestar. See no. 4032. See no. 4075
Werther: Je ne sais si je veille...O natur; Un autre est son epoux...J'airais sur ma poitrine; Qui ce qu'elle m'ordonne... Lorsque l'enfant. See no. 3689
Werther: O nature; Un autre est son epoux; Pourquoi me reveiller. See no. 3839
Werther: Pourquoi me reveiller. See no. 3754. See no. 3757. See no. 3838
Werther: Va laisse les couler mes larmes. See no. 3710. See no. 3713
Werthe: Was bin ich aufgewacht O wie suss...O natur. See no. 4022
MASTERPIECES OF THE AMERICAN SYNAGOGUE. See no. 3919
MATEJ, Josef
Concerto, flute and harpsichord. See no. 2085
MATHER, Bruce
Fantasy. See no. 1751
In memoriam Alexandre Uninsky. See no. 1751
MATHIAS, William
Quintet, winds, op. 22. See no. 742
Songs: The law of the Lord, op. 61, no. 2; Make a joyful noise unto the Lord. See no. 3632
Symphony, no. 1. See no. 1935
Toccata giocosa, op. 36, no. 2. See no. 3619
MATTEIS, Nicola
Ayres with divisions. See no. 4056
MATTHESON, Johann
2184 Suites, harpsichord, nos. 1, 6, 8, 11. Bradford Tracey, hpd. Harmonia Mundi 1C 065 99875
+-FF 1/2-81 p146 +HFN 1-81 p97
+-Gr 1-81 p967 +MT 6-81 p388
MATTHUS, Siegfried
2185 Concerto, violoncello. Symphony, no. 2. Josef Schwab, vlc; Berlin Comic Opera Orchestra; Siegfried Matthus. Nova 885 163
+FF 9/10-81 p135
Symphony, no. 2. See no. 2185
MATTON, Roger
Mouvement symphonique, no. 1. See no. 2013
MAULDIN, Michael
Petroglyph. See no. 1895
MAW, Nicholas
2186 Life studies, nos. 1-8. AMF; Neville Marriner. Argo ZRG 899
+FF 1/2-81 p146 ++RR 12-79 p62
++Gr 1-80 p1152 +ST 8-80 p267

+HFN 12-79 p165 +STL 12-2-79 p37
++MT 3-80 p180 ++Te 3-80 p29

2187 Songs: The voice of love; La vita nuova. Sarah Walker, ms; Roger Vignoles, pno; Nan Christie, s; Nash Ensemble; Lionel Friend. Chandos ABR 1037 Tape (c) ABT 1037
+Gr 11-81 p738 +-STL 10-11-81 p41
+HFN 11-81 p95

MAXWELL DAVIES, Peter

2188 Renaissance and Baroque realisations: Bach: Preludes and fugues, C sharp major, C sharp minor. Dunstable: Veni sancte: Veni creator spiritus; Three early Scottish motets; Kinloch his fantassie. Purcell: Fantasias upon one note. Fantasia and 2 pavans. Fires of London; Peter Maxwell Davies. Unicorn KP 8005
+HFN 12-81 p97

St. Thomas wake. See no. 62

2189 Songs: Ave maris stella; Tenebrae super Gesualdo. Mary Thomas, s; Timothy Walker, gtr; Fires of London; Peter Maxwell Davies. Unicorn KP 8002
+Gr 8-81 p303 +HFN 10-81 p89

MAYER

Valse etude, op. 83, D flat major. See no. 3920

MAYER, William

2190 Dream's end. STOKES: Eldey Island. On the badlands, parables. St. Paul Chamber Orchestra; William McGlaughlin, Dennis Russell Davies, Cynthia Stokes, flt, pic. CRI SD 415
+FF 3/4-81 p153 +-NR 5-81 p2

MAYS, Bill

Suite, flute and piano. See no. 3730

MAYUZUMI, Toshiro

2191 Mandala. Nirvana. NHK Symphony Orchestra; Japan Chorus Union; Kazuo Yamada. Philips 9500 762 Tape (c) 7300 841
+ARG 2-81 p22 +NR 11-80 p3
++FF 9/10-80 p158 +SFC 9-28-80 p21
+HF 3-81 p56 +St 11-80 p92

Nirvana. See no. 2191

MAZZOCHI, Domenico

Songs: Ottave; Per la nativita di N.S. See no. 3630

MCCLEAN

Wonderful baby. See no. 4114

MCCUNN, Hamish

The land of the mountain and the flood, op. 8. See no. 3722

MCDADE, Carolyn

2192 Original songs (9). TRAD.: Spiritual songs (3). Carolyn McDade, vocals, autoharp, dulcimer; Eve Minkoff, Joan Minkoff, vocals; Instrumentalists and Chorus. Sonory 4631
+FF 3/4-81 p34

MCFREDERICK, Michael

2193 Duo, alto flute and piano. Rhapsody, solo piano. Sextet, woodwinds, strings and piano. Trio, piano, bass and drums. New City Ensemble. Golden Age 1015
+-FF 3/4-81 p153 -NR 6-80 p8

Rhapsody, solo piano. See no. 2193

Sextet, woodwinds, strings and piano. See no. 2193

Trio, piano, bass and drums. See no. 2193

MCGUIRE, James
Suite, no. 2, in popular style. See no. 785
MCKIE, William
We wait for thy loving kindness. See no. 4061
MCLEAN, Barton
Dimensions III and IV. See no. 1739
MCLEOD, John
The song of Icarus. See no. 4062
MEFANO, Paul
Melodies. See no. 866
MEGLI, Domenico
Se di farmi morire. See no. 3946
MEHUL, Etienne-Nicolas
Joseph en Egypt: Ainement Pharaon...Champs paternals. See no. 3688
Joseph en Egypt: Champs paternels. See no. 3967
MEIJERING, Chiel
Electric blue. See no. 3943
MELICHAR
Nanon: Heut' ist der schonste Tag in meinem Leben. See no. 4083
MELLNAS, Arne
Bossa buffa. See no. 1930
MENDELSSOHN, Felix
2194 Allegro brillant, op. 92, A major. RAVEL: Ma mere l'oye. SCHUBERT: Andantino varie, op. 84, no. 1, D 823, B minor. Allegro, op. 144, D 947, A minor. Dallas Weekley, Nancy Arganbright, pno. Golden Crest CRS 4204
+-NR 12-81 p15
Allegro brillant, op. 92, A major. See no. 1497
Athalia, op. 74: March of the priests. See no. 2229. See no. 3699
2195 Die Beiden Padagogen. Krisztina Laki, Gabriele Fuchs, s; Adolf Dallapozza, t; Dietrich Fischer-Dieskau, Klaus Hirte, bar; Gunter Wewel, bs; Bavarian Radio Chorus; Munich Radio Orchestra; Heinz Wallberg. EMI 1C 065 45416
+ARG 9-81 p48 +Gr 2-81 p1115
+FF 1/2-81 p147
Calm sea and prosperous voyage, op. 27. See no. 2210. See no. 2231
2196 Cantatas: Ach Gott vom Himmel sieh darein; Jesu meine Freude. Songs: Christe du Lamm Gottes; Wer nur den lieben Gott. Krisztina Laki, s; Roland Hermann, bar; Stuttgart Chamber Chorus; Wurttemberg Chamber Orchestra; Frieder Bernius. EMI 1C 065 46221
+FF 11/12-81 p195 +-Gr 8-81 p303
2197 Cantatas: Ach Gott vom Himmel sieh darein; Jesu meine Freude; O Haupt voll Blut und Wunden; Verleih uns Frieden gnadiglich; Wir glauben all an einen Gott. Albrecht Ostertag, bar; Marburg Bach Choir, Hesse Bach Collegium; Wolfgang Wehnert. Fono FSM 68 101
+HF 11-81 p88
2198 Concert pieces, op. 113, nos. 1 and 2. Nocturne, C major. Sonata, clarinet and piano, E flat major. Dieter Kocker, clt; Waldemar Wandel, basset hn; Werner Genuit, pno; VSO Wind Ensemble. Musical Heritage Society MHS 4327

+FF 7/8-81 p132

Concert pieces, op. 113, F minor; op. 114, D minor. See no. 1036

2199 Concerto, piano, no. 1, op. 25, G minor. Concerto, piano, no. 2, op. 40, D minor. Valentin Gheorghiu, pno; Leipzig Radio Symphony Orchestra; Herbert Kegel. DG 2535 416 Tape (c) 3335 416 (From 2736 002)

++Gr 7-81 p154 +HFN 5-81 p91

2200 Concerto, piano, no. 1, op. 25, G minor. Concerto, piano, no. 2, op. 40, D minor. Kristin Merscher, pno; Salzburg Mozarteum Orchestra; Leopold Hager. Eurodisc SQ 200 152-366

++SFC 11-8-81 p18

Concerto, piano, no. 2, op. 40, D minor. See no. 2199. See no. 2200

2201 Concerto, violin and piano, D minor. Robert Stoyanov, vln; Artur Stoyanov, pno; Denver Chamber Orchestra; Carl Topilow. Orion ORS 81401

-ARG 10-81 p33 /NR 5-81 p7
/FF 7/8-81 p132

2202 Concerto, violin, op. 64, E minor. TCHAIKOVSKY: Concerto, violin, op. 35, D major. Isaac Stern, vln; PO; Eugene Ormandy. CBS MY 36724

+FF 11/12-81 p257

2203 Concerto, violin, op. 64, E minor. TCHAIKOVSKY: Concerto, violin, op. 35, D major. Erick Friedman, vln; LSO; Seiji Ozawa. RCA AGL 1-3884 Tape (c) AGK 1-3884

+-FF 7/8-81 p180

Concerto, violin, op. 64, E minor. See no. 563. See no. 896. See no. 1037. See no. 1038. See no. 1039. See no. 3969. See no. 4122

Elijah: Ist nicht das Herrn Wort wie ein Feuer. See no. 3639

Elijah, op. 7: It is enough. See no. 4074

Elijah, op. 70: Lord God of Abraham; Is not his word like a fire; It is enough; For the mountain shall depart. See no. 4047

2204 Die erste Walpurgisnacht, op. 60. A midsummer night's dream, opp. 21/61: Scherzo; Intermezzo; Dance of the clowns. Norma Hirsh, ms; William Brown, t; Abraham Lindoquendo, bar; North Texas State University A Capella Choir; RPO; Paul Freeman. Musical Heritage Society MHS 4240

+ARG 4-81 p29 +FF 1/2-81 p148

Etudes, op. 104 (3). See no. 1159

Hebrides overture, op. 26. See no. 1549. See no. 2210. See no. 2230. See no. 2238. See no. 3656. See no. 3722. See no. 3792. See no. 3998

2205 Die Heimkehr aus der Fremde. Helen Donath, s; Hanna Schwarz, con; Peter Schreier, t; Dietrich Fischer-Dieskau, bar; Benno Kusche, bs; Bavarian Radio Choir; Munich Radio Orchestra; Heinz Wallberg. EMI 1C 065 30741

+Gr 2-81 p1115

Laudate pueri dominum. See no. 3616

Lord of Burleigh: Agitato; Allegro vivace. See no. 3840

May breezes. See no. 3969

A midsummer night's dream, opp. 21/61: Overture. See no. 2210. See no. 3726

A midsummer night's dream, opp. 21/61: Scherzo. See no. 2695

A midsummer night's dream, opp. 21/61: Scherzo; Intermezzo; Dance

of the clowns. See no. 2204
A midsummer night's dream, opp. 21/61: Wedding march. See no. 3725
Nocturne, C major. See no. 2198
2206 Octet, op. 20, E flat major. SPOHR: Quartet, op. 65, D minor. Melos Ensemble. Arabesque 8017 Tape (c) 8017
+-ARG 2-81 p22 +-NR 10-80 p7
+FF 11/12-80 p135
2207 Octet, op. 20, E flat major. Israel Philharmonic Orchestra Strings; Zubin Mehta. Decca SXDL 7506 Tape (c) KSXDC 7506 (also London LDR 10009)
+-Audio 11-81 p68 +HFN 9-80 p105
+FF 5/6-81 p105 +-NR 1-81 p7
+-Gr 9-80 p334 +-ST 2-81 p733
+Gr 12-80 p889 tape
2208 Octet, op. 20, E flat major. Smetana and Panocha Quartets. Denon OX 7219
+-FF 11/12-81 p196 ++St 12-81 p120
2209 Octet, op. 20, E flat major. Symphony, strings, no. 10, B minor. Symphony, strings, no. 12, G minor. I Musici. Philips 6527 076 Tape (c) 7311 076 (From 6580 103)
+Gr 4-81 p1339 +-HFN 4-81 p80
+Gr 7-81 p196 tape +-HFN 7-81 p83 tape
Overture, op. 10, C major. See no. 2236
2210 Overtures: Calm sea and prosperous voyage, op. 27. Hebridés, op. 26. Die schone Melusine, op. 32. A midsummer night's dream, op. 21. Ruy Blas, op. 95. LSO; Gabriel Chmura. DG 2535 460 Tape (c) 3335 460 (From 2530 782)
+Gr 2-81 p1091 +HFN 8-81 p92 tape
Pieces, string quartet, op. 81. See no. 2213
Prelude and fugue, D minor. See no. 182
Prelude and fugue, G minor. See no. 3627
2211 Preludes and fugues, op. 37, nos. 1-3. Sonatas, organ, op. 65, nos. 1-6. Hans Fagius, org. BIS LP 156/7 (2)
+-FF 9/10-81 p135 +-NR 8-81 p13
+Gr 6-81 p60
2212 Preludes and fugues, op. 37. REUBKE: Sonata on Psalm, no. 94. Martin Haselbock, org. Pape 203
+FF 7/8-80 p169 +NR 4-81 p14
Preludes and fugues, op. 37, no. 3, D minor. See no. 198
2213 Quartets, strings, nos. 1-6. Pieces, string quartet, op. 81 (4). Bartholdy Quartet. Acanta JB 23075 (4) (From HA 21815, HA 21966)
+Gr 3-81 p1210 ++STL 5-10-81 p41
+-HFN 2-81 p90
Quartet, strings, no. 1, op. 12, E flat major. See no. 1416
2214 Quartet, strings, no. 2, op. 13, A minor. Quartet, strings, no. 3, op. 44, D major. Composers Quartet. Musical Heritage Society MHS 4272
++St 12-81 p120
Quartet, strings, no. 3, op. 44, D major. See no. 2214
2215 Quintet, strings, no. 1, op. 18, A major. Quintet, strings, no. 2, op. 87, B flat major. Vienna Philharmonia Quintet. Decca SDD 562
+-Gr 10-80 p512 +-MT 6-81 p390
+HFN 10-80 p106 +ST 2-81 p733

Quintet, strings, no. 2, op. 87, B flat major. See no. 2215

2216 Rondo capriccioso, op. 14, E major. SCHUBERT: Fantasia, op. 15, D 760, C major. SCHUMANN: Sonata, piano, no. 2, op. 22, G minor. David Bar-Illan, pno. Connoisseur Society Tape (c) InSync 4061
+Audio 10-81 p24 tape
+-CL 5/6-81 p9 tape
+HF 4-81 p93 tape
++St 4-81 p110 tape

Ruy Blas, op. 95. See no. 2210

St. Paul: How lovely are the messengers. See no. 3824

2217 Scherzo a capriccio, F sharp minor. RACHMANINOFF: Sonata, piano, no. 2, op. 36, B flat minor. SCHUMANN: Fantasiestucke, op. 111. Nachtstucke, op. 23, nos. 3 and 4. Vladimir Horowitz, pno. RCA ARL 1-3775 Tape (c) ARK 1-3775
-CL 4-81 p14
+-Gr 7-81 p176
+Gr 10-81 p614 tape
+-HFN 6-81 p82
+/HFN 9-81 p95 tape
+MUM 5/6-81 p32
+NR 4-81 p11
+-NYT 3-22-81 pD23
+-SFC 2-22-81 p19

Scherzo a capriccio, F sharp minor. See no. 2700

Die schone Melusine overture, op. 32. See no. 2210

Sonata, clarinet and piano, E flat major. See no. 2198

Sonatas, organ, op. 65, nos. 1-6. See no. 2211

Sonatas, organ, op. 65, no. 2, C minor. See no. 1082. See no. 3811

Sonatas, organ, op. 65, no. 3, A major. See no. 198

Sonatas, organ, op. 65, no. 6, D minor. See no. 179

2218 Sonata, violin and piano, A major. SCHUMANN, C.: Romances, op. 22 (3). SCHUMANN, R.: Sonata, violin and piano, no. 1, op. 105, A minor. Sergiu Luca, vln; Anne Epperson, pno. Nonesuch D 79007
+FF 7/8-81 p219
+HF 7-81 p71
+NR 7-81 p7
++SFC 3-1-81 p19
+St 6-81 p124

2219 Sonata, violin and piano, no. 1, op. 4, F minor. SCHUBERT: Sonata, violin and piano, op. 162, D 574, A major. Jaap Schroder, vln; Christopher Hogwood, fortepiano. L'Oiseau-Lyre DSLO 571
+Gr 4-81 p1339
+HFN 3-81 p87
+ST 10-81 p431

Songs, op. 48 (6). See no. 955

2220 Songs: Allnachtlich im Traume, op. 86, no. 4; Gruss, op. 19, no. 5; Die Liebende schreibt, op. 86, no. 3; Der Mond, op. 86, no. 5; Nachtlied, op. 71, no. 6; Neue Liebe, op. 19, no. 4; Pagenlied; Scheidend, op. 9, no. 6; Suleika, op. 57, no. 3. WOLF: An den Schlaf; Begegnung; Der Genesene an die Hoffnung; Frage und Antwort; Heimweh; Lebe wohl; Nimmersatte Liebe; Peregrina, I and II; Um Mitternacht. Brigitte Fassbaender, s; Erik Werba, pno. EMI 1C 065 30950
+FF 5/6-81 p192

2221 Songs: Psalm, no. 115, op. 31, Nicht unsern Namen Herr; Psalm, no. 98, op. 91, Singet dem Herrn ein neues Lied; Lauda Sion, op. 73. Evelyn Brunner, s; Naoko Ihara, con; Alejandro Ramirez, t; Philippe Huttenlocher, bar; Gulbenkian Foundation Symphony Orchestra and Chorus; Michel Corboz. Erato STU 71223
+Gr 10-79 p689
+HFN 10-79 p157
+MQ 7-81 p445
+-MT 6-80 p383
+RR 10-79 p137

2222 Songs: Psalms, no. 4, op. 42, Wie der Hirsch schreit; no. 95, op. 46, Kommt lasst uns anbeten. Christiane Baumann, Joana Silva, s; Pierre-Andre Blaser, t; Gulbenkian Foundation Orchestra and Chorus; Michel Corboz. Erato STU 71101 (also Musical Heritage Society MHS 4185)

++ARG 10-79 p44 +HFN 7-78 p97
++FF 9/10-79 p106 +MQ 7-81 p445
+-FF 11/12-80 p136 -MT 2-79 p134
+Gr 7-78 p236 +NYT 10-7-79 pD24
+HF 11-79 p102 +RR 7-78 p87

2223 Songs (cantatas, sacred songs, hymns): Christe du Lamm Gottes; Hor mein Bitten Herr neige dich zu mir; Lass o herr mich Hilfe finden; Wer nur den lieben Gott lasst walten. Uta Spreckelsen, s; Dorothea Brinkmann, alto; Martin Weyer, org; Marburg Instrumental and Vocal Ensembles; Rolf Beck. Musicaphon BM 30 SL 1336

+FF 11/12-79 p99 +MQ 7-81 p445
+Gr 1-81 p981

Songs: Above all praise and majesty. See no. 3824
Songs: Ave Maria, op. 23, no. 2. See no. 3638
Songs: Fruhlingslied. See no. 3626
Songs: Hear my prayer. See no. 3614
Songs: Hear my prayer; O for the wings of a dove. See no. 4107
Songs: On wings of song, op. 34, no. 2. See no. 3847
Songs: Rise up arise. See no. 3700

2224 Songs without words, op. 19, nos. 1, 3, 6; op. 30, nos. 7, 10, 12; op. 38, nos. 14, 17-18; op. 53, nos. 20; op. 62, nos. 25-26, 29-30; op. 67, nos. 32, 34; op. 102, nos. 43, 45, 47. Daniel Adni, pno. HMV ESD 7113 Tape (c) TC ESD 7113 (From SLS 862)

+-Gr 11-81 p724 +HFN 12-81 p109

2225 Songs without words, op. 19, nos. 1, 5-6; op. 30, nos. 3-4, 6; op. 38, nos. 2-3, 5; op. 53, nos. 2-3; op. 62, nos. 1, 5-6; op. 67, nos. 2, 4-6; op. 85, nos. 3, 6; op. 102, nos. 1, 4, 6. Daniel Barenboim, pno. DG 2531 260

+ARG 5-81 p22 ++NR 11-80 p9
+CL 1-81 p14 ++RR 7-80 p81
+FF 1/2-81 p148 +St 12-80 p129
+Gr 8-80 p242 +STL 7-13-80 p38
+-HFN 7-80 p117

Songs without words, op. 109, D major. See no. 3667. See no. 3686

2226 Symphony, no. 2, op. 52, B flat major. Symphony, no. 3, op. 56, A minor. Margaret Price, Sally Burgess, s; Siegfried Jerusalem, t; LPO and Chorus, LSO; Riccardo Chailly. Philips 6769 042 (2) Tape (c) 7699 128

+-FF 5/6-81 p106 +-NR 4-81 p3
+-Gr 12-80 p835 ++St 5-81 p68
+HFN 12-80 p141

2227 Symphony, no. 3, op. 56, A minor. Symphony, no. 4, op. 90, A major. AMF; Neville Marriner. Argo ZRG 926 Tape (c) KZRC 926

+Gr 6-81 p42 +HFN 7-81 p74
+Gr 8-81 p324 tape

2228 Symphony, no. 3, op. 56, A minor. Symphony, no. 4, op. 90, A major. St. John's Orchestra; John Lubbock. ASV ACM 2012

+-HFN 11-81 p95

2229 Symphony, no. 3, op. 56, A minor. Athalia, op. 74: War march of the priests. VPO; Christoph von Dohnanyi. Decca SXL 6954 Tape (c) KSXC 6954 (also London CS 7184)

+FF 1/2-81 p149
+Gr 7-80 p141
+HF 1-81 p75
+HFN 7-80 p109
+NR 2-81 p5
+-RR 7-80 p57
++St 3-81 p90

2230 Symphony, no. 3, op. 56, A minor. Hebrides overture, op. 26. Israel Philharmonic Orchestra; Leonard Bernstein. DG 2531 256 Tape (c) 3301 256

+-ARG 9-81 p26
+FF 1/2-81 p149
+Gr 9-80 p335
+Gr 12-80 p889 tape
+HF 1-81 p75
+-HFN 10-80 p106
+-HFN 11-80 p131 tape
+St 3-81 p90

2231 Symphony, no. 3, op. 56, A minor. Calm sea and prosperous voyage, op. 27. LPO; Bernard Haitink. Philips 9500 535 Tape (c) 7300 678

+ARG 9-80 p32
+HF 9-80 p91
+-HFN 12-81 p97
+-NR 6-80 p5
++SFC 3-2-80 p41

2232 Symphony, no. 3, op. 56, A minor. Symphony, strings, no. 10. op. posth., B minor. Leipzig Gewandhaus Orchestra, Lucerne Festival Strings; Kurt Masur, Rudolf Baumgartner. RCA GL 2-5330 Tape (c) GK 2-5330 (From RCA LRL 1-5005)

+-Gr 8-81 p274
+-Gr 8-81 p324 tape
+-HFN 8-81 p92 tape

Symphony, no. 3, op. 56, A minor. See no. 2226

2233 Symphony, no. 4, op. 90, A major. SCHUMANN: Symphony, no. 4, op. 120, D minor. BPhO; Klaus Tennstedt. Angel DS 37760 Tape (c) 4ZS 37760 (also HMV ASD 3963 Tape (c) TC ASD 3963)

+-ARG 7/8-81 p23
+FF 3/4-81 p154
+Gr 4-81 p1318
+HF 10-81 p86
+-HFN 4-81 p72
+-MUM 7/8-81 p32
+MUM 9/10-81 p37 tape
-NR 3-81 p4
+St 4-81 p106
+STL 3-8-81 p38

2234 Symphony, no. 4, op. 90, A major. SCHUBERT: Symphony, no. 8, D 759, B minor. BPhO; Herbert von Karajan. DG 2531 291 Tape (c) 3301 291

+-HFN 9-80 p115
++NR 3-81 p4

2235 Symphony, no. 4, op. 90, A mjor. Symphony, no. 5, op. 107, D minor. Leipzig Gewandhaus Orchestra; Kurt Masur. RCA GL 2-5307 Tape (c) GK 2-5307

+-HFN 3-81 p95
/HFN 3-81 p97 tape

2236 Symphony, no. 4, op. 90, A major. Overture, op. 101, C major. Warsaw Philharmonic Orchestra; Stanislaw Wislicki. Stolat SZM 0111

-FF 11/12-81 p211

Symphony, no. 4, op. 90, A major. See no. 2227. See no. 2228

Symphony, no. 4, op. 90, A major: Tarantella. See no. 3662

2237 Symphony, no. 5, op. 107, D major. SCHUMANN: Symphony, no. 1, op. 38, B flat major. PhO; Riccardo Muti. HMV SQ ASD 3781 Tape (c) TC ASD 3781 (also Angel SZ 37601)

+-Gr 10-79 p643
+-HF 1-81 p75
+-NYT 5-11-80 pD24
+RR 10-79 p104

+-HFN 11-79 p141 ++SFC 7-20-80 p34
+-HFN 1-80 p123 tape +St 11-80 p94
+NR 7-80 p80 p3

2238 Symphony, no. 5, op. 107, D minor. Hebrides overture, op. 26. LPO; Bernard Haitink. Philips 9500 713 Tape (c) 7300 804
+ARG 1-81 p35 +NR 9-80 p2
++FF 11/12-80 p136 ++St 11-80 p94
+Gr 6-81 p42 +STL 5-10-81 p41
++HF 1-81 p75

Symphony, no. 5, op. 107, D minor. See no. 2235

2239 Symphonies, strings, nos. 2-3, 5-6. Polish Chamber Orchestra; Jerzy Maksymiuk. HMV ESD 7123 Tape (c) TCC ESD 7123
+Gr 8-81 p274 ++HFN 8-81 p85
+Gr 11-81 p783 tape

2240 Symphonies, strings, nos. 6-7, 10. Baden Baden Ensemble 13; Manfred Reichert. Harmonia Mundi 1C 065 99823 (aso Pro Arte PAL 1007)
-FF 11/12-81 p197 +-RR 4-80 p68
+-Gr 4-80 p1557 +-ST 6-80 p118
+HFN 3-80 p93

2241 Symphony, strings, no. 8, D major. Symphony, strings, no. 9, C major. New York Pro Arte Chamber Orchestra; Raffael Adler. Musical Heritage Society MHS 4252
+FF 3/4-81 p154

Symphony, strings, no. 9, C major. See no. 2241
Symphony, strings, no. 10, B minor. See no. 2209. See no. 2232
Symphony, strings, no. 12, G minor. See no. 2209

2242 Te deum, A major. Elizabeth Lane, Rosemary Hardy, s; Jean Temperley, Gloria Jennings, alto; Paul Taylor, Peter Hall, t; Paul Hillier, David Wilson-Johnson, bs; Christopher Bowers-Broadbent, org; London Schutz Choir; Roger Norrington. Fono FSM 63 105
-HF 11-81 p88

2243 Trio, piano, no. 1, op. 49, D minor. Trio, piano, no. 2, op. 46, C minor. Istomin-Stern-Rose Trio. CBS M 35835 Tape (c) MT 35835
+-FF 9/10-81 p136 ++SR 10-81 p86
+NR 8-81 p7 +St 11-81 p88
+NYT 6-21-81 pD23

2244 Trio, piano, no. 1, op. 49, D minor. Trio, piano, no. 2, op. 66, C minor. Anne Queffelec, pno; Pierre Amoyal, vln; Frederic Lodeon, vlc. Erato STU 71025
+Gr 5-81 p1488 +RR 4-80 p87
+HFN 9-79 p108

2245 Trio, piano, no. 1, op. 49, D minor. SCHUMANN: Trio, piano, no. 1, op. 63, D minor. Kyung Wha Chung, vln; Paul Tortelier, vlc; Andre Previn, pno. HMV ASD 3894 Tape (c) TC ASD 3894
+Gr 9-80 p360 +-ST 1-81 p647
+Gr 1-81 p1001 tape +STL 11-9-80 p40
+HFN 9-80 p105

Trio, piano, no. 1, op. 49, D minor. See no. 1000. See no. 1457
Trio, piano, no. 2, op. 66, C minor. See no. 2243. See no. 2244
Variations concertantes, op. 17. See no. 949
Variations serieuses, op. 54, D minor. See no. 717
Wedding march. See no. 3924

MENDELSSOHN-HENSEL, Fanny
Bergeslust. See no. 3814
Italien. See no. 3814
2246 Melodies, piano, op. 4, nos. 4-6, op. 5, nos. 2, 4. SCHUMANN, C.: Impromptu, op. 9. Polonaise, op. 1 (4). Romance, no. 1, op. 21, no. 1, A minor. Scherzo, no. 2, op. 14, C minor. Variations on a theme by Robert Schumann, op. 20. Judith Alstadter, pno. Musical Heritage Society MHS 4163
+-CL 3-81 p15 +FF 3/4-81 p193
Songs: Die Nonne; Du bist die Ruh; Im Herbste; Nachtanderer; Rosenkranz; Verwurf. See no. 1989
MENOTTI, Giancarlo
Overture and caccia. See no. 3817
2247 The unicorn, the gorgon and the manticore. Colgate University Chamber Ensemble and Chorus; Marietta Cheng. Redwood Records ES 15
+-FF 1/2-81 p150 +-NR 1-81 p8
MERCANDANTE, Giuseppe Saverio
2248 Concerti, flute, D major, E major. Variations, flute, A major. Jean-Pierre Rampal, flt; ECO; Claudio Scimone. RCA ARL 1-3727 Tape (c) ARK 1-3727
+FF 3/4-81 p155 +SFC 3-29-81 p18
+-NR 3-81 p6 ++St 6-81 p121
Le due illustri rivali: Leggio gia nel vostro cor. See no. 723
Variations, flute, A major. See no. 2248
MERIKANTO, Oskar
A fairy story by the fire. See no. 3967
Passacaglia, op. 80. See no. 3804
MERTZ, Johann
Fantasie hongroise, op. 65, no. 1. See no. 1591
Kindermarchen, op. 13, no. 8. See no. 1591
Liebeslied, op. 13, no. 4b. See no. 1591
Polacca, op. 5, no. 3. See no. 1591
Romance, op. 13, no. 1b. See no. 1591
Tarantelle, op. 13, no. 6. See no. 1591
MERULA, Tarquinio
Un cromatico ovvero capriccio. See no. 3622. See no. 4012
Toccata im 2 ton. See no. 3832
MERULO, Claudio
Toccata. See no. 4094
MESSAGER, Andre
Fortunio: J'aimais le vieille maison grise. See no. 3967
Fortunio: J'aimais le vieille maison grise; Je suis tendre; Si vous croyez. See no. 4051
Fortunio: Je sus tres tendre; Ma vieille maison grise. See no. 4049
Fortunio: La maison grise. See no. 4043
The two pigeons: Entrance of the gipsies; Entrance of Pepio; Dance of two pigeons; Theme and variations. See no. 3840
MESSE VON BARCELONA. See no. 3994
MESSIAEN, Oliver
2249 L'Ascension. Hymne. Les offrandes oubliees. ORTF; Marius Constant. Erato STU 70673 (also Musical Heritage Society MHS 3685)
+-FF 5/6-78 p60 +HFN 2-81 p79
+-Gr 4-77 p1550 +MT 9-77 p736
+-HFN 4-77 p138

2250 Les corps glorieux. Jennifer Bate, org. Unicorn DKP 9004
++Gr 9-81 p412 +-HFN 9-81 p81
Les corps glorieux: Joie et clarte des corps glorieux. See no. 4118
Diptyque. See no. 4110
Hymne. See no. 2249
Le merle noir. See no. 3668
Messe de la pentecote: Communion; Sortie. See no. 3811
2251 La nativite du Seigneur. Theodore Gillen, org. Liturgical Press 7131
+-FF 9/10-81 p137 +MU 9-81 p14
+HF 11-81 p87
La nativite du Seigneur: Dieu parmi nous. See no. 310. See no. 4113. See no. 4118
Les offrandes oubliees. See no. 2249
2252 Poemes pour mi. TIPPETT: Songs for Dov. Felicity Palmer, s; BBC Symphony Orchestra; Robert Tear, t; London Sinfonietta; David Atherton, Pierre Boulez. Argo ZRG 703
++Gr 5-73 p2072 ++MQ 1-76 p139
+-HF 7-74 p94 ++NR 6-74 p9
+HFN 5-73 p986 +NYT 2-17-74 pD33
+HFN 2-81 p79 +RR 5-73 p25
+-MJ 12-74 p46 ++SFC 4-7-74 p25
++St 9-74 p126
2253 Quatuor pour la fin du temps. Vera Beths, vln; George Pieterson, clt; Anner Bylsma, vlc; Reinbert de Leeuw, pno. Philips 9500 725
+Gr 7-81 p168 +-ST 9-81 p352
+-HFN 3-81 p89
2254 Songs: Harawi; Chants de terre et de ciel; Poemes pour mi; Trois melodies. Michele Command, s; Marie-Madeleine Petit, pno. EMI 2C 167 16226/8 (3)
+Gr 5-81 p1504
Songs: O sacrum convivium. See no. 3925
Theme and variations. See no. 1473
2255 La transfiguration de notre Seigneur Jesus Christ. Michael Sylvester, t; Paul Acquino, bar; Yvonne Loriod, pno; Janos Starker, vlc; Wallace Mann, flt; Loren Kitt, clt; Frank Ames, marimba; John Kane, xylorimba; Ronald Barnett, vibraphone; Westminster Symphonic Choir; Washington National Symphony Orchestra; Antal Dorati. Decca HEAD 1-2 (2) (also London HEAD 1-2)
++Gr 5-74 p2050 ++NR 1-75 p10
+-HF 4-75 p88 +-RR 5-74 p19
+HFN 2-81 p79 ++SFC 11-3-74 p22
++MJ 10-75 p45
2256 Turangalila symphony. Michel Beroff, pno; Jeanne Loriod, ondes martenot; LSO; Andre Previn. HMV SQ SLS 5117 (2) Tape (c) TC SLS 5117 (also Angel SB 3853)
-FF 9/10-78 p77 ++MJ 12-78 p45
++Gr 6-78 p51 +MT 3-79 p228
+Gr 10-78 p748 ++NR 9-78 p4
++HF 12-78 p116 ++RR 6-78 p51
+HFN 6-78 p124 ++RR 12-78 p114 tape
++HFN 9-78 p157 tape ++SFC 6-11-78 p49
+HFN 2-81 p79 ++St 9-78 p123

METCALF
Absent. See no. 4046
MEYERBEER, Giacomo
L'Africaine: C'est de la que mon canto fragile...Combein tu m'es chere; Erreur fatale...O ma Selika. See no. 3689
L'Africaine: Di qui si vede il mar...Qual soave concento. See no. 4041
L'Africaine: Figlia di regi. See no. 4034
L'Africaine: Mi batte il cor...O paradiso. See no. 3757. See no. 3995
L'Africaine: O paradiso. See no. 3754. See no. 3838. See no. 3839. See no. 3972. See no. 3987. See no. 4053. See no. 4075
L'Africaine: O paradiso; Combien tu m'es chere; Erreur fatal. See no. 1676
L'Africaine: O Selika io t'adora. See no. 4035
L'Africaine: Pays merveilleux...O paradiso. See no. 3769
L'Africaine: Sur me genoux; Hirtenlied. See no. 3531
2257 Il crociato in Egitto. Yvonne Kenny, Felicity Palmer, s; Rockwell Blake, t; Justino Diaz, bs; Sacred Music Society Orchestra and Chorus; West Point Military Band; Gianfranco Masini. VOCE 36 (3)
+NR 11-81 p11
2258 Dinorah. Deborah Cook, s; Della Jones, ms; Alexander Oliver, t; Christian du Plessis, bar; PhO; James Judd. Opera Rara OR 5 (3)
+ARG 10-80 p23
+FF 9/10-80 p163
+-Gr 8-80 p266
+-MT 6-81 p390
+NYT 6-29-80 pD20
+OC Fall 1981 p51
+ON 8-80 p36
+-Op 9-80 p911
+RR 7-80 p20
+STL 6-8-80 p38
Dinorah: En chasse. See no. 4029
Dinorah: Les bles sont beaux a faucher. See no. 1676
Dinorah: Ombra leggiera. See no. 4040
L'Etoile du nord: O jours heureux. See no. 4045
Les Huguenots: Ah qual soave vision...Bianca al par di neve alpina. See no. 3996
Les Huguenots: Ah quel spectacle enchanteur...Plus blanche que la blanche hermine. See no. 4028
Les Huguenots: Bianca al par. See no. 4075
Les Huguenots: Nobles seigneurs salut. See no. 3710
Les Huguenots: O qual soave...Bianca al par. See no. 4035
Les Huguenots: Piff paff. See no. 4029
Les Huguenots: Plus blanche que la blanche hermine. See no. 1676
Le prophete: Coronation march. See no. 3699
Le prophete: Pretres de baal. See no. 3713
Le prophete: Prison scene. See no. 4039
Le prophete: Roi du ciel; Pour Bertha moi je souspire. See no. 1676
Robert le diable: Invocation. See no. 4025
Robert le diable: Le rovine son queste...Suore che riposte. See no. 3968
Songs: Guide au bord ta nacelle. See no. 3758
Songs: Hirtenlied. See no. 3954
MIASKOVSKY, Nikolai
2259 Sonata, piano, no. 2, op. 13, F sharp minor. Sonata, piano, no.

3, op. 19. RACHMANINOFF: Prelude, op. 3, no. 2, C sharp minor. SCRIABIN: Preludes, op. 74. Idil Biret, pno. Finnadar SR 9029
-CL 10-81 p10 +-NR 6-81 p14
+FF 7/8-81 p133 ++ST 7-81 p84
Sonata, piano, no. 3, op. 19. See no. 2259
MICHALSKY, Donal
Fantasia alla marcia. See no. 1271
Fantasia sopra M.F.V. See no. 1271
MIDDLETON, Owen
Processional and Virginia reel. See no. 3870
MIKULI, Karol
Etude. See no. 3912
Lied. See no. 3912
MILAN, Luis de
Fantasia del quarto tono. See no. 3883
Pavane. See no. 4094
Perdid tenyo la color. See no. 3828
Poys dezeys que me quereys ben. See no. 3828
Songs: Aquel caballero madre. See no. 4063
Toda mi vida os ame. See no. 3828
MILANO, Francesco da
Fantasia. See no. 3766
Fantasias. See no. 3883
Ricercare. See no. 3766. See no. 3883
Spagna, 2 lutes. See no. 3661
MILES
Anchor's away. See no. 3699
MILFORD
2260 Pastoral dance. VAUGHAN WILLIAMS: Greensleeves. ZACHAU: Vom himmel hoch. Trad: Christmas carols arranged by Robert Edward Smith. John Rose, org; Rebecca Flannery, Gail Sacco, hp; Steve Agritelley, Edward Wrobel, perc. Towerhill T 1009
+MU 4-81 p22
MILFORD, Robin
Songs: If it's ever spring again; The colour; So sweet love seemed. See no. 3874
MILHAUD, Darius
Autumne: Alfama. See no. 1278
La boeuf sur le toit. See no. 1131
2261 Cantate de l'enfant et de la mere. La muse menagere. Madeleine Milhaud, narrator; Leonid Hambro, Darius Milhaud, pno; Juilliard Quartet; Darius Milhaud. CBS 61130
+-Gr 8-81 p286 +HFN 8-81 p85
2262 La cheminee de Roi Rene, op. 205. Divertissement en trois parties, op. 299b. Pastorale, op. 147. Sketches, op. 227b (2). Suite d'apres Corrette, op. 161b. Athena Ensemble. Chandos ABR 1012 Tape (c) ABT 1012
++FF 1/2-81 p150 +HFN 11-80 p121
++Gr 8-80 p239 +RR 8-80 p63
+Gr 12-80 p889 tape ++St 3-81 p91
+HFN 10-80 p117 tape
La cheminee du Roi Rene, op. 205. See no. 562. See no. 574. See no. 3934
Concerto, marimba and vibraphone. See no. 3678
Concerto, piano, no. 1, op. 127. See no. 1278

Divertissement en trois parties, op. 299b. See no. 2262
La muse menagere. See no. 2261
Pastorale, op. 147. See no. 2262
Le printemps. See no. 3984
Saudades do Brasil: Paysandu. See no. 1278
Saudades do Brasil: Tijuca. See no. 3789
Scaramouche: Braziliera. See no. 3789
Sketches, op. 227b. See no. 2262
Songs: L'Aurore; Poemes de Jean Cocteau. See no. 3687
Suite d'apres Corrette, op. 161b. See no. 2262
Suite provencale, op. 152a. See no. 2013

MILLOCKER, Carl

2263 Der Bettelstudent. Rita Streich, Renate Holm, s; Nicolai Gedda, t; Gerhard Unger, t; Hermann Prey, bar; Bavarian Radio Orchestra; Franz Allers. Arabesque 8065-2 (2) (also EMI 1C 175 30162/3)

+FF 1/2-81 p151 +ON 12-20-80 p52
+Gr 12-81 p940 +SFC 12-7-80 p33
+NR 12-80 p9

Der Bettelstudent, excerpts. See no. 3975
Du Dubarry: Ja so ist sie die Dubarry. See no. 4083
Gasparone: Komm mia bella. See no. 4083

MIRON-HAGIZ

Ura Dor. See no. 3897

MIRZOVAN, Edward

Poem. See no. 3917

MISEK, Adolf

Sonata, double bass and piano, no. 2, op. 6, E minor. See no. 863

MISSA, Edmond de

Muguette: Entr'acte. See no. 4122

MITCHELL, Roscoe

2264 Prelude. Variations on sketches from Bamboo, nos. 1 and 2. OSHITA: Marche. Textures. Roscoe Mitchell, sax, clt; Tom Buckner, voice; Gerald Oshita, sarrusophone, sax, Conn-o-sax. 1750 Arch S 1785

*NR 11-81 p6

Variations on sketches from Bamboo, nos. 1 and 2. See no. 2264

MIYASHITA

Yoru no shirabe (Nocturne). See no. 4106

MOERAN, Ernest

Ludlow town: When smoke stood up from Ludlow; Farewell to barn and stack and tree; Say lad have you things to do; The lads in their hundreds. See no. 3893
Maltworms. See no. 3973
Pieces, orchestra (2). See no. 3856
Shakespeare songs: The lover and his lass; Where the bee sucks; When daisies pied; When icicles hang by the wall. See no. 956
Songs: Tis time I think by Wenlock town. See no. 3893
Songs: When daisies pied; When icicles hang by the wall; Where the bee sucks. See no. 3878
Trio, strings, G major. See no. 1018

MOLINARO, Simone

Ballo detto "Il Conte Orlando". See no. 4016
Fantasia. See no. 4016
Saltarellos (2). See no. 4016

MOLINS, Pierre de
Amis tout dous. See no. 3846
MOLLER
Presto, C major. See no. 3627
MOLLICONE, Henry
2265 The face on the barroom floor. FOSS: Thirteen ways of looking at a blackbird. Leanne McGiffin, s; Rosemarie Freni, ms; Barry McCauley, t; David Holloway, bar; Alice Lenicheck, Robert Dick, flt; Jan Williams, perc; George Banks, vlc; Henry Mollicone, Ivar Mikhashoff, pno. CRI SD 442
+-ARG 10-81 p52
*FF 9/10-81 p138
+NR 7-81 p10
+ON 4-11-81 p52
++St 10-81 p127
MOLLOY
The Kerry dance. See no. 3967
MOLTER, Johann
2266 Concerto, clarinet, no. 4, A major. STAMITZ, C.: Concerto, clarinet, E flat major. STAMITZ, J.: Concerto, clarinet and 2 horns, B flat major. Laszlo Horvath, clt; Liszt Ferenc Chamber Orchestra; Janos Rolla. Hungaroton SLPX 11954
++ARG 6-79 p44
+FF 1/2-80 p109
+Gr 4-81 p1318
+-HFN 2-81 p95
+NR 7-79 p6
Concerto, flute and strings, G major. See no. 4008
Concerto, trumpet, no. 2, D major. See no. 1483
MONCAYO GARCIA, Jose
Huapango. See no. 1133. See no. 1134
MONDONVILLE, Jean-Joseph Cassanaea de
2267 Songs (motets): Venite exultemus; Domius regnavit. Colette Alliot-Lugaz, Daniele Borst, s; Michael Goldthorpe, Jean Buclet, t; Philippe Huttenlocher, bs; A Coeur Joie, Adam de la Halle d'Arras Vocal Ensemble; Jean-Francois Paillard Chamber Orchestra; Jean-Francois Paillard. Erato STU 71323
+Gr 1-81 p981
2268 Songs (motets): Benefac Domine; Domino laudabitur; Cantate Deo; In decachordo psalterio; In Domino laudabitur; Laudate Dominum; Paratum cor meum; Protector meus; Quare tristis es; Regna terrae; Spera in Deo. Judith Nelson, s; William Christie, hpd; Stanley Ritchie, vln. Harmonia Mundi HM 1045
+FF 11/12-80 p136
+-Gr 7-80 p158
/-HFN 8-80 p99
+MT 6-81 p390
MONIUSZKO, Stanislaw
Halka: The wind wails in the hills. See no. 4030
MONN, Georg
Quartet, strings, no. 1, B flat major. See no. 1558
MONRAD-JOHANSEN, David
2269 Pan, op. 22. NYSTEDT: The burnt sacrifice, op. 36. SAEVERUD: Symphony, no. 6. Claes Gill, narrator; Bergen Symphony Orchestra and Chorus; Karsten Andersen. Philips 6507 007
+FF 7/8-81 p159
Suite, no. 2, op. 9. See no. 1981
MONTECLAIR, Michel Pignolet de
Le beau berger Tircis. See no. 4067
Brunetes ancienes et modernes: Je suis charme d'une brune. See no. 4067
Je sens naitre en mon coeur. See no. 4067

MONTEVERDI, Claudio

Arianna: Lasciatemi morire. See no. 3839

Il combattimento di Tancredi e Clorinda. See no. 1493

2270 Christmas vespers. Motets: Ab aeterno ordinata sum; Salve regina; Audi caelum, Salve regina. Julie Kennard, Elisabeth Harrison, s; Shirley Minty, alto; Peter Hall, Edgar Fleet, t; David Wilson-Johnson, bar; Roderick Earle, bs; Trinity Boys Choir; Accademia Monteverdiana Orchestra and Chorus; Denis Stevens. Nonesuch HB 73032 (2)
+-FF 3/4-81 p156 +SFC 12-21-80 p22

2271 Madrigals, Bk 8. Soloists; Glyndebourne Chorus Members, Ambrosian Singers Members; ECO; Raymond Leppard. Philips 6768 175 (3)
+FF 5/6-81 p107 +-St 8-81 p98
+NR 4-81 p8

2272 Madrigals: Al lume della stelle; Alcun non consigli; Altri canti d'amor; Ardo avvampo; Dolcissimo uscignolo; Eri gia tutta mia; La fiera vista; Gira il nemico; Interrotte speranze; Io son pur vezzosetta; Le lagrime d'amante al sepolcro dell'amata; Ninfa che scalza; Non giacinti; Non sono in queste rive; O come sei gentile; O viva fiamma; Qual si puo; Quel sguardo; Raggi dov'e'l mio bene; Romancesca; S'andasse amor; S'el vostro cor; Soave libertate; Su pastorelli; Tempro la cetra; Tornate o cari baci; Zefiro torna. Lausanne Instrumental and Vocal Ensemble; Michel Corboz. Musical Heritage Society MHS 4196/8 (3)
+FF 5/6-81 p107

2273 Madrigals: Altri canti di Marte; Chiomo d'oro; Amor che deggio far; Hor ch'el ciel; Gira il nemico; Perche t'en fuggi; Tirsi e Clori. Les Arts Florissants Vocal and Instrumental Ensemble; William Christie. Harmonia Mundi HM 1068 Tape (c) HM 40-1068
+FF 11/12-81 p197 +HFN 9-81 p81
++Gr 9-81 p421 +STL 9-13-81 p41

2274 Madrigals: Ardo e scoprir; Bel pastor; Di far sempre gioire; Ecco mormorar l'onde; Eccomi pronto ai baci; Hor ch'l ciel e la terra; Io mi son giovinetta; Lamento della ninfa; Lasciatemi morire; Maledetto sia l'aspetto; La mia Turca; Non e di gentil core; Perche fuggi; Presso un fiume tranquillo; Ohime ch'io cado; Questi vaghi concenti; Si ch'io vorrei morire; Si dolce e il tormento; Sfogava con le stelle; Tirsi e Clori; Vorrei baciarti. Lausanne Vocal and Chamber Ensemble; Michel Corboz. Musical Heritage Society MHS 824283 (2)
+FF 5/6-81 p107 +St 8-81 p98

2275 Madrigals, Bk 6, Lasciatemi morire; O Teseo o Teseo mio; Dove dove la fede; Ahi che non pur rispondi; Una donna fra l'altre. Bk 7: Eccomi pronti ai baci; Tu dormi. Bk 8: Lamento della ninfa; Ardo e scoprir. Bk 9: Alcun non mi consigli; Bel pastor; Ohime ch'io cado; Eri gia tutta mia. Marjanne Kweksilber, s; Rene Jacobs, alto; Marius van Altena, Michiel ten Houte de Lange, t; Floris Rommerts, bs; Gustav Leonhardt, hpd. RCA RL 3-0390
+-Gr 7-81 p185 +-HFN 8-81 p86

2276 Magnificat a 6 voci. Mass, In illo tempore. Vespro della beata vergine. Paul Esswood, Kevin Smith, c-t; Ian Partridge, John Elwes, t; David Thomas, Christopher Keyte, bs; Regensburger Domspatzen; Instrumental Ensemble; Hanns-Martin Schneidt. DG 2723 043 Tape (c) 3376 010

+Gr 12-81 p945 tape

Mass, In illo tempore. See no. 2276

2277 L'Orfeo (arr. Orff). Lucia Popp, s; Rose Wagemann, ms; Hermann Prey, bar; Karl Ridderbusch, bs; Bavarian Radio Orchestra; Kurt Eichhorn. Acanta EA 23378

+-ON 4-4-81 p28

2278 L'Orfeo. Wally Stampfli, s; Magali Schwartz, ms; Eric Tappy, t; Jakob Stampfli, bs; Philippe Huttenlocher, bar; Lausanne Instrumental and Vocal Ensembles; Michel Corboz. Erato STU 70440/2 (3) (From World Records SOC 237/9)

+Gr 1-81 p989 +-HFN 1-81 p97

2279 L'Orfeo. Bad Hersfeld Festival, 1980, Soloists and Chorus; Hesse Chamber Orchestra; Siegfried Heinrich. Jubilate JU 85810/12 (3)

+-STL 11-8-81 p40

2280 Il ritorno d'Ulisse in patria. Frederica von Stade, s; Anne Murray, ms; Richard Lewis, Alexander Oliver, t; Richard Stilwell, bar; Glyndebourne Festival Chorus; LPO; Raymond Leppard. CBS 79332

+FF 3/4-81 p157 +Op 12-80 p1214
+-Gr 12-80 p878 +SFC 12-7-80 p33
+HFN 12-80 p141 +SR 7-81 p90
+NR 4-81 p8 ++St 4-81 p102
+ON 4-4-81 p28

2281 Songs (motets): Ab aeterno ordinata sum Confitebor tibi Domine (3); Deus tuorum militum sors et corona; Iste confessor Domini sacratus; Laudate dominum O omnes gentes; La Maddalena: Prologue: Su le penne de veint; Nisi Dominus aedifica verit Domum. Emma Kirkby, s; Ian Partridge, t; David Thomas, bs; Parley of Instruments; Roy Goodman, vln; Peter Holman, chamber org. Hyperion A 66021

+Gr 10-81 p594 ++STL 11-8-81 p40
++HFN 10-81 p89 tape

Songs (motets): Ab aeterno ordinata sum; Salve regina; Audi caelum, Salve regina. See no. 2270

Songs: Adoramus te Christe; Cantate domino. See no. 3633

Songs: Beatus vir; O Rosetta che Rosetta. See no. 3692

Songs: Gloria in excelsis. See no. 3845

Songs (motets): Exultata filia Sion. See no. 3808

Songs: Lamento d'Arianna. See no. 4114

Songs: Lamento d'Arianna; Lamento d'Olimpia. See no. 1493

Songs: Lamento d'Arianna; Lamento della ninfa. See no. 3677

Songs (motets): Laudate Dominum. See no. 3808

Songs: O come sei gentile. See no. 3947

Songs (motets): Salve o regina; Salve regina; Sancta Maria. See no. 3808

Suite, brass instruments. See no. 4002

2282 Vespro della beata vergine. Pro Cantione Antiqua Montserrat Escolania and Capella de Musica; Collegium Aureum; Ireneu Segarra. BASF JA 228 576 (20 (also Harmonia Mundi SQ 1C 165 99681-2)

+-FF 5/6-78 p61 +-Gr 10-78 p718
+FF 5/6-81 p108 +-HFN 9-78 p145

Vespro della beata vergine. See no. 2276

MONTI

Czardas. See no. 3645. See no. 4066

MONTSALVATGE, Xavier
Canciones negras: Cancion de cuna para dormir un negrito. See no. 3703
MORALES, Cristobal de
2283 Lamentations a 4, 5 and 6. Ensemble A Sei Voci. Le Chant du Monde LDS 78680
-Gr 2-81 p1110 +RR 8-80 p85
+HFN 8-80 p99
MORAN, Robert
In memoriam Maurice Ravel. See no. 3942
MOREL, Francois
2284 Alleluia. Esquisse. Rituel de l'espace. Me duele Espana. Soloists; National Arts Centre Orchestra, Toronto Symphony Orchestra; Mario Bernardi, Ernest MacMillan. RCA ACM 6 (5)
+MUM 1/2-81 p33
Esquisse. See no. 2284
Me duele Espana. See no. 2284
Rituel de l'espace. See no. 2284
MOREL, Jorge
Danza. See no. 1076
Malambo. See no. 1076
MORES, Mariano
Danza brasilera. See no. 1076
Milonga. See no. 1076
MORGAN, Robert
Trio, flute, violoncello and harpsichord. See no. 1128
MORLEY, Thomas
False love did me inveigle. See no. 3845
Fantasia "La torello". See no. 4092
Fantasia of 2 parts. See no. 4092
Fyer fyer. See no. 4114
Introduction, nos. 3, 5-6. See no. 1880
Joyne hands. See no. 3762
Lachrymae pavan and galliard. See no. 4090
Pavan. See no. 3883
The sacred end pavan. See no. 4059
La sampogna. See no. 1880
Songs: Die now my heart; Hark jolly shepherds; You black bright stars. See no. 4085
Il torello. See no. 1880
La volta. See no. 3734
MORRILL, Dexter
Fantasy quintet. See no. 1554
No. See no. 1554
Six dark questions. See no. 873
MORTARI, Virgilio
Canzone. See no. 3953
MORTHENSON, Jan
Wechselspiel I. See no. 3690
MOROSS, Jerome
The big country: Main theme. See no. 4105
MORTON, Robert
Songs: N'aray je jamais mieulx; Le souvenir de vous me tue. See no. 3948
MOSCHELES, Ignaz
2285 Allegro di bravura, op. 51, no. 1. Etudes, op. 70, nos. 5, 8, 12,

17; op. 95, nos. 3, 4, 7, 9. Rondeau brillant, op. 54. Sonate melancolique, op. 49, F sharp minor. Noel Lee, pno. Arion ARN 38559
+Gr 6-81 p60

Etudes, op. 70, nos. 5, 8, 12, 17. See no. 2285
Etudes, op. 95, nos. 3, 4, 7, 9. See no. 2283
Grand duo concertante, piano and bassoon. See no. 1399
Rondeau brillant, op. 54. See no. 2285

2286 Sonata concertante, op. 44. SCHUBERT: Sonata, arpeggione and piano, D 821. Jean-Pierre Rampal, flt; John Stelle Ritter, pno. CBS M 36706
++FF 9/10-81 p168 +NR 8-81 p7
+-MUM 11/12-81 p32 +SFC 5-31-81 p22

Sonate melancolique, op. 49, F sharp minor. See no. 2285

MOSS
The floral dance. See no. 3654

MOSS, Lawrence
Hear this touch. See no. 1269
Omaggio II. See no. 461

MOSZKOWSKI, Moritz
Etude, no. 6, op. 72, F major. See no. 4018
Serenata. See no. 3967

2287 Suite, op. 71, G minor. PROKOFIEV: Sonata, 2 violins, op. 56, C major. SHOSTAKOVICH: Duets, violin (3). Itzhak Perlman, Pinchas Zukerman, vln; Samuel Sanders, pno. HMV ASD 3861 (also Angel SZ 37668)
+-FF 11/12-80 p210 +MT 3-81 p184
++Gr 7-80 p153 ++NR 8-80 p8
+HF 10-81 p80 +NYT 7-6-80 pD15
+HFN 7-80 p114 +St 11-80 p94

Waltz, E flat major. See no. 20

MOTOORI
Nanatsu no ko. See no. 3696

MOULINIE, Etienne
2288 Cantique de Moyse. Espoir de toute ame affligee. Fantasies, 4 viols (3). O bone Jesu. Veni sponsa mea. Les Arts Florissants Vocal and Instrumental Ensemble; William Christie. Harmonia Munid (France) HM 1055
+FF 5/6-81 p110 +MT 6-81 p391
+-Gr 8-81 p303

Espoir de toute ame affligee. See no. 2288
Fantasies, 4 viols. See no. 2288
O bone Jesu. See no. 2288
Veni sponsa mea. See no. 2288

MOURANT, Walter
Aria for orchestra. See no. 1750

MOURET, Jean-Joseph
Rondeau. See no. 3746
Sinfonies de fanfares. See no. 3629

MOUTON, Charles
2289 Pieces, lute, A minor, A major, F sharp minor. Hopkinson Smith, lt. Astree AS 52
+FF 3/4-81 p158

MOZART, Franz Xaver
Sonata, op. 19, E major. See no. 720

MOZART, Leopold

2290 Cassation, G major: Toy symphony. PROKOFIEV: Peter and the wolf, op. 67. Jacqueline du Pre, narrator; ECO; Daniel Barenboim. DG 2531 275 Tape (c) 3371 275
+FF 3/4-81 p98
+-Gr 10-80 p498
+Gr 1-81 p1001
+-HF 4-81 p81
+HFN 10-80 p107
+-HFN 11-80 p131 tape
+NR 12-80 p2
+-NYT 12-14-80 pD38

Concerto, trumpet, D major. See no. 36

MOZART, Wolfgang

2291 Adagio, K 261, E major. Concerti, violin, nos. 1-7. Rondo, violin, K 373, C major. Rondo, violin, K 269, B flat major. Mayumi Fujikawa, vln; RPO; Walter Weller. Decca D239D4 (4)
+HFN 11-81 p96
+STL 12-13-81 p39

Adagio, K 261, E major. See no. 2487

Adagio, K 410 (484d), F major. See no. 2292

2292 Adagio, K 411 (484a), B flat major. Adagio, K 410 (484d), F major. Adagio, K 580, F major. Divertimento, K 439b, F major. Duo, 2 clarinets, B flat major (after Sonata, violin, K 317d). Karl Leister, Hans Rudolf Stalder, Peter Geisler, clt; Hans Rudolf Stalder, Heinz Hofer, Elmar Schmid, basset horn; Paul Meyer, bsn. Jecklin 549
+-FF 1/2-81 p155

Adagio, K 540, B minor. See no. 2391. See no. 2392

Adagio, K 580a, C major. See no. 125. See no. 227. See no. 2292

Adagio and allegro, K 594, F minor. See no. 471

2293 Adagio and fugue, K 546, C minor. Quintet, strings, no. 4, K 516, G minor. Quartour Danois; Serge Collot, vla. Valois MB 323
+-FF 11/12-81 p231

Adagio and fugue, K 546, C minor. See no. 2486

Adagio and rondo, K 617, C minor. See no. 117. See no. 3881

Allegro, K 3, B flat major; K 312, G minor; K 400, B major. See no. 2392

Allegro, K 312, G minor. See no. 233

2294 Allegro, K 580b, F major: Fragment (completed Gerhard Mass). Quintet, clarinet, K 581, A major. Rondo, K 581a, A major (completed Otto Bach). Kurt Birsak, basset clt; Jean Engel, basset hn; Divertimento Salzburg. Claves D 8007
+-FF 9/10-81 p142
+Gr 3-81 p1210

Allegro and andante, K 533, F major. See no. 913. See no. 2423

Alleluia. See no. 4100

2295 Andante, K 315, C major. Concerto, flute and harp, K 299, C major. Valentin Zverev, flt; Vera Doulova, hp; Soloists Ensemble. Chant du Monde LDX 78664
/HFN 1-81 p97

2296 Andante, K 315, C major. Concerto, flute, no. 1, K 313, G major. Concerto, flute, no. 2, K 314, D major. Jean-Pierre Rampal, flt; Israel Music Centre Chamber Orchestra; Isaac Stern. Erato STU 71144 (also Musical Heritage Society MHS 4238 Tape (c) MHC 6238. From RCA 1-3084)
+FF 3/4-81 p167
+HF 12-81 p76
+HFN 4-80 p107

2297 Andante, K 315, C major. Concerto, flute, no. 1, K 313, G major. Concerto, flute, no. 2, K 314, D major. John Solum, Baroque flt; Hanoverian Orchestra; John Holloway. HMV ASD 4056 Tape(c)

TC ASD 4056
+Gr 11-81 p693 +-HFN 12-81 p100

2298 Andante, K 315, C major. Concerto, flute, no. 1, K 313, G major. Concerto, flute, no. 2, K 314, D major. Concerto, flute and harp, K 299, C major. Rondo, flute, K Anh 184, D major. Frans Vester, flt; Edward Witsenburg, hp; Mozart Ensemble Amsterdam; Frans Bruggen. Pro Arte PAL 2004 (2) Tape (c) PAC 2004
+-FF 7/8-81 p133 +-NYT 8-9-81 pD19
+HF 12-81 p76 +SFC 7-19-81 p19
+-MUM 7/8-81 p35 /-St 10-81 p192

2299 Andante, K 315, C major. Concero, flute, no. 1, K 313, C major. Concerto, flute, no. 2, K 314, D major. Concerto, flute and harp, K 299, C major. Rondo, flute, K Anh 184 (K 373), C major. Frans Vester, flt; Edward Witsenburg, hp; Amsterdam Mozart Ensemble; Frans Bruggen. RCA RL 3-0386 (2)
-Gr 10-81 p558 +-HFN 8-81 p86

2300 Andante, K 616, F major. Church sonatas, nos. 1-17. Fantasia, K 594, F minor. Fantasia, K 608, F minor. Lionel Rogg, org; Lausanne Chamber Orchestra; Arpad Gerecz. HMV SLS 5218 (2)
+Gr 7-81 p156 +HFN 7-81 p74

Andante, K 616, F major. See no. 471. See no. 2392
Andante with variations, K 501, G major. See no. 449
Andantino, K 236, E flat major. See no. 2392

2301 Arias (concert): Ah se in ciel benigne stelle, K 538; Mia speranza adorata...Ah non sai qual pena, K 416; Nehmt meinen Dank ihr holden Gonner, K 383; No no che non sei capace, K 419; Popoli di Tessaglia...Io non chiedo eterni Dei, K 316; Vado ma dove o Dei, K 583; Vorrei spiegarvi oh Dio...Ah conte partite, K 418. Rita Streich, s; Bavarian Radio Symphony Orchestra; Charles Mackerras. DG 2535 465 Tape (c) 3335 465 (From SLPEM 136208)
+Gr 10-81 p594

2302 Arias (concert): Ma che vi fece o stelle...Sperai vicino il lido, K 368; Popoli di Tessaglia...Io non chiedo eterni Dei, K 316. Don Giovanni, K 527: Crudele...Non mi dir. Die Entfuhrung aus dem serail, K 384: Martern aller Arten. Die Zauberflote, K 620: O zittre nicht; Der Holle Rache. Edda Moser, s; Bavarian State Opera Orchestra; Leopold Heger, Wolfgang Sawallisch. EMI 1C 063 29082
+Gr 11-81 p753

2303 Arias: Ch'io mi scordi di te...Non temer amato bene, K 505; Vorrei spiegarvi o Dio, K 418. Exsultate jubilate, K 165: Alleluia. Le nozze di Figaro, K 492: Porgi amor; Voi che sapete; E Susanna non vien...Dove sono; Giunse alfin il momento...Deh vieni non tardar. Il Re pastore, K 208: L'amero saro costante. Die Zauberflote, K 620: Ach ich fuhl's. Joan Sutherland, s; National Philharmonic Orchestra; Richard Bonynge. London OS 26613 (also Decca SXL 6933 Tape (c) KSXC 6933)
+-FF 11/12-80 p142 +-MUM 5/6-81 p30
+-Gr 11-80 p732 +-NYT 6-15-80 pD29
-HF 9-80 p102 -ON 12-13-80 p44
+-HFN 11-80 0121 -Op 8-81 p823

2304 Arias: Ascanio in Alba, K 111: Padre...o numi...Si ma d'un altro amore; Ferma aspetta...Infelici affetti miei. Ezio, K 369: Misera dove son...Ah non son'io che parlo. La finta giardiniera, K 196: Geme la tortorella. La finta semplice, K 51:

Senti l'eco ove t'aggiri; Amoretti. Il Re pastore, K 208: Aer tranquillo e di sereni; L'amero saro costante. Zaide, K 344: Trostlos schluchzet Philomele. Rotraud Hansmann, s; VSO; Marinus Voorberg. Musical Heritage Society MHS 4338
+-FF 9/10-81 p141

Arias: Cosi dunque tradisci...Aspri rimorsi atroci, K 432; Ich mochte wohl der Kaiser sein, K 539; Manner suchen stets zu naschen; Mentre ti lascio, K 513; Un bacio di mano, K 541. See no. 1752

Arias: Ich mochte wohl der Kaiser sein, K 539; Manner suchen stets zu naschen, K 433; Musst ich auch durch tausend Drachen, K 435; Schon lacht der holde Fruhling, K 580; Welch angstliches Beben, K 389. See no. 2377

Arias: Ma che vi fece o stelle...Sperai vicino il lido, K 368. See no. 2302

Arias: Popoli di Tessaglia...Io non chiedo eterni dei, K 316. See no. 2302

2305 Ascanio in Alba, K 111. Lilian Sukis, Edith Mathis, Arleen Auger, s; Agnes Baltsa, ms; Peter Schreier, t; Salzburg Chamber Choir; Salzburg Mozarteum Orchestra; Leopold Hager. DG 2740 181 (3)
+-Gr 8-81 p310 +HFN 9-81 p83

Ascanio in Alba, K 111: Padre...o numi...Si ma d'un altro amore; Ferma aspetta...Infelici affetti miei. See no. 2304

Ave verum corpus, K 618. See no. 3615. See no. 3619. See no. 4061

2306 Bastien und Bastienne, K 50. Edith Mathis, s; Claes Ahnsjo, t; Walter Berry, bs; Salzburg Mozarteum Orchestra; Leopold Hager, hpd and cond. DG 2537 038 Tape (c) 3306 038
+Gr 9-78 p538 +ON 10-81 p52
+Gr 11-78 p969 tape +RR 10-78 p44
+HFN 10-78 p127

Bourree. See no. 3816

Capriccio, K 395, C major. See no. 2392

Church sonatas, nos. 1-17. See no. 2300

Church sonatas, no. 1, K 67, E flat major; no. 17, K 336, C major. See no. 3807

Church sonatas, no. 7, K 224/241a, F major. See no. 2385.

Church sonatas, no. 17, K 336, C major. See no. 233

2307 La clemenza di Tito, K 621. Cosi fan tutte, K 588. Don Giovanni, K 527. Die Entfuhrung aus dem Serail, K 384. Idomeneo, Re di Creta, K 366. Le nozze di Figaro, K 492. Der Schauspieldirektor, K 486. Die Zauberflote, K 620. Teresa Berganza, Edith Mathis, Julia Varady, Marga Schmall, Gundula Janowitz, Brigitte Fassbaender, Reri Grist, Birgit Nilsson, Martina Arroyo, Arleen Auger, Tàtiana Troyanos, Evelyn Lear, Robert Peters, Peter Schreier, Theo Adam, Hermann Prey, Rolando Panerai, Dietrich Fischer-Dieskau, Ezio Flagello, Martti Talvela, Harald Neukirch, Kurt Moll, Wieslaw Ochman, Fritz Wunderlich Franz Crass, Hans Hotter, soloists; VPO, Prague National Theatre Orchestra, Staatskapelle Dresden, Deutsch Oper Orchestra, BPhO; Karl Bohm. DG 2740 (22)
+-FF 9/10-81 p138

La clemenza di Tito, K 621: Ah perdona al primo affetto; Saltro che lacrime. See no. 1610

La clemenza di Tito, K 621: Overture. See no. 2486

La clemenza di Tito, K 621: Parto, parto. See no. 4039

2308 Concerto, bassoon, K 191, B flat major (arr.). Concerto, clarinet, K 622, A major. Richard Stoltzman, clt; ECO; Alexander Schneider. RCA ARL 1-3934 Tape (c) ARL 1-3934
+FF 11/12-81 p198 +-HFN 12-81 p112 tape
+-Gr 10-81 p557 ++NR 9-81 p4
+HFN 10-81 p90 ++NYT 8-9-81 pD19

2309 Concerto, bassoon, K 191, B flat major. Concerto, flute, no. 2, K 314, C major. Jurg Schaeftlein, ob; Milan Turkovic, bsn; Mozarteum Orchestra; Leopold Hager. Telefunken 6-43261
++FF 3/4-81 p159

Concerto, bassoon, K 191, B flat major. See no. 2485

2310 Concerto, clarinet, K 622, A major. Concerto, flute and harp, K 299, C major. Jacques Lancelot, clt; Jean-Pierre Rampal, flt; Lily Laskine, hp; Jean-Francois Paillard Chamber Orchestra. Erato EF 28011
-MUM 11/12-81 p32

2311 Concerto, clarinet, K 622, A major. Concerto, horn, no. 3, K 447, E flat major. Hans Deinzer, clt; Hubert Cruts, hn; Collegium Aureum; Franzjosef Maier. Harmonia Mundi 1C 065 99829
+FF 5/6-80 p111 ++MT 4-81 p246
+HFN 4-80 p119 +-RR 5-80 p66

2312 Concerto, clarinet, K 622, A major. Sinfonia concertante, KA 9 (K 297b), E flat major. Bernard Walton, clt; Sidney Sutcliffe, ob; Cecil James, bsn; Dennis Brain, hn; PhO; Herbert von Karajan. HMV SXLP 60004 Tape (c) XLP 60004 (From 33CX 1178, 33CS 1361)
+-FF 7/8-81 p139 +STL 2-8-81 p40
+-Gr 1-81 p952

2313 Concerto, clarinet, K 622, A major. Concerto, flute and harp, K 299, C major. Jack Brymer, clt; Hubert Barwahser, flt; Osian Ellis, hp; LSO; Colin Davis. Philips 6570 146 Tape (c) 7310 146 (From SAL 3535)
+Gr 3-81 p1200 +HFN 4-81 p81 tape
+HFN 2-81 p97

2314 Concerto, clarinet, K 622, A major (ed. Galway). Concerto, flute and harp, K 299, C major. James Galway, flt; Marisa Robles, hp; LSO; Eduardo Mata. RCA RL 2-5171 Tape (c) RK 2-5171 (also RCA 1-3353 Tape (c) ARK 1-3353)
+-FF 1/2-80 p111 +-NYT 5-4-80 pD24
+-Gr 12-78 p1103 +NYT 9-27-81 pD24
+Gr 5-79 p1940 tape ++RR 12-78 p62
+HF 12-79 p110 tape ++SFC 11-11-79 p45
+HFN 3-79 p127 +St 12-79 p154
+NYT 9-23-79 pD28

Concerto, clarinet, K 622, A major. See no. 2308. See no. 2485

2315 Concerto, flute, no. 1, K 313, G major. Concerto, flute, no. 2, K 314, D major. William Bennett, flt; ECO; George Malcolm. Argo ZRG 910 Tape (c) KZRC 910
++FF 3/4-81 p159 +HFN 10-79 p159
++Gr 12-79 p1017 ++RR 10-79 p98
+HF 12-81 p76 ++St 3-81 p92

2316 Concerto, flute, no. 1, K 313, G major. Concerto, flute and harp, K 299, C major. Andreas Blau, James Galway, flt; Fritz Helmis, hp; BPhO; Herbert von Karajan. HMV ASD 2993 (als Angel S 36857)

+-NR 10-74 p5 +-RR 8-74 p39
-NYT 9-27-81 pD24

Concerto, flute, no. 1, K 313, G major. See no. 2296. See no. 2297. See no. 2298. See no. 2299. See no. 2485

2317 Concerto, flute, no. 2, K 314, D major. Serenade, no. 13, K 525, G major. Serenade, no. 6, K 239, D major. James Galway, flt; Gunars Larsens, Jan Milewski, vln; Max Lesueur, vla; Alfred Steinauer, bs; Dieter Dyk, timpani; Lucerne Festival Strings; Rudolf Baumgartner. Eurodisc SQ 200 341-250
+FF 11/12-81 p208 +NYT 7-26-81 pD23

Concerto, flute, no. 2, K 314, D major. See no. 335. See no. 2296. See no. 2297. See no. 2298. See no. 2299. See no. 2309. See no. 2315. See no. 2319. See no. 2485

2318 Concerto, flute and harp, K 299, C major. Sinfonia concertante, K 297b, E flat major. Wolfgang Schulz, flt; Nicanor Zabaleta, hp; Walter Lehmayer, ob; Peter Schmidl, clt; Gunther Hogner, hn; Fritz Faltl, bsn; VPO; Karl Bohm. DG 2530 715 Tape (c) 3300 715
++ARG 10-77 p38 +NR 9-77 p4
+-Gr 11-76 p798 -NYT 9-27-81 pD24
+HFN 10-76 p175 +RR 10-76 p61

2319 Concerto, flute and harp, K 299, C major. Concerto, flute, no. 2, K 314, D major. Rondo, violin, K 373b, C major (arr.). Jean-Pierre Rampal, flt; Pierre Pierlot, ob; Marielle Nordmann, hp; ECO; Jean-Pierre Rampal. Erato STU 71321 (also CBS M 35875 Tape (c) 35875)
+FF 7/8-81 p134 +-Gr 10-80 p500
+HF 12-81 p76 +St 10-81 p129

2320 Concerto, flute and harp, K 299, C major. Divertimento, no. 2, K 131, D major. Rene le Roy, flt; Lili Laskine, hp; RPO; Thomas Beecham. World Records SH 316 (From HMV DB 6485/7, DB 6649/51)
+ARSC Vol. 12, no. 3, 1980 p247 ++Gr 5-80 p1666
+HFN 6-80 p108
+-FF 5/6-81 p110 +RR 6-80 p55

Concerto, flute and harp, K 299, C major. See no. 2295. See no. 2298. See no. 2299. See no. 2310. See no. 2313. See no. 2314. See no. 2316. See no. 2485. See no. 4008

2321 Concerti, horns, nos. 1-4, K 412, 417, 447, 495. Gunter Hogner, hn; VPO; Karl Bohm. DG 2531 274 Tape (c) 3301 274
+Audio 6-81 p14 +HFN 3-81 p89
+-FF 1/2-81 p154 +HFN 4-81 p81 tape
+Gr 4-81 p1320 +NR 1-81 p4

2322 Concerti, horn, nos. 1-4, K 412, 417, 447, 495. Milos Petr, hn; Musici di Praga; Libor Hlavacek. Supraphon 110 2628
+FF 11/12-81 p198 ++NR 5-81 p7

Concerti, horn, nos. 1-4, K 412, 417, 447, 495. See no. 2485. See no. 2486

Concerto, horn, no. 3, K 447, E flat major. See no. 2311

Concerto, piano, K 107, D major. See no. 98

2323 Concerto, piano, no. 8, K 246, C major. Concerto, piano, no. 22, K 482, E flat major. ECO; Murray Perahia, pno, cond. CBS M 35869 Tape (c) MT 35869 (also CBS 76966 Tape (c) 40-76966)
+ARG 1-81 p36 +HFN 3-81 p89
+Gr 3-81 p1198 +OV 12-81 p39

+Gr 8-81 p324 ++St 11-80 p76
+-HF 7-81 p63

2324 Concerto, piano, no. 8, K 246, C major. Concerto, piano, no. 26, K 537, D major. Jorg Demus, pno; Collegium Aureum. Harmonia Mundi 1C 065 99699 Tape (c) Pro Arte 1023 (From BASF BAC 3003)
*FF 11/12-81 p208 +HFN 2-79 p115
+-Gr 3-79 p1566 +RR 2-79 p69
+HF 9-81 p46 tape

2325 Concerto, piano, no. 9, K 271, E flat major. Concerto, piano, no. 17, K 453, G major. Maria-Joao Pires, pno; Gulbenkian Foundation Chamber Orchestra; Theodor Guschlbauer. Erato STU 70763 (also Musical Heritage Society MHS 4345)
+-FF 9/10-81 p140 +-HFN 6-73 p1180
+Gr 6-73 p56 +RR 6-73 p54

2326 Concerto, piano, no. 12, K 414, A major. Concerto, piano, no. 27, K 595, B flat major. ECO; Murray Perahia, pno and cond. CBS M 35828 Tape (c) MT 35828
+ARG 1-81 p36 +HF 7-81 p63

2327 Concerto, piano, no. 12, K 414, A major. Concerto, piano, no. 18, K 456, B flat major. Lili Kraus, pno; BSO; Pierre Monteux. RCA Musique GM 43276 (From LM 1783)
+FF 5/6-81 p111

Concerto, piano, no. 12, K 414, A major. See no. 228

2328 Concerto, piano, no. 14, K 449, E flat major. Concerto, piano, no. 26, K 537, D major. Tamas Vasary, pno; BPhO; Tamas Vasary. DG 2531 207 Tape (c) 3301 207
++CL 9-80 p16 +NR 6-80 p7
+-FF 7/8-80 p113 +NYT 5-4-80 pD24
++Gr 1-80 p1157 +RR 2-80 p59
++HF 7-81 p63 ++St 6-80 p77
+HFN 3-80 p95

Concerto, piano, no. 15, K 450, B flat major. See no. 2467

2329 Concerti, piano, nos. 17, 19, 27. Pavel Stepan, pno; Musica de Praga; Libor Hlavacek. Supraphon 110 2701/2 (2)
-FF 9/10-81 p140 ++NR 8-81 p6

2330 Concerto, piano, no. 17, K 453, G major. Concerto, piano, no. 27, K 595, B flat major. Walter Klien, pno; Minnesota Orchestra; Stanislaw Skrowaczewski. Candide CE 31119 Tape (c) CT 2275
-FF 3/4-81 p160 ++SFC 2-15-81 p19
+HF 7-81 p63

2331 Concerto, piano, no. 17, K 453, G major. Concerto, piano, no. 18, K 456, B flat major. Murray Perahia, pno; ECO. CBS 36686 Tape (c) 40-36686
+Gr 10-81 p557 +HFN 10-81 p89

Concerto, piano, no. 17, K 453, G major. See no. 2325

2332 Concerto, piano, no. 18, K 456, B flat major. Concerto, piano, no. 25, K 503, C major. Michel Dalberto, pno; Lausanne Chamber Orchestra; Armin Jordan. Erato STU 71421
+-Gr 12-81 p886

Concerto, piano, no. 18, K 456, B flat major. See no. 2327. See no. 2331

2333 Concerto, piano, no. 19, K 459, F major. Concerto, piano, no. 24, K 491, C minor. Vladimir Ashkenazy, pno; PhO. Decca SXL 6947 Tape (c) KSXC 6947 (also London 7174 Tape (c) 5-7174)
+-ARG 9-81 p14 +HFN 2-81 p91

+-CL 12-81 p10 +NR 5-81 p8
+-FF 7/8-81 p134 +NYT 8-9-81 pD19
+Gr 2-81 p1091

2334 Concerto, piano, no. 20, K 466, D minor. Concerto, piano, no. 21, K 467, C major. Geza Anda, pno; VSO; Geza Anda. Eurodisc 86947
+FF 11/12-81 p204 +-St 11-75 p128

2335 Concerto, piano, no. 20, K 466, D minor. Concerto, piano, no. 23, K 488, A major. Clara Haskil, pno; VSO; Bernhard Paumgartner, Paul Sacher. Philips 6527 093 Tape (c) 7311 093 (From ABL 3129)
+Gr 11-81 p693 +HFN 12-81 p109
+HFN 9-81 p93 tape

2336 Concerto, piano, no. 20, K 466, D minor. Concerto, piano, no. 23, K 488, A major. Alfred Brendel, pno; AMF; Neville Marriner. Philips 6570 023 Tape (c) 7310 023 (From 6833 119, 6500 283)
+Gr 2-81 p1092 +HFN 5-81 p93 tape
+HFN 3-81 p95

2337 Concerto, piano, no. 20, K 466, D minor. Concerto, piano, no. 23, K 488, A major. Stephen Bishop-Kovacevich, pno; LSO; Colin Davis. Philips 9500 570 Tape (c) 7300 703
+-ARG 9-79 p34 +NR 7-79 p6
+FF 11/12-79 p103 +-SFC 9-9-79 p45
+Gr 6-81 p42 ++St 8-79 p111
+HFN 5-81 p81

2338 Concerto, piano, no. 20, K 466, D minor. Concerto, piano, no. 22, K 482, E flat major. Emanuel Ax, pno; Dallas Symphony Orchestra; Eduardo Mata. RCA ARL 1-3457 Taep (c) ARK 1-3457
+-ARG 2-81 p24 +-HFN 3-81 p89
+-Audio 3-81 p62 -NR 1-81 p4
-FF 3/4-81 p160 +NYT 8-9-81 pD19
+Gr 3-81 p1198 +St 2-81 p108
+HF 7-81 p63

Concerto, piano, no. 20, K 466, D minor. See no. 2476

Concerto, piano, no. 20, K 466, D minor: 1st movement, excerpt. See no. 3998

2339 Concerto, piano, no. 21, K 467, C major. Concerto, piano, no. 23, K 488, A major. Ilana Vered, pno; LPO; Uri Segal. Contour CC 7507 Tape (c) CCT 7505
+-Gr 8-81 p316

2340 Concerto, piano, no. 21, K 467, C major. Concerto, piano, no. 27, K 595, B flat major. Friedrich Gulda, pno; VSOO; Hans Swarowsky. Pearl SHE 560
+Gr 11-81 p693 +-HFN 12-81 p100

Concerto, piano, no. 21, K 467, C major. See no. 223. See no. 2334. See no. 3749. See no. 4017

Concerto, piano, no. 21, K 467, C major: Andante. See no. 3695

2341 Concerto, piano, no. 22, K 482, E flat major. Rondo, piano, K 382, D major. Vladimir Ashkenazy, pno; PhO; Valdimir Ashkenazy. Decca SXL 6982 Tape (c) KSXC 6982
+Gr 11-81 p694 +HFN 11-81 p95

Concerto, piano, no. 22, K 482, E flat major. See no. 2323. See no. 2337

Concerto, piano, no. 23, K 488, A major. See no. 495. See no. 2335. See no. 2336. See no. 2337. See no. 2339

Concerto, piano, no. 24, K 491, C minor. See no. 2333

2342 Concerto, piano, no. 25, K 503, C major. Rondo, piano, K 382, D

major. Alfred Brendel, pno; AMF: Neville Marriner. Philips 6527 085 Tape (c) 7311 085 (From 6768 050, 9500 145)
+Gr 9-81 p388

Concerto, piano, no. 25, K 503, C major. See no. 2332. See no. 2486

2343 Concerto, piano, no. 26, K 527, D major. Concerto, piano, no. 27, K 595, B flat major. Raphael Orozco, pno; ECO; Charles Dutoit. Classics for Pleasure CFP 40357
+-HFN 11-81 p96

Concerto, piano, no. 26, K 537, D major. See no. 2324. See no. 2328

Concerto, piano, no. 27, K 595, B flat major. See no. 2326. See no. 2330. See no. 2340. See no. 2343

Concerti, violin, nos. 1-7. See no. 2291. See no. 2487

2344 Concerto, violin, no. 1, K 207, B flat major. Concerto, violin, no. 3, K 216, G major. Josef Suk, vln; PCO; Libor Hlavacek. Eurodisc Tape (c) 440 053
+HF 11-81 p103 tape

2345 Concerto, violin, no. 1, K 207, B flat major.* Concerto, violin, no. 3, K 216, G major.* Rondos, violin, K 269, B flat major; K 373, C major. Josef Suk, vln; PCO; Josef Suk. RCA GL 2-5288 Tape (c) GK 2-5288 (*From LR 1-5084, 1-5046)
+-Gr 10-80 p498 +HFN 1-81 p109 tape
+HFN 11-80 p129 +ST 7-81 p124

Concerto, violin, no. 1, K 207, B flat major. See no. 151

2346 Concerto, violin, no. 2, K 211, D major. Rondo, violin, K 373b, C major. Sinfonia concertante, K 364, E flat major. NPhO; Henrik Szeryng, vln; Bruno Giuranna, vla; Alexander Gibson. Philips 6570 175 Tape (c) 7310 175 (From 6707 011)
+Gr 4-81 p1320 +HFN 5-81 p93 tape
+HFN 2-81 p97 +ST 7-81 p206

2347 Concerto, violin, no. 3, K 216, G major. Concerto, violin, no. 4, K 218, D major. Iona Brown, vln; AMF; Iona Brown. Argo ZRG 880 Tape (c) KZRC 880
++FF 3/4-81 p161 +NR 1-81 p4
+Gr 7-80 p142 +RR 7-80 p59
+HFN 7-80 p109

2348 Concerto, violin, no. 3, K 216, G major. Concerto, violin, no. 5, K 219, A major. Anne-Sophie Mutter, vln; BPhO; Herbert von Karajan. DG 2531 049 Tape (c) 3301 049
+ARG 11-79 p41 +NYT 7-15-79 pD22
+-FF 9/10-79 p110 +RR 10-78 p77
+Gr 9-78 p479 ++RR 1-79 p91 tape
+HFN 10-78 p127 ++SFC 6-10-79 p45
+HFN 2-79 p118 ++SR 5-12-79 p35
++NR 6-79 p8 +SR 11-81 p62

2349 Concerto, violin, no. 3, K 216, G major. Concerto, violin, no. 5, K 219, A major. Bath Festival Chamber Orchestra; Yehudi Menuhin, vln. HMV SXLP 30449 Tape (c) TC SXLP 30449 (From ASD 473)
+Gr 3-81 p1200 +HFN 3-81 p95

Concerto, violin, no. 3, K 216, G major. See no. 2344. See no. 2345. See no. 2484

2350 Concerto, violin, no. 4, K 218, D major. Concerto, violin, no. 7, K 271, D major. Bath Festival Orchestra; Yehudi Menuhin, vln. HMV SXLP 30454 Tape (c) TC SXLP 30454 (From ASD 533)
+-Gr 10-81 p558 +-HFN 10-81 p95

2351 Concerto, violin, no. 4, K 218, D major. SZYMANOWSKI: Concerto, violin, no. 1, op. 35. Piotr Janowski, vln; Warsaw National Philharmonic Orchestra; Stanislaw Wislocki. Stolat SZM 0105
+FF 11/12-81 p199
Concerto, violin, no. 4, K 218, D major. See no. 2347
Concerto, violin, no. 5, K 219, A major. See no. 565. See no. 900. See no. 2348. See no. 2349
Concerto, violin, no. 7, K 271a, D major. See no. 2350
Concertone, 2 violins, K 190 (K 166b), C major. See no. 2487
2352 Contredanses, K 267 (4); K 610. Contredanses with overture, K 106. Minuets, K 122; K 164, nos. 3-4; K 461 (5). Minuets with contredanses, K 463. Marches, K 290, K 445. Paul Angerer Ensemble; Paul Angerer. Saga SAGA 5478
++Gr 5-81 p1476 +-HFN 5-81 p81
Contredanses with overture, K 106. See no. 2352
2353 Cosi fan tutte, K 588. Soloists; Glyndebourne Festival Orchestra and Chorus; Fritz Busch. Turnabout 65126/8 (3)
++FF 1/2-81 p255
Cosi fan tutte, K 588. See no. 2307. See no. 2486
2354 Cosi fan tutte, K 588, excerpts. Sena Jurinac, s; Blanche Thebom, ms; Richard Lewis, t; Erich Kunz, Mario Borriello, bar; Glyndebourne Festival Orchestra and Chorus; Fritz Busch. World Records SH 397
+HFN 12-81 p97 +Op 12-81 p1263
Cosi fan tutte, K 588, excerpts. See no. 2416
Cosi fan tutte, K 588: Come scoglio. See no. 3850
2355 Cosi fan tutte, K 588: Come scoglio; Per pieta ben mio perdono. Don Giovanni, K 527: Or sai chi l'onore; Non mi dir bel idol mio. Le nozze di Figaro, K 492: Porgi amor; Dove sono. Die Zauberflote, K 620: Ach ich fuhl's. Teresa Stich-Randall, s; Vienna Orchestra; Laszlo Somogyi. Westminster MCA 1416 (From XWN 19046)
+ARG 4-81 p29 +FF 1/2-81 p151
Cosi fan tutte, K 588: In uomini in soldati; Una donna quindici anni. See no. 3748
2356 Cosi fan tutte, K 588: La mia Dorabella; Ah guarda sorella; Soave sia il vento; Come scoglio; Non siate ritrosi...E voi ridete; Dove son; Prendero quel brunettino; Per pieta ben mio; E amore un ladroncello; Fra gli amplessi; Richiamati da regio contrordine. Elisabeth Schwarzkopf, s; Christa Ludwig, ms; Hanny Steffek, s; Alfredo Kraus, t; Giuseppe Taddei, bar; Walter Berry, bs; PhO; Karl Bohm. HMV SXLP 30457 Tape (c) TC SXLP 30457 (From SAN 103/3)
+Gr 6-81 p93 tape +NR 3-81 p1233
+HFN 4-81 p81
Cosi fan tutte, K 588: Un'aura amorosa. See no. 1363
2357 Deutsche Tanze, K 509, 586, 600, 605. Jean-Francois Paillard Chamber Orchestra; Jean-Francois Paillard. Musical Heritage Society MHS 4289
+FF 5/6-81 p114
Deutsche Tanze, K 509. See no. 2392
2358 Divertimento, K 136, D major. Rondo, violin, K 269 (K 261a), B flat major. Serenade, no. 12, K 388, C minor. Pinchas Zukerman, vln; LAPO Members, ECO; Pinchas Zukerman, Daniel Barenboim. CBS M 35870

+-FF 11/12-81 p206 -NR 11-81 p2

3859 Divertimento, K 136, D major. Divertimento, K 137, B flat major. Berlin Philharmonic Octet Members. HMV SQS 1432
+Gr 9-80 p360 +-ST 1-81 p649

Divertimento, K 136, D major. See no. 2470

Divertimento, K 136, D major: Presto. See no. 3666

2360 Divertimento, K 137, B flat major. Divertimento, no. 15, K 287, B flat major. Vienna Mozart Ensemble; Willi Boskovsky. Decca JB 90 Tape (C) KJBC 90
+Gr 12-80 p836 +HFN 11-80 p121
++Gr 2-81 p1122 tape

Divertimento, K 137, B flat major. See no. 2359

2361 Divertimento, no. 1, K 113, E flat major. Divertimento, no. 2, K 131, D major. Vienna Mozart Ensemble; Willi Boskovsky. Decca JB 67 Tape (c) KJBC 67 (From SXL 6366)
+Gr 9-81 p386

Divertimento, no. 2, K 131, D major. See no. 2320. See no. 2361

Divertimento, no. 5, K 187, C major. See no. 3979

Divertimento, no. 6, K 188, C major. See no. 3979

2362 Divertimenti, no. 8, K 213, F major; no. 9, K 240, B major; no. 13, K 253, F major; no. 14, K 270, B flat major. VPO Wind Soloists. DG 2531 296
+FF 5/6-81 p127 ++NR 5-81 p10
++Gr 12-80 p846 +SFC 3-8-81 p19
+HFN 12-80 p143

Divertimento, no. 9, K 240, B flat major. See no. 840. See no. 2362

2363 Divertimento, no. 10, K 247, F major. Serenade, no. 13, K 525, G major. Capella Academica, Vienna; Eduard Melkus, vln and cond. Denon OX 7211
+FF 11/12-81 p208 +-St 11-80 p86

Divertimento, no. 12, K 252, E flat major. See no. 840

Divertimento, no. 13, K 253, F major. See no. 2362

Divertimento, no. 14, K 270, B flat major. See no. 562. See no. 574. See no. 2362

Divertimento, no. 15, K 287, B flat major. See no. 2360

2364 Divertimento, no. 17, K 334, D major. Camerata de Lucerne. Accord 140 038
+HFN 9-81 p83

Divertimento, no. 17, K 334, D major: Minuet. See no. 336

Divertimento, K 439b, F major. See no. 2292

2365 Divertimento, K 563, E flat major. Trio strings, K 562 (K Anh 66), G major. Kalafusz Trio. Intercord 120 888
+FF 3/4-81 p162

2366 Divertimento, K 563, E flat major. Trio a Cordes Francais. Musical Heritage Society MHS 4360
+FF 11/12-81 p200

2367 Divertimento, K 563, E flat major. Grumiaux Trio. Philips 802 803LY (From SAL 3664)
++Gr 1-81 p960 +HFN 1-81 p97

2368 Don Giovanni, K 527 (arr. Triebensee). Athena Ensemble. Chandos ABR 1015 Tape (c) ABT 1015
+ARG 10-81 p54 +Gr 4-81 p1376 tape
++ARG 12-81 p49 +HFN 2-81 p91
+FF 7/8-81 p135 +HFN 3-81 p97 tape
+Gr 2-81 p1096

2369 Don Giovanni, K 527. Urszula Koszut, Jill Gomez, s; Lutz Harder, t; Granz Grundheber, bar; Matthias Holle, bs; Ludwigsburg Festival Orchestra and Chorus; Wolfgang Gonnenwein. EMI 1C 155 99810/13 (4)
+-FF 11/12-81 p200
2370 Don Giovanni, K 527. Hilde Zadek, Sena Jurinac, Graziella Sciutti, s; Eberhard Waechter, bar; George London, bs-bar; Walter Berry, Ludwig Weber, bs; Vienna Chamber Chorus; VSO; Rudolf Moralt. Philips 6768 033 (3) (From ABL 3069/71)
+-Gr 10-81 p604 +-Op 11-81 p1150
+-HFN 10-81 p95
2371 Don Giovanni, K 527. Hilde Zadek, Maud Cunitz, Rita Streich, s; Leopold Simoneau, t; George London, bar; Ludwig Weber, Benno Kusche, bs; Cologne Radio Orchestra and Chorus; Otto Klemperer. Bruno Walter Society RR 478 (3)
+-FF 11/12-81 p254
2372 Don Giovanni, K 527. Soloists; Glyndebourne Festival Orchestra; Fritz Busch. Turnabout THS 65084/6
++FF 1/2-81 p255 +NYT 10-9-77 pD21
Don Giovanni, K 527. See no. 2307. See no. 2486
Don Giovanni, K 527: Ah fuggi il traditor; Mi tradi. See no. 3713
Don Giovanni, K 527: Crudele...Non mir dir. See no. 2302
Don Giovanni, K 527: Crudele...Non mir dir; In quali eccessi... Mi tradi quell'alma ingrata. See 3844
Don Giovanni, K 527: Dalla sua pace. See no. 3747. See no. 3966
Don Giovanni, K 527: Dalla sua pace; Il mio tesoro. See no. 4032
Don Giovanni, K 527: Deh vieni alla finestra. See no. 3968
Don Givoanni, K 527: Don Ottavio son morta; Il mio tesoro. See no. 3972
Don Giovanni, K 527: Don Ottavio son morta...Or sai chi l'onore. See no. 3755
Don Giovanni, K 527: Duet, Act 1; Il mio tesoro. See no. 1207
Don Giovanni, K 527: Finch'han dal vino; Serenata. See no. 4031
Don Giovanni, K 527: Il mio tesoro. See no. 3836
Don Giovanni, K 527: Il mio tesoro; Ridente la calma. See no. 3967
Don Giovanni, K 527: La ci darem la mano. See no. 1891
2373 Don Giovanni, K 527: Madamina il catalogo e questo; Ho capito signor si; La ci darem la mano; Or sai chi l'onore...Della sua pace; Finch'han dal vino; Batti batti; Venite pur avante; Deh vieni alla finestra; Vedrai carino; In quali eccessi...Mi tradi; Non mi dir; Don Giovanni a cenar teco; Questo e il fin. Edda Moser, Kiri Te Kanawa, s; Kenneth Riegel, t; Ruggero Raimondi, John Macurdy, Jose Van Dam, Malcolm King, bs; Teresa Berganza, ms; Paris Opera Orchestra and Chorus; Lorin Maazel. Columbia M 35859 Tape (c) MT 35859 (also CBS 73888 Tape (c) 40-73888. From 79321)
+Gr 1-81 p989 +HFN 1-81 p109 tape
+-HFN 11-80 p129 -NR 4-80 p10
Don Giovanni, K 527: Madamina il catalogo. See no. 4064
Don Giovanni, K 527: Or sai chi l'onore. See no. 472
Don Giovanni, K 527: Or sai chi l'onore; Non mi dir bel idol mio. See no. 2355
Don Giovanni, K 527: Overture. See no. 3760
Don Giovanni, K 527: Troppo mi spiace...Non mi dir. See no. 3850
Duo, 2 clarinets, B flat major. See no. 2292

2374 Duos, violin and viola, K 423, G major; K 424, B flat major. Toshiya Eto, vln; Michael Tree, vla. Nonesuch N 78005
+ARG 7/8-81 p26
+Audio 8-81 p67
+FF 3/4-81 p167
++SFC 2-15-81 p19

2375 Duo, violin and viola, K 423, G major. Duo, violin and viola, K 424, B flat major. Regis Pasquier, vln; Bruno Pasquier, vla. Harmonia Mundi HM 1052
+Gr 5-81 p1488
+HFN 6-81 p75
+STL 7-12-81 p40

Duo, violin and viola, K 424, B flat major. See no. 2374. See no. 2375

2376 Die Entfuhrung aus dem Serail, K 384. Edita Gruberova, Gudrun Ebel, s; Francisco Araiza, Norbert Orth, t; Roland Bracht, bs; Harald Leipnitz, speaker; Bavarian Radio Chorus; Munich Radio Orchestra; Heinz Wallberg. Eurodisc 300 027 400 (3)
+-FF 11/12-81 p201
+HFN 12-81 p97
+NYT 8-9-81 pD19
+-ON 10-81 p52
+OV 12-81 p36
++St 12-81 p122

2377 Die Entfuhrung aus dem Serail, K 384. Arias: Ich mochte wohl der Kaiser sein, K 539; Manner suchen stets zu naschen, K 433; Musst ich auch durch tausend Drachen, K 435; Schon lacht der holde Fruhling, K 580; Welch angstliches Beben, K 389. Christiane Eda-Pierre, Norma Burrowes, s; Stuart Burrows, Robert Tear, t; Robert Lloyd, bs; AMF; Colin Davis. Philips 6769 026 Tape (c) 7699 111 (also Philips 9500 625/7)
+-ARG 5-81 p47
+FF 1/2-81 p152
+-Gr 9-80 p397
+-HF 3-81 p72
+HFN 9-80 p109
+HFN 11-80 p131 tape
+MT 5-81 p318
+NR 11-80 p7
++NYT 10-19-80 pD24
+OC Summer 1981 p50
+-ON 12-13-80 p44
+Op 9-80 p910
+-OV 12-81 p40
++SFC 10-5-80 p21
++St 1-81 p85

Die Entfuhrung aus dem Serail, K 384. See no. 2307

Die Entfuhrung aus dem Serail, K 384: Hier soll ich dich denn sehen. See no. 3648

Die Entfuhrung aus dem Serail, K 384: Hier soll ich dich denn sehen; Constance O wie Angslicht; Ich baue ganz. See no. 1363

Die Entfuhrung aus dem Serail, K 384: Konstanze dich wiederzusehen. See no. 3747

Die Entfuhrung aus dem Serail, K 384: Martern aller Arten. See no. 2302

Die Entfuhrung aus dem Serail, K 384: Overture. See no. 2486

Die Entfuhrung aus dem Serail, K 384: Overture; March of the Janissaries. See no. 1605

Die Entfuhrung aus dem Serail, K 384: Traurigkeit; Martern aller Arten; Welch ein Geschick. See no. 3748

Die Entfuhrung aus dem Serail, K 384: Welcher Kummer...Traurigkeit ward mir zum Lose; Martern aller Arten. See no. 3844

Exsultate jubilate, K 165. See no. 2484

Exsultate jubilate, K 165: Alleluia. See no. 2303

Ezio, K 369: Misera dove son...Ah non son'io che parlo. See no. 2304

Fantasia, K 396, C minor. See no. 171. See no. 2392

2378 Fantasia, K 397, D minor. Fantasia, K 475, C minor. Rondo, piano,

K 511, A minor. Sonata, piano, no. 14, K 457, C minor. Variations on "Ah vous dirai'je Maman", K 265, C major. Jos van Immersel, fortepiano. Accent ACC 8018
+FF 7/8-81 p136 +HFN 4-81 p73

Fantasia, K 397, D minor. See no. 205. See no. 233. See no. 2391. See no. 2392. See no. 3764

Fantasia, K 475, C minor. See no. 2378. See no. 2392. See no. 2423. See no. 2425. See no. 2427

Fantasia, K 594, F minor. See no. 2300

Fantasia, K 608, F minor. See no. 251. See no. 471. See no. 2300

Fantasia and fugue, K 394, C major. See no. 2391

2379 La finta giardiniera, K 196. Julia Conwell, Lilian Sukis, Jutta Renate Ihloff, s; Brigitte Fassbaender, ms; Ezio di Cesare, Thomas Moser, t; Barry McDaniel, bar; Salzburg Mozarteum Orchestra; Leopold Hager. DG 2740 234 (4)
+-ARG 9-81 p48 ++NR 5-81 p11
+/FF 5/6-81 p112 +NYT 8-9-81 pD19
+Gr 2-81 p1115 +-ON 7-81 p36
+-HF 7-81 p50 +-Op 7-81 p716
+HFN 4-81 p73 /St 5-81 p78

La finta giardiniera, K 196: Geme la tortorella. See no. 2304

La finta giardiniera, K 196: Nach der weischen art. See no. 1752

La finta semplice, K 51: Senti l'eco ove t'aggiri; Amoretti. See no. 2304

Fugue, K 401, G minor. See no. 117. See no. 233. See no. 2392

Gigue, K 574, G major. See no. 2391. See no. 2392

Gloria in excelsis Deo. See no. 3700

2380 Idomeneo, Re di Creta, K 366. Rachel Yakar, Felicity Palmer, s; Trudeliese Schmidt, alto; Werner Hollweg, Kurt Equiluz, Robert Tear, t; Simon Estes, bs; Zurich Mozart Orchestra and Chorus; Nikolaus Harnoncourt. Telefunken 6-35547 (4) Tape (c) 4-35547
++Gr 5-81 p1510 +ON 7-81 p36
+-HF 7-81 p52 +St 7-81 p90
++HFN 8-81 p86 +STL 3-8-81 p38
+-NYT 3-15-81 pD25

Idomeneo, Re di Creta, K 366. See no. 2307

2381 Idomeneo, Re di Creta, K 366: Ballet music. Sinfonia concertante, KA 9 (K 297b), E flat major. Randall Wolfgang, ob; Jane Hamborsky, clt; Frank Morelli, bsn; William Purvis, hn; Orpheus Chamber Orchestra. Nonesuch D 79009 Tape (c) DI 79009
+-FF 5/6-81 p115 ++NYT 3-29-81 pD31
+HF 7-81 p65 ++SFC 2-15-81 p19
+HF 7-81 p71 tape ++St 6-81 p122
+NR 7-81 p2

Idomeneo, Re di Creta, K 366: Zeffiretti lusinghieri. See no. 3748

Jubilate Deo. See no. 3822

Laudate dominum. See no. 3634

Litaniae, K 195, D major: Sancta Maria. See no. 2484

2382 Litaniae de venerabili altaris sacramento, K 243, E flat major. Vesperae de Dominica, K 321. Margaret Marshall, s; Margaret Cable, con; Wynford Evans, t; Stephen Roberts, bs; St. John's College Choir; Wren Orchestra; David Hill, org; George Guest. Argo ZRG 933 Tape (c) KZRC 933
+-Gr 11-81 p738 +HFN 11-81 p95

Little funeral march, K 453a, C minor. See no. 2392. No. 2391
March, K 249, D major. See no. 2414
March, K 290. See no. 2352
March, K 385a, D major. See no. 2460
March, K 408, C major. See no. 2479
March, K 445. See no. 2352
Masonic funeral music, K 477. See no. 2456. See no. 2486

2383 Masonic music: Maurerische Trauermusik, K 477; Zur Eroffnung der Freimaurerloge, K 483; Zum Schluss der Freimaurerloge, K 484; Die ihr des unermesslichen Weltalls Schopfer Ehrt, K 619; Dir Seele des Weltalls, K 429; Laut verkunde unsre Freude, K 623; O heiliges Band, K 148; Gesellenreise, K 468; Die Maurerfreude, K 471; Kleine Freimaurer Kantatae, K 623. Werner Hollweg, Ian Partridge, t; Stafford Dean, bs; Irwin Gage, pno; Simon Lindley, org; Ambrosian Singers; NPhO; Edo de Waart. Philips 6570 063 Tape (c) 7310 063 (From 6500 020)
+-ARG 12-78 p34 +HFN 5-81 p93
+Gr 5-81 p1509 +NR 12-78 p9
*HF 6-79 p96 tape ++SFC 2-25-79 p41

2384 Mass, no. 4, K 139, C minor. Sebastian Hennig, s; Rafael Harten, alto; John Elwes, t; Stephen Varcoe, bs; Knabenchor Hannover; Collegium Aureum; Heinz Hennig. Harmonia Mundi 1C 065 99910
+-FF 11/12-81 p204

2385 Mass, no. 6, K 192, F major. Church sonata, no. 7, K 224/241a, F major. Vesperae solennes de confessore, K 339, C major. Maria Zadori, s; Paul Esswood, alto; Alexander Oliver, t; Laszlo Polgar, bs; Istvan Ella, org; Jeunesses Musicales Chorus; Budapest Philharmonic Orchestra; Ivan Fischer. Hungaroton SLPX 12235
+-Gr 4-81 p1355

Mass, no. 7, K 194, D major. See no. 4060

2386 Mass, no. 10, K 220, C major. Mass, no. 16, K 317, C major. Robert Behan, t; Walter Raninger, bs; Vienna Boys Choir, Vienna Choir; Vienna Cathedral Orchestra; Ferdinand Grossmann. Philips 6527 097 Tape (c) 7311 097 (From 6747 384)
+-Gr 11-81 p738 +-HFN 12-81 p109

2387 Mass, no. 12, K 258, C major. Vesperae solennes de confessore, K 339, C major. Felicity Palmer, s; Margaret Cable, ms; Philip Langridge, t; Stephen Roberts, bs; St. John's College Chapel Choir; Wren Orchestra; George Guest. Argi ZRG 924 Tape (c) KZRC 924
+Gr 4-81 p1355 +HFN 4-81 p73

Mass, no. 15, K 337, C major: Agnus Dei. See no. 2484
Mass, no. 16, K 317, C major. See no. 2386

2388 Mass, no. 19, K 626, D minor. Hans Buchhierl, treble; Mario Kramer, alto; Werner Krenn, t; Barry McDaniel, bar; Tolzer Boys Choir; Collegium Aureum; Gerhard Schmidt-Gaden. Pro Arte PAL 1027 (From Harmonia Mundi 065 99694)
++FF 11/12-81 p205

Mass, no. 19, K 626, D minor: Introit and kyrie. See no. 4061
Minuets, K 1-2, 4-5, 94, 355. See no. 2392
Minuets, K 122, K 164, nos. 3-4, K 461. See no. 2352
Minuets, K 355, D major. See no. 2391
Minuet and trio, K 315a. See no. 2392
Minuets with contredanses, K 463. See no. 2352

2389 Ein musicalischer Spass, K 522, F major. Quintet, horn, K 407,

E flat major. Serenade, no. 13, K 525, G major. Berlin Philharmonic Octet Members. Philips 6570 147 Tape (c) 7310 147 (From SAL 3710, 3691, LY 802909)
+-Gr 2-81 p1098 +HFN 5-81 p93 tape
+HFN 2-81 p97

Le nozze di Figaro, K 492. See no. 2307. See no. 2486

Le nozze di Figaro, K 492, excerpts. See no. 2416

Le nozze di Figaro, K 492: Cosa mi narri...Sull' aria. See no. 723

Le nozze di Figaro, K 492: Hai gia vinta la causa. See no. 4079

Le nozze di Figaro, K 492: Hai gia vinta la causa...Verdro mentr' is sospiro. See no. 1752

Le nozze di Figaro, K 492: Non piu andrai...Hai gia vinta la causa ...Vedro mentr'io sospiro. See no. 1891

Le nozze di Figaro, K 492: Non so piu; Deh vieni non tardar. See no. 3713

Le nozze di Figaro, K 492: Non so piu; Voi che sapete; Sull'aria; Deh vieni non tardar. See no. 3748

2390 Le nozze di Figaro, K 492: Overture; Cinque...dieci...; Se vuol ballare; Non so piu cosa son; Non piu andrai; Voi che sapete; Crudel perche finora; Hai gia vinta la causa...Vedro mentro io sospiro; E Susanna non vien...Dove sono i bei momenti; Sull aria; Ricevete o padroncina; L'ho perduta me meschina; Tutto e disposto...Aprite un po quegl'occhi; Giunse alfin il momento... Deh vieni non tardar; Pace pace mio dolce tesoro. Jessye Norman, Mirella Freni, s; Yvonne Minton, ms; Ingvar Wixell, bar; Wladimiro Ganzarolli, bar; BBC Symphony Orchestra and Chorus; Colin Davis. Philips 6570 164 Tape (c) 7310 164 (From 6707 014)
+Gr 6-81 p82 +HFN 5-81 p93

Le nozze di Figaro, K 492: Porgi amor. See no. 3642

Le nozze di Figaro, K 492: Porgi amor; Dovo sono. See no. 2355. See no. 3651

Le nozze di Figaro, K 492: Porgi amor; E Susanna non vien...Dove sono; Giunse alfin il momento...Deh vieni non tardar. See no. 3844

Le nozze di Figaro, K 492: Porgi amor; Voi che sapete; E Susanna non vien...Dove sono; Giunse alfin il momento...Deh vieni non tardar. See no. 2303

Le nozze di Figaro, K 492: Voi che sapete. See no. 4026

Le nozze di Figaro, K 492: Wedding march. See no. 3959

2391 Piano works: Adagio, K 540, B minor. Fantasia, K 397 (K 385g), D minor. Fantasia and fugue, K 394, C minor. Gigue, K 574, G major. Marche funebre, K 453a, C minor. Minuet, K 355 (K 376b), D major. Rondo, piano, K 511, A minor. Variations on "Ah vous dirai-je Maman", K 265, C major. Paul Badura Skoda, pianoforte. Astree AS 40
+FF 1/2-81 p156 +HFN 4-81 p73

2392 Piano works: Adagio, K 540, B minor. Allegros, K 3, B flat major; K 312, G minor; K 400, B major (fragment). Andante, K 616, G major. Andantino, K 236, E flat major. Capriccio, K 395, C major. Deutsche Tanze, K 509 (6). Fantasias, K 396, C minor; K 397, D minor (fragment); K 475, C minor. Fugue, K 501, G minor (fragment). Little funeral march, K 453a, C minor. Gigue, K 574, G major. Minuets, K 1, G major; K 2, F major; K 4, F major; K 5, F major; K 94, D major; K 355, D major. Min-

uet and trio, K 315a (8). Prelude and fugue, D 394, C major. Rondos, piano, K 485, D major; K 511, A minor. Sonata-movement and minuet, K 498a/K Anh 136, B major. Suite, K 399, C minor. Variations on an allegretto, K 500, B flat major (12). Variations on a Dutch song by Graaf, K 24, G major (8). Variations on a minuet by Duport, K 573, D major. Variations on a minuet by Fischer, K 179, C major. Variations on an aria by Salieri, K 180, G major (6). Variations on "Ah vous dirai'je Maman", K 265, C major (12). Variations on an allegretto, K 54, F major (6). Variations on "Come un'agnello", K 460, A major. Variations on "Ein Weib ist das herrlichste Ding", K 613, F major (8). Variations on "Je suis Lindor", K 354 (12). Variations on "La belle Francaise", K 353, E flat major (12). Variations on "Les mariages samnites", K 352, F major (8). Variations on "Lison dormait", K 264 (9). Variations on the song "Willem von Nassau", K 25 (7). Variations on "Salve tu Domine", K 398, F major (6). Variations on "Unser Dummer Pobel meint", K 455 (10. Walter Gieseking, pno. EMI 1C 197 43020/4 (5) (Reissues)
+Gr 12-81 p903

Prelude and fugue, K 394, C major. See no. 2392

2393 Quartets, flute, K 285, K 294 (4). Aurele Nicolet, flt; Munich Trio. Tudor 73019
+Gr 8-81 p288 +HFN 8-81 p86

2394 Quartet, flute, K 285, D major. Quartet, oboe, K 370, F major. Trio, clarinet, K 498, E flat major. Bela Kovacs, clt; Peter Pongracz, ob; Attila Lajos, flt; Peter Komlos, vln; Geza Nemeth, vla; Karoly Botvay, vlc; Ferenc Rados, pno. Budapest FX 12298
+Gr 6-81 p50 +HFN 5-81 p81

2395 Quartet, oboe, K 370, F major. SCHUBERT: Quartet, strings, no. 14, D 810, D minor. Ian Wilson, ob; Gabrieli Quartet. Classics for Pleasure CFP 40356 Tape (c) TC CFP 40356 (From World ST 573, CFP 171)
+Gr 7-81 p167 +HFN 7-81 p79
+Gr 9-81 p460 tape +HFN 8-81 p92 tape

2396 Quartet, oboe, K 370, F major. Quintet, clarinet, K 581, A major. Quintet, horn, K 407, E flat major. Antony Pay, clt; Timothy Brown, hn; Neil Black, ob; Iona Brown, Malcolm Matchem, vln; Stephen Shingles, Anthony Jenkins, vla; Denis Vigay, vlc. Philips 9500 772 Tape (c) 7300 848
+-FF 9/10-81 p143 +HFN 9-81 p93 tape
+Gr 6-81 p50 -NR 8-81 p5
+Gr 9-81 p460 +STL 10-11-81 p41
+-HFN 6-81 p75

Quartet, oboe, K 370, F major. See no. 11. See no. 2394

2397 Quartet, piano, K 478, G minor. Quartet, piano, K 493, E flat major. Jorg Demus, pno; Wiener Kammerensemble Members. Eurodisc 200 481-366
+FF 11/12-81 p204

2398 Quartet, piano, K 478, G minor. Quartet, piano, K 493, E flat major. Dezso Ranki, pno; Pal Eder, vln; Zoltan Toth, vla; Gyorgy Eder, vlc. Telefunken 6-42523 Tape (c) 4-42523
++FF 11/12-80 p141 ++HF 6-81 p69 tape

Quartet, piano, K 493, E flat major. See no. 716. See no. 2397. See no. 2398

2399 Quartet, strings, no. 3, K 156, G major. Quintet, clarinet, K 581, A major. Bohuslav Zahradnik, clt; Quatuor Talich. Calliope CAL 1628
/FF 7/8-81 p137
Quartet, strings, no. 6, K 159, B major: Andante. See no. 543
2400 Quartets, strings, nos. 14-19. Chilingirian Quartet. CRD CRD 1062/4 (3) Tape (c) CRD 4062/3
+Gr 12-80 p846 ++HFN 12-80 p143
++Gr 10-81 p614 tape ++HFN 10-81 p95 tape
2401 Quartets, strings, nos. 14-19. Melos Quartet. DG 2740 249 (3) (From 2530 898, 2530 800, 2530 981)
+Gr 11-81 p719 +HFN 12-81 p109
2402 Quartet, strings, no. 18, K 464, A major. Quartet, strings, no. 19, K 465, C major. Musikverein Quartet. Decca SDD 560
+Gr 4-81 p1339 +-ST 7-81 p206
-HFN 3-81 p90
2403 Quartet, strings, no. 19, K 465, C major. Quartet, strings, no. 20, K 499, D major. Gabrieli Quartet. Decca SDD 561
+Gr 6-81 p50 +HFN 5-81 p81
Quartet, strings, no. 19, K 465, C major. See no. 2402
2404 Quartets, strings, nos. 20-22. Melos Quartet. Intercord INT 180 800 (2)
+HFN 12-81 p100
2405 Quartets, strings, nos. 20-23. Quartetto Italiano. Philips 6770 042 (2) (From 6500 241, 6500 225)
+Gr 8-81 p286 +ST 12-81 p589
+HFN 7-81 p79
2406 Quartets, strings, nos. 20-23. Prague Quartet. Supraphon 111 2601/2 (2)
++NR 9-81 p8 ++St 12-81 p123
Quartet, strings, no. 20, K 499, D major. See no. 2403
2407 Quartet, strings, no. 22, K 589, B flat major. Quartet, strings, no. 23, K 590, F major. Melos Quartet. DG 2531 320 Tape (c) 3301 320
++FF 9/10-81 p142 +HFN 8-81 p86
+Gr 8-81 p286 ++HFN 8-81 p92 tape
++Gr 9-81 p460 tape ++St 12-81 p123
Quartet, strings, no. 23, K 590, F major. See no. 2407
2408 Quintet, clarinet, K 581, A major. Trio, clarinet, K 498, E flat major. Bob Wilber, clt; Bjorn Sjogren, vla; Janos Solyom, pno; Crafoord Quartet. Artemis ARTE 7109
+-Gr 6-81 p50
2409 Quintet, clarinet, K 581, A major. Serenade, no. 13, K 525, G major. Guy Deplus, clt; Quatuor Danois; Johan Poulsen, double bs. Astree MB 325
/FF 7/8-81 p137 ++SFC 9-19-81 p18
Quintet, clarinet, K 581, A major. See no. 1977. See no. 2294. See no. 2396. See no. 2399
Quintet, clarinet, K 581, A major: Allegretto con variazioni. See no. 543
Quintet, horn, K 407, E flat major. See no. 989. See no. 1834. See no. 2389. See no. 2396
Quintet, strings, no. 4, K 516, G minor. See no. 2293
2410 Il Re pastore, K 208. Reri Grist, Lucia Popp, Arlene Saunders, s; Nicola Monti, Luigi Alva, t; Denis Vaughan, hpd; Naples Orch-

estra; Denis Vaughan. Arabesque 8050 (2) (From RCA PVL 2-9086, SER 5567/8)
+NR 12-81 p8 +OV 12-81 p36

Il Re pastore, K 208. See no. 2460

Il Re pastore, K 208: Aer tranquillo e di sereni; L'amero saro costante. See no. 2304

Il Re pastore, K 208: L'amero saro costante. See no. 2303. See no. 3844

Rondo, K 581a, A major. See no. 2294

Rondo, flute, K Anh 184, D major. See no. 2298. See no. 2299

Rondo, piano, K 382, D major. See no. 2341. See no. 2342

Rondo, piano, K 485, D major. See no. 609. See no. 2392

Rondo, piano, K 494, F major. See no. 912. See no. 2423. See no. 2425

Rondo, piano, K 511, A minor. See no. 171. See no. 300. See no. 609. See no. 2378. See no. 2391. See no. 2392. See no. 3697

Rondo, violin, K 269, B flat major. See no. 2291. See no. 2345 See no. 2358. See no. 2487

Rondo, violin, K 373, C major. See no. 2291. See no. 2319. See no. 2345. See no. 2246. See no. 2482. See no. 2487

Der Schauspieldirektor, K 486. See no. 2307

2411 Die Schuldigkeit des ersten Gebotes, K 35. Arleen Auger, Krisztina Laki, Sylvia Geszty, s; Werner Hollweg, Claes Ahnsjo, t; Berlin Cathedral Orchestra; Roland Bader, hpd and cond. Schwann Musica Sacra AMS 714/5
+ARG 10-81 p53

Serenades, nos. 6, 10-13. See no. 2486

2412 Serenade, no. 6, K 239, D major. Serenade, no. 12, K 388, C minor. Serenade, no. 13, K 525, G major. DBS; Helmut Winschermann. Arabesque 8077 Tape (c) 9077
+-ARG 7/8-81 p24 /NR 5-81 p8
+-FF 3/4-81 p163

Serenade, no. 6, K 239, D major. See no. 2317. See no. 2480. See no. 2484

2413 Serenade, no. 7, K 250, D major. LAPO Members; Pinchas Zukerman, vln and cond. CBS M 35871 Tape (c) MT 35871
+FF 1/2-81 p157

2414 Serenade, no. 7, K 250, D major. March, K 249, D major. RIAS Sinfonietta; Gustav Kuhn. HMV ASD 4013
-Gr 8-81 p274 +-HFN 9-81 p83

Serenade, no. 7, K 250, D major. See no. 2460

Serenade, no. 9, K 320, D major. See no. 2460

2415 Serenades, nos. 10-12. NWE; Edo de Waart. Philips 6770 047 (2) (From 838734, 802907)
+-Gr 7-81 p158 +STL 10-11-81 p41
+HFN 7-81 p79

2416 Serenades, nos. 10-12. Cosi fan tutte, K 588, excerpts (arr. Wendt). Le nozze di Figaro, K 492, excerpts (arr. Wendt). New York Philomusica Winds. Vox SVBX 5114 (3)
+FF 7/8-81 p138 ++SFC 3-8-81 p13
+NYT 8-9-81 pD19

2417 Serenade, no. 10, K 361, B flat major. Vienna Wind Soloists. Decca SDD 579
+Gr 10-81 p558 +HFN 10-81 p90

2418 Serenade, no. 10, K 361, B flat major. Jean-Francois Paillard Wind Ensemble; Jean-Francois Paillard. Erato STU 71335
+Gr 3-81 p1198

2419 Serenade, no. 10, K 361, B flat major. HSO Wind Ensemble; Ervin Lukacs. Hungaroton SLPX 12224
-FF 9/10-81 p143 +-NR 9-81 p2

2420 Serenade, no. 11, K 375, E flat major. Serenade, no. 12, K 388, C minor. Danzi Quintet; Frans Vester. RCA RC 3-0342
+-Gr 8-81 p286 +HFN 8-81 p86

Serenade, no. 12, K 388, C minor. See no. 2358. See no. 2412. See no. 2420

2421 Serenade, no. 13, K 525, G major. SCHUBERT: Symphony, no. 8, D 759, B minor. STRAUSS, J. II: Polkas. Orchestra; Karl Bohm. DG Tape (c) 3583 021
+Gr 8-81 p324 tape

Serenade, no. 13, K 525, G major. See no. 164. See no. 336. See no. 782. See no. 1647. See no. 2317. See no. 2363. See no. 2389. See no. 2409. See no. 2412. See no. 2479. See no. 2484. See no. 3792

Sinfonia concertante, KA 9 (K 297b), E flat major. See no. 2312. See no. 2318. See no. 2381

Sinfonia concertante, K 364, E flat major. See no. 241. See no. 2346. See no. 2484. See no. 2487

2422 Il sogno di Scipione, K 126. Lucia Popp, Edita Gruberova, Edith Mathis, s; Peter Schreier, Claes Ahnsjo, Thomas Moser, t; Salzburg Chamber Choir; Salzburg Mozarteum; Leopold Hager. DG 2709 098 (3) (also DG 2740 218)
+-ARG 10-80 p26 +NR 7-80 p9
+-FF 3/4-81 p164 +-NYT 5-4-80 pD23
+-Gr 3-80 p1437 +-ON 7-81 p36
+-HF 10-80 p84 +RR 4-80 p48
+HFN 3-80 p93 +-SFC 4-27-80 p35
+-MT 12-80 p787 +-SR 11-80 p94
+-MUM 11/12-80 p34 ++St 8-80 p100

Sonata, flute and harpsichord, no. 4, K 13, F major. See no. 571
Sonata, flute and harpsichord, no. 5, K 14, C major. See no. 3820

2423 Sonatas, piano, nos. 1-17. Allegro and andante, K 533, F major. Fantasia, K 475, C minor. Rondo, piano, no. 2, K 494, F major. Andras Schiff, pno. Decca D222D6 (6)
+-Gr 11-81 p724 +STL 11-8-81 p40
+HFN 10-81 p90

2424 Sonatas, piano, nos. 1-18. Sonata, piano, K 547a, F major. Walter Gieseking, pno. DaCapo 1C 19703 133/7 (5)
+-ARSC Vol X, no. 1 1978 p74 ++FF 9/10-81 p144
+Gr 12-81 p903

2425 Sonatas, piano, nos. 1-18. Fantasia, K 475, C minor. Rondo, piano, K 494, F major. Christoph Eschenbach, pno. DG 2720 092 (7)
+-FF 9/10-81 p144 +SR 10-81 p86

2426 Sonatas, piano, nos. 1-18. Paul Badura-Skoda, pno and fortepiano. Eurodisc 301 609-460 (8)
+HFN 12-81 p100

2427 Sonatas, piano, nos. 1, 3, 7, 10-11, 14, 16-18. Fantasia, K 475, C minor. Zoltan Kocsis, pno. Hungaroton SLPX 12219/22 (4)
+Gr 7-81 p176

2428 Sonata, piano, no. 1, K 279, C major. Sonata, piano, no. 2, K 280, F major. Sonata, piano, no. 3, K 281, B flat major. Maria Joao Pires, pno. Denon OX 7051
+HFN 6-81 p75

2429 Sonatas, piano, nos. 2, 5-6, 8-9, 12-13, 15. Deszo Ranki, pno. Hungaroton 11835/7 (3)
+-Gr 5-81 p1498 +SR 10-81 p86
+HFN 6-81 p75

Sonata, piano, no. 2, K 280, F major. See no. 2428
Sonata, piano, no. 3, K 281, B flat major. See no. 2428
Sonata, piano, no. 4, K 282, E flat major. See no. 475

2430 Sonata, piano, no. 7, K 309, C major. Sonata, piano, no. 9, K 311, D major. Maria Joao Pires, pno. Denon OX 7053
+HFN 8-81 p86

Sonata, piano, no. 8, K 310, A minor. See no. 298. See no. 475. See no. 3749
Sonata, piano, no. 9, K 311, D major. See no. 2430
Sonata, piano, no. 10, K 330, C major. See no. 3857
Sonata, piano, no. 11, K 331, A major. See no. 1555. See no. 3866
Sonata, piano, no. 11, K 331, A major: Rondo alla turca. See no. 3695. See no. 3764

2431 Sonata, piano, no. 12, K 332, F major. Sonata, piano, no. 13, K 333, B flat major. Malcolm Bilson, fortepiano. Nonesuch N 78004 Tape (c) N 1-78004
+Audio 10-81 p30 +SR 10-81 p86
+FF 3/4-81 p163 +St 6-81 p121
+HF 2-81 p61

2432 Sonata, piano, no. 12, K 332, F major. Sonata, piano, no. 13, K 333, B flat major. Steven Lubin, fortepiano. Spectrum SR 125 Tape (c) SC 225
+-ARG 10-81 p34 +-St 6-81 p121
+HF 9-81 p46 tape

Sonata, piano, no. 13, K 333, B flat major. See no. 2431. See no. 2432
Sonata, piano, no. 14, K 457, C minor. See no. 2378
Sonata, piano, no. 15, K 545, C major. See no. 171. See no. 1344
Sonata, piano, K 547a, F major. See no. 2424

2433 Sonatas, violin and piano, K 58, 304, 481. Sigiswald Kuijken, Baroque vln; Gustav Leonhardt, pianoforte. Pro Arte PAL 1021
*FF 11/12-81 p88

2434 Sonatas, violin and piano, K 58, K 304, K 481. Sigiswald Kuijken, vln; Gustav Leonhardt, fortepiano. RCA RL 3-0335
-FF 9/10-81 p145 +HFN 8-81 p86
+-Gr 7-81 p167

2435 Sonata, violin and piano, K 296, C major. Sonata, violin and piano, K 303, C major. Sonata, violin and piano, K 306, D major. Jean-Jacques Kantorow, vln; Alain Planes, pno. Denon OX 7144
+HFN 6-81 p75

2436 Sonatas, violin and piano, K 303, 304, 379, 404. Jean-Jacques Kantorow, vln; Alain Planes, pno. Denon OX 7169
+HFN 6-81 p75

Sonata, violin and piano, K 303, C major. See no. 2435

Sonatas, violin and piano, K 304, 376-377, 526. See no. 636
Sonata, violin and piano, K 306, D major. See no. 2435
2437 Sonatas, violin and piano, K 454, K 481, K 526, K 547. Annegret Diedrichsen, vln; Desmond Wright, pno. Acanta HA 23200/1 (2)
-Gr 1-81 p962 +ST 6-81 p123
+-HFN 1-81 p99
2438 Sonata, violin and piano, K 454, B flat major. Sonata, violin and piano, K 526, A major. Rainer Kussmaul, vln; Rolf Junghanns, fortepiano. Toccata FSM 53631
+-Gr 10-81 p574
Sonata, violin and piano, K 526, A major. See no. 2438
Sonata-movement and minuet, K 498a/K Anh 136, B major. See no. 2392
2439 Songs (vocal trios and quartets): Bona Nox bist a rechta Ox, K 561; Caro bell idol mio, K 562; Caro mio Druck und Schluck, K App 5; D'Baurin hat d'Katz verlorn, K App 188; Due pupille amabili, K 439; Das gestorte Standchen, K 441b; Ecco quel fiero istante, K 436; Grazie agl' inganni tuoi, K 532; Lacrimoso son io, K 555; Liebes Mandel wo is's Bandel, K 441; Luci care luci belle, K 346; Mi lagnero tacendo, K 437; Nascoso e il mio sol, K 557; Nun liebes Weibchen, K 625; Piu non si trovano, K 549; Sie ist da hin, K 229; Weibchen, K 625; Piu non si trovano, K 549; Sie ist da hin, K 229; Se lontan ben mio tu sei, K 438. Ana Maria Miranda, s; Clara Wirz, ms; Marcel Quillevere, t; Udo Reinemann, bar; Marie-Claude Arbaretaz, pno; Jean-Noel Crocq, Alain Damien, basset horns, clt; Jean-Marc Volta, basset horn. Arion ARN 38490 (also Musical Heritage Society MHS 4318)
-FF 9/10-81 p148 +Gr 12-79 p1034
+RR 12-79 p113
2440 Songs: Abendempfidung, K 523; Als Luise die Briefe, K 520; Die kleine Friedrichs Geburtstag, K 529; Das Kinderspiel, K 598; Die kleine Spinnerin, K 531; Sehnsucht nach dem Fruhling, K 596; Die Verschweigung, K 518; Das Veilchen, K 476; Der Zauberer, K 472. STRAUSS, R.: Begegnung; Breit uber mein Haupt, op. 19, no. 2; Die erwachte Rose; Du meines Herzens Kronelein, op. 21, no. 2; Meinem Kinde, op. 37, no. 3; Schon sind doch kalt, op. 19, no. 3; Sie wissen's nicht, op. 49, no. 5; Die Verschwiegenen, op. 10, no. 6; Zueignung, op. 10, no. 1. Helen Donath, s; Klaus Donath, pno. EMI 1C 065 45417
+-Gr 11-81 p738
2441 Songs: Abendempfidung, K 523; Als Luise die Briefe, K 520; Die Alte, K 517; An Chloe, K 524; Dans un bois solitaire, K 308; Das Kinderspiel, K 598; Das Traumbild, K 530; Das Veilchen, K 476; Im Fruhlingsanfange, K 597; Die kleine Spinnerin, K 531; Das Lied der Trennung, K 519; Oiseaux si tous les ans, K 307; Ridente la calma, K 152; Sehnsucht nach dem Fruhling, K 596; Der Zauberer, K 492; Die Zufriedenheit, K 349. Elizabeth Schwarzkopf, s; Walter Gieseking, pno. HMV ASD 3858 Tape (c) TD ASD 3858 (From 33CX 1321)
+FF 3/4-81 p166 +HFN 6-80 p119
+Gr 5-80 p1706 +HFN 9-80 p116 tape
+Gr 9-80 p413 tape
2442 Songs: Als Luise die Briefe ihres Ungetreuen, K 520; An Chloe, K 524; Abendempfindung, K 523; Das Lied der Trennung, K 519;

Warnung, K 433. SCHUBERT: Auf dem Wasser zu singen, D 774; Fischer, D 225; Fischerweise, D 881; Die Forelle, D 550; Ganymed, D 544; Gretchen am Spinnrade, D 118; Gretchens Bitte, D 564; Liebhaber in allen Gestalten, D 558; Im Fruhling, D 882; Der Jungling und der Tod, D 545; Das Lied im Grunen, D 917; Der Konig von Thule, D 367; Seligkeit, D 433; Der Tod und das Madchen, D 531; Schafers Klagelied, D 121; Szene aus Faust, D 126; Der Wanderer an den Mond, D 870; Wanderers Nachtlied, D 768; Widerschein, D 949. SCHUMANN: Frauenliebe und Leben, op. 42. WOLF: Goethe Lieder: Mignon I-III. Irmgard Seefried, s; Erik Werba, Walter Klien, pno. Pearl SHE 556/7 (2)
+Gr 4-81 p1358

2443 Songs: Abendempfidung, K 523; Als Luise die Briefe Verbrannte, K 520; Die Alte, K 517; An Chloe, K 524; Dans un bois solitaire, K 308; Das Lied der Trennung, K 519; Die Kleine Spinnerin, K 531; Komm liebe Zither komm, K 351; Un moto di gioia, K 579; Oiseau si tous les ans, K 307; Ridente la calma, K 152; Sehnsucht nach dem Fruhling, K 596; Sei du mein Trost, K 391; Das Traumbild, K 530; Das Veilchen, K 476; Die Verschweignung, K 518; Warnung, K 433; Der Zauberer, K 472; Die Zufriedenheit, K 473. Elly Ameling, s; Jorg Demus, fortepiano; Willi Rosenthal, mand. Seraphim S 60334
+ARG 2-81 p23 +ON 12-13-80 p44
+NR 9-80 p8 +St 11-80 p79

Songs: Abendempfidung, K 523; Die Zauberer, K 472. See no. 3844
Songs: An Chloe, K 524. See no. 3657
Songs: Cor sincerum amore plenum, K 505; Mens sancta Deo chara (attrib.). See no. 3790
Songs: Misero o sogno o son desto. See no. 3838
Songs: Ninna Nanna, K 350. See no. 3753
Songs: Per pieta, K 420. See no. 1363
Suite, K 399, C major. See no. 2392

2444 Symphonies (41). BPhO; Karl Bohm. DG 2720 044 (15) Tape (c) 3378 016/17 (12) (also DG SKL 2721 013, 2721 007)
++FF 9/10-81 p145 +-RR 9-72 p66
+-Gr 11-73 p1015 tape

Symphonies, K 121, D major; K 203, D major; K 204, D major. See no. 2453

2445 Symphonies, nos. 1, 4-20, 42-47, 55; G major; K 126/163 (K 141a), D major; K 208/102 (K 213c), C major; K 111/120 (K 111a), D major; K 196/121 (K 207a), D major. AMF; Neville Marriner. Philips 6769 054 (3) (From 6747 099)
++Gr 7-81 p156 +HFN 8-81 p91

2446 Symphonies, nos. 9, 14-17. Symphonies, K 35, C major; K 38, D major; K 62a/K 100, D major; K 74c/K 118, D major; K 75, F major; K 75b/K110, G major. Academy of Ancient Music; Christopher Hogwood, hpd; Jaap Schroder, vln. L'Oiseau-Lyre D168D3 (3) Tape (c) K168K3
+-Gr 8-81 p276 +NYT 10-11-81 pD31
+HFN 8-81 p86

2447 Symphonies, nos. 18-27. Academy of Ancient Music; Jaap Schroder, vln; Christopher Hogwood, hpd. L'Oiseau-Lyre D169D3 (3) Tape (c) K169K33 (r) B-C W/D 169D3
++FF 5/6-80 p120 +RR 12-79 p63
+Gr 12-79 p1008 +SFC 6-1-80 p34

+Gr 5-80 p1717 tape +SR 11-80 p94
+-HF 5-80 p61 ++St 5-80 p72
+HF 4-81 p93 tape +STL 2-10-80 p40
+-HFN 1-80 p107

Symphony, K 19a, F major. See no. 1326

2448 Symphonies, nos. 21-24. AMF; Neville Marriner. Philips 9500 888 Tape (c) 7300 888
+NR 5-81 p6 +-NYT 8-9-81 pD19

2449 Symphonies, nos. 21-41. AMF; Neville Marriner. Philips 6769 043 (8)
+ARG 11-81 p37 ++HFN 11-80 p106
+Gr 9-80 p338

2450 Symphony, no. 21, K 134, A major. Symphony, no. 31, K 297, D major. RIAS Sinfonietta; Gustav Kuhn. EMI 1C 067 99884 (also HMV ASD 4014)
-FF 11/12-81 p209 +-HFN 7-81 p74
+Gr 7-81 p158

2451 Symphonies, nos. 25-27. AMF; Neville Marriner. Philips 9500 587 Tape (c) 7300 710
+ARG 12-81 p19 +-NYT 8-9-81 pD19
++NR 8-81 p5

2452 Symphonies, nos. 25, 28-29, 33. Stuttgart Chamber Orchestra; Karl Munchinger. Intercord INT 185852 (2)
+-FF 7/8-81 p139 +-NYT 3-29-81 pD31

2453 Symphonies, nos. 25, 28-30. Symphony, K 121, D major; K 203, D major; D 204, D major. Academy of Ancient Music; Christopher Hogwood. L'Oiseau-Lyre D170D3 (3) Tape (c) K170K3
+FF 5/6-81 p116 +HF 12-81 p93 tape
+Gr 9-80 p338 +HFN 9-80 p109
+Gr 2-81 p1122 tape +St 4-81 p106
+-HF 6-81 p58 +STL 11-9-80 p40

Symphonies, nos. 25, 29, 31, 33-36, 38-41. See no. 2486

2454 Symphony, no. 25, K 183, G minor. Symphony, no. 29, K 201, A major. Symphony, no. 32, K 318, G major. LSO; Colin Davis. Philips 6570 207 Tape (c) 7310 207 (From PHS 900133)
++FF 1/2-81 p158 ++HF 2-81 p68
++Gr 10-81 p558 +HFN 9-81 p89

2455 Symphony, no. 25, K 183, G minor. Symphony, no. 29, K 201, A major. BRSO; Lorin Maazel. Quintessence PMC 7149
+FF 1/2-81 p158 +SFC 8-31-80 p31

Symphony, no. 25, K 183, G minor. See no. 1814. See no. 2118. See no. 2484

2456 Symphony, no. 29, K 201, A major. Symphony, no. 35, K 385, D major. Masonic funeral music, K 477. VPO; Karl Bohm. DG 2531 335 Tape (c) 3301 335
-FF 11/12-81 p209 +HFN 10-81 p95 tape
+Gr 9-81 p388 +HFN 9-81 p83

2457 Symphony, no. 29, K 201, A major. Symphony, no. 39, K 543, E flat major. VSO; Ferenc Fricsay. DG 2535 130 Tape (c) 3335 130 (From 138125/709)
++FF 1/2-81 p159 +-HF 2-81 p68

Symphony, no. 29, K 201, A major. See no. 1814. See no. 2454. See no. 2455. See no. 2484

2458 Symphony, no. 31, K 297, D major. Symphony, no. 32, K 318, G major. Symphony, no. 39, K 543, E flat major. LPO; Zdenek

Macal. Classics for Pleasure CFP 40354 Tape (c) TC CFP 40354
+Gr 7-81 p158 +-HFN 8-81 p92 tape
+HFN 7-81 p74 +-STL 7-12-81 p40

2459 Symphony, no. 31, K 297, D major. Symphony, no. 32, K 318, G major. Symphony, no. 35, K 385, D major. Stuttgart Philharmonic Orchestra; Karl Munchinger. London STS 15529 (From CS 6625)
-FF 3/4-81 p167 +NR 12-80 p4
+-HF 2-81 p68

Symphony, no. 31, K 297, D major. See no. 2450

2460 Symphonies, nos. 32-36. March, K 385a, D major. Il Re pastore, K 208, C major. Serenade, no. 7, K 250, D major. Serenade, no. 9, K 320, D major. Christopher Hogwood, hpd; Academy of Ancient Music; Jaap Schroder. L'Oiseau-Lyre D171D4 (4) Tape (c) K171K44
+FF 9/10-81 p146 ++MUM 11/12-81 p32
+Gr 1-81 p951 ++NYT 8-9-81 pD19
+HF 12-81 p93 tape ++St 11-81 p86
+HFN 1-81 p97 +STL 4-12-81 p40

Symphony, no. 32, K 318, G major. See no. 2454. See no. 2458. See no. 2459

2461 Symphony, no. 33, B flat major. Symphony, no. 40, K 550, G minor. Collegium Aureum; Franzjosef Maier. Quintessence PMC 7159 Tape (c) 7159 (From BASF KHB 21511)
+-ARG 2-81 p24 ++SFC 10-5-80 p21
+FF 11/12-80 p142

Symphony, no. 33, K 319, B flat major. See no. 1447

2462 Symphony, no. 34, K 338, C major. Symphony, no. 35, K 385, D major. COA; Nikolaus Harnoncourt. Telefunken 6-42703 Tape (c) 4-42703
+FF 11/12-81 p209 +NYT 8-9-81 pD19
+Gr 7-81 p158 +OV 12-81 p36
++Gr 10-81 p614 tape -St 11-81 p86
+NR 11-81 p2

2463 Symphony, no. 35, K 385, D major. Symphony, no. 36, K 425, C major. Collegium Aureum. Harmonia Mundi (Germany) C 065 99903
+-FF 5/6-81 p115 +HFN 5-81 p81
+Gr 3-81 p1200

2464 Symphony, no. 35, K 385, D major. Symphony, no. 41, K 551, C major. Klassiche Philharmonic Orchestra, Sutttgart; Karl Munchinger. Intercord INT 160835
+-HFN 9-81 p83

Symphony, no. 35, K 385, D major. See no. 2456. See no. 2459. See no. 2462

2465 Symphony, no. 36, K 425, C major. SCHUBERT: Symphony, no. 3, D 200, D major. Rosamunde, op. 26, D 797: Ballet music; Entr'acte, no. 3. North German Radio Orchestra, South German Radio Orchestra; Erich Kleiber. Bruno Walter Society RR 521
+-FF 7/8-81 p164 +NR 4-81 p2

2466 Symphony, no. 36, K 425, C major. Symphony, no. 38, K 504, D major. Mostly Mozart Orchestra; Jean-Pierre Rampal. CBS M 35840 Tape (c) MT 35840
+-ARG 3-81 p37 +-HF 2-80 p68
+-FF 11/12-80 p142 -SFC 10-19-80 p20

2467 Symphony, no. 36, K 425, C major. Concerto, piano, no. 15, K 450,

B flat major. VPO; Leonard Bernstein, pno and cond. Decca JB 95 Tape (c) KJBC 95 (From SET 332)
+-Gr 10-81 p557

2468 Symphony, no. 36, K 425, C major. Symphony, no. 38, K 504, D major. NHK Orchestra; Otmar Suitner. Denon OX 7156
+Audio 9-81 p82

2469 Symphony, no. 36, K 425, C major. Symphony, no. 39, K 543, E flat major. AMF; Neville Marriner. Philips 9500 653 Tape (c) 7300 756
-ARG 10-81 p35 +-NYT 8-9-81 pD19
++NR 7-81 p2 ++St 8-81 p95

2470 Symphony, no. 36, K 425, C major. Divertimento, K 136, D major. Mozart Festival Orchestra; George Cleve. Sonic Arts LS 19 Tape (c) Audible Image A1-107
+-Audio 12-81 p68 tape +SFC 12-9-80 p33

Symphony, no. 36, K 425, C major. See no. 2463

2471 Symphonies, nos. 38-41. BPhO; Karl Bohm. DG 2725 104 (2) Tape (c) 3374 104
+-Gr 1-81 p952 +-HFN 1-81 p109 tape
+-HFN 1-81 p107

2472 Symphony, no. 38, K 504, D major. Symphony, no. 39, K 543, E flat major. VPO; Karl Bohm. DG 2531 206 Tape (c) 3301 206
+FF 7/8-80 p116 +NR 6-80 p3
++Gr 11-79 p833 +RR 11-79 p88
+-HF 2-81 p68 +-RR 4-80 p127 tape
+HFN 12-79 p166

2473 Symphony, no. 38, K 504, D major. Symphony, no. 41, K 551, C minor. BBC Symphony Orchestra; Colin Davis. Philips 6570 087 Tape (c) 7310 087
+HF 8-78 p98 tape +HFN 4-81 p81 tape
+HFN 2-81 p97

Symphony, no. 38, K 504, D major. See no. 2466. See no. 2468

2474 Symphony, no. 39, K 543, E flat major. Symphony, no. 40, K 550, G minor. BPhO; Herbert von Karajan. HMV SXLP 30527 Tape (c) TC SCLP 30527 (From SLS 809)
+Gr 9-81 p388 +HFN 9-81 p89

2475 Symphony, no. 39, K 543, E flat major. Symphony, no. 40, K 550, G minor. LSO; Colin Davis. Philips 6570 143 Tape (c) 7310 143 (From 835113)
+Gr 11-80 p672 +-HFN 1-81 p109 tape
+-HFN 12-80 p153

Symphony, no. 39, K 543, E flat major. See no. 2457. See no. 2458. See no. 2469. See no. 2472. See no. 3781

Symphony, no. 39, K 543, E flat major: 3rd movement. See no. 4122

2476 Symphony, no. 40, K 550, C minor. concerto, piano, no. 20, K 466, D minor. Yvonne Lefebure, pno; BPhO; Wilhelm Furtwangler. Bruno Walter Society RR 395
-FF 9/10-81 p141 -NR 4-81 p3

2477 Symphony, no. 40, K 550, G minor. Symphony, no. 41, K 551, C major. Bavarian Radio Orchestra; Rafael Kubelik. CBS IM 36703
++SFC 10-25-81 p21

2478 Symphony, no. 40, K 550, G minor. Symphony, no. 41, K 551, C major. CO; Georg Szell. CBS MY 37220
+FF 11/12-81 p210

2479 Symphony, no. 40, K 550, G minor. Serenade, no. 13, K 525, G

major. March, K 408, C major. VPO; Istvan Kertesz. Contour CC 7507 Tape (c) CCT 7507
+Gr 8-81 p316

2480 Symphony, no. 40, K 550, G minor. Serenade, no. 6, K 239, D major. ECO; Benjamin Britten. Decca JB 107 Tape (c) KJBC 107 (From SXL 6372)
+Gr 11-81 p694

2481 Symphony, no. 40, K 550, G minor. Symphony, no. 41, K 551, C major. LSO; Claudio Abbado. DG 2531 273 Tape (c) 3301 273
++FF 1/2-81 p159 +HFN 11-80 p121
+-Gr 11-80 p672 +HFN 12-80 p159 tape
+Gr 12-80 p889 +-NR 12-80 p4
+-HF 6-81 p58 +-ST 6-81 p123

Symphony, no. 40, K 550, G minor. See no. 2461. See no. 2474. See no. 2475

2482 Symphony, no. 41, K 551, C major. Rondo, violin, K 373, C major. Franzjosef Maier, vln; Collegium Aureum; Franzjosef Maier. Harmonia Mundi 065 99673 Tape (c) 1C 265 99673 (also Pro Arte PAL 1009 Tape (c) PAC 1009)
+FF 7/8-81 p111 +NR 5-81 p6
+Gr 2-79 p1422 +-RR 9-78 p62
-HF 8-81 p61 -RR 9-79 p134 tape
+HFN 9-78 p145 ++St 8-81 p95
+HFN 7-79 p119 tape

Symphony, no. 41, K 551, C major. See no. 2464. See no. 2473. See no. 2477. See no. 2478. See no. 2481

Symphony, no. 41, K 551, C major: 1st movement. See no. 4122

Trio, clarinet, K 498, E flat major. See no. 2394. See no. 2408

2483 Trios, piano (6). Beaux Arts Trio. Philips 6768 032 (2) Tape (c) 7650 017 (From SAL 3681/2)
+-Gr 7-80 p148 ++RR 7-80 p18
+Gr 2-81 p1122 tape ++SFC 9-9-79 p45
+HFN 8-80 p107 +STL 7-13-80 p38

Trio, piano, K 564, G major: Allegretto. See no. 543

Trio, strings, K 562 (K Anh 66), G major. See no. 2365

Variations on a Dutch song by Graaf, K 24, G major. See no. 2392

Variations on a minuet by Duport, K 573, D major. See no. 2392

Variations on a minuet by Fischer, K 179, C major. See no. 2392

Variations on "Ah vous dirai'je, Maman", K 265, C major. See no. 2378. See no. 2391. See no. 2392

Variations on an allegretto, K 54, F major. See no. 2392

Variations on an allegretto, K 500, B flat major. See no. 2392

Variations on an aria by Salieri, K 180, G major. See no. 2392

Variations on "Come un agnello" by Sarti, K 460, A major. See no. 2392

Variations on "Ein Weib ist das herrlichste Ding", K 613, F major. See no. 2392

Variations on "Je suis Lindor", K 354. See no. 2392

Variations on "La belle Francaise", K 353, E flat major. See no. 2392

Variations on "Les mariages samnites", K 352, F major. See no. 2392

Variations on "Lison dormait", K 264. See no. 2392

Variations on "Salve tu Domine", K 398, F major. See no. 2392

Variations on the song "Willem von Nassau", K 25. See no. 2392

Variations on "Unser Dummer Pobel", K 455. See no. 717. See no. 2392

Vesperae de Dominica, K 321. See no. 2382

Vesperae solennes de confessore, K 339, C major. See no. 2385. See no. 2387

Vorrei spiegarvi o Dio, K 418. See no. 2303

2484 Works, selections: Concerto, violin, no. 3, K 216, G major. Exsultate jubilate, K 165. Litaniae, K 195, D major: Sancta Maria. Mass, no. 15, K 337, C major: Agnus Dei. Serenade, no. 6, K 239, D major. Serenade, no. 13, K 525, G major. Sinfonia concertante, K 364, E flat major. Symphony, no. 25, K 183, G minor. Symphony, no. 29, K 201, A major. Alan Loveday, vln; Erna Spoorenberg, Ileana Cotrubas, s; Helen Watts, con; Robert Tear, t; John Shirley-Quirk, bar; Oxford Schola Cantorum; AMF; Neville Marriner. Argo D243D3 (3) Tape (c) K243K33 (From ZRG 679, 554, 706, 729, 524, 677)

+Gr 11-81 p694

2485 Works, selections: Concerto, bassoon, K 191, B flat major. Concerto, clarinet, K 622, A major. Concerto, flute, no. 1, K 313, G major. Concerto, flute and harp, K 299, C major. Concerti, horn, nos. 1-4. Concerto, flute, no. 2, K 314, C major. Sinfonia concertante, K 297b, E flat major. Alfred Prinz, clt; Dietmar Zeman, Peter Schmidl, clt; Fritz Faltl, bsn; Werner Tripp, Wolfgang Schulz, flt; Gerhard Turetschek, Walter Lehmayer, ob; Nicanor Zabaleta, hp; Gunther Hogner, hn; VPO; Karl Bohm. DG 2740 231 (4) (From 2530 441, 2530 527, 2530 715)

+-FF 5/6-81 p111 +-HFN 11-80 p121
+-Gr 12-80 p836

2486 Works, selections: Adagio and fugue, K 546, C minor. Concerti, horn, nos. 1-4. Concerto, piano, no. 25, K 503, C major. Cosi fan tutte, K 588. Don Giovanni, K 527. Masonic funeral music, K 477. Le nozze di Figaro, K 492. Die Entfuhrung aus dem Serail, K 384: Overture. Serenades, nos. 6, 10-13. Symphonies, nos. 25, 29, 31, 33-36, 38-41. La clemenza di Tito, K 621: Overture. Die Zauberflote, K 620. Various soloists; Daniel Barenboim, pno; Alan Civil, hn; PhO, NPhO; Otto Klemperer. Electrola 1C 197 53714/38 (25)

+FF 9/10-81 p149

2487 Works, selections: Adagio, K 261, E major. Concerti, violin, nos. 1-7. Concertone, 2 violins, K 190 (K 166b), C major. Rondo, violin, K 373, C major. Rondo, violin, K 269, B flat major. Sinfonia concertante, K 364, E flat major. Josef Suk, Vaclav Snitil, vln; Josef Kodousek, vla; PCO; Libor Hlavacek. Supraphon 110 1521/5 (5)

+-FF 5/6-81 p117 ++SFC 3-29-81 p18
++NR 3-81 p7

Zaide, K 344: Trostlos schluchzet Philomele. See no. 2304

2488 Die Zauberflote, K 620. Kiri Te Kanawa, Edita Gruberova, Kathleen Battle, Helena Dose, Ann Murray, s; Naoka Ihara, con; Peter Hofmann, t; Philippe Huttenlocher, bar; Kurt Moll, Jose Van Dam, bs; Zurich Boys Choir, Rhine Opera Chorus; Strasbourg Philharmonic Orchestra; Alain Lombard. Barclay 960012/4 (3) Tape (c) 4-960012/4

+-FF 11/12-81 p203 -Op 8-79 p780
+Gr 5-79 p1929 -RR 7-79 p36

2489 Die Zauberflote, K 620. Rita Streich, Maria Stader, Marianne Schech, Liselotte Losch, Lisa Otto, s; Margarete Klose, con; Ernst Hafliger, Howard Vandenburg, Martin Vantin, t; Dietrich Fischer-Dieskau, bar; Josef Greindl, Kim Borg, bs; RIAS Chamber Choirs, Berlin Motet Choir; RIAS Symphony Orchestra; Ferenc Fricsay. DG 2701 015 (3) (also DG 2728 009, DG 2701 003) (From DG 18267/9)

+ARSC Vol 12, no. 1-2 1980 p124
/FF 3/4-81 p163
+-Gr 1-79 p1324
+-HFN 2-79 p117
+ON 12-13-80 p44
+RR 2-79 p49

2490 Die Zauberflote, K 620. Edith Mathis, Karen Ott, Janet Perry, s; Francisco Araisa, t; Gottfried Hornik, bar; Jose van Dam, bs; Deutsch Oper Chorus; BPhO; Herbert von Karajan. DG 2741 001 (3) Tape (c) 3382 001 (alsO DG 2560 001/3, DG 2810 076)

+-ARG 4-81 p48
+FF 1/2-81 p155
+Gr 10-80 p534
+Gr 2-81 p1122 tape
+HF 12-80 p76
+-HF 5-81 p53 tape
+HFN 11-80 p121
+HFN 1-81 p109 tape
+-MT 6-81 p391
+-MUM 2-81 p32
+-NR 1-81 p9
+NYT 10-26-80 pB33
+-ON 12-13-80 p44
+Op 11-80 p1109
++SFC 10-19-80 p20
+St 11-80 p71
+STL 12-14-80 p38

2491 Die Zauberflote, K 620. Helen Donath, Sylvia Geszty, Renate Hoff, Peter Schreier, Gunther Lieb, Harald Neukirch, Theo Adam; Leipzig Radio Chorus; Dresden State Orchestra; Otmar Suitner. Eurodisc 80 584 (3)

+-HFN 12-81 p97

2492 Die Zauberflote, K 620. Edith Gruberova, Lucia Popp, Marilyn Richardson, s; Doris Soffel, ms; Ortrun Wenkel, con; Siegfried Jerusalem, Waldemar Kmentt, t; Wolfgang Brendel, bar; Norman Bailey, bs-bar; Erich Kunz, Roland Bracht, bs; Tolzer Boys Choir; Bavarian Radio Orchestra and Chorus; Bernard Haitink. HMV SLS 5223 (3) Tape (c) TCC SLS 5223 (also Angel DSX 3918)

+Gr 11-81 p753
+-NYT 11-1-81 pD21

2493 Die Zauberflote, K 620. Zdislawa Donat, Rachel Yakar, Ileana Cotrubas, s; Eric Tappy, t; Christian Boesch, bar; Horst Hiestermann, t; Jose Van Dam, bs-bar; Martti Talvela, bs; Vienna State Opera Orchestra; James Levine. RCA CTC 4-4124 (4) (also RL 0-3728)

+Gr 11-81 p753
+HFN 11-81 p95
+NR 11-81 p9
+NYT 11-1-81 pD21
+ON 11-81 p68
+SFC 9-20-81 p18

Die Zauberflote, K 620. See no. 2307. See no. 2486
Die Zauberflote, K 620: Ach ich fuhl's. See 2303. See no. 2355
Die Zauberflote, K 620: Bei Mannern. See no. 1891
Die Zauberflote, K 620: Dies Bildnis ist bezaubernd schon. See no. 1363. See no. 3747. See no. 3966
Die Zauberflote, K 620: Dies Bildnis ist bezaubern schon; Zum Ziele fuhrt dich. See no. 3972
Die Zauberflote, K 620: O zittre nicht; Der Holle Rache. See no. 2302. See no. 3748
Die Zauberflote, K 620: Possenti numi. See no. 3968
Die Zauberflote, K 620: Que sdegno; Possenti numi. See no. 4029

Die Zauberflote, K 620: Schnelle Fusse. See no. 4122
2494 Die Zauberflote, K 620: Zu Hilfe zu Hilfe; Der Vogelfanger bin ich ja; Dies Bildnis ist bezaubernd schon; O zittre nicht mein lieber Sohn; Bei Mannern welche Liebe fuhlen; O Isis und Osiris; Alles fuhlt der Liebe Freuden; Der Holle Rache kocht in meinem Herzen; In diesen heil'gen Hallen; Seid uns zum zweiten Mal wilkommen; Ach ich fuhl's es ist verschwunden; O Isis und Osiris; Ein Madchen oder Weibchen; Pa-pa-pa; Die Strahlen der Sonne...Heil sei euch Geweihten. Edith Mathis, Karen Ott, s; Jose van Dam, bs-bar; Francisco Araiza, t; Gottfried Hornik, bar; Berlin Opera Chorus; BPhO; Herbert von Karajan. DG 2532 004 Tape (c) 3302 004 (From 2741 007)
+Gr 6-81 p82 +HFN 6-81 p88
+Gr 6-81 p93 tape +-HFN 6-81 p87 tape

MUCZYNSKI, Robert
Dance movements, op. 17. See no. 809
2495 Maverick pieces (12). Preludes, op. 6 (6). Sonatas, piano, nos. 1, 3. Robert Muczynski, pno. Laurel LR 114
++FF 5/6-81 p118 +NR 6-81 p14
Preludes, op. 6. See no. 2495
Serenade for summer, op. 38. See no. 809
Sonatas, piano, nos. 1, 3. See no. 2495

MUDARRA, Alonso de
Claros y frescos rios. See no. 3853
Fantasia. See no. 3701. See no. 4016
Tiento para harpa. See no. 3778

MUFFAT, Georg
Fugue, G minor. See no. 3622. See no. 4012
2496 Toccatas, nos. 2-3, 7, 9-10, 12. Rene Saorgin, org. Harmonia Mundi HM 966
+-FF 3/4-81 p167 +HFN 9-80 p109
+Gr 9-80 p376

MULET, Henri
Esquisses byzantines: Noel. See no. 3894

MULLER
Kossuth march. See no. 3863

MUNDY, William
O Lord the maker of all things. See no. 3636
Vox patris caelestis. See no. 54

MUNROW, David
The king's hunt. See no. 3853
The six days of Grenoble. See no. 3853

MURRILL, Herbert
Nunc dimittis. See no. 3618
The souls of the righteous. See no. 3637

MUSCHEL, Georgi
Air and toccata. See no. 3910

MUSET, Colin
Quand je voy iver retorner. See no. 3853

MUSGRAVE, Thea
2497 A Christmas carol. Claudette Peterson, Kathryn Montgomery, s; Carolyne James, ms; Jerold Norman, t; Frederick Burchinal, Howard Bender, Robert Randolph, bar; Virginia Opera Orchestra; Peter Mark. Moss Music Group MMG 302 (3)
+-FF 7/8-81 p141 +-ON 11-22-80 p44
+HF 5-81 p60

MUSIC OF THE MID-1800s. See no. 4099
MUSSORGSKY, Modest
Album leaf: Meditation. See no. 2504
2498 Boris Godunov: Prologue; In the courtyard of the Novodievich Monastery; Coronation scene; Pimen's monologue; Vaarlam's song; I have attained the highest power; Clock scene; Polonaise; Revolutionary scene; Farewell and death of Boris. Robert Cauwet, treble; Lawrence Mason, t; Nicola Rossi-Lemeni, bs; San Francisco Opera Chorus; San Francisco Symphony Orchestra; Leopold Stokowski. Dell'Arte DA 9002
+Gr 11-81 p754 +-HFN 12-81 p100
2499 Boris Godunov: Prologue, Coronation scene; I have attained supreme power; Clock scene; Pimen's narrative; Death of Boris. Andrei Sokolov, t; Evgeny Nesterenko, bs; Bolshoi Theatre Orchestra and Chorus; Yuri Simonov. HMV ASD 4006 Tape (c) TC ASD 4006
+Gr 7-81 p192 +-HFN 7-81 p74
Capriccio "In the Crimea". See no. 2503
Capricious woman. See no. 2503
The Capture of Kars march. See no. 2517
Children's games: A children's joke. See no. 2504
The dressmaker. See no. 2504
The fair at Sorochinsk: Gopak. See no. 3693
Hopak. See no. 2504
Impressions of a voyage in the Crimea. See no. 2503
Impromptu passione. See no. 2503
In the village. See no. 2503
Intermezzo. See no. 2503
Khovanschina: Intermezzo, Act 4. See no. 3787
Khovanschina: Prelude. See no. 2513
Khovanschina: Prelude; Introduction, Act 4. See no. 2517
2500 The marriage. Jean Mollien, t; Charlotte Desmazures, con; Nicolas Agroff, bs-bar; Alexandre Popovitzky, bs; Paris Philharmonic Orchestra; Rene Leibowitz. Olympic 9105 (From Oceanic)
-NR 10-74 p10 +-Op 4-81 p384
Memories of childhood. See no. 2504
2501 A night on the bare mountain (arr. Rimsky-Korsakov). Pictures at an exhibition. NYP; Leonard Bernstein. CBS MY 36726
-FF 11/12-81 p222
2502 Night on the bare mountain (arr. Rimsky-Korsakov). Pictures at an exhibition (orch. Ravel). COA; Colin Davis. Philips 9500 744 Tape (c) 7300 829
+-ARG 9-81 p27 +HFN 4-81 p73
++FF 7/8-81 p141 +NYT 7-19-81 pD23
+-Gr 3-81 p1200 +St 7-81 p85
+HF 7-81 p71 tape
Night on the bare mountain. See no. 856. See no. 1390. See no. 2517. See no. 2710
Oedipus in Athens: Chorus of people in the temple. See no. 2517
2503 Piano works: Capricious woman. Impressions of a voyage in the Crimea. Impromptu passionne. Capriccio "In the Crimea". In the village. Intermezzo. Scherzo. Kun Woo Paik, pno. Arabesque Tape (c) 9093
+-NR 6-81 p14 -St 11-81 p90
+-SFC 7-28-81 p18
2504 Piano works: Album leaf: Meditation. Children's games: A child-

ren's joke. Hopak. The dressmaker. Memories of childhood (rev. Karatygin). Memories of childhood: The first punishment; Nanni and I. Reverie. A tear. Kun Woo Paik, pno. Arabesque 8094 Tape (c) 9094
+NR 11-81 p13
2505 Pictures at an exhibition. Kun Woo Paik, pno. Arabesque 8073 Tape (c) 9073
+-FF 3/4-81 p168 +-NR 4-81 p11
2506 Pictures at an exhibition. PROKOFIEV: Sonata, piano, no. 3, op. 28, A minor. Visions fugitives, op. 22, nos. 1, 3, 5-6, 8, 10, 14, 16-18. Oxana Yablonskaya, pno. Connoisseur Society Tape (c) InSync C 4034
+ARG 9-81 p17 +NR 9-80 p10
+HFN 9-80 p105
2507 Pictures at an exhibition. RACHMANINOFF: Preludes, op. 23, nos. 2, 4-5, 7. Preludes, op. 32, nos. 1 and 2. Rudolf Firkusny, Sviatoslav Richter, pno. Contour CC 7516 Tape (c) CCT 7516
+Gr 8-81 p316
2508 Pictures at an exhibition. RACHMANINOFF: Preludes, nos. 3, 5-6. Takahiro Sonoda, pno. Denon OX 7004
-HFN 6-81 p75
2509 Pictures at an exhibition (orch. Ravel). RAVEL: Pavane pour une infante defunte. Tokyo Metropolitan Symphony Orchestra; Louis Fremaux. Denon PCM OX 7072
+-Audio 1-78 p98 +-HFN 6-81 p75
+-HF 10-77 p112
2510 Pictures at an exhibition (trans. Wills). Arthur Wills, org. Hyperion AS 66006 Tape (c) KA 66006
+Gr 12-80 p854 +HFN 6-81 p87 tape
+HFN 12-80 p143
2511 Pictures at an exhibition. RAVEL: Le tombeau de Couperin. CSO; Georg Solti. London LDR 10040 Tape (c) LDR 5-10040 (also Decca SXDL 7520 Tape (c) KSXDC 7520)
++FF 5/6-81 p119 +NR 3-81 p4
+Gr 12-80 p836 +-NYT 7-19-81 pD23
++Gr 4-81 p1376 tape ++SFC 11-23-80 p21
+HF 7-81 p71 tape +St 4-81 p106
+-HFN 12-80 p143
2512 Pictures at an exhibition. Piotr Paleczny, pno. Stolat SZM 0114
+-FF 11/12-81 p211
2513 Pictures at an exhibition (arr. Ravel). Khovanschina: Prelude. NPhO; Charles Mackerras. Vanguard VSD 71188 (Q) VSQ 30032 (also VCS 10116 Tape (r) 47118)
+Gr 12-74 p1143 +NR 3-77 p3
+HF 11-74 p117 +-RR 12-74 p36
+HF 5-81 p53 tape +St 9-74 p127
Pictures at an exhibition. See no. 1467. See no. 2501. See no. 2502
Pictures at an exhibition: Hut on fowl's legs; Ballet of the chicks in their shells. See no. 4003
Pictures at an exhibition: Ballet of the unhatched chicks. See no. 4007
Reverie. See no. 2504
2514 Salammbo (Pesko). Ludmila Schemchuk, ms; Gheorghi Seleznev, Giorgio Tieppo, t; William Stone, bar; Giorgio Surjan, bs;

Verona Arena Male Choir, Choir of the Oratorio dell'Immacolata di Bergamo, Italian Radio and Television Symphony Orchestra and Choir; Zoltan Pesko. CBS 79253(2)
+Gr 12-81 p930 +-STL 12-13-81 p39
+-HFN 12-81 p100

Salammbo: Chorus of the priestesses. See no. 2517
Scherzo. See no. 2503
Scherzo, B flat major. See no. 2517
Songs: Mephistopheles song of the flea. See no. 2516
Songs: The destruction of Sennacherib; Joshua. See no. 2517
Songs: Sunless. See no. 2515

2515 Songs and dances of death. Songs: Sunless. Anton Diakov, bs; Gerard Wyss, pno. Accord ACC 14035
+HFN 9-81 p83

2516 Songs and dances of death. Songs: Mephistopheles' song of the flea. RACHMANINOFF: Songs: Christ is risen, op. 26, no. 6; The harvest of sorrow, op. 4, no. 5; How fair this spot, op. 21, no. 7; A dream, op. 8, no. 5; Night is mournful, op. 26, no. 12; Oh stay my love, op. 4, no. 1; Oh never sing to me again, op. 4, no. 4; When yesterday we met, op. 26, no. 13. Martti Talvela, bs; Ralf Gothoni, pno. Decca SXL 6974
+-Gr 7-81 p185 +STL 10-11-81 p41
+HFN 7-81 p74

A tear. See no. 2504

2517 Works, selections: The capture of Kars march. Khovanschina: Prelude; Introduction, Act 4. Oedipus in Athens: Chorus of people in the temple. Night on the bare mountain (orig. version). Salammbo: Chorus of the priestesses. Scherzo, B flat major. Songs: The destruction of Sennacherib; Joshua. Zehava Gal, con; LSO and Chorus; Claudio Abbado. RCA RL 3-1540 (also RCA ARL 1-3988 Tape (c) ARK 1-3988)
+ARG 12-81 p20 +NR 8-81 p3
+FF 9/10-81 p105 *NYT 7-19-81 pD23
+-Gr 2-81 p1116 +ON 12-19-81 p44
+Gr 7-81 p196 tape ++SFC 7-28-81 p18
+HFN 2-81 p91 ++St 10-81 p75
+HFN 6-81 p87 tape +STL 4-12-81 p40
+MT 8-81 p540

MUTHEL, Johann
Sonata, flute, D major. See no. 112

MYSLIVECEK, Josef

2518 Abramo ed Isacco. Gianfranca Ostini, Jana Jonasova, s; Anna Viganoni, alto; Choichiro Tahara, t; Gianni Matteo, bar; CPhO, Prague Chamber Orchestra; Peter Maag. Supraphon 112 1021/2 (2)
+Gr 9-74 p571 +NR 4-74 p8
+-Gr 3-81 p1233 +RR 2-74 p56
-HF 5-74 p91 +SFC 10-19-75 p33
/HFN 2-74 p341 ++St 11-74 p131
+HFN 3-81 p97

Suite, strings. See no. 3826

NAGY
Songs: The orphan bird. See no. 380

NAPRAVNIK, Eduard
Dubrovsky: Oh give me oblivion. See no. 4028. See no. 4030
Dubrovsky: Vladimir's recitative and romance. See no. 3854

Nizhgorbdtsy: Hail Kremlin. See no. 4028
NARDELLO
Chiove. See no. 3641
NARES, James
Introduction and fugue, F major. See no. 3625
Lesson, op. 2, D major. See no. 3733. See no. 4103
The souls of the righteous. See no. 3633
NARVAEZ, Luis de
Con que la lavare. See no. 3828
NAUMANN, Johann
Sonata, glass harmonica, no. 11. See no. 3881
Wie ein Hirt sein Volk zu weiden. See no. 3881
NAUMANN, Siegfried
Vita vinum est. See no. 1461
NAUWACH, Johann
Songs: Ach Liebste lass uns eilen. See no. 24
NEAR, Gerald
Arise my love my fair one. See no. 3818
Christ hath a garden. See no. 4060
Songs for celebration: Alleluia, Allelu. See no. 4060
NEDBAL, Oskar
Sonata, violin and piano, op. 9, B minor. See no. 1529
NEGRI MILANESI, Cesare
La nizzarda. See no. 3938
NEIDHART VON REUENTHAL
Meye dein lichter schein. See no. 3896
NERUDA, Johann
Concerto, trumpet, E flat major. See no. 783. See no. 1483
NEUMANN, Alfred
Truly we shall be in paradise with him. See no. 3818
NEUSIDLER, Hans
Hie folget ein welscher Tantz. See no. 4016
Ich klag den Tag. See no. 4016
Der Judentanz. See no. 4016
Mein Herz hat sich mit Lieb verpflicht. See no. 4016
Songs: Preaembulum; Wascha mesa. See no. 3896
NEVIN, Ethelbert
Ein Liedchen. See no. 4104
Mighty lak a rose. See no. 3931. See no. 4076
NEW NONESUCH GUIDE TO ELECTRONIC MUSIC. See no. 3941
NEWMAN
Airport: Main theme. See no. 4105
NEWMAN (16th century England)
Pavan. See no. 3622. See no. 4012
NEWMAN, Alfred
Conquest. See no. 3976
NEWMAN, Anthony
2519 Piano cycle, no. 1. Sonata, violin and piano. Sonata, violoncello and piano. Variations and grand contrapunctus. Bruce Berg, vln; Frederic Zlotkin, vlc; Benjamin Verdery, gtr; Anthony Newman, pno. Cambridge CRS B 2833 (2)
+ARG 6-79 p29 ++NR 6-79 p9
+FF 5/6-81 p121
Sonata, violin and piano. See no. 2519
Sonata, violoncello and piano. See no. 2519

Variations and grand contrapunctus. See no. 2519

NEXUS

Amazing space; An African song; Kobina; Passage; Unexpected pleasures. See no. 3931

NICHOLSON, Richard

Fair the day that sees him rise. See no. 3636

NICOLAI, Otto

Die lustigen Weiber von Windsor: Horch die Lerche singt im Hain. See no. 3800. See no. 4022

Die lustigen Weiber von Windsor: Nein das ist wirklich. See no. 3748

Die lustigen Weiber von Windsor: Overture. See no. 3656. See no. 3792

NIEDERMEYER

Pieta signore. See no. 4036

NIELSEN, Carl

Aftenstemning. See no. 3691

2520 Canto serioso. Fantasias, op. 2. The mother, op. 41. Quintet, op. 43. Serenata in vano. Athena Ensemble. Chandos ABR 1003 Tape (c) ABT L003

+FF 1/2-81 p159 +HFN 2-80 p97
+Gr 3-80 p1411 +RR 2-80 p67
+Gr 7-81 p196 tape

Canto serioso. See no. 3683

Chaconne, op. 32. See no. 2522

The children play. See no. 3683

Commotio, op. 58. See no. 2156

2521 Concerto, flute. NORBY: Illuminations. Jean-Pierre Rampal, flt; Sjaellands Symphony Orchestra; John Frandsen. Erato STU 71273

+Audio 2-80 p47 +-MUM 1/2-81 p33
+-Gr 11-79 p834 +-RR 10-79 p101
+HFN 9-79 p109

A dream of "Silent night". See no. 2522

Fantasias, op. 2. See no. 2520

Festival prelude. See no. 2522

Humoresque bagatelles, op. 11. See no. 2522

Little suite, op. 1, A minor. See no. 1646

Maskarade: Overture. See no. 2527

The mother, op. 41. See no. 2520

Piano music for young and old, op. 53. See no. 2522

2522 Piano works: Chaconne, op. 32. A dream of "Silent night". Festival prelude. Humoresque bagatelles, op. 11. Piece, piano, C major. Pieces, piano, op. 3 (5). Pieces, piano, op. 59 (3). Piano music for young and grown-up, op. 53. Symphonic suite, op. 8. Suite, op. 45. Theme and variations, op. 40. Elisabeth Westenholz, pno. BIS LP 167/8 (2)

+FF 9/10-81 p150 *NR 9-81 p13
+-Gr 11-81 p764 +St 9-81 p98
+-HFN 9-81 p83 ++STL 9-13-81 p41

Piece, piano, C major. See no. 2522

Pieces, piano, op. 3 (5). See no. 2522

Pieces, piano, op. 59 (3). See no. 2522

Quintet, op. 43. See no. 781. See no. 2520

Serenato in vano. See no. 2520

Suite, op. 45. See no. 1931. See no. 2522

Symphonic suite, op. 8. See no. 2522
2523 Symphony, no. 1, op. 7, G minor. Symphony, no. 3, op. 27. LSO; Ole Schmidt. Unicorn Tape (c) UKC 7130
+Gr 7-81 p196 +HFN 8-81 p92
2524 Symphony, no. 2, op. 16. Symphony, no. 5, op. 50. LSO; Ole Schmidt. Unicorn Tape (c) UKC 7250
+Gr 7-81 p196 +HFN 6-81 p87
Symphony, no. 3, op. 27. See no. 2523
2525 Symphonies, nos. 4-6. LSO; Ole Schmidt. Unicorn KPM 7004/6 (3) (From RHS 324/30)
+Gr 2-81 p1092 ++MUM 7/8-81 p33
+HFN 1-81 p107
2526 Symphony, no. 4, op. 29. Symphony, no. 6. LSO; Ole Schmidt. Unicorn Tape (c) 7460
+Gr 7-81 p196 ++HFN 8-81 p92
2527 Symphony, no. 4, op. 29. Maskarade: Overture. Cincinnati Symphony Orchestra; Max Rudolf. Westminster MCA 1419
+-FF 1/2-81 p160
Symphony, no. 5, op. 50. See no. 2524
Symphony, no. 6. See no. 2526
Theme and variations, op. 40. See no. 2522

NIEMANN
Evening in Seville, op. 55, no. 2. See no. 1003

NIEMANN, Alfred
Meditation on "Paradise regained". See no. 1980

NILES, John
Songs: Evening; For my brother reported missing in action, 1943; Love winter when the plant says nothing. See no. 3932

NILSSON, Bo
Deja connu. See no. 2024
Deja connu deja entendu. See no. 2024
Deja-vu. See no. 2024

NILSSON, Torsten
Concertino, trombone and organ. See no. 1670

NIN-CULMELL, Joaquin
Pano murciano. See no. 3703
Songs: Villancico castellano; Villancico vasco. See no. 3702

NIN Y CASTELLANOS, Joaquin
Chants d'Espagne. See no. 3686

NIXON
Fiesta del pacifico. See no. 3817

NOBRE, Marlos
Ago lona. See no. 3911

NOLA, Gian Domenico da
Chi la gagliarda. See no. 3766

NOLTE
In dir ist Freude. See no. 3806

NONO, Luigi
Como una ola de fuerza y luz. See no. 3785
Sofferte onde serene. See no. 3785

NOORDT, Anthoni van
Psalm, no. 116. See no. 3786

NORBY, Erik
Illuminations. See no. 2521

NORDENSTROM, Gladys
Zeit XXIV. See no. 1974

NORDHEIM, Arne
2528 The tempest: Suite. Susan Campbell, s; Christopher Keyte, bar; South German Radio Orchestra and Chorus; Charles Darden; Electronic realisation by Bohdan Mazurek. Philips 9598 043
++FF 7/8-81 p142 +HFN 8-80 p99
+Gr 8-80 p225
NORMIGER, August
Tantz Adelich und from. See no. 3676
Viel Freuden mit sich bringet. See no. 3676
Von Gott will ich nicht lassen. See no. 3676
NOTARI, Angelo
Songs: Intenerite voi lagrime mie. See no. 3947
NOUGES, Jean
Quo Vadis: Amica l'ora. See no. 4024
NOVA, Sayat
Songs (2). See no. 3912
NOVACEK, Ottokar
Perpetuum mobile. See no. 4007
NOVAK, Vitezslav
2529 Marysa, op. 18. South Bohemian suite, op. 64. Brno Philharmonic Orchestra; Jiri Pinkas. Supraphon 110 2486
+FF 3/4-81 p169 +NR 2-81 p3
+Gr 4-81 p1320 +STL 1-11-81 p38
+HFN 4-81 p73
Sonata, violin and piano, D minor. See no. 1529
South Bohemian suite, op. 64. See no. 2529
NOVELLO
Keep the home fires burning. See no. 3967
When it's spring in Vienna. See no. 3653
NUCKOLLS
CHACONNE. See no. 3740
NUTILE
Mamma mia che vo sapete. See no. 3996
NYSTEDT, Knut
The burnt sacrifice, op. 36. See no. 2269
Velsignet vaere han. See no. 3618
OBRADORS, Fernando
Songs: Aquel sombrero de monte; Del cabello mas sutil; El molondron; El vito. See no. 3889
Songs: Corazon porque pasais; Del cabello mas sutil; Chiquitita la novia. See no. 3838
OBRECHT, Jacob
Ic draghe de mutze clutze. See no. 3945
Vavilment. See no. 3777
OCKEGHEM, Johannes
2530 Missa cuiusvis toni. Frankfurter Madrigal Ensemble; Siegfried Heinrich. Jubilate JU 15211
+FF 11/12-81 p212
Songs: L'Autre d'antan l'auterier passa; Ma bouche rit. See no. 3948
ODDONE
Capelli d'oro. See no. 4041
OFFENBACH, Jacques
2531 Arias: Barbe-bleue: Y'a des bergers; Faut-il y aller...V'la d'encor de croi's de jeunesses. La belle Helene: C'est le

devoir des jeunes filles; Amours divins ardentes flammes; On me nomme Helene la blonde. La grande Duchesse de Gerolstein: Vous aimez le danger...Ah que j'aime les militaires; Voici le sabre de mon pere; Dites-lui qu'on l'a remarque; Il etait de mes mieux. La perichole: Ah quel diner je viens de faire; Oh mon cher amant je te jure; Que veulent dire ces coleres...Ah que les hommes sont betes; Tu n'est pas beau tu n'es pas riche. La vie parisienne: Vous souvient-il ma belle; C'est ici l'endroit redoute. Jane Rhodes, ms; Ellane Lavall Aquitaine Vocal Ensemble; Bordeau Aquitaine Orchestra; Roberto Benzi. EMI 2C 069 16386
-FF 9/10-81 p152 +-HFN 11-80 p122
+Gr 9-80 p398 -NYT 6-14-81 pD23

Barbe-bleue: Couplets de la rosiere. See no. 2546
Barbe-bleue: Overture. See no. 2542
Barbe-bleue: Y'a des bergers; Faut-il aller...V'la d'encor de droi's de jeunesses. See no. 2531

2532 La belle Helene (in German). Anneliese Rothenberger, s; Brigitte Fassbaender, con; Nicolai Gedda, Norbert Orth, t; Ferry Gruber, bar; Bavarian Radio Orchestra; Willi Mattes. Electrol 1C 157 45832/3
+-ON 2-28-81 p36 +-NYT 6-14-81 pD23

La belle Helene, excerpts. See no. 2010
La belle Helene: Amours divine. See no. 2546
La belle Helene: C'est le devoir des jeunes filles; Amours divins ardentes flammes; On me nomme Helene la blonde. See no. 2531
La belle Helene: Overture. See no. 2542

2533 Les brigands, excerpts. Daniele Perriers, Helene Vanura, s; Christophe Kotlarski, t; Robert Manuel, Jacques Leleux, Jean Kriff, bar; Jacques Duby, bar; Orchestra and Chorus; Daniel Mourruau. SPI Milan SLP 84
+-Gr 4-81 p1377 +NYT 6-14-81 pD23

Les brigands: Couplets de Fiorella. See no. 2546
La chanson de Fortunio. See no. 81
La chanson de Fortunio: Si vous croyez. See no. 2546

2534 Les contes d'Hoffmann. Ruth Welting, Ashley Putnam, s; Judith Forst, Rosalind Elias, ms; Nicolai Gedda, James Atherton, t; Jose van Dam, bar; Steven Willermann, bs; Orchestra and Chorus; Antonio de Almeida. Historical Recordings HRE 330 (3)
+FF 5/6-81 p122

Les contes d'Hoffmann: Ah vivre deux; O dieux. See no. 4049
Les contes d'Hoffmann: Barcarolle. See no. 3787. See no. 3967
Les contes d'Hoffmann: C'est une chanson d'amour. See no. 4044
Les contes d'Hoffmann: Doll's song. See no. 3649. See no. 4122
Les contes d'Hoffmann: Epilogue; Barcarolle; Entr'acte; Duet, Giulietta and Hoffmann; Intermezzo, Act 1. See no. 4121
Les contes d'Hoffmann: Ha wie in meiner Seel'. See no. 3747
Les contes d'Hoffmann: Legend von Kleinsach; Ha wie in meiner Seele. See no. 3966
Les contes d'Hoffmann: Overture. See no. 2542

2535 La course en traineaux. Deux ames au ciel, op. 25. Introduction et valse melancolique, op. 14. Reverie au bord de la mer. STRAUSS, J. II: Romances, nos. 1-3. Imke Heitmann, vlc; Heinz Geese, pno. Acanta DC 23274
+-Gr 10-81 p574 +HFN 9-81 p83

Deux ames au ciel, op. 25. See no. 2535

2536 Duos, violoncello, op. 54: Suites, nos. 1 and 2. Roland Pidoux, Etienne Peclard, vlc. Harmonia Mundi HM 1043 Tape (c) HM 40-1043
+Audio 6-81 p20
++FF 9/10-80 p176
+Gr 6-80 p44
+HF 11-80 p70
+HFN 4-81 p75
+MT 1-81 p35
++NYT 6-14-81 pD23

2537 Duos 2 violoncelli, opp. 52 and 53. Alain Meunier, Philippe Muller, vlc. Arion ARN 38564
+Gr 4-81 p1339

La fille du Tambour-Major: Chanson de la fille. See no. 2546

2538 Gaite parisienne (arr. Rosenthal). STRAUSS, J. II: Graduation ball, op. 97 (arr. Dorati). PhO; Charles Mackerras. Arabesque 8020 (also DBX dbx SS 3021)
+FF 11/12-80 p149
+FF 9/10-81 p153
+St 7-80 p82

Gaite parisienne, excerpts. See no. 1391

La grande Duchesse de Gerolstein: Ah que j'aime les militaires... Dites-lui; Legende de la verre. See no. 2546

La grande Duchesse de Gerolstein: Dites lui. See no. 3710. See no. 3713

La grande Duchesse de Gerolstein: Overture. See no. 2542

La grande Duchesse de Gerolstein: Vous aimez le danger...Ah que j'aime les militaires; Voici le sabre de mon pere; Dites-lui qu'on l'a remarque; Il etait de mes aieux. See no. 2531

Harmonies du soir. See no. 3789

Introduction et valse melancolique, op. 14. See no. 2535

La jolie parfumeuse: La famille. See no. 2546

Kakadu. See no. 2542

Madame Favart: Ronde des vignes. See no. 2546

2539 Offenbachiana (arr. Rosenthal). BRSO; Manuel Rosenthal. Varese VC 81088
+FF 1/2-81 p160
+NYT 6-14-81 pD23
+St 3-81 p92

2540 Orphee au enfers. Jane Rhodes, Mady Mesple, Michele Pena, Michele Command, s; Jane Berbie, ms; Michel Senechal, Charles Burles, Andre Mallabrera, Bruce Brewer, t; Michel Trempont, bar; Toulouse Capitole Orchestra and Chorus; Michel Plasson. Angel SZCX 3886 (3) Tape (c) 4Z3X 3886 (also HMV SLS 5175)
+-ARG 12-79 p46
+FF 1/2-80 p120
+Gr 3-80 p1437
+HFN 3-80 p95
++MT 10-80 p635
++NR 12-79 p9
+NYT 9-30-79 pD22
+ON 2-28-81 p36
+Op 6-80 p620
+RR 3-80 p41
+-SFC 11-25-79 p46
++St 12-79 p147
+STL 3-9-80 p41

2541 Orphee au enfers. Anneliese Rothenberger, Gisela Litz, Kari Lovaas, s; Adolf Dallapozza, t; Ferry Gruber, Benno Kusche, bar; Theo Lingen, bs; Cologne Opera Chorus; Philharmonia Hungarica; Willi Mattes. EMI 157 30 802/3 (2)
+-ARG 12-79 p46
+-NYT 6-14-81 pD23

Orphee au enfers, excerpts. See no. 2010

Orphee au enfers: Overture. See no. 2542

Orphee au enfers: Overture. See no. 3656. See no. 3768

2542 Overtures; Barbe-bleue. La belle Helene. Les contes d'Hoffmann.

La grande Duchesse de Gerolstein. Orfee au enfers. Kakadu. BPhO; Herbert von Karajan. DG 2532 006 Tape (c) 3302 006
/+FF 11/12-81 p213
+Gr 5-81 p1476
+Gr 7-81 p196 tape
++HFN 5-81 p81
++HFN 6-81 p87 tape
++SFC 8-16-81 p19

Pariser Leben: Pas de six. See no. 3788

La perichole: Ah quel diner je viens de faire. See no. 3710

La perichole: Ah quel diner je viens de faire; Oh mon cher amant je te jure; Que veulent dire ces coleres...Ah que les hommes ont betes; Tu n'est pas beau tu n'es pas riche. See no. 2531

La perichole: Duo de l'espagnol et al jeune indienne...Tu n'es pas beau; La lettre...Couplets de l'aveu. See no. 2546

La perichole: Je t'adore, excerpt. See no. 3653

La perichole: O mon cher amant. See no. 4026

Reverie au bord de la mer. See no. 2535

2543 Robinson Crusoe. Marilyn Hill-Smith, s; Sandra Browne, ms; John Brecknock; RPO; Alun Francis. Opera Rara OR 7 (3)
+STL 11-8-81 p40

2544 Songs: Barcarolle; Chanson de Fortunio; Ballade a la lune; Doux menestrel; Fables de la Fontaine (6); Ma belle amie est mort; La rose foulee. Bruno Laplante, bar; Marc Durand, pno. Calliope CAL 1881
+Gr 4-81 p1355
+HFN 4-81 p73
+NYT 6-14-81 pD33

2545 La vie parisienne. Danielle Chlostawa, Renee Auphan, Daniele Millet, Patrick Minard, Jacques Tayles, Jacques Trigeau, Christian Jean, Jean-Christoph Benoit, Michel Roux, Michele Pena; Concerts Colonne Orchestra; Laurent Petitgirard. Tristan Polydor 267 6904 (2)
+FF 9/10-81 p153

La vie parisienne, excerpts. See no. 1020

La vie parisienne: Cancan. See no. 3645

La vie parisienne: Je suis veuve. See no. 2546

La vie parisienne: Vous souvient-il ma belle; C'est ici l'endroit redoute. See no. 2531

2546 Works, selections: Barbe bleue: Couplets de la rosiere. La belle Helene: Amours divins. Les brigands: Couplets de Fiorella. Le chanson de Fortunio: Si voux croyez. La fille du Tambour-Major: Chanson de la fille. La grande Duchesse de Gerolstein: Ah que j'aime les militaires;...Dites-lui. La perichole: Duo de l'espagnol et la jeune indienne; ...Tu n'es pas beau. La vie parisienne: Je suis veuve. Anna Tariol-Bauge, s. La belle Helene: Amours divins. La grande Duchesse de Gerolstein: Legende de la verre;...Dites-lui. La jolie parfumeuse: La famille. La perichole: La lettre;...Couplets de l'aveu. Madame Favart: Ronde des vignes. Juliette Simon-Girard, ms. Rubini GV 600
+-ARG 11-81 p12
+Gr 2-81 p1121
+HFN 1-81 p99
+NYT 6-14-81 pD23

OFFICUM FESTI FATUORUM--Office des fous, messe de l'Ane. See no. 3797

O'HARA, Geoffrey

The perfect melody. See no. 4104

OLAN, David

Composition, clarinet and tape. See no. 1532

Octet. See no. 3933

Sonata, violin and piano. See no. 1532

OLANDER, Per August

Symphony, E major. See no. 48

OLIVIERI

Garibaldi hymn. See no. 4036

OLSEN, Poul Rovsing

Inventions, op. 38. See no. 1931

OLSEN, Sparre

Aubade, op. 57, no. 3. See no. 3683

Poem, op. 11. See no. 3683

OLSSON, Otto

Fantasy, op. 29. See no. 3992

Meditation, op. 14. See no. 2547

Prelude and fugue, op. 39, C sharp minor. See no. 2547

Romance, op. 24. See no. 3681

2547 Sinfonia, organ, no. 2, op. 50. Meditation, op. 14. Stucke, organ, op. 17: Cantilena; Pastorale. Prelude and fugue, op. 39, C sharp minor. Erik Lundkvist, org. Proprius 7825/6 (2)

+FF 1/2-81 p161

Songs: Canticum Simeonis; Jag lyfter mina ogon; Jesu dulcis memoria. See no. 3991

Stucke, organ, op. 17: Cantilena; Pastorale. See no. 2547

We praise thee great Lord. See no. 3992

ONSLOW, Georges

2548 Quintet, op. 81, no. 3, F major. Septet, op. 79, B major. Ursula Burkhard, flt; Peter Fuchs, ob; Hans Rudolf Stalder, clt; Bernard Leguillon, hn; Paul Meyer, bsn; Werner Bartschi, pno; Rudolf Frei, bs. Jecklin 554

+FF 1/2-81 p161 +Gr 1-81 p962

Septet, op. 79, B major. See no. 2543

ORD, Boris

Adam lay ybounden. See no. 3685

ORFF, Carl

2549 Carmina burana. Arleen Auger, s; Jonathan Summers, bar; John Van Kesteren, t; Southend Boys Choir, PhO and Chorus; Riccardo Muti. Angel SZ 37666 Tape (c) 4ZS 37666

+ARG 1-81 p37 ++MUM 2-81 p33

2550 Carmina burana. Janice Harsanyi, sl Rudolf Petrak, t; Harve Presnell, bar; Rutgers University Choir; PO; Eugene Ormandy. CBS MY 37217

+-FF 11/12-81 p214

2551 Carmina burana. Judith Blegen, s; Kenneth Riegel, t; Peter Binder, bar; Cleveland Orchestra Chorus and Boys Choir; CO; Michael Tilson Thomas. CBS HM 43172 (From Columbia MX 33172)

-St 9-81 p90

2552 Carmina burana. Soloists; Leipzig Radio Children's Choruses; Leipzig Radio Orchestra; Herbert Kegel. DG 2535 275

+FF 7/8-81 p32

2553 Carmina burana. Sheila Armstrong, s; Gerald English, t; Thomas Allen, bar; St. Clement Danes Grammar School Boys Choir; LSO and Chorus; Andre Previn. Mobile Fidelity MFSL 1-506 (From HVM ASD 3117)

+FF 5/6-81 p123 +NR 5-81 p12
+FF 7/8-81 p32 -St 9-81 p90
+Gr 4-81 p1355

2554 Carmina burana. Barbara Hendricks, s; John Aler, t; Hakan Hagegard, bar; St. Paul's Cathedral Boys Choir; LSO; Eduardo Mata. RCA ATC 1-3925 Tape (c) ATK 1-3925
+FF 7/8-81 p32
+Gr 9-81 p421
++HF 10-81 p91 tape
+-HFN 10-81 p90
+-MUM 7/8-81 p33
+NR 9-81 p8
+-St 9-81 p90

2555 Carmina burana. Lucia Popp, s; John Van Kesteren, Karl Kreil, t; Anton Rosner, Heinrich Weber, Hermann Prey, bar; Paul Hansen, Gunter Haussler, Josef Weber, bs; Bavarian Radio Orchestra and Chorus; Kurt Eichorn. RCA GL 2-5196 Tape (c) GK 2-5196 (also Eurodisc 86827)
+-FF 11/12-81 p214
+-Gr 11-79 p895
-HFN 10-79 p171
+-HFN 1-80 p123 tape
+-RR 10-79 p142
+-RR 3-80 p104 tape
++St 11-81 p90

2556 Carmina burana. HINDEMITH: Symphonic metamorphosis on themes by Weber. Judith Blegen, s; William Brown, t; Hakan Hagegard, bar; Atlanta Boys Choir; Atlanta Symphony Orchestra and Chorus; Robert Shaw. Telarc DG 10056/7 (2)
+FF 7/8-81 p32
+-Gr 9-81 p421
+HFN 7-81 p73
+NR 7-81 p9
+-SFC 7-12-81 p18
+St 9-81 p90

2557 Die Kluge. Lucia Popp, s; Thomas Stewart, bar; Gottlob Frick, bs; Bavarian Radio Orchestra; Kurt Eichhorn. Eurodisc 80485 (2)
+-HFN 12-81 p100

ORNSTEIN, Leo
Preludes. See no. 1675

2558 Quartet, strings, no. 3, New Boston Quartet. Serenus SRS 12089
+FF 11/12-81 p214
++HF 10-81 p84
+NR 6-81 p6
+St 8-81 p96

ORR, Charles
Songs: Along the field; The lent lily; Oh when I was in love with you. See no. 3893
Song: Along the field; Bahnhofstrasse; Farewell to barn and stack and tree; In valleys green and still; Is my team ploughing; The lads in their hundreds; When I watch the living meet; When smoke stood up from Ludlow; With rue my heart is laden; While summer on is stealing. See no. 1884

ORTIZ, Diego
Recercadas prima e segunda sobre "O felici occhi miei". See no. 4010
Recercadas segonda y tercera sobre Doulce memoire. See no. 3835

OSHITA, Gerald
Marche. See no. 2264
Textures. See no. 2264

OSTRCIL, Otakar

2559 Calvary, op. 24. The orphan's tale, op. 9. Libuse Marova, ms; CPhO; Vaclav Neumann. Supraphon 110 2548
+Gr 3-81 p1200
+HFN 4-81 p75
+NR 7-81 p11

The orphan's tale, op. 9. See no. 2559
Suite, op. 14, C minor. See no. 2092

OSWALD VON WOLKENSTEIN
Songs: Ain graserin; Du auserwahltes; Freu dich du; Wer die augen; Wohl auf gesell. See no. 3896
OTHEGRAVEN, August von
Vom Himmel hoch ihr Engel kommt. See no. 3963
OTTO, Luigi
Concerto, trumpet, E flat major. See no. 29
OUSELEY, Frederick
Songs: It came even to pass; When all thy mercies o my God. See no. 3616
OYENS, Tera de Marez
Safed. See no. 3728
PACHELBEL, Johann
Alle Menschen mussen sterben. See no. 3622. See no. 4012
Aria con variazioni, A major. See no. 3783
Aria sebaldina variations, F minor. See no. 2560
Canon. See no. 170
Canon, D major. See no. 4066
Canon and gigue, D major. See no. 1612. See no. 3783. See no. 3980
Chaconne, C major. See no. 4084
Chaconne, F minor. See no. 249. See no. 2560
Chorale preludes: Da Jesus an dem Kreuze stund; Christus der ist mein Leben; Vom Himmel hoch; Wir glauben all an einen Gott; Wie schon leuchtet der Morgenstern; Vater unser im Himmelreich; O Lamm Gottes unschuldig. See no. 2560
Du haut du ciel je decends, chant de Noel. See no. 3901
Fantasie, G major. See no. 1347. See no. 3720
Magnificat: Fugues, nos. 4, 5, 10, 13. See no. 3622
Magnificat: Fugues, nos. 4-5, 10, 13. See no. 4012

2560 Organ works: Aria sebaldina variations, F minor. Chaconne, F minor. Chorale preludes: Da Jesus an dem Kreuze stund; Christus der ist mein Leben; Vom Himmel hoch; Wir glauben all an einen Gott; Wie schon leuchtet der Morgernstern; Vater unser im Himmelreich; O Lamm Gottes unschuldig. Ricercar. Toccata, E minor. Bernard Lagace, org. Arion ARN 38273 (also Musical Heritage Society MHS 4353)
/-FF 11/12-81 p216 +RR 11-75 p82

Partita, no. 2, C minor. See no. 3867
Ricercar, C minor. See no. 2560
Songs: Nun danket alle Gott. See no. 3633
Suites, G major, E minor. See no. 3783
Toccata, E minor. See no. 2560
Toccata, G minor. See no. 3720
Toccata and fugue, B flat major. See no. 3622. See no. 4012
Vom Himmel hoch. See no. 3673. See no. 3786. See no. 3901
Vom Himmel kam der Engel Schar. See no. 3961
PACIUS, Frederik

2561 Konig Karl: Ahvenanmaalaisen laulu; Balladi. Prinzessin von Zypern: Jauhajan laulu; Kylikin kosijat; Laps Suomen. Songs: Autio; Kevatlaulu; Meriminen morsian; Oi ma naan sun tanti kaunokainen; Oi onnen sain; Paaskyset; Seitsentoistavuotias; Sotilespoika; Tuutulaulu. Jorma Hynninen, Margareta Haverinen, Viking Smeds, vocals; Pentti Koskimies, pno. Finlandia FA 902
+FF 9/10-81 p154

Prinzessin von Zypern : Jauhajan laulu; Kylikin kosijat; Laps Suomen. See no. 2561
Songs: Autio; Kevatlaulu; Meriminen morsian; Oi ma naan sun tanti kaunokainen; Oi onnen sain; Paaskyset; Seitsentoistavuotias; Sotilespoika; Tuutulaulu. See no. 2561
PADEREWSKI, Jan
Manru: Come al sol cocentre. See no. 4027
Un moment musical, op. 16, no. 6. See no. 3920
PADILLA, Jose
Songs: Princesita. See no. 4054
Songs: Princesita; Valencia. See no. 3983
PAER, Ferdinando
Beatus vir. See no. 3790
PAGANINI, Niccolo
Cantabile, op. 17, D major. See no. 1130. See no. 3704
2562 Caprices, op. 1, nos. 1-24. Concerto, violin, no. 1, op. 6, D major. Michael Rabin, vln; PhO; Lovro von Matacic. Electrola C 147 81323/4 (2)
+FF 7/8-81 p143
2563 Caprices, op. 1, nos. 1-24. Caprice, no. 25. Duo, solo violin. Ruggiero Ricci, vln. Ultra Fi ULDD 11 (2)
+-Gr 2-81 p1104 ++MUM 1/2-80 p35
+-HFN 1-81 p99
Caprices, op. 1, nos. 1-3, 5, 9, 11, 17, 20, 24. See no. 1130
Caprice, op. 1, no. 14, E flat major. See no. 3693
Caprice, op. 1, no. 24, A minor. See no. 3682
Caprice, no. 25. See no. 2563
Concerto, violin, no. 1, op. 6, D major. See no. 2562
Concerto, violin, no. 2, op. 7, B minor: La campanella. See no. 1130
Concerto, violin, no. 2, op. 7, B minor: La clochette. See no. 3847
2564 Concerto, violin, no. 6, op. posth., E minor. Salvatore Accardo, vln; LPO; Charles Dutoit. DG 2535 421 Tape (c) 3335 421 (From 2530 467)
+Gr 3-81 p1202 ++HFN 3-81 p95
+HFN 11-80 p131 tape ++ST 2-81 p734
Duo, solo violin. See no. 2563
Moses fantasy, op. 24. See no. 1130
Moto perpetuo, op. 11. See no. 1130
Romanza e andantino variato. See no. 3886
Sonata, violin and guitar, op. 3, nos. 1, 6. See no. 1208
Variations on a theme from Rossini's "Moses in Egypt". See no. 1381
PAINE, John Knowles
Variations on the Austrian hymn. See no. 3674
PAISIELLO, Giovanni
Accensa clare face fidelis. See no. 3790
2565 Il maestro ed i sui due scolari. SUSSMAYR: Das Namensfest. Margit Laszlo, s; Zsuzsa Barlay, ms; Jozsef Dene, bar; Hungarian Radio and Television Children's Chorus and Orchestra; Budapest Madrigal Choir; Hungarian State Orchestra; Laszlo Csanyi, Ferenc Szekeres. Serenus SRS 12088 (also Budapest FX 12294)
+-ARG 10-81 p38 +-HFN 6-81 p88
++FF 11/12-81 p216 +NR 5-81 p12
+Gr 8-81 p303 +St 7-81 p87

Songs: Nel cor piu non mi sento. See no. 3756

PAIX, Jacob

Der Keyserin Tantz. See no. 3676

PALADILHE, Emile

Psyche. See no. 3653

PALARDI

Santa Lucia. See no. 3641

PALERO, Francisco

Paseasbase el rey moro. See no. 3778

Pues no me querreis hablar. See no. 3778

PALESTRINA, Giovanni

2566 Adoramus te Christ; Canticum canticorum; Quinque salutationes in passione domini; Stabat mater dolorosa; Vexilla regis prodeunt. Societa Cameristic di Lugano; Edwin Loehrer. Accord ACC 140031
+HFN 12-81 p100

Compline. See no. 2090

Domine quando veneris, motet. See no. 2090

Gloria. See no. 4061

Haec dies. See no. 3619

Missa Benedicta es. See no. 1939

2567 Missa Hodie Christus natus est. Motets: Ave Maria; Canite tuba; Hodie Christus natus est; Jubilate Deo; O magnum mysterium; Tui sunt caeli. King's College Choir; Philip Ledger. HMV ASD 3559 Tape (c) TC ASD 3559 (also Angel S 37514)
+Gr 12-81 p945 tape
+Gr 10-78 p721
++FF 9/10-79 p119
+HFN 9-78 p145
+HFN 11-78 p187 tape
+NR 5-79 p8
+RR 10-78 p106
+RR 1-79 p92 tape
+St 5-79 p104

2568 Missa Papae Marcelli. Motets: Alma redemptoris mater; Dominus Jesus in qua nocte; Peccantem me quotidie. Stabat mater. Pro Cantione Antiqua; Bruno Turner. ASV ACM 2009 (From Enigma K 5 3560)
+-Gr 6-81 p70
+HFN 5-81 p83

Missa Papae Marcelli. See no. 54

Ricercar primo tono. See no. 4071. See no. 4088

2569 Songs (choral works): Hodie beata virgo. Litaniae de beata Vergine Maria a 8 vocum. Magnificat a 8 voci (primi toni). Senex puerum portabat. Stabat mater. King's College Choir; David Willcocks. Argo ZK 4 Tape (c) KZKS 4 (From ZRG 5398)
+-Gr 12-76 p1034
+Gr 12-81 p945 tape
+HFN 1-77 p121
+-HFN 4-77 p155 tape
+RR 1-77 p82

2570 Songs (choral works): Exultate Deo; Hymnus in adventu Dei; Jesu rex admirabilis; Magnificat VI toni; Tua Jesu dilectio; Veni sponsa Christi, antiphon; Veni sponsa Christi, motet; Veni sponsa Christi, mass. St. John's College Choir; George Guest. Argo ZK 69 (From ZRG 578)
+-Gr 7-81 p185
+HFN 7-81 p81
++STL 6-14-81 p40

Songs (motets): Alma redemptoris mater. See no. 3634

Songs (motets): Alma redemptoris mater; Dominus Jesus in quo nocte; Peccantem me quotidie. See no. 2568

Songs (motets: Ave Maria; Canite tuba; Hodie Christus natus est; Jubilate Deo; O magnum mysterium; Tui sunt caeli. See no. 2567

Songs (motets): Hodie Christus natus est. See no. 3775
Songs: Matribus suis. See no. 3909
Songs (motets): Sicut cervus. See no. 3906
Stabat mater. See no. 2568

PALIASHVILI, Zachary

2571 Absalom and Etery. Lamara Chkoniya, Zisana Tatishvili, s; Liana Tatishvili, Olga Kuszenova, ms; Surab Sotkilava, Abrek Pirzchalava, Aedischer Gelashvili, t; Shota Kiknadze, bar; Irakli Shushaniya, Nikolay Kapanadze, bs; USSR Radio Orchestra and Chorus; Didim Mirzchulava. DG 2709 094 (3) (also Melodiya 33CM 02831-36)

+ARG 6-80 p28
+FF 5/6-80 p127
+FF 7/8-80 p120
+Gr 11-79 p908
+HFN 11-79 p143
+NR 2-80 p10
+NYT 12-16-79 pD21
+-ON 3-14-81 p44
+RR 12-79 p41
+-SFC 1-6-80 p43
+St 4-80 p137

PALMGREN, Selim

Songs: Jaguaren; En latmansmelodi; Hilden orjien laulu. See no. 3805

PANIAGUA, Gregorio

La begognette. See no. 3828
La Edoarda. See no. 3828
Fermata. See no. 3828

PANUFNIK, Andrzej

2572 Autumn music. Heroic overture. Nocturne. Tragic overture. LSO; Jascha Horenstein. Unicorn RHS 306

+FF 11/12-80 p152
++NR 8-75 p5
+RR 3-80 p57
+SFC 2-8-81 p21

Dreamscape. See no. 1345
Heroic overture. See no. 2572
Nocturne. See no. 2572
Tragic overture. See no. 2572

PAPELYAN, Stepan

La fin d'un reve. See no. 3912

PAPINEAU-COUTURE, Jean

Concerto grosso. See no. 2573

2573 Le debat du coeur et du corps de Villon. Concerto grosso. Mouvement perpetuel. Prelude. Psaume CL. Quatrains. Various performers. RCA ACM 4 (6)

+MUM 1/2-81 p33

Mouvement perpetuel. See no. 2573
Prelude. See no. 2573
Psalm CL. See no. 2573
Quatrains. See no. 2573

PARADIES, Pietro Domenico

Sonata, harpsichord, no. 6, A major. See no. 3733. See no. 4103

PARADIS, Maria Theresia von

Sicilienne. See no. 3814. See no. 3841

PARCHAM, Andrew

Solo, G major. See no. 1099

PARISH-ALVARS, Elias

2574 Concerto, harp, op. 81 G minor (rev. Zabaleta). RODRIGO: Concierto de Aranjuez (arr. for harp). Nicanor Zabaleta, hp; Spanish National Orchestra; Rafael Fruhbeck de Burgos. HMV ASD

3034 (also Angel S 37042)
+Gr 10-74 p703 +RR 10-74 p56
++NYT 9-27-81 pD24

PARMEGIANI, Bernard
2575 De natura sonorum. INA/Collection GRM AM 714.01
+CMJ Summer 1981 p68

PARRY, Charles Hubert
Fantasia on the old 104th. See no. 4112
Jerusalem, op. 208. See no. 3721. See no. 3852
Songs: Dear Lord and father of mankind. See no. 3618
Songs: I was glad when they said unto me. See no. 3873. See no. 4116
Songs: Love is a bable. See no. 3654
Songs: O never say that I was false of heart; A sea dirge, op. 21, no. 5; Willow willow willow. See no. 3878
Songs: O praise the Lord. See no. 4107
Songs of farewell: My soul there is a country. See no. 3824
When I survey the wondrous cross, chorale fantasia. See no. 4120

PARRY, John
Calening. See no. 2576
Dafudd gareg wen with variations. See no. 2576
Gavotta in the 10th solo of Corelli. See no. 2576
2576 Harp works: Calening. Dafudd gareg wen with variations. Gavotta in the 10th solo of Corelli. Of noble race was Shenkin. Torried y dydd. Sonatas, harp, nos. 1-4. Sioned Williams, hp. Meridian E 45002
+Gr 12-81 p904 +HFN 10-81 p90
Of noble race was Shenkin. See no. 2576
Sonatas, harp, nos. 1-4. See no. 2576
Torried y dydd. See no. 2576

PARSCH, Arnost
2577 The bird flew above the clouds. REZAC: Sinfonietta. Jiri Kaniak, ob; PSO, Brno Philharmonic Orchestra; Jindrich Rohan, Jiri Belohlavek. Supraphon 110 2339
+FF 1/2-81 p174 ++NR 8-80 p3
+HFN 2-81 p91

PARSONS, Robert
Ave Maria. See no. 3685

PARVIAINEN, Jarmo
Toccata and fugue. See no. 3804

PASADAS
Noche feliz. See no. 4036

PASCULLI, Antonio
Concerto on themes from Donizetti's "La favorita". See no. 4007

PASQUINI, Bernardo
Canzone francese, no. 7. See no. 3622. See no. 4012
Ricercare, no. 4. See no. 3622. See no. 4012

PASSEREAU, Pierre
El est bel et bon. See no. 3677

PATACHICH, Ivan
Metamorphoses. See no. 3865

PATAVINO, Francesco
Vrai dieu d'amour. See no. 3661

PATERSON, Wilma
Casida del llanto. See no. 4062

PAULLI, Holger
The Kermesse in Bruges: Slovanka; Pas de deux. See no. 1836
PEEBLES
Si quis diligit me. See no. 4101
PEEL, Graham
Songs: In summertime on Bredon; Reveille; When the lad for longing sighs. See no. 3893
PEERSON, Martin
The fall of the leaf. See no. 3676
The primrose. See no. 3676
PEETERS, Flor
Aria. See no. 3673. See no. 4100
Konzertstuck, op. 52a. See no. 1565
Passacaglia and fugue, op. 42. See no. 1936
Variations on an original theme, op. 58. See no. 4116
PEHKONEN, Elis
A boy is born. See no. 3818
PELLIGRINI, Anthony
Songs: Salve regina. See no. 3634
PELLEGRINI, Vincenzo
La serpentina. See no. 4094
PELLMAN, Samuel
Horizon. See no. 1383
Silent night. See no. 3915
PENDERECKI, Krzystztof
Anaklasis. See no. 369
Awakening of Jacob. See no. 369
Miniatures, violin and piano. See no. 4072
Quartet, strings, no. 1. See no. 2089
PENN, William
Fantasy, solo harpsichord. See no. 4068
PENNINO
Pecche. See no. 4075
PENNYCOOK, Bruce
If carillons grew wings. See no. 873
PEPIN, Clermont
2578 Cycle-Eluard. Guernica. Quartet, strings, no. 1. Suite, piano. Parlow Qaurtet; Pierrette Alarie, singer; John Newmark, pno; Toronto Symphony Orchestra; Jean Deslauriers. RCA ACM 5 (4)
+MUM 1/2-81 p33
Guernica. See no. 2578
Quartet, strings, no. 1. See no. 2578
Suite, piano. See no. 2578
PEPPING, Ernst
Songs: Ich steh an deiner Krippe hier. See no. 3809
PEPUSCH, John
Corydon cantata. See no. 3949
Sonata, recorder, D minor. See no. 3927
Sonata, recorder, no. 4, F major. See no. 1099
PERERA, Ronald
Poems of Gunter Grass. See no. 25
PERGOLESI, Giovanni
Concerto, flute, no. 1, G major. See no. 3980
Songs: Se tu m'ami. See no. 3756
Songs: Tre giorni son che nina. See no. 3836

2579 Stabat mater. WASSENAER: Concerto armonico, no. 2, G major (attrib. Ricciotti). Felicity Palmer, s; Alfreda Hodgson, con; David Hill, org; St. John's College Choir; Argo Chamber Orchestra; George Guest. Argo ZRG 913 Tape (c) KZRC 913
-FF 5/6-81 p124 +Gr 2-81 p1122 tape
/-Gr 11-80 p724 +HFN 11-80 p107

2580 Stabat mater. Ileana Cotrubas, s; Lucia Valentini Terrani, con; I Solisti Veneti; Claudio Scimone. Erato STU 71179 Tape (c) MCE 71197
+-HFN 1-81 p99

PERKIN, Helen
Carnival suite: Burlesque. See no. 3717

PERLE, George
Quintet, woodwinds, no. 3. See no. 3815

PEROTINUS LE GRAND
Viderunt omnes. See no. 3779

PERSICHETTI, Vincent
Chorale prelude. See no. 40
Concerto, English horn, op. 137. See no. 1851
Concerto, piano, 4 hands. See no. 1979
Concerti, violin, F major, B flat major. See no. 3572

2581 Harmonium, op. 50. Quintet, piano, op. 66. Vincent Persichetti, pno; Darleen Kliewer, s; Lois McLeod, Vincent Persichetti, pno; New Art String Quartet. Arizona State University JMP 102679 (2)
/ARG 7/8-81 p27 +FF 11/12-81 p217

Parable, no. 9. See no. 2087
Parable, no. 11. See no. 3819
Parable, no. 16, op. 130. See no. 90
Quintet, piano, op. 66. See no. 2581
Sonata, organ, op. 86. See no. 40
Symphony, band. See no. 3817

PERSICO
E pallume. See no. 3641

PESENTI, Martino
Che faralla. See no. 3661

PESTALOZZA
Ciribiribin. See no. 4083

PETERSEN, Wilhelm

2582 Quartets, strings, nos. 1-3. Gunter Kehr Quartet. Da Camera SM 92419/20 (2)
/FF 11/12-81 p218

PETERSMA, Wim
Quartet, saxophone. See no. 3729

PETERSON-BERGER, Olof Wilhelm
A walk in the mountains, op. 6. See no. 2583

2583 Songs, op. 11 (8). A walk in the mountains, op. 6. Malmo Kammarkor; Lunds Studentsangare; Dan-Olof Stenlund. BIS LP 139
+ARG 3-81 p39 ++FF 11/12-80 p153

2584 Symphony, no. 2. Swedish Radio Orchestra; Stig Westerberg. Swedish EMI C 061 35455
+FF 7/8-78 p63 +Gr 7-81 p158

PETRASSI, Goffredo
Nonsense songs of Edward Lear. See no. 4114

PETROVICS, Emil
Movement in ragtime. See no. 1384

Nocturne. See no. 1384

PETRUS, Frater

Ave Maria virgo serena. See no. 4011

PETTERSSON, Gustaf Allan

2585 Concerto, violin, no. 2. Ida Haendel, vln; Swedish Radio Orchestra; Herbert Blomstedt. Caprice CAP 1200
+-FF 5/6-81 p125 +Gr 4-81 p1320

PEUERL, Paul

Canzon, no. 1. See no. 3898

PEZEL, Johann

Compositions for brass instruments. See no. 1557

Sonata, no. 22: Suite. See no. 4002

PFEYLL, Baltsaro

Sonata, G major. See no. 4115

PFITZNER, Hans

2586 Der arme Heinrich: Dietrich's Erzahlung. Songs: An den Mond, op. 18; An die Mark, op. 15, no. 3; Herr Oluf, op. 12; Lethe, op. 37; Sie haben heut abend Gesellschaft, op. 4, no. 2; Zorn, op. 15, no. 2. Dietrich Fischer-Dieskau, bar; Bavarian Radio Orchestra; Wolfgang Sawallisch. EMI 1C 065 45616
+-FF 1/2-81 p163 +RR 7-80 p93
+-Gr 5-80 p1706

2587 Concerto, violin,op. 34, B minor. Susanne Lautenbacher, vln; PH; Gunther Wich. Intercord 120 918
/FF 3/4-81 p176 +-HFN 12-81 p101

Das Katchen von Heilbronn overture. See no. 2529

Palestrina: Preludes. See no. 677

2588 Songs: Abbitte, op. 28, no. 1; An den Mond, op. 18; An die Mark, op. 15, no. 3; Gewalt der Minne, op. 24, no. 2; Hussens Kerker, op. 32, no. 1; Ich aber weiss, op. 11, no. 2; In Danzig, op. 22, no. 1; Lass scharren einer Rosse Huf, op. 32, no. 4; Michaelskirchplatz, op. 19, no. 2; Saerspruch, op. 32, no. 2; Sehnsucht, op. 10, no. 1; Willkommen und Abschied, op. 29, no. 3; Zorn, op. 15, no. 1. Robert Holl, bs-bar; Konrad Richter, pno. Preiser SPR 3294
+-ARG 3-81 p41

Songs: An den Mond, op. 18, An die Mark, op. 15, no. 3; Herr Oluf, op. 12; Lethe, op. 37; Sie haben heut abend Gesellschaft, op. 4, no. 2; Zorn, op. 15, no. 2. See no. 2586

Songs: Mailied; Trauerstille. See no. 3547

2589 Symphony, no. 1, C sharp minor. Das Katchen von Heilbronn overture. German Opera House Orchestra, VPO; Hans Schmidt-Isserstedt, Hans Pfitzner. Varese VC 81094 (Reissues)
+ARG 3-81 p42 +-FF 1/2-81 p164

Symphony, op. 46, C major. See no. 3791

PHILIDOR, Andre

2590 Le sorcier. Peggy Bouveret, Judith Monk, Chantal Reyjal, s; Jean-Claude Orliac, Bernard Boudier, t; Udo Reinemann, bar; Rennes Orchestra; Marc Soustrot. Arion ARN 238027 (2)
+-Gr 6-81 p82

PHILIPP

Feux follets, op. 24, no. 3. See no. 3920

PHILIPPE DE CHANCELIER

Mundus a munditia. See no. 4009

PHILIPS, Peter
Ascendit Deus. See no. 3636. See no. 3685
Cromatica pavana. See no. 3883
Galliard and chromatic pavan. See no. 4016
Songs: Ecce tu pulchra es; O beatum et sacrosanctum diem. See no. 3620
PHILLIPS
Nightfall at sea. See no. 4033
PHILLIPS, Burrill
Sonatas, piano, nos. 1 and 2. See no. 41
PIAZZA, Gaetano
Sonata, F major. See no. 4115
PICCHI, Giovanni
Canzoni, nos. 3, 12. See no. 1103
Toccata. See no. 1103. See no. 3832
PICCININI, Alessandro
Corrente, nos. 5-6, 10. See no. 1944
Gagliarda, no. 3. See no. 1944
Intavolatura di liuto e di chitarrone, 1623: Toccata, no. 6. See no. 4067
Partite variate sopra la folia aria romanesca. See no. 1944
Passacaglia. See no. 1944
Ricercar, no. 1. See no. 1944
Toccata. See no. 3937
Toccatas, nos. 2, 8, 11-13. See no. 1944
PICCININI, Nicolo
O notte a dea del mistero. See no. 3718
PICHL
Concertino con pastorella, F major. See no. 4078
PICKER, Tobias
2591 Rhapsody. Romance. Sextet, no. 3. When soft voices die. Speculum Musicae Members. CRI SD 427
++ARG 2-81 p25
+FF 1/2-81 p164
+NR 10-80 p6
+NYT 6-7-81 pD23
+St 2-81 p110
Romance. See no. 2591
Sextet, no. 3. See no. 2591
When soft voices die. See no. 2591
PIERNE, Gabriel
2592 Cantilene. Prelude. Scherzando. VIERNE: Symphony, no. 4, op. 32, G minor. John Rose, org. Towerhille T 1003
+ARG 1-81 p51
+Audio 6-80 p113
+FF 9/10-80 p266
++MU 3-81 p10
Canzonetta. See no. 3738
2593 Les cathedrales: Prelude. Images, op. 49. Paysages Franciscains, op. 43. Orchestre Philharmonique des Pays de Loire; Pierre Dervaus. Pathe Marconi C 069 16302
+ARG 9-80 p45
++FF 5/6-81 p126
+Gr 1-81 p952
+HFN 4-81 p75
2594 Cydalise et le chevre-pied: Suites, nos. 1 and 2. Ramuntcho, overture on Basque themes. Paris Opera Orchestra; Jean-Baptiste Mari. Pathe Marconi 2C 069 14140
++Gr 2-81 p1202
Images, op. 49. See no. 2593
Paysages Franciscains, op. 43. See no. 2593

Prelude, G minor. See no. 2592
Ramuntcho, overture on Basque themes. See no. 2594
Scherzando. See no. 251. See no. 2592
Sophie Arnould: J'ai six moutons; Dorval jeune ingenu. See no. 4044

PIERS, Edward
Hey trola trola. See no. 4093

PILKINGTON, Francis
Songs: Care for thy soul; Diapheia; Down-a-down. See no. 4085
Songs: My choice is made. See no. 3871

PILSS, Karl
Adagio. See no. 4100

PINKHAM, Daniel
Songs: Henry was a worthy king; The leaf; Piping Anne and husky Paul; Agnus Dei. See no. 3951
Songs: The kings and shepherds. See no. 3809
The other voices of the trumpet. See no. 3740

PINTO, Octavio
Scenas infantis. See no. 4018

PISTON, Walter
Symphony, no. 6. See no. 2171

PIXIS, Johann
Variations on a theme from Seyfried's "Niklas am Scheidewege", op. 19. See no. 3669

PIZZETTI, Ildebrando
Concerto, violoncello, C major. See no. 1841

PLANQUETTE, Robert

2595 Les cloches de Corneville. Mady Mesple, Christiane Stutzmann, Annie Tallard, Arta Verlen, s; Charles Burles, Jean Giraudeau, Jean Bussard, t; Bernard Sinclair, Jean-Christoph Benoit, bar; Charles Roeder, bs; Paris Opera Chorus; Opera-Comique Orchestra; Jean Doussard. Connoisseur Society CS 2-2107 (also EMI 2C 163 12275/6)

+ARG 11-76 p35
++Gr 4-81 p1377
+-HF 9-76 p95
*MJ 12-76 p28
+-ON 1-29-77 p44
+SFC 10-24-76 p35
+-St 11-76 p152

PLATTI, Giovanni
Concerto, flute, G major. See no. 4008
Concerto, oboe, G major. See no. 2148
THE PLAY OF DANIEL. See no. 3659. See no. 3892. See no. 3940

PLAYFORD, John

2596 The English dancing master: Hyde Park; Jenny pluck pears; Bobbing Joe; Mayden Lane; Halfe Hannikin; Rufty tuffty; The fine companion; Hearts ease; Confesse; The maid peept out at the window; An old man is a bed full of bones; Boate man; Petticoat wag; Grimstock; Stingo; Jack pudding; Kettle drum; Lulle me beyond thee; Dissembling love; The beggar boy; The glory of the west; Parsons farewell. John Wright, vln; Jew's harp, vocal; Denis Gasser, hpd; Janine Rubinlicht, vln; Yvonne Guicher, rec, tin whistle, 3-holed flute, bodhran; Dominique Paris, Northumbrian pipes. Le Chant du Monde LDX 74690

+Gr 1-81 p962
+HFN 8-80 p101
+RR 8-80 p65

PLEYEL, Ignaz
Rondeau, C major. See no. 4096
2597 Serenade, no. 1, F major. Sextet, 2 clarinets, 2 horns, 2 bassoons, E flat major. Strasbourg Philharmonic Wind Octet. Musical Heritage Society MHS 4269
+FF 5/6-81 p127
Sextet, 2 clarinets, 2 horns, 2 bassoons, E flat major. See no. 2597
Symphony concertante, op. 57, A major. See no. 3794
Variations, G major. See no 4096
PLOG, Anthony
Sierra scenes. See no. 1271
PLUMSTEAD, Mary
Songs: Close thine eyes; A grateful heart. See no. 3852
Songs: Sigh no more ladies; Take o take those lips away. See no. 3878
POISSL, Johann Nepomuk von
Lieder to tests by Prince Ludwig of Bavaria. See no. 3907
POLDOWSKI, Irene
Impression Fausse. See no. 3814
POLLOCK, Robert
Voilament. See no. 90
PONCE, Manuel
Scherzino mexicano. See no. 3765
Songs: Estrellita. See no. 3983
Variations and fugue on "Las folias de Espana". See no. 785. See no. 3929
PONCHIELLI, Amilcare
2598 Capriccio. Elegie funebre. Gavotte poudree. Paolo and Virginia. Prelude "A Gaetano Donizetti". Quartet, flute, oboe, piccolo and clarinet. Syrinx Ensemble. Accord ACC 140024
+Gr 5-81 p1488
Elegie funebre. See no. 2598
Il figliuol prodigo: Opening prayer; Amenofi's aria; Azaele's aria. See no. 2602
Gavotte poudree. See no. 2598
2599 La gioconda. Montserrat Caballe, s; Agnes Baltsa, ms; Alfreda Hodgson, con; Luciano Pavarotti, t; Sherrill Milnes, bar; Nicolai Ghiaurov, bs; London Opera Chorus; Finchley Children's Music Group; National Philharmonic Orchestra; Bruno Bartoletti. Decca D232D3 (3) Tape (c) K232K3 (also London LDR 73005)
+Gr 12-81 p930 ++SFC 11-15-81 p18
++HFN 12-81 p101
2600 La gioconda. Montserrat Caballe, s; Patricia Payne, alto; Maria Luisa Nave, ms; Jose Carreras, t; Matteo Manuguerra, bar; Bonaldo Giaiotti, bs; Geneva Grand Theatre Orchestra and Chorus; Jesus Lopez-Cobos. Legendary Recordings LR 116 (3)
+FF 11/12-81 p218
2601 La gioconda. Elena Suliotis, s; Oralia Dominguez, alto; Rosalind Elias, ms; Richard Tucker, t; Cornell MacNeil, bar; Paolo Washington, bs; Teatro Colon Buenos Aires; Bruno Bartoletti. Teatro Dischi TD 505 (3)
+FF 11/12-81 p218
La gioconda: Badoer questa notte...O grido. See no. 3657
La gioconda: Cielo e mar. See no. 3750. See no. 3754. See no.

3759. See no. 3944. See no. 3982. See no. 3987. See no. 3996. See no. 4027. See no. 4035. See no. 4037. See no. 4075
La gioconda: Cielo e mar; Deh non tremar. See no. 3839
La gioconda: Enzo Grimaldo. See no. 3965. See no. 4045
La gioconda: O grido di quest anima. See no. 3967
La gioconda: Suicidio. See no. 2602. See no. 3623. See no. 4076
La gioconda: Trio, Act 4; Deh non turbare, Duet, Act 2. See no. 3890
2602 I Lituani. Il figliuol prodigo: Opening prayer, Amenofi's aria; Azaele's aria. La gioconda: Suicidio, Act 4. I promessi sposi: Lucia's prayer. Yasuko Hayashi, Susanna Ghione, Magda Oliviera, s; Margarete Matzenauer, ms; Ottavio Garaventa, t; Alessandro Cassis, bar; Carlo de Bortoli, Ambrogio Riva, bs; RAI Orchestra and Chorus, Turin; Gianandrea Gavazzeni; Various unidentified orchestras and conductors (excerpts). MRF Records MRF 168 (3)
++FF 5/6-81 p128
I promessi sposi: Lucia's prayer. See no. 2602
Paolo and Virginia. See no. 2598
Prelude "A Gaetano Donizetti". See no. 2598
Quartet, flute, oboe, piccolo and clarinet. See no. 2598
Songs: Il trovatore. See no. 3758
POPP, Wilhelm
Scherzo fantastique, op. 423. See no. 4065
POPPER, David
Elfentaz, op. 39. See no. 3667
Mazurka, op. 11, no. 3, G major. See no. 3686
POPULAR TUNES IN 17TH CENTURY ENGLAND. See no. 3829
PORPORA, Nicola
Or che una nube ingrata. See no. 1091
PORTER, Cole
Miss Otis regrets. See no. 4114
PORTUGAL
Adeste fidelis. See no. 3967
POSTON, Elizabeth
Jesus Christ the apple tree. See no. 3618
POULENC, Francis
Aubade. See no. 1872
2603 Les biches: Suite. Bucolique for "Variations sur le nom de Marguerite Long". Matelote provencale for "La guirlande de Campra". Pastourelle for "L'Eventail de Jeanne". Ambrosian Singers; PhO; Georges Pretre. HMV ASD 4067 Tape (c) TCC ASD 4067
+Gr 9-81 p388 +HFN 9-81 p84
Les biches: Suite. See no. 1876
Bucolique for "Variations sur le nom de Marguerite Long". See no. 2603
Concerto, flute. See no. 1118
Elegie, horn and piano. See no. 2606
Elegie in memory of Dennis Brain. See no. 3986
Matelote provencale for "La guirlande de Campra". See no. 2603
Mouvements perpetuels. See no. 4007
Pastourelle for "L'Eventail de Jeanne". See no. 2603
Petites prieres de Saint-Francois d'Assise (4). See no. 3691
Sextet, piano and winds. See no. 1915
Sonata, clarinet and bassoon. See no. 1846. See no. 2606
Sonata, clarinet and piano. See no. 1846. See no. 2606

Sonata, 2 clarinets. See no. 2606
Sonata, flute. See no. 1915
Sonata, flute and piano. See no. 2606. See no. 3668. See no. 3914. See no. 3928
Sonata, horn, trumpet and trombone. See no. 2606. See no. 3671. See no. 3741
Sonata, oboe and piano. See no. 2606
Sonata, violin and piano. See no. 2606
Sonata, violoncello and piano. See no. 2099. See no. 2606

2604 Songs: A sa guitare; Airs chantes; Banalites; Bestiare; Bleuet; Ce doux petit visage; Calligrammes; Chansons (3); Chanson de porcelaine (Une); Chansons gaillardes; Chanson polonaises (8); Chansons pour enfants (4); Chansons villageoises; Cocardes; Colloque; Courte paille (La); Derniere poeme; Disparu (13); Epitaphe; Fancy; Fraicheur et le fue (La); Fiancailles pour rire; Grenouillere (La); Hyde Park; Hymne; Main dominee par le coeur; Mais mourir; Mazurka; Melodies (Apollinaire) (2); Melodies (Apollinaire; De Beylie) (2); Metamorphoses; Miroirs brulants; Montparnasse; Parisiana; Paul et Virginie; Poemes (Apollinaire) (2); Poemes (Aragon) (2); Poemes (De Vilmorin)(3); Poemes (Eluard) (5); Poemes (Jacob) (5); Poemes de Louis Lelanne (3); Poemes de Ronsard (5); Portrait; Priez pour paix; Rosemonde; Tel jour telle nuit; Toreador; Travail du peintre (Le). Elly Ameling, s; Nicolai Gedda, Michel Senechal, t; Gerard Souzay, William Parker, bar; Dalton Baldwin, pno. EMI France 2C 165 16231/5 (5)
++HF 5-81 p51 +STL 6-8-80 p38

Songs: Chanson Bretonne; Hier; La petite servante; Poemes de Ronsard. See no. 3687
Songs: Les chemins de l'amour. See no. 3703
Songs: Un soir de neige. See no. 4005

2605 Trio, oboe, bassoon and piano. SAINT-SAENS: Sonata, bassoon and piano, op. 168. SCHUMANN: Romances, op. 94 (3). TANSMAN: Sonatine, bassoon and piano. Ray Still, ob; Milan Turkovic, bsn; John Perry, pno. Telefunken 6-42081
+FF 5/6-80 p194 ++SFC 1-11-81 p17

2606 Works, selections: Elegie, horn and piano. Sonata, clarinet and piano. Sonata, clarinet and bassoon. Sonata, 2 clarinets. Sonata, flute and piano. Sonata, horn, trumpet and trombone. Sonata, oboe and piano. Sonata, violin and piano. Sonata, violoncello and piano. Michel Portal, Maurice Gabai, clt; Jacques Fevrier, pno; Alan Civil, hn; John Wilbraham, tpt; John Iveson, trom; Amaury Wallez, bsn; Yehudi Menuhin, vln; Pierre Fournier, vlc; Michael Debost, flt; Michael Borgue, ob. EMI 2C 165 12519/22 (4) (From EMSP 553)
+Gr 2-81 p1098

POWELL
Appreciation. See no. 3955

POWELL, Mel
Little companion pieces. See no. 2935

POWER, Lionel
Credo. See no. 4085

PRADO, Almeida
Magnificat. See no. 3911

PRAETORIUS, Jakob
Was kann uns kommen an fur Not. See no. 3903

PRAETORIUS, Michael
A solis ortus cardine. See no. 2607
Bourrees. See no. 4071
Courantes. See no. 4071
Deutsch et in terra. See no. 4071
Es ist ein Ros entspringen. See no. 3775
Eulogodia sionia, 1611: Resonet in laudibus; Musae Sionae IV, 1607: Christus der uns selig macht; Musae Sionae I, 1605: Gott der Vater wohn uns bei. See no. 3853
Gavottes. See no. 4071
Mass, 8 parts: Kyrie, Agnus Dei. See no. 3720
Nun lob mein Seel den Herren. See no. 2607
O lux beata trinitas. See no. 1347. See no. 2607. See no. 4094
2607 Organ works: A solis ortus cardine. Nun lob mein Seel den Herren. O lux beata trinitas. Sumo parenti gloria. Te mane laudum carmine. Wir glauben all an einen Gott. Wolfgang Dallman, org. Musical Heritage Society MHS 4281 (From Da Camera)
+FF 5/6-81 p129 +MU 9-81 p16
Psallite, In natali domini. See no. 3963
2608 Songs (choral works): Canticum trium puerorum; Ecce Maria; Gelobet und gepreiset; Hort zu ihr lieben Leute; In dulci jubilo; Puer natus in Bethlehem. Paris Audite Nova Chorale; Les Saquebout-iers; Paris Recorder Ensemble; Marcello Ardizzone, viol; Marie-Francoise Bloch, Anne-Catherine Huraut, Francoise Leger, bs viol; Georges Delvalee, org; Jean Sourisse. Erato STU 71408
-Gr 10-81 p594
Sumo parenti gloria. See no. 2607
Te mane laudum carmine. See no. 2607
2609 Terpsichore: Dances. SCHEIN: Banchetto musicale: Suites, nos. 3-5. WIDMANN: Daentze und Galliarden. Collegium Terpsichore; Fritz Neumeyer. DG 2547 005 Tape (c) 3347 005 (From SAPM 198166)
+Gr 4-80 p1595 +HFN 6-80 p117
+Gr 12-81 p944 tape +RR 5-80 p67
Terpsichore: La bouree; Pavane de Spaigne; La sarabande; Bransles doubles; Bransle double de Poictou; Bransle gay double; Bransle simple. See no. 3853
Wir glauben all an einen Gott. See no. 2607

PRAGER, Heinrich
Introduction, theme and variations, op. 21. See no. 1555

PRATELLA, F. Balilla
Songs: Ninna Nanna di Modigliana: Ninanana. See no. 3753

PREMRU, Raymond
Music for Harter Fell. See no. 76

PRICHARD
Ye that know the lord is gracious. See no. 3632
PROCESSION WITH CAROLS UPON ADVENT SUNDAY. See no. 3848

PROCH, Heinrich
Air and variations. See no. 3649

PROKOFIEV, Serge
1610 Alexander Nevsky, op. 78. Elena Obraztsova, ms; LSO and Chorus; Claudio Abbado. DG 2531 202 Tape (c) 3301 202
+FF 9/10-80 p180 +-NR 7-80 p9
+Gr 4-80 p1579 +RR 4-80 p116
+HF 7-80 p71 +RR 7-80 p98 tape
+HF 11-81 p103 tape +SFC 6-22-80 p36
++HFN 4-80 p108

2611 Alexander Nevsky, op. 78. Ivan the Terrible, op. 116. Lieutenant Kije, op. 60. Claudine Carlson, ms; Arnold Voketaitis, narrator and bass; Samuel Timberlake, bs; St. Louis Symphony Orchetra and Chorus; Leonard Slatkin. Vox VCL 9004 (3)
+SFC 11-8-81 p18

2612 Alexander Nevsky, op. 78: Russia under the Mongolian yoke; Song of Alexander Nevsky; Crusaders in Pskov; Rise up Russians; Ice battle; The field of the dead; Alexander Nevsky enters Pskov. War and Peace, op. 91, excerpts. Larissa Avdeyeva, ms; Russian Republican Chorus; USSR Academy Symphony Orchestra; Yevegni Svetlanov. Galina Vishnevskaya, s; Valentina Klepatskaya, ms; Yevgeny Kibkalo, bar; Aleksei Krivchenya, Leonid Ktitorov, bs; Boris Shapenko, t; Bolshoi Theatre Orchestra and Chorus; Alexander Melik-Pashayev. Musical Heritage Society MHS 824351 (2)
/ARG 12-81 p22 ++St 10-81 p130

2613 The betrothal in a monastery (The duenna). Nina Isakova; Ivan Petrov; Moscow Musical Theatre Orchestra and Chorus; Kemal Abdullayev. Everest S 465/3 (3)
+Op 6-81 p607

Cinderella, op. 87: Waltz; Midnight. See no. 3840

Cinderella suite. See no. 3715

2614 Concerto, piano, no. 3, op. 26, D major. Concerto, violin and piano, no. 1, op. 19, D major. Lyubov Timofeyeva, pno; Victor Tretyakov, vln; MSO; Dmitri Kitayenko. Bruno Walter Society IGI 377
+-NR 4-81 p6

2615 Concerto, piano, no. 3, op. 26, C major. RAVEL: Concerto, piano, G major. Martha Argerich, pno; BPhO; Claudio Abbado. DG 2542 149 Tape (c) 3342 149 (From 139349)
+Gr 4-81 p1320 +-HFN 6-81 p87 tape
+HFN 5-81 p91

Concerto, piano, no. 4, op. 53, B flat major. See no. 2635

2616 Concerto, violin, no. 1, op. 19, D major. Concerto, violin, no. 2, op. 63, G minor. Erik Friedman, Itzhak Perlman, vln; BSO; Erich Leinsdorf. RCA GL 4-2917 Tape (c) GK 4-2917
+-HFN 3-81 p97 tape

Concerto, violin, no. 1, op. 19, D major. See no. 2614

2617 Concerto, violin, no. 2, op. 63, G minor. SIBELIUS: Concerto, violin, op. 47, D minor. Henryk Szeryng, vln; LSO; Gennady Rozhdestvensky. Quintessence PMC 7150 (also Philips 6527 041 Tape (c) 7311 041 (From SAL 3571)
+FF 9/10-80 p206 +HFN 10-81 p95 tape
+Gr 7-81 p276 +ST 12-81 p590
+-HFN 6-81 p85

Concerto, violin, no. 2, op. 63, G minor. See no. 2616

The dazzling cylinder that crashed in Tunguska Siberia. See no. 4003

Ivan the Terrible, op. 116. See no. 2612

2618 Lieutenant Kije, op. 60. The love for three oranges, op. 33. Symphony, no. 1, op. 25, D major. LSO; Neville Marriner. Philips 9500 930 Tape (c) 7300 903
-FF 9/10-81 p154 +NYT 7-19-81 pD23
+Gr 4-81 p1320 ++SFC 8-9-81 p18
+-HFN 7-81 p75 +St 10-81 p131

2619 Lieutenant Kije, op. 60. STRAVINSKY: Chant du rossignol. CSO;

Fritz Reiner. RCA AGL 1-3881 Tape (c) AGK 1-3881
+-FF 7/8-81 p99 +MUM 7/8-81 p35

2620 Lieutenant Kije, op. 60: Suite. Scythian suite, op. 20. CSO; Claudio Abbado. DG 2530 967 Tape (c) 3300 967
+ARG 10-79 p47 +HFN 2-79 p118 tape
+-FF 11/12-79 p110 +NYT 7-29-79 pD24
+Gr 11-78 p884 ++RR 12-78 p65
+-HF 9-79 p123 ++SFC 5-13-79 p43
+HF 11-81 p103 tape ++St 8-79 p112
+HFN 1-79 p120

Lieutenant Kije, op. 60. See no. 2612

The love for three oranges, op. 33. See no. 2618

The love for three oranges, op. 33: March. See no. 3699. See no. 3704

The love for three oranges, op. 33: Suite. See no. 1492. See no. 3232

March, op. 99. See no. 3817

2621 Peter and the wolf, op. 67. SAINT-SAENS: Carnival of the animals. Angela Rippon, reader; Anthony Goldstone, Ian Brown, pno; RPO; Owain Arwel Hughes. ASV ACM 2005 Tape (c) ZCAC 2005 (From Enigma VAR 1047)
+-Gr 4-81 p1378 +HFN 6-81 p87 tape
+Gr 7-81 p196 tape

2622 Peter and the wolf, op. 67. PROTO: Casey at the bat. SOUSA: Stars and stripes forever. Tom Seaver, Johnny Bench, narrators; Cincinnati Pops Orchestra; Erich Kunzel. MMG 1127 Tape (c) CMB 1127
+HF 4-81 p81 +SFC 1-4-81 p18

Peter and the wolf, op. 67. See no. 1030. See no. 1031. See no. 2290

Pieces, piano, op. 4, no. 4: Suggestion diabolique. See no. 3723

Prelude, op. 12, no. 7, C major. See no. 3643

Romeo and Juliet, op. 64: Aubade. See no. 3643

2623 Romeo and Juliet, op. 64: Ballet suite. PhO; Efrem Kurtz. Seraphim S 60340
+-ARG 1-81 p37

2624 Romeo and Juliet, op. 64: Introduction; Juliet and young girl; Masques; Dance of the knights; Gavotte; Romeo resolves to avenge Mercutio's death; Finale, Act 2; Introduction; Interlude; Again at Juliet's home; Dance of the maidens with lilies; Juliet's funeral; Death of Juliet. LAPO; Erich Leinsdorf. Sheffield LAB 8
+Audio 9-78 p116 +-HFN 1-81 p99
+Gr 11-78 p900 +SFC 12-3-78 p55
+-HFN 1-79 p73 ++St 8-78 p134

Romeo and Juliet, op. 64: Montagues and Capulets; Dance; Romeo at Juliet's grave; Dance of the girls from Antilles; Tybalt's death. See no. 764

Romeo and Juliet, op. 64: Suite. See no. 3241

2625 Romeo and Juliet, op. 64: Suites, nos. 1 and 2, excerpts. Rotterdam Philharmonic Orchestra; Edo de Waart. Philips 6539 070 (also FH 21. From Philips 6500 640)
+-FF 7/8-81 p143 +MUM 5/6-81 p31

Romeo and Juliet, op. 75: Suite. See no. 2628

2626 Russian folksongs, op. 104: White snowflakes; The dream; The monk; Wedding song; Katerina; Green grove. RIMKSY-KORSAKOV: Songs:

The dying glow of the sunset, op. 39, no. 2; In the silence of the night, op. 40, no. 3; The heavy clouds scatter, op. 42, no. 3; More sonorous than the lark's singing, op. 43, no. 1; Not the wind, op. 43, no. 2; The nymph, op. 56, no. 1; Octave, op. 45, no. 3; The rose and the nightingale, op. 2, no. 2. Galina Vishnevskaya, s; Mstislav Rostropovich, pno. EMI 1C 065 03504
++Gr 11-81 p738

2627 Sarcasms, op. 17. Sonata, piano, no. 3, op. 28, A minor. Sonata, piano, no. 6, op. 82, A major. Staffan Scheja, pno. BIS LP 155
+FF 5/6-81 p130 +NR 4-81 p11
+HFN 5-81 p83 +-St 6-81 p122

Scythian suite, op. 20. See no. 1549. See no. 2020

Sonata, piano, no, 3, op. 38, A minor. See no. 1295. See no. 2506. See no. 2627

Sonata, piano, no. 6, op. 82, A major. See no. 2627

Sonata, piano, no. 7, op. 83, B flat major. See no. 3785

2628 Sonata, piano, no. 8, op. 84, B flat major. Romeo and Juliet, op. 75: Suite. Steven de Groote, pno. Finlandia FA 309
+-FF 5/6-81 p130 +NR 4-81 p11

Sonata, violin, op. 115, D major. See no. 450. See no. 3984

2629 Sonata, 2 violins, op. 56, C major. SCHNITTKE: Prelude to the memory of Dmitri Shostakovich. SHOSTAKOVICH: Sonata, violin and piano, op. 134. Gidon Kremer, Tatiana Gridenko, vln; Andrei Gavrilov, pno. HMV ASD 3547
+ARG 4-81 p45 +HFN 8-78 p99
+FF 11/12-80 p220 +RR 12-78 p98
+Gr 9-78 p492

Sonata, 2 violins, op. 56, C major. See no. 2287

2630 Sonata, violin and piano, no. 1, op. 80, F minor. Sonata, violin and piano, no. 2, op. 94, D major. Itzhak Perlman, vln; Vladimir Ashkenazy, pno. RCA AGL 1-3912
+-FF 7/8-81 p144

Sonata, violin and piano, no. 2, op. 94, D major. See no. 2630

2631 Sonata, violoncello and piano, op. 119. RACHMANINOFF: Sonata, violoncello and piano, op. 19, G minor. Arto Noras, vlc; Eero Heinonen, pno. Finlandia FA 317
+FF 7/8-81 p147

2632 Sonata, violoncello and piano, op. 119. SHOSTAKOVICH: Sonata, violoncello and piano, op. 40, D minor. Mstislav Rostropovich, vlc; Sviatoslav Richter, Dmitri Shostakovich, pno. Monitor MC 2021
++FF 1/2-81 p255

Songs without words, op. 35 (5). See no. 1319

2633 Suite of waltzes by Schubert. SCRIABIN: Etudes, op. 8 (12). TANEYEV: Prelude and fugue, op. 29, G sharp minor. Vladimir Leyetchkiss, pno. Orion ORS 80378
+ARG 3-81 p44 +FF 5/6-81 p204
+CL 2-81 p13 +-St 6-81 p127

2634 Symphony, no. 1, op. 25, D major. Symphony, no. 7, op. 13, C sharp minor. MRSO; Gennady Rozhdestvensky. Quintessence PMC 7138
+Audio 8-81 p66 +FF 9/10-80 p181

Symphony, no. 1, op. 25, D major. See no. 799. See no. 2618

2635 Symphony, no. 4, op. 47. Concerto, piano, no. 4, op. 53, B flat major.* Rudolf Serkin, pno; PO; Eugene Ormandy. CBS 61435 Tape (c) 40-61435 (*From SBRG 72109)

+Gr 4-81 p1323 +-HFN 5-81 p91

2636 Symphony, no. 5, op. 100, B flat major. Israel Philharmonic Orchestra; Leonard Bernstein. CBS IM 35877 Tape (c) HMT 35877
+-ARG 1-81 p38 +-MUM 5/6-81 p31
-HF 4-81 p93 tape +-ST 5-81 p44
+-HFN 4-81 p81 tape

Symphony, no. 7, op. 13, C sharp minor. See no. 2634

Visions fugitives, op. 22, nos. 1, 3, 5-6, 8, 10, 14, 16-18. See no. 2506

War and peace, op. 91, excerpts. See no. 2612

PROTO, Frank

Case at the bat. See no. 2622

Quartet, strings, no. 1, B minor. See no. 1586

PRYOR, Arthur

Air varie. See no. 1263

PUCCINI, Giacomo

2637 Arias: La boheme: Quando m'en vo. Edgar: Addio mio dolce amore. Madama Butterfly: Un bel di vedremo. Manon Lescaut: In quelle trine morbide. La rondine: Che il bel sogno di Doretta. Suor Angelica: Senza mamma. Tosca: Vissi d'arte. Turandot: Signore ascolta; In questa reggia. Raina Kabaivanska, s; Emilio Stabile Orchestra; Nino Sanzogno. RCA RL 3-1475
+-Gr 10-81 p604

2638 La boheme. Renata Scotto, Carol Neblett, s; Alfredo Kraus, Paul Crook, t; Sherrill Milnes, Matteo Manuguerra, bar; Paul Plishka, Renato Capecchi, Italo Tajo, bs; Trinity Boys Choir, Ambrosian Opera Chorus; National Philharmonic Orchestra; James Levine. HMV SLS 5192 (2) Tape (c) TC SLS 5192 (also Angel SZBX 3900 Tape (c) 4Z2X 3900)
+-ARG 3-81 p45 +NYT 6-29-80 pD18
+-Gr 7-80 p162 +ON 9-80 p68
+-HF 11-80 p57 +-Op 10-80 p1015
+HFN 9-80 p109 +-RR 8-80 p29
+HFN 10-80 p117 tape +SFC 7-27-80 p34
+-NR 9-80 p7 +-St 11-80 p98

2639 La boheme. Anna Moffo, s; Mary Costa, ms; Richard Tucker, t; Robert Merrill, bar; Giorgio Tozzi, Fernando Corena, bs; Rome Opera House Orhcestra and Chorus; Erich Leinsdorf. RCA AGL 2-3969 (2) Tape (c) AGK 2-3969 (also LSC 6095)
+-FF 9/10-81 p155

La boheme: Che gelida manina. See no. 3657. See no. 3759. See no. 3839. See no. 3885. See no. 3890. See no. 3987. See no. 4033. See no. 4037. See no. 4054

La boheme: Che gelida manina; Mi chiamano Mimi. See no. 4081

La boheme: Che gelida manina; O Mimi tu piu non torni; O soave fanciulla; Addio dolce svegliare. See no. 3995

La boheme: Che gelida manina; O soave fanciulla; Ah Mimi tu piu non torni. See no. 3967

La boheme: Donde lieta usci. See no. 3844

La boheme: In un coupe O Mimi tu piu non torni. See no. 4045

La boheme: Mi chiamano Mimi; Duet, Act 3; Donde lieta usci. See no. 3837

La boheme: Mi chiamano Mimi; O soave fanciulla. See no. 3748

La boheme: Musetta' waltz. See no. 4000

La boheme: O Mimi tu piu non torni. See no. 3965

2640 La boheme: O soave fanciulla. Gianni Schicchi: Lauretta mia. Madama Butterfly: Bimba dagli occhi. Manon Lescaut: Tu tu amore tu. VERDI: Otello: Gia nella notte densa. La traviata: Parigi o cara. Mirella Freni, s; Franco Bonisolli, t; Hamburg State Philharmonic Orchestra, Berlin State Chamber Orchestra; Leone Magiera, Lamberto Gardelli. Acanta DC 22007 (From BAC 31011/2, DC 29384)
+-Gr 4-81 p1362 +-HNF 2-81 p91

La boheme: O soave fanciulla. See no. 2640
La boheme: O soave fanciulla: O Mimi tu piu non torni. See no. 4048
La boheme: Quando m'en vo' soletta. See no. 2637. See no. 3711
La boheme: Si, mi chiamano Mimi. See no. 3623. See no. 3850
La boheme: Si, mi chiamano Mimi; Donde lieta usci. See no. 3642
La boheme: Si, mi chiamano Mimi; O soave fanciulla; Donde lieta usci. See no. 2018
La boheme: Vecchia zimarra. See no. 3752
Edgar: Addio mio dolce amor. See no. 2637

2641 La fanciulla del West: Arias. Madama Butterfly: Arias. Tosca: Arias. Turandot: Arias. VERDI: Don Carlo: Arias. Macbeth: Arias. Rigoletto: Arias. La traviata: Arias. Mirella Freni, Raina Kabaivanska, Katia Ricciarelli, s; Luciano Pavarotti, Gianna Raimondi, t; Renato Bruson, bar; Verona Orchestra del Teatro Arena; Bruno Martinotti, Armando Gatto. Decca SDD 570 (From Ars Nova ANC 25003)
+-Gr 4-81 p1372

La fanciulla del West: Ch'ella mi creda libero. See no. 3757
La fanciulla del West: Ch'ella mi creda; Or son sei mesi. See no. 4023
La fanciulla del West: Or son sei mesi; Ch'ella mi creda. See no. 3839
La fanciulla del West: Una parola...Or son sei mesi; Ch' elle mi creda libero. See no. 3843

2642 Gianni Schicchi. Suor Angelica. Il tabarro. Renata Scotto, Ileana Cotrubas, s; Marilyn Horne, ms; Placido Domingo, t; Tito Gobbi, Ingvar Wixell, bar; PhO, NPhO, LSO; Lorin Maazel. CBS 79312 (3) (also CBS M3 35913) (From 76641, 76570, 76563)
+FF 3/4-81 p171 +Op 11-78 p1094
+Gr 8-78 p378 +-RR 8-78 p49
+-HFN 8-78 p113

Gianni Schicchi: Avete torto. See no. 3843
Gianni Schicchi: Firenze e come un albero fiorito. See no. 3707
Gianni Schicchi: Lauretta mia. See no. 2640
Gianni Schicchi: O mio babbino caro. See no. 3711. See no. 3713. See no. 3844. See no. 4007. See no. 4042

2643 Madama Butterfly. Maria Chiara, s; Trudeliese Schmidt, ms; James King, Perry Gruber, t; Hermann Prey, Anton Rosner, bar; Richard Kogel, bs; Bavarian Radio Orchestra and Chorus; Giuseppe Patane. Eurodisc 86515 (3)
+-HF 1-74 p76 +-ON 1-11-75 p35
+-HFN 12-81 p101 +St 4-74 p115

2644 Madama Butterfly. Hungarian State Opera Orchestra; Veronica Kincses, s; Klara Takacs, ms; Peter Dvorsky, Istvan Kozsos, t; Lajos Miller, bar; Giuseppe Patane. Hungaroton SLPJ 1 11256/8 (3)
+ON 12-5-81 p60

Madama Butterfly: Addio fiorita asil. See no. 3752. See no. 4075
Madama Butterfly: Amore o grillo; Non ve l'avevo detto. See no. 3996
Madama Butterfly: Arias. See no. 2641
Madama Butterfly: Bimba bimba non piangere. See no. 1374
Madama Butterfly: Bimba dagli occhi. See no. 2640
Madama Butterfly: Dovunque al mondo; Amore o grillo. See no. 4033
Madama Butterfly: Entrance of Butterfly; Un bel di. See no. 3642
Madama Butterfly: Love duet. See no. 3707. See no. 4023
Madama Butterfly: Love duet; Addio fiorito asil. See no. 3966
Madama Butterfly: Love duet, Act 1. See no. 3748
Madama Butterfly: Love duet, Act 1; Un bel di; Con onor muore. See no. 2018
Madama Butterfly: Non ve l'avelo detto. See no. 4048
Madama Butterfly: Tu tu piccolo addio. See no. 3755
Madama Butterfly: Un bel di. See no. 2637. See no. 3623. See no. 3713. See no. 3844. See no. 3850. See no. 4041. See no. 4042
Madama Butterfly: Un po do vero c'e. See no. 3995
Manon Lescaut: Donna non vidi ami. See no. 3965. See no. 3982. See no. 3987. See no. 4028. See no. 4053
Manon Lescaut: Donna non vidi mai; Tra voi belle. See no. 4035
Manon Lescaut: In quelle trine morbide. See no. 2637. See no. 3647
Manon Lescaut: In quella trine morbide; Sola perduta abbandonata. See no. 3711
Manon Lescaut: Intermezzo. See no. 3644
Manon Lescaut: Intermezzo, Act 3. See no. 3787
Manon Lescaut: Ma se vi talenta...Tra voi belle; Donna non vidi mai; Ah non v'avvicinate...No no pazzo son. See no. 3757
Manon Lescaut: Sola perduta abbandonata. See no. 1588. See no. 3755
Manon Lescaut: Tra voi belle brune e bionde; Donna non vidi mai; Ah Manon mi tradisce. See no. 842
Manon Lescaut: Tra voi belle; Donna non vidi mai; Tu tu amore; Ah Manon mi tradisce; Guardate pazzo son. See no. 4033
Manon Lescaut: Tu tu amore tu. See no. 2640
La rondine: Chi il bel sogno di Doretta. See no. 2637. See no. 3711
Suor Angelica. See no. 2642
Suor Angelica: Intermezzo. See no. 2637. See no. 3644. See no. 3711. See no. 3713. See no. 3755
Il tabarro. See no. 2642

2645 Tosca. Katia Ricciarelli, s; Jose Carreras, Heinz Zednik, t; Ruggero Raimondi, Gottfried Hornik, Fernando Corena, Victor von Halem, bs; Berlin Opera Chorus; BPhO; Herbert von Karajan. DG 2707 121 (2) Tape (c) 3370 033

+-ARG 3-81 p46
+-FF 1/2-81 p166
++Gr 7-80 p162
++Gr 10-80 p548 tape
+-HF 11-80 p57
+HF 7-81 p71 tape
++HFN 9-80 p109
++HFN 10-80 p117 tape
+NR 10-80 p10
+-NYT 9-14-80 pD26
+OC Spring 1981 p51
+-Op 9-80 p953
+-RR 8-80 p31
++SFC 8-24-80 p36
+-St 12-80 p130

2646 Tosca. Zinka Milanov, s; Franco Corelli, David Tree, t; Giangiacomo Guelfi, bar; Michael Langdon, Forbes Robinson, Leonardo Monreale, sb; Orchestra and Chorus; Alexander Gibson. Historical Recordings HRE 366 (2) (also Unique Opera Records UORC 157)
+FF 3/4-81 p170

2647 Tosca, excerpts. Maria Callas, s; Amsterdam Concert, Hamberg Concert, Stuttgart Concerto. VOCE 34 (3)
-FF 9/10-81 p210

2648 Tosca: Ah finalmente...Recondita armonia; Mario Mario...Non la sospiri la nostra cassetta...Qual occhio al mondo; Tre sbirri... Una carrozza...Te deum laudamus; Vittoria Vittoria...La povera mia cena fu interrotta...Gia mi dicon venal...Vissi d'arte vissi d'amore; E lucevan le stelle...Ah Franchigia a Floria Tosca...O dolci mani...Trionfal di nova speme...Presto su Mario Mario. Montserrat Caballe, s; Jose Carreras, Piero de Palma, t; Ingar Wixell, Domenico Trimarchi, bar; Samuel Ramey, William Elvin, bs; ROHO and Chorus; Colin Davis. Philips 6570 158 Tape (c) 7310 158 (From 6700 108)
+Gr 1-81 p989 ++HFN 5-81 p93 tape
++HFN 2-81 p97

Tosca: Arias. See no. 2641

Tosca: Dammi i colori...Recondita armonia; E lucevan le stelle. See no. 842

Tosca: E lucevan le stelle. See no. 3657. See no. 3843. See no. 4022

Tosca: Non la sospiri;...Vissi d'arte; Amara sol per te;...trionfal di nova speme. See no. 1167

Tosca: Recondita armonia. See no. 3885. See no. 3965. See no. 4032. See no. 4053

Tosca: Recondita armonia; E lucevan le stelle. See no. 1363. See no. 3759. See no. 3839. See no. 3987. See no. 3995

Tosca: Recondita armonia; E lucevan le stelle: O dolci mani. See no. 4075

Tosca: Recondita armonia; E lucevan le stelle; O dolci mani...Amaro sol per te;...Trionfal di nuovo speme. See no. 4054

Tosca: Scene, Act 2. See no. 1588

Tosca: Tu di tua mano...O dolci mani. See no. 4045

Tosca: Und es blitzten die Sterne; Wie sich die Bilder gleichen. See no. 3747

Tosca: Vissi d'arte. See no. 2637. See no. 3623. See no. 3755. See no. 4021. See no. 4042

2649 Turandot. Birgit Nilsson, Renata Tebaldi, s; Jussi Bjorling, t; Giorgio Tozzi, bs; Rome Opera House Orchestra and Chorus; Erich Leinsdorf. RCA AGL 3-3970 (3) (From LSC 6149)
++FF 9/10-81 p155

Turandot: Arias. See no. 2641

Turandot: In questa reggia. See no. 3647

Turandot: Nessun dorma. See no. 3646. See no. 3750. See no. 3759. See no. 3838. See no. 3885. See no. 3982

Turandot: Nessun dorma; Signore ascolta. See no. 3751

Turandot: Non piangere Liu. See no. 4022

Turandot: Non piangere Liu; Nessun dorma. See no. 3839. See no. 3843

Turandot: Scene of Liu's death including Tu che di gel sei cinto. See no. 3837

Turandot: Signore ascolta; In questa reggia. See no. 2637
Turandot: Signore ascolta; Tu che di gel sei cinta. See no. 2018. See no. 3844

2650 Le Villi. Renata Scotto, s; Placido Domingo, t; Leo Nucci; Tito Gobbi, speaker; National Philharmonic Orchestra; Lorin Maazel. CBS M 36669 Tape (c) MT 36669 (also CBS GL 0149, CBS 76890)
+FF 3/4-81 p171
+Gr 5-81 p1510
+HF 2-81 p71
+HFN 7-81 p75
+-MT 12-81 p828
+Op 7-81 p718
+SFC 12-7-80 p33
++St 3-81 p92
++STL 6-14-81 p40

2651 Le Villi. Marilyn Richardson, s; David Parker, t; James Christiansen, bar; Adelaide Festival Chorale, Corinthian Singers; Adelaide Symphony Orchestra; Myer Fredman. Chandos ABR 1019 Tape (c) ABT 1019
+-Gr 2-81 p1116
+HFN 2-81 p91
+HFN 3-81 p97 tape
+-MT 7-81 p481
+-ON 9-81 p60
+Op 3-81 p271

Le Villi: Non ti scordar di me. See no. 3711

PUI FAN CHAN
The pedlar. See no. 3860
To spring. See no. 3860

PUJOL VILARRUBI, Emilio
Guajira. See no. 3694. See no. 3701. See no. 3795
Tango. See no. 3795

PUNTO, Giovanni (Jan Vaclav Stich)

2652 Concerti, horn, nos. 5-6, 10-11. Barry Tuckwell, hn; AMF; Neville Marriner. Angel SZ 37781 (also HMV ASD 4008)
++FF 9/10-81 p179
++Gr 6-81 p42
++HF 8-81 p61
++HFN 5-81 p83
++NR 6-81 p7
++St 10-81 p131
+STL 6-14-81 p40

PURCELL, Henry
Abdelazer: Overture. See no. 2665
Abdelazer: Rondeau. See no. 3818

2653 Amphitryon. The old bachelor. The virtuous wife. Judith Nelson, s; Martyn Hill, t; Christopher Keyte, bs; Academy of Ancient Music; Christopher Hogwood. L'Oiseau-Lyre DSLO 550
++ARG 9-80 p35
++FF 7/8-80 p123
+-Gr 12-79 p1034
+-HF 1-81 p62
+HFN 2-80 p97
+MT 9-80 p567
+NYT 11-25-79 pD15
+ON 4-19-80 p28
+RR 10-79 p143

Bonduca: Overture. See no. 2665
Celebrate the festival: Crown the altar. See no. 2677
Chacony, G minor. See no. 4066
Come ye sons of art: Sound the trumpet; See nature rejoicing; Ritornello and chorus. See no. 3853
Comus: Overture and minuet. See no. 3840

2654 Dido and Aeneas. Emma Kirkby, Judith Nelson, Judith Rees, s; Jantina Noorman, ms; David Thomas, bs; Taverner Players and Choir; Andrew Parrott. Chandos ABRD 1034 Tape (c) ABRD 1034
+Gr 12-81 p930
+-HFN 11-81 p96
+STL 10-11-81 p41

2655 Dido and Aeneas. Victoria de los Angeles, Heather Harper, s; Sybil Michelow, ms; Patricia Johnson, con; Robert Tear, t; Peter

Glossop, bar; Ambrosian Singers; ECO; John Barbirolli. Classics for Pleasure CFP 40359 Tape (c) TCC CFP 40359 (From HMV SAN 169)
/Gr 9-81 p428 +HFN 8-81 p92

2656 Dido and Aeneas (edit. Britten and I. Holst). Norma Burrowes, Felicity Palmer, Felicity Lott, s; Janet Baker, Anna Reynolds, ms; Peter Pears, Robert Tear, t; George Malcolm, hpd; Kenneth Heath, vlc; London Opera Chorus; Aldeburgh Festival Strings; Steuart Bedford. Decca SET 615 Tape (c) KCET 615 (also London OSA 1170 Tape (c) OSA 5-1170)
+-ARG 2-79 p26 +-MT 12-78 p1052
+FF 3/4-79 p95 +-NR 6-79 p11
+-Gr 7-78 p243 +-NYT 3-4-79 pD23
++Gr 12-81 p945 tape +ON 3-31-79 p40
+-HF 12-78 p118 +-Op 9-78 p896
+HFN 6-78 p125 ++RR 6-78 p38
+HFN 9-78 p159 tape +RR 5-79 p110 tape
+Gr 11-78 p970 tape +SFC 10-1-78 p53
-MJ 5/6-79 p53 ++St 1-79 p110

2657 Dido and Aeneas. Tatiana Troyanos, Sheila Armstrong, Margaret Baker-Genovesi, s; Patricia Johnson, Margaret Lensky, con; Paul Esswood, alto; Nigel Rogers, t; Barry McDaniel, bar; Hamburg Monteverdi Choir; North German Radio Chamber Orchestra; Charles Mackerras. DG 2547 032 Tape (c) 3347 032 (From SAPM 198424)
+-Gr 11-80 p735 +-HFN 6-81 p88
+HFN 1-81 p109 tape

2658 Dido and Aeneas. Kirsten Flagstad, Elisabeth Schwarzkopf, Eilidh McNab, Sheila Rex, Anna Pollack, s; Arda Mandikian, ms; David Lloyd, t; Thomas Hemsley, bar; Mermaid Singers and Orchestra; Geraint Jones. EMI 2C 051 03613 (also Seraphim 60346)
+-ARG 7/8-81 p47 +ARSC Vol 12, nos. 1-2, 1980, p107

2659 Dido and Aeneas. Nancy Armstrong, Susan Klebanow, Roberta Anderson, s; D'Anna Fortunato, ms; Bruce Fithian, t; Mark Baker, bs; Boston Camerata; Joel Cohen. Harmonia Mundi HM 10067
-FF 11/12-80 p158 +HFN 8-80 p101
+Gr 7-80 p162 +NYT 8-10-80 pD17
+HF 1-81 p62

Dido and Aeneas: Overture. See no. 2665
Dido and Aeneas: When I am laid in earth. See no. 3653
Distressed innocence: Overture. See no. 2665

2660 Don Quixote. Emma Kirkby, Judith Nelson, s; James Bowman, c-t; Martyn Hill, t; David Thomas, bs; Academy of Ancient Music; Christopher Hogwood, hpd and cond. L'Oiseau-Lyre DSLO 534 Tape (c) DSLC 534
+FF 3/4-80 p131 +NYT 11-25-79 pD15
+Gr 11-78 p944 +ON 4-19-80 p28
++Gr 12-81 p945 tape +RR 11-78 p104
++Gr 5-79 p1940 tape ++SFC 1-13-80 p40
+HFN 11-78 p173 ++St 10-79 p144
+MT 3-79 p228

2661 Double dealer; Cynthia frowns; Orchestra excerpts. Henry II: In vain 'gainst love I strove. Richmond heiress: Behold the man. The rival sisters: Overture; Celia has a thousand charms; Take not a woman's anger ill; How happy is she. Tyrannic love:

Hark my Damilcar; Ah how sweet it is to love. Judith Nelson, Emma Kirkby, s; Martyn Hill, t; David Thomas, bs; Academy of Ancient Music; Christopher Hogwood, hpd. L'Oiseau-Lyre DSLO 561

+Gr 4-81 p1356 +HFN 3-81 p90

2662 Fairy Queen, excerpts. Julianne Baird, s; Peter Becker, c-t; Stephen Sturck, t; Wilbur Pauley, bs; New York Ensemble for Early Music; Frederick Renz. Musical Heritage Society MHS 4237

+-FF 7/8-81 p144 +HF 1-81 p62

Fairy Queen: Overture. See no. 2665
Fantasia, D major. See no. 2677
Fantasia, no. 13, F major. See no. 3842
Fantasia in 3 parts on a ground, F major. See no. 4101
Fantasia on one note, F major. See no. 4101
Funeral music for Queen Mary. See no. 2668
The Gordian knot untied: Rondeau minuet. See no. 215
Grounds: Minuet. See no. 2674
Henry II: In vain 'gainst love I strove. See no. 2661

2663 The Indian Queen. Jennifer Smith, s; Martyn Hill, John Elwes, t; Stephen Varcoe, bar; David Thomas, bs; Monteverdi Choir; English Baroque Soloists; John Eliot Gardiner. Erato STU 71275 Tape (c) 71275

+FF 7/8-81 p145 +HFN 8-80 p101
+Gr 9-80 p398 +HFN 10-80 p117 tape
+-Gr 12-81 p945 tape +MT 2-81 p112

The Indian Queen: Overture. See no. 2665

2664 King Arthur. Deller Consort, King's Musik; Alfred Deller. Harmonia Mundi HM 252/3 (2) (also Musical Heritage Society MHS 4188/9 Tape (c) MHC 6188/9)

+ARG 2-81 p26 +-HFN 5-79 p124
+FF 1/2-80 p128 +NYT 11-25-79 pD15
+FF 11/12-80 p159 +-ON 4-19-80 p28
++Gr 5-79 p1925 +-RR 5-79 p44
+-HF 1-81 p60 +-St 12-80 p132
+HF 6-81 p70 tape

King Arthur: Allegro and air. See no. 4002
King Arthur: Overture. See no. 2665
King Arthur: Trumpet tune. See no. 3959
Love's goddess sure: May she to heaven. See no. 3853
The married beau: Overture. See no. 2665
Music for Queen Mary II. See no. 4002
Musick's handmaid: March; Song tune; Air; Minuet; New minuet; New Scotch tune; Minuet; Sefauchi's farewell; Minuet rigadoon; A new ground; Minuet; A new Irish tune; Suite, G minor; Toccata; Hornpipe; Air. See no. 3926
Musick's handmaid: Minuets (2). See no. 4084
Musick's handmaid: Sefauchi's farewell; A new ground, E minor. See no. 2677
A new ground. See no. 2674. See no. 3949
A new Irish tune. See no. 3733. See no. 4103
The old bachelor. See no. 2653
The old bachelor: Overture. See no. 2665
Overtures, D minor, G minor. See no. 2677

2665 Overtures: Abdelazer. Bonduca. Dido and Aeneas. Distressed innocence. The fairy queen. The Indian queen. King Arthur

I and II. The married beau. The old bachelor. The rival sisters. Timon of Athens. Bournemouth Sinfonietta; Ronald Thomas. Chandos ABR 1026 Tape (c) ABT 1026
+FF 9/10-81 p156 +HFN 6-81 p77
+-Gr 7-81 p160 +HFN 7-81 p83 tape

Pavans, A major, B flat major. See no. 4101

Pavans, A major, B major, G minor. See no. 2677

Prelude, recorder. See no. 3949

The queen's epicedium. See no. 3842

Richmond heiress: Behold the man. See no. 2661

The rival sisters: Overture. See no. 2665

The rival sisters: Overture; Celia has a thousand charms; Take not a woman's anger ill; How happy is she. See no. 2661

Round O. See no. 2674

Sonata, trumpet, D major. See no. 1211

2666 Songs: Ah cruel nymph; As Amoret and Thirsis lay; I lov'd fair Celia; Incassum Lesbia; The fatal hour comes on a pace; Musick for awhile; Pious Celinda goes to prayers; Retir'd from any mortal's sight; Since from my dear Astrea's sight; Sweeter than roses; Tis nature's voice; Young Thirsis fate. Rene Jacobs, c-t; Wieland Kuijken, vla da gamba; Konrad Junghanel, theorbo. Accent ACC 7802
+FF 3/4-80 p132 +HFN 6-80 p101
+-HF 1-81 p62 +RR 6-80 p31

2667 Songs (choral): Canticles: Evening service, G minor: Magnificat; Nunc dimittis. Te deum and jubilate, D major. Service, B flat major: Benedicite omnia opera; Cantate domino; Deus misereatur; Magnificat; Nunc dimittis. Full anthems: O God thou hast cast us out; O Lord God of hosts; Remember not Lord our offences; Lord how long wilt thou be angry; O God thou art my God. Funeral sentences: Man that is born of a woman; In the midst of life; Thou knowest Lord; Thou knowest Lord. Latin psalm: Jehova quam multi sunt hostes mei. Verse anthems: My heart is inditing; O sing unto the Lord; My beloved spake; They that go down to the sea in ships; Praise the Lord O Jerusalem. David Thomas, bs; Christ Church Cathedral Choir; English Concert; Francis Grier, org; Simon Preston. DG 2723 076 (3)
+Gr 7-81 p185 +STL 7-12-81 p40
+HFN 7-81 p75 +STL 6-14-81 p40
++SFC 12-20-81 p18

2668 Songs: Come ye sons of art (Birthday ode for Queen Mary). Funeral music for Queen Mary. Felicity Lott, s; Charles Brett, John Williams, c-t; Thomas Allen, bs; Monteverdi Orchestra and Choir, Equale Brass Ensemble; John Eliot Gardiner. Erato STU 70911 Tape (c) MCE 70911
+ARG 11-79 p46 +HFN 11-77 p179
++FF 1/2-80 p128 ++HFN 10-80 p117 tape
+-Gr 8-77 p331 +-MM 4-78 p40
+Gr 12-81 p945 tape ++NR 10-79 p7
+-HF 8-78 p84 +RR 8-77 p77

2669 Songs: Celestial music; Ode for Queen Mary's birthday, 1689. Monteverdiana Accademia Orchestra and Chorus; Denis Stevens. Everest 3470
+ARG 5-81 p23 +NR 1-81 p11
+FF 3/4-81 p172

2670 Songs: Blow up the trumpet in Sion; Hear my prayer; My song shall be alway; O give thanks; O Lord God of hosts; O solitude. Deller Consort and Choir; Alfred Deller. Harmonia Mundi HM 247

+FF 1/2-80 p128
+HF 1-81 p62
+HFN 8-78 p106
+RR 7-78 p87

2671 Songs: Evening hymn; Fairest isle; From rosy bowr's; I attempt from love's sickness to fly; If music be the food of love; Music for a while; Not all my torments; The plaint; O lead me to some peaceful gloom; Retired from any mortal's sight; Since from my dear Astrea's sight; Sweeter than roses; Thrice happy lovers. Alfred Deller, c-t; Wieland Kuijken, bs viol; William Christie, hpd; Roderick Skeaping, baroque vln. Harmonia Mundi HM 249 Tape (c) 40 249

+ARG 10-80 p45
+FF 5/6-80 p135
+-Gr 8-79 p364
+HF 1-81 p62
+HFN 12-79 p167
+-MT 3-80 p181
+-NR 5-80 p10
+ON 4-19-80 p28
++RR 12-79 p115

2672 Songs: Come let us drink; A health to the nut brown lass; I gave her cakes and I gave her ale; If ever I more riches did desire; Laudate ceciliam; The miller's daughter; Of all the instruments; Once twice thrice I Julia tried; Prithee ben't so sad and serious; Since time so kind to us does prove; Sir Walter enjoying his damsel; Tis woman makes us love; Under this stone; Young John the gard'ner. Deller Consort; Alfred Deller. Musical Heritage Society MHS 4124

+ARG 7/8-80 p36
++FF 9/10-80 p181
+HF 1-81 p62

2673 Songs (odes): Come ye sons of art; High on a throne of glittering ore. Elegies: O dive Custos auriacae domus; Incassum Lesbia. BLOW: No Lesbia no. Julianne Baird, s; James Bowman, Peter Becker, c-t; Stephen Sturck, t; Wilbur Pauley, bs; New York Ensemble for Early Music; Frederic Renz. Musical Heritage Society MHS 4234

+-FF 7/8-81 p144
+HF 1-81 p62

2674 Songs: An evening hymn on a ground; Bess of Bedlam; The fatal hour; I attempt from love's sickness to fly; If music be the food of love; More love or more disdain; Not all my torments; A song on a ground; Solitude; Sweeter than roses; Urge me no more. Grounds: Minuet. A new ground. Round O. Anna Carol Dudley, s; Laurette Goldberg, hpd. 1750 Arch Records S 1776

++ARG 12-80 p42
+-FF 11/12-80 p158
+-HF 1-81 p62
+NR 1-81 p11

Songs: Come ye sons of art; High on a throne of glitt'ring ore; O dive custos Auricae Domus; Incassum Lesbia incassum rogas. See no. 814

Songs: Evening hymn. See no. 3614

Songs (anthems): Hear my prayer; My beloved spake; O God thou hast cast us out. See no. 815

Songs: Here's that will challenge all the fair; I spy Celia; Lost is my quiet; Since time so kind to us does prove; Sweeter than roses; When the cock begins to crow. See no. 4058

Songs: If music be the food of love. See no. 3653

Songs (motets): Jehova quam multi sunt. See no. 815. See no. 3620

Songs: Let mine eyes. See no. 3621

Songs (anthems): O God thou art my God. See no. 4116
Songs: Once twice thrice would you know how we meet; Since time so kind. See no. 4093
Songs: Passing by. See no. 3657
Songs: Thou knowest Lord. See no. 3634
Suites, nos. 1-8. See no. 4084
Suite, no. 2, G minor. See no. 3733. See no. 4103
Suite, no. 6, D major. See no. 2677

2675 Te deum et jubilate Deo, D major. Yorkshire Feast song. Pro Cantione Antiqua Soloists; St. Mary of Warwick Choir; La Grande Ecurie et Chambre du Roy; Jean-Claude Malgoire. CBS 76925 Tape (c) 40-76925
+Gr 10-80 p528
-HFN 10-80 p107
+-HFN 12-80 p159
/-MT 4-81 p247
+STL 9-14-80 p40

2676 The tempest. Jennifer Smith, Rosemary Hardy, s; Carol Hall, ms; John Elwes, t; Stephen Varcoe, bar; David Thomas, Roderick Earle, bs; Monteverdi Orchestra and Choir; John Eliot Gardiner. Erato STU 71274 Tape (c) MCE 71274
++Gr 4-80 p1579
+HFN 4-80 p108
+HFN 10-80 p117 tape
++MT 6-81 p391
+RR 5-80 p48
+STL 4-13-80 p39

Timon of Athens: Overture. See no. 2665
Trumpet tune. See no. 3629. See no. 4100
Trumpet tune and air, D major. See no. 1211
Trumpet tune and almand. See no. 3959
Trumpet tunes and ayre. See no. 4002
Trumpet voluntary. See no. 3798. See no. 4100
Tyrannic love: Hark my Damilcar; Ah how sweet it is to love. See no. 2661
The virtuous wife. See no. 2653
Voluntary, C major. See no. 3625
Voluntary, 2 trumpets, C major. See no. 1211

2677 Works, selections: Celebrate the festival: Crown the altar. Fantasia, D major. Musick's handmaid: Sefauchi's farewell; A new ground, E minor. Overtures, G major, D minor, G minor. Pavans, A major, B major, G minor. Suite, flute, no. 6, D major. Leonhardt Consort; Gustav Leonhardt. Telefunken AQ 6-41222 Tape (c) CQ 4-41222
++Gr 9-81 p460 tape
++HFN 3-81 p97

Yorkshire feast song. See no. 2675

PYCARD, (15th century)
Gloria. See no. 4085

QUAGLIATI, Paolo
La sfera armoniosa: O primavera gioventa dell'anno; Soavissimi fiori; Amore il mio tormento e la mia fede. See no. 4067

QUANTZ, Johann
Concerto, flute, G major. See no. 123
Sonata, flute, F major. See no. 111

QUARANTA
Songs: O ma charmante. See no. 4024
Songs: Lasciali dir tu m'ami; Si dice. See no. 4041

QUELDRYK (15th century England)
Gloria in excelsis. See no. 3845

QUILTER, Roger
Children's overture, op. 17. See no. 3652

Songs: Blow blow thou winter wind, op. 6, no. 3; Come away death, op. 6, no. 1; Hark hark the lark; Hey ho the wind and the rain, op. 23, no. 5; O mistress mine, op. 6, no. 2. See no. 3878
Songs: Now sleeps the crimson petal, op. 3, no. 2. See no. 3967

QUINTERO, Juan
Morucha. See no. 3983

RABAUD, Henri
2678 Divertissement sur des chansons russes, op. 2. Eglogue, op. 7. Marouf, Savetier du Caire: Ballet music. La procession nocturne, op. 6. Orchestre Philharmonique des Pays de Loire; Pierre Dervaux. Pathe Marconi C 069 16303
+ARG 9-80 p45 +Gr 1-81 p952
+FF 5/6-81 p131 +HFN 4-81 p75
Eglogue, op. 7. See no. 2678
La fille de Roland: Chanson des epees. See no. 3688
Marouf, Savetier du Caire: Ballet music. See no. 2678
La procession nocturne, op. 6. See no. 2678

RABBATH, Francois
2679 Briez. Embruns. Equation. Incantation pour Junon. L'Odysee d'eau. Horda. Mutants d'eau pale. Poucha-dass. Papa Georges. Thyossane. Francois Rabbath, double-bs; with percussion. QCA RM 394
+ARG 9-81 p28 +-NR 8-80 p8
+IN 11-81 p94
Embruns. See no. 2679
Equation. See no. 2679
Horda. See no. 2679
Incantation pour Junon. See no. 2679
Mutants d'eau pale. See no. 2679
L'Odysee d'eau. See no. 2679
Papa Georges. See no. 2679
Poucha-dass. See no. 2679
Thyossane. See no. 2679

RACHMANINOFF, Sergei
Aleko: Intermezzo and women's dance. See no. 2704
Barcarolle, op. 10, no. 3. G minor. See no. 2046
2680 The bells, op. 35. Galina Pisarenko, s; Alexei Maslennikov, t; Sergei Yakovenko, bar; RSFSR Academic Russian Choir; USSR Symphony Orchestra; Yevgeny Svetlanov. HMV ASD 4005 Tape (c) TC ASD 4005
-Gr 5-81 p1509 +-HFN 7-81 p75
2681 The bells, op. 35. Yelizaveta Shumskaya, s; Mikhail Dovenman, t; Aleksei Bolshakov, bar; RSFSR Russian Chorus; MPO; Kiril Kondrashin. Quintessence PMC 7173
++FF 5/6-81 p131
2682 Concerto, piano, no. 2, op. 18, C minor. Rhapsody on a theme by Paganini, op. 43. Gary Graffman, pno; NYP; Leonard Bernstein. CBS MY 36772
+FF 11/12-81 p220
2683 Concerto, piano, no. 2, op. 18, C minor. Rhapsody on a theme by Paganini, op. 43. Jean-Philippe Collard, pno; Toulouse Capitole Orchestra; Michel Plasson. Connoisseur Tape (c) EC 7004
+HF 8-81 p69 tape
2684 Concerto, piano, no. 2, op. 18, C minor. SCHUMANN: Concerto, piano, op. 54, A minor. Alicia de Larrocha, pno; RPO; Charles Dutoit. Decca SXL 6978 Tape (c) KSXC 6978

+Gr 12-81 p886

2685 Concerto, piano, no. 2, op. 18, C minor. Rhapsody on a theme by Paganini, op. 43. Jean-Philippe Collard, pno; Toulouse Capitole Orchestra; Michel Plasson. HMV SQ ESD 7076 Tape (c) ESD 7076
+-FF 7/8-81 p146
+-Gr 7-79 p210
+-HFN 7-79 p111
+-HFN 8-79 p123 tape
+-RR 7-79 p66

2686 Concerto, piano, no. 2, op. 18, C minor. Artur Rubinstein, pno; PO; Eugene Ormandy. RCA RL 1-0031 Tape (c) RK 1-0031 (From ARD 1-0031)
+-Gr 3-81 p1202
+-HFN 6-81 p85
+-HFN 6-81 p87 tape

2687 Concerto, piano, no. 2, op. 18, C minor. Rhapsody on a theme by Paganini, op. 43. Benno Moisewitsch, pno; PhO; Hugo Rignold. World Records SH 380
+Gr 1-81 p998
+-HFN 12-80 p153

Concerto, piano, no. 2, op. 18, C minor. See no. 4017

2688 Concerto, piano, no. 3, op. 30, D minor. Alexis Weissenberg, pno; Orchestre National de France; Leonard Bernstein. Angel SZ 3772 (also HMV ASD 4082)
-Gr 10-81 p558
-HFN 11-81 p96
-NR 9-81 p4
++St 11-81 p91

2689 Concerto, piano, no. 3, op. 30, D minor. Andrei Gavrilov, pno; USSR State Academic Orchestra; Alexander Lazarev. CBS/Melodiya M 36685 Tape (c) MT 36685
+FF 9/10-81 p156
+St 6-81 p126

2690 Concerto, piano, no. 3, op. 30, D minor. Jean-Philippe Collard, pno; Capitole de Toulouse Orchestra; Michel Plasson. Connoisseur Society Tape (c) Sync C 4003
+-ARG 7-79 p42 tape
+-Audio 12-79 p121 tape
+-FF 11/12-79 p19
+Gr 8-81 p324
+-HF 7-79 p157 tape
+HF 9-79 p131 tape
++SFC 3-25-79 p41 tape
+St 7-79 p108 tape

2691 Concerto, piano, no. 3, op. 30, D minor. Alexis Weissenberg, pno; CSO; Georges Pretre. RCA AGL 1-3366
+FF 7/8-81 p147

2692 Concerto, piano, no. 3, op. 30, D minor. Earl Wild, pno; RPO; Jascha Horenstein. RCA GL 2-5292 Tape (c) GK 2-5292 (From Readers Digest RDS 6253)
+Gr 8-81 p276
+-HFN 8-81 p92 tape

2693 Concerto, piano, no. 4, op. 40, G minor. Rhapsody on a theme by Paganini, op. 43. Earl Wild, pno; RPO; Jascha Horenstein. RCA GL 2-5293 Tape (c) GK 2-5293 (also Readers Digest RDS 6251/4)
+-Gr 12-81 p886

Danses tziganes, op. 6, no. 2. See no. 3872
Etudes tableaux, op. 33. See no. 2696
Etudes tableaux, op. 33, nos. 1 and 2. See no. 589
Etudes tableaux, op. 33, no. 7, E flat major. See no. 3869
Etudes tableaux, op. 39. See no. 2696
Etudes tableaux, op. 39, nos. 3, 5, 9. See no. 1967
Etudes tableaux, op. 39, no. 5. See no. 589
Floods of spring, op. 14, no. 11. See no. 3952
Fragments. See no. 2696

Humoreske, op. 10, no. 5, G major. See no. 2046
Lilacs, op. 21, no. 5. See no. 589

2694 Moments musicaux, op. 16. Pieces, piano, op. 10 (7). Ruth Laredo, pno. CBS M 35836 Tape (c) MT 35836
+-ARG 9-80 p36 +-FF 1/2-81 p167

Moments musicaux, op. 16. See no. 2696
Morceau de fantaisie, nos. 1-2. See no. 2696

2695 Morceau de fantaisie, op. 3, no. 3, E major. Variations on a theme by Chopin, op. 22. Variations on a theme by Corelli, op. 42. MENDELSSOHN (trans. Rachmaninoff): A midsummer night's dream, opp. 21/61: Scherzo. Howard Shelley, pno. Hyperion A 66009
+-Gr 4-81 p1346 +HFN 4-81 p75

Morceau de salon, op. 10. See no. 2696
Oriental sketch. See no. 2696

2696 Piano works: Etudes tableaux, op. 33. Etudes tableaux, op. 39. Fragments. Morceau de fantaisie, nos. 1-2. Morceau de salon, op. 10. Moments musicaux, op. 16. Oriental sketch. Pieces, piano, op. 3. Polka de V.R. Prelude. Preludes, op. 23 (10). Preludes, op. 32 (13). Sonata, no. 1, op. 28, D minor. Sonata, no. 2, op. 36, B flat minor. Variations on a theme by Chopin, op. 22. Variations on a theme by Corelli, op. 42. Transcriptions: Bach: Partita, violin, E major: Prelude; Gavotte; Gigue. Bizet: L'Arlesienne suite, no. 1: Minuet. Kreisler: Liebesfreud. Liebesleid. Mendelssohn: A midsummer night's dream: Scherzo. Mussorgsky: Fair at Sorochinsk: Gopak. Rachmaninoff: Daisies. Lilacs. Rimsky-Korsakov: Flight of the bumblebee. Tchaikovsky: Lullaby. Ruth Laredo, pno. CBS 79700 (7)
+Gr 12-81 p904 +-HFN 12-81 p101

Pieces, piano, op. 3. See no. 2696
Pieces, piano, op. 10. See no. 2694
Polichinelle. See no. 3993
Polka de V.R. See no. 2696. See no. 2698
Prelude. See no. 2696
Preludes, nos. 3, 5-6. See no. 2508

2697 Preludes, op. 3, no. 2, C sharp minor; op. 23, no. 1, F sharp minor; op. 23, no. 4, D major; op. 32, no. 12, G sharp minor; op. 32, no. 10, B minor; op. 23, no. 2, B flat major. Variations on a theme by Corelli, op. 42. Lazar Berman, pno. DG 2531 276 Tape (c) 3301 276
+CL 3-81 p15 +-HFN 11-80 p122
+-FF 5/6-81 p202 ++MT 6-81 p392
+Gr 11-80 p703 ++St 3-81 p93
+HF 4-81 p90

Prelude, op. 3, no. 2, C sharp minor. See no. 1295. See no. 1967. See no. 2259
Preludes, op. 23. See no. 2696
Preludes, op. 23, nos. 1, 2, 4. See no. 2697
Preludes, op. 23, nos. 2, 4-5, 7. See no. 2507
Preludes, op. 23, nos. 6-7. See no. 1967
Preludes, op. 32. See no. 2696
Preludes, op. 32, nos. 1 and 2. See no. 2507
Preludes, op. 32, nos. 2, 5, 10-12. See no. 1967
Preludes, op. 32, nos. 3, 9. See no. 3869
Preludes, op. 32, nos. 10, 12. See no. 2697

Rhapsody on a theme by Paganini, op. 43. See no. 2682. See no. 2683. See no. 2685. See no. 2687. See no. 2693

2698 Sonata, piano, no. 1, op. 28, D minor. Sonata, piano, no. 2, op. 36, B flat minor. Polka de V. R. Ruth Laredo, pno. CBS M 35881 Tape (c) MT 35881
++ARG 3-81 p48 ++NR 1-81 p15
++FF 1/2-81 p168 ++St 1-81 p74

2699 Sonata, piano, no. 1, op. 28, D minor. Sonata, piano, no. 2, op. 36, B flat minor. Francois-Joel Thiollier, pno. RCA RL 3-7142
+-CL 1-81 p14

Sonata, piano, no. 1, op. 28, D minor. See no. 2696

2700 Sonata, piano, no. 2, op. 36, B flat minor. MENDELSSOHN: Scherzo a capriccio, F sharp minor. SCHUMANN: Fantasiestucke, op. 111. Nachtstucke, op. 23, nos. 3, 4. Vladimir Horowitz, pno. RCA ARL 1-3775 Tape (c) ARK 1-3775
+-FF 5/6-81 p132

Sonata, piano, no. 2, op. 36, B flat minor. See no. 2217. See no. 2696. See no. 2698. See no. 2699

2701 Sonata, violoncello and piano, op. 19, G minor. Stephen Kates, vlc; Carolyn Kobler, pno. Audible Images Tape (c) A1-107
+Audio 11-81 p69 tape

Sonata, violoncello and piano, op. 19, G minor. See no. 2631

Sonata, violoncello and piano, op. 19, G minor: Slow movement. See no. 3667

2702 Songs: All things depart, op. 26, no. 15; As fair as day in blaze of noon, op. 14, no. 9; By the gates of the holy dwelling; Did you hiccough; Do you remember the evening; A flower fell; From St. John's gospel; Let me rest here alone, op. 26, no. 9; Letter to S. Stanislavsky from S. Rachmaninoff; Lilacs, op. 21, no. 5 (piano solo); Love's flame, op. 14, no. 2; Night; O do not grieve, op. 14, no. 8; Song of disappointment; The soul's concealment, op. 34, no. 2; Thy pity I implore, op. 26, no. 8; Tis time, op. 14, no. 12; When yesterday we met, op. 26, no. 13; With holy banner firmly held, op. 34, no. 11. Elisabeth Soderstrom, s; Vladimir Ashkenazy, pno. Decca SXL 6940 (also London OS 26615)
++FF 3/4-81 p173 +HFN 9-80 p110
+Gr 10-80 p528 ++NYT 4-5-81 pD33

Songs: Before my window, op. 26, no. 10; O cease thy singing maiden fair, op. 4, no. 4; To the children, op. 26, no. 7; When night descends, op. 43, no. 3. See no. 3967

Songs: Christ is risen, op. 26, no. 6; The harvest of sorrow, op. 4, no. 5; How fair this spot, op. 21, no. 7; A dream, op. 8, no. 5; Night is mournful, op. 26, no. 12; Oh stay my love, op. 4, no. 1; Oh never sing to me again, op. 4, no. 4; When yesterday we met, op. 26, no. 13. See no. 2516

Songs: Georgian song. See no. 4028

Songs: To the children, op. 26, no. 7. See no. 4043

Songs: To thee O Lord do I lift up my soul. See no. 3636

2703 Suite, 2 pianos, no. 1, op. 5. Suite, 2 pianos, no. 2, op. 17. Guber and Suher Pekinel, pno. DG 2531 345
++FF 11/12-81 p220 ++OV 12-81 p36
+-Gr 8-81 p296 +St 11-81 p92
+-HFN 8-81 p86

Suite, 2 pianos, no. 2, op. 17. See no. 2703

2704 Symphonies, nos. 1-3. Aleko: Intermezzo; Women's dance. LSO; Andre Previn. HMV SLS 5225 (3) Tape (c) TC SLS 5225 (From ASD 3137, 2889, 3369)
++Gr 7-81 p160 ++HFN 10-81 p95 tape
++HFN 7-81 p79

2705 Symphonies, nos. 1-3. St. Louis Symphony Orchestra; Leonard Slatkin. Vox QSVBX 5152 (3) Tape (c) CBX 5152
+ARG 12-79 p51 +-NYT 7-1-79 pD22
+-FF 11/12-79 p113 ++St 9-79 p98
+HF 5-81 p53 tape

2706 Symphony, no. 2, op. 27, E minor. PhO; Ling Tung. ASV ACM 2016 (From Enigma K 53568)
+Gr 4-81 p1323 +-HFN 5-81 p91

2707 Symphony, no. 2, op. 27, E minor. Scottish National Orchestra; Alexander Gibson. Chandos ABRD 1021 Tape (c) ABTD 1021
+-FF 9/10-81 p157 +-HFN 3-81 p90
+Gr 3-81 p1202 +-HFN 5-81 p93 tape
+Gr 6-81 p93 tape

2708 Symphony, no. 2, op. 27, E minor. Rotterdam Philharmonic Orchestra; Edo de Waart. Philips 9500 309 Tape (c) 7300 610 (r) G 9500 309
++ARG 1-79 p27 ++HFN 2-79 p118 tape
+-Gr 12-78 p1109 ++NR 2-79 p2
+HF 5-79 p90 +-RR 12-78 p65
+HF 6-81 p70 tape +St 2-79 p133
+HFN 12-78 p159

2709 Symphony, no. 3, op. 44, A minor. Vocalise, op. 34, no. 14. PO; Eugene Ormandy. CBS 61994 Tape (c) 40-61994 (From 72674) (also Columbia MS 6110)
++Gr 1-81 p952 +-HFN 1-81 p107
+Gr 6-81 p93 tape +-HFN 3-81 p97 tape

2710 Symphony, no. 3, op. 44, A minor. MUSSORGSKY: A night on the bare mountain. OSR; Paul Kletzki. London STS 15530
+/FF 9/10-81 p157

Transcriptions: Bach: Partita, violin, E major; Prelude; Gavotte; Gigue. Bizet: L'Arlesienne suite, no. 1: Minuet. Kreisler: Liebesfreud. Liebesleid. Mendelssohn: A midsummer night's dream: Scherzo. Mussorgsky: Fair at Sorochinsk: Gopak. Rachmaninoff: Daisies. Lilacs. Rimsky-Korsakov: Flight of the bumblebee. Tchaikovsky: Lullaby. See no. 2696

Variations on a theme by Chopin, op. 22. See no. 2695. See no. 2696

Variations on a theme by Corelli, op. 42. See no. 2695. See no. 2696. See no. 2697

2711 Vespers, op. 37. TCHAIKOVSKY: Vespers, op. 52. Maria-Luise Gilles, alto; Gunter Schmitz, t; Johannes Damascenus Chor for Ostkirchliche Liturgie Essen, Romanes Chor fur Estkirchliche Liturgie Essen, Chor des Missions Priesterseminars der Spiritaner in Knechtsteden, Knaben Schola St. Elisabeth Essen, Chor der Monche der Benediktiner Abtei Chevetogne Belgien; Karl Linke, Winfried Pentek, Josef Wipper, Theo Schafer, Philippe Baer. Schwann AMS 1921 (4) (also Musical Heritage Society MHS 1656)
+FF 1/12-81 p217

Vocalise, op. 34, no. 14. See no. 589. See no. 1954. See no. 2709

RAFF, Joachim

2712 Octet, op. 176, C major. SPOHR: Quartet, op. 65, D minor. Die Kammermusiker Zurich. Jecklin 547
/FF 3/4-81 p197

Serenade. See no. 3967

RAIMBAUT DE VAQUEIRAS

Kalenda maia. See no. 4086

RAMEAU, Jean

2713 Le berger fidele. Hippolyte et Aricie: Air du rossignol. Orphee. Colette Herzog, s; I Solisti Veneti; Claudio Scimone. Erato STU 71214
+-HFN 4-80 p108 +-RR 5-80 p99
-MT 3-81 p184

2714 Castor et Pollux: Overture; Venus o Venus c'est a toi; Venus que ta gloire reponde; Venus o Venus; D'un spectacle nouveau; Que tout gemisse; Tristes apprets pales flambeaux; Votre amour pour mon frere...Que l'enfer applaudisse; Nature amour qui partagez mon coeur; Tout l'eclat de l'Olympe; Air pour Hebe et ses suivantes; Un malheureux amour...Qu' Hebe de fleurs; Rassemblez-vous; Sortez sortez d'esclavage; Air des demons; Brisons tous nos fers; Sejour de l'eternelle paix; Ritournelle; Castor revoit le jour; Tonnerre--Qu'ai-je entendu; Palais de ma grandeur...Tant de vertus; Brillez astres nouveaux; Que le ciel que la terre et l'onde. Jeanette Scovotti, Marta Schele, s; Norma Lerer, ms; Zeger Vandersteene, t; Gerard Souzay, bar; Jacques Villisech, bs; Stockholm Chamber Choir; VCM; Nikolaus Harnoncourt. Telefunken 6-42024 Tape (c) CQ 4-42024 (From HF 6-35048)
+Gr 3-81 p1234 +HFN 7-81 p81
+Gr 9-81 p460 tape

2715 Concerts en sextour (6). Caen Chamber Orchestra. Calliope CAL 1838
+-HFN 1-81 p99

2716 Concerts en sextour (6). Stuttgart Soloists; Marcel Couraud. Philips 6537 007
+-MUM 3/4-81 p31

2717 Dardanus. Frederica von Stade, s; Georges Cautier; Roger Soyer, bar; Paris Opera Orchestra and Chorus; Raymond Leppard. Erato STU 71416 (2)
+Gr 5-81 p1515 ++MUM 9/10-81 p32
+-HFN 9-81 p84 +STL 3-8-81 p38

L'Enharmonique, G minor. See no. 3916

2718 Les fetes d'Hebe: La danse, Act 3. Jill Gomez, Anne-Marie Rodde, s; Jean-Claude Orliac, t; Marilyn Sansom, vlc; Nicholas Kramer, hpd; Monteverdi Orchestra and Choir; John Eliot Gardiner. Erato STU 71089 (also Musical Heritage Society MHS 4247)
++ARG 3-81 p49 ++MT 1-80 p35
+Gr 5-79 p1925 +RR 3-79 p52
+-FF 1/2-81 p168

Hippolyte et Aricie: Air du rossignol. See no. 2713

2719 Hippolyte et Aricie: Suite. La Petite Bande; Sigiswald Kuijken. Harmonia Mundi 1C 065 99837
++Gr 5-80 p1671 ++RR 5-80 p68
+-HFN 6-80 p111 +STL 6-8-80 p38
+-MT 10-81 p677

Hymne a la nuit. See no. 3796

2720 Les Indes galantes: Airs and dances. Kenneth Gilbert, hpd. Harmonia Mundi HM 1028
+FF 5/6-80 p135
+Gr 2-80 p1282
+HFN 3-80 p97
+MT 1-81 p35
+St 6-80 p119

2721 Les Indes galantes: Ballet suite. Collegium Aureum. Harmonia Mundi 1C 065 99864
+FF 11/12-80 p122
+-HFN 11-81 p103

Les Indes galantes: Concert, no. 3. See no. 2727

2722 Nais. Lynda Russell, s; Ann Mackay, ms; Ian Caley, t; Ian Caddy, bar; John Tomlinson, bs; English Bach Festival Singers and Baroque Orchestra; Nicolas McGegan. Erato STU 71439 (2)
+-Gr 10-81 p609
+-HFN 12-81 p101

2723 Nouvelles suites de pieces de clavecin. Alan Curtis, hpd. Harmonia Mundi 1C 065 99918
+Gr 11-81 p724
+-HFN 12-81 p101

Orphee. See no. 2713

Pieces de clavecin: L'Entretien des muses; Le lardon; La triomphante. See no. 3877

2724 Pieces de clavecin: Suites (4). Trevor Pinnock, hpd. Vanguard VSD 71270/1
+FF 9/10-80 p182
+NR 10-80 p15
+SFC 3-29-81 p18

2725 Pieces de clavecin: Suites, E minor, G major. Alan Curtis, hpd. Harmonia Mundi 1C 065 99918
+-FF 11/12-81 p221

2726 La Princesse de Navarre. Marilyn Hill-Smith, Eiddwen Harrhy, Frances Chambers, Judith Rees, s; Michael Goldthorpe, alto; Peter Savidge, bar; Ian Caddy, Richard Wigmore, bs; English Bach Festival Singers; Baroque Orchstra; Nicolas McGegan. Erato STU 71283 Tape (c) MCE 71283
+-Gr 6-81 p84

2727 Pygmalion. Les Indes galantes: Concert, no. 3. Andree Esposito, Claudine Collart, Edith Selig, s; Eric Marion, t; Raymond Saint-Paul Choir; Lamoureux Chamber Orchestra; Marcel Couraud. DG 2547 047 Tape (c) 3347 047 (From 198302)
+-Gr 4-81 p1362
+Gr 9-81 p460 tape
+-HFN 7-81 p81
+-HFN 7-81 p83 tape

Suite. See no. 3715

Suite, E major. See no. 1253

Suite, E minor. See no. 3916

RAMSEY, Robert

What tears dear prince can serve. See no. 3807

RAMSOE, Wilhelm

Quartet, no. 5. See no. 3662

RANGSTROM, Ture

King Erik's songs. See no. 2728

Songs in antique style (2). See no. 2728

2728 Symphony, no. 3. King Erik's songs. Songs in antique style (2). Hakan Hagegard, bar; Helsingborg Symphony Orchestra; Janos Furst, John Frandsen. EMI (Sweden) 7C 061 35774
+FF 9/10-81 p157
+-Gr 11-81 p764

RAPOPORT-HAMEIRI

Jerusalem. See no. 3897

RATCLIFFE, Philip
Mary walked through a wood of thorns. See no. 3634
RATHBONE, Christopher
October music. See no. 4118
RATHGEBER, Valentin
Aria pastorella. See no. 3816
RAUTAVAARA, Einojuhani
A requiem for our time. See no. 3129
Songs: Huojuva heula; Sa var det. See no. 3805
RAVEL, Maurice
A la maniere de Borodine. See no. 2745. See no. 2746
A la maniere de Chabrier. See no. 2745. See no. 2746

2729 Berceuse sur le nom de Faure. Sonata, violin and piano. Sonata, violin and piano, op. posth. Tzigane. Charles Libove, vln; Nina Lugovoy, pno. Finnadar SR 9028
+-ARG 1-81 p39 +FF 1/2-81 p171

2730 Bolero. Daphnis et Chloe: Suite, no. 2. Pavane pour une infante defunte. LSO; Andre Previn. Angel SZ 37670 Tape (c) 4ZS 37670 (also HMV ASD 3912 Tape (c) TC ASD 3912)
+-FF 1/2-81 p169 +-NR 1-81 p2
++Gr 11-80 p674 ++SFC 11-30-80 p21
-HF 7-81 p66 +St 3-81 p93
++HFN 11-80 p122

2731 Bolero. Daphnis and Chloe: Suite, no. 2. Miroirs: Alborada del gracioso. La valse. Orchestre National de France; NYP; Leonard Bernstein. CBS MY 36714
+-FF 11/12-81 p222

2732 Bolero. Pavane pour une infante defunte. La valse. RPO; Claude Monteux. Contour CC 7521 Tape (c) CCT 7521
+Gr 8-81 p316

2733 Bolero. Daphnis et Chloe: Suite, no. 2. La valse. Halle Orchestra; John Barbirolli. Everest SDBR 3741 (From Vanguard 177)
-FF 9/10-81 p158 *NR 12-80 p5
-HF 7-81 p66

2734 Bolero. La valse. TCHAIKOVSKY: Nutcracker, op. 71: Suite. COA; Eduard van Beinum. Philips 6570 183 (From SABL 130, 2001)
+FF 7/8-81 p148 +-HFN 6-81 p85
+Gr 6-81 p89

2735 Bolero. Daphnis et Chloe: Suite, no. 2. Ma mere l'oye. Pavane pour une infante defunte. Isao Tomita, electronics. RCA ARL 1-3412 Tape (c) RK 1-3412 (also CRD 1-3412)
-Audio 1-81 p81 +*HFN 2-81 p91
-FF 7/8-80 p124 +NR 5-80 p15
+-HFN 10-80 p117

2736 Bolero. Pavane pour une infante defunte. La valse. BSO; Charles Munch. RCA AGL 1-3653
+-FF 7/8-81 p148

2737 Bolero. Miroirs: Alborada del gracioso. Rapsodie espagnole. Dallas Symphony Orchestea; Eduardo Mata. RCA ARC 1-3686 Tape (c) ARK 1-3686
++ARG 2-81 p26 +MUM 2-81 p35
+FF 1/2-81 p168 ++NR 11-80 p2
+Gr 4-81 p1323 ++SFC 10-26-80 p20
+HF 7-81 p66 +SR 1-81 p92
++HFN 2-81 p90 ++St 2-81 p76

2738 Bolero. Daphnis et Chloe: Suite, no. 2. Pavane pour une infante defunte. St. Louis Symphony Orchestra and Chorus; Leonard Slatkin. Telarc 10052
+/FF 5/6-81 p133 +-HFN 6-81 p77
+-Gr 4-81 p1323 ++NR 5-81 p2
+HF 7-81 p66 ++St 3-81 p93
Bolero. See no. 750. See no. 1303. See no. 4003
2739 Concerto, piano, G major. Concerto, piano, for the left hand, D major. Jean-Philippe Collard, pno; French National Orchestra; Lorin Maazel. HMV ASD 3845 Tape (c) TC ASD 3845 (also Angel SZ 37730)
+-CL 3-81 p14 +HFN 6-80 p111
+FF 1/2-81 p170 ++HFN 9-80 p116 tape
+FF 3/4-81 p174 +NR 3-81 p6
+Gr 6-80 p38 +RR 6-80 p58
++Gr 9-80 p413 ++SFC 11-30-80 p21
++Gr 3-81 p1171 +STL 7-13-80 p38
Concerto, piano, G major. See no. 1278. See no. 2615
Concerto, piano, for the left hand, D major. See no. 2739. See no. 3709
2740 Daphnis et Chloe. Montreal Orchestra and Chorus; Charles Dutoit. London LDR 71028 (also Decca SXDL 7526 Tape (c) SXDC 7526)
+FF 11/12-81 p222 ++HFN 7-81 p75
++Gr 6-81 p44 ++MUM 7/8-81 p33
++Gr 9-81 p460 tape ++SFC 11-29-81 p18
2741 Daphnis et Chloe. Dallas Symphony Orchestra and Chorus; Eduardo Mata. RCA ARC 1-3458 Tape (c) ARK 1-3458
++ARG 9-80 p38 +-HFN 7-80 p109
+-FF 7/8-80 p135 ++NR 5-80 p2
+Gr 7-80 p142 +-RR 7-80 p63
+HF 8-80 p79 +SFC 3-23-80 p35
+-HF 3-81 p80 tape
2742 Daphnis et Chloe: Suite, no. 2. Pavane pour une infante defunte. Songs: Melodies hebraiques. Nadine Denize, s; Lille Philharmonic Orchestra; Jean-Claude Casadesus. Harmonia Mundi HM 10064 Tape (c) 40064
++FF 9/10-80 p183 +-HFN 6-80 p111
+-Gr 5-80 p1672 +RR 5-80 p69
+HF 7-81 p66
2743 Daphnis et Chloe: Suite, no. 2. Ma mere l'oye: Suite. Pavane pour une infante defunte. La valse. Orchestra; Sergiu Celibidache. Rococo 2141
+NR 3-81 p1
Daphnis et Chloe: Suite, no. 2. See no. 1300. See no. 2730. See no. 2731. See no. 2733. See no. 2735. See no. 2738
Don Quichotte a Dulcinee. See no. 4119
Forlane. See no. 17
Frontispiece. See no. 2746
2744 Gaspard de la nuit. SCRIABIN: Preludes, op. 11 (24). Walter Gieseking, pno. Rococo 2090
++CL 9-81 p18 ++NR 3-80 p14
Gaspard de la nuit. See no. 627. See no. 2745. See no. 2746
Gaspard de la nuit: Ondine. See no. 1290
Introduction and allegro. See no. 1499
Jeux d'eau. See no. 1290. See no. 2745. See no. 2746

Ma mere l'oye. See no. 1282. See no. 1301. See no. 2194. See no. 2735. See no. 2745. See no. 2746. See no. 3665
Ma mere l'oye: Pavane. See no. 3730
Ma mere l'oye: Suite. See no. 2743
Menuet antique. See no. 2745. See no. 2746. See no. 2747
Menuet sur le nom de Haydn. See no. 2745. See no. 2746
Miroirs. See no. 2745. See no. 2746. See no. 2747
Miroirs: Alborada del gracioso. See no. 2731. See no. 2737. See no. 3749
Miroirs: Noctuelles; Oiseaux tristes; La vallee des cloches. See no. 3723
Pavane. See no. 2746
Pavane pour une infante defunte. See no. 250. See no. 1282. See no. 1499. See no. 2730. See no. 2732. See no. 2735. See no. 2736. See no. 2738. See no. 2742. See no. 2743. See no. 2745. See no. 2747. See no. 3666. See no. 4001

2745 Piano works: A la maniere de Borodine. A la maniere de Chabrier. Gaspard de la nuit. Jeux d'eau. Menuet sur le nom de Haydn. Ma mere l'oye. Menuet antique. Pavane pour une infante defunte. Prelude. Miroirs. Les sites auriculaires: Habanera. La tombeau de Couperin. Valses nobles et sentimentales. Robert Casadesus, Gaby Casadesus, pno. CBS 77346 (3)
+Gr 11-80 p703 +-HFN 1-81 p107

2746 PIano works: A la maniere de Borodine. A la maniere de Chabrier. Frontispiece. Gaspard de la nuit. Jeux d'eau. Ma mere l'oye. Menuet antique. Menuet sur le nom de Haydn. Miroirs. Pavane. Prelude. Serenade grotesque. Les sites auriculaires. Sonatine. Le tombeau de Couperin. La valse. Valses nobles et sentimentales. Jean-Philippe Collard, Michel Beroff, Katia Labeque, pno. Pathe Marconi EMI 2C 167 73025/7 (3)
+-FF 7/8-81 p148 +STL 7-12-81 p40
+Gr 5-81 p1501

2747 Piano works: Menuet antique. Miroirs. Prelude. Pavane pour un infante defunte. Le tombeau de Couperin. Valses nobles et sentimentales. Kun Woo Paik, pno. Quintessence 2PCM 2712 (2)
+-FF 7/8-81 p149

Piece en forme de habanera. See no. 2750
Piece en forme de habanera, op. 21, no. 2. See no. 3841. See no. 3847
Prelude. See no. 2745. See no. 2746. See no. 2747
Quartet, strings, F major. See no. 440. See no. 1315
Rhapsodie espagnole. See no. 1114. See no. 1301. See no. 2737
Serenade grotesque. See no. 2746
Sheherazade. See no. 758. See no. 2752
Sheherazade: Asie. See no. 3713
Les sites auriculaires. See no. 2746
Les sites auriculaires: Habanera. See no. 2745

2748 Sonata, violin. Trio, violin, violoncello and piano. Caecilian Trio. Turnabout TVC 37007 Tape (c) CT 7007
+-FF 3/4-81 p175

2749 Sonata, violin and piano. Sonata, violin and piano, op. posth. Trio, piano, A minor. Augustin Dumay, vln; Frederic Lodeon, vlc; Jean-Philippe Collard, pno. EMI 2C 069 73024
+Gr 6-81 p50

2750 Sonata, violin and piano. Piece en forme de habanera. SAINT-SAENS:

Fantaisie, op. 124. James Carter, vln; Marilyn Thompson, pno; Anne Adams, hp. Sound Storage SSR 2030
+FF 11/12-81 p223

Sonata, violin and piano. See no. 1319. See no. 2729. See no. 2984. See no. 4072

2751 Sonata, violin and piano, G major. Trio, piano, A minor.* Tzigane. Beaux Arts Trio; Arthur Grumiaux, vln; Istvan Hajdu, pno. Philips 6570 177 Tape (c) 7310 177 (*From SAL 3619)
+Gr 10-80 p512
-Gr 2-81 p1122 tape
+HFN 11-80 p129
+HFN 1-81 p109 tape
+NYT 6-21-81 pD23

Sonata, violin and piano, op. posth. See no. 2729. See no. 2749

Sonatine. See no. 1289. See no. 2746. See no. 4020

Sonatine en trio. See no. 1317

2752 Songs: Chansons madecasses; Melodies hebraiques (2); Melodies populaires Grecques, excerpts. Sheherazade. Frederica von Stade, ms; Doriot Anthony Dwyer, flt; Jules Eskind, vlc; Martin Katz, pno; BSO; Seiji Ozawa. CBS IM 36665 Tape (c) HMT 36665
+FF 7/8-81 p151
+Gr 7-81 p186
++Gr 10-81 p614 tape
+-HFN 7-81 p75
+HFN 9-81 p93 tape
++MUM 9/10-81 p37 tape
++SFC 9-19-81 p18
+SR 7-81 p90
+St 9-81 p100
+STL 7-12-81 p40

Songs: Melodies hebraiques. See no. 2742

Songs: Melodies hebraiques: Kaddisch. See no. 3

Songs: Nicolette; Trois beaux oiseaux de Paradis; Ronde. See no. 4005

2753 Le tombeau de Couperin. STRAVINSKY: Petrouchka: Movements (3). Piano rag music. David Lively, pno. DG 2535 009
-CL 2-81 p12
+FF 1/2-81 p81
+HF 1-81 p58
+-NR 1-81 p14
+-NYT 3-8-81 pD34
+St 2-81 p54

Le tombeau de Couperin. See no. 1499. See no. 2511. See no. 2745. See no. 2746. See no. 2747

Trio, piano, A minor. See no. 2749. See no. 2751

Trio, violin, violoncello and piano. See no. 2748

Tzigane. See no. 1130. See no. 2729. See no. 2751. See no. 3841

La valse. See no. 1113. See no. 1492. See no. 2731. See no. 3732. See no. 2733. See no. 2734. See no. 2736. See no. 2743. See no. 2746

Valses nobles et sentimentales. See no. 2745. See no. 2746. See no. 2747

RAVENSCROFT, Thomas

Hornpipe. See no. 3959

Now Robin lend to me thy bow. See no. 3670

Songs: By a bank as I lay; He that will an alehouse keep; Jinkin the jester; The maid she went a-milking; Malt's come down; What I hap had to marry a shrow. See no. 3973

Songs: By a bank as I lay; We be three poor mariners. See no. 4058

Songs: Canst thou love and lie alone; Hey ho nobody at home; Give us once a drink; Hey ho to the greenwood; I cannot come every day; Long have we been perplext; Tomorrow the fox will come; Who liveth so merry; Who's the fool now; Yonder comes a courteous knight. See no. 4093

RAZZI, Serafino
Songs: Crucifixum in carne; Jesu dulcis memoria; O Maria diana stella; O signor mio. See no. 4011
REA, John
Reception and offering music. See no. 1101
READ, Daniel
Songs: Expression; He is king of kings; I believe this is Jesus; Star in the East; Rise up shepherd and follow; Sherburne. See no. 3911
READ, Gardner
Los dioses aztecas, op. 107. See no. 2091
REBEL, Jean-Fery
Les elements. See no. 1342
REDOLFI, Michel
2754 Immersion. Pacific. Tubular waves. Electronic sound, Groupe de Musique de Marseille. Harmonia Mundi INA GRM 3D 833.12 (HM 57)
*+FF 3/4-81 p30
Pacific. See no. 2754
Tubular waves. See no. 2754
REED, Alfred
2755 Armenian dances, Pt 1. Symphony, no. 1. Symphony, no. 2. Tennessee Tech Symphonic Band; R. Winston Morris, Alfred Reed. USC Sound Enterprises KM 4971
+-FF 1/2-81 p171
Symphony, no. 1. See no. 2755
Symphony, no. 2. See no. 2755
REEVE
I am a friar of orders grey. See no. 4077
REGER, Max
Albumblatt, E flat major. See no. 2771
2756 An die Hoffnung, op. 24. Romantische suite, op. 125. Cornelia Wulkopf, con; Landesjungendorchester Nordrhein-Westfalen; Martin Stephani. Da Camera SM 91607
+FF 11/12-81 p223
2757 Aus meinem Tagebuch, op. 82. Richard Laugs, pno. Da Camera SM 93124/6 (3)
-FF 9/10-81 p158
Caprice, op. 79, no. 1, Aminor. See no. 2771
Choral fantasies, op. 67: Meinen Jesum lass ich nicht; Wachet auf ruft uns die Stimme. See no. 198
2758 Concerto, piano, op. 114, F minor. Rudolf Serkin, pno; PO; Eugene Ormandy. CBS 61711 (From SBRG 72399)
++Gr 8-81 p276 +STL 10-11-81 p41
+-HFN 8-81 p91
2759 Concerto, violin, op. 101, A major. Suzanne Lautenbacher, vln; BeSO; Gunther Wich. Intercord INT 160817
/FF 3/4-81 p176 +St 6-81 p123
+-HFN 9-81 p84
2760 Fantasia, op. 27. Fantasia and fugue, op. 135b, D minor. Pieces, organ, op. 59: Toccata; Fugue. Kjell Johnsen, org. Polyhymnia PRC 7812
+FF 9/10-81 p159
2761 Fantasia, op. 40, no. 1. Monologue, op. 63: Ave Maria; Introduction; Passacaglia; Scherzo. Pieces, organ, op. 145: Weihnachten. Rosalinde Hass, org. Motette M 1027
+FF 9/10-81 p159

Fantasia on "Wachet auf ruft uns die Stimme", op. 52, no. 2. See no. 1990
Fantasia and fugue, op. 135b, D minor. See no. 2760
2762 From the 52 easy preludes to the most popular Lutheran chorales, op. 67. Rolf Schonstedt, org. Musical Heritage Society MHS 3790
+FF 11/12-78 p104 +/MU 11-81 p16
2763 Konzert im alten Stil, op. 123, F major. Suite im alten Stil, op. 93. Nurnberg Symphony Orchestra; Gunter Neidlinger. Colosseum SM 542
/FF 9/10-81 p160
Monologue, op. 63: Ave Maria; Introduction; Passacaglia; Scherzo. See no. 2761
Motets, op. 138: Unser lieben Frauen Traum. See no. 3963
Pieces, organ, op. 59: Benedictus. See no. 3725. See no. 3806
Pieces, organ, op. 59: Benedictus; Toccata. See no. 1990
Pieces, organ, op. 59: Pastorale. See no. 4110
Pieces, organ, op. 59: Toccata. See no. 3930
Pieces, organ, op. 59: Toccata; Fugue. See no. 2760
Pieces, organ, op. 65: Scherzo. See no. 4110
2764 Pieces, organ, op. 76 (12). Andreas Schroder, org. Musical Heritage Society MHC 5563
++MU 4-81 p22
Pieces, organ, op. 80: Perpetuum mobile. See no. 4110
Pieces, organ, op. 80: Prelude and fugue, E minor. See no. 2031
Pieces, organ, op. 129: Prelude and fugue, B minor. See no. 2031
Pieces, organ, op. 145: Weihnachten. See no. 2761
2765 Pieces, violoncello and piano, op. 79 (2). Suites, op. 131c (3). Rama Jucker, vlc; Gerard Wyss, pno. Accord ACC 140013
+HFN 9-81 p84
Quartet, strings, D minor. See no. 2771
Quartet, strings, op. 109, E flat major. See no. 2771
2766 Requiem, op. 145a. Requiem, op. 145a: Dies irae. Yoko Kawahara, s; Marga Hoffgen, alto; Hans-Dieter Bader, t; Nikolaus Hillebrand, bs; North German Radio Orchestra and Chorus; Roland Bader. Schwann AMS 3527
+ARG 9-81 p53 +-FF 7/8-81 p152
Romantische suite, op. 125. See no. 2756
Romanze. See no. 1856
Romanze, op. 79, no. 2. See no. 2771
Scherzino. See no. 3655
2767 Serenades, flute, nos. 1, op. 77a, D major; no. 2, op. 141, G major. Peter-Lukas Graf, flt; Sandor Vegh, vln; Rainer Moog, vla. Claves D 8104
++FF 11/12-81 p223 ++Gr 9-81 p402
2768 Sextet, op. 118, F major. Kammermusiker Zurich. Jecklin 543
+FF 1/2-81 p172
Songs: Es waren zwei Konigskinder; Ich hab heut Nacht getraumet. See no. 955
Songs: Maria Wiegenlied, op. 76, no. 52. See no. 3702. See no. 3753
Songs: Wiegenlied, op. 97, no. 2. See no. 2079
Suite, op. 131c. See no. 2765
Suite im alten Stil, op. 93. See no. 2763
Tarantella, G minor. See no. 2771

2769 Trio, strings, op. 77b, A minor. Trio, strings, op. 141b, D minor. New String Trio. Acanta EA 21642
+-Gr 11-80 p692 +RR 7-80 p73
+HFN 8-80 p101 -ST 1-81 p648
Trio, strings, op. 141b, D minor. See no. 2769
2770 Variations and fugue on a theme by Beethoven, op. 86. STRAUSS, R.: Burleske, op. 11, D minor. Hanae Nakajima, pno; Nurnberg Symphony Orchestra; Erich Kloss. Colosseum SM 512
/-FF 9/10-81 p160
Variations and fugue on a theme by Hiller, op. 100. See no. 3684
Variations and fugue on a theme by Mozart, op. 132, A major. See no. 3791
Variations and fugue on a theme by Telemann, op. 134. See no. 1002
Variations on "Heil dir im Siegerkranz". See no. 3950
2771 Works, selections: Albumblatt, E flat major. Caprice, op. 79, no. 1, A minor. Romanze, op. 79, no. 2. Quartet, strings, op. 109, E flat major. Quartet, strings, D minor. Tarantella, G minor. Keller Quartet; Lux Brahn, clt; Philippe Muller, vlc; Richard Laugs, pno. Musical Heritage Society MHS 4287
*FF 5/6-81 p133
REGIS, Johannes
S'il vous plaist que vostre je soye. See no. 3948
REICH, Steve
2772 Music for a large ensemble. Octet. Violin phase. Various performers; Shem Guibbory, vln. ECM 1-1168 Tape (c) M5E 1168 (ct) M8E 1168
+ARG 7/8-81 p28 +-HF 3-81 p74
++FF 3/4-81 p177 +MUM 3/4-81 p33
2773 Music for mallet instruments, voices and organ. Six pianos. Steve Reich and Ensemble. DG 2535 463 Tape (c) 3335 463 (From 2740 106)
*Gr 9-81 p402 +HFN 9-81 p93 tape
+HFN 9-81 p90
Octet. See no. 2772
Six pianos. See no. 2773
Violin phase. See no. 2772
REICHA, Anton
2774 Quartet, flute, op. 98, no. 1, G minor. Quartet, flute, op. 98, no. 2, C major. Aurele Nicolet, flt; Deutsches Streichtrio. Intercord INT 160 833
+HFN 12-81 p102
Quartet, flute, op. 98, no. 2, C major. See no. 2774
2775 Symphony, no. 3, op. 41, E flat major. VORISEK: Symphony, D major. PCO; Frantisek Vajnar. EMI 1C 065 036660
+-Gr 10-81 p563
2776 Trios, horn, op. 82. Bedrich Tylsar, Emanuel Hrdina, Zdenek Tylsar, hn. Supraphon 111 2617
+FF 3/4-81 p179 +SFC 5-31-81 p22
+HFN 10-80 p107 +STL 9-14-80 p40
++NR 3-81 p7
REICHARDT, Johann
Heilige Nacht. See no. 3775
Rondo, B major: Grazioso. See no. 3881

REICHE, Johann
Sonata, no. 19. See no. 4002
REIMANN, Aribert
2777 Lear. Helga Dernesch, Colette Lorand, Julia Varady, s; Karl Helm, George Paskuda, Richard Holm, t; Dietrich Fischer-Dieskau, bar; Hans Wilbrink, Hans Gunter Nocker, bs-bar; Bavarian State Opera Orchestra and Chorus; Gerd Albrecht. DG 2709 089 (3)
+ARG 12-79 p52
++FF 1/2-80 p130
+FU 2-80 p50
+Gr 9-79 p518
+HF 12-81 p90
+HFN 9-79 p109
+MM 12-79 p28
+MT 2-80 p107
+NR 12-79 p9
++ON 12-1-79 p44
+Op 10-79 p976
++RR 9-79 p29
++St 11-80 p108
+STL 12-2-79 p37
REINCKEN
Fugue, G minor. See no. 3951
REINCKEN, Johann
Sonatas, A minor, E minor. See no. 3783
REINECKE, Carl
2778 Concerto. flute, op. 283, D major. Sonata, flute and piano, op. 167, E minor. James Galway, flt; Phillip Moll, pno; LPO; Hiroyuki Iwaki. RCA ATC 1-4034 (also RCA RL 2-5373 Tape (c) RK 2-5373)
+Gr 10-81 p563
++NR 11-81 p6
2779 Sonata, flute and piano, op. 167, E minor. Trio, op. 88, A minor. Mario Venzago, pno; Heinrich Keller, flt; Omar Zabali, ob; Francesco Raselli, hn. Accord ACC 140019
+-HFN 12-81 p102
Sonata, flute and piano, op. 167, E minor. See no. 2778
Trio, op. 88, A minor. See no. 2779
2780 Trio, op. 274. SCHMIDT: Concerto, trumpet and piano. Anthony Plog, tpt; Sharon Davis, pno; David Atkins, clt; Calvin Smith, hn; Pasadena Chamber Orchestra; Robert Duerr. WIM WIMR 20
+FF 9/10-81 p167
+NR 8-81 p9
REINER, Jacob
Behuet euch Gott zu aller Zeit. See no. 3675
Mane nobiscum domine. See no. 3675
REINER, Karel
Drawings. See no. 803
REISSIGER, Carl
Duo brillant, op. 130. See no. 3669. See no. 3793
RENEE
Passions in paint. See no. 3817
RESPIGHI, Ottorino
2781 Ancient airs and dances: Suite, no. 2. Gli uccelli. New Koto Ensemble; Sho Kukumori. Angel SZ 37830 Tape (c) 4SX 37830 (also Toshiba TA 80002)
+FF 9/10-81 p160
*HF 11-81 p103 tape
+NR 8-81 p15
Antiche danze ed arie per liuto: Suite, no. 3. See no. 373
2782 Feste romane. Fountains of Rome. LAPO; Michael Tilson Thomas. CBS M 35846 Tape (c) MT 35846
+FF 1/2-81 p173
+NR 11-80 p2
+NYT 9-7-80 pD26
+SFC 2-8-81 p21
2783 Festa romane. Pines of Rome. CO; Lorin Maazel. Mobile Fidelity

MFSL 1-507
++SFC 9-13-81 p17

2784 Festa romane. Pines of Rome. Baltimore Symphony Orchestra; Sergiu Comissiona. Vanguard VA 25004 Tape (c) CVA 25004
+ARG 12-81 p23 +-HF 12-81 p93 tape
-FF 7/8-81 p152 +NR 6-81 p2

2785 Fountains of Rome. Pines of Rome. OSR; Ernest Ansermet. London STS 15524
+-FF 1/2-81 p173

2786 Fountains of Rome. Pines of Rome. CSO; Fritz Reiner. RCA ATL 1-4040
++FF 11/12-81 p224 +NR 9-81 p3
++MUM 11/12-81 p34 ++SFC 8-9-81 p18

Fountains of Rome. See no. 2782
Gli uccelli. See no. 2781
Pines of Rome. See no. 749. See no. 2783. See no. 2784. See no. 2785. See no. 2786
Siciliana. See no. 3643

2787 Songs: Deita silvane; Lauda per la nativita del Signore. Trittico Botticelliano. Jill Gomez, s; Meriel Dickinson, ms; Robert Tear, t; London Chamber Orchestra, Argo Chamber Orchestra; Laszlo Heltay. Argo ZRG 904
++FF 3/4-81 p180 ++MT 12-80 p787
+Gr 2-80 p1287 ++MT 1-81 p35
+HFN 12-79 p167 ++RR 11-79 p90

Songs: I tempi assai lontani. See no. 3758
Trittico Botticelliano. See no. 2787

REUBKE, Julius
Sonata on the 94th psalm. See no. 2212. See no. 3959

REUSNER, Esaias
Suite, A minor. See no. 1225

REVEULTAS, Silvestre
Sensemaya. See no. 1133

REYER, Ernest
Sigurd: J'ai garde mon ame ingenue; Esprits gardiens. See no. 3689
Sigurd: Le bruit des champs. See no. 4050
Sigurd: Prince du Rhin; J'ai garde mon ame ingenue; Oui Sigurd est vainqueur; Esprits gardiens; Un souvenir poignant. See no. 1676
Sigurd: Un souvenir poignant; Le bruit des chants...Esprits gardiens. See no. 3688

REZAC, Ivan
sinfonietta. See no. 2577

REZNICEK, Emil Nikoalus von
Donna Diana: Overture. See no. 3964

2788 Serenade, G major. STRAUS, O: Serenade, op. 35, G minor. Hans Maile, vln; RIAS Sinfonietta; Jiri Starek. Schwann VMS 2080
+ARG 7/8-81 p55

RHEINBERGER, Joseph

2789 Sonata, horn and piano, op. 178, E flat major. RIES: Sonata, horn and piano, op. 34, F major. STRAUSS, R.: Andante, op. posth., C major. Douglas Hill, hn; Karen Zaczek Hill, pno. Crystal S 373
+-ARG 10-81 p49 +NR 7-81 p5
+-FF 9/10-81 p269 +SFC 4-12-81 p21

Sonata, organ, no. 5, op. 111, F sharp minor. See no. 3627

2790 Sonatas, organ, nos. 7-8, 14, 16. Robert Munns, Roger Fisher, Timothy Farrell, org. Musical Heritage Society MHS 824295 (2) (From Vista VPS 1016/7)
+FF 5/6-81 p134

2791 Sonata, organ, no. 8, op. 132, E minor. Sonata, organ, no. 15, op. 168, D major. Heinz Lohmann, org. Da Camera DM 93269
+FF 5/6-81 p134

Sonata, organ, no. 15, op. 168, D major. See no. 2791
Suite, op. 150: Gigue; Theme and variations. See no. 1856
Suite, op. 166, C major. See no. 1856
Trios, op. 46, nos. 5 and 7. See no. 3950

RHENE-BATON (Rene Baton)
Heures d'ete. See no. 3653

RHODES, Philip
Visions of remembrance. See no. 464

RICCI, Federico
Prigione d'Edinburgo, excerpts. See no. 4077

RICCIARDI
Amor mio. See no. 4036
Luna lu. See no. 4032

RICCIO, Giovanni
Primo libro delle divina lodi, 1612: Canzona. See no. 4067
Terzo libro delle divini lodi, 1612: Canzona. See no. 4067

RICHARD I, King
Ja nuns hons pris. See no. 3670

RICHARDS
Got bless the Prince of Wales. See no. 3721

RICHARDSON
Mary. See no. 4033

RICHTER, Franz
Concerto, flute, E minor. See no. 3782
Symphony, B flat major. See no. 3782

RIDOUT, Alan
I turn the corner. See no. 3621

RIEDEL, Karl
Songs: Freu dich Erd und Sternezelt; Kommet ihr Hirten; Lasst alle Gott uns loben. See no. 3963

RIES, Fernando
Sonata, horn and piano, op. 34. See no. 2789

RILEY, Terry
A rainbow in curved air. See no. 378

RIMMER
Harlequin. See no. 3955
Ravenswood. See no. 3955

RIMSKY-KORSAKOV, Nikolai
Antar, op. 9. See no. 856

2792 Capriccio espagnol, op. 34. Snow maiden: Dance of the tumblers. TCHAIKOVSKY: Capriccio italien, op. 45. Eugen Onegin, op. 24: Polonaise and waltz. NYP; Leonard Bernstein. CBS MY 36728
+FF 9/10-81 p161

2793 Capriccio espagnol, op. 34. TCHAIKOVSKY: Capriccio italien, op. 45. BPO; Arthur Fiedler. Crystal Clear CCS 7003 Tape (c) Ultragroove EC 7011 (also Platinum PS 1021 dbx 1021)
+ARG 5-80 p40
+Audio 12-81 p24
+HF 6-79 p94
+-HF 8-81 p69 tape

+-FF 3/4-79 p14 +NR 12-78 p2
+FF 9/10-81 p161 +SFC 6-3-79 p49
+-Gr 7-78 p259 ++St 10-79 p131

2794 Capriccio espagnol, op. 34. Le coq d'or: Suite. Russian Easter Festival overture, op. 36. CO; Lorin Maazel. Decca SXL 6966 Tape (c) KSXC 6966 (also London 7196)
++FF 3/4-81 p181 +-HFN 11-80 p122
++Gr 11-80 p674 ++NR 2-81 p5
+Gr 2-81 p1122 tape +NYT 7-19-81 pD23

2795 Capriccio espagnol, op. 34. TCHAIKOVSKY: Capriccio italien, op. 45. BPO; Arthur Fiedler. Ulgragroove UG 7003
+HFN 6-81 p77

Capriccio espagnol, op. 34. See no. 750. See no. 1112. See no. 1297

2796 Le coq d'or: Introduction, Act 1; Procession, Act 3. The legend of the invisible city of Kitezh: Eulogy; Battle of Kerzhenets. Mlada: Procession of the nobles. The tale of the Tsar Sultan, op. 57: Suite. State Academic Symphony Orchestra; Yevgeny Svetlanov. Quintessence PMC 7189
+FF 7/8-81 p153

Le coq d'or: Suite. See no. 2794

Fantasia, op. 33. See no. 3872

The legend of Sadko, op. 5. See no. 1601

The legend of Sadko, op. 5: Song of India. See no. 4030. See no. 4042. See no. 4064

The legend of the invisible city of Kitezh: Eulogy; Battle of Kerzhenets. See no. 2796

The legend of the invisible city of Kitezh: O vain illusion. See no. 4064

May night. See no. 2064

Mlada: Procession of the nobles. See no. 2796

Mlada: Procession of the nobles; Dance of the tumblers. See no. 3956

Russian Easter Festival overture, op. 36. See no. 858. See no. 1954. See no. 2021. See no. 2794

2797 Scheherazade, op. 35. Winnipeg Symphony Orchestra; Piero Gamba. CBC SM 5005
+-MUM 11/12-81 p36

2798 Scheherazade, op. 35. Irvine Arditti, vln; LSO; Loris Tjeknavorian. Chalfont SDG 304 Tape (c) EC 7009
++ARG 5-81 p24 +HF 8-81 p69 tape
-FF 1/2-81 p174 +HFN 10-80 p107
+Gr 11-80 p677 +St 3-81 p94
+HF 12-80 p84

2799 Scheherazade, op. 35. OSR; Ernest Ansermet. Contour CC 7501 Tape (c) CCT 7501
+Gr 8-81 p316

2800 Scheherazade, op. 35. Henrik Fridheim, vln; USSR Symphony Orchestra; Yevgeny Svetlanov. Musical Heritage Society MHS 4096 (also Quintessence PMC 7171) (From Melodiya/Angel SR 40112)
+-ARG 7/8-80 p37 +FF 3/4-81 p182
+FF 7/8-80 p125 +-HF 6-80 p83

2801 Scheherazade, op. 35. Rodney Friend, vln; LPO; Bernard Haitink. Philips 6500 410 Tape (c) 7300 226 (r) G 6500 410
+Gr 1-74 p1382 /NR 1-74 p6
+Gr 9-74 p592 tape ++RR 1-74 p47

++HF 3-74 p94
+HF 4-81 p93 tape
++SFC 2-3-74 p26

2802 Scheherazade, op. 35. COA; Kiril Kondrashin. Philips 9500 681 Tape (c) 7300 776
+FF 1/2-81 p174
+Gr 11-80 p677
+-HF 12-80 p84
++HFN 11-80 p122
++HFN 1-81 p109 tape
+-NR 12-80 p3
+NYT 9-7-80 pD29
+St 12-80 p133

Serenade, op. 37. See no. 1423
Servilia: Servilia's aria. See no. 3854
Snow maiden: Chanson de Lehl. See no. 4038
Snow maiden: Dance of the tumblers. See no. 2792
Snow maiden: Leh's songs. See no. 4042
Snow maiden: So full of wonders. See no. 4030
Snow maiden: Tsar Berendey's aria. See no. 4028
Songs: I waited for thee at the appointed hour, op. 40, no. 4. See no. 3801
Songs: The dying glow of the sunset, op. 39, no. 2; In the silence of the night, op. 40, no. 3; The heavy clouds scatter, op. 42, no. 3; More sonorous than the lark's singing, op. 43, no. 1; Not the wind, op. 43, no. 2; The nymph, op. 56, no. 1; Octave, op. 45, no. 3; The rose and the nightingale, op. 2, no. 2. See no. 2626
The tale of the Tsar Sultan, op. 57: Flight of the bumblebee. See no. 3714. See no. 3872. See no. 4000
The tale of the Tsar Sultan: Suite. See no. 2796
Variations on a romance by Glinka. See no. 3891

RIPPE, Albert de

2803 Fantasies, nos. 1 and 2. Gaillarde. Gaillarde l'Amirale. Lute settings: O passi sparse; Verbum iniquum; Douce memoire; On en dira ce qu'on youdra. Tavblatvre de levt: Fantasies, nos. 13, 16, 18, 22, 25. Hopkinson Smith, lt, gtr. Astree AS 18
+FF 7/8-81 p153

Gaillarde. See no. 2803
Gaillarde l'Amirale. See no. 2803
Lute settings: O passi sparse; Verbum iniquum; Douce memoire; On en dira ce qu'on youdra. See no. 2803
Tavblatvre de levt: Fantasies, nos. 13, 16, 18, 22, 25. See no. 2803

RITTER, August

Symphony concertante, F major. See no. 3794

RITTER, Christian

Sonata, organ, no. 3, A minor. See no. 2071

RIVIER, Jean

Grave et presto. See no. 3737

ROBB, John

Symphony, no. 1: Elegy. See no. 1895

ROBBINS

Mont Saint-Michel. See no. 4100

ROBINSON

Psalm, no. 122, I was glad when they said unto me. See no. 3895

ROCHBERG, George

2804 Concerto, violin. Isaac Stern, vln; Pittsburg Symphony Orchestra; Andre Previn. Columbia M 35149 (also CBS 76797)
+ARG 9-79 p34
+MT 11-81 p755

+FF 7/8-79 p80 ++NR 6-79 p7
+Gr 3-80 p1392 +NYT 4-18-79 pD28
+HF 9-79 p123 +RR 3-80 p57
+HFN 2-80 p97 +SFC 4-1-79 p44
++MJ 5/6-79 p44 +St 7-79 p103

Electrikaleidoscope. See no. 4068

2805 Quintet, piano and strings. Alan Marks, pno; Concord String Quartet. Nonesuch N 78011
+ARG 12-81 p24 +St 11-81 p92
+-FF 9/10-81 p162

Slow fires of autumn. See no. 1741

RODGERS, Richard

South Pacific: Scenario. See no. 3817

RODRIGO, Joaquin

Bajando de la meseta. See no. 2811

2806 Concierto de Aranjuez. Fantasia para un gentilhombre. John Williams, gtr; PO, ECO; Eugene Ormandy, Charles Groves. CBS MY 36717
+FF 9/10-81 p163

2807 Concierto de Aranjeuz. Fantasia para un gentilhombre. Carlos Bonell, gt; Montreal Symphony Orchestra; Charles Dutoit. Decca SXDL 7525 Tape (c) KSXDC 7525 (also London LDR 71027)
+Gr 7-81 p160 +HFN 7-81 p75
++Gr 9-81 p460 tape

2808 Concierto de Aranjuez. Concierto madrigal. Narciso Yepes, Godelieve Monden, gr; PhO; Garcia Navarro. DG 2531 208 Tape (c) 3301 208
+-FF 1/2-81 p175 +-HFN 9-80 p116 tape
+-Gr 6-80 p38 +NR 1-81 p4
+Gr 8-80 p275 tape +-RR 7-80 p63
+-HFN 7-80 p109

2809 Concierto de Aranjuez. Fantasia para un gentilhombre. Narciso Yepes, gtr; Spanish RTV Symphony Orchestra; Odon Alonso. DG 2542 150 Tape (c) 3342 150 (From 139440)
+-Gr 4-81 p1323 +HFN 6-81 p87 tape
+HFN 6-81 p87 +HFN 8-81 p92 tape

2810 Concierto de Aranjuez. Fantasia para un gentilhombre. Alexandre Lagoya, gtr; Monte Carlo National Orchestra; Antonio de Almeida. Philips 6527 058 Tape (c) 7311 058 (From 6500 454)
-Gr 4-81 p1323 +HFN 7-81 p83 tape
+HFN 5-81 p91

Concierto de Aranjuez. See no. 1105. See no. 2574. See no. 3712

Concierto madrigal. See no. 2808

En los trigales. See no. 2811. See no. 3727. See no. 4001

Fandango. See no. 2811. See no. 3795

Fantasia para un gentilhombre. See no. 2806. See no. 2807. See no. 2809. See no. 2810. See no. 3712

Junto al Generalife. See no. 2811

Little pieces. See no. 2811

Madrigales amatorios. See no. 3642. See no. 3889

Nocturne. See no. 3694

Pequenas sevillanas. See no. 3795

Prelude. See no. 3694

Romance de Durandarte. See no. 2811

Scherzino. See no. 3694

Sonata a la espanola. See no. 2811
Songs: Verde verderol; Pajaro del agua. See no. 3953
Tiento antiguo. See no. 2811
2811 Works, selections: Bajando de la meseta. En los trigales. Fandango. Junto al Generalife. Little pieces (3). Romance de Durandarte. Sonata a la espanola. Tiento antiguo. Pepe Romero, gtr. Philips 9500 915 Tape (c) 7300 915
+FF 11/12-81 p225
Ya se van los pastores. See no. 3795

RODRIGUES COELHO, Manuel
Susanne un jour. See no. 3835

RODRIGUEZ, Jorge
Toccata, no. 2. See no. 3778

ROGNONI, Riccardo
Un gay bergier. See no. 3835

ROGNONI TAEGGIO, Francesco
Pulchra es amica mea. See no. 3835

ROIG
La gracia de Dios. See no. 3981

ROLAND-MANUEL, Alexis
Elegies: Charmant rossignol; Chanson. See no. 3953

ROLLA, Alessandro
2812 Concerto, viola, F major. SCHUBERT, J.: Concerto, viola, C major. Vidor Nagy, vla; Wurttemberg Chamber Orchestra; Jorg Faerber. Carus FSM 63109
+ST 7-81 p207

ROMAN, Johann
Concerto, oboe d'amore, D major. See no. 79
2813 Drottingholmsmusik. Drottningholm Theatre Chamber Orchestra; Ulf Bjorlin. EMI 4E 063 34404
+-Gr 8-81 p317

ROMBERG, Sigmund
2814 The student prince. Celia Jeffreys, s; Erik Geisen, t; Dieter Honig, bs-bar; Hamburg State Opera Orchestra and Chorus Members; Stefan Gyarto. Kanon 01 132
+/FF 11/12-81 p12
LA RONDE ANTOUR DE L'EUROPE (French version of the Carl Orff method). See no. 3831

RONTANI, Raffaello
Nerinda bella. See no. 3945
Or ch'io non seguo piu. See no. 3823

RONTGEN, Julius
Sonata, oboe, no. 1. See no. 1029

ROPARTZ, Joseph Gay (Gay-Ropartz, Joseph)
Andante and allegro. See no. 3741
Theme varie. See no. 3901

ROQUELAY
Ta bonne grace. See no. 3766

RORE, Cipriano de
Anchor che col partire. See no. 3766. See no. 3938
Contrapunto sopra "Non mi toglia il ben mio". See no. 3937
Madrigals: Anchor che col partire (2); Come la notte ogni fiammella e viva; Datemi pace; Hor che l'aria; Non e lasso martire. See no. 4010

ROREM, Ned
2815 Miss Julie, excerpts. Judith James, s; Veronica August, ms; Ronald Madden, bar; Orchestra; Peter Leonard. Painted Smiles PS 1388
+-ARG 10-80 p35 +St 6-80 p120
+-ON 4-11-81 p52
Morning scene. See no. 3932
2816 Serenade on five English poems. STARER: Quartet, piano. Elaine Bonazzi, ms; The Cantilena Chamber Players. Grenadilla GS 1031
+-ARG 3-80 p36 +NR 1-80 p6
++FF 9/10-79 p126 ++St 2-81 p108
Songs: Motets on poems of Manley Hopkins (3). See no. 3810
Songs: Sing my soul. See no. 3951
ROSA
To be near thee. See no. 3823
ROSA, Salvator
Quand on aime. See no. 4026
ROSE, Bernard
Behold I make all things new. See no. 3637
ROSENBERG, Hilding
Fantasie e fuga. See no. 2817
2817 Hymnus: Lover gud i himmelshod. Fantasie e fuga. Preludium e fuga. Toccata, aria pastorale, ciaconna. Alf Linder, org. Caprice CAP 1064
+ARG 7/8-81 p54 ++NR 9-80 p9
+FF 11/12-80 p163
Preludium e fuga. See no. 2817
Small piece, violoncello. See no. 79
Toccata, aria pastorale, ciaconna. See no. 2817
ROSENMULLER, Johann
Sonatas, C major, E minor, B flat major. See no. 3783
Sonata, 2 violins, no. 2, E minor. See no. 3833
ROSENTHAL, Moriz
Carnival de Vienne. See no. 3920
ROSETTI, Francisco (Rossler, Franz)
Concerto, horn, D minor. See no. 1276
Concerto, horn, no. 1, E flat major. See no. 783
Quartet, 4 violoncelli, B major. See no. 3788
ROSS, Walter
Divertimento. See no. 3815
ROSSETER
When Laura smiles. See no. 3973
ROSSI, Salomone de
Les cantiques de Salomon. See no. 1669
ROSSINI, Gioacchino
2818 Adina. Il Signor Bruschino. Mariella Adani, Alda Noni, s; Mario Spina, Antonio Spruzzola, t; Sesto Bruscantini, Afro Poli, bar; Giorgio Tadeo, bs; Milan Orchestra dell' Angelicum, RAI Orchestra, Milan; Bruno Rigacci, Carlo Maria Giulini. Voce 32 (3)
/FF 9/10-81 p163
Armida: Overture. See no. 2834
L'Assedio di Corinto: Che vedo; Ohime tu piangi; Giusto ciel... Parmi vederlo ahi misero. See no. 3640
L'Assedio di Corinto: L'ora fatal s'appressa...Giusto ciel; In tal periglio. See no. 4014

Assez de memento. See no. 2838
Barcarolle. See no. 2838
2819 Il barbiere di Siviglia. Mercedes Capsir, Cesira Ferrari, s; Dino Borgioli, t; Riccardo Stracciari, bar; Salvatore Baccaloni, bs-bar; Vincenzo Bettoni, bs; La Scala Orchestra and Chorus; Lorenzo Molajoli. Arabesque 8029-3 (3) Tape (c) 8029
+ARG 10-80 p30
+-FF 9/10-80 p188
-HF 4-81 p81
+HF 2-81 p81
+NYT 7-13-80 pD20
+ON 8-80 p36
Il barbiere di Siviglia: All' idea. See no. 3966
Il barbiere di Siviglia: Des rayons de l'aurore. See no. 4049
Il barbiere di Siviglia: D'un metal di precieux. See no. 4051
Il barbiere di Siviglia: Ecco ridente. See no. 4027. See no. 4054
Il barbiere di Siviglia: Ecco ridente; Se il mio nome. See no. 4047
Il barbiere di Siviglia: La calunnia. See no. 3968
Il barbiere di Siviglia: Largo al factotum. See no. 4000. See no. 4031. See no. 4034. See no. 4079
Il barbiere di Siviglia: O il meglio mi scordavo. See no. 3967
Il barbiere di Siviglia: O il meglio me scordaro...Numero quindici. See no. 3657
Il barbiere di Siviglia: Overture. See no. 2832. See no. 2829. See no. 2835. See no. 2836
Il barbiere di Siviglia: Se il mio nome; Ecco ridente in cielo; Numero quindici; All'idea di quel metallo; Ah qual colpo; Se il mio nome; Ah qual colpo; Ecco ridente in cielo. See no. 4032
2820 Il barbiere di Siviglia: Una voce poco fa; Contro un cor. La cenerentola; Non piu mesta. L'Italiana in Algeri: Cruda sorte; Per lui che adoro; Amici in ogni evento. Semiramide: Bel raggio. Stabat mater: Fac ut portem. Teresa Berganza, ms; LSO; Alexander Gibson. London STS 15533
+FF 3/4-81 p183
Il barbieri di Siviglia: Una voce poco fa. See no. 3642. See no. 3649. See no. 3748. See no. 3850
Il barbieri di Siviglia: Una voce poco fa; Dunque io son. See no. 3640
Il barbiere di Siviglia: Una voce poco fa; Io son docile. See no. 4021
Bianca e Faliero: Overture. See no. 2833
2821 La boutique fantasque (arr. Respighi). Toronto Symphony Orchestra; Andrew Davis. CBS IM 35842 Tape (c) HMT 35842
+HF 11-81 p103 tape
+MUM 9/10-81 p33
+St 9-81 p100
La boutique fantasque: Suite. See no. 1392
Cavatina. See no. 3715
2822 La cenerentola. Bianca Casoni, ms; Giovanna Di Rocco, s; Teresa Rocchino, ms; Ugo Benelli, t; Sesto Bruscantini, bar; Alfredo Mariotti, Federico Davia, bs; Berlin State Opera Chorus; Berlin Radio Orchestra; Piero Bellugi. Acanta JB 23271/3 (3)
+-FF 9/10-80 p187
+-Gr 1-81 p990
+-ON 8-80 p36
La cenerentola: Nacqui all affanno...Non piu mesta. See no. 1362
La cenerentola: Non piu mesta. See no. 2820
La cenerentola: Overture. See no. 2832. See no. 4081
La danza. See no. 3645. See no. 3759. See no. 3885

Demetrio e Polibio: Overture. See no. 2833
La donna del lago: Mura felici. See no. 3890
2823 Duet, violoncello and double bass, D major. Un mot a Paganini. Une larme. Sonate a quattro (6). Salvatore Accardo, Sylvia Gazeau, vln; Alain Meunier, vlc; Franco Petracchi, double bass; Bruno Canino, pno. Philips 6769 024 (2)
++Gr 4-81 p1340 ++HFN 5-81 p83
Edipo a Colona: Overture. See no. 2834
Edoardo e Cristina: Overture. See no. 2833
Egle ed Irene. See no. 2828
Ermione: Overture. See no. 2833
Fantasia, E flat major. See no. 3669
2824 Fantasia, clarinet and piano. SPOHR: Fantasie and variations, op. 81. WEBER: Introduction, theme and variations, B major. Theme and variations concertante, op. 33, B major. Hans Rudolf Stalder, clt; Jurg von Vintschger, pno; B. Langbein, R. Pezzani, vln; O. Corti, vla; R. Altwegg, vlc. Jecklin 536
+FF 1/2-81 p161
La gazza ladra: Overture. See no. 2830. See no. 2832. See no. 2836. See no. 3726
2825 Guillaume Tell. Mirella Freni, s; Elizabeth Connell, ms; Luciano Pavarotti, t; Sherrill Milnes, bar; Nicolai Ghiaurov, Richard van Allan, bs; Ambrosian Opera Chorus; NPhO; Riccardo Chailly. London OSA 1446 (4) Tape (c) OSA 5-1446 (also Decca D219D4 Tape (c) K219K44)
+FF 3/4-81 p184 +ON 1-10-81 p29
+-Gr 1-81 p990 +Op 2-81 p159
+Gr 4-81 p1376 tape ++SFC 11-30-80 p21
+-HF 5-81 p62 +-SR 5-81 p96
+MT 6-81 p392 ++St 4-81 p74
+OC Winter 1981 p55
Guillaume Tell: Ils s'eloignent enfin...Sombre foret. See no. 1362
Guillaume Tell: Overture. See no. 2829. See no. 2830. See no. 2832. See no. 2835. See no. 2836. See no. 3626. See no. 3760
Guillaume Tell: Sombre foret. See no. 3647
L'Inganno felice: Una voce m'ha colpito. See no. 1378
2826 L'Italiana in Algeri. Graziella Sciutti, s; Mafalda Masini, Giulietta Simionato, ms; Cesare Valletti, t; Marcello Cortis, bar; Mario Petri, Enrico Campi, bs; La Scala Orchestra and Chorus; Carlo Maria Giulini. HMV RLS 747 (2) (From Columbia 33CX 1215/6) (also Seraphim IB 6119)
+-FF 1/2-81 p176 +NYT 10-26-80 pB33
+-Gr 8-80 p269 +-ON 5-81 p44
+-HFN 7-80 p119 -Op 1-81 p53
+NR 1-81 p9 +RR 7-80 p46
2827 L'Italiana in Algeri. Kathleen Battle, Clara Foti, s; Marilyn Horne, ms; Ernesto Palacio, t; Domenico Trimarchi, bar; Samuel Ramey, Nicola Zaccaria, bs; Prague Chorus; I Solisti Veneti; Claudio Scimone. RCA ARL 3-3855 Tape (c) ARK 3-3855 (also Erato STU 71394)
+FF 7/8-81 p155 +NYT 5-3-81 pD19
+Gr 3-81 p1234 +-ON 5-81 p44
+HF 8-81 p62 +SFC 3-15-81 p18
+-NR 6-81 p11 +St 7-81 p71
L'Italiana in Algeri: Cruda sorte; Per lui che adoro; Amici ogni evento. See no. 2820

L'Italiana in Algeri: Overture. See no. 2830. See no. 2831. See no. 2832. See no. 2836
Une larme. See no. 2823
Maometto II: Overture. See no. 2831. See no. 2834
Marche et reminiscences pour mon dernier voyage. See no. 2838
Melodie candide. See no. 2838
Memento homo. See no. 2838
Mon prelude hygienique du matin. See no. 2838
Un mot a Paganini. See no. 2823

2828 L'Occasione fa il ladro. Egle ed Irene. Serenata per piccolo complesso. Gino Sinimberghi, Cecilia Fusco, Pietro Bottazzo, Italo Tajo, Miti Truccato, Renzo Gonzales; RAI Scarlatti Orchestra; Luigi Colonna; Anastasia Tomaszewska-Schepia, s; Elena Zilio, ms; Giorgio Favaretto, pno. Voce 29 (2)
-FF 7/8-81 p156

Otello: Overture. See no. 2831. See no. 2833
Ouf les petits pois. See no. 2838

2829 Overtures: Il barbiere di Siviglia. Guillaume Tell. La scala di seta. Semiramide. Le siege de Corinthe. Il viaggio a Reims. PO; Riccardo Muti. Angel SZ 37750 (also HMV ASD 3903 Tape (c) TC ASD 3903)
+ARG 9-81 p29
+-FF 5/6-81 p135
+-Gr 3-81 p1202
+HF 5-81 p62
+-HFN 4-81 p75
+/NR 4-81 p5
+ON 5-81 p44
-Op 6-81 p652
+St 4-81 p120

2830 Overtures: Guillaume Tell. La gazza ladra. L'Italiana in Algeri. La scala di seta. Il signor Bruschino. Il Turco in Italia. Il viaggio a Reims. NPhO; Riccardo Chailly. Decca SXDL 7534
++HFN 10-81 p90

2831 Overtures: L'Assedio de Corinth. L'Italian in Algeri. Maometto II. Otello. Semiramide. PhO; Claudio Scimone. Erato STU 71178
*Gr 3-81 p1202

2832 Overtures: Il barbiere di Siviglia. La cenerentola. L'Italiana in Algeri. Semiramide. La gazza ladra. Guillaume Tell. RPO; Carlos Paits. Lodia LOD 775 (From Decca PFS 4386)
+HFN 6-81 p85

2833 Overtures: Bianca e Faliero. Demetrio e Polibio. Edoardo e Cristina. Ermione. Otello. Torvaldo e Dorliska. Ambrosian Singers; AMF: Neville Marriner. Philips 9500 886 Tape (c) 7300 886
++ARG 9-81 p29
++FF 5/6-81 p135
+HF 12-81 p93 tape
+NR 5-81 p6
++SFC 3-15-81 p18
++St 6-81 p120

2834 Overtures: Armida. Edipo a Colono. Maometto II. Ricciardo e Zoraide. Sinfonia "Al conventello". Sinfonia di Bologna. Ambrosian Singers; AMF; Neville Marriner. Philips 9500 887 Tape (c) 7300 887
+ARG 11-81 p38
++FF 9/10-81 p164

2835 Overtures: Il barbiere di Siviglia. Guillaume Tell. La scala di seta. Semiramide. Tancredi. Il Turco in Italia. LSO; Claudio Abbado. RCA ARL 1-3634 Tape (c) ARK 1-3634
+-ARG 9-81 p29
+FF 3/4-81 p182
+NR 4-81 p5
+ON 5-81 p44

+HF 5-81 p62 +St 6-81 p120

2836 Overtures: Il barbiere di Siviglia. La gazza ladra. Guillaume Tell. L'Italiana in Algeri. Semiramide. CPhO; Gaetano Delogu. Supraphon 110 2637

/ARG 6-81 p33 +-HF 5-81 p62
+FF 3/4-81 p182 -NR 1-81 p9

Les peches de vieillesse: Une caresse a ma femme; Prelude inoffensif; L'innocence italienne; La candeur francaise; Tarantelle pur sang; Specimen de l'ancien regime. See no. 2838

La pesarese. See no. 2838

Petite caprice. See no. 2838

Un petit train de plaisir. See no. 2838

2837 Petite messe solennelle. Mirella Freni, s; Lucia Valentini, ms; Luciano Pavarotti, t; Ruggero Raimondi, bs; La Scala Coro Polifonico; Leone Magiera, pno; Vittorio Rosetta, harmonium; Romano Gandolfo. London Cime Ars Nova C3S/134 (2) (also Decca SDD 567/8)

+-FF 3/4-79 p106 +-HFN 3-81 p90
+-Gr 3-80 p1428 +-ON 2-9-80 p37
+-Gr 4-81 p1352 +SFC 10-22-78 p53
-HF 3-79 p100 +St 12-78 p162

Petite messe solennelle: Crucifixus. See no. 4036

2838 Piano works: Assez de memento. Barcarolle. Les peches de vieillesse: Une caresse a ma femme; Prelude inoffensif; L'innocence italienne; La candeur francaise; Tarantelle pur sang; Specimen de l'ancien regime. Marche et reminiscences pour mon dernier voyage. Melodie candide. Memento homo. Mon prelude hygienique de matin. Ouf les petits pois. La pesarese. Petit caprice. Un petit train de plaisir. Prelude pretentieux. Un reve. Bruno Mezzena, pno. Dischi Ricordi ARCL 327 003 (3)

-FF 11/12-81 p225 +-Gr 11-80 p704

La pietra del paragone: Quell'alme pupille. See no. 3838

Prelude pretentieux. See no. 2838

2839 Ouartets, flute, nos. 1-4. Aurele Nicolet, flt; Kalafusz Trio. Intercord 160 825

+FF 3/4-81 p162 +HFN 12-81 p102

Un reve. See no. 2838

Ricciardo e Zoraide: Overture. See no. 2834

La scala di seta: Overture. See no. 2829. See no. 2830. See no. 2835

Semiramide: Bel raggio lusinghier. See no. 1362. See no. 2820. See no. 3713

Semiramide: Overture. See no. 2829. See no. 2831. See no. 2832. See no. 2835. See no. 2836

Serenata per piccolo complesso. See no. 2828

Le siege de Corinth: Overture. See no. 2829. See no. 2831

Il Signor Bruschino. See no. 2818

Il Signor Bruschino: Overture. See no. 2830

Sinfonia "Al conventello". See no. 2834

Sinfonia di Bologna: Overture. See no. 2834

2840 Sonatas, strings, nos. 2-5. Polish Chamber Orchestra; Jerzy Maksymiuk. HMV SQ ASD 3464 Tape (c) TC ASD 3464 (also Seraphim S 60351)

+-FF 7/8-81 p157 +-HFN 10-78 p139 tape
+-Gr 7-78 p199 +RR 7-78 p59
+HFN 7-78 p101 +RR 11-78 p113 tape

Sonate a quattro (6). See no. 2823
Songs: A me innocente e misero; Alle voci della gloria; Mi lagnero tacendo. See no. 1378
Songs: Arietta all'antica; Chanson de Zora; Les soirees musicales: La promessa; Il rimprovera; La partenza; L'orgia; L'invito; La pastorella dell'Alpi; La gita in gondola; La danza; Adieux a la vie. See no. 3758
Songs: Li marinari; Mira la bianca luna. See no. 3967
Songs: Pieta signore. See no. 4032
Songs: Trois choeurs religieux: La carita. See no. 3753
Stabat mater: Fac ut portem. See nol 2820
Stabat mater: Inflammatus. See no. 1167
Stabat mater: Pro peccatis. See no. 4025. See no. 4029
2841 Tancredi. Lella Cuberli, Lucia Rizzi, s; Fiorenza Cossotto, Helga Muller, ms; Werner Hollweg, t; Nicolai Ghiuselev, bs; Georg Fischer, fortepiano; West German Radio Choir; Capella Coloniensis; Gabriele Ferro. Italia ITL 70070 (3)
-Gr 4-81 p1362
Tancredi: Overture. See no. 2835
2842 Torvaldo e Dorliska. Pietro Bottazzo, t; Lella Cuberli, s; Siegmund Nimsgern, bs-bar; Enzo Dara, Gianni Socci, Lucia Valentini-Terrani, soloists; RAI Symphony Orchestra and Chorus, Milan; Alberto Zedda. Voce 25 (3)
+ARG 2-81 p27
Torvaldo e Dorliska: Overture. See no. 2833
Il Turco in Italia: Overture. See no. 2830. See no. 2835
Il viaggio a Reims: Overture. See no. 2829. See no. 2830
ROTOLI
Songs: La gondola nera; Mia sposa sara la mia bandiera. See no. 4024
ROUCAIROL, Joseph
Honneur et louange a Dieu. See no. 3634
ROUSSEAU
Dormez amours. See no. 4051
ROUSSEAU, Marcel
Le bon Roi Dagobert: Majeste madame mon enfant. See no. 4044
ROUSSEL, Albert
2843 Bacchus et Ariane, op. 43: Suite, no. 2. Psalm, no. 80, op. 37. John Mitchinson, t; Stephane Caillat Chorale; Orchestre de Paris; Serge Baudo. Connoisseur Society CS 2124 Tape (c) In Sync C 4008
+ARG 5-77 p31
+Audio 12-79 p121
+FF 11/12-79 p19 tape
+Gr 8-81 p324 tape
+HF 8-79 p53 tape
+MJ 10-78 p24
+NR 8-77 p8
+SFC 6-12-77 p41
++St 7-77 p119
++St 7-79 p108 tape
Concertino, violoncello and orchestra, op. 57. See no. 2160
Concerto, piano, op. 36, G major. See no. 1872
2844 Evocations, op. 15. CPhO and Chorus; Zdenek Kosler. Supraphon 112 2454
+-ARG 7/8-81 p29
+-FF 3/4-81 p185
+-Gr 10-80 p528
+HFN 12-80 p143
+NR 1-81 p2
+STL 9-14-80 p40
Fanfare pour un sacre paien. See no. 3624
Flute players, op. 27. See no. 1400. See no. 3668. See no. 3923

Petite suite. See no. 1305
Poemes de Ronsard: Rossignol mon mignon; Ciel aer et vens. See no. 3953
Psalm, no. 80, op. 37. See no. 2843
Segovia, op. 29. See no. 4001
Songs: Adieu; A flower given to my duaghter; Jazz dans la nuit; Light; Melodies, op. 20; Poemes chinois, op. 12; Poemes chinois, op. 35; Odes anacreontiques, nos. 1, 5; Odelette. See no. 1486

2845 Symphony, no. 4, op. 53, A major.* STRAVINSKY: Jeu de cartes. PhO; Herbert von Karajan. HMV SLP 60003 Tape (c) TC SXP 60003 (*From Columbia LX 1348/51)
++Gr 5-81 p1476 +-HFN 6-81 p77

ROVETTA, Giovanni
Songs: Chi vuol haver felice e lieto il core; Io mi sento morir. See no. 3947

ROYER, Joseph-Nicolas-Pancrace
2846 Pieces de clavecin, Bk 1. William Christie, hpd. Harmonia Mundi HM 1037
+Gr 6-81 p62

ROYLLART, Philippe de
Rex Karole: Leticie. See no. 3779

ROZSA, Miklos
That Hamilton woman: Love theme. See no. 4105
Tribute to a badman: Suite. See no. 4105

RUBBRA, Edmund
Duo, op. 156. See no. 1029
Fanfare for Europe, op. 142. See no. 4006
Introduction and fugue, op. 19. See no. 2847
Introduction, aria and fugue, op. 104. See no. 2847
Little pieces, op. 74 (9). See no. 2847

2847 Piano works: Introduction and fugue, op. 19. Introduction, aria and fugue, op. 104. Little pieces, op. 74 (9). Preludes, op. 131 (8). Prelude and fugue, op. 69. Studies, op. 139 (4). Edward Moore, pno. Phoenix DGS 1009
+Gr 8-81 p296

Preludes, op. 131. See no. 2847
Prelude and fugue, op. 69. See no. 2847
Sonata, oboe, op. 100, C minor. See no. 1029
Sonnets, op. 87. See no. 956
Studies, op. 139. See no. 2847

2848 Symphony, no. 5, op. 63, B flat major. BLISS: Checkmate: Dances (5). Melbourne Symphony Orchestra, West Australian Symphony Orchestra; Hans-Hubert Schonzeler. Chandos ABR 1018 Tape (c) ABT 1018
+FF 7/8-81 p158 +-HFN 3-81 p80
++Gr 3-81 p1184 +-HFN 4-81 p81 tape

RUBINSTEIN, Anton
2849 Concerto, piano, no. 1, op. 25, E minor. Michael Fardink, pno; RPO; Paul Freeman. Orion ORS 79347
+ARG 6-80 p38 +FF 5/6-80 p144
+-CL 1-81 p12 +NR 5-80 p6

The demon: Deh non plorar. See no. 4031
The demon: Prince Sinodal's aria. See no. 4030
The demon: Tamara's song. See no. 3854

2850 Sonata, piano, no. 1, op. 12, E minor. Sonata, piano, no. 3, op. 41, F major. Leslie Howard, pno. Hyperion A 66017
++Gr 9-81 p412 +MT 12-81 p828
+-HFN 8-81 p86 +SFC 12-13-81 p18
Sonata, piano, no. 3, op. 41, F major. See no. 2850
2851 Sonata, violin and piano, op. 49, F minor. JOACHIM: Hebrew melodies, op. 9, nos. 1 and 3. Lubomir Maly, vla; Libuse Krepelova, pno. Supraphon 111 2475
+FF 1/2-81 p176 ++SFC 1-18-81 p21
++NR 11-80 p5 ++St 11-80 p99
Songs: Der Wanderers Nachtlied. See no. 4039
RUDIGER
Songs: Still o Himmel; Es bluhen die Maien. See no. 3775
RUDOLF, Archduke of Austria
Theme and variations, clarinet and piano. See no. 3793
RUE, Pierre de la
Fors seulement. See no. 3777
RUFFO, Vincenzo
O felici occhi miei. See no. 4010
RUGGLES, Carl
Angels. See no. 2852
Evocations. See no. 2852
Exaltation. See no. 2852
Men. See no. 2852
Men and mountains. See no. 2852
Organum. See no. 2852
Portals. See no. 2852
Sun-treader. See no. 2852
Toys. See no. 2852
Vox clemens in deserto. See no. 2852
2852 Works, selections: Angels (2 versions). Evocations (2). Exaltation. Men. Men and mountains. Organum. Portals. Sun-treader. Toys. Vox clemens in deserto. Judith Blegen, s; Beverly Morgan, ms; Michael Tilson Thomas, John Kirkpatrick, pno; Leonard Raver, org; Gerard Schwarz Brass Ensemble; Gregg Smith Singers; Speculum Musicae, Buffalo Philharmonic Orchestra; Michael Tilson Thomas. Columbia M2 34591 (2) (also CBS 79225)
+-ARG 12-80 p43 +MT 12-81 p838
+-FF 9/10-80 p189 +-MUM 7/8-81 p34
+Gr 1-81 p953 +-NYT 8-17-80 pD15
-HF 10-80 p69 ++SFC 8-3-80 p33
+HFN 1-81 p100 +St 10-80 p80
+MQ 10-80 p604
RUIFROK, Henri
Minuet, op. 4, no. 1. See no. 4104
Song without words, op. 5, no. 2. See no. 4104
RUSSIAN ORTHODOX MUSIC: Liturgy for All Saints Day. See no. 3772
RUSSO, John
Essay, band, no. 1. See no. 1938
Variations on a yank. See no. 1938
Winchester overture. See no. 1938
RUTTER, John
A Gaelic blessing. See no. 3818
Nativity carol. See no. 3632

Psalm, no. 150. See no. 4107
RYBA, Jakub Jan
Concerto, horn, D sharp major. See no. 783
RZEWSKI, Frederic
2853 Ballad, no. 3 "Which side are you on". Pieces, piano (4). Frederic Rzewski, pno. Vanguard VA 25001 Tape (c) CVA 25001
+ARG 10-81 p37 *NR 5-81 p13
++FF 11/12-81 p227 *NYT 6-7-81 pD23
+HF 8-81 p65 ++St 10-81 p128
North American ballads. See no. 844
2854 The people united will never be defeated. Ursula Oppens, pno. Vanguard VSD 71248
+-ARG 7-79 p44 +NR 4-79 p12
+FF 5/6-79 p117 +St 4-79 p148
++HF 4-79 p90 +Te 3-81 p24
Pieces, piano (4). See no. 2853
SABBATINI, Galeazzo
Songs: Udite o selve; Fulmina de la bocca. See no. 3947
SAEVERUD, Harald
2855 Peer Gynt, op. 28: Suites, nos. 1 and 2. Oslo Philharmonic Orchestra; Militiades Caridis. Phonogram 6507 006 (also Philips 6507 006)
+FF 7/8-81 p159 +RR 7-77 p59
Symphony, no. 6. See no. 2269
SAEVERUD, Ketil
2856 Concerto, flute and guitar. Kvartoni. Mi-Fi-Li. Solveig Faringer, s; Clas Pehrsson, rec; Cecilia Peijel, gtr; Carl-Axel Dominique, pno; Gunilla von Bahr, flt; Diego Blanco, gtr; Stockholm Chamber Orchestra, RPO; Per Dreier, Ketil Saeverud. BIS LP 129
+FF 3/4-81 p186 ++HFN 1-81 p100
Kvartoni. See no. 2856
Mi-Fi-Li. See no. 2856
SAGRERAS, Julio
El colibri. See no. 3929
Merengue. See no. 3929
SAHL, Michael and Eric Salzman
2857 Civilization and its discontents. Candice Earley, William Parry, Paul Binotto, Karl Patrick Krause; Michael Sahl, pno and org; Cleve Pozar, perc. Nonesuch N 78009 Tape (c) 78009
+ARG 12-81 p46 *NR 7-81 p11
+-HF 11-81 p94 ++St 10-81 p133
SAINT-SAENS, Camille
Adagio and variation on "Airs de ballet d'Ascanio". See no. 3682
Africa, op. 89. See no. 2862
Allegro appassionato, op. 43. See no. 3667
Allegro appassionato, op. 70, C sharp minor. See no. 2861
Benediction nuptiale, op. 9. See no. 4120
Berceuse, op. 105. See no. 3665
Le carnaval des animaux. See no. 1031. See no. 2621
Le carnaval des animaux: Suite. See no. 3717
Le carnaval des animaux: The swan. See no. 3667. See no. 3993. See no. 4007
2858 Cavatine, op. 114. Romance, op. 36. Sonata, clarinet and piano, op. 167, E flat major. Sonata, bassoon and piano, op. 168, G

major. Sonata, oboe and piano, op. 166, D major. Maurice Bourgue, ob; Maurice Allard, Gilbert Coursier, Jacques Toulon, tromb; Maurice Gabai, clt; Annie d'Arco, pno. Calliope CAL 1819
+-Gr 9-80 p367 +RR 7-80 p83
+MT 2-81 p112

2859 Concerti, piano, nos. 1-5. La jeunesse d'Hercule, op. 50, E flat major. Pascal Roge, pno; PhO, RPO, LPO; Charles Dutoit. Decca D244D3 (3)
+Gr 10-81 p563 ++STL 12-13-81 p39
+HFN 10-81 p90

Concerti, piano, nos. 1-5. See no. 2862

2860 Concerto, piano, no. 2, op. 22, G minor. Concerto, piano, no. 4, op. 44, C minor. Francois-Rene Duchable, pno; Strasbourg Philharmonic Orchestra; Alain Lombard. Erato STU 71460
+Gr 12-81 p891

Concerto, piano, no. 4, op. 44, C minor. See no. 2860
Concerto, violin, no. 1, op. 20, A major. See no. 1985
Concerto, violoncello, no. 1, op. 33, A minor. See no. 1983
Cypres et Lauriers, op. 156. See no. 2874
Danse macabre, op. 40. See no. 746. See no. 1390. See no. 1391. See no. 1392. See no. 2873
Le deluge, op. 45: Prelude. See no. 746
Etudes, op. 52. See no. 2861
Etudes, op. 111. See no. 2861
Fantaisie, E flat major. See no. 4116
Fantaisie, op. 124. See no. 2750. See no. 2874
Havanaise, op. 83. See no. 1130. See no. 1984. See no. 1986
Introduction and rondo capriccioso, op. 28. See no. 1130. See no. 1984. See no. 1986. See no. 3109
Le jeunesse d'Hercule, op. 50, E flat major. See no. 2859. See no. 2873
Konzertstuck, op. 94. See no. 2874
Marche heroique, op. 34. See no. 2873
Marche militaire francaise. See no. 3817. See no. 3955
Mazurkas, op. 66. See no. 2861
La muse et le poete, op. 132. See no. 2874
Phaeton, op. 39. See no. 2873

2861 Piano works: Etudes, opp. 52 and 111. Allegro appassionato, op. 70, C sharp minor. Mazurka, op. 66, B minor. Valse gaie, op. 139. Valse mignonne, op. 104, E flat major. Francoise-Rene Duchable, pno. Pathe Marconi EMI 6 069 16423
+FF 9/10-81 p164 +Gr 12-81 p911

2862 Piano works: Africa, op. 89. Concerti, piano, nos. 1-5. Rapsodie d'Auvergne, op. 73. Wedding cake, op. 76. Gabriel Tacchino, pno; Luxembourg Radio Orchestra; Louis de Froment. Turnabout TV 37106/8 (3) Tape (c) KTVC 37106/8 (c) Vox CBX 5143
+Gr 6-78 p56 +-HFN 7-78 p111 tape
+Gr 10-78 p751 tape +-HFN 9-78 p159 tape
+HF 5-81 p53 tape +-RR 5-78 p36
+-HFN 5-78 p139 +-RR 8-78 p102 tape

Prelude and fugue, B major. See no. 833

2863 Preludes and fugues, op. 99, nos. 1-3; op. 109, nos. 1-3. Odile Pierre, org. RCA 26-41145
+FF 5/6-81 p135

Rapsodie d'Auvergne, op. 73. See no. 2862

Romance, op. 36. See no. 2858. See no. 2874
Romance, op. 37, D flat major. See no. 4065
Le rouet d'Omphale, op. 31. See no. 2873

2864 Samson et Dalila. Elena Obraztsova, ms; Placido Domingo, t; Renato Bruson, bar; Pierre Thau, Robert Lloyd, bs; Orchestre and Choir de Paris; Daniel Barenboim. DG 2531 167/9 (3) Tape (c) 3371 050 (also DG 2709 095 Tape (c) 3371 050)
+ARG 5-80 p32 +-NYT 12-23-79 pD28
++FF 3/4-80 p139 +OC Summer 1980 p47
+-FU 5-80 p49 +-ON 3-15-80 p45
+Gr 10-79 p710 +Op 2-80 p167
+Gr 12-79 p1065 tape ++RR 11-79 p59
+HF 4-80 p93 +-RR 6-80 p94 tape
+-HF 8-80 p87 tape +-SFC 11-25-79 p46
+-MT 4-81 p247 +St 2-80 p130
-NR 1-80 p10

Samson et Dalila: Amour viene aidor ma faiblesse. See no. 3970

2865 Samson et Dalila: Arretez o mes freres; Dance of the priestesses of Dagon; Printemps que commence; Mon coeur s'ouvre a ta voix; Vois ma misere; Samson qu'as-tu fait du Dieu de tes peres; Bacchanale; Allons Samson divertisnous. Elena Obraztsova, ms; Placido Domingo, t; Renato Bruson, bar; Orchestre and Chorus de Paris; Daniel Barenboim. DG 2537 056
+-FF 11/12-81 p288 +-HFN 6-81 p88
+-Gr 6-81 p84

Samson et Dalila: Arretez o mes freres; En ces lieux malgre moi... Mon coeur s'ouvre. See no. 3689
Samson et Dalila: Arretez mes freres; Scene de la meule. See no. 4050
Samson et Dalila: Bacchanale. See no. 746
Samson et Dalila: J'ai gravi la montagne. See no. 3968
Serenade d'hiver. See no. 4114
Sonata, bassoon and piano, op. 168, G major. See no. 1399. See no. 2605. See no. 2858
Sonata, clarinet and piano, op. 167, E flat major. See no. 2858
Sonata, oboe and piano, op. 166, D major. See no. 2858

2866 Sonata, violin and piano, no. 1, op. 75, D major. Sonata, violin and piano, no. 2, op. 102, E flat major. Michel Benedetto, vln; Annie d'Arco, pno. Calliope CAL 1817
+-MT 6-81 p392 +-ST 1-81 p648

Sonata, violin and piano, no. 2, op. 102, E flat major. See no. 2866
Songs: Aimons-nous. See no. 3758
Songs: Calme des nuits; Les fleurs et les arbres. See no. 4005
Songs: Il canto del cigno. See no. 4045

2867 Symphony, no. 3, op. 78, C minor. Noel Rawsthorne, org; Royal Liverpool Orchestra; Loris Tjeknavorian. Chalfont SDG 312
+-ARG 12-81 p26 +-HFN 3-81 p86
+Gr 7-81 p160 +St 12-81 p126
-FF 11/12-81 p229

2868 Symphony, no. 3, op. 78, C minor. Feike Asma, org; Hague Philharmonic Orchestra; Roberto Benzi. Philips 6570 149 Tape (c) 7310 149 (From 6580 070)
+-Gr 5-81 p1479 +-HFN 6-81 p85

2869 Symphony, no. 3, op. 78, C minor. Virgil Fox, org; PO; Eugene

Ormandy. RCA AGL 1-3711 (From ARL 1-0484)
++FF 7/8-81 p160
2870 Symphony, no. 3, op. 78, C minor. Berj Zamkochian, org; BSO; Charles Munch. RCA ATL 1-4039 Tape (c) ATK 1-4039
+FF 11/12-81 p228 +St 12-81 p126
+MUM 11/12-81 p34
2871 Symphony, no. 3, op. 78, C minor. Michael Murray, org; PO; Eugene Ormandy. Telarc 10051
++Audio 3-81 p64 +HFN 8-80 p101
+FF 9/10-80 p194 +-RR 8-80 p51
+-Gr 9-80 p349 +SFC 8-17-80 p36
+HF 8-80 p81 ++St 8-80 p73
2872 Symphony, no. 3, op. 78, C minor. Baltimore Symphony Orchestra; Sergiu Commissiona. Vanguard VA 25008
+-SFC 12-20-81 p18
Le timbre d'Argent: Le bonheur est une chose legere. See no. 4038
Trio, piano, no. 1, op. 18, F major. See no. 1508. See no. 1987
Valse gaie, op. 139. See no. 2861
Valse mignonne, op. 104, E flat major. See no. 2861
Wedding cake, op. 76. See no. 2862
2873 Works, selections: Danse macabre, op. 40. La jeunesse d'Hercule, op. 50, E flat major.* Marche heroique, op. 34. Phaeton, op. 39. Le rouet d'Omphale, op. 31. PhO; Charles Dutoit. Decca SXL 6975 Tape (c) KSXC 6975 (*From D244D3)
+Gr 12-81 p891
2874 Works, selections: Cypres et Lauriers, op. 156. Fantaisie, op. 124. Konzertstuck, op. 94. La muse et le poet, op. 132. Romance, op. 36. Ruggiero Ricci, vln; Francis Orval, hn; Susanna Mildonian, hp; George Mallach, vlc; Luxembourg Radio Orchestra; Louis de Froment. Turnabout QTV 34723
+SFC 4-12-81 p21

SAINTE-COLOMBE, Sieur de
2875 Concerts a deux violes esgales, nos. 27, 41, 44, 48, 54. Wieland Kuijken, Jordi Savall, vla da gamba. Telefunken AW 6-42123 (also Astree 10)
+FF 7/8-81 p159 +HFN 1-78 p133
+Gr 2-78 p1425 +RR 12-77 p72
+-HF 4-78 p108

SAINZ DE LA MAZA, Eduardo
Campanas del alba. See no. 19

SALADIN, Louis
Canticum Hebraicum. See no. 1669

SALIERI, Antonio
2876 Concerti, piano, B flat major, C major. Aldo Ciccolini, pno; I Solisti Veneti; Claudio Scimone. Italia ITL 70028
+NYT 3-1-81 pD31
O mortales festinate. See no. 3790
2877 La scuola de gelos, overture (rev. Spada). Symphony "Il giorno onomastico". Variations on the aria "La follia de Spagna" (26). Richard Studt, vln; Renata Schefel-Stein, hp; LSO; Zoltan Pesko. Italia ITL 70052
+Gr 6-79 p53 +NYT 3-1-81 pD31
Symphony "Il giorno onomastico". See no. 2877
Variations on the aria "La follia de Spagna". See no. 2877

SALLINEN, Aulis
Mauermusik. See no. 3127
2878 The red line. Taru Valjakka, s; Usko, Viitanen, Antti Salmen, t; Jorma Hynninen, bar; Erkki Aalot, bs-bar; Jaakko Heitikko, bs; Finnish National Opera Orchestra and Chorus; Okko Kamu. Finlandia FA 102 (3)
+FF 3/4-81 p187 +NR 3-81 p11
+Gr 2-81 p1116 +ON 4-4-81 p28
++HFN 1-81 p100 +Op 2-81 p204
+MT 11-81 p755 +STL 1-11-81 p38
SALMENHAARA, Erkki
Preludium, schlager and fuga. See no. 3679
SALONEN, Sulo
Sen suuven suloisuutta. See no. 3804
SALZEDO, Carlos
Piece concertante. See no. 3742
SALZEDO, Leonard
Capriccio, op. 90. See no. 76
SALZMAN, Eric
2879 Civilization and its discontents. Candice Early, s; Karl Patrick Krause, Paul Binotto, t; William Parry, bar; Michael Sahl, pno, org; Cleve Pozar, perc, drums. Nonesuch N 78009 Tape (c) 78009
+ARG 12-81 p46 *NR 7-81 p11
+-FF 9/10-81 p165 ++St 10-81 p133
+-HF 11-81 p94
SAMMARTINI, Guiseppe
Concerto, recorder, F major. See no. 1693
Sonata, 2 violoncelli, no. 3, A minor. See no. 63
SANDERS, John
Toccata. See no. 4112
SANDERSON, Wilfred
Beyond the dawn. See no. 3852
SANDRIN, Pierre
Doulce memoire. See no. 3677
SANDSTROM, Sven-David
A cradle song/The Tyger. See no. 1930
Effort. See no. 3690
SANDVOLD, Arild
2880 Introduction and passacaglia, op. 4, B minor. Variations on the Norwegian folk tune "Herre jeg hjertelig onsker a fremme din aere". EGGEN: Ciaconna, G minor. Kjell Johnsen, org. Ansgar ANS 3030
+-FF 9/10-81 p166
Variations on the Norwegian folk tune "Herre jeg hjertelig onsker a fremme din aere". See no. 2880
SANG TUNG
Eastern Mongolian folk songs. See no. 3861
SANTA MARIA, Tomas de
Fantasias (3). See no. 4088
Fantasias (8). See no. 4094
SANTORO, Claudio
Sonata, solo violin. See no. 1522
SANZ, Gaspar
Canarios. See no. 3795
Espanoleta. See no. 3795

Instruccion de musica: Pavanas. See no. 4015
Suite espanola: Canarios. See no. 4015

SARASATE, Pablo de
Caprice basque, op. 24. See no. 1491
Danzas espanolas, nos. 1 and 2, op. 21; no. 5, op. 23; no. 8, op. 26. See no. 1491
Danzas espanolas, op. 23: Zapateado. See no. 3847
Zigeunerweisen, op. 20, no. 1. See no. 3872. See no. 4106

SARJEANT
Blow blow thou winter wind. See no. 4074

SARTI, Giuseppe
Si tranquilla. See no. 3790

SARY, Laszlo
Sonata, percussion, no. 2. See no. 3865

SATIE, Erik
Avant dernieres pensees. See no. 2883
Choses vues a droite et a gauche. See no. 3984
Danses gothiques. See no. 2884
Embryons desseches. See no. 2883
Fete donnee par des Chevaliers Normands en l'honneur d'une jeune demoiselle. See no. 2884

2881 Genevieve de Brabant. Mass for the poor, op. posth. Songs: Le Chapelier; La diva de l'empire; Dapheneo; Three songs of 1886; Three other songs. Mady Mesple, s; Jean-Christoph Benoit, bar; Rene Duclos Choir; Gaston Litaize, org; Aldo Ciccolini, pno; National Theatre Opera Chorus; Orchestre de Paris; Pierre Dervaux. Arabesque 8053 Tape (c) 9053
+HF 10-80 p98 tape +ON 2-28-81 p36
+NYT 1-6-80 pD18 +St 6-80 p124

Gnossienes (6). See no. 2884
Gnossiennes, nos. 1-5. See no. 2883
Gnossiennes, no. 2. See no. 2887
Gymnopedies. See no. 1876

2882 Gymnopedies (2). Mercure. Parade. Relache. Utah Symphony Orchestra; Maurice Abravanel. Vanguard 71275 Tape (c) CA 471275
+HF 6-81 p69 tape ++SFC 10-25-81 p21
+NR 12-81 p4

Gymnopedies (2). See no. 1499
Gymnopedies (3). See no. 1279. See no. 2883. See no. 2884
Gymnopedie, no. 1. See no. 2887. See no. 4066
Gymnopedies, nos. 1, 3. See no. 751. See no. 3840. See no. 4082
Mass for the poor, op. posth. See no. 2881
Mercure. See no. 2882
Monotones. See no. 3840
Morceaux en forme de poire. See no. 3665
Musique d'ameublement: Tenture de cabinet prefectoral; Carrelage phonique; Tapisserie enfer orge. See no. 2886
Nocturne, no. 1. See no. 2883
Nouvelles pieces froides. See no. 2884
Ogives. See no. 2884
Parade. See no. 2882
Petite ouverture a danser. See no. 2884

2883 Piano works: Avant dernieres pensees. Gnossiennes, nos. 1-5. Gymnopedies, nos. 1-3. Embryons desseches. Nocturne, no. 1. Sarabandes, nos. 1, 3. Sonatine bureaucratique. Valses du

precieux degoute. Daniel Varsano, pno. CBS M 36694 Tape (c) MT 36694 (also CBS 61874)
+FF 3/4-81 p188 +HFN 3-81 p90
+Gr 3-81 p1214 +-MJ 10-81 p677
++HF 8-81 p56 +-NR 7-81 p13
+HF 11-81 p103 tape

2884 Piano works: Danses gothiques. Fete donnee par des Chevaliers Normands en l'honneur d'une jeune demoiselle. Gnossienes (6). Gymnopedies (3). Petite ouverture a danser. Nouvelles pieces froides. Priere. Prelude d'Eginhard. Preludes du Nazareen (2). Prelude de la porte heroique du ciel. Ogives. Sarabandes (3). Sonneries de la Rose Croix (3). Reinbert de Leeuw, pno. Philips 6768 269 (3)
+Gr 9-81 p412 ++HFN 11-81 p96

Le piccadilly. See no. 2887
Pieces froides: Airs a faire fuir. See no. 2887
Poudre d'or. See no. 2887
Prelude d'Eginhard. See no. 2884
Prelude de la porte heroique du ciel. See no. 2884
Preludes du Nazareen. See no. 2884
Priere. See no. 2884
Relache. See no. 2882
Relache: Entr'acte cinematographique. See no. 2886
Sarabandes (3). See no. 2884
Sarabandes, nos. 1, 3. See no. 2883

2885 Socrate. Hughes Cuenod, t; Geoffrey Parsons, pno. Nimbus QS 2104
++Gr 1-78 p1278 +-St 6-81 p123
+-RR 11-78 p36

Sonatine bureaucratique. See no. 2883
Songs: Chanson; Chanson medievale; La diva de l'empire; Elegie; Hymne: Salut drapeau; Genevieve de Brabant: Air de Genevieve; Je te veux; Petit air; Les anges, Les fleurs, Sylvie; Tendrement. See no. 2887
Songs: La diva de l'empire; Dapheneo; Le chapelier; Je te veux; La statue de bronze; Tendrement. See no. 1877
Songs: Le Chapelier; La diva de l'empire; Dapheneo; Three songs of 1886; Three other songs. See no. 2881
Sonnerie pour reveillier le roi des singes. See no. 2886
Sonneries de la Rose Croix. See no. 2884
Valses du precieux degoute. See no. 2883
Vexations. See no. 2886. See no. 2887

2886 Works, selections: Musique d'ameublement: Tenture de cabinet prefectoral; Carrelage phonique; Tapisserie enfer orge. Relache: Entr'acte cinematographique. Sonnerie pour reveillier le roi des singes. Vexations. Pierre Thibaud, Bernard Jeannoutot, tpt; Michel Dalberto, pno; Ars Nova Ensemble; Marius Constant. Erato STU 71336 Tape (c) MCE 71336
*Gr 4-81 p1323 +HFN 4-81 p87

2887 Works, selections: Pieces froides: Airs a faire fuir. Gnossienne, no. 2. Gymnopedie, no. 1. Poudre d'or. Le piccadilly. Vexations. Songs: Chanson; Chanson medievale; La diva de l'empire; Elegie; Hymne: Salut drapeau; Genevieve de Brabant: Air de Genevieve; Je te beux; Petit air. Songs: Les anges, Les fleurs, Sylvie; Tendrement. Peter Dickinson, pno; Meriel Dickinson, ms.

Unicorn RHS 338
+FF 9/10-81 p166
+Gr 11-76 p858
+-HFN 11-76 p167
+HFN 3-79 p129
+NYT 7-22-79 pD21
++RR 11-76 p101
+RR 2-79 p92
+St 2-77 p120

SAUGUET, Henri
2888 Concerto, piano, no. 1, A mainor. Les forains. Vasso Devetzi, pno; USSR Radio Orchestra, Lamoureux Orchestra; Gennady Rozhdestvensky, Henri Sauguet. Le Chant du Monde LDX 78300
+-Gr 8-81 p278
+HFN 5-81 p83

Les forains. See no. 2888

SAUTER, Ed
Arrangements of Moonlight sonata; Tchaikovsky's piano concerto; Midnight sleighride; Azure-te; Rain; Nina never knew; When hearts are young. See no. 2023
Doddletown fifers. See no. 2023

SAYLOR, Bruce
Psalms (4). See no. 1513

SCARLATESCU
Bagatelle. See no. 3841

SCARLATTI
Sonatas, D minor, E major. See no. 3801

SCARLATTI, Alessandro
Cantata pastorale per la nativita. See no. 3702
2889 Concerti grossi, nos. 1-6. I Musici. Philips 9500 603 Tape (c) 7300 725
+FF 5/6-80 p145
++Gr 9-80 p349
+HFN 5-80 p123
+HFN 10-80 p107
+MT 4-81 p247
++NR 5-80 p5
+NYT 5-25-80 pD21

2890 E pur vuole il cielo e amore. No non ti voglio Cupido. Mentre su'l car aurato. Questo silenzio ambroso. Five Centuries Ensemble. Italia ITL 70065
+-Gr 1-81 p981

Flavio Cuniberto: Chi vuole innamorarsi. See no. 3836
2891 Il giardino di amore. Catherine Gayer, s; Brigitte Fassbaender, con; Munich Chamber Orchestra; Hans Stadlmair. DG 2535 361 Tape (c) 3335 361 (From DG 73244) (also DG 2547 033 Tape (c) 3347 033. From SAPM 198344)
+ARG 6-80 p39
+FF 5/6-80 p145
+Gr 11-80 p724
+Gr 2-81 p1122 tape
-HFN 1-81 p109
++HFN 1-81 p109 tape
++NR 4-80 p12

Mentre su'l caro aurato. See no. 2890
No non ti voglio Cupido. See no. 2890
Pompeo: O cessate di piagarmi. See no. 3836
Questo silenzio ambroso. See no. 2890
2892 St. Cecilia mass. Elizabeth Harwood, Wendy Eathorne, s; Margaret Cable, con; Wynford Evans, t; Christopher Keyte, bs; St. John's Colege Chapel Choir; Wren Orchestra; George Guest. Argo ZRG 903 Tape (c) KZRC 903
+Audio 10-81 p28
+FF 1/2-81 p177
+Gr 7-80 p161
+HFN 7-80 p110
+RR 8-80 p88
++St 5-81 p74
++STL 9-14-80 p40

Sinfonia di concerto grosso, no. 3. See no. 3980
Songs: Le violette; Toglietemi la vita ancor; Viene a stringermi; Gia il sol dal gange; O cessate di piagarmi. See no. 3838
SCARLATTI, Domenico
2893 Essercizi per gravicembalo (12). Ton Koopman, hpd. Philips 9502 034
+HFN 12-81 p102
2894 Le quattro stagioni. Kari Lovaas, s; Ria Bollen, ms; Regina Marheineke, s; Heiner Hopfner, t; Munich Vokalsolisten; Munich Chamber Orchestra; Hans Hirsch. Tudor 73014
+-Gr 2-81 p981 -HFN 12-80 0145
Sonatas, guitar. See no. 765
Sonatas, guitar (5). See no. 301
Sonatas, guitar, E minor (2). See no. 4001
Sonata, guitar, K 9, E minor. See no. 3879
Sonata, guitar, K 380, A major. See no. 3879
Sonata, harpsichord. See no. 4007
2895 Sonatas, harpsichord (14). Tom Pixton, hpd. Titanic TI 18
+AR 11-81 p133
2896 Sonatas, harpsichord (3). Blandine Verlet, hpd. Philips 6768 650 (2) Tape (c) 7650 650
+FF 1/2-81 p178 ++HFN 6-81 p77
+Gr 6-81 p62 +NR 11-80 p11
Sonatas, harpsichord, B minor, C minor, D minor, D major. See no. 213
Sonatas, harpsichord, D major, D minor, G major. See no. 3698
Sonatas, harpsichord, E major, D minor. See no. 3749
Sonata, harpsichord, E flat major. See no. 4020
2897 Sonatas, harpsichord, K 3, 52, 183, 184, 192, 193, 208, 209, 227, 238, 239, 252, 253. Gustav Leonhardt, hpd. Pro Arte PAL 1022
+FF 11/12-81 p230
2898 Sonatas, harpsichord, Kk 3, A minor; Kk 184/5, F minor; Kk 227, B minor; Kk 238/9, F minor; Kk 52, D minor; Kk 192/3, E flat major; Kk 208/9, A major; Kk 252/3, E flat major; Kk 191, D minor. Gustav Leonhardt, hpd. RCA RL 3-0334
+Gr 4-80 p1572 ++MT 3-81 p184
+HFN 4-80 p109 +-RR 5-80 p89
2899 Sonatas, harpsichord, L 5, 14, 23, 33, 41, 58, 103, 104, 263, 281, 288, 366, 413. Aldo Ciccolini, pno. Seraphim S 60341
++NR 2-81 p14
2900 Sonatas, harpsichord, nos. 6, 8-11, 13, 28. SOLER: Sonatas, harpsichord, D major, C sharp minor, D minor, G minor, F sharp minor, F major. Alicia de Larrocha, pno. London CS 7177 (also Decca SXL 6949)
+FF 11/12-81 p230 +Gr 12-81 p911
2901 Sonatas, harpsichord, L 17/K 450; L 120/K 541; L 459/K 270; L 155/K 271; L 441/K 314; L 235/K 315; L 399/K 228; L 199/K 299; L 67/K 294; L 270/K 295; L 491/K 456; L 292/K 457. Gilbert Rowland, hpd. Keyboard KGR 1003
+HFN 1-77 p115 +RR 1-77 p74
+MT 8-81 p540
2902 Sonatas, harpsichord, K 28, 43, 69, 105, 133, 215, 259, 426, 460, 490, 517, 518. John McCabe, pno. Hyperion A 66025
+-HFN 11-81 p96
Sonata, harpsichord, Kk 39, A major. See no. 3723

2903 Sonatas, harpsichord, Kk 46, 87, 95, 99, 124, 201, 204, 490, 491, 492, 513, 520, 521. Trevor Pinnock, hpd. CRD CRD 1068 Tape (c) CRDC 4068
++Gr 5-81 p1501 +HFN 4-81 p75
++Gr 9-81 p460 tape +HFN 9-81 p93 tape
Sonatas, harpsichord, K 87, 238, 239, 401. See no. 1689
2904 Sonatas, harpsichord, Kk 98, 123, 124, 147, 198, 326, 327, 454, 466, 467, 428, 429. Colin Tilney, hpd. L'Oiseau-Lyre DSLO 567
+-Gr 4-81 p1346 +HFN 3-81 p91
2905 Sonatas, harpsichord, K 108, 156, 157, 240, 241, 197, 215, 216, 364, 365, 468, 469. Gilbert Rowland, hpd. Keyboard KGR 1012
+-HFN 4-81 p75
2906 Sonatas, harpsichord, Kk 109, 110, 127, 130, 170, 189, 190, 390, 391, 343, 435, 436. Gilbert Rowland, hpd. Keyboard KGR 1011
+-HFN 12-80 p145 +MT 8-81 p540
2907 Sonatas, harpsichord, K 112, B flat major; K 137/138, D major; K 152/153, G major; S 201, G major; K 296/297, F major; K 466/467, F minor; K 532, A minor; K 533, A major. Gilbert Rowland, hpd. Keyboard KGR 1009
+HFN 9-79 p111 ++RR 9-79 p109
+MT 8-81 p540
2908 Sonatas, harpsichord, Kk 117, 121, 123, 128, 139, 158/159, 169, 201, 244/245, 256/257, 308/9, 333, 341/2, 345/346, 354/355, 356/357, 382, 385, 388/389, 396/397, 400/401, 410/411, 431/433, 443/444, 451, 439/440, 452, 453, 449/450, 458/459, 468/469, 472/473, 488/489, 493/494, 497/500, 501/502, 505/506, 538/539, 548/549. Luciano Sgrizzi, hpd. Erato ERA 9232 (4)
+Gr 10-81 p584 +HFN 12-81 p102
2909 Sonatas, harpsichord, K 142, 162-163, 167-168, 183-184, 227, 258, 304, 305, 484. Gilbert Rowland, hpd. Keyboard KGR 1010
+-HFN 5-80 p123 +RR 7-80 p84
+MT 8-81 p540
Sonatas, harpsichord, Kk 144, 149, 193, 274. See no. 3807
2910 Sonatas, harpsichord, K 176, D minor; K 187, F minor; K 198, E minor; K 265, A minor; K 283, G major; K 284, G major; K 339, C major; K 340, C major; K 368, A major; K 269, A major; K 507, E flat major; K 508, E flat major. Gilbert Rowland, hpd. Keyboard KGR 1005
+Gr 2-78 p1447 +MT 8-81 p540
+HFN 1-78 p1133 +RR 1-78 p73
2911 Sonatas, harpsichord, K 188, A minor; K 173, B minor; K 384, C major; K 385, C major; K 285, A major; K 286, A major; K 538, G major; K 539, G major; K 194, F major; K 195, F major; K 351, B flat major; K 203, E mionr. Gilbert Rowland, hpd. Keyboard KGR 1006
+HFN 7-78 p101 +RR 7-78 p81
+MT 8-81 p540
2912 Sonatas, harpsichord, K 199, 200, 279, 280, 298, 299, 337, 338, 349, 350, 464, 465. Gilbert Rowland, hpd. Keyboard KGR 1008
+HFN 7-79 p111 +-RR 6-79 p109
+MT 8-81 p540
Sonatas, harpsichord, Kk 212, A major; Kk 144, G major. See no. 3877
2913 Sonatas, harpsichord, K 215/6, K 263/4; K 52, K 490/2, K 308/9.

Gustav Leonhardt, hpd. Harmonia Mundi 065 99615 Tape (c) Pro Arte 2PAC 2005 (From BASF)
+HF 9-81 p46 tape +-RR 3-79 p115
+HFN 2-79 p115
Sonata, harpsichord, K 288, D major. See no. 4111
2914 Sonatas, harpsichord, K 378/379, F major; K 281/282, D major; K 451, A minor; K 174, C minor; K 196, G minor; K 172, B flat major; K 219/220, A major; K 412/413, G major. Gilbert Rowland, hpd. Keyboard KGR 1007
-Gr 11-78 p933 +MT 8-81 p540
+HFN 10-78 p129 +-RR 10-78 p97
Sonatas, harpsichord, K 441-442, 490-492, 501-502. See no. 1713
2915 Sonatas, harpsichord, K 447/L 294, F sharp minor; K 448/L 485, F sharp minor; K 232/L 62, E minor; K 233/L 467, E minor; K 396/L 110, D minor; K 397/L 208, D major; K 225/L 351, C major; K 226/L 112, C minor; K 300/L 92, A major; K 546/L 312, G minor; K 547/L 28, G major. Gilbert Rowland, hpd. Keyboard KGR 1004
++HFN 8-81 p119 +RR 7-77 p83
+MT 8-81 p540
Sonatas, harpsichord, K 490/L 206, D major; K 292/L 24, E minor; K 380/L 23, E major; K 208/L 238, A major; K 209/L 428, A major. See no. 1208
Sonatas, violin, Kk 208, A major, 209, A major, 380, E major, 545, B flat major. See no. 3643
SCELSI, Giacinto
2916 Songs: Ho Khoom; Pranam I. Michiko Hirayama. Ananda 3
+MT 10-81 p678
2917 Songs: Cante del capricorno, excerpts; Sauh; Taiagaru. Michiko Hirayama. Ananda 5
+MT 10-81 p678
SCHAFER, R. Murray
2918 Concerto, harpsichord and 8 wind instruments. Epitaph for moonlight.*. Minnelieder. Quartet, strings, no. 1. Requiems for a party girl.* Purcell String Quartet; Various other performers. RCA ACM 3 (5) (*From RCI 299, CBC BR SM 274)
+MUM 1/2-81 p33
Epitaph for moonlight. See no. 2918
Minnelieder. See no. 2918
Quartet, strings, no. 1. See no. 2918
Requiems for a party girl. See no. 2918
SCHAFFER, Boguslaw
2919 Jazz concerto, orchestra. Movimenti, piano (4). S'alto, saxophone. Aleksandra Utrecht, pno; Milton Wimmer, sax; Polish Radio Orchestra, Rochester Chamber Orchestra, New England Conservatory Orchestra; Zdzislaw Szostak, Prad Robertson, Gunther Schuller. Muza SX 1594
++FF 1/2-81 p178
Movimenti, piano (4). See no. 2919
S'alto, saxophone. See no. 2919
SCHAFFRATH, Christoph
Duetto, 2 bass viols, D minor. See no. 2078
SCHAT, Peter
Entelechie I. See no. 3943
SCHEIDEMANN, Heinrich
Ballett. See no. 3832

In dich hab ich gehoffet Herr. See no. 3960
Preambulum, D minor. See no. 3903
Prelude, G minor. See no. 3960
Prelude on "Jesu wollst uns weisen". See no. 4117

SCHEIDLER, Christian
Sonata, flute and guitar, D major. See no. 381

SCHEIDT, Samuel
Battle suite. See no. 3762
Battle suite: Galliard battaglia; Courant dolorosa; Canzon bergamasque. See no. 3798
Benedicamus domino; Canzon gallicam. See no. 3898
Bergamasque. See no. 4090
Canzon cornetto a 4. See no. 3936

2920 Cum ergo fleret. Hosanna filio David. In dulci jubilo. Puer natus in Bethlehem. Sic Deus dilexit. Tulerunt dominum meum. SCHEIN: Da Jakob vollendet hatte. Die mit Tranen saen. Psalm, no. 116. Zion spricht. Audite Noa Chorale, Paris; Ars Nova Brass Ensemble; Jean Sourisse. Musical Heritage Society MHS 4288 (also Erato STU 71196)
+FF 5/6-81 p137

Hosanna filio David. See no. 2920
In dulci jubilo. See no. 2920
Magnificat noni toni. See no. 3903
Modus ludendi pleno. See no. 3720
Modus ludendi organo pleno. See no. 4117
O Jesulein zart. See no. 3775
Puer natus in Bethlehem. See no. 2920
Sic Deus dilexit. See no. 2920
Tulerunt dominum meum. See no. 2920
Variations on a galliard of John Dowland. See no. 3812

SCHEIN, Johann
Banchetto musicale: Suites, nos. 3-5. See no. 2609
Da Jakob vollendet hatte. See no. 2920
Die mit Tranen saen. See no. 2920
Psalm, no. 116. See no. 2920
Songs: Amor das blinde Gottelein; Der edle Schafer Coridon; Einsmals wett Coridon; O Scheiden o bitter Scheiden; O Sternenaugelein in grosser Traurigkeit. See no. 24
Zion spricht. See no. 2920

SCHENCK, Johann
L'Echo du Danube: Sonata, no. 2. See no. 3813
Le nymphe di Rheno, op. 8: Chaconne, G major. See no. 3833
Le nymphe di Rheno: Sonata, 2 viols, op. 8, no. 10, G major. See no. 2070
Suite, D major. See no. 3783

SCHICKELE, Peter
Diversions. See no. 3815

SCHILLING
Canzona uber "Christ ist erstanden". See no. 3740

SCHILLINGS, Max von

2921 Glockenlieder, op. 22: Die Fruhglocke, Die Nachzugler; Ein Bildchen; Mittagskonig und Glockenherzog. STRAUSS, R.: Songs: Morgen, op. 27, no. 4; Standchen, op. 17, no. 2; Traum durch die Dammerung, op. 29, no. 1; Verfuhrung, op. 33, no. 1; Waldseligkeit, op. 49, no. 1. Peter Anders, t; Orchestra; Joseph Keil-

berth; Artur Rother, Arthur Gruber, Robert Heger. Acanta BB 23185
+-ARG 12-80 p45 +-HFN 8-81 p88

SCHLICK, Arnolt
Da pacem domine. See no. 3960
Maria zart von edler Art. See no. 3720

SCHMELZER, Johann
Balletto a cavallo. See no. 3979

SCHMID, Bernard
Alemando novelle: Ein guter neuer Dantz. See no. 3676
Der Imperial: Ein Furtlicher Hofdantz; Ein schoner Englischer Dantz; Wie schon Bluet uns der Maye. See no. 3676

SCHMIDT
Concerto, trumpet and piano. See no. 2780

SCHMIDT, Franz
2922 Fantasia and fugue, D major. Little preludes and fugues (4). Prelude and fugue, A major. Toccata and fugue, A flat major. Variations and fugue on an original theme. Kurt Rapf, org. Musical Heritage Society MHS 834329 (3)
++FF 7/8-81 p160
Little preludes and fugues (4). See no. 2922
Notre Dame: Intermezzo. See no. 3644. See no. 3787
Prelude and fugue, A major. See no. 2922
Prelude and fugue, A flat major. See no. 2922
Variations and fugue on an original theme. See no. 2922

SCHMIDT, William
2923 Concertino, 2 trumpets and organ. Sonata, trumpet and piano. Variants with solo cadenzas. Anthony Plog, Donald Green, Russell Kidd, Lloyd Lippert, tpt; Orpha Ochse, org; Sharon Davis, pno. WIM WIMR 17
++ARG 12-81 p28 +NR 8-81 p9
+FF 9/10-81 p166
Sonata, trumpet and piano. See no. 2923
Variants with solo cadenzas. See no. 2923

SCHMITT, Florent
Antony and Cleopatra, op. 69: Le camp de Pompee. See no. 3624
Songs: Chants, op. 98 (3); Poemes de Ronsard, op. 100 (4). See no. 1877

SCHNEIDER, Georg
Symphony concertante, op. 19, D major. See no. 3794

SCHNITTKE, Alfred
Prelude to the memory of Dmitri Shostakovich. See no. 2629

SCHNITZER, Franz
2924 Alma redemptoris mater, E flat major. Mass, C major: Gloria; Agnus dei. Sonatas, organ, op. 1, nos. 5 and 6. Franz Lehrndorfer, org; Hans Pizka, hn; Sebastian Ludwig, vlc; Werner Booz, contrabass; Augsburg Vocal Ensemble; Convivium Musicum Munich; Franz Lehrndorfer. Musica Bavarica MB 70308
+ARG 9-81 p55 +-FF 9/10-81 p151
Mass, C major: Gloria; Agnus dei. See no. 2924
Sonatas, organ, op. 1, nos. 5 and 6. See no. 2924

SCHOECK, Othmar
2925 Nocturne, op. 47. Niklaus Tuller, bs; Berne String Quartet. Accord ACC 140021
+HFN 12-81 p102

SCHOENBERG, Arnold

2926 Das Buch der hangenden Garten, op. 15. Songs, op. 6 (8). Erika Sziklay, s; Jeno Jando, pno. Hungaroton SLPX 12040
-Gr 2-81 p1110
+HFN 2-81 p93

2927 Chamber symphony, no. 1, op. 9, E major. Pieces, orchestra, op. 16 (5). Los Angeles Chamber Orchestra; Gerard Schwarz. Nonesuch D 79001
+-ARG 7/8-81 p30
++FF 3/4-81 p188
+NYT 3-29-81 pD31
++St 4-81 p107

2928 Chamber Symphony, no. 1, op. 9, E major (arr. Webern). WEBERN: Quintet, piano. Quintetto Italiano. Ricordi RCL 27012
+FF 11/12-81 p279

2929 Concerto, piano, op. 42, C major. STRAVINSKY: Concerto, piano and wind instruments. Movements, piano and orchestra. Adam Fellegi, pno; Budapest Symphony Orchestra; Ivan Fischer. Hungaroton SLPX 12021
+HFN 2-81 p93
+-RR 7-80 p67

2930 Erwartung, op. 17. Lieder, op. 8. Anja Silja, s; VPO; Christoph von Dohnanyi. Decca SXDL 7509 Tape (c) KSXDC 7509
+-Gr 6-81 p70
+Gr 9-81 p460 tape
+HFN 6-81 p77
+Op 11-81 p1150

2931 Fantasy, op. 47. Suite, op. 29. BSO Chamber Players; Joseph Silverstein, vln; Gilbert Kalish, pno. DG 2531 277
+FF 3/4-81 p190
+Gr 9-80 p367
+HFN 9-80 p110
+NR 1-81 p6
+ST 1-81 p649

2932 Gurrelieder. Jessye Norman, s; Tatiana Troyanos, con; James McCracken, t; Tanglewood Chorus; BSO; Seiji Ozawa. Philips 6769 038 Tape (c) 7699 124 (r) R 6769 038
+-ARG 6-80 p13
+FF 3/4-80 p142
++FU 4-80 p44
+Gr 1-80 p1193
+-HF 3-80 p84
+-HF 5-80 p90 tape
+HF 2-81 p81 tape
+-HFN 1-80 p109
+-HFN 2-80 p107 tape
+-MT 3-80 p181
++MUM 7/8-80 p32
+NR 2-80 p8
+NYT 11-18-79 pD24
+ON 2-9-80 p37
++RR 1-80 p108
+RR 3-80 p105 tape
++SFC 12-2-79 p53
++SR 1-5-80 p39
++St 3-80 p83
+STL 12-2-79 p37

2933 Music for a cinematographic scene, op. 34. Pieces, orchestra, op. 16 (5). A survivor from Warsaw, op. 46. Variations, op. 31. BBC Symphony Orchestra; Pierre Boulez. CBS 35882 Tape (c) 35882
+FF 11/12-80 p167
++HF 1-81 p69
++MUM 7/8-81 p35
+NR 1-81 p3
+SFC 11-30-80 p21
++St 3-81 p95

Pelleas und Melisande, op. 5. See no. 1500

Pieces, orchestra, op. 16. See no. 2927. See no. 2933

Pieces, piano, op. 11 (3); op. 19 (6); op. 23 (5); op. 33 (2). See no. 3785

Pieces, piano, op. 33a. See no. 3869

2934 Pierrot Lunaire, op. 21. Maureen McNalley, reciter; Orchestra of Our Time; Joel Thome. Moss Music Group D MMG 111
+FF 9/10-81 p167
+NR 8-81 p3
+St 11-81 p94

2935 Quartet, strings, no. 2, op. 10, F sharp minor. POWELL: Little companion pieces. Bethany Beardslee, s; Sequoia Quartet. Nonesuch D 79005
+-ARG 6-81 p33 +-FF 3/4-81 p189
2936 Serenade, op. 24. Louis-Jacques Rondeleux, bs; Guy Deplus, Louis Montaigne, clt; Paul Grund, mand; Paul Stingl, gtr; Luben Yordanoff, vln; Serge Collot, vla; Jean Huchot, vlc; Pierre Boulez. Wergo WER 60002
+Gr 9-81 p402 +HFN 9-81 p90
Serenade, op. 24: 4th movement. See no. 810
Songs, op. 6. See no. 2926
Songs, op. 8. See no. 2930
Suite, op. 25. See no. 3785
Suite, op. 29. See no. 2931
A survivor from Warsaw, op. 46. See no. 2933
Variations, op. 31. See no. 2133. See no. 2933
Variations on a recitative, op. 40. See no. 2156
Verklarte Nacht, op. 4. See no. 1849
SCHOLZ
Menuett. See no. 3816
SCHOLZ, Viktor
In paradisum. See no. 196
SCHONTHAL, Ruth
2937 Songs of death. WEILL: Frauentanz, op. 10. ZAIMONT: Songs, soprano and harp (2). Edith Ainsberg, Bernice Bramson, s; Sara Cutler, hp; Ruth Schonthal, pno; Bronx Arts Ensemble. Leonarda LP 106
+ARG 9-81 p44 +NR 6-81 p12
+FF 5/6-81 p186 +St 7-81 p88
+-HF 8-81 p64
SCHREKER, Franz
2938 Songs: Funf Gesange, nos. 1, 4; Die gluhende Krone; Das fuerige Mannlein; Lieder, op. 2; Lieder, op. 7, nos. 2-7; Lieder auf den Tod eines Kindes, op. 5; Die Rosen und der Flieder. Steven Kimbrough, bar; Martin Katz, pno. Acanta 68 23389
+-FF 5/6-81 p139 +NYT 4-5-81 pD33
SCHROEDER
In dulci jubilo. See no. 3809
SCHROTER, Johann
Concerto, fortepiano, F major. See no. 1247
SCHUBACK, Peter
Burro. See no. 3690
Poemas. See no. 3690
SCHUBERT, Franz
2939 Alfonso und Estrella overture, D 732. Rosamunde, op. 26, D 797: Incidental music. Die Zauberharfe overture, D 644. Ileana Cotrubas, s; Leipzig Radio Chorus; Dresden State Orchestra; Willi Boskovsky. Seraphim S 60338
+St 1-81 p86
2940 Allegretto, D 915, C minor. Deutsche Tanze, D 366. Scherzo, D 593 (2). Sonata, piano, no. 18, D 894, G major. Jeremy Menuhin, pno. Ades 14017
+-HFN 8-81 p87
Allegretto, D 915, C minor. See no. 2986
Allegro, op. 144, D 947, A minor. See no. 2194

Andantino varie, op. 84, no. 1, D 823, B minor. See no. 2194. See no. 2959
Ave Maria, D 839. See no. 3700. See no. 3759. See no. 3847. See no. 3999
Deutsche Tanze, D 366. See no. 2940. See no. 3020
Der Erlkonig, D 328. See no. 3693
Fantasia, D 605, C major. See no. 2989
Fantasia, op. 15, D 760, C major. See no. 205. See no. 2216
Fantasia, op. 103, D 940, F minor. See no. 2959. See no. 2990
2941 Fantasia, op. 159, D 934, C major. Sonata, violin and piano, op. 162, D 574, A major. Sonatinas, violin and piano, op. 137, nos. 1-3. Szymon Goldberg, vln; Radu Lupu, pno. Decca D195D2 (2)
+Gr 3-81 p1212 +ST 7-81 p206
2942 Fantasia, op. 159, D 934, C major. Quartet, strings, no. 8, D 112, B flat major. Quartet, strings, no. 14, D 810, D minor. Quartet, strings, no. 15, D 887, G major. Trio, no. 2, op. 100, D 929, E flat major. Busch Quartet; Busch-Serkin Trio; Adolph Busch, vln; Rudolf Serkin, pno. World Records SHB 53
++FF 3/4-81 p190
Fantasia, op. 159, D 934, C major. See no. 720
2943 Die Freunde von Salamanka, D 326. Der Spiegelritter, D 11, fragment. Edith Mathis, Christine Weidlinger, s; Carol Wyatt, ms; Thomas Moser, Eberhard Buchner, Norbert Orth, t; Hermann Prey, bar; Robert Holl, Kurt Rydl, bs; Austrian Radio Orchestra and Chorus; Theodor Guschlbauer. DG 2707 126 (2)
+Gr 8-81 p310 +-HFN 8-81 p87
Galopp, D 735, G major. See no. 3020
Grand duo sonata, op. 140, D 812, C major. See no. 2959
2944 Grande marche heroique, op. 66, D 885, A minor. Marches, op. 40, no. 5, D 819, E flat minor. Marches, op. 121, nos. 1-2, D 886. Karl-Heinz and Michael Schluter, pno. Da Camera SM 93146
+-FF 5/6-81 p140
2945 Impromptus, op. 90, D 899 and op. 142, D 935. Andreas Schiff, pno. Decca SDD R 563
/Gr 3-81 p1217 +HFN 5-81 p83
2946 Impromptus, op. 90, D 899 and op. 142, D 935. Moments musicaux, op. 94, D 780. Klavierstucke, D 946 (3). Rudolf Buchbinder, pno. Telefunken 6-48132 (2) Tape (c) 4-48132
++FF 1/2-81 p179 ++NR 1-81 p15
+-HF 11-80 p75
Impromptus, op. 90, no. 1, D 899, C minor. See no. 2987
Impromptus, op. 90, no. 2, D 899, E flat major. See no. 298
Impromptus, op. 90, nos. 2-3, D 899. See no. 3749
Impromptus, op. 90, no. 3, D 899, G flat major. See no. 298. See no. 3020
2947 Impromptus, op. 90, no. 4, D 899, A flat major. Sonata, piano, no. 12, D 784, A major. SCHUMANN: Carnaval, op. 9. Alicia de Larrocha, pno. Decca SXL 6910 Tape (c) KSXC 6910 (also London CS 7134 Tape (c) CS5-7134)
+-CL 2-81 p12 +-RR 2-80 p80
+-FF 11/12-80 p170 +-St 10-80 p121
+Gr 2-80 p1282 +STL 3-9-80 p41
+HFN 2-80 p97
Impromptus, op. 142, no. 4, D 935, F minor. See no. 3869
Introduction and variations, op. 160, D 802, E minor. See no. 571. See no. 3040

2948 Klavierstuck, D 946. Moments musicaux, op. 94, D 780. Alfred Brendel, pno. Philips 6527 110 Tape (c) 7311 110 (From 6500 418, 6500 928)
+Gr 11-81 p724 +HFN 11-81 p105
Klavierstuck, D 946. See no. 2946. See no. 2985
2949 Konzertstuck, D 345, D major. SCHUMANN: concerto, violin, D minor. Vaclav Snitil, vln; PSO; Libor Hlavacek. Supraphon 110 2288
+FF 11/12-80 p171 +-HFN 5-81 p84
+-HF 11-80 p78 +-NR 10-80 p5
2950 Lazarus, D 689. Mass, no. 2, D 167, G major. Sheila Armstrong, s; Ruth Welting, Jocelyne Chamonin, s; Anthony Rolfe Johnson, Martyn Hill, t; Martin Egel, bar; French Radio Chorus; French Radio New Philharmonic Orchestra; Theodor Guschlbauer. Erato STU 71442 (2)
+-Gr 10-81 p594 +-HFN 12-81 p102
2951 Magnificat, D 486, C major. Offertorium, D 963. Stabat mater, D 383, F minor. Sheila Armstrong, s; Hanna Schaer, ms; Alejandro Ramirez, t; Philippe Huttenlocher, bar; Lausanne Vocal Ensemble; Lausanne Orchestra; Michel Corboz. Erato STU 71262 (also Musical Heritage Society MHS 4239)
+-ARG 7/8-81 p32 +MU 6-81 p14
+FF 1/2-81 p180 +RR 5-80 p100
+Gr 4-80 p1580 +St 6-81 p118
+-HFN 4-80 p109
Marches, op. 40, no. 5, D 819, E flat minor. See no. 2944
Marches, op. 121, nos. 1-2, D 886. See no. 2944
Mass, no. 2, S 167, G major. See no. 2950
Mass, no. 2, K 167, G major: Kyrie. See no. 3618
2952 Mass, no. 4, op. 48, D 452, C major. Salve regina, D 386; D 811. Delcina Stevenson, s; Nina Hinson, ms; Keith Wyatt, t; Richard Wagner, bar; Los Angeles Camerata; H. Vincent Mitzelfelt. Grand Prix GP 9004
+-ARG 11-80 p28 +NR 3-81 p11
-FF 7/8-80 p127
Minuet and finale, D 72, F major. See no. 1429
2953 Moments musicaux, op. 94, D 780. SCHUMANN: Nachtstucke, op. 23. Emil Gilels, pno. Quintessence PMC 7187
+FF 7/8-81 p161
2954 Moments musicaux, op. 94, D 780. SCHUMANN: Carnival, op. 9. Lee Luvisi, pno. Rivergate LP 1004
+-CL 3-80 p15 ++St 1-81 p78
Moments musicaux, op. 94, D 780. See no. 2946. See no. 2948
Moments musicaux, op. 94, no. 2, D 780, A flat major. See no. 2959. See no. 3020
Moments musicaux, op. 94, no. 3, D 780, F minor. See no. 3645. See no. 3764. See no. 3993. See no. 4066
2955 Nocturne, op. 148, D 897, E flat major. Trio, piano, no. 1, op. 99, D 989, B flat major. Ferenc Rados, pno; Denes Kovacs, vln; Ede Banda, vlc. Hungaroton SLPX 11966
-NR 9-81 p5
2956 Nocturne, op. 148, D 897, E flat major. Trio, piano, no. 1, op. 99, D 898, B flat major. Suk Trio. Supraphon 111 1896 (also Denon 7043)
+FF 5/6-81 p143 +-HFN 4-81 p76
+Gr 4-81 p1340 ++NR 6-81 p5
++HF 9-81 p76

2957 Octet, op. 166, D 803, F major. Music Group of London. ASV ACA 1004 Tape (c) ZCACA 1004 (From Enigma K 53590)
-Gr 4-81 p1340
+HFN 4-81 p81
+HFN 6-81 p81 tape
2958 Octet, op. 166, D 803, F major. Vienna Chamber Ensemble. DG 2531 278 Tape (c) 3301 278
++FF 7/8-81 p162
+-Gr 5-81 p1488
+Gr 9-81 p460 tape
+-HFN 5-81 p83
+HFN 6-81 p87 tape
-NR 7-81 p7
++SFC 7-19-81 p19
++St 8-81 p100
Offertorium, D 136. See no. 3790
Offertorium, D 963. See no. 2951
Overture, D 470, B flat major. See no. 3003
Overture, D 556, D major. See no. 3003
Overture in the Italian style, D 591, C major. See no. 3003
2959 Piano works: Andantino varie, D 823, B minor. Fantasia, op. 103, D 940, F minor. Grand duo sonata, op. 140, D 812, C major. Moments musicaux, op. 94, no. 2, D 780, A flat major. Sonata, piano, no. 6, D 566, E minor. Variations on an original theme, op. 35, D 813, A flat major. Sviatoslav Richter, pno; Benjamin Britten, fortepiano. Rococo 2121 (8)
-NR 3-81 p13
2960 Quartets, strings (complete). Melos Quartet. DG 2740 123 (7)
+FF 11/12-81 p230
2961 Quartet, strings, no. 7, D 94, D major. Quartet, strings, no. 13, D 804, A minor. Allegri Quartet. Argo ZK 88
+Gr 4-81 p1340
+HFN 3-81 p91
2962 Quartet, strings, no. 8, D 112, B flat major. Quartet, strings, no. 10, D 87, E flat major. Amadeus Quartet. DG 2531 336 Tape (c) 3301 336
+Gr 7-81 p168
+Gr 9-81 p460 tape
+-HFN 9-81 p84
+-HFN 10-81 p95 tape
Quartet, strings, no. 8, D 112, B flat major. See no. 2942
Quartet, strings, no. 8, D 112, B flat major: Menuetto. See no. 543
Quartet, strings, no. 10, D 87, E flat major. See no. 2962
2963 Quartet, strings, no. 12, D 703, C minor. Quartet, strings, no. 14, D 810, D minor. Heutling Quartett. EMI 1C 037 29292
+FF 11/12-81 p231
2964 Quartet, strings, no. 12, D 703, C minor. Quartet, strings, no. 14, D 810, D minor. Quartetto Italiano. Philips 6570 180 Tape (c) 7310 180 (From SAL 3618)
+Gr 10-81 p574
2965 Quartet, strings, no. 12, D 703, C minor. Quartet, strings, no. 14, D 810, D minor. Quartetto Italiano. Philips 9500 751
+-FF 5/6-81 p139
+Gr 4-81 p1340
-HF 9-81 p76
+-HFN 4-81 p75
+HFN 10-81 p95
+-MUM 5/6-81 p32
++NR 4-81 p7
+ST 12-81 p589
Quartet, strings, no. 12, D 703, C minor. See no. 1417. See no. 1419
Quartet, strings, no. 13, D 804, A minor. See no. 2961
Quartet, strings, no. 13, D 804, A minor: Andante. See no. 543
Quartet, strings, no. 14, D 810, D minor. See no. 2395. See no. 2942. See no. 2963. See no. 2964. See no. 2965
2966 Quartet, strings, no. 15, D 887, G major. Juilliard Quartet.

Columbia M 35827 Tape (c) MT 35827 (also CBS 76908)
+-FF 9/10-80 p198 ++NR 5-80 p6
+Gr 12-80 p847 +-SFC 3-23-80 p35
++HF 6-80 p85 ++St 7-80 p84
+HFN 2-81 p93

2967 Quartet, strings, no. 15, op. 161, D 887, G major. Alban Berg Quartet. EMI 1C 065 03832 (also HMV ASD 3882)
++FF 1/2-81 p179 +MT 10-81 p678
++Gr 3-81 p1212 ++STL 9-13-81 p41
+HFN 3-81 p91

Quartet, strings, no. 15, D 887, G major. See no. 2942

Quintet, piano, op. 44, E flat major. See no. 2109

2968 Quintet, piano, op. 114, D 667, A major. Sviatoslav Richter, pno; Borodin Quartet Members; Georg Hortnagel, double bass. HMV ASD 4032 Tape (c) TCC ASD 4032 (also Angel DS 37846)
+Gr 9-81 p402 ++HFN 9-81 p84

2969 Quintet, piano, op. 114, D 667, A major. Songs: Die Forelle, D 550. Beaux Arts Trio; Samuel Rhodes, vla; Georg Hortnagel, double bass; Hermann, Prey, bar; Leonard Hokanson, pno. Philips 6527 075 Tape (c) 7311 075 (From 9500 071, 6584 050)
+Gr 4-81 p1340 +HFN 4-81 p81
++Gr 7-81 p196 tape +HFN 7-81 p83 tape

Quintet, piano, op. 114, D 667, A major. See no. 710

2970 Quintet, strings, op. 163, D 956, C major. Allegri Quartet; Moray Welsh, vlc. Argo ZK 83
+-Gr 10-80 p512 +-ST 1-81 p648
+HFN 9-80 p110

2971 Quintet, strings, op. 163, D 956, C major. Chilingirian Quartet. Classics for Pleasure CFP 40355 Tape (c) TC CFP 40355
+-Gr 7-81 p168 +HFN 7-81 p76
+-Gr 9-81 p460 tape +HFN 8-81 p92 tape

2972 Quintet, strings, op. 163, D 956, C major. Amadeus Quartet; William Pleeth, vlc. DG 2542 139 Tape (c) 3342 139 (From SLPM 139105)
++Gr 12-80 p847 +HFN 12-80 p159 tape
+Gr 2-81 p1122

2973 Quintet, strings, op. 163, D 956, C major. Collegium Aureum Members. Harmonia Mundi 1C 065 99911
+FF 11/12-81 p231 +Gr 10-81 p574

2974 Quintet, strings, op. 163, D 956, C major. Stuttgart Soloists. Intercord INT 160816
+HFN 12-81 p102

2975 Quintet, strings, op. 163, D 956, C major. Arthur Grumiaux, Arpad Gerecz, vln; Max Lesueur, vla; Paul Szabo, Philippe Mermoud, vlc. Philips 9500 752
+FF 1/2-81 p180 ++NR 1-81 p6
+Gr 2-81 p1098 ++St 2-81 p112
+HF 9-81 p76 +ST 7-81 p207
+HFN 2-81 p93 ++STL 4-12-81 p40

Rosamunde, op. 26, D 797: Ballet music, nos. 1, 2. See no. 3001

Rosamunde, op. 26, D 797: Ballet music; Entr'acte, no. 3. See no. 2465

Rosamunde, op. 26, D 797: Entr'acte, D major; Ballet, G major. See no. 3666

2976 Rosamunde, op. 26, D 797: Incidental music. Katherine Montgomery,

s; St. Hedwig's Cathedral Choir; BRSO; Gustav Kuhn. HMV ASD 4012
+-Gr 7-81 p186 +HFN 7-81 p76
Rosamunde, op. 26, D 797: Incidental music. See no. 2939. See no. 3005
Rosamunde, op. 26, D 797: Overture. See no. 3760
Rosamunde, op. 26, D 797: Overture; Ballet music, nos. 1 and 2. See no. 3000
Rosamunde, op. 26, D 797: Overture; Ballet music, no. 2; Entr' acte, no. 3. See no. 3792
Salve regina, D 386; D 811. See no. 2952
Scherzi, D 593 (2). See no. 2940
2977 Die schone Mullerin, op. 25, D 795. Schwanengesang, D 957: Am Meer; Das Fischermadchen; Der Doppelganger; Die Taubenpost. Die Winterreise, op. 89, D 911. Songs: Abschied, D 578; An die Musik, D 547; Der Erlkonig, D 328; Der Musensohn, D 764; Der Wanderer, D 489; Liebeslauchen, D 898; Lied eines Schiffers; Horch horch die Lerch; Standchen; Wer nie sein Brot mit Tranen; Wer sich der Einsamkeit ergibt; Widerschien, D 949. Gerhard Husch, t; Hanns Udo Muller, Gerald Moore, pno. Arabesque 8107/3 (3) (also World Records SHB 65)
+Gr 1-81 p994 ++NR 11-81 p12
2978 Die schone Mullerin, op. 25, D 795. Aksel Schiotz, t; Gerald Moore, pno. EMI 6C 053 39145
-FF 9/10-81 p168
2979 Die schone Mullerin, op. 25, D 795. Peter Schreier, t; Konrad Ragossnig, gtr. Odeon 065 30995
+FF 7/8-81 p162
Die schone Mullerin, op. 25, D 795: Ungeduld. See no. 3844
Die schone Mullerin, op. 25, D 795: Ungeduld; Wohin. See no. 3988
2980 Schwanengesang, D 957. Hermann Prey, bar; Leonard Hokanson, pno. DG 2531 325
+-FF 11/12-81 p232 +-HFN 4-81 p87
+-Gr 8-81 p303 +St 11-81 p70
2981 Schwanengesang, D 957. Peter Schreier, t; Walter Olbertz, pno. DG 2542 144 Tape (c) 3342 144 (From 2530 469)
+Gr 12-80 p866 +HFN 12-80 p153
++Gr 2-81 p1122 tape
Schwanengesang, D 957: Am Meer. See no. 3966. See no. 3988
Schwanengesang, D 957: Am Meer; Das Fischermadchen; Der Doppelganger; Die Taubenpost. See no. 2977
Schwanengesang, D 957: Die Taubenpost. See no. 3547
2982 Sonata, arpeggione and piano, D 821, A minor. Trio, strings, no. 1, D 471, B flat major. Trio, strings, no. 2, D 581, B flat major. Regis Pasquier, vln; Bruno Pasquier, vla; Roland Pidoux, vlc; Jean-Claude Pennetier, pno. Harmonia Mundi (France) HM 1035 Tape (c) 40-1035
+-FF 5/6-81 p143 ++HFN 4-81 p76
+-Gr 7-81 p168
Sonata, arpeggione and piano, D 821, A minor. See no. 2286
2983 Sonatas, piano, complete. Wilhelm Kempff, pno. DG 2740 132 (2) (From 2720 024)
++CL 1-81 p12 +-HFN 12-75 p171
+-FF 5/6-81 p140 ++NYT 10-5-80 pD24
+Gr 4-76 p1640 +RR 2-76 p53

Sonata, piano, no. 4, D 537, A minor. See no. 875. See no. 986
Sonata, piano, no. 6, D 566, E minor. See no. 2959
Sonata, piano, no. 8, D 571, F sharp minor. See no. 986
2984 Sonatas, piano, nos. 11, 13-21. Noel Lee, pno. Valois CMB (5)
+-FF 11/12-81 p234
Sonata, piano, no. 12, D 784, A major. See no. 2947
Sonata, piano, no. 13, D 664, A major. See no. 986
2985 Sonata, piano, no. 15, D 840, C major. Klavierstucke, D 946 (3). Gilbert Kalish, pno. Nonesuch H 71386
+ARG 3-281 p51 +HF 11-80 p73
+FF 11/12-80 p168 ++St 11-80 p100
Sonata, piano, no. 18, D 894, G major. See no. 245. See no. 2940
2986 Sonata, piano, no. 19, D 958, C minor. Allegretto, D 915, C minor. Claudio Arrau, pno. Philips 9500 755 Tape (c) 7300 836
-ARG 9-81 p31 +-MUM 7/8-81 p34
+CL 9-81 p18 ++NR 5-81 p14
++FF 9/10-81 p168 +NYT 3-22-81 pD23
2987 Sonata, piano, no. 20, D 959, A major. Impromptu, op. 90, no. 1, D 899, C minor. Ludwig Olshansky, pno. Monitor MCS 2164
+-ARG 11-81 p39 +NR 8-81 p12
+FF 7/8-81 p163
2988 Sonata, piano, no. 21, D 960, B flat major. Rudolf Serkin, pno. CBS 61946 Tape (c) 40-61946 (From 79216)
+Gr 4-81 p1346 +STL 3-8-81 p38
+-HFN 4-81 p81
2989 Sonata, piano, no. 21, D 960, B flat major. Fantasia, D 605, C major. Jorg Ewald Dahler, hammerflugel. Claves D 8011
+FF 11/12-81 p233
Sonata, piano, no. 21, D 960, B flat major. See no. 947
2990 Sonata, piano, 4 hands, op. 140, D 812, C major. Fantasia, op. 103, D 940, F minor. Alfons and Aloys Kontarsky, pno. DG 2531 050
+-CL 3-81 p10 -NR 11-80 p9
+-FF 1/2-81 p180 +-NYT 9-21-80 pD22
+Gr 6-80 p53 +RR 6-80 p31
+HFN 6-80 p112
2991 Sonata, violin and piano, op. 162, D 574, A major. Sonatinas, violin and piano, op. 137, nos. 1-3. Arthur Grumiaux, vln; Paul Crossley, pno. Philips 9500 394
+Gr 5-81 p1493 ++SFC 7-30-78 p49
+HFN 5-81 p83 +St 7-78 p96
+MJ 1-79 p46 ++ST 10-81 p431
+NR 7-78 p8
Sonata, violin and piano, op. 162, D 574, A major. See no. 2219. See no. 2941
2992 Sonatinas, violin and piano, op. 137, nos. 1-3. Bohuslav Matousek, vln; Petr Adamec, pno. Supraphon 111 2619
+ARG 6-81 p34 +NR 12-80 p7
+FF 3/4-81 p192 ++St 2-81 p108
2993 Sonatinas, violin and piano, op. 137, nos. 1-3. Jaap Schroder, vln; Christopher Hogwood, fortepiano. L'Oiseau-Lyre DSLO 565
+FF 3/4-81 p165 ++MUM 11/12-81 p32
++Gr 11-80 p697 ++St 2-81 p108
Sonatinas, violin and piano, op. 137, nos. 1-3. See no. 2941. See no. 2991

Sonatina, violin and piano, no. 1, D 384, D major. See no. 947. See no. 1102

Sonatina, violin and piano, no. 3, K 408, G minor. See no. 636

2994 Songs: Abendbilder, D 650; Das Lied im Grunen, D 917; Das war ich, D 174; Der blinde Knabe, D 833; Die Gotter Griechensland, D 677; Ihr Grab, D 736; Der Winterabend, D 938. WOLF: Beherzigung; Bei einer Trauung; Die du Gott gebarst; Fuhr mich Kind; Fruhling ubers Jahr; Ganymed; Der Gartner; Sankt Nepomukz Vorabend; Schlafendes Jesuskind; Der Scholar; Spottlied; Wenn ich dein gedenke; Wie sollt ich heiter bleiben. Peter Pears, t; Benjamin Britten, pno. BBC REGL 410 Tape (c) ZCF 410

++Gr 7-81 p186 ++STL 5-10-81 p41
+NYT 8-16-81 pD19

2995 Songs: Abschied, D 578; Alinde, D 904; An den Tod, D 518; An die Musik, D 547; Atys, D 585; Geheimes, D 719; Gesange des Harfners, D 480; Der Kreuzzug, D 932; Greisengesang, D 778; Die Liebe hat gelogen, D 751; Liedesend, D 473; Meerstille, D 216; Orest auf Tauris, D 548; Orpheus, D 474; Pilgerweise, D 789; Der Schafer und der Reiter, D 517; Sangers habe; Schiffers Scheidelied, D 912; Tiefes Lied, D 876; Todtengrabers Heimweh, D 842; Der Wanderer, D 946; Wanderers Nachtlied, D 768; Der Wanderer, D 649; Das Zugenglocklein, D 871. Hans Hotter, bs-bar; Michael Raucheisen, pno. Discocorp IGI 386 (2) (also Bruno Walter Society IGI 386)

+-FF 9/10-81 p169 +-St 12-81 p126
+NR 6-81 p11

2996 Songs: An die Musik, D 547; An Sylvia, D 891; Auf dem Wasser zu singen, D 774; Ganymed, D 544; Gretchen am Spinnrade, D 118; Im Fruhling, D 882; Die junge Nonne, D 828; Das Lied in Grunen; Der Musensohn, D 764; Nachtviolen, D 752; Nahe des Geliebten, D 162b; Wehmut, D 772. Elisabeth Schwarzkopf, s; Edwin Fischer, pno. EMI ALP 3843

+FF 3/4-81 p166

2997 Songs: Das Dorfchen, D 598; Ellens Gesang II, D 838; Gebet, D 815; Mirjams Siegesgesang, D 942; Nachtgesang im Walde, D 913; Nachthelle, D 892; Standchen, D 920. Lucia Popp, s; Ernesto Palacio, t; La Scala Chorus; Antonio Beltrami, pno; Various other accompaniments. Fonit Cetra LIC 9002

-Gr 10-81 p594

2998 Songs: An die Musik, D 547; An Sylvia, D 891; Auf dem Wasser zu singen, D 774; Du bist die Ruh, D 776; Die Forelle, D 550; Fruhlingsglaube, D 686; Gretchen am Spinnrade, D 118; Heidenroslein, D 257; Die junge Nonne, D 828; Litanei, D 343; Musensohn, D 764; Nacht und Traume, D 827; Rastlose Liebe, D 183; Der Tod und das Madchen, D 531. Janet Baker, ms; Geoffrey Parsons, pno. HMV ASD 4054 Tape (c) TC ASD 4054

++Gr 7-81 p186 ++HFN 9-81 p84
++Gr 10-81 p614 tape

2999 Songs: Du liebst mich nicht, D 756; Gretchen am Spinnrade, D 118; Heimliches Lieben, D 922; Der Hirt auf den Felsen, D 965; Der jungling an der Quelle, D 300; Im Fruhling, D 822; Landler, op. 171 (12); Der Musensohn, D 764; Seligkeit, D 433; Die Vogel, D 691. SCHUMANN: Auftrage, op. 77, no. 5; Er ist's, op. 79, no. 23; Ersters Grun, op. 34, no. 4; Frage, op. 35, no. 9; Jasminenstrauch, op. 27, no. 4; Kauzlein, op. 79, no. 11; Die

Kartenlegerin, op. 21, no. 2; Die letzten Blumen starben; Lorelei, op. 53, no. 2; Marienwurmchen, op. 79, no. 14; Die Meerfee, op. 125, no. 1; Mein schoner Stern, op. 101, no. 4; Der Nussbaum, op. 26, no. 3; Der Sandmann, op. 79, no. 13; Schneeglockchen, op. 79, no. 27; Sehnsucht, op. 51, no. 1; Sehnsucht nach der Waldegegend, op. 35, no. 5; Schmetterling, op. 71, no. 2; Die Sennen, op. 90, no. 4; Waldesgesprach, op. 39, no. 3; Widmung, op. 25, no. 1. Elly Ameling, s; Jorg Demus, hammerflugel; Hans Deinzer, clt. Quintessence 2PMC 2710 (22
++FF 7/8p81 p166

Songs: Abendstern, D 806; Ach um deine feuchten Schwingen, D 717; Auf dem Strom, D 943; Auflosung, D 807; Ave Maria, D 839; Die Forelle, D 550; Dass sie hier gewesen, D 775; Fruhlingsglaube, D 686; Heidenroslein, D 257; Der Hirt auf dem Felsen, D 965; Im Fruhling, D 882; Jager Ruhe, D 838; Lachen und Weinen, D 777; Liebesbotschaft, D 957; Lob der Tranen, D 711; Nachtviolen, D 752; Raste Krieger, D 837; Seligkeit, D 433; Was Bedeutet die Bewegnung, D 702. See no. 3020

Songs: Abschied, D 578; An die Musik, D 547; Der Erlkonig, D 328; Der Musensohn, D 764; Der Wanderer, D 489; Liebeslauche, D 898; Lied eines Schiffers; Horch horch die Lerch; Standchen; Wer nie sein Brot mit Tranen; Wer sich der Einsamkeit ergibt; Widerschien, D 949. See no. 2977

Songs: An die Musik, D 547. See no. 3642

Songs: An die Musik, D 547; Du bist die Ruh, D 776; Im Abendrot, D 799; Der Jungling an der Quelle, D 300; Der Lindenbaum; Litanie, D 343; Der Musensohn, D 764; Nacht und Traume, D 824; Standchen, D 967. See no. 3988

Songs: An die Musik, D 547; Die Allmacht, D 852; Du bist die Ruh, D 776; Der Jungling and der Quelle, D 300; Lachen und Weinen, D 777; Nacht und Traume, D 827; Nachtviolen, D 752; Rastlose Liebe, D 138. See no. 637

Songs: Auf der Bruck, D 853; Im Fruhling, D 882. See no. 3842

Songs: Ave Maria, D 839; Farewell, D 957; Hark hark the lark, D 889; Hurdy gurdy man, D 911; Nights and dreams, D 827; Serenade, D 957; To the lyre, D 905; Who is Sylvia, D 891. See no. 4043

Songs: Ave Maria, D 839; Schwanengesang, D 957, no. 4: Serenade; Du bist die Ruh, D 776; Farewell, D 957; Hark hark the lark, D 889; Holy night, D 827; The hurdy gurdy man, D 911; Die liebe hat gelogen, D 751; To the lyre, D 737; Whi is Sylvia, D 891. See no. 3967

Songs: Ave Maria, D 839; Wiegenlied, D 498. See no. 3753

Songs: Der Hirt auf dem Felsen, D 965. See no. 3957

Songs: Die Forelle, D 550. See no. 2969

Songs: Du bist die Ruh, D 776; Die liebe hat gelogen, D 755; Who is Sylvia, D 891. See no. 3657

Songs: Erlkonig, D 328; Lodas Gespenst; Der Zwerg, D 771. See no. 2079

Songs: Erlkonig, D 328; Der Tod und das Madchen, D 531. See no. 4039

Songs: Im Walde, D 834. See no. 958

Songs: Litanei, D 343; Die Forelle, D 550; Seligkeit, D 433. See no. 3844

Songs: Mignons Gesang, op. 19, no. 2; Der Konig in Thule, D 367. See no. 465

Songs: Rastlose Liebe, D 138; Wasserfluth. See no. 3654
Songs: Standchen. See no. 3736
Songs: Standchen; Der Wanderer. See no. 3639
Der Spiegelritter, D 11, fragment. See no. 2943
3000 Symphonies, nos. 1-6, 8-9. Rosamunde, op. 26, D 797: Overture; Ballet music, nos. 1 and 2. BPhO; Karl Bohm. DG 2740 127 (5) Tape (C) 3378 082 (also DG 2720 097)
+FF 7/8-81 p163 +-HFN 10-75 p152
+-Gr 1-76 p1204 +-RR 10-75 p49
+Gr 6-79 p109 tape ++SFC 12-9-80 p33
3001 Symphonies, nos. 1-6, 8-9. Rosaumunde, op. 26, D 797: Overture; Ballet music, nos. 1 and 2. BPhO; Herbert von Karajan. EMI 1C 157 03285/9 (5)
+FF 11/12-81 p234
3002 Symphony, no. 1, D 82, D major. Symphony, no. 2, D 125, B flat major. Cologne Radio Orchestra; Gunter Wand. Harmonia Mundi 1C 065 99772
+Gr 4-81 p1324
Symphony, no. 2, D 125, B flat major. See no. 3002
3003 Symphony, no. 3, D 200, D major. Overtures, D 470, B major; D 556, D major. Overture in the Italian style, D 591, C major. Winterthur State Orchestra; Moshe Atzmon. Intercord INT 120936
/HFN 12-81 p102
Symphony, no. 3, D 200, D major. See no. 2465
3004 Symphony, no. 4, D 417, C minor. Symphony, no. 8, D 759, B minor. Dresden State Orchestra; Wolfgang Sawallisch. Philips 6570 150 Tape (c) 7310 150 (From SABL 40)
+Gr 1-81 p953 +-HFN 10-81 p95
+-HFN 5-81 p93 tape
3005 Symphony, no. 5, D 485, B flat major. Symphony, no. 6, D 589, C major. Symphony, no. 8, D 759, B minor. Symphony, no. 9, D 944, C major. Rosamunde, op. 26, D 797: Incidental music. Lucia Popp, s; Naples Orchestra; Denis Vaughan. Arabesque 8046/3 (3) Tape (c) 9046
+ARG 6-81 p35 +-NR 12-80 p4
+-FF 3/4-81 p192
3006 Symphony, no. 5, D 485, B flat major. SCHUMANN: Symphony, no. 4, op. 120, D minor. VPO; Karl Bohm. DG 2531 279 Tape (c) 3301 279
+-FF 7/8-81 p163 +HFN 1-81 p109 tape
++Gr 11-80 p677 -NR 4-81 p3
+HF 10-81 p86 +ST 3-81 p820
+-HFN 12-80 p145
Symphony, no. 6, D 589, C major. See no. 3005
3007 Symphony, no. 7, D 729, E major (arr. Weingartner). BRSO; Heinz Rogner. Spectrum SR 116 Tape (c) SC 216 (r) B-G D 116
+FF 9/10-80 p201 +HF 10-80 p98 tape
++HF 8-80 p68 +HF 6-81 p70 tape
Symphony, no. 8, D 759, B minor. See no. 670. See no. 694. See no. 973. See no. 978. See no. 2234. See no. 2421. See no. 3004. See no. 3005. See no. 3781. See no. 3855
3008 Symphony, no. 9, D 944, C major. Bavarian Radio Orchestra; Eugen Jochum. Contour CC 7512 Tape (c) CCT 7512
++Gr 8-81 p316
3009 Symphony, no. 9, D 944, C major. Berlin Radio Orchestra; Heinz

Rogner. Denon PCM OB 7350/1 (2)
+Audio 9-81 p82 +St 2-80 p132

3010 Symphony, no. 9, D 944, C major. BPhO; Wilhelm Furtwangler. DG 2535 808 Tape (c) 3335 808 (From DG 18015/6)
+-FF 9/10-79 p135 ++NR 7-79 p2
++Gr 5-77 p1690 +NYT 3-18-79 pD23
+-HF 2-81 p81 tape +RR 5-77 p56
+HFN 6-77 p137

3011 Symphony, no. 9, D 944, C major. BSO; Colin DAvis. Philips 9500 890 Tape (c) 7300 890
+FF 11/12-81 p235 +HFN 7-81 p75
+-Gr 7-81 p160 +HFN 10-81 p95 tape
+-HF 12-81 p80 ++NR 9-81 p2

3012 Symphony, no. 9, D 944, C major. BSO; William Steinberg. RCA ARG 1-3789 (From LSC 3115)
-FF 7/8-81 p165

3013 Symphony, no. 9, D 944, C major. North German Radio Orchestra; Erich Kleiber. Rococo 2068
+NR 4-81 p3

Symphony, no. 9, D 944, C major. See no. 3005. See no. 3781

Tanze, op. 9, D 365. See no. 1555

3014 Trio, piano, no. 1, op. 99, D 898, B flat major. Trio, piano, no. 2, op. 100, D 929, E flat major. Regis Pasquier, vln; Roland Pidoux, vlc; Jean Claude Pennetier, pno. Harmonia Mundi HM 1047/8 (2)
+FF 1/2-81 p181 +HFN 1-81 p100
+-Gr 12-80 p846 +St 6-81 p123
++HF 9-81 p76

Trio, piano, no. 1, op. 99, D 898, B flat major. See no. 946. See no. 2955. See no. 2956

3015 Trio, piano, no. 2, op. 100, D 929, E flat major. Odeon Trio. Musicaphon BM 30 SL 4000
+-HFN 1-81 p100

Trio, piano, no. 2, op. 100, D 929, E flat major. See no. 2942. See no. 3014

Trio, strings, no. 1, D 471, B flat major. See no. 2982

Trio, strings, no. 2, D 581, B flat major. See no. 2982

Valse, D 145, no. 2, B major. See no. 3020

Valses nobles, op. 77, D 969. See no. 3866

Variations on an original theme, op. 35, D 813, A flat major. See no. 2959

3016 Variations on Trockne Blumen, D 802. SCHUMANN: Quartet, piano, op. 47, E flat major. Paula Robison, flt; Richard Goode, pno; Goode-Laredo-Trampler-Parnas Quartet. Musicmasters MM 20006 Tape (c) MMC 40006
+FF 7/8-81 p165 -NR 12-81 p11
*HF 12-81 p93 tape +-NYT 4-12-81 pD28

Die Verschworenen, D 787: Romanze. See no. 3954

3017 Winterreise, op. 89, D 911. Ernst Haefliger, t; Jorg Ewald Dahler, pno. Claves D 8008/9 (2)
+Gr 2-81 p1110

3018 Winterreise, op. 89, D 911. Dietrich Fischer-Dieskau, bar; Daniel Barenboim, pno. DG 2707 118 (2) Tape (c) 3301 237
+ARG 7/8-81 p31 ++HFN 12-80 p159 tape
+Gr 11-80 p724 +NR 1-81 p11
+Gr 2-81 p1122 tape +NYT 12-14-80 pD38

++HFN 11-80 p122 ++St 2-81 p77

3019 Winterreise, op. 89, D 911. Shura Gehrman, bs; Nina Walker, pno. Nimbus 2130/1

+-HFN 10-81 p90

Winterreise, op. 89, D 911. See no. 2977

Winterreise, op. 89, D 911: Die Post. See no. 3988

3020 Works, selections: Deutsche Tanze, D 366 (6). Galopp, D 735, G major. Impromptu, op. 90, no. 3, D 899, G flat major. Moment musicaux, op. 94, no. 2, D 780, A flat major. Songs: Abendstern, D 806; Ach um deine feuchten Schwingen, D 717; Auf dem Strom, D 943; Auflosung, D 807; Ave Maria, D 839; Die Forelle, D 550; Dass sie hier gewesen, D 775; Fruhlingsglaube, D 686; Heidenroslein, D 257; Der Hirt auf dem Felsen, D 965; Im Fruhling, D 882; Jager Ruhe, D 838; Lachen und Weinen, D 777; Liebesbotschaft, D 957; Lob der Tranen, D 711; Nachtviolen, D 752; Raste Krieger, D 837; Seligkeit, D 433; Was Bedeutet die Bewegnung, D 720. Valse, D 145, no. 2, B major. Judith Nelson, s; Jorg Demus, pno; Alfred Prinz, clt; Franz Sollner, hn. Harmonia Mundi HM 1023/4 (2)

+-FF 12-79 p116 +-MT 4-81 p247
-FU 5-80 p49 ++NR 6-80 p11

Die Zauberharfe, D 644: Overture. See no. 2939. See no. 3858

SCHUBERT, Joseph

Concerto, viola, C major. See no. 2812

SCHULHOFF, Erwin

Bass Nachtigall. See no. 3739

SCHULLER

Meditation. See no. 3817

SCHULZ, Johann

Largo. See no. 3881

SCHUMAN, William

3021 In sweet music. Time to the old. The young dead soldiers. Rosalind Rees, s; Robin Graham, hn; Thomas Muraco, pno; Orpheus Trio, White Mountains Festival Orchestra; Gerard Schwarz. CRI SD 439

+-FF 11/12-81 p236 *NYT 9-27-81 pD24
+-HF 11-81 p96 ++St 8-81 p97
+NR 8-81 p10

3022 Symphony, no. 3. Symphony, strings, no. 5. NYP; Leonard Bernstein. CBS MS 7442

+FF 7/8-81 p255

Symphony, strings, no. 5. See no. 3022

Time to the old. See no. 3021

The young dead soldiers. See no. 3021

SCHUMANN, Camillo

Sonata, organ, no. 5, op. 40, G minor. See no. 877

SCHUMANN, Clara

Das ist ein Tag. See no. 3814

Impromptu. See no. 1119. See no. 3814

Impromptu, op. 9. See no. 2246

Liebst du um Schonheit. See no. 3814

Piece fugitive, op. 15, no. 1. See no. 1119

Polonaises, op. 1 (4). See no. 2246

Prelude and fugues, op. 16. See no. 1119

Romances, op. 21. See no. 2218

Romance, op. 21, no. 1, A minor. See no. 2246

Scherzo, op. 14, C minor. See no. 1119. See no. 2246
Songs: Das ist ein Tag der klingen mag; Die stille Lotosblume; Er ist gekommen in Sturm und Regen; Liebst du um Schonheit; Ich stand in dunkeln Traumen; Warum willst du And're fragen; Was weinst du Blumlein. See no. 1989
Variations on a theme by Robert Schumann, op. 20. See no. 2246

SCHUMANN, Robert

Adagio and allegro, op. 70, A flat major. See no. 1197. See no. 3056. See no. 3057. See no. 3058. See no. 3655

3023 Andante and variations, op. 46, B flat major. Spanische Liebeslieder, op. 138. Kathleen Battle, s; D'Anna Fortunato, con; John Aler, t; Dominic Cossa, bar; Charles Wadsworth, Richard Goode, pno; Leslie Parnas, Laurence Lesser, vlc; John Barrows, French hn. Musicmasters MM 20007
+NR 12-81 p14

3024 Arabesque, op. 18, C major. Sonata, piano, no. 1, op. 11, F sharp minor. Variations on A-B-E-G-G, op. 1. Ferenc Rados, pno. Hungaroton LSPX 12080
+FF 3/4-81 p194

Arabesque, op. 18, C major. See no. 17. See no. 3039
Bunte Blatter, op. 99. See no. 4020
Bunte Blatter, op. 99: Novellette. See no. 3039

3025 Bunte Blatter, op. 99: Pieces (3). Kinderscenen, op. 15. Sonata, piano, no. 2, op. 22, G minor. Variations on A-B-E-G-G, op. 1. Brigitte Engerer, pno. Chant du Monde LDX 78696
+-HFN 9-81 p84

3026 Carnaval, op. 9. Humoresque, op. 20, B flat major. Bella Davidovich, pno. Philips 9500 667 Tape (c) 7300 765
+-CL 9-80 p14
+FF 7/8-80 p132
+Gr 10-81 p582
+-HF 5-80 p81
++HFN 11-81 p96
+-NR 7-80 p12
++St 10-80 p121

3027 Carnaval, op. 9. STRAUSS, R.: Burleske, op. 11, D minor (orch. Horvat). Shura Cherkassky, pno. Rococo 2119
+-NR 3-81 p13

Carnaval, op. 9. See no. 1162. See no. 2947. See no. 2954

3028 Concerto, piano, op. 54, A minor. WEBER: Konzertstuck, op. 79, F minor. Alfred Brendel, pno; LSO; Claudio Abbado. Philips 9500 677 Tape (c) 7300 772
-FF 1/2-81 p182
+-Gr 11-80 p677
+-HF 4-81 p86
+-HFN 10-80 p109
+HFN 12-80 p159 tape
+-NR 12-80 p6

Concerto, piano, op. 54, A minor. See no. 1153. See no. 1644. See no. 1645. See no. 2684. See no. 3749. See no. 4017
Concerto, violin, D minor. See no. 2949

3029 Davidsbundlertanze, op. 6. Humoreske, op. 20. Lydia Artymiw, pno. Chandos ABR 1029 Tape (c) ABT 1029
+-FF 11/12-81 p237
+Gr 6-81 p62
+Gr 10-81 p614 tape
+HFN 8-81 p87
+HFN 9-81 p93 tape

3030 Dichterliebe, op. 48. Liederkreis, op. 24. Peter Schreier, t; Norman Shetler, pno. DG 2530 353 Tape (c) 3342 156
+HFN 11-81 p105 tape

3031 Dichterliebe, op. 48. Liederkreis, op. 39. Dietrich Fischer-Dieskau, bar; Christoph Eschenbach, pno. DG 2531 290 Tape (c)

3301 290 (From 2740 185, 2740 167)
+ARG 9-81 p32 +HFN 12-80 p145
+FF 5/6-81 p144 +-NR 5-81 p12
++Gr 11-80 p724

Etude in form freier Varitionen uber ein Beethovensches Thema. See no. 1159

Fantasia, op. 17, C major. See no. 1311. See no. 2065

Fantasiestucke, op. 12: Warum; Grillen. See no. 3041

Fantasiestucke, op. 73. See no. 1544. See no. 3056. See no. 3058. See no. 3793

Fantasiestucke, op. 75. See no. 3704

Fantasiestucke, op. 88. See no. 3056. See no. 3057

Fantasiestucke, op. 111. See no. 2217. See no. 2700

3032 Faschingsschwank aus Wien, op. 26. Sonata, piano, no. 2, op. 22, G minor. Waldscenen, op. 82: Vogel als prophet; Abschied. Kenneth van Barthold, pno. Argo ZK 91
+-Gr 1-81 p967 +HFN 1-81 p100

Frauenliebe und Leben, op. 42. See no. 465. See no. 2442. See no. 3043. See no. 3045

Fugues, op. 60. See no. 3962

Gedichte und Requiem, op. 90. See no. 3038

Genoveva overture, op. 81. See no. 3053

Genoveva overture, op. 81: Duets. See no. 4022

3033 Humoresque, op. 20, B flat major. Variations on ABEGG op. 1. Waldscenen, op. 82. Michel Dalberto, pno. Erato STU 71332
+Gr 1-81 p970

Humoresque, op. 20, B flat major. See no. 2046. See no. 3026. See no. 3029

Julius Caesar overture, op. 128. See no. 3048

3034 Kinderscenen, op. 15. Kreisleriana, op. 16. Karl Engel, pno. Astree Valois MB 367
/FF 11/12-81 p237

3035 Kinderscenen, op. 15. Sonata, piano, no. 2, op. 22, G minor. Wilhelm Kempff, pno. DG 2542 155 Tape (C) 3342 155 (From 2740 133)
+Gr 9-81 p417 +HFN 11-81 p115

3036 Kinderscenen, op. 15. Kreisleriana, op. 16. Alfred Brendel, pno. Philips 9500 964 Tape (c) 7300 964
+FF 11/12-81 p238 +HFN 10-81 p91
+Gr 10-81 p582

Kinderscenen, op. 15. See no. 1161. See no. 3025. See no. 3039. See no. 3680

Kinderscenen, op. 15: Traumerei. See no. 3764

Klavierstucke, op. 85: Abendlied. See no. 3058

Kreisleriana, op. 16. See no. 3034. See no. 3036

Lieder, op. 40. See no. 3038

3037 Liederalbum fur die Jugend, op. 79. Liederkreis, op. 39. Elly Ameling, s; Jorg Demus, pno. Philips 6769 037 (2)
+ARG 5-81 p25 +-MT 1-81 p35
+FF 1/2-81 p183

Liederkreis, op. 24. See no. 3030

3038 Liederkreis, op. 39. Gedichte und Requiem, op. 90. Lieder, op. 40. Peter Pears, t; Murray Perahia, pno. CBS 76815 Tape (c) 40-76815 (also CBS 36668)
+ARG 6-81 p38 +MUM 3/4-81 p33

++FF 1/2-81 p184
+Gr 2-80 p1288
+Gr 8-80 p275 tape
+HFN 2-80 p97
+HFN 8-80 p109 tape
+OV 12-81 p40
+RR 2-80 p91
+RR 8-80 p95 tape
+-STL 3-9-80 p41

Liederkreis, op. 39. See no. 3031. See no. 3037. See no. 3043
Manfred overture, op. 115. See no. 961. See no. 3055
Marchenbilder, op. 113. See no. 3056
Marchenerzahlungen, op. 132. See no. 3056
Myrthen Lieder, op. 25: Der Nussbaum. See no. 3844
Nachtstucke, op. 23. See no. 2217. See no. 2953
Nachtstucke, op. 23, nos. 3, 4. See no. 2700
Overture, scherzo and finale, op. 52, E major. See no. 3048
Papillons, op. 2. See no. 4018

3039 Piano works: Arabesque, op. 18, C major. Bunte Blatter, op. 99: Novellette. Kinderscenen, op. 15. Romances, op. 28. Waldscenen, op. 82: The phrophet bird. Wilhelm Kempff, pno. DG 2531 297

+CL 9-81 p18
+-FF 5/6-81 p144
++NR 4-81 p11
++NYT 3-22-81 pD23

3040 Quartet, piano, op. 47, E flat major. SCHUBERT: Introduction and variations, op. 160, D 802, E minor. Jaime Laredo, vln; Walter Trampler, vla; Leslie Parnas, vlc; Richard Goode, pno; Paula Robison, flt. Musicmasters MM 20006 Taep (C) MMC 40006 (also Musical Heritage Society MHS 4299 Tape (c) MHC 6299)

+HF 11-81 p94
+St 8-81 p98

Quartet, piano, op. 47, E flat major. See no. 3016. See no. 3056
Quartets, strings, nos. 1-3. See no. 920. See no. 3056
Quintet, piano, op. 44, E flat major. See no. 1788. See no. 3056
Romances, op. 28. See no. 3039
Romance, op. 28, no. 2, F sharp major. See no. 3764
Romances, op. 94. See no. 2605. See no. 3056. See no. 3057. See no. 3058
Sonata, piano, no. 1, op. 11, F sharp minor. See no. 3024

3041 Sonata, piano, no. 2, op. 22, G minor. Fantasiestucke, op. 12: Warum; Gillen. LISZT: Paraphrases: Schubert: Ave Maria; Der Erlkonig; Die Junge Nonne; Der Leiermann; Tauschung; Wohin. Lazar Berman, pno. Quintessence PMC 7155 Tape (4C 7155 (also Musical Heritage Society MHS 4066 Tape (c) MHC 6066)

+-FF 11/12-80 p173
-HF 4-81 p90

Sonata, piano, no. 2, op. 22, G minor. See no. 2216. See no. 3025. See no. 3032. See no. 3035

3042 Sonata, violin and piano, no. 1, op. 105, A minor. Sonata, violin and piano, no. 2, op. 121, D minor. Ronald Gorevic, vln; Cary Lewis, pno. Crystal S 131

+-ARG 9-81 p33
+-FF 5/6-81 p146
+NR 5-81 p11

Sonata, violin and piano, no. 1, op. 105, A minor. See no. 2218. See no. 3056
Sonata, violin and piano, no. 2, op. 121, D minor. See no. 3042. See no. 3056
Sonata, violin and piano, op. posth., A minor. See no. 3057

3043 Songs: Der frohe Wandersmann, op. 77, no. 1. Frauenliebe und Leben, op. 42. Liederkreis, op. 39. Evelyn Lear, s; Roger Vignoles, pno. Chandos ABR 1009 Tape (c) ABT 1009

-FF 1/2-81 p183 +HFN 8-80 p102
-Gr 8-80 p257 +HFN 5-81 p93 tape

3044 Songs: Bedeckt mich mit Blumen, op. 138, no. 4; Blaue Augen hat das Madchen, op. 138, no. 9; Duette, op. 34 (4); Duette, op. 78 (4); Fruhlingslied, op. 79, no. 19; Das Gluck, op. 79, no. 16; Ich bin dein Baum, op. 101, no. 3; In der Nacht, op. 74, no. 4; Intermezzo, op. 74, no. 2; Landliches Lied, op. 29, no. 1; Liebesgram, op. 74, no. 3; Die Lotosblume, op. 33; Mailied, op. 79, no. 10; Schon ist das Fest des Lenzes, op. 37, no. 7; Die Schwalben, op. 79, no. 21; So wahr die Sonne scheinet, op. 37, no. 12; Sommerruh; Die tausend Grusse, op. 101, no. 7; Zweistimmige Lieder, op. 43 (3). Julia Varady, s; Peter Schreier, t; Dietrich Fischer-Dieskau, bar; Christoph Eschenbach, pno. DG 2531 204

+ARG 6-81 p36 +-MT 12-80 p787
++FF 3/4-81 p194 ++St 1-81 p87
++Gr 8-80 p257 +NYT 9-21-80 pD22
+HFN 8-80 p102 +STL 8-10-80 p30

3045 Songs: Die Blume der Ergebung, op. 83, no. 2; Frauenliebe und Leben, op. 42; Fruhingslust, op. 125, no. 5; Hinaus ins Freie, op. 79, no. 11; Kinderwacht, op. 79, no. 2; Die Letzten Blumen, op. 104, no. 6; Liebeslied, op. 51, no. 5; Lieder der Suleika, op. 25, no. 9; Mond meiner Seele Liebling, op. 104, no. 1; Reich mir die Hand, op. 104, no. 5; Der Sandmann, op. 79, no. 12; Schmetterling, op. 71, no. 2; Singet nicht in Trauertonen, op. 98a, no. 7; Weit weit, op. 25, no. 20. Edith Mathis, s; Christopher Eschenbach, pno. DG 2531 323 Tape (C) 3301 323

++ARG 12-81 p27 +HFN 10-81 p95 tape
+FF 11/12-81 p237 ++SFC 9-13-81 p17
+Gr 8-81 p306 ++SFC 9-27-81 p18
+Gr 11-81 p783 tape ++St 10-81 p134
+HFN 4-81 p87 +STL 9-13-81 p41

3046 Songs (choral): Gedichte, op. 29 (3); Gesange, op. 59 (4); Gesange, op. 141 (4); Lieder, op. 55 (4); Lieder fur drei Frauenstimmen, op. 114 (3); Romanzen, op. 69, 91; Romanzen und Balladen, opp. 145, 146. Stuttgart Chamber Choir; Frieder Bernius. EMI 1C 06530 807, 1C 06545 617 (2)

+-Gr 2-81 p1110

3047 Songs: Lieder und Gesange aus Wilhelm Meister, op. 98a, nos. 1, 3, 5, 7, 9; Requiem, op. 90, no. 7; Stille Tranen, op. 35, no. 10. STRAUSS, R.: Befreit, op. 39, no. 4; Fruhlingsfeier, op. 56, no. 5; Lieder der Ophelia, op. 67; Schlechtes Wetter, op. 69, no. 5; Standchen, op. 17, no. 2. Edda Moser, s. EMI 1C 065 45418

+-FF 1/2-81 p197 +ON 3-7-81 p28

Songs: Auftrage, op. 77, no. 5; Er ist's, op. 79, no. 23; Ersters Grun, op. 34, no. 4; Frage, op. 35, no. 9; Jasminenstrauch, op. 27, no. 4; Kauzlein, op. 79, no. 11; Die Kartenlegerin, op. 21, no. 2; Die letzten Blumen starben; Lorelei, op. 53, no. 2; Marienwurmchen, op. 79, no. 14; Die Meerfee, op. 125, no. 1; Mein schoner Stern, op. 101, no. 4; Der Nussbaum, op. 26, no. 3; Der Sandmann, op. 79, no. 13; Schneeglockchen, op. 79, no. 27; Sehnsucht, op. 51, no. 1; Sehnsucht nach der Waldegegend, op. 25, no. 5; Schmetterling, op. 71, no. 2; Die Sennen, op. 90, no. 4; Waldesgesprach, op. 39, no. 3; Widmung, op. 25, no. 1. See no. 2999

Songs: Der Hidalgo, op. 30, no. 3; Provencalisches Lied. See no. 3547
Songs: Der Konig von Thule, op. 67, no. 1; Im Walde, op. 75, no. 2. See no. 955
Songs: Die beiden Greandiere, op. 49, no. 1. See no. 3639
Songs: Die beiden Granadiere, op. 49, no. 1; Die Feindlichen Bruder, op. 49, no. 2; Belsazar, op. 57; Der Soldat; Die Wandelnde Glocke, op. 79, no. 17. See no. 2079
Songs: Mondnacht, op. 39, no. 5; Nussbaum, op. 25, no. 3. See no. 3988
Songs: Myrthen, op. 25; Der Nussbaum; Lieder und Gesange, op. 77: Auftrage. See no. 3844
Songs: Sangers Trost, op. 127, no. 1. See no. 3967
Songs: The two grenadiers, op. 49, no. 1. See no. 4025
Spanisches Liederslieder, op. 138. See no. 3023
Stucke im Volkston, op. 102. See no. 1544. See no. 3056. See no. 3058
Symphonic etudes, op. 13. See no. 17. See no. 718

3048 Symphonies, nos. 1-4. Overture, scherzo and finale, op. 52, E major. Julius Caesar overture, op. 128. VPO; Georg Solti. Decca D190D3 (3) (From SXL 6486, 6486, 6356)
+Gr 10-81 p563 +-HFN 10-81 p95

3049 Symphonies, nos. 1-4. PO; James Levine. RCA ARL 3-3907 (3) Tape (c) CRK 2-3908
/FF 7/8-81 p166 +HF 12-81 p93 tape
+HF 10-81 p86 +NR 6-81 p2

3050 Symphony, no. 1, op. 38, B major. Symphony, no. 4, op, 120, D minor. BPhO; Rafael Kubelik. Contour CC 7532 Tape (c) CCT 7532
+Gr 8-81 p316

3051 Symphony, no. 1, op. 38, B flat major. Symphony, no. 4, op. 120, D minor. Dresden State Orchestra; Wolfgang Sawallisch. HMV SXLP 30526 Tape (c) RC SXLP 30526 (From SLS 867)
++Gr 8-81 p278 +-HFN 8-81 p91
+Gr 11-81 p783 tape

Symphony, no. 1, op. 38, B flat major. See no. 2237
Symphony, no. 1, op. 38, B flat major: 1st movement. See no. 3998

3052 Symphony, no. 2, op. 61, C major. Bamberg Symphony Orchestra; Dietrich Fischer-Dieskau. Acanta DC 227 049
+-Gr 1-81 p954 +-ST 3-81 p820
-HFN 1-81 p100

3053 Symphony, no. 2, op. 61, C major. Genoveva overture, op. 81. VPO; Zubin Mehta. Decca SXL 6976 Tape (c) KSXC 6976
+-Gr 12-81 p886 +-HFN 12-81 p102

3054 Symphony, no. 3, op. 97, E flat major. VERDI: La forza del destino: Overture. Harvard-Radcliffe Orchestra; James Yannatos. AFKA SK 4638
*FF 3/4-81 p34

3055 Symphony, no. 4, op. 120, D minor.* Manfred overture, op. 115. WEBER: Euryanthe: Overture. BPhO; Wilhelm Furtwangler. DG 2535 805 Tape (c) 3335 805 (*From 16063)
+-FF 5/6-80 p149 +HFN 6-78 p121
+Gr 7-78 p199 +NR 8-80 p6
+HF 2-81 p81 tape +RR 6-78 p60

Symphony, no. 4, op. 120, D minor. See no. 2233. See no. 3006. See no. 3050. See no. 3051. See no. 3684. See no. 3781

Toccata, op. 7, C minor. See no. 627
Trios, piano, nos. 1-3. See no. 3056. See no. 3057
Trio, piano, no. 1, op. 63, D minor. See no. 2245
Variations on A-B-E-G-G, op. 1. See no. 3024. See no. 3025. See no. 3033. See no. 4020
Waldscenen, op. 82. See no. 3033
Waldscenen, op. 82: The prophet bird. See no. 3039
Waldscenen, op. 82: The prophet bird; Abschied. See no. 3032

3056 Works, selections: Adagio and allegro, op. 70, A flat major. Fantasiestucke, op. 73. Fantasiestucke, op. 88. Marchenbilder, op. 113. Marchenerzahlungen, op. 132. Quartet, piano, op. 47, E flat major. Quartets, strings, nos. 1-3. Quintet, piano, op. 44, E flat major. Romances, op. 94 (3). Sonatas, violin and piano, no. 1, op. 105, A minor; no. 2, op. 121, D minor. Stucke in Volkston, op. 102. Trios, piano, nos. 1-3. Jean Jubeau, Daria Hovora, pno; Jean Mouillere, Jean-Pierre Sabouret, vln; Claude Naveau, Gerard Causse, vla; Jean-Marie Gamard, Frederick Lodeon, vlc; Pierre del Vescovo, hn; Pierre Pierot, ob; Walter Boeykines, clt; Via Nova Quartet. Erato STU 71252 (7)
+Gr 11-80 p692 +-HFN 1-81 p100

3057 Works, selections: Allegro and adagio, op. 70, A flat major. Fantasiestucke, op. 88. Romances, op. 94. Sonata, violin and piano, op. posth., A minor. Trios, nos. 1-3. Trio Ravel. Musical Heritage Society MHS 4230/2 (3)
+-FF 1/2-81 p181

3058 Works, selections: Adagio and allegro, op. 70, A flat major. Fantasiestucke, op. 73. Klavierstucke, op. 85: Abendlied (arr. Joachim). Romances, op. 94. Stucke in Volkston, op. 102. Heinz Holliger, ob; Alfred Brendel, pno. Philips 9500 740 Tape (c) 7300 847
+FF 5/6-81 p145 ++NR 6-81 p4
+Gr 3-81 p1212 +St 8-81 p98
++HFN 3-81 p91 +STL 4-12-81 p40
++HFN 4-81 p81 tape

SCHURMANN, Gerard

3059 Studies of Francis Bacon (6). Variants. BBC Symphony Orchestra; Gerard Schurmann. Chandos ABR 1011 Tape (c) ABT 1011
++FF 1/2-81 p185 +HFN 10-80 p122
++Gr 8-80 p229 +MT 11-80 p711
+-HFN 10-80 p117 tape +RR 8-80 p53

Variants. See no. 3059

SCHUTZ, Heinrich

3060 Cantiones sacrae, S 53, 54, 56-60, 73-77. Gachinger Kantorei; Helmuth Rilling. Musical Heritage Society MHS 3954 (From Barenreiter 30 SL 1310)
+FF 1/2-81 p186 +MU 9-79 p16

3061 Cantiones sacre, S 61-66, 68-69, 78-81, 83. Gachinger Kantorei; Helmuth Rilling. Musical Heritage Society MHS 4161
+FF 1/2-81 p186

Danket dem Herren denn er ist freundlich. See no. 3066
Dialogues: Es gingen zweene Menschen hinauf; Weib was weinest du; Ich beschwore euch ihr Tochter zu Jerusalem; Mein Sohn warum hast du uns das getan. See no. 3068
Die Himmel erzahlen. See no. 3619

3062 Historia der Auferstehung Jesu Christi. Kurt Widmer, bar; Musica Polyphonica of Belgium; Louis Devos. Erato STU 71390 (also RCA ZL 30758)
+MUM 9/10-81 p33

3063 Magnificat, S 468. Songs (choral): Aus der Tiefe; Ich hebe meine Augen; Wie lieblich. Westfallen Kantorei Soloists; Wilhelm Ehmann. Musical Heritage Society MHS 4334
+FF 11/12-81 p239 +-MU 11-81 p16

3064 Motets: Ich weiss dass mein Erloser lebt; Selig sind die Toten; So fahr ich hin; Ich bin die Auferstehung und das Leben. VICTORIA: Ascendens Christus, motet. Cambridge University Chamber Choir; Richard Marlow. Cambridge CCRS 1003
+Gr 5-81 p1509

3065 Motets and psalms, SWV Anh 5, 9, 24, 39, 415, 455, 456, 471. Philippe Caillard Instrumental and Vocal Ensemble; Philippe Caillard. Musical Heritage Society MHS 4082 (From Erato STU 70723)
+FF 1/2-81 p186

3066 Musikalische Exequien. Danket dem Herren denn er ist freundlich. Nigel Rogers Vocal Ensemble, Basel Boy Singers; Schola Cantorum Basiliensis Instrumental Ensemble. EMI 1C 065 03828
++Gr 10-81 p596

3067 Musikalische Exequien. Friedemann Jackel, Andreas Gohler, treble; Johannes Oelsner, alto; Peter Schreier, Hans-Joachim Rotzsch, t; Hermann Christian Polster, Siegfried Vogel, bs; Werner Jaroslawski, vla da gamba; Wilhelm Neumann, violone; Hans Otto, org; Dresden Kreuzchor; Rudolf Mauersberger. Philips 9502 025 (From 6580 039)
-ARG 5-81 p27 +-HFN 4-81 p81
+FF 3/4-81 p195 +NR 1-81 p7
+-Gr 7-81 p186

3068 Die sieben Worte Jesu Chrsti am Kreuz. Dialogues: Es gingen zweene Menschen hinauf; Weib was weinest du; Ich beschwore euch ihr Tochter zu Jerusalem; Mein Sohn warum hast du uns das getan. Collegium Sagittarii, London Bach Society Choir, Monteverdi Choir; Paul Steinitz, John Eliot Gardiner. Musicaphon BM 30 SL 1946
+Gr 1-81 p981

3069 Songs (choral): Domini est terra, S 476 (From Psalm 24); Erbarm dich mein, S 447; Heute ist Christus der Herr geboren, S 439; O bone Jesu, S 471; Song of Simeon, S 433; Vater Abraham, S 477. Ars Europea Choeur National; Jacques Grimbert. Harmonia Mundi HMU 958
++FF 1/2-81 p186 +-HFN 9-80 p110
+-HFN 5-76 p109 +RR 3-76 p71

3070 Songs (polychoral sacred works): Es erhub sich ein Streit im Himmel. Psalmen Davids: Herr unser Herrscher; Wie lieblich sind deine Wohnungen; Nicht uns Herr sondern deinem Namen gib Ehre. Symphoniae sacrae III: Komm heiliger Geist Herre Gott; Nun danket alle Gott. Munich Motet Choir; Munich Wind Ensemble; Munich Instrumental Collegium; Christian Kroll, org; Hans Rudolf Zobeley. Musical Heritage Society MHS 4226 (From Christophorus SCGLX 73769)
+ARG 5-81 p27 +FF 1/2-81 p186

Songs (choral): Aus der Tiefe; Ich hebe meine Augen; Wie lieblich. See no. 3063

SCHWANTNER, Joseph
...Amid the mountains rising nowhere. See no. 1233
Elixir. See no. 4068
Sparrows. See no. 4068
SCHWARTZ
Godspell: On the willows; Day by day. See no. 3816
SCHWARTZ, Elliott
3071 Chamber concerto II. Cycles and gongs. Extended clarinet. Souvenir. Leonard Raver, org; Allan Dean, tpt; Jerome Bunke, clt; Elliott Schwartz, pno; Paul Zonn, clt; University of Illinois Contemporary Chamber Ensemble; Edwin London. Orion ORS 80384
+FF 7/8-81 p167 *NR 2-81 p15
Cycles and gongs. See no. 3071
Extended clarinet. See no. 3071
Extended oboe. See no. 1109
Extended piano. See no. 3072
3072 Grand concerto. Extended piano. Mirrors. Prince Albert. Elliott Schwartz, pno. Folkways FSS 33431
*NR 2-81 p14
Mirrors. See no. 3072
Prince Albert. See no. 3072
Souvenir. See no. 3071
SCIORTINO, Patrice
3073 Arc. Ciels pour d'autres hommes. La mecanique sunaturelle. Musique de la Police National; Pierre Bigot. Corelia CC 78020
+FF 11/12-81 p240
Ciels pour d'autres hommes. See no. 3073
La mecanique sunaturelle. See no. 3073
SCOTT
Think on me. See no. 3703
SCOTT, Alicia
Annie Laurie. See no. 4076
SCOTT, Cyril
Water wagtail, op. 71, no. 3. See no. 4055
SCOTTO
Vieni vieni. See no. 4083
SCRIABIN, Alexander
Etude, C sharp minor. See no. 3730
Etude, op. 2, no. 1, C sharp minor. See no. 1295
Etudes, op. 8. See no. 2633
3074 Etude, op. 8, no. 2, F minor. Mazurka, op. 40, no. 2, F major. Preludes, op. 11, nos. 1-2, 13-14. Preludes, op. 22, no. 1, G minor. TCHAIKOVSKY: Souvenir de Florence, op. 70. Genrikh Talalyan, vla; Mstislav Rostropovich, vlc; Alexander Scriabin, pno; Borodin Quartet. Musical Heritage Society MHS 4159
+FF 5/6-81 p164
Etudes, op. 65, nos. 1-3. See no. 1521
Mazurka, op. 40, no. 2, F major. See no. 3074
3075 Poem. Preludes, op. 11, nos. 2-3, 5, 9-12, 15-17, 19, 29; op. 13, nos. 1, 4; op. 37, nos. 1-4; op. 39, nos. 3-4, op. 59 (2); op. 74, nos. 1, 3-4. Sonatas, piano, no. 2, op. 19, G sharp minor; no. 5, op. 53, F sharp major; no. 9, op. 68, F major. Sviatoslav Richter, pno. Rococo 2144
+NR 3-81 p13

Poem, op. 32, no. 1, F sharp minor. See no. 1295
Poeme de l'extase, op. 54. See no. 3076
Preludes, op. 11. See no. 2744
Preludes, op. 11, nos. 1-2, 13-14. See no. 3074
Preludes, op. 11, nos. 2-3, 5, 9-12, 15-17, 19, 29. See no. 3075
Preludes, op. 13, nos. 1, 4. See no. 3075
Preludes, op. 22, no. 1, G minor. See no. 3074
Preludes, op. 37, nos. 1-4. See no. 3075
Preludes, op. 39, nos. 3-4. See no. 3075
Preludes, op. 57. See no. 3698
Preludes, op. 59. See no. 3075
Preludes, op. 74. See no. 2259
Preludes, op. 74, nos. 1, 3-4. See no. 3075
Prometheus, poem of fire, op. 60. See no. 3076
Sonata, piano, no. 2, op. 19, G sharp minor. See no. 3075
Sonata, piano, no. 5, op. 53, F sharp major. See no. 3075
Sonata, piano, no. 9, op. 68, F minor. See no. 1295. See no. 3075
Sonata, piano, no. 10, op. 70, C major. See no. 1521

3076 Symphonies, nos. 1-3. Poeme de l'extase, op. 54. Prometheus, poem of fire, op. 60. Frankfurt Radio Orchestra; Eliahu Inbal. Philips 6769 041 (4)
+FF 9/10-81 p170 +-HFN 9-80 p111
+Gr 9-80 p349 +-MT 10-81 p678

Waltz, op. 38. See no. 3920

SCRONX, Gherardus (Gerard)
Echo, F major, C major. See no. 92
Echo fantasia. See no. 3950

SEAVER
Just for today. See no. 3967

SEIBER, Matyas
Permutazioni a cinque. See no. 1531

SEIFEN, Wolfgang
3077 Symphonie in 4 Satzen. Maria zu lieben. Gegrusset seist du Konigin. Maria Maienkonigin. Wolfgang Seifen, org. Motette M 1022
+/FF 9/10-81 p173

SEIXAS, Jose
Toccata, C minor. See no. 4115

SELMA Y SALAVERDE, Bartolome de
Canzona a due II. See no. 1103
Festiva i colli passaggiato a 2. See no. 1103
Susanne un jour. See no. 3835

SEMEGEN, Daria
Spectra. See no. 1637

SENFL, Ludwig
Das D'laut zu Speyer. See no. 3675
Es taget vor dem Walde. See no. 3675
Es wollt' ein Frau zum Weine gehn. See no. 3675
Ich armes Kauzlein Klein. See no. 3675
Patiencia muss ich han. See no. 3675
Songs: Carmen in la; Carmen in re; Nasci pati mori. See no. 3777
Songs: Chiara luce; Ich steund an einem Morgen; Nun gruss dich Gott. See no. 3896

SERMISY, Claude de
A douce amour. See no. 3766
La je m'y plains. See no. 3945
Languir me fais. See no. 3677
Songs: Candidiores Nazarei. See no. 3909
Tant que vivray. See no. 3862
3078 Tota pulchra es mass. TALLIS: Mass, 4 voices. Harvard Glee Club; F. John Adams. Musical Heritage Society MHS 4261
+ARG 9-81 p34 +-FF 9/10-81 p226
SEROV, Alexander
The power of evil: Yeromka's song. See no. 3854
SERRANO, Jose
La dolorosa: La roca fria del Calvario. See no. 3836
Los de Aragon: Cuantas veces solo. See no. 3888
El trust de los tenorios: Jota. See no. 3888
El trust de los tenorios: Te quiero. See no. 3836. See no. 3838
SESSIONS, Roger
Black maskers suite: Finale. See no. 3817
Sonata, piano, no. 3. See no. 91
3079 Symphony, no. 3. LEES: Concerto, string quartet. RPO; Igor Buketoff. CRI SD 451
+FF 11/12-81 p241 +-NR 9-81 p2
Waltz. See no. 3942
SEVERAC, Deodat Joseph de
Chanson melancolique. See no. 3901
SHAN TE-TING
Childrens suite. See no. 3860
Dance Sinkiang, no. 1. See no. 3860
Sinkiang dance, no. 2. See no. 1887
Toccata. See no. 3860
SHAPEY, Ralph
3080 Fromm variations. Robert Black, pno. CRI SD 428
+FF 7/8-81 p168 +NYT 6-7-81 pD23
+NR 6-81 p14
SHARP
The wayside cross (arr.). See no. 4077
SHAW, Woody
Epilogue. See no. 378
Katrina ballerina. See no. 378
Specs. See no. 378
SHCHEDRIN, Rodion
3081 Carmen ballet (after Bizet). Bolshoi Theatre Orchestra; Gennady Rozhdestvensky. Musical Heritage Society MHD 4319 (also Odyssey/Melodiya Y 34613)
+FF 7/8-81 p76
SHEN CHUAN SHIN
Yunnan suite. See no. 3861
SHEPHERD, Richard
And when the builders. See no. 3895
SHEPPERD, John
3082 Cantate mass. Respond Spiritus sanctus. Clerkes of Oxenford; David Wulstan. Calliope CAL 1621 (also Nonesuch H 71396)
++Gr 2-79 p1454 ++St 12-81 p127
+Gr 1-81 p982
Jesu salvator saeculi verbum. See no. 3637

Respond, Spiritus sanctus. See no. 3082
Verbum caro factum est. See no. 3083
3083 The western wind mass. Verbum caro factum est. TALLIS: Salve intemerata Virgo, mass. Antiphons: Clarifica me pater i, ii and iii. St. John's College Choir; Ian Shaw, org; George Guest.
+-Gr 12-81 p924 +STL 11-8-81 p40
+-HFN 12-81 p103

SHOSTAKOVICH, Dmitri
The age of gold, op. 22. See no. 1601. See no. 3099. See no. 3100
Concerto, piano, no. 2, op. 101, F major. See no. 401
3084 Concerto, violin, no. 1, op. 99, A minor. Concerto, violoncello, no. 1, op. 107, E flat major. David Oistrakh, vln; Paul Tortelier, vlc; NPhO, Bournemouth Symphony Orchestra; Maxim Shostakovich, Paavo Berglund. HMV ASD 4046 Tape (c) TC ASD 4046 (From ASD 2924, 2936)
++Gr 6-81 p44 +HFN 9-81 p93 tape
+HFN 7-81 p79 ++ST 10-81 p431
Concerto, violoncello, no. 1, op. 107, E flat major. See no. 1873. See no. 3084
Duets, violin (3). See no. 2287
Festive overture, op. 96. See no. 3101. See no. 3098
The gadfly, op. 97: Folk festival. See no. 3891
The gadfly, op. 97: Romance. See no. 3101
3085 The gamblers. Boris Tarknov, Nikolai Kurpe, t; Yaroslav Radivonik, bar; Vladimir Ribassenko, Valerii Byelikh, Ashot Sarkissov, bs; Leningrad Philharmonic Orchestra; Gennady Rozhdestvensky. Melodiya/Eurodisc 200 370405 (also HMV ASD 3880)
+FF 9/10-80 p204 +MT 8-81 p540
++Gr 9-80 p399 ++Op 4-81 p384
The golden gate: Polka. See no. 3678
Overture, op. 23. See no. 3801
Prelude, op. 34, no. 17, A flat major. See no. 3693
3086 Quartets, strings, nos. 1-15. Fitzwilliam Quartet. Decca D188D7 (7)
++Gr 2-81 p1099 ++STL 2-8-81 p40
3087 Quartet, strings, no. 1, op. 49, C major. Quintet, piano, op. 57, G minor. Miroslav Langer, pno; Talich Quartet. Supraphon 111 2484
+-ARG 7/8-81 p33 -HFN 1-81 p101
+-FF 9/10-81 p173 -NR 4-81 07
+Gr 1-81 p962 ++SFC 2-1-81 p18
3088 Quartet, strings, no. 8, op. 110, C minor. Quartet, strings, no. 15, op. 144, E flat minor. Fitzwilliam Quartet. L'Oiseau-Lyre DSLO 11 Tape (r) DLE 11
++ARG 12-76 p40 +NYT 2-15-81 pD21 tape
++Gr 4-76 p1624 ++RR 4-76 p61
++HF 2-77 p102 +SR 11-13-76 p52
++HFN 4-76 p113 +St 5-77 p117
+MJ 7-77 p70 +STL 4-11-76 p36
++MT 9-76 p748 +Te 9-76 p26
+NYT 8-7-77 pD13
Quartet, strings, no. 15, op. 144, E flat minor. See no. 3088
3089 Quintet, piano, op. 57, G minor. STRAVINSKY: Pieces, string quartet (3). Borodin Quartet; Lyubov Yedlina, pno. Musical Heri-

tage Society MHS 4321
-FF 7/8-81 p169
Quintet, piano, op. 57, G minor. See no. 1025. See no. 3087
Sonata, violin and piano, op. 134. See no. 2629
Sonata, violoncello and piano, op. 40, D minor. See no. 2632
3090 Symphony, no. 1, op. 10, F minor. Symphony, no. 9, op. 70, E flat major. LPO; Bernard Haitink. Decca SXDL 7515 Tape (c) KSXDC 7515 (also London LDR 71017)
+-FF 11/12-81 p242
+Gr 5-81 p1479
+Gr 6-81 p93
+-HFN 5-81 p84
+NYT 9-20-81 pD29
++ST 10-81 p429
3091 Symphony, no. 1, op. 10, F major. Symphony, no. 9, op. 70, E flat major. Cincinnati Symphony Orchestra; Walter Susskind. Vox VCL 9003
++SFC 10-18-81 p18
3092 Symphony, no. 4, op. 43, C minor. LPO; Bernard Haitink. Decca SXL 6927 Tape (c) KSXC 6927 (also London CS 7160)
+FF 9/10-80 p204
+-Gr 11-79 p840
+HF 11-80 p79
+-HFN 12-79 p170
+MT 2-81 p113
+NYT 9-20-81 pD29
++RR 12-79 p75
+STL 12-2-79 p37
3093 Symphony, no. 5, op. 47, D minor. NYP; Leonard Bernstein. CBS MY 37218 (From MS 6115)
+FF 11/12-81 p242
3094 Symphony, no. 5, op. 47, D minor. NYP; Leonard Bernstein. CBS IM 35854, DGTM 6000 Tape (c) HMT 35854, 40-35854
+-ARG 3-81 p51
++FF 11/12-80 p173
+Gr 12-80 p836
+Gr 1-81 p1001 tape
+-HF 9-80 p78
+HFN 12-80 p145
+HFN 4-81 p81 tape
+MUM 1/2-81 p35
++MUM 9/10-81 p37 tape
++SFC 10-26-80 p20
+ST 6-81 p121
3095 Symphony, no. 5, op. 47, D minor. MPO; Kiril Kondrashin. Quintessence PMC 7156 (also Melodiya/Angel 4004)
+-ARG 2-81 p29
+-FF 11/12-80 p174
3096 Symphony, no. 5, op. 47, D minor. PO; Eugene Ormandy. RCA AGL 1-3886 Tape (c) AGK 1-3886
+FF 7/8-81 p172
Symphony, no. 5, op. 47, D minor. See no. 3855
3097 Symphony, no. 6, op. 54, B minor. Symphony, no. 11, op. 103, G minor. Bournemouth Symphony Orchestra; Paavo Berglund. HMV SLS 5177 (2)
+FF 1/2-81 p188
++Gr 2-80 p1270
+HFN 3-80 p99
++MT 10-80 p635
+RR 4-80 p79
++STL 2-10-80 p40
3098 Symphony, no. 6, op. 54, B minor. Festive overture, op. 96. Plovdiv Bulgarian Philharmonic Orchestra; Dobrin Petrov. Monitor MCS 2163
-FF 9/10-81 p174
+NR 8-81 p4
3099 Symphony, no. 6, op. 54, B minor. The age of gold, op. 22. CSO; Leopold Stokowski. RCA GL 4-2916 Tape (c) GK 4-2916 (From SB 6839)
++Gr 10-81 p563
3100 Symphony, no. 7, op. 60. The age of gold, op. 22. LPO; Bernard Haitink. Decca D213D2 (2) (also London LDR 10015 Tape (c) LDR

5-10015)
+FF 5/6-81 p146
+Gr 11-80 p678
++HF 9-81 p73
+HF 7-81 p71 tape
++HFN 2-81 p93
+NYT 9-20-81 pD29
++SFC 2-8-81 p21
+St 6-81 p125
+ST 7-81 p207

3101 Symphony, no. 9, op. 70, E flat major. Festive overture, op. 96. The gadfly, op. 97: Romance. Tahiti trot, op. 16. USSR Symphony Orchestra; Yevgeny Svetlanov. Chant du Monde LDX 78687
+-HFN 6-81 p77

Symphony, no. 9, op. 70, E flat major. See no. 3090. See no. 3091

3102 Symphony, no. 10, op. 93, E minor. NYP; Dmitri Mitropoulos. CBS 61457 (From ABL 3052)
+-Gr 2-81 p1092
+-HFN 3-81 p95

Symphony, no. 11, op. 103, G minor. See no. 3097

3103 Symphony, no. 13, op. 113. Dimiter Petkov, bs; LSO and Chorus; Andre Previn. Angel SZ 37661 (also HMV ASD 3911 Tape (c) TC ASD 3911)
+-ARG 7/8-81 p33
++FF 1/2-81 p188
++Gr 4-81 p1324
+HF 2-81 p71
+HFN 4-81 p76
++MUM 3/4-81 p34
+NR 2-81 p3
++NYT 9-20-81 pD29
++St 3-81 p79
+STL 4-12-81 p40

Tahiti trot, op. 16. See no. 3101

The tale of the priest and his servant Baldaj: Suite, op. 36. See no. 3801

Trio, piano, op. 67, E minor. See no. 2172

Two fables of Krilov, op. 4: The dragonfly and the ant; The ass and the nightingale. See no. 3801

SIBELIUS, Jean

3104 Bagatelles, op. 34 (10). Pieces, piano, op. 24 (10). Erik Tawastjerna, pno. BIS LP 169
+Gr 9-81 p417
+-HFN 9-81 p85

Bagatelles, op. 34: The harp player. See no. 3678

The bard, op. 64. See no. 3115. See no. 3133

3105 Concerto, violin, op. 47, D minor. SINDING: Suite, op. 10, A minor. Itzhak Perlman, vln; Pittsburgh Symphony Orchestra; Andre Previn. Angel SZ 37663 (also HMV ASD 3933 Tape (c) TC ASD 3933)
+-ARG 7/8-81 p34
+FF 1/2-81 p189
+Gr 10-80 p502
+Gr 4-81 p1376 tape
+HF 7-81 p68
+HFN 12-80 p146
+HFN 12-80 p159 tape
+NR 1-81 p3
+NYT 11-30-80 p35B
++SFC 1-4-81 p18
+ST 5-81 p46

3106 Concerto, violin, op. 47, D minor. Finlandia, op. 26. Karelia suite, op. 11. Eugene Sarbu, vln; Halle Orchestra; Ole Schmidt. Classics for Pleasure CFP 40360 Tape (c) TC CFP 40360
+-Gr 9-81 p388
+-HFN 9-81 p85

3107 Concerto, violin, op. 47, D minor. Melodies, op. 77 (2). Serenades, op. 69 (2). Boris Belkin, vln; PhO; Vladimir Ashkenazy. Decca SXL 6953 Tape (c) KSXC 6953 (also London CS 7181)
+-ARG 3-81 p52
+FF 1/2-81 p189
++HFN 6-80 p112
+NYT 11-30-80 p35B

+Gr 6-80 p43 +RR 8-80 p65
+-HF 10-80 p86

3108 Concerto, violin, op. 47, D minor. Humoresques (6). Salvatore Accardo, vln; LSO; Colin Davis. Philips 9500 675 Tape (c) 7300 770
++FF 9/10-80 p206 +NR 9-80 p5
++FF 11/12-80 p174 tape +NYT 7-6-80 pD15
+Gr 10-80 p502 +-NYT 11-30-80 p35B
+HF 10-80 p86 +SFC 7-27-80 p34
+-HFN 11-80 p123 +St 11-80 p100
+-HFN 12-80 p157 tape +-ST 5-81 p45
++MUM 10-80 p132

3109 Concerto, violin, op. 47, D minor. SAINT-SAENS: Introduction and rondo capriccioso, op. 28. Dylana Jenson, vln; PO; Eugene Ormandy. RCA ATC 1-3972 Tape (c) TK 1-3972
+-FF 7/8-81 p170 +NR 5-81 p7
+HF 7-81 p68 +St 7-81 p85
++HF 10-81 p91 tape

Concerto, violin, op. 47, D minor. See no. 1041. See no. 2617. See no. 3132. See no. 3841

The Dryad, op. 45, no. 1. See no. 3133

3110 Finlandia, op. 26. Karelia suite, op. 11. En saga, op. 9. Legends, op. 22: Swan of Tuonela. VPO; Malcolm Sargent. Arabesque 8010 Tape (c) 9010
+ARG 6-81 p39 +NR 2-81 p4
+FF 3/4-81 p195

3111 Finlandia, op. 26. The tempest: Prelude. Tapiola, op. 112. LSO; Adrian Boult. Everest 3472
-ARG 6-81 p40 -NR 1-81 p3
/-FF 3/4-81 p196

Finlandia, op. 26. See no. 741. See no. 1652. See no. 1656. See no. 3106. See no. 3121. See no. 3128. See no. 3132. See no. 3133

3112 Finnish folk songs (6). Impromptus, op. 5 (6). Kalevala, op. 41: Kyllikki. Sonata, piano, op. 12, F major. Erik Tawaststjerna, pno. BIS LP 153
+ARG 5-81 p28 +-Gr 4-81 p1341
+FF 1/2-81 p190 +HFN 12-80 p146
+FF 11/12-81 p244 +St 5-81 p78

Humoresques. See no. 3108

Impromptus, op. 5. See no. 3112

Impromptu, op. 5, no. 1. See no. 1966

Kalevala, op. 41: Kyllikki. See no. 3112

Karelia suite, op. 11. See no. 3106. See no. 3110

Kuolema, op. 44: Valse triste. See no. 1646. See no. 1652. See no. 1656. See no. 3126. See no. 3132

3113 Legends, op. 22. OSR; Horst Stein. Decca SXL 6973
+-Gr 1-81 p953 +-ST 6-81 p123
+HFN 1-81 p101

Legends, op. 22: Lemminkainen and the maidens of Saari. See no. 741

Legends, op. 22: Swan of Tuonela. See no. 1652. See no. 1656. See no. 3110. See no. 3117. See no. 3132

Luonnotar, op. 70. See no. 3128. See no. 3133

Masonic ritual music, op. 113: Hymn; Marche funebre. See no. 1966

Melodies, op. 77. See no. 3107
Night ride and sunrise, op. 55. See no. 3133
The oceanides, op. 73. See no. 3133
Pelleas and Melisande, op. 46. See no. 1500
Pieces, organ, op. 111: Funeral; Intrada. See no. 1966
Pieces, piano, op. 24. See no. 3104
Pohjola's daughter, op. 49. See no. 3133
Quartet, strings, op. 56, D minor. See no. 1333
Rakastava, op. 14. See no. 1646
Romance, op. 24, no. 9, D flat major. See no. 3764
En saga, op. 9. See no. 3110. See no. 3115. See no. 3133
Serenades, op. 69. See no. 3107
Sonata, piano, op. 12, F major. See no. 3112

3114 Songs: Flickan kom ifran sin alsklings mote, op. 38, no. 5; Illalle, op. 17; Kaiutar, op. 72, no. 4; Norden, op. 90; Sav sav susa, op. 36, no. 4; Svarta rosor, op. 36, no. 1; Var det en drom, op. 37, no. 4; Songs, op. 13 (7); op. 50 (6); op. 57 (8); Two songs from Shakespeare's "Twelfth Night', op. 60; Vilse, op. 17, no. 4. Jorma Hynninen, bar; Ralf Gothoni, pno. Finlandia FA 202 (2)
+FF 9/10-81 p175 +NR 7-81 p12

Spring song, op. 16. See no. 3133

3115 Symphonies, nos. 1-3. The bard, op. 64. En saga, op. 9. Helsinki Radio Orchestra, BPhO; Okko Kamu. DG 2535 457/9 (3) Tape (c) 3335 457/9 (From 2530 455, 2530 021)
+Gr 7-81 p162 +-HFN 8-81 p91
+Gr 11-81 p783 tape +-HFN 9-81 p95 tape

3116 Symphony, no. 1, op. 39, E minor. Symphony, no. 7, op. 105, C major. Bournemouth Symphony Orchestra; Paavo Berglund. HMV ESD 7095 Tape (c) TC ESD 7095 (From ASD 3216, 2874)
+Gr 7-81 p162 +HFN 7-81 p79
+Gr 11-81 p783 tape

3117 Symphony, no. 1, op. 39, E minor. Legends, op. 22: The swan of Tuonela. LPO; Loris Tjeknavorian. RCA RL 2-5316
+HFN 9-81 p85

3118 Symphony, no. 2, op. 43, D major. BPhO; Herbert von Karajan. Angel DS 37816 (also HMV ASD 4060 Tape (c) TCC ASD 4060)
+Gr 10-81 p564 +-NYT 10-18-81 pD21
+HFN 10-81 p91 +SFC 10-18-81 p18
+NR 12-81 p5

3119 Symphony, no. 2, op. 43, D major. Tokyo Metropolitan Symphony Orchestra; Moshe Atzmon. Denon OX 7190
+-FF 5/6-81 p148 +HF 9-81 p76

3120 Symphony, no. 2, op. 43, D major. PhO; Vladimir Ashkenazy. London LDR 10014 (also Decca SXDL 7513 Tape (c) KSXDC 7513)
+-ARG 7/8-81 p37 +HFN 11-80 p123
-FF 3/4-81 p196 +NR 2-81 p4
++Gr 11-80 p678 +NYT 11-30-80 p35B
+-Gr 12-80 p889 tape +SR 1-81 p92
++HF 9-81 p76 +-ST 2-81 p734

3121 Symphony, no. 2, op. 43, D major. Finlandia, op. 26. COA; Georg Szell, Eduard van Beinum. Philips 6527 111 Tape (c) 7311 111 (From SAL 3515, SABE 2002)
+Gr 11-81 p694 +-HFN 11-81 p103

3122 Symphony, no. 2, op. 43, D major. BSO; Colin Davis. Philips 9500

141 Tape (c) 7300 518 (r) 9500 141
++ARG 10-77 p41
+Gr 4-77 p1556
+Gr 8-77 p349 tape
+HF 9-77 p119 tape
++HF 12-77 p98
+HF 8-81 p69 tape
++HFN 4-77 p145
+HFN 8-77 p99 tape
+MJ 9-77 p35
++NR 7-77 p2
+RR 4-77 p59
++RR 9-77 p99
+St 11-77 p156

3123 Symphony, no. 2, op. 43, D major. PO; Eugene Ormandy. RCA GL 4-2868 Tape (c) GK 4-2868 (From ARD 1-0018) (also AGL 1-3785)
+-FF 7/8-81 p172
+Gr 4-80 p1558
-HFN 4-80 p119
-HFN 8-80 p109 tape
+-RR 4-80 p80

Symphony, no. 4, op. 43, D major. See no. 4122

3124 Symphony, no. 3, op. 52, C major. Symphony, no. 5, op. 82, E flat major. Bournemouth Symphony Orchestra; Paavo Berglund. HMV ESD 7094 Tape (c) TC ESD 7094 (From SLS 5129, ASD 3038)
-FF 11/12-81 p245
+Gr 2-81 p1092
+HFN 3-81 p95

3125 Symphony, no. 3, op. 52, C major. Symphony, no. 5, op. 82, B flat major. MRSO; Gennady Rozhdestvensky. Quintessence PMC 7188
-FF 7/8-81 p172
-NR 8-81 p4

Symphonies, nos. 4-7. See no. 3132

3126 Symphony, no. 4, op. 63, A minor. Kuolema, op. 44: Valse triste. BPhO; Herbert von Karajan. DG 2535 359 Tape (c) 3335 359
+FF 9/10-81 p178

3127 Symphony, no. 4, op. 63, A minor. SALLINEN: Mauermusik. Finnish Radio Orchestra; Paavo Berglund. Finlandia FA 312 (From Decca SXL 6431)
*FF 5/6-81 p149
+Gr 1-81 p953
+HFN 1-81 p101
+NR 3-81 p2

3128 Symphony, no. 4, op. 63, A minor. Finlandia, op. 26. Luonnotar, op. 70. Elisabeth Soderstrom, s; PhO; Vladimir Ashkenazy. London LDR 71019 (also Decca SXDL 7517 Tape (c) KSDC 7517)
+-FF 9/10-81 p176
+Gr 5-81 p1480
+HF 9-81 p76
+-HFN 5-81 p84
+-MT 11-81 p755
+NR 8-81 p4
+NYT 9-20-81 pD29
++St 10-81 p72
++STL 5-10-81 p41

3129 Symphony, no. 5, op. 82, E flat major. RAUTAVAARA: A requiem for our time. Helsinki Philharmonic Orchestra; Jorma Panula. Finlandia FA 313
+FF 5/6-81 p149
-FF 11/12-80 p175
+-Gr 1-81 p953
+-HFN 1-81 p101
+NR 3-81 p2

3130 Symphony, no. 5, op. 82, E flat major. Symphony, no. 7, op. 105, C major. PhO; Herbert von Karajan. HMV SXLP 30430 Tape (c) TC SXLP 30430 (From Columbia SAX 2392, 33CX 1341)
+-FF 1/2-81 p191
+Gr 7-80 p147
+-HFN 7-80 p115
+HFN 10-80 p117 tape
+-RR 7-80 p65

Symphony, no. 5, op. 82, E flat major. See no. 3124. See no. 3125

3131 Symphony, no. 6, op. 104, D minor. Symphony, no. 7, op. 105, C major. BPhO; Herbert von Karajan. DG 2542 137 Tape (c) 3342

137 (From 139032)
+Gr 4-81 p1324 ++HFN 3-81 p95
+HFN 12-80 p159 tape

Symphony, no. 7, op. 105, C major. See no. 3116. See no. 3130. See no. 3131

Tapiola, op. 112. See no. 1963. See no. 3111. See no. 3132. See no. 3133

The tempest: Prelude. See no. 3111

3132 Works, selections: Concerto, violin, op. 47, D minor. Finlandia, op. 26. Symphonies, nos. 4-7. Legends, op. 22: The swan of Tuonela. Tapiola, op. 112. Kuolema, op. 44: Valse triste. Christian Ferras, vln; BPhO; Herbert von Karajan. DG 2740 255 (4) (From SLPM 138974, 138973, 139032, 138961, 139016)
+Gr 9-81 p388 +HFN 10-81 p95

3133 Works, selections: The bard, op. 64. The Dryad, op. 45, no. 1. Finlandia, op. 26. Luonnotar, op. 70. Night ride and sunrise, op. 55. The oceanides, op. 73. Pohjola's daughter, op. 49. En saga, op. 9. Spring song, op. 16. Tapiola, op. 112. Phyllis Bryn-Julson, s; Scottish National Orchestra; Alexander Gibson. RCA RL 2-5136 (2)
+Audio 9-78 p111 +-HFN 6-78 p129
+-FF 9/10-81 p174 +RR 7-78 p62
+-Gr 6-78 p62

SILVERS/DESYLVA/ENGELMAN

April showers. See no. 3931

SIMONDS

Prelude on "Iam sol". See no. 3806

SIMPSON

Allemande. See no. 3762

I sent my love two roses. See no. 4046

SIMPSON, Christopher

Divisions on a ground, G major, F major, E minor. See no. 1526

SIMPSON, Robert

Canzona for brass. See no. 4006

Volcano. See no. 3716

SINDING, Christian

3134 Quintet, piano, op. 5. Eva Knardahl, pno; Arne Monn-Iversen Quartet. NKF 30033
+FF 5/6-81 p150 +HFN 8-81 p87
+Gr 8-81 p317

Suite, op. 10, A minor. See no. 3105

SINIGAGLIA

Song and humoreske, op. 28. See no. 3736

SKALKOTTAS, Nikolaos

Bolero, op. 63. See no. 3135

Duo, violin and viola, op. 44. See no. 3135

Greek dances, op. 11. See no. 3135

Largo, op. 66. See no. 3135

Little serenade, op. 64. See no. 3135

Pieces, piano, no. 20: Berceuse. See no. 3135

Quartet, strings, no. 3, op. 34. See no. 3135

Sketches, op. 8. See no. 3135

Sonatina, op. 62. See no. 3135

Sonatina, no. 3, op. 48. See no. 3135

Sonatina, no. 4, op. 49. See no. 3135

Suite, piano, no. 3: 2nd and 3rd movements. See no. 3135
Tender melody, op. 65. See no. 3135
Variations on a Greek folk tune, op. 43. See no. 3135
3135 Works, selections: Bolero, op. 63. Duo violin and viola, op. 44. Greek dances, op. 11 (5). Largo, op. 66. Little serenade, op. 64. Pieces, piano, op. 20: Berceuse. Quartet, strings, no. 3, op. 34. Sketches, op. 8 (10). Sonatina, op. 62. Sonatinas, no. 3, op. 48; no. 4, op. 49. Suite, no. 3: 2nd and 3rd movements. Tender melody, op. 65. Variations on a Greek folk tune, op. 43 (8). Little String Orchestra, Greek Quartet; Nina Patrikidou, vln; Diana Vranoussi, Nelly Semitecolo, pno; Dimitris Vraskos, vln; Christos Sfetsas, vlc; Tatsis Apostolidis, vln; Yannis Vatikiotis, vla; Sotiris Tachiatis, vlc; John Papaioannou, pno; Tatsis Apostolidis. EMI 14C 163 70981/4 (4)
+-Gr 9-81 p406

SKOLD, Sven
Sommar. See no. 48

SLATER
From Oberon in fairyland. See no. 4074

SLOGEDAL
Cantate domino. See no. 3991

SLONIMSKY, Nicolas
My toy balloon. See no. 3880

SMETANA, Bedrich
3136 The bartered bride (in German). Teresa Stratas, Janet Perry, Margarethe Bence, s; Gudrun Wewezow, ms; Rene Kollo, Heinz Zednik, t; Jorn Wilsing, Walter Berry, Karl Donch, bar; Alexander Malta, Theodor Nicolai, bs; Bavarian Radio Orchestra and Chorus; Jaroslav Krombholc. Eurodisc 89036 XGF (3) Tape (c) 57640
+FF 11/12-81 p245 +NYT 7-26-81 pD23
+-HF 3-76 p94 +-ON 3-20-76 p56
+HF 11-81 p103 tape +St 11-81 p90
The bartered bride: Marie's aria, Act 3. See no. 3748
The bartered bride: Nun in Lust und Leide; Armer Narr...Es muss gelingen. See no. 3966
The bartered bride: Overture. See no. 1484. See no. 3656
Brandenburgers in Bohemia: Tvuj obraz divko. See no. 4079
3137 Dreams, excerpts. Sketches, opp. 4 and 5 (8). Frantisek Rauch, pno. Supraphon 111 2587
++ARG 2-81 p50 +NR 8-80 p13
+-FF 9/10-80 p208 ++SFC 7-20-80 p34
Esquisses. See no. 1162
3138 Ma Vlast. CPhO; Vaclav Talich. Quintessence PMC 7168
+FF 3/4-81 p196
Ma Vlast: Vltava. See no. 1264. See no. 1484. See no. 3792
3139 Polkas (16). Radoslav Kvapil, pno. Da Camera SM 93117
++NR 11-81 p13
3140 Quartet, strings, no. 1, E minor. SUK: Quartet, strings, no. 1, op. 11, B flat major. Bohemian String Quartet. Parnassus 1001
+FF 11/12-81 p247
Quartet, strings, no. 1, E minor. See no. 1918
Reves. See no. 1162
Revolutionary marches. See no. 3817
The secret: Jsem zebrak. See no. 4079

Sketches, opp. 4 and 5. See no. 3137

SMITH, Glenn

Mood music 2. See no. 1268

SMITH, Michael

3141 The inferno, excerpts. Michael Smith, pno. Golden Crest CRDG 4197

+-ARG 5-81 p29 +NR 5-81 p13

SMITH, Peter

Etude, no. 1. See no. 3728

SMITH, William

Tribute to the bassoon. See no. 3739

SNOW, David

3142 The passion and transfiguration of the postapolcalyptic eunuch. Mark Campellone, voice, guitars, bass, piano, percussion and violin; David Snow, voice, pno; Synthesizer, tpt; perc; Electronic effects; Rachel Back, voice. Opus One 55

+-HF 11-81 p94

SOJO, Vicente

Aguinaldo. See no. 3929

Mi Teresa, estrella del mar, mi Teresa. See no. 3929

SOLA, Andres de

Tiento de primer tono, no. 2. See no. 4098

SOLAGE (14th century France)

Femeux fume. See no. 3853

SOLER, Antonio

3143 Fandango. Sonatas, harpsichord, D major, B minor, E minor, A minor, C minor, C major. Igor Kipnis, hpd. Nonesuch D 79010 Tape (c) D 1-79010

+FF 7/8-81 p173 +HF 7-81 p71 tape
+-Gr 8-81 p299 ++St 5-81 p82

Quintet, strings, no. 1, C major. See no. 3978

Rondo, F major. See no. 4098

Sonata, clarino, C major. See no. 4098. See no. 4115

3144 Sonatas, harpsichord, C major (2), A minor, D major (2), C minor, D flat major, G minor, B flat major. Gilbert Rowland, hpd. Nimbus 2128

+-Gr 1-81 p970 ++RR 8-80 p75
+HFN 9-80 p111 +-STL 8-10-80 p30

Sonatas, harpsichord, D major, C sharp minor, D minor, G minor, F sharp minor, F major. See no. 2900

Sonatas, harpsichord, D major, B minor, E minor, A minor, C minor, C major. See no. 3143

Sonata, harpsichord, D major. See no. 4018

SOMERVELL, Arthur

Jesus the very thought of thee. See no. 3636

Quintet, clarinet. See no. 1904

A Shropshire lad: Loveliest of trees; When I was one and twenty; There pass the careless people; In summertime on Bredon; The street sounds to the soldiers tread; On the idle hill of summer; White in the moon the long road lies; Think no more lad laugh be jolly; Into my heart an air that kills; The lads in their hundreds. See no. 3893

Songs: Orpheus with his lute. See no. 3787

SOMMERFELDT, Oisten

Divertimento, op. 9. See no. 3679

Sonatina, no, 3, op. 14. See no. 1981

SOR, Fernando

Etude, no. 17. See no. 3701

Etude, op. 6, no. 11, E minor. See no. 1590

Etudes, op. 29, nos. 12, 23. See no. 1590

Fantasias, op. 7; op. 30. See no. 10

Fantasia, op. 7, C minor. See no. 1590

Fantasia and minuet. See no. 4015

Fantasia elegiaca, op. 59. See no. 3795

Introduction and variations on a theme by Mozart, op. 9. See no. 3701

Minuet, op. 11, no. 6. See no. 3701

Minuet, op. 22. See no. 3701

3145 Sonata, guitar, op. 22, C major. Sonata, guitar, op. 25, C major. Pepe Romero, gtr. Philips 9500 586 Tape (c) 7300 709

+FF 5/6-80 p139 +NR 7-80 p14
+-Gr 8-81 p299 +NYT 6-1-80 pD19
+HFN 6-81 p78 ++St 8-80 p101

Sonata, guitar, op. 25, C major. See no. 3145

Variations on a theme by Mozart, op. 9. See no. 10. See no. 3765

SORABJI, Kaikhosru

Fantaisie espagnole. See no. 3146

Fragment. See no. 3146

In the hothouse. See no. 3146

Opus Clavicembalisticum: Introito and Preludio corale. See no. 3146

Pastiche: "Habanera" from Bizet's Carmen. See no. 3146

Toccata. See no. 3146

3146 Works, selections: Fantaisie espagnole. Fragment. In the hothouse. Opus Clavicembalisticum: Introito and Preludio corale. Pastiche on "Habanera" from Bizet's Carmen. Toccata. Michael Habermann, pno. Musical Heritage Society MHS 4271 (also Musicmasters MM 20015)

++FF 5/6-81 p151 +Te 6-81 p51
++St 12-81 p128

SORIANO, Perez

El guitarrico: Serenata. See no. 3888. See no. 3983

SOUSA, John Philip

The free lance. See no. 3817

The gallant Seventh. See no. 3891

George Washington bicentennial march. See no. 3817

Hands across the sea. See no. 3699

Semper fidelis. See no. 3699

A Sousa collection. See no. 4000

Stars and stripes forever. See no. 2622. See no. 3626. See no. 3699. See no. 3817

The thunderer. See no. 3699

Under the double eagle. See no. 3699

Washington post. See no. 778. See no. 3699

SOUTULLO Y VERT, Reveriano

La leyenda del beso: Hecho di un rayo de luna. See no. 3888

Puenteareas. See no. 3981

El ultimo romantico: Bella enamorada. See no. 3836. See no. 3888

SOWERBY, Leo

Songs: I was glad when they said unto me. See no. 3810

SPADI, Giovanni
Anchor che col partire. See no. 4010
SPEARS, Jared
3147 Alleluias. Divertimento. Symphony, band, no. 1. Woven tales. Tennessee Tech Symphonic Band, Tennessee Tech Percussion Ensemble, Tennessee Tech Tuba Ensemble; Wayne Pegram, Jared Spears, Joseph Rasmussen, R. Winston Morris. USC Sound Enterprises unnumbered
+FF 11/12-81 p249
Divertimento. See no. 3147
Symphony, band, no. 1. See no. 3147
Woven tales. See no. 3147
SPEER, Daniel
Sonatas, brass quintet (2). See no. 3762
Sonata, 4 trombones. See no. 3936
SPENTIARIAN, Alexandre
Enzeli. See no. 3912
Lullaby. See no. 3912
SPIES, Claudio
3148 Bagatelle. Dadivas (4). Songs: Animula vagula, blandula; Songs on poems by May Swenson (3); Sonnet-settings (5). Christine Whittlesey, s; Johana Arnold, alto; David Ronis, t; Jan Opalach, bs; Henry Martin, Alan Feinberg, pno; Claudio Spies. CRI SD 445
+ARG 12-81 p29 +NR 8-81 p11
+FF 9/10-81 p179
Dadivas. See no. 3148
Songs: Animula vagula blandula; Songs on poems by May Swenson; Sonnet-settings. See no. 3148
SPIRIDION
Toccatina, no. 1. See no. 3808
SPOHR, Ludwig (Louis)
Concertante, harp and violin. See no. 3150
3149 Concerto, clarinet, no. 1, op. 26, C minor. Concerto, clarinet, no. 2, op. 57, E flat major. Anthony Pay, clt; London Sinfonietta; David Atherton. Argo ZRG 920
++Gr 3-81 p1202 +HFN 4-81 p76
Concerto, clarinet, no. 2, op. 57, E flat major. See no. 3149
3150 Concerto, violin, no. 8, op. 47, A major. Concertante, harp and violin. Pierre Amoyal, vln; Marielle Nordmann, hp; Lausanne Chamber Orhcestra; Armin Jordan. Erato STU 71318
+Gr 1-81 p954 +-HFN 12-80 p146
Fantasie and variations, op. 81. See no. 2824. See no. 3669
3151 Nonet, op. 31, F major. Octet, op. 32, E minor. Quintet, op. 52, C minor. Septet, op. 147, A minor. Consortium Classicum, Danzi Quintet Members; Werner Genuit, pno; Anner Bylsma, vlc; Jaap Schroder, vln. Musical Heritage Society MHS 824364 (2) (From BASF 23132, MPS 88014)
+FF 11/12-81 p251
Octet, op. 32, E minor. See no. 3151
Quartet, op. 65, D minor. See no. 2206. See no. 2712
Quintet, op. 52, C minor. See no. 1277. See no. 3151
Septet, op. 147, A minor. See no. 3151
Sonata, harp, op. 113, E flat major. See no. 1377
Sonata, violoncello and harp, op. 115, G major. See no. 56

SPONTINI, Gaspare
3152 Fernando Cortez. Renata Tebaldi, s; Gino Penno, Aldo Protti, Italo Tajo, Afro Poli, Piero de Palma, Antonio Casinelli, Augusto Romano, Gerardo Gaudioso, Gianni Avalanti, Luigi Paolico; Orchestra and Chorus; Gabriele Santini. Historical Recordings HRE 286 (2)
+FF 1/2-81 p191
La vestale: O nume tutelar. See no. 4014
SQUIRE
Like stars above. See no. 4046
STAINER, John
The crucifixion: God so loved the world. See no. 3616
Evening canticles, B flat major. See no. 3873
Lord Jesus think on me. See no. 3824
Songs: Awake awake put on thy strength; How beautiful the mountains. See no. 3637
STAMITZ, Anton (Jan Antonin)
3153 Concerto, violin B flat major. STAMITZ, C.: Sinfonia concertante, D major. Josef Suk, vln; Josef Kodousek, vla; Suk Chamber Orchestra; Hynek Farkac. Supraphon 110 2626
+FF 3/4-81 p197 +-HFN 10-80 p109
+Gr 11-80 p679 +NR 1-81 p5
++HF 6-81 p61
STAMITZ, Carl
Concerto, clarinet, E flat major. See no. 2266
Concerti, flute, D major, G major. See no. 113
Concerto, flute, op. 29, G minor. See no. 94
Concerto, horn, E major. See no. 1832
Concerto, organ, no. 6, F major. See no. 1032
Concerto, viola d'amore, no. 1, D major. See no. 1136
Duet, D major. See no. 3867
Quartet, oboe, op. 8, no. 2, E flat major. See no. 1515
Sinfonia concertante, D major. See no. 3153
STAMITZ, Johann
Concerto, clarinet and 2 horns, B flat major. See no. 2266
Concerto, violin, C major. See no. 3782
Trio, op. 1, no. 5, B flat major. See no. 3782
STANFORD, Charles
Concerto, clarinet, op. 80, A minor. See no. 1517
Evening canticles, G major. See no. 3873
Fantasia and toccata, op. 57, D minor. See no. 4120
Jubilate Deo. See no. 4061
Magnificat and nunc dimittis, G major. See no. 3614
Prelude, G major: Conclusion. See no. 3895
Sonata, clarinet and piano, op. 129. See no. 1514
Songs: Bible songs, op. 113: O for a closer walk with God. See no. 3875
Songs: Drake's drum. See no. 4057
Songs: The blue bird, op. 119, no. 3. See no. 4005
Songs: The Lord is my shepherd. See no. 3621
Songs: The Lord is my shepherd; Te deum, op. 115, C major. See no. 3632
STANKOVYCH, Yevhen
Triptych "In the highlands". See no. 1885

STANLEY, John
Prelude and fugue, G major. See no. 4115
Trumpet tune and aires: Voluntaries (3). See no. 3746
Trumpet voluntary. See no. 3959
Voluntary, A minor. See no. 3992
Voluntary, C major. See no. 4111
Voluntary, D major. See no. 3629. See no. 4112
Voluntary, no. 7. See no. 117

STARER, Robert
Fantasia concertante. See no. 1979
The ideal self. See no. 3957
Quartet, piano. See no. 2816

STAROKADOMSKY, Michail
Passacaglia. See no. 3910

STEFANI, Giovanni
Pargoletra che non sai. See no. 3938

STEFFANI, Agostino
Stabat mater. See no. 1274

STEFFE
Battle hymn of the republic. See no. 3699

STEIN, Leon
Quintet, saxophone and string quartet. See no. 2087

STENHAMMER, Wilhelm
Concerto, piano, no. 2, op. 23, D minor. See no. 2070

STEPANIAN
Prelude. See no. 3917

STEPTOE, Roger
3154 Quartet, strings, no. 1. Songs: The looking glass; Shelley songs (2). David Wilson-Johnson, bar; Roger Steptoe, pno; Hunt Trio, Coull Quartet. Phoenix DGS 1001
+-Gr 8-81 p306
Songs: The looking glass; Shelley songs. See no. 3154

STEVENS, Halsey
Sonata, trumpet and piano. See no. 1636
Songs: Go lovely rose; Like as the culver; Weepe O mine eyes. See no. 3951

STEWART
Crown him with many crowns. See no. 3615

STIRLING, Ian
Horncore. See no. 3731
Suite of four pieces: Namepiece; Improvisation. See no. 3986
Variations on a Tyrolean theme. See no. 3731

STOCK, David
Inner space. See no. 1740

STOCKHAUSEN, Karlheinz
3155 Formel. Inori. Suzanne Stephens, Japanese rin; Maria Bergmann, pno; Southwest German Radio Orchestra; Karlheinz Stockhausen. DG 2707 111 (2)
+FF 5/6-81 p155 +HFN 5-80 p125
+Gr 4-80 p1563
3156 Hymnen Region I-IV. Electronic realization, WDR Cologne. DG 2707 039 (2)
++FF 3/4-81 p198
Inori. See no. 3155
3157 Intensitat. Kommunion. Johannes Fritsch, vla; Rolf Gelhaar, Alfred Alings, tamtam; Carlos Roque Alsina, pno, org; Jean-

Francois Jenny-Clark, contrabass; Michel Portal, sax, flt, pno; Jean-Pierre Drouet, perc; Karlheinz Stockhausen, voice, short wave receiver, glass with stones, nails, hammer, timber, sandpaper, file, rasp, four car horns, siren, filter, volume control, sound direction. DG 2530 256
++FF 3/4-81 p198
Kommunion. See no. 3157
3158 Prozession. Harald Boje, elektronium; Christoph Caskel, tamtam; Joachim Krist, microphone; Peter Eotvos, electrochord with synthesizer; Aloys Kontarsky, pno; Karlheinz Stockhausen, filters, potentiometers, supervison of sound system. DG 2530 582
++FF 3/4-81 p198
Set sail for the sun. See no. 868
3159 Sirus. Markus Stockhausen, tpt; Annette Meriweather, s; Boris Carmeli, bs; Suzanne Stephens, clt; Electronic tape; Karlheinz Stockhausen. DG 2707 122 (2)
+FF 1/2-81 p192 +HFN 11-80 p123
+Gr 9-80 p367 *NR 3-81 p15
+HF 3-81 p56
Spiral. See no. 1109
3160 Sternklang. Various artists; Karlheinz Stockhausen. DG 2707 123 (2) (From Polydor 2612 031)
+FF 1/2-81 p192 +HFN 11-80 p123
+Gr 8-80 p1230 *NR 3-81 p15
+HF 3-81 p60
Zeitgeist. See no. 868
Zyklus. See no. 2007

STOELZEL, Gottfried
Bist du bei mir. See no. 3629
Concerto, trumpet, D major. See no. 3774

STOKES, Eric
Eldey Island. See no. 2190
On the badlands, parables. See no. 2190

STOLTZER, Thomas
Songs: Es mut vil leut; Ich klag den tag; Man sicht nun wol. See no. 3862

STOLZ, Robert
Songs: Im Prater bluh'n wieder die Baume. See no. 3823

STONE
The Lord's prayer. See no. 3895

STORACE, Bernardo
Ballo della battaglia aus. See no. 3622. See no. 4012

STORL
Sonata, brass quintet. See no. 3762

STOUT, Alan
For prepared piano. See no. 3915
Waltz. See no. 3942

STRAESSER, Joep
Intersections V. See no. 3729

STRANGE
Damon. See no. 4076

STRAUBE, Karl
Sonatas, nos. 1-3. See no. 1777

STRAUSS
Orchesterlieder. See no. 640

Schatz waltz. See no. 1327

STRAUSS, Johann I

Alice Polka, op. 238. See no. 3161

Cachucha galop, op. 97. See no. 3166

Einzugs galop, op. 35. See no. 3169

Exotische Pflanzen, op. 109. See no. 3161

Frederica Polka, op. 239. See no. 3161

Furioso Galopp, op. 114. See no. 3161

Gabrielen Walzer, op. 68. See no. 3161

Indianer Galopp, op. 111. See no. 3161

Jubel Quadrille, op. 130. See no. 3161. See no. 3169

Loreley Rhein Klange, op. 154. See no. 3169

Marien Walzer, op. 212. See no. 3161

Mittel gegen den Schlaf, op. 65. See no. 3161

Radetzky Marsch, op. 228. See no. 3161. See no. 3168. See no. 3617. See no. 3699. See 3768

Rosen ohne Dornen, op. 166. See no. 3161

Die Schwalben, op. 208. See no. 3161

Sorgenbrecher, op. 230. See no. 3161

Themis-Klange, op. 201. See no. 3161

Wiener Carnevals Quadrille, op. 124. See no. 3161

Wiener Kreuzer Polka, op. 220. See no. 3161

3161 Works, selections: Alice Polka, op. 238. Exotische Pflanzen, op. 109. Frederica Polka, op. 239. Furioso Galopp, op. 114. Gabrielen Walzer, op. 69. Indianer Galopp, op. 111. Jubel Quadrille, op. 130. Marien Walzer, op. 212. Mittel gegen den Schlaf, op. 65. Radetzky Marsch, op. 228. Rosen ohne Dornen, op. 166. Die Schwalben, op. 208. Sorgenbrecher, op. 230. Themis-Klange, op. 201. Wiener Carnevals Quadrille, op. 124. Wiener Kreuzer Polka, op. 220. Vienna Chamber Orchestra; Paul Angerer. Intercord INT 180828 (2)

++HFN 11-81 p100

STRAUSS, Johann II

Accelerationen, op. 234. See no. 3162. See no. 3168. See no. 3169. See no. 3170

3162 An der schonen blauen Donau, op. 314. Accelerationen, op. 234. Kaiserwalzer, op. 437. Rosen aus dem Suden, op. 388. STRAUSS, Johann II/Josef: Pizzicato polka. VPO; Josef Krips. Contour CC 7522 Tape (c) CCT 7522

+Gr 8-81 p316

An der schonen blauen Donau, op. 314. See no. 3165. See no. 3166. See no. 3167. See no. 3168. See no. 3175. See no. 3768. See no. 4083

Annen Polka, op. 117. See no. 3166. See no. 3167. See no. 3168. See no. 3169. See no. 3175

Auf der Jagd, op. 373. See no. 3166. See no. 3168. See no. 3175

Ballstrausschen, op. 380. See no. 3171

Banditen, op. 378. See no. 3170. See no. 3174. See no. 3768

3163 Cinderella: Ballet (arr. Bayer, Rev. and ed. Gamley). Ritter Passman, op. 441: Ballet music. National Philharmonic Orchestra; Richard Bonynge. Decca D225D2 (2) Tape (c) K225K22 (also London LDR 72005)

+Gr 5-81 p1479 +SFC 10-4-81 p17

++HFN 7-81 p76

Egyptischer Marsch, op. 335. See no. 3173

Eljen a Magyar, op. 332. See no. 3168. See no. 3173. See no. 3863
Explosionen, op. 43. See no. 3170
Fata Morgana, op. 330. See no. 3166. See no. 3768
Feenmarchen, op. 312. See no. 3171
Die Fledermaus, op. 363, excerpts. See no. 2010
Die Fledermaus, op. 363: Dieser Anstand. See no. 3966
Die Fledermaus, op. 363: Mein Herr Marquis spiel ich die Unschuld vom Lande. See no. 4083
Die Fledermaus, op. 363: Mein Herr was dachten Sie von mir; Klange der Heimat. See no. 3844
Die Fledermaus, op. 363: Overture. See no. 3175. See no. 3212. See no. 3817. See no. 3964. See no. 4122
Die Fledermaus, op. 363: Overture; Czardas. See no. 3768
Die Fledermaus, op. 363: Overture; Quadrille. See no. 3168
Flugschriften, op. 300. See no. 3171
Freikugeln, op. 326. See no. 3173
Freut' euch des Lebens, op. 340. See no. 3173
Fruhlingstimmen, op. 410. See no. 3165. See no. 3174. See no. 3175. See no. 4083
Geschichten aus dem Wienerwald, op. 325. See no. 3165. See no. 3167. See no. 3168. See no. 3173. See no. 3175
Graduation ball, op. 97. See no. 2538
Gruss an Wien, op. 225. See no. 3171
Heiligenstad Rendez-vous, op. 78. See no. 3169
Helenen Polka, op. 203. See no. 3171
Im Krapfenwald, op. 336. See no. 3174
Im Sturmschritt, op. 348. See no. 3170
Indigo Marsch, op. 349. See no. 3169. See no. 3173
Juristenball Tanze, op. 177. See no. 3171
Juz Polka, op. 17. See no. 3171
Kaiserwalzer, op. 437. See no. 3162. See no. 3165. See no. 3166. See no. 3168. See no. 3172. See no. 3174. See no. 3175. See no. 3768. See no. 4083
Kreuzfidel, op. 301. See no. 3171
Kunstlerleben, op. 316. See no. 3165. See no. 3168. See no. 3175
Lagunen, op. 411. See no. 3170. See no. 3174
Leichtes Blut, op. 319. See no. 3168. See no. 3170
Licht und Schatten, op. 374. See no. 3171
Man lebt nur einmal, op. 167. See no. 3171
Morgenblatter, op. 279. See no. 3166. See no. 3169. See no. 3170. See no. 3175
Eine Nacht in Venedig: Annina...Rondinella pellegrina; Was mir der Zufall gab. See no. 3844
Napoleon Marsch, op. 156. See no. 3168
Neue Pizzicato Polka, op. 449. See no. 3768
Nur fort, op. 383. See no. 3171
Perpetuum Mobile, op. 257. See no. 3168. See no. 3169. See no. 3768.
Persischer Marsch, op. 289. See no. 3168. See no. 3169
Polkas. See no. 2421
Ritter Pasman, op. 441: Ballet music. See no. 3163
Ritter Pasman, op. 441: Csardas. See no. 3174
Romances, nos. 1-3. See no. 2535

Rosen aus dem Suden, op. 388. See no. 3162. See no. 3165. See no. 3168. See no. 3169. See no. 3172. See no. 3174. See no. 3175. See no. 4083
Russischer Marsch, op. 426. See no. 3174
Schatz, op. 418. See no. 3170. See no. 3172. See no. 3174
Spitzentuch Quadrille, op. 392. See no. 3171
Die Tanzerin Fanny Eisler: Drausen in Sievering. See no. 4083
Tausend und eine Nacht, op. 346. See no. 3165. See no. 3173
Tritsch Tratsch, op. 214. See no. 3166. See no. 3167. See no. 3168. See no. 3169
Unter Donner und Blitz, op. 324. See no. 3167. See no. 3168. See no. 3169. See no. 3170. See no. 3175. See no. 3212. See no. 3721
Vergnugungszug, op. 281. See no. 3801
Waldine, op. 385. See no. 3171
Wien, Weib und Gesang, op. 333. See no. 3165. See no. 3168. See no. 3169. See no. 3172. See no. 3212
Wellen und Wogen, op. 141. See no. 3171

3164 Wiener Blut, op. 354. Hilde Gueden, Margit Schramm, Wilma Lipp, s; Rudolf Schock, t; Benno Kusche, Erich Kunz, bs; Vienna State Opera Chorus; VSO; Robert Stolz. Eurodisc 72751 (2)
+FF 11/12-81 p252

Wiener Blut, op. 354. See no. 3165. See no. 3167. See no. 3168. See no. 3173. See no. 3175. See no. 3768
Wiener Blut, op. 354: Es hat Grafen...Gruss dich Gott; Ah ha na Warte du Schwindler. See no. 3844
Wiener Bonbons, op. 307. See no. 3166
Wo die Zitronen, bluhn, op. 364. See no. 3169

3165 Works, selections: An der schonen blauen Donau, op. 314. Fruhlingstimmen, op. 410. Geschichten aus dem Wienerwald, op. 325. Kaiserwalzer, op. 437. Kunstlerleben, op. 316. Rosen aus dem Suden, op. 388. Tausend und eine Nacht, op. 346. Wiener Blut, op. 354. Wein, Weib und Gesang, op. 333. STRAUSS, Josef: Delirien, op. 212. Dorfschwalben aus Oesterreich, op. 164. PO, NYP; Eugene Ormandy, Leonard Bernstein, Georg Szell. CBS MG 35918 (2)
+-FF 9/10-81 p180 +NR 6-81 p4

3166 Works, selections: An der schonen blauen Donau, op. 314. Annen polka, op. 117. Auf der Jagd, op. 373. Fata Morgana, op. 330. Kaiserwalzer, op. 437. Morgenblatter, op. 279. Tritsch Tratsch, op. 214. Wiener Bonbons, op. 307. STRAUSS, J. I: Cachucha Galopp, op. 97. STRAUSS, Josef: Aquarellen, op. 258. Moulinet, op. 57. Ohne Sorgen, op. 271. Johann Strauss Orchestra; Jack Rothenstein. Chandos ABRD 1039 Tape (c) ABTD 1039
+HFN 12-81 p103

3167 Works, selections: An der schonen blauen Donau, op. 314. Annen polka, op. 117. Geschichten aus dem Wiener Wald, op. 325. Tritsch Tratsch, op. 214. Unter Donner und Blitz, op. 324. Wiener Blut, op. 354. BPhO; Herbert von Karajan. DG 2542 143 Tape (c) 3342 143 (From 139014, 2530 027)
+Gr 6-81 p89 +-HFN 6-81 p87 tape
+-HFN 6-81 p85

3168 Works, selections: Accelerationen, op. 234. An der schonen blauen Donau, op. 314. Annen Polka, op. 117. Auf der Jagd, op. 373. Eljen a Magyar, op. 332. Die Fledermaus, op. 363: Overture;

Quadrille. Geschichten aus dem Wienerwald, op. 325. Kaiserwalzer, op. 437. Kunstlerleben, op. 316. Leichtes Blut, op. 319. Napoleon Marsch, op. 156. Perpetuum Mobile, op. 257. Persischer Marsch, op. 289. Rosen aus dem Suden, op. 388. Tritsch Trasch, op. 214. Unter Donner und Blitz, op. 324. Wein, Weib und Gesang, op. 333. Wiener Blut, op. 354. Die Zigeunerbaron, op. 420: Overture. STRAUSS, J. I: Radetzky Marsch, op. 228. STRAUSS, Josef: Delirien, op. 212. Spharenklange, op. 235. BPhO; Herbert von Karajan. DG 2741 003 (3) Tape (c) 3382 003

+FF 11/12-81 p251 ++HFN 8-81 p87
+Gr 8-81 p318 ++HFN 10-81 p95 tape
+Gr 10-81 p614 tape +St 10-81 p116

3169 Works, selections: Accelerationen, op. 234. Annen Polka, op. 117. Heiligenstradter Rendez-vous, op. 78. Indigo Marsch, op. 349. Morgenblatter, op. 279. Perpetuum Mobile, op. 257. Persischer Marsch, op. 289. Rosen aus dem Suden, op. 388. Tritsch Tratsch, op. 214. Unter Donner und Blitz, op. 324. Wein, Weib und Gesang, op. 333. Wo di Citroen Bluhn, op. 364. STRAUSS, J. I: Einzugs Galopp, op. 35. Jubel Quadrille, op. 130. Loreley Rhein Klange, op. 154. STRAUSS, Josef: Feuerfest, op. 269. Frauenherz, op. 166. STRAUSS, Johann/Josef: Pizzicato Polka. LANNER: Hofballtanze, op. 161. Die Schonbrunner, op. 200. BeSO, VSO; Robert Stolz. Eurodisc 87360 (2)

+FF 11/12-81 p251 +St 10-81 p116

3170 Works, selections: Acellerationen, op. 234. Banditen, op. 378. Im Sturmschritt, op. 348. Explosionen, op. 43. Lagunen, op. 411. Leichtes Blut, op. 319. Morgenblatter, op. 279. Schatz, op. 418. Unter Donner und Blitz, op. 324. STRAUSS, Josef: Feuerfest, op. 269. Johann Strauss Orchestra; Willi Boskovsky. HMV ASD 4041 Tape (c) TCC ASD 4041

+-Gr 9-81 p451 +HFN 10-81 p91

3171 Works, selections: Ballstrausschen, op. 380. Feenmarchen, op. 312. Flugschriften, op. 300. Gruss an Wien, op. 225. Helenen Polka, op. 203. Juristenball Tanze, op. 177. Jux Polka, op. 17. Kreuzfidel, op. 301. Licht und Schatten, op. 374. Man lebt nur einmal, op. 167. Nur fort, op. 383. Spitzentuch Quadrille, op. 392. Waldine, op. 385. Wellen und Wogen, op. 14. Zeitgeister, op. 25. Vienna Chamber Orchestra; Paul Angerer. Intercord INT 180816 (2)

++HFN 11-81 p100

3172 Works, selections: Kaiserwalzer, op. 437 (arr. Schoenberg). Rosen aus dem Suden, op. 388 (arr. Schoenberg). Schatz, op. 418 (arr. Webern). Wein, Weib und Gesang, op. 333 (arr. Berg). Ensemble 13, Baden-Baden; Manfred Reichert. Pro Arte PAL 1011

+FF 7/8-81 p173 +St 8-81 p99
+SFC 4-26-81 p18

3173 Works, selections: Egyptischer Marsch, op. 335. Eljen a Magyar, op. 332. Freut euch des Lebens, op. 340. Freikugeln, op. 326. Geschichten aus dem Wienerwald, op. 325. Indigo Marsch, op. 349. Ein Tausend und eine Nacht, op. 346. Wiener Blut, op. 354. BeSO, VSO; Robert Stolz. RCA GL 2-5264 Tape (c) GK 2-5264 (From World Records SM 113/8)

+Gr 11-80 p739 +HFN 1-81 p109 tape
+HFN 11-80 p131

3174 Works, selections: Banditen, op. 378. Fruhlingsstimmen, op. 410.* Im Krapfenwald, op. 336.* Kaiserwalzer, op. 437. Lagunen, op. 411. Ritter Pasman, op. 411: Csardas. Rosen aus dem Suden, op. 388. Schatz, op. 418. Russischer Marsch, op. 426. BeSO, VSO; Robert Stolz. RCA GL 2-5265 Tape (c) GK 2-5265 (*From BASF 3069/70)
+Gr 8-81 p318 +-HFN 8-81 p92

3175 Works, selections: An der schonen blauen Donau, op. 314. Annen Polka, op. 117. Auf der Jagd, op. 373. Die Fledermaus, op. 363: Overture. Fruhlingsstimmen, op. 410. Geschichten aus dem Wienerwald, op. 325. Kaiserwalzer, op. 347. Kunstlerleben, op. 316. Morgenblatter, op. 279. Rosen aus dem Suden, op. 388. Unter Donner und Blitz, op. 324. Wiener Blut, op. 354. STRAUSS, Josef: Feuerfest, op. 269. PO; Eugene Ormandy. RCA RL 4-2846 (2)
+NR 11-81 p3

Zeitgeister, op. 25. See no. 3171
Der Zigeunerbaron, op. 420, excerpts. See no. 2010
Der Zigeunerbaron, op. 420: Overture. See no. 3168. See no. 3858
Der Zigeunerbaron, op. 420: Wers uns getraut. See no. 3844

STRAUSS, Johann II/Joseph
Pizzicato polka. See no. 3162. See no. 3169. See no. 3792

STRAUSS, Josef
Aquarellen, op. 258. See no. 3166
Bouquet, op. 188. See no. 3176
Delirien, op. 212. See no. 3165. See no. 3168
Dorfschwalben aus Oesterreich, op. 164. See no. 3165
Eingesendent, op. 240. See no. 3768
Die Emancipierte, op. 282. See no. 3176
Ernst und Humor, op. 254. See no. 3176
Fashion, op. 165. See no. 3176
Feuerfest, op. 269. See no. 3169. See no. 3170. See no. 3891
Frauenherz, op. 166. See no. 3169. See no. 3176
Freudengrusse, op. 128. See no. 3176
Gedenkblatter, op. 178. See no. 3176
Geheime Anziehungskrafte, op. 173. See no. 3176
Herbstrosen, op. 232. See no. 3176
Jokey, op. 278. See no. 3176
Mairosen, op. 34. See no. 3176
Memento, op. 178. See no. 3176
Moulinet, op. 57. See no. 3166
Neckerei, op. 262. See no. 3176
Ohne Sorgen, op. 271. See no. 3166
Spharenklange, op. 235. See no. 3168
Sport, op. 170. See no. 3176
Die Tanzende Muse, op. 266. See no. 3176
Wiener Leben, op. 218. See no. 3176

3176 Works, selections: Bouquet, op. 188. Die Emancipierte, op. 282. Ernst und Humor, op. 254. Fashion, op. 165. Frauenherz, op. 166. Freudengrusse, op. 128. Gedenkblatter, op. 178. Geheime Anziehungskrafte, op. 173. Herbstrosen, op. 232. Jokey, op. 278. Mairosen, op. 34. Memento, op. 178. Neckerei, op. 262. Sport, op. 170. Die tanzende Muse, op. 266. Wiener Leben, op. 218. Vienna Chamber Orchestra; Paul Angerer. Intercord INT 180814

/FF 7/8-81 p174 ++HFN 11-81 p100

STRAUSS, Oscar

The chocolate soldier: My hero. See no. 3640

Serenade, op. 35, G minor. See no. 2788

3177 Ein Walzertraum. Anneliese Rothenberg, Edda Moser, s; Brigitte Fassbaender, ms; Nicolai Gedda, Willi Brokmeier, t; Wolfgang Annheisser, bar; Bavarian State Opera Chorus; Graunke Symphony Orchestra; Willy Mattes. Arabesque 8063/2 (From EMI)
+ARG 5-81 p48
+FF 1/2-81 p193
+NR 12-80 p9
+St 3-81 p95

STRAUSS, Richard

3178 Alpine symphony, op. 64. David Bell, org; BPhO; Herbert von Karajan. DG 2532 015 Tape (c) 3302 015
++Gr 12-81 p891
+HFN 12-81 p103

3179 Alpine symphony, op. 64. Bavarian Radio Orchestra; Georg Solti. London CS 7189 (aso Decca SXL 6959 Tape (c) KSXC 6959)
+FF 1/2-81 p193
+Gr 9-80 p349
+Gr 12-80 p889 tape
+HF 1-81 p77
+HFN 10-80 p109
+MT 6-81 p392
++NR 2-81 p4
+OV 12-81 p42
++SFC 10-5-80 p21
++St 3-81 p96
++ST 3-81 p819

3180 Also sprach Zarathustra, op. 30. Glenn Dicterow, vln; NYP; Zubin Mehta. CBS IM 35888 Tape (c) HMT 35888
+-FF 3/4-81 p200
+Gr 5-81 p1479
+HF 6-81 p61
+-HFN 5-81 p84
+St 4-81 p107

3181 Also sprach Zarathustra, op. 30. Schlagobers, op. 70: Waltzes. VPO; Richard Strauss. Everest 3475 (From Olympia 8111)
+-FF 3/4-81 p201
-HF 6-81 p61
+-NR 2-81 p3

3182 Also sprach Zarathustra, op. 30. PO; Eugene Ormandy. HMV ASD 3897 Tape (c) TC ASD 3897 (also Angel DS 37744 Tape (c) 4ZS 37744)
+ARG 6-81 p42
+-FF 3/4-81 p200
+-Gr 12-80 p841
-HF 6-81 p61
+-HFN 12-80 p146
+MUM 9/10-81 p37
+NR 2-81 p3
+SFC 12-7-80 p33
++St 4-81 p107

3183 Also sprach Zarathustra, op. 30. CSO; Fritz Reiner. Mobile Fidelity Sound Lab MFSL 1-522 (From RCA LSC 2609)
+FF 9/10-81 p181
++NR 6-81 p3
++SFC 5-3-81 p22
+St 11-81 p94

3184 Also sprach Zarathustra, op. 30. Don Juan, op. 20. Ein Heldenleben, op. 40. CSO; Fritz Reiner. RCA VL 4-2267 (2)
+-FF 7/8-81 p175

Also sprach Zarathustra, op. 30: Introduction. See no. 3645

Also sprach Zarathustra, op. 30: Opening fanfare. See no. 3746

Andante. See no. 2789

3185 Arabella, op. 79. Julia Varady, Helen Donath, s; Helga Schmidt, ms; Adolf Dallapozza, Hermann Winkler, t; Dietrich Fischer-Dieskau, bar; Walter Berry, bs; Bavarian State Opera Chorus; Bavarian State Orchestra; Wolfgang Sawallisch. HMV SLS 5220 (3) (also Angel SX 3917)
++Gr 10-81 p610
+HFN 1-81 p91
+-Op 12-81 p1305

3186 Arabella, op. 79: Du sollst mein Gebieter sein; Er ist der Richtige nicht...Aber der Richtige. Ariadne auf Naxos, op. 60: Querschnitt. Capriccio, op. 85: Du Spiegelbild der verliebten Madeleine; Holla ihr Streiter in Apoll. Daphne, op. 82: Gotter Bruder im hohen Olympos; O wie gern blieb ich bei dir. Die Frau ohne Schatten, op. 65: Intermezzo, Act 1; Falke du wiedergefundener; Sie haben es mir gesagt. Salome, op. 54: Salomes Tanz. Soloists; Staatskapelle, VSOO; Karl Bohm. Acanta DE 23280/1 (2)
+-HFN 6-80 p112 +Op 8-80 p800
+-ON 3-7-81 p28 +-RR 5-80 p49

3187 Arabella, op. 79: Ich danke Fraulein; Welko das Bild; Mein Elemer; Sie wolln mich heiraten; Und jetzt sag ich adieu; Das war sehr gut. Capriccio, op. 85: Morgen mittag um elf. Vier letzte Lieder, op. posth. Elisabeth Schwarzkopf, s; PhO; Otto Ackermann, Lovro von Matacic. HMV RLS 751 (2) (From Columbia 33CX 1107, 33CS 1226)
+-FF 7/8-81 p177 +-HFN 11-80 p131
+Gr 11-80 p735 +Op 3-81 p311

Arabella, op. 79: Ich mochte meinen fremden Mann; So wie Sie sind. See no. 3651

3188 Ariadne auf Naxos, op. 60. Maria Reining, Alda Noni, Irmgaard Seefried, s; Max Lorenz, Peter Klein, t; Erich Kunz, Paul Schoffler, bar; Richard Sallaba, Marjan Rus, bs; VSOO; Karl Bohm. Bruno Walter Society IGI 378 (2)
+-FF 7/8-81 p176 +NR 6-81 p10

3189 Ariadne auf Naxos, op. 60. PhO; Herbert von Karajan. HMV RLS 760 (3) Tape (c) TC SLS 760 (From Columbia 33CX 1292/4)
++Gr 5-81 p1515 +Op 7-81 p718
+HFN 5-81 p93

Ariadne auf Naxos, op. 60: Querschnitt. See no. 3186

3190 Le bourgeois gentilhomme, op. 60, nos. 1-6, 9. Feuersnot, op. 50: Love scene. Intermezzo, op. 72: Interlude. RPO; Thomas Beecham. World Records SH 378
+FF 5/6-81 p157 +HFN 12-80 p146
+Gr 12-80 p880

Burleske, op. 11, D minor. See no. 2770. See no. 3027

3191 Capriccio, op. 85. WAGNER: Siegfried Idyll. Lausanne Chamber Orchestra; Armin Jordan. Erato STU 71333
+Gr 5-81 p1479

3192 Capriccio, op. 85. Songs (5). Die Tageszeiten, op. 76. Vier letzte Lieder, op. posth. Viorica Ursuleac, s; Hertha Topper, ms; Rudolf Schock, t; Karl Schmitt-Walter, Hans Braun, bar; Hans Hotter, bs; Hermann Prey, bar; Sena Jurinac, s; Bavarian Radio Orchestra, VPO; French Radio Orchestra; Orchestra; Clemens Krauss, Robert Heger, Milan Horvat. Rococo 1021 (4)
+-NR 3-81 p11

Capriccio, op. 85: Du Spiegelbild der verliebten Madeleine; Holla ihr Streiter in Apoll. See no. 3186

Daphne, op. 82: Gotter Bruder im hohen Olympos; O wie gern blieb ich bei dir. See no. 3186

3193 Don Juan, op. 20. Till Eulenspiegels lustige Streiche, op. 28. Tod und Verklarung, op. 24. CO; Lorin Maazel. CBS IM 35826, DGTM 6002 Tape (c) HMT 35826, 40-35826)
+FF 11/12-80 p178 +-HFN 4-81 p81 tape

+Gr 12-80 p841 ++MUM 2-81 p35
+Gr 1-81 p1001 tape ++SFC 8-24-80 p36
+-HF 1-81 p77 +St 12-80 p118
+HFN 12-80 p146

3194 Don Juan, op. 20. Till Eulenspiegels lustige Streiche, op. 28. Tod und Verklarung, op. 24. CO; Georg Szell. CBS MY 36721
+-FF 9/10-81 p182

3195 Don Juan, op. 20. TCHAIKOVSKY: Romeo and Juliet: Fantasy overture. VPO; Herbert von Karajan. Contour CC 7528 Tape (c) CCT 7528
+Gr 8-81 p316

3196 Don Juan, op. 20. Vier letzte Lieder, op. posth. Montserrat Caballe, s; Strasbourg Philharmonic Orchstra; Alain Lombard. Erato STU 71054 (also Musical Heritage Soicety MHS 4298)
-FF 5/6-81 p157 -ON 3-3-79 p41
+-FF 5/6-80 p155

3197 Don Juan, op. 20. Till Eulenspiegels lustige Streiche, op. 28. Tod und Verklarung, op. 24. VPO; Andre Previn. HMV ASD 3913 Tape (c) TC ASD 3913 (also Angel DS 37753)
+-FF 9/10-81 p183 +Gr 8-81 p324 tape
+Gr 2-81 p1092 +HFN 2-81 p94

3198 Don Juan, op. 20. Der Rosenkavalier, op. 59: 1st waltz sequence. Salome, op. 54: Dance of the seven veils. Till Eulenspiegels lustige Streiche, op. 28. Cincinnati Symphony Orchestra; Thomas Schippers. Turnabout QTV 34666, DBX SS 3005 Tape (c) CT 2138
+Audio 12-81 p67 +NYT 11-27-77 pD15
+HF 1-79 p54 tape +SFC 6-5-77 p45
+NR 7-77 p2

Don Juan, op. 20. See no. 685. See no. 695. See no. 3184. See no. 3781. See no. 3791

3199 Don Quixote, op. 35. Der Rosenkavalier, op. 59: Waltzes (arr. Reiner). Antonio Janigro, vlc; CSO; Firtz Reiner. RCA AGL 1-3367
-FF 7/8-81 p98

Duet-concertino. See no. 1874

3200 Elektra, op, 58: Allein; Weh ganz Allein; Was willst du fremder Mensch; Elektra Schwester komm mit uns. Inge Borkh, s; Paul Schoeffler, bs; CSO; Fritz Reiner. RCA AGL 1-3879 Tape (c) AGK 1-3879
+FF 7/8-81 p98 +MUM 7/8-81 p35

Elektra, op. 58: Allein Weh ganz allein. See no. 3989

Fanfare. See no. 3220

Fanfare fur die Wiener Philharmoniker. See no. 3220

Feierlicher Einzug der Titter des Johanniterordens. See no. 3220

Festmusik der Stadt Wien. See no. 3220. See no. 3660

Feuersnot, op. 50: Love scene. See no. 3190

Die Frau ohne Schatten, op. 65: Intermezzo, Act 1; Falke du wiedergefundener; Sie haben es mir gesagt. See no. 3186

3201 Ein Heldenleben, op. 40. LAPO; Zubin Mehta. Decca JB 101 Tape (c) KJBC 101 (From SXL 6382)
++Gr 1-81 p954

3202 Ein Heldenleben, op. 40. Michel Schwalbe, vln; BPhO; Herbert von Karajan. DG 2535 194 (From 138025)
+-FF 1/2-81 p195 +RR 8-76 p53
++Gr 8-76 p299

3203 Ein Heldenleben, op. 40. Gerhart Hetzel, vln; VPO; Karl Bohm.

DG 2542 153 Tape (c) 3342 153 (From 2530 781)
+Gr 5-81 p1479 +-HFN 6-81 p87 tape

3204 Ein Heldenleben, op. 40. Hermann Krebbers, vln; COA; Bernard Haitink. Philips 6500 048 Tape (c) B-CG 6500 048
++Gr 1-71 p1165 ++NR 5-71 p2
+HF 7-71 p91 ++SFC 4-25-71 p32
+HF 4-81 p93 tape ++St 8-71 p85
+HFN 1-71 p117 +SR 5-29-71 p48
+MJ 6-71 p7

3205 Ein Heldenleben, op. 40. PO; Eugene Ormandy. RCA ARL 1-3581 Tape (c) ARK 1-3581
++ARG 4-81 p32 +NYT 9-7-80 pD29
/FF 11/12-80 p179 ++SFC 8-24-80 p36
+NR 9-80 p3 +St 12-80 p135

Ein Heldenleben, op. 40. See no. 3184. See no. 4122

3206 Intermezzo, op. 72. Lucia Popp, Gabriele Fuchs, Gudrun Greindl-Rosner, s; Adolf Dallapozza, Martin Finke, t; Dietrich Fischer-Dieskau, Klaus Hirte, Raimund Grumbach, bar; Kurt Moll, bs; Philipp Brammer, speaker; Bavarian Radio Orchestra; Wolfgang Sawallisch. HMV SLS 5204 (3) (also Electrola 1C 165 30983/5)
+FF 3/4-81 p203 +NYT 4-5-81 pD33
+Gr 11-80 p735 +ON 3-7-81 p28
+HFN 2-81 p93 +Op 2-81 p202
+MT 6-81 p393 +STL 12-14-80 p38

Intermezzo, op. 72: Interlude. See no. 3190

Olympische hymne. See no. 3220

Parade marches, nos. 1 and 2. See no. 3220

3207 Quartet, piano, op. 13, C minor. Milan Piano Quartet. Accord ACC 140016
+-HFN 12-81 p103 +STL 9-13-81 p41

3208 Der Rosenkavalier, op. 59. Soloists; Dresden State Opera Ensemble and Chorus; Rudolf Kempe. Acanta JA 23039 (4)
-HFN 2-81 p93

3209 Der Rosenkavalier, op. 59. Marianne Schech, Erika Koth, Hertha Topper, s; Lorenz Fehenberger, t; Otto Edelmann, bs; Bavarian State Opera Orchestra and Chorus; Hans Knappertsbusch. Bruno Walter Society RR 482 (3)
+-FF 11/12-81 p253 +-NR 9-81 p11

3210 Der Rosenkavalier, op. 59 (film). Ensemble 13, Baden Baden; Manfred Reichert. Harmonia Mundo (Germany) 065 99904/5 (2)
+FF 5/6-81 p158 +-HFN 9-81 p85
-Gr 9-81 p394

3211 Der Rosenkavalier, op. 59. Evelyn Lear, Ruth Welting, Nelly Morpurgo, Renee van Haarlem, s; Frederica von Stade, Sophia van Sante, ms; Jose Carreras, James Atherton, Wouter Goedhardt, Matthijs Coppens, Adriaan van Limpt, t; Derek Hammond Stroud, Henk Smit, bar; Jules Bastin, bs; Netherlands Opera Chorus; Rotterdam Philharmonic Orchestra; Edo de Waart. Philips 6707 030 (4) Tape (c) 7699 045
+-ARG 10-77 p43 +NR 8-77 p10
++FF 9-77 p56 +-NYT 7-10-77 pD13
+Gr 8-77 p339 +ON 8-77 p56
+HF 9-77 p110 +-OR 9/10-77 p29
-HF 11-77 p138 tape +RR 7-77 p40
+HFN 7-77 p103 +-RR 10-77 p99 tape

+HFN 9-77 p155 tape +SFC 6-5-77 p45
+-MJ 9-77 p34 +SR 7-81 p90
+MT 11-77 p924 +St 10-77 p146

Der Rosenkavalier, op. 59: Di rigori armato. See no. 3648. See no. 3759. See no. 3885

Der Rosenkavalier, op. 59: First waltz sequence. See no. 3198

Der Rosenkavalier, op. 59: Herr Gott im Himmel; Presentation of the silver rose. See no. 3844

3212 Der Rosenkavalier, op. 59: Suite. STRAUSS, J. II: Die Fledermaus, op. 363: Overture. Unter Donner und Blitz, op. 324. Wein, Weib und Gesang, op. 333. Cincinnati Symphony Orchestra; Max Rudolf. Westminster MCA 1421
-FF 1/2-81 p197

Der Rosenkavalier, op. 59: Suite. See no. 796

Der Rosenkavalier, op. 59: Waltzes. See no. 3199

3213 Der Rosenkavalier, op. 59: Wie du warst, Wie du bist; Di rigori armato il seno; Da geht er hin...Ach du bist wieder da; Ein ernster Tag; Mir ist die Ehre widerfahren; Da lieg ich; Marie Theres; Hab mir's gelobt...Ist ein Traum. Evelyn Lear, Ruth Welting, s; Frederica von Stade, ms; Jose Carreras, t; Derek Hammond Stroud, bar; Jules Bastin, bs; Netherlands Opera Chorus; Rotterdam Philharmonic Orchestra; Edo de Waart. Philips 6570 101 Tape (c) 7310 101 (From 6707 030)
+Gr 1-81 p990 +-HFN 3-81 p97

3214 Salome, op. 54. Walburga Wegner, s; Georgine von Milinkovic, ms; Dagmar Hermann, con; Laszlo Szemere, Waldemar Kmentt, t; Josef Metternich, bar; Oskar Czerwenka, Walter Berry, bs; VSO; Rudolf Moralt. Philips 6747 406 (2) (From ABL 3003/4)
+Gr 11-81 p757

Salome, op. 54; Dance of the seven veils. See no. 3198.

Salome, op. 54: Salomes Tanz. See no. 3186

Schlagobers, op. 70: Waltzes. See no. 3181

3215 Serenade, op. 7, E flat major. Sonatina, no. 1, F major. Suite, op. 4, B flat major. Symphony, wind instruments (1945). NWE; Edo de Waart. Philips 6770 048 (2) (From 6500 097, 6500 297)
++Gr 2-81 p1101 +-HFN 3-81 p97

3216 Sinfonia domestica, op. 53. Songs: Liebeshymnus, op. 32, no. 3; Waldseligkeit, op. 49, no. 1; Verfuhrung, op. 33, no. 1; Winterliebe, op. 48, no. 5. Peter Anders, t; BPhO; Wilhelm Furtwangler. Arabesque 8082
+NR 11-81 p3 -NYT 9-20-81 pD29

3217 Sonata, violin and piano, op. 18, E major. Sonata, violoncello and piano, op. 6, F major. Rudolf Koeckert, vln; Gerhard Mantel, vlc; Erika Frieser, pno. Da Camera SM 93709
+-MT 3-81 p184 +-ST 12-80 p575

Sonata, violin and piano, op. 18, E major. See no. 3841

Sonata, violoncello and piano, op. 6, F major. See no. 1199. See no. 3217

Sonatina, no. 1, F major. See no. 3215

3218 Songs: Ach Lieb ich muss nun Scheiden, op. 21, no. 3; Ach weh mir ungluckhaftem Mann, op. 21, no. 4; Breit uber mein Haupt, op. 19, no. 2; Cacilie, op. 27, no. 2; Fur funfzehn Pfennige, op. 36, no. 2; Fruhlingsgedrange, op. 26, no. 1; Geduld, op. 10, no. 5; Heimlich Afforderung, op. 27, no. 3; Ich trage meine Minne, op. 32, no. 1; Morgen, op. 27, no. 4; Die Nacht,

op. 10, no. 3; Nachtgang, op. 29, no. 3; Nichts, op. 10, no. 2; O Susser Mai, op. 32, no. 4; Ruhe meine Seele, op. 27, no. 1; Traum durch die Dammerung, op. 29, no. 1; Wie Sollten wir geheim sie halten, op. 19, no. 4; Winternacht, op. 15, no. 2; Zueignung, op. 10, no. 1. Bernd Weikl, bar; Cord Garben, pno. DG 2531 076
+NR 2-81 p11 ++St 6-81 p125

3219 Songs: Am Ufer, op. 41, no. 3; Befreit, op. 39, no. 4; Breit uber mein Haupt, op. 19, no. 2; Freundliche Vision, op. 48, no. 1; Heimliche Aufforderung, op. 27, no. 3; Ich Schwebe, op. 48, no. 2; Lieder der Ophelia aus Hamlet (3); Nichts, op. 10, no. 2; Schlechtes Wetter, op. 69, no. 5; Standchen, op. 17, no. 2; Wie sollten wir geheim, op. 19, no. 4; Wiegenlied, op. 41, no. 1; Wozu noch Madchen, op. 19, no. 1; Die Zeitlose. Helen-Kay Eberly, s; Donald Isaak, pno. Eb-Sko 1005
+-ARG 2-81 p30 +ON 3-7-81 p28
+-Audio 11-80 p85 ++St 10-81 p134
+FF 11/12-80 p180

Songs (5). See no. 3192

Songs: Allerseelen. See no. 4000

Songs: Allerseelen, op. 10, no. 8; Du meines Herzens Kronelein, op. 21, no. 2; Morgen, op. 27, no. 4. See no. 3657

Songs: Befreit, op. 39, no. 4; Fruhlingsfeier, op. 56, no. 5; Lieder der Ophelia, op. 67; Schlechtes Wetter, op. 69, no. 5; Standchen, op. 17, no. 2. See no. 3047

Songs: Begegnung; Breit uber mein Haupt, op. 19, no. 2; Die erwachte Rose; Du meines Herzens Kronelein, op. 21, no. 2; Meinem Kinde, op. 37, no. 3; Schon sind doch kalt, op. 19, no. 3; Sie wissen's nicht, op. 49, no. 5; Die Verschwiegenen, op. 10, no. 6; Zueignung, op. 10, no. 1. See no. 2440

Songs: Du meines Herzens Kronelein, op. 21, no. 2. See no. 4043

Songs: Freundliche Vision, op. 48, no. 1; Ich trage meine Minne, op. 32, no. 1; Morgen, op. 27, no. 4; Standchen, op. 17, no. 2; Traum durch die Dammerung, op. 29, no. 1; Zueignung, op. 10, no. 1. See no. 3988

Songs: Hat gesagt bleibt's nich dabei, op. 36, no. 3; Schlechtes Wetter, op. 69, no. 5. See no. 3844

Songs: Liebeshymnus, op. 32, no. 3; Verfuhrung, op. 33, no. 1; Waldseligkeit, op. 49, no. 1; Winterliebe, op. 48, no. 4. See no. 2107

Songs: Liebeshymnus, op. 32, no. 3; Waldseligkeit, op. 49, no. 1; Verfuhrung, op. 33, no. 1; Winterliebe, op. 48, no. 5. See no. 3216

Songs: Morgen, op. 27, no. 4; Du meines Herzens Kronelein, op. 21, no. 2; Allerseelen, op. 10, no. 8. See no. 3967

Songs: Morgen, op. 27, no. 4; Standchen, op. 17, no. 2. See no. 3823

Songs: Morgen, op. 27, no. 4; Standchen, op. 17, no. 2; Traum durch die Dammerung, op. 29, no. 1; Verfuhrung, op. 33, no. 1; Waldseligkeit, op. 49, no. 1. See no. 2921

Songs: Ophelia Lieder, op. 67, nos. 1-3. See no. 3698

Songs: Standchen, op. 17, no. 2. See no. 4076

Songs: Weihnachtsegefuhl. See no. 3702

Suite, op. 4, B flat major. See no. 3215

Symphony, wind instruments (1945). See no. 3215

Die Tageszeiten, op. 76. See no. 3192
Till Eulenspiegels lustige Streiche, op. 28. See no. 1390. See no. 3193. See no. 3194. See no. 3197. See no. 3198. See no. 3781. See no. 3791
Tod und Verklarung, op. 24. See no. 2131. See no. 3193. See no. 3194. See no. 3197
Vier letzte Lieder, op. posth. See no. 3187. See no. 3192. See no. 3196. See no. 3684
Vier letzte Lieder, op. posth.: Beim Schlafengehen. See no. 3713
3220 Works, selections: Fanfare. Fanfare fur die Wiener Philharmoniker. Feierlicher Einzug der Titter des Johanniterordens. Festmusik der Stadt Wien (original version). Olympische hymne. Parade marches, nos. 1 and 2 (arr. Locke). Locke Brass Consort; James Stobart. Chandos ABR 1002 Tape (c) ABT 1002
++FF 1/2-81 p195 +Gr 8-80 p275 tape
+Gr 2-80 p1270 +RR 2-80 p61

STRAVINSKY, Igor
Agon. See no. 733
3221 Apollon musagete. Orpheus. St. John's Orchestra; John Lubbock. ASV ACM 2025 Tape (c) ZCAC 2025 (From Enigma K 53585)
+Gr 9-81 p394 +HFN 9-81 p89
+Gr 11-81 p783 tape
Apollon musagete. See no. 429
3222 Apollon musagete: Ballet suite. Pulcinella: Ballet suite. ECO; Charles Dutoit. Musical Heritage Society MHS 4270
-FF 11/12-81 p255
Chant du rossignol. See no. 2619
Les cinq doigts. See no. 3238
3223 Concerto, piano and wind instruments. Serenade, A major. Sonata, piano, C major. Zdenek Kozina, pno; Dvorak Chamber Orchestra; Vladimir Valek. Supraphon 110 2419
++FF 3/4-81 p204 +HFN 10-80 p109
+-Gr 10-80 p504 +NR 9-80 p5
Concerto, piano and wind instruments. See no. 2929
Concerto, 2 pianos. See no. 448
Concerto, 2 solo pianos. See no. 448
Concerto, violin, D major. See no. 736
3224 Concerto, 16 instruments, E flat major. Danses concertantes. Ragtime. Tango. London Sinfonietta; Riccardo Chailly. Dischi Ricordi RCL 27037
+FF 11/12-81 p255 +RR 7-80 p68
+-Gr 7-80 p147 ++SFC 11-1-81 p18
Danses concertantes. See no. 3224
Divertimento. See no. 1490
Duo concertante. See no. 3954
Etudes, op. 7. See no. 3238. See no. 3321
3225 L'Histoire du soldat (English version by Michael Flanders and Kitty Black). John Gielgud, narrator; Tom Courtenay, soldier; Ron Moody, the devil; Boston Symphony Chamber Players. DG 2535 456 Tape (c) 3335 456 (From 2530 609)
+Gr 10-81 p574 ++HFN 8-81 p92 tape
L'Histoire du soldat. See no. 1852
Jeux de cartes. See no. 2845
Movements, piano and orchestra. See no. 2929
3226 Oedipus Rex. Martha Modl, ms; Peter Pears, Helmut Krebs, t; Heinz

Rehfuss, bar; Otto von Rohr, bs; Jean Cocteau, narrator; Cologne Radio Orchestra and Chorus; Igor Stravinsky. CBS 61131 (From Philips ABL 3054)
+Gr 8-81 p315

3227 L'Oiseau de feu. NYP; Pierre Boulez. CBS HM 43508, M 33508
+SFC 12-20-81 p18

3228 L'Oiseau de feu. NPhO; Ernest Ansermet. Contour CC 7500 Tape (c) CCT 7500
+Gr 8-81 p316 ++HFN 8-81 p91

3229 L'Oiseau de feu. VPO; Christoph von Dohnanyi. Decca SXDL 7511 Tape (c) KSXDC 7511 (also London LDR 10012 Tape (c) LDR 5-10012)
+FF 5/6-81 p159 +HFN 11-80 p123
+-Gr 11-80 p678 +-NYT 7-19-81 pD23
+-Gr 2-81 p1122 tape +St 6-81 p72

L'Oiseau de feu. See no. 857

L'Oiseau de feu: Dance of the firebird; Scherzo; Infernal dance. See no. 4122

L'Oiseau de feu: Danse infernale. See no. 3709

L'Oiseau de feu: Finale. See no. 4003

3230 L'Oiseau de feu: Suite. Petrouchka. NYP; Leonard Bernstein. CBS MY 37221
+-FF 11/12-81 p106

3231 L'Oiseau de feu: Suite. Symphony in 3 movements. Dallas Symphony Orchestra; Eduardo Mata. RCA ARC 1-3459 Tape (c) ARK 1-3459
+-ARG 7/8-80 p41 +-HFN 7-80 p110
+-FF 7/8-80 p135 +NR 5-80 p3
+Gr 7-80 p148 +RR 7-80 p68
+HF 8-80 p79 +St 7-80 p84
+-HF 3-81 p80 tape

L'Oiseau de feu: Suite. See no. 2021

Orpheus. See no. 3221

3232 Petrouchka. PROKOFIEV: Love for three oranges, op. 33: Suite. Minnesota Orchestra; Stanislaw Skrowaczewski. Candide QCE 31103 DBX SS 3006
+Audio 12-81 p67 +NR 12-78 p6
++FF 3/4-79 p120 +St 5-79 p110
+HF 12-80 p42

3233 Petrouchka. NYP; Zubin Mehta. CBS IM 35823 DGTM 6001 Tape (c) HMT 35823, 40-35823
+-ARG 2-81 p32 ++HFN 12-80 p146
++FF 11/12-80 p181 +HFN 4-81 p83 tape
+Gr 12-80 p841 /-MUM 2-81 p35
+Gr 1-81 p1001 tape ++SFC 8-17-80 p36
+-HF 9-80 p78 ++St 12-80 p118
+HF 10-80 p98 tape

3234 Petrouchka (1947 version). Detroit Symphony Orchestra; Antal Dorati. Decca SXDL 7521 Tape (c) KSXDC 7521 (also London LDR 71023)
+Gr 10-81 p564 ++SFC 11-1-81 p18
++HFN 11-81 p96

3235 Petrouchka (1911 version). Leslie Howard, pno; LSO; Claudio Abbado. DG 2532 010 Tape (c) 3302 010
+Gr 11-81 p694 +HFN 12-81 p112 tape
++HFN 11-81 p97

3236 Petrouchka (1911 version). LPO; Bernard Haitink. Philips FH 27

+FF 7/8-81 p178

3237 Petrouchka (1911 version). LSO; Charles Mackerras. Vanguard VSD 7117 Tape (c) ZCVSM 7117 (r) CA 47177 (Q) VSQ 30021 Tape (r) VSS 23 (also VCS 10113)
+-Gr 2-74 p1566 ++NR 2-77 p2
+-HF 8-73 p104 ++RR 11-73 p53
+HF 5-76 p114 Quad tape +-RR 2-75 p76
+HF 5-81 p53 tape ++St 6-73 p123

Petrouchka. See no. 2330

Petrouchka: Movements (3). See no. 2753. See no. 3238. See no. 3785

Piano rag music. See no. 2753. See no. 3238

3238 Piano works: Les cinq doigts. Etudes, op. 7 (4). Petrouchka: Movements (3) (trans. composer). Piano rag music. Scherzo. Sonatas, piano, nos. 1 and 2. Serenade, A major. Souvenir d'une marche boche. Tango. Valse pour les enfants. Michel Beroff, pno. Pathe Marconi 2C 069 73031/2 (2)
+-Gr 1-81 p970 +-HFN 2-81 p94

Pieces, solo clarinet (3). See no. 3793

Pieces, string quartet (3). See no. 422. See no. 3089

Pieces faciles (3). See no. 3243

Pieces faciles (5). See no. 3243

Pulcinella: Ballet suite. See no. 3222

Ragtime. See no. 3224

3239 Le sacre du printemps. National Youth Orchestra; Simon Rattle. ASV ACM 2030 Tape (c) ZCACM 2030 (From Enigma MID 5001)
+Gr 9-81 p394 +-HFN 10-81 p95

3240 Le sacre du printemps. Dag Achatz, pno. BIS LP 188
+-NYT 12-6-81 pD27

3241 Le sacre du printemps. PROKOFIEV: Romeo and Juliet, op. 64: Suite, no. 2. Minnesota Orchestra; Stanislaw Skrowaczewski. Candide QCE 31108
+-FF 3/4-81 p207 +HF 8-80 p81
+-FU 2-80 p51

3242 Le sacre du printemps. CO; Pierre Boulez. CBS HM 47293
+-FF 7/8-81 p178 +NYT 7-19-81 pD23
+MUM 9/10-81 p34 +SFC 4-5-81 p18

3243 Le sacre du printemps (arr. Stravinsky). Pieces faciles (3). Pieces faciles (5). Bracha Eden, Alxander Tamir, pno. London STS 15531 (From CS 6626)
+-FF 3/4-81 p205 -HF 4-81 p86

3244 Le sacre du printemps. LSO; Colin Davis. Philips 6539 012
-MUM 9/10-81 p34

3245 Le sacre du printemps. BSO; Seiji Ozawa. Philips 9500 781 Tape (c) 7300 855
/FF 7/8-81 p179 +NR 5-81 p5
+Gr 12-80 p841 +NYT 7-19-81 pD23
+-HFN 12-80 p146 +SFC 2-1-81 p18
+-MUM 9/10-81 p34

3246 Le sacre du printemps (trans. Raphling). Dickran Atamian, pno. RCA ARC 1-3636 Tape (c) ARK 1-3636
+-ARG 2-81 p31 +NR 11-80 p10
+Audio 5-81 p62 +NYT 10-19-80 pD24
+-FF 3/4-81 p204 +OV 12-81 p42
+HF 3-81 p80 tape -SFC 11-30-80 p21
+HF 4-81 p86

3247 Le sacre du printemps. BSO; Pierre Monteux. RCA Musique GM 4-3274 (From LM 1149)
+FF 5/6-81 p159 ++NYT 7-19-81 pD23
3248 Le sacre du printemps. CO; Lorin Maazel. Telarc DG 10054
++FF 3/4-81 p181 +-NYT 7-19-81 pD23
+-Gr 4-81 p1324 +OV 12-81 p42
+-HF 4-81 p86 ++SFC 11-30-80 p21
+-HFN 6-81 p78 +SR 1-81 p92
+MUM 9/10-81 p34 ++St 1-81 p86
++NR 3-81 p4
Scherzo. See no. 3238
Serenade, A major. See no. 3223. See no. 3238
Sonata, piano, C major. See no. 3223
Sonatas, piano, nos. 1 and 2. See no. 3238
Souvenir d'une marche boche. See no. 3238
Suites, nos. 1 and 2. See no. 3998
Suite italienne. See no. 3704
Symphony in 3 movements. See no. 3231
Symphony of psalms. See no. 260
Tango. See no. 3224. See no. 3238
Valse pour les enfants. See no. 3238
STRICKLAND, William
3249 An electronic visit to the zoo. Sound hypnosis. Moog Synthesizer. Spectrum SR 118
+-FF 3/4-81 p30
Sound hypnosis. See no. 3249
STUNTZ, Josef
Agnus Dei. See no. 3908
STURMS, Arnolds
3250 Little suite, piano. Sonatas, piano, nos. 2, 3. Sonata da chiesa. David Volckhausen, pno. Desto DC 7202
+-FF 5/6-81 p160
Sonatas, piano, nos. 2, 3. See no. 3250
Sonata da chiesa. See no. 3250
SUBOTNIK, Morton
3251 After the butterfly. A sky of cloudless sulphur. Mario Gaurneri, tpt; Twentieth Century Players; Morton Subotnik. Nonesuch N 78001
+-ARG 4-81 p33 +FF 11/12-80 p181
+CMJ Winter 1981 p81 +HF 11-80 p80
A sky of cloudless sulphur. See no. 3251
SUDERBURG, Robert
Concerto (Voyage de nuit d'apres Baudelaire). See no. 1022
SUK, Josef
3252 Fairy tale (Pohadka), op. 16. Fantastic scherzo, op. 25. PSO; Josef Suk, vln; Jiri Belohlavek. Supraphon 410 2699
+Gr 11-81 p701 +HFN 12-81 p103
Fantastic scherzo, op. 25. See no. 3252
Pieces, violin and piano, op. 17 (4). See no. 85. See no. 3841
Quartet, strings, no. 1, op. 11, B flat major. See no. 3140
SULLIVAN, Arthur
3253 The gondoliers (without dialogue). Mavis Bennett, Winifred Lawson, Sybil Gordon, Beatrice Elburn, s; Doris Hemingway, ms; Bertha Lewis, Gwladys Gowrie, con; Arthur Hosking, Derek Oldham, Herbert Aitken, t; Henry Lytton, Leo Sheffield, George Baker,

Richard Walker, bar; Ronald Stear, bs; Orchestra and Chorus; Harry Norris. Pearl GEM 141/2 (From HMV D 1334-45) (also Arabesque 8058)

+ARG 6-78 p14
+ARG 4-81 p35
+FF 9/10-78 p52
+FF 3/4-81 p119
+Gr 5-78 p1953
+NR 2-81 p12
+-RR 4-78 p39

The gondoliers: Take a pair of sparkling eyes. See no. 3972

3254 H.M.S. Pinafore. Trial by jury. Winifred Lawson, Elsie Griffin, s; Nellie Briercliffe, ms; Bertha Lewis, con; Derek Oldham, Charles Goulding, t; Arthur Hosking, George Baker, Henry Lytton, bar; Leo Sheffield, Sydney Granville, bs-bar; Darrell Fancourt, Stuart Robertson, bs; Orchestra and Chorus; Harry Norris, Malcolm Sargent. Arabesque 8052-2L (2) Tape (c) 9052-2L (From HMV originals)

+ARG 4-81 p35
+-HF 5-80 p68
+NYT 1-6-80 pD18

3255 H.M.S. Pinafore. Trial by jury. Violet Essex, Bessie Jones, Pamela Baselow, Winifred Lawson, s; Bertha Lewis, Nellie Walker, con; James Hay, Walter Glynne. Arthur Hosking, Derek Oldham, t; Frederic Ranalow, Sydney Granville, Leo Sheffield, George Baker, bar; Darrell Fancourt, Frederick Hobbs, Edward Halland, T. Penry Hughes, bs; Orchestra and Chorus. Pearl GEMM 148/9 (2) (From HMV D 724/31, D 1469/72)

+ARG 8-79 p28
+ARG 4-81 p35
+Gr 11-78 p974
+HFN 11-78 p177
-RR 10-78 p50

3256 Iolanthe. Nellie Briercliffe; Nellie Walker, con; Winifred Lawson, s; Bertha Lewis, con; George Baker, Derek Oldham, Sydney Granville, bar; Darrell Fancourt, Leslie Rands, bs; D'Oyly Carte Opera Orchestra and Chorus; Malcolm Sargent. Arabesque 8066/2 (2)

+ARG 4-81 p35
+-FF 3/4-81 p119
+NR 12-80 p9

3257 Iolanthe (without dialogue). Trial by jury. Nellie Briercliffe, Alice Moxon, Winifred Lawson, Beatrice Elburn, s; Nellie Walker, Bertha Lewis, con; Derek Oldham, t; George Baker, Leslie Rands, Arthur Hosking, bar; Sydney Granville, Leo Sheffield, bs; Orchestra and Chorus; L'Oyly Carte Opera Chorus; Harry Norris. World Records SHB 64 (2) (From HMV D 1785/95)

+ARG 4-81 p35
+-ARSC Vol 12, no. 1-2 1980, p108
+-FF 3/4-81 p119
+Gr 4-80 p1596
+-HFN 5-80 p125
++RR 4-80 p50

The light of the world: God shall wipe away all tears. See no. 3650

3258 The Mikado. Brenda Bennett, Marjorie Eyre, Elizabeth Nickell-Lean, s; Josephine Curtis; Radley Flynn, bar; Darrell Fancourt, bs; Derek Oldham, Martyn Green, Sydney Granville, bar; Leslie Rands, bs; D'Oyly Carte Orchestra and Chorus; Isidore Godfrey. Arabesque 8051/2 (2)

+ARG 4-81 p35
+FF 3/4-81 p120
+NR 10-80 p12

3259 The Mikado. Elsa Sinclair, Maude Perry, s; Ada Florence, con; Walter Hyde, t; Harry Thornton, bs; Harry Dearth, Walter Passmore; D'Oyly Carte Company. Pearl GEMM 198

+-Gr 1-81 p994 +HFN 1-81 p101

3260 Pineapple poll (arr. Mackerras). RPO; Charles Mackerras. Arabesque 8016
++FF 1/2-81 p197

3261 The pirates of Penzance. The sorcerer, abridged. Soloists; D'Oyly Carte Opera Company; Malcolm Sargent, Isidore Godfrey. Arabesque 8068 (2)
+NR 8-81 p11 +ON 8-81 p36
+NYT 5-17-81 pD37

3262 The pirates of Penzance. Linda Ronstadt, Alexandra Korey, Marcie Shaw, Wendy Wolfe, Estelle Parsons, Rex Smith, George Rose, Stephen Hanan, Tony Azito, Kevin Kline, soloists; New York Shakespeare Festival Ensemble; William Elliott, arr. and cond. Elektra VE 601 Tape (c) VC 601
-HF 9-81 p51 -NYT 5-17-81 pD37

3263 The pirates of Penzance (without dialogue). Elsie Griffin, Nellie Briercliffe, s; Nellie Walker, Dorothy Gill, con; Derek Oldham, t; George Baker, Stuart Robertson, bar; Peter Dawson, bs-bar; Leo Sheffield, bs; Orchestra and Chorus; Malcolm Sargent. Pearl GEMM 171/2 (2) (From HMV D 1678/8)
+ARG 4-81 p35 +-HFN 6-80 p112
+Gr 4-80 p1596 +-RR 5-80 p49

Songs: Onward Christian soldiers. See no. 3700
Songs: The lost chord; Onward Christian soldiers. See no. 3967
The sorcerer, abridged. See no. 3261
Trial by jury. See no. 3254. See no. 3255. See no. 3257
Victoria and merrie England: Suite, no. 1. See no. 3264

3264 The yeomen of the guard. Victoria and merrie England: Suite, no. 1. Barbara Lilley, Jane Metcalfe, s; Patricia Leonard, Suzanne O'Keefe, ms; Geoffrey Shovelton, Meston Reid, Barry Clark, t; Michael Rayner, John Ayldon, John Reed, Kenneth Sandford, Gareth Jones, bar; D'Oyly Carte Opera Chorus; RPO; Royston Nash. Decca SKL 5307/8 (2) Tape (c) K157K22 (also London OSA 12117 Tape (c) OSA 5-12117)
+-ARG 4-81 p35 +-Gr 11-79 p921
+-FF 3/4-81 p120 +St 11-80 p87

SULLIVAN, Timothy
Luckeystone. See no. 1554
Numbers, names. See no. 873

SUMNER, John
Child of the king. See no. 4100

SUPPE, Franz von
Boccaccio, excerpts. See no. 3975
Boccaccio: Overture. See no. 3265
Light cavalry: Overture. See no. 3265
Morning, noon and night: Overture. See no. 3265

3265 Overtures: Boccaccio. Light cavalry. Morning, noon and night. Pique dame. Poet and peasant. Die schone Galatea. LPO; Alexander Cameron, vlc; Neville Marriner. Philips 9500 399 Tape (c) 7300 612 (r) 9500 399
++FF 5/6-79 p93 ++NR 10-79 p1
+Gr 5-78 p1949 ++RR 5-78 p39
+HF 6-81 p70 tape ++SFC 10-22-78 p53
+HFN 5-78 p143 ++St 2-79 p136
+-MJ 12-78 p45

Pique Dame: Overture. See no. 3265
Poet and peasant: Overture. See no. 3265. See no. 3726. See no. 4000
3266 Die schone Galatea. Anna Moffo, s; Rose Wagemann, ms; Rene Kollo, Ferry Gruber, t; Bavarian Radio Chorus; Munich Radio Orchestra; Kurt Eichhorn. RCA RL 2-5108 (also Eurodisc 87583)
+FF 11/12-81 p256 +HFN 4-78 p124
+-Gr 2-78 p1478 +-RR 2-78 p34
Die schone Galatea: Overture. See no. 3265
SURINACH, Carlos
Ritmo jondo. See no. 3817
SUSATO, Tielman
Dances (3). See no. 4002
La Mourisque. See no. 3853
Pavane la bataille. See no. 3853
SUSSMAYR, Franz
Das Namensfest. See no. 2565
SUTERMEISTER, Heinrich
Romeo and Juliet: Balcony scene. See no. 3989
SVENDSEN, Johan
3267 Andante funebre. Carnival in Paris, op. 9. Icelandic melodies (2). Polonaise, no. 2, op. 28. Romance, op. 26, G major. Ornulf Boye Hansen, vln; Oslo Philharmonic Orchestra; Kjell Ingebretsen, Oivin Fjeldstad. Norsk Kulturrads NFK 30028
+FF 5/6-81 p161 +Gr 1-80 p1167
+-FF 5/6-79 p93 +Gr 9-80 p408
Carnival in Paris, op. 9. See no. 3267
3268 Concerto, violin, op. 6, A major. Concerto, violoncello, op. 7, D major. Arve Tellefsen, vln; Hege Waldeland, vlc; Oslo Philharmonic Orchestra, Bergen Symphony Orchestra; Karsten Andersen. NKF 30002
+FF 5/6-81 p160 +Gr 9-80 p408
+Gr 3-77 p1457 +HFN 3-77 p109
+-Gr 1-80 p1167 +RR 1-77 p64
Concerto, violoncello, op. 7, D major. See no. 3268
Icelandic melodies. See no. 3267
3269 Norwegian rhapsodies, nos. 1-4. Bergen Symphony Orchestra; Karsten Andersen. NKF 30006
+FF 5/6-81 p161 +HFN 3-77 p109
+Gr 3-77 p1457 +-HFN 7-80 p110
+Gr 9-80 p408 +RR 1-77 p64
Polonaise, no. 2, op. 28. See no. 3267
Romance, op. 26, G major. See no. 3267
SWEELINCK, Jan
Da pacem Domine in diebus nostris. See no. 3270
Fantasia, D minor. See no. 309
Fantasia, no. 4, D major. See no. 3270
Fantasia, no. 5. See no. 3270
Fantasia, no. 12, A minor. See no. 3270
Fantasia en echo. See no. 3786
Malle symen. See no. 3832
Motets: De profundis. See no. 3906
3270 Organ works: Da pacem Domine in diebus nostris. Fantasia, no. 12, A minor. Fantasia, no. 4, D major. Fantasia, no. 5. Puer nobis nascitur. Toccata, no. 17, A minor. Gustav Leonhardt,

org. Harmonia Mundi 065 99608
+Gr 9-80 p379 ++RR 8-80 p75
+-HFN 1-81 p105
Pavana lachrimae. See no. 184
Praeludium toccata. See no. 4090
Puer nobis nascitur. See no. 3270
Rimes francoises et italiennes a deux parties. See no. 3949
Toccata no. 17, A minor. See no. 3270
Under der Linden grune. See no. 4111
Variations on "Allein Gott in der Hoh sei Ehr". See no. 184
Von der fortuna werd' ich getrieben. See no. 4088

SYMONDS, Norman
A diversion. See no. 3898

SZARZYNSKI, Stanislav
Sonata, 2 violins, D major. See no. 3978

SZERVANSZKY
Songs: The river has overflown. See no. 380

SZOKOLAY, Sandor
Playing with intervals. See no. 1384

SZYMANOWSKI, Karol
Berceuse, op. 52. See no. 3276

3271 Concerto, violin, no. 1, op. 35. Concerto, violin, no. 2, op. 61. Konstanty Kulka, vln; Polish Radio Orchestra; Jerzy Maksymiuk. EMI 1C 065 03597
+Gr 11-81 p701

Concerto, violin, no. 1, op. 35. See no. 2351
Concerto, violin, no. 2, op. 61. See no. 3271

3272 Etude, op. 4, no. 3, B flat minor. Masques, op. 34 (ed. Feder). Sonata, piano, no. 3, op. 36 (rev. Feder). Valse romantique. Donn-Alexandre Feder, pno. Protone PR 149
+-ARG 7/8-81 p37 +NR 11-80 p10
+FF 11/12-80 p183 +-St 11-81 p94

Harnasie, op. 51: Dance. See no. 3276
King Roger: Roxanna's song. See no. 1543
Masques, op. 34. See no. 3272

3273 Mythes, op. 30. Quartet, strings, op. 56, no. 2. Wilanow Quartet; Konstanty Kulka, vln; J. Marchwinski, pno. Aurora AUR 7004
+Gr 1-80 p1168 +MT 2-81 p113
+-HFN 12-79 p177 +-RR 12-79 p90

Mythes, op. 30. See no. 1543
Notturno e tarantella, op. 28. See no. 3276
Quartet, strings, no. 2. See no. 2089. See no. 3273
Romance, op. 23. See no. 3276
Sonata, piano, no. 3, op. 36. See no. 3272
Sonata, violin, op. 9, D minor. See no. 3276

3274 Symphony, no. 2, op. 19, B flat major. Symphony, no. 3, op. 27. Ryszard Karczykowski, t; Kenneth Jewell Chorale; Detroit Symphony Orchestra; Antal Dorati. London LDR 71026 (also Decca SXDL 7524 Tape (c) KSXDC 7524)
+FF 9/10-81 p183 ++NYT 9-20-81 pD29
+Gr 7-81 p162 +SFC 6-7-81 p19
+Gr 10-81 p614 tape ++St 12-81 p128
+HFN 7-81 p76 +STL 7-12-81 p40
+NR 8-81 p4

3275 Symphony, no. 3, op. 27. Stabat mater, op. 53. Warsaw Philharmonic Orchestra and Chorus; Witold Rowicki. Aurora AUR 7003 (From Muza XLO 149)
+Gr 1-80 p1193 +MT 2-81 p113
+-HFN 12-79 p177 +-RR 12-79 p116
Symphony, no. 3, op. 27. See no. 3274
Stabat mater, op. 53. See no. 3275
Valse romantique. See no. 3272
Variations on a Polish folk tune, op. 10. See no. 1075
3276 Works, selections: Berceuse, op. 52. Harnasie, op. 51: Dance. Notturno e tarantella, op. 28. Romance, op. 23. Sonata, violin, op. 9, D minor. Wanda Wilkomirska, vln; Tadeusz Chmielewski, pno. Connoisseur Society Tape (c) InSync 4059
+Audio 5-81 p58 tape +St 4-81 p110 tape
+HF 4-81 p93 tape

TACKETT, Fred
The yellow bird. See no. 1974

TAFFANEL, Claude
Fantasy on "Der Freischutz". See no. 3682

TAGLIAFERRI, E.
Songs: Piscatore e pusilecco. See no. 3641. See no. 3843

TAILLEFERRE, Germaine
Ballade. See no. 61
Partita, perpetuum mobile. See no. 3918
Pastorale. See no. 3884
Quatuor. See no. 3814
Songs: Chansons francaises. See no. 3687

TAKEMITSU, Toru
3277 A flock descends into the pentagonal garden. Quatrain. Tashi, BSO; Seiji Ozawa. DG 2531 210
+FF 1/2-81 p198 +MUM 3/4-81 p34
+Gr 8-80 p230 ++NR 12-80 p3
++HF 3-81 p56 ++ST 5-81 p43
Quatrain. See no. 3277
3278 Quatrain II. Water ways. Waves. Tashi. RCA ARL 1-3843 Tape (c) 1-3843
+ARG 1-81 p40 +NR 10-80 p6
++FF 11/12-80 p184 +SFC 9-28-80 p21
++HF 3-81 p56 ++St 11-80 p102
+-MUM 3/4-81 p34
Water ways. See no. 3278
Waves. See no. 3278

TAKI
Kohmoh no Tsuki. See no. 3696

TALLIS, Thomas
Antiphons: Clarifica me pater i, ii and iii. See no. 3083
In jejunio et fletu. See no. 3620
Lamentations of Jeremiah. See no. 3691
Mass, 4 voices. See no. 3078
O ye tenderest babes. See no. 3734
3279 Puer natus est, mass. Motets: Salvator mundi; Suscipe quaeso domine. Clerkes of Oxenford; David Wulstan. Nonesuch H 71378 (also Calliope CAL 1623)
+ARG 12-80 p46 +Gr 1-81 p982
++FF 9/10-80 p213 +-NYT 8-10-80 pD17

+FU 6-80 p50 +St 10-80 p122
++Gr 2-79 p1454

Salve intemerata Virgo, mass. See no. 3083
Songs: If ye love me. See no. 3634
Songs: O nata lux. See no. 3685
Songs (motets): Salvator mundi. See no. 1245
Songs (motets): Salvator mundi; Suscipe quaeso domine. See no. 3279
Songs: Veni redemptor. See no. 3625

TALMA, Louise
Sonata, piano, no. 1. See no. 3918

TANEYEV, Sergei
3280 The Oresteia (The temple of Apollo in Delphi). Nelly Tkachenko, Lyudmila Ganestova, Tamara Shimko, s; Lidiya Galushkina, con; Ivan Dubrovin, t; Anatoly Bokov, Arkady Savchenko, bar; Victor Chernobayev, bs; Belorussian State Opera and Ballet Theatre Orchestra and Chorus; Tatyana Kolomyzeva. DG 2709 097 (3)
+-ARG 6-80 p29 +NYT 12-16-79 pD21
+Gr 11-79 p911 +-ON 3-14-81 p44
+HF 5-80 p83 +-Op 4-80 p375
+HFN 11-79 p143 ++RR 11-79 p61
+MT 2-80 p109 +-St 4-80 p139
+NR 3-80 p12

Prelude and fugue, op. 29, G sharp minor. See no. 2633
3281 Quartet, strings, no. 8, C major. Taneyev Quartet. Melodiya S10 12411
+FF 9/10-81 p184
3282 Quartet, strings, no. 9, A major. Taneyev Quartet. Melodiya S10 12333
+FF 9/10-81 p184
3283 Symphony, no. 4, op. 12, C minor. LSO; Yuri Ahronovitch. Arabesque 8074 Tape (c) 8074 (From RCA RL 3-0372)
+ARG 2-81 p33 /NR 2-81 p3
+FF 3/4-81 p208

TANG, Jordan Cho-Tung
A little suite. See no. 3815

TANNER, Jerre, Leon Siu and Malia Elliott
3284 Boy with goldfish. Leon Siu, singer and gtr; Malia Elliott, singer; Timothy Farrell, org; Nigel Brooks Chorale; LSO; Lee Holdridge. Varese VCDM 1000 30 (also PS 1010)
+*FF 5/6-81 p161 +-HF 2-81 p72

TANSMAN, Alexandre
Berceuse d'Orient. See no. 3870
Cavatina. See no. 3870
Sonatina, bassoon and piano. See no. 2605

TARREGA, Francisco
Alborada. See no. 3727
Capricho arabe. See no. 3701. See no. 3727. See no. 3795
Estudio brillante. See no. 3765
Etude (Dream). See no. 3694
Gran jota. See no. 3701. See no. 3795
Grand waltz. See no. 3694
Introduction and fantasia on themes from "La traviata". See no. 3886
Maria. See no. 3795

Recuerdos de la Alhambra. See no. 3765
Sueno. See no. 3701. See no. 3795
Two little sisters. See no. 3694
Variations on the theme "Carnival in Venice". See no. 3694
Waltz. See no. 3694

TARTINI, Giuseppe
Concertino. See no. 3714
Concerto, flute, F major. See no. 4008
3285 Concerti, flute, nos. 1-4. Jean-Pierre Rampal, flt; I Solisti Veneti; Claudio Scimone. Musical Heritage Society MHS 3761 (also CBS M 36688)
+FF 1/2-79 p110 +NR 7-81 p4
+FF 9/10-81 p185
Concerto, trumpet, D major. See no. 33
Concerto, violoncello, A major. See no. 816
3286 Sonatas, violin and piano, G minor, A minor, A major; op. 1, no. 10, G minor. Roberto Michelucci, vln; Franz Walter, vlc; Marjke Smit Sibinga, hpd. Philips 9502 099
+Gr 7-81 p168 +HFN 7-81 p81
Sonata, violin and piano, no. 10, G minor. See no. 1735. See no. 3286. See no. 4106
Variations on a theme by Corelli. See no. 3704. See no. 3841

TAUSINGER, Jan
Au dernier amour. See no. 803
Nonet of Hukvaldy. See no. 1674

TAVERNER, John
Dum transisset Sabbatum. See no. 3685
In nomine. See no. 4092

TAYLOR, Silas
Pavan and galliard. See no. 3622. See no. 4012

TCHAIKOVSKY, Peter
3287 Capriccio italien, op. 45. Eugene Onegin, op. 24: Polonaise. Overture, the year 1812, op. 49. H.M. Royal Marines Band, Bournemouth Symphony Orchestra; Constantin Silvestri. EMI 1C 037 04538
+-FF 11/12-81 p257
3288 Capriccio italien, op. 45. The nutcracker, op. 71: Suite. Eugene Onegin, op. 24: Waltz and polonaise. LPO; Leopold Stokowski. Philips 6527 079 Tape (c) 7311 079 (From 6500 766)
+Gr 4-81 p1378 +-HFN 7-81 p83 tape
+-HFN 4-81 p80
3289 Capriccio italien, op. 45. Mazeppa: Cossack dance. Overture, the year 1812, op. 49. Cincinnati Symphony Orchestra; Erich Kunzel. Telard DG 10041
-ARG 5-80 p40 +-NR 10-80 p2
+Audio 7-81 p62 +RR 4-80 p82
+FF 3/4-80 p164 +SFC 12-7-80 p33
+Gr 4-80 p1597 +St 1-80 p96
+-HFN 4-80 p111
Capriccio italien, op. 45. See no. 2792. See no. 2793. See no. 2795
3290 Concerto, piano, no. 1, op. 23, B flat minor. BACH, J.S.: Das wohltemperierte Klavier, Bk I: Prelude, B minor (arr. Siloti). Emil Gilels, pno; NYP; Zubin Mehta. CBS IM 36660 Tape (c) HMT 36660

+FF 5/6-81 p162
+Gr 5-81 p1480
+-HFN 5-81 p84
++SFC 1-4-81 p18
++St 5-81 p82

3291 Concerto, piano, no. 1, op. 23, B flat minor. Andre Gavrilov, pno; Moscow Radio and Television Orchestra; Dimitri Kitaenko. CBS M 36693

-FF 7/8-81 p179

3292 Concerto, piano, no. 1, op. 23, B flat minor. Variations on a rococo theme, op. 33. Myung-Whun Chung, pno; Myung-Wha Chung, vlc; LAPO; Charles Dutoit. Decca SXL 6955

+Gr 3-81 p1206
+HFN 3-81 p91

3293 Concerto, piano, no. 1, op. 23, B flat minor. Hans Lang, pno; North German Philharmonic Orchestra; Hans Zanotelli. Intercord INT 120838

-HFN 12-81 p104

3294 Concerto, piano, no. 1, op. 23, B flat minor. Van Cliburn, pno; Symphony Orchestra; Kyril Kondrashin. RCA ATL 1-4099

++SFC 10-4-81 p17

Concerto, piano, no. 1, op. 23, B flat minor. See no. 1546. See no. 4017

3295 Concerto, violin, op. 35, D major. Serenade melancolique, op. 26, B minor. Gidon Kremer, vln; BPhO; Lorin Maazel. DG 2532 001 Tape (c) 3302 001

+ARG 9-81 p35
-FF 3/4-81 p208
++FF 9/10-81 p186
+Gr 12-80 p841
+Gr 2-81 p1122 tape
+HF 2-81 p72
+HFN 12-80 p146
+HFN 1-81 p109 tape
++MUM 9/10-81 p37 tape
++NR 5-81 p4
++SFC 3-1-81 p19
+St 4-81 p114
+ST 3-81 p820

3296 Concerto, violin, op. 35, D major. Arthur Grumiaux, vln; COA; Bernard Haitink. Philips 6527 067 Tape (c) 7311 067 (From SABL 176)

+-FF 11/12-81 p256
+Gr 8-81 p278

3297 Concerto, violin, op. 35, D major. Serenade melancolique, op. 26, B flat minor. Shizuka Ishikawa, vln; CPhO; Zdenek Kosler. Supraphon 110 2460

+FF 1/2-81 p199
+HF 2-81 p72
++NR 12-80 p5

Concerto, violin, op. 35, D major. See no. 896. See no. 900. See no. 1405. See no. 1408. See no. 2202. See no. 2203

Coronation march. See no. 3976

3298 Eugene Onegin, op. 24. Galina Vishnevskaya, s; Tamara Sinyavskaya, alto; Vladimir Atlantov, t; Yuri Mazurok, bar; Alexander Ognivtsev, bs; Bolshoi Opera Orchestra and Chorus; Mstislav Rostropovich. Musical Heritage Society MHS 834278 (3) (also Melodiya Angel)

+ARG 7/8-81 p48
-FF 5/6-81 p163

Eugene Onegin, op. 24: Faint echo of my youth. See no. 1363. See no. 3648

Eugene Onegin, op. 24: Gremin's aria. See no. 4064

Eugene Onegin, op. 24: I love you Olga; Whither whither have you gone. See no. 4030

Eugene Onegin, op. 24: Lensky's aria. See no. 3966

3299 Eugene Onegin, op. 24: Polonaise. Sleeping beauty, op. 66: Suite.

Swan Lake, op. 20: Suite. Warsaw National Philharmonic Orchestra; Witold Rowicki. DG 2548 125 Tape (c) 3348 125 (From 136 036) (also 2535 371)
+FF 1/2-81 p199 -RR 4-75 p1867
+Gr 4-75 p1867 +-RR 9-76 p92 tape

Eugene Onegin, op. 24: Polonaise. See no. 3287
Eugene Onegin, op. 24: Polonaise and waltz. See no. 2792
Eugene Onegin, op. 24: Se dell'imen la dolce cura. See no. 4031

3300 Francesca da Rimini, op. 32. Romeo and Juliet: Overture. COA; Edo de Waart. Philips 9500 745 Tape (c) 7300 830
+-ARG 9-81 p36 +-NR 5-81 p4
+FF 5/6-81 p163 +NYT 7-19-81 pD23
+HFN 5-81 p87 +SFC 3-1-81 p19
+HFN 9-81 p95 tape ++St 10-81 p135
+-MUM 9/10-81 p37 tape

Francesca da Rimini, op. 32. See no. 861. See no. 3330
Humoresque. See no. 3969
Maid of Orleans, excerpts. See no. 3970

3301 Manfred symphony, op. 58. LSO; Michael Tilson Thomas. CBS 36673 Tape (c) MT 36673
+-ARG 5-81 p30 +-HF 12-81 p84
+-FF 3/4-81 p209 +-NYT 7-19-81 pD23

3302 Manfred symphony, op. 58. COA; Bernard Haitink. Philips 9500 778 Tape (c) 7300 852
+FF 11/12-81 p258 +HF 12-81 p84
+Gr 6-81 p44 +HFN 6-81 p78
+Gr 10-81 p614 tape +HFN 9-81 p95 tape

Manfred symphony, op. 58. See no. 3327. See no. 3328

3303 Marche slav, op. 31. Overture the year 1812, op. 49. Romeo and Juliet: Overture. NYP; Leonard Bernstein. CBS MY 36723
+FF 11/12-81 p222

3304 Marche slav, op. 31. Mozartiana, op. 61. Romeo and Juliet: Fantasy overture. N. Y. Stadium Orchestra, VSO; Leopold Stokowski, Jonel Perlea. Everest SDBR 3463
+-ARG 1-81 p43 -NR 4-80 p4
-FF 9/10-80 p218

3305 Marche slav, op. 31. Overture, the year 1812, op. 49. Romeo and Juliet: Overture. LSO; Andre Previn. Mobile Fidelity MFSL 1-502 (From Angel 36890) (also MFSL 10002. From HMV ASD 2898)
++FF 11/12-80 p185 ++Gr 1-81 p1002

3306 Marche slav, op. 31. Overture, the year 1812, op. 49.* Romeo and Juliet: Overture.* VSOO; Hermann Scherchen. Westminster MCA 1423 (*From WST 14005)
+-ARG 6-81 p44

Marche slav, op. 31. See no. 3699

3307 Mazeppa. V. Davydova, Alexei Ivanov, Ivan Petrov, N. Pokrovskaya, G. Bolshakov; Bolshoi Theatre Orchestra and Chorus; Vasili Nebolsin. Melodiya D 014757/62 (also Bruno Walter Society IGI 376)
+-ARG 10-77 p56 +-NR 4-81 p9

Mazeppa: Cossack dance. See no. 3289
Meditation, op. 42. See no. 1264
The months (The seasons), op. 37: January. See no. 3723
Mozartiana. See no. 3304
Nocturne, op. 19, no. 4. See no. 1399. See no. 1423

3308 The nutcracker, op. 71. COA; St. Bavo Cathedral Boys' Choir;

Antal Dorati. Philips 6747 257 (2) Tape (c) 7505 076 (r) R 6747 257 (also 6747 364)
+Audio 6-77 p133
+Gr 1-77 p1148
++HF 1-77 p128
+HF 2-81 p81 tape
++HFN 1-77 p117
++HFN 5-77 p138 tape
+MJ 1-77 p26
++NR 12-76 p5
++RR 1-77 p64
++SFC 10-24-76 p35
+St 2-77 p123

3309 The nutcracker, op. 71: Ballet suite. Romeo and Juliet: Fantasy overture. Sleeping beauty, op. 66: Ballet suite. Swan Lake, op. 20: Ballet suite. BPhO; Herbert von Karajan. DG 2725 105 (2) Tape (c) 3374 105 (From 2530 295, SKL 927, 104811)
+-Gr 1-81 p1002
+HFN 1-81 p107
+-HFN 6-81 p87 tape

3310 The nutcracker, op. 71: Suite. Swan Lake, op. 20: Valse; Scene; Dance of the swans; Scene pas d'action; Hungarian dance; La Czardas; Scene. Israel Philharmonic Orchestra; Zubin Mehta. Decca SXDL 7505 Tape (c) KSXDC 7505 (also London LDR 10008)
+FF 3/4-81 p211
+-Gr 12-80 p842
+-Gr 2-81 p1122
+-HFN 12-80 p146
+-NR 3-81 p3
+SFC 12-14-80 p20

3311 The nutcracker, op. 71: Suite. Swan Lake, op. 20: Suite. Minnesota Symphony Orchestra; Leonard Slatkin. Pro Arte PAD 121
+-SFC 11-1-81 p18

The nutcracker, op. 71: Suite. See no. 2734. See no. 3288

3312 The nutcracker, op. 71: Suites, nos. 1 and 2. COA; Antal Dorati. Philips FH 23 (also Philips 9500 697 Tape (c) 7300 788)
+FF 7/8-81 p180
+HFN 1-81 p109 tape

3313 Overture, the year 1812, op. 49. Romeo and Juliet: Fantasy overture. LAPO; Zubin Mehta. Decca JB 96 Tape (c) KJBC 96 (From SXL 6448)
+-Gr 1-81 p1002
+-HFN 11-80 p129

Overture, the year 1812, op. 49. See no. 858. See no. 3287. See no. 3289. See no. 3303. See no. 3305. See no. 3306. See no. 3316

Pezzo capriccioso, op. 62. See no. 1423. See no. 1465

Pieces, piano, op. 16, no. 6, F major: Theme and variations. See no. 3723

3314 Quartet, strings, no. 1, op. 11, D major. VERDI: Quartet, strings, E minor. Amadeus Quartet. DG 2531 283 Tape (c) 3301 283
+ARG 5-81 p32
+FF 3/4-81 p209
+Gr 9-80 p367
+HFN 9-80 p111
+HFN 10-80 p117 tape
*NR 1-81 p6
+SFC 1-11-81 p17
++ST 1-81 p648

Quartet, strings, no. 1, op. 11, D major: Andante cantabile. See no. 1423. See no. 3788. See no. 3851. See no. 4066

3315 Romeo and Juliet: Fantasy overture. Suite, no. 3, op. 55, G major: Theme and variations. Boris Simsky, vln; MPO; Kiril Kondrashin. Quintessence PMC 7175
+-FF 7/8-81 p181

Romeo and Juliet: Fantasy overture. See no. 748. See no. 764. See no. 3195. See no. 3309. See no. 3313. See no. 3331

Romeo and Juliet: Overture. See no. 777. See no. 3300. See no. 3303. See no. 3304. See no. 3305. See no. 3306

3316 Serenade, op. 48, C major. Overture, the year 1812, op. 49. PO; Riccardo Muti. HMV ASD 3956 Tape (c) TC ASD 3956 (also Angel

DS 37777)
+Gr 12-81 p891 ++HFN 12-81 p104

3317 Serenade, op. 48, C major. GRIEG: Holberg suite, op. 40. Elegaic melodies, op. 34: Heart wounds; The last spring. Polish Chamber Orchestra; Jerzy Maksymiuk. Seraphim S 60355
+-FF 9/10-81 p187

Serenade, op. 48, C major. See no. 374. See no. 1424. See no. 1426. See no. 1427. See no. 1647

Serenade, op. 48, C major: Waltz. See no. 3343

Serenade, op. 48, C major: Waltz and finale. See no. 3792

Serenade melancolique, op. 26, B flat minor. See no. 3295. See no. 3297

3318 Sleeping beauty, op. 66. BBC Symphony Orchestra; Gennady Rozhdestvensky. BBC Artium 3001 (3) Tape (c) ZCBC 3001 (also Eurodisc 300 575-435)
++Gr 9-80 p350 ++SFC 11-8-81 p18
+RR 8-80 p56

3319 Sleeping beauty, op. 66. Theo Olof, vln; Jean Decroos, vlc; COA; Antal Dorati. Philips 6769 036 (3) Tape (c) 7699 125
+-Gr 11-81 p701 +HFN 12-81 p104

3320 Sleeping beauty, op. 66, excerpts. Hugh Maguire, vln; Kenneth Heath, vlc; LSO; Anatole Fistoulari. Quintessence PMC 7167
+-FF 5/6-81 p165

Sleeping beauty, op. 66: Ballet suite. See no. 3309

Sleeping beauty, op. 66: Suite. See no. 3299

3321 Sonata, piano, op. 37, G major. STRAVINSKY: Etudes, op. 7 (4). Nikita Magaloff, pno. Ricordi RCL 27024
+/FF 11/12-81 p258

Songs: None but the lonely heart, op. 6, no. 6. See no. 3967

3322 The sorceress. Rimma Glushkova, Lev Kuznetsov, Loeg Klenov, Liudmilly Simonova, Evgeny Vladimirov, Vladimir Makhov, Andre Sokolov, Pyotr Gluboky, Sergei Strukachev, Galina Molodsova, Lev Bliseyev, Vladimir Matorin, Boris Dobrin, Nina Derbina, Victor Rybinsky; MRSO and Chorus; Gennady Provatorov. CBS M4X 35182 (4)
++ARG 1-81 p41 +-ON 3-14-81 p44

The sorceress: Mein los ist seltsam. See no. 3651

Souvenir de Florence, op. 70. See no. 3074

Souvenir d'un lieu cher, op. 42: Melodie. See no. 3693

Suite, no. 3, op. 55, G major: Theme and variations. See no. 3315

3323 Swan Lake, op. 20, excerpts. Mikhail Chernyakhovsky, vln; Viktor Simon, vlc; Olga Erdeli, hp; MRSO; Gennady Rozhdestvensky. Quintessence PMC 7174
+FF 5/6-81 p165

Swan Lake, op. 20: Ballet suite. See no. 3309

3324 Swan Lake, op. 20: Scene; Waltz; Pas d'action; Dance of the goblets; Scene; Dance of the swans; Hungarian dance; Russian dance; Dance of the little swans; Final scene. BSO; Seiji Ozawa. DG 2531 351 Tape (c) 3301 351
+-Gr 11-81 p701 +-HFN 12-81 p104

3325 Swan Lake, op. 20: Scene; Waltz scene; Dance of the goblets; Dance of the swans; Dance of the queen of the swans; Dance of the little swans; Scene and waltz; Spanish dance; Hungarian dance; Pas de deux; Dance of the little swans; Final scene. Hugh Maguire, vln; LSO; Pierre Monteux. Philips 6570 187 Tape (c) 7310

187 (From Philips 9500 089)
-FF 11/12-80 p186 +HFN 3-81 p95
+Gr 1-81 p1002 +-HFN 5-81 p93 tape

Swan Lake, op. 20: Suite. See no. 3299. See no. 3311

Swan Lake, op. 20: Valse; Scene; Dance of the swans; Scene pas d'action; Hungarian dance: La Czardas; Scene. See no. 3310

3326 Symphonies, nos. 1-3. BPhO; Herbert von Karajan. DG 2709 101 (3) Tape (c) 3371 053 (also DG 2531 284/5 Tape (c) 3301 284/6)
+FF 3/4-80 p166 +-NR 2-80 p2
+Gr 10-80 p502 ++NYT 12-9-79 pD25
+Gr 12-80 p889 tape +-St 5-80 p92
+HF 2-80 p98 +ST 3-81 p819
+-HF 11-80 p82 tape +STL 11-9-80 p40
+-HFN 12-80 p153

3327 Symphonies, nos. 1-6. Manfred symphony, op. 58. VPO; Lorin Maazel. Decca D8D6 (6) Tape (c) K164K64
+Gr 9-76 p477 ++HFN 10-76 p181
+Gr 2-81 p122 tape +RR 9-76 p67

3328 Symphonies, nos. 1-6. Manfred symphony, op. 58. COA; Bernard Haitink. Philips 6768 267 (7) (From 9500 777, 9500 444, 9500 776, 9500 622, 6500 922, 9500 610, 9500 778)
+Gr 9-81 p394 ++HFN 11-81 p103

3329 Symphony, no. 1, op. 13, G minor. COA; Bernard Haitink. Philips 9500 777 Tape (c) 7300 851
++ARG 12-81 p30 +HFN 4-81 p76
+-FF 9/10-81 p188 ++NR 8-81 p3
+Gr 4-81 p1324 ++SFC 8-2-81 p17

3330 Symphony, no. 2, op. 17, C minor. Francesca da Rimini, op. 32. PhO; Carlo Maria Giulini. HMV SXLP 30509 Tape (c) TC SXLP 30509 (From SAX 2416 2483)
++Gr 7-81 p162 +HFN 7-81 p79

3331 Symphony, no. 2, op. 17, C minor. Romeo and Juliet: Fantasy overture. LAPO; Zubin Mehta. London CS 7149 (From CSP 10, 6670)
+-ARG 5-81 p30 +NR 3-81 p3
+FF 3/4-81 p211

3332 Symphony, no. 2, op. 17, C minor. USSR Symphony Orchestra; Yevgeny Svetlanov. Quintessence PMC 7090 Tape (c) 7090
+-ARG 10-81 p42

3333 Symphony, no. 2, op. 17, C minor. LIADOV: Russian folksongs, op. 58 (8). LSO; Andre Previn. RCA GL 4-2960 Tape (c) GK 4-2960 (From SB 6670)
+-Gr 9-80 p413 tape +-HFN 10-80 p117 tape
+Gr 8-80 p222 +-HFN 3-81 p95

3334 Symphony, no. 3, op. 29, D major. COA; Bernard Haitink. Philips 9500 776 Tape (c) 7300 850
++ARG 5-81 p30 ++HFN 8-81 p87
+-FF 3/4-81 p212 +NR 3-81 p3
++Gr 8-81 p278 ++SFC 1-4-81 p18

3335 Symphonies, nos. 4-6. LSO; Karl Bohm. DG 2740 248 (3) (From 2531 078, 2532 005, 2531 212)
++Gr 8-81 p278 +-HFN 8-81 p91

3336 Symphonies, nos. 4-6. USSR Symphony Orchestra, NPhO, CPhO; Yevgeny Svetlanov, Jascha Horenstein, Lovro von Matacic. Quintessence BL 3702 (3)
+-FF 5/6-81 p166

3337 Symphony, no. 4, op. 36, F minor. Orchestre de Paris; Seiji Ozawa. Arabesque 8079 Tape (c) 9079 (also Classics for Pleasure CFP 40351 Tape (c) TC CFP 40351)
+ARG 5-81 p30
+-FF 3/4-81 p211
+Gr 4-81 p1324
+-NR 3-81 p3
++SFC 1-4-81 p18
3338 Symphony, no. 4, op. 36, F minor. Vancouver Symphony Orchestra; Kazuyoshi Akiyama. CBS SM 5006
+MUM 11/12-81 p36
3339 Symphony, no. 4, op. 36, F minor. BeSO; Kurt Sanderling. Denon/ PCM OX 7137
-FF 5/6-79 p11
+Gr 5-81 p1480
+-HF 3-79 p109
+HFN 6-81 p78
+-St 6-79 p142
3340 Symphony, no. 4, op. 36, F minor. BPhO; Herbert von Karajan. DG 2542 152 Tape (c) 3342 152 (From 139017)
+Gr 8-81 p278
+-HFN 6-81 p85
+HFN 6-81 p87 tape
3341 Symphony, no. 4, op. 36, F minor. BPhO; Herbert von Karajan. HMV SXLP 30433 Tape (c) TC SXLP 30433 (From Columbia SAX 2357)
+FF 1/2-81 p199
+Gr 7-80 p148
+-HFN 7-80 p117
+RR 7-80 p68
3342 Symphony, no. 4, op. 36, F minor. LAPO; Zubin Mehta. London CS 7155 (From CSA 2406)
+-NR 2-81 p4
3343 Symphony, no. 4, op. 36, F minor. Symphony, no. 5, op. 64, E minor. Serenade, op. 48, C major: Waltz. COA; Willem Mengelberg. Pearl GEMM 212/3
+HFN 12-81 p103
3344 Symphony, no. 4, op. 36, F minor. COA; Bernard Haitink. Philips 9500 622 Tape (c) 7300 738 (r) G 9500 622
+ARG 2-80 p44
+-FF 5/6-80 p161
++Gr 11-79 p842
+-HF 3-80 p88
+HF 8-81 p69 tape
++HFN 1-80 p111
++HFN 1-80 p123 tape
++NR 2-80 p2
+RR 11-79 p99
3345 Symphony, no. 4, op. 36, F minor. Baltimore Symphony Orchestra; Sergiu Comissiona. Vanguard VA 25006 Tape (c) CVA 25006
+ARG 10-81 p38
+-FF 7/8-81 p181
+-HF 12-81 p93 tape
+NR 5-81 p6
+SFC 4-5-81 p18
Symphony, no. 4, op. 36, F minor: Finale. See no. 3956
3346 Symphony, no. 5, op. 64, E minor. Stokowski in rehearsal. International Festival Youth Orchestras; Leopold Stokowski. Cameo GOCL 9007
+FF 7/8-81 p182
+Gr 10-79 p654
-HFN 1-80 p111
-RR 1-80 p89
3347 Symphony, no. 5, op. 64, E minor. VPO; Riccardo Chailly. Decca SXDL 7533 Tape (c) KSXDC 7533 (also London LDR 71033)
+-Gr 12-81 p891
3348 Symphony, no. 5, op. 64, E minor. BeSO; Kurt Sanderling. Denon OX 7186
+Gr 5-81 p1480
+HFN 6-81 p78
++St 5-81 p84
3349 Symphony, no. 5, op. 64, E minor. LSO; Karl Bohm. DG 2532 005

Tape (c) 3302 005
+ARG 12-81 p31 +-HFN 4-81 p76
+-FF 5/6-81 p169 +HFN 4-81 p83 tape
+FF 7/8-81 p182 +-MUM 9/10-81 p34
+Gr 3-81 p1206 -NR 8-81 p3

3350 Symphony, no. 5, op. 64, E minor. Bamberg Symphony Orchestra; Gary Bertini. Pro Arte PAD 101
+-FF 11/12-81 p259

3351 Symphony, no. 5, op. 64, E minor. Symphony, no. 6, op. 74, B minor. La Scala Orchestra, PhO; Guido Cantelli. World Records SHB 52 (2) Tape (c) TC 2-SHB 52 (From DB 21187/91, ALP 1042)
+ARSC Vol 12, no. 1-2 1980 p117 ++Gr 4-79 p1720
++FF 5/6-81 p167 ++Gr 6-79 p109 tape

Symphony, no. 5, op. 64, E minor. See no. 3343. See no. 3855

3352 Symphony, no. 6, op. 74, B minor. BeSO; Kurt Sanderling. Denon PCM OX 7183
-FF 11/12-80 p188 +Gr 5-81 p1480
+-FF 1/2-81 p199 +St 5-81 p84

3353 Symphony, no. 6, op. 74, B minor. LAPO; Carlo Maria Giulini. DG 2532 013 Tape (c) 3302 013
+-ARG 12-81 p32 +-HFN 9-81 p85
/Gr 10-81 p564 +HFN 12-81 p112 tape

3354 Symphony, no. 6, op. 74, B minor. BPhO; Wilhelm Furtwangler. DG 2535 165 Tape (c) 3335 165
+-FF 5/6-80 p161 +NR 8-80 p6
+-Gr 5-76 p1772 +RR 5-76 p22
+HF 7-80 p76 +STL 1-9-77 p35
+HF 2-81 p81 tape

3355 Symphony, no. 6, op. 74, B minor. BPhO; Herbert von Karajan. DG 2542 154 Tape (c) 3342 154 (From SLPM 138921)
++Gr 9-81 p394

3356 Symphony, no. 6, op. 74, B minor. PhO; Riccardo Muti. HMV ASD 3901 Tape (c) TC ASD 3901 (also Angel SZ 37626)
+ARG 6-81 p30 +HFN 11-80 p123
+-FF 3/4-81 p213 ++NR 3-81 p3
+Gr 11-80 p683 +St 5-81 p84
+Gr 2-81 p1122 tape

3357 Symphony, no. 6, op. 74, B minor. National Philharmonic Orchestra; Carlos Paita. Lodia LOD 778 Tape (c) LOC 778
+-Gr 6-81 p44 ++HFN 6-81 p87 tape
+-HFN 6-81 p78

3358 Symphony, no. 6, op. 74, B minor. PhO; Vladimir Ashkenazy. London CS 7170 (also Decca SXL 6941 Tape (c) KSXC 6941)
++FF 11/12-81 p259 +HFN 7-81 p76
++Gr 8-81 p278

3359 Symphony, no. 6, op. 74, B minor. BPhO; Herbert von Karajan. Mobile Fidelity Sound MFSL 1-512 (From Angel S 36886, HMV SLS 833)
-FF 5/6-81 p169 ++NR 6-81 p3
+-Gr 4-81 p1326

3360 Symphony, no. 6, op. 74, B minor. Orchestre de Paris; Seiji Ozawa. Philips 6527 094 (From 6500 094)
+FF 11/12-81 p260 ++SFC 10-4-81 p18
+-HFN 11-81 p103

Symphony, no.6, op. 74, B minor. See no. 3351

Symphony, no. 6, op. 74, B minor: Andante. See no. 3626

3361 Trio, piano, op. 50, A minor. Vladimir Ashkenazy, pno; Itzhak Perlman, vln; Lynn Harrell, vlc. Angel SZ 37678 Atpe (c) 4XS 37678 (also HMV ASD 4036)

+FF 9/10-81 p188 +MUM 9/10-81 p34
+Gr 7-81 p168 ++NR 6-81 p5
-HF 11-81 p97 +NYT 6-21-81 pD23
+HF 11-81 p103 tape ++St 8-81 p99
+HFN 7-81 p76 ++ST 12-81 p590

3362 Trio, piano, op. 50, A minor. Yehudi Menuhin, vln; Maurice Gendron, vlc; Hephzibah Menuhin, pno. Arabesque 8014 Tape (c) 9014

++FF 9/10-80 p221 -NYT 6-21-81 pD23
+HF 11-81 p97 ++SFC 7-27-80 p34

3363 Trio, piano, op. 50, A minor. Mikhail Pletnyov, pno; Elmar Oliveira, vln; Nathaniel Rosen, vlc. CBS M 35855 Tape (c) MT 35855

+FF 11/12-81 p260 ++NYT 6-21-81 pD23
++HF 11-81 p97 +SFC 8-2-81 p17
+-NR 9-81 p5 +St 11-81 p94

3364 Trio, piano, op. 50, A minor. Mirecourt Trio. Grand Prix GP 9006

+FF 5/6-81 p170 +-NYT 6-21-81 pD23
-HF 11-81 p97 +St 8-81 p99
++NR 6-81 p5

3365 Trio, piano, op. 50, A minor. Eastman Trio. Turnabout TVC 37017 Tape (c) CT 37017

+FF 11/12-81 p260 +NYT 6-21-81 pD23
+-HF 11-81 p97 +St 11-81 p96
+-NR 7-81 p8

Variations on a rococo theme, op. 33. See no. 1410. See no. 1465. See no. 3292

Vespers, op. 52. See no. 2711

TCHEREPNIN, Alexander

Sonata, violin and piano, F major. See no. 948

Trio, op. 34, D major. See no. 1236

TCHEREPNIN, Ivan

Valse perpetuelle. See no. 3942

TEIXIDOR

Amparito roca. See no. 3981

TELEMANN, Georg

Ach Herr strafe mich nicht. See no. 124

Air de trompette. See no. 3629

Air de trompette, C major. See no. 3905

Allein Gott in der Hoh sei Ehr. See no. 3905

Canons, F major. See no. 4096

3366 Concerti, flute (6). Paula Robison, flt; Anthony Newman, hpd. Musicmasters MM 20014

+NR 12-81 p11

3367 Concerto, flute, D major. Concerto, violin, A minor. Overture, A minor. Eva Legene, rec; Nels Lindeblad, flt; Ole Bohn, vln; Societas Musica Chamber Orchestra Copenhagen; Jorgen Hansen. Denon OX 7074

+HFN 6-81 p78

3368 Concerti, flute, B minor, E major. Concerto, 2 flutes, E minor. Concerto, 2 flutes, oboe and violin, B flat major. Jean-Michel Tanguy, Jerry Felmlee, flt; Enrico Raphaelis, ob; Peter Rundel, vln; Heidelberg Chamber Orchestra. Da Camera SM 91044 (also

Spectrum SR 124)
+FF 5/6-80 p164 +-FF 11/12-81 p263
+FF 9/10-81 p189
Concerto, flute, oboe d'amore and viola d'amore, E major. See no. 3767
3369 Concerto, flute, violin and viola da gamba, D major. Quartet, flute, violin and violoncello, E minor. Quartet, oboe, violin and viola da gamba, G minor. Trio sonata, oboe and harpsichord, E flat major. Aulos Ensemble. Musicmasters MM 20009 Tape (c) MMC 40009
++HF 12-81 p62
3370 Concerto, flute, violin and violoncello, A major. Concerto, 2 flutes, A minor. Jiri Valek, Frantisek Cech, flt; Vaclav Snitil, vln; Frantisek Slama, vlc; Ars Rediviva Ensemble Prague; Milan Munclinger. Musicaphon BM 30 SL 4204
+HFN 5-81 p84
Concerto, 2 flutes, A minor. See no. 3370
Concerto, 2 flutes, E minor. See no. 3368
Concerto, 2 flutes and 2 oboes, B flat major. See no. 3373
Concerto, 2 flutes, oboe and violin, B flat major. See no. 3368
Concerto, horn, D major. See no. 384
Concerto, 2 horns, E flat major. See no. 1527
Concerto, 3 horns, D major. See no.384
Concerto oboe, E flat major. See no. 3373
3371 Concerto, oboe, F minor. Concerto, recorder and oboe, B flat major. Concerto, viola, G major. Overture, G major. Eva Legene Anderson, rec; Jorgen Skyttegard, ob; Bjarne Boie Rasmussen, vla; Societas Musica Chamber Orchestra Copenhagen; Jorgen Hansen. Denon OX 7068
+-HFN 6-81 p78
Concerto, oboe, F minor. See no. 36
Concerto, 3 oboes and 3 violins, B major. See no. 4091
Concerto, oboe d'amore, A major. See no. 1136. See no. 3373
Concerto, recorder, C major. See no. 1693. See no. 1694
3372 Concerto, recorder, no. 4, E minor. Suites, orchestra, no. 83, G major; no. 112, A minor. Friedrich Tilegant, Frans Bruggen, rec; Frans Vester, flt; Gustav Leonhardt, hpd; Amsterdam Chamber Orchestra, Sudwestern Chamber Orchestra; Gustav Leonhardt. Telefunken AQ 6-41342 Tape (c) CQ 41-41342
++Gr 9-81 p460 tape
3373 Concerto, recorder and flute, E minor. Concerto, oboe, E flat major. Concerto, 2 flutes and 2 oboes, B flat major. Concerto, oboe d'amore, A major. Aurele Nicolet, Christiane Nicolet, flt; Michael Copley, rec; Louise Pellerin, ob; Heinz Holliger, ob and ob d'amore; Camerata Bern; Jorg Dahler, hpd; Thomas Furi. DG 2533 454 Tape (c) 3310 454
++FF 9/10-81 p189 +HF 12-81 p62
+Gr 3-81 p1206 ++SFC 12-13-81 p18
+Gr 9-81 p460 tape ++St 10-81 p136
Concerto, recorder and oboe, B flat major. See no. 3371
3374 Concerto, recorder, bassoon and strings, F major. Suite, A minor. Laszlo Czidra, rec; Jozsef Vajda, bsn; Ferenc Liszt Chamber Orchestra; Frigyes Sandor. Hungaroton SLPX 12119
+FF 9/10-80 p223 -HFN 6-81 p78
Concerto, trumpet, D major. See no. 28. See no. 32. See no. 1483. See no. 3761. See no. 3774

Concerto, viola, G major. See no. 3371
Concerto, violin, A minor. See no. 3367
3375 Du aber Daniel gehe hin. Ertrage nur das Joch der Mangel. Hochselige Blicke voll heiliger Wonne. Liselotte Rebmann, s; Kurt Equiluz, t; William Reimer, bs; Helga Rehm, vln; Burghard Schaeffer, Erdmuthe Boehr, flt; Uwe Peter Rehm, vlc; Karl Grebe, hpd; Hamburg Monteverdi Choir; Hamburg Telemann Society Chamber Ensemble; Jurgen Jurgens. Philips 9502 026 Tape (c) 7313 026
+-Gr 3-81 p128
+HFN 8-81 p92
Entrage nur das Joch der Mangel. See no. 3375
3376 Essercizii musici: Sonatas, A minor, D minor. Der Getreue Musik-Meister: Duet, B flat major. Sonata, F minor. Trio sonatas, recorder, F major, A minor, G minor, D minor, F major, C major. Kees Boeke, rec; Alice Harnoncourt, vln, pardessus de viole, violino, piccolo; Bob van Asperen, hpd. Telefunken EK 6-35451 (2)
+AR 2-81 p187
+FF 3/4-80 p168
++Gr 11-79 p866
+HF 6-80 p88
++HFN 5-79 p127
++RR 4-79 p105
+St 2-80 p134
3377 Essercizii musici: Trios, recorder, F major, D minor, B flat major, A major, C minor, E major. Der Getreue Musik-Meister: Introduzione a tre, C major. Trios, recorder, D minor, A minor. Scherzo, 2 German flutes, E major. Frans Bruggen, rec and German flt; Walter van Hauwe, rec; Barthold Kuijken, German flt; Paul Dombrecht, ob; Wieland Kuijken, pardessus de viole; Sigiswald Kuijken, vln; Bob van Asperen, hpd; Anner Bylsma, vlc; Anthony Woodrow, double bs; Brian Pollard, bsn; Gustav Leonhardt, hpd. Musical Heritage Society MHS 4172/3 (2)
++FF 1/2-81 p201
Fantasies, G minor, G major. See no. 4095
3378 Fantasies, flute, nos. 1-12. Alexandre Magnin, flt. Da Camera SM 92922
+FF 7/8-81 p184
3379 Fantasies, flute, nos. 1-12. Maxence Larrieu, flt. Tudor TUD 73013
+Gr 6-81 p62
+HFN 6-81 p79
3380 Fantasies, recorder, nos. 4, 6. Partita, recorder, no. 2, G major. Sonatas, recorder, C major, F major. Sonata, recorder, op. 13, no. 4. Trio sonata, B flat major. Michala Petri, rec; David Petri, vlc; Hanne Petri, hpd. Philips 9500 941 Tape (c) 7300 941
+FF 11/12-81 p263
+-Gr 7-81 p170
+HF 12-81 p62
+HFN 7-81 p77
+HFN 10-81 p95 tape
+NR 9-81 p6
++SFC 9-6-81 p18
3381 Fantasies, violin, nos. 1-12. Hans Kalafusz, vln. Intercord INT 180838
+HFN 12-81 p104
3382 Der Getreue Musik-Meister. Edith Mathis, s; Hertha Topper, con; Ernst Hafliger, Gerhard Unger, t; Barry McDaniel, bar; Wurzburg Bach Choir; Archiv Production Soloists; Josef Ulsamer. DG 2723 073 (5)(From SKL 943/7)
+Gr 2-81 p1113
+HFN 9-81 p90
Der Getreue Musik-Meister: Duet, B flat major; Sonata, F minor.

See no. 3376
Der Getreue Musik-Meister: Introduzione a tre, C major. See no. 3377
Heidenmusik, excerpts. See no. 3391
Hochselige Blicke voll heiliger Wonne. See no. 3375
Introductione a tre, C major. See no. 3397
Marches (4). See no. 3905

3383 Musique de table: Concerti, flute, A major; 3 violins, F major; 2 horns, E flat major. Frans Vester, flt; Jaap Schroder, Jacques Holtman, Marie Leonhardt, vln; Adriaan van Woudenberg, Hermann Baumann, hn; Gustav Leonhardt, hpd; Anner Bylsma, vlc; Concerto Amsterdam; Frans Bruggen. Telefunken AQ 6-41152 Tape (c) CQ 4-41152 (From SAWT 9449/54)
+Gr 11-81 p702

3384 Musique de table; Conclusions, oboe, D major; 2 flutes, E minor; 2 oboes, B flat major. Solos, flute, B minor; violin, A major; oboe, G minor. Maurice Andre, tpt; Frans Vester, Joost Tromp, flt; Ab Mater, Lilian Lagaay, ob; Jaap Schroder, vln; Concerto Amsterdam; Frans Bruggen. Telefunken AQ 6-42557 Tape (c) CQ 4-42557 (From SAWT 9449/54)
+Gr 11-81 p702

3385 Musique de table: Trios, flute, E minor; 2 violins, E flat major; 2 flutes, D major. Frans Vester, Joost Tromp, flt; Ad Mater, ob; Jaap Schroder, Jacques Holtman, vln; Brian Pollard, bsn; Anner Bylsma, vlc; Gustav Leonhardt, hpd. Telefunken AQ 6-42700 Tape (c) CQ 4-42700 (From SAWT 9449/54)
++Gr 11-81 p719

Overture, A minor. See no. 3367
Overture, G major. See no. 3371

3386 Overtures, 3 oboes and strings, D major, G minor, D minor, C major. VCM; Nikolaus Harnoncourt. Telefunken 6-35498 (2)
+FF 3/4-81 p214 +STL 10-11-81 p41
++Gr 12-81 p892

3387 Partitas, nos. 1-2, 6, 9. Narciso Yepes, Godelieve Monden, gtr. DG 2531 350 Tape (c) 3301 350
++Gr 12-81 p897 +HFN 12-81 p104

3388 Partita, no. 2, G major. Sonatas, B flat major, G minor. Suite, G minor. Paul Dombrecht, ob; Wieland Kuijken, vlc; Robert Kohnen, hpd. Accent ACC 8013
+Audio 10-81 p24 +HFN 9-80 p111
+FF 1/2-81 p201 ++RR 8-80 p76
+Gr 8-80 p239

Partita, no. 2, G major. See no. 3380
Psalm, no. 111: Ich danke dem Herrn, Er sendent eine Erlosung seinen Volk. See no. 159
Quartet, G major. See no. 3763
Quartet, flute, violin and violoncello, E minor. See no. 3369
Quartet, oboe, violin and viola da gamba, G minor. See no. 3369

3389 St. Lukas Passion 1744. Uta Spreckelsen, s; Theo Altmeyer, Adalbert Kraus, Gerd Beusker, t; Gerhard Faulstich, bar; Frankfurt Chamber Orchestra and Madrigal Ensemble; Siegfried Heinrich. Cantate 658 203/4 (2)
/Gr 2-81 p982 +HFN 10-80 p109

3390 St. Mark Passion. Agnes Giebel, s; Ira Malaniuk, con; Theo Altmeyer, t; Heinz Rehfuss, Horst Gunter, bar; Lausanne Youth Choir; Munich Pro Arte Orchestra; Leonard Hokanson, hpd; Lionel

Rogg, org; Kurt Redel. Philips 6768 027 (2) (From SAL 3494/5)
+Gr 7-81 p191

Scherzo, 2 flutes, E major. See no. 3377. See no. 3397

Sonatas, B flat major, G minor. See no. 3388

Sonata, bassoon, A flat major. See no. 840

Sonata, flute, G major. See no. 121

3391 Sonatas, oboe and harpsichord, B flat major, C minor. Heldenmusik, excerpts. Roy Smedvig, tpt; Sherman Walt, bsn; Joyce Lindorff, hpd. Digitech DIGI 106 Tape (c) GIDI C 106
+-ARG 10-81 p40 +-HF 12-81 p62
+-FF 7/8-81 p184 +St 7-81 p88

Sonata, recorder, C major. See no. 3949

Sonatas, recorder, C major, F major. See no. 3380

Sonata, recorder, op. 5, no. 6, A minor/A major. See no. 1880

Sonata, recorder, op. 13, no. 4. See no. 3380

Sonata, recorder, Anh 1, no. 5, A major/C major. See no. 1880

Sonata, viola da gamba, D major. See no. 1689

Songs: Die Frau; Gluck; Neues; Uber das niedersachsische Versapeh; Die vergesserne Phillis. See no. 3985

Songs: Les plaisirs. See no. 3853

3392 Suite, A minor. VIVALDI: Concerti, flute, D minor, C minor. Jean-Pierre Rampal, flt; Jerusalem Center Chamber Orchestra; Isaac Stern, vln and cond. CBS HM 45133
+-FF 11/12-81 p272

Suite, A minor. See no. 3374

Suite, G minor. See no. 3388

Suite, flute, A minor. See no. 333

Suite, flute, D minor. See no. 121

Suite, 2 horns, F major. See no. 384

Suite, 2 horns, F major. See no. 1527

Suite, 2 horns, 2 oboes, bassoon and strings, D major. See no. 3767

Suite, orchestra, no. 63, F major. See no. 1511

Suite, orchestra, no. 83, G major. See no. 3372

Suite, orchestra, no. 112, A minor. See no. 3372

Suite, sopranino recorder. See no. 1136

3393 Suite, trumpet, D major. Suite, 2 trumpets, D major. Suite, 3 trumpets, D major. Wolfgang Basch, Albert Oesterle, Otto Blas-aditsch, tpt; DBS; Helmut Winschermann. Musical Heritage Society MHS 4275
+-HF 5/6-81 p171

Suite, trumpet, D major. See no. 3978

Suite, 2 trumpets, D major. See no. 3393

Suite, 3 trumpets, D major. See no. 3393

3394 Tafelmusik, nos. 1-3. Schola Cantorum Basiliensis; August Wenzinger. DG 2723 074 (4) (From SAPM 198334/5, 198336/7, 198338/9)
+Gr 3-81 p1208 +-HFN 9-81 p90

3395 Tafelmusik, nos. 1-3. Jaap Schroder; Gustav Leonhardt, hpd; Concerto Amsterdam; Frans Bruggen. Telefunken 6-35298 (6)
+FF 5/6-81 p256

Trio, no. 78, B flat major. See no. 3867

Trio, flute and harpsichord, A major. See no. 3397

Trio, flute and oboe, D minor. See no. 3397

3396 Trios, recorder. Frans Bruggen, rec; Gustav Leonhardt, hpd; Barthold Kuijken, flt; Sigiswald Kuijken; Wieland Kuijken, vla da gamba. Pro Arte PAL 2002

++MUM 9/10-81 p34

Trios, recorder, D minor, A minor. See no. 3377
Trio, recorder and harpsichord, B flat major. See no. 3397
Trio, recorder and oboe, C minor. See no. 3397
Trio, recorder and pardessus de viole, D minor. See no. 3397
Trio, recorder and viola da gamba, F major. See no. 3397
Trios, recorder and violin, A minor, A major. See no. 3397
Trio sonata, B flat major. See no. 3380
Trio sonata, E minor. See no. 3631
Trio sonata, oboe and harpsichord, E flat major. See no. 3369
Trio sonatas, recorder, F major, A minor, G minor, D minor, F major, C major. See no. 3376
Vater unser im Himmelreich. See no. 3905

3397 Works, selections: Introductione a tre, C major. Scherzo, 2 flutes, E major. Trio, recorder and viola da gamba, F major. Trio, flute and harpsichord, A major. Trio, flute and oboe, D minor. Trio, recorder and harpsichord, B flat major. Trio, recorder and oboe, C minor. Trio, recorder and pardessus de viole, D minor. Trio, recorder and violin, E major, A minor. Frans Bruggen, rec and flt; Walter van Hauwe, rec; Berthold Kuijken, flt; Paul Dombrecht, ob; Wieland Kuijken, vla da gamba, pardessus de viole; Bob van Asperen, Gustav Leonhardt, hpd; Anner Bylsma, vlc; Anthony Woodrow, double bs; Brian Pollard, bsn. RCA RL 3-0343 (2)

+Gr 5-80 p1689 +MT 3-81 p185
+HFN 6-80 p112 +RR 5-80 p79

TENAGLIA

Begli occhi merce. See no. 3838

TEN HOLT, Simeon

I am Sylvia but somebody else. See no. 3728

TENTH CENTURY LITURGICAL CHANTS. See no. 3935

TERZIAN, Alicia

Danza criolla. See no. 3913
Juegos para Diana. See no. 3913
Toccata. See no. 3913

TESCHEMACHER-GARTNER

Love is mine. See no. 3997

TESSIER, Georg

In a grove most rich of shade. See no. 3946

TEYBER, Anton

Concerto, horn, E flat major. See no. 1832

THAYER

My laddie. See no. 4042

THIBAUT IV OF NAVARRE

Chanson pieuse "Dou tres doux non". See no. 3853

THIEL, Carl

Songs: Adeste fideles; Freu dich Erd und Sternenzelt. See no. 3775

THIEME, Karl

Invocation. See no. 196

THOMA, Annette

3398 German peasant mass. Die Fischbachauer Sangerinnen; Der Darchinger Viergesang; Instrumentalists. Intercord 160807

+-HFN 12-81 p104

THOMAS, Ambroise

La Caid: Air du Tambour-major. See no. 3968. See no. 4025

3399 Hamlet. Christine Barbaux, s; Josephine Veasey, ms; Gordon Christie, Thomas Allen, bar; Paul Hudson, bs; Buxton Festival Chorus; Manchester Camerata; Anthony Hose. MRF MRF 169 (3)
+FF 7/8-81 p185
Hamlet: Come romito fior. See no. 4034
Mignon: Addio Mignon fa core; Ah non credevi tu. See no. 3843
Mignon: Ah non credivi tu; La tua bell alma; Addio Mignon. See no. 4032
Mignon: Ah que ton ame; Je suis heureuse. See no. 4051
Mignon: C'est moi...Me voici; Connais-tu le pays. See no. 3713
Mignon: Connais-tu le pays. See no. 3710
Mignon: Connais-tu le pays; Elle est aimee. See no. 4038
Mignon: Del suo cor calmai. See no. 3968
Mignon: Elle ne croyait pas. See no. 3972
Mignon: Elle ne croyait pas; Adieu Mignon courage. See no. 3966
Mignon: Gavotte. See no. 3626
Mignon: In her simplicity. See no. 3657
Mignon: Ninna nanna. See no. 4029
Mignon: Wie ihre Unschuld. See no. 3747
Songs: Le soir. See no. 3758

THOMAS-MIFUNE, Werner
Drunken rag. See no. 3789
Tango peleado. See no. 3789

THOME, Diane
3400 Anais. WILSON: The ballad of Longwood Glen. Eclogue. YANNAY: At the end of the parade. Lawrence Weller, bar; Paul Sperry, t; Bianca Uribe, Diane Thome, pno; Nancy Allen, hp; Michael Finckel, vlc; Electronic tape; Orchestra of Our Time Members; Joel Thome. CRI SD 437
*FF 5/6-81 p186
-NR 7-81 p5

THOMPSON, David
The knight of Bethlehem. See no. 3852

THOMPSON, Randall
Songs: Felices ter; The paper reeds. See no. 3951

THOMSON, Virgil
3401 Etudes. Portraits: Cantabile; Catalan waltz; Bugles and birds; An old song; In a bird cage; Alternation. Arthur Tollefson, pno. Finnadar SR 9027
+ARG 2-81 p34
+CL 2-81 p13
+FF 11/12-80 p188
+HF 10-80 p91
+NR 12-80 p10
++SFC 1-25-81 p17
+St 1-81 p87
For a happy occasion. See no. 3942
Portraits: Cantabile; Catalan waltz; Bugles and birds; An old song; In a bird cage; Alternation. See no. 3401
Symphony, no. 3. See no. 1835

THORLEY
Piece, flute. See no. 3627

THYBO, Leif
Aria con variatzione. See no. 3679

TIBURTINO, Giuliano
Ricercare "La sol fa ni fa". See no. 3945

TIGRANIAN
Et-Arhaj. See no. 3912

TINCTORIS, Johannes de
Missa 3 vocum: Kyrie. See no. 3853
TING SHAN-TE
3402 Long march symphony. Nagoya Philharmonic Orchestra; Kek-Tjian Lim. Hong Kong HK 1004 (also Arioa 300 400-450)
+/ARG 6-81 p56
TIPPETT, Michael
Fanfare, brass, no. 1. See no. 4006
3403 King Priam. Felicity Palmer, Heather Harper, s; Anne Murray, ms; Yvonne Minton, con; Robert Tear, Philip Langridge, t; Norman Bailey, Thomas Allen, Stephen Roberts, bar; London Sinfonietta Orchestra and Chorus; David Atherton. Decca D246D3 (3) Tape (c) K246K33 (also London LDR 73006)
+Gr 11-81 p757 +STL 11-8-81 p40
++HFN 11-81 p91
The midsummer marriage: Ritual dances. See no. 1024
Negro spirituals. See no. 951
3404 Shires suite. YOUNG: Virages: Region one. Leicestershire Schools Symphony Orchestra; Leicestershire Chorale; Rohan de Saram, vlc; Douglas Young, Peter Fletcher. Unicorn UNS 267
++Gr 6-81 p44 +Te 9-81 p62
+HFN 6-81 p79
Songs of Dov. See no. 2252
Suite for the birthday of Prince Charles, D major. See no. 3405
3405 Symphony, no. 4. Suite for the birthday of Prince Charles, D major. CSO; Georg Solti. Decca SXDL 7546 Tape (c) KSXDC 7546 (also London LDR 71046)
+Gr 8-81 p280 ++HFN 8-81 p87
+Gr 11-81 p783 tape +STL 9-13-81 p41
TISCHTSCHENKO, Boris
Invention, no. 3. See no. 3910
TISDALE, William
Coranto. See no. 4090
TISNE, Antoine
Soliloques. See no. 3739
TJEKNAVORIAN, Loris
Armenian dance, no. 2. See no. 3913
TOCH, Ernst
Burlesken, op. 31. See no. 1075
TODD, George
Satan's sermon. See no. 1637
Variations on a bagatelle. See no. 1637
TOESCHI, Karl
Symphony, D major. See no. 1326
TOLLEY, Dick
Meditation. See no. 4100
O come o come Emanuel. See no. 4100
TOMASI, Henri
Fanfares liturgiques: Procession du Vendredi-Saint. See no. 3660
Triptyque. See no. 3741
TOMKINS, Thomas
Barafostus dream. See no. 3734
A sad pavan for these distracted times. See no. 3807
Songs: O let me die for true love; Oyez has any found a lad. See no. 4085

TOMOANA
E pari ra. See no. 3956
Pokarekare. See no. 3956
TORELLI, Giuseppe
Concerto, trumpet, D major. See no. 33. See no. 3774
Concerti, trumpet, nos. 1 and 2. See no. 2076
Concerto grosso, op. 8, no. 6, G minor. See no. 1241
Sinfonia, trumpet. See no. 3740
Sonata, trumpet, D major. See no. 28. See no. 33
Sonata, trumpet, no. 1, G major. See no. 3761
TORRE, Francesco de la
Adoramos te senor; La Spagna. See no. 3945
Pampano verde. See no. 3828
TORROBA, Federico
Aires de la Mancha. See no. 3407
Burgalesa. See no. 3795
La chulapona: Tienes razon amigo. See no. 3888
3406 Concierto iberico. Dialogos. Los romeros; AMF: Neville Marriner. Philips 9500 749 Tape (c) 7300 834
++FF 5/6-81 p172 +HFN 12-80 p147
++Gr 12-80 p842 +NR 6-81 p7
Dialogos. See no. 3406
Luisa Fernanda: De este apacible rincon de Madrid. See no. 3888
Madronos. See no. 3407. See no. 3727
Nocturne, A minor. See no. 3407
Piezas caracteristicas. See no. 3407
Sonatina. See no. 3407
Suite castellana. See no. 3407
Torija. See no. 3694
3407 Works, selections: Aires de la Mancha. Madronos. Nocturne, A minor. Piezas caracteristicas. Sonatina. Suite castellana. Eric Hill, fleta gtr. Saga SAGA 5462
+FF 9/10-81 p190 +HFN 10-78 p127
+Gr 7-79 p234 +RR 2-79 p82
TOSELLI, Enrico
Serenade. See no. 4051
Serenade, no. 1, op. 6. See no. 3965
TOSTI, Francesco
Songs: A vucchella; L'ultima canzone. See no. 3839
Songs: Addio. See no. 3997
Songs: Ancora; Amour amour; Ideale; La serenata. See no. 4031
Songs: Aprile; Vorrei morire; Ideale; Non t'amo piu; Malia. See no. 3838
Songs: Ideale. See no. 3987. See no. 4075
Songs: Ideale; Merechiare; La serenata. See no. 4032
Songs: Ideale; Pour un baiser. See no. 3995
Songs: L'alba separa dalla luce l'ombra. See no. 4036
Songs: L'ultima canzone. See no. 3718
Songs: Marechiare. See no. 3641
Songs: Parted. See no. 3966
Songs: Pour un baiser. See no. 4051
TOURNEMIRE, Charles
Pater dimite illis nesciunt enim quid faciunt, op. 67, no. 1. See no. 1936

TOWER, Joan
Red garnet waltz. See no. 3942
TOWNSEND, Douglas
3408 Chamber concerti, nos. 2-3. Fantasy on motives of Burt Bacharach. Suite, strings, no. 1. Per Brevig, trom; Karl Kraber, flt; Martin Smith, hn; Velma Richter, pno; Garden State Chamber Orchestra; Frederick Storfer. Musical Heritage Society MHS 4223
+ARG 7/8-81 p39 +FF 1/2-81 p202
Fantasy on motives of Burt Bacharach. See no. 3408
Suite, strings, no. 1. See no. 3408
TOYE, Geoffrey
The haunted ballroom. See no. 3652
TROMBONCINO, Bartolomeo
Ave Maria gratia plena. See no. 4011
3409 Forttole. Consorte of Musicke; Anthony Rooley. L'Oiseau-Lyre DSLO 593
+HFN 12-81 p105
Hor ch'el ciel e la terra; Ostinato vo seguire. See no. 3945
Songs: Ostinato vo seguire; Vergine bella. See no. 3692
TROTERE
Asthore. See no. 3967
TSCHISCHKO, Oles
Ukrainian rhapsody. See no. 3910
TSINTSADZE, Sulkhan
Fantasy, quartet. See no. 88
TULOU, Jean-Louis
L'Angelus, op. 46. See no. 4065
TUMA, Frantisek
Parthia, D major. See no. 3826
TUNDER, Franz
In dich hab ich gehoffet Herr. See no. 3903
TURINA, Joaquin
Danza de la seduccion. See no. 3857
Danzas andaluzas, op. 8: Zapateado. See no. 3410
Danzas fantasticas, op. 22. See no. 3410
Danzas fantasticas, op. 22: Orgia. See no. 1297
Danzas gitanas, op. 55: Sacro-Monte. See no. 3410
Fandanguillo, op. 36. See no. 18. See no. 19
Homenaje a Lope de Vega. See no. 3838
3410 Piano works: Danzas fantasticas, op. 22. Danzas andaluzas, op. 8: Zapateado. Danzas gitanas, op. 55: Sacro-Monte. Sonata pintoresca, op. 24. Alicia de Larrocha, pno. Moss Music Group TV 34773 Tape (c) CT 4773 (From Hispavox CT 4773). (also Musical Heritage Society MHS 1408)
-ARG 12-81 p34 +NYT 7-12-81 pD21
+HF 9-81 p46 tape
Sonata, guitar, op. 61, D major. See no. 18
Sonata pintoresca, op. 24. See no. 3410
Songs: Las locas por amor. See no. 3703
Trio, piano, no. 2, op. 74, B minor. See no. 1236
TYE, Christopher
In nomine "Trust". See no. 4092
Songs: Laudate nomen Domini; Praise ye the Lord ye children. See no. 3618

UHL, Alfred
Festfanfare. See no. 3660
ULEHLA, Ludmilla
Elegy for a whale. See no. 3884
VALDERRABANO, Enriquez de
Fantasia primero grado. See no. 4094
Songs: De donde venis amore; Senora si te olvidare. See no. 4063
VALEN, Olav Faartein
Gavotte and musette, op. 24. See no. 3411
Intermezzo, op. 36. See no. 3411
Legende, op. 1. See no. 3411
Pieces, piano, op. 22. See no. 3411
Preludes, op. 29. See no. 3411
Prelude and fugue, op. 28. See no. 3411
Sonata, piano, no. 1, op. 2. See no. 3411
Sonata, piano, no. 2, op. 38. See no. 3411
Variations, op. 23. See no. 3411
3411 Works, selections: Gavotte and musette, op. 24. Intermezzo, op. 36. Legende, op. 1. Pieces, piano, op. 22 (4). Preludes, op. 29 (2). Prelude and fugue, op. 28. Sonata, piano, no. 1, op. 2. Sonata, piano, no. 2, op. 38. Variations, op. 23. Robert Riefling, pno. BIS LP 173/4 (2)
+FF 11/12-81 p264 +HFN 9-81 p85
+Gr 11-81 p764
VALENTE, Antonio
Passione. See no. 3641
VALENTINE, Robert
Concerto, flute, D major. See no. 3978
VALENTINI, Giovanni
Songs: Vanne o carta amorosa. See no. 3947
VALLET, Nicolas
Bourees (2). See no. 3937
La chaconna. See no. 3937
Sarabanda. See no. 3937
VALLIER, John
Witches ride. See no. 1168
VALLS, Francisco
3412 Scala Aretina, mass. Mavis Beattie, Valerie Hill, Nancy Long, s; Christopher Robson, Ashley Stafford, alto; Edgar Fleet, t; Anthony Shelley, bar; London Oratory Choir; Thames Chamber Orchestra; John Hoban. CRD CRD 1071 Tape (c) CRDC 4071
+-Gr 11-80 p724 +-HFN 3-81 p97 tape
+-HFN 11-80 p123 +-MT 4-81 p248
VALVERDE, Joaquin
Songs: Clavelitos. See no. 3642. See no. 3886
VAN BERGEIJK, Gilius
D.E.S. See no. 3728
VAN CAMPEN, Tony
Sintering. See no. 3728
VANDERPOOL
Values. See no. 4042
VAN DE VATE, Nancy
Music, viola, percussion and piano. See no. 1897
VAN DOORN, Frans
Minnuet. See no. 3728

VAN EYCK, Jacob
Amarilli mia bella. See no. 1880
Blyndschap van mign vliedt. See no. 1880
Boffons. See no. 3927
Doen Daphne. See no. 1099
Engels Nachtegaeltje. See no. 1099. See no. 3927
O slaep o zoete slaep. See no. 1880
Pavane lachrymae. See no. 1099
VAN GHIZEGHEM, Hayne
De tous biens plaine. See no. 3948
VANHAL, Jan
Sonata, flute and violin, op. 3, G major. See no. 1515
VAN VLIJMEN, Jan
3413 Quarterni. Quintet, winds, no. 2. COA, Danzi Quintet; Lucas Vis. Composers Voice CVS 1981/3
+FF 11/12-81 p265
Quintet, winds, no. 2. See no. 3413
VARNEY, Louis
3414 Les mousquetaires au couvent. Mady Mesple, Christiane Chateau, Michele Command, s; Charles Burles, t; Michel Trempont, bar; Jules Bastin, bs; Theatre Royal de Monnaie Chorus; Belgian Radio-Television Orchestra and Chorus; Edgar Doneux. EMI 2C 167 16361/2 (2)
+Gr 9-80 p399 +HFN 2-81 p94
VASQUEZ, Juan
Con que la lavare. See no. 3828
Morenica dame un beso. See no. 4063
VAUGHAN WILLIAMS, Ralph
Concerto, tuba, F minor. See no. 3423
3415 Concerto, oboe, A minor. Concerto grosso. WARLOCK: Capriol suite. Serenade, strings. Celia Nicklin, ob; AMF; Neville Marriner. Argo ZRG 881 Tape (c) KZRC 881
+FF 5/6-80 p166 ++RR 9-79 p98
+Gr 9-79 p473 +-RR 3-80 p104 tape
+-HF 6-81 p69 tape +ST 1-80 p692
+HFN 9-79 p115
Concerto accademico, D minor. See no. 3423
Concerto grosso. See no. 1328. See no. 3415
The England of Elizabeth: Suite. See no. 3423
3416 English folk song suite (arr. Jacob). Fantasia on "Greensleeves" (arr. Greaves). TRAD. (arr. Hazel): John Peel. Sumer is icumen in. The turtle dove. (arr. Pearson): The British grenadiers. Early one morning. I will give my love an apple. The keeper. The jolly miller. The oak and the ash. AMF; Neville Marriner. Argo ZRG 931 Tape (c) KZRC 931
+Gr 11-81 p702 ++HFN 11-81 p97
English folk song suite. See no. 69. See no. 1859
Fantasia on a theme by Thomas Tallis. See no. 4082
Fantasia on "Greensleeves". See no. 3416. See no. 3666
Folk-song arrangements: Just as the tide was flowing; The lover's ghost; Wassail song. See no. 3685
The 49th parallel: Prelude and fugue. See no. 4105
Greensleeves. See no. 2260
In Windsor forest. See no. 1477
The lark ascending. See no. 1331. See no. 3421

Let all the world. See no. 3615
Mystical songs: Come my way. See no. 3615
3417 On Wenlock edge. WARLOCK: The curlew. Ian Partridge, t; London Music Group. Arabesque 8018 Tape (c) 9018
+ARG 5-81 p34 +NR 11-80 p7
++FF 3/4-81 p218 +St 3-81 p60
3418 On Wenlock edge. Gerald English, t; West Australian Symphony Orchestra; David Measham. Unicorn KP 8001
+St 3-81 p60
On Wenlock edge. See no. 1077. See no. 1673. See no. 1900
Prelude and fugue, C minor. See no. 3422
Prelude on hymn tune, no. 13. See no. 3857
Preludes on Welsh hymn tunes: Rhosymedre. See no. 1021. See no. 3666
3419 Songs (Folksongs): As I walked out; Ballade de Jesus Christ; The brewer; Bushes and briars; The captain's apprentice; Chanson de Quete; The cuckoo; Geordie; How cold the wind doth blow; Joseph and Mary; The lawyer; The maiden's lament; The morning dew; On board a 98; The ploughman; Reveillez-vous, Piccars; Rolling in the dew; The saviour's love; Searching for lambs; she's like the swallow; The truth sent from above. Robert Tear, t; Philip Ledger, pno; Hugh Bean, vln. HMV SQ HQS 1412 Tape (c) TC HQS 1412 (also Angel S 50003)
+Gr 3-78 p1605 +MUM 5/6-81 p32
++HFN 3-78 p149 ++RR 3-78 p66
Songs: A clear midnight; Four nights; How can the tree but wither; Joy shipmate joy; Motion and stillness; The new ghost; Nocturne; Twilight people; The water mill. See no. 1336
Songs: Linden Lea; Silent noon; Songs of travel. See no. 4057
Songs: O how amiable are thy dwellings; Linden Lea. See no. 3618
Songs: Poems by Fredegond Shove. See no. 1272
Songs: Rhosymedre; Lord thou hast been our refuge. See no. 3809
Songs: Silent noon. See no. 3703
Songs: The call. See no. 3852
Songs: The cloud-capp'd towers; Full fathom five; Over hill over dale. See no. 4005
Songs: Vocalises. See no. 3957
Suite be ballet: Passepied. See no. 1021
Symphonies, nos. 1-9. See no. 3423
3420 Symphony, no. 1. Sheila Armstrong, s; John Carol Case, bar; LPO and Chorus; Adrian Boult. HMV ESD 7104 Tape (c) TC ESD 7104 (From ASD 2439/40)
+Gr 4-81 p1326 +HFN 5-81 p93
+Gr 7-81 p196 tape
3421 Symphony, no. 4, F minor. The lark ascending. Barry Griffiths, vln; RPO; Paavo Berglund. HMV ASD 3904 Tape (c) TC ASD 3904
+-Gr 2-81 p1092 +-HFN 2-81 p94
3422 Symphony, no. 6, E minor. Prelude and fugue, C minor. David Bell, org; LPO; Vernon Handley. Classics for Pleasure CFP 40334 Tape (c) 40334
+-Gr 9-80 p350 +HFN 5-81 p93 tape
+HFN 9-80 p111
Toccata marziale. See no. 69. See no. 1859
The wasps. See no. 1858
The wasps: Overture. See no. 3423

3423 Works, selections: Concerto accademico, D minor. Concerto, tuba, F minor. England of Elizabeth: Suite. Symphonies, nos. 1-9. The wasps: Overture. LSO and Chorus; Andre Previn; Heather Harper, s; John Shirley-Quirk, bar; John Fletcher, tuba; James Oliver Buswell, vln. RCA GL 4-3576/83 (8) Tape (c) GK 4-3576/83 (From SER 5585, GL 43577, SB 6860, GL 43578, SB 16856, GL 43579, SB 6769, GL 43580, 43581, SB 6861, 6801, GL 43582, 43583, SB 6736, 6842)
+Gr 12-81 p892

VECCHI, Orfeo Orazio
Il bianco e dolce cigno. See no. 4010
So ben mi chi ha bon tempo. See no. 3692. See no. 3938

3424 Le veglie de Siena. Societa Cameristica di Lugano; Edwin Loehrer. Accord ACC 140037
+HFN 12-81 p105

VEJVANOVSKY, Paul
Serenade. See no. 3979
Sonata italica. See no. 3979

VELLONES
Le posson volant. See no. 3823

VELLUTI
Venetian barcarolle. See no. 3907

VENTO, Ivo de
Frisch ist mein Sinn. See no. 3675
Herr dein Wort mich getroestet hat. See no. 3675
Ich weiss ein Maidlein. See no. 3675
So wuensch ich ihr ein gute Nacht. See no. 3675

VERACINI, Francesco Maria

3425 Sonatas, op. 1, nos. 1-3, 6-8, 10-12. Piero Toso, vln; Gianni Chiampan, vlc; Edoardo Farina, hpd. Musical Heritage Society MHS 824293 (2)
+FF 7/8-81 p187

Sonata, violin, E minor. See no. 1735

VERBEN, Johannes
O domine gloriosa. See no. 3896

VERCOE, Barry
Synapse. See no. 1638

VERCOLIER
Quant les papillons. See no. 4051

VERDELOT
Italia mia. See no. 3692

VERDELOT, Philippe
Madrigals: Amor quanto piu lieto; La bella donna; Donna se fera stella; Madonna non so dir tante parole; Madonna per voi ardo; O dolce notte; Quella che sospirand'ogn hor deseo; Se l'ardor foss equale; Trist Amarilli mia dunqu'e pur vero. See no. 4010

VERDI, Giuseppe

3426 Aida. Mirella Freni, Katia Ricciarelli, s; Agnes Baltsa, ms; Jose Carreras, t; Piero Cappuccilli, bar; Ruggero Raimondi, Jose van Dam, bs; VSOO Chorus; VPO; Herbert von Karajan. HMV SLS 5205 (3) Tape (c) TC SLS 5205 (also Angel SZ 3888)
+-ARG 7/8-81 p49
+FF 1/2-81 p203
++Gr 9-80 p399
++Gr 12-80 p889 tape
+MT 4-81 p248
++MUM 3/4-81 p35
+-NR 1-81 p8
+-ON 2-14-81 p44

+-HF 4-81 p85 +-SFC 1-18-81 p21
+-HFN 11-80 p124 +St 2-81 p106
+HFN 1-81 p109 tape

Aida: Ahime di guerra fremere;...Fu la sorte...Ebben qual nuovo fremito...Pieta ti prenda...La tra foreste vergine;...Morir si pur e bella...O terra addio. See no. 1167

Aida: Celeste Aida. See no. 3657. See no. 3750. See no. 3759. See no. 3839. See no. 3987. See no. 3995. See no. 4050

Aida: Celeste Aida...Gia i sacerdoti;...Misero appien;...La fatal pietra...O terra addio. See no. 1361

Aida: Celeste Aida; Tutto e finito...O terra addio. See no. 3967

3427 Aida: Dance of the little Moorish slaves; Grand march and ballet. Macbeth: Ballet; Chorus of witches; Dance of the spirits. I vespri siciliani: The four seasons. PhO; Riccardo Muti. Angel SZ 37801 (also HMV ASD 4015 Tape (c) TC ASD 4015. From SLS 992, 977)

+Gr 8-81 p280 +-HFN 8-81 p88
+Gr 11-81 p783 tape +NR 11-81 p4

Aida: Gia i sacerdoti...Misera appien. See no. 3966

Aida: Gia i sacerdote adunansi; Misero appien mi festi; Se quel guerrier io fossi; Celeste Aida. See no. 3997

Aida: Gloria all'Egitto; Grand march. See no. 3474

Aida: Grand march. See no. 3699

Aida: La fatal pietra...O terra addio. See no. 3849. See no. 3996

Aida: Mortal diletto ai numi; Nume custode e vindice. See no. 3968

Aida: O patria mia. See no. 3430

Aida: O terra addio. See no. 4023

Aida: Ojime morir mi sento. See no. 4080

Aida: Overture. See no. 3447. See no. 3448

Aida: Quest assisa. See no. 4034

Aida: Qui Radames verra...O patria mia. See no. 3647. See no. 3850

Aida: Ritorna vincitor. See no. 1588. See no. 3623. See no. 3752. See no. 4041

Aida: Ritorna vincitor; O patria mia. See no. 3989

3428 Aida: Se quel guerrier io fossi...Celeste Aida; Or di Vulcano al tempio muovi...Ritorna vincitor; Gloria all'Egitto...O re pei sacri numi; O patria mia...Ciel mio padre; Gia i sacerdoti; Morir si pura e bella. Mirella Freni, s; Agnes Baltsa, ms; Jose Carreras, Thomas Moser, t; Piero Cappuccilli, bar; Ruggero Raimondi, Jose van Dam, bs; Vienna State Opera Chorus; VPO; Herbert von Karajan. HMV ASD 3983 Tape (C) TC ASD 3983 (From SLS 5205)

+Gr 6-81 p84 ++HFN 6-81 p88

Aida: Se quel guerrier io fossi...Celeste Aida. See no. 842. See no. 3433. See no. 3646. See no. 3769

Alzira: Overture. See no. 3475

3429 Arias: Un ballo in maschera: Alla vita che t'arride; Eri tu. Don Carlo: O Carlo ascolta. La forza del destino: Morir; Tremenda cosa. Macbeth: Perfidi; All' anglo contro me venite. Otello: Credo. Rigoletto: Cortigiani vil razza dannata. La traviata: Di provenza il mar. Il trovatore: Il balen del suo sorriso. Bernd Weikl, bar; Munich Radio Orchestra; Heinz Wallberg. Acanta DC 23237

+-FF 7/8-81 p188 +-ON 3-28-81 p36

3430 Arias: Aida: O patria mia. Il Corsaro: Non so le tetre imagini. Falstaff: Sul fil d'un suffio etesio. La forza del destino: Pace pace mio Dio. I Lombardi: La mia letizia infondere. Macbeth: Ah la paterna mano. Otello: Gia nella notte densa. La traviata: De miei bollenti spiriti. Katia Ricciarelli, s; Luciano Pavarotti, t; Teatro Regio di Parma Orchestra; Giuseppe Patane. Decca SDD 569 (From Ars Nova ANC 25001)
+Gr 4-81 p1366 +-Op 7-81 p719
+HFN 3-81 p93

3431 Arias: Un ballo in maschera: Ecco l'orrido campo...Ma dall'arido stelo; Morro ma prima in grazia. Il Corsaro: Non so le tetre immagini. Don Carlo: O don fatale. Ernani: Surta e le notte ...Ernani Ernani involami. Nabucco: Ben io t'invenni...Anch'io dischiuso un giorno...Salgo gia del trono aurato. Fiorenza Cossotto, ms; RPO; Nello Santi. Fonit Cetra LIC 9003
+-Gr 9-81 p445

3432 Arias: Un ballo in maschera: Eri tu. Don Carlo: Prison scene. La forza del destino: Urna fatale. Macbeth: Pieta rispetto amore. Otello: Credo in un Dio crudel. I vespri siciliani: In braccio alle dovizie. Renato Bruson, bar; Orchestras; Armando Gatto, Riccardo Muti, Francesco Molinari-Pradelli, Claudio Abbado. Legendary Recordings LR 134
++FF 5/6-81 p174

3433 Arias: Aida: Se quel guerrier io fossi...Celeste Aida. Un ballo in maschera: Di tu se fedele. Ernani: Merce diletti amici... Come rugiada al cespite. La forza del destino: La vita e inferno all'infelice...Oh tu che in seno agli angeli. Luisa Miller: Oh fede negar potessi...Quando le sere al placido. Macbeth: O figli...Ah la paterna mano. Otello: Dio mi potevi scagliar; Niun mi tema. Rigoletto: Questa o quella; La donna e mobile. La traviata: Lunge da lei...De miei; Bollenti spiriti. Il trovatore: Il presagio funesto...Ah si ben mio; Di quella pira. Carlo Bergonzi, t; Ambrosian Singers; NPhO; Nello Santi. Philips MS 6570 045 (From 6747 193)
+-Gr 8-81 p315 ++HFN 6-81 p88

3434 Aroldo. Montserrat Caballe, s; Gianfranco Cecchele, t; Juan Pons, bar; Louis Lebherz, bs; New York Opera Orchestra; Eve Queler. CBS 79328 (3) (also CBS M3X 35906)
+-FF 5/6-81 p175 +-ON 4-11-81 p52
+Gr 9-80 p400 +-Op 10-80 p1014
+-HFN 10-80 p109 -RR 8-80 p32
+-MT 12-80 p788 +SFC 3-15-81 p18
+-NYT 5-3-81 pD19 +-STL 8-10-80 p30
+OC Fall 1981 p51

Aroldo: Ciel ch'io respiri; Ah dagli scanni eterei...Cabaletta. See no. 3713

3435 Un ballo in maschera. Don Carlo. Macbeth. Rigoletto. Simon Boccanegra. La traviata. Il trovatore. Antonietta Stella, Renata Scotto, Mirelli Freni, s; Fiorenza Cossotto, Shirley Verrett, ms; Flaviano Labb, Placido Domingo, Carlo Bergonzi, Jose Carreras, t; Ettore Bastianini, Piero Cappuccilli, Dietrich Fischer-Dieskau, bar; Boris Christoff, Ivo Vinco, Nicolai Ghiaurov, Jose van Dam, bs; Gianni Poggi; La Scala Orchestra and Chorus; Gianandrea Gavazzeni, Gabriele Santini, Claudio Abbado, Rafael Kubelik, Antonino Votto, Tullio Serafin. DG 2562 (21)
+FF 9/10-81 p191

3436 Un ballo in maschera. Katia Ricciarelli, Edita Gruberova, s; Elena Obraztsova, ms; Placido Domingo, t; Renato Bruson, bar; Ruggero Raimondi, bs; La Scala Orchestra and Chorus; Claudio Abbado. DG 2740 251 (3) Tape (c) 3378 111
+FF 11/12-81 p266
+Gr 9-81 p428
+HFN 11-81 p105 tape
+HFN 12-81 p105
+-ON 12-19-81 p44
+-Op 10-81 p1040
++SFC 10-18-81 p18
+St 11-81 p96
+-STL 9-13-81 p41

3437 Un ballo in maschera. Antonietta Stella, Eugenia Ratti, s; Ebe Stignani, ms; Giuseppe di Stefano, t; Ettore Bastianini, bar; La Scala Orchestra and Chorus; Gianandrea Gavazzeni. Historical Recordings HRE 353/3 (3)
+NR 11-81 p10

3438 Un ballo in maschera. Zinka Milanov, Stella Andreva, s; Bruna Castagna, ms; Jussi Bjoerling, John Carter, Lodovico Oliviero, t; Alexander Sved, Arthur Kent, bar; Norman Cordon, Nicola Moscona, bs; Metropolitan Opera Orchestra and Chorus; Ettore Panizza. MET 8 (3)
+HF 6-81 p63
+ON 3-81 p36

Un ballo in maschera: Alla vita che t'arride; Eri tu. See no. 3429

Un ballo in maschera: Barcarola; La rivedro nell' estasi. See no. 3944

Un ballo in maschera: Di tu se fedele. See no. 3433. See no. 3987. See no. 4075

Un ballo in maschera: Di tu se fedele; Forse la soglia attinse; Ma se m'e forza perderti. See no. 3997

Un ballo in maschera: E scherzo; La rivedra. See no. 4037

Un ballo in maschera: Ecco l'orrido campo...Ma dall'arido stelo. See no. 4021

Un ballo in maschera: Ecco l'orrido campo; Ma dall'arido stelo; Morro ma prima in grazia. See no. 3431

Un ballo in maschera: Eri tu. See no. 3432

Un ballo in maschera: La rivedra See no. 4023

Un ballo in maschera: La rivedra nell'estasi; Di tu se fedele; Forse la soglia a attinse...Ma se m'e forza perderte... See no. 842

Un ballo in maschera: Ma se m'e forza perderti. See no. 3750

Un ballo in maschera: Morro ma prima in grazia. See no. 3751

3439 Un ballo in maschera: Posa in pace; Sire...Che leggo il bando ad una donna; Ecco l'ordo campo; Alzati la tuo figlio...Eri tu; Ah perche que fuggite. Christina Deutekom, Patricia Hay, s; John Robertson, Charles Craig, t; Jan Derksen, bar; William McCue, Pieter van den Berg, bs; Scottish Opera Chorus; Scottish National Orchestra; Alexander Gibson. Classics for Pleasure CFP 40252
+-FF 9/10-80 p227
+-Gr 1-77 p1174
+HFN 12-76 p149
+-ON 2-14-81 p44
+RR 1-77 p40

La battaglia di Legnano: Voi lo diceste...Quante volte. See no. 3711

Il Corsaro: Non so le tetre immagini. See no. 3430. See no. 3431

3440 Don Carlo (4 act version). Edita Gruberova, Mirella Freni, s; Agnes Baltsa, ms; Jose Carreras, Horst Nitsche, t; Jose van Dam, Piero Cappuccilli, bar; Nicolai Ghiaurov, Ruggero Raimondi, bs;

German Opera Chorus; BPhO; Herbert von Karajan. HMV SLS 5154 (7) Tape (c) TC SLS 5154 (Also Angel SCLX 3875 Tape (c) 4Z4X 3875)

+-ARG 6-80 p30
+-FF 1/2-80 p169
+Gr 10-79 p711
++Gr 3-80 p1446 tape
+-HF 4-80 p97
+HFN 12-79 p171
+HFN 1-80 p123 tape
+-MT 2-81 p113
+-NR 2-80 p10
+NYT 12-23-79 pD28
+-ON 12-15-79 p36
+-Op 2-80 p165
+-RR 10-79 p66
+RR 6-80 p95 tape
++SFC 1-20-80 p47
+-St 4-80 p136

3441 Don Carlo (in French). Marie Tremblay, Gillian Knight, s; Michele Vilma, ms; Andre Turp, t; Robert Savoie, bar; Joseph-Alfred Rouleau, Richard van Allen, bs; BBC Singers, BBC Concerto Orchestra; John Matheson. VOCE 23 (4)

+FF 9/10-81 p193

Don Carlo. See no. 3435
Don Carlo: Arias. See no. 2641
Don Carlo: Dio che nell'alma infondere. See no. 3849. See no. 4048
Don Carlo: Dormiro sol. See no. 3968
Don Carlo: Ella giammai m'amo. See no. 4064
Don Carlo: Fontainebeau; Foresta immense...Io la vidi e al suo sorriso. See no. 842
Don Carlo: Io la vidi. See no. 3839
Don Carlo: Monologue of Philip. See no. 4025
Don Carlo: O Carlo ascolta. See no. 3429
Don Carlo: O don fatale. See no. 795. See no. 3431. See no. 3970. See no. 4080
Don Carlo: Per me giunto; Morro ma lieta in corre. See no. 4024
Don Carlo: Prison scene. See no. 3432
Don Carlo: Tu che la vanita. See no. 1588. See no. 3623. See no. 3647. See no. 3755. See no. 4014
I du Foscari: O vecchio cor. See no. 4034

3442 Ernani. Il trovatore: Act 4, Scene 1. Raina Kabaivanska, s; Milena Pauli, ms; Placido Domingo, Heinz Zednik, t; Carlo Meliciani, bar; Nicolai Ghiaurov, Alfredo Giacomotti, bs; La Scala Orchestra and Chorus; Orchestra; Antonino Votto, Herbert von Karajan. Legendary Recordings LR 135 (3)

+FF 7/8-81 p189

Ernani: Che mai vegg'io...Infelice. See no. 3968
Ernani: Come rugiada. See no. 3839
Ernani: Grand trio finale, Act 4. See no. 3890
Ernani: Infelice. See no. 4064
Ernani: Merce diletti amici...Come rugiada al cespite. See no. 3433
Ernani: Merce diletti amici...Come rugiada al cespito...O tu che l'alma adora. See no. 3769
Ernani: O dei verd'anni miei; Lo vedremo o veglio audace. See no. 4034
Ernani: Solingo errante e misero; Come rugiada al cespite. See no. 3944
Ernani: Surta e la notte...Ernani involami. See no. 1365. See no. 3431

3443 Falstaff. Elisabeth Schwarzkopf, Anna Moffo, s; Nan Merriman,

Fedora Barbieri, ms; Luigi Alva, t; Tito Gobbi, Rolando Panerai, bar; PhO and Chorus; Herbert von Karajan. HMV SLS 5211 (2) Tape (c) TC SLS 5211 (From Columbia 33CS 1410-2, SAX 2254/6)
+FF 7/8-81 p190
+Gr 12-80 p880
+HFN 2-81 p97
+STL 2-8-81 p40

3444 Falstaff. Raina Kabaivanska, Janet Perry, s; Christa Ludwig, Trudeliese Schmidt, ms; Francisco Araiza, Piero de Palma, Heinz Zednik, t; Giuseppe Taddei, Rolando Panerai, Federico Davia, bs-bar; VSOO Chorus; VPO; Herbert von Karajan. Philips 6769 060 Tape (c) 7654 060
-FF 5/6-81 p176
+Gr 2-81 p1121
+-HF 6-81 p63
+HF 7-81 p71 tape
++HFN 3-81 p91
++HFN 5-81 p93 tape
+MUM 9/10-81 p35
+-NR 4-81 p8
+ON 3-28-81 p36
+-Op 3-81 p271
++SFC 1-18-81 p21
+St 5-81 p54
+-STL 2-8-81 p40

Falstaff: Dal labbro tinto. See no. 4054
Falstaff: Sul fil d'un suffio etesio. See no. 3430
La forza del destino: Dalla natal dua terra...O tu che in seno angeli. See no. 3996
La forza del destino: Invano Alvaro; Le minaccie i fieri accenti. See no. 3997
La forza del destino: Invan Alvaro...Le mannacie; Solenne in quest'ora. See no. 4048
La forza del destino: La vergine degli angeli. See no. 1167
La forza del destino: La vita e inferno...O tu che in seno agli angeli. See no. 3433. See no. 3843
La forza del destino: Madre pietosa vergine; Pace pace mio Dio. See no. 1588
La forza del destino: Morir; Tremenda cosa. See no. 3429
La forza del destino: O tu che in seno agli angeli. See no. 3839
La forza del destino: O tu che in seno agli angeli. See no. 3944. See no. 4053
La forza del destino: Overture. See no. 748. See no. 3054. See no. 3447. See no. 3475
La forza del destino: Pace pace mio Dio. See no. 3430
La forza del destino: Solenne in quest'ora. See no. 3849. See no. 3965. See no. 3966. See no. 3995. See no. 4045. See no. 4075
La forza del destino: Son giunta grazie o Dio. See no. 3080
La forza del destino: Urna fatale. See no. 3432
Giovanna d'Arco: Overture. See no. 3448
Giovanna d'Arco: Sempre all'alba. See no. 3647
Giovanna d'Arco: Sotto un quercia parvemi...Pondo e letal martiro. See no. 842
Jerusalem: Je veux encore entendre. See no. 3689
I Lombardi: Dove sola m'inoltro...Per dirupi e per foreste. See no. 1374
I Lombardi: La mia letizia infondere. See no. 3430
I Lombardi: O madre...Se vano e il pregare. See no. 3711
I Lombardi: O signore dal tetto natio. See no. 3474
I Lombardi: Qual vo'uta transcorrere. See no. 3997

3445 Luisa Miller. Katia Ricciarelli, s; Elena Obraztsova, Audrey Michael, ms; Placido Domingo, Luigi de Corato, t; Gwynne Howell, Wladimiro Ganzarolli, Renato Bruson, bar; ROHO and Chorus;

Lorin Maazel. DG 2709 096 (3) Tape (c) 3370 035 (also DG 2531 229/31)

+-ARG 10-80 p33
+-FF 9/10-80 p229
+Gr 6-80 p65
+Gr 8-80 p275 tape
+-HF 10-80 p92
+HF 7-81 p71 tape
++HFN 7-80 p111
+HFN 8-80 p109 tape
+MT 12-80 p788
++NR 7-80 p8
+NYT 6-29-80 pD20
+-ON 9-80 p68
+-Op 7-80 p685
+-RR 6-80 p37
+St 9-80 p73
+-STL 5-11-80 p39

Luisa Miller; Ah fede negar potessi...Quando le sere al placido. See no. 3433. See no. 4027

3446 Luisa Miller: Lo vidi e'l primo palpito; Ah fu giusto il mio sospetto; Il mio sangue la vita darei; Duchessa...Duchessa tu m'appelli; Fra i mortali ancora oppressa e tanto l'innocenza; Tu puniscimi o Signore; A brani o perfido; Quando le sere al placido; L'ara o l'avello apprestami; Andrem raminghi e poveri; Ah l'ultima preghiera; Scampo non resta. Katia Ricciarelli, s; Elena Obraztsova, ms; Placido Domingo, t; Wladimir Ganzarolli, Renato Bruson, bar; Gwynne Howell, bs; ROHO and Chorus; Lorin Maazel. DG 2537 055 (From 2709 096)

+Gr 8-81 p315
++HFN 6-81 p88

Luisa Miller: Overture. See no. 3447. See no. 3475. See no. 3448
Luisa Miller: Overture; Quando le sere al placido. See no. 4081
Luisa Miller: Quando le sere al placido. See no. 4032
Macbeth. See no. 3435
Macbeth: Ah la paterna mano. See no. 3430
Macbeth: Ambizioso spirto tu sei. See no. 3623
Macbeth: Arias. See no. 2641
Macbeth: Ballet music. See no. 3722
Macbeth: Ballet music; Chorus of witches; Dance of the spirits. See no. 3427
Macbeth: Che faceste; Dite su; S'allontanarone; Chi v'impose unirvi a noi; Tre volte miagola la gatta in fregola; Patri oppressa. See no. 3474
Macbeth: La luce langue; Una macchia e qui tutt'ora. See no. 795
Macbeth: O figli...Ah la paterna mano. See no. 3433
Macbeth: Overture. See no. 3448
Macbeth: Perfidi; All' anglo contro me venite. See no. 3429. See no. 4079
Macbeth: Pieta rispetto amore. See no. 3432
Macbeth: Vegliammo invan due notti. See no. 4122
Macbeth: Vien t'affretta. See no. 4021
I Masnadieri: Tu del mio Carlo. See no. 3890
Nabucco: Anch'io dischiuso...Salgo gia del trono. See no. 2018
Nabucco: Ben io t'invenni...Anch'io dischiuso. See no. 4021
Nabucco: Ben io t'invenni...Anch'io dischiuso un giorno; Salgo gia del trono aurato. See no. 3431. See no. 3711
Nabucco: Gli arredi festivi; E l'assiria un regina; Va pensiero. See no. 3474
Nabucco: Overture. See no. 3447. See no. 3475
Nabucco: Sperate o figli. See no. 4074
Otello: Ave Maria. See no. 3713. See no. 3751
Otello: Canzone di salce...Ave Maria. See no. 3711
Otello: Credo. See no. 3429. See no. 3432

Otello: Dio mi potevi scagliar; Niun mi tema. See no. 3433
Otello: Gia nella notte densa. See no. 2640. See no. 3430. See no. 3890. See no. 4081
Otello: Mia madre aveva una povera ancella; Ave Maria. See no. 3642
Otello: Nell'ora arcane...Ora e per sempre addio. See no. 3996
Otello: Niun mi tema; Si pel ciel. See no. 4023
Otello: Ora e per sempre addio. See no. 1361
Otello: Vanne la tua meta gia vedo. See no. 3752

3447 Overtures: Aida. La forza del destino. Luisa Miller. Nabucco. La traviata, Act 1 and 3. I vespri siciliano. Budapest Philharmonic Orchestra; Karolos Trikolidis. Hungaroton SLPX 12142
-FF 7/8-81 p191 -NR 4-81 p5

3448 Overtures: Aida. Giovanna d'Arco. Luisa Miller. Macbeth. La traviata. I vespri siciliani. NPhO; Igor Markevitch. Philips 6527 078 Tape (c) 7311 078 (From SFM 23023)
+Gr 4-81 p1378 +HFN 7-81 p83 tape
+HFN 5-81 p91

3449 Pezzi sacre (4). Janet Baker, ms; PhO and Chorus; Carlo Maria Giulini. HMV SXLP 30508 Tape (c) TC SXLP 30508 (From SAN 120)
++Gr 6-81 p75 +HFN 8-81 p92

3450 Pezzi sacri (4). Kvetoslava Nemeckova, s; CPhO and Chorus; Gaetano Delogu. Pro Arte PAL 1013 (From Supraphon 112 2433)
+-FF 11/12-81 p269

3451 Pezzi sacre (4). Patricia Brooks, s; Musica Aeterna Orchestra and Chorus; Frederic Waldman. Westminster 1420 (From Decca DL 79429)
+ARG 7/8-81 p40 -FF 1/2-81 p203

Quartet, strings, E minor. See no. 821. See no. 3314

3452 Requiem. BRUCKNER: Symphony, no. 8, C minor: Finale. Hilde Zadek, s; Margarete Klose, ms; Helge Roswange, t; Boris Christoff, bs; Wiener Singverein; VPO, Berlin Staatskapelle; Herbert von Karajan. Bruno Walter Society RR 391 (2)
+-FF 9/10-81 p195 +-NR 4-81 p10

3453 Requiem. Montserrat Caballe, s; Bianca Berini, ms; Placido Domingo, t; Paul Plishka, bs; Musica Sacra Chorus; NYP; Zubin Mehta. CBS 36927 (2)
++ON 12-19-81 p44 ++SFC 9-20-81 p18
*NR 11-81 p8

3454 Requiem. Katia Ricciarelli, s; Shirley Verrett, ms; Placido Domingo, t; Nicolai Ghiaurov, bar; La Scala Orchestra and Chorus; Claudio Abbado. DG 2707 120 Tape (c) 3370 032
+FF 1/2-81 p204 +HFN 1-81 p109 tape
+-Gr 11-80 p727 ++NR 12-80 p8
-HF 3-81 p75 +ON 2-14-81 p44
-HF 11-81 p103 tape ++STL 11-9-80 p40
+HFN 11-80 p124

3455 Requiem. Gwyneth Jones, s; Grace Bumbry, ms; Franco Corelli, t; Ezio Flagello, bs; Orchestra and Chorus; Zubin Mehta. Legendary Recordings LR 125 (2)
+FF 5/6-81 p179

3456 Requiem. Heather Harper, s; Josephine Veasey, ms; Carlo Bini, t; Hans Sotin, bs; London Philharmonic Chorus; RPO; John Alldis, Carlos Paita. Lodia Tape (c) LOC 772/3
+HFN 6-81 p87 tape

Requiem, excerpts. See no. 3817

Requiem: Confutatis maledictis. See no. 3968
Requiem: Ingemisco. See no. 3707. See no. 3759
3457 Rigoletto. Ileana Cotrubas, s; Elena Obraztsova, ms; Placido Domingo, t; Piero Cappuccilli, bar; Nicolai Ghiaurov, Kurt Moll, bs; VPO; Carlo Maria Giulini. DG 2740 225 Tape (c) 3371 054 (also DG 2531 2134/6)
-ARG 5-81 p49
+-FF 1/2-81 p205
+Gr 12-80 p889 tape
+Gr 10-80 p541
+-HF 4-81 p88
+-HF 7-81 p71 tape
++HFN 10-80 p109
+HFN 11-80 p131
++HFN 10-81 p95 tape
+MT 4-81 p248
/NYT 10-26-80 pB33
+-ON 11-22-80 p44
++SFC 9-21-80 p21
++SFC 11-2-80 p22
+St 1-81 p73
+STL 11-9-80 p40
3458 Rigoletto. Gianna D'Angelo, s; Alfredo Kraus, t; Aldo Protti, bar; Giorgio Tadeo, bs; Trieste Teatro Communale Orchestra and Chorus. Movimento Musica 02 003 (2)
+-HFN 12-81 p105
3459 Rigoletto. Mercedes Capsir, s; Anna Masetti Bassi, ms; Dino Borgioli, t; Duilio Baronti, Ernesto Dominici, bs; Riccardo Stracciari, Aristide Baracchi; La Scala Orchestra and Chorus; Lorenzo Molajoli. Pearl GEMM 177/8
+Gr 4-81 p1374
+-Op 8-81 p824
3460 Rigoletto. Gianna d'Angelo, s; Miriam Pirazzini, ms; Richard Tucker, Vittorio Pandano, t; Renato Capecchi, Vito Susca, Giorgio Giorgetti, bar; Ivan Sardi, bs; San Carlo Teatro di Napoli Orchestra and Chorus; Francesco Molinari-Pradelli. Philips 6770 016 (2) Tape (c) 7650 016 (also Philips 6747 407. From ABL 3307/8, Fontana SFL 14005/6)
+-FF 5/6-79 p100
+-Gr 11-81 p763
+-Op 10-81 p1070
+SFC 6-3-79 p48
+-St 8-79 p117
Rigoletto. See no. 3435
3461 Rigoletto, excerpts. Maria Gyurkovics, s; Olga Szonyi, ms; Josef Simandy, Erno Kenez, t; Alexander Sved, bar; Mihaly Szekely, bs; HSOO; Miklos Lukacs, Andras Korodi, Francesco Molinari-Pradelli, Vilmos Komor, Janos Kulka. Hungaroton LPX 12344
-FF 9/10-81 p195
Rigoletto: Arias. See no. 2641
Rigoletto: Bella figlia dell'amore; La donna e mobile; Questa o quella. See no. 3995
Rigoletto: Caro nome. See no. 3713
Rigoletto: Caro nome; Si vendetta. See no. 3748
Rigoletto: Cortigiani vil razza dannata. See no. 3429. See no. 4079
Rigoletto: E il sol dell'anima. See no. 4033. See no. 4081
Rigoletto: E il sol dell'anima; Caro nome; Bella figlia dell' amore; V'ho ingannato. See no. 3640
Rigoletto: E il sol dell'anima; Caro nome; Tutte le feste; Si vendetta; Quartet. See no. 4040
Rigoletto: Ella mi fu rapita; Parmi veder le lagrime; La donna e mobile. See no. 3972
Rigoletto: Freundlich blick ich; O wie so trugerisch. See no. 3747
Rigoletto: La donna e mobile. See no. 3836. See no. 3838. See

no. 3987. See no. 4028

Rigoletto: La donna e mobile; Bella figlia dell'amore; Questa o quella. See no. 3657

Rigoletto: La donna e mobile; E il sol dell anima. See no. 4032

Rigoletto: Pari siamo; Cortigiani vil razza dannata. See no. 4034

3462 Rigoletto: Prelude; Questa o quella; Pari siamo...Figlia...Mio padre; Caro nome che il mio cor festi primo palpitar; Ella mi fu rapita...Parmi veder le lagrime; Povero Rigoletto; Cortigiani vil razza dannata; Tutte le feste al tempio... and following scene; La donna e mobile; Un di se ven rammentomi...Bella figlia dell'amore...and following scene; V'ho ingannato colpevole fui. Ileana Cotrubas, s; Elena Obraztsova, Audrey Michael, ms; Placido Domingo, Luigi DeCorato, t; Piero Cappuccilli, bar; Nicolai Ghiaurov, Kurt Moll, bs; Vienna State Opera Chorus; VPO; Carlo Maria Giulini. DG 2537 057 Tape (c) 3306 057 (From 2740 225)

+Gr 8-81 p315 ++HFN 6-81 p88

Rigoletto: Questa o quella; La donna e mobile. See no. 3433. See no. 3759. See no. 3839. See no. 3966. See no. 4047. See no. 4054

Rigoletto: Questa o quella; La donna e mobile; Bella figlia dell' amore. See no. 3967

Rigoletto: Questa o quella; Parmi veder le lagrime; La donna e mobile; Quartet. See no. 1361

Simon Boccanegra. See no. 3435

Simon Boccanegra: A te l'estremo addio...Il lacerato spirito. See no. 3968

Simon Boccanegra: Il lacerato spirito. See no. 3752

3463 Songs: Album di sei romanze; L'Esule; Il poveretto; La seduzione; Sei romanze. Klara Takacs, ms; Sandor Falvai, pno. Hungaroton SLPX 12197

+ARG 1-81 p44 +HFN 12-80 p147
+-FF 9/10-80 p230 ++NR 10-80 p11
+Gr 12-80 p871 +SFC 8-10-80 p29
+HF 12-80 p86 +STL 4-12-81 p40

Songs: Il poveretto. See no. 3758

Songs: La seduzione; Non t'accostare all'urna; Brindisi. See no. 3718

3464 Stiffelio. Sylvia Sass, s; Jose Carreras, t; ORTF; Vienna Chorus; Lamberto Gardelli. Philips 6769 039 (2) Tape (c) 7699 127

+-ARG 2-81 p34 +MT 6-81 p393
+FF 1/2-81 p205 +OC Spring 1981 p51
+-Gr 10-80 p542 ++ON 10-80 p42
/+HF 2-81 p74 +Op 10-80 p1014
+HFN 10-80 p109 +-SFC 9-7-80 p32
+-NR 10-80 p10 ++St 12-80 p135
++NYT 9-14-80 pD42

3465 La traviata. Renata Scotto, Giuliana Tavolaccini, s; Armanda Bonato, ms; Gianni Raimondi, t; Ettore Bastianini, bar; Silvio Maionica, bs; La Scala Orchestra and Chorus; Antonino Votto. DG 2726 049 (2) Tape (c) 3372 049 (From SLPM 138832/4)

+-ARG 10-79 p30 +-HFN 1-81 p109 tape
+-Gr 8-76 p333 +-NYT 8-5-79 pD20
+-HF 10-79 p126 tape +RR 8-76 p24
+-HFN 8-76 p91

3466 La traviata. Teresa Stratas, Mimi Rosencrantz, s; Hanna Handulmann, ms; Fritz Wunderlich, Murray Dickie, t; Hermann Prey, bar; Helmut Kahn, bs; Munich National theater Orchestra and Chorus; Antonino Votto. Historical Recording HRE 334 (2)
+-FF 3/4-81 p215
-MUM 7/8-81 p34

3467 La traviata. Maria Callas, s; Mario Sereni, bar; Alfredo Kraus, t; San Carlo OPera Orchestra and Chorus; Franco Ghione. HMV RLS 757 (2) Tape (c) TC SLS 757 (also Angel ZBX 3910 Tape (c) 4Z2X 3910)
+ARG 2-81 p36
+FF 1/2-81 p207
+Gr 10-80 p541
+-HFN 1-81 p109 tape
+MT 6-81 p393
+-MUM 3/4-81 p34
+-NR 1-81 p10
+NYT 9-4-80 pD26
+-ON 2-14-81 p44
+-Op 1-81 p53
+St 12-80 p117
+STL 11-9-80 p40

3468 La traviata. Valerie Masterson, s; Della Jones, Shelagh Squires, ms; John Brecknock, Geoffrey Pogson, t; Christian du Plessis, Dennis Dowling, John Gibbs, John Kitchiner, bar; English National Opera Orchestra and Chorus; Charles Mackerras. HMV SLS 5216 (2) Tape (c) TC SLS 5216
+Gr 10-81 p609
+HFN 12-81 p105
+Op 12-81 p1263
+STL 10-11-81 p41

3469 La traviata. Joan Sutherland, Marjon Lambrinks, s; Della Jones, ms; Luciano Pavarotti, Alexander Oliver, t; Matteo Manuguerra, Jonathan Summers, bar; John Tomlinson, Giorgio Tadeo, bs; London Opera Chorus; National Philharmonic Orchestra; Richard Bonynge. London LDR 73002 (2) (also Decca D212D3 Tape (c) K212K32)
+-FF 11/12-81 p267
+Gr 4-81 p1362
+-HFN 4-81 p76
+MT 9-81 p608
+-NYT 5-3-81 pD19
+-OC Winter 1981 p55
-ON 6-81 p44
+-Op 6-81 p607
-SFC 5-31-81 p22
+-St 8-81 p99
+STL 5-10-81 p41

La traviata. See no. 3435

La traviata: Addio del passato. See no. 3711. See no. 3844

La traviata: Ah fors'e lui...Sempre libera. See no. 4040

La traviata: Ah fors'e lui...Sempre libera; Libiamo libiamo ne lieta calici. See no. 4081

La traviata: Ah si da un anno...Un di felice eterea; Parigi o cara; De miei bollenti spiriti. See no. 4032

La traviata: Arias. See no. 2641

La traviata: Brindisi; E strano...Ah fors'e lui...Sempre libera; Parigi o cara. See no. 3604

La traviata: Brindisi; Parigi o cara. See no. 3754

La traviata: De miei bollenti spiriti. See no. 3430. See no. 3965. See no. 4028

La traviata: Di provenza il mar. See no. 3429. See no. 4034. See no. 4079

La traviata: Finale, Act 1. See no. 3748

La traviata: Lunge da lei...De miei; Bollenti spiriti. See no. 3433. See no. 3843

La traviata: Lunge da lei...De miei bollenti spiriti; Parigi o cara. See no. 3967

La traviata: Noi siamo zingarelle; Di Madride noi siam. See no. 3474

La traviata: Parigi o cara. See no. 2604
La traviata: Parigi o cara; Gran dio. See no. 4023
La traviata: Parigi o cara; Lunge da lei...De miei bollenti spiriti. See no. 4035
La traviata: Prelude. See no. 3448
La traviata: Preludes, Act 1 and Act 3. See no. 3447
La traviata: Prelude, Act 3. See no. 3787
La traviata: Sempre libera. See no. 4000
La traviata: Sempre libera; Dite all giovine; Close of Act 3. See no. 3837
La traviata: Tenesta la promessa...Addio del passato. See no. 3642

3470 Il trovatore. Katia Ricciarelli, s; Stefania Toczynska, Phyllis Cannan, ms; Jose Carreras, Robin Leggate, t; Yuri Mazurok, bar; Robert Lloyd, bs; ROHO and Chorus; Colin Davis. Philips 6769 063 (3) Tape (c) 7654 063
+Gr 12-81 p933 ++HFN 12-81 p105

Il trovatore. See no. 3435
Il trovatore: Act 4, Scene 1. See no. 3442
Il trovatore: Ah si ben mio. See no. 3750. See no. 4053
Il trovatore: Ah si ben mio; Deserto sulla terra. See no. 3944
Il trovatore: Ah si ben mio; Di quella pira. See no. 3646. See no. 3769. See no. 4037
Il trovatore: Ah si ben mio; Di quella pira; Miserere. See no. 3987
Il trovatore: Ah si ben mio; Di quella pira; Miserere; Ai nostri monti. See no. 3966
Il trovatore: Ah si ben mio; Se m'ami ancor; Ai nostri monti; Di quella pira. See no. 3995
Il trovatore: Ai nostri monti. See no. 4023
Il trovatore: Ballet music, excerpts. See no. 3475

3471 Il trovatore: Che piu t'arresti...Tacea la notte; Vedi le fosche ...Stride la vampa; Tutto e deserto...Il balen; Or co dadi... Squilli echeggi; Di qual tetra...Ah si ben mio; Di quella pira; Siam giunti...Timor di me...D'amor sull'ali rosee; Miserere; Ti scosta. Joan Sutherland, s; Marilyn Horne, ms; Luciano Pavarotti, Graham Clark, t; Ingvar Wixell, bar; Nicolai Ghiaurov, bs; London Opera Chorus; National Philharmonic Orchestra; Richard Bonynge. Decca SET 631 Tape (c) KCET 631 (From D82D3)
+-Gr 4-81 p1366 +HFN 4-81 p81

Il trovatore: Dass nur fur mich dein Herz erbebt; Lodern zum Himmel. See no. 3747
Il trovatore: Deserto sulla terra; Mal reggendo; Aria, Act 3, Sc. 2. See no. 3839
Il trovatore: Di due figli...Abietta zingara. See no. 3968
Il trovatore: Di qual tetra...Ah si ben mio...Di quella pira. See no. 3759
Il trovatore: Di qual tetra...Ah si ben mio; Di quella pira. See no. 3885
Il trovatore: Finale, Act 4. See no. 3890
Il trovatore: Il balen del suo sorriso. See no. 3429. See no. 4079
Il trovatore: Il balen del suo sorriso; Condotta ell'era in ceppi. See no. 3752
Il trovatore: Il presagio funesto...Ah si ben mio; Di quella pira. See no. 3433

Il trovatore: Mal reggendo; Se m'ami ancor; Ai nostri monti. See no. 3997
Il trovatore: Mira d'acerbe; Vivra contende. See no. 4024
Il trovatore: Miserere. See no. 3996
Il trovatore: Stride la vampa. See no. 4080
Il trovatore: Tacea la notte placida; D'amor sull'ali rosee. See no. 3651
Il trovatore: Tacea la notte placida; Miserere. See no. 4076
Il trovatore: Vanne; Lasciami...D'amor sull'ali rosee. See no. 4021
Il trovatore: Vedi; Le fosche notturno; Squilli echeggi la tromba guerriera. See no. 3474

3472 I vespri siciliani. Antonietta Stella, s; Mario Filippeschi, t; Giuseppe Taddei, bar; Bernard Ladysz, bs; Palermo Opera Orchestra and Chorus; Tullio Serafin. Historical Recordings HRE 346/3 (3)
-NR 11-81 p11

3473 I vespri siciliani. Anita Cerquetti, s; Mario Ortica, t; Carlo Tagliabue, bar; Boris Christoff, bs; RAI Orchestra and Chorus; Mario Rossi. Replica 11 2433/5 (3)
/FF 11/12-81 p269

I vespri siciliani: Arrigo, ah parli a un core; Merce dilette amiche. See no. 3711
I vespri siciliani: Bolero. See no. 3754
I vespri siciliani: The four seasons. See no. 3427. See no. 3475
I vespri siciliani: In braccio alle dovizie. See no. 3432
I vespri siciliani: Merce dilette amiche. See no. 1365
I vespri siciliani: O patria...O tu Palermo. See no. 3968
I vespri siciliani: O tu Palermo. See no. 4074
I vespri siciliani: Overture. See no. 3447. See no. 3448
Le villi: Roberto's aria. See no. 3707

3474 Works, selections: Aida: Gloria all'Egitto; Grand march. I Lombardi: O signore dal tetto natio. Macbeth: Che faceste; Dite su; S'allontanarone; Chi v'impose unirvi a noi; Tre volte miagola la gatta in fregola; Patri oppressa. Nabucco: Gli arredi festivi; E l'assiria un regina; Va pensiero. La traviata: Noi siamo zingarelle; Di Madride noi siam. Il trovatore: Vedi; Le fosche notturne; Squilli echeggi la tromba guerriera. Ambrosian Opera Chorus, ROHO Chorus; NPhO; Riccardo Muti. Angel SZ 37795 (also HMV ASD 3979 Tape (c) TC ASD 3979)
+-FF 9/10-81 p192 +-HFN 9-81 p95 tape
+HFN 7-81 p81 +NR 11-81 p12

3475 Works, selections: Alzira: Overture. La forza del destino: Overture. Luisa Miller: Overture. Nabucco: Overture. Il trovatore: Ballet music, excerpts. I vespri siciliani: Four seasons ballet. PhO; Charles Mackerras. Seraphim S 60354
+FF 9/10-81 p194

VERNE, Adela
H. M. Queen Elizabeth's march. See no. 1168

VERSTOVSKY, Alexis
Askold's tomb: Near the town of Slavyansk. See no. 4030
Askold's tomb: Strangers aria and chorus. See no. 3854

VIARDOT-GARCIA, Pauline
Dites que faut-il aire. See no. 3814
Fluestern athemscheues Lauschen. See no. 3814

Songs: Das Voglein; Des Nachts; Die Beschworung. See no. 1989
Die Sterne. See no. 3814

VICTORIA, Tomas Luis de
Jesu dulcis memoria. See no. 3822
Jesu the very thought of thee. See no. 3614
The lamentations of Jeremiah for holy Saturday: Lessons, 1-3. See no. 1398
Magnificat primi toni. See no. 3638
Motet: Ascendens Christus. See no. 3064
Motets: O quam gloriosum. See no. 3636. See no. 3906

VIDAL, Peire
Barons de mon dan covit. See no. 4086

VIERNE, Louis
Cathedrales. See no. 3901
Fantasiestucke, op. 53: Clair de lune. See no. 4069
Fantasiestucke, op. 53: Clair de lune; Toccata. See no. 833
Fantasiestucke, op. 53: Toccata, B minor. See no. 3902
Fantasiestucke, op. 54: Carillon de Westminster. See no. 3616. See no. 3799. See no. 4069

3476 Pieces en style libre, op. 31. Pierre Labric, org. Grand Orgue LVM 801243
+FF 7/8-81 p191 +MU 11-81 p18

Pieces in free style, op. 31: Canon; Divertissement. See no. 3477
Suite, no. 2, op. 53: Toccata, B flat minor. See no. 3799
Suite, no. 4, op. 55: Naiades. See no. 3822

3477 Symphony, no. 4, op. 32, G minor. Pieces in style libre, op. 31: Canon; Divertissement. David Sanger, org. Meridian E 77033
++Gr 3-81 p1217 ++HFN 3-81 p91

Symphony, no. 4, op. 32, G minor. See no. 2592
Symphony, no. 6, op. 59, B major: Final. See no. 3744

VIEUXTEMPS, Henri
Ballade et polonaise, op. 38. See no. 2015
Fantasia appassionata, op. 35. See no. 1131
Romance, op. 7, no. 2. See no. 3693

VILLA-LOBOS, Heitor
A prole do bebe: Polichinelle. See no. 3680

3478 Chamber choros, nos. 1-5, 7. Choros, violin and violoncello (2). Various soloists; Ensembles; Mario Tavares. Kuarup KLP 002
+FF 11/12-81 p270

Choros, violin and violoncello. See no. 3478
Choros, no. 1, E minor. See no. 3727. See no. 3765

3479 Choros, no. 12. Liege Philharmonic Orchestra; Pierre Bartholomee. Ricercare RIC 007
++FF 7/8-81 p192

Concerto, guitar. See no. 3712
Etude, guitar, no. 1, E minor. See no. 3727
Etude, guitar, no. 11. See no. 3886
Preludes, nos. 1-2. See no. 3886
Prelude, no. 2. See no. 3727
Trio, piano, no. 2. See no. 1955

VILLETTE, Paul
Complainte. See no. 4113

VINCENET, Johannes
Fortune par tu cruaulte. See no. 3948

VINTER, Gilbert
Hunter's moon. See no. 3731
John O'Gaunt. See no. 3716
Lisbon carnival. See no. 3717
VIOLA, Anselmo
Sonata, A major. See no. 4115
VIOLETTE, Andrew
Black tea. See no. 1882
Piece, piano, no. 2. See no. 1882
VIOTTI, Giovanni
3480 Concerto, violin, no. 22, A minor. Ulf Hoelscher, vln; Nuremburg Symphony Orchestra; Othmar Maga. Acanta 63 23157
+-ST 12-81 p590
VISEE, Robert de
Suite, D minor. See no. 4015
VITRY, Philippe de
Impudenter: Virtutibus laudabilis. See no. 3779
VITTORIA
Responsaries for tenebrae. See no. 3634
VIVALDI, Antonio
Amor hai vinto, RV 651. See no. 3808
Armida al campo d'Egitto: Overture. See no. 3521
Arsilda Regina di Ponto: Overture. See no. 3521
L'Ateneide: Un certo non so che. See no. 3756
Bajazet: Overture. See no. 3521
Bajazet: Sposa son disprezzata. See no. 3756
3481 Concerti, op. 3. Janos Rolla, Kalman Kostyal, Zoltan Tfirst, Gyorgy Lovas, Peter Gazda, vln; Maria Frank, vlc; Zsuzsa Pertis, hpd, org; Liszt Chamber Orchestra; Janos Rolla. Hungaroton SLPX 12171/3 (3)
+FF 5/6-81 p180 ++NR 4-81 p6
3482 Concerti, op. 3. Piero Toso, Nane Calabrese, Kazuki Sasaki, Ronald Valpreda, vln; I Solisti Veneti; Claudio Scimone. Musical Heritage Society MHS 834341
++ARG 11-81 p40 +FF 9/10-81 p196
3483 Concerti, op. 3. Academy of Ancient Music; Christopher Hogwood. L'Oiseau-Lyre D245D2 (2) Tape (c) K245K22
++Gr 12-81 p892 ++STL 12-13-81 p39
++HFN 12-81 p105
Concerti, op. 3. See no. 3529
3484 Concerti, op. 3, nos. 2 and 11. Concerto, flute, RV 439, G minor. Concerti, strings, RV 120, C major; RV 129, D minor. Concerto, oboe, RV 461, A minor. Richard Chester, flt; Susan Tyte, ob; Angus Anderson, Andrew Martin, vln; Adrian Shepherd, vlc; Cantilena; Adrian Shepherd. Chandos ABR 1008 Tape (c) ABT 1008
+-FF 1/2-81 p208 +HFN 10-80 p117 tape
+-Gr 8-80 p233 -RR 8-80 p58
+-HFN 8-80 p103
3485 Concerti, op. 3, nos. 3, 6, 8-9, 12. Josef Suk, Gunars Larsens, vln; Lucerne Festival Strings; Rudolf Baumgartner. Eurodisc 27896
+FF 11/12-81 p271 +-NYT 7-26-81 pD23
3486 Concerti, op. 3, nos. 5-8, 10-12. BPhO; Thomas Brandis, Leon Spierer, vln and cond. DG 2531 334 Tape (c) 3301 334 (From 2709 100)

+-Gr 7-81 p162 +-HFN 8-81 p91
+HFN 10-81 p95 tape +-ST 12-81 p591

3487 Concerto, op. 3, no. 10. Concerto, op. 10, no. 5. Concerto, bassoon, RV 481, D minor. Concerto, 2 oboes, RV 534, C major. Concerto, 2 violins, RV 524, B flat major. Jerzy Chudyba, flt; Stefan Sutkowski, Janusz Banaszek, ob; Kazimierz Piwkowski, bsn; Igor Iwanow, Janusz Kucharski, Zenon Bakowski, Edmund Komosinski, Ludwik Radek, vln; Warsaw Chamber Orchestra; Stefan Sutkowski. Stolat SZM 0103 (also Muza SXL 0504)
++FF 11/12-81 p271

Concerto, op. 3, no. 10, B minor. See no. 1612. See no. 3528

Concerti, op. 4 (12). See no. 3529

3488 Concerti, op. 8. Concerto, flute, RV 429, D major. Concerto, violoncello, RV 424, B minor. Simon Standage, vln; Stephen Preston, flt; Anthony Pleeth, vlc; English Concert; Trevor Pinnock, hpd. CRD CRD 1092/4 (3) (From CRD 1052, 1048/9)
+Gr 4-81 p1326 +HFN 4-81 p76

Concerti, op. 8. See no. 3529

3489 Concerti, op. 8, nos. 1-4. Yehudi Menuhin, vln; Camerata Lysy; Alberto Lysy. Angel DS 37755 Tape (c) 4XS 37755 (also HMV ASD 3964 Tape (c) TC ASD 3964)
+-FF 9/10-81 p197 +HFN 7-81 p77
+-Gr 6-81 p55 +-MUM 9/10-81 p33
+Gr 8-81 p324 tape /-NR 6-81 p7
+Gr 11-81 p783 tape ++St 9-81 p101
+HF 10-81 p91 tape

3490 Concerti, op. 8, nos. 1-4. Christian Altenburger, vln; DBS; Helmut Winschermann. Arabesque 8085 Tape (c) 9085
+ARG 12-81 p35 +NR 7-81 p4

3491 Concerti, op. 8, nos. 1-4. Pinchas Zukerman, vln; St. Paul Chamber Orchestra; Pinchas Zukerman. CBS IM 36710
+-FF 11/12-81 p272 +NR 11-81 p4

3492 Concerti, op. 8, nos. 1-4. Ronald Thomas, vln; Linnhe Robertson, hpd; Bournemouth Sinfonietta; Ronald Thomas. Chandos ABR 1004
++FF 1/2-81 p209 +-HFN 3-80 p101
+Gr 12-79 p1023 +-RR 1-80 p92

3493 Concerti, op. 8, nos. 1-4. Astorre Ferrari, vln; Stuttgart Soloists; Marcel Couraud. Contour CC 7527 Tape (c) 7527
+Gr 8-81 p316 +-HFN 9-81 p90

3494 Concerti, op. 8, nos. 1-4. Elmar Oliveira, vln; Los Angeles Chamber Orchestra; Gerard Schwarz. Delos DMS 3007
+Audio 9-81 p83 ++NR 1-81 p5
+-FF 3/4-81 p217 +-NYT 3-29-81 pD31
+-HF 2-81 p74 ++St 2-81 p109

3495 Concerti, op. 8, nos. 1-4. Gunars Larsens, vln; Lucerne Festival Strings; Rudolf Baumgartner. Denon OX 7174
+Audio 9-81 p82 +HFN 6-81 p79
+FF 5/6-80 p168

3496 Concerti, op. 8, nos. 1-4. Emanuel Borok, vln; Cambridge Chamber Orchestra; Rolf Smedvig. Digitech DIGI 107
+ARG 10-81 p40 /FF 5/6-81 p181

3497 Concerti, op. 8, nos. 1-4. Felix Ayo, vln; I Musici. Philips 6527 088 Tape (c) 7311 088 (From SABL 117)
+Gr 11-81 p702 +HFN 11-81 p103

3498 Concerti, op. 8, nos. 1-4. Iona Brown, vln; AMF; Iona Brown.

Philips 9500 717 Tape (c) 7300 809
+FF 3/4-81 p217 +HFN 12-80 p147
+-Gr 12-80 p842 ++NR 12-80 p5
+HF 2-81 p75 ++St 2-81 p108

3499 Concerti, op. 8, nos. 1-4. La Petite Bande; Sigiswald Kuijken, vln. RCA RL 3-0397
+-Gr 8-81 p280 +HFN 8-81 p88

Concerto, op. 8, no. 2, G minor. See no. 3767

3500 Concerto, op. 8, nos. 5-12. Concerto, flute, D major. Concerto, violoncello, B minor. Simon Standage, vln; Stphen Preston, flt; Anthony Pleeth, vlc; English Consort; Trevor Pinnock, hpd and cond. CRD CRD 1048/9 Tape (C) CRDC 1048/9 (also Vanguard VSD 71273/4)
+ARG 5-81 p33 +HFN 10-78 p139 tape
+Audio 12-81 p24 ++MT 5-79 p409
+-FF 1/2-81 p209 ++NR 12-80 p5
+Gr 7-78 p206 +-RR 8-78 p72
+Gr 11-78 p969 tape +RR 1-79 p92 tape
++HF 2-81 p75 ++St 4-81 p108
+HFN 7-78 p107

Concerti, op. 9. See no. 3529

3501 Concerti, op. 10. Aurele Nicolet, flt; Wurttemberg Chamber Orchestra; Jorg Faerber. Intercord INT 160814
+HFN 12-81 p105

3502 Concerti, op. 10. Michala Petri, rec; AMF; Iona Brown. Philips 9500 942 Tape (c) 7300 942
+Gr 10-81 p564 +HFN 10-81 p91

3503 Concerti, op. 10. Frans Bruggen, flt; Eighteenth Century Orchestra Members. RCA RL 3-0392
+HFN 8-81 p88 +STL 7-12-81 p40

Concerti, op. 10. See no. 3529

Concerto, op. 10, no. 2, G minor. See no. 782. See no. 2076

Concerto, op. 10, no. 3, D major. See no. 94. See no. 3767

Concerto, op. 10, no. 5. See no. 3487

Concerto, op. 11, no. 2, E minor. See no. 3529

3504 Concerto, bassoon, A minor. Concerto, flute, C minor. Concerto, oboe, F major. Concerto, 2 oboes, bassoon, 2 horns and violin, F major. Neil Black, Celia Nicklin, ob; Martin Gatt, bsn; Timothy Brown, Robin Davis, hn; Iona Brown, vln; William Bennett, flt; AMF; Neville Marriner. Argo ZRG 839 Tape (c) KZRC 839
+AR 8-81 p79 ++HF 1-79 p54 tape
+Audio 6-78 p127 +HFN 11-77 p183
+FF 5/6-79 p135 +MT 4-78 p336
+Gr 11-77 p853 +RR 11-77 p74
++Gr 2-78 p1471 tape +RR 1-78 p15
+HF 8-78 p90 +St 10-78 p169

3505 Concerti, bassoon, RV 472, 480, 498, 504. Robert Thompson, bsn; London Mozart Players; Philip Ledger, hpd. Musical Heritage Society MHS 4323 Taep (c) MHC 6323
+ARG 10-81 p42 +HF 9-81 p46 tape
+FF 7/8-81 p193

3506 Concerti, bassoon, RV 475, 480, 484, 492, 496, 501. Gabor Janota, bsn; Liszt Ferenc Chamber Orchestra; Frigyes Sandor. Budapest FX 12297
+FF 11/12-81 p271 +HFN 5-81 p84
+Gr 4-81 p1326

Concerto, bassoon, K 481, D minor. See no. 3486
Concerto, bassoon, RV 484, E minor. See no. 3529
3507 Concerto, bassoon, RV 501, B flat major. Concerto, oboe, RV 461, A minor. Frantisek Herman, bsn; Jiri Krejci, ob; Pardubice State Chamber Orchestra; Libor Pesek. Supraphon 110 2666
+NR 5-81 p8
Concerto, flautino, RV 445, A minor. See no. 3529
Concerto, flute, C minor. See no. 3504
Concerto, flute, D major. See no. 3500
Concerti, flute, D minor, C minor. See no. 3392
3508 Concerti, flute, RV 89, D major; RV 102, G major. Concerto, recorder, RV 108, A minor. Sonatas, 2 violins, RV 84, D major; RV 63, D minor. Wilbert Hazelzet, flt; Gudrun Heyens, rec; Cologne Musica Antiqua; Rheinhard Goebel. DG 2533 463
++Gr 11-81 p719 +STL 10-11-81 p41
++HFN 12-81 p106
3509 Concerti, flute, RV 108, A minor; RV 438, G major; RV 431, E minor; RV 432, E minor. Concerto, 2 flutes, RV 533, C major. Concerti, piccolo, RV 443, C major; RV 444, C major. Jean-Pierre Rampal, flt and pic; Joseph Rampal, flt; I Solisti Veneti; Claudio Scimone. Musical Heritage Society MHS 4190 Tape (c) MHC 6190
+FF 11/12-80 p190 +HF 9-81 p46 tape
3510 Concerti, flute, RV 108, A minor; RV 438, G major; RV 441, C minor; RV 533, C major; RV 570, F major. Severino Gazzelloni, Marja Steinberg, flt; Bernard Schenkel, ob; Jiri Stavicek, bsn; I Musici. Philips 6570 185 Tape (c) 7310 186 (From SAL 3705, 6500 820)
+Gr 1-81 p954 +HFN 4-81 p83 tape
++HFN 3-81 p95
Concerto, flute, RV 427, D major. See no. 3529
Concerto, flute, RV 429, D major. See no. 3488
Concerto, flute, RV 439, G minor. See no. 3484
Concerto, flute, RV 441, C minor. See no. 3529
Concerto, flute, RV 443, C major. See no. 3808
Concerto, 2 flutes, RV 533, C major. See no. 3509. See no. 3529
Concerti, guitar, D major, A major. See no. 3712
Concerto, 2 horns, P 321. See no. 2076
Concerto, lute, RV 93, D major. See no. 1961
Concerto, mandolin, no. 2, G major. See no. 3980
Concerto, mandolin, RV 425, C major. See no. 215. See no. 3528
Concerto, 2 mandolins, RV 532, G major. See no. 3528. See no. 3529
3511 Concerti, oboe, A minor, C major, D major, D minor, F major, C major. Han de Vries, ob; I Solisti di Zagreb. Angel SZ 37741
++ARG 2-81 p37 +NR 9-80 p6
Concerto, oboe, A minor. See no. 227
3512 Concerti, oboe, C major, D minor, F major, A minor (2). Heinz Holliger, Maurice Bourgue, ob; I Musici. Philips 9500 742 Tape (c) 7300 827
++FF 1/2-81 p210 +NR 12-80 p5
Concerto, oboe, F major. See no. 3504
Concerto, oboe, RV 447, C major; RV 457, F major. See no. 2148
Concerto, oboe, RV 461, A minor. See no. 1755. See no. 3484. See no. 3507. See no. 3529

Concerto, oboe and violin, RV 548, B flat major. See no. 36
Concerto, 2 oboes, RV 534, C major. See no. 3487
Concerto, 2 oboes, RV 535, D minor. See no. 3529
Concerto, 2 oboes, bassoon, 2 horns and violin, F major. See no. 3504
Concerto, piccolo, RV 443, C major. See no. 3767. See no. 3509
Concerto, piccolo, RV 444, C major. See no. 3509
Concerto, recorder, op. 44, no. 11, C major. See no. 3528
Concerto, recorder, RV 108, A minor. See no. 3508
Concerto, recorder, RV 443, C major. See no. 1693
Concerto, recorder, RV 445, C major. See no. 1694

3513 Concerti, recorder and flute, op. 10, nos. 1-6. Frans Bruggen, rec and flt; Orchestra of the Eighteenth Century. Pro Arte PAL 1014 Tape (c) PAC 1014 (also RCA RL 3-0392)
+-ARG 11-81 p41 +HFN 8-81 p88
+FF 7/8-81 p193 +STL 7-12-81 p40
+HF 9-81 p78

3514 Concerto, recorder, oboe and bassoon, RV 103, G minor. Concerto, recorder, violin and bassoon, RV 100, F major. Concerto, 2 recorders, RV 533, D major. Sonatas, recorder, F major, A major. Laszlo Czidra, Zsolt Harsanyi, rec; Gergely Sarkozy, lt, vla bastarda; Jozsef Vajda, bsn; Janos Rolla, vln; Peter Pongracz, ob; Zsuzsa Pertis, hpd, org; Liszt Chamber Orchestra; Janos Rolla. Hungaroton SLPX 12161
+FF 5/6-81 p180 +-NR 5-81 p8

Concerto, recorder, violin and bassoon, RV 100, F major. See no. 3514
Concerto, 2 recorders, RV 533, C major. See no. 3514
Concerti, strings, RV 29, 134, 153, 158. See no. 3529
Concerti, strings, RV 120, C major; RV 129, D minor. See no. 3484
Concerto, trumpet, A flat major. See no. 28
Concerto, trumpet, C major. See no. 3761
Concerto, trumpet, G minor. See no. 75
Concerto, 2 trumpets, C major. See no. 1211. See no. 3774
Concerto, 2 trumpets, RV 537, C major. See no. 1612. See no. 3528. See no. 3529

3515 Concerti, viola d'amore, A major, D minor (3), D major. Laszlo Barsonyi, vla d'amore; Maria Frank, vlc; Zsuzsa Pertis, hpd; Liszt Chamber Orchestra; Janos Rolla. Hungaroton SLPX 12162
/ARG 7/8-81 p40 ++NR 2-81 p6
++FF 3/4-81 p216

Concerto, viola d'amore, RV 540, D minor. See no. 1961
Concerti, violin, RV 199, 234, 270, 271, 552. See no. 3529
Concerto, violin and organ, RV 542, F major. See no. 3529
Concerto, violin and violoncello, RV 547, B flat major. See no. 3529

3516 Concerto, violin and 2 violoncelli, P 58, C major. Concerti, violoncelli, P 30, 180, 434. Concerto, 2 violoncelli, P 411, G minor. Jacques Manzone, vln; Philip Ledger, hpd; Paul Tortelier, Maud Tortelier, vlc; London Mozart Players. HMV ASD 3914
+Gr 5-81 p1480 +-ST 10-81 p432
+-HFN 4-81 p77

Concerto, 2 violins, RV 93, D major. See no. 215
Concerti, 2 violins, RV 523, 527. See no. 3529
Concerto, 2 violins, RV 524, B flat major. See no. 3487

Concerto 2 violins and 2 violoncelli, RV 564, D major. See no. 3529
Concerto, 3 violins, F major. See no. 241
Concerto, 3 violins, RV 551, F major. See no. 3529
Concerto, violoncello, B minor. See no. 3500
Concerti, violoncello, G minor, G major. See no. 102
Concerti, violoncello, P 30, 180, 434. See no. 3516
Concerto, violoncello, RV 401, C minor. See no. 816. See no. 3529
Concerto, violoncello, RV 424, B minor. See no. 3488
Concerto, 2 violoncelli, P 411, G minor. See no. 3516
Concerto, 2 violoncelli, RV 531, G minor. See no. 3529
Concerto grosso, no. 5, PV 342, G minor. See no. 4091

3517 Credo, RV 591. Gloria, RV 589, D major. Maria Stader, s; Alberta Pellegrini, s; Anna Maria Rota, con; Maggio Musicale Orchestra and Chorus Fiorentino; Bruno Bartoletti. DG 2535 411 Tape (c) 3335 411 (From 138788)
+-ARG 1-81 p45 +-FF 1/2-81 p211

3518 Dixit dominus. Stabat mater. Marilyn Hill Smith, Anna Bernardin, s; Helen Watts, con; Ian Partridge, t; Ian Caddy, bs; John Toll, org; English Bach Festival Orchestra and Chorus; Jean-Claude Malgoire. CBS M 35847 Tape (c) MT 35847
+-FF 1/2-81 p211

3519 Dixit dominus. O qui coeli, RV 631. Uta Spreckelsen, s; Hanna Schaer, alto; Jean-Pierre Maurer, t; Michel Brodard, bs; Daniel Grosgurin, vlc; Christiane Jaccottet, hpd; Philippe Corboz, org; Lausanne Vocal Ensemble and Chamber Orchestra; Michel Corboz. Musical Heritage Society MHS 4112 (also Erato 71005)
++FF 7/8-80 p151 +MU 10-81 08

3520 Dixit dominus. Gloria. Nisi dominus. Stabat mater. Elsa Saque, Joana Silva, Jennifer Smith, Anna Bernardin, s; Helen Watts, Naoka Ihara, con; Fernando Serafim, Edmund Barham, t; Jose Oliviera Lopes, bs; John Toll, org; Michael Laird, tpt; Clare Shanks, Sophie Wilson, ob; Jeremy Ward, bsn; Charles Medlam, vld; Gulbenkian Foundation Orchestra and Chorus, English Bach Festival Orchestra and Chorus; Michel Corboz. Musical Heritage Society MHS 804248 (2) (also Erato 71018, 71200)
+FF 5/6-81 p183 +-St 5-81 p84
+MU 6-81 p14

Dorilla in tempe: Overture. See no. 3521
Ercole sul Termodonte: Onde chiare. See no. 3756
Farnace: Overture. See no. 3521
Giustino: Overture. See no. 3521
Gloria. See no. 3520
Gloria, RV 589, D major. See no. 3517
Griselda: Agitata da due venti; Da due venti. See no. 3756
Griselda: Overture. See no. 3521
L'Incoronazione di Dario: Overture. See no. 3521
Nisi dominus. See no. 3520
O qui coeli, RV 631. See no. 3519
L'Olimpiade: Overture. See no. 3521
Ottone in Villa: Overture. See no. 3521
Ottone in Villa: Vieni vieni o mio diletto. See no. 3756

3521 Overtures: Armida al campo d'Egitto. Arsilda Regina di Ponto. Bajazet. Dorilla in tempe. Farnace. Giustino. Griselda. L'Incoronazione di Dario. L'Olimpiade. Ottone in Villa. La

verita in cimento. I Solisti Veneti; Claudio Scimone. Erato STU 71215 (also Musical Heritage Society MHS 4134)
++FF 5/6-81 p182 +Gr 4-80 p1564

3522 Serenata a tre. Petya Grigorova, Marjorie Vance, s; Kurt Spanier, t; Clemencic Consort; Rene Clemencic. Harmonia Mundi HM 1066/7 (2) Tape (c) HM 40-1066/7
++HFN 12-81 p106

Sinfonia, G major. See no. 3719

Sonata, RV 57, G major. See no. 215

3523 Sonatas, flute, C major, D minor, E minor, G minor. Stephen Preston, flt; Hans Ludwig Hirsch, hpd; Hannelore Muller, vlc. Jecklin 5002
+FF 3/4-81 p218

Sonata, harpsichord, F major. See no. 3763

Sonata, oboe, RV 53, C major. See no. 319

Sonata, recorder, F major, A major. See no. 3514

Sonata, recorder, op. 13, no. 6, G minor. See no. 4056

Sonata, strings, RV 130, E flat major. See no. 3529

Sonata, trombone, no. 1. See no. 1670

3524 Sonatas, violin, op. 2 (12). Sonatas, violin, RV 29, A major; RV 10, D major. Piero Toso, vln; Gianni Chiampan, vlc; Edoardo Farina, hpd. Musical Heritage Society MHS 4218/9 (2)
+FF 1/2-81 p212

Sonatas, violin, RV 29, A major; RV 10, D major. See no. 3524

Sonatas, 2 violins, RV 84, D major; RV 63, D minor. See no. 3508

3525 Sonatas, violoncello, op. 14. Arto Noras, vlc; Marketta Valve, hpd. Finlandia FA 316
++FF 5/6-81 p184

3526 Sonatas, violoncello, RV 40-41, 43-47, 50-51. Claude Starck, vlc; Mischa Frey, vlc; Isolde Ahlgrimm, hpd. Tudor 74005/6 (2)
+-Gr 1-81 p962

3527 Songs (choral): Beatus vir, RV 598; Credo, RV 592; Gloria, RV 588; Dixit dominus, RV 595; Introduction to Gloria, RV 693; Introduction to Dixit dominus, RV 635; Laudate pueri, RV 602; Magnificat, RV 610, RV 611. Margaret Marshall, Felicity Lott, Sally Burgess, s; Susan Daniel, ms; Linda Finnie, Anne Collins, con; Anthony Rolf-Johnson, t; Thomas Tomaschke, bs; John Constable, org; John Alldis Choir; ECO; Vittorio Negri. Philips 6769 046 (3) (From 6768 149)
+Gr 12-80 p871 ++St 5-81 p84
+HFN 12-80 p147

Stabat mater. See no. 3518. See no. 3520

Trio, violin and lute, RV 82, C major; RV 85, G minor. See no. 215

Trio sonata, RV 63, D minor. See no. 3808

La verita in cimento: Overture. See no. 3521

3528 Works, selections: Concerto, op. 3, no. 10, B minor. Concerto, mandolin, RV 425, C major. concerto, 2 mandolins, RV 532, G major. Concerto, 2 trumpets, RV 537, C major. Concerto, recorder, op. 44, no. 11, C major. Georges Armand, Oreste Giordano, Klaus Muhlberger, Aimee Auriacombe, vln; Michel Debost, flt; Andre Saint-Clivier, Christian Schneider, mand; Albert Calvayrac, Andre Bernes, tpt; Michel Sanvoisin, rec; Toulouse Chamber Orchestra; Louis Auriacombe. Classics for Pleasure CFP 40353 Tape (c) TC CFP 40353 (From HMV SXLP 30144)

+Gr 8-81 p280 +HFN 7-81 p77

3529 Works, selections: Concerti, op. 3 (12). Concerti, op. 4 (12). Concerti, op. 8 (12). Concerti, op. 9 (12). Concerti, op. 10 (6). Concerto, op. 11, no. 2, E minor. Concerto, bassoon, RV 484, E minor. Concerti, flute, RV 427, D major; RV 441, C minor. Concerto, 2 flutes, RV 533, C major. Concerto, flautino, RV 445, A minor. Concerto, 2 mandolins, RV 532, G major. Concerto, oboe, RV 461, A minor. Concerto, 2 oboes, RV 535, D minor. Concerti, strings, RV 129, 158, 153, 134. Concerto, 2 trumpets, RV 537, C major. Concerti, violin, RV 199, C major; 234, D major; 270, D major, RV 271, E major, RV 522, A major. Concerto, 2 violins, RV 523, A minor; RV 527, B flat major. Concerto, 3 violins, RV 551, F major. Concerto, violin and violoncello, RV 547, B flat major. Concerto, violin and organ, RV 542, F major. Concerto, 2 violins and 2 violoncelli, RV 564, D major. Concerto, violoncello, RV 401, C minor. Concerto, 2 violoncelli, RV 531, G minor. Sonata, strings, RV 130, E flat major. Various soloists; I Musici. Philips 6747 029 (18)

+FF 9/10-81 p196

VIVES, Amadeo

La dona Franscisquita: Por el humo se sabe. See no. 3836. See no. 3888

Songs: El amor y los ojos; El retrato de Isabela; Valgame Dios que los ansares vuelan. See no. 3889

VIVIANI, Giovanni

Sonata, trumpet, no. 1, C major. See no. 3774

Sonata, trumpet, no. 2, D major. See no. 3629

VOELCKEL, Samuel

Courantes. See no. 3853

VOGEL, Johann

3530 Quartet, clarinet, B flat major. Sinfonia concertante, no. 1, B flat major. Dieter Klocker, clt; Karl-Otto Harmann, bsn; Concerto Amsterdam; Jaap Schroder. Acanta EA 23140

+-HFN 10-80 p110 +MT 10-81 p679

Sinfonia concertante, no. 1, B flat major. See no. 3530

VOGLER, Georg

3531 Gustav Adolf och Ebba Brahe. MEYERBEER: L'Africaine: Sur me genoux; Hirtenlied. WEBER: Euryanthe: Glockenlein im Thale; So bin ich nun verlassen. Montserrat Caballe, Beverly Sills, Joan Sutherland, s; Placido Domingo, t; Royal Opera Orchestra and Chorus, Sweden; Charles Farncombe. MRF MRF 156 (3)

+FF 7/8-81 p194

Preludes, B minor, E flat major. See no. 183

Preludes, organ, nos. 1-2, 32. See no. 3908

VOIGTLANDER, Gabriel

Zum Lobe der Musik. See no. 3985

VOLPI, Adamo

Oremus pro pontifice. See no. 3634

VON BRUCK, Arnold

Motets: Gott der Vater wohn uns bei; Mitten wir im Leben sind. See no. 3906

VORISEK, Jan

Symphony, D major. See no. 2775

VRANICKY (Wranitzky), Paul

3532 Great characteristic symphony, op. 31. Prague Radio Orchestra;

Vaclav Smetacek. Schwann VMS 1207
+ARG 12-81 p49
Quartet, flute, no. 3, F major. See no. 1515
Quartet, strings, D major. See no. 1790

VRIES, Klaas de
Bewegingen. See no. 3533
Chorales. See no. 3729

3533 Follia. Bewegingen. WAGEMANS: Muziek II. Rotterdam Philharmonic Orchestra, Resident Orchestra Members, Sudwestfunk Orchestra; Otto Ketting, Ernest Bour. Composers Voice CV 8004
+-FF 9/10-81 p198

VYSHNEGRADSKIY, Ivan
Study on the rotatory movements. See no. 4072

WAGEMANS, Peter-Jan
Muziek II. See no. 3533
Quartet, saxophone. See no. 3729

WAGENSEIL, Georg
Concerto, trombone, E flat major. See no. 1558
Divertimento, F major. See no. 4084
Suite of pieces, 3 violoncelli and bass. See no. 3789

WAGNER, J. F.
Under the double eagle. See no. 3976

WAGNER, Richard

3534 Die Feen, excerpts. Jill Gomez, s; Miroslav Frydlewicz, t; Christopher Davies, bar; Hans-Rainer Schwarzbeck, bs; Bayreuth Youth Festival Orchestra and Chorus, 1967; John Bell. Colosseum SM 4002
+FF 9/10-81 p199

3535 Die fliegende Hollander: Viorica Ursuleac, s; Luise Willer, alto; Franz Klarwein, t; Hans Hotter, bar; George Hann, bs; Karl Ostertag; Bavarian State Opera Orchestra and Chorus; Clemens Krauss. Acanta HA 23135/7 (3) (also Bruno Walter Society IGI 381)
+-FF 7/8-80 p152
+Gr 6-80 p66
+-HFN 5-80 p127
+-NR 4-81 p9
+ON 4-5-80 p29
+-Op 8-80 p799
+-RR 7-80 p39

3536 Der fliegende Hollander. Marianne Schech, s; Sieglinde Wagner, ms; Fritz Wunderlich, Rudolf Schock, t; Dietrich Fischer-Dieskau, bar; Gottlob Frick, bs; Berlin State Opera Orchestra and Chorus; Franz Konwitschny. HMV SLS 5226 (3) Tape (c) TC SLS 5226 (From ASD 385/7)
+Gr 7-81 p192
+-Gr 11-81 p783 tape
+-HFN 7-81 p81

3537 Der fliegende Hollander; Overture. Die Meistersinger von Nurnberg: Overture. Rienzi: Overture. Tannhauser: Overture. PhO; Lorin Maazel. CBS 76883 Tape (c) 40-76883 (also CBS 36699)
-FF 9/10-81 p201
+Gr 3-80 p1398
+HFN 3-80 p107 tape
+NR 7-81 p1
+RR 7-80 p97 tape
++SFC 7-26-81 p19

3538 Der fliegende Hollander: Overture. Lohengrin: Preludes, Acts 1 and 3. Tristan und Isolde: Prelude and Liebestod. VPO; Karl Bohm. DG 2531 288 Tape (c) 3301 288
-FF 9/10-81 p199
-Gr 4-81 p1326
+HFN 6-81 p79
+-HFN 7-81 p83 tape

3539 Der fliegende Hollander: Overture. Lohengrin: Prelude, Act 1. Rienzi: Overture. Tannhauser: Overture. PhO; Otto Klemperer. HMV SXLP 30436 Tape (c) SXLP 30436 (From Columbia SAX 2347) (also Angel S 36187)
+-FF 1/2-81 p213 +Gr 10-80 p548 tape
++Gr 8-80 p233 +HFN 10-80 p117 tape

Der fliegende Hollander: Overture. See no. 3858

3540 Gotterdammerung: Dawn and Rhine journey; Siegfried's funeral music and final scene. Das Rheingold: Entrance of the gods into Valhalla. Siegfried: Forest murmurs. Die Walkure: Ride of the Valkyries; Magic fire music. CO; Georg Szell. CBS MY 36715
+-FF 9/10081 p182

3541 Gotterdammerung: Dawn and Siegfried's Rhine journey; Siegfried's funeral march; Brunnhilde's immolation and finale. LSO; Leopold Stokowski. RCA AGL 1-3709 (From ARL 1-1317)
+-FF 9/10-81 p200

Gotterdammerung: Dawn and Siegfried's Rhine journey. See no. 1264

Gotterdammerung: Ho ho. See no. 4122

3542 Gotterdammerung: Siegfried's funeral march. Die Meistersinger von Nurnberg: Overture; Dance of the apprentices. Lohengrin: Prelude, Act 3. Tristan und Isolde: Prelude and Liebestod. PhO; Otto Klemperer. HMV SXLP 30525 Tape (c) TC SXLP 30525 (From SAX 2347)
+Gr 9-81 p394 +-HFN 9-81 p89
+Gr 11-81 p783 tape

3543 Gotterdammerung: Siegfried's funeral music. Siegfried: Forest murmurs. Tristan und Isolde: Prelude, Act 1. Die Walkure: Ride of the Valkyries. LAPO; Erich Leinsdorf. Sheffield LAB 7
+HFN 1-81 p103

3544 Gotterdammerung: Siegfried's Rhine journey; Siegfried's death and funeral march. Das Rheingold: Entry of the Gods into Valhalla. Siegfried: Forest murmurs. Die Walkure: Ride of the Valkyries; Magic fire music. BPhO; Klaus Tennstedt. HMV ASD 3985 Tape (c) TCC ASD 3985 (also Angel DS 37808)
+Gr 10-81 p567 +-NYT 11-22-81 pD23
+-HFN 12-81 p106

Gotterdammerung: Siegfried's Rhine journey. See no. 3561

Gotterdammerung: Starke Scheite schichet mir. See no. 795

3545 Lohengrin. Renata Tebaldi, s; Elena Nicolai, ms; Gino Penno, t; Giangiacomo Guelfi, bar; Giulio Neri, bs; Naples Teatro San Carlo Orchstra and Chorus; Gabriele Santini. Historical Recordings HRE 295 (3)
+FF 7/8-81 p195

3546 Lohengrin. Leonie Rysanek, Astrid Varnay, s; Sandor Konya, t; Ernest Blanc, Eberhard Waechter, bar; Keith Engen, bs; Bayreuth Festival Orchestra and Chorus; Andre Cluytens. Replica 20 2489/92 (4)
+FF 11/12-81 p275

3547 Lohengrin. Songs: PFITZNER: Mailied; Trauerstille. SCHUBERT: Schwanengesang: Die Taubenpost. SCHUMANN: Der Hidalgo, op. 30, no. 3; Provencalisches Lied. WOLF: Liebesfruhling; Nachtgruss; Der Musikant; Wohin mit der Freud. Trude Eipperle, s; Helena Braun, con; Peter Anders, t; Carl Kronenberg, bar; Josef Greindl, bs; Cologne Radio Orchestra and Chorus; Richard Kraus. Rococo 1015 (4)

+FF 11/12-81 p274 +NR 10-75 p7

Lohengrin: Bridal chorus. See no. 3924

Lohengrin: Das susse Lied erhalt. See no. 3651

Lohengrin: Einsam in truben Tagen. See no. 3642. See no. 3755

Lohengrin: Elsa's processional to the cathedral. See no. 3817

Lohengrin: Entweihte Gotter. See no. 4080

Lohengrin: In fernem Land. See no. 4028

Lohengrin: In fernem Land; Mein lieber Schwan. See no. 3648

Lohengrin: Ma confiance; Aus bords lointain; Mon cygne aime. See no. 4050

Lohengrin: Merce merce cigno gentil; Di non t'incanta; S'el torna alfin; Cessaro i canti alfin; Mio salvatore...Mai devi domandarmi; Merce merce cigno gentil. See no. 4032

3548 Lohengrin: Prelude, Act 1. Die Meistersinger von Nurnberg: Prelude, Act 1. Siegfried Idyll. Tristan und Isolde: Prelude and Liebestod. BPhO; Rafael Kubelik. DG 2535 212 Tape (c) 3335 212 (From DG 136228)

-FF 9/10-81 p201 ++SFC 7-26-81 p19

Lohengrin: Prelude, Act 1. See no. 3539

Lohengrin: Prelude, Acts 1 and 3. See no. 3538

Lohengrin: Prelude, Act 3. See no. 3542

3549 Die Meistersinger von Nurnberg. Elisabeth Grummer, s; Marga Hoffgen, con; Horst Wilhelm, Manfred Schmidt, Leopold Clam, Herold Kraus, Rudolf Schock, Gerhard Unger, t; Ferdinand Frantz, Gottlob Frick, Walter Stoll, Benno Kusche, Gustav Neidlinger, Robert Koffmane, Anton Metternich, Hans Pick, Hermann Prey, bs; German State Opera Chorus, St. Hedwig's Cathedral Choir; BPhO; Rudolf Kempe. HMV RLS 740 (5) Tape (c) TC RLS 740 (From ALP 1506/10)

+-FF 7/8-81 p197 +HFN 11-79 p155
+Gr 10-79 p715 +-RR 10-79 p69

3550 Die Meistersinger von Nurnberg. Gyorgy Losonczy, Mihaly Szekely, Jozsef Simandy, soloists; Budapest Opera Orchestra; Otto Klemperer. HMV SXLP 30525

+Gr 11-81 p764

Die Meistersinger von Nurnberg: Am stillen Herd; Morgandlich leuchtend im rosigen Schein. See no. 3966

Die Mesitersinger von Nurnberg: Morgenlich leuchtend. See no. 3688

Die Meistersinger von Nurnberg: Overture; Dance of the apprentices. See no. 3542

Die Meistersinger von Nurnberg: Preizlied. See no. 3967

3551 Die Mesitersinger von Nurnberg: Prelude. Siegfried Idyll. WAGNER, S.: Der Barenhauter: Overture. Konzertstuck, flute. Gerhard Weisner, flt; Nurnberg Symphony Orchestra; Erich Kloss, Gilbert Graf Gravina. Colosseum SM 513

+FF 9/10-81 p200

3552 Die Meistersinger von Nurnberg: Prelude; Da zu dir der Heiland kam; Am stillen Herd in Winterszeit; Fanget an So rief der Lenz in den Wald; Was duftet doch der Flieder; Wahn Wahn Unberall Wahn; Die selige Morgentraum Deutwise; Selig wie die Sonne; Wach auf, Es nahet gen den Tag; Morgenlich leuchtend; Verachtet mir die Meister nicht. Catarina Ligendza, s; Christa Ludwig, ms; Placido Domingo, Horst Laubenthal, t; Dietrich Fischer-Dieskau, bar; Peter Lagger, Roland Hermann, Gerd Feldhoff, Miomir Nikolic, Victor von Halem, bs; German Opera Orchestra and Chorus; Eugen

Jochum. DG 2537 041 (From 2740 149)
+FF 11/12-81 p276 +-RR 9-78 p39
+Gr 9-78 p550

Die Meistersinger von Nurnberg: Prelude. See no. 970. See no. 3537. See no. 3781

Die Meistersinger von Nurnberg: Prelude, Act 1. See no. 3548. See no. 3709

O tu bell'astro. See no. 4031

3553 Parsifal. Dunja Vejzovic, Hanna Schwarz, ms; Peter Hofmann, Claes Ahnsjo, t; Siegmund Nimsgern, Jose van Dam, bar; Victor von Halem, Kurt Moll, Kurt Rydl, bs; German Opera Chorus; BPhO; Herbert von Karajan. DG 2741 002 (5) Tape (c) 3382 002
+-ARG 11-81 p54 ++MUM 9/10-81 p35
+FF 7/8-81 p198 +NR 7-81 p10
+Gr 4-81 p1366 +ON 6-81 p44
+-HF 8-81 p63 ++Op 5-81 p495
++HF 10-81 p91 tape ++SFC 5-3-81 p22
+HFN 4-81 p69 ++SR 8-81 p68
++HFN 5-81 p93 tape ++St 8-81 p66
+MT 9-81 p608 +-STL 4-12-81 p40

3554 Parsifal, excerpts. Gotthelf Pistor, Max Lorenz, t; Herbert Janssen, bar; Ivan Andresen, Alexander Kipnis, bs; Various Orchestras; Frieder Weissman, Karl Muck, Wilhelm Furtwangler, Richard Strauss. Bruno Walter Society IGI 379
+-FF 11/12-81 p254 +-NR 12-81 p10

Parsifal: Amfortas die Wunde. See no. 3800

Parsifal: Good Friday music. See no. 3781

Parsifal: Nur eine Waffe taugt. See no. 3688

Parsifal: Prelude, Act 1. See no. 3651

3555 Das Rheingold. Marita Napier, Lucia Popp, Uta Priew, s; Yvonne Minton, ms; Ortrun Wenkel, Hanna Schwarz, alto; Eberhard Buchner, Peter Schreier, Christian Vogel, t; Siegmund Nimsgern, Karl-Heinz Stryczek, bar; Theo Adam, bs-bar; Roland Bracht, Matti Salminen, bs; Dresden State Orchestra; Marke Janowski. Eurodisc 301 137 (3) Tape (c) 501 137
+FF 11/12-81 p276 +ON 11-81 p68
+Gr 11-81 p757 +Op 12-81 p1264
+-HF 12-81 p86 +SFC 9-27-81 p18
+-HFN 12-81 p106

Das Rheingold: Abendlich straht der Sonne Auge. See no. 3639

Das Rheingold: Entrance of the Gods into Valhalla. See no. 3540. See no. 3544. See no. 3561

Rienzi: Allmacht'ger Vater. See no. 3800

Rienzi: Gerechter Gott. See no. 4039

Rienzi: Overture. See no. 521. See no. 964. See no. 3537. See no. 3539

3556 Der Ring des Nibelungen: Gotterdammerung. Gwyneth Jones, Jeannine Altmeyer, s; Gwendolyn Killebrew, ms; Ilse Gramatzki, ms; Marga Schiml, con; Manfred Jung, t; Franz Mazura, Fritz Hubner, bs; Hermann Becht, bs-bar. Das Rheingold. Hanna Schwarz, Carmen Reppel, ms; Ortrun Wenkel, con; Norma Sharp, Ilse Gramatzki, s; Marga Schiml, con; Siegfried Jerusalem, Heinz Zednik, Helmut Pampuch, t; Donald McIntyre, Martin Egel, bar; Matti Salminen, Fritz Hubner, bs; Hermann Becht, bs-bar. Siegfried. Gwyneth Jones, Norma Sharp, s; Ortrun Wenkel, con; Manfred Jung, Heinz

Zednik, t; Donald McIntyre, bar; Hermann Becht, bs-bar; Fritz Hubern, bs. Die Walkure. Jeannine Altmeyer, Gwyneth Jones, s; Hanna Schwarz, Carmen Reppel, ms; Peter Hofmann, t; Donald McIntyre, bar; Matti Salminen, bs; Bayreuth Festival Orchestra and Chorus; Pierre Boulez. Philips 6769 074 (16)
+-Gr 11-81 p757 +NYT 11-22-81 pD23
+-HFN 11-81 p93 ++SFC 10-25-81 p19

Siegfried: Auf wolkigan Hoh'n wohnen die Gotter. See no. 3639
Siegfried: Forest murmurs. See no. 3540. See no. 3543. See no. 3544. See no. 3561
Siegfried: Nothung Nothung; Hoho, hoho, hohei. See no. 3688
Siegfried: Scene de la forge. See no. 4050
Siegfried Idyll. See no. 3191. See no. 3548. See no. 3551. See no. 3851
Songs: Der Engel. See no. 4030
Songs: Traume. See no. 3703

3557 Tannhauser. Victoria de los Angeles, Grace Bumbry, s; Wolfgang Windgassen, Gerhard Stolze, Georg Paskuda, t; Dietrich Fischer-Dieskau, bar; Joseph Greindl, Franz Crass, Theo Adam, bs; Bayreuth Festival Orchestra and Chorus; Wolfgang Sawallisch. Teatro Dischi TD 503
+-FF 7/8-81 p200

Tannhauser: Als du in kuhnem Sange...Blick ich umher...Wohl wusst ich hier; Wie Todesahnung...O du mein holder Abendstern. See no. 1891
Tannhauser: Dich teure Halle. See no. 3642
Tannhauser: Fest march. See no. 3699
Tannhauser: Geliebter komm. See no. 4080
Tannhauser: Grand march. See no. 3626
Tannhauser: O du mein holder Abendstern; Als dir in Kuhnem Sange. See no. 3639
Tannhauser: Overture. See no. 3537. See no. 3539
Tannhauser: Pilgrim's chorus. See no. 3721
Tannhauser: Prelude, Act 3. See no. 3561
Tannhauser: Wie Todesahnung...O du mein holder Abendstern. See no. 4079

3558 Tristan und Isolde. Linda Esther Gray, s; Anne Wilkens, ms; John Mitchinson, t; Phillip Joll, bs-bar; Gwynne Howell, bs; Welsh National Opera Orchestra and Chorus; Reginald Goodall. Decca D250D5 (5) Tape (c) K250K53 (also London LDR 75001)
++Gr 9-81 p445 +HFN 10-81 p91
+Op 10-81 p996

Tristan und Isolde: Liebestod. See no. 3817
Tristan und Isolde: Mild und leise. See no. 795. See no. 4076
Tristan und Isolde: Prelude, Act 1. See no. 3543
Tristan und Isolde: Prelude and Liebestod. See no. 3538. See no. 3542. See no. 3548

3559 Die Walkure, Act 1. Lotte Lehmann, s; Lauritz Melchior, t; Orchestra; Bruno Walter. EMI 2C 051 03032
++Gr 6-81 p84

3560 Die Walkure, Act 1. Birgit Nilsson, s; Set Svanholm, t; Josef Greindl, bs; Hamburg Radio Orchestra; Hans Schmidt-Isserstedt. Historical Recordings HRE 347/1
+NR 12-81 p10

Die Walkure: Chanson du printemps. See no. 4050

Die Walkure: Du schuf'st ihm die Noth. See no. 4080
Die Walkure: Ho-jo-to-ho. See no. 4076
Die Walkure: Ho-jo-to-ho...Tanto fu triste. See no. 4041
Die Walkure: Ride of the Valkyries. See no. 3543. See no. 3561
Die Walkure: Ride of the Valkyries; Magic fire music. See no. 3540. See no. 3544
Die Walkure: Wintersturme. See no. 3688

3561 Works, selections: Gotterdammerung: Siegfried's Rhine journey. Parsifal: Prelude, Act 1. Das Rheingold: Entry of the Gods into Valhalla. Siegfried: Forest murmurs. Tannhauser: Prelude, Act 3. Die Walkure: Ride of the Valkyries. PhO; Otto Klemperer. HMV SXLP 30528 Tape (c) SXLP 30528 (From Columbia SAX 2464)
+-Gr 11-81 p702

WAGNER, Siegfried

3562 An allem ist Hutchen schuld: Prelude. Concerto, violin. Der Heidenkonig: Intermezzo. Jenny Abel, vln; Nurnberg Chamber Orchestra; Gilbert Graf Gravina. Colosseum SM 532
+FF 9/10-81 p200

Der Barenhauter: Overture. See no. 3551
Concerto, violin. See no. 3562
Der Heidenkonig: Intermezzo. See no. 3562
Konzertstuck, flute. See no. 3551

WALCHA, Helmut

O Mensch bewein. See no. 3786

WALDTEUFEL, Emile

Estudiantina, op. 191. See no. 3563
Je t'aime. See no. 3563
Mon reve, op. 151. See no. 3563
Les patineurs, op. 183. See no. 3563
Pluie de diamants. See no. 3563
Les sirenes. See no. 3563

3563 Works, selections: Estudiantina, op. 191. Je t'aime. Mon reve, op. 151. Les patineurs, op. 183. Pluie de diamants. Les sirenes. BeSO; Robert Stolz. RCA GL 2-5281 Tape (c) GK 2-5281
+Gr 11-80 p739 +HFN 1-81 p109 tape
+HFN 10-80 p113

WALKER

I will lift up mine eyes. See no. 3822

WALKER, Ernest

Sonata, viola and piano, C major. See no. 867

WALLACE, William Vincent

Maritana: There is a flower that bloometh. See no. 3967
Maritana: Hear me gentle Maritana...The mariner in his barque. See no. 4074

WALLIS

Gentil galant de France. See no. 3653

WALLOWITCH, John

Snappy pieces. See no. 1010

WALOND, William

Voluntary, no. 3, D minor. See no. 3905

WALTERS

English folk songs. See no. 3721
Iona. See no. 3721
The national anthem. See no. 3721

WALTHER, Johann
Chorus, 4 parts. See no. 3720
3564 Concerti, F major (after Albinoni); B major (after Taglietti); A minor (after Meck); D minor (after Torelli); A major (after Gentili). Hanns-Christoph Schuster, org. Pape 2
+NR 4-81 p14
Concerto del Sigr. Albinoni. See no. 3735
Concerto del Signor Meck, B minor. See no. 3735
Mit Fried und Freud ich fahr dahin. See no. 3720
Motets: Nun bitten wir den heiligen Geist. See no. 3906
WALTON, William
3565 Belshazzar's feast. Te deum. Sherrill Milnes, bar; Scottish National Orchestra and Chorus; Scottish Festival Brass Bands; Alexander Gibson. RCA GL 1-3368 Tape (c) GK 1-3368 (From RL 2-5105)
++Gr 10-81 p596
Chichester service: Magnificat; Nunc dimittis. See no. 744
Concerto, violoncello. See no. 1463
3566 Facade I and II. Cathy Berberian, Robert Tear, speakers; Various instrumentalists; Steuart Bedford. Peters PLG 135 Tape (c) PCE 135 (also Oxford OUP 201)
+-FF 9/10-80 p234
+-Gr 1-80 p1194
+HF 6-80 p91
+HFN 1-80 p111
+-MT 5-81 p318
+RR 1-80 p111
+SFC 6-8-80 p36
++St 8-80 p102
+STL 5-11-80 p39
Fanfare "Hamlet". See no. 4006
Orb and sceptre. See no. 3976
Pieces, violin and piano (2). See no. 1473
Queen's fanfare. See no. 4006
Songs: All this time. See no. 3685
Songs: Make we joy now in this fest. See no. 3921
Spitfire: Prelude and fugue. See no. 4105
3567 Symphony, no. 1, B flat minor. Royal Liverpool Philharmonic Orchestra; Vernon Handley. ASV Tape (c) ZCACM 2006
+HFN 6-81 p87 tape
3568 Symphony, no. 1, B flat minor. Royal Liverpool Orchestra; Vernon Handley. Nonesuch H 71394 Tape (c) N5-71394
-FF 5/6-81 p185
+HF 10-81 p91 tape
+NR 7-81 p2
+SFC 2-8-81 p21
3569 Symphony, no. 1, B flat minor. LSO; Andre Previn. RCA GL 4-2707 Tape (c) GK 4-2707 (From SB 6691, LSC 2927)
++FF 11/12-81 p278
++Gr 1-79 p1292
+Gr 3-79 p1614 tape
+HFN 1-79 p128 tape
Te deum. See no. 3565
The wise virgins: Ballet suite (Bach). See no. 1331
WARD, John
3570 Fantasias, nos. 3-4, 8, 14. First set of English madrigals, 1613. Consort of Musicke; Anthony Rooley, Trevor Jones. L'Oiseau-Lyre D238D2 (2)
+Gr 9-81 p422
+HFN 7-81 p77
Fantasia a 5. See no. 4092
First set of English madrigals, 1613. See no. 3570
Songs: O my thoughts surcease; Retire my troubled soul. See no. 4085

WARLOCK, Peter
Capriol suite. See no. 3415. See no. 3856
Captain Stratton's fancy. See no. 4057
The curlew. See no. 3417
Serenade, strings. See no. 1331. See no. 3415
Serenade for the 60th birthday of Delius. See no. 1328
Songs: After two years; Away to Twivver; Balulalow; The frostbound wood; Jillian of Berry; My own country; Passing by; Pretty ring time; Rest sweet nymphs; Sleep; Sweet and twenty; Yarmouth fair. See no. 1336
Songs: Away to Twivver; Fill the the cup Philip; Capriol suite: Tordion; Mattachins; Hey troly loly lo; I asked a thief to steal me a peach; In an arbour green; Jillian of Berry; My ghostly fader; Piggesine; Sweet content; Peter Warlock's fancy. See no. 3973
Songs: Balulalow. See no. 3852
Songs: Pretty ringtime; Sigh no more ladies; Take o take those lips away. See no. 3878
WASHBURN
Quintet, winds. See no. 4019
WASSENAER, Unico Wilhelm Graf van
3571 Concerti armonici, nos. 1-6 (attrib. Pergolesi, Ricciotti). Camerata Bern; Thomas Furi, vln. DG 2533 456
+Gr 7-81 p162 ++SFC 12-27-81 p18
++HFN 7-81 p77
3572 Concerti armonici, nos. 1-6. PERGOLESI (attrib.): Concerti, violin, F major, B flat major. Pina Carmirelli, vln; I Musici. Philips 6768 163 (2) Tape (c) 7699 146
+FF 9/10-81 p202 +SFC 7-19-81 p19
Concerto arminico, no. 2, G major. See no. 2579
WATTS, John
3573 Elegy to a chimney: In memoriam. Mots d'heures: Gousses, Rames. Piano for te. Robert Levy, tpt; John Watts, Robert Levy, synthesizer, electronics, tape; Wesleyan Singers; Neely Bruce. Serenus SRS 12080
+-ARG 1-80 p43 +NR 10-79 p6
*FF 9/10-81 p203
Mots d'heures: Gousses, Rames. See no. 3573
Piano for te. See no. 3573
Signals for soprano and chamber orchestra. See no. 1009
Sonata, piano. See no. 41
WEBER, Carl Maria von
3574 Abu Hassan. Edda Moser, s; Nicolai Gedda, t; Kurt Moll, bs; Bavarian State Opera Orchestra and Chorus; Wolfgang Sawallisch. EMI Electrola 1C 065 30148
+FF 7/8-81 p203
Abu Hassan: Overture. See no. 3577
Air russe and rondo. See no. 3847
Andante and rondo ungarese, op. 35. See no. 3863
Aufforderung zum Tanz, op. 65. See no. 1075. See no. 3577
3575 Concerto, clarinet, no. 1, op. 73, E minor. Concerto, clarinet, no. 2, op. 74, E flat major. Benny Goodman, clt; CSO; Jean Martinon. RCA AGL 1-3788 Tape (c) AGK 1-3788
+FF 3/4-81 p219
Concerto, clarinet, no. 2, op. 74, E flat major. See no. 3575

Duets, op. 31. See no. 3907
Euryanthe: Glockenlein im Thale; So bin ich nun verlassen. See no. 3531
Euryanthe: Overture. See no. 3055. See no. 3577. See no. 3792
3576 Der Freischutz. Hildegard Behrens, Helen Donath, s; Rene Kollo, t; Hermann Sapell, Raimund Grumbach, Wolfgang Brendel, bar; Peter Meven, Kurt Moll, bs; Bavarian Radio Orchestra and Chorus; Rafael Kubelik. London OSA 13136 (3) Tape (C) OSA 5-13136 (also Decca D235D3 Tape (c) K235K32)

++FF 7/8-81 p202 +NYT 5-31-81 pD23
+Gr 1-81 p992 +ON 9-81 p60
+Gr 6-81 p93 tape +Op 2-81 p158
/-HF 9-81 p78 ++SFC 5-3-81 p22
++HFN 1-81 p103 +St 6-81 p72
+-MT 7-81 p482 +STL 1-11-81 p38

Der Freischutz: Durch die Walder durch die Auen. See no. 3800
Der Freischutz: Nein langer trag ich nicht die Qualen. See no. 3747
Der Freischutz: Nein langer trag ich nicht...Durch die Walder. See no. 3648
Der Freischutz: Overture. See no. 3577. See no. 3644. See no. 3792
Der Freischutz: Wer legt auf in strengen Bann. See no. 3639
Der Freischutz: Wie nahte mir der Schlummer...Leise, leise; Und ob die Wolke. See no. 3651
Introduction, theme and variations, B major. See no. 2824
Konzertstuck, op. 79, F minor. See no. 3028
Oberon: Overture. See no. 3577. See no. 3656. See no. 3792. See no. 3855. See no. 4122
Oberon: Ozean du Ungeheuer. See no. 472. See no. 3830. See no. 3989
Oberon: Seit fruhster Jugend; Du der diese Profung schickt. See no. 3648
Oberon: Von Jugend auf in dem Kampfgefild. See no. 3800
Oberon: Von Jugend auf. See no. 4022
3577 Overtures: Abu Hassan. Aufforderung zum Tanz, op. 65 (orch. Berlioz). Euryanthe. Der Freischutz. Oberon. Preziosa. Budapest MAV Symphony Orchestra; Geza Oberfrank. Hungaroton SLPX 12175

-HFN 8-81 p88 ++NR 8-81 p6

Preciosa: Overture. See no. 3577
Quintet, clarinet, op. 34, B flat major. See no. 1976
Romanze appassionata. See no. 1670
3578 Sonata, piano, no. 1, op. 24, C major. Sonata, piano, no. 2, op. 39, A flat major. Dino Ciano, pno. Ricordi RCL 27003

/-FF 11/12-81 p278

Sonata, piano, no. 1, op. 24, C major: Rondo. See no. 3920
Sonata, piano, no. 2, op. 39, A flat major. See no. 3578
3579 Sonata, piano, no. 3, op. 49, D minor. Sonata, piano, no. 4, op. 70, E minor. Dino Ciano, pno. Ricordi RCL 27004

/-FF 11/12-81 p278

Sonata, piano, no. 4, op. 70, E minor. See no. 3579
Songs: Duets, op. 31. See no. 2079
Theme and variations concertante, op. 33, B major. See no. 2824
Turandot: Overture. See no. 747

Variations, op. 9, F major. See no. 1159
Variations on a theme from Silvana. See no. 926. See no. 3669. See no. 3715

WEBERN, Anton
Bagatelles, op. 9 (6). See no. 422
Kinderstuck. See no. 1019
Passacaglia, op. 1. See no. 3580
Pieces, orchestra, op. 6. See no. 3580
Pieces, orchestra, op. 10. See no. 3580
Piece, piano. See no. 1019
Pieces, violin and piano, op. 7. See no. 2020
Quintet, piano. See no. 2928
Sonata movement, piano. See no. 1019
Songs (Richard Dehmel). See no. 1272
Symphony, op. 21. See no. 3580
Variations, op. 27. See no. 3785
Variations, op. 30. See no. 3580

3580 Works, selections: Passacaglia, op. 1. Pieces, op. 6 (6). Pieces, op. 10 (5). Symphony, no. 21. Variations, op. 30. BACH: Ein musikalische Opfer, S 1079: Fugue (orch. Webern). LSO; Pierre Boulez. CBS 76911 Tape (c) 40-76911 (From 79402)
+Gr 11-80 p233 +HFN 11-80 p129
+Gr 10-80 p548 tape +MT 3-81 p185
++HFN 10-80 p117 tape

WECKERLIN
Tambourin. See no. 3703

WECKMANN, Matthias
Fantasia, D minor. See no. 3720
Nun freut euch lieben Christen g'mein. See no. 3960

WEELKES, Thomas
Songs: All people clap your hands. See no. 3637
Songs: As Vesta was; Hark all ye lovely saints. See no. 3876
Songs: Come sirrah Jack ho; Come let's begin to revel out; Some men desire spouses; Those sweet delightful lilies. See no. 4085
Songs: Give ear O Lord. See no. 3621
Songs: Hark all ye lovely saints. See no. 3677
Songs: Hark I hear some dancing. See no. 3762
Songs: Why are you ladies staying. See no. 3762

WEGNER, August
Something, flute and piano. See no. 3915

WEIGL, Karl
3581 Pieces, violoncello and piano. Sonata, piano and violoncello. Sonata, viola and piano. Songs, male voice and piano (3). Paul Doktor, vla; Kermit Moore, vlc; David Holloway, bar; Richard Woitach, pno. Orion ORS 80389
-NR 4-81 p7
Sonata, piano and violoncello. See no. 3581
Sonata, viola and piano. See no. 3581
Songs, male voice and piano. See no. 3581

WEIGL, Vally
3582 Brief encounters. Dear earth. Songs of love and leaving. Shirley Love, ms; Robert Shiesley, David Holloway, bar; Marilyn Dubow, vln; David Moore, vlc; Peter Gordon, French hn; Lawrence Sobol, clt; Ilse Sass, Richard Woitach, pno; City Winds. Orion ORS 80393

+-NR 6-81 p12

Dear earth. See no. 3582

Songs of love and leaving. See no. 3582

WEILL, Kurt

3583 Die Dreigroschenoper. Caroline Kava, Blair Brown, Ellen Greene, Elizabeth Wilson, Raul Julia, C. K. Alexander, David Shabin, Roy Brocksmith, soloists; Orchestra; Stanley Silverman. CBS 61138

+-HFN 9-81 p85 +op 12-81 p1306

3854 Die Dreigroschenoper. Karin Huebner, Ursula Dirichs, Edith Teichmann, Anita Mey, Hans Korte, Franz Kutschera, Albert Hoermann, Dieter Brammer, soloists; Frankfurt Opera Orchestra; Wolfgang Rennert. Philips 6768 700 (2)

+HFN 10-81 p91 +-Op 12-81 p1306
+-NYT 9-13-81 pD41

Die Dreigroschenoper: Suite. See no. 695

Frauentanz, op. 10. See no. 2937

3585 Der Ozeanflug. Karl Markus, t; Uwe Freibott, bar; Gottfried Schwartz, bs; Gottingen University Chorus; Academic Orchestra Union; Hermann Fuchs. Thorofon MTH 118

+FF 9/10-81 p203

3586 Der Silbersee. Elizabeth Hynes, s; Elaine Bonazzi, ms; Joel Grey, William Neill, Jack Harrold, t; New York City Opera Orchestra; Julius Rudel. Nonesuch DB 79003 (2)

+ARG 7/8-81 p50 +ON 12-20-80 p52
+FF 1/2-81 p213 ++St 2-81 p116
-HF 2-81 p58

Der Silbersee: Suite. See no. 1964

Sonata, violoncello and piano. See no. 1354

3587 Songs: Der Abschiedsbrief; Berlin im Licht song; Buddy on the nightshift; Complainte de la Seine; Es Regnet; Je ne t'aime pas; Klops Lied; Das Lied von den Braunen Inseln; Die Muschel von Margate, the petroleum song; Nannas Lied; Schickelgruber; Und was Bekam des Soldaten Weib; Wie Lange Noch; Youkali, Tango habanera. Teresa Stratas, s; Richard Woitach, pno. Nonesuch D 79019

+NYT 9-13-81 pD41 +OV 12-81 p36
+ON 12-19-81 p44 +St 11-81 p68

WEINBERGER, Jaromir

3588 Schwanda the bagpiper (sung in German). Lucia Popp, s; Gwendolyn Killebrew, ms; Siegfried Jerusalem, Karl Kreile, t; Hermann Prey, bar; Siegmund Nimsgern, bs; Bavarian Radio Chorus; Munich Radio Orchestra; Heinz Wallberg. CBS 79344 (3)

+Gr 12-81 p933 /HFN 12-81 p106

Schwanda the bagpiper: Fantasia. See no. 3993

Schwanda the bagpiper: Ich bin der Schwanda; Wie kann ich denn vergessen. See no. 3639

Schwanda the bagpiper: Polka and fugue. See no. 3817

The way to Emmaus. See no. 3821

WEINER, Leo

Sonata, violin and piano, no. 2, op. 11, F sharp minor. See no. 1490. See no. 2020

WEINER, Stanley

Fantasy, no. 1, op. 57. See no. 1110

WEISGALL, Hugo
3589 The golden peacock. Translations. Judith Raskin, s; Morey Ritt, pno. CRI SD 417
+ARG 11-80 p37
+FF 7/8-81 p203
+NR 5-80 p11
+NYT 2-24-80 pD20
+St 9-80 p84
Translations. See no. 3589
WEISMANN, Julius
Concertino, op. 118, E flat major. See no. 3655
WEISS, Sylvius Leopold
Chaconne, A major. See no. 3886
Fantasie, E minor. See no. 4015
Passacaglia. See no. 4015
Suite, D major. See no. 312
Suite, D minor. See no. 3927
Tombeau sur la mort de M. Comte de Logy. See no. 4015
WELIN, Karl-Erik
Frammenti. See no. 3690
WELLS
Electronic music. See no. 1637
WENTINK, Victor
Discours. See no. 3728
WERLE, Lars
Trees. See no. 1930
WERNER, Fritz
Duo, op. 53. See no. 1110
WERNER, Joseph
Musical calendar: May. See no. 3767
WERT, Giaches de
Vezzosi augelli. See no. 3692
WESLEY, Samuel
Behold how good and joyful. See no. 3615
Fugue, G major. See no. 3625
WESLEY, Samuel Sebastian
An air composed for Holsworthy church bells with variations. See no. 4112
Andante cantabile. See no. 3930
Larghetto, F sharp minor. See no. 3625
Songs: Blessed be the God and father. See no. 3873
Songs: Thou wilt keep him in perfect peace. See no. 3618. See no. 4107
WESTERLUND
Songs: Host-Vinter. See no. 3805
WESTHOFF, Johann Paul von
Sonata, a major. See no. 3783
WHEAR, Paul
3590 Celebration XXV. Enterprise overture. Of this time. Symphony, no. 4. Youngstown State University Wind Ensemble; Robert Fleming, Joseph Lapinski. Golden Crest 5071
+-ARG 5-81 p35
*NR 7-81 p14
Enterprise overture. See no. 3590
Of this time. See no. 3590
Symphony, no. 4. See no. 3590
WHITE, L.J.
Prayer of St. Richard at Chichester. See no. 3615

WHITE, Robert
3591 Songs (choral): Lamentations of Jeremiah. Motets: Domine quis habitavit; Christe qui lux es; Portio mea Domine; Regina coeli. Clerkes of Oxenford; David Wulstan. Calliope CAL 1622
+Gr 4-79 p1761 +Gr 1-81 p982
Songs: Lamentations of Jeremiah. See no. 1245
WHITLOCK, Percy
3592 Fantasie-chorals, nos. 1-2. March for the "Phoebe". Sketches (2). Sonata, organ, C minor: Canzona. Robert Gower, org. Wealden WS 196
+Gr 7-81 p176
March for the "Phoebe". See no. 3592
Sketches (2). See no. 3592
Sonata, organ, C minor: Canzona. See no. 3592
Songs: Here O my lord I see thee. See no. 3633
Songs: Jesu grant me this I pray. See no. 3615
WHYTHORNE, Thomas
As thy shadow itself apply'th. See no. 3973
WIDMANN, Erasmus
Canzona, galliard, intrada. See no. 3719
Daentze und Galliarden. See no. 2609
WIDOR, Charles
3593 Nouvelles pieces, op. 87 (3). Suite latine. Jane Parker-Smith, org. L'Oiseau-Lyre SOL 352
+-Gr 8-80 p242 +-MT 3-81 p197
+HFN 7-80 p111 -RR 7-80 p85
Salve regina. See no. 3806
Suite latine. See no. 3593
3594 Symphony, organ, no. 3, op. 13, no. 3, E minor: Prelude; Adagio; Finale. Symphony, organ, no. 4, op. 13, no. 4, F major. Symphony, organ, no. 6, op. 42, no. 2, B major. Symphony, organ no. 9, op. 70, C minor. Marie-Claire Alain, org. Eratu STU 71165 (2)
++Gr 5-80 p1693 +-MU 3-81 p12
+-HFN 4-80 p112 +RR 4-80 p104
+MT 3-81 p197
3595 Symphony, organ, no. 4, op. 13, no. 4, F major. Symphony, organ, no. 10. Odile Pierre, org. RCA RL 3-7394
++MU 9-81 p14
Symphony, organ, no. 4, op. 13, no. 4, F major. See no. 3594
Symphony, organ, no. 5, op. 42, no. 1, F minor: 1st movement. See no. 4120
Symphony, organ, no. 5, op. 42, no. 1, F minor: Toccata. See no. 251. See no. 3725. See no. 3744. See no. 3746. See no. 3799
Symphony, organ, no. 6, op. 42, no. 2, G major. See no. 3594
Symphony, organ, no. 6, op. 42, no. 2, G major: Allegro moderato. See no. 3786
Symphony, organ, no. 6, op. 42, no. 2, G major: Finale. See no. 251. See no. 3725
3596 Symphony, organ, no. 9, op. 70, C minor. Marie-Andree Morisset-Balier, org. Grand Orgue MBM 800100
+FF 7/8-81 p191 +MU 11-81 p18
Symphony, organ, no. 9, op. 70, C minor. See no. 3594
Symphony, organ, no. 10. See no. 3595
Toccata. See no. 3673

WIENIAWSKI, Henryk
Capriccio valse. See no. 3597
Concerto, violin, no. 1, op. 14, F sharp minor. See no. 1044
Konzertstucke, op. 19: Obertass mazurka. See no. 3597
Kuyawiak. See no. 3597
Legende, op. 17, G major. See no. 564. See no. 3597. See no. 3704
Polonaise, D major, A major. See no. 3597
Scherzo tarantelle, op. 16. See no. 3597
Souvenir de Moscow, op. 6. See no. 3597
Variations on an original theme. See no. 3597

3597 Works, selections: Capriccio valse. Kuyawiak. Legende, op. 17, G major. Konzertstucke, op. 19: Obertass mazurka. Polonaise, D major, A major. Scherzo tarantelle, op. 16. Souvenir de Moscow, op. 6. Variations on an original theme. Ruggiero Ricci, vln; Joanna Gruenberg, pno. Unicorn DKP 9003
+-ARG 12-81 p36 ++HFN 6-81 p79
+FF 9/10-81 p204 ++SFC 7-12-81 p18
+Gr 7-81 p170 ++St 12-81 p129

WIKLUND, Adolf
3598 Concerto, piano, no. 2, op. 17, B flat minor. Pieces, strings and harp. Little suite: Sang til varen. Greta Erikson, pno; Swedish Radio Orchestra; Stig Westerberg. Caprice CAP 1165
++ARG 2-81 p39 +NR 9-80 p4
+HFN 2-81 p94 +RR 8-80 p58
Little suite: Sang til varen. See no. 3598
Pieces, strings and harp. See no. 3598

WIKMANSON, Johann
Quartet, strings, op. 1, no. 2, E minor. See no. 779

WILBYE, John
Songs: Adieu sweet Amaryllis. See no. 3845
Songs: As matchless beauty; Lady when I behold; Weep o mine eyes. See no. 4085
Songs: The Lady Oriana. See no. 3876
Songs: Weep weep mine eyes. See no. 4114

WILDBERGER, Jacques
3599 Diario. Double refrain. Tod und Verklarung. Kurt Widmer, bar; Aurele Nicolet, flt; Heinz Holliger, ob; Bernhard Wulff, gtr; Hans-Rudolf Stadler, clt; Camerata Zurich; Rato Tschupp. Musicaphon BM 30 SL 1714
+HFN 1-81 p103
Double refrain. See no. 3599
Tod und Verklarung. See no. 3599

WILDING-WHITE, Raymond
Band music. See no. 1938

WILKINSON, R.
Salve regina. See no. 1033

WILLAERT, Adrian
Songs: A quand; Allons allons gay; Ricercari (2); Villanelle. See no. 3862

WILLCOCKS
Fanfare on "Gopsal". See no. 3959
Saraband. See no. 3955

WILLIAMS, David
Songs: Dearest thou now O soul; In the year that King Uzziah died.

See no. 3818

WILLIAMS, Grace

3600 Carillons, oboe and orchestra. Concerto, trumpet. Fairest of stars. Fantasia on Welsh nursery tunes. Howard Snell, tpt; Anthony Camden, ob; Janet Price, s; LSO; Charles Groves. Oriel ORM 1005 (From HVM ASD 3006)
+Gr 9-81 p422

Concerto, trumpet. See no. 3600

Fairest of stars. See no. 3600

Fantasia on Welsh nursery tunes. See no. 3600

WILLIAMS, John

Midway march. See no. 3976

Star wars: Main theme. See no. 4105

WILLIAMS, R. V.

God be with you. See no. 4061

WILLIAMS, William

Sonata in imitation of birds. See no. 3853

WILLIAMSON

Epiphany carol. See no. 3822

WILLIAMSON, Malcolm

Wrestling Jacob. See no. 3621

WILSON, Mark

Sappho. See no. 1269

WILSON, Meredith

The music man: 76 trombones. See no. 3976

WILSON, Richard

The ballad of Longwood Glen. See no. 3400

Eclogue. See no. 3400

WILSON, Thomas

Cancion. See no. 4062

WINHAM, Godfrey

N. P. See no. 1638

WINTER, Peter

German Te deum. See no. 3908

Symphony concertante, B flat major. See no. 3794

WIREN, Dag

Serenade, op. 11. See no. 1646

WISE, Michael

Prepare ye the way. See no. 3637

WITT, Friedrich

Concertino, 2 horns, E flat major. See no. 1511

WOLF, Hugo

3601 Intermezzo, string quartet. Italian serenade, G major. Pieces, piano (3). Songs from the Schenkenbuch (5). Songs from the Book of Suleika (5). Raimund Gilvan, t; Elisabeth Schwarz, Frederic Capon, pno; Keller String Quartet. Musical Heritage Society MHS 1868 (also Da Camera SM 92723)
-HFN 6-81 p79 +St 7-75 p106

Italian serenade, G major. See no. 1046. See no. 3601

Pieces, piano. See no. 3601

3602 Songs: (Record no. 1) Ach des Knaben Augen; Auch kleine Dinge; Auf einer Wanderung; Begegnung; Das Standchen; Das verlassene Magdelein; Die ihr schwebet; Du denkst mir einem Fadchen; Gesang Weylas; Heimweh; Herr was tragt der Boden hier; Ihr jungen Leute; In dem Schatten meiner Locken; Lied vom Winde; Nien junger Herr; Nun wandre Maria; Rat einer Alten; Und steht ihr fruh; Wenn du zu den Blumen gehst. (Record, no. 2) Anakreons Grab; Beherzigung; Die Bekehrte; Blumengruss; Coptisches Lied II; Epiphanias; Fruhling ubers Jahr; Ganymed; Genialisch Treiben; Gleich und gleich; Harfenspieler: Wer sich der Einsamkeit ergibt, An die Turen will ich schleichen, Wer nie sein Brot; Prometheus; Der Rattenfanger; Die Sprode. (Record, no. 3) Alles endet was entstehet; Benedit die sel'ge Mutter; Bitt ich o Mutter; Ertes Liebeslied eines Madchens; Fuhlt meine Seele; Grenzen der Menscheit; Klinge klinge mein Pandero; Kopfchen Kopfchen nich gewimmert; Meine Liebster hat zu Tische mich geladen; Mogen alle bosen zungen; Der Mond hat eine schwere Klag erhoben; Nixe Binsefuss; Schwieg einmal still; Schon streckt ich aus im Bett; Um Mitternacht; Wer rief dich denn; Wohl denk ich oft. (Record, no. 4) Dass doch gemalt all deine Reize waren; Du sagts mir; Gesegnet sei das Grun; Gesegnet sei durch den die Welt entstand; Geselle woll'n wir uns in Kutten hullen; Heb aur dein blondes Haupt; Heut Nacht erhob ich mich; Hoffartig seid ihr schones Kind; Ich esse nun mein Brot; Ich hab in Penna; Ich liess mir sagen; Ihr seid die Allerschonste; Man sagt mir; Mein Liebster ist so klein; Mein Libster singt am Haus; Mir ward gesagt; Nun lass uns Frieden schliessen; O war dein Haus; Ein Standchen Euch zu bringen; Sterb ich so hullt in Blumen meine Glieder; Und willst du deinen Liebsten sterben sehen; Was fur ein Lied; Was soll der Zorn; Wenn du mein Liebster; Wenn du mich mit dein Augen streifst; Wie soll ich frohlich sein; Wie lange schon war immer mein verlangen; Wie viele Zeit verlor ich; Wir haben beide lange Zeit geschwiegen; Wohl kenn ich Euren stand. (Record, no. 5) An die Geliebte; Auf dem grunen Balkon; Auf ein altes Bild; Biterolf; Bei einer Trauung; Coptisches Lied I; Denk es o Seele; Elfenlied; Gebet; Muhvoll komm ich und beladen; Der Musikant; Der Schreckenberger; Seufzer; Der Soldat I; Ein Stundlein wohl vor Tag; Sie blasen zum Abmarsch; Trau nicht der Liebe; Treibe nur mit Lieben Spott; Seufzer; Verborgenheit; Wie glanzt der Helle Mond. (Record, no. 6) Ach im Maien war's; Alle gingen Herr zu Ruh; An der Schlaf; Dereinst dereinst; Der Feuerreiter; Gesellenlied; Herz verzage nicht geschwind; Komm o Tod; Lebewohl; Mignon I: Heiss mich nicht; Mignon III: So lasst mich scheinen; Neue Liebe; Storchenbotschaft; Tief im Herzen Trag ich Pein; Wiegenlied im Sommer; Zur Ruh zur Ruh. (Record, no. 7) Auftrag; Fussreise; Geh Geliebter; Der Gartner; Die Geister am Mummelsee; In der Fruhe; Jagerlied; Keine gleicht von allen Schonen; Lied eines Verliebten; Nimmerstatte Liebe; Ritter Kurts Brautfahrt; Sankt Nepomuks Vorabend; Der Sanger; Schlafendes Jesukind; Der Scholar; Sonne der Schlummerlosen; Unfall; Der verzweifelte Liebhaber; Wiegenlied im Winter; Wo wird einst. Alexandra Trianti, Elisabeth Rethberg, Ria Ginster, Marta Fuchs, Tiana Lemnitz, s; Elena Gerhardt, ms; John McCormack, Helge Roswaenge, Karl Erb, t; Herbert Hanssen, Gerhard Husch, Friedrich Schorr, bar; Alexander Kipnis, Ludwig Weber, bs; Coenrad Bos, Edwin Schnieder, Michael Raucheisen, Hanns Udo Muller, Ernst Victor Wolff, Gerald Moore, pno; LSO; Robert Heger. HMV RLS 759 (7)

++FF 9/10-81 p205 +NR 7-81 p11
++Gr 3-81 p1218 +ON 8-81 p36

+HF 11-81 p98 +STL 3-8-81 p38
+HFN 4-81 p77

3603 Songs: Als ich auf dem Euphrat schiffte; Anakreons Grab; Blumengruss; Du milchunger Knabe; Epiphanias; Fruhling ubers Jahr; Ganymed; Hoch begluckt in deiner Liebe; Das Kohlerweib ist trunken; Kennst du das Land; Maufallenspruchlein; Mignon, I-III; Morgentau; Nimmer will ich dich verlieren; Philine; St. Nepomuks Vorabend; Singt mein Schatz; Die Spinnerin; Sonne der Schlummerlosen; Tretet ein hoher Krieger; Das Voglein; Wandl ich in dem Morgentau; Wie glantz der Helle Mond; Wiegenlied in Sommer; Wiegenlied in Winter. Elisabeth Schwarzkopf, s; Gerald Moore, pno. HMV SLS 5197 (2)
+-FF 7/8-81 p204 +STL 11-9-80 p40
++Gr 9-80 p386

Songs: An den Schlaf; Begegnung; Der Genesene an die Hoffnung; Frage und Antwort; Heimweh; Lebe wohl; Nimmersatte Liebe; Peregrina, I and II; Um Mitternacht. See no. 2220

Songs: Anakreons Grab; Bedeckt mich mit Blumen; Im Fruhling; Mogen alle Bosen zungen; Die Zigeunerin. See no. 2107

Songs: Auch kleine Dinge; Schlafendes Jesuskind; Wo find' ich Trost. See no. 3657

Songs: Auf ein altes Bild; Bei einer Trauung; Elfenlied; Fussreise; Heimweh; Jagerlied; Selbstgestandnis; Mausfallenspruchlein; Nixe Binsefuss; Nimmersatte Liebe; Storchenbotschart; Das verlassene Magdlein. See no. 952

Songs: Beherzigung; Bei einer Trauung; Die du Gott gebarst; Fuhr mich Kind; Fruhling ubers Jahr; Ganymed; Der Gartner; Sankt Nepomuks Vorabend; Schlafendes Jesuskind; Der Scholar; Spottlied; Wenn ich dein gedenke; Wie sollt ich heiter bleiben. See no. 2994

Songs: Epiphanias. See no. 3702

Songs: Geistliche Lieder. See no. 951

Songs: Goethe Lieder: Mignon I-III. See no. 2442

Songs: Liebesfruhling; Nachtgruss; Der Musikant; Wohin mit der Freud. See no. 3547

Songs: Mignon. See no. 3653

Songs: Morike Lieder: Verborgenheit. See no. 3988

Songs: Schlafendes Jesuskind; Wo find ich trost. See no. 3967

Songs: Verschwiegene Liebe. See no. 3988

Songs: Wiegenlied; Maufallenspruchlein. See no. 3844

Songs from the Book of Suleika (5). See no. 3601

Songs from the Schenkenbuch (5). See no. 3601

3604 Spanisches Liederbuch. Elisabeth Schwarzkopf, s; Dietrich Fischer-Fieskau, bar; Gerald Moore, pno. DG 2726 071 (2) Tape (c) 3372 071 (From SLPM 139329/30)
+ARG 8-79 p45 +-HFN 1-81 p109 tape
+-FF 1/2-80 p160 ++NYT 8-5-79 pD19
+Gr 4-79 p1762 +RR 5-79 p92
+HFN 4-79 p133

WOLF-FERRARI, Ermanno

Il gioelli della Madonna: T'eri un giorno ammalato. See no. 3657. See no. 3967

Der Schmuck der Madonna: Madonna unter Tranen. See no. 3747

WOLPE, Stefan

Chamber piece, no. 2. See no. 3933

Form for piano. See no. 740
Piece in two parts, solo violin. See no. 740

WOLSTENHOLME, William
Allegretto, op. 17, no. 2, E flat major. See no. 3971

WOOD, Charles
Songs: Expectans, expectavi. See no. 4107
Songs: O thou the central orb. See no. 3873
Songs: Oculi omnium. See no. 3618

WOTJA
Introduzione et aria. See no. 3826

WRIGHT
Carol-prelude on "Greensleeves". See no. 3921

WRIGHT, Maurice
Chamber symphony. See no. 4068

WUORINEN, Charles
Pieces, violin and piano. See no. 2014
The winds. See no. 3933

WYTON, Alec
Songs: A hymne to God the father. See no. 3810

XIMENO, Fabian
Ay ay galeguinos. See no. 3911

YAMADA
Chugokuchiho no komoruta. See no. 3696
Sunayama. See no. 3696

YAN PING JIN
Dance. See no. 3859

YANNATOS, James
3605 Cycles: A musical entertainment. Minicycle I (Moods). Prieres dans l'arche. Sonata, clarinet and piano. Thomas Hill, clt; Lucy Shelton, Joan Heller, s; Lawrence Berman, Christopher Oldfather, pno; Chamber Ensemble, Contemporary Music Ensemble, Boston; James Yannatos. AFKA 4628-1
+-FF 3/4-81 p34
Minicycle I (Moods). See no. 3605
Prieres dans l'arche. See no. 3605
Sonata, clarinet and piano. See no. 3605

YANNAY, Yehuda
At the end of the parade. See no. 3400

YARDUMIAN, Richard
3606 Come creator spirit, mass. Lili Chookasian, ms; Philadelphia Chorale Chamber Symphony, Philadelphia Chamber Symphony; Fordham University Glee Club, Thomas More College Women's Chorale; Anshel Brusilow. CRI SD 430 (also RCA LSC 2979)
+FF 3/4-81 p219 +NR 3-81 p8
Preludes (2). See no. 3913

YATSUHASHI
Rokudan no Shirabe. See no. 3696

YI KEUNG SUN
Rice threshing dance. See no. 3860

YIAO XIAN MA ZHONG HAN LI
Spring in Sinkiang. See no. 3859

YODER
Relax. See no. 3817

YON, Pietro
L'organo primitivo: Humoresque. See no. 4116

YONG CHEN QIN
Romance. See no. 3859
YOSHIZAWA
Chidori no kyoku (Tune of the plovers). See no. 3696. See no. 4106
YOUMANS
Tea for two. See no. 3801. See no. 4114
YOUNG, Douglas
Virages: Region one. See no. 3404
YOUNG, Gayle
3607 According to the moon. In motion. Theorein. Billie Bridgman, s; Karen Skidmore, con; Gayle Young, columbine; Reinhard Reitzenstein, speaker. WRC 1-1265
+MUM 5/6-81 p33
In motion. See no. 3607
Theorein. See no. 3607
YOUNG, Victor
Stella by starlight. See no. 4007
YSAYE, Eugene
Reve d'enfant, op. 14. See no. 2015. See no. 3704
Sonata, solo violin, no. 3, op. 27, D minor. See no. 1319
YTTREHUS, Rolv
Quintet. See no. 1839
YUEN MAO
Dance of the Yao people. See no. 1887
ZACH, Johan
Fugue, A minor. See no. 3962
Sonata a tre, A major. See no. 3826
ZACHAU, Friedrich
Prelude and fugue, G major. See no. 3622. See no. 4012
Suite, B minor. See no. 4087
Vom Himmel hoch da komm ich her. See no. 2260
ZAIMONT, Judith
3608 A calendar set. Chansons nobles et sentimentales. La fin de siecle. Charles Bressler, t; Gary Steigerwalt, Judith Zaimont, pno. Leonarda LPl 101
+ARG 3-80 p52
+-FF 9/10-80 p237
+NR 4-80 p12
++NYT 6-7-81 pD26
+St 3-81 p96
Chansons nobles et sentimentales. See no. 3608
La fin de siecle. See no. 3608
Songs, soprano and harp. See no. 2937
ZALDIVAR, E.
Carnavalito. See no. 1076
ZANDONAI, Riccardo
3609 I cavalieri di Ekebu. Rina Malatrasi, s; Fedora Barbieri, ms; Mirto Picchi, t; Giampiero Malaspina, bar; Antonio Zaccaria, bs; RAI Orchestra and Chorus, Milan; Alfredo Simonetto. MRF Records MRF 167 (2)
+FF 5/6-81 p187
Una partita: Non svegliarti. See no. 4022
ZANNETTI, Gasparo
Aria del Gran Duca. See no. 3938
Fuggi, fuggi, fuggi. See no. 3938
La montovana. See no. 3938

ZAVALA
Viva el rumbo. See no. 3981
ZEHLE
Wellington. See no. 3955
ZELENKA, Johann Dismas
Cavalry fanfare, no. 5. See no. 3979
Concerto grosso, G major. See no. 3978
3610 Hipocondrie, A major. Overture, F major. Sonata, 2 oboes, bassoon and violoncello, no. 2, G minor. Jurg Schaeftlein, Paul Hailperin, ob; Milan Turkovic, bsn; Eduard Hruza, violone; Herbert Tachezi, hpd; VCM. Telefunken 6-42415 Tape (c) 4-42415
+FF 5/6-81 p188 +HF 1-81 p79
3611 Magnificat, D major. Psalms, no. 110, Confitebor tibi Domine; no. 111, Beatus vir; no. 113, In exitu Israel. Ute Fruhhaber, s; Dorothea Brinkmann, alto; Alejandro Ramirez, t; Hanns-Friedrich Kunz, bs; Marburg Bach Choir, Hesse Bach Collegium; Wolfram Wehnert. Fono FSM 63108
-HF 11-81 p99
Overture, F major. See no. 3610
Psalms, no. 110, Confitebor tibi Domine; no. 111, Beatus vir; no. 113, In exitu Israel. See no. 3611
Sonata, 2 oboes, bassoon and violoncello, no. 2, G minor. See no. 3610
ZELLER, Karl
3612 Der Vogelhandler, complete. Anneliese Rothenberger, Renate Holm, s; Gisela Litz, con; Gerhard Unger, Adolf Dallapozza, t; Walter Berry, bs; VSOO and Chorus; Willi Boskovsky. EMI 1C 157 30194/9
+Gr 12-81 p940
ZEUNER
Fugue, D minor. See no. 3627
ZIEHRER, Carl
Loslassen, op. 386. See no. 3768
ZIMMERMANN, Heinz
Monologue. See no. 2027
Perspectives. See no. 2027
ZIPOLI, Domenico
Canzone, no. 5, G minor. See no. 4088
Improvisation on "Heiland reiss die Himmel auf". See no. 3961
Pastorale, C major. See no. 3905. See no. 3961
ZUPKO, Ramon
3613 Fluxus II. Masques. Nocturnes. Abraham and Arlene Stokman, pno; Western Brass Quintet. CRI SD 425
+ARG 1-81 p45
Masques. See no. 3613
Nocturnes. See no. 3613

Section II

MUSIC IN COLLECTIONS

ABBEY

APR 301
3614 BACH: Praise the Lord all ye heathen. BRITTEN: Te deum, C major. FARRANT: Call to remembrance. HUMFREY: Hymne to God the father. JACKSON: Magnificat and nunc dimittis (St. David's service). LANGLAIS: Salve regina. MENDELSSOHN: Hear my prayer. PURCELL: Evening hymn. STANFORD: Magnificat and nunc dimittis, G major. VICTORIA: Jesu the very thought of thee. ANON.: Lord for thy tender mercy's sake. Philip Raymond, treble; Sian Phillips, s; Brian Birks, bar; Sue Handscombe, flt; Carol Watts, hpd; Geoffrey Warrington, double-bs; Nicholas Jackson, hpd, org; Malcolm Watts, org; St. David's Cathedral Choir; Nicholas Jackson.
+-HFN 7-79 p113 +-NR 3-81 p8
+-MT 8-79 p661 ++RR 7-79 p112

APR 302
3615 ASHFIELD: The fair chivalry. BACH: Toccata and fugue, S 540, F major. BRIDGE: God's goodness. FERGUSON: Death and darkness get you packing; Psalm, no. 137, Verses 1-6; Reverie. HEATH: Verse service: Mangnificat. MOZART: Ave verum corpus, K 618. STEWART: Crown him with many crowns. VAUGHAN WILLIAMS: Mystical songs: Come my way. Let all the world. WESLEY, S.: Behold how good and joyful. WHITE: Prayer of St. Richard at Chichester. WHITLOCK: Jesu grant me this I pray. Richard Paul, bar; David Poulter, org. Rochester Cathedral Choir; Barry Ferguson.
+Gr 5-80 p1706 +NR 3-81 p8
+HFN 5-80 p129 +RR 7-80 p92
+MT 10-80 p638

APR 303
3616 BRITTEN: Antiphon. BYRD: From virgin's womb this day did spring. Laudibus in sanctis. DERING: Factum est silentium. GIBBONS: The secret sins. MENDELSSOHN: Laudate pueri dominum. OUSELEY: It came even to pass; When all thy mercies o my God. STAINER: The crucifixion: God so loved the world. VIERNE: Fantasiestucke, op. 54: Carillon de Westminster. St. Michael's College Choir; Andrew Millington, org; Roger Judd.
+Gr 5-80 p1711 ++NR 3-81 p9
+HFN 5-80 p129 ++RR 5-80 p94
+MT 10-80 p638

APR 304
3617 BACH: Brandenburg concerto, no. 3, S 1048, G major: 1st movement.

CORELLI (Barbirolli): Concerto, oboe: Prelude-gavotte. ELGAR: Enigma variations, op. 36: Nimrod. In the south overture, op. 50. GOUNOD: Petite symphony, B flat major: 1st movement. STRAUSS, J I: Radetzky march, op. 222. Soloists; Lancashire Schools Symphony Orchestra; Malcolm Doley.
+-HFN 5-80 p133 +RR 8-80 p47
+NR 7-81 p2

APR 305
3618 BAIRSTOW: Let all mortal flesh keep silence. BRITTEN: Jubilate Deo, C major. GARDNER: Fight the good fight; Tomorrow shall be may dancing day. GERMAN: My bonnie lass. HAYNE: Loving shepherd of thy sheep. HOVLAND: Og ordet ble kjob. MURRILL: Nunc dimittis. NYSTEDT: Velsignet vaere han. PARRY: Dear Lord and father of mankind. POSTON: Jesus Christ the apple tree. SCHUBERT: Mass, no. 2, D 167, G major: Kyrie. TYE: Laudate nomen Domini; Praise ye the Lord ye children. VAUGHAN WILLIAMS: O how amiable are thy dwellings; Linden lea (arr. Somervell). WESLEY, S.S.: Thou wilt keep him in perfect peace. WOOD, C.: Oculi omnium. TRAD. De battle ob Jerico. De virgin Mary. I will give my love an apple. King Edward VI School Choir; Jeremy Blandford, org; Eric Merriman.
-Gr 5-80 p1706 +-NR 3-81 p9
+-HFN 5-80 p127

APR 306
3619 BAIRSTOW: Though I speak with the tongues of men. BRITTEN: Hymn to the virgin. BRUCKNER: Locus iste. BULLOCK: Give us the wings of faith. ELGAR: Ave verum corpus, op. 2, no. 1. FAURE: Tantum ergo, op. 65, no. 2. FRESCOBALDI: Aria with variations. HOWELLS: Gloucester service: Magnificat. All my hope on God is founded. JONGEN: Chant de mai, op. 53. LANG: Tuba tune, op. 15, D major. LIDON: Sonata para trompeta real. MATTHIAS: Toccata giocosa, op. 36, no 2. MOZART: Ave verum corpus, K 618. PALESTRINA: Haec dies. SCHUTZ: Die Himmel erzahlen. Jonathan Newell, Keith Rhodes, org; Bradford Cathedral Choirs; Keith Rhodes.
+Gr 5-80 p1706 +NR 2-81 p8
+HFN 4-80 p112 +RR 6-80 p84
+MT 10-80 p638

ABY 814
3620 BLOW: Salvator mundi. BRITTEN: Festival Te deum, op. 32. BYRD: Sing joyfully unto God. DERING: Contristatus est Rex David; Quem vidistis pastores. EAST: When David heard that Absalom was slain. HOWELLS: Jubilate Deo. PHILIPS: Ecce tu pulchra es; O beatum et sacrosanctum diem. PURCELL: Jehova quam multi sunt hostes mei. TALLIS: In jejunio et fletu. TRAD. (Italian): Once as I remember (C. Wood, arr. Williams). St. Peter ad Vincula Choir; John Williams, Joseph Sentance, org.
+Gr 8-80 p258 +-MT 3-81 p197
+-HFN 8-80 p103

ABY 817
3621 BROWN: Laudate dominum. BYRD: Laudibus in sanctis. DAVIES: Magdalen at St. Michael's gate. GIBBONS: Hosanna to the son of David. PURCELL: Let mine eyes. RIDOUT: I turn the corner. STANFORD: The Lord is my shepherd. WEELKES: Give ear O Lord. WILLIAMSON: Wrestling Jacob. ANON.: Doxology (arr. Ridout).

Canterbury Cathedral Choir; David Flood, org; Allan Wicks.
+Gr 8-80 p258 +MT 1-81 p36
+-HFN 8-80 p103

ABC

ABCL 67008 (2) (also RCA RL 3-0381)
3622 AMMERBACH: Wer das Tochterlein haben will. BLITHEMAN: Eterne rerum. EBERLIN: Toccata sexta. Toccata e fuga tertia. FISCHER: Preludes and fugues, B minor, D major, E flat major, C minor. FROBERGER: Capriccio, no. 8. Ricercare, no. 1. FUX: Sonata quinta. KERLL: Canzona, G minor. Toccata con durezza e ligature. KREBS: Jesu meine Freude. Jesus meine Zuversicht. Von Gott will ich nicht lassen. MERULA: Un cromatico ovvero capriccio. MUFFAT: Fugue, G minor. NEWMAN: Pavan. PACHELBEL: Alle Menschen mussen sterben. Magnificat: Fugues, nos. 4, 5, 10, 13. Toccata and fugue, B flat major. PASQUINI: Canzone francese, no. 7. Ricercare, no. 4. STORACE: Ballo della battaglia aus. TAYLOR: Pavan and galliard. ZACHAU: Prelude and fugue, G major. ANON.: Gagliarda "Cathaccio". Gagliarda "Lodesana". Pavan and galliard. Gustav Leonhardt, org.
+FF 9/10-81 p246 +NR 4-77 p15
++HF 3-77 p108 +PRO 5-77 p25
+-MJ 2-77 p30 ++St 5-77 p54

ACANTA

DC 23325
3623 GIORDANO: Andrea Chenier: La mamma morta. MASCAGNI: Cavalleria rusticana: Voi lo sapete. PONCHIELLI: La Gioconda: Suicidio. PUCCINI: La boheme: Si mi chiamano Mimi. Madama Butterfly: Un bel di. Tosca: Vissi d'arte. VERDI: Aida: Ritorna vincitor. Don Carlo: Tu che la vanita. Macgeth: Ambizioso spirto tu sei. Martina Arroyo, s; Munich Radio Orchestra; Kurt Eichorn.
+-FF 9/10-81 p207 *ON 3-28-81 p36

ACCORD

ACC 140015 (also RCA ZL 30668)
3624 DEBUSSY: Martyre de Saint-Sebastian: Fanfare. DUKAS: La Peri: Fanfare. JOLIVET: Fanfares pour Britannicus. ROUSSEL: Fanfare pour un sacre paien. SCHMITT: Antony and Cleopatra, op. 69: Le camp de Pompee. Cuivres Guy Touvron Ensemble; Sylvain Cambreling.
+-HFN 10-81 p93

AERCO

AERL 30
3625 BAIRSTOW: Toccata prelude on "Pange lingua". BULL: Salve regina. BYRD: Fantasia, C major. FORBES: Capriccio. HOWELLS: Master Tallis' testament. NARES: Introduction and fugue, F major. PURCELL, H.: Voluntary, C major. TALLIS: Veni redemptor. WESLEY, S.: Fugue, G major. WESLEY, S.S.: Larghetto, F sharp minor. Margaret Phillips, org.
++Gr 6-81 p65

AFKA

SK 277
3626 BACH: Anna Magdalena notebook, S 508: Bist du bei mir. MASSENET: Thais: Meditation. MENDELSSOHN: Fruhlingslied. ROSSINI: Guillaume Tell: Overture. SOUSA: Stars and strieps forever. TCHAIKOVSKY: Symphony, no. 6, op. 74, B minor: Andante. THOMAS: Mignon: Gavotte. WAGNER: Tannhauser: Grand march. Thomas Murray, org.
+-FF 9/10-81 p245 +HF 11-81 p87

S 3640/1
3627 BACH: Fugue, G minor. BOYCE: Volunatry, A minor. CAMIDGE: Gavotte, G minor. MENDELSSOHN: Prelude and fugue, G major. MOLLER: Presto, C major. RHEINBERGER: Sonata, organ, no. 5, op. 111, F sharp minor. THORLEY: Piece, flute. ZEUNER: Fugue, D minor. Thomas Murray, org.
+ARG 2-81 p49 +FF 3/4-81 p35

S 3650
3628 Christmas service of lessons and carols. St. Paul's Cathedral Choir, Boston; Thomas Murray, org and cond.
*+FF 3/4-81 p36

SK 4634
3629 CLARKE: Trumpet voluntary (Prince of Denmark march). HANDEL: Alcina: Verdi prati. HOVHANESS: Prayer of St. Gregory. KREBS: Wachet auf. MOURET: Sinfonies de fanfares. PURCELL: Trumpet tune. STANLEY: Voluntary, D major. STOELZEL: Bist du bei mir. TELEMANN: Air de trompette. VIVIANI: Sonata, trumpet, no. 2, D major. Walter Chestnut, tpt; Ernest May, org.
++FF 3/4-81 p34 +MU 3-80 p8

ALPHA

BNB 1
3630 CACCINI: Nell amoroso ciel dei vostro volto. FRESCOBALDI: Aria detta "La Frescobalda". Toccata seconda. Toccata terza, da sonarsi alla levatione. d'INDIA: O primavera gioventu dell' anno; Vostro fui vostro son e saro vostro. KAPSBERGER: Io amo io ardo io moro; Io mi parto cor mio; O cor sempre dolente. MAZZOCHI: Ottave; Per la nativita di N.S. Rene Jacobs, alto;

Johan Huys, org, hpd.
+Gr 6-81 p75

DB 248
3631 BOISMORTIER: Concerto, op. 37, no. 6, E minor. DORNEL: Sonate en quatuor, D minor. FUX: Sinfonia, F major. GEMINIANI, F.: Concerti grossi, op. 2, no. 4, D major. TELEMANN: Trio sonata, E minor. Parnassus Ensemble.
+-FF 3/4-81 p235 +HFN 10-80 p111
+Gr 10-80 p504

APS 307
3632 BYRD: Justorum animae. DARKE: Creed; Gloria. HARRIS: King of glory, king of peace. JACKSON: Magnificat and nunc dimittis, G major. MATHIAS: The law of the lord, op. 61, no. 2; Make a joyful noise unto the lord. PRICHARD: Ye that know the lord is gracious. RUTTER: Nativity carol. STANFORD: The lord is my shepherd; Te deum, op. 115, C major. Llandaff Cathedral Choir; Michael Smith, org and cond.
+HFN 9-80 p113 +NR 2-81 p8

APS 308
3633 ALBINONI: Concerto, oboe, D major. CAMPBELL: Sing we merrily unto God. DYSON: Lauds; Poet's hymn; Praise. HOWELLS: Like as the hart desireth the waterbrooks. JOUBERT: O lord the maker of all things. MONTEVERDI: Adoramus te Christ; Cantata domino. PACHELBEL: Nun danket alle Gott. NARES: The souls of the righteous. WHITLOCK: Here o my lord I see thee. Wells Cathedral Choir and String Ensemble; Anthony Crossland.
+HFN 9-80 p113 +NR 2-81 p8

APS 132
3634 BERCHAM: O Jesu Christe. BYRD: Sacerdotes domini. BURCKNER: Ave Maria. CARTER: A maiden most gentle (Lourdes hymn). DURUFLE: Ubi caritas. MOZART: Laudate dominum. PALESTRINA: Alma redemptoris mater. PELLEGRINI: Salve regina. PURCELL: Thou knowest Lord. RATCLIFFE: Mary walked through a wood of thorns. ROUCAIROL: Honneur et louange a Dieu. TALLIS: If ye love me. VITTORIA: Responsaries for tenebrae. VOLPI: Oremus pro pontifice. GREGORIAN CHANT: Salve regina. Boy Singers of Our Lady of Grace, Chiswick, London; Denis Chochrane; Anthony Pellegrini, org.
+-HFN 10-81 p111 +-NR 3-81 p10

APS 313
3635 Christmas from St. Anne's Cathedral, Belfast: Hark the herald angels sing; Shepherd's pipe carol; The first noel; There is no rose; Sir Christemas; Still the night; Good King Wenceslas; Away in a manger; Sussex carol; A hymn to the virgin; O little town of Bethlehem; I sing of a maiden; Tomorrow shall be my dancing day; Bethlehem; Adeste fideles; In dulci jubilo. Cathedral Choir; Christopher Boodle, org; Jonathan Gregory.
/NR 12-81 p1 +-HFN 12-80 p147

APS 314
3636 BAINTON: And I saw a new heaven. BLITHEMAN: In pace. BYRD: Non vos relinquam orphanos. DERING: Duo seraphim; Gaudent in coelis. GIBBONS: This is the record of John. HARWOOD: O how glorious is the kingdom. IVES: O sing joyfully. MUNDY: O Lord the maker of all things. NICHOLSON: Fair the day that sees him rise. PHILIPS: Ascendit Deus. RACHMANINOFF: To thee,

O Lord do I lift up my soul. SOMERVELL: Jesus the very thought of thee. VICTORIA: O quam gloriosum. ANON.: Aeterne Rex altissime. Tewkesbury Abbey Schoool Choir; David Angus, org; Michael Peterson.
+-Gr 1-81 p982 +-NR 3-81 p10
+HFN 11-80 p125

APS 317
3637 ALBRIGHT: Chichester mass: Sanctus, Benedictus and Agnus Dei. BATTEN: Out of the deep. CARISSIMI: Beatus vir. BLITHEMAN: In pace. IVES, C.: Listen sweet dove. HAWES: Magnificat, D major. HARRIS, W.: Benedicite, A major. LIONCOURT: Quid retribuam Domino. MURRILL: The souls of the righteous. ROSE: Behold I make all things new. SHEPPARD: Jesu salvator saeculi verbum. STAINER: Awake awake put on thy strength: How beautiful upon the mountains. WEELKES: All people clap your hands. WISE: Prepare ye the way. Chichester Cathedral Choir; Kenneth Sweetman, Jeremy Suter, org; Alan Thurlow.
+-Gr 8-81 p309 +HFN 7-81 p78

ACA 501 Tape (c) CACA 501
3638 BRUCKNER: Motets: Tota pulchra es; Virga Jesse. LASSUS: Stabat mater. LISZT: Ave Maria, S 20; Salve regina, S 66. MENDELSSOHN: Ave Maria, op. 23, no. 3. VICTORIA: Magnificat primi toni. Westminster Cathedral Choir; Andrew Wright, org; Stephen Cleobury.
+-Gr 11-81 p748 +HFN 11-81 p99

ALTE MEISTER

AM 1
3639 BEETHOVEN: Ich liebe dich. HUMPERDINCK: Der Konigskinder: Verdorben Gestorben. Hansel und Gretel: Gesenbinderlied. MENDELSSOHN: Elijah: Ist nicht das Herrn Wort wie ein Feuer. SCHUBERT: Standchen; Der Wanderer. SCHUMANN: Die beiden Grenadiere, op. 49, no. 1. WAGNER: Das Rheingold: Abendlich strahlt der Sonne Auge. Siegfried: Auf wolkigan Hoh'n wohnen die Gotter. Tannhauser: O du mein holder Abendstern; Als du in kuhnem Sange. WEBER: Der Freischutz: Wer legt auf in strengen Bann. WEINBERGER: Schwanda the bagpiper: Ich bin der Schwanda; Wie kann ich denn vergessen. Karl Hammes, Gerhard Husch, Hans Hermann Nissen, Herbert Janssen, Friedrich Schorr, Heinrich Schlusnus, bar; VSOO and Chorus, Berlin State Opera Orchestra, NSL; Karl Alwin, Hans Udo Muller, Bruno Seidler-Winkler, Albert Coates; Michael Raucheisen, Franz Rupp, pno.
+FF 9/10-81 p218

ANGEL

SZCX 3911 (3)
3640 BELLINI: I Capuleti ed i Montecchi: Oh quante volte; Ah crudel d'onor ragioni. CHARPENTIER: Louise: Depuis le jour. DONIZETTI: Don Pasquale: Quel guardo il cavaliere...So anch'io la

virtu magica; Pronto io son; Tornami a dir che m'ami. HERBERT: Eileen: Thine alone. Naughty Marietta: Italian street song; Ah sweet mystery of life. Sweethearts: Sweethearts. LEHAR: Die lustige Witwe: Vilia; Waltz. MASSENET: Thais: Dis-moi que je suis belle; Death of Thais. ROSSINI: Il barbiere di Siviglia: Una voce poco fa; Dunque io son. L'Assedio di Corinto: Che vedo; Ohime tu piangi; Giusto ciel...Parmi vederlo ahi misero. STRAUSS, R.: The chocolate soldier: My hero. VERDI: Rigoletto: E il sol del anima; Caro nome; Bella figlia dell'amore; V'ho ingannato. La traviata: Brindisi; E strano...Ah fors'e lui... Sempre libera; Parigi o cara. Beverly Sills, s; Various assisting artists, orchestras and conductors.

+-FF 5/6-81 p190 +SFC 2-8-81 p21
+-NR 2-81 p10

SZ 3913
3641 d'ANNIBALE: Paese d' 'o sole. BELLINI: Fenesta che lucive. CAPUA: Maria mari; I te vurria vasa; O sole mio. CARDILLO: Core 'ngrato. CIOFFI: Na sera e maggio. CURTIS: Autunno; Senza nisciuno; Torna a Surriento; Tu ca nun chiagne; Voce e notte. FALVO: Dicitencello vuie. GAMBARDELLA: O Marenariello. LAMA: Silenzio cantatore. MARIO: Santa Lucia luntana. NARDELLO: Chiove. PALARDI/N.N.: Santa Lucia. PERSICO: E pallume. TAGLIAFERRI: Piscatore e pusilecco. TOSTI: Marechiare. VALENTE: Passione. Giuseppe de Stefano, t; Orchestra; Dino Olivieri.

-FF 7/8-81 p205 +NYT 8-16-81 pD19
++NR 5-81 p13

SCLX 3914 (3)
3642 BARRERA Y CALLEJA: Adios Granada (arr. de los Angeles). BIZET: Carmen: Habanera; Seguidilla. BRAHMS: Dein blaues Auge, op. 59, no. 8; Vergebliches Standchen, op. 84, no. 4. CANTELOUBE: Songs of the Auvergne: Bailero. CHAPI Y LORENTE: La chavale: Cancion de la gitana. Las hijas del Zebedeo: Carceleras. La patria chica: Cancion de pastora. CORNAGO: Que es mi vida preguntais. DUPARC: L'Invitation au voyage. FALLA: La vida breve: Vivan los que rien, Alli esta riyendo. FAURE: Clair de lune, op. 46, no 2. GOUNOD: Faust: Jewel song. GRANADOS: Goyescas: La maja y el ruisenor. Tonadillas: La maja dolorosa. HAHN: Le rossignol des lilas. MASSENET: Manon: Adieu notre petite table. Werther: Air des lettres. MOZART: Le nozzi di Figaro, K 492: Porgi amor. PUCCINI: La boheme: Si mi chiamano Mimi; Donde lieta usci. Madama Butterfly: Entrance of Butterfly; Un bel di vedremo. RODRIGO: Madrigales amatorios (4). ROSSINI: Il barbiere di Siviglia: Una voce poco fa. SCHUBERT: An die Musik, D 547. VALVERDE: Clavelitos. VERDI: Otello: Mia madre aveva una povera ancella; Ave Maria. La traviata: Teneste la promessa...Addio del passato. WAGNER: Lohengrin: Einsam in truben Tagen. Tannhauser: Dich teure Halle. Victoria de los Angeles, s.

+NR 9-81 p11 +NYT 8-16-81 pD19

DG 37334 Tape (c) 4ZS 37334
3643 BACH: French suite, no. 6, S 817, E major: Allemande and courante. Sonata, violin, no. 2, S 1003, A minor: Andante. COUPERIN: Livres de clavecin, Bk II, no. 6: Les barricades mysterieuses. DAQUIN: La coucou. FRANCISQUE: Bransles. Courante. Pavane. LOEILLET: Toccata. PROKOFIEV: Prelude, op. 12, no. 7, C major. Romeo and Juliet, op. 64: Aubade. RESPIGHI: Siciliana.

SCARLATTI, D.: Sonatas, violin, Kk 20, A major; Kk 209, A major; Kk 380, E major; Kk 545, B flat major. Nancy Allen, hp.
+MUM 7/8-81 p35 ++SFC 5-31-81 p22
+NR 6-81 p15 +St 9-81 p10.
+NYT 9-27-81 pD24

DS 37810

3644 CHERUBINI: Anacreon: Overture. HUMPERDINCK: Hansel und Gretel: Overture. MASCAGNI: L'Amico Fritz: Intermezzo. MASSENET: Thais: Meditation. PUCCINI: Manon Lescaut: Intermezzo. Suor Angelica: Intermezzo. SCHMIDT: Notre Dame: Intermezzo. WEBER: Der Freischutz: Overture. BPhO; Anne-Sophie Mutter, vln; Herbert von Karajan.
-NR 12-81 p4

DS 37812

3645 BRAHMS: Waltz, op. 39, no. 15, A major.* DEBUSSY: Children's corner suite: Golliwog's cakewalk (arr. Caplet). FAURE: Pelleas et Melisande: Sicilienne. GALAS: Lake Como.* HANDEL: Serse: Largo.* KHACHATURIAN: Gayaneh: Sabre dance. LISZT: Liebestraum, no. 3, S 541, A flat major.* MONTI: Czardas.* OFFENBACH: La vie parisienne: Cancan.* ROSSINI: La danza.* SCHUBERT: Moment musicaux, op. 94, no. 3, D 780, F minor.* STRAUSS, R.: Also sprach Zarathustra, op. 30: Introduction. LSO; Frank Pourcel. (*arr. Pourcel)
+-FF 9/10-81 p289 -NR 7-81 p2

S 37834

3646 BELLINI: Norma: Meco all'altar di venere...Me protegge me difende. GIORDANO: Andrea Chenier: Colpito que m'avete...Un di all' azzurro spazio; Credo a una possanza arcana; Si fui soldato; Come un bel di di maggio. GOUNOD: Romeo et Juliette: L'amour; Oui son ardeur; Ah leve toi soleil. LEONCAVALLO: I Pagliacci: Recitar...Vesti la giubba. MASCAGNI: Cavalleri rusticana: Mamma quel vino e generoso. PUCCINI: Turandot: Nessun dorma. VERDI: Aida: Se quel guerrier io fossi...Celeste Aida. Il trovatore: Ah si ben mio; Di quella pira. Franco Corelli, t; Orchestral accompaniments.
+NR 9-81 p12

S 37840

3647 BELLINI: Il pirata: Col sorriso d'innocenza. I puritani: Vien diletto. BOITO: Mefistofele: L'altra notte. MASCAGNI: Cavalleria rusticana: Voi lo sapete o mamma. PUCCINI: Manon Lescaut: In quelle trini morbide. Turandot: In questa reggia. ROSSINI: Guillaume Tell: Sombre foret. VERDI: Aida: Qui Radames verra ...Oh patria mia. Don Carlo: Tu che le vanita. Giovanna d'Arco: Sempre all'alba. Montserrat Caballe, s; PhO, RTI Orchestra Rome, LSO, NPhO, Strasbourg Philharmonic Orchestra, RPO, ROHO: Ricardo Muti, Gianandrea Gavazzeni, Julius Rudel, Bruno Bartoletti, Alain Lombard, Lamberto Gardelli, Carlo Maria Giulini, James Levine.
+FF 11/12-81 p284

ARABESQUE

8003 Tape (c) 9003 (From HMV originals)
3648 ADAM: Le postillon de Longjumeau: Mes amis ecoutez l'histoire. AUBER: Fra Diavolo: Pour toujours disait-elle. BEETHOVEN: Fidelio, op. 27: Gott welch Dunkel hier...In des Lebens Fruhlingstagen. LEHAR: Giuditta: Du bist meine Sonne; Freunde das Leben ist lebenswert. MOZART: Die Entfuhrung aus dem Serail, K 384: Hier soll ich dich denn sehen. STRAUSS, R.: Der Rosenkavalier, op. 59: Di rigori armato. TCHAIKOVSKY: Eugen Onegin, op. 24: Faint echo of my youth. WAGNER: Lohengrin: In fernem Land; Mein lieber Schwan. WEBER: Der Freischutz: Nein langer trag ich nicht...Durch die Walder. Oberon: Seit fruhster Jugned; Du der diese Profung schickt. Helge Roswange, t; Various accompaniments.

+ARG 7/8-80 p48 +HF 2-81 p81 tape
+-FF 11/12-80 p196 +MUM 11/12-80 p35
+-HF 10-80 p94 +NYT 1-6-80 pD18

8013 Tape (c) 9013
3649 ADAM: Le toreador: Ah vous dirai-je Maman. ALABIEV: The nightingale. BENEDICT: Il carnevale di Venezi. DELIBES: Lakme: Air des clochettes; Blanche Dourga; D'ou viens tu...C'est la Dieu; Les filles de Cadiz. DONIZETTI: Lucia di Lammermoor: O giusto cielo...Il dolce suono. La Zingara: Fra l'erbe cosparse. OFFENBACH: Les contes d'Hoffman: Doll's song. PROCH: Air and variations. ROSSINI: Il barbiere di Siviglia: Una voce poco fa. Miliza Korjus, s.

+ARG 6-80 p47 +HF 2-81 p81 tape
+-HF 7-80 p79 +NYT 1-6-80 pD18

8027 Tape (c) 8027
3650 BROADWOOD: The keys of heaven. DONIZETTI: Lucrezia Borgia: Il segreto. DVORAK: Biblical songs, op. 99. ELGAR: Dream of Gerontius, op. 35: Softly and gently. Sea pictures, op. 37: Where corals lie. Coronation ode, op. 44: Land of hope and glory. GLUCK: Orfeo ed Euridice: Sposa Euridice...Che faro senza Euridice. GOODHART: A fairy went a-marketing. HANDEL: Alessandro: Ne trionfa d'Alessandro...Lusinghe...piu care. Sosarme: Rendi'l sereno al ciglio. HATTON: The enchantress. HULLAH: Three fishers went sailing. LEHMANN: The birth of the flowers. SULLIVAN: The light of the world: God shall wipe away all tears. Clara Butt, con; Instrumental accompaniments.

+ARG 1-81 p47 +NR 9-80 p8
+FF 5/6-81 p192

8028 Tape (c) 9028 (From HMV originals)
3651 MOZART: Le nozze di Figaro, K 492: Porgi amor; Dove sono. STRAUSS, R.: Arabella, op. 79: Ich mochte meinen fremden Mann; So wie Sie sind. TCHAIKOVSKY: The sorceress: Mein los ist seltsam. VERDI: Il trovatore: Tacea la notte; D'amor sull'ali rosee (in German). WAGNER: Lohengrin: Das susse Lied verhalt. WEBER: Der Freischutz: Wie nahte mir der Schlummer...Leise leise fromme Weise; Und ob die Wolke. Tiana Lemnitz, s; Torsten Ralf, Helge Roswange, t; Gerhard Husch, bar; Walter Lutz, vlc.

+ARG 4-80 p47 +-HF 7-80 p78
+FF 5/6-80 p179 +HF 2-81 p81 tape

8037
3652 GARDINER: Shepherd Fennel's dance. GIBBS: Fancy dress: Dusk. GRAINGER: Country gardens. Handel in the Strand. Mock Morris. Molly on the shore. Londonderry air. Shepherd's hey. QUILTER: Children's overture, op. 17. TOYE: The haunted ballroom. Light Music Society Orchestra; Vivian Dunn.
+FF 3/4-81 p129 +NR 2-81 p5

8069
3653 BRAHMS: Songs: Dein blaues Auge. DEBUSSY: Songs: Le faune; Je tremble en voyant ton visage. HAHN: Si mes vers avaient des ailes. NOVELLO: When it's spring in Vienna. OFFENBACH: Le perichole: Je t'adore, excerpt. PALADILHE: Psyche. PURCELL: Dido and Aeneas: When I am laid in earth. Songs: If music be the food of love. RHENE-BATON: Heures d'ete. WALLIS: Gentil galant de France. WOLF: Mignon. TRAD.: Vielle chanson de chasse. (Interviews). Maggie Teyte, s; Felix Aprahamian, narrator.
+ARG 10-81 p44 +NR 1-81 p11
+FF 5/6-81 p191

8070 Tape (c) 8070
3654 BERKELEY: Poems of St. Teresa of Avila (4). BRAHMS: Auf dem See, op. 59, no. 2; Es Schauen die Blumen, op. 96, no. 3; Der Jager, op. 95, no. 4; Ruhe Sussliebchen im Schatten. BRITTEN: Rape of Lucretia, op. 37: Duet. GLUCK: Orfeo ed Euridice: Recitative; Che faro senza Euridice. MOSS: The floral dance. PARRY: Love is a bable. SCHUBERT: Rastlose Liebe, D 138; Wasserfluth. TRAD.: The Spanish lady. Kathleen Ferrier, con; Owen Brannigan, bs.
+-ARG 1-81 p48 +NYT 8-16-81 pD19
+-FF 1/2-81 p215

8084
3655 CHERUBINI: Sonatas, horn, nos. 1 and 2. KALLIWODA: Introduction and rondo, F minor/F major. REGER: Scherzino. SCHUMANN: Adagio and allegro, op. 70, A flat major (orch. Ansermet). WEISMANN: Concertino, op. 118, E flat major. Hermann Baumann, French hn; Munich Philharmonic Orchestra Members; Marinus Voorberg
-NR 12-81 p11

8100
3656 BERLIOZ: Le carnival romain, op. 9. MENDELSSOHN: Hebrides overture, op. 26. NICOLAI: Die lustigen Weiber von Windsor: Overture. OFFENBACH: Orphee au Enfers: Overture. SMETANA: The bartered bride: Overture. WEBER: Oberon: Overture. VPO; Rudolf Kempe
++NR 8-81 p2

3105-2 (2)
3657 ARNE: The lass with a delicate air. BIZET: Carmen: Il fior che avevi a me; Flower song. BRAHMS: Die Mainacht, op. 43, no. 2; In Waldeinsamkeit. DONIZETTI: La favorita: Spirto gentil. HANDEL: Il pastor Fido: Caro amor. MASCAGNI: Cavalleria rusticana: Siciliana. MOZART: An Chloe, K 524. PONCHIELLI: La gioconda: Badoer questa notte...O grido. PUCCINI: La boheme: Che gelida manina. Tosca: E lucevan le stelle. PURCELL: Passing by. ROSSINI: Il barbiere di Siviglia: Or il meglio me scordaro...Numero quindici. SCHUBERT: Du bist die Ruh, D 776;

Die liebe hat gelogen, D 755; Who is Sylvia, D 891. STRAUSS, R.: Songs: Allerseelen, op. 10, no. 8; Du meines Herzens Kronelien, op. 21, no. 2; Morgen, op. 27, no. 4. THOMAS: Mignon: In her simplicity. VERDI: Aida: Celeste Aida. Rigoletto: La donna e mobile; Bella figlia dell'amore; Questa o quella. WOLF: Auch kleine Dinge; Schlafendes Jesuskind; Wo find' ich Trost. WOLF-FERRARI: Il gioelli della Madonna: T'eri un giorno ammalato. John McCormack, t.

+ARG 10-81 p45 *NR 6-81 p12

8124

3658 Irish melodies: Believe me if all those endearing young charms; Blind ploughman; Cloths of heaven; Come back to Erin; Dawn will break; Garden where the praties grow; Green Isle of Erin; The harp that once through Tara's halls; Kerry dance; Killarney; Little boats; O promise me; Song to the seals; Star of the County Down; Still as the night; Terence's farewell to Kathleen; Waiting for you; When I awake. John McCormack, t.

+ARG 10-81 p47 *NR 6-81 p12

ARGO

ZRG 900 Tape (c) KZRC 990 (r) B-C F 900

3659 The play of Daniel. Pro Cantione Antiqua, Landini Consort.

+FF 5/6-80 p182 +MT 1-80 p36
+Gr 7-79 p234 ++NYT 8-17-80 pD20
+Gr 9-79 p534 tape +RR 9-79 p124
+HF 1-80 p65 +SR 12-81 p64
+HF 2-81 p81 tape +St 1-80 p110
++HFN 7-79 p113

ZRG 912 Tape (c) KZRC 912

3660 BLISS: Fanfare for the Lord Mayor of London. BOURGEOIS: Wine symphony: Hock theme. BRITTEN: The eagle has two heads. Russian funeral. CASALS: O vos omnes (trans. Stokowski). COPLAND: Fanfare for the common man. FRANCK: Piece heroique (trans. Fuller). JANACEK: Sinfonietta: Allegretto. STRAUSS, R.: Festmusik der Stad Wien. TOMASI: Fanfares liturgiques: Procession du Vendredi-Saint. UHL: Festfanfare. Philip Jones Brass Ensemble.

+Gr 3-80 p1398 +HFN 3-80 p103
+Gr 1-81 p1001 tape +RR 3-80 p64

ZRG 923

3661 BROCHUS: Tienalora. CAPIROLA: Balletto. Padoana. CARA: Per fuggir d'amor le punte. Poiche in van. DALZA: Piva. GHISELIN: La spagna a 4. JOSQUIN DES PRES: Fortuna d'un gran tempo. Scaramella. JUDENKUNIG: Rosina. MILANO: Spagna, 2 lutes. PATAVINO: Vrai dieu d'amour. PESENTI: Che faralla. ANON.: Basela un tratto. London Early Music Group; James Tyler.

+Gr 1-81 p985 ++HFN 1-81 p105

ZRG 928 Tape (c) KZRC 928

3662 DVORAK: Humoresques, op. 101, no. 7, G flat major (arr. Hazell). Terzetto, op. 74: Scherzo (arr. Wallace). EWALD: Quintet, no. 3, op. 7. GLAZUNOV: In modo religioso, op. 38. LEONTOVYCH: Ukrainian folktunes (2). MENDELSSOHN: Symphony, no. 4, op.

90, A major: Tarantella (arr. Civil). RAMSOE: Quartet, no. 5. Philip Jones Brass Ensemble.
+FF 7/8-81 p223 +HFN 1-81 p105
+Gr 1-81 p959

ZRG 932 Tape (c) KZRC 932 (also London CS 7221)
3663 BANCHIERI: Udite ecco le trombe fantasia (arr. Jones). BYRD: The battel (arr. Howarth). HANDEL: La rejoussance (arr. Howarth). JENKINS: Newark siege fantasia (arr. Reeve). KUHNAU: The battle between David and Goliath. (Bibilical sonata, no. 1). (arr. Hazell). Philip Jones Brass Ensemble; Elgar Howarth, Philip Jones.
+-FF 11/12-81 p296 +HFN 6-81 p81
+Gr 6-81 p46

ARION

ARN 336024 (3)
3664 Gregorian chant: Gregorian chant in Kergonan Abbey; The joy of Easter; Mary Mother of God. Kergonan Monks Choir of the Benedictine Abbey; Dom le Feuvre.
+-Gr 5-81 p1509

ARN 336025 (3)
3665 BIZET: Jeux d'enfants, op. 22. CAPLET: Un tas de petites choses. CHABRIER: Cortege burlesque. Souvenirs de Munich. DEBUSSY: Epigraphes antiques (6). FAURE: Dolly suite, op. 56. FAURE: Souvenirs de Bayreuth (arr. Messager). GOUNOD: Sonata, piano, E flat major: 1st movement. MASSENET: Suite, no. 1, op. 11. L'Annee passee. RAVEL: Ma mere l'oye. SAINT-SAENS: Berceuse, op. 105. SATIE: Morceaux en forme de poire (3). Christian Ivaldi, Noel Lee, pno.
++Gr 4-81 p1351

ASV

DCS 503 Tape (c) ZCDCA 503
3666 DELIUS: On hearing the first cuckoo in spring. FAURE: Masques et bergamasques, op. 112: Overture. Dolly suite, op. 56: Berceuse. GRIEG: Peer Gynt, op. 46: Suite, no. 1: Morning. MOZART: Divertimento, K 136, D major: Presto. RAVEL: Pavane pour une infante defunte. SCHUBERT: Rosamunde, D 797: Entracte, D major: Ballet, G major. VAUGHAN WILLIAMS: Fantasia on "Greensleeves". Preludes on Welsh hymn tunes: Rhosymedre (orch. Foster). St. John's Smith Square Orchestra; John Lubbock.
+-Gr 5-81 p1485 +HFN 6-81 p87 tape
+-HFN 5-81 p89

ACM 2002 Tape (c) ACACM 2002 (From Enigma K 23524)
3667 CHOPIN: Introduction and polonaise, op. 3, C major. DELIUS: Romance. ELGAR: Salut d'amour, op. 12. FAURE: Apres un reve, op. 7, no. 1. MENDELSSOHN: Song wihtout words, op. 109, D major. POPPER: Elfentanz, op. 39. RACHMANINOFF: Sonata,

violoncello and piano, op. 19, G minor: Slow movement. SAINT-SAENS: Allegro appassionato, op. 43. Carnival of the animals: The swan. Julian Lloyd Webber, vlc; Yitkin Seow, pno.
+Gr 4-81 p1343 +HFN 4-81 p80
+Gr 7-81 p196 tape +-HFN 6-81 p87 tape

ACM 2010 Tape (c) ZCACM 2010 (From Enigma K 23538)
3668 BOZZA: Agrestide. DEBUSSY: Syrinx. FAURE: Fantasie, op. 79, C major. IBERT: Piece, flute. MESSIAEN: Le merle noir. POULENC: Sonata, flute and piano. ROUSSEL: Joueurs de flute, op. 27. Susan Milan, flt; Clifford Benson, pno.
++Gr 4-81 p1378 +HFN 5-81 p91
+Gr 7-81 p196 tape +HFN 6-81 p87 tape

ACM 2011
3669 DONIZETTI: Etude, no. 1, solo clarinet. PIXIS: Variations on a theme from Seyfried's "Niklas am Scheidewege", op. 19. REISSIGER: Duo brillant, op. 130. ROSSINI: Fantasy, E flat major. SPOHR: Fantasy and variations, op. 81. WEBER: Variations on a theme from Silvana. Colin Bradbury, clt; Oliver Davies, pno.
+Gr 10-81 p579 +-HFN 10-81 p93

ACM 2017 (From Enigma VAR 1020)
3670 BLONDEL DE NESLE: Quant je plus. CORNYSHE: Ah Robin. ADAM DE LA HALLE: The play of Robin and Marion, excerpts. RAVENSCROFT: Now Robin lend to me thy bow. RICHARD I, King: Je nus hons pris. ANON/TRAD.: A la fontenella; Bonny sweet Robin; English estampie; Greenwood/Dargason; Fanfare; The maid in the moon; My Robin; The nutting girl; The parson's farewell/Goddesses; Redit aetas aurea; Robin Hood and the tanner; Sally's fancy/The maiden's blush; Shepherd's hey; Stingo; Tristan's lament; Two-voices estampie. St. George's Canzona; John Sothcott.
+Gr 6-81 p75 +-HFN 4-81 p81

AUDITE

FSM 53175
3671 BACH: Cantata, no. 112, Der Herr ist mien getreuer Hirt. Magnificat, S 243, D major: Sicut locatus est. Prelude and fugue, S 555, E minor. BEACH: Music brass quintet. CALVERT: Suite from the Monteregian Hills. CRESPO: American suite, no. 1: Ragtime; Son de Mexico. FINCK: Greiner Zanner. POULENC: Sonata, horn, trumpet and trombone. ANON.: Sonata, B flat major. German Brass Quintet.
-FF 5/6-81 p214

AUGSBURG

23 1317
3672 Christmas carols: Angels and the shepherds; Benedicamus domino (Warlock); Away in a manger; Bring a torch Jeanette, Isabella; Child of peace (Van); First Nowell; How still he rests (Pierce); Make we joy (Figginger); Of the father's love begotten; Personent hodie; Shepherd's carol (Billings); Still still still;

Tomorrow shall be my dancing day; What child is this; What is the fragrance. Dale Warland Singers; Dale Warland.
+FF 11/12-81 p288

23 1783
3673 BACH: Chorale prelude, S 643, Alle Menschen mussen Sterben. BUXTEHUDE: Toccata and fugue, F major. DURUFLE: Variations on "Veni creator", op. 4. MANZ: Improvisations on St. Anne. Blessed Jesus at thy word. PACHELBEL: Vom Himmel hoch. PEETERS: Aria. WIDOR: Toccata. Paul Mang, org
+FF 9/10-81 p246 ++MU 5-81 p23

BARCLAY

40234
3674 BACH: Prelude and fugue, S 532, D major. BINGHAM: Passacaglia, op. 40. COUPERIN, F.: Messe pour les couvents: Elevation. Recit tierce en taille. DURUFLE: Variations on "Veni creator spiritus", op. 4. PAINE: Variations on the Austrian hymn. Robert Plimpton, org.
+NR 6-81 p6

BASF

KBF 21192 (2)
3675 DASER: Benedictus Dominus. Dominus regit me. FOSSA: Missa super theutonicam cantionem. GOSSWIN: Am Abend spat lieb Breuderlein. HOYOUL: Wenn mein Stundlein vorhanden ist. LASSUS: A voi Guglielmo. Am Abend spat beim buehlen Wein. Bicinium. Die fasstnacht ist ein schoene Zeit. Im Mayen hoert man die hanen krayen. Kombt her zu mir spricht gottes son. Magnificat sexti toni. Matona mia cara. Missa sexta, 8 voices. La nuict froide et sombre. O fugace dolcezza. Schaff mir doch Recht in Sachen mien. Sybilla Europea. Der Tag ist so freudenreich. Timor Domini principium. Timor et tremor, Exaude Deus. Vedi l'aurora. LECHNER: Allein zu dir Herr Jesu Christ. Nach meiner Lieb viel hundert Knaben trachten. REINER: Behuet euch Gott zu aller Zeit. Mane nobiscum Domine. SENFL: Es taget vor dem Walde. Es wollt' ein Frau zum Weine gehn. Das G'laut zu Speyer. Ich armes Kauzlein Klein. Patiencia muss ich han. VENTO: Herr dein Wort mich getroestet hat. Frisch ist mein Sinn. Ich weiss ein Maidlein. So wuensch' ich ihr ein gute Nacht. Munich Capella Antiqua; Konrad Ruhland.
+AR 8-81 p77 ++St 2-74 p128
+NR 11-73 p13

BIS

LP 126
3676 AMMERBACH: Ich sag ade. ATTAIGNANT: Gaillard. CABEZON: Ave maris

stella. CARLETON: Praeludium. FACOLI: Padoana terza dita la finetta. Aria della comedia nuovo. Hor ch'io son gionto quivi. S'io m'accorgo ben mio. GERLE: Ach Elslein, liebes Elselein. KLEBER: Die Brunnlein die da fliessen. Zucht Ehr und Lob. LOFFELHOLTZ: Es het ein Baur sein freylein verlohren. Die kleine Schacht. NORMIGER: Tanz Adelich und from. Viel Freuden mit sich bringet. Von Gott will ich nicht lassen. PAIX: Der Keyserin Tantz. PEERSON: The fall of the leaf. The primrose. SCHMID: Alemando novelle: Ein guter neuer Dantz. Der Imperial: Ein Furtlicher Hofdantz; Ein schoner Englischer Dantz; Wie schon Bluet uns der Maye. ANON.: Entlaubet ist der Walde. Ich armes Kauzlein kleine. My delyght. The nightingale. The Scots marche. Wanton season, a galyarde. Lena Jackson, org.

-ARG 11-80 p39
+-FF 9/10-80 p271
+Gr 4-81 p1351
+HFN 7-80 p113
+-NR 4-80 p14
+-RR 8-80 p68

LP 148

3677 BENNET: Weep o mine eyes. CLEMENS NON PAPA: Iuvons beau lieu. DOWLAND: A shepherd in the shade. JANEQUIN: Le chant des oyseaux; Au joli jeu. MONTEVERDI: Lamento d'Arianna; Lamento della ninfa. PASSEREAU: El est bel et bon. SANDRIN: Doulce memoire. SERMISY: Languir me fais. WEELKES: Hark all ye lovely saints. Copenhagen Chamber Choir Camerata; Per Enevold.

+FF 9/10-81 p228
+-HFN 4-81 p78
/NR 2-81 p9
/St 8-81 p98

LP 149

3678 FISSINGER: Suite, marimba. LEMBA: Estonian cradle song (arr. Pachla). MILHAUD: Concerto, marimba and vibraphone. SHOSTAKOVICH: The golden gate: Polka (arr. Ljubimov). SIBELIUS: Bagatelles, op. 34: The harp player (arr. Ljubimov). Rainer Kuisma, marimba, vibraphone; Norrkoping Symphony Orchestra; Jorma Panula.

+NR 12-81 p2

LP 150

3679 KOCH: Monologue, no. 1. LIDHOLM: Sonata, solo flute. SALMENHAARA: Preludium, schlager and fuga. SOMMERFELDT: Divertimento, op. 9. THYBO: Aria con variatzione. Gunilla von Bahr, flt.

++Gr 11-81 p764
+HFN 9-81 p87
+NR 8-81 p14

LP 158

3680 BARTOK: For children: Children at play; Play; Old Hungarian tune; Andante con moto; Teasing song; Farewell. BEETHOVEN: Bagatelle, no. 25, A minor. DEBUSSY: Children's corner suite. SCHUMANN: Kinderscenen, op. 15. VILLA-LOBOS: A prole do bebe: Polichinelle. Dag Achatz, pno.

+ARG 12-81 p39
/FF 9/10-81 p235
+-HFN 9-81 p86
+NR 8-81 p12

LP 160

3681 BADINGS: Dialogues. FRUMERIE: Aria, op. 77. HARTMANN: Prelude, G minor. MARTIN: Sonata da chiesa. OLSSON: Romance, op. 24. Gunilla von Bahr, flt; Hans Fagius, org.

+FF 9/10-81 p265
+HFN 6-81 p83
+NR 2-81 p7

LP 166

3682 BOHM: Grand polonaise, op. 16. KUHLAU: Le colporteur, op. 98.

PAGANINI (Callimahos): Caprice, op. 1, no. 24, A minor. SAINT-SAENS: Adagio and variation on "Airs de ballet d'Ascanio". TAFFANEL: Fantasy on "Der Freischutz". Robert Aitken, flt; Elisabeth Westenholz, pno.
+FF 11/12-81 p293

LP 171
3683 ALFVEN: Notturno elegiaco, op. 5. BERGH: Pan. GROVEN: Sun mood. JEPPESEN: Little trio, D minor. KVANDAL: Introduction and allegro, op. 30. NIELSEN: Canto serioso. The children play. OLSEN: Audabe, op. 57, no. 3. Poem, op. 11. Per Oien, flt; Ingegard Oien, hn; Geir Henning Braaten, pno.
+FF 9/10-81 p277 +HFN 4-81 p79
+Gr 8-81 p317 +NR 2-81 p7

BRUNO WALTER SOCIETY

RR 487 (2)
3684 BEETHOVEN: Concerto, piano, no. 4, op. 58, G major: 1st movement. BERLIOZ: Benvenuto Cellini, op. 23: Overture. REGER: Variations and fugue on a theme by Hiller, op. 100. SCHUMANN: Symphony, no. 4, op. 120, D minor. STRAUSS, R.: Vier letzte Lieder, op. posth. Northwest German Radio Orchestra, Danish Radio Orchestra, Stockholm Philharmonic Orchestra; Rudolf Serkin, pno; Sena Jurinac, s; Fritz Busch.
+-NR 9-81 p16

CABALLETA

CDN 5001
3685 BENNETT: Out of your sleep. BERKELEY: I sing of a maiden. BEST: Make we joy now in this fest. BRITTEN: A hymn to the virgin. BYRD: Laetentur coeli; Lullaby my sweet baby, part 1. GIBBS, D.: I heard a maiden softly sing. LEIGHTON: Lully lulla thou little tiny child. ORD: Adam lay ybounden. PARSONS: Ave Maria. PHILIPS Ascendit Deus. TALLIS: O nata lux. TAVERNER: Dum transisset Sabbatum. VAUGHAN WILLIAMS: Folk-song arrangements: Just as the tide was flowing; The lover's ghost; Wassail song. WALTON: All this time. Corydon Singers; Matthew Best.
+Gr 10-81 p596 +-HFN 9-81 p85

CALLIOPE

CAL 1676
3686 DVORAK: Songs: Op. 55: Songs my mother taught me. Humoresque, op. 101, no. 7, G flat major. Rondo, op. 94, G minor. Silent woods, op. 68. FALLA: Suite populaire espagnole (trans. Marechal). FAURE: Apres un reve, op. 7, no. 1 (trans. Casals). GRANADOS: Goyescas: Intermezzo (trans. Cassado). MENDELSSOHN:

Song without words, op. 10, D major. NIN Y CASTELLANOS: Chants d'Espagne. POOPER: Mazurka, op. 11, no. 3, G major. Andre Navarra, vlc; Erika Kilcher, pno.
++Gr 7-81 p170 +HFN 8-81 p89

CAMBRIDGE

CRS 2777
3687 AURIC: Chansons de Lise Hirtz (5); Printemps. DUREY: La boule de neige; La metempsychose; La grenade. HONEGGER: Les cloches; Clotilde; Le delphinium. MILHAUD: L'Aurore; Poems de Jean Cocteau(3). POULENC: Chanson Bretonne; Hier; La petite servante; Poemes de Ronsard. TAILLEFERRE: Chansons francaises (6). Carole Bogard, s; John Moriarty, pno.
+ARG 11-81 p42 +NR 5-81 p12
+-FF 7/8-81 p205 ++NYT 4-5-81 pD33
+-HF 10-81 p88 ++St 8-81 p100

CANTILENA

6243
3688 ADAM: Minuits. Chretiens. BERLIOZ: La damnation de Faust: Nature immense. FAURE: Les rameaux. GRANIER: Hosanna. MASSENET: Le Cid: O noble lame etincelante; O souverain o juge o pere. Herodiade: Ne pouvant reprimer...Adieu donc vains objets. MEHUL: Joseph en Egypt: Ainement Pharaon...Champs paternals. RABAUD: La fille de Roland: Chanson des epees. REYER: Sigurd: Un souvenir poignant; Le bruit des chants...Esprits gardiens. WAGNER: Die Meistersinger von Nurnburg: Morgenlich leuchtend. Parsifal: Nur eine Waffe taugt. Siegfried: Nothung Nothung; Hoho, hoho, hohei. Die Walkure: Wintersturme. Paul Franz, t; Instrumental accompaniments.
+NR 2-81 p10

6244
3689 GOUNOD: Reine de Saba: Faibless de la race humaine...Inspirez-moi race divine. MASSENET: Herodiade: Jean je te revois. Werther: Je ne sais si je veille...O natur; Un autre est son epoux... J'airais sur ma poitrine; Qui ce qu'elle m'ordonne...Lorsque l'enfant. MEYERBEER: L'Africaine: C'est de la que mon canto fragile...Combine tu m'es chere; Erreur fatale...O ma Selika. REYER: Sigurd: J'ai garde mon ame ingenue; Esprits gardiens. SAINT-SAENS: Samson et Dalila: Arretez o mes freres; En ces lieux malgre moi...Mon coeur s'ouvre. VERDI: Jerusalem: Je veux encore entendre. Cesar Vezzani, t; Instrumental accompaniments.
+-NR 2-81 p10

CAPRICE

CAP 1190
3690 ELIASSON: Disegno. MORTHENSON: Wechselspiel I. SANDSTROM: Effort. SCHUBACK: Burro. Poemas. WELIN: Frammenti. Peter Schuback, vlc.
+NR 1-81 p4

CAP 1230
3691 LIDHOLM: Kort ar rosornas tid. LYNE: There was a naughty boy. NIELSEN: Aftenstemning. POULENC: Petites prieres de Saint-Francois d'Assise (4). TALLIS: Lamentations of Jeremiah. TRAD.: The mermaid; The old whiff song. Lamentabile Consort.
+FF 9/10-81 p224 +-NR 8-81 p10

CBS

M 35554
3692 CACCINI: Amarilli mia bella. CALESTANI: Damigella tutta bella. DALZA: Pavana alla venetiana. Passa e mezzo. Piva. FRESCOBALDI: Capriccio sopra l'Aria di Ruggiero. GABRIELI: Ecco l'aurora. LUZZASCHI: Quivi sospire. MANTUANUS: Lirum bililirum. MONTEVERDI: Geatus vir; O Rosetta che Rosetta. TROMBONCINO: Ostinato vo'seguiere; Vergine bella. VECCHI: So ben mi chi ha bon tempo. VERDELOT: Italia mia. WERT: Vezzosi augelli. ANON.: Dances, harpsichord (3). Waverly Consort; Michael Jaffee.
+FF 5/6-81 p201

M 35838 Tape (c) MT 35838
3693 BEETHOVEN: Deutsche Tanze, WoO 42 (6). BRAHMS: Hungarian dance, no. 5, G minor (arr. Joachim). FIBICH: Poeme, op. 41, no. 6 (arr. Kubelik). FISCHER: Amoroso. DINICU: Hora staccato (arr. Heifetz). KHANDOSHKIN: Sentimental aria (arr. Yampolsky). KREISLER: March miniature Viennoise. LISZT: La lugubre gondola, S 200. MUSSORGSKY: The fair at Sorochinsk: Gopak (arr. Rachmaninoff). PAGANINI: Caprice, op. 1, no. 14, E flat major (arr. Schumann). SCHUBERT: Der Erlkonig, D 328 (trans. Ernst). SHOSTAKOVICH: Prelude, op. 34, no. 17, A flat major (arr. Tsyganov). TCHAIKOVSKY: Souvenir d'un lieu cher, op. 42: Melodie. VIEUXTEMPS: Romance, op. 7, no. 2. Gidon Kremer, vln; Oleg Maisenberg, pno.
+-FF 3/4-81 p231 +-St 11-80 p104

M 35857 (also CBS 76946 Tape (c) 40-76946)
3694 ALBENIZ (Lagoya): Suite espanola, op. 47: Cadiz. PUJOL VILARRUBI: Guajira. RODRIGO: Nocturne. Prelude. Scherzino. TARREGA: Etude (Dream). Grand waltz. Variations on the theme "Carnival in Venice". Two little sisters. Waltz. TORROBA: Torija. Alexandre Lagoya, gtr.
+FF 9/10-80 p275 +Gr 3-81 p1217

IM 35858 Tape (c) HMT 35858
3695 BEETHOVEN: Minuet, G major. The ruins of Athens, op. 113: Turkish march. Bagatelle, no. 25, A minor. BOCCHERINI: Quintet, strings, A major: Minuet. GLUCK: Orfeo ed Euridice: Dance of the blessed spirits. GOSSEC: Gavotte. HAYDN: Quartet, strings, op. 3, no. 5, F major: Andante cantabile. Concerto, trumpet,

E flat major: Finale. MOZART: Concerto, piano, no. 21, K 467, C major: Andante. Sonata, piano, no. 11, K 331, A major: Rondo alla turca. Chick Corea, pno; Edward Carroll, tpt; Hubert Laws, flt; Philharmonia Virtuosi of New York; Richard Kapp.
+FF 3/4-81 p233 +-HFN 9-81 p87
-HF 4-81 p93 tape ++St 4-81 p109

M 35872
3696 HIROTA: Shikararete. MOTOORI: Nanatsu no ko. TAKI: Kohjoh no Stuki. YAMADA: Chugokuchiho no Komoruta. Sunayama. YATSUHASHI: Rokudan no Shirabe. YOSHIZAWA: Chidori no kyoku. TRAD.: Imayoh. Sakura Sakura. Tohryanse. Zuizuizukhorobashi. Isaac Stern, vln; Hozan Yamamoto, shakuhachi; Ensemble Nipponia.
+NR 8-81 p13

I2M 35903 (2)
3697 BEETHOVEN: Sonata, piano, no. 8, op. 13, C minor. CHOPIN: Nocturne, op. 72, E minor. Sonata, piano, no. 2, op. 35, B flat minor. CLEMENTI: Sonata, piano, op. 40, no. 2, B minor. GERSHWIN: Prelude, no. 2. LISZT: Rhapsodie espagnole, S 254. Trauervorspiel und Trauermarsch, S 206. MOZART: Rondo, piano, K 511, A minor. Lazar Berman, pno.
+-FF 5/6-81 p202 +-HF 4-81 p90

M2X 35914 (2) (also CBS 76983)
3698 BACH, C.P.E.: Sonata, harpsichord, no. 1, op. 2, A minor. BEETHOVEN: Symphony, no. 6, op. 68, F major: 1st movement (arr. Liszt). GOULD: A Glenn Gould fantasy. So you want to write a fugue. SCARLATTI, D.: Sonatas, D major, D minor, G major. SCRIABIN: Preludes, op. 57 (2). STRAUSS, R.: Ophelia Lieder, op. 67, nos. 1-3. Elisabeth Schwarzkopf, Elizabeth Benson-Guy, s; Anita Darian, ms; Charles Bressler, t; Donald Gramm, bar; Glenn Gould, voice, pno; Juilliard Quartet; Vladimir Golschmann.
+FF 3/4-81 p227 +MUM 5/6-81 p33
+Gr 6-81 p65 ++St 6-81 p126

MG 35919 (2)
3699 ALFORD: Colonel Bogey march. ARNE: British Grenadiers. Rule Britannia. BAGLEY: National emblem. BERLIOZ: La damnation de Faust, op. 24: Rakoczy march. BIZET: Carmen: March of the toreadors. ELGAR: Pomp and circumstance march, op. 39, no. 1, D major. GRIEG: Lyric pieces, op. 54: March of the dwarfs. IPPOLITOV-IVANOV: Caucasian sketches, op. 10: Procession of the Sardar. de LISLE: La Marseillaise. MEYERBEER: Le prophete: Coronation march. MENDELSSOHN: Athalia, op. 74: War march of the priests. MILES: Anchors aweigh. PROKOFIEV: Love for three oranges: March. SOUSA: Hands across the sea. Semper fidelis. Stars and stripes forever. The thunderer. Under the double eagle. Washington post. STEFFE: Battle hymn of the republic. STRAUSS, J. I: Radetzky march, op. 228. TCHAIKOVSKY: Marche slav. VERDI: Aida: Grand march. WAGNER: Tannhauser: Festmarch. NYP; Leonard Bernstein.
-FF 9/10-81 p291 +-NR 6-81 p4

IM 36661 Tape (c) HMT 36661
3700 BACH: Cantata, no. 147, Jesu joy of man's desiring. A mighty fortress is our God. HANDEL: Messiah: Hallelujah chorus. HAYDN: Awake the harp. MALOTTE: The Lord's prayer. MENDELSSOHN: Rise up arise. MOZART: Gloria in excelsis Deo. SCHUBERT: Ave Maria,

D 839. SULLIVAN: Onward Christian soldiers. TRAD. (arr. Wilhousky): The battle hymn of the republic. Mormon Tabernacle Choir; Columbia Symphony Orchestra; Jerold Ottley.
+Gr 7-81 p195 ++St 9-81 p102

36675
3701 ALBENIZ, M.: Sonata, guitar. MUDARRA: Fantasia. PUJOL VILARRUBI: Guajira. SOR: Etude, op. 17. Introduction and variations on a theme by Mozart, op. 9. Minuet, op. 11, no. 6. Minuet, op. 22. TARREGA: Capricho arabe. Gran jota. Sueno. Liona Boyd, gtr.
+-FF 7/8-81 p215 +NR 7-81 p16
+MUM 1/2-81 p34

M 36677
3702 CORNELIUS: Weihnachtslieder, op. 8. DIEPENBROCK: Berceuse. NIN-CULMELL: Villancico castellano; Villancico vasco. REGER: Maria Wiegenlied, op. 76, no. 52. SCARLATTI, A.: Cantata pastorale per la nativita. STRAUSS, R.: Weihnachtsgefuhl. WOLF: Epiphanias. Ely Ameling, s; Dalton Baldwin, pno; Instrumental Ensemble.
+NR 12-81 p2 +SR 12-81 p65
+SFC 12-13-81 p18

M 36682 Tape (c) MT 36682
3703 BRAHMS: Songs: Mein Madel hat einen Rosenmund. DVORAK: Als die alte Mutter. GERSHWIN: By Strauss. GRANADOS: Tonadillas: El majo discreto. GUASTAVINO: La rosa y el sauce. HAHN: Le rossignol des lilas. LISZT: Es muss ein Wunderbares sein. MONTSALVATGE: Canciones negras: Cancion de cuna para dormir un negrito. NIN-CULMELL: Pano murciano. POULENC: Les chemins de la'mour. SCOTT: Think on me. TURINA: Las locas por amor. VAUGHAN WILLIAMS: Silent noon. WAGNER: Traume. WECKERLIN: Tambourin. Elly Ameling, s; Dalton Baldwin, pno.
+NR 8-81 p11 +St 8-81 p100

36689
3704 BARTOK: Rumanian folk dances. PAGANINI: Cantabile, op. 17, D major. PROKOFIEV (trans. Heifetz): The love for three oranges, op. 33: March. STRAVINSKY: Suite italienne (trans. Stravinsky & Dushkin). SCHUMANN: Fantasiestucke, op. 75. TARTINI: Variations on a theme by Corelli (trans. Kreisler). WIENIAWSKI: Legende, op. 17. YSAYE: Reve d'enfant, op. 14. Pinchas Zukerman, vln; Marc Neikrug, pno.
+NR 8-81 p13

M 37205
3705 Christmas music: Jingle bells; What child is this; Deck the halls; Il est ne le divin enfant; Silent night. LEGRAND: Pastorales. Jean-Pierre Rampal, flt; Alexandre Lagoya, gtr; Michel Legrand, keyboards; LSO; Michel Legrand.
+NR 12-81 p2

IM 37206
3706 Greatest hits of Christmas: Joy to the world; O little town of Bethlehem; Adeste fideles; Carol of the bells; White Christmas; Winter wonderland; Carol of the drum; Messiah: Hallelujah, for unto us a child is born; Silver bells; O Tannenbaum; Silent night. Mormon Tabernacle Chorus; Columbia Brass and Percussion Ensemble; Jerold Ottley.
+NR 12-81 p1 +SFC 12-13-81 p18

M 37207
3707 CILEA: Adriana Lecouvreur: La dolcissima effigie. DONIZETTI: L'Elisir d'amore: Una furtiva lagrima; Venti scudi. MASSENET: Le Cid: O noble lame etincelante; O souverain o juge o pere. PUCCINI: Gianni Schicchi: Firenze e come un albero fiorito. Madama Butterfly: Love duet. Le villi: Roberto's aria. VERDI: Requiem: Ingemisco. Placido Domingo, t; Orchestral accompaniments.
+NR 11-81 p12

M 37245
3708 Christmas with Placido Domingo: Joy to the world; God rest ye merry gentlemen; Good King Wenceslas; O little town of Bethlehem; The first noel; O joyful children; La virgen lava panales; It's Christmas time this year; White Christmas; I'll be home for Christmas; Mary's boy child; Cantique de Noel; I heard the bells on Christmas day; Silent night. Placido Domingo, t; VSO; Lee Holdridge.
+NR 12-81 p2 *SFC 12-13-81 p18

61432 Tape (c) 40-61432 (From CBS 73333)
3709 BERG: Seven early songs: Die Nachtigall. BERLIOZ: Le carnival romain, op. 9. DEBUSSY: Prelude a l'apres-midi d'un faune. RAVEL: Concerto, piano for the left hand. STRAVINSKY: L'Oiseau de feu: Infernal dance. WAGNER: Die Meistersinger von Nurnberg: Prelude, Act 1. Philippe Entremont, pno; Heather Harper, s; NYP, CO, NPhO, BBC Symphony Orchestra; Pierre Boulez.
+Gr 4-81 p1378 +HFN 6-81 p87 tape
+-HFN 5-81 p89

76522 Tape (c) 40-76522 (also Columbia M 34206)
3710 BERLIOZ: Beatrice et Benedict: Dieu, Que viens-je d'entendre...Il m'en souvient. La damnation de Faust, op. 24: D'amour l'ardente flamme. GOUNOD: Romeo et Juliette: Depuis hier je cherche en vain. MASSENET: Cendrillon: Enfin je suis ici. Werther: Va laisse les couler mes larmes. MEYERBEER: Les Huguenots: Nobles seigneurs, salut. OFFENBACH: La grand Duchesse de Gerolstein: Dites lui. La perichole: Ah quel diner je viens de faire. THOMAS: Mignon: Connais-tu le pays. Frederica von Stade, ms; LPO; John Pritchard.
++Gr 7-76 p212 +ON 1-29-77 p44
+-HF 2-77 p114 +RR 7-76 p28
+HFN 7-76 p83 +SR 7-81 p90
++HFN 10-76 p185 tape +St 2-77 p83
+-NR 1-77 p10 +STL 9-19-76 p36

79230 (2) (From 76407, 76426)
3711 CATALANI: La Wally: Ebben ne andro lontana. CILEA: Adriana Lecouvreur: Io son l'umile ancella; Poveri fiori. MASCAGNI: Lodoletta: Ah il suo nome; Flammen perdonami. Iris: Un di al tempio. PUCCINI: La boheme: Quando m'en vo'soletta. Gianna Schichhi: O mio babbino caro. Manon Lescaut: In quelle trine morbide; Sola perduta abbandonata. La rondine: Ch'il bel sogno di Doretta. Suor Angelica: Senza mamma o bimbo tu sei morto. Le villi: Non ti scordar di me. VERDI: La battaglia di Legnano: Voi lo diceste...Quante volte. I Lombardi: O madre...Se vano e il pregare. Nabucco: Ben io t'invenni... Anch'io dischiuso...Salgo gia. Otello: Canzone di salce...Ave Maria. La traviata: Addio del passato. I vespri siciliani:

Arrigo, Ah parli a un core; Merce dilette amiche. Renata Scotto, s; LPO, LSO; Gianandrea Gavazzeni.
+Gr 4-81 p1372 ++HFN 4-81 p78

79334 (3) Tape (c) 40-79334 (From 72798, 76369, 72661, 76634)
3712 CASTELNUOVO-TEDESCO: Concerto, guitar, op. 99, D major. GIULIANI: Concerto, guitar, op. 30, A major. RODRIGO: Concierto de Aranjuez. Fantasia para un gentilhombre. VILLA-LOBOS: Concerto, guitar. VIVALDI: Concerti, guitar, D major, A major. John Williams, gr; ECO; Charles Groves, Daniel Barenboim.
+Gr 11-80 p683 +HFN 4-81 p81 tape
+HFN 11-80 p129

79343 (3)
3713 BELLINI: Norma: Casta diva. CHARPENTIER: Louise: Depuis le jour. CILEA: Andriana Lecouvreur: Io sono l'umile ancella. DONIZETTI: Gemma di Vergy: Eccomi sola alfine. DURUFLE: Requiem, op. 9: Pie Jesu. FALLA: El amor brujo: Air. HANDEL: Rinaldo: Lascia ch'io piangi. HUMPERDINCK: Hansel und Gretel: Der kleine Sandmann; Children's prayer. MASSENET: Cendrillon: Ah que mes soeurs sont heureuses. Werther: Va laisse couler mes larmes. MEYERBEER: Le prophete: Pretres de baal. MOZART: Don Giovanni, K 527: Ah fuggi il traditor; Mi tradi. Le nozze di Figaro, K 492: Non so piu cosa son; Deh vieni non tardar. OFFENBACH: La grande Duchesse de Gerolstein: Dites-lui. PUCCINI: Gianni Schicchi: O mio babbino caro. Madama Butterfly: Un bel di. Suor Angelica: Senza Mamma. RAVEL: Sheherazade: Asie. ROSSINI: Semiramide: Bel raggio. STRAUSS, R.: Vier letzte Lieder, op. posth.: Beim Schlafengehen. THOMAS: Mignon: C'est moi... Me voici; Connais-tu le pays. VERDI: Aroldo: Ciel ch'io respiri; Ah dagli scanni eterei...Cabaletta. Otello: Ave Maria. Rigoletto: Caro nome. Kiri Te Kanawa, Ileana Cotrubas, Montserrat Caballe, Marilyn Horne, Renata Scotto, s; Frederica von Stade, ms; Instrumental and orchestral accompaniments.
+Gr 12-81 p934 +-HFN 12-81 p108

CHALUMEAU

EBY 001
3714 ARNOLD: Sonatina, op. 29. GIAMPIERI: Variations on "The carnival of Venice". LOVREGLIO: Concert fantasia on Verdi's "La traviata". RIMSKY-KORSAKOV: The tale of the Tsar Sultan, op. 57: Flight of the bumblebee. TARTINI: Concertino. Mark Walton, clt; Paul Bateman, pno.
+/Gr 9-81 p451 +-RR 12-78 p91

EBY 003
3715 BASSI: Fantasia di concerto on Verdi's "Rigoletto". HOROVITZ: Majorcan pieces (2). PROKOFIEV: Cinderella suite (Prorvich). RAMEAU: Suite (Ettlinger). ROSSINI: Cavatina. WEBER: Variations on a theme from Silvana (7). Paul Bateman, pno; Mark Walton, clt.
+/Gr 9-81 p451

CHANDOS

BBR 1004 Tape (c) BBT 1004
3716 CALVERT: Introduction, elegy and caprice. GREGSON: Connotations. HUBER: Symphonic music. SIMPSON: Volcano. VINTER: John O' Gaunt. Black Dyke Mills Band; Peter Parkes.
+FF 1/2-81 p228 +RR 6-80 p59
+Gr 6-80 p69

BBR 1004
3717 ALBENIZ: Iberia: Carnival in Seville (arr. Newsome). BERLIOZ: Le carnaval romain, op. 9 (arr. Wright). DVORAK: Carnival overture, op. 92 (arr. Newsome). SAINT-SAENS: Carnival of the animals: Suite (arr. Langofrd). PERKIN: Carnival suite: Burlesque. VINTER: Lisbon carnival. Sun Life Stanshaw Band; Brian Howard, Roy Newsome.
+FF 1/2-81 p229 -RR 8-80 p38

ABR 1016 Tape (c) ABT 1016
3718 CAPUA: I te vurria vasa. DONIZETTI: La conocchia; La tradimiento; Me voglia fa'na casa. GLUCK: Paride ed Elena: O del mio dolce ardor. MARTINI IL TEDESCO: Plaisir d'amour. PICCININI: O notte a dea del mistero. TOSTI: L'ultima canzone. VERDI: La seduzione; Non t'accostare all'urna; Brindisi. Renato Bruson, bar; Craig Sheppard.
+Gr 6-81 p76 +HFN 8-81 p92 tape
+HFN 6-81 p81 +STL 4-12-81 p40

ABR 1024 Tape (c) ABT 1024 (From Grange SGR 1124)
3719 CORELLI: Concerto grosso, op. 6, no. 8, G minor. FARINA: Pavane. FERRABOSCO: Pavane, no. 4. VIVALDI: Sinfonia, G major. WIDMANN: Canzona. Galliard. Intrada. Cantilena; Adrian Shepherd.
+-Gr 2-81 p1095 +-HFN 3-81 p97 tape
-HFN 2-81 p97

ABA 1028
3720 BOHM: Vater unser im Himmelreich. BRUHNS: Toccata, G major. BUXTEHUDE: Mensch wilt du leben seliglich. Toccata, D major. ISAAC: Innsbruck ich muss dich lassen. Choruses (2). LECHNER: Nun schein du Glanz der Herrlichkeit; O Tod du bist ein bitter Gallen. PACHELBEL: Fantasia, G minor. Toccata, G minor. PRAETORIUS: Mass, 8 parts: Kyrie, Agnus Dei. SCHEIDT: Modus ludendi pleno. SCHLICK: Maria zart von edler Art. WALTHER: Mit Fried und Freud ich fahr dahin. Chorus, 4 parts. WECKMANN: Fantasia, D minor. Nicholas Danby, org; Lemgo Church of our Lady Choir; Walther Schmidt.
+Gr 6-81 p65 +-HFN 6-81 p79

ABRD 1030
3721 ARDITI: Il bacio. ARNOLD: Little suite, brass. DAVIES: Close thine eyes. ELGAR: Enigma variations, op. 36: Nimrod. GOUNOD: Faust: Soldier's chorus. JONES: Morte Christe. HUGHES: Royal Doulton march. KNIPPER: Cavalry of the Steppes. PARRY: Jerusalem, op. 208. RICHARDS: God bless the Prince of Wales. STRAUSS, J. II: Unter Donner und Blitz, op. 324. WAGNER: Tannhauser: Pilgrim's chorus. WALTERS: Iona. The national anthem. English folksongs (3). Massed English Male Choirs; Royal Doulton Band; Edmund Walters, Ted Gray.
+FF 11/12-81 p284

ABRD 1032 Tape (c) ABRD 1032

3722 ARNOLD: Tam O'Shanter, op. 51. BERLIOZ: Waverly overture, op. 2. MACCUNN: Land of the mountain and the flood, op. 8. MENDELSSOHN: Hebrides overture, op. 26. VERDI: Macbeth: Ballet music. Scottish National Orchestra; Alexander Gibson.
+Gr 11-81 p713 +HFN 11-81 p101

DBR 3001 (3)

3723 BALAKIREV: Islamey. BARBER: Sonata, piano, op. 26, E minor. CHOPIN: Nocturne, op. 32, no. 1, B major. GINASTERA: Sonata, piano. HAYDN: Sonata, no. 33, C minor. LIADOV: Musical snuff box, op. 32. LISZT: Annees de pelerinage, 2nd year, S 161: Sposalizio; Supplement, S 162. Annees de pelerinage, 3rd year, S 163: Les jeux d'eaux a la Villa d'Este. Hungarian rhapsody, no. 11, S 244, A minor. PROKOFIEV: Pieces, piano, op. 4, no. 4: Suggestion diabolique. RAVEL: Miroirs: Noctuelles; Oiseaux tristes; La vallee des cloches. SCARLATTI, D.: Sonata, harpsichord, Kk 39, A major. TCHAIKOVSKY: Pieces, piano, op. 19, F major: Theme and variations. The months, op. 37: January. Terence Judd, pno.
+-FF 7/8-81 p211 +-HFN 12-80 p151
+Gr 12-80 p859 +MT 4-81 p248

CHANT DU MONDE

LDX 78691/2 (2)

3724 Divine orthodox liturgy: Easter; Pentecost and Assumption; Matins for Pentecost; Divine liturgy for the Feast of St. Sergius of Radoneje. Holy Trinity-St. Sergius Monastery Choir; Moscow Ecclesiastic Academy Choir; Archimandrite Nikolai Vassilievich Matfei.
+Gr 8-81 p307 ++HFN 4-81 p77

CLASSICS FOR PLEASURE

CFP 40324 Tape (c) TC CFP 40324 (From Music for Pleasure MFP 57006)

3725 BACH: Cantata, no. 147, Jesu joy of man's desiring. Toccata and fugue, S 565, D minor. Ave Maria (Gounod). BOELLMANN: Suite gothique, op. 25: Priere a Notre Dame. MENDELSSOHN: A midsummer night's dream, opp. 21/61: Wedding march. REGER: Pieces, organ, op. 59: Benedictus. WIDOR: Symphony, organ, no. 5, op. 42, no. 1, F major: Toccata. Symphony, organ, no. 8, op. 42, no. 4, B minor: Finale. Jane Parker-Smith, org.
+Gr 1-80 p1172 +HFN 5-81 p93 tape
+HFN 1-80 p121 -RR 12-79 p97

CFP 40358 Tape (c) TC CFP 40358 (From HMV ALP 1596, ASD 287, Columbia 33CS 1429, HMV HQS 1143, ALP 1533, ASD 420)

3726 BEETHOVEN: Die Ruinen von Athen, op. 113: Overture. BERLIOZ: Le Corsaire, op. 21: Overture. BRAHMS: Academic festival overture, op. 80. MENDELSSOHN: A midsummer night's dream, opp. 21/61: Overture. ROSSINI: La gazza ladra. SUPPE: Poet and peasant: Overture. RPO; Thomas Beecham.

+Gr 8-81 p396 +HFN 8-81 p91

CFP 40362 Tape (c) TC CFP 40362

3727 ALBENIZ: Piezas caracteristicas: Torre bermeja. Recuerdos de viaje, op. 71: Rumores de la caleta. Suite espanola, op. 47: Asturias. BORGES (arr. Riera): Vals venezolano. FALLA: El sombrero de tres picos: Danza del corregidor; Danza del molinero. GRANADOS: Danzas espanolas, op. 37: Andaluza. LAURO: Vals criollo. MALATS: Serenata espanola. RODRIGO: En los trigales. TARREGA: Alborada. Capricho arabe. TORROBA: Madronos. VILLA-LOBOS: Choro, no. 1, E minor. Etude, no. 1, E minor. Prelude, no. 2. Julian Byzantine, gtr.

+Gr 12-81 p911 +-HFN 12-81 p108

COMPOSERS VOICE

CV 7903 (2)

3728 ANDRIESSEN: In memoriam. ARRAS: A.B.C. CATS: Cadence 1. KUNST: Exterieur. OYENS: Safed. SMITH: Etude, no. 1. TEN HOLT: I am Sylvia but somebody else. VAN BERGEIJK: D.E.S. VAN CAMPEN: Sintering. VAN DOORN: Minnuet. WENTINK: Discours. Electronic tape music.

+CMJ Spring 1981 p74 *FF 3/4-81 p30

CV 8002

3729 HEPPENER: Canzona. KEURIS: Quartet, saxophone. Petersma: Quartet, saxophone. STRAESSER: Intersections V. VRIES: Chorales (2). WAGEMANS: Quartet, saxophone. Leo van Oostrom, soprano saxophone; Ed Bogaard, alto saxophone; Adri van Velsen, tenor saxophone; Jacques Landa, baritone saxophone.

++FF 9/10-81 p276

CONCORD CONCERTO

CC 2002

3730 BACH: Sonata, flute and harpsichord, A minor. DEBUSSY: Preludes, Bk I: La fille aux cheveux de lin. MAYS: Suite, flute and piano. RAVEL: Ma mere l'oye: Pavane. SCRIABIN: Etude, C sharp minor. Bud Shank, flt; Bill Mays, pno.

*NR 11-81 p6

CORNUCOPIA

IJ 100

3731 BAKER: Cantilena. COOKE: Rondo, B flat major. DUNHILL: Cornucopia. ECCLES: Sonata, horn, G minor (arr. Eger). GWILT: Sonatina. STIRLING: Horncore. Variations on a Tyrolean theme. VINTER: Hunter's moon. TRAD.: Carnival in Venice (arr. Stirling). Ifor James, hn; John McCabe, Wilfrid Parry, pno.

+Gr 10-80 p157 +HFN 2-81 p95

CRD

CRD 1007 (also Vanguard 71272)
3732 ARNE: Sonata, harpsichord, no. 3, G major. BACH, J.C.: Sonata, harpsichord, op. 5, no. 6, C minor. BYRD: The Queens alman. The bells. CROFT: Sonata, harpsichord, no. 3, C minor. HANDEL: Suite, harpsichord, no. 5, E major. ANON.: Lady Wynkfylds rownde. Trevor Pinnock, hpd, spinet.
+ARG 7/8-81 p42 +HFN 3-74 p121
+FF 5/6-81 p206 +RR 3-74 p50
+HF 5-78 p116

CRD 1047 Tape (c) CRDC 4047
3733 ARNE: Sonata, harpsichord, no. 6, G major. BLOW: Mortlack's ground. DRAGHI: Ground, C minor. GIBBS: The Lord Monck's march. GREENE: Overture, D major. LOCKE: Suite, no. 4, D major. NARES: Lesson, op. 2, D major. PARADIES: Sonata, harpsichord, no. 6, A major. PURCELL: A new Irish tune. Suite, no. 2, G minor. ANON.: Gerard's mistress. The Grange. Trevor Pinnock, hpd.
+Gr 9-78 p513 +MT 5-79 p410
+Gr 12-81 p944 tape ++RR 8-78 p84
+HFN 10-78 p133

CRD 1050 Tape (c) CRDC 4050
3734 BULL: My grief. My self. The king's hunt. BYRD: Carmans whistle. Lord Willoughby's welcome home. Watkin's ale (attrib. Byrd). DOWLAND: Can she excuse. FARNABY: Loath to depart. Muscadin. GIBBONS: The fairest nymph. Lord of Salisbury his pavan and galliard. The woods so wild. MORLEY: La volta. TALLIS: O ye tenderest babes. TOMKINS: Barafostus dream. ANON.: My Lady Careys dompe. Trevor Pinnock, hpd and virginals.
++Gr 11-78 p934 +HFN 12-80 p159 tape
+Gr 12-81 p944 tape +MT 5-79 p410
+HFN 10-78 p135 +RR 11-78 p89

CRESCENT

ARS 109 Tape (c) LRS 109
3735 BACH, C.P.E.: Sonata, organ, no. 5, D major. BACH, J.S.: Fantasia, S 573, C major. DAQUIN: Noel Suisse. KREBS: Chorale preludes: Allein Gott in der Hoh sei Ehr; Von Gott will ich nicht lassen; Jesu meine Freud. WALTHER: Concerto del Sigr. Albinoni. Concerto del Sigr. Meck, B minor. Gerald Gifford, org.
+Gr 4-77 p1577 +HFN 8-77 p81
+Gr 6-81 p94 tape +RR 3-77 p83
+Gr 7-81 p196 tape

CRYSTAL

S 126
3736 BACH: Suite, orchestra, S 1068, D major: Air on the G string.

CUI: Perpetual motion. KELLAWAY: Dance of the ocean breeze. Sonoro. SCHUBERT: Standchen. SINIGAGLIA: Song and humoreske, op. 28. Roger Bobo, tuba and bs horn; Froydis Ree Wekre, hn; Zita Carno, pno; Roger Kellaway, pno.
+ARG 5-81 p36 +NR 2-81 p7
+-FF 1/2-81 p225

S 155
3737 BACH: Fugue, G minor. BOZZA: Nuages. DESENCLOS: Quartet, saxophones. GLAZUNOV: Quartet, saxophones, op. 109, B flat major. JOPLIN: The cascades. RIVIER: Grave et presto. Harvey Pittel Saxophone Quartet; Monty Budwig, bs.
-NR 4-81 p7

S 336
3738 BOZZA: Aria. DEBUSSY: Petite piece. Rhapsody, clarinet. GADE: Fantasy pieces. LUTOSLAWSKI: Dance preludes. PIERNE: Canzonetta. James Campbell, John York, pno.
+NR 12-81 p11

S 342
3739 DUISBERG: Relativity's rainbow. Airs and divisions. GELBRUN: Miniature. SCHULHOFF: Bass Nachtigall. SMITH: Tribute to the bassoon. TISNE: Soliloques. Arthur Grossman, bsn, contrabassoon, narration; Donald McInnes, vla; Silvia Kind, hpd; Daniel Dunbar, perc.
+FF 9/10-81 p269 +NR 2-81 p7

S 365
3740 HOVHANESS: Prayer of St. Gregory. LANGLAIS: Chorale preludes: Aus tiefer Not schrei ich zu dir; Ein feste Burg ist unser Gott. NUCKOLLS: Chaconne. PINKHAM: The other voices of the trumpet. SCHILLING: Canzona uber "Christ ist erstanden". TORELLI: Sinfonia, tromba. Byron Pearson, tpt; Arthur Vidrich, org.
+-HF 3-81 p77 +NR 3-81 p13

S 367
3741 BOZZA: Badinage. Caprice. Lied. IBERT: Impromptu. POULENC: Sonata, trumpet, horn and trombone. ROPARTZ: Andante and allegro. TOMASI: Triptyque. Thomas Stevens, tpt; Zita Carno, pno; John Cerminaro, hn; Ralph Sauer, trom.
++ARG 10-81 p50 ++St 8-81 p105
++NR 7-81 p5

S 385 (also Crystal 90065)
3742 BOUTRY: Pieces a quatre (5). CASTEREDE: Sonatina. CHAYNES: Impulsions. DEFAYE: Danses (2). SALZEDO: Piece concertante. Miles Anderson, trom; Los Angeles Slide Trombone Ensemble; Virko Baley, pno.
+Audio 10-81 p28 +NR 5-80 p16
+-FF 5/6-80 p187 +NYT 5-18-80 pD42

CRYSTAL CLEAR

CCS 6004/5
3743 Flamenco: Tango antiguo; Levante; Caribe aflamencao; Fandango; Taranto; Variaciones; Aires de Genil; Malaga; Jerez; Macarena en tango; Saeta; Solea-Cana; Zambra; Zapateao. Carlos Montoya, gtr.
++HFN 5-81 p87 ++St 10-80 p129

CCS 7001/2 (2)
3744 ALAIN: Litanies, op. 79. BACH: Toccata, adagio and fugue, S 564, C major. Toccata and fugue, S 565, D minor. DUPRE: Prelude and fugue, G minor. FRANCK: Piece heroique. GIGOUT: Toccata. JONGEN: Symphonie concertante: Toccata. VIERNE: Symphony, no. 6, op. 59, B major: Finale. WIDOR: Symphony, organ, no. 5, op. 42, no. 1, F major: Toccata. Virgil Fox, org.
+-ARG 4-80 p51 +-HFN 6-81 p83
++Audio 1-79 p108 +MU 2-79 p12
++Audio 8-79 p86 +NR 10-78 p15
+-FF 3/4-79 p14 -SFC 6-3-79 p49
+Gr 6-78 p90 +St 11-79 p98

CCS 7010 dbx 2021
3745 BACH: Toccata and fugue, S 565, D minor. BLISS: Salute (arr. Tulan). BRAHMS: Let nothing ever grieve thee, op. 30 (arr. Morris). COPLAND: Fanfare for the common man. GIGOUT: Grand choeur dialogue (arr. Morris). Richard Morris, org; Atlanta Brass Ensemble; Jere Flint.
+ARG 11-79 p30 +NR 6-80 p14
+Audio 12-79 p120 +SFC 12-23-79 p40
+Audio 12-81 p67 +St 2-80 p141
+-HFN 5-81 p89

CCS 7011 dbx GS 2022
3746 COUPERIN, L.: Chaconne (arr. Morris). DUPRE: Poeme heroique. MOURET: Rondeau (arr. Morris). STANLEY: Trumpet tune and aires: Voluntaries (3). STRAUSS, R.: Also sprach Zarathustra, op. 30: Opening fanfare. WIDOR: Symphony, organ, no. 5, op. 42, no. 1, F major: Toccata. Richard Morris, org; Atlanta Brass Ensemble; Jere Flint.
+ARG 11-79 p31 +-HFN 5-81 p89
+Audio 12-79 p120 +NR 6-80 p14
+-FF 7/8-81 p223 +SFC 12-23-79 p40

DA CAPO

C 047 28559
3747 d'ALBERT: Tiefland: Schau her das ist ein Taler. BIZET: Carmen: La fleur que tu m'avais jetee. KIENZL: Der Evangelimann: Selig sind die Verfolgung leiden. Der Kuhreigen: Lud Dursel lug. MOZART: Don Giovanni, K 527: Dalla sua pace. Die Entfuhrung aus dem Serail, K 384: Konstanze dich wiederzusehen. Die Zauberflote, K 620: Dies Bildnis ist bezaubernd schon. OFFENBACH: Les contes de Hoffmann: Ha wie in meiner Seel'. PUCCINI: Tosca: Und es blitzten die Sterne; Wie sich die Bilder gleichen. THOMAS: Mignon: Wie ihre Unschuld. VERDI: Rigoletto: Freundlich blick ich; O wie so trugerisch. Il trovatore: Dass nur fur mich dein Herz erbebt; Lodern zum Himmel. WEBER: Der Freischutz: Nein langer trag ich nicht die Qualen. WOLF-FERRARI: Der Schmuck der Madonna: Madonna unter Tranen. Richard Tauber, t; Various orchestras and conductors.
++FF 5/6-81 p195

1C 137 46104/5 (2)
3748 DONIZETTI: Don Pasquale: Quel guardo il cavaliere. NICOLAI: Die lustigen Weiber von Windsor: Nein das ist wirklich. MOZART: Cosi fan tutte, K 588: In uomini in soldati; Una donna a quindici anni. Die Entfuhrung aus dem Serail, K 384: Traurigkeit; Martern aller Arten; Welch ein Geschick. Idomeneo, Re di Creta, K 366: Zeffiretti lusinghieri. Les nozze di Figaro, K 492: Non so piu; Voi che sapete; Sull'aria; Deh vieni non tardar. Die Zauberflote, K 620: O zittre nicht; Der Holle Rache. PUCCINI: La boheme: Mi chiamano Mimi; O soave fanciulla. Madama Butterfly: Love duet, Act 1. ROSSINI: Il barbiere di Siviglia: Una voce poco fa. SMETANA: The bartered bride: Marie's aria, Act 3. VERDI: Rigoletto: Caro nome; Si vendetta. La traviata: Finale, Act 1. Erna Berger, s.
+-FF 9/10-81 p212

1C 197 53780/6 (7)
3749 BACH: Cantata, no. 148, Jesus bleibet meine freude. Chorlae preludes, S 599, Nun komm der Heiden Heiland; S 639, Ich ruf zu dir Herr Jesu Christ. Partita, harpsichord, no. 1, S 825, B flat major. Sonata, flute and harpsichord, S 1031, E flat major: Siciliano. BRAHMS: Waltzes, op. 39. CHOPIN: Barcarolle, op. 60, F sharp major. Concerto, piano, no. 1, op. 11, E minor. Mazurka, op. 50, no. 3, C sharp minor. Nocturne, op. 27, no. 2, D flat major. Sonata, piano, no. 3, op, 58, B minor. Waltzes (14). ENESCO: Sonata, piano, no. 3, op. 24, D major. GRIEG: Concerto, piano, op. 16, A minor. LISZT: Annees de pelerinage, 2nd year, S 161: Sonetto del Petrarch. MOZART: Concerto, piano, no. 21, K 467, C major. Sonata, piano, no. 8, K 310, A minor. RAVEL: Miroirs: Alborada del gracioso. SCARLATTI: Sonatas, harpsichord, E major, D minor. SCHUBERT: Impromptus, op. 90, nos. 2-3, D 899. SCHUMANN: Concerto, piano, op. 54, A minor. Dinu Lipatti, Nadia Boulanger, pno; PhO, Lucerne Festival Orchestra, Orchestra; Alceo Galliera, Herbert von Karajan.
++FF 9/10-81 p234

DECCA

JB 99 Tape (c) KJBC 99 (From SXL 6451)
3750 CILEA: Adriana Lecouvreur: La dolcissima effigie. DONIZETTI: Lucia di Lammermoor: Tombe degli' ave miei...Fra poco a me recovero. GIORDANO: Andrea Chenier: Un di all'azzurro spazio. Fedora: Amor ti vieta. LEONCAVALLO: I Pagliacci: Recitar... Vesti la giubba. MASCAGNI: Cavalleria rusticana: Mamma quel vino e generoso. PONCHIELLI: La gioconda: Cielo e mar. PUCCINI: Turandot: Nessun dorma. VERDI: Aida: Celeste Aida. Un ballo in maschera: Ma se m'e forza perderti. Il trovatore: Ah si ben mio. Placido Domingo, t; German Opera Orchestra; Nello Santi.
+Gr 10-81 p610

SDD 571 (From Ars Nova ANC 25004)
3751 Le grandi voci dell'arena di Verona: CILEA: Adriana Lecouvreur: Io son l'umile ancella. DONIZETTI: L'Elisir d'amore: Una

furtiva lagrima. GIORDANO: Andrea Chenier: Son sessant'anni; Nemico della patria. GOUNOD: Faust: O santa medaglia; Vous que faites l'endormie; Le veau d'or. PUCCINI: turandot: Nessun dorma; Signore ascolta. VERDI: Un ballo in maschera: Morro ma prima in grazia. Otello: Ave Maria. Raina Kabaiwanska, Katia Ricciarelli, s; Luciano Pavarotti, t; Piero Cappuccilli, bar; Ruggero Raimondi, bs; Verona Teatro Arena Orchestra.

+-Gr 4-81 p1372 +-Op 7-81 p719
+-HFN 3-81 p93

SDD 572
3752 BIZET: Carmen: L'amour est un oiseau rebelle. CILEA: Adriana Lecouvreur: Io son l'umile ancella. GOUNOD: Faust: Salut demeure chaste et pure. PUCCINI: La boheme: Vecchia zimarra senti. Madama Butterfly: Addio fiorito asil. VERDI: Aida: Ritorna vincitor. Otello: Vanne la tua meta gia vedo. Simon Boccanegra: Il lacerato spirito. Il trovatore: Il balen del suo sorriso; Condotta ell'era in ceppi. Mirella Freni, s; Viorica Cortez, ms; Luis Lima, t; Garbis Boyagian, bar; Verona Arena Orchestra; Leone Magiera.

+-Gr 4-81 p1372 -Op 7-81 p719
+-HFN 3-81 p93

SDD 573 (From Ars Nova 25006)
3753 BACH: Ave Maria (Gounod). BRAHMS: Ninna Nanna. DVORAK: Songs, op. 55: Als die alte Mutter. HANDEL: Serse: Ombra mai fu. MOZART: Ninna Nanna, K 350 (attrib.). PRATELLA: Ninna Nanna di Modigliani; Ninanana. REGER: Maria Wiegenlied, op. 76, no. 52. ROSSINI: Trois choeurs religieux: La carita. SCHUBERT: Ave Maria, D 839; Wiegenlied, D 498. Mirella Freni, s; Bologna Teatro Comunale Orchestra and Chorus; Leone Magiera.

+-Gr 4-81 p1358 -Op 7-81 p719
-HFN 3-81 p93

SDD 578 Tape (c) KSDC 578
3754 BOITO: Mefistofele: L'altra notte. DONIZETTI: La fille du regiment: Convien partir. L'Elisir d'amore: Una parola...Chiedi all'aura. MASCAGNI: L'Amico Fritz: Suzel buon di. MASSENET: Werther: Pourquoi me reveiller. MEYERBEER: L'Africaine: O paradiso. PONCHIELLI: La gioconda: Cielo e mar. VERDI: La traviata: Brindisi; Parigi o cara. I vespri siciliani: Bolero. Mirella Freni, s; Luciano Pavarotti, t; Orchestra dell'Ater; Leone Magiera.

+Gr 3-81 p1237 +-Op 7-81 p719
+HFN 3-81 p93

SXL 6923 (also London OS 26611)
3755 FALLA: La vida breve: Vivan los que rien; Alli esta riyendo junto a esa mujer. GRANADOS: Goyescas: La maja y el ruisenor. MOZART: Don Giovanni, K 527: Don Ottavio son morta...Or sai chi l'onore. PUCCINI: Madama Butterfly: Tu tu piccolo addio. Manon Lescaut: Sola perduta abbandonata. Suor Angelica: Senza mamma. Tosca: Vissi d'arte. VERDI: Don Carlo: Tu che le vanita. WAGNER: Lohengrin: Einsam in truben Tagen. Pilar Lorengar, s; LPO; Jesus Lopez Cobos.

-FF 1/2-81 p215 +NYT 9-14-80 pD42
+-Gr 8-80 p270 -Op 11-80 p1148
+-HFN 8-80 p103 +RR 8-80 p29
+-NR 1-81 p9

SXL R 6936 (also London OS 26618)
3756 COSTANZI: Eupatra: Lusinga la speme. GIORDANI: Caro mio ben. LOTTI: Pur dicesti. MARCELLO: Quella fiamma che m'accende. PAISIELLO: Nel cor piu non mi sento. PERGOLESI: Se tu m'ami. VIVALDI: Bajazet: Sposa son disprezzata. L'Ateneide: Un certo non so che. Ercole sul Termodonte: Onde chiare. La Griselda: Agitata da due venti; Da due venti. Ottone in Villa: Vieni vieni o mio diletto. Montserrat Caballe, s; Miguel Zanetti, pno.

+ARG 4-81 p46
+FF 9/10-80 p240
+-Gr 3-80 p1445
+HF 8-80 p84
++HRN 3-80 p101
+-NYT 6-15-80 pD29
++RR 4-80 p51
+St 9-80 p84

SXDL 7504 Tape (c) KSXDC 7504 (also London LDR 10020)
3757 BOITO: Mefistofele: Dai campi dai prati; Ogni mortal mister gustai...Giunto sul passo estremo. CILEA: Adriana Lecouvreur: La dolcissima effigie; L'anima ho stanca. GIORDANO: Andrea Chenier: Colpito qui m'avete...Un di all'azzurro spazio; Come un bel di di maggio; Si fui soldato. Fedora: Amor ti vieta. MASCAGNI: Iris: Apri la tua finestra. MASSENET: Werther: Pourquoi me reveiller. MEYERBEER: L'Africaine: Mi batte il cor... O paradiso. PUCCINI: La fanciulla del West: Ch'ella mi creda. Manon Lescaut: Ma se vi talenta...Tra voi belle; Donna non vidi mai; Ah non v'avvicinate...No no pazzo son. Luciano Pavarotti, t; Neil Howlett, bar; National Philharmonic Orchestra; Oliviero de Fabritis, Riccardo Chailly.

*ARG 7/8-81 p43
+-FF 5/6-81 p194
+Gr 12-80 p878
+Gr 6-81 p93 tape
+HFN 12-80 p149
+-NR 2-81 p11
+Op 3-81 p311
+SFC 12-7-80 p33
+St 3-81 p80

D125D3 (3)
3758 ADAM: Mariquita. BELLINI: Dolente immagine di fille mia; Malinconia ninfa gentile; Vaga luna che inargenti. BIZET: Pastorale. CAMPANA: L'ultima speme. CHAMINADE: Berceuse. CIMARA: Stornello. DALAYRAC: Nina ou le folle par amour: Quand le bienaime reviendra. DAVID: Les hirondelles. DELIBES: Les filles de Cadiz. DONIZETTI: A mezzanotte; J'attends toujours; Il sospiro. FAURE: Le papillon et la fleur. GOUNOD: Au printemps; Chanson de Florian. HAHN: Aimons-nous. LALO: L'esclave. LEONCAVALLO: Serenata francese. MASCAGNI: La tua stella. MASSENET: Pensee d'automne; Puisqu'elle a pris ma vie; Oh si les fleurs avaient des yeux. MEYERBEER: Guide au bord ta nacelle. PONCHIELLI: Il trovatore. RESPIGHI: I tempi assai lontani. ROSSINI: Arietta all'antica; Chanson de Zora; Les soirees musicales: La promessa; Il rimprovera; La partenza; L'orgia; L'invito; La pastorella dell'Alpi; La gita in gondola; La danza; Adieux a la vie. SAINT-SAENS: Aimons-nous. THOMAS: Le soir. VERDI: Il poveretto. Joan Sutherland, s; Richard Bonynge, pno.

+Gr 8-81 p307
+-HFN 8-81 p89

D236D2 Tape (c) K236K22
3759 BELLINI: I puritani: A te o cara. Songs: Vanne o rosa fortunata. BIZET: Carmen: La fleur que tu m'avais jetee. CURTIS: Torna a Surriento. DENZA: Funiculi funicula (arr. Chiaramello). DONIZETTI: L'Elisir d'amore: Una furtiva lagrima. La favorita:

Spirto gentil. La fille du regiment: O mes amis...Pour mon ame. FRANCK: Panis Angelicas. GOUNOD: Faust: Salut demeure chaste e pure. LEONCAVALLO: I Pagliacci: Vesti la giubba. Songs: Mattinata. PONCHIELLI: La gioconda: Cielo e mar. PUCCINI: La boheme: Che gelida manina. Tosca: Recondita armonia; E lucevan le stelle. Turandot: Nessun dorma. ROSSINI: La danza. SCHUBERT: Ave Maria, D 839. STRAUSS, R.: Der Rosenkavalier, op. 59: Di rigori armato. VERDI: Aida: Celeste Aida. Requiem: Ingemisco. Rigoletto: Questa o quella; La donna e mobile. Il trovatore: Di qual tetra...Ah si ben mio...Di quella pira. Luciano Pavarotti, t; LPI, BPhO, NPhO, PhO, VPO, Teatro Comunale Orchestra, ROHO, ECO, Vienna Volksoper Orchestra, LSO; Zubin Mehta, Nicola Rescigno, Herbert von Karajan, Georg Solti, Piero Gamba, Richard Bonynge, Gian Carlo Chiaramello, Leone Magiera, Giuseppe Patane, Kurt Adler, Anton Guadagno.

+Gr 1-81 p994 +HFN 1-81 p109
+Gr 6-81 p93 tape

DELL'ARTE

DA 9003 (From Pye PCNNX 6)

3760 BEETHOVEN: Leonore overture, no. 3, op. 72. BERLIOZ: Le carnival romain, op. 9. MOZART: Don Giovanni, K 527: Overture. ROSSINI: Guillaume Tell: Overture. SCHUBERT: Rosamunde, op. 26, D 797: Overture. National Philharmonic Orchestra; Leopold Stokowski.

+Gr 11-81 p713 +HFN 12-81 p109

DELOS

DMS 3002

3761 ALTENBURG: Concerto, trumpet, D major. BIBER: Sonata, trumpet, C major. TELEMANN: Concerto, trumpet, D major. TORELLI: Sonata, no. 1, G major. VIVALDI: Concerto, trumpet, C major. Gerard Schwarz, Mark Gould, Ed Carroll, Robert Sirinek, Norman Smith, James Miller, Neil Balm, Raymond Mase, tpt; Sayoko Aki, vln; Frederick Zlotkin, vlc; Loren Glickman, bsn; Linda Skernick, hpd; Gordon Gottlieb, timpani; New York Y Chamber Symphony Orchestra.

+Audio 9-81 p83 +NR 12-79 p5
+-FF 11/12-79 p15 +NYT 5-18-80 pD32
+HF 2-80 p100 +-RR 4-80 p60
++HFN 4-80 p113 ++St 2-80 p136

D/DMS 3003

3762 BACH: Die Kunst der Fuge, S 1080: Contrapunctus, nos. 3 and 9. COPRARIO: Al primo giorno. Fancie a 5. DOWLAND: Volta. FERRABOSCO: Almayne. Dovehouse pavan. GABRIELI, A.: Ricercar del sesto tuono. GABRIELI, G.: Canzona per sonare, nos. 4 and 5. Canzona per sonare "La spiritata". HOLBORNE: The widows myte. MORLEY: Joyne hands. SCHEIDT: Battle suite. SIMPSON: Allemande. SPEER: Sonatas, brass quintet (2). STORL:

Sonata, brass quintet. WEELKES: Why are you ladies staying. Hark I hear some dancing. American Brass Quintet.
+Audio 3-81 p64 ++NYT 5-18-80 pD32
+HFN 4-80 p115 +-RR 4-80 p60
++NR 3-80 p7 ++St 7-80 p84

DENON

OX 7026
3763 BACH: Sonata, 2 violins and harpsichord, S 1038, G major. BALBASTRE: La d'Hericourt. COUPERIN, F.: Piece de clavecin, G minor. Sonata, B flat major. TELEMANN: Quartet, G major. VIVALDI: Sonata, harpsichord, F major. Robert Veyron-Lacroix, hpd; Maxence Larrieu, flt; Pierre Pierlot, ob; Robert Gendre, vln; Paul Hongne, bsn.
+-HFN 5-81 p85

OX 7177
3764 BEETHOVEN: Bagatelle, no. 25, A minor. CHOPIN: Nocturnes, op. 9, no. 2, E flat major; op. 27, E minor. DEBUSSY: Suite bergamasque: Clair de lune. HANDEL: Air and variations (The harmonious blacksmith). MOZART: Sonata, piano, no. 11, K 331, A major: Turkish march. Fantasia, K 397, D minor. SCHUBERT: Moment musicaux, op. 94, no. 3, D 780, F minor. SCHUMANN: Kinderscenen, op. 15: Traumerei. Romance, op. 28, no. 2, F sharp major. SIBELIUS: Romance, op. 24, no. 9, D flat major. John O'Connor, pno.
+-FF 9/10-80 p263 +-HFN 7-81 p78

OX 7191
3765 ALBENIZ: Mallorca, op. 202. BARRIOS MANGORE: Choro de Saudade. PONCE: Scherzino mexicano. SOR: Variations on a theme by Mozart, op. 9. TARREGA: Estudio brillante (Alard). Recuerdos de la Alhambra. VILLA-LOBOS: Choro, no. 1, E minor. Machiko Kikuchi, gtr.
-FF 7/8-81 p216

DESTO

DC 7194 (also CMS/Oryx 82)
3766 ARCADELT: Ancidetimi pur. Da si felice sorte. Donna quando pietosa. ATTAIGNANT: Branles (5). DALLA CASA: Ancor che col partire. CRECQUILLON: Toutes les nuictz. FONTANA: Madonna mia pieta. MILANO: Fantasia. Ricercar. NOLA: Chi la gagliarda. LASSUS: Bonjour mon coeur. La nuit froide et sombre. ROQUELAY: Ta bonne grace. RORE: Anchor che col partire. SERMISY: A douce amour. London Pro Musica.
*ARG 2-81 p48 +St 10-80 p128
+FF 5/6-81 p198

DC 7197/8 (2)
3767 ALBINONI: Concerto, op. 5, no. 5, A minor. BACH: Brandenburg concerto, no. 3, S 1048, G major. TELEMANN: Concerto, flute, oboe d'amore, viola d'amore and strings, E major. Suite, 2 horns,

2 oboes, bassoon and strings, D major. VIVALDI: Concerto, op. 8, no. 2, G minor. Concerto, op. 10, no. 3, D major. Concerto, piccolo, RV 443, C major. WERNER: Musical calendar: May. Theodora Sommer, pic; Rainer Kussmaul, vln, vla d'amore; Doris Ziegenfelder, Alexander Magnin, flt; Marga Scheurich, hpd; Lola Bobesco, vln; Kietmar Keller, ob d'amore; Heidelberg Chamber Orchestra.
+-ARG 4-81 p42 +-FF 5/6-81 p214

DEUTSCHE GRAMMOPHON

2532 002 Tape (c) 3302 002
3768 OFFENBACH: Orpheus in the underworld: Overture. STRAUSS, J. I: Radetzky march, op. 228. STRAUSS, J. II: An der schonen blauen Donau, op. 314. Banditen, op. 378. Fata morgana, op. 330. Die Fledermaus, op. 363: Overture; Czardas. Kaiserwalzer, op. 437. Neue Pizzicato, op. 449. Perpetuum mobile, op. 257. Wiener Blut, op. 354. STRAUSS, Josef: Eingesendent, op. 240. ZIEHRER: Loslassen, op. 386. VPO; Lorin Maazel.
+-ARG 11-81 p50 +HFN 4-81 p83 tape
+-FF 3/4-81 p181 +NR 5-81 p6
+-Gr 1-81 p1002 +SFC 4-5-81 p18
+HF 10-81 p91 tape ++St 5-81 p88
+HFN 1-81 p105 +St 8-81 p105

2532 009 Tape (c) 3302 009
3769 BIZET: Carmen: La fleur que tu m'avais jetee. Les pecheurs de perles: Je crois entendre encore. DONIZETTI: L'elisir d'amore: Una furtiva lagrima. Lucia di Lammermoor: Tombe degl'avi miei. HALEVY: La Juive: Rachel quand du seigneur. MEYERBEER: L'Africaine: Pays merveilleux...O paradis. VERDI: Aida: Se quel guerrier io fossi...Celeste Aida. Ernani: Merce diletti amici ...Come rugiada al cespite...O tu che l'alma adora. Il trovatore: Ah si ben mio...Di quella pira. Placido Domingo, t; Roger Wagner Chorale; LAPO; Carlo Maria Giulini.
+Gr 10-81 p610 ++Op 11-81 p1152
+-ON 11-81 p68

DG 2533 443
3770 Easter on Mount Athos: Morning liturgy on Good Friday and Holy Saturday. Xenophontos Monastery Monks; Abbot Alexios.
+Gr 1-81 p985

2533 446
3771 Easter on Mount Athos: Office of Easter. Xenophontos Monastery Community; Abbot Alexios.
+-Gr 1-81 p985 +-RR 5-80 p95
+HFN 6-80 p113

2533 451
3772 Russian orthodox music: Liturgy for All Saints Day. Trinity St. Sergius Monastery Priests Choir.
+-FF 3/4-81 p222 +HFN 11-80 p125
+-Gr 11-80 p731 +NR 3-81 p10

2533 457
3773 Celebration of the Feast of St. Ivan of Rila: Evening service; Morning service. St. Ivan Rilski Monastery Monks.
++Gr 8-81 p307 +HFN 7-81 p77

2535 385 Tape (c) 3335 385 (From 2530 792)
3774 STOELZEL: Concerto, trumpet, D major. TELEMANN: Concerto, trumpet, D major. TORELLI: Concerto, trumpet, D major. VIVALDI: Concerto, 2 trumpets, C major. VIVIANI: Sonata, trumpet, no. 1, C major. Maurice Andre, tpt; Maurits Sillem, hpd; Hedwig Bilgram, org; ECO; Charles Mackerras.
+Gr 10-81 p567

2536 410 Tape (c) 3336 410
3775 ECCARD: Over the mountains Mary goes; Von der Geburt Christi. FREUNDT: Wie schon singt uns der Engel Schar. GABRIELI, G.: Benedixisti domine. GUMPELZHAIMER: Vom Himmel hoch. GRUBER: Stille Nacht heilige Nacht. HASSLER: Verbum caro factum est. LOEWE: Quem pastores laudavere. PALESTRINA: Hodie Christus natus est. PRAETORIUS: Est is ein Ros entsprungen. REICHARDT: Heilige Nacht. RUDIGER: Still o Himmel; Es bluhen die Maien. SCHEIDT: O Jesulein zart. THIEL: Adeste fideles; Freu dich Erd und Sternenzelt. TRAD.: Auf dem Berge da geht der Wind; O sanctissima; O schlafe gottlicher Knabe. Regensburger Domspatzen; Georg Ratzinger.
+FF 11/12-81 p286
+Gr 12-80 p889 tape
+HFN 11-80 p124
+HFN 12-80 p159 tape
+NR 11-80 p1
+SFC 12-14-80 p20

2547 028 Tape (c) 3347 028 (From APM 14002)
3776 Gregorian chant: Prima missa in commemoratione omnium fidelium defunctorum. Benedictine Abbey of St. Martin Monks Choir; Maurus Pfaff.
+-Gr 11-80 p728
+Gr 2-81 p1122 tape
+-HFN 1-81 p109

2547 029 Tape (c) 3347 029 (From SAPM 198323)
3777 BRUMEL: Noe noe; Tandernac. FESTA: Quis dabit oculis nostris. HOFHAIMER: Tandernaken. ISAAC: A la bataglia; An buos; Carmen in fa; Fortuna in mi; Imperii proceres; Innsbruck ich muss dich lassen; J'ay pris amours; La morra; San Sancti spiritus assit nobis gratia. JOSQUIN DES PRES: Comment peult. OBRECHT: Vavilment. RUE: Fors seulement. SENFL: Carmen in la; Carmen in re; Nasci pati mori. ANON.: Carmen Hercules; En l'ombre d'un buissonet; Naves pont; Si je perdu. Vienna Boys Choir, Vienna Chorus; VCM; Nikolaus Harnoncourt.
+Gr 11-80 p731
+HFN 1-81 p109 tape

2547 049 Tape (c) 3347 049 (From 198458)
3778 ALBERTO: Piece, 3 parts. CABEZON: Diferencias sobre la gallarda milanesa. Diferencias sobre el canto llano del caballero. Pavana con su glosa. Pavana italiana. FERNANDEZ DE HUETE: Cancion italiana con diferencias. Cancion francesa, Monsieur de la boleta. MUDARRA: Tiento para harpa. PALERO: Paseababase el rey moro. Pues no me querreis hablar. RODRIGUEZ: Toccata, no. 2. ANON.: Bacas. Folias. Pabanas. Paraderas. Hachas. Ribayas. Seguidillas. Nicanor Zabaleta, hp.
+Gr 4-81 p1351
+Gr 9-81 p460
+HFN 7-81 p83 tape
+HFN 8-81 p92

2547 951 Tape (c) 3347 051 (From 2723 045)
3779 LEONIN: Viderunt omnes. MACHAUT: Christi qui lux es: Veni creator spiritus. Hoquetus David. Lasse: Se j'aim mon loyal ami; Pour quoy. PEROTINUS LE GRAND: Viderunt omnes. ROYLLART: Rex Karole: Leticie. VITRY: Impudenter; Virtutibus laudabilis.

ANON.: Clap clap; Sus Robin. Early Music Consort; David Munrow.
+Gr 6-81 p81 ++HFN 7-81 p81
+Gr 9-81 p460 tape +HFN 7-81 p83 tape

2547 059 Tape (c) 3347 059 (From SAPM 139431)

3780 Christmas in the holy land: Liturgical music from different rites. Various artists.
+Gr 12-81 p924

2721 202 (10)

3781 BEETHOVEN: Egmont, op. 84: Overture. Symphony, no. 5, op. 67, C minor. BRAHMS: Symphony, no. 1, op. 68, C minor. BRUCKNER: Symphony, no. 7, E major. FURTWANGLER: Symphony, no. 2, E minor. HAYDN: Symphony, no. 88, G major. MOZART: Symphony, no. 39, K 543, E flat major. SCHUBERT: Symphony, no. 8, D 759, B minor. Symphony, no. 9, D 944, C major. SCHUMANN: Symphony, no. 4, op. 120, D minor. STRAUSS, R.: Don Juan, op. 20. Till Eulenspiegel's lustige Streiche, op. 28. WAGNER: Die Meistersinger von Nurnberg: Prelude. Parsifal: Good Friday music. BPhO; Wilhelm Furtwangler.
+-FF 7/8-81 p228

2723 068 (3)

3782 CANNABICH: Sinfonia concertante, C major. Sinfonia, B flat major. FILTZ: Concerto, violoncello, G major. HOLZBAUER: Sinfonia, op. 4, no. 3, E flat major. Sinfonia concertante, A major. LEBRUN: Concerto, oboe, D minor. RICHTER: Concerto, flute, E minor. Symphony, B flat major. STAMITZ, J.: Concerto, violin, C major. Trio, op. 1, no. 5, B flat major. Thomas Furi, vln; Jorg Dahler, hpd; Heinz Holliger, ob; Berne Camerata; Thomas Furi.
+Audio 9-81 p84 +HFN 11-80 p128
+FF 7/8-81 p224 +NR 4-81 p4
++Gr 11-80 p684 +St 9-81 p100
++HF 6-81 p49

2723 078 (3)

3783 BACH: Sonata, harpsichord, S 965, A minor. BUXTEHUDE: Sonatas, op. 1, nos. 2-4. PACHELBEL: Aria con variazioni, A major. Canon and gigue, D major. Suites, G major, E minor. REINCKEN: Sonatas, A minor, E minor. ROSENMULLER: Sonatas, C major, E minor, B flat major. SCHENCK: Suite, D major. WESTHOFF: Sonata, A major. Cologne Musica Antiqua.
+Gr 10-81 p574 +HFN 10-81 p93

2726 004 (2) Tape (c) 3372 004

3784 Gregorian chant: Alta trinita beata; Chants for the Feast of Corpus Christi. Chants for the penitential season. Concordi laetitia. Cristo risusciti in tutti i cuori. De la crudel morte di Cristo. Laude nouvelle sia cantata. Laudar vollio. Martir glorioso aulente flore. O spea mea cara. O Virgo pulcherrima. Omne omo ad alta voce. Plainsong melodies for the commemoration of the Lord's supper on Maundy Thursday. Puer natus in Bethlehem. Troppo perde 'l tempo. Venite a laudare. Capella Papale di San Francesco d'Assisi Choir; Alfonso del Ferraro.
-Gr 5-73 p2092 +HFN 1-81 p109 tape
+-HFN 4-73 p789 +-RR 4-73 p80

2740 229 (5) (From 2530 225, 2530 901, 2530 531, 2530 803, 2530 436, 2531 004)

3785 BARTOK: Concerti, piano, nos. 1 and 2. BOULEZ: Sonata, piano, no.

2. NONO: Como una ola de fuerza y luz. Sofferte onde serene. PROKOFIEV: Sonata, piano, no. 7, op. 83, B flat major. SCHOENBERG: Pieces, piano, op. 11 (3); op. 19 (6); op. 23 (5); op. 33 (2). Suite, op. 25. STRAVINSKY: Petrouchka: Movements (3). WEBERN: Variations, op. 27. Slava Taskova, s; Maurizio Pollini, pno; CSO, Bavarian Radio Orchestra; Claudio Abbado.

+CL 9-81 p18
+FF 9/10-81 p230
+Gr 8-80 p242
++HF 3-81 p56
+HFN 10-80 p115
+NR 2-81 p15
++SFC 2-1-81 p18
+SR 5-81 p96
+STL 8-10-80 p30

DORDT COLLEGE

Unnumbered

3786 EBEN: Sonntagsmusik: Moto ostinato. KRAPF: Fantasy on Psalm CL. LISZT: Prelude and fugue on the name B-A-C-H, S 260. PACHELBEL: Vom Himmel hoch. SWEELINCK: Fantasia en echo. NOORDT: Psalm, no. 116. WALCHA: O Mensch bewein. WIDOR: Symphony, organ, no. 6, op. 42, no. 2, G major: Allegro moderato. Joan Ringerwole, org.

+-MU 3-81 p12

EMI

1C 037 00422

3787 BERLIOZ: Les Troyens: Royal hunt and storm. GRANADOS: Goyescas: Intermezzo. LEONCAVALLO: I Pagliacci: Intermezzo. MASCAGNI: L'Amico Fritz: Intermezzo. MUSSORGSKY: Khovanschina: Intermezzo, Act 4. OFFENBACH: Les contes de Hoffmann: Barcarolle. PUCCINI: Manon Lescaut: Intermezzo, Act 3. SCHMIDT: Notre Dame: Intermezzo. VERDI: La traviata: Prelude, Act 3. PhO; Herbert von Karajan.

+-FF 9/10-81 p289

1C 063 45713

3788 FRANCAIX: Serenade. LACHNER: Elegy, op. 160. OFFENBACH: Pariser Leben: Pas de six. ROSETTI: Quartet, 4 violoncelli, B major. TCHAIKOVSKY: Quartet, strings, no. 1, op. 11, D major: Andante cantabile. Cologne Philharmonic Cellists; Werner Thomas.

+FF 9/10-81 p280

1C 063 46134

3789 BALAKIREV: Romance. BIALAS: Puss in boots. LOPEZ BUCHARDO: Bailecito. FRANCHOMME: Valse de Chopin. GINASTERRA: Danza de la moza donosa. MILHAUD: Saudades du Brasil: Tijuca. Scaramouche: Braziliera. OFFENBACH: Harmonies du soir. THOMAS-MIFUNE: Drunken rag. Tango peleado. WAGENSEIL: Suite of pieces, 3 violoncelli and bass. Cologne Philharmonic Cellists; Werner Thomas.

+FF 9/10-81 p280

1C 065 30992

3790 CHERUBINI: Ave Maria. GUGLIELMI: Gratias agimus. MOZART: Songs:

Cor sincerum amore plenum, K 505; Mens sancta Deo chara (attrib.). PAER: Beatus vir. PAISIELLO: Accensa clare face fidelis. SARTI: Si tranquilla. SALIERI: O mortales festinate. SCHUBERT: Offertorium, D 136. Rachel Yakar, s; Dieter Klocker, clt; Berlin RIAS Sinfonietta; Erno Sebestyen.
+Gr 9-81 p422

1C 137 53508/13 (6)
3791 BEETHOVEN: Symphony, no. 9, op. 125, D minor. BERGER: Rondino giocoso, op. 4. BRAHMS: Symphony, no. 4, op. 98, E minor. BRUCKNER: Symphony, no. 4, E flat major. Symphony, no. 5, B flat major. PFITZNER: Symphony, op. 46, C major. REGER: Variations and fugue on a theme by Mozart, op. 132, A major. STRAUSS, R.: Till Eulenspiegels lustige Streiche, op. 28. Don Juan, op. 20. Margarete Teschemacher, s; Elisabeth Hongen, con; Torsten Ralf, t; Josef Hermann, bar; Dresden State Opera Chorus; Dresden Staatskapelle; Karl Bohm.
+ARG 1-81 p52 +FF 9/10-80 p291

1C 149 03584/6 (3)
3792 BEETHOVEN: Fidelio, op. 72: Overture. BERLIOZ: La damnation de Faust, op. 24: Rakoczy march. BRAHMS: Hungarian dances, nos. 1, 3, 10. CHERUBINI: Anacreon: Overture. GLUCK: Alceste: Overture. Iphigenie in Aulis: Overture. LISZT: Les preludes, S 97. MENDELSSOHN: Hebrides overture, op. 27. MOZART: Serenade, no. 13, K 525, G major. NICOLAI: The merry wives of Windsor: Overture. SCHUBERT: Rosamunde, op. 26, D 797: Overture; Ballet music, no. 2; Entr'acte no. 3. SMETANA: Ma Vlast: Vltava. STRAUSS, J. II/Joseph: Pizzicato polka. TCHAIKOVSKY: Serenade, op. 48, C major: Waltz and finale. WEBER: Der Freischutz: Overture. Euryanthe: Overture. Oberon: Overture. VPO; Wilhelm Furtwangler.
++FF 9/10-81 p293 +Gr 12-80 p881

1C 151 45392/3 (2)
3793 BAERMANN: Quintet, clarinet, op. 23: Adagio. BOCHSA: Sonata, clarinet and piano. DEBUSSY: Petite piece, clarinet and piano. Rhapsody, clarinet, no. 1. LUTOSLAWSKI: Dance preludes. REISSIGER: Duo brillant, op. 130. RUDOLF, Archduke of Austria: Theme and variations, clarinet and piano. SCHUMANN: Fantasiestucke, op. 73. STRAVINSKY: Pieces, solo clarinet (3). Dieter Klocker, clt; Werner Genuit, pno.
+FF 5/6-81 p210

1C 157 30762/6 (5)
3794 ABEL: Symphony concertante, B flat major. CRUSELL: Symphony concertante, op. 3, B flat major. DANZI: Symphony concertante, op. 41, B major. HOFFMEISTER: Symphonie concertante, E flat major, B flat major. KOZELUCH: Symphony concertante, E flat major. PLEYEL: Symphony concertante, op. 57, A major. RITTER: Symphony concertante, F major. SCHNEIDER: Symphony concertante, op. 19, D major. WINTER: Symphony concertante, B flat major. Consortium Classicum, AMF; Iona Brown.
+Gr 4-81 p1328

ENIGMA

VAR 1015 (also Nonesuch H 71390, also ASV ACM 2003 Tape (c) ZCACM 2003)
3795 PUJOL VILARRUBI: Guajira. Tango. RODRIGO: Fandango. Pequenas sevillanas. Ya se van los pastores. SANZ: Espanoleta. Canarios. SOR: Fantasia elegiaca, op. 59. TARREGA: Capricho arabe. Gran jota. Maria. Sueno. TORROBA: Burgalesa. TRAD.: Brincan y bailan. Don Gato. La serrana. Ya se van la paloma. (all. arr. Bonell). Carlos Bonell, gtr.
+Audio 6-81 p14 +Gr 6-81 p65
+-FF 7/8-81 p216 +HFN 1-77 p107
+Gr 12-76 p1027 +RR 12-76 p84

ERATO

STU 70662 (also Musical Heritage Society MHS 3591 Tape (c) MHC 5591)
3796 BACH: Magnificat, S 243, D major: Arioso, fanfare and fugue. Cantata, no. 147, Jesus bleibet meine Freude. COLOMBIER: Sextet, op. 335. FAURE: Cantique de Racine. HANDEL: Water music: Suite. Messiah: Alleluia. RAMEAU: Hymne a la nuit. ANON.: Cortege en fauxbourdon. Ars Nova Brass Quintet; Xavier Darasse, org.
+Gr 3-72 p1546 +MU 10-81 p8 tape
+-MU 9-81 p14

STU 71285
3797 Officium festi fatuorum: Office des fous, messe de l'Ane. Guillaume Dufay Ensemble Vocal et Instrumental; Arsene Bedois.
+FF 3/4-81 p225

STU 71410
3798 ARNOLD: Quintet, brass, op. 37. FARNABY: Fancies toyes and dreames: The old spagnoletta; His rest; Tell me Daphne; A toye; His dreame; The new Sa-Hoo (arr. Howarth). HOLBORNE: Suite of Elizabethan dances: The honie-suckle; Wanton; The fruit of love; The choise; The fairie-round. Galliards, nos. 1 and 2. PURCELL (trans. Corley): Trumpet voluntary. SCHEIDT, S.: (arr. Jones): Battle suite: Galliard battaglia; Courant dolorosa; Canzon bergamasque. Budapest Brass Quintet.
+Gr 10-81 p579

STU 71415
3799 ALAIN: Toccata on "Cantemus domino". BACH: Toccata and fugue, S 565, D minor. BOELLMANN: Suite, no. 2, op. 27: Toccata, C minor. BOELY: Fantasy, B flat major. DUBOIS: Toccata, G major. GIGOUT: Toccata, B minor. VIERNE: Fantasiestucke, op. 54: Carillon de Westminster. Suite, no. 2, op. 53: Toccata, B minor. WIDOR: Symphony, organ, no. 5, op. 42, no. 1, F minor: Toccata. Marie-Claire Alain, org.
+Gr 9-81 p417

EURODISC

200 089 Tape (c) 400 089
3800 d'ALBERT: Tiefland: Wolfserzahlung. GLUCK: Iphigenie en Tauride:

Nur einen Wunsch nur ein verlangen. FLOTOW: Martha: Ach so fromm ach so traut. KORNGOLD: Die tote Stadt: Gluck das mir verblieb. NICOLAI: Die lustigen Weiber von Windsor: Horch die Lerche singt im Hain. WAGNER: Parsifal: Amfortas die Wunde. Rienzi: Allmacht'ger Vater. WEBER: Der Freischutz: Durch die Walder durch die Auen. Oberton: Von Jugend auf in dem Kampfgefild. Siegfried Jerusalem, t; Munich Radio Orchestra; Heinz Wallberg.

+-Gr 12-81 p934 +HFN 12-81 p107
+HF 11-81 p103 tape ++St 12-81 p132

201 974-366 (From Melodiya S 10 11415/6)

3801 BEETHOVEN: There once was a king, op. 75, no. 3 (arr. Shostakovich). RIMSKY-KORSAKOV: I waited for thee at the appointed hour, op. 40, no. 4 (arr. Shostakovich). SCARLATTI: Sonatas, D minor, E major (arr. Shostakovich). SHOSTAKOVICH: Overture, op. 23. The tale of the priest and his servant Baldaj: Suite, op. 36 (film score). Two fables of Krilov, op. 4: The dragonfly and the ant; The ass and the nightingale. STRAUSS, J. II: Vergnugungszug, op. 281 (arr. Shostakovich). YOUMANS: Tea for two (arr. Shostakovich). Galina Borissova, ms; Alla Abladerdizheva, s; USSR Chamber Orchestra, MPO; Leningrad Philharmonic Orchestra, USSR Symphony Orchestra; Moscow Conservatory Women's Chorus; Yevgeny Nesterenko, bs; Gennady Rozhdestvensky.

+FF 11/12-81 p243

EVEREST

SDBR 3469

3802 Christmas songs: Silent night; Hark the herald angels sing; See amid the winter snow; We three kings; Away in a manger; The first noel; Good King Wencelas; The holly and the ivy; While shepherds watched; God rest ye merry gentlemen. St. Paul's and St. Mary's Cathedral Choirs.

*FF 11/12-81 p287 +NR 12-80 p1

3474

3803 Gregorian chants, vol. 4. Benedictine Abbey of En Calcat Monks and Trappist Monks.

-FF 5/6-81 p195 +NR 3-81 p10

FINLANDIA

FA 308 (From Finnlevy SFX 32)

3804 ENGLUND: Passacaglia. KOKKONEN: Lux aeterna. MERIKANTO: Passacaglia, op. 80. KUUSISTO: Ramus virens olivarum, op. 55, no. 1. PARVIAINEN: Toccata and fugue. SALONEN: Sen suuven suloisuutta. Tauno Aikaa, org.

+FF 11/12-80 p210 +NR 4-81 p13
+-HFN 12-80 p151

FA 321

3805 BERGMAN: Junibastu. DONNER: En liten konstnar; Etude for sommarvind. FOUGSTEDT: Det gar en liten speleman; Marsbjorkar;

Naktergalen. MADETOJA: Solta somer. PALMGREN: Jaguaren; En latmansmelodi; Hilden orjien laulu. RAUTAVAARA: Huojuva heula; Se var det. WESTERLUND: Host-Vinter. TRAD.: Les compagnons de la Marjolaine (arr. Fougstedt). Etelapohjalainen kansanlaulu (arr. Bergman). Helsink University Academic Male Choir; Markus Westerlund.

+FF 9/10-81 p221 +HFN 10-80 p110
+-FF 11/12-80 p20 +NR 3-81 p8

FIRST PRESBYTERIAN CHURCH

Kilgore, TX unnumbered

3806 BACH: Prelude and fugue, S 552, E flat major. BAIRSTOW: Allegro giocoso. BINGHAM: Roulade. CALLAHAN: Aria. DAQUIN: Noel, no. 10. DAVIES: A solemn melody. KARG-ELERT: Ach bleib mit deiner Gnade, op. 65, no. 1. LIDON: Sonata da primo tono. MANZ: God of grace. NOLTE: In dir ist Freude. REGER: Pieces, organ, op. 59: Benedictus. SIMONDS: Prelude on "Iam sol". WIDOR: Salve regina. Neal Campbell, James Lynn Culp, Stephen Farrow, William Teague, org.

+MU 10-81 p12

FOLIO SOCIETY

FS 1001/2 (2)

3807 BACH, C.P.E.: Sonata, no. 5, C major. BACH, J.S.: Ein musicalischer Opfer, S 1079: Ricercar a 3 voci. Canon perpetuo. Trio sonata. BYRD: La volta. COUPERIN, F.: Concert Royaux IV. DOWLAND: Queen Elizabeth her galliard. FREDERICK II, King: Sonata, flute, B minor. IVES, S.: The virgin: Fancy. Pavan. Ayre. Coranto. JOHNSON, E.: Eliza is the fairest queen. LANIER: Mark how the blushful morn. MOZART: Church sonatas, no. 1, K 67, E flat major; no. 17, K 336, C major. RAMSEY: What tears dear prince can serve. SCARLATTI, D.: Sonatas, harpsichord, Kk 144, 149, 193, 274. TOMKINS: A sad pavan for these distracted times. ANON.: The Queen of Bohemia's dumpe. La royne d'Ecosse galliard. Paul Elliot, t; Academy of Ancient Music; Christopher Hogwood, hpd.

+Gr 4-81 p1361 +HFN 12-80 p149

1007/8 (2)

3808 CAVALLI: Canzon a 3. CIMA: Canzona. La novella. GABRIELI, A.: Intonatione del primo tono. GABRIELI, G.: Intonatione del primo tono. Fuga del nono tono. Sonata con tre violini. GRANDI: O intemerata. LEGRENZI: La pezzoli, op. 4, no. 6. MARCELLO, A.: Concerto, oboe, D minor. MARINI: Sonata a tre, op. 22. MONTEVERDI: Exulta filia Sion. Laudate Dominum. Sancta Maria. Salve Regina. Salve o Regina. SPIRIDION: Toccatina, no. 1. VIVALDI: Amor hai vinto, RV 651. Concerto, flute, RV 443, C major. Trio sonata, RV 63, D minor. Academy of Ancient Music; Christopher Hogwood.

+Gr 6-81 p81 +HFN 2-81 p97

FOURTH PRESBYTERIAN CHURCH

Chicago, unnumbered

3809 ANDERSON (ar.): How firm a foundation. DARKE: In the bleak midwinter. FRANCK: Domine non secundum. HOWELLS: A spotless rose. PEPPING: Ich steh an deiner Krippe hier. PINKHAM: The kings and shepherds. SCHROEDER: In dulci jubilo. VAUGHAN WILLIAMS: Rhosymedre; Lord thou hast been our refuge. HYMN (arr. Johnson): Guide me O thou great Jehovah; The lone wild bird; Lovely child. Morgan Simmons, org and choirmaster; Morning Choir Fourth Presbyterian Church.
+MU 3-81 p12

GAMUT

UT 7501

3810 BRISTOL: Let your bearing in life. DAWSON (arr.): Good news. Hymn settings; Amazing grace; At the river; Copland; Furnivall. DIRKSEN: Rejoice ye pure in heart (arr. Dawson). ROREM: Motets on poems of Manley Hopkins (3). SOWERBY: I was glad when they said unto me. WYTON: A hymne to God the father. Trinity Church Choir, Princeton; Harold Pysher, Irene Willis, org; James Litton.
+FF 9/10-81 p223 +NR 3-81 p8
+Gr 3-81 p1224

UT 7502

3811 BACH: Chorale prelude, S 63, Liebster Jesu wir sind hier. Fantasia and fugue, S 542, G minor. COUPERIN: Messe pour les couvents: Movements. DUPRE: Prelude and fugue, op. 7, no. 1, B major. MENDELSSOHN: Sonata, organ, op. 65, no. 2, C minor. MESSIAEN: Messe de la pentecote: Communion; Sortie. Francis Grier, org.
+-FF 9/10-81 p249 +Gr 2-81 p1104
+FF 11/12-81 p291 +NR 3-81 p14

UT 7503

3812 BACH: Passacaglia and fugue, S 582, C minor. BALBASTRE: Au jo deu de pubelle. Grand dei ribon ribeine. CORRETTE: Livre de orgue, no. 3: Suite, D minor. BUXTEHUDE: Prelude, A minor. GUILAIN: Pieces d'orgue pour le Magnificat sur les huit tons differens de l'Eglise: Suite, G minor. SCHEIDT: Variations on a galliard of John Dowland. John Kitchen, org.
+-Gr 9-81 p417 +-HFN 9-81 p87

GASPARO

GS 206

3813 ARIOSTI: Le profezie d'Eliseo nel'assedio di Samaria: Ma per destin peggiore...Prole tenera. BIBER: Sonata, solo violin, no. 6. FUX: Gli ossequi della notte: Caro mio ben. LIDL: Trio, violin, violoncello and viola da gamba, E major.

SCHENCK: L'Echo du Danube: Sonata, no. 2. Oberlin Baroque Performance Institute Members; August Wenzinger.

+Audio 6-81 p16 +FF 9/10-80 p284
+IN 7-81 p28 ++St 9-80 p84
++NR 10-80 p7

GEMINI HALL

RAP 1010 (2)

3814 AMALIA, Princess of Prussia: Regimental marches (3). ANNA AMALIA, Duchess of Saxe-Weimar: Erwin and Elmire, excerpt. ANDREE: Quintet, E major: Allegro molto vivace. BOULANGER, L.: Clairieres dans le ciel, excerpts. Nocturne. BRONSART: Jery und Bately: Lied and duet. CACCINI, F.: La liberazione di Ruggiero dall'Isola d'Alcina, excerpta. CHAMINADE: Caprice espagnole. FARRENC: Quintet: Scherzo. JACQUET DE LA GUERRE: Jacob et Rachel: Air. Susanne: Recitative and air. HERITTE-VIARDOT: Quartet: Serenade. LANG: Sie liebt mich. MALIBRAN: Le reveil d'un beau jour. MENDELSSOHN-HENSEL: Bergeslust. Italien. PARADIS: Sicilienne. POLDOWSKI: Impression fausse. SCHUMANN, C.: Das ist ein Tag. Impromptu. Liebst du um Schonheit. TAILLEFERRE: Quatuor. VIARDOT-GARCIA: Dites que fait-il faire. Fluestern athemscheues Lauschen. Die Sterne. Berenice Bramson, Marton Johns, s; Thomas Theis, bs; Michael May, pno, hpd; Vieuxtemps String Quartet; Roger Rundle, pno; Yvonne Cable, vlc.

+AR 8-81 p79 +NR 4-76 p15
*MJ 11-76 p44 +St 5-76 p124

GOLDEN CREST

CRS 4191

3815 GIBSON: Quintet, winds. IANNACONNE: Parodies. PERLE: Quintet, woodwinds, no. 3. ROSS: Divertimento. SCHICKELE: Diversions. TANG: A little suite. Clarion Wind Quintet.

+ARG 11-80 p49 +FF 9/10-81 p278

CRS 4196

3816 ANDERSON: Blue tango. Forgotten dreams. Syncopated clock. BACH (Parker): Joy. BEETHOVEN: Sonata, piano, no. 14, op. 27, no. 2, C sharp minor. BRAHMS: Intermezzo. DEBUSSY: Suite bergamasque: Clair de lune. DUSSEK: Sonatina. HANDEL: Sarabande. LAI: A man and a woman. MOZART: Bourree. RATHGEBER: Aria pastorella. SCHOLZ: Menuett. SCHWARTZ: Godspell: On the willows, Day by day. Martin Ringers; Richard Litterst.

+Audio 10-81 p26 +NR 6-81 p15
+MU 11-81 p16

CRS 4202 (6)

3817 ALBENIZ (arr. Caillet): Iberia: Fete Dieu a Seville. ALEXANDER (arr. Bainum): The southerner march. ALFORD: A step ahead. BACH (arr. Leidzen): Toccata and fugue, D minor. BENNETT: Symphonic songs. BERLIOZ (arr. Smith): Damnation of Faust,

OP. 24: March hongroise. BILLINGS: When Jesus wept. DELLO JOIO: Variants from a medieval tune. ELGAR (arr. Slocum): Enigma variations, op. 36. GIANNINI: Praeludium and allegro. Variations and fugue. GOLDMAN: March on the Hudson. GOULD (arr. Lang): American salute. Folk suite. St. Lawrence suite. HANDEL (arr. Kay): Water music: Suite. KING: The huntress. LALO (arr. Godfrey): Le Roi d'Ys: Overture. MASSENET (arr. Harding): Thais: Meditation. MENOTTI (arr. Lang): Overture and caccia. NIXON: Fiesta del pacifico. PERSICHETTI: Symphony, band. PROKOFIEV (arr. Yoder): March, op. 99. RENEE (arr. Werle): Passions in paint. RODGERS (arr. Werle): South Pacific: Scenario. SAINT-SAENS (arr. Godfrey): March militaire francaise. SCHULLER: Meditation. SESSIONS (arr. Bancroft): Black maskers suite: Finale. SMETANA (arr. Nelhybel): Revolutionary marches (3). SOUSA: The free lance. Stars and stripes forever. George Washington bicentennial march. STRAUSS, J. II (arr. Cailliet): Die Fledermaus, op. 363: Overture. SURINACH: Ritmo jondo. VERDI: Requiem (Manzini), excerpts. WAGNER (arr. Cailliet): Lohengrin: Elsa's processional to the cathedral. Tristan und Isolde: Liebestod. WEINBERGER (arr. Bainum): Schwanda the bagpiper: Polka and fugue. YODER: Relax. University of Michigan Symphony Band; William Revelli.

++ARG 9-81 p40

CRDG 4203

3818 DIRKSEN: Welcome all wonders, excerpt. HOLST: Christmas day. MAHLER: Symphony, no. 2, C minor: Finale. NEAR: Arise my love my fair one. NEUMANN: Truly we shall be in paradise with him. PEHKONEN: A boy is born. PURCELL: Abdelazar: Rondeau (arr. Gordon). RUTTER: A Gaelic blessing. WILLIAMS: Darest thou now O soul; In the year that King Uzziah died. ANON.: (Flemish): O leave your sheep. Christ Congregational Church, Silver Spring, Md, Orchestra and Chorus; Alfred Neumann.

+NR 11-81 p9

RE 7091

3819 BOZZA: Pulcinella, op. 53, no. 1. CRESTON: Sonata, saxophone and piano. DEL BORGO: Canto. ECCLES (trans. Rascher): Sonata, G minor. IBERT: Aria. PERSICHETTI: Parable XI. Dale Underwood, saxophone; Kate Lewis, pno.

+-FF 5/6-81 p211

RE 7099

3820 DEBUSSY: Suite bergamasque: Clair de lune. GODARD: Idylle. GIOVANNINI: Morocco. LEGRAND: Brian's song. KOSINS: Love letters. MARCELLO, B.: Sonata, flute, F major. MOZART: Sonata, flute and piano, no. 5, K 14, C major. Mark Thomas, flt; Christine Croshaw, pno.

+NR 11-81 p7

GOTHIC

2797 9802

3821 FARNHAM: Toccata on "O filii et filiae". GIGOUT: Grand choeur

dialogue. KARG-ELERT: Abide O dearest Jesus. LANGLAIS: Te deum. WEINBERGER: The way to Emmaus. Frederick Swann, org.
+-NR 1-81 p12

2797 9803

3822 BYRD: Sacerdotes domini. DRISCHNER: Chorale partita on "Praise to be Lord the almighty". DUPRE: Preludes and fugues, op. 7: Prelude, B major. DURUFLE: Suite, organ, op. 2, no. 5: Prelude. ELGAR: Ave verum. HEWITT-JONES: Fanfare. arr. MACDONALD: Lourdes hymn. Salve regina coelitum. MOZART: Jubilate deo. VICTORIA: Jesu dulcis memoria. VIERNE: Suite, no. 4, op. 55: Naiades. WALKER: I will lift up mine eyes. WILLIAMSON: Epiphany carol. GREGORIAN CHANT, 13th century: Divinum mysterium. KATHOLISCHES GESANGBUCH: Holy God we praise thy name. Soloists; Chorus; Robert MacDonald, org.
++NR 1-81 p12

GRAND PRIX

GP 9003

3823 BENATZKY: Ich muss wieder einmal. BLECH: Telefonische Bestellung. DEBUSSY: Songs: Ballade des femmes de Paris; C'est l'extase langoureuse. DUPARC: Phidyle. DVORAK: Songs, op. 55: Songs my mother taught me. GRIEG: Thanks for advice. KALMAN: Komm Zigany. RONTANI: Or ch'io non seguo piu. ROSA: To be near thee. STOLZ: Im Prater bluh'n wieder die Baume. STRAUSS, R.: Morgen, op. 27, no. 4; Standchen, op. 17, no. 2. VELLONES: Le posson volant. TRAD.: Echo song; Eriskay love lilt; Let us break bread together; Malurous qu'o uno fenno. Dorothy Warenskjold, s; Rolin Jensen, pno.
+FF 9/10-80 p241 +NR 2-81 p12

GUILD

GRS 7008

3824 ATTWOOD: Turn thee again O Lord at the last. BATTEN: O sing joyfully. BATTISHILL: O Lord look down from heaven. BOYCE: I have surely built thee an house. GOSS: Psalms, nos. 127, 128. GREENE: Lord let me know mine end. MACPHERSON: A little organ book: Andante, G major. MENDELSSOHN: Above all praise and majesty. St. Paul: How lovely are the messengers. PARRY: Songs of farewell: My soul there is a country. STAINER: Lord Jesus think on me. St. Paul Cathedral Choir; Barry Rose, org; Christopher Dearnley.
+-Gr 6-77 p90 +MT 1-81 p36
+HFN 6-77 p131 +-RR 6-77 p90

HARMONIA MUNDI

HM 248

3825 Chants a la vierge. Deller Consort.

+FF 5/6-81 p196 +-HFN 6-79 p113
+-Gr 7-79 p234 +-RR 6-79 p111

HM 509

3826 CERNOHORSKY: Fuga moderato. LINEK: Concerto, organ, D major. Fanfares nos. 1-3, 5-6, 13-14. MYSLIVECEK: Suite, strings. TUMA: Parthia, D major. WOTJA: Introduzione et aria. ZACH: Sonata a tre, A major. Pro Arte Antiqua Prague.
+-FF 9/10-80 p285 +HFN 7-78 p95
+FF 1/2-81 p227 ++RR 7-78 p52

1003 Tape (c) 40-1003

3827 Danse anciennes de Hongrie et de Transylvanie. Clemencic Consort; Rene Clemencic.
+ARG 4-81 p54 +HFN 4-79 p134 tape
+FF 5/6-80 p193 +RR 12-78 p92
+HFN 1-79 p124

HM 1025 Tape (c) HM 40-1025

3828 ENCINA: Amor con fortuna contrefacon de Halcon que se atreve. MILAN: Poys dezeys que me quereys ben. Perdid tenyo la color. Toda mi vida hos ame. NARVAEZ: Con que la lavare. PANIAGUA: La begognette. La Edoarda. Fermata. TORRE: Panpano verde. VASQUEZ: Con que la lavare. ANON.: A los banos del amor. A su alvedrio. Con que la lavare. Daca bailemos. Dindirindin. E la don don verges Maria. La mas graciosa serrana (arr. E. and G. Paniagua). Pase el agoa. Pues no mejora mi suerte. Quien vos avia de llevar. Riu riu chiu. So ell enzina. Sola me dexaste. Vesame y abracame. Madrid Atrium Musicae; Gregoria Paniagua.
+FF 5/6-81 p201 +HFN 11-80 p125
+-Gr 3-81 p1224

HM 1039

3829 Popular tunes in 17th century England: London tunes: Hyde Park; Mayden Lane; St. Paul's wharf; Tower Hill; Gray's Inn. Country dances: Cuckolds all in a row; Merry milkmaids we; Woodick; Newcastle. Ballads mentioned by Shakespeare: Callino Casturame; Come live with me and be my love; Light o love; Jog on. 17th century top three-greensleeves: Fortune my foe; Packington's pound. Across the Channel: Chi passa; All in a garden green; La folia; Quarte branles. Across the border: The clean contrary way; Gilderoy; Gillecrankie; The miller of the Dee. Broadside Band; Jeremy Barlow.
+FF 9/10-80 p257 +RR 7-80 p60
+HFN 6-80 p113 ++SFC 12-21-80 p22
*NYT 8-10-80 pD17 ++St 3-81 p98

HM 1044

3830 Gregorian chant: Alleluias and offertories of the Gauls; Alleluia Sancta Michael defende nos; Alleluia non vos relinquam; Offertory Scapulis suis; Alleluia ego sum pastor bonus; Alleluia Martinus; Offertory Martinus igitur; Alleluia Oculis; Alleluia Candor; Alleluia concussum est; Offertory stetit angelus; Alleluia confitebor. Iegor Reznikoff.
+-Gr 1-81 p986 ++HFN 11-80 p124

HM 30010

3831 La ronde autour de l'Europe (French version of the Carl Orff method). D. Pannetier, flt; J. Scortani, M. Janssens, rec; C. Villevieille, ob; P-A. Begou, bsn; M. Mouquin, bs; B. Pornon-

Michelon, gtr; A. Schillinger, narrator and perc; P. Fanise, L. Claesens, M-C. Molin, perc; La Cigale; Christian Wagner.
-FF 1/2-81 p227

027 99795

3832 BACH, C.P.E.: Sonata, no. 1, A minor. BACH, J.S.: Adagio, S 968, G major. Prelude, fugue and allegro, S 998, E major. KERLL: Ciacona, C major. MACQUE: Gagliarden, nos. 1 and 2. MERULA: Toccata im 2 ton. PICCHI: Toccata. SCHEIDEMANN: Balletto. SWEELINCK: Malle Symes. Gustav Leonhardt, hpd.
+-HFN 10-80 p113 ++MT 7-81 p481

1C 065 99824

3833 BIBER: Harmonia artificiosa ariosa, no. 1, D minor. BUXTEHUDE: Sonata, 2 violins, op. 1, no. 5, C major. KUHNEL: Sonata, 2 viola da gamba, E minor. ROSENMULLER: Sonata, 2 violins, no. 2, E minor. SCHENK: La nymphe di Rheno, op. 8: Chaconne, G major. Janine Rubinlicht, vln; Sigiswald Kuijken, vln, vla da gamba; Wieland Kuijken, vla, vla da gamba; Robert Kohnen, hpd.
+FF 5/6-80 p195 +MT 6-81 p394
+HFN 5-80 p133 ++RR 6-80 p72

1C 065 99847

3834 Gregorian chant: Vir Dei benedictus. Benedictine Abbey of Munsterschwarzach Choir; Godehard Joppich.
+-FF 5/6-81 p196 +HFN 4-81 p78

1C 165 99895/6 (2)

3835 BASSANO: Anchor che co'l partire; La bella netta ignuda e bianca mano; Frais et gaillard; Io canterei d'amor; Ricercata prima; Susanne un jour; Tirsi morir volea; Un gay bergier. BOVICELLI: Anchor che co'l partire; Angelus ad pastores ait; Io son ferito. CABEZON: Un gay bergier; Pour un plaisir. LUZZASCHI: Ch'io non t'ami; Aura soave; O primavera. ORTIZ: Recercadas segonda y tercera sobre Doulce memoire. RODRIGUES COELHO: Susanne un jour. ROGNONI, R.: Un gay bergier. ROGNONI TAEGGIO, F.: Pulchra es amica mea. SELMA Y SALAVERDE: Susanne un jour. Schola Cantorum Basiliensis.
+Gr 9-81 p427

HISTORICAL RECORDING ENTERPRISES

HRE 247

3836 DONIZETTI: L'Elisir d'amore: Una furtiva lagrima. GIORDANI: Marcella; Dolce notte misteriosa. Songs: Caro mio ben. GLUCK: Paride ed Elena: O del mio dolce ardor. GOUNOD: Romeo et Juliette: Ah leve toi soleil. LUNA Y CARNE: La mancha: El pan el queso el vino; En el fondo de la mina. MOZART: Don Giovanni, K 527: Il mio tesoro. PERGOLESI: Tre giorni son che nina. SCARLATTI, A.: Pompeo: O cessate di piagarmi. Flavio Cuniberto: Chi vuole innamorarsi. SERRANO: La dolorosa: La roca fria del Calvario. El triest de los tenorios: Te quiero. SOUTILLO Y VERT: El ultimo romantico: Bella enamorada. VERDI: Rigoletto: La donna e mobile. VIVES: La dona Francisquita: Por el humo se sabe. ANON.: Spanish song. Alfredo Kraus, t; Miguel Zanetti, pno.
++FF 1/2-81 p216

HRE 331

3837 BIZET: Carmen: Je dis que rien ne m'epouvante. GOUNOD: Faust: Ah je ris de me voir si belle; Il m'aime il m'aime quel trouble en mon coeur. LEHAR: Giuditta: Meine Lippen sie Kussen so heiss. LEONCAVALLO: I Pagliacci: Balatella; Non mi tentar. PUCCINI: La boheme: Mi chiamano Mimi; Duet, Act 3; Donde lieta usci. Turandot: Scene of Liu's death including Tu che di gel sei cinto. VERDI: La traviata: Sempre libera; Dite alla giovine; Close of Act 3. Diana Soviero, s; Pablo Elvira, bar; Orchestral accompaniments.

+FF 3/4-81 p220

349/3 (3)

3838 BELLINI: I Capuleti ed i Montecchi: Deh tu bell'anima. Songs: Dolente immagine di fille mia; Vaga luna che inargenti. BONONCINI: Vado ben spesso. CARDILLO: Cor 'ngrato. DONIZETTI: Il sospiro; Le crepuscule. FAURE: Apres un reve; Toujours. GIORDANO: Andrea Chenier: Improviso. GOUNOD: Romeo et Juliette: Ah leve-toi soleil. HANDEL: Serse: Ombra mai fu. LARA: Granada. LEONCAVALLO: Lady Chatterton: Tu sola mi rimani. LUNA Y CARNE: En el fondo de la nina; En toda la quintana. MASSENET: Elegie; Ouvre tes yeux bleus. Werther: Pourquoi me reveiller. MEYERBEER: L'Africaine: O paradiso. MOZART: Misero, O sogno o son desto. PUCCINI: Turandot: Nessun dorma. OBRADORS: Corazon porque pasais; Del cabello mas sutil; Chiquitita la novia. ROSSINI: La pietra del paragone: Quell'alme pupille. SCARLATTI, A.: Le violette; Toglietemi la vita ancor; Vieni a stringermi; Gia il sole dal gange; O cessate di piagarmi. SERRANO: El trust de los tenorios: Te quiero. TENAGLIA: Begli occhi merce. TOSTI: Aprile; Vorrei morire; Ideale; Non t'amo piu; Malia. TURINA: Homenage a Lope de Vega. VERDI: Rigoletto: La donna e mobile. ANON.: Pueblita mi pueblo. Alfredo Kraus, Jose Carreras, t; Instrumental accompaniments.

+NR 12-81 p13

352/3 (3)

3839 BELLINI: Norma: Meco al altar. BIZET: Carmen: Flower song: Finale, Act 3. CARDILLO: Core 'ngrato. CAPUA: O sole mio. CILEA: Adriana Lecouvreur: La dolcissima effigie; L'anima ho stanca. CURTIS: Tu ca nun chiagne. DONIZETTI: Lucia di Lammermoor: Fra poco a me ricovero. GIORDANO: Andrea Chenier: Improviso; Credi al destino; Si fui soldato; Come un bel di. GRIEG: I love thee. LEONCAVALLO: I Pagliacci: Un tal gioco; Vesti la giubba; Non Pagliaccio non son. MASCAGNI: Cavalleria rusticana: Siciliana: Addio alla madre; Brindisi. MASSENET: Le Cid: O souverain o juge o pere. Werther: O nature; Un autre est son epoux; Pourquoi me reveiller. MEYERBEER: L'Africaine: O paradiso. MONTEVERDI: Arianna: Lasciatemi morire. PONCHIELLI: La gioconda: Cielo e mar; Deh non tremar. PUCCINI: La boheme: Che gelida manina. La fanciulla del West: Or son sei mesi; Ch'ella mi creda. Tosca: Recondita armonia; E lucevan le stelle. Turandot: Non piangere Liu; Nessun dorma. TOSTI: A vucchella; L'ultima canzone. VERDI: Aida: Celeste Aida. Don Carlo: Io la vidi. Ernani: Come rugiada. La forza del destino: O tu che in seno. Rigoletto: Questa o quella; La donna e mobile. Il

Trovatore: Deserto sulla terra; Mal reggendo; Aria, Act 3, Scene 2. Neapolitan song: I te vurria vasa. ANON.: Italian song. Franco Corelli, t; Instrumental accompaniments.
+NR 12-81 p9

HMV

ESDW 713 (2) Tape (c) TC ESDW 713
3840 ADAM: Giselle: Myrtha's appearance; Giselle's appearance; Giselle's dance; Scene; Albrecht's appearance and scene with Giselle; Willis' scene. AUBER (arr. Lambert): Les rendezvous: Allegro non troppo; Allegro. BERNERS: Wedding bouquet: Tango and waltz. BLISS: Adam Zero: Dance of summer. BOYCE (arr. Lambert): The prospect before us: Fugue, D major. CHOPIN (arr. Lanchbery): A month in the country: Alla Polacca; Andantino; Largo non troppo; Presto, lento quasi adagio, molto piu mosso. COUPERIN, F. (arr. Jacob): Harlequin in the street: Allegro. GORDON: The rake's progress: Sarabande and orgy. LAMBERT: Horoscope: Valse for the Gemini. LANCHBERY: Tales of Beatrix Potter: The mouse waltz. LISZT (orch. Jacob/Lambert): Apparitions: Consolation; Galop. MENDELSSOHN (orch. Jacob): Lord of Burleigh: Agitato; Allegro vivace. MESSAGER: The two pigeons: Gypsies entry; Pepio's entry; Dance of the two pigeons; Theme and variations. PROKOFIEV: Cinderella: Waltz; Midnight. PURCELL (arr. Lambert): Comus: Overture and minuet. SATIE (orch. Debussy): Monotones. Gymnopedies, nos. 1, 3. ROHO; Robert Irving, Yuri Fayer, John Lanchbery, Charles Mackerras.
+-Gr 6-81 p46 +-HFN 9-81 p93 tape

RLS 739 (4)
3841 BACH. W.F.: Air (arr. Kreisler). BRAHMS: Concerto, violin, op. 77, D major. CHAUSSON: Poeme, op. 25, E major. CHOPIN: Nocturne, op. posth, C sharp minor (arr. Rodionov) (2). DEBUSSY: Sonata, violin and piano, G minor. DINICU: Hora staccato (arr. Heifetz). FALLA: La vida breve: Danse espagnole (arr. Kreisler). GLUCK: Orfeo ed Euridice: Melodie. PARADIS: Sicilienne (arr. Dushkin). RAVEL: Piece en forme de habanera, op. 21, no. 2. Tzigane. SCARLATESCU: Bagatelle. SIBELIUS: Concerto, violin, op. 47, D minor. STRAUSS, R.: Sonata, violin and piano, op. 18, E flat major. SUK: Pieces, op. 17. TARTINI: Variations on a theme by Corelli (arr. Kreisler). Ginette Neveu, vln; Jean Neveu, Gustaf Beck, pno; PhO; Walter Susskind.
+Gr 9-80 p354 ++ST 3-81 p817

RLS 748
3842 BRITTEN: Songs: Come you not from Newcastle; The foggy foggy dew; The holy sonnets of John Donne, op. 35; The king is gone a-hunting; O waly waly; The ploughboy; Sonnets of Michelangelo, op. 22 (7). COPLAND: Old American songs. GRAINGER: The jolly-sailor song; Six dukes went a-fishing. PURCELL (arr. Britten): The queen's epicedium. Fantasia, no. 13, F major. SCHUBERT: Auf der Bruck, D 853; Im Fruhling, D 882. Peter Pears, t; Benjamin Britten, pno; Zorian Quartet.

++FF 9/10-81 p215 +NYT 9-21-80 pD22
++Gr 6-80 p60 ++RR 6-80 p83
++HFN 6-80 p113 +STL 7-13-80 p38
+MT 1-81 p36

RLS 756 (2) Tape (C) TC RLS 756

3843 d'ANNIBALE: O paese d'o sole. BELLINI: Fenesta che lucive. BIXIO: Vola vola; Canto ma sotto voce. CILEA: L'Arlesiana: E la solita storia. CURTIS: Voce e notte. DONIZETTI: L'Elisir d'amore: Una furtiva lagrima. Lucia di Lammermoor: Io di te memoria viva...Verrano a te. GAMBARDELLA: O Marinariello. MASCAGNI: L'Amico Fritz: E anche Beppe...O amore. Iris: Oh come al tuo sottice corpo. MASSENET: Manon: Ah dispar vision; Oh dolce incanto...Chiudo gli occhi. PUCCINI: La fanciulla del West: Una parola...Or son sei mesi; Ch' elle mi creda libero. Gianni Schicchi: Avete torto. Tosca: E lucevan le stelle. Turandot: Non piangere Liu; Nessun dorma. TAGLIA-FERRI: Piscatore e pusilecco. THOMAS: Mignon: Addio Mignon fa core; Ah non credevi tu. VERDI: La forza del destino: La vita e inferno ...O tu che in seno angeli. La traviata: Lunge da lei...De miei bollenti spirti. Folksongs: A la Barcillunsia; Cantu a timuni; Abballati; Mutteti di lu Paliu. Giuseppe di Stefano, t; Maria Callas, Rosanna Carteri, s; Various orchestras and accompaniments.

++FF 9/10-81 p216 +HFN 3-81 p93
+-Gr 3-81 p1234 +NYT 8-16-81 pD19
+-Gr 6-81 p93 tape +-Op 6-81 p608

RLS 763 (4) Tape (c) TC RLS 763

3844 ARNE: Songs: When daisies pied; Where the bee sucks. BACH: Anna Magdalena Notebook, S 508: Bist du bei mir. BRAHMS: Songs: Vergebliches Standchen, op. 84, no. 4. CHARPENTIER: Louise: Depuis le jour. GLUCK: Le rencontre imprevue: Einmen Bach der flieset. HUMBERDINCK: Hansel und Gretel: Suse liebe Suse...Bruderchen komm tanz mit mir; Dance duet; Der kleine Sandmann bin ich; Sandman's song; Abends will ich schlafen geh'n; Evening prayer. LEHAR: Das land des Lachelns: Da kommt Lisa...Ich danke fur die Huldigung...Flirten bisschen flirten; Guten Abend, Hoheit...Bei einem Tee ne daux. Die lustige Witwe: Frau Glawari darf keinen...Bitte meine Herr'n; Nun lasst uns aber daheim...Vilja o Vilja; Heia Madel auf geschaut...Dummer dummer Reitersmann. MOZART: Don Giovanni, K 527: Crudele...Non mi dir; In quali eccessi...Mi tradi quell'alma ingrata. Die Entfuhrung aus dem Serail, K 384: Welcher Kummer...Traurigkeit ward mir zum Lose; Martern aller arten. Le nozze di Figaro, K 492: Porgi amor; E Susanna non vien...Dove sono; Giunse alfin il momento...Deh vieni non tardar. Il re pastore, K 208: L'amero saro costante. Songs: Abendempfidung, K 523; Die Zauberer, K 472. PUCCINI: La boheme: Donde lieta usci. Gianni Schicchi: O mio babbino caro. Madama Butterfly: Un bel di. Turandot: Signore ascolta; Tu che di gel sei cinta. SCHUBERT: Die schone Mullerin, D 795: Ungeduld. Songs: Litanei, D 343; Die Forelle, D 550; Seligkeit, D 433. SCHUMANN: Myrthen Lieder, op. 25: Der Nussbaum. Lieder und Gesange, op. 77: Auftrage. STRAUSS, J. II (arr. Korngold): Ene Nacht in Venedit: Annina...Rondinella pellegrina; Was mir der Zufall gab. Die Feldermaus, op. 363:

Mein Herr was dachten Sie von mir; Klange der Heimat. Wiener Blut, op. 354: Es hat Grafen...Gruss dich Gott; Ah ha na Warte du Schwindler. Der Ziguenerbaron, op. 420: Wers uns getraut. STRAUSS, R.: Der Rosenkavalier, op. 59: Herr Gott im Himmel; Presentation of the silver rose. Songs: Hat gesagt bleibt's nich dabei, op. 36, no. 3; Schlechtes Wetter, op. 69, no. 5. VERDI: La traviata: Addio del passato. WOLF: Wiegenlied; Mausfallenspruchlein. TRAD. (arr. Brahms): Da unten im Tale; Och Mod'r ich well en Ding han. Elisabeth Schwarzkopf, s; Various accompaniments.

+Gr 11-81 p763 +-HFN 12-81 p107

HQS 1434 Tape (c) TC HQS 1434

3845 BEETHOVEN: Nei campi e nelle selve. DUNSTABLE: Veni sancte spiritus. FARMER: A little pretty bonny lass. GABRIELI, A.: Ricercar. GABRIELI, G.: In ecclesiis, motet. LASSUS: Fuyons tous d'amour; Quand mon mari. MONTEVERDI: Gloria in excelsis. MORLEY: False love did me inveigle. QUELDRYK: Gloria in excelsis. WILBYE: Adieu sweet Amaryllis. ANON.: Sanctus and benedictus; Salve sancta parens. Ursula Connors, Patricia Clark, Mary Thomas, s; Christopher Keyte, bar; Edgar Fleet, Leslie Fyson, Ian Partridge, t; Shirley Minty, con; John Frost, bs; Ambrosian Singers; Accademia Monteverdiana, String and Brass Enesemble; Barry Rose, org; Philip Jones, tpt; Geraint Jones, org; Ambrosian Consort; Denis Stevens.

+Gr 6-81 p75 +HFN 7-81 p81 tape
+-Gr 12-81 p944 tape +MT 10-81 p680

ASD 3454 Tape (c) TCA SD 3454 (From SLS 863)

3846 DANDRIEU: Armes amours O flour des flours. LESCUREL: A vous douce debonaire. MACHAUT: Amours me fait desirer; Dame se vous m'estes; De bon espoir, Puis que la douce; De toutes flours; Douce dame jolie; Hareu hareu helas ou sera pris confors; Ma fin est mon commencement; Mes esperis se combat; Phyton le merveilleus serpent; Quant j'ay l'espart; Quant je sui mis; Quant Theseus, Ne quier veoir; Trop plus est bell-Biaute paree, Je ne sui; Se je souspir. MOLINS: Amis tout dous. ANON.: La septime estampie real. Early Music Consort; David Munrow.

+Gr 8-78 p366 +-RR 9-78 p81
+Gr 12-81 p944 tape +RR 1-79 p90 tape

ASD 3785

3847 BARTOK: Rumanian folk dances (trans. Szekeley). COPLAND: Rodeo: Hoe-down. DVORAK: Songs, op. 55: Songs my mother taught me (trans. Kreisler). HALFFTER: Danza de la gitana (trans. Heifetz). MENDELSSOHN: On wings of song, op. 34, no. 2 (trans. Larsen). PAGAININI: Concerto, violin, no. 2, op. 7, B minor: La clochette (ed. Kreisler). RAVEL: Piece en forme de habanera, op. 21, no. 2. SARASATE: Danza espanol, op. 23: Zapateado (ed. Francescatti). SCHUBERT: Ave Maria, D 839 (trans. Wilhelmj). WEBER: Air russe and rondo (trans. Szigeti). Ida Haendel, vln; Geoffrey Parsons, pno.

+Gr 5-80 p1689 +NR 5-81 p15
++HFN 5-80 p134 ++RR 5-80 p88

ASD 3907 Tape (c) TCC ASD 3907

3848 Procession with carols upon Advent Sunday. King's College Choir; Adrian Partington, org; Philip Ledger.

++Gr 11-81 p748 +HFN 12-81 p107

ASD 3908 Tape (c) TC ASD 3908 (From SLS 5113, 943, 956, 977, 5170, 5187, SAN 242/3, Columbia SAX 2412/4)

3849 BELLINI: Norma: Mira O Norma. BIZET: Les pecheurs de perles: C'etait le soir...Au fond du temple saint. GOUNOD: Faust: Il se fait tard. LEONCAVALLO: I Pagliacci: E fra quest'ansie... Decido il mio destino. MASCAGNI: L'Amico Fritz: Suzel buon di. VERDI: Aida: La fatal pietra...O terra addio. Don Carlo: Dio che nell'anima infondere. La forza del destino: Solenne in quest'ora. Maria Callas, Montserrat Caballe, Mirella Freni, Renata Scotto, s; Christa Ludwig, Fiorenza Cossotto, ms; Alain Vanzo, Carlo Bergonzi, Placido Domingo, Luciano Pavarotti, t; Guillermo Sarabia, Piero Cappuccilli, Sherrill Milnes, Thomas Allen, bar; Paris Opera Orchestra, La Scala Orchestra, RPO, ROHO, PhO; Georges Pretre, Tullio Serafin, Lamberto Gardelli, Carlo Maria Giulini, Riccardo Muti, Gianandrea Gavazzeni.

+Gr 9-80 p407 +HFN 1-81 p109 tape

ASD 3915 Tape (c) TC ASD 3915 (From SAN 184/6, 103/6, 114/6, 131/2, SAX 2369/72, 2284, 2316/7, SLS 5113, 977)

3850 BIZET: Les pecheurs de perles: Me voila seule dans la nuit... Comme autrefois. DONIZETTI: Lucia di Lammermoor: Sparsa e di rose...Il dolce suono...Spargi d'amaro pianto. MOZART: Cosi fan tutte, K 588: Come scoglio. Don Giovanni, K 527: Troppo mi spiace...Non mi dir. PUCCINI: La boheme: Si mi chiamano Mimi. Madame Butterfly: Un bel di vedremo. ROSSINI: Il barbiere di Siviglia: Una voce poco fa. VERDI: Aida: Que Radames verra...O patria mia. WEBER: Oberon; Ozean du Ungeheuer. Renata Scotto, Elisabeth Schwarzkopf, Joan Sutherland, Birgit Nilsson, Victoria de los Angeles, Mirella Freni, Maria Callas, Ileana Cotrubas, Montserrat Caballe, Rome Opera Orchestra, PhO, RPO, Paris Opera Orchestra, NPhO; John Barbirolli, Karl Bohm, Carlo Maria Giulini, Heinz Wallberg, Vittorio Gui, Thomas Schippers, Tullio Serafin, Georges Pretre, Riccardo Muti.

+Gr 11-80 p736 +-HFN 11-80 p129
+Gr 4-81 p1376 tape

ASD 3943 Tape (c) TC ASD 3943 (also Angel DS 37758)

3851 BOCCHERINI: Quintet, strings, op. 13, no. 5, E major: Minuet (arr. Woodhouse). DVORAK: Nocturne, op. 40, B minor. FAURE: Pavane, op. 50. GRIEG: Elegiac melodies, op. 34 (2). TCHAIKOVSKY: Quartet, strings, no. 1, op. 11, D major: Andante cantabile. WAGNER: Siegfried Idyll. AMF; Neville Marriner.

+Gr 6-80 p43 ++HFN 10-80 p117 tape
+Gr 12-80 p889 tape +NR 8-80 p5
+Gr 10-81 p614 tape +-RR 6-80 p64
++HFN 6-80 p114

ASD 8981 Tape (c) TC ASD 3981

3852 BACH (Gounod): Ave Maria. BRAHE: Bless this house. DAVIES: God be in my head. FORD: A prayer to our lady. LIDDLE: How lovely are thy dwellings; The lord is my shepherd; Abide with me. MARTIN: The holy child. PARRY: Jerusalem, op. 208 (arr. Thalben-Ball). PLUMSTEAD: Close thine eyes; A grateful heart. SANDERSON: Beyond the dawn. THOMPSON: The night of Bethlehem. VAUGHAN WILLIAMS: The call. WARLOCK: Balulalow. TRAD.:

Were you there. Janet Baker, ms; Philip Ledger, org.
+Gr 4-81 p1358 ++STL 5-10-81 p41

HMV SLS 5136 (3) Tape (c) TC SLS 5136

3853 ARNE: Under the greenwood tree. BACH: Cantatas, no. 106: Sonatina. Cantata, no. 208: Schafe konnen sicher weiden. Magnificat, S 243: D major: Esurientes. BARBIREAU: Eeen vrolic Wesen. BUSATTI: Surrexit pastor bonus. CORELLI: La folie d' Espagne. DONATI: In te Domine speravi. DUFAY: Se la face ay pale, mass: Sanctus. Ce moys de may lamentationsanctae matris ecclesiae Constantinopolitanae. HANDEL: Acis and Galatea: O ruddier than the cherry. HENRY VIII, King: Pastime with good company. HOLBORNE: Dances (5). JOSQUIN DES PRES: El grillo; Inviolata integra et casta es Maria; Scaramella. MACHAUT: Douce dame jolie. MAINERIO: Il primo libro di balli, 1578: Dances (5). MUDARRA: Claros y frescos rios. MUNROW: Six days of Grenoble. The king's hunt. MUSET: Quand je voy yver retorner. PRAETORIUS: Eulogodia sionia, 1611: Resonet in laudibus; Musae Sionae IV, 1607: Christus der uns selig macht; Musae Sionae 1, 1605: Gott der Vater wohn uns bei. Terpsichore: La bouree; Pavane de Spaigne; La sarabande; Bransles doubles (3); Bransle double de Poictou; Bransle gay double; Bransle simple. PURCELL: Come ye sons of art: Sound the trumpet; See nature rejoicing; Ritornello and chorus. Love's goddess sure: May she to heaven. SOLAGE: Fumeux fume. SUSATO: La Mourisque. Pavane la bataille. TELEMANN: Les plaisirs. TINCTORIS: Missa tre vocum: Kyrie. THIBAUT IV of Navarre: Chanson pieuse "Dou tres doux non". VOELCKEL: Courantes (2). WILLIAMS: Sonata in imitation of birds. ANON.: English dance. Istampitta tre fontaine. Saltarello (14th century). The dream. O death rock me asleep. St. Alban Abbey Church Boys Choir; Early Music Consort, AMF; David Munrow, Neville Marriner.
+-Gr 6-81 p76 ++HFN 7-81 p81
++Gr 9-81 p460 ++HFN 9-81 p93 tape
+Gr 12-81 p944 tape +STL 6-14-81 p40

SLS 5196 (2)

3854 DARGOMIZHSKY: Russalka: Miller's aria. The stone guest (Cui, orch. Rimsky-Korsakov). NAPRAVNIK: Dubrovsky: Vladimir's recitative and romance. RIMSKY-KORSAKOV: Servilia: Servilia's aria. RUBINSTEIN: The demon: Tamara's song. SEROV: The power of evil: Yeromka's song. VERSTOVSKY: The tomb of Askold: Stranger's aria and chorus. Tamara Milashkina, Maria Beishu, Zoe Khristich, s; Tamara Sinyavskaya, ms; Vladimir Atlantov, Vitaly Nartov, Mark Reshetin, bs; Vladimir Valaitis, Nicolay Kondratyuk, bar; Bolshoi Theatre Orchestra and Chorus; Mark Ermler, Boris Khaikin.
+Gr 12-80 p872 +*MT 8-81 p539
+-HFN 2-81 p86 +Op 5-81 p496

SLS 5212

3855 BRAHMS: Symphony, no. 2, op. 73, D major. SCHUBERT: Symphony, no. 8, D 759, B minor. SHOSTAKOVICH: Symphony, no. 5, op. 47, D minor. TCHAIKOVSKY: Symphony, no. 5, op. 64, E minor. WEBER: Oberon: Overture. Leningrad Philharmonic Orchestra; Yevgeny Mravinsky.
+-Gr 4-81 p1330 +-HFN 5-81 p87

ESD 7101 Tape (c) TC ESD 7101 (From CSD 3705)
3856 BUTTERWORTH: English idylls, nos. 1, 2. IRELAND: Songs: The holy boy. LEIGH: Concertino. MOERAN: Pieces, orchestra (2). WARLOCK: Capriol suite. Neville Dilkes, hpd; English Sinfonia.
+Gr 2-81 p1095 +HFN 3-81 p95

HLM 7128 (From various EMI 78's)
3857 BACH: Concerto, harpsichord, no. 1, S 1052, D minor. BAX: Morning songs. CHOPIN: Etude, op. posth., no. 25, F minor. Etude, op. posth., no. 26, A flat major. FALLA: Piezas espanolas: Andaluza. MOZART: Sonata, piano, no. 10, K 330, C major. TURINA: Danza de la seduccion. VAUGHAN WILLIAMS: Prelude on hymn tune, no. 13. Harriet Cohen, pno.
+FF 5/6-81 p204

SXLP 30506 Tape (c) TC SXLP 30506 (From ASD 3775, 3160, 3132, SLS 5127, SEOM 18)
3858 BEETHOVEN: Fidelio, op. 72: Overture. BRAHMS: Tragic overture, op. 81. DVORAK: Slavonic dance, op. 46, no. 8, G minor. SCHUBERT: Die Zauberharfe, D 644. STRAUSS, J. II: Die Zigeunerbaron, op. 420: Overture. WAGNER: Der fliegende Hollander: Overture. BPhO; Herbert von Karajan.
+Gr 5-81 p1474 +-HFN 5-81 p91

HONG KONG

HK 1003
3859 CHAN HAO HO, KANG CHEN: Concerto, violin. GUO QUAN LI: Singing the night among fishing boats. JIAN CHEN: Song of the five fingers mountain. YAN PING JIN: Dance. YIAO XIAN MA ZHONG HAN LI: Spring in Sinkiang. YONG CHENG QIN: Romance. Takako Nichizaki, vln; Yitkin Seow, pno; Nagoya Philharmonic Orchestra; Kek-Tjiang Lim.
+-FF 1/2-81 p231

HK 2001
3860 CHIEN HUA CHEN: Adagio, klavier. CHIH HUNG KUO: Sinkiang dance. CHIN YE CHU: Prelude. CHUN WAI YEUNG: The peacock. PUI FAN CHAN: The pedlar. To spring. SHAN TE-TING: Children suite. Dance Sinkiang, no. 1. Toccata. YI KEUNG SUN: Rice threshing dance. Yitkin Seow, pno.
+-FF 1/2-81 p231

HK 6-240034
3861 CHAN PUI FAN: Cantonese scenes (4). HUANG HU WEI: Szechuan suite. HUANG TSEN JUNG: North Shansi scenes. SANG TUNG: Eastern Mongolian folk songs. SHEN CHUAN SHIN: Yunnan suite. Koo Kowk Kuen, pno.
+-FF 1/2-81 p231

HUNGAROTON

SLPX 11983/4 (2)
3862 GREFINGER: Ach Gott; Ich stel leicht ab; Wol kumbt der mey. FINCK: Greiner zanner; Ich stund an einem morgen; Ich wird

erlost; Der Ludel und der Hensel. Instrumental pieces (3). HOFHAIMER: Carmen in re; Carmen magistri Pauli; Cupido; Der Hundt; Man hat bisher; Greiner zanner; Nach willen dein. LUBLIN: Dances. Mon mary. SERMISY: Tant que vivray. STOLTZER: Es mut vil leut; Ich klag den Tag; Man sicht nun vol. WILLAERT: A quand; Allons allons gay; Ricercari (2); Villanelle. Ars Renata; Camerata Hungarica; Laszlo Czidra.
++ARG 9-80 p49 +-HFN 2-81 p95
++FF 7/8-80 p179 +NR 12-80 p9
+Gr 2-81 p1113

SLPX 12041
3863 BERLIOZ: La damnation de Faust, op. 24: Rakoczy march. DELIBES: Coppelia: Csardas. ERKEL: Festival overture. Hunyadi Laszlo: Palotas dance. LANNER: Pest Waltz, op. 93. MULLER: Kossuth march. STRAUSS, J. II: Eljen a Magyar, op. 332. WEBER: Andante and rondo ungarese, op. 35. HSO; Janos Ferencsik.
+NR 3-81 p4

SLPX 12050
3864 Gregorian chant: Magyar Gregorianum 4: Easter. Schola Hungarica; Laszlo Dobsay, Janka Szendrei.
+FF 11/12-81 p289

SLPX 12065
3865 DUBROVAY: Duets, violin and percussion. KALMAR: Anera. KOSA, Gyorgy: Divertimento. KOSA, Gabor: Two. PATACHICH: Metamorphoses. SARY: Sonata, percussion, no. 2. Gabor Kosa, perc.
+FF 1/2-81 p226 -NR 12-80 p11

LPX 12085/6 (2)
3866 BEETHOVEN: Sonata, piano, no. 8, op. 13, C minor. Sonata, piano, no. 14, op. 27, no. 2, C sharp minor. Sonata, piano, no. 28, op. 101, A major: Allegretto ma non troppo. BRAHMS: Pieces, op. 117: Intermezzo. CHOPIN: Impromptu, no. 2, op. 36, F sharp major. Mazurka, op. 56, no. 2, C major. Nocturne, op. 62, no. 1, B major. DOHNANYI: Cascades, op. 41, no. 4. Humoresque, op. 17, no. 1. Pastorale. Rhapsody, op. 11, no. 2, F sharp minor. LISZT: Consolation, no. 3, S 172, D flat major. MOZART: Sonata, piano, no. 11, K 331, A major. SCHUBERT (Dohnanyi): Valses nobles, op. 77, D 969. Erno Dohnanyi, pno.
+-FF 9/10-80 p261 +-HFN 2-81 p95

SLPX 12117
3867 ABEL: Sonata, G major. BOISMORTIER: Trio sonata, E minor. LECLAIR: Forlane and tambourin, op. 8, F major. PACHELBEL: Partita, no. 2, C minor. STAMITZ, C.: Duet, D major. TELEMANN: Trio, no. 78, B flat major. Marta Fabian, cimb; Imre Kovacs, flt; Bela Sztankovits, gtr.
+FF 9/10-81 p274 ++NR 5-81 p9

SLPX 12169
3868 Gregorian chant: Magyar Gregorianum 5: Hungarian Saints. Schola Hungarica; Laszlo Dobsay, Janka Szendrei.
+FF 11/12-81 p289

SLPX 12239
3869 BARTOK: Etudes, op. 18 (3). CHOPIN: Ballade, no. 1, op. 23, G minor. LISZT: Annees de pelerinage, 2nd year, S 162: Venezia e Napoli. Csardas obstine. RACHMANINOFF: Preludes, op. 32, nos. 3, 9. Etudes-Tableaux, op. 33, no. 7, E flat major.

SCHOENBERG: Pieces, piano, op. 33a. SCHUBERT: Impromptu, op. 142, no. 4, D 935, F minor. Zoltan Kocsis, pno.
+-FF 7/8-81 p211 +-SFC 9-19-81 p18
+NR 5-81 p14

HYPERION

A 66002 (From Gemini GME 1019)
3870 DUARTE: Variations on a Catalan folksongs, op. 25. EASTWOOD: Ballade phantasy. FALLA: Homenaje a Debussy. HENZE: Kammermusik, 1958: Tentos (3). MIDDLETON: Processional and Virginia reel. TANSMAN: Berceuse d'Orient. Cavatina. Alice Artzt, gtr.
+Gr 1-81 p970 ++HFN 1-81 p105

A 66003 Tape (c) KA 66003
3871 CAMPIAN: If thou long'st so much to learn; Shall I come sweet love. DANYEL: Eyes look no more. DOWLAND: Come away come sweet love; Fine knacks for ladies; Flow my tears; Humour say what mak'st thou here; In darkness let me dwell; Now o now I needs must part; Time's eldest son; Old age. FERRABOSCO: Tell me o love. HUME: Tobacco tobacco. JONES, R.: Now what is love. PILKINGTON: My choice is made. ANON.: Earl of Essex galliard. Piper's galliard. Camerata of London.
+-Gr 4-81 p1356 +HFN 3-81 p93
+Gr 12-81 p944 tape

A 66007
3872 CALACE: Prelude, no. 2, op. 49. HOWARD: Ramble on a Russian theme. KAUFMANN: Burletta. Mitoka dragomirna. KREISLER: Liebesfreud (trans.). Liebesleid (trans.). Schon Rosmarin (trans.). RACHMANINOFF: Danses tziganes, op. 6, no. 2 (trans.). RIMSKY-KORSAKOV: Fantasia, op. 33. The tale of the Tsar Sultan, op. 57: The flight of the bumble bee (trans.). SARASATE: Zigeunerweisen, op. 20, no. 1 (trans.). Keith Harris, mand and domra; Leslie Howard, pno.
+Gr 8-81 p299 +HFN 4-81 p79

A 66012 Tape (c) KA 66012
3873 ATTWOOD: Come holy ghost. PARRY: I was glad. STAINER: Evening canticles, B flat major. STANFORD: Evening canticles, G major. WESLEY, S.: Exultate deo. WESLEY, S.S.: Blessed be the God and father. WOOD: O thou the central orb. Ely Cathedral Choir; Stephen le Prevost, org; Arthur Wills.
+Gr 12-80 p871 ++HFN 7-81 p83 tape
+HFN 11-80 p125

A 66015
3874 FARRAR: O mistress mine. FINZI: Oh fair to see, op. 13b; To a poet, op. 13a. GILL: In memoriam. GURNEY: Down by the salley gardens; Hawk and buckle; Sleep. MILFORD: If it's ever spring again; The colour; So sweet love seemed. Ian Partridge, t; Stephen Roberts, bar; Clifford Benson, pno.
+-Gr 9-81 p422 +STL 10-11-81 p41
+-HFN 9-81 p85

A 66018
3875 BAIRSTOW: Lord I call upon thee. BRIDGE: Adagio, E major. ELGAR:

The apostles, op. 49: The spirit of the Lord. HOWELLS: Rhapsody, op. 17, no. 3, C sharp minor. Songs: I love all beauteous things. KELLY: Te deum. LEIGHTON: Paean. STANFORD: Bible songs, op. 113: O for a closer walk with God. St. Alban's Cathedral Choir; Andrew Parnell, Stephen Darlington, org.
+Gr 11-81 p747 +HFN 11-81 p99

A 66019
3876 BENNET: All creatures. CAMPIAN: Move now; Now hath Flora; Woo her. CAVENDISH: Come gentle swains. COPRARIO: Go happy man; Come ashore; While dancing rests. DOWLAND: Welcome black night. EAST: Hence stars; You meaner beauties. GIBBONS: Long live fair Oriana. GILES: Triumph now. LANIER: Bring away; Mark how the blushful morn. LUPO: Shows and nightly revels; Time that leads. WEELKES: As Vesta was; Hark all ye lovely saints. WILBYE: The Lady Oriana. Emma Kirkby, s; David Thomas, bs; Consort of Musicke; Anthony Rooley.
+FF 11/12-81 p284 +HFN 9-81 p86
+Gr 9-81 p427

A 66020
3877 ARNE: Sonata, harpsichord, no. 1, F major. BACH: French suite, S 814, B minor. FROBERGER: Suite, G minor. RAMEAU: Pieces de clavecin: L'Entretien des muses; Le lardon; La triomphante. SCARLATTI, D.: Sonata, harpsichord, Kk 212, A major; Kk 144, G major. Maggie Cole, hpd.
++FF 11/12-81 p290 +HFN 11-81 p101
++Gr 9-81 p418

A 66026
3878 COATES: Orpheus with his lute; Tell me where is fancy bred. FINZI: Let us garlands bring, op. 18; Love's labour's lost, op. 28: Riddle song; Sigh no more ladies. GURNEY: Under the greenwood tree. MOERAN: When daisies pied; When icicles hang by the wall; Where the bee sucks. PARRY: O never say that I was false of heart; A sea dirge, op. 21, no. 5; Willow willow willow. PLUMSTEAD: Sigh no more ladies; Take o take those lips away. QUILTER: Blow blow thou winter wind, op. 6, no. 3; Come away death, op. 6, no. 1; Hark hark the lark; Hey ho the wind and the rain, op. 23, no. 5; O mistress mine, op. 6, no. 2. SOMERVELL: Orpheus with his lute. WARLOCK: Pretty ringtime; Sigh no more ladies; Take o take those lips away. Graham Trew, bar; Roger Vignoles, pno.
+Gr 12-81 p924 +STL 11-8-81 p40
+HFN 12-81 p107

ICARUS

1002
3879 ALBENIZ: Cantos de Espana, op. 232: Baja la palmera; Cordoba. (trans. Llobet and Pujol). BROUWER: Micro piezas. GALLES: Sonata, guitar, E minor (trans. Castellani-Andriaccio). GRANADOS: Goyescas; Intermezzo (trans. Pújol). SCARLATTI, D.: Sonata, guitar, K 9, E minor (trans. Pujol). Sonata, guitar, K 380, E major (trans. Castellani-Andriaccio). Joanne Castellani, Michael Andriaccio, gtr.
+NR 8-80 p15 +St 6-81 p126

INTER-AMERICAN MUSICAL EDITIONS

OAS 007

3880 DIEMER: Youth overture. GUARNIERI: Suite Vila Rica. CHAVEZ Y RAMIREZ: Caballos de vapor: Danza agil; Tango of the sirens. KOHN: Castles and kings. SLONIMSKY: My toy balloon. D.C. Youth orchestra; Lyn McLain.

+-FF 9/10-81 p290

INTERCORD

INT 160 830

3881 BACH: Cantata, no. 98, Was Gott tut das ist wohlgetan. St. Matthew Passion, S 244: Wenn ich einmal soll scheide. FRESCOBALDI: Corrente. GLUCK: Orfeo ed Euridice: Reigen seliger Geister. Paride ed Elena: Gavotte. HANDEL: Aylesford pieces: Gavotte and passepied. MOZART: Adagio and rondo, K 617, C minor. NAUMANN: Sonata, glass harmonica, no. 11. Wie ein Hirt sein Volk zu weiden. REICHARDT: Rondo, B major: Grazioso. SCHULZ: Largo. Bruno Hoffmann, glass harmonica; Stuttgart Chamber Ensemble.

+FF 5/6-81 p212

I.P.G.

(Japan) ULX 3341 PG

3882 Gregorian chant: Messe et office de Sainte Cecile. Abbey of St. Pierre de Solesmes Choir; Jean Claire.

+FF 5/6-81 p196

LACHRIMAE

LR 1034

3883 BYRD: The woods so wild. MILANO: Fantasias (2). Ricercare. DOWLAND: Fantasie. Farewell. Lachrimae pavan. Queen Elizabeth's galliard . Earl of Essex galliard. Sir John Smith's almain. MILAN: Fantasia del quarto tono. MORLEY: Pavan. PHILIPS: Cromatica pavana. ANON.: Greensleeves. Brian Whitehouse, lt.

+-Gr 9-81 p418 +-HFN 8-81 p90

LEONARDA

LPL 104

3884 BOULANGER: D'un matin de printemps. Nocturne. FARRENC: Trio, op. 45, E minor. HOOVER: On the betrothal of Princess Isabelle

of France, aged six. TAILLEFERRE: Pastorale. ULEHLA: Elegy for a whale. Katherine Hoover, flt; Carter Brey, vlc; Barbara Weintraub, Virginia Eskin, pno.
+ARG 2-81 p42 +-NR 8-80 p10
+-FF 9/10-80 p287 +St 10-80 p126

LONDON

PAV 2006
3885 BELLINI: I puritani: A te o cara. BIZET: Carmen: Flower song. CURTIS: Torna a Surriento. DONIZETTI: La fille du regiment: O mes amis...Pour mon ame. La favorita: Spirto gentil. LEONCAVALLO: Mattinata. PUCCINI: La boheme: Che gelida manina. Tosca: Recondita armonia. Turandot: Nessun dorma. ROSSINI: La danza. STRAUSS, R.: Der Rosenkavalier: Di rigori armato. VERDI: Il trovatore: Di qual tetra...Ah si ben mio; Di quella pira. Luciano Pavarotti, t; Orchestral accompaniment.
++NR 6-81 p9
CS 7178 (also Decca SXL 6950 Tape (C) KSXC 6950)
3886 ALBENIZ: Suite espanola, op. 47: Asturias (Bonell). CHAPI Y LORENTE: Serenata morisca (Bonell). CHOPIN: Prelude, op. 28, no. 7, A major (Bonell). LLOBET: Scherzo. Vals. PAGANINI: Romanze e andantino variato. VALVERDE (Llobet): Clavelitos. TARREGA: Introduction and fantasia on themes from "La traviata". VILLA-LOBOS: Etude, no. 11. Preludes, nos. 1-2. WEISS: Chaconne, A major (Bonell). Carlos Bonell, gtr.
+-FF 11/12-81 p248 +HFN 3-81 p94
+Gr 4-81 p1351
LDR 10028
3887 Christmas carols: Angelus ad virginem; Ding dong merrily on high; Gabriels' message; God rest ye merry gentlemen; Hark the herald angels sing; Hush my dear lie still and slumber; In dulci jubilo; O come all ye faithful; One in Royal David's city; Shepherd's pipe carol; Silent night; Star carol; Sussex carol; Unto us is born a son; A virgin most pure. Bach Choir; Philip Jones Brass Ensemble; David Willcocks.
+FF 11/12-81 p286
OS 26434 (also Decca SXL 6988)
3888 GUERRERO: El huesped del sevillano: Canto a la Espada. LUNA Y CARNE: La picara molinera: Paxarin tu que vuelas. SERRANO: Los de Aragon: Cuantas veces solo. El trust de los tenorios: Jota. SORIANO: El guitarrico: Serenata. SOUTULLO Y VERT: El ultimo romantico: Bella enamorada. La leyenda del beso: Hecho de un rayo de luna. TORROBA: La chulapona: Tienes razon amigo. Luisa Fernanda: De este apacible rincon de Madrid. VIVES: Dona Francisquite: Por el humo. Placido Domingo, t; Orquesta Sinfonica de Barcelona; Louis Garcia Navarro.
+FF 9/10-81 p213 ++SFC 9-7-80 p32
+Gr 4-81 p1367 ++St 2-81 p111
+NYT 9-14-80 pD42 ++STL 5-10-81 p41
OS 26617 (also Decca SXLR 6935)
3889 ALBENIZ: Besa el aura; Del salon. FALLA: Oracion de las madres que tienen a sus hijos en brazos; Tus ojillos negros. GRAN-

ADOS: Tonadillas: La maja dolorosa. OBRADORS: Aquel sombrero de monte; Del cabello mas sutil; El molondron; El vito. RODRIGO: Madrigales amatorios: Con que la lavare; Vos me matasteis; De donde venis amore; De los alamos vengo madre. VIVES: El amor y los ojos; El retrato de Isabela; Valgame Dios que los ansares vuelan. Montserrat Caballe, s; Miguel Zanetti, pno.

+FF 5/6-81 p191 ++HFN 3-81 p91
+Gr 4-81 p1358 ++St 5-81 p86

LDR 72009 (2) Tape (c) LDRS 72009 (also Decca D255D2 Tape (c) K255K22)
3890 BELLINI: Beatrice di Tenda: Angiol de pace. Norma: Scena and duet, Act 1; Finale, Act 1. PONCHIELLI: La gioconda: Trio, Act 4; Deh non turbare, Duet, Act 2. PUCCINI: La boheme: Che gelida manina. ROSSINI: La donna del lago: Mura felici. VERDI: Ernani: Finale grand trio, Act 4. I Masnadieri: Tu del mio Carlo. Otello: Gia nella notte. Il trovatore: Finale, Act 4. Joan Sutherland, s; Marilyn Horne, ms; Luciano Pavarotti, t; Jake Bardner, bar; New York City Opera Orchestra; Richard Bonynge.

+FF 11/12-81 p282 +-ON 11-81 p68
+-Gr 9-81 p446 +-Op 10-81 p1071
+-HF 12-81 p89 ++SFC 7-26-81 p19
+NR 12-81 p7 +-St 9-81 p82

MARLBOROUGH COLLEGE

SM 237
3891 KHACHATURIAN: The battle of Stalingrad. Gayaneh: Lezghinka (arr. Peel). RIMSKY-KORSAKOV: Variations on a theme by Glinka. SHOSTAKOVICH: The gadfly, op. 97: Folk festival. SOUSA: The gallant Seventh. STRAUSS, Josef: Feuerfest, op. 269 (arr. Peel). Marlborough College Wind Orchestra; Robert Peel.

+Gr 6-81 p44

MELODIYA

33C 10 07015-6 (also Chant du Monde 78660)
3892 The play of Daniel. Hortus Musicus Ensemble; Andres Mustonen.

+FF 3/4-81 p224 +HFN 1-81 p107

MERIDIAN

E 77031/2 (2)
3893 BAX: Far in a western brookland. BUTTERWORTH: A Shropshire lad: Loveliest of trees; When I was one and twenty; Look not in my eyes; Think no more lad; The lads in their hundreds; Is my team ploughing. GIBBS: When I was one and twenty. GURNEY: The western playland: Reveille; Loveliest of trees; Golden friends; Twice a week; The aspens; Is my team ploughing; The

far country; March. IRELAND: The boys are up in the woods all day. MOERAN: Ludlow town: When smoke stood up from Ludlow; Farewell to barn and stack and tree; Say lad have you things to do; The lads in their hundreds. Songs: Tis time I think by Wenlock town. ORR, C.W.: Songs: Along the field; The lent lily; Oh when I was in love with you. PEEL: In summertime on Bredon; Reveille; When the lad for longing sighs. SOMERVELL: A Shropshire lad: Loveliest of trees; When I was one and twenty; There pass the careless people; In summertime on Bredon; The street sounds to the soldiers tread; On the idle hill of summer; White in the moon the long road lies; Think no more lad laugh be jolly; Into my heart an air that kills; The lads in their hundreds. Graham Trew, bar; Roger Vignoles, pno; Coull Quartet.

++Gr 4-80 p1583 +HFN 4-80 p113
++Gr 3-81 p1172 ++STL 5-11-80 p39

E 77036
3894 DANDRIEU: Allons voir de divin Gage. DAQUIN: Noel Suisse. DUBOIS: Pieces nouvelles: Noel. DUPRE: Variations sur un noel, op. 20. EDMUNDSON: Von Himmel hoch, toccata. GUILMANT: Noel Brabancon. Introduction et variations sur an ancien Noel polonais. Offertoire sur des Noels. MULET: Esquisses byzantines: Noel. Christopher Herrick, org.

+Gr 12-81 p911 +-HFN 12-81 p108

E 77044
3895 AYLEWARD/GITTINS: Preces and responses. BREWER: Magnificat and nunc dimittis, D major. BOSSI: Entree pontificale. BRUCKNER: Locus iste a Deo factus est. ELVEY: Psalm, no. 84, How lovely are thy dwellings. CROFT: Lords of the world above. ROBINSON: Psalm, no. 122, I was glad when they said unto me. STANFORD: Prelude, G major: Conclusion. SHEPHERD, R.: And when the builders. STONE: The Lord's prayer. Readings: First lesson: First book of Kings, Chapter 8, vv 22-30; Second Lesson: The revelation of St. John the Divine, Chapter 21 vv 1-6, 22-26. Creed. Prayers. Blessing. Salisbury Cathedral Choir; Colin Walsh, org; Richard Seal.

+Gr 10-81 p596 +HFN 10-81 p93

MIRROR MUSIC

00001
3896 BINCHOIS: Deuil angouisseux. DUFAY: Donnez l'assault. DUNSTABLE: Specialis virgo. HOFHAIMER: Herzliebstes pild; Maecenas atavis; Ohn freud. HERMANN DER MONCH VON SALZBURG: Das Taghorn. ISAAC: Intradas (2); Carmen; J'ai pris amour; O Venus bant. NEUSIDLER: Preaembulum; Wascha mesa. NEIDHART VON REUENTHAL: Meye dein lichter schein. SENFL: Chiara luce; Ich steund an einem Morgen; Nun gruss dich Gott. VERBEN: O domine gloriosa. OSWALD VON WOLKENSTEIN: Ain graserin; Du auserwahltes; Freu dich du; Wer die augen; Wohl auf gesell. Les Menestrels.

+FF 9/10-81 p225

MOSS MUSIC GROUP

MMG 1114
3897 BELARSKY-KACERGINSKY: Zol Shoin Kumin di Geula. CONTINELLO-ALOGON: Lo Teday Milhama. ELLSTEIN: V'liyerushalayim Ir'cha. GLANTZ-KRAUSS: Sim Shalom. GOLUB-FRUG: Der Becher. KRAUSS: Yehi Ratzon. LOW: A Din-Toire mit Gott. MIRON-HAGIZ: Ura Dor. RAPOPORT-HAMEIRI: Jerusalem. Misha Raitzin, t; Arr. and conducted by Bob Reisenman.
+ARG 1-81 p49

MMG 1123
3898 ARNOLD: Quintet, brass. BACH: Die Kunst der Fuge, S 1080: Contrapunctus, no. 9. Cantata, no. 147, Jesu joy of man's desiring. GABRIELI, G.: Canzon, no. 3. PEUERL: Canzon, no. 1. SCHEIDT: Benedicamus domino; Canzon gallicam. SYMONDS: A diversion. Canadian Brass.
-NR 3-81 p7

MMG 1124
3899 Christmas music: Away in a manger; Bel astre que j'adore; Canzone d'i Zampognare; Christams song; Deck the halls; El noi de la mare; Es ist ein Ros entsprungen; First Nowell; Go tell it on the mountain; God rest you merry gentlemen; Hajej nynej jezisku; The holly and the ivy; Il est ne le divin enfant; Jingle bells; Komt verwondert u hier Mensen; Les angels donas nos campagnes; O ful med din glaede; O Tannenbaum; Pastores a Belen; Schedrifka; Stille Nacht; What child is this. Swingle Singers.
/FF 11/12-81 p287

MMG 1126
3900 Christmas with the King's Singers: Christmas song; De virgin Mary had a baby boy; Do you hear what I hear; Gloria (Heilige Nacht auf Engelswingen); God rest ye merry gentlemen; Have yourselves a merry little Christmas; Il est ne le divin enfant; In dulci jubilo; Jingle bells; Little drummer boy; O du Frohliche; Somerset wassail; Stille Nacht; Twelve days of Christmas; We wish you a merry Christmas. King's Singers.
/FF 11/12-81 p287

MOTETTE

M 1003
3901 BACH: Chorale prelude, S 648. BRAHMS: Chorale preludes, op. 122, no. 2. DUPRE: Placare. LANGLAIS: Mon ame cherche un fin paisible. Notre Dieu est une puissante fortress. Kyrie (orbis factor). Kyrie Dieu pere eternel. PACHELBEL: Vom Himmel hoch. Chant de Noel "Du haut du ciel je decends". ROPARTS: Theme varie. SEVERAC: Chanson melancolique. VIERNE: Cathedrales. Marie Ducrot, org.
-FF 1/2-81 p122

M 1026
3902 BACH: Toccata, adagio and fugue, S 564, C major. KERLL: Passacaglia, D minor. LEMMENS: Invocation, F minor. LISZT: Pre-

lude and fugue on B-A-C-H, S 260. VIERNE: Fantasiestucke, op. 3: Toccata, B minor. Klemens Schnorr, org.
+-FF 1/2-81 p222 ++MU 3-81 p12

M 1028
3903 BOHM: Ach wie nichtig ach wie fluchtig. Prelude and fugue, C major. LUBECK: Prelude, G minor. PRAETORIUS, J.: Wass kann uns kommen an fur Not. SCHEIDEMANN: Preambulum, D minor. SCHEIDT: Magnificat noni toni. TUNDER: In dich hab ich gehoffet Herr. Philip Swanton, org.
+ARG 5-81 p37 -MU 11-81 p16
+-FF 9/10-81 p249

M 1032
3904 Improvisations on "Serdeczna Matko", "Maria breit den Mantel aus". Heinz Bernhard Orlinski, org.
+FF 1/2-81 p222

M 2001
3905 ALCOCK: Voluntary, D major. BUXTEHUDE: Erschienen ist der herrlich Tag. MARTINI: Largo, E major. TELEMANN: Allein Gott in der Hoh sei Ehr. Air de trompette, C major. Marches (4). Vater unser im Himmelreich. WALOND: Voluntary, no. 3, D minor. ZIPOLI: Pastorale, C major. Wolfgang Brasch, tpt; Johannes Ricken, org.
-FF 1/2-81 p222 +MU 11-80 p17

M 5002
3906 COMPERE: O vos omnes. GESUALDO: Ave regina coelorum; Ave dulcissima Maria. JOSQUIN DES PRES: Ave Maria. LASSUS: Justorum animae. PALESTRINA: Sicut cervus. SWEELINCK: De profundis. VICTORIA: O quam gloriosum. VON BRUCK: Gott der Vater wohn uns bei; Mitten wir im Leben sind. WALTHER: Nun bitten wir den heiligen Geist. Gerresheimer Madrigal Choir; Heinz Odenthal.
+ARG 7/8-81 p43 +MU 6-81 p14
-FF 1/2-81 p220

MUSIC BAVARICA

MB 70908
3907 BUCHWIESER: Canzonettas: Cavatina, no. 2. FRANZL: Quartet, op. 9, no. 2: Andante con moto. LINDPAINTNER: Fantasy, variations and rondo, op. 49. POISSL: Lieder to texts by Prince Ludwig of Bavaria (3). VELLUTI: Venetian barcarolle. WEBER: Duets, op. 31 (3). Karin Hautermann, Isolde Mitternacht, s; Claude-France Journes, pno; Klaus Wallendorf, Rolf Jurgen Eisermann, Fr hn; Sinnhoffer Quartet.
+ARG 4-81 p56

MB 70909
3908 DANZI: Latin vesper psalms (5). GLEISSNER: Sinfonia, op. 2, no. 4. STUNTZ: Agnus Dei. VOGLER: Preludes, organ, nos. 1-2, 32. WINTER: German Te deum. Erika Ruggeberg, Gertrud Freedmann, s; Julia Falk, alto; Albert Gassner, t; Carlo Schmid, Keith Engen, bs; Franz Lehrndorfer, org; Heart-of-Jesus-Church Choir, Passion Church Choir; Convivium Musicum, Musica Bavarica Chamber Orchestra; Josef Schmidhuber, Eric Keller, Wilhelm Walter.
+ARG 4-81 p56

MUSICAL HERITAGE SOCIETY

MHS 3291
3909 ARCADELT: Defecerunt. BRUMEL: Cogitavit...Defecerunt. BYRD: Cogitavit dominus. GENET: Omnis populus ejus. PALESTRINA: Matribus suis. SERMISY: Candidiores Nazarei. Harvard Glee Club; F. John Adams.
+FF 9/10-81 p226

MHS 3301 (also Pelca PRS 40551)
3910 BALANCHIVADZE: Fugue. KALNIN: Pastorale, no. 2, G major. MUSCHEL: Air and toccata. TSCHISCHKO: Ukrainian rhapsody. TISCHTSCHENKO: Invention, no. 3. STAROKADOMSKY: Passacaglia. Konrad Voppel, org.
+-MU 9-81 p14

MHS 4077 Tape (c) 6077
3911 ARAUJO: Los cofla desde la estleya. BELCHER: Carol. BILLINGS: Bethlehem; Boston; Judea. DENNIS: Of a rose. FRANCO: Salve regina. IVES: A Christmas carol. NOBRE: Ago lona. PRADO: Magnificat. READ: Expression; He is king of kings; I believe this is Jesus; Star in the East; Rise up shepherd and follow; Sherburne. XIMENO: Ay ay galeguinos. Western Wind.
+AR 8-80 p85 +MU 6-81 p14
+ARG 12-79 p14

MHS 4080
3912 BERBERIAN: Prelude. CHUKHADJIAN: Impromptus. ELMAS: Nocturne. GHORGHANIAN: Bayati. KOMITAS: Dances. MANAS: Petite suite. MIKULI: Etude. Lied. NOVA: Songs (2). PAPELYAN: La fin d'un reve. SPENTIARIAN: Enzeli. Lullaby. TIGRANIAN: Et-Arhaj. Sahan Arzruni, pno.
+ARG 11-81 p47 +FF 5/6-80 p184

MHS 4110
3913 ARZRUNI: Invocation. Mentations, no. 1. Heterophonic suite, excerpts. BARTEVIAN: For children. GAZARROSIAN: Prelude. GELALIAN: Andantino. HOVHANESS: Achtamar. Farewell to the mountains. Mystic flute. Vanadour. KARAMANUK: Admiration. KALAJIAN: Song. TERZIAN: Danza criolla. Juegos para Diana. Toccata. TJEKNAVORIAN: Armenian dance, no. 2. YARDUMIAN: Preludes (2). Sahan Arzruni, pno.
+ARG 11-81 p47 +FF 9/10-80 p262

MHS 4180 Tape (c) MHS 6180
3914 DEBUSSY: Syrinx. ENESCO: Cantabile et presto. FAURE: Fantaisie, op. 79, C major. Morceau de concours, F major. GAUBERT: Sonata, flute and piano, no. 1, A major. HONEGGER: Danse de la chevre. POULENC: Sonata, flute and piano. Carol Wincenc, flt; Andreas Schiff, pno.
+ARG 4-81 p43 +HF 10-80 p96
+-FF 11/12 p212 +St 10-80 p127

MHS 4187
3915 BUNGER: Mirrors, piano and tape recordist. CAGE: Bacchanal. HARRISON: May rain. PELLMAN: Silent night. STOUT: For prepared piano. WEGNER: Something, flute and piano. Joan La Barbara, voice; Richard Bunger, pno, tam-tam, tape recordist; John Heitmann, flt; Delores Stevens, pno.
++St 3-81 p98

MHS 4206

3916 d'ANGLEBERT: Tombeau de M. de Chambonnieres. Chaconne, D major. CHAMBONNIERES: Chaconne, F major. Rondeau. COUPERIN, L.: Passacaille, C major. La Piemontaise, A minor. DUMONT: Pavane, D minor. RAMEAU: Suite, E minor. L'Enharmonique, G minor. Kenneth Gilbert, hpd.

+FF 9/10-81 p345

MHS 4229

3917 ASTVATSATRIAN: Prologue and motet. BABAJANIAN: Dance of Vagharshapat. Images: Chorale; Dance of the people of Sassoun. Prelude. BARKHUDARIAN: Naz-Par. CHEBOTARIAN: Prelude. KHACHATURIAN: Dance. Poem. Sonatina. Toccata. Valse caprice. MIRZOVAN: Poem. MANSURIAN: Short suite. STEPANIAN: Prelude. Sahan Arzruni, pno.

+ARG 11-81 p47 +FF 5/6-81 p205

MHS 4236

3918 BAUER: Pieces, piano (4). BEACH: Variations on Balkan themes, op. 60. BACEWICZ: Ten studies, nos. 2 and 8. Triptych. TAILLEFERRE: Partita, perpetuum mobile. TALMA: Sonata, piano, no. 1. Virginia Eskin, pno.

++FF 9/10-81 p236

MHS 4245

3919 Masterpieces of the American synagogue: Max Janowski, Ben Steinberg, Max Helfman, Gershon Kingsley, Abraham Elistein (Thou shalt love). Kenneth Jewell Chorale and Chamber Orchestra; Eric Freudigman, Cantor Harold Orbach.

+-MU 4-81 p20

MHS 4246

3920 CHOPIN: Nouvelles etudes, no. 1, F minor. DOHNANYI: Postludium, op. 13, no. 10. FRIEDMAN (Gartner): Viennese dance, no. 3. GLUCK (Sgambati): Orfeo ed Euridice: Melody. JOSEFFY: At the spring. LISZT: Paraphrase: Verdi: Rigoletto. MAYER: Valse etude, op. 83, D flat major. LEVITZKI: Arabesque valsante, op. 6. PADEREWSKI: Un moment musical, op. 16, no. 6. PHILIPP: Feux follets, op. 24, no. 3. ROSENTHAL:Carnival de Vienne. SCRIABIN: Waltz, op. 38. WEBER: Sonata, piano, no. 1, op. 24, C major: Rondo. David Dubal, Stanley Waldoff, pno.

+-FF 9/10-81 p240

MHS 4257

3921 BACH: Chorale preludes, In dulci jubilo; Meine Seele erhebet den Herrn. BANCHIERI: Fantasia. BERLIOZ: L'Enfance du Christ, op. 25: Dance of the Ishmaelites. BUXTEHUDE: Magnificat. DANDRIEU: Magnificat. Noel de Saintonge. JACQUES: When Christ was born. WALTON: Make we joy now in this fest. WRIGHT: Carol-prelude on "Greensleeves:. TRAD.: Coventry carol. Now unto Bethlehem. Joy to the world. Lo how a rose e'er blooming. Once in Royal David's city. Colorado State University Chamber Singers; Colorado State Brass Choir; Robert Cavarra, org; Edward Anderson, Jacob Larson.

+/FF 11/12-81 p287

MHS 4276

3922 Carols for brass (arr. by Richard Price): Angels we have heard on high; Away in a manger; Carol of the bells; Coventry carol; The first noel; Gloucestershire carol; God rest ye merry gentlemen; Good King Wencelas; Greensleeves; I saw three ships; Lo how a

rose e'er blooming; O come O come Emmanuel; O Maria diana stella; O Tannenbaum; Silent night; Sing we now of Christmas; Tantum ergo/Let all mortal flesh keep silence; We three kings; We wish you a merry Christmas. Galliard Brass Ensemble.
+FF 11/12-81 p287

MHS 4339
3923 BOULANGER: A spring morning. DOHNANYI: Aria, flute and piano, op. 48, no. 1. Passacaglia, op. 48, no. 2. HUE: Fantasy, flute and piano. IBERT: Piece, solo flute. ROUSSEL: Flute players, op. 27. Eleanor Lawrence, flt; Joseph Seiger, Morey Ritt, pno.
+FF 9/10-81 p263

MHS 4349
3924 ALBINONI: Adagio, G minor. BACH: Ave Maria. Cantata, no. 147, Jesus bleibet meine Freude. FAURE: Messe basse. Motet: Maria mater gratiae, op. 47, no. 2. FRANCK: Panis angelicus. MENDELSSOHN: Wedding march. WAGNER: Lohengrin: Bridal chorus. Jorgen Ernst Hansen, Marie-Claire Alain, Jean Langlais, org; Maurice Andre, tpt; Camille Maurane, bar; Jocelyne Chamonin, s; Stephane Caillat Vocal Ensemble; Stephane Caillat.
+-FF 9/10-81 p299

MHS 4358 (also Augsburg 23 1454)
3925 ARGENTO: Trio carmina paschalia. BACH: Lobet den Herrn. BRAHMS: Motets: Warum ist das Licht gegeben, op. 74, no. 1. GINASTERA: The lamentations of Jeremiah. MESSIAEN: O sacrum convivium. Dale Warland Singers.
+FF 9/10-81 p220

MUSICAPHON

BM 30 SL 1209 (From Cantate 047704, Oryx 3C 301)
3926 BULL: Fantasia. In nomine. BYRD: Coranto. Galliard. Pavan. FARNABY: A toye. Loth to depart. GIBBONS: Pavan. PURCELL: Musick's hand-maid; March; Song tune; Air; Minuet; New minuet; New Scotch tune; Minuet; Sefauchi's farewell; Minuet rigadoon; A new ground; Minuet; A new Irish tune; Suite, G minor; Toccata; Hornpipe; Air. Fitzwilliam virginal book: Pieces. ANON.: Nowells galliard. Why aske you. George Malcolm, hpd.
+Gr 2-81 p1104 +-RR 8-80 p73
+HFN 8-80 p101

BM 30 SL 1911
3927 FINGER: Division on a ground. FRESCOBALDI: La bernardina. La donatina. GAULTIER, E.: Tombeau de Mezangeau. Canaries. GAULTIER, D.: Corante. Prelude. LEFEVRE: Suites faciles: Allemande de Mr. le Fevre; Passecaille de Mr. le Fevre. PEPUSCH, J.C.: Sonata, recorder, D minor. VAN EYCK: Boffons. Engels nachtegaeltje. WEISS: Suite, D minor. ANON.: The bird fancyer's delight: Tune for the canary bird; Second tune for the canary bird; A tune for the woodlark; A tune for the East India nightingale. Suites faciles: Gavottes, nos. 1 and 2; Rondeau; Sarabande; Rondeau. Manfred Harras, rec; Anthony Bailes, lt.
+-Gr 1-81 p966 +HFN 10-80 p112

MUSICMASTERS

MM 20004 Tape (c) MMC 40004 (also Musical Heritage Society MHS 4180 Tape (c) MHS 6180)

3928 DEBUSSY: Syrinx. ENESCO: Cantabile et presto. FAURE: Fantaisie, op. 79, C major. Morceau de concours, F major. GAUBERT: Sonata, flute and piano, no. 1, A major. HONEGGER: Danse de la chevre. POULENC: Sonata, flute and piano. Carol Wincenc, flt; Andras Schiff, pno.

+ARG 4-81 p43
+-FF 11/12-80 p212
+FF 9/10-81 p263
+HF 10-81 p91 tape
+HF 10-80 p96
++NYT 4-12-81 pD28
+St 10-80 p127

MM 20008 Tape (c) MC 40008

3929 BARRIOS MANGORE: Aire de zamba. Danza paraguaya. Maxixe. LAURO: Angostura. Carora. El marabino, El totumo de Guarenas. El nino. Seis por derecho. PONCE: Variations and fugue on "La folias de la Espana". SAGRERAS: El colibri. Merengue. SOJO: Aguinaldo. Mi Teresa, Estrella del mar, Mi Teresa. Eliot Fisk, gtr.

+FF 9/10-81 p254
+HF 10-81 p91 tape
+-NYT 4-12-81 pD28
+St 8-81 p102

MW RECORDS

MW 920

3930 BRAHMS: Fugue, A flat minor. ELGAR: Enigma variations, op. 36: Nimrod. HANDEL: Judas Maccabeaus: See the conquering hero comes (arr. Best). Concerto, organ, op. 4, no. 1, G major: Finale (arr. Dearnley). FLETCHER: Festival toccata. LISZT: Prelude and fugue on the name B-A-C-H, S 260. REGER: Pieces, organ, op. 59: Toccata. WESLEY, S.S.: Andante cantabile. Christopher Dearnley, org.

+Gr 11-80 p710
+HFN 1-81 p104

NEXUS

NE 01

3931 CAHN: The birds. NEVIN/BECKER: Mighty lak a rose. NEXUS: Amazing space; An African song; Kobina; Passage; Unexpected pleasures. SILVERS/DESYLVA/ENGELMAN: April showers. Nexus.

+MUM 11/12-81 p34

NEW WORLD

NW 305

3932 BACON: Billy in the Darbies. EVETT: Billy in the Darbies. GRIFFES: An old song resung; Das ist ein Brausen und Heulen; Des

Muden Abendlied; The first snowfall; Wo ich bin mich rings Umdunkelt; Zwei Konig. HOIBY: Summer and smoke: Anatomy lesson and scene. NILES: Evening; For my brother reported missing in action, 1943; Love winter when the plant says nothing. ROREM: Mourning scene. William Parker, bar; William Huckaby, pno; Virgil Blackwell, clt; Columbia String Ouartet.
++ARG 11-81 p43 +NYT 4-12-81 pD29
+-FF 1/2-81 p216 ++St 6-81 p128

NW 306
3933 DAVIDOVSKY: Pennplay. LUNDBORG: Soundsoup. OLAN: Octet. WOLPE: Chamber piece, no. 2. WUORINEN: The winds. Parnassus; Anthony Korf.
+NYT 4-12-81 pD29 ++St 5-81 p80

NIMBUS

2134
3934 AURIC: Trio, oboe, clarinet and bassoon. FRANCAIX: Quintet, woodwinds. HONEGGER: Danse de la chevre. IBERT: Pieces breves (3). MILHAUD: La cheminee du Roi Rene, op. 205. Pro Arte Quintet, Zurich.
+-HFN 11-81 p101

NONESUCH

H 71348
3935 Tenth century liturgical chant: Masses for Christmas day and Easter day. Schola Antiqua; R. John Blackley.
++FF 3/4-79 p137 +NR 8-78 p10
+Gr 12-78 p1162 +RR 12-78 p31
++HFN 1-79 p125 +SR 12-81 p64

H 71385
3936 BIBER: Sonata sancti polycarpi. GABRIELI, G.: Canzon, nos. 1-2, 28. Canzon primi toni, septimi toni. GUAMI: Canzon, no. 25. LAPPI: La negrona. LOCKE: Music for His Majesty's sackbuts and cornetts. SCHEIDT: Canzon cornetto a 4. SPEER: Sonata, 4 trombones. Edward Tarr Brass Ensemble; Edward Tarr.
++FF 3/4-81 p235 ++St 1-81 p87

H 71389
3937 ALISON: Sharp pavin. BERNIA: Toccata chromatica. BORRONO DO MILANO: Casteliono book: Pieces (3). CASTELLO: Sonata. CORBETTA: Chiacconi. Preludio. Sarabanda. Sinfonia. RORE (Gerzi): Contrapunto sopra "Non mi toglia il ben mio". DOWLAND: Fantasia. FERRABOSCO: Spanish pavane. KAPSBERGER: Toccata. PICCININI: Toccata. VALLET: Bourees (2). La chaconna. Sarabanda. ANON.: Zouch, his march. James Tyler, lt; Baroque gtr, mandora; Nigel North, lt, theorbo, cittern; Douglas Wooton, lt, bandora; Jane Ryan, bs viol.
+FF 5/6-81 p200 ++St 7-81 p91

H 71392 Tape (c) N5 71392
3938 BANCHIERI: Sonata sopra l'aria musicale del Gran Duca. CALVI:

La bertazzina. GARSI DA PARME: La Lisfeltina. FARINA: Pavana. NEGRI MILANESI: La nizzarda. RORE (Rogniono): Anchor che col partire. STEFANI: Pargoletta che non sai. VECCHI: So ben mi chi ha bon tempo. ZANNETTI: Aria del Gran Duca. Fuggi, fuggi, fuggi. La mantovana. ANON: Pavaniglia. Spagnoletta. Va pur superba va. London Early Music Group; James Tyler.
++FF 9/10-81 p228 +SR 10-81 p86
+HF 10-81 p91 tape ++St 9-81 p102

H 72085
3939 Floating petals...Wild geese...The moon on high: Music of the Chinese pipa. Lui Pui-yuen, pipa.
++FF 1/2-81 p233

N 78003
3940 The play of Daniel. Clerkes of Oxenford; David Wulstan.
+ARG 4-81 p8 +FF 3/4-81 p233/224
++Audio 12-80 p86 ++SFC 9-28-80 p23

NB 78007
3941 New Nonesuch guide to electronic music: Once below a time; Etude in sine; Triangle wave; Sawtooth over San Onofre; Very square wave; White on white; FM; AM; Timber modulation; V. Gates; Twist of fate; C'est la fin des haricots. Music and text by Bernard Krause.
+FF 9/10-81 p300 +-NR 9-81 p15

D 79011
3942 ASHFORTH: Sentimental waltz. BABBITT: Minute waltz (or 3/4 ± 1/8). CAGE: Waltzes for the five boroughs (49). CONSTANTEN: Deja-valse. FELCIANO: Two hearts. FENNIMORE: Titles waltz: After Max Steiner. GENA: Valse. GLASS: Modern love waltz. HARRISON: A waltz for Evelyn Hinrichsen. HELPS: Valse mirage. KRAUZE: Music box waltz. MORAN: In memoriam Maurice Ravel. SESSIONS: Waltz. STOUT: Waltz. TCHEREPNIN, I.: Valse perpetuelle. THOMSON: For a happy occasion. TOWER: Red garnet waltz. Robert Moran, John Cobb, Alan Feinberg, Yvar Mikhashoff, pno; Robert Moran, vocalist.
++FF 9/10-81 p241 ++NR 7-81 p13
+HF 9-81 p81 +NYT 6-7-81 pD26

NOS

1980/1-2 (2)
3943 BEETHOVEN: Symphony, no. 7, op. 92, A major. JANSSEN: Toonen. KOX: Dorian Gray suite. MEIJERING: Electric blue. SCHAT: Entelechi I. Hilversum Radio Chamber Orchestra; Ernest Bour.
+FF 9/10-81 p285

O.A.S.I.

644
3944 BIZET: Carmen: Flower song. DONIZETTI: Lucia di Lammermoor: Hai tradito il ciel. GIORDANO: Andrea Chenier: Colpito qui mi avete. Fedora: Vedi io piango. MASCAGNI: Cavalleria rusti-

cana: Addio alla madre. PONCHIELLI: La gioconda: Cielo e mar. VERDI: Un ballo in maschera: Barcarola; La rivedro nell'estasi. Ernani: Solingo errante e misero; Come rugiado al cespite. La forza del destino: O tu che in seno. Il trovatore: Ah si ben mio; Deserto sulla terra. Giuseppe Radaelli, t.
+FF 9/10-81 p213

L'OISEAU-LYRE

SPA 547 Tape (c) KCSP 547
3945 ALISON: Doloroso pavan. AZZAIOLO: Sentemi la formicula. BUSNOIS: Spinacino: Je ne fay plus. COMPERE: Virgo celesti. DALZA: Pavana and piva ferrarese. FORSTER: Vitrum nostrum gloriosum. FAYRFAX: I love loved. GUAMI: La brillantina. ISAAC: La la ho ho. JEUNE: Fiere cruelle. OBRECHT: Ich draghe de mutse clutse. RONTANI: Nerinda bella. SERMISY: La je m'y plains. TIBURTINO: Ricercare "La sol fa ni fa". TORRE: Adoramos te senor; La Spagna. TROMBONCINO: Hor ch'el ciel e la terra; Ostinato vo sequire. ANON.: La bella Franceschina (Pacoloni). Belle tenez moy, La triquotee. Blame not my lute (Wyatt). Christ ist erstanden. Elslein liebes Elslein. Mignonne allons. Where grypinge griefs (Edwards). Shooting the guns pavan. Le rossignol. Consort of Musicke; Anthony Rooley.
+Gr 12-81 p944 tape +RR 12-79 p82
+HFN 12-79 p173

DSLO 555 Tape (c) KDSLC 555
3946 CACCINI: Amarilli mia bella; Dovro dunque morire. BATCHELAR: To plead my faith. DOWLAND: Far from triumphing court; In darkness let me dwell; Lady if you spite me. GUEDRON: Ce penser qui sans fin tirannise ma vie; Si le parler et le silence; Vous que le bonheur rappelle. HALES: O eyes leave off your weeping. HOLBORNE: My heavy sprite oppressed with sorrow's might. MARTIN: Change thy mind since she doth change. MEGLI: Se di farmi morire. TESSIER: In a grove most rich of shade. ANON.: Go my flock go get you hence; O bella piu; O dear life when shall it be; Passava amor su arco desarmado; Sta notte mi sognava; Vuestros ojos tienen d'amor. Consort of Musicke; Anthony Rooley.
++FF 1/2-81 p108 +RR 12-79 p109
+Gr 12-79 p1033

DSLO 588
3947 FONTEI: Fortunato cantore. FRESCOBALDI: Maddalena alla Croce. GRANDI: Spine care e soavi. d'INDIA: Alla guerra d'amore; La mia filli crudel; La virtu. MONTEVERDI: O come sei gentile. NOTARI: Intenerite voi lagrime mie. ROVETTA: Chi vuol haver felice e lieto il core; Io mi sento morir. SABBATINI: Udite o selve; Fulmina de la bocca. VANENTINI: Vanne o carta amorosa. Emma Kirkby, Judith Nelson, s; Consort of Musicke; Anthony Rooley.
+Gr 8-81 p307 +HFN 7-81 p77

D186D4 (4)
3948 BARBINGANT: L'Omme bany de sa plaisance. BEDYNGHAM: Mon seul

plaisir ma doulce joye; Gentil madona. BINCHOIS (?): Je ne veis onques la pareille. BUSNOIS: Est il mercy de quoy l'on puest finer; J'ay moins de bien. CARON: Cent mille escus. DUFAY: Dona gentile; Le serviteur hault guerdonne; Vostre bruit et vostre grant fame. DUNSTABLE (? Bedyngham): O rosa bella. FRYE: Tout a par moy. MORTON: N'aray je jamais mieulx; Le souvenir de vous me tue. OCKEGHEM: L'autre d'antan l'autrier passa; Ma bouche rit. REGIS: S'il vous plaist que vostre je soye. VAN GHIZEGHEM: De tous biens plaine. VINCENET: Fortune par tu cruaulte. ANON.: Adieu vous dy; Ben lo sa Dio; Chiara fontana; Comme femme desconfortee; De mon povoir vous veul complaire; Faites moy scavoir de la belle; Finir voglio la mia vita; La gracia de voi; Helas je n'ay pas ose dire; Helas n'aray je jamais mieulx; Hora gridar oime; J'ay pris amours; L'aultre jour par ung matin; Ma bouche plaint; Mort merce; O meschin inamorati; O pelegrina luce; Or ay je perdu; Perla mia cara; Terriblement suis fortunee; Vray dieu d'amours. Consort of Musicke; Anthony Rooley.

+FF 7/8-81 p209 +HF 7-81 p69
+Gr 11-80 p727 +NYT 2-22-81 pD30

OPUS

3 7804
3949 BACH: Toccata, S 916, G major. GASPARINI: Prelude, recorder. PEPUSCH: Corydon cantata. PURCELL: A new ground. Prelude, recorder. SWEELINCK: Rimes francoises et italiennes a deux parties (4). TELEMANN: Sonata, recorder, C major. Ingrid Grave-Muller, rec; Eva Nassen, ms; Leif Grave-Muller, hpd; Erik Hammarberg, vlc.

+FF 9/10-81 p274

ORGAN HISTORICAL SOCIETY

OHS 78
3950 BUCK: Grande sonata, op. 22, E flat major: Finale. Fugue "Hail Columbia". On the coast. DANDRIEU: Michau qui causoit de grand bruit. FRANCK: Prelude, fugue and variation. KARG-ELERT: Choral improvisations, op. 65: Herzlich tut mich verlangen. REGER: Variations on "Heil dir im Siegerkranz". REINCKEN: Fugue, G minor. RHEINBERGER: Trios, op. 46, nos. 5 and 7. SCRONX: Echo fantasia. ANON.: Dances (2). George Bozeman, Lois Regestein, Brian Jones, James David Christie, John Skelton, Rosiland Mohnsen, M. Kenneth Wolf, Samuel Walter, Harold Knight, Donald Paterson, org.

+FF 3/4-81 p36 +MU 4-81 p18

ORION

ORS 75205

3951 ADLER: A kiss; Strings in the earth. BARBER: Reincarnation, op. 16. BERGER, J.: Snake baked a hoe-cake; The Frisco whale. CHORBAJIAN: Bitter for sweet. HENNAGIN: Crossing the Han River; Walking on the green grass. PINKHAM: Henry was a worthy king; The leaf; Piping Anne and husky Paul; Agnus Dei. ROREM: Sing my soul. STEVENS: Go lovely rose; Like as the culver; Weepe O mine eyes. THOMPSON, R.: Felices ter; The paper reeds. The King Chorale; Gordon King.

+-Audio 7-76 p71
+Gr 8-81 p307
+HF 11-76 p136
+NR 4-76 p8
+St 7-76 p113

ORS 79352

3952 CUI: Causerie, op. 40. HAYDN: Sonata, piano, E flat major. IBERT: Little white donkey. GRIFFES: Roman sketches, op. 7. RACHMANINOFF: Floods of spring, op. 14, no. 11 (arr. Stearns). Duncan Stearns, pno.

+-ARG 1-81 p51
+-FF 7/8-81 p167
+-NR 7-80 p11
+-St 11-80 p104

ORS 80371

3953 BERLINSKY: Psalm, no. 23. CAPLET: Ecoute. DRAGANSKI: The bestiary: Weathervane cock; Fish and the river; Fish eggs; Ic ane geseah idese sittan; Book worm. IBERT: Steles orientees: Mon amant a la vertus dans l'eau; On me dit. Aria (Vocalise). MORTARI: Canzone. ROLAND-MANUEL: Elegies: Charmant rossignol; Chanson. RODRIGO: Verde verderol; Pajaro del agua. ROUSSEL: Poemes de Ronsard: Rossignol mon mignon; Ciel aer et vens. Yolanda Marcoulescou, s; Robert Goodberg, flt.

+ARG 2-81 p44
+-FF 9/10-80 p199
+NR 8-80 p12
++St 12-81 p132

ORS 80388

3954 ADAMS: Nightingales. GAVEAUX: Le tromperer trompee: Polacca. JACOB: Songs: Of all the birds that I do know; Flow my tears; Ho who comes here. LAURIDSEN: Be still my soul be still. MEYERBEER: Hirtenlied. SCHUBERT: Die Verschworenen, D 787: Romanze. Yehuda Gilad, clt; Juliane Gondek, s; Michael Mathews, vlc; Arlene Shrut, pno.

+FF 9/10-81 p275
+-NR 1-81 p5

ORS 80391

3955 BARROCLOUGH: Simoraine. CALVERT: Challenge. GERMAN: The president. GREGSON: Swedish march. LITHGOW: Invercargill. POWELL: Appreciation. RIMMER: Harlequin. Ravenswood. SAINT-SAENS: Marche militaire francaise. WILLCOCKS: Saraband. ZEHLE: Wellington. New Zealand National Band; Rodney Sutton.

+ARG 11-81 p49
+FF 9/10-81 p82
+NR 4-81 p15

ORS 80392

3956 ELLIS: Coronation Scot. FREEDMAN: Hoko Hoki. GOODWIN: Where eagles dare. LUSHER: Concert variations. MARKOPOULOS: Who pays the ferryman. RIMSKY-KORSAKOV: Mlada: Procession of the nobles; Dance of the tumblers. TCHAIKOVSKY: Symphony, no. 4, op. 36, F minor: Finale. TOMOANA: E pari ra. Pokare-

kare. New Zealand National Band; Rodney Sutton; Barrie Aldredge, soloist.
+FF 9/10-81 p82 +NR 4-81 p15
+ARG 11-81 p49

ORS 81411

3957 BARAB: Bits and pieces. GOTTLIEB: Downtown blues for uptown halls. SCHUBERT: Der Hirt auf dem Felsen, D 965. STARER: The ideal self. VAUGHAN WILLIAMS: Vocalises. Julia Lovett, s; Jerome Bunke, clt; Michael Fardink, pno.
+NR 12-81 p12

ORPHEUS

ORP 0802

3958 ARAUJO: Batalha de 7th tono. BRUNO: Tiento lleno por Cesolfami. CABANILLES: Batalla imperial del 5th tono. CORREA DE ARAUXO: Tiento de baxon del 5th tono. AGUILERA DE HEREDIA: Tiento de falsas 4th tono. Tiento lleno por Gsolreut. Ensalada del 8th tono alto. MARTIN Y COLL: Entrada y tres canciones de clarin. ANON.: Tiento lleno del 3rd tono. Pere Casulleras, org.
+Gr 6-81 p66 +-HFN 9-81 p88

OXFORD UNIVERSITY PRESS

OUP 154

3959 CLARKE: Trumpet voluntary (arr. Hurford). HANDEL: Rigadoon. HAYDN: Pieces, musical clock: March. HURFORD: Fanfare on "Old 100th". JACKSON: The Archbishop's fanfare. MOZART: Le nozze de Figaro, K 492: Wedding march. PURCELL: King Arthur: Trumpet tune (arr. Jackson). Trumpet tune and almand. RAVENSCROFT: Hornpipe. REUBKE: Sonata on the 94th psalm. STANLEY: Trumpet voluntary (arr. Willcocks). WILLCOCKS: Fanfare on "Gopsal". ANON.: The Lord Mayor's swan hopping trumpet tune. Prince Eugen's march. Southwark Grenadiers march. Trumpet tune. Christopher Dearnley, org.
+FF 9/10-81 p250 ++HFN 11-80 p127
+-FF 11/12-81 p290 +MU 11-81 p17
++Gr 10-80 p523

PAPE

9

3960 BUCHNER: Christ ist erstanden. Sancta Maria won unss bey. ISAAC: Herr Gott lass dich erbarmen. Innsbruck ich muss dich lassen. Inssbruck ad equalis. LUBECK: Prelude and fugue, C minor. KOTTER: Prelude, D major. LUBLIN: Tabulatur: De profundis. SCHEIDEMANN: In dich hab ich gehoffett Herr. Prelude, G minor. SCHLICK: Da pacem domine. WECKMANN: Nun freut euch lieben Christen g'mein. Gunter Maurischat, org.

/NR 4-81 p13

12
3961 BACH: Chorale prelude, S 642, Wer nur den lieben Gott lasst walten. Prelude and fugue, S 553, C major. FISCHER: Christ ist erstanden. PACHELBEL: Vom Himmel kam der Engel Schar. ZIPOLI: Improvisation on "Heiland reiss die Himmel auf". Pastorale, C major. Walter Bibo, org.
+-NR 3-81 p15

13
3962 BRAHMS: Choralvorspiele, op. 122, no. 6. CERNOHORSKY: Fugue, C minor. KUCHAR: Fantasia, D minor. SCHUMANN: Fugue, op. 60. ZACH: Fugue, A minor. Jan Hora, org.
-NR 3-81 p15

201 (also Pape FSM 43771)
3963 BODENSCHATZ: Joseph lieber Joseph mein. BRUCH: Lasst uns das Kindlein wiegen. BRUCKNER: Ave Maria. BURKHARD: Die Verkundigung Mariae, op. 51. DISTLER: Choral motet, op. 12: Singet frisch und wohlgemut. FREUNDT: Wie schon singt uns der Engel Schar. FUCHS: O freudenreicher Tag. OTHEGRAVEN: Vom Himmel hoch ihr Engel kommt. PRAETORIUS: Psallite, In natali domini. REGER: Motets, op. 138: Unser lieben Frauen Traum. RIEDEL: Freu dich Erd und Sternezelt; Kommet ihr Hirten; Lasst alle Gott uns loben. ANON.: Schlaf wohl du Himmelsknabe du. Heinrich-Schutz Kreis; Wolfgang Matkowitz.
+/FF 9/10-81 p223 +-NR 12-81 p2

PAST MASTERS

PM 30
3964 BEETHOVEN: Symphony, no. 8, op. 93, F major: Allegretto. Deutsche Tanze, no. 12. BERLIOZ: La damnation de Faust, op. 24: Rakoczy march. HEUBERGER: Der Opernball: Overture. JANACEK: Lachian dance, no. 1. LISZT: Annees de pelerinage, 2nd year, S 162: Venezia e Napoli. Tarantelle. REZNICEK: Donna Diana: Overture. STRAUSS, J. II: Die Fledermaus, op. 363: Overture. BPhO; Erich Kleiber.
+FF 5/6-81 p220 +NR 10-80 p3

PEARL

GEMM 146
3965 BOITO: Mefistofele: Dai campi dai prati; Giunto sul passo estremo. DONIZETTI: L'Elisir d'amore: Quanto e bella. Lucia di Lammermoor: Tombe degl'avi miei; Giusto cielo rispondete; Tu che a Dio. PONCHIELLI: La gioconda: Enzo Grimaldo. PUCCINI: La boheme: O Mimi tu piu non torni. Manon Lescaut: Donna non vidi mai. Tosca: Recondita armonia. TOSELLI: Serenade, no. 1, op. 6. VERDI: La forza del destino: Solenne in quest'ora. La traviata: De miei bollenti. Beniamino Gigli, t; Ezio Pinza, bs; Giuseppe de Luca, bar; Orchestral accompaniment.
+Gr 11-78 p963 +NYT 6-28-81 pD19
+HFN 11-78 p181 +RR 10-78 p42

GEMM 153/4 (2) (Reissues)

3966 d'ALBERT: Tiefland: Schau her das ist ein Taler. BIZET: Carmen: Parle-moi di ma mere; Flower song. FLOTOW: Martha: Ach so fromm. GRIEG: Last spring. LISZT Es muss ein Wunderbares sein, S 314. LORTZING: Undine: Vater, Mutter, Schwestern, Bruder. MOZART: Don Giovanni, K 524: Dalla sua pace. Die Zauberflote, K 620: Dies Bildnis ist bezaubernd schon. OFFENBACH: Les contes de Hoffmann: Legend von Kleinsach; Ha wie in meiner Seele. PUCCINI: Madama Butterfly: Love duet; Addio fiorito asil. ROSSINI: Il barbiere di Siviglia: All'idea. SCHUBERT: Schwanengesang, D 957: Am Meer. SMETANA: The bartered bride: Nun in Lust und Leide; Armer Narr...Es muss gelingen. STRAUSS, J. II: Die Fledermaus, op. 363: Dieser Anstand. TCHAIKOVSKY: Eugene Onegin, op. 24: Lensky's aria. THOMAS: Mignon: Elle ne croyait pas; Adieu Mignon courage. TOSTI: Parted. VERDI: Aida: Gia i sacerdoti...Misera appien. La forza del destino: Solenne in quest'ora. Rigoletto: Questa o quella; La donna e mobile. Il trovatore: Ah si ben mio; Di quella pira; Miserere; Ai nostri monti. WAGNER: Die Meistersinger von Nurnberg: Am stillen Herd; Morgenlich leuchtend. Richard Tauber, t; Orchestral accompaniment.

+Gr 10-79 p716 ++Op 10-79 p1010
+NYT 6-28-81 pD19 ++RR 10-79 p45

GEMM 155/60 (6)

3967 ADAMS: Thora. ALLITSEN: Psalm, no. 27. AITKEN: Maire, my girl. BACH: Ave Maria (Gounod). BALFE: The bohemian girl: When other lips. BANTOK: Love's secret; Songs from the Chinese poets, op. 2: A dream of spring; Desolation. BENEDICT: The lily of Kilarney: The moon hath raised her lamp above. BENNETT: Take o take those lips away. BIZET: Carmen: Parle-moi de ma mere; Il fior che avevi. Les pecheurs de perles: Del tempio al limitar (2); Mi par d'udir ancora. BOHM: Still as the night. BOITO: Mefistofele: Dai campi prati; Giunto sul passo estremo. BRAGA: Angel's sereande. BRAHMS: Feldeinsamkeit, op. 86, no. 2; Im Waldeseinsamkeit, op. 85, no. 6; Komm bald; Die Mainacht, op. 43, no. 2. BUZZI-PECCIA: Lolita. CHAMINADE: The little silver ring. CURTIS: Carme. DELIBES: Lakme: Vieni al contento profondo. DONIZETTI: L'Elisir d'amore: Una furtiva lagrima. La favorita: Spirto gentil. La figlia del reggimento: Per viver vicino a Maria. Lucia di Lammermoor: Fra poco a me ricovero; Tu che a Dio. DONAUDY: O del mio amato ben; Luoghi sereni e cari. FAURE, J.B.: The crucifix; The palms. FORD: Since first I saw your face. FRANCK: La procession; Panis angelicus. FRANZ: Widmung, op. 14, no. 1. GODARD: Jocelyn: Beneath the quivering leaves. GOUNOD: Faust: Salve dimora casta e pura; Alerte alerte. HAGEMAN: Christ went up into the hills alone. HANDEL: Atalanta: Come my beloved. Semele: O sleep why dost thou leave me. HERBERT: Natoma: No country can my own outvie. JUDGE/WILLIAMS: It's a long way to Tipperary. KRAMER: The last hour; Swans. LOTTI: Pur dicesti. LEROUX: Le nil. LARCHET: Padraic the fiddler. MARSHALL: I hear you calling me; When shadows gather. MARTIN: The holy child. MASCAGNI: Cavalleria rusticana: Ave Maria. MASSENET: Manon: Chiudo gli occhi. MEHUL: Joseph en Egypt: Champs paternals. MERIKANTO: A fairy story by the fire. MESSAGER: Fortunio: J'aimais le vielle maison grise. MOLLOY: The Kerry dance. MOSZKOWSKI: Serenata. MOZART: Don Giovanni, K 527: Il mio tesoro; Ridente la calma. NOVELLO: Keep the home fires burning. OFFENBACH: Tales of Hoffman: Barcarolle. PONCHIELLI: La gioconda: O grido di quest anima. PORTUGAL (atrib.): Adeste fidelis. PUCCINI: La boheme: Che gelida manina; O soave fanciulla; Ah Mimi tu piu non torni. QUILTER: Now sleeps the crimson petal, op. 3, no. 2. RACHMANINOFF: Before my window, op. 26, no. 10; O cease thy singing maiden fair, op. 4, no. 4; To the children, op. 26, no. 7; When night descends, op. 43, no. 3. RAFF: Serenade. ROSSINI: Il barbiere di Siviglia: O il meglio mi scordavo. Songs: Li marinari: Mira la bianca luna. SCHUBERT: Ave Maria, D 839; Schwanengesang, D 957, no. 4: Serenade; Du bist die Ruh, D 776; Farewell, D 957; Hark hark the lark, D 889; Holy night, D 827; The hurdy gurdy man, D 911; Die liebe hat gelogen, D 751; To the lyre, D 737; Who is Sylvia, D 891. SCHUMANN: Sangers Trost, op. 127, no. 1. SEAVER: Just for today. STRAUSS, R.: Morgen; Du meines Herzens Kronelein, op. 21, no. 2; Allerseelen, op. 10, no. 8. SULLIVAN: The lost chord; Onward Christian soldiers. TCHAIKOVSKY: None but the lonely heart, op. 6, no. 6. TROTERE: Asthore. VERDI: Aida: Celeste Aida; Tutto e finito...O terra addio. Rigoletto: Questa o quella; La donna e mobile; Bella figlia dell'amore. La traviata: Lunga da lei...De'miei bollenti spiriti; Parigi o cara. WAGNER: Die Meistersinger von Nurnberg: Prize song. WOLF: Schlafendes Jesuskind; Wo find ich trost. WOLF-FERRARI: I gioielli dell madonna: T'eri un giorno ammalato. WALLACE: Maritana: There is a flower that bloometh. TRAD.: All mein gedanken (arr. Karg-Elert); Believe me of all those endearing young charms; I saw from the beach; Drink to me only. John McCormack, t; Emmy Destin, Lucy March, Lucrezia Bori, Nelli Melba, s; Edna Thornton, Josephine Jacoby, Louise Kirkby-Lunn, con; Mario Sammarco, Reinald Werrenrath, bar; Instrumental and orchestral accompaniments.

+Gr 8-79 p372 +NYT 6-28-81 pD19
+HFN 9-79 p116

162/3 (2)

3968 BELLINI: Norma: Al del tebro. I Puritani: Cinta de fiori. BIZET: Carmen: Toreador song. BOITO: Mefistofele: Ave Signor, Son lo spirito. DONIZETTI: La favorita: Non sai tu; Splendon piu belle. Lucia di Lammermoor: Dalle stanze. GOUNOD: Faust: Le veau d'or; Ebben che ti pare...Io voglio il piacer. HALEVY: La juive: Se oppressi ognor; Voi che del Dio vivante. MOZART: Don Giovanni, K 527: Finch han dal vino; Deh vieni alla finestra. Die Zauberflote, K 620: Possenti numi. ROSSINI: Il barbiere di Siviglia: La calunnia. SAINT-SAENS: Samson et Dalila: J'ai gravi la montagne. THOMAS: Le Caid: Drum major's aria. Mignon: Del suo cor calmai. MEYERBEER: Roberto il diavolo: Le rovine son queste...Suore che riposte. VERDI: Aida: Mortal diletto ai numi; Nume custode e vindice. Don Carlo: Dormiro sol nel manto mio regal. Ernani: Che mai vegg'io... Infelice. Requiem: Confutatis maledictis. Simon Boccanegra: A te l'estremo addio...Il lacerato spirito. Il trovatore: Di due figli...Abietta zingara. I vespri siciliani: O patria ...O tu Palermo. Ezio Pinza, bs.

+Gr 5-80 p1712 +NR 5-80 p9
+HF 2-81 p77 +RR 3-80 p26
+HFN 2-80 p101

GEMM 190

3969 BIZET: L'Arlesienne: Intermezzo. CHOPIN: Mazurka, op. 33, no. 2, D major. DVORAK: Songs, op. 55: Songs my mother taught me. KREISLER (Dittersdorf): Scherzo. MENDELSSOHN: Concerto, violin, op. 64, E minor. May breezes. TCHAIKOVSKY: Humoresque. Fritz Kreisler, vln; BSOO; Leo Blech.
+-FF 11/12-81 p196 +Gr 1-81 p998

GEMM 193

3970 DONIZETTI: La favorita: O mio Fernando. GIORDANI: Caro mio ben. HANDEL: Messiah: He was despised. MARTINI IL TEDESCO: Plaisir d'amour. SAINT-SAENS: Samson et Dalila: Amour viene aidor ma faiblesse. TCHAIKOVSKY: The maid of Orleans, excerpts. VERDI: Don Carlo: O don fatale. TRAD.: Heav'n heav'n; Sometimes I feel like a motherless child. Marian Anderson, s.
+-Gr 6-81 p84 +HFN 8-81 p88

GEMM 201

3971 BAX: Sonata, viola and piano. BEETHOVEN: Duo, viola and violoncello, E flat major. DALE: Romance. GALUPPI: Aria amorosa. MARTINI: Allegro. WOLSTENHOLME: Allegretto, op. 17, no. 2, E flat major. Lionel Tertis, vla; Lillian Tertis, vlc; Arthur Woodward, Arnold Bax, pno.
+Gr 7-81 p192

GEMM 210

3972 BALFE: Bohemian girl: When other lips. CAREY: Sally in the alley. DONIZETTI: L'Elisir d'amore: Una furtiva lagrima. GOUNOD: Faust: Salut demeure chaste et pure. LEONCAVALLO: I Pagliacci: O Colombina. MEYERBEER: L'Africaine: O paradiso. MOZART: Don Giovanni, K 527: Don Ottavio son sorta; Il mio tesoro. Die Zauberflote, K 620: Dies Bildnis ist bezaubern schon; Zum Ziele fuhrt dich. SULLIVAN: The gondoliers: Take a pair of sparkling eyes. THOMAS: Mignon: Elle ne croyait pas. VERDI: Rigoletto: Ella mi fu rapita; Parmi veder le lagrime; La donna e mobile. Heddle Nash, t.
+Gr 1-81 p994 +HFN 1-81 p104

SHE 525 (From Unicorn UNS 249)

3973 DOWLAND: Mrs. White's nothinge. My Lady Hunsdon's puffe. (trans. Warlock). MOERAN: Maltworms (Warlock). RAVENSCROFT: By a bank as I lay; He that will an alehouse keep; Jinkin the jester; The maid she went a-milking; Malt's come down; Whay I hap had to marry a shrow. ROSSETER: When Laura smiles. WARLOCK: Away to Twivver; Fill the cup Philip; Capriol suite: Tordion; Mattachins; Hey troly loly lo; I asked a thief to steal me a peach; In an arbour green; Jillian of Berry; My ghostly fader; Piggesine (arr. Tomlinson); Sweet content; Peter Warlock's fancy. WHYTHORNE (ed. Warlock): As thy shadow itself apply'th. ANON.: Have you seen but a white lily grow; The lady's birthday; One more river; Wine versus women. READINGS: Aristotle: An observation on beer drinkers. Beldaminis, P. de, Jr: (Pseud. of Warlock): Prosdorinus de Beldaminis Senior. Blunt: The drunken wizard. Beaumont/Fletcher: The night of the burning pestle, excerpt. Oinophilus: In good company. Nash: Eight kinds of drunkenness.

Rab Noolas (pseud. of Warlock): Drunken song in the Saurian mode; Mother's ruin. Ian Partridge, t; Neilson Taylor, bar; Jennifer Partridge, s and pno; Peter Gray, speaker; Fred Tomlinson, bar, pno and cond; Singers.
+FF 1/2-81 p256 +-Gr 3-76 p1053
+-RR 5-76 p73

SHE 558
3974 Armenian sacred songs: Havoun; Havoun; Havig mi baydzar desi; I Gerezman; Ov Kerahrash dzaghig; Badz mez der zdur'n voghormutyan; Sal'n ayn itchaner; Sourp sourp; Yes dzayn zarudzun asem; Sird im sasini sarsap zis uni vass'n Hutayi; Urakhatzir Sirpuhi. Lousine Zakarian, s.
++Gr 4-81 p1352 +-HFN 6-81 p81

PENTACLES

PR 10
3975 FALL: Die Kaiserin, excerpts. KALMAN: Die Csardasfurstin, excerpts. LEHAR: Paganini, excerpts. LORTZING: Undine, excerpts. Der Waffenschmied, excerpts. Der Wildschutz, excerpts. Zar und Zimmerman, excerpts. MILLOCKER: Der Bettelstudent, excerpts. SUPPE: Boccaccio, excerpts. Anni Frind, s; Walther Ludwig, t; Wilhelm Strienz, bs; Marcel Wittrisch, t; Gerhard Husch, bar; Orchestral accompaniments.
+NR 6-81 p13 +ON 12-1-79 p44

PHILIPS

6302 082 Tape (c) 7144 082
3976 BAUDAC/HAGGART: South Rampart Street parade. ELGAR: Pomp and circumstance march, op. 39, no. 4, G major. GERSHWIN: Strike up the band. HANDY: St. Louis blues march. NEWMAN: Conquest. TCHAIKOVSKY: Coronation march. WAGNER, J.F.: Under the double eagle. WALTON: Orb and sceptre march. WILLIAMS: Midway march. WILSON: The music man: 76 trombones. BPO; John Williams.
+ARG 11-81 p52 +NR 5-81 p5
+-FF 7/8-81 p233 +SFC 4-5-81 p18
+-HFN 9-81 p95 tape ++St 7-81 p88
+-HFN 6-81 p82

6527 073 Tape (c) 7311 074 (From 6580 061)
3977 Gregorian chant: Salva festa dies. Benedictine Monks of the Abbey St. Maurice and St. Maur of Clairvaux.
+Gr 4-81 p1358 +HFN 7-81 p83 tape
+HFN 4-81 p81 ++STL 6-14-81 p40

6701 011 (2)
3978 BARSANTI: Concerto grosso, op. 3, no. 10, D major. FESCH: Concerto, oboe, op. 3, no. 2, B flat major. LULLY: Le divertissement de Chambord. SOLER: Quintet, strings, no. 1, C major. SZARZYNSKI: Sonata, 2 violins, D major. TELEMANN: Suite, trumpet, D major. VALENTINE: Concerto, flute, D major. ZELENKA: Concerto grosso, G major. Maurice Andre, tpt; Gernot Schmal-

fuss, Gunther Zorn, ob; Saschko Gawriloff, Rainer Kussmaul, vln; Peter Hahn, vlc; Klaus Thunemann, bsn; Gottfried Bach, hpd; Zdenek Bruderhans, flt; German Bach Soloists; Helmut Winschermann.

+Gr 1-81 p959 +HFN 12-80 p151

6769 056 (2)

3979 ALTENBERG: Concerto a 7. BIBER, C.H.: Sonatas, trumpet (2). BIBER, H.: Sonata a 5, no. 4. Sonata a 7. Sonata "Sancti polycarpi". MOZART: Divertimenti, no. 5, K 187, C major; no. 6, K 188, C major. SCHMELZER: Balletto a cavallo. VEJVANOVSKY: Serenade. Sonata italica. ZELENKA: Cavalry fanfare, no. 5. Don Smithers, tpt; Clarion Consort; Ton Koopman.

+FF 11/12-81 p293 ++SFC 9-6-81 p18
+NR 9-81 p5 +St 11-81 p56

6770 057 Tape (c) 7650 057

3980 ALBINONI: Adagio, G minor. BACH: Brandenburg concerto, no. 3, S 1048, G major. DURANTE: Concerto, strings, F minor. GALUPPI: Concerto a 4, no. 2, G major. HANDEL: Concerto, organ, no. 6, B flat major. LOCATELLI: Concerto grosso, op. 1, no. 11. PACHELBEL: Canon and gigue, D major. PERGOLESI: Concerto, flute, no. 1, G major. SCARLATTI, A.: Sinfonia di concerto grosso, no. 3. VIVALDI: Concerto, mandolin, no. 2, G major. Severino Gazzelloni, flt; Gino del Vescovo, Tommaso Ruta, mand; Ursula Holliger, hp; Maria Teresa Garatti, org; I Musici.

++Gr 9-81 p460 tape +-HFN 7-81 p81 tape
+HFN 4-81 p80

9500 764

3981 ALVAREZ: Suspiros de Espana. CHOVI: Pepite greus. JAVALOYES: El abanico. LOPE: Gallito. Gerona. MARQUINA: Espana cani. ROIG: La gracia de Dios. SOUTULLO Y VERT: Puenteareas. TEIXIDOR: Amparito roca. ZAVALA: Viva el rumbo. ECO; Enrique Garcia Asensio.

+-FF 5/6-81 p217 +NR 11-80 p4

9500 771 Tape (c) 7300 846

3982 CILEA: L'Arlesiana: E la solita storia. GIORDANO: Andrea Chenier: Un di all'azzurro spazio. GOMES: Fosca: Intenditi con Dio. LEONCAVALLO: La boheme: Testa adorata. I Pagliacci: Vesti la giubba. Zaza: O mio piccolo tavolo. I Zingari: Principe, Radu io son. MASCAGNI: L'Amico Fritz: Ed anche Beppe amo. PONCHIELLI: La gioconda: Cielo e mar. PUCCINI: Manon Lescaut: Donna non vidi mai. Turandot: Nessun dorma. Jose Carreras, t; LSO; Jesus Lopez Cobos.

*ARG 7/8-81 p43 +-NR 1-81 p9
+FF 5/6-81 p193 +Op 6-81 p608
++Gr 3-81 p1237 +SFC 12-7-80 p33
+HFN 3-81 p93 ++St 5-81 p88

9500 894 Tape (c) 7300 894

3983 ALONSO: Maitechu mia. ALVAREZ: La partida. FREIRE: Ay ay ay. GREVER: Jurame. LACALLE: Amapola. PADILLA: Princesita; Valencia. PONCE: Estrellita. QUINTERO: Morucha. SORIANO: El guitarrico: Serenata. Jose Carreras, t; ECO; Robin Stapleton.

+-Gr 6-81 p75 +HFN 9-81 p95 tape
+HFN 6-81 p81

9500 912 Tape (c) 7300 912

3984 MILHAUD: Le printemps. PROKOFIEV: Sonata, violin, op. 115, D

major. RAVEL: Sonata, violin and piano. SATIE: Choses vues a droite et a gauche (sans lunettes). STRAVINSKY: Duo concertane. Gidon Kremer, vln; Elena Kremer, pno.
+FF 9/10-81 p255 ++St 9-81 p78
+NR 7-81 p6

9502 500
3985 ALBERT: Herbstlied. BACH, C.P.E.: Der Fruhling; Passionalied. BACH, J.S.: Anna Magdalena notebook, S 508: Bist du bei mir; Erbauliche Gedanken eines Tabakrauchers. Songs: Lasset uns mit Jesu ziehan, S 481. GLUCK: Die fruhen Graber; Die Sommernacht; Der Jungling. GORNER: Das Heidelberger Fass. HANDEL: Songs (German arias): Die ihr aus dunkeln Gruften; Kunst'ger Zeiten eitler Kummer. HAMMERSCHMIDT: Der Verfuhrer. KRIEGER: Der Rheinsche Wein. TELEMANN: Die Frau; Gluck; Neues; Uber das niedersachische Versapeh; Die vergesserne Phillis. VOIGTLANDER: Zum Lobe der Musik. Hermann Prey, bar; Eduard Melkus, vln; Marcal Cervera, vla da gamba; Leonard Hokanson, hpd, org; Vienna Capella Academica Members.
+-Gr 4-81 p1356 +HFN 4-81 p77

PHOENIX

DGS 1003
3986 ALBAN: Variations on a German theme. BELLINI/ALBAN: "Norma" variations. DAMASE: Pavane variee. JAMES: Merry-go-round. Phoenix. MARAIS: Le basque. POULENC: Elegie in memory of Dennis Brain. STIRLING: Suite of four pieces: Name piece; Improvisation. Ifor James, hn; Jennifer Partridge, pno.
+Gr 7-81 p170

PREISER

LV 271
3987 LEONCAVALLO: I Pagliacci: Vesti la giubba. MASCAGNI: Serenata. MEYERBEER: La Africaine: O paradiso. PONCHIELLI: La gioconda: Cielo e mar. PUCCINI: La boheme: Che gelida manina. Tosca: Recondita armonia; E lucevan le stelle. Manon Lescaut: Donna non vidi mai. TOSTI: Ideale. VERDI: Aida: Celeste Aida. Un ballo in maschera: Di tu se fedele. Rigoletto: Le donna e mobile. Il trovatore: Ah si ben mio; Di quella pira; Miserere. Giovanni Martinelli, t; Emmy Destinn, s.
+ARG 2-81 p44

LV 20002 (2)
3988 BRAHMS: Feldeinsamkeit, op. 86, no. 2; Standchen. HILDACH: Der Lenz. LOEWE: Tom der Reimer, op. 135. SCHUBERT: An die Musik, D 547; Du bist di Ruh, D 776; Im Abendrot, D 799; Der Jungling an der Quelle, D 300; Der Lindenbaum; Litanie, D 343; Der Musensohn, D 764; Nacht und Traume, D 824; Standchen, D 967. Die schone Mullerin, D 795: Ungeduld; Wohin. Schwanengesang, D 957: Am Meer. Winterreise, D 911: Die Post. SCHUMANN: Mondnacht, op. 39, no. 5; Nussbaum, op. 25, no. 3.

STRAUSS, R.: Freundliche Vision, op. 48, no. 1; Ich trage meine Minne, op. 32, no. 1; Morgen, op. 27, no. 4; Standchen, op. 17, no. 2; Traum durch die Dammerung, op. 29, no. 1; Zueignung, op. 10, no. 1. WOLF: Morike Lieder: Verborgenheit. Verschwiegene Liebe. Leo Slezak, t.

+Gr 1-81 p998

PR 135005

3989 BEETHOVEN: Fidelio, op. 72: Abscheulicher. GLUCK: Alceste: Divinites du Styx. GOETZ: Taming of the shrew: Die Kraft versagt. STRAUSS, R.: Elektra, op. 58: Allein Weh ganz allein. SUTERMEISTER: Romeo and Juliet: Balcony scene. VERDI: Aida: Ritorna vincitor; O patria mia. WEBER: Oberon: Ozean du Ungeheuer. Christel Goltz, s; Various orchestras and conductors.

+-FF 11/12-80 p198 +-Gr 1-81 p998

PRIVATE LABEL

HTM 580

3990 Hymns of the Russian orthodox church. Holy Trinity Seminary Choir; Sergey Lukianov.

+FF 3/4-81 p222

PROPRIUS

PROP 7831

3991 BACK: Som hjorten torstar. BERG, G.: Ave Maria; Miserere; Sig frojde nu var kristen man; Veni creator spiritus. GRIEG: Hvad est du dog skjon; I himmelen. KLEMETTI: Angelus emittitur; Ave maris stella. LINDBERG: Pingst. LEWKOVITCH: Cantabo domino; O bone Jesu. OLSSON: Canticum Simeonis; Jag lyfter mina ogon; Jesu dulcis memoria. SLOGEDAL: Cantate domino. Vasteras Domkyrkas Gosskor.

+FF 11/12-81 p285

PROP 7832

3992 BACH: Cantata, no. 147, Jesu bleibet meine Freude. BUXTEHUDE: Prelude and fugue, E major. BRAHMS: Prelude and fugue, G minor. HEMBERG: Epitaffio per organo, op. 34. OLSSON: Fantasy, op. 29. We praise thee great Lord. STANLEY: Voluntary, A minor. Erik Lundqvist, org.

+/FF 7/8-81 p215

PROTONE

PR 148

3993 ALBENIZ: Espana, op. 165: Tango (arr. Godowsky). CHOPIN: Waltz, op. 42, A flat major. GLUCK: Orfeo ed Euridice: Melodie (arr. Chasins). LISZT: Etudes de concert, nos. 1-2, S 145: Waldesrauschen; Gnomenreigen. Paraphrases: Chopin: My joys; The maiden's wish. RACHMANINOFF: Polichinelle. SAINT-SAENS: Le carnival des animaux: The swan (arr. Godowsky). SCHUBERT: Moment musicaux, op. 94, no. 3, D 780 (arr. Godowsky). WEINBERGER: Schwanda the bagpiper: Fantasia (arr. Chasins). Constance Keene, pno.

+-ARG 5-81 p39 +NR 10-80 p13
+FF 3/4-81 p230

PSALLITE

38/100 267

3994 ANON.: Messe von Barcelona. GREGORIAN CHANT: Proper of the third Mass of Christmas. Capella Antiqua Stuttgart; Eberhard Hofmann.

+FF 11/12-81 p187

RCA

ARM 1-2766/7 Tape (c) RK 12766/7 (From Victor originals)

3995 BARTHELEMY: Adorables tourments; Triste ritorno. BIZET: Les pecheurs de perles: Del tempio al limitar. BUZZI-PECCIA: Lolita. DONIZETTI: La favorita: Spirto gentil. Lucia di Lammermoor: Chi mi frena. Don Sebastien: Deserto in terra (2 versions). FLOTOW: Martha: M'appari. GIORDANO: Andrea Chenier: Un di all'azzurro spazio. GOUNOD: Faust: Salut demeure. LEONCAVALLO: I Pagliacci: Recitar...Vesti la giubba. MEYERBEER: L'Africaine: Mi batte il cor...O paradiso. PUCCINI: La boheme: Che gelida manina; O Mimi tu piu non torni; O soave fanciulla; Addio dolce svegliare. Madama Butterfly: Un po di vero c'e. Tosca: Recondita armonia: E lucevan le stella. TOSTI: Ideale; Pour un baiser. VERDI: Aida: Celeste Aida (2). La forza del destino: Solenne in quest'ora. Rigoletto: Bella figlia dell'amore (2); La donna e mobile; Questa o quella. Il trovatore: Ah si ben mio; Se m'ami ancor...Ai nostri monti; Di quella pira. Enrico Caruso, t; Orchestral accompaniment.

+ARG 11-78 p53 +-HFN 11-80 p124
++FF 11/12-78 p134 +HFN 1-81 p109 tape
++Gr 9-80 p407 +MJ 9/10-79 p50
+Gr 11-80 p736 +MUM 7/8-80 p30
+HF 10-78 p96 +-NR 10-78 p9
+HFN 8-80 p109 tape +ON 10-78 p68
+HFN 7-80 p111 +RR 8-80 p12

ARM 1-3373/4 (From Victor originals, 1909-1910)

3996 BIZET: Carmen: La fleur que tu m'avais jetee; Il fior che avevi a me dato. FLOTOW: Martha: Solo profugo reietto. FRANCHETTI: Germania: Studenti udite; Ah vieni qui...No non chiuder gli occhi vaghi. GEEHL: For you alone. GOLDMARK: Die Konigin von Saba: Magische note. GOUNOD: Faust: Seigneur Dieu que voisje; Eh quoi toujours seule; Il se fait tard...Eternelle o nuit d'amour; O merveille; Que voulez-vous messieurs; Mon coeur est penetre d'epouvante; Attends; Voici la rue; Alerte ou vous etes perdus. LEONCAVALLO: I Pagliacci: No Pagliaccio non son. MASCAGNI: Cavalleria rusticana: Siciliana. MEYERBEER: Les Huguenots: Ah qual soave vision...Bianca al par di neve alpina. NUTILE: Mamma mia che vo sapete. PONCHIELLI: La gioconda: Cielo e mar. PUCCINI: Madama Butterfly: Amore o grillo; Non ve l'avevo detto. VERDI: Adia: La fatal pietra; O terra addio. La forza del destino: Dalla natal sua terra... O tu che in seno agli angeli. Otello: Nell'ore arcane...Ora e per sempre addio. Il trovatore: Miserere. Enrico Caruso, t; Various accompaniments.

++FF 11/12-79 p149 +HFN 4-81 p83 tape
+-Gr 4-81 p1374 +HFN 3-81 p93
+Gr 8-81 p317 +MUM 7/8-80 p30
+-HF 12-79 p106 ++NR 10-79 p9
+HFN 11-81 p105 tape +ON 8-80 p36

ARM 1-3570 (2) Tape (c) ARK 1-3570/1

3997 CARDILLO: Core 'ngrato. CRESCENZO: Tarantella sincera. CURTIS: Cante pe me. DONIZETTI: L'Elisir d'amore: Una furtiva lagrima. FAURE: Crucifix. FLOTOW: Martha: Siam giunti o giovinette; Questo cameo e per voi; Che vuol dir cio; Presto presto andiam; T'ho raggiunta sciagurata. GOMES: Lo schiavo: L'importuna insistenza; Quando nascesti tu. LEONCAVALLO: La boheme: Musette; O gioia della mia dimora; Io non ho che una povera stanzetta; Testa adorata. MASCHERONI: Eternamente. MASSENET: Manon: Je sus seul; Ah fuyez douce image. TESCHEmacher-Gartner: Love is mine. TOSTI: Addio. VERDI: Aida: Gia i sacerdoti adunansi; Misero appien mi festi; Se quel guerrier io fossi; Celeste Aida. Un ballo in maschera: Di tu se fedele; Forse la soglia attinse; Ma se m'e forza perderti. La forza del destino: Invano Alvaro; Le minaccie i fieri accenti. I Lombardi: Qual vo'uta transcorrere. Il trovatore: Mal reggendo; Se m'ami ancor; Ai nostri monti. Enrico Caruso, tenor; Orchestral accompaniment.

+ARG 1-81 p6 +NR 9-80 p6
+-FF 3/4-81 p221 +NYT 8-3-80 pD20
+HF 2-81 p81 tape

XRC 1-3624

3998 BRAHMS: Hungarian dances, nos. 11-16. MENDELSSOHN: Hebrides overture, op. 26. MOZART: Concerto, piano, no. 20, K 466, D minor: 1st movement, excerpt. SCHUMANN: Symphony, no. 1, op. 38, B flat major: 1st movement. STRAVINSKY: Suites, nos. 1 and 2. Emanuel Ax, pno; PO, Dallas Symphony Orchestra; James Levine, Eugene Ormandy, Eduardo Mata.

+FF 11/12-80 p226 +NR 8-80 p5
+HFN 4-81 p79 +St 12-80 p138

ARL 1-3835 Tape (c) ARK 1-3835 (also RL 3-0469)

3999 BACH: Ave Maria (Gounod). BIZET: Agnus Dei. EYBLER: Omnes de Saba venient. FAURE: Crucifix. FRANCK: Panis angelicus. HANDEL: Serse: Ombra mai fu. HERBECK: Pueri concinite. KIENZL: Der Evangelimann: Selig sind die Verfolgung leiden. LUTHER: A mighty fortress is our God. SCHUBERT: Ave Maria, D 839. TRAD.: Adeste fideles. Placido Domingo, t; Vienna Boys Choir; VSO; Helmuth Froschauer.

+NR 2-81 p11 +St 6-81 p126
+SFC 12-14-80 p20

ATC 1-3924 Tape (c) ATK 1-3924

4000 FOSTER: A Stephen Foster treasury. PUCCINI: La boheme: Musetta's waltz. RIMSKY-KORSAKOV: The tale of the Tsar Sultan, op. 57: Flight of the bumble bee. ROSSINI: Il barbiere di Siviglia: Largo al factotum. SOUSA: A Sousa collection. STRAUSS, R.: Allerseelen. SUPPE: Poet and peasant: Overture. VERDI: La traviata: Sempre libera. TRAD.: Carnival of Venice. The war between the states. Canadian Brass.
+FF 9/10-81 p282 ++St 8-81 p101

AGL 1-3964 (From LSC 2448)

4001 ALBENIZ, M.: Sonata, guitar, D major. BERKELEY: Sonatina. CIMAROSA: Sonatas, guitar, A major, C sharp minor. FRESCOBALDI: Aria detta "La Frescobaldi". RAVEL: Pavane pour une infante defunte. RODRIGO: En los trigales. ROUSSEL: Segovia, op. 29. SCARLATTI, D.: Sonatas, guitar, E minor (2). Julian Bream, gtr.
+FF 9/10-81 p253

AGL 1-3968

4002 ADSON: Ayres (2). BACH: Die Kunst der Fuge, S 1080: Contrapunctus I and IX. GABRIELI: Canzona per sonare, no. 2. HOLBORNE: Galliard. Honiesuckle. Muy linda. Night watch. Pavan. JOSQUIN DESPRES: Royal fanfare. MONTEVERDI: Suite, brass instruments (arr. Beck). PEZEL: Sonata, no. 22; Suite. PURCELL: King Arthur: Allegro and air. Music for Queen Mary II. Trumpet tunes and ayre (2). REICHE: Sonata, no. 19. SUSATO: Dances (3). ANON.: Die Bankelsangerlieder: Sonata. Carmina (16th century): Ich sag ade; Als ich anschau das frohlich Gsicht; Carmen in la; Greiner zanner. New York Brass Quintet.
+-FF 9/10-81 p252

ARL 1-4019

4003 BACH: The sea named solaris (arr. Tomita). DEBUSSY: Reverie. Suite bergamasque: Passepied. Preludes, Bk I: La fille aux cheveux de lin. HONEGGER: Pacific 231. HOLST: The planets, op. 32: Mercury; Venus. MUSSORGSKY: Pictures at an exhibition: Hut on fowls' legs; Ballet of the chicks in their shells. PROKOFIEV: The dazzling cylinder that crashed in Tunguska Siberia (arr. Tomita). RAVEL: Bolero. STRAVINSKY: L'Oiseau de feu: Finale. Isao Tomita, electronics.
+NR 9-81 p16

ARL 1-4136

4004 Christmas with Renata Scotto: Angels we have heard on high; Messiah: He shall feed his flock. Tu scendi dalle stelle; Joy to the world; Silent night. BACH (Gounod): Ave Maria. Christmas at the cloisters; Adeste fideles. FRANCK: Panis angelicus. SCHUBERT: Ave Maria. What child is this; Coventry carol; Virgin's slumber song; Cantique de Noel. Renata Scotto, s; Orchestra; St. Patrick's Cathedral Choir.
+NR 12-81 p1 +-ON 12-5-81 p60

RL 2-5112 Tape (c) RK 2-5112

4005 BRITTEN: Hymn to St. Cecilia, op. 27. DEBUSSY: Chansons de Charles d'Orleans: Dieu qu'il la fait bon regarder; Quant j'ai ouy le tambourin; Yver vous n'estes qu'un villian. ELGAR: The shower, op. 71, no. 1. POULENC: Un soir de neige. RAVEL: Songs: Nicolette; Trois beaux oiseaux de Paradis; Ronde. SAINT-SAENS: Songs: Calme des nuits; Les fleurs et les arbres.

STANFORD: The blue bird, op. 119, no. 3. VAUGHAN WILLIAMS: The cloud-capp'd towers; Full fathom five; Over hill over dale. Swingle II.

++FF 9/10-81 p224 ++HFN 11-78 p133
++Gr 10-77 p685 ++HFN 5-78 p147 tape
+Gr 2-78 p1473 tape +RR 11-77 p101; 1-78 p15

GL 2-5308 Tape (c) GK 2-5308 (From 2-5081)

4006 BLISS: Fanfare for a coming of age. Fanfare for a dignified occasion. Fanfare for the bride. Fanfare for heroes. Fanfare for the Lord Mayor of London. Fanfare, homage to Shakespeare. Interlude. Royal fanfare. Royal fanfare, no. 1: Sovereign's fanfare. Royal fanfares, nos. 5, 6. BENJAMIN: Fanfare for a festive occasion. Fanfares: For a state occasion; For a brilliant occasion; For a gala occasion. BRIAN: Festival fanfare. ELGAR: Civic fanfare. JACOB: Music for a festival: Interludes for trumpets and trombones, no. 1, Intrada; no. 2, Round of seven parts; no. 3, Interlude; no. 4, Saraband; no. 5, Madrigal. RUBBRA: Fanfare for Europe, op. 142. SIMPSON: Canzona for brass. TIPPETT: Fanfare, brass, no. 1. WALTON: Fanfare "Hamlet" (arr. Sargent). A queen's fanfare. TRAD.: National anthem (arr. Coe). Locke Consort of Brass; James Stobart.

+Gr 1-81 p1001 tape +HFN 10-80 p115
+Gr 10-80 p533

RL 2-5367 Tape (c) RK 2-5367

4007 DEBUSSY: Reverie (arr.). DELERUE: Adagio. JOSEPHS: Song of freedom (arr.). KREISLER: Caprice viennois, op. 2 (arr.). MUSSORGSKY: Pictures at an exhibition: Ballet of the unhatched chickens (arr.). NOVACEK: Perpetuum mobile (arr.). PASCULLI: Concerto on themes from Donizetti's "La favorita". POULENC: Mouvements perpetuels (arr.). PUCCINI: Gianni Schicchi: O mio babbino caro (arr.). SAINT-SAENS: Carnival of the animals: The swan (arr.). SCARLATTI, D.: Sonata, harpsichord (arr.). YOUNG: Stella by starlight. Malcolm Messiter, ob, ob d'amore, cor anglais; National Philharmonic Orchestra; Ralph Mace.

+Gr 11-81 p713 +HFN 10-81 p93

CRL 2-7003 (2) (also Erato)

4008 CIMAROSA: Concertante, 2 flutes, G major. HANDEL: Concerto, harp, op. 4, no. 5, F major. MOLTER: Concerto, flute, G major. MOZART: Concerto, flute and harp, K 299, C major. PLATTI: Concerto, flute, G major. TARTINI: Concerto, flute, F major. Jean-Pierre Rampal, Clementine Scimone, flt; Lily Laskine, hp; Jean-Francois Paillard Chamber Orchestra; I Solisti Veneti; Jean-Francois Paillard, Claudio Scimone.

+-HF 5-75 p94 +NYT 9-27-81 pD24
++NR 10-74 p6 ++SFC 6-1-75 p21

RL 3-0336

4009 ABAELARD: O quanta qualia. GAUTIER DE CHATILLON: Ver pacis aperit. GUIDO OF AREZZO: Ut queant laxis resonare. PHILIPPE DE CHANCELIER: Mundus a munditia. ANON.: Ave Maris stella; Cum animaadverterem; De ramis cadunt folia; Flos in monte cernitur; In saeculum viellatoris; Magne deus potencie; Mater summi domini; Novus miles sequitur; O Roma nobilis; Olim in armonia; Quinte estampie real; Stantipes; Veris ad imperia. Munich Capella Antiqua; Konrad Ruhland.

+Gr 4-80 p1583 +MT 6-81 p394

+-HFN 4-80 p113 +RR 6-80 p87

RL 3-0354 (2)

4010 ARCADELT: Madrigals: Ahime ahime dov' e'l bel viso; Il bianco e dolce cigno; Il ciel rado virtu tenta mostra; O felici occhi miei; Ver' infern' e'l mio petto; Voi mi ponest in foco; Voi ve n'andat al cielo. BERNARDI, S.: Il bianco e dolce cigno. GALILEI: Anchor che col partire. GARDANE: Anchor che col partire. HOYOUL: Anchor che col partire. MANCINUS: Anchor che col partire. ORTIZ: Recercadas prima e segunda sobre "O felici occhi miei". RORE: Madrigals: Anchor che col partire (2); Come la notte ogni fiammella e viva; Datemi pace; Hor che l'aria; Non e lasso martire. RUFFO: O felici occhi miei. SPADI: Anchor che col partire. VECCHI: Il bianco e dolce cigno. VERDELOT: Madrigals: Amor quanto piu lieto; La bella donna; Donna se fera stella; Madonna non so dir tante parole; Madonna per voi ardo; O dolce notte; Quella che sospirand'ogn hor deseo; Se l'ardor foss equale; Trist Amarilli mia dunq'e pur vero. ANON.: Anchor ch'io possa dire. Munich Capella Antiqua; Konrad Ruhland.

+-Gr 11-81 p747

RL 3-0376

4011 DAMMONIS: Amor Jesu divino; Jesu dulcis memoria; O gloriosa vergine Maria; Tutti debiam cantare. LYMBURGIA: Recordare frater pie. PETRUS: Ave Maria virgo serena. RAZZI: Crucifixum in carne; Jesu dulcis memoria; O Maria diana stella; O signor mio. TROMBONCINO: Ave Maria gratia plena. ANON.: Anima Christi sanctifica me; Ave mater o Maria; Dilecto Jesu Christo; Lauda Sion salvatorem; Laudiamo Jesu; Virgene benedeta. Niederaltaich Scholars; Konrad Ruhland.

+Gr 11-81 p748

RL 3-0381 (2)(From Philips 6775 006)

4012 AMMERBACH: Wer das Tochterlein haben will. BLITHEMAN: Eterne rerum conditor. EBERLIN: Toccata sexta. Toccata and fugue tertia. FISCHER: Preludes and fugues, B minor, D major, E flat major, C minor. FROBERGER: Ricercar, no. 1. Capriccio, no. 8. FUX: Sonata, organ, no. 5. KERLL: Canzona, G minor. Toccata con durezza e ligature. KREBS: Klavierubung: Praeambulum sopra "Jesu meine Freude". MERULA: Un cromatico ovvero capriccio. MUFFAT: Fugue, G minor. NEWMAN: Pavan. PACHELBEL: Chorale prelude, Alle Menschen mussen sterben. Magnificat fugues, nos. 4, 5, 10, 13. Toccata and fugue, B flat major. PASQUINI: Canzone francese, no. 7. Ricercar, no. 4. STORACE: Ballo della battaglia. TAYLOR: Pavan and galliard. ZACHAU: Prelude and fugue, G major. ANON.: Cathaccio, gagliarda. Lodensana, gagliarda. Pavan and galliard. Gustav Leonhardt, org.

+Gr 12-81 p911

RL 3-0383

4013 Gregorian chant: Te decet laus; Gloria in excelsis Deo; Aeterne rerum conditor; Inventor rutili; Mediae noctis tempus est; A solis ortus cardine; Gloria laus et honor; Sancti venite; Congregavit nos in unum; Pange lingua; Hic est dies verus dei; Beata nobis gaudia; Ave maris stella; Ut queant laxis; Aurea luce; Urbs beata Jerusalem; O quanta qualia; Alleluia dulce carmen. Munich Capella Antiqua; Konrad Ruhland.

+Gr 11-81 p747

RL 3-1555
4014 BELLINI: La straniera: Sono all'ara...Ciel pietoso...Or sei pago. CHERUBINI: Medea: Dei tuoi figli. DONIZETTI: Roberto Devereux: E Sara...Vivi ingrato...Quel sangue versato. ROSSINI: L'Assedio di Corinto: L'ora fatal s'appressa...Giusto ciel; In tal periglio. SPONTINI: La vestale: O nume tutelar. VERDI: Don Carlo: Tu che le vanita. Raina Kabaivanska, s; Bulgarian Radio Chorus; Sofia Philharmonic Orchestra; Maurizio Arena.
+-Gr 10-81 p604

RL 4-2936
4015 BACH: Fugue, lute, S 1000, G minor. Prelude, S 999, C minor. DOWLAND: Dowland's first galliard. Earl of Derby his galliard. Earl of Essex galliard. Frogg galliard. Lachrimae antiquae. Lachrimae verae. Lord d'Lisle's galliard. Lady Rich galliard. Melancholie galliard. My Lady Hunsdon's puffe. Mrs. Vaux's gigge. The shoemaker's wife. Sir Henry Gifford's almaine. Sir John Smith's almaine. Semper Dowland semper dolens. Unnamed piece. SANZ: Suite espanola: Canarios. Instruccion de musica: Pavanas. SOR: Fantasie and minuet. VISEE: Suite, D minor. WEISS: Fantasie, E minor. Passacaglia. Tombeau sur la mort de M. Comte de Logy. Julian Bream, lt, gtr.
+NR 11-81 p15

GL 4-2952 (From SB 6698)
4016 BAKFARK: Fantasia. BESARD: Air de cour. Branle. Guillemette. Volte. Dlugoraj: Fantasia. Finales (2). Villanellas, nos. 1 and 2. DOWLAND: Fantasia. Queen Elizabeth's galliard. FERRABOSCO: Pavan. HOWETT: Fantasia. LANDGRAVE OF HESSE: Pavan. MOLINARO: Ballo detto "Il Conte Orlando". Fantasia. Saltarellos (2). MUDARRA: Fantasia. NEUSEIDLER: Hie folget ein welscher Tanz. Ich klag den Tag. Der Judentanz. Mein Herz hat sich mit Lieb verpflicht. PHILIPS: Galliard and chromatic pavan. Julian Bream, lt.
+Gr 4-80 p1575 +HFN 2-81 p97
+-HFN 4-80 p119 +-RR 4-80 p97
+HFN 8-80 p109 tape

RL 4-3195 (5) (From SB 6532, 6797, 6747, 2112, 6869, 6551, CRL 5-1415, ARD 100031)
4017 BEETHOVEN: Concerto, piano, no. 5, op. 73, E flat major. BRAHMS: Concerto, piano, no. 2, op. 83, B flat major. CHOPIN: Concerto, piano, no. 2, op. 21, F minor. GRIEG: Concerto, piano, op. 16, A minor. MOZART: Concerto, piano, no. 21, K 467, C major. RACHMANINOFF: Concerto, piano, no. 2, op. 18, C minor. SCHUMANN: Concerto, piano, op. 54, A minor. TCHAIKOVSKY: Concerto, piano, no. 1, op. 23, B flat minor. Artur Rubinstein, pno; PO, LPO, CSO, BSO, RCA Victor Orchestra, Orchestra; Alfred Wallenstein, Eugene Ormandy, Carlo Maria Giulini, Daniel Barenboim, Erich Leinsdorf.
++Gr 1-81 p954

REDWOOD

ES 11
4018 CHOPIN: Nocturne, op. 15, no. 1, F major. Nocturne, op. 27, no.

2, D flat major. LISZT: Etude d'execution transcendente d'apres Paganini, S 140: La campanella. Etudes d'execution transcendente, S 139: Ricordanza. MOSKOWSKI: Etude, no. 6, op. 72, F major. PINTO: Scenas infantis. SCHUMANN: Papillons, op. 2. SOLER: Sonata, harpsichord, D major. Valery Lloyd-Watts, pno.
/NR 2-81 p14

ES 16
4019 BARTHE: Passacaille (ed. Voxman). COLOMER: Menuet. DEBUSSY: Arabesque, no. 2 (arr. Rosenthal). LEFEVBRE: Suite, op. 57. WASHBURN: Quintet, winds. Wisconsin Arts Quintet.
+NR 2-81 p7

ROCOCO

2089
4020 BACH: Toccata, S 914, E minor. HINDEMITH: Four temperaments: Theme and variations. RAVEL: Sonatine. SCARLATTI, S.: Sonata, harpsichord, E flat major. SCHUMANN: Bunte Blatter, op. 99. Variations on ABEGG, op. 1. Clara Haskil, pno.
-NR 3-81 p13

5369
4021 BELLINI: Norma: Duet. DONIZETTI: Lucia di Lammermoor: Scena della pazzia. PUCCINI: Tosca: Vissi d'arte. ROSSINI: Il barbiere di Siviglia: Una voce...Io son docile. VERDI: Un ballo in maschera: Ecco l'orrido campo...Ma dall'arido stelo. Macbeth: Vien t'affretta. Nabucco: Ben io t'invenni...Anch' io dischiuso. Il trovatore: Vanne lasciami...D'amor sull' ali. Maria Callas, s.
+-NR 7-81 p10

5392
4022 BIZET: Les pecheurs de perles: Mi par d'udir. BOITO: Mefistofele: Dai campi; Giunto sul passo. CILEA: L'Arlesiana: E la solita storia. FLOTOW: Martha: M'appari. GOUNOD: Faust: Recitative and cavatina. MASSENET: Werther: Was bin ich aufgewacht O wie suss...O natur. NICOLAI: Die lustigen Weiber von Windsor: Horch die lerche. PUCCINI: Tosca: E lucevan le stelle. Turandot: Non piangere Liu. SCHUMANN: Genoveva: Duets (2). WEBER: Oberon: Von Jugend auf. ZANDONAI: Una partita: Non svegliarti. Petre Munteanu, t; Instrumental accompaniments.
*NR 2-81 p10

RUBINI

GV 27 (From Fonotipia 33973, 92759, 39819, 92813, 92814, 92809, 92332, 39825, 92830, 92829, 92852, 92851, 92815/6, 92205, 92204)
4023 BOITO: Mefistofele: Dai campi dai prati; Giunto sul passo. DONIZETTI: Lucia di Lammermoor: Sulla tomba. LEONCAVALLO: La boheme: Questa e Mimi. I Pagliacci: O Columbina. PUCCINI:

La fanciulla del west: Ch'ella mi creda; Or son sei mesi. Madama Butterfly: Love duet. VERDI: Aida: O terra addio. Un ballo in maschera: La rivedra. Otello: Niun mi tema; Si pel ciel. La traviata: Parigi o cara; Gran dio. Il trovatore: Ai nostri monti. Giovanni Zenatello; Orchestra accompaniment.

+ARG 11-81 p7 +Gr 5-78 p1933

GV 34

4024 COCCIA: Per la patria: Bella Italia. DENZA: Culto; Occhi di fata. HEROLD: Zampa: Perche tremar. NOUGUES: Quo Vadis: Amica l'ora. QUARANTA: O ma charmante. ROTOLI: La gondola nera; Mia sposa sara la mia bandiera. VERDI: Don Carlo: Per me giunto; Morro ma lieta in corre. Il trovatore: Mira d'acerbe; Vivra contende. Mattia Battistini, bar.

+FF 1/2-81 p49 +RR 8-77 p20
+NYT 8-3-80 pD20

GV 39

4025 ADAM: Le chalet: Vallons de l'Helvetie. BERLIOZ: La damnation de Faust, op. 24: Serenade. FLOTOW: Martha: Canzone del porter. GODARD: Embarquez-vous. GOUNOD: Faust: Serenade; Le veau d'or. Romeo et Juliette: Allons jeunes gens. MEYERBEER: L'Etoile du nord: O jours heureux. Robert le diable: Invocation. ROSSINI: Stabat mater: Pro peccatis. SCHUMANN: Les deux grenadiers, op. 49, no. 1. THOMAS: Le Caid: Air du Tambour-major (2 versions). VERDI: Don Carlo: Monologue of Philip. Pol Plancon, bs.

+FF 1/2-81 p48 +RR 8-77 p20
+NYT 8-3-80 pD20

GV 57

4026 BEETHOVEN: In quest tomba oscura (in Italian). BELLINI: Norma: Casta diva (in Italian). DAVID: La perle du Bresil: Charmant oiseau. DE LARA: Partir c'est mourir un peu. EMMETT: Dixie (in English). GODARD: La vivandiere: Viens avec nous petit. GORING (Thomas): Ma voisine. GOUNOD: Barcarolle; Serenade. HAHN: Dernier voeu; L'heure exquise. LULLY: Amadis de Gaule: Amour que veux-tu. MASCAGNI: Cavalleria rusticana: Voi lo sapete. MASSENET: Sapho: Pendant un an je fus ta femme. MOZART: Le nozze di Figaro, K 492: Voi che sapete. OFFENBACH: La perichole: O mon cher amant. ROSA: Quand on aime. Emma Calve, s.

+-ARG 11-81 p6 +RR 8-77 p20

GV 64 (From Edison 83004, Edison unpublished, Fonotipia 625159/60, 62289, 62187, 62186, 62168, 62473, 62268, 74038, 62406, 62275, 62274, 62407)

4027 ANSELMI: Su l'ocean, fragment; La villanella; La serenata; Pater noster. BIZET: Les pecheurs de perles: Mi par d'udir ancora. COCIUBEI: Ditele. DAVIDOV: Che felicita. GIORDANO: Marcella: O santa liberta. HANDEL: Serse: Va godendo. LEOPARDI/ANSELMI: L'infinito. PADEREWSKI: Manru: Come al sol cocentre. PONCHIELLI: La gioconda: Cielo e mar. ROSSINI: Il barbiere di Siviglia: Ecco ridente. VERDI: Luisa Miller: Ah fede negar potesi...Quando le sere al placido. Giuseppe Anselmi, t; Piano and orchestral accompaniments.

+FF 1/2-81 p48 +ON 3-28-81 p36
+Gr 5-78 p1933 +RR 8-78 p37

GV 74
4028 GRETCHANINOV: Dobrynia Nikitich: Flowers are blooming; Alecha's aria. KASCHEVAROV: Tranquility. KAZACHANKO: Pan Sotnik: Peter's aria. MEYERBEER: Les Huguenots: Ah quel spectacle enchanteur...Plus blanche que la blanche hermine. NAPRAVNIK: Dubrovsky: Oh give me oblivion. Nizhgorodtsy: Hail Kremlin. PUCCINI: Manon Lescaut: Donna non vidi mai. RACHMANINOFF: Georgian song. RIMSKY-KORSAKOV: The snow maiden: Tsar Berendey's aria. VERDI: Rigoletto: La donna e mobile. La traviata: Dei mioi bollenti spiriti. WAGNER: In fernem Land. Dmitri Smirnov, t.
+-FF 1/2-81 p48 +-RR 8-78 p37

GV 76
4029 BELLINI: La sonnabmula: Va ravviso. BEMBERG: Le soupir. BERLIOZ: La damnation de Faust: Une puce gentille; Voici des roses; Serenade. BIZET: Carmen: Air du toreador. GOUNOD: Faust: Le veau d'or. Philemon et Baucis: Aux bruit des lourds. HAYDN: Die Jahreszeiten: Air du laboureur. MASSENET: Si tu veux Mignonne. MEYERBEER: Dinorah: En chasse. Les Huguenots: Piff paff. MOZART: Die Zauberflote, K 620: Qui sdegno; Possenti numi. ROSSINI: Stabat mater: Pro peccatis. THOMAS: Mignon: Ninna nanna. Pol Plancon, bs; Orchestral accompaniment.
+ARG 11-81 p9 ++Gr 7-79 p256

GV 84
4030 ABT: Serenade. BORODIN: Prince Igor: Vladimir's cavatina. DARGOMIZSHKY: Russalka: Unwillingly to these sad shores...Everything here reminds me. GLINKA: Ivan Sussanin: Brother in the snowstorm. KASCHEVAROFF: Tranquility. KROKTOV: The poet: Aria of Luiidy. MONIUSZKO: Halka: The wind wails in the hills. NAPRAVNIK: Dubrovsky: O give me oblivion. RIMSKY-KORSAKOV: Snow maiden: So full of wonders. The legend of Sadko, op. 5: Song of India. RUBINSTEIN: The demon: Prince Sinodal's aria. TCHAIKOVSKY: Eugen Onegin: I love you Olga; Whither whither have you gone. VERSTOVSKY: Askold's tomb: Near the town of Slavyansk. WAGNER: Der Engel. Andreii Labinskii, t.
+FF 1/2-81 p38

GV 99
4031 ALVAREZ: La mantilla. DENZA: Occhi di fata. DONIZETTI: La favorita: Ah l'alto ardor. GOUNOD: Faust: Dio possente. Songs: Le soir. MOZART: Don Giovanni: Finch'han dal vino; Serenata. ROSSINI: Il barbiere di Siviglia: Largo al factotum. RUBINSTEIN: Demon: Deh non plorar. TCHAIKOVSKY: Eugen Onegin: Se dell'imen la dolce cura. TOSTI: Ancora; Amour amour; Ideale; La serenata. WAGNER: O tu bell'astro. Mattia Battistini, bar.
+-ARG 11-81 p9 +Gr 2-81 p1121

RS 305 (5)
4032 BALDELLI: A suon di baci. BARTHELEMY: Sulla bocca amorosa; Triste ritorno; Serenamente. BELLINI: La sonnambula: Ah perche non posso odiarti; Prendi l'anel ti dono; Son geloso. BIZET: Carmen: Il fior che avevi a me (2); La tua madre... Mia madre vedo ancor. Les pecheurs de perles: Della mia vita; Mi par d'udir ancora; Non hai compreso. CAPUA: O sole mio. CILEA: Adriana Lecouvreur: L'anima ho stanca. Songs:

Lontananza. COSTA: Napulitanata; Tu sei morta nella vita mia; Oili oila; Era de maggio. COTTRAU: Fenesta che lucive. CURTIS: Carmela; A surrentina. DENZ: Occhi de fata. DONIZETTI: L'Elisir d'amore: Ecco il magico liquore...Obbligato obbligato. La favorita: Una vergine un angel di Dio. GAMBARDELLA: Nun me guardate chiu. GIORDANO: Fedora: Amor ti vieta; Mia madre la mia vecchia madre; Vedi io piangi. GOUNOD: Faust: Tardi si fa; Salve dimora casta e pura; Tardi si fa. Romeo et Juliette: Deh sorgi il luce in ciel. MASCAGNI: Cavalleria rusticana: O Lola ch' hai di latti. MASSENET: Manon: Chiudo gli occhi (2). Werther: Ah non mi ridestar. MOZART: Don Giovanni, K 527: Dalla sua pace; Il mio tesoro. PUCCINI: Tosca: Recondita armonia. RICCIARDI: Luna lu. ROSSINI: Il barbiere di Siviglia: Se il mio nome; Ecco ridente in cielo; Numero quindici; All' idea di quel metallo; Ah qual colpo; Se il mio nome; Ah qual colpo; Ecco ridente in cielo. Songs: Pieta signore. THOMAS: Mignon: Ah non credivi tu; La tua bell'alma; Addio Mignon. TOSTI: Ideale; Marechiare; La serenata. VERDI: Luisa Miller: Quando le sere al placido. Rigoletto: La donna e mobile; E il sol dell anima. La traviata: Ah si da un anno...Un di felice eterea; Parigi o cara; De miei bollenti spiriti. WAGNER: Lohengrin: Merce merce cigno gentil; Di non t'incanta; S'el torna alfin; Cessaro i canti alfin; Mio salvatore...Mai devi domandarmi; Merce merce cigno gentil. Fernando de Lucia, t; Various accompaniments.

+FF 1/2-81 p47 | +HFN 1-81 p103
++Gr 3-80 p1442 | ++NYT 8-3-80 pD20
++Gr 3-81 p1170 | ++RR 2-80 p20
++HF 12-80 p62

RS 308 (2)

4033 CADMAN: At dawning, op. 29, no. 1. COATES: I heard you singing. ELGAR: Violet. GEEHL: For you alone. MASSENET: Manon: En fermant les yeux; Ah fuyez douce image. PHILLIPS: Nightfall at sea. PUCCINI: La boheme: Che gelida manina. Madama Butterfly: Dovunque al mondo; Amore o grillo. Manon Lescaut: Tra voi belle; Donna non vidi mai; Tu tu amore; Ah Manon mi tradisce; Guardate pazzo son. RICHARDSON: Mary. VERDI: Rigoletto: E il sol dell'anima. TRAD.: Eriskay love lilt. Herding song. My love is like a red red rose. The loves of Robert Burns (from film): Spoken introduction and Loch Lomand, Ye banks and braes and Mary of Argyle; Annie Laurie; Flow gently sweet Afton. Turn ye to me. Of a' the airts the wind can blaw. Joseph Hislop, t; Greta Soderman, Lotte Schoene, s.

+ARG 11-81 p4 | +HFN 4-81 p78

RV 501

4034 BERLIOZ: Damnation de Faust, op. 24: Serenade. CATALANI: La wally: T'amo ben mio. DONIZETTI: La favorita: A tanto amor; Vien Leonora. Lucia di Lammermoor: Cruda funesta smania. MEYERBEER: L'Africaine: Figlia di regi. ROSSINI: Il barbiere di Siviglia: Largo al factotum. THOMAS: Hamlet: Come romito fior. VERDI: Aida: Quest assisa. I due Foscari: O vecchio cor. Ernani: O dei verd'anni miei; Lo vedremo o veglio audace. Rigoletto: Pari siamo; Cortigiani vil razza

dannata. La traviata: Di provenza il mar. Riccardo Stracciari, bar; Various accompaniments.
++FF 1/2-81 p49 +NYT 8-3-80 pD20
+Gr 2-79 p1466 +ON 10-80 p42

GV 502
4035 DONIZETTI: Don Pasquale: Com'e gentile; Cerchero lontano. L' Elisir d'amore: Quanto e bella; Adina credimi; Una furtiva lagrima. LEONCAVALLO: I Pagliacci: Vesti la giubba. MARCHETTI: Ruy Blas: O dolce volutta. MEYERBEER: L'Africaine: O Selike io t'adora. Les Huguenots: O qual soave...Bianca al par. PONCHIELLI: La gioconda: Cielo e mar. PUCCINI: Manon Lescaut: Donna non vidi mai; Tra voi belle. VERDI: La traviata: Parigi o cara; Lunge da lei...De miei bollenti spiriti. Fernando da Lucia, t.
+FF 1/2-81 p38 +Gr 9-80 p407

GV 504
4036 COHEN: Over there. CHAPI Y LORENTE: El milagro de la virgen: Flores purisimas. COTTRAU: Addio a Napoli. CURTIS: Tu ca non chiagne; Senza nisciuno; Canta pe'me. FUCITO: Scordame. LEONCAVALLO: Lasciata amar; Mattinata. NIEDERMEYER: Pieta signore. OLIVIERI: Garibaldi hymn. PASADAS: Noche feliz. RICCIARDI: Amor mio. ROSSINI: Petite messe solennelle: Crucifixus. TOSTI: L'alba separa dalla luce l'ombra. Enrico Caruso, t; Orchestral accompaniment.
+-FF 1/2-81 p48 +NYT 8-3-80 pD20
+Gr 3-80 p1445 +ON 8-80 p36
+-HFN 9-80 p113

GV 505
4037 BOITO: Nerone: Queste ad un lido; Ecco la Dea. DONIZETTI: Lucia di Lammermoor: Fra poco a me; Tu che a dio. MASCAGNI: Cavalleria rusticana: Siciliana. Iris: Apri la tua finestra. PONCHIELLI: La gioconda: Cielo e mar. PUCCINI: La boheme: Che gelida manina. VERDI: Un ballo in maschera: E scherzo; La rivedra. Il trovatore: Ah si ben mio; Di quella pira. Aureliano Pertile, t; Orchestral accompaniment.
+-FF 1/2-81 p48 +NYT 8-3-80 pD20
++Gr 8-79 p374 +-RR 4-80 p30

GV 509
4038 BACHELET: Chere nuit. CHARPENTIER: Louise: Depuis le jour. DUPARC: Chanson triste, op. 2, no. 2. FALLA: El amor brujo: Cancion de amor dolido; Cancion de fuego fatuo; Danza del jungo de amor. GOUNOD: Faust: Il etait un Roi de Thule; Air des Bijoux. MASSENET: Heroidade: Il est doux il est bon. RIMSKY-KORSAKOV: Snegurochka (Snow maiden): Chanson de Lehl. SAINT-SAENS: Le timbre d'Argent: Le bonheur est une chose legere. THOMAS: Mignon: Connais tu le pays; Elle est aimee. Ninon Vallin, s.
+-FF 1/2-81 p49 +-RR 4-80 p30
+Gr 9-80 p408

GV 514
4039 DELIBES: Good morning Sue. DONIZETTI: Lucrezia Borgia: Brindisi. GOUNOD: Sapho: O ma lyre immortelle. MEYERBEER: Le prophete: Prison scene. MOZART: La clemenza di Tito: Parto parto ma tu ben mio. RUBINSTEIN: Der Wanderers Nachtlied. SCHUBERT: Der Erlkonig, D 328; Der Tod und das Madchen, D 531. WAGNER: Rienzi: Gerechter Gott; Traume. TRAD.: Die

Lorelei. Ernestine Schumann-Heink, con.
+FF 1/2-81 p38

GV 515
4040 DAVID: La perle du Bresil: Charmant oiseau. DELIBES: Lakme: Ou va jeune indoue. FLOTOW: Martha: Qui sola vergin rose. GOUNOD: Mireille: Valse. MEYERBEER: Dinorah: Ombra leggiera. VERDI: Rigoletto: E il sol dell anima; Caro nome; Tutte le feste; Si vendetta; Quartet. La traviata: Ah fors'e lui...Sempre libera. Maria Barrientos, s; Orchestral accompaniment.
+FF 1/2-81 p49 +Gr 1-81 p994
+Gr 8-79 p372

GV 519 (From Fonotipias, 1906-8)
4041 BOITO: Mefistofele: L'altra notte. CATALANI: Loreley: Da che tutta. La Wally: Ebben ne andro lontana. CILEA: Adriana Lecouvreur: Io sono l'umile ancella; Poveri fiori. MEYERBEER: L'Africaine: Di qui si vede...Qual soave concento. ODDONE: Capelli d'oro. QUARANTA: Lasciali dir tu m'ami; Si dice. PUCCINI: Madama Butterfly: Un bel di vedremo. VERDI: Aida: Ritorna vincitor. WAGNER: Die Walkure: Ho jo to ho...Tanto fu triste. Salomea Kruszelnicka, s.
+-ARG 11-81 p8

GV 520
4042 BIZET: Carmen: Micaela's aria. GOUNOD: Faust: Air des bijoux. Songs: Ave Maria; O divine redeemer. GRIEG: Pier Gynt, op. 23: Solveig's song. HERBERT: Mlle Modiste: Kiss me again. Leoncavallo: I Pagliacci: Balatella. PUCCINI: Gianni Schicchi: O mio babbino daro. Madama Butterfly: Un bel di. Tosca: Vissi d'arte. RIMSKY-KORSAKOV: Snow maiden: Lehl's song. The legend of Sadko, op. 5: Song of India. THAYER: My laddie. VANDERPOOL: Values. Florence Easton, s.
+-FF 1/2-81 p38

GV 523
4043 BANTOCK: Desolation; A dream of spring. CHAMINADE: The little silver ring. COATES: Bird songs of eventide. DONAUDY: Luoghi sereni e cari. HAMBLEN: Tick tick tock. MESSAGER: Fortunio: La maison grise. RACHMANINOFF: To the children, op. 26, no. 7. SCHUBERT: Ave Maria, D 839; Farewell, D 957; Hark hark the lark, D 889; Hurdy gurdy man, D 911; Nights and dreams, D 827; Serenade, D 957; To the lyre, D 905; Who is Sylvia, D 891. STRAUSS, R.: Du meines Herzens Kronelein, op. 21, no. 2. John McCormack, t; Edwin Schneider, pno; Orchestra; Nathaniel Shilkret.
+FF 1/2-81 p47 +Gr 8-79 p373

GV 525
4044 GOUNOD: Mireille: Mon coeur ne peut changer. MASSENET: Manon: Je suis encore toute entourdie; Voyons Manon; Duo de la lettre; Adieu notre petite table; Je marche sur tous les chemins; Gavotte. Thais: Air du Miroir. OFFENBACH: Les contes d'Hoffmann: C'est une chanson d'amour. PIERNE: Sophie Arnould: J'ai six moutons; Dorval jeune ingenu. ROUSSEAU: Le bon Roi Dagobert: Majeste madame mon enfant. Emma Luart, s.
+FF 1/2-81 p38 +Gr 9-80 p407

GV 531 (From Pearl GEMM 146, 165, HMV HQM 1194, COLH 146)
4045 BIZET: Les pecheurs de perles: Mi par d'udir ancora. BOITO:

Mefistofele: Dai campi dai prati; Giunto sui passo. CAPUA: Mari Mari. CATALANI: Loreley: Nel verde maggio. DENZA: Funiculi funicula. DONIZETTI: Lucia di Lammermoor: Tombe degli...Fra poco; Tu che a dio. PONCHIELLI: La gioconda: Enzo Grimaldo. PUCCINI: La boheme: In un coupe O Mimi tu piu non torni. Tosca: Tu di tua mano...O dolci mani. SAINT-SAENS: Il canto del cigno. VERDI: La forza del destino: Solenne in quest'ora. Beniamino Gigli, t; Various accompaniments.

+FF 1/2-81 p48 +NYT 8-3-80 pD20
+Gr 3-80 p1441 +RR 3-80 p30

GV 532
4046 ALLITSEN: The Lord is my light. BALFE: Killarney. BARNARD: Come back to Erin. BUZZI-PECCIA: Lolita. CLAY: I'll sing thee songs of Araby. DAVEY: The Bay of Biscay. DAVIS: A nation once again. MACMURROUGH: Eileen Aroon. MARSHALL: A child's song; When shadows gather. METCALF: Absent. SIMPSON: I sent my love two roses. SQUIRE: Like stars above. TRAD.: The croppy boy; God save Ireland; The boys of Wexford. John McCormack, t.

+-ARG 11-81 p2 +NYT 6-28-81 pD19
+HFN 1-81 p104

GV 537
4047 BELLINI: La sonnambula: Prendi l'anel; Son geloso; D'un pensiero. BIZET: Les pecheurs de perles: Del tempio al limitar; Mi par d'udir ancora; Della mia vita. DONIZETTI: Don Pasquale: Com'e gentile; Tornami a dir. GOUNOD: Faust: Salve dimora; Tardi si fa. ROSSINI: Il barbiere di Siviglia: Ecco ridente; Se il mio nome. VERDI: Rigoletto: Questa o quella; La donna e mobile. Dino Borgioli, t.

+FF 1/2-81 p38 +-ON 10-80 p42
+Gr 1-81 p994

GV 542
4048 BIZET: Les pecheurs de perles: Del tempio al limitar. DONIZETTI: L'Elisir d'amore: Venti scudi. GOMES: Il Guarany: Sento una forza indomita. GOUNOD: Faust: O Merveille. PUCCINI: La boheme: O soave fanciulla; O Mimi tu piu non torni. Madama Butterfly: Non ve l'avelo detto. VERDI: Don Carlo: Dio che nell'alma infondere. La forza del destino: Invan Alvaro... Le minnacie; Solenne in quest'ora. Enrico Caruso, t; Emmy Destin, s; Nellie Melba, s; Antonio Scotti, Pasquale Amato, Mario Ancona, bar; Marcel Journet, bs.

+FF 1/2-81 p38 +HFN 9-80 p113
+Gr 9-80 p407

GV 547
4049 BAZIN: Maitre Pathelin: Je pense a vous. BOIELDIEU: La dame blanche: Ah quel plaisir; Viens gentille dame. GOUNOD: Mireille: Anges du paradis. LALO: Le Roi d'Ys: Le salut nous est promis; Vainement. MASSENET: Griselidis: Voir Griselidis ...Je suis l'oiseau. Le jongleur de Notre Dame: Il fait beau voir; Mon beau seigneur. MESSAGER: Fortunio: Je suis tres trende; Ma vieille maison grise. OFFENBACH: Les contes de Hoffmann: Ah vivre deux; O dieux. ROSSINI: Il barbiere di Siviglia: Des rayons de l'aurore. Miguel Villabella, t.

+-ARG 11-81 p6

GV 548
4050 BIZET: Carmen: La fleur. GOUNOD: Romeo et Juliet: Salut tombeau. MASSENET: Herodiade: Ne pouvant reprimer. REYER: Sigurd: Le bruit des champs. SAINT-SAENS: Samson et Dalila: Arretez o mes freres; Scene de la meule. VERDI: Aida: Celeste Aida. WAGNER: Lohengrin: Ma confiance; Aus bords lointain; Mon cygne aime. Siegfried: Scene de la forge. Die Walkure: Chanson du printemps. Paul Franz, t.
+-FF 1/2-81 p38 +Gr 2-81 p1121

GV 556/7 (2)
4051 (Louis Cazette) MAINGUENEAU: Mon coeur est un oiseau. MALDEREN: Le tango du reve. MASSENET: Griselidis: Je suis l'oiseau. Manon: Le reve; Ah fuyez douce image. MESSAGER: Fortunio: J'aimais la vieille maison grise. ROUSSEAU: Dormez amours. THOMAS: Mignon: Ah que ton ame; Je suis heureuse. TOSELLI: Serenade. TOSTI: Pour un baiser. (Eugene de Creus) AUDRAN: La mascotte: Couplets de Fritellini; Couplets du tambour. DAVID: Le desert: Chant du muezzin. HALEVY: La Juive: Loin de son amie. HEROLD: Le pre aux clercs: Enfin me voila donc dans cette ville. HERVE: Mam'zelle Nitouche: Couplets de l'inspecteur. MESSAGER: Fortunio: Je suis tendre; Si vous croyez. ROSSINI: Il barbiere di Siviglia: D'un metal di precieux. VERCOLIER: Quant les papillons. (Leon Beyle) BORDESE: David chantant devant Saul. GOUNOD: Romeo et Juliette: Duo de la chambre; Duo final. MAILLART: Les dragons de Villars: Duo de Rose et Sylvain. MASSENET: Le Cid: A St. Jacques de Compostelle; Priere et vision de St. Jacques. THOMAS: Mignon: Je suis heureuse. Louis Cazette, Eugene de Creus, Leon Beyle, t; Leon Elain, bar; Lucette Korsoff, s; Suzanne Brohly, ms.
+ARG 11-81 p5 +-HFN 8-81 p89
+Gr 11-81 p764

GV 558
4053 BIZET: Carmen: La fleur. DONIZETTI: Don Sebastiano: Deserto in terra. GOMES: Salvator Rosa: Mia piccirella. HALEVY: La juive: Rachel quand du seigneur. LEONCAVALLO: I Pagliacci: No Pagliaccio non son; Vesti la giubba. MASSENET: Le Cid: O souverain. Manon: Il sogno. MEYERBEER: L'Africaine: O paradiso. PUCCINI: Manon Lescaut: Donna non vidi mai. Tosca: Recondita armonia. VERDI: La forza del destino: O tu che in sono. Il trovatore: Ah si ben mio. Enrico Caruso, t.
+ARG 11-81 p10 +NYT 6-28-81 pD19
+HFN 4-81 p77

GV 564
4054 BARRERA Y SAAVEDRA: Granadinas. CILEA: L'Arlesiana: Lamento di Federico. FRANCK: Panis angelicus. LEONCAVALLO: I Pagliacci: O Columbina. MASCAGNI: Cavalleria rusticana: O Lola. MASSENET: Manon: Il sogno. PADILLA: Princesita. PUCCINI: La boheme: Che gelida manina. Tosca: Recondita armonia...E lucevan le stelle;...O dolci mani;...Amaro sol per te;...Trionfal di nuovo speme. ROSSINI: Il barbiere di Siviglia: Ecco ridente. VERDI: Falstaff: Dal labbro. Rigoletto: Questa o quella;...La donna e mobile. Tito Schipa, t.
*ARG 11-81 p3

SAGA

5445
4055 BAX: Burlesque. BOWEN: Sonata, op. 35. BRIDGE: Sketches (3). GOOSSENS: Kaleidoscope, op. 18. IRELAND: Aubade. SCOTT: Water wagtail, op. 71, no. 3. Richard Deering, pno.
+-FF 9-77 p68 /MM 10-77 p44
+-Gr 5-77 p1717 +MT 11-77 p921
+-HFN 6-77 p123 +-RR 5-77 p68
+-HFN 6-81 p85

SAGA 5465 (also Nonesuch H 71393)
4056 BARSANTI: Sonata, recorder, G minor. BONONCINI, G.B.: Divertimento, F major. CORELLI: Sonata, op. 5, no. 4, F major. MARCELLO, B.: Sonata, recorder, op. 2, no. 2, D minor. MATTEIS: Ayres with divisions. VIVALDI: Sonata, recorder, op. 13, no. 6, G minor (attrib.). Philip Pickett, rec; Anthony Pleeth, vlc; David Roblou, hpd.
+-FF 9/10-81 p261 ++MT 3-80 p180
/FF 7/8-81 p220 /NR 8-81 p9
+Gr 9-79 p484 +-RR 9-79 p110
+-HFN 9-79 p119

5473 (From XIP 7011, STXID 5211, 5260, 5207)
4057 BUTTERWORTH: A Shropshire lad: Songs (6). IRELAND: I have twelve oxen; Love and friendship; My fair; The Sally gardens; Sea fever. KEEL: Sea water ballads: Trade winds. STANFORD: Drake's drum. VAUGHAN WILLIAMS: Linden Lea; Silent noon; Songs of travel. WARLOCK: Captain Stratton's fancy. John Shirley-Quirk, bar; Viola Tunnard, Martin Isepp, Eric Parkin, pno.
+FF 9/10-81 p217 +-HFN 6-80 p119
+Gr 11-80 p728

SAGA 5477
4058 ARNE: The street intrigue; Which is the properest day to drink. BLOW: Chloe found Amyntas. BOYCE: On the banks gentle Stour; Orpheus and Euridice. ECCLES: So well Corinna likes the joy; My man John. LANIER: Tho I am young. PURCELL: Here's that will challenge all the fair; I spy Celia; Lost is my quiet; Since time so kind to us does prove; Sweeter than roses; When the cock begins to crow (attrib.). RAVENSCROFT: By a bank as I lay; We be three poor mariners. Hilliard Ensemble.
+Gr 6-81 p70 +MT 10-81 p679
+HFN 5-81 p85 +STL 5-10-81 p41

5479
4059 ALISON: Lady Frances Sidneys goodmorowe. Mr. Allisons knell. Go from my windoe. BACHILLER: The Lady Walsinghams conceites. DOWLAND (attrib.): What if a day. Sir John Smith his almaine. JOHNSON: Chi passa. The Quadrone pavene. MORLEY: The sacred end pavan. ANON.: Duncomes galiarde. Dargesson. Mall Symes. Galliard after Laveche. Packingtoune galiarde. James Tyler, lt; London Early Music Group Members.
++Gr 6-81 p55 +HFN 6-81 p81

ST. JOHN THE DIVINE EPISCOPAL CHURCH

Houston, Texas unnumbered

4060 BACH: Chorale preludes, Drauf schliess ich mich; Lobet den Herrn. CROCE: Cantate domino. DURUFLE: Motets: Ubi caritas. FRANCK: Psalm, no. 150. HANDEL: Sing unto god; Hallelujah amen. MOZART: Mass, no. 7, K 194, D major. NEAR: Christ hath a garden. Songs for celebration: Alleluia, Allelu. Joseph Golden, org; St. John Choir; Richard Woods.
++MU 5-81 p23

SCARSDALE CONGREGATIONAL CHURCH

Unnumbered

4061 BERTALOT: Lord of the dance. BRITTEN: Jubilate Deo, C major. BYRD: Ave verum corpus. Psallite domino. DURUFLE: Motets: Ubi caritas. GOSS: Praise my soul the king of heaven. McKIE: We wait for thy loving kindness. MOZART: Mass, no. 19, K 626, D minor: Introit and kyrie. Motets: Ave verum, K 618. PALESTRINA: Gloria. STANFORD: Jubilate Deo. WILLIAMS: God be with you. Frederick Schuder, org and conductor.
+MU 11-81 p17

SCOTTISH SOCIETY OF COMPOSERS

SSC 001

4062 BEAT: Dancing on moonbeams. GEDDES: Callandish IV. McLEOD: The song of Icarus. PATERSON: Casida del llanto. WILSON: Cancion.
*MT 11-81 p755

SERAPHIM

S 60349

4063 CORNAGO: Gentil dama non se gana. DALZA: Dame acogida en tu hato; Enfermo estaba Antioco. ENRIQUE: Mi querer tanto vos quiere. ENCINA: Ay triste que vengo. FUENLLANA: De antequera salio el Moro; De los diamos vengo madre; Duelete de mi senora. GABRIEL: No soy yo quien la descubre. MILAN: Aquel caballero madre. VALDERRABANO: De donde vénis amore; Senora si te olvidare. VASQUEZ: Morenica dame un beso. ANON.: Pastorcico non te aduermas; Si la noche se hace oscura; Una hija tiene el rey; Una matica de ruda. Victoria de los Angeles, s; Ars Musicae Ensemble Barcelona; Jose Lamana.
+-FF 9/10-81 p208 +NR 5-81 p12

60350

4064 BOITO: Mefistofele: Ave signor; Son lo spirito che nega. BORODIN: Prince Igor: Galitzky's aria; Kontchak's aria. GLINKA:

A life for the Tsar: They guess the truth. MOZART: Don Giovanni, K 527: Madama. RIMSKY-KORSAKOV: The legend of Sadko, op. 5: Song of the Viking guest. The legend of the invisible city of Kitez: O vain illusion. TCHAIKOVSKY: Eugen Onegin, op. 24: Gremin's aria. VERDI: Don Carlo: Ella giammai m'amo. Ernani: Infelice. Boris Christoff, bs; PhO; Various conductors.
+FF 9/10-81 p219 +-ON 5-81 p44
+NR 6-81 p9

S 60356
4065 DOPPLER: L'Oiseau des bois, op. 21. FURSTENEAU: Rondo brillant, op. 38. KUMMER: Divertissement, op. 13. POPP: Scherzo fantastique, op. 423. SAINT-SAENS: Romance, op. 37, D major. TULOU: L'Angelus, op. 46. John Solum, flt; PhO; Neville Dilkes.
+FF 9/10-81 p265

1750 ARCH

1783
4066 DINICU (Heifetz): Hora staccato. DVORAK: Humoresques, op. 101. GABRIEL-MARIE: La cinquantaine. HAYDN: Quartet, strings, op. 3, no. 5, F major: Andante cantabile. KREISLER: Schon Rosmarin. MONTI: Czardas. PACHELBEL: Canon, D major. PURCELL: Chacony, G minor. SATIE: Gymnopedie, no. 1. SCHUBERT: Moment musicaux, op. 94, no. 3, D 780, F minor. TCHAIKOVSKY: Quartet, strings, no. 1, op. 11, D major: Andante cantabile. San Francisco String Quartet.
+NR 12-80 p7 ++St 1-81 p88

SIMAX

PS 1006
4067 BARRE: Meslanges de musique: Tendres plaisirs. Suite, no. 3, E minor: Sarabande. Suite, no. 7, E minor. COUPERIN, L.: Prelude, harpsichord, G minor. MONTECLAIR: Brunetes ancienes et modernes: Je suis charme d'une brune. Le beau berger Tircis. Je sens naitre en mon coeur. PICCININI: Intavolatura di liuto e di chitarrone, 1623: Toccata, no. 6. QUAGLIATI: La sfera armoniosa: O primavera gioventa dell' anno; Soavissimi fiori; Amore il mio tormento e la mia fede. RICCIO: Primo libro delle divina lodi, 1612: Canzona. Terzo libro delle divini lodi, 1612: Canzona. Oslo Consort.
+-Gr 8-81 p288

SMITHSONIAN COLLECTION

N 022 (2)
4068 CHENOWETH: Candles. PENN: Fantasy, solo harpsichord. ROCHBERG: Electrikaleidoscope. SCHWANTNER: Elixir. Sparrows. WRIGHT: Chamber symphony. Twentieth Century Consort; Christopher

Kendall.
+FF 9/10-81 p279

SOLIST

1186
4069 FRANCK: Final, op. 21, B major. GIGOUT: Grand choeur dialogue. LISZT: Orpheus, S 98. LITAIZE: Stucke, organ: Prelude et danse fugue. VIERNE: Fantasiestucke, op. 54: Carillon de Westminster. Fantasiestucke, op. 53: Clair de lune. Gunther Kaunzinger, org.
+-FF 9/10-81 p247

SPECTRUM

SR 110 Tape (c) SC 210 (From Omega 153011)
4070 Gregorian chant: Laudes Mariae. Cathedral of St. Salvator Scola Gregoriana; Roger Deruwe.
+FF 9/10-80 p253 ++HF 9-81 p46 tape

SR 129 Tape (c) SC 229
4071 FRANCK: Courante-Gagliarda. Intrada. FRESCOBALDI: Fugue. FROBERGER: Tombeau. GUMPELZHAIMER: Sacred songs (3). HASSLER: Cantate domino. Domine Deus. LUBLIN: Chorea. PALESTRINA: Ricercar primo tono. PRAETORIUS: Bourrees. Courantes. Deutsch et in terra. Gavottes. Pohlert Renaissance Ensemble, Ensemble for Early Music, Ensemble of the Weinheim School of Music; Werner Pohlert.
+FF 9/10-81 p227 +HF 9-81 p46 tape

SR RECORDS

SRLP 1320/2 (3)
4072 ALLDAHL: Biceps. BACK: Time present. Tollo. BARTOK: Sonata, solo violin. BENTZON: Variations on "Volga boatmen's song". GABRIELI, G.: Canzona, nos. 5, 6. HALLNAS: Epitaph for strings. HALFFTER: Introduction, fugue and finale. PENDERECKE: Miniatures, violin and piano (3). LUCIUK: Lirica di timbre. RAVEL: Sonata, violin and piano. VYSHNEGRADSKIY: Study on the rotatory movements. Jose Ribera, Bella Horn, pno; Jennifer Nuttall, Endre Wolf, vln; Erling Blondal Bengtsson, vlc; Sven-Erik Back.
+-FF 9/10-81 p294

STUDIO

SM 30977
4073 Gregorian chant: Saint Benoit. Abbey of St. Pierre de Solesmes

Choir; Jean Claire.
+-FF 5/6-81 p196

SUNDAY OPERA

SYO 1
4074 BREVELLE-SMITH: The witch of Bowden. ELLIOTT: Hybrius the Cretan. GOUNOD: Faust: The calf of gold. GOULD: The curfew. HANDEL: Alexander's feast: Behold a ghastly band...Revenge Timotheus cries. Scipio: Hear me ye winds and waves. JUDE: The mighty deep. LEHMANN: Myself when young. MENDELSSOHN: Elijah, op. 70: It is enough. SARJEANT: Blow blow thou winter wind. SLATER: From Oberon in fairyland. VERDI: Nabucco: Sperate o figli. I vespri siciliani: O tu Palermo. WALLACE: Maritana: Hear me gentle Maritana...The mariner in his barque. Malcolm McEachern, bs; Various orchestras and accompanists.
+Gr 4-81 p1374 +RR 1-80 p62

SYO 2
4075 DONIZETTI: Don Sebastiano: Deserto sulla terra. L'Elisir d' amore: Una furtiva lagrima. La favorita: Spirto gentil. GOLDMARK: Regina de Saba: Magiche note. MASSENET: Werther: Ah non mi ridestar. MEYERBEER: L'Africaine: O paradiso. Les Huguenots: Bianca al par. PENNINO: Pecche. PONCHIELLI: La gioconda: Cielo e mar. PUCCINI: Madama Butterfly: Addio fiorito asil. Tosca: Recondita armonia; E lucevan le stelle; O dolci mani. TOSTI: Ideale. VERDI: Un ballo in maschera: Di tu se fedele. La forza del destino: Solenne in quest'ora. Costa Milona, t; Various orchestras.
+-Gr 4-81 p1374 +-RR 4-80 p47

SYO 6
4076 CADMAN: From the land of sky blue water. DEBUSSY: Mandoline. ERKEL: Hunyadi Laszlo, excerpt. GOMES: Salvator Rosa: Mia piccarella. NEVIN: Mighty lak a rose. PONCHIELLI: La gioconda: Suicidio. SCOTT: Annie Laurie. STRAUSS, R.: Standchen, op. 17, no. 2. STRANGE: Damon. VERDI: Il trovatore: Tacea la notte; Miserere. WAGNER: Tristan und Isolde: Mild und leise. Die Walkure: Ho-jo-to-ho. Lillian Nordica, s.
+-Gr 1-81 p994

SYO 7
4077 HANDEL: Messiah: Why do the nations; The trumpet shall sound. HATTON: Simon the cellerer. HAYDN: Die Schopfung: Now heaven in fullest glory. HENSEL: Young Dietrich. LEONCAVALLO: I Pagliacci, excerpts. MENDELSSOHN: Elijah, op. 70: Lord God of Abraham; Is not his word like a fire; It is enough; For the mountain shall depart. REEVE: I am a friar of orders grey. RICCI: Prigione d'Edinburgo, excerpts. Arr. SHARP: The wayside cross. Horace Stevens, bs.
+Gr 1-81 p994

SUPRAPHON

111 2616

4078 FIALA: Divertimento pastorale, B flat major. HAVEL: Allegro and pastorella, B flat major. MASEK: Partita, D major. PICHL: Concertino con pastorella, F major. ANON.: Partita pastoralis, G major. Collegium Musicum Prague.
++NR 8-81 p9 ++St 7-81 p89

116 2535

4079 LEONCAVALLO: I Pagliacci: Si puo. MOZART: Le nozze di Figaro, K 492: Hai gia vinta la causa. ROSSINI: Il barbiere di Siviglia: Largo al factotum. SMETANA: Brandenburgers in Bohemia: Tvuj obraz divko. The secret: Jsem zebrak. VERDI: Macbeth: Perfidi; All' anglo contro me v'unite. Rigoletto: Cortigiani vil razza dannata. La traviata: Di provenza il mar. Il trovatore: Il balen del suo sorriso. WAGNER: Tannhauser: Wie Todesahnung...O du mein holder Abendstern. Rene Tucek, bar; Brno Janacek Opera Orchestra; Josef Chaloupka.
+-NR 6-81 p9

116 2696

4080 CAJKOVSKIJ: Panna Orleanska: Prasite vy chalmy palja radnyje. DVORAK: Rusalka: Cury mury fuk. MASCAGNI: Cavalleria rusticana: Voi lo sapete. VERDI: Aida: Ohime morir mi sento. Don Carlo: O don fatale. La forza del destino: Son giunta grazie o Dio. Il trovatore: Stride la vampa. WAGNER: Lohengrin: Entweihte Gotter. Tannhauser: Geliebter komm. Die Walkure: Du schuf'st ihm die Noth. Eva Randova, s; Orchestral accompaniments.
+NR 6-81 p9 -SFC 5-24-81 p19

TEATRO DISCHI

TD 506 (2)

4081 CILEA: Adriana Lecouvreur: Prelude, Act 4. DONIZETTI: Don Pasquale: Quel guardo il cavaliere...So anch'io la virtu magica. L'Elisir d'amore: Duet, Act 1. HALEVY: La juive: Rachel quand du seigneur. MASSENET: Manon: Toi vous...N'est-ce plus ma main que cette main presse. PUCCINI: La boheme: Che gelida manina; Mi chiamano Mimi. ROSSINI: La cenerentola: Overture. VERDI: Luisa Miller: Overture; Quando le sere al placido. Otello: Gia nella notte densa. Rigoletto: E il sol del anima. La traviata: Ah fors'e lui...Sempre libera; Libiamo libiamo ne lieta calici. Ileana Cotrubas, s; Placido Domingo, t; Orchestra; Gianfranco Masini.
+FF 7/8-81 p208

TELARC

DG 10059

4082 BARBER: Adagio. FAURE: Pavane, op. 50. GRAINGER: Irish tune from County Derry. SATIE: Gymnopedies, nos. 1, 3. VAUGHAN

WILLIAMS: Fantasia on a theme by Thomas Tallis. St. Louis Symphony Orchestra; Leonard Slatkin.
+SFC 12-20-81 p18

TELEFUNKEN

6-28024
4083 ARDITI: Parla. BLUME (Lons): Grun ist die Heide. BUZZI-PECCIA: El morenito. CLEWING (Ferdinands): Alle Tag ist kein Sonntag. CZERNIK: Chi sa. DENZA: Funiculi funicula. DVORAK: Humoreske, op. 10. no. 7, G flat major. Symphony, no. 9, op. 95, E minor: Heimatlied. FELIX (Klischnegg-Niedt): Die Katzchen: Unter dem Lindenbaum. KAPELLER (Wilhelm): Ich hab a mal a Rauscherl g'habt. LEHAR: Gold und Silber, op. 79. LINCKE (Bolten-Baeckers): Lysystrata: Gluhwurmchen-Idyll. MELICHAR (Baumann): Nanon: Heut is der schonste Tag in meinem Leben. MILLOCKER: Die Dubarry: Ja so is sie die Dubarry. Gasparone: Komm mia bella. PESTALOZZA: Ciribiribin. SCOTTO (Nachmann): Vieni vieni. STRAUSS, J. II: An die schonen blauen Donau, op. 314. Fruhlingstimmen, op. 410. Die Fledermaus, op. 363; Mein Herr Marquis spiel ich die Unschuld vom Lande. Kaiserwalzer, op. 437. Rosen aus dem Suden, op. 388. Die Tanzerin Fanny Eisler: Drausen in Sievering. Erna Sack, s; Orchestral Accompaniments.
+NR 1-81 p12

EK 6-35488 (3) (*From Toccata FSM 53626, 53614, 53627)
4084 FARNABY: Fantasias, nos. 10, 27. The flatt pavan. Farmer's pavan. Lachrymae pavan. Mal Sims. Muscadin. Meridian alman. The old spagnoletta. Praeludium. Rosasolis. Tell me Daphne. Tower Hill. A toye. Up tails all.* Why aske you. FUX: Parthie, G minor. KERLL: Canzona, no. 1, D minor. Ciacona, C major. Toccatas, nos. 1, 3. PACHELBEL: Chaconne, C major. PURCELL: Musick's handmaid: Minuets (2). Suites, nos. 1-8.* WAGENSEIL: Divertimento, F major.* Bradford Tracey, hpd, org, spinet.
+Gr 12-81 p912

6-35494 (3)
4085 BYRD: Come woeful Orpheus. CAMPIAN: Never weather-beaten sail; Jack and Jone, A secret love. CHIRBURY: Agnus Dei. COOKE: Alma proles. DAMETT: Salve porta paradisi. DOWLAND: Fine knacks for ladies; I must complain; Mr. Dowland's midnight; Now oh now I needs must part; A shepherd in a shade; Sweet stay awhile; Where sin sore wounding. DUNSTABLE: Albanus roseo rutilat; Crux fidelis O crux gloriosa; Gaude virgo. FORD: Since first I saw; There is a lady. FOREST: Qualis est dilectus. JONES: Thinkst thou Kate. MORLEY: Die now my heart; Hark jolly shepherds; You black bright stars. PILKINGTON: Care for thy soul; Diaphenia; Down-a-down. POWER: Credo. PYCARD: Gloria. TOMKINS: O let me die for true love; Oyez has any found a lad. WARD: O my thoughts surcease; Retire my troubled soul. WEELKES: Come sirrah Jack ho; Come let's begin to revel out; Some men desire spouses; Those sweet delightful lilies. WILBYE: As matchless beauty; Lady

when I behold; Weep o mine eyes. Pro Cantione Antiqua; Bruno Turner, Geoffrey Mitchell, Ian Patridge.
+FF 5/6-81 p199 +NYT 2-22-81 pD30
+-Gr 8-81 p306

6-35519 (2) (From AS 6-41126, AW 6-41275)

4086 BERNARD DE VENTADORN: Can vei la lauzeta mover. BRULE: Biaus m'est estez. DIA: A chanter m'er de so qu'eu no volria. ETIENNE DE MEAUX: Trop est mes maris jalos. GILLEBERT DE BERNEVILLE: De moi doleros vos chant. GUIOT DE DIJON: Chanterai por mon coraige. GUIRAUT DE BORNELH: Leu chansonet e vil. JACQUES DE CAMBRAI: Retrowange novelle. RAIMBAUT DE VAQUEIRAS: Kalenda maia. VIDAL: Barons de mon dan covit. ANON.: A l'entrada del temps clar. Saltarello. Veris ad imperia. Li joliz temps d'estey. Lasse pour quoi refusai. Studio de Fruhen Musik; Thomas Binkley.
+Gr 7-81 p191

EK 6-35521 (3)

4087 BACH, J.C.: Air and 15 variations, A minor. BACH, J.S.: Capriccio, S 992, B flat major. French suite, no. 5, S 816, G major. Toccata, S 913, D minor. Toccata, S 916, C major. Trio sonata, S 525, E flat major. Trio sonata, S 526, C minor. Das wohltempierte Klavier, S 846-869: Preludes and fugues, C major, B flat major. FISCHER: Musicalisches Blumenbuschlein: Suite, no. 6, D major. BUXTEHUDE: Prelude and fugue, no. 22, G minor. HANDEL: Suite, harpsichord, no. 2, D minor. ZACHAU: Suite, B minor. Bradford Tracey, Rolf Junghanns, hpd, cld.
+Gr 9-81 p418

AP 6-41036 Tape (c) CR 4-41036

4088 BUXTEHUDE: Wie schon leuchtet der Morgenstern. CASANOVAS: Sonata, organ, no. 5. CORRETTE: Vous qui desirez sans fin. COUPERIN, L.: Chaconne, D minor. FRESCOBALDI: Ave maris stella. GIBBONS, O.: Fancy, A major. The king's juell. PALESTRINA: Ricercare primi toni. SWEELINCK: Von der fortuna werd' ich getrieben. SANTA MARIA: Fantasias primi toni, tertii toni, octavi toni. ZIPOLI: Canzona, no. 5, G minor. Albert de Klerk, org.
+FF 1/2-80 p170 +Gr 12-81 p944 tape
+Gr 9-81 p418

AO 6-41214 Tape (c) CQ 4-41214 (From SAWT 9493)

4089 Gregorian chant: Conditor alme siderum; Nato canunt omnia; Cum natus esset Jesus; Nunc dimittis; Mittit ad virginem; O redemptor sume carmen; Surrexit dominus vere; Ad coenam agni providi; Veni sancte spiritus; Kyrie fons bonitatis; Aeterne rerum conditor; Te deum laudamus. Munich Capella Antiqua; Konrad Ruhland.
+-Gr 11-81 p748

AP 6-42074 Tape (c) CR 4-42074

4090 BULL: Lord Lumley's pavan and galliard. Prince's galliard. Prelude and fantasia. GIBBONS: Fantasia, A minor. Ground, A minor. LASSUS: Susanne un jour. MORLEY: Lachrymae pavan and galliard. SCHEIDT: Bergamasque. SWEELINCK: Prealudium toccata. TISDALE: Coranto. Bradford Tracey, virginal.
+Gr 10-81 p584 +HFN 9-81 p90
+Gr 12-81 p944 tape

6-42166
4091 BACH: Concerto, violin and strings, S 1042, E major. BIBER: Battalia, D major. HANDEL: Concerto, organ, op. 7, no. 13, F major. TELEMANN: Concerto, 3 oboes and 3 violins, B major. VIVALDI: Concerto grosso, no. 5, PV 342, G minor. Soloists; VCM; Nikolaus Harnoncourt.
+Gr 9-81 p460 tape +HFN 3-81 p95

AW 6-42356
4092 BRADE: Pavan and galliard a 6. BULL: In nomine. COPRARIO: Fantasias a 4, a 5, a 6. CORNYSHE: Fa la sol. FERRABOSCO: Four note pavan. HENRY VIII, King: Consorts IV, XII. En vray amoure. If love now reigned. HOLBORNE: The choise. Fairie-round. As it fell on a holie eve. Gaillard. "Lullabie". Pavan. LUPO: Fantasia a 5. MORLEY: Fantasia "La torello". Fantasia of 2 parts. TAVERNER: In nomine. TYE: In nomine "Trust". WARD: Fantasia a 5. Vienna Recorder Ensemble.
/-Gr 11-79 p873 +NR 1-81 p7
+HFN 8-79 p117 +RR 7-79 p77

6-42554
4093 BENNETT: Luer falconer; Round about a fair ring. BROWN: We cats when assembled. COLEMAN: The glories of our birth and state. ISHAM (Isum): Celia learning. PIERS: Hey trola trola. PURCELL: Once twice thrice would you know how we meet; Since time so kind. RAVENSCROFT: Canst thou love and lie alone; Hey ho nobody at home; Give us once a drink; Hey ho to the greenwood; I cannot come every day; Long have we been perplext; Tomorrow the fox will come; Who liveth so merry; Who's the fool now; Yonder comes a courteous knight. Pro Cantione Antiqua; Mark Brown.
+FF 5/6-81 p199

6-42587
4094 CABEZON: Diferencias sobre el canto Llano de cavallero. ERBACH: Ricercare secundi toni. HOFHAIMER: Recordare. KOTTER: Salve regina. MERULO: Toccata. MILAN: Pavane. PELLEGRINI: La serpentina. PRAETORIUS: O lux beati trinitas. SANTA MARIA: Fantasies (8). VALDERRABANO: Fantasia primero grado. Herbert Tachezi, org.
+-FF 1/2-81 p223

6-42811
4095 BABELL: Concerto a 7, D major. COUPERIN: Livres de clavecin, Bk III, Ordre no. 14: Le rossignol en amour. DIEUPART: Sonata, A major. LOEILLET: Sonata, op. 2, G major. TELEMANN: Fantasies, B major, G minor. Frans Bruggen, rec.
++AR 11-81 p134 +FF 1/2-81 p224

6-42827
4096 ANTONIOTTI: Sonata, no. 9, C minor. BENDA: Sonata, violoncello and bass, F major. BOCCHERINI: Fugues, C major, E major, E flat major. HAYDN: Andantino and minuet, C minor. HAYDN, M.: Polonáise, C major. MASSENET: Duo, D major. PLEYEL: Rondeau, C major. Variations, G major. TELEMANN: Canons, F major (2). Jorg Baumann, vlc; Klaus Stoll, bs.
+FF 7/8-81 p220

TITANIC

TI 40

4097 BESARD: Branles de village (4). CORBETTA: Sinfonia. Sinfonia a 2. CAROSO: Canario. Gagliarda. Nido d'amore. Rotta. Spagnoletta nuovo al modo di madrigalia. FOSCARINI: Sinfonias, nos. 1-2. GAULTIER, E. Les larmes de Boisset. L'Immortelle. Canaries. GAULTIER, D.: Narcisse. Sarabande. GRANATA: Sinfonia a dui. LAWES: Alman. Corant (2). Catherine and Robert Strizich, lt, baroque gtr.
+ARG 6-81 p47

TI 41

4098 ALVARADO: Tiento por delasolrre, fa e ut no mesmo signo. CABANILLES: Batalla imperial. CABEZON: Tiento del quinto tono. CORREA DE ARAUXO: Tiento, no. 5. DURON: Gaitilla de mano izquierda. SOLA: Siento de primer tono, no. 2. SOLER: Rondo, F major. Sonata de clarines, C major. ANON.: Cancion para la corneta con el eco. Piezas de clarines (4). Esteban Elizando-Iriarte, org.
+ARG 12-81 p38 +FF 9/10-81 p247

TI 81

4099 Music of the Mid-1800's. The Brass Band Journal: Ellen Bayne quick step; Rainbow Schottisch; The jewel waltz; Massa's in the cold ground; Farewell my Lilly dear; Wedding schottisch; Prima donna waltz; Lilly Bell quick step. Dodworth's Brass Band School: The star-spangled banner; Gift polka; Auld lange syne. Stephen Foster's The Social Orchestra: Quadrilles, nos. 3 and 4; Would I were with thee; Happy land; Oh summer night; Old folks at home. Band of the 26th North Carolina Regiment: Empire quick step; To thee oh country; Dixie's land; Washington's march; Hosanna; Mocking bird quick step. American Brass Quintet; John Stevens, bs horn.
++FF 5/6-81 p213

TOLLEY

Dick Tolley, Dept. of Music, Texas Tech. University

4100 ADAMS: Holy city. BACH: Air. KNAPP: Open the gates. MALOTTE: Lord's prayer. MARTINI: Toccata. MOZART: Alleluia. PEETERS: Aria. PURCELL (Clarke): Trumpet voluntary. Trumpet tune. PILSS: Adagio. ROBBINS: Mont Saint-Michel. SUMNER: Child of the king. TOLLEY: Meditation. O come O come Emanuel. Dick Tolley, tpt; Julie Wyrick, org.
+MU 4-81 p21

UNICORN

KP 8005

4101 ANGUS: Our father which in heaven art. BACH: Prelude and fugue, S 848, C sharp major. Prelude and fugue, S 849, C sharp

minor. DUNSTABLE: Veni sancte/Veni creator spiritus. KINLOCH: Kinloch his fantassie. PEEBLES: Si quis diligit me. PURCELL: Fantasia on one note, F major. Fantasia in 3 parts on a ground, F major. Pavans, A major, B flat major. ANON: All sons of Adam. Fires of London; Peter Maxwell Davies.
+Gr 12-81 p896

UNIVERSITY OF EAST ANGLIA

UEA 78001
4102 BARTOLINO DA PADOVA: Per un verde boschetto. GIOVANNI DA CASCIA: De' come dolcemente. DONATO DA FIRENZE: Come in sul fonte. JACOPO DA BOLOGNA: Vola el bel sparver. I'Senti'za. LANDINI: Caro signor pales. Donna i prego. In somm' alteca. Ochi dolenti mie. ANON.: Istampitta Isabella. La Manfredina. Su la Rivera. Landini Consort; Peter Syrus.
+Gr 2-81 p1113 +RR 2-80 p91

VANGUARD

VSD 71263
4103 ARNE: Sonata, harpsichord, no. 6, G major. BLOW: Mortlack's ground. DRAGHI (attrib.): Ground, C minor. GIBBS (attrib.): The Lord Monck's march. GREENE: Overture, D major. LOCKE: Suite, no. 4, D major. NARES: Lesson, no. 2, D major. PARADIES: Sonata, no. 6, A major. PURCELL: A new Irish tune. Suite, no. 2, G minor. ANON.: Gerard's mistress. The grange. Trevor Pinnock, hpd.
+FF 5/6-81 p206 ++St 3-81 p98
++NR 5-81 p15

VSD 79429
4104 ARNDT: Marionette. AUFDERHEIDE: Pelham waltzes. EUROPE: Castles half and half. FARWELL: Wa-Wan choral. JOPLIN: Bethena. Solace. MACDOWELL: Woodland sketches, op. 51: To a wild rose. NEVIN: Ein Liedchen. O'HARA: The perfect melody. RUIFROK: Song without words, op. 5, no. 2. Minuet, op. 4, no. 1. Max Morath, pno.
+ARG 10-80 p51 +-HF 8-81 p65
+-FF 7/8-80 p165

VARESE

DBX VCDM 1000.20/PS 1008
4105 BLISS: Things to come: Epilogue. COPLAND: The red pony: Morning on the ranch. GOULD: Windjammer: Main theme. MOROSS: The big country: Main theme. NEWMAN: Airport: Main theme. ROZSA: That Hamilton woman: Love theme. Tribute to a badman: Suite. VAUGHAN WILLIAMS: The 49th parallel: Prelude

and fugue. WALTON: Spitfire: Prelude and fugue. WILLIAMS: Star wars: Main theme. LSO; Morton Gould.

+-FF 7/8-80 p193 +-St 11-80 p94
-FF 7/8-81 p233

VCDM 1000.60

4106 DVORAK (Kreisler): Symphony, no. 9, op. 95, E minor: Largo. Slavonic dance, op. 72, no. 2, E minor. Songs, op. 55: Songs my mother taught me. MIYASHITA: Yoru no shirabe (Nocturne). SARASATE: Zigeunerweisen, op. 20, no. 1. TARTINI (Kreisler): Sonata, violin and piano, no. 10, G minor. YOSHIZAWA (Miyashita): Chidori no kyoku (Tune of the plovers). Vaclav Hudecek, vln; Josef Hala, pno; Susumu Miyashita, koto.

+FF 9/10-81 p256 +-HFN 7-81 p78

VISTA

VPS 1066

4107 BACH (Teschner): All glory laud and honour. BYRD: Sing joyfully. EWING: Jerusalem the golden. FRANCK: Psalm, no. 150. HORSLEY: There is a green hill far away. KING: Songs of praise the angels sang. LOOSEMORE: O Lord, increase our faith. MENDELSSOHN: Hear my prayer; O for the wings of a dove. PARRY: O praise the Lord. RUTTER: Psalm, no. 150. WESLEY, S.S.: Thou wilt keep him in perfect peace. WOOD: Expectans expectavi. Nicholas Hayes, bar; Norwich Cathedral Choir; Michael Nicholas.

+Gr 8-78 p367 ++MU 10-78 p10
+HFN 7-78 p96 +NR 7-81 p8

VPS 1077

4108 BROUWER: Etudes simples. CANONICO (arr. Lauro): Aire de Joropa. GIULIANI: Variations on a theme by Handel, op. 107. GRANADOS: Valses poeticas (trans. Brightmore). HUNT: The barber of Baghdad. LAURO: Venezuelan waltzes (2). Robert Brightmore, gtr.

+Gr 4-81 p1346 +-HFN 9-81 p86

VPS 1085

4109 Christmas songs: People look East; Sans day carol; Wexford carol; All bells in paradise; In Bethlehem city; Sussex carol; Kings of the orient; Rise up shepherd; Angels from the realm of glory; Ding dong merrily on high; Today maiden Mary; The holly and the ivy; Through Gabriel his message mild; Adam and his helpmate; Joy joy from every steeple; The birds; It came upon the midnight clear. Norwich Cathedral Choir; Michael Nicholas.

+NR 12-81 p2

VPS 1091

4110 BACH: Fantasia, S 562, C minor. Trio sonata, no. 4, S 528, E minor. GERMANI: Toccata. KARG-ELERT: Valse mignonne, op. 142, no. 2. MESSIAEN: Diptyque. REGER: Pieces, organ, op. 59: Pastorale. Pieces, organ, op. 80: Perpetuum mobile. Pieces, organ, op. 65: Scherzo. Graham Barber, org.

+HFN 1-80 p117 +/MU 11-81 p12
+MT 11-80 p712 +RR 4-80 p99

VPS 1095

4111 BACH: Toccata and fugue, S 565, D minor. BREMNER: Miscellany: Tunes from Colonial Williamsburg. FRANCK: Piece heroique. HAYDN: Pieces, flute clock (3). LEMMENS: Sonate pontificale. SCARLATTI, D.: Sonata, harpsichord, K 288, D major. STANLEY: Voluntary, C major. SWEELINCK: Unter der Linden grune. Eileen Morris Guenther, org.
+Gr 9-81 p417 ++MU 10-81 p10
+-HFN 9-81 p87 -NR 3-81 p14

VPS 1097

4112 BREWER: Marche heroique. CORRETTE: Magnificat du 3 and 4 ton. DUBOIS: Toccata, G major. GUILMANT: Marche funebre et chant seraphique. LLOYD, C.H.: Allegretto. PARRY: Fantasia on the old 104th. SANDERS: Toccata. STANLEY: Trumpet voluntary, D major. WESLEY, S.S.: An air composed for Holsworthy church bells with variations. John Sanders, org.
+Gr 11-80 p704 ++MU 11-81 p17
+HFN 9-81 p87 +NR 1-81 p13

VPS 1098

4113 ALAIN: Litanies, op. 79: Trois movements. BACH: Prelude and fugue, S 542, G minor. Sonata, flute and harpsichord, S 1031, E flat major: Siciliano (attrib.). FAURE: Apres un reve, op. 7, no. 1 (arr.). MARTIN: Sonata da chiesa. MESSIAEN: La nativite du Seigneur: Dieu parmi nous. VILLETTE: Complainte. Edward Beckett, flt; Nicholas Jackson, org.
+Gr 9-81 p406 +HFN 9-81 p87

VPS 1102

4114 BACHARACH: Wives and lovers (arr. Chilcott). CERTON: La la la je ne l'oise dire. LASSUS: Bonjour mon coeur. MACLEAN: Wonderful baby (arr. Chilcott). MONTEVERDI: Lamento d'Arianna. MORLEY: Fyer fyer. PETRASSI: Nonsense songs of Edward Lear (5). PORTER: Miss Otis regrets (arr. Pickard). SAINT-SAENS: Serenade d'hiver. WILBYE: Weep weep mine eyes. YOUMANS: Tea for two (arr. Chilcott). The Bright Blues.
++Gr 7-81 p191 +HFN 9-81 p86

VPS 1921

4115 ALBINONI (arr. Giazotto): Adagio, G minor. COUPERIN, L.: Chaconne, F major. GOEURY (arr. van Marion): Entrada, C major. HANDEL (arr. van Marion): Gavotte, B flat major. PFEYLL (arr. van Marion): Sonata, G major. PIAZZA (arr. van Marion): Sonata, F major. ELIAS: Minuet, D major. SEIXAS: Toccata, C minor. SOLER: Sonata, clarino, C major. STANLEY: Prelude and fugue, G major. VIOLA: Sonata, A major. Sander van Marion, org.
++Gr 6-81 p62

WEALDEN

WS 202

4116 BACH: Prelude and fugue, S 541, G major. BAIRSTOW: Scherzo. KARG-ELERT: Triptych, op. 141: Legend. PARRY: I was glad. PEETERS: Variations on an original theme, op. 58. PURCELL: O God thou art my God. SAINT-SAENS: Fantasia, no. 2, op.

101, E flat major. YON: L'Organo primitivo: Humoresque. St. Andrew's Cathedral Choir Aberdeen; Geoffrey Pearce, Andrew Morrisson, org.
+Gr 7-81 p178

WS 204
4117 ALBINONI (arr. Walther): Concerto, organ, B flat major. BACH: Chorale preludes, S 599, 600, 603, 607, 618-619. Prelude and fugue, S 547, C major. BUXTEHUDE: Prelude on "Ach wir armen Sunder". FROBERGER: Toccata, no. 6. SCHEIDEMANN: Prelude on "Jesu wollst uns weisen". SCHEIDT: Modus ludendi organo pleno. Paul Kenyon, org.
+Gr 6-81 p66

WS 206
4118 BLISS: Prelude. DURUFLE: Suite, op. 5: Toccata. HOWELLS: Siciliano for a high ceremony. MESSIAEN: La nativite du Seigneur: Dieu parmi nous. Les corps glorieux: Joi et clarte. RATHBONE: October music. Christopher Rathbone, org.
+-Gr 10-81 p584

WERGO

WER 60083
4119 BARTOK: Hungarian folksongs (8). BIALAS: Haiku, Bk 2. FALLA: Spanish popular songs (7). HILLER: Muspilli. RAVEL: Don Quichotte a Dulcinee. Spyros Sakkas, bar; Georg Kouropos, pno; Karl Peinkofer, Edith Salmen, perc; Berner String Quartet.
+-FF 9/10-81 p217 +HFN 9-81 p86

WOODWARD

MW 924
4120 DUPRE: Variations sur un noel, op. 20. GOWERS: Toccata. PARRY: When I survey the wondrous cross. SAINT-SAENS: Benediction nuptiale, op. 9. STANFORD: Fantasia and toccata, op. 57, D minor. WIDOR: Symphony, organ, no. 5, op. 42, no. 1, F major: 1st movement. Catherine Ennis, org.
+Gr 12-81 p912

WORLD RECORDS

SHB 55 (5) Tape (c) TGSHB 55 (From Columbia LX 880, 823/4, 541/2, 614, 317/8, 885, 530, 805, 702/3)
4121 BERLIOZ: La damnation de Faust, op. 24: Hungarian march; Dance of the sylphs; Minuet of the will o' the wisps. BIZET: L' Arlesienne: Suites, nos. 1 and 2. Carmen: Suite, no. 1. La jolie fille de Perth: Suite. CHABRIER: Espana: Rhapsody. DEBUSSY: Prelude a l'apres midi d'un faune. GRETRY: Zemire et Azor: Air de ballet. OFFENBACH: The tales of Hoffmann:

Epilogue; Barcarolle; Entr'acte: Duet, Giulietta and Hoffmann; Intermezzo, Act 1. LPO; Thomas Beecham.

+ARSC Vol. 12, no. 3, 1980 p246
+FF 3/4-81 p234
++Gr 9-79 p474
+HFN 12-79 p173
++RR 1-80 p74

SHB 100 (8)

4122 d'ALBERT: Tiefland, excerpts. ATTERBERG: Symphony, no. 6, op. 31, C major. BEETHOVEN: Concerto, piano, no. 4, op. 58, G major. BERLIOZ: Le carnival romain, op. 9. BORODIN: Prince Igor: Polovtsian dances (arr. Rimsky-Korsakov, Glazunov). DEBUSSY: Printemps. DELIUS: On hearing the first cuckoo in spring. DVORAK: The golden spinning wheel, op. 109. GERMAN: Have you news of my boy Jack. HANDEL: The origin of design: Ballet suite (arr. Beecham). Israel in Egypt: But as for his people; Moses and the children of Israel; The Lord is a man of war. Solomon: Arrival of the Queen of Sheba. HAYDN: Symphony, no. 40, F major. MASSENET: La vierge: Le dernier sommeil de la vierge. MENDELSSOHN: Concerto, violin, op. 64, E minor. MISSA: Muquette: Entr'acte. MOZART: Symphony, no. 39, K 543, E flat major: 3rd movement. Symphony, no. 41, K 551, C major: 1st movement. Die Zauberflote, K 620: Schnelle Fusse. OFFENBACH: Les contes de Hoffmann: Doll's song. SIBELIUS: Symphony, no. 2, op. 43, D major. STRAUSS, J. II: Die Fledermaus, op. 363: Overture. STRAUSS, R.: Ein Heldenleben, op. 40. STRAVINSKY: L'Oiseau de feu: Dance of the firebird; Scherzo; Infernal dance. VERDI: Macbeth: Vegliammo invan due notti. WAGNER: Gotterdammerung: Ho ho. WEBER: Oberon: Overture. TRAD.: The national anthem "God save the Queen". Tiana Lemnitz, Margherita Grandi, Vera Terry, Caroline Hatchard, s; Clara Butt, con; Heinrich Tessmer, Helge Roswaenge, t; Gerhard Husch, bar; Wilhelm Strienz, bs; Ernest Frank, bar; Herbert Janssen, bar; Ludwig Weber, bs; Jascha Heifetz, vln; Artur Rubinstein, pno; Beecham Symphony Orchestra, RPO, LPO, BPhO; Thomas Beecham.

++ARG 3-81 p58
++Gr 5-79 p1905
+HFN 5-79 p117
+-NYT 7-22-79 pD19
+RR 8-79 p21

SECTION III

ANONYMOUS WORKS

A la fontenele. See no. 3670
A l'entrada del temps clar. See no. 4086
A los banos del amor. See no. 3828
A su alvedrio. See no. 3828
Adeste fideles. See no. 3999
Adieu vous dy. See no. 3948
Aeterne Rex altissime. See no. 3636
All mein gedanken. See no. 3967
All sons of Adam. See no. 4101
Amor mi fa cantar. See no. 1580
Anchor ch'io possa dire. See no. 4010
Anima Christi sanctifica me. See no. 4011
Auf dem Berge da geht der Wind. See no. 3775
L'aultre jour par ung matin. See no. 3948
Ave maris stella. See no. 4009
Ave mater O Maria. See no. 4011
Bacas. See no. 3778
Die Bankelsangerlieder: Sonata, excerpts. See no. 4002
Basela un tratto. See no. 3661
Battle hymn of the republic. See no. 3700
Believe me of all those endearing young charms. See no. 3967
La bella Franceschina. See no. 3945
Belle tenes mo. See no. 3945
Ben lo sa Dio. See no. 3948
Bird fancyers delight: Tune for the canary bird; Second tune for the canary bird; A tune for the woodlark; A tune for the East India nightingale. See no. 3927
Blame not my lute. See no. 3945
Bonny sweet Robin. See no. 3670
Boys of Wexford. See no. 4046
Brincan y bailan. See no. 3795
British Grenadiers. See no. 3416
Cancion para la corneta con el eco. See no. 4098
Carmen Hercules. See no. 3777
Carmina (16th century): Ich sag ade; Als ich anschau das frohlich Gsicht; Carmen in la; Greiner zanner. See no. 4002
Carnival in Venice. See no. 3731. See no. 4000
Cathaccio, gagliarda. See no. 4012
Chanter's song. See no. 1021
Che ti cova. See no. 1580
Chiara fontana. See no. 3948
Christ der ist erstanden. See no. 3945
Clap clap: Sus Robin. See no. 3779
Comme femme desconfortee. See no. 3948
Les compagnons de la Marjolaine. See no. 3805
Con que la lavare. See no. 3828
Cortege en fauxbourdon. See no. 3796
Coventry carol. See no. 3921
The croppy boy. See no. 4046
The cuckoo. See no. 1021
Cum animadverterem. See no. 4009
Da unten im Tale. See no. 3844
Daca bailemos. See no. 3828
Dances. See no. 3950
Dances, harpsichord (3). See no. 3692
Dargesson. See no. 4059
De battle ob Jerico. See no. 3610
De mon povoir vous veul complaire. See no. 3948
De ramis cadunt folia. See no. 4009
De virgin Mary. See no. 3618

Dilecto Jesu Christo. See no. 4011
Dindirindin. See no. 3828
Don Gato. See no. 3795
Donna tu pur in vecchi. See no. 1580
Doxology. See no. 3621
The dreams. See no. 3853
Drink to me only. See no. 3967
Duncomes galiarde. See no. 4059
E la don don verges Maria. See no. 3828
Earl of Essex galliard. See no. 3871
Early one morning. See no. 3416
Echo song. See no. 3823
Elslein liebes Elslein. See no. 3945
En l'ombre d'un buissonet. See no. 3777
English dance. See no. 3853
English estampie. See no. 3670
Entlaubet ist der Walde. See no. 3676
Eriskay love lilt. See no. 3823. See no. 4033
Etelapohjalainen kansanlaulu. See no. 3805
Faites moy scavoir de la belle. See no. 3948
Finir voglio la mia vita. See no. 3948
Flos in monte cernitur. See no. 4009
Folias. See no. 3778
Gagliarda "Cathaccio". See no. 3622
Gagliarda "Lodesana". See no. 3622
Galliard after Laveche. See no. 4059
Gerard's mistress. See no. 3733. See no. 4103
Go my flock go get you hence. See no. 3946
God save Ireland. See no. 4046
La gracia de voi. See no. 3948
The Grange. See no. 3733. See no. 4103
Greensleeves. See no. 1021. See no. 3883
Greenwood/Dargason: Fanfare. See no. 3670
Gregorian chant: Salve regina. See no. 3634
Gregorian chant, 13th century: Divinum mysterium. See no. 3822
Hachas. See no. 3778
Heav'n heav'n. See no. 3970
Helas je n'ay pas ose dire. See no. 3948
Helas n'aray je jamais mieulx. See no. 3948
Herding song. See no. 4033
Una hija tiene el rey. See no. 4063
Hora gridar oime. See no. 3948
How unto Bethlehem. See no. 3921
Hymns: Guide me O thou great Jehovah; The lone wild bird; Lovely child. See no. 3809
I saw from the beach. See no. 3967
I te vurria vasa. See no. 3839
I will give my love an apple. See no. 3416. See no. 3618
Ich armes Kauzlein kleine. See no. 3676
Imayoh. See no. 3696
In saeculum viellatoris. See no. 4009
Istampitta Isabella. See no. 4102
Istampitta tre fontaine. See no. 3853
J'ay pris amours. See no. 3948
John Peel. See no. 3416
The jolly miller. See no. 3416
Joy to the world. See no. 3921
Katholisches Gesangbuch: Holy God we praise thy name. See no. 3822
The keeper. See no. 3416
Lady Wynkfyldes rownde. See no. 3732
Lasse pour quoi refusai. See no. 4086
Lauda Sion salvatorem. See no. 4011
Laudiamo Jesu. See no. 4011
Let us break bread together. See no. 3823
Li joliz temps d'estey. See no. 4086
Lo how a rose e'er blooming. See no. 3921
Lodensana, gagliarda. See no. 4012
Lord for thy tender mercy's sake. See no. 3614
Lord Mayor's swan hopping trumpet tune. See no. 3959

Die Lorelei. See no. 4039
Lucente Stella. See no. 1580
Ma bouche plaint. See no. 3948
Magne deus potencie. See no. 4009
Maid in the moon. See no. 3670
Mall Symms. See no. 4059
Malurous qu'o uno fenno. See no. 3823
La Manfredina. See no. 4102
La mas graciosa serrana. See no. 3828
Mater summi domini. See no. 4009
Una matica de ruda. See no. 4063
The mermaid. See no. 3691
Messe de Tournai. See no. 2093
Mignonne allons. See no. 3945
Mort merce. See no. 3948
My delyght. See no. 3676
My Lady Carey's dompe. See no. 3734
My love is like a red red rose. See no. 4033
My Robin. See no. 3670
National anthem. See no. 4006. See no. 4122
Naves pont. See no. 3777
The nightingale. See no. 3676
Novus miles sequitur. See no. 4009
Nowells galliard. See no. 3926
Nutting girl. See no. 3670
O bella piu. See no. 3946
O dear life when shall it be. See no. 3946
O death rock me to sleep. See no. 3853
O leave your sheep. See no. 3818
O meschin inamorati. See no. 3948
O pelegrina luce. See no. 3948
O Roma nobilis. See no. 4009
O sanctissima. See no. 3775
O schlafe Gottlicher Knabe. See no. 3775
The oak and the ash. See no. 3416
Och Mod'r ich well en Ding han. See no. 3844
The old whiff song. See no. 3691
Olim in armonia. See no. 4009
Once as I remember. See no. 3620
Once in Royal David's city. See no. 3921
Or ay je perdu. See no. 3948
Pabanas. See no. 3778
Packingtoune galiarde. See no. 4059
Paraderas. See no. 3778
Parson's farewell/Goddesses. See no. 3670
Partita pastoralis, G major. See no. 4078
Pase el agoa. See no. 3828
Passava amor su arco desarmado. See no. 3946
Pastorcico non te aduermas. See no. 4063
Pavan and galliard. See no. 3622. See no. 4012
Pavaniglia. See no. 3938
Per tropo fede. See no. 1580
Perla mia cara. See no. 3948
Piezas de clarines (4). See no. 4098
Piper's galliard. See no. 3871
The plough boy. See no. 1021
Prince Eugen's march. See no. 3959
Pueblita mi pueblo. See no. 3838
Pues no mejora mi suerte. See no. 3828
Queene of Bohemia's dumpe. See no. 3807
Quien vos avia de llevar. See no. 3828
Quinte estampie real. See no. 4009
Redit aetas aurea. See no. 3670
Ribayas. See no. 3778
Riu riu chiu. See no. 3828
Robin Hood and the tanner. See no. 3670
Le rossignol. See no. 3945
La royne d'Ecosse galliard. See no. 3807
Sakura Sakura. See no. 3696
Sally's fancy/The maiden's blush. See no. 3670
Saltarello. See no. 3853. See no. 4086
Sanctus and benedictus; Salve sancte parens. See no. 3845
Scarborough fair. See no. 1021
Schlaf wohl du Himmelsknabe du. See no. 3963
Scottish dance tunes. See no. 1021
Scots marche. See no. 3676
Seguidillas. See no. 3778
Septime estampie real. See no. 3846
Serrana, La. See no. 3795
Shepherd's hey. See no. 3670

Shooting the guns pavan. See no. 3945
Si je perdu. See no. 3777
Si la noche se hace oscura. See no. 4063
So ell enzina. See no. 3828
Sola me dexaste. See no. 3828
Sometimes I feel like a motherless child. See no. 3970
Southwark Grenadiers march. See no. 3959
Spagnoletta. See no. 3938
Spanish lady. See no. 3654
Spanish song. See no. 3836
Spiritual songs. See no. 2192
Sta notte mi sognava. See no. 3946
Stabat mater. See no.1274
Stantipes. See no. 4009
Stingo. See no. 3670
Su la Rivera. See no. 4102
Suites faciles: Gavottes, nos. 1 and 2; Rondeau; Sarabande; Rondeau. See no. 3927
Sumer is icumen in. See no. 3416
Sweet Jane. See no. 1021
Terriblement suis fortunee. See no. 3948
Tiento lleno del 3rd tono. See no. 3958
Tohryanse. See no. 3696
Tomorrow shall be my dancing day. See no. 1021
Tristan's lament. See no. 3670
Trumpet tune. See no. 3959
The turtle dove. See no. 3416
Two-voices estampie. See no. 3670
Va pur superba va. See no. 3938
Veris ad imperia. See no. 4009. See no. 4086
Vesame y abracame. See no. 3828
Vielle chanson de chasse. See no. 3653
Virgene benedeta. See no. 4011
Vray dieu d'amours. See no. 3948
Vuestros ojos tienen d'amor. See no. 3946
Wanton season, a galyarde. See no. 3676
The war between the states. See no. 4000
Were you there. See no. 3852
Where griping griefs. See no. 3945
Why aske you. See no. 3926
Ya se van la paloma. See no. 3795
Zouch, his march. See no. 3937
Zuizuizukkorobashi. See no. 3696